Household Spending

Household
Spending

Who Spends How Much on What

BY THE EDITORS OF NEW STRATEGIST PUBLICATIONS

New Strategist Publications, Inc.
Ithaca, New York

New Strategist Publications, Inc.
P.O. Box 242, Ithaca, New York 14851
800/848-0842
www.newstrategist.com

ISBN 1-885070-67-5

Printed in the United States of America

Contents

List of Tables

Chapter 10. Spending on Personal Care, Reading, Education, and Tobacco, 2002

Chapter 11. Spending on Transportation, 2002

Introduction

Welcome to the ninth edition of *Household Spending: Who Spends How Much on What*. This edition provides a comprehensive analysis of the spending of American households in the year 2002.

Since we published the first edition of *Household Spending* in 1991, the economy has cycled through good times and bad. The nation pulled out of a severe recession in the early 1990s, enjoyed a stunning economic recovery in the mid- to late 1990s, and then experienced another recession in 2001—a recession from which we are still recovering. Through the ups and downs, the average household has held a surprisingly steady course. While spending grew strongly at the national level during the decade, it rose more moderately at the household level. This caution served Americans well, insulating their day-to-day lives from the economy's wild gyrations.

During the 1990s, consumer spending at the national level showed strong gains not only because of population and household growth but also because the baby-boom generation entered the peak-spending age groups. While spending at the aggregate level soared, spending by the average household rose more slowly. In 2002, spending by the average household was only 5 percent greater than in 1997, after adjusting for inflation. The average household spent $40,677 in 2002, up from $38,904 in 1997.

Between 1997 and 2002, average household spending increased in a number of discretionary categories. Spending on food away from home (primarily restaurant and carry-out meals) rose 6 percent. Spending on alcoholic beverages was up 9 percent. Spending on "other lodging" (primarily hotels and motels) increased 6 percent. Entertainment spending climbed 3 percent. Spending on new cars and trucks was up a substantial 28 percent in response to low- and no-interest loans. But some discretionary spending categories experienced declines. Average household spending on furniture was down 7 percent between 1997 and 2002, after adjusting for inflation. Spending on clothes fell 9 percent.

Average household spending on life's necessities also increased over the five-year period. The average household spent 14 percent more on property taxes in 2002 than in 1997, 3 percent more on water and other public services, 6 percent more on vehicle insurance, 19 percent more on out-of-pocket health insurance costs, 36 percent more on drugs, and 18 percent more on education. Property tax is now Americans' fifth biggest expenditure, and health insurance ranks seventh. (See Appendix D for a ranking of expenditures in 2002.)

Analyzing spending trends at the individual household level, as *Household Spending* does, provides deeper insight into the nation's economic ups and downs than any examination of aggregate figures. Unfortunately, the complexity of household spending statistics discourages many from tackling the job of analyzing the data. It's much easier to analyze spending at the national level because it requires an examination of only two figures—today's and yesterday's. But analyzing trends in spending at the household level requires delving into the who, what, and why of spending—the mindset and motivations of individual consumers. The ninth edition of *Household Spending* is for those who want to know the who, what, and why.

Consumer spending is the result of a complex mix of wants and needs, hopes and fears. This mix determines the success of individual businesses and the health of our economy. Knowing how consumers spend their dollars is key to understanding the our economy is headed, an insight of immense value as the nation copes with uncertainty.

How to Use This Book

Household Spending is based on unpublished data collected by the Bureau of Labor Statistics' Consumer Expenditure Survey, an ongoing, nationwide survey of household spending. The editors of New Strategist start with the average spending figures collected by the Bureau of Labor Statistics and analyze them in a variety of ways, calculating household spending indexes, aggregate (or total) spending, and market shares. We do this for hundreds of spending categories by age of householder, household income, household type, race and Hispanic origin of householder, region of residence, and educational attainment of householder.

The Bureau of Labor Statistics' Consumer Expenditure Survey, a complete accounting of household expenditures, includes everything from big-ticket items such as homes and cars to small purchases like laundry detergent and film. The survey does not include expenditures by government, business, or institutions. The lag time between data collection and publication is about two years. The data in this book are from the 2002 Consumer Expenditure Survey, unless otherwise noted.

The Consumer Expenditure Survey uses "consumer unit" as its sampling unit. The Bureau of Labor Statistics defines consumer unit as "a single person or group of persons in a sample household related by blood, marriage, adoption, or other legal arrangement or who share responsibility for at least two out of three major types of expenses—food, housing, and other expenses." For convenience, consumer units are referred to as households in the text of this book. For more information about the Consumer Expenditure Survey and consumer units, see Appendix A.

Chapter 1 of *Household Spending* is devoted to summary household spending statistics. These are shown for the following consumer segments: age, income, age by income, household type, region, region by income, metros by region, race and Hispanic origin, education, household size, homeowners and renters, number of earners, and occupation.

Chapters 2 through 11 present detailed spending statistics organized by major product and service category (food, housing, transportation, and so on) and include all typical household expenditures. Within each chapter, spending statistics are shown by age of householder, household income, household type, race and Hispanic origin of householder, region of residence, and educational attainment of householder. For each of the demographic variables, tables show average spending, indexed spending, total (or aggregate) spending, and share of spending.

How to Use the Tables in This Book

The data in *Household Spending* reveal how American households allocate their spending dollars. The starting point for all calculations in *Household Spending* are the unpublished detailed average household spending data collected by the Consumer Expenditure Survey. These are shown in the average spending tables in chapters 2 through 11. The remaining tables in each chapter were produced by New Strategist's statisticians and are based on the average figures. The indexed spending tables reveal whether spending by households in a given segment is above or below the average for all households (or for all households in that segment), and by how much. The total (or aggregate) spending tables show the overall size of a particular market. The market share tables reveal how much spending in a market is accounted for by a household segment. These four types of tables are described in detail below.

• **Average Spending Tables** The average spending tables report the average annual spending of households on each item or category of items in 2002. The Consumer Expenditure Survey produces average spending data for all households in a segment, e.g., all households with a householder aged 25 to 34, not just for those who purchased an item. When reviewing the spending data, it is important to remember that by including both purchasers and nonpurchasers in the calculation, the average is diluted—especially for infrequently purchased items. For example, the average household spent $211 on day care centers in 2002. Since only a small percentage of households spend money on day care, this figure greatly underestimates the amount spent on day care centers by those who make use of them. To get a more realistic idea of how much buyers spend on an item, Appendix C shows the percentage of households purchasing individual products and services during an average quarter of 2002, and the amount spent by purchasers per quarter. According to Appendix C, only 6 percent of households spent on day care centers during an average quarter of 2002. The purchasers spent an average of $883 per quarter, for an estimated annual cost of $3,534— a much more realistic figure than the average of $211 for all households.

For frequently purchased items—such as bread—the average spending figures give a fairly accurate account of actual spending. But for most of the products and services examined in *Household Spending*, the average spending figures are less revealing than the indexes and market shares.

Average spending figures are useful in determining the market potential of a product or service in a local area. By multiplying the average amount married couples spend on children's clothing by the number of married couples in the Pittsburgh metropolitan area, for example, marketers can estimate the size of the market for children's clothing in Pittsburgh. The Pittsburgh media could show those figures to potential advertisers as evidence of the local demand for children's clothing.

Note that because of sampling errors, average values can vary—especially for infrequently purchased items. To examine the standard errors associated with summary average spending figures (Chapter 1), go to http://www.bls.gov/cex/csxstnderror.htm. To examine the standard errors associated with detailed average spending data, contact the Bureau of Labor Statistics Consumer Expenditure Survey statisticians by phone at 202-691-6900 or by email at cexinfo@bls.gov.

• **Indexed Spending Tables** The indexed spending tables compare the spending of each household segment with that of the average household. To compute the indexes, New Strategist's statisticians divide the average amount each household segment spends on a particular item by how much the average household spends on the item, then multiply the resulting figure by 100. An index of 100 is thus the average for all households. An index of 125 means the spending of a household segment is 25 percent above average (100 plus 25). An index of 75 indicates spending that is 25 percent below the average for all households (100 minus 25). Indexed spending figures identify the best customers for a product or service. Households with an index of 177 for outdoor furniture, for example, are a strong market for that product. Those with an index below 100 are either a weak or an underserved market.

Spending indexes can reveal hidden markets—household segments with a high propensity to buy a particular product or service but which are overshadowed by larger household segments that account for a bigger share of the total market. Householders aged 55 to 64, for example, spend 40 percent more than the average household on magazine subscriptions (with an index of 140). This is a higher index than that of any other age group, making householders aged 55 to 64 the best customers of this item. Householders aged 35 to 44 spend 14 percent less than average on magazine subscriptions (with an index of 86), meaning they are a weaker or underserved market for this product. But the market share of 35-to-44-year-olds is equally as large as that of 55-to-64-year-olds (19 percent) because there are more households in the younger age group. Using the indexed spending tables, marketers can see that older householders are in fact their better customers and adjust their business strategy accordingly.

Note that because of sampling errors, small differences in index values usually are not statistically significant. But the broader patterns revealed by indexes can guide marketers to the best customers.

• **Total Spending Tables** To produce the total spending tables, New Strategist's statisticians multiplied average spending figures by the number of households in a segment. The result is the dollar size of the total household market and of each market segment. All totals are shown in thousands of dollars. To convert the numbers in the total spending tables to dollars, you must append "000" to the number. For example, households headed by people aged 45 to 54 spent approximately $10.6 billion ($10,559,938,000) on alcoholic beverages in 2002.

When comparing the total spending figures in *Household Spending* with total spending estimates from the Bureau of Economic Analysis, other government agencies, or trade associations, keep in mind that the Consumer Expenditure Survey includes only household spending, not spending by businesses or institutions. Sales data also will differ from household spending totals because sales figures for consumer products include the value of goods sold to industries, government, and foreign markets, which can be a significant proportion of sales.

• **Market Share Tables** New Strategist's statisticians produced the market share tables by converting total spending data to percentages. To calculate the percentage of total spending on an item that is controlled by a demographic segment—i.e., its market share—each segment's total spending on the item was divided by aggregate household spending on the item.

Market shares reveal the biggest customers—the demographic segments that account for the largest share of household spending on a particular product or service. In 2002, for example, married couples without children at home (most of them empty-nesters) accounted for 56 percent of total household spending on ship fares. The cruise industry could reach most of its customers if it targeted only this demographic segment. Of course, by single-mindedly targeting the biggest customers, businesses cannot nurture potential growth markets. An additional danger of focusing only on the biggest customers is that businesses can end up ignoring their best customers. This is especially problematic because market shares are unstable, thanks to baby booms and busts over the past half-century. Right now, for example, the biggest customers of new cars are householders aged 35 to 44. They account for 25 percent of total household spending on this item because the age group is filled with the large baby-boom generation. But in fact the best customers of new cars are older householders. Those aged 55 to 64 spend 30 percent more than average on this item versus an index of 113 for 35-to-44-year-olds. Although the older age group accounts for a smaller 18 percent of the market today, as the large baby-boom generation ages that share will expand. The best customers of new cars will then become the biggest customers as well. Marketers who ignore their best customers in favor of the biggest customers may end up with no customers.

For More Information

The ninth edition of *Household Spending* offers researchers a detailed analysis of the voluminous and unpublished spending data collected by the Bureau of Labor Statistics. It provides a convenient way to compare and contrast spending on goods and services by demographic characteristics such as age of householder or household type. For more about the Consumer Expenditure Survey, visit the Bureau of Labor Statistics web site (http://www.bls.gov/cex/), where summary average spending figures (as shown in chapter 1 of this book) are available online. The detailed average spending numbers (as shown in chapters 2 through 11) are available only by special request.

To examine spending by individual product category, see the new third edition of New Strategist's *Best Customers: Demographics of Consumer Demand*, which profiles household spending on more than three-hundred product and service categories, including an analysis of past and future trends. To see household spending trends for single product categories, see New Strategist's *Who's Buying* reports.

To find out more about these books and reports, including examination of tables of contents and sample pages, visit New Strategist's web site at http://www.newstrategist.com. All New Strategist books and reports are available as downloads or in print.

Spending Overview

Spending Trends: 1997 to 2002

Between 1997 and 2002, spending by the average household grew 5 percent to $40,677, after adjusting for inflation. The increase in spending was much less than the 11 percent growth in household income during those years. While the media frequently claim that consumers spend beyond their means, in fact the steady rise in consumer spending at the national level is primarily the result of demographic change—the combination of population growth and the aging of the baby-boom generation into its peak earning and spending years.

American households have been cutting their spending on discretionary items for years as nondiscretionary expenses claim an ever-growing share of the household budget. The food-away-from-home category is one of the few bright spots. Average household spending on restaurant and take-out meals rose 6 percent between 1997 and 2002, after adjusting for inflation. But spending on groceries (food at home) fell 4 percent during that time. Spending on apparel dropped 9 percent between 1997 and 2002, furniture was down 7 percent, public transportation (mostly airfares) declined 11 percent, and reading material plummeted 24 percent.

Americans cut back on many discretionary purchases because their nondiscretionary expenses—the spending they cannot control—was on the rise. After adjusting for inflation, the average household spent 14 percent more on property taxes in 2002 than in 1997. Mortgage interest expenses were up 19 percent despite falling interest rates because of the surge in homeownership. Out-of-pocket spending on health insurance increased 19 percent, and drug spending climbed 36 percent. Spending on vehicle insurance rose 6 percent. Spending on water and other public services increased 3 percent. Spending on education saw an 18 percent increase.

Contrary to popular perception, Americans are cautious spenders at the individual household level. Older Americans learned the lesson of caution during the Depression. Boomers learned to be cautious during the recession of the early 1990s, and the booming economy that followed failed to convince most of them to spend beyond their means. The recession of 2001 and the sluggish recovery have reinforced the economic conservatism of the average household, hurting the bottom line of many businesses that provide discretionary products and services.

During the next few years, the United States will experience yet another dramatic demographic shift as the enormous baby-boom generation will become empty-nesters and move out of the peak earning and spending age groups. The aging of boomers will tighten household budgets even more, and the U.S. economy will have to adapt.

Table 1.1 Spending Trends, 1997 to 2002

(average annual spending of consumer units (CU) by product and service category, 1997, 2000, and 2002; percent change 1997–2002 and 2000–2002; in 2002 dollars)

	2002	2000	1997	percent change 2000–2002	percent change 1997–2002
Number of consumer units (in thousands, add 000)	112,108	109,367	105,576	2.5%	6.2%
Average income before taxes	$49,430	$46,625	$44,610	6.0	10.8
Average annual spending	40,677	39,729	38,904	2.4	4.6
FOOD	$5,375	$5,386	$5,364	−0.2%	0.2%
Food at home	3,099	3,155	3,218	−1.8	−3.7
Cereals and bakery products	450	473	506	−4.9	−11.1
Cereals and cereal products	154	163	180	−5.5	−14.4
Bakery products	296	310	326	−4.6	−9.3
Meats, poultry, fish, and eggs	798	830	830	−3.9	−3.9
Beef	231	249	250	−7.1	−7.7
Pork	167	174	175	−4.2	−4.8
Other meats	101	105	107	−4.2	−5.8
Poultry	144	151	162	−4.9	−11.1
Fish and seafood	121	115	99	5.3	21.7
Eggs	34	36	37	−4.2	−7.8
Dairy products	328	339	351	−3.4	−6.5
Fresh milk and cream	127	137	143	−7.2	−11.2
Other dairy products	201	202	208	−0.3	−3.3
Fruits and vegetables	552	544	532	1.5	3.8
Fresh fruits	178	170	168	4.6	6.2
Fresh vegetables	175	166	160	5.4	9.5
Processed fruits	116	120	114	−3.4	1.8
Processed vegetables	83	88	89	−5.4	−7.1
Other food at home	970	968	1,000	0.2	−3.0
Sugar and other sweets	117	122	127	−4.2	−8.1
Fats and oils	85	87	91	−1.9	−6.1
Miscellaneous foods	472	456	450	3.4	4.8
Nonalcoholic beverages	254	261	274	−2.7	−7.2
Food prepared by CU on trips	41	42	58	−1.8	−29.4
Food away from home	2,276	2,232	2,146	2.0	6.0
ALCOHOLIC BEVERAGES	376	388	345	−3.2	8.9
HOUSING	13,283	12,864	12,594	3.3	5.5
Shelter	7,829	7,429	7,088	5.4	10.4
Owned dwellings	5,165	4,806	4,397	7.5	17.5
Mortgage interest and charges	2,962	2,756	2,486	7.5	19.1
Property taxes	1,242	1,189	1,085	4.4	14.5
Maintenance, repair, insurance, other expenses	960	862	825	11.4	16.4
Rented dwellings	2,160	2,124	2,216	1.7	−2.5
Other lodging	505	499	476	1.2	6.1
Utilities, fuels, and public services	2,684	2,599	2,695	3.3	−0.4
Natural gas	330	321	336	2.9	−1.9
Electricity	981	951	1,016	3.1	−3.4
Fuel oil and other fuels	88	101	121	−13.1	−27.1
Telephone	957	916	904	4.5	5.9
Water and other public services	328	309	320	6.1	2.6

	2002	2000	1997	percent change 2000–2002	percent change 1997–2002
Household services	**$706**	**$714**	**$612**	**−1.2%**	**15.3%**
Personal services	331	340	294	−2.8	12.6
Other household services	375	374	318	0.3	17.8
Housekeeping supplies	**545**	**503**	**508**	**8.3**	**7.2**
Laundry and cleaning supplies	131	137	130	−4.2	1.1
Other household products	283	236	235	19.9	20.6
Postage and stationery	131	132	144	−0.4	−9.1
Household furnishings and equipment	**1,518**	**1,618**	**1,689**	**−6.2**	**−10.1**
Household textiles	136	111	88	22.9	54.1
Furniture	401	408	432	−1.8	−7.3
Floor coverings	40	46	87	−12.9	−54.1
Major appliances	188	197	189	−4.7	−0.4
Small appliances, misc. housewares	100	91	103	10.1	−2.7
Miscellaneous household equipment	652	763	790	−14.6	−17.5
APPAREL AND RELATED SERVICES	**1,749**	**1,938**	**1,932**	**−9.8**	**−9.5**
Men and boys	**409**	**459**	**455**	**−11.0**	**−10.1**
Men, aged 16 or older	319	359	361	−11.2	−11.6
Boys, aged 2 to 15	90	100	94	−10.2	−4.1
Women and girls	**704**	**757**	**760**	**−7.0**	**−7.3**
Women, aged 16 or older	587	634	641	−7.4	−8.5
Girls, aged 2 to 15	117	123	118	−5.0	−1.2
Children under age 2	**83**	**86**	**86**	**−3.1**	**−3.5**
Footwear	**313**	**358**	**352**	**−12.6**	**−11.1**
Other apparel products and services	**240**	**278**	**279**	**−13.6**	**−14.1**
TRANSPORTATION	**7,759**	**7,745**	**7,215**	**0.2**	**7.5**
Vehicle purchases	**3,665**	**3,569**	**3,057**	**2.7**	**19.9**
Cars and trucks, new	1,753	1,676	1,373	4.6	27.7
Cars and trucks, used	1,842	1,848	1,636	−0.3	12.6
Other vehicles	70	45	48	55.9	45.7
Gasoline and motor oil	**1,235**	**1,348**	**1,227**	**−8.4**	**0.7**
Other vehicle expenses	**2,471**	**2,382**	**2,492**	**3.7**	**−0.8**
Vehicle finance charges	397	343	327	15.9	21.3
Maintenance and repairs	697	652	762	7.0	−8.5
Vehicle insurance	894	812	844	10.0	6.0
Vehicle rentals, leases, licenses, other charges	483	575	560	−16.1	−13.7
Public transportation	**389**	**446**	**439**	**−12.8**	**−11.4**
HEALTH CARE	**2,350**	**2,157**	**2,057**	**8.9**	**14.2**
Health insurance	1,168	1,027	984	13.8	18.7
Medical services	590	593	593	−0.5	−0.6
Drugs	487	434	358	12.1	36.2
Medical supplies	105	103	121	1.6	−13.0
ENTERTAINMENT	**2,079**	**1,945**	**2,026**	**6.9**	**2.6**
Fees and admissions	542	538	526	0.8	3.0
Television, radio, sound equipment	692	650	645	6.5	7.3
Pets, toys, and playground equipment	369	349	365	5.8	1.0
Other entertainment products and services	476	410	491	16.0	−3.0
PERSONAL CARE PRODUCTS AND SERVICES	**526**	**589**	**590**	**−10.7**	**−10.8**
READING	**139**	**152**	**183**	**−8.8**	**−24.1**
EDUCATION	**752**	**660**	**638**	**13.9**	**17.9**

	2002	2000	1997	percent change 2000–2002	percent change 1997–2002
TOBACCO PRODUCTS AND SMOKING SUPPLIES	$320	$333	$295	−3.9%	8.5%
MISCELLANEOUS	792	810	946	−2.3	−16.3
CASH CONTRIBUTIONS	1,277	1,245	1,118	2.6	14.2
PERSONAL INSURANCE AND PENSIONS	3,899	3,514	3,601	11.0	8.3
Life and other personal insurance	406	417	423	−2.6	−4.1
Pensions and Social Security	3,493	3,097	3,178	12.8	9.9
PERSONAL TAXES	2,496	3,255	3,621	−23.3	−31.1
Federal income taxes	1,843	2,516	2,758	−26.7	−33.2
State and local income taxes	506	587	721	−13.8	−29.8
Other taxes	147	152	144	−3.6	2.0
GIFTS FOR NON–HOUSEHOLD MEMBERS	1,036	1,131	1,183	−8.4	−12.4
Food	82	73	76	12.2	7.9
Alcoholic beverages	13	15	–	−11.1	–
Housing	259	304	305	−14.8	−15.1
Housekeeping supplies	42	41	41	3.1	1.6
Household textiles	14	14	9	3.1	56.6
Appliances and misc. housewares	24	29	30	−17.9	−20.4
Major appliances	8	8	7	−4.2	19.3
Small appliances and misc. housewares	16	22	23	−27.0	−31.8
Miscellaneous household equipment	65	73	74	−11.1	−11.9
Other housing	114	146	151	−22.0	−24.4
Apparel and services	237	255	282	−7.0	−15.8
Males, aged 2 or older	64	71	68	−9.9	−6.1
Females, aged 2 or older	82	89	91	−7.6	−9.4
Children under age 2	40	43	37	−6.6	8.5
Other apparel products and services	52	53	86	−2.4	−39.6
Jewelry and watches	24	21	55	14.9	−56.2
All other apparel products and services	28	31	32	−10.6	−13.6
Transportation	44	73	64	−39.8	−30.9
Health care	33	40	34	−16.8	−1.6
Entertainment	78	98	111	−20.5	−29.5
Toys, games, hobbies, and tricycles	30	31	46	−4.2	−34.5
Other entertainment	48	67	65	−28.2	−25.9
Personal care products and services	21	20	–	5.8	–
Reading	1	2	–	−52.1	–
Education	184	158	173	16.7	6.2
All other gifts	84	93	140	−9.6	−39.9

Note: The Bureau of Labor Statistics uses consumer unit rather than household as the sampling unit in the Consumer Expenditure Survey. For the definition of consumer unit, see the glossary. Spending by category will not add to total spending because gift spending is also included in the preceding product and service categories and personal taxes are not included in the total. (−) means data not available.
Source: Bureau of Labor Statistics, 1997, 2000, and 2002 Consumer Expenditure Surveys, Internet site http://www.bls.gov/cex/; calculations by New Strategist

Spending by Age, 2002

The average household spent $40,677 in 2002, but some spent more while others spent less. Because spending rises with income, affluent householders spend the most. Householders aged 45 to 54 are in their peak earning years, which explains why they spent 20 percent more than the average household in 2002, the highest level of spending among all age groups. Householders aged 35 to 44 were not far behind, with spending 19 percent above average.

Households headed by people under age 25 and aged 75 or older spend the least because their incomes are lowest. Householders under age 25 spend just 60 percent as much as the average household, while householders aged 75 or older spend 58 percent as much as the average.

Householders aged 45 to 54 spend more than other age groups on many products and services, including alcoholic beverages, household furnishings, men's clothing, education, and gifts for non–household members.

Householders aged 35 to 44 spend the most on food, entertainment, and children's clothes. Householders aged 25 to 34 spend the most on infants' apparel. Spending on other lodging and public transportation is highest in the 55-to-64 age group. Households headed by people aged 65 or older spend the most on health care, including the individual categories of health insurance and drugs.

With the early retirement trend coming to an end, look for the two-earner couples of the baby-boom generation to boost spending by householders aged 55 to 64 in the years ahead.

Table 1.2 Average spending by age of householder, 2002

(average annual spending of consumer units (CU) by product and service category and age of consumer unit reference person, 2002)

	total CUs	under 25	25 to 34	35 to 44	45 to 54	55 to 64	aged 65 or older total	65 to 74	75 or older
Number of consumer units (in thousands, add 000)	112,108	8,737	18,988	24,394	22,691	15,314	21,983	11,216	10,767
Average number of persons per CU	2.5	1.9	2.9	3.2	2.7	2.1	1.7	1.9	1.5
Average income before taxes	$49,430	$20,773	$49,133	$61,532	$64,974	$53,162	$29,711	$35,118	$23,890
Average annual spending	40,677	24,229	40,318	48,330	48,748	44,330	28,105	32,243	23,759
FOOD	$5,375	$3,621	$5,471	$6,314	$6,228	$5,559	$3,910	$4,479	$3,302
Food at home	3,099	1,926	3,093	3,601	3,528	3,114	2,548	2,877	2,195
Cereals and bakery products	450	287	442	542	500	423	386	418	352
Cereals and cereal products	154	113	163	191	169	133	120	128	112
Bakery products	296	174	279	351	332	290	266	290	240
Meats, poultry, fish, and eggs	798	460	817	918	929	807	641	745	529
Beef	231	131	253	271	273	216	174	208	138
Pork	167	95	162	198	188	169	144	169	117
Other meats	101	52	96	122	117	103	84	97	70
Poultry	144	96	159	164	168	134	110	123	96
Fish and seafood	121	61	113	126	146	154	98	115	79
Eggs	34	24	34	38	37	32	30	33	28
Dairy products	328	200	324	392	367	325	274	301	244
Fresh milk and cream	127	87	130	153	136	121	107	112	102
Other dairy products	201	113	195	238	232	204	167	189	142
Fruits and vegetables	552	338	522	597	627	591	510	556	461
Fresh fruits	178	105	154	191	204	207	169	185	152
Fresh vegetables	175	100	162	185	205	191	163	176	149
Processed fruits	116	81	118	128	127	113	103	108	97
Processed vegetables	83	53	88	93	91	81	75	87	63
Other food at home	970	640	988	1,153	1,106	967	738	858	609
Sugar and other sweets	117	64	104	139	130	125	108	125	90
Fats and oils	85	47	81	93	99	90	78	90	66
Miscellaneous foods	472	344	512	572	531	434	340	392	283
Nonalcoholic beverages	254	160	260	303	296	265	178	207	148
Food prepared by CU on trips	41	25	31	46	49	54	33	45	22
Food away from home	2,276	1,696	2,378	2,712	2,700	2,445	1,362	1,602	1,107
ALCOHOLIC BEVERAGES	376	394	395	367	465	420	237	324	144
HOUSING	13,283	7,436	13,727	16,350	15,476	13,831	9,176	10,052	8,257
Shelter	7,829	4,851	8,470	9,902	9,223	7,667	4,834	5,299	4,350
Owned dwellings	5,165	830	4,701	7,105	6,787	5,595	3,162	3,849	2,447
Mortgage interest and charges	2,962	443	3,286	4,608	4,061	2,712	897	1,366	408
Property taxes	1,242	281	823	1,473	1,557	1,540	1,199	1,299	1,095
Maintenance, repair, insurance, other expenses	960	106	592	1,024	1,169	1,343	1,066	1,183	944
Rented dwellings	2,160	3,644	3,476	2,351	1,733	1,303	1,259	905	1,627
Other lodging	505	377	293	446	704	770	413	545	275
Utilities, fuels, and public services	2,684	1,348	2,503	3,026	3,106	2,953	2,371	2,590	2,142
Natural gas	330	108	288	369	383	355	338	336	339
Electricity	981	471	864	1,105	1,138	1,112	894	985	799
Fuel oil and other fuels	88	21	55	86	90	127	119	115	123
Telephone	957	641	1,032	1,096	1,109	981	689	794	579
Water and other public services	328	108	263	369	387	378	331	360	302

	total CUs	under 25	25 to 34	35 to 44	45 to 54	55 to 64	aged 65 or older total	65 to 74	75 or older
Household services	**$706**	**$198**	**$895**	**$1,010**	**$613**	**$561**	**$602**	**$486**	**$723**
Personal services	331	99	650	580	165	79	218	79	363
Other household services	375	99	245	430	448	481	384	407	360
Housekeeping supplies	**545**	**226**	**389**	**589**	**633**	**838**	**466**	**547**	**379**
Laundry and cleaning supplies	131	77	125	152	147	139	110	132	85
Other household products	283	95	173	295	333	538	213	250	172
Postage and stationery	131	54	92	142	153	161	143	164	121
Household furnishings and equipment	**1,518**	**812**	**1,469**	**1,823**	**1,900**	**1,811**	**903**	**1,131**	**663**
Household textiles	136	93	128	137	152	183	106	127	84
Furniture	401	170	472	524	453	484	186	242	127
Floor coverings	40	8	30	44	59	53	30	33	27
Major appliances	188	88	148	252	219	220	139	168	108
Small appliances, misc. housewares	100	76	109	88	124	134	68	93	42
Miscellaneous household equipment	652	377	583	776	893	738	374	467	274
APPAREL AND RELATED SERVICES	**1,749**	**1,365**	**1,989**	**2,101**	**2,029**	**1,791**	**972**	**1,252**	**674**
Men and boys	**409**	**266**	**486**	**562**	**477**	**337**	**208**	**285**	**126**
Men, aged 16 or older	319	230	367	383	391	297	182	252	108
Boys, aged 2 to 15	90	36	119	179	85	40	26	33	18
Women and girls	**704**	**609**	**647**	**787**	**850**	**840**	**450**	**558**	**335**
Women, aged 16 or older	587	559	511	540	732	788	424	523	318
Girls, aged 2 to 15	117	50	136	247	118	52	26	35	17
Children under age 2	**83**	**102**	**188**	**97**	**51**	**49**	**21**	**27**	**15**
Footwear	**313**	**246**	**385**	**382**	**365**	**290**	**160**	**208**	**108**
Other apparel products and services	**240**	**142**	**283**	**273**	**286**	**276**	**133**	**175**	**90**
TRANSPORTATION	**7,759**	**5,102**	**8,423**	**9,400**	**9,173**	**8,449**	**4,481**	**5,731**	**3,178**
Vehicle purchases	**3,665**	**2,635**	**4,269**	**4,592**	**4,203**	**3,882**	**1,818**	**2,430**	**1,180**
Cars and trucks, new	1,753	664	1,739	2,394	1,966	2,080	1,038	1,352	712
Cars and trucks, used	1,842	1,917	2,454	2,115	2,109	1,763	761	1,043	468
Other vehicles	70	54	75	83	128	39	18	35	–
Gasoline and motor oil	**1,235**	**903**	**1,257**	**1,473**	**1,495**	**1,292**	**777**	**970**	**575**
Other vehicle expenses	**2,471**	**1,339**	**2,505**	**2,935**	**3,055**	**2,735**	**1,586**	**1,945**	**1,212**
Vehicle finance charges	397	217	516	529	479	370	153	217	87
Maintenance and repairs	697	394	609	843	848	832	482	553	408
Vehicle insurance	894	479	872	987	1,125	991	666	799	528
Vehicle rentals, leases, licenses, other charges	483	249	508	576	603	542	284	376	189
Public transportation	**389**	**225**	**392**	**400**	**421**	**540**	**300**	**386**	**211**
HEALTH CARE	**2,350**	**640**	**1,417**	**1,980**	**2,550**	**3,007**	**3,586**	**3,588**	**3,584**
Health insurance	1,168	285	762	1,023	1,180	1,356	1,886	1,921	1,849
Medical services	590	196	391	556	768	863	582	635	527
Drugs	487	130	209	303	490	659	955	884	1,028
Medical supplies	105	30	55	99	112	129	163	148	179
ENTERTAINMENT	**2,079**	**1,212**	**2,027**	**2,685**	**2,565**	**2,297**	**1,139**	**1,371**	**896**
Fees and admissions	542	313	490	743	662	584	301	382	216
Television, radio, sound equipment	692	457	750	817	806	717	461	546	372
Pets, toys, and playground equipment	369	193	368	463	466	420	200	262	135
Other entertainment products and services	476	249	420	662	631	577	177	181	173
PERSONAL CARE PRODUCTS AND SERVICES	**526**	**329**	**488**	**615**	**588**	**557**	**451**	**509**	**390**
READING	**139**	**57**	**103**	**135**	**167**	**181**	**147**	**161**	**134**
EDUCATION	**752**	**1,664**	**571**	**738**	**1,208**	**589**	**202**	**289**	**112**

	total CUs	under 25	25 to 34	35 to 44	45 to 54	55 to 64	aged 65 or older total	65 to 74	75 or older
TOBACCO PRODUCTS AND SMOKING SUPPLIES	$320	$286	$315	$376	$415	$361	$152	$220	$81
MISCELLANEOUS	792	422	678	841	989	930	686	794	572
CASH CONTRIBUTIONS	1,277	319	743	1,247	1,571	1,520	1,679	1,620	1,740
PERSONAL INSURANCE AND PENSIONS	3,899	1,382	3,972	5,183	5,323	4,838	1,286	1,853	696
Life and other personal insurance	406	51	230	409	559	595	407	521	287
Pensions and Social Security	3,493	1,331	3,742	4,774	4,764	4,243	880	1,332	409
PERSONAL TAXES	2,496	567	2,259	3,075	4,051	2,856	1,037	1,556	479
Federal income taxes	1,843	402	1,642	2,258	3,052	2,136	725	1,111	310
State and local income taxes	506	149	546	680	798	493	144	230	51
Other taxes	147	16	71	136	201	227	169	215	118
GIFTS FOR NON–HOUSEHOLD MEMBERS	1,036	437	688	868	1,604	1,531	832	1,089	560
Food	82	27	34	60	153	152	49	61	37
Alcoholic beverages	13	15	13	16	14	13	10	17	3
Housing	259	104	213	231	387	334	206	268	139
Housekeeping supplies	42	24	32	41	51	55	43	56	29
Household textiles	14	2	13	11	14	29	12	18	5
Appliances and misc. housewares	24	13	12	17	28	54	22	32	11
Major appliances	8	–	2	7	9	27	5	8	2
Small appliances and misc. housewares	16	13	10	9	20	27	16	23	9
Miscellaneous household equipment	65	24	45	65	94	85	53	75	29
Other housing	114	42	111	98	199	111	76	88	65
Apparel and services	237	170	249	208	257	341	193	251	132
Males, aged 2 or older	64	55	56	63	69	74	62	89	34
Females, aged 2 or older	82	37	72	56	89	158	77	88	65
Children under age 2	40	34	57	45	40	41	20	26	15
Other apparel products and services	52	44	65	44	59	68	33	48	18
Jewelry and watches	24	13	44	20	23	33	11	15	6
All other apparel products and services	28	32	21	23	36	35	23	33	12
Transportation	44	15	22	45	80	70	17	11	24
Health care	33	1	11	21	55	55	39	40	37
Entertainment	78	30	60	86	106	107	56	73	38
Toys, games, hobbies, and tricycles	30	11	20	29	36	50	27	38	15
Other entertainment	48	19	40	57	69	57	29	35	23
Personal care products and services	21	13	16	27	26	17	21	31	10
Reading	1	–	1	1	1	2	3	3	3
Education	184	43	27	108	415	293	146	194	96
All other gifts	84	18	42	67	112	145	93	140	43

Note: Spending by category will not add to total spending because gift spending is also included in the preceding product and service categories and personal taxes are not included in the total. (–) means sample is too small to make a reliable estimate.
Source: Bureau of Labor Statistics, 2002 Consumer Expenditure Survey, Internet site http://www.bls.gov/cex/

Table 1.3 Indexed spending by age of householder, 2002

(indexed average annual spending of consumer units (CU) by product and service category and age of consumer unit reference person, 2002; index definition: an index of 100 is the average for all consumer units; an index of 132 means that spending by consumer units in that group is 32 percent above the average for all consumer units; an index of 68 indicates spending that is 32 percent below the average for all consumer units)

	total CUs	under 25	25 to 34	35 to 44	45 to 54	55 to 64	aged 65 or older total	65 to 74	75 or older
Average spending of CU, total	$40,677	$24,229	$40,318	$48,330	$48,748	$44,330	$28,105	$32,243	$23,759
Average spending of CU, index	100	60	99	119	120	109	69	79	58
FOOD	100	67	102	117	116	103	73	83	61
Food at home	100	62	100	116	114	100	82	93	71
Cereals and bakery products	100	64	98	120	111	94	86	93	78
Cereals and cereal products	100	73	106	124	110	86	78	83	73
Bakery products	100	59	94	119	112	98	90	98	81
Meats, poultry, fish, and eggs	100	58	102	115	116	101	80	93	66
Beef	100	57	110	117	118	94	75	90	60
Pork	100	57	97	119	113	101	86	101	70
Other meats	100	51	95	121	116	102	83	96	69
Poultry	100	67	110	114	117	93	76	85	67
Fish and seafood	100	50	93	104	121	127	81	95	65
Eggs	100	71	100	112	109	94	88	97	82
Dairy products	100	61	99	120	112	99	84	92	74
Fresh milk and cream	100	69	102	120	107	95	84	88	80
Other dairy products	100	56	97	118	115	101	83	94	71
Fruits and vegetables	100	61	95	108	114	107	92	101	84
Fresh fruits	100	59	87	107	115	116	95	104	85
Fresh vegetables	100	57	93	106	117	109	93	101	85
Processed fruits	100	70	102	110	109	97	89	93	84
Processed vegetables	100	64	106	112	110	98	90	105	76
Other food at home	100	66	102	119	114	100	76	88	63
Sugar and other sweets	100	55	89	119	111	107	92	107	77
Fats and oils	100	55	95	109	116	106	92	106	78
Miscellaneous foods	100	73	108	121	113	92	72	83	60
Nonalcoholic beverages	100	63	102	119	117	104	70	81	58
Food prepared by CU on trips	100	61	76	112	120	132	80	110	54
Food away from home	100	75	104	119	119	107	60	70	49
ALCOHOLIC BEVERAGES	100	105	105	98	124	112	63	86	38
HOUSING	100	56	103	123	117	104	69	76	62
Shelter	100	62	108	126	118	98	62	68	56
Owned dwellings	100	16	91	138	131	108	61	75	47
Mortgage interest and charges	100	15	111	156	137	92	30	46	14
Property taxes	100	23	66	119	125	124	97	105	88
Maintenance, repair, insurance, other expenses	100	11	62	107	122	140	111	123	98
Rented dwellings	100	169	161	109	80	60	58	42	75
Other lodging	100	75	58	88	139	152	82	108	54
Utilities, fuels, and public services	100	50	93	113	116	110	88	96	80
Natural gas	100	33	87	112	116	108	102	102	103
Electricity	100	48	88	113	116	113	91	100	81
Fuel oil and other fuels	100	24	63	98	102	144	135	131	140
Telephone	100	67	108	115	116	103	72	83	61
Water and other public services	100	33	80	113	118	115	101	110	92

							aged 65 or older		
	total CUs	under 25	25 to 34	35 to 44	45 to 54	55 to 64	total	65 to 74	75 or older
Household services	**100**	**28**	**127**	**143**	**87**	**79**	**85**	**69**	**102**
Personal services	100	30	196	175	50	24	66	24	110
Other household services	100	26	65	115	119	128	102	109	96
Housekeeping supplies	**100**	**41**	**71**	**108**	**116**	**154**	**86**	**100**	**70**
Laundry and cleaning supplies	100	59	95	116	112	106	84	101	65
Other household products	100	34	61	104	118	190	75	88	61
Postage and stationery	100	41	70	108	117	123	109	125	92
Household furnishings and equipment	**100**	**53**	**97**	**120**	**125**	**119**	**59**	**75**	**44**
Household textiles	100	68	94	101	112	135	78	93	62
Furniture	100	42	118	131	113	121	46	60	32
Floor coverings	100	20	75	110	148	133	75	83	68
Major appliances	100	47	79	134	116	117	74	89	57
Small appliances, misc. housewares	100	76	109	88	124	134	68	93	42
Miscellaneous household equipment	100	58	89	119	137	113	57	72	42
APPAREL AND RELATED SERVICES	**100**	**78**	**114**	**120**	**116**	**102**	**56**	**72**	**39**
Men and boys	**100**	**65**	**119**	**137**	**117**	**82**	**51**	**70**	**31**
Men, aged 16 or older	100	72	115	120	123	93	57	79	34
Boys, aged 2 to 15	100	40	132	199	94	44	29	37	20
Women and girls	**100**	**87**	**92**	**112**	**121**	**119**	**64**	**79**	**48**
Women, aged 16 or older	100	95	87	92	125	134	72	89	54
Girls, aged 2 to 15	100	43	116	211	101	44	22	30	15
Children under age 2	**100**	**123**	**227**	**117**	**61**	**59**	**25**	**33**	**18**
Footwear	**100**	**79**	**123**	**122**	**117**	**93**	**51**	**66**	**35**
Other apparel products and services	**100**	**59**	**118**	**114**	**119**	**115**	**55**	**73**	**38**
TRANSPORTATION	**100**	**66**	**109**	**121**	**118**	**109**	**58**	**74**	**41**
Vehicle purchases	**100**	**72**	**116**	**125**	**115**	**106**	**50**	**66**	**32**
Cars and trucks, new	100	38	99	137	112	119	59	77	41
Cars and trucks, used	100	104	133	115	114	96	41	57	25
Other vehicles	100	77	107	119	183	56	26	50	–
Gasoline and motor oil	**100**	**73**	**102**	**119**	**121**	**105**	**63**	**79**	**47**
Other vehicle expenses	**100**	**54**	**101**	**119**	**124**	**111**	**64**	**79**	**49**
Vehicle finance charges	100	55	130	133	121	93	39	55	22
Maintenance and repairs	100	57	87	121	122	119	69	79	59
Vehicle insurance	100	54	98	110	126	111	74	89	59
Vehicle rentals, leases, licenses, other charges	100	52	105	119	125	112	59	78	39
Public transportation	**100**	**58**	**101**	**103**	**108**	**139**	**77**	**99**	**54**
HEALTH CARE	**100**	**27**	**60**	**84**	**109**	**128**	**153**	**153**	**153**
Health insurance	100	24	65	88	101	116	161	164	158
Medical services	100	33	66	94	130	146	99	108	89
Drugs	100	27	43	62	101	135	196	182	211
Medical supplies	100	29	52	94	107	123	155	141	170
ENTERTAINMENT	**100**	**58**	**97**	**129**	**123**	**110**	**55**	**66**	**43**
Fees and admissions	100	58	90	137	122	108	56	70	40
Television, radio, sound equipment	100	66	108	118	116	104	67	79	54
Pets, toys, and playground equipment	100	52	100	125	126	114	54	71	37
Other entertainment products and services	100	52	88	139	133	121	37	38	36
PERSONAL CARE PRODUCTS AND SERVICES	**100**	**63**	**93**	**117**	**112**	**106**	**86**	**97**	**74**
READING	**100**	**41**	**74**	**97**	**120**	**130**	**106**	**116**	**96**
EDUCATION	**100**	**221**	**76**	**98**	**161**	**78**	**27**	**38**	**15**

| | total CUs | under 25 | 25 to 34 | 35 to 44 | 45 to 54 | 55 to 64 | aged 65 or older | | |
							total	65 to 74	75 or older
TOBACCO PRODUCTS AND SMOKING SUPPLIES	**100**	**89**	**98**	**118**	**130**	**113**	**48**	**69**	**25**
MISCELLANEOUS	**100**	**53**	**86**	**106**	**125**	**117**	**87**	**100**	**72**
CASH CONTRIBUTIONS	**100**	**25**	**58**	**98**	**123**	**119**	**131**	**127**	**136**
PERSONAL INSURANCE AND PENSIONS	**100**	**35**	**102**	**133**	**137**	**124**	**33**	**48**	**18**
Life and other personal insurance	100	13	57	101	138	147	100	128	71
Pensions and Social Security	100	38	107	137	136	121	25	38	12
PERSONAL TAXES	**100**	**23**	**91**	**123**	**162**	**114**	**42**	**62**	**19**
Federal income taxes	100	22	89	123	166	116	39	60	17
State and local income taxes	100	29	108	134	158	97	28	45	10
Other taxes	100	11	48	93	137	154	115	146	80
GIFTS FOR NON–HOUSEHOLD MEMBERS	**100**	**42**	**66**	**84**	**155**	**148**	**80**	**105**	**54**
Food	**100**	**33**	**41**	**73**	**187**	**185**	**60**	**74**	**45**
Alcoholic beverages	**100**	**115**	**100**	**123**	**108**	**100**	**77**	**131**	**23**
Housing	**100**	**40**	**82**	**89**	**149**	**129**	**80**	**103**	**54**
Housekeeping supplies	100	57	76	98	121	131	102	133	69
Household textiles	100	14	93	79	100	207	86	129	36
Appliances and misc. housewares	100	54	50	71	117	225	92	133	46
Major appliances	100	–	25	88	113	338	63	100	25
Small appliances and misc. housewares	100	81	63	56	125	169	100	144	56
Miscellaneous household equipment	100	37	69	100	145	131	82	115	45
Other housing	100	37	97	86	175	97	67	77	57
Apparel and services	**100**	**72**	**105**	**88**	**108**	**144**	**81**	**106**	**56**
Males, aged 2 or older	100	86	88	98	108	116	97	139	53
Females, aged 2 or older	100	45	88	68	109	193	94	107	79
Children under age 2	100	85	143	113	100	103	50	65	38
Other apparel products and services	100	85	125	85	113	131	63	92	35
Jewelry and watches	100	54	183	83	96	138	46	63	25
All other apparel products and services	100	114	75	82	129	125	82	118	43
Transportation	**100**	**34**	**50**	**102**	**182**	**159**	**39**	**25**	**55**
Health care	**100**	**3**	**33**	**64**	**167**	**167**	**118**	**121**	**112**
Entertainment	**100**	**38**	**77**	**110**	**136**	**137**	**72**	**94**	**49**
Toys, games, hobbies, and tricycles	100	37	67	97	120	167	90	127	50
Other entertainment	100	40	83	119	144	119	60	73	48
Personal care products and services	**100**	**62**	**76**	**129**	**124**	**81**	**100**	**148**	**48**
Reading	**100**	**–**	**100**	**100**	**100**	**200**	**300**	**300**	**300**
Education	**100**	**23**	**15**	**59**	**226**	**159**	**79**	**105**	**52**
All other gifts	**100**	**21**	**50**	**80**	**133**	**173**	**111**	**167**	**51**

Note: (–) means sample is too small to make a reliable estimate.
Source: Calculations by New Strategist based on the Bureau of Labor Statistics 2002 Consumer Expenditure Survey

Spending by Income, 2002

Among households reporting their incomes to Consumer Expenditure Survey interviewers, average spending was $42,557 in 2002. Not surprisingly, the most affluent households, those with incomes of $70,000 or more, spend the most—80 percent more than the average household. The highest income group spends the most on almost every product and service category, with a few exceptions such as rented dwellings and tobacco.

Households with incomes below $20,000 spend less than the average household on almost every category. One of the few exceptions is rent. Many low-income households spend more money than they make. The income they report to government interviewers is less than their reported expenditures. These households make up the difference through borrowing, the use of savings, and unreported income.

Income makes a bigger difference in the purchasing of some products than others. Everyone has to buy food, but only those who can afford to do so will buy a new car. The most affluent households spend close to the average on items such as eggs, prescription drugs, and tobacco. They spend well over twice what the average household spends on other lodging (a category that includes hotel and motel expenses as well as housing for children in college), mortgage interest, and fees and admissions to entertainment events.

Table 1.4 Average spending by household income, 2002

(average annual spending of consumer units (CU) by product and service category and before-tax income of consumer unit, 2002; complete income reporters only)

	complete income reporters	under $10,000	$10,000– $19,999	$20,000– $29,999	$30,000– $39,999	$40,000– $49,999	$50,000– $69,999	$70,000 or more
Number of consumer units (in thousands, add 000s)	92,388	10,933	15,075	12,312	10,727	8,873	13,521	20,947
Average number of persons per CU	2.5	1.7	1.9	2.3	2.5	2.6	2.8	3.1
Average income before taxes	$49,430	$5,555	$14,724	$24,495	$34,423	$44,443	$58,933	$115,629
Average annual spending	42,557	17,628	22,839	28,836	35,095	41,787	50,406	76,627
FOOD	**$5,612**	**$3,085**	**$3,486**	**$4,349**	**$4,881**	**$5,502**	**$6,548**	**$8,874**
Food at home	**3,217**	**1,969**	**2,395**	**2,768**	**3,006**	**3,241**	**3,555**	**4,524**
Cereals and bakery products	471	289	364	403	431	454	519	666
Cereals and cereal products	161	113	127	140	147	156	174	219
Bakery products	310	177	236	264	284	298	345	447
Meats, poultry, fish, and eggs	815	526	628	729	782	807	896	1,099
Beef	238	148	175	213	251	220	263	325
Pork	172	126	142	165	164	168	191	210
Other meats	103	63	91	95	87	103	115	136
Poultry	146	87	109	130	137	155	163	200
Fish and seafood	121	77	82	89	108	126	127	188
Eggs	35	25	31	36	34	35	36	40
Dairy products	345	219	253	294	315	371	377	481
Fresh milk and cream	134	90	109	129	127	136	145	171
Other dairy products	210	129	144	164	189	235	232	309
Fruits and vegetables	568	338	432	502	527	559	612	807
Fresh fruits	181	109	134	161	168	176	184	264
Fresh vegetables	181	105	137	166	164	175	200	256
Processed fruits	119	70	91	104	112	114	131	170
Processed vegetables	87	52	70	72	84	93	97	117
Other food at home	1,018	597	717	840	951	1,050	1,151	1,471
Sugar and other sweets	125	74	96	105	117	134	132	179
Fats and oils	88	59	70	83	82	84	100	113
Miscellaneous foods	495	278	339	403	456	522	571	719
Nonalcoholic beverages	266	169	194	220	254	269	302	373
Food prepared by CU on trips	44	17	18	30	42	41	45	87
Food away from home	**2,395**	**1,116**	**1,093**	**1,581**	**1,875**	**2,261**	**2,994**	**4,350**
ALCOHOLIC BEVERAGES	**415**	**182**	**172**	**275**	**346**	**433**	**453**	**780**
HOUSING	**13,481**	**6,323**	**7,775**	**9,595**	**11,240**	**13,159**	**15,276**	**23,695**
Shelter	**7,854**	**3,745**	**4,482**	**5,368**	**6,451**	**7,671**	**8,581**	**14,212**
Owned dwellings	5,148	1,285	1,859	2,511	3,547	4,720	6,047	11,502
Mortgage interest and charges	2,947	569	612	1,167	1,841	2,728	3,641	7,125
Property taxes	1,209	403	654	690	846	1,030	1,335	2,515
Maintenance, repair, insurance, other expenses	992	313	592	654	860	962	1,070	1,862
Rented dwellings	2,197	2,195	2,435	2,640	2,601	2,604	2,082	1,461
Other lodging	509	264	188	217	304	346	452	1,249
Utilities, fuels, and public services	**2,683**	**1,520**	**1,973**	**2,316**	**2,526**	**2,749**	**3,126**	**3,782**
Natural gas	323	162	229	279	319	340	342	485
Electricity	973	601	772	883	931	999	1,130	1,273
Fuel oil and other fuels	90	54	89	83	84	71	93	122
Telephone	968	553	647	800	899	999	1,169	1,405
Water and other public services	329	152	238	271	293	339	392	497

	complete income reporters	under $10,000	$10,000–$19,999	$20,000–$29,999	$30,000–$39,999	$40,000–$49,999	$50,000–$69,999	$70,000 or more
Household services	**$736**	**$196**	**$309**	**$477**	**$575**	**$688**	**$753**	**$1,571**
Personal services	352	53	116	228	306	340	359	775
Other household services	384	144	193	249	270	348	394	796
Housekeeping supplies	**606**	**317**	**349**	**432**	**490**	**523**	**1,046**	**847**
Laundry and cleaning supplies	140	97	104	129	127	134	165	186
Other household products	322	140	161	192	240	242	697	441
Postage and stationery	144	79	84	111	122	147	184	220
Household furnishings and equipment	**1,602**	**544**	**662**	**1,001**	**1,198**	**1,529**	**1,770**	**3,283**
Household textiles	144	54	71	130	115	144	135	268
Furniture	399	104	118	240	261	343	425	928
Floor coverings	42	10	26	23	25	16	35	107
Major appliances	199	66	104	112	147	204	241	383
Small appliances, misc. housewares	108	44	53	81	102	122	105	194
Miscellaneous household equipment	708	267	291	415	547	699	829	1,403
APPAREL AND RELATED SERVICES	**1,872**	**939**	**1,058**	**1,176**	**1,497**	**1,692**	**2,043**	**3,469**
Men and boys	**436**	**188**	**213**	**236**	**361**	**387**	**453**	**880**
Men, aged 16 or older	342	145	138	182	288	312	349	709
Boys, aged 2 to 15	94	42	75	54	73	75	103	171
Women and girls	**757**	**419**	**467**	**501**	**573**	**673**	**809**	**1,368**
Women, aged 16 or older	628	385	383	414	473	529	660	1,141
Girls, aged 2 to 15	129	35	84	88	100	144	149	227
Children under age 2	**88**	**28**	**48**	**63**	**99**	**96**	**94**	**147**
Footwear	**338**	**197**	**206**	**199**	**296**	**304**	**426**	**562**
Other apparel products and services	**252**	**106**	**123**	**177**	**167**	**232**	**261**	**512**
TRANSPORTATION	**7,984**	**2,727**	**4,327**	**5,275**	**7,041**	**8,651**	**10,555**	**13,487**
Vehicle purchases	**3,778**	**1,189**	**2,223**	**2,323**	**3,343**	**4,292**	**5,191**	**6,198**
Cars and trucks, new	1,767	374	900	762	1,446	2,054	2,264	3,433
Cars and trucks, used	1,939	815	1,311	1,525	1,860	2,174	2,811	2,601
Other vehicles	72	–	12	37	37	64	116	164
Gasoline and motor oil	**1,252**	**536**	**718**	**987**	**1,261**	**1,289**	**1,592**	**1,927**
Other vehicle expenses	**2,550**	**835**	**1,216**	**1,734**	**2,172**	**2,688**	**3,302**	**4,527**
Vehicle finance charges	403	88	141	226	372	452	593	734
Maintenance and repairs	732	297	385	571	614	759	918	1,228
Vehicle insurance	920	324	520	707	877	1,024	1,160	1,465
Vehicle rentals, leases, licenses, other charges	494	126	170	229	310	453	631	1,099
Public transportation	**404**	**167**	**170**	**231**	**264**	**382**	**471**	**834**
HEALTH CARE	**2,410**	**1,111**	**1,978**	**2,289**	**2,379**	**2,598**	**2,672**	**3,230**
Health insurance	1,185	570	1,018	1,109	1,180	1,276	1,313	1,550
Medical services	605	198	338	455	590	716	734	974
Drugs	508	289	521	629	506	495	502	549
Medical supplies	112	54	101	95	103	112	124	157
ENTERTAINMENT	**2,167**	**773**	**926**	**1,187**	**1,561**	**1,924**	**2,641**	**4,457**
Fees and admissions	562	189	191	233	303	477	592	1,364
Television, radio, sound equipment	710	357	432	532	651	740	876	1,110
Pets, toys, and playground equipment	397	130	190	249	319	413	552	701
Other entertainment products and services	498	98	112	173	289	294	620	1,282
PERSONAL CARE PRODUCTS AND SERVICES	**562**	**269**	**367**	**432**	**464**	**551**	**655**	**915**
READING	**145**	**59**	**85**	**106**	**109**	**140**	**170**	**262**
EDUCATION	**771**	**851**	**410**	**311**	**388**	**536**	**619**	**1,653**

	complete income reporters	under $10,000	$10,000–$19,999	$20,000–$29,999	$30,000–$39,999	$40,000–$49,999	$50,000–$69,999	$70,000 or more
TOBACCO PRODUCTS AND SMOKING SUPPLIES	$334	$225	$272	$364	$390	$401	$422	$302
MISCELLANEOUS	846	344	451	675	808	778	1,035	1,417
CASH CONTRIBUTIONS	1,366	406	644	981	1,093	1,182	1,560	2,704
PERSONAL INSURANCE AND PENSIONS	4,593	333	886	1,822	2,898	4,239	5,756	11,382
Life and other personal insurance	425	131	212	259	324	385	469	867
Pensions and Social Security	4,169	202	674	1,563	2,574	3,854	5,287	10,515
PERSONAL TAXES	2,496	1	20	476	831	1,934	2,585	7,802
Federal income taxes	1,843	–46	–59	251	481	1,333	1,880	6,022
State and local income taxes	506	10	36	132	224	466	540	1,464
Other taxes	147	38	42	93	126	135	165	317
GIFTS FOR NON–HOUSEHOLD MEMBERS	1,095	403	516	652	780	952	1,207	2,267
Food	87	28	33	36	67	44	92	210
Alcoholic beverages	14	9	4	16	5	6	22	25
Housing	275	128	123	197	212	285	313	509
Housekeeping supplies	48	22	26	40	36	44	71	75
Household textiles	17	9	7	13	17	22	23	23
Appliances and misc. housewares	29	13	10	23	25	43	20	53
Major appliances	10	1	1	7	8	10	7	24
Small appliances and misc. housewares	19	12	9	17	17	33	13	29
Miscellaneous household equipment	71	33	25	44	47	83	88	133
Other housing	112	52	54	76	88	93	111	226
Apparel and services	258	125	136	204	186	220	278	481
Males, aged 2 or older	71	35	48	59	49	61	70	130
Females, aged 2 or older	88	51	37	75	46	52	88	186
Children under age 2	43	19	22	27	45	48	45	75
Other apparel products and services	56	20	29	43	44	59	75	90
Jewelry and watches	25	10	10	15	10	53	30	40
All other apparel products and services	31	11	19	28	34	6	45	50
Transportation	43	4	54	9	25	36	101	49
Health care	34	9	15	20	16	45	35	72
Entertainment	80	27	38	52	67	82	102	148
Toys, games, hobbies, and tricycles	31	9	17	26	29	32	45	49
Other entertainment	49	18	20	26	38	50	57	99
Personal care products and services	24	13	20	19	20	20	25	38
Reading	1	1	1	2	1	1	2	2
Education	189	34	52	49	96	150	142	546
All other gifts	88	23	41	49	86	64	95	186

Note: Spending by category will not add to total spending because gift spending is also included in the preceding product and service categories and personal taxes are not included in the total. (–) means sample is too small to make a reliable estimate.
Source: Bureau of Labor Statistics, 2002 Consumer Expenditure Survey, Internet site http://www.bls.gov/cex/; calculations by New Strategist

Table 1.5 Indexed spending by household income, 2002

(indexed average annual spending of consumer units (CU) by product and service category and before-tax income of consumer unit reference person, 2002; complete income reporters only; index definition: an index of 100 is the average for all consumer units; an index of 132 means that spending by consumer units in that group is 32 percent above the average for all consumer units; an index of 68 indicates spending that is 32 percent below the average for all consumer units)

	complete income reporters	under $10,000	$10,000– $19,999	$20,000– $29,999	$30,000– $39,999	$40,000– $49,999	$50,000– $69,999	$70,000 or more
Average spending of CU, total	$42,557	17,628	22,839	$28,836	$35,095	$41,787	$50,406	$76,627
Average spending of CU, index	100	41	54	68	82	98	118	180
FOOD	**100**	**55**	**62**	**77**	**87**	**98**	**117**	**158**
Food at home	**100**	**61**	**74**	**86**	**93**	**101**	**111**	**141**
Cereals and bakery products	100	61	77	86	92	96	110	141
Cereals and cereal products	100	70	79	87	91	97	108	136
Bakery products	100	57	76	85	92	96	111	144
Meats, poultry, fish, and eggs	100	64	77	89	96	99	110	135
Beef	100	62	74	89	105	92	111	137
Pork	100	73	82	96	95	98	111	122
Other meats	100	61	88	92	84	100	112	132
Poultry	100	59	74	89	94	106	112	137
Fish and seafood	100	63	68	74	89	104	105	155
Eggs	100	72	89	103	97	100	103	114
Dairy products	100	64	73	85	91	108	109	139
Fresh milk and cream	100	68	81	96	95	101	108	128
Other dairy products	100	61	69	78	90	112	110	147
Fruits and vegetables	100	59	76	88	93	98	108	142
Fresh fruits	100	60	74	89	93	97	102	146
Fresh vegetables	100	58	76	92	91	97	110	141
Processed fruits	100	59	77	87	94	96	110	143
Processed vegetables	100	60	81	83	97	107	111	134
Other food at home	100	59	70	83	93	103	113	144
Sugar and other sweets	100	59	77	84	94	107	106	143
Fats and oils	100	67	80	94	93	95	114	128
Miscellaneous foods	100	56	68	81	92	105	115	145
Nonalcoholic beverages	100	64	73	83	95	101	114	140
Food prepared by CU on trips	100	38	41	68	95	93	102	198
Food away from home	**100**	**47**	**46**	**66**	**78**	**94**	**125**	**182**
ALCOHOLIC BEVERAGES	**100**	**44**	**42**	**66**	**83**	**104**	**109**	**188**
HOUSING	**100**	**47**	**58**	**71**	**83**	**98**	**113**	**176**
Shelter	**100**	**48**	**57**	**68**	**82**	**98**	**109**	**181**
Owned dwellings	100	25	36	49	69	92	117	223
Mortgage interest and charges	100	19	21	40	62	93	124	242
Property taxes	100	33	54	57	70	85	110	208
Maintenance, repair, insurance, other expenses	100	32	60	66	87	97	108	188
Rented dwellings	100	100	111	120	118	119	95	66
Other lodging	100	52	37	43	60	68	89	245
Utilities, fuels, and public services	**100**	**57**	**74**	**86**	**94**	**102**	**117**	**141**
Natural gas	100	50	71	86	99	105	106	150
Electricity	100	62	79	91	96	103	116	131
Fuel oil and other fuels	100	60	99	92	93	79	103	136
Telephone	100	57	67	83	93	103	121	145
Water and other public services	100	46	72	82	89	103	119	151

	complete income reporters	under $10,000	$10,000– $19,999	$20,000– $29,999	$30,000– $39,999	$40,000– $49,999	$50,000– $69,999	$70,000 or more
Household services	100	27	42	65	78	93	102	213
Personal services	100	15	33	65	87	97	102	220
Other household services	100	37	50	65	70	91	103	207
Housekeeping supplies	100	52	58	71	81	86	173	140
Laundry and cleaning supplies	100	69	75	92	91	96	118	133
Other household products	100	44	50	60	75	75	216	137
Postage and stationery	100	55	58	77	85	102	128	153
Household furnishings and equipment	100	34	41	62	75	95	110	205
Household textiles	100	38	49	90	80	100	94	186
Furniture	100	26	29	60	65	86	107	233
Floor coverings	100	25	62	55	60	38	83	255
Major appliances	100	33	53	56	74	103	121	192
Small appliances, misc. housewares	100	41	49	75	94	113	97	180
Miscellaneous household equipment	100	38	41	59	77	99	117	198
APPAREL AND RELATED SERVICES	100	50	57	63	80	90	109	185
Men and boys	100	43	49	54	83	89	104	202
Men, aged 16 or older	100	43	40	53	84	91	102	207
Boys, aged 2 to 15	100	45	80	57	78	80	110	182
Women and girls	100	55	62	66	76	89	107	181
Women, aged 16 or older	100	61	61	66	75	84	105	182
Girls, aged 2 to 15	100	27	65	68	78	112	116	176
Children under age 2	100	32	54	72	113	109	107	167
Footwear	100	58	61	59	88	90	126	166
Other apparel products and services	100	42	49	70	66	92	104	203
TRANSPORTATION	100	34	54	66	88	108	132	169
Vehicle purchases	100	31	59	61	88	114	137	164
Cars and trucks, new	100	21	51	43	82	116	128	194
Cars and trucks, used	100	42	68	79	96	112	145	134
Other vehicles	100	–	17	51	51	89	161	228
Gasoline and motor oil	100	43	57	79	101	103	127	154
Other vehicle expenses	100	33	48	68	85	105	129	178
Vehicle finance charges	100	22	35	56	92	112	147	182
Maintenance and repairs	100	41	53	78	84	104	125	168
Vehicle insurance	100	35	56	77	95	111	126	159
Vehicle rentals, leases, licenses, other charges	100	25	35	46	63	92	128	222
Public transportation	100	41	42	57	65	95	117	206
HEALTH CARE	100	46	82	95	99	108	111	134
Health insurance	100	48	86	94	100	108	111	131
Medical services	100	33	56	75	98	118	121	161
Drugs	100	57	102	124	100	97	99	108
Medical supplies	100	49	90	85	92	100	111	140
ENTERTAINMENT	100	36	43	55	72	89	122	206
Fees and admissions	100	34	34	41	54	85	105	243
Television, radio, sound equipment	100	50	61	75	92	104	123	156
Pets, toys, and playground equipment	100	33	48	63	80	104	139	177
Other entertainment products and services	100	20	23	35	58	59	124	257
PERSONAL CARE PRODUCTS AND SERVICES	100	48	65	77	83	98	117	163
READING	100	41	58	73	75	97	117	181
EDUCATION	100	110	53	40	50	70	80	214

	complete income reporters	under $10,000	$10,000– $19,999	$20,000– $29,999	$30,000– $39,999	$40,000– $49,999	$50,000– $69,999	$70,000 or more
TOBACCO PRODUCTS AND SMOKING SUPPLIES	100	67	81	109	117	120	126	90
MISCELLANEOUS	100	41	53	80	96	92	122	167
CASH CONTRIBUTIONS	100	30	47	72	80	87	114	198
PERSONAL INSURANCE AND PENSIONS	100	7	19	40	63	92	125	248
Life and other personal insurance	100	31	50	61	76	91	110	204
Pensions and Social Security	100	5	16	37	62	92	127	252
PERSONAL TAXES	100	0	1	19	33	77	104	313
Federal income taxes	100	–	–	14	26	72	102	327
State and local income taxes	100	2	7	26	44	92	107	289
Other taxes	100	26	28	63	86	92	112	216
GIFTS FOR NON–HOUSEHOLD MEMBERS	100	37	47	60	71	87	110	207
Food	100	32	38	41	77	51	106	241
Alcoholic beverages	100	67	29	114	36	43	157	179
Housing	100	47	45	72	77	104	114	185
Housekeeping supplies	100	46	54	83	75	92	148	156
Household textiles	100	54	40	76	100	129	135	135
Appliances and misc. housewares	100	46	36	79	86	148	69	183
Major appliances	100	6	15	70	80	100	70	240
Small appliances and misc. housewares	100	65	47	89	89	174	68	153
Miscellaneous household equipment	100	46	35	62	66	117	124	187
Other housing	100	46	48	68	79	83	99	202
Apparel and services	100	49	53	79	72	85	108	186
Males, aged 2 or older	100	49	67	83	69	86	99	183
Females, aged 2 or older	100	58	42	85	52	59	100	211
Children under age 2	100	45	52	63	105	112	105	174
Other apparel products and services	100	37	51	77	79	105	134	161
Jewelry and watches	100	39	38	60	40	212	120	160
All other apparel products and services	100	34	62	90	110	19	145	161
Transportation	100	10	126	21	58	84	235	114
Health care	100	25	43	59	47	132	103	212
Entertainment	100	34	47	65	84	103	128	185
Toys, games, hobbies, and tricycles	100	30	55	84	94	103	145	158
Other entertainment	100	37	42	53	78	102	116	202
Personal care products and services	100	54	82	79	83	83	104	158
Reading	100	100	100	200	100	100	200	200
Education	100	18	28	26	51	79	75	289
All other gifts	100	27	46	56	98	73	108	211

Note: (–) means sample is too small to make a reliable estimate.
Source: Calculations by New Strategist based on the Bureau of Labor Statistics 2002 Consumer Expenditure Survey

Spending by High-Income Households, 2001–02

Fully 36 percent of consumer units had an income of $50,000 or more in 2001–02, and 13 percent had an income of $90,000 or more. A more detailed look at the spending of high-income households reveals interesting patterns. Spending surges as income rises, in part because affluent households have more earners and more expenses than the average household. In 2001–02, the average household had 1.4 earners. Households with incomes of $90,000 or more had an average of 2.1 earners.

The most affluent households, those with incomes of $90,000 or more, spend the most—more than twice as much as the average household ($87,292 versus $41,988 in 2001–02). On many products, the most affluent consumer units spend more than three times the average. These items include "other lodging" (motels, hotels, vacation homes, college dorms) and fees and admissions to entertainment events. The most affluent households spend more than four times the average on federal income taxes.

The most affluent households spend close to the average on items such as eggs and prescription drugs. They spend less than average on rent and tobacco.

Table 1.6 Average spending by high-income households, 2001–02

(average annual spending of consumer units (CU) by product and service category and before-tax income of consumer unit, 2001–02; complete income reporters and consumer units with incomes of $50,000 or more)

	total complete reporters	$50,000– $59,999	$60,000– $69,999	$70,000– $89,999	$90,000 or more
Number of consumer units (in thousands, add 000s)	90,559	7,220	5,779	8,195	11,723
Average number of persons per CU	2.5	2.8	2.9	3.1	3.2
Average income before taxes	$48,484	$54,507	$64,478	$78,619	$140,150
Average annual spending	41,988	47,668	53,567	60,740	87,292
FOOD	$5,637	$6,395	$7,087	$7,736	$9,805
Food at home	3,235	3,568	3,749	4,271	4,729
Cereals and bakery products	476	517	549	618	712
Cereals and cereal products	163	173	183	202	236
Bakery products	312	344	366	416	476
Meats, poultry, fish, and eggs	842	924	948	1,082	1,147
Beef	251	280	278	332	337
Pork	180	202	192	227	219
Other meats	105	111	127	138	141
Poultry	153	174	191	198	210
Fish and seafood	117	120	123	146	200
Eggs	36	37	37	40	41
Dairy products	348	385	404	484	504
Fresh milk and cream	140	150	157	180	179
Other dairy products	209	235	247	304	325
Fruits and vegetables	557	595	624	723	824
Fresh fruits	174	184	187	222	273
Fresh vegetables	175	187	199	227	258
Processed fruits	120	129	137	163	172
Processed vegetables	88	96	101	111	120
Other food at home	1,013	1,147	1,224	1,365	1,543
Sugar and other sweets	124	132	142	165	187
Fats and oils	89	103	101	113	113
Miscellaneous foods	488	554	607	664	756
Nonalcoholic beverages	270	315	322	359	388
Food prepared by CU on trips	42	43	52	64	99
Food away from home	2,402	2,827	3,338	3,465	5,076
ALCOHOLIC BEVERAGES	401	399	504	597	840
HOUSING	13,304	14,674	16,107	18,454	27,290
Shelter	7,721	8,298	9,355	10,853	16,320
Owned dwellings	5,029	5,740	6,710	8,273	13,384
Mortgage interest and charges	2,886	3,513	4,021	5,193	8,305
Property taxes	1,193	1,232	1,503	1,759	2,977
Maintenance, repair, insurance, other expenses	950	995	1,186	1,322	2,102
Rented dwellings	2,197	2,137	2,042	1,849	1,347
Other lodging	495	421	603	731	1,589
Utilities, fuels, and public services	2,710	3,016	3,239	3,395	4,100
Natural gas	362	386	418	443	590
Electricity	981	1,092	1,133	1,187	1,349
Fuel oil and other fuels	100	87	110	120	148
Telephone	943	1,084	1,159	1,228	1,470
Water and other public services	324	367	418	417	543

	total complete reporters	$50,000–$59,999	$60,000–$69,999	$70,000–$89,999	$90,000 or more
Household services	**$705**	**$703**	**$745**	**$964**	**$1,910**
Personal services	324	330	340	487	893
Other household services	380	373	405	477	1,017
Housekeeping supplies	**586**	**1,002**	**763**	**767**	**966**
Laundry and cleaning supplies	144	166	191	183	194
Other household products	302	670	386	404	503
Postage and stationery	141	166	186	179	270
Household furnishings and equipment	**1,582**	**1,655**	**2,005**	**2,474**	**3,995**
Household textiles	136	138	156	175	347
Furniture	394	383	491	597	1,136
Floor coverings	43	21	55	60	141
Major appliances	194	240	247	291	434
Small appliances, misc. housewares	100	91	121	143	225
Miscellaneous household equipment	716	781	936	1,208	1,712
APPAREL AND RELATED SERVICES	**1,859**	**1,884**	**2,395**	**2,545**	**4,117**
Men and boys	**447**	**475**	**600**	**662**	**1,046**
Men, aged 16 or older	355	372	477	522	860
Boys, aged 2 to 15	93	103	123	141	186
Women and girls	**738**	**709**	**969**	**1,010**	**1,571**
Women, aged 16 or older	611	568	823	837	1,314
Girls, aged 2 to 15	126	142	146	173	256
Children under age 2	**89**	**102**	**112**	**123**	**166**
Footwear	**330**	**354**	**448**	**400**	**653**
Other apparel products and services	**256**	**244**	**266**	**349**	**681**
TRANSPORTATION	**7,953**	**9,955**	**10,589**	**12,104**	**14,780**
Vehicle purchases	**3,778**	**4,910**	**4,923**	**5,681**	**6,808**
Cars and trucks, new	1,750	2,218	2,143	2,672	4,077
Cars and trucks, used	1,969	2,590	2,687	2,906	2,578
Other vehicles	59	103	93	102	153
Gasoline and motor oil	**1,271**	**1,535**	**1,690**	**1,872**	**2,046**
Other vehicle expenses	**2,500**	**3,065**	**3,486**	**3,942**	**4,871**
Vehicle finance charges	385	513	638	697	683
Maintenance and repairs	720	838	940	1,053	1,332
Vehicle insurance	876	1,076	1,192	1,281	1,479
Vehicle rentals, leases, licenses, other charges	519	638	716	911	1,377
Public transportation	**404**	**446**	**490**	**609**	**1,055**
HEALTH CARE	**2,318**	**2,557**	**2,644**	**2,731**	**3,319**
Health insurance	1,123	1,235	1,274	1,330	1,514
Medical services	599	757	760	766	1,107
Drugs	485	450	475	492	531
Medical supplies	111	114	135	143	167
ENTERTAINMENT	**2,098**	**2,468**	**2,850**	**3,298**	**4,888**
Fees and admissions	551	525	694	852	1,722
Television, radio, sound equipment	693	817	869	946	1,220
Pets, toys, and playground equipment	380	499	512	577	766
Other entertainment products and services	475	627	776	923	1,181
PERSONAL CARE PRODUCTS AND SERVICES	**538**	**575**	**697**	**690**	**975**
READING	**146**	**163**	**189**	**211**	**308**
EDUCATION	**706**	**619**	**760**	**941**	**1,913**

	total complete reporters	$50,000–$59,999	$60,000–$69,999	$70,000–$89,999	$90,000 or more
TOBACCO PRODUCTS AND SMOKING SUPPLIES	$330	$385	$414	$330	$293
MISCELLANEOUS	808	982	917	1,103	1,631
CASH CONTRIBUTIONS	1,345	1,393	1,831	1,793	3,371
PERSONAL INSURANCE AND PENSIONS	4,545	5,220	6,583	8,207	13,762
Life and other personal insurance	424	417	562	617	1,023
Pensions and Social Security	4,121	4,803	6,021	7,589	12,739
PERSONAL TAXES	2,704	2,643	3,362	4,648	11,209
Federal income taxes	2,036	1,944	2,533	3,453	8,912
State and local income taxes	530	541	684	983	1,945
Other taxes	138	158	146	212	353
GIFTS FOR NON–HOUSEHOLD MEMBERS	1,087	1,167	1,281	1,492	2,806
Food	81	64	119	114	268
Alcoholic beverages	15	13	19	21	33
Housing	275	275	387	367	628
Housekeeping supplies	47	53	84	61	92
Household textiles	16	16	25	28	36
Appliances and misc. housewares	27	21	32	46	56
Major appliances	8	9	8	20	19
Small appliances and misc. housewares	19	13	24	27	37
Miscellaneous household equipment	68	86	104	93	140
Other housing	117	100	141	140	304
Apparel and services	259	271	296	335	572
Males, aged 2 or older	70	68	78	102	132
Females, aged 2 or older	92	81	111	136	236
Children under age 2	44	51	56	55	87
Other apparel products and services	52	70	51	43	118
Jewelry and watches	22	29	18	17	54
All other apparel products and services	30	41	32	25	63
Transportation	63	144	35	58	125
Health care	35	59	29	54	85
Entertainment	80	96	89	126	172
Toys, games, hobbies, and tricycles	32	41	45	48	55
Other entertainment	48	55	44	78	117
Personal care products and services	24	14	45	25	39
Reading	1	2	2	2	3
Education	170	119	172	256	676
All other gifts	85	110	88	132	206

Note: Spending by category will not add to total spending because gift spending is also included in the preceding product and service categories and personal taxes are not included in the total.
Source: Bureau of Labor Statistics, 2001 and 2002 Consumer Expenditure Surveys, Internet site http://www.bls.gov/cex/

Table 1.7 Indexed spending by high-income households, 2001–02

(indexed average annual spending of consumer units (CU) by product and service category and before-tax income of consumer unit reference person, 2001–02; complete income reporters and consumer units with incomes of $50,000 or more; index definition: an index of 100 is the average for all consumer units; an index of 132 means that spending by consumer units in that group is 32 percent above the average for all consumer units; an index of 68 indicates spending that is 32 percent below the average for all consumer units)

	total complete reporters	$50,000–$59,999	$60,000–$69,999	$70,000–$89,999	$90,000 or more
Average spending of CU, total	**$41,988**	**$47,668**	**$53,567**	**$60,740**	**$87,292**
Average spending of CU, index	**100**	**114**	**128**	**145**	**208**
FOOD	**100**	**113**	**126**	**137**	**174**
Food at home	**100**	**110**	**116**	**132**	**146**
Cereals and bakery products	100	109	115	130	150
Cereals and cereal products	100	106	112	124	145
Bakery products	100	110	117	133	153
Meats, poultry, fish, and eggs	100	110	113	129	136
Beef	100	112	111	132	134
Pork	100	112	107	126	122
Other meats	100	106	121	131	134
Poultry	100	114	125	129	137
Fish and seafood	100	103	105	125	171
Eggs	100	103	103	111	114
Dairy products	100	111	116	139	145
Fresh milk and cream	100	107	112	129	128
Other dairy products	100	112	118	145	156
Fruits and vegetables	100	107	112	130	148
Fresh fruits	100	106	107	128	157
Fresh vegetables	100	107	114	130	147
Processed fruits	100	108	114	136	143
Processed vegetables	100	109	115	126	136
Other food at home	100	113	121	135	152
Sugar and other sweets	100	106	115	133	151
Fats and oils	100	116	113	127	127
Miscellaneous foods	100	114	124	136	155
Nonalcoholic beverages	100	117	119	133	144
Food prepared by CU on trips	100	102	124	152	236
Food away from home	**100**	**118**	**139**	**144**	**211**
ALCOHOLIC BEVERAGES	**100**	**100**	**126**	**149**	**209**
HOUSING	**100**	**110**	**121**	**139**	**205**
Shelter	**100**	**107**	**121**	**141**	**211**
Owned dwellings	100	114	133	165	266
Mortgage interest and charges	100	122	139	180	288
Property taxes	100	103	126	147	250
Maintenance, repair, insurance, other expenses	100	105	125	139	221
Rented dwellings	100	97	93	84	61
Other lodging	100	85	122	148	321
Utilities, fuels, and public services	**100**	**111**	**120**	**125**	**151**
Natural gas	100	107	115	122	163
Electricity	100	111	115	121	138
Fuel oil and other fuels	100	87	110	120	148
Telephone	100	115	123	130	156
Water and other public services	100	113	129	129	168

	total complete reporters	$50,000–$59,999	$60,000–$69,999	$70,000–$89,999	$90,000 or more
Household services	**100**	**100**	**106**	**137**	**271**
Personal services	100	102	105	150	276
Other household services	100	98	107	126	268
Housekeeping supplies	**100**	**171**	**130**	**131**	**165**
Laundry and cleaning supplies	100	115	133	127	135
Other household products	100	222	128	134	167
Postage and stationery	100	118	132	127	191
Household furnishings and equipment	**100**	**105**	**127**	**156**	**253**
Household textiles	100	101	115	129	255
Furniture	100	97	125	152	288
Floor coverings	100	49	128	140	328
Major appliances	100	124	127	150	224
Small appliances, misc. housewares	100	91	121	143	225
Miscellaneous household equipment	100	109	131	169	239
APPAREL AND RELATED SERVICES	**100**	**101**	**129**	**137**	**221**
Men and boys	**100**	**106**	**134**	**148**	**234**
Men, aged 16 or older	100	105	134	147	242
Boys, aged 2 to 15	100	111	132	152	200
Women and girls	**100**	**96**	**131**	**137**	**213**
Women, aged 16 or older	100	93	135	137	215
Girls, aged 2 to 15	100	113	116	137	203
Children under age 2	**100**	**115**	**126**	**138**	**187**
Footwear	**100**	**107**	**136**	**121**	**198**
Other apparel products and services	**100**	**95**	**104**	**136**	**266**
TRANSPORTATION	**100**	**125**	**133**	**152**	**186**
Vehicle purchases	**100**	**130**	**130**	**150**	**180**
Cars and trucks, new	100	127	122	153	233
Cars and trucks, used	100	132	136	148	131
Other vehicles	100	175	158	173	259
Gasoline and motor oil	**100**	**121**	**133**	**147**	**161**
Other vehicle expenses	**100**	**123**	**139**	**158**	**195**
Vehicle finance charges	100	133	166	181	177
Maintenance and repairs	100	116	131	146	185
Vehicle insurance	100	123	136	146	169
Vehicle rentals, leases, licenses, other charges	100	123	138	176	265
Public transportation	**100**	**110**	**121**	**151**	**261**
HEALTH CARE	**100**	**110**	**114**	**118**	**143**
Health insurance	100	110	113	118	135
Medical services	100	126	127	128	185
Drugs	100	93	98	101	109
Medical supplies	100	103	122	129	150
ENTERTAINMENT	**100**	**118**	**136**	**157**	**233**
Fees and admissions	100	95	126	155	313
Television, radio, sound equipment	100	118	125	137	176
Pets, toys, and playground equipment	100	131	135	152	202
Other entertainment products and services	100	132	163	194	249
PERSONAL CARE PRODUCTS AND SERVICES	**100**	**107**	**130**	**128**	**181**
READING	**100**	**112**	**129**	**145**	**211**
EDUCATION	**100**	**88**	**108**	**133**	**271**

	total complete reporters	$50,000–$59,999	$60,000–$69,999	$70,000–$89,999	$90,000 or more
TOBACCO PRODUCTS AND SMOKING SUPPLIES	100	117	125	100	89
MISCELLANEOUS	100	122	113	137	202
CASH CONTRIBUTIONS	100	104	136	133	251
PERSONAL INSURANCE AND PENSIONS	100	115	145	181	303
Life and other personal insurance	100	98	133	146	241
Pensions and Social Security	100	117	146	184	309
PERSONAL TAXES	100	98	124	172	415
Federal income taxes	100	95	124	170	438
State and local income taxes	100	102	129	185	367
Other taxes	100	114	106	154	256
GIFTS FOR NON–HOUSEHOLD MEMBERS	100	107	118	137	258
Food	100	79	147	141	331
Alcoholic beverages	100	87	127	140	220
Housing	100	100	141	133	228
Housekeeping supplies	100	113	179	130	196
Household textiles	100	100	156	175	225
Appliances and misc. housewares	100	78	119	170	207
Major appliances	100	113	100	250	238
Small appliances and misc. housewares	100	68	126	142	195
Miscellaneous household equipment	100	126	153	137	206
Other housing	100	85	121	120	260
Apparel and services	100	105	114	129	221
Males, aged 2 or older	100	97	111	146	189
Females, aged 2 or older	100	88	121	148	257
Children under age 2	100	116	127	125	198
Other apparel products and services	100	135	98	83	227
Jewelry and watches	100	132	82	77	245
All other apparel products and services	100	137	107	83	210
Transportation	100	229	56	92	198
Health care	100	169	83	154	243
Entertainment	100	120	111	158	215
Toys, games, hobbies, and tricycles	100	128	141	150	172
Other entertainment	100	115	92	163	244
Personal care products and services	100	58	188	104	163
Reading	100	200	200	200	300
Education	100	70	101	151	398
All other gifts	100	129	104	155	242

Source: Calculations by New Strategist based on the Bureau of Labor Statistics 2001 and 2002 Consumer Expenditure Surveys

Spending by Age and Income, 2001–02

Within age groups, spending on most categories of products and services rises with income. There are some interesting exceptions, however. Among householders under age 25, those with incomes below $10,000 spend the most on education—fully $2,231 in 2001–02. These young adults are attending college. Their incomes will rise when their schooling is complete and they embark on a career.

Only 7 percent of householders aged 65 or older have incomes of $70,000 or more. The proportion is a much larger 24 percent among householders aged 55 to 64 and peaks at 33 percent among those aged 45 to 54. Thirty-one percent of householders aged 35 to 44 have incomes of $70,000 or more.

Householders aged 45 to 54 with incomes of $70,000 or more spent the most in 2001–02, fully $80,663. Close behind are affluent householders aged 35 to 44, spending $79,369 in 2001–02. Householders aged 45 to 54 with incomes of $70,000 or more spent 97 percent as much on eating out as on groceries in 2001–02. For the average household, the ratio is 74 percent. Affluent householders aged 45 to 54 spent fully $4,371 on entertainment in 2001–02 compared to the $2,098 spent by the average household.

Table 1.8 Under age 25: Average spending by income, 2001–02

(average annual spending of consumer units (CU) headed by people under age 25 by product and service category and before-tax income of consumer unit, 2001–02; complete income reporters only)

	complete income reporters under age 25	under $10,000	$10,000–$19,999	$20,000–$29,999	$30,000–$39,999	$40,000 or more
Number of consumer units (in thousands, add 000s)	7,153	2,844	1,653	938	684	1,033
Average number of persons per CU	1.8	1.3	1.9	2.1	2.3	2.7
Average income before taxes	$20,771	$4,638	$14,231	$23,897	$33,850	$64,142
Average annual spending	24,699	14,803	22,111	26,937	32,472	46,419
FOOD	**$3,828**	**$2,578**	**$3,231**	**$3,951**	**$4,511**	**$6,273**
Food at home	**1,910**	**1,104**	**1,747**	**2,218**	**2,270**	**2,949**
Cereals and bakery products	286	165	278	325	327	426
Cereals and cereal products	115	73	112	132	128	158
Bakery products	171	92	166	193	199	268
Meats, poultry, fish, and eggs	451	215	400	559	553	754
Beef	141	63	124	160	179	255
Pork	91	48	77	130	109	131
Other meats	55	26	47	69	75	86
Poultry	87	43	83	112	101	139
Fish and seafood	52	24	49	60	61	94
Eggs	24	10	20	28	29	49
Dairy products	202	125	177	214	241	326
Fresh milk and cream	89	50	84	96	105	141
Other dairy products	114	74	94	118	136	186
Fruits and vegetables	319	171	281	362	402	522
Fresh fruits	97	50	92	101	117	165
Fresh vegetables	93	41	73	111	130	168
Processed fruits	80	56	67	91	90	123
Processed vegetables	48	25	48	59	64	66
Other food at home	653	428	612	758	747	921
Sugar and other sweets	65	44	62	75	80	85
Fats and oils	48	29	43	56	62	70
Miscellaneous foods	345	230	310	430	364	487
Nonalcoholic beverages	171	110	161	176	214	252
Food prepared by CU on trips	24	15	36	21	28	26
Food away from home	**1,917**	**1,475**	**1,483**	**1,733**	**2,241**	**3,324**
ALCOHOLIC BEVERAGES	**415**	**278**	**403**	**411**	**552**	**605**
HOUSING	**7,606**	**4,469**	**7,005**	**8,608**	**10,095**	**14,335**
Shelter	**4,868**	**2,990**	**4,414**	**5,339**	**6,554**	**9,218**
Owned dwellings	778	170	420	558	1,088	3,019
Mortgage interest and charges	422	49	116	277	632	1,927
Property taxes	261	108	268	145	274	768
Maintenance, repair, insurance, other expenses	96	13	37	136	182	324
Rented dwellings	3,742	2,312	3,687	4,597	5,335	5,934
Other lodging	348	508	306	185	131	265
Utilities, fuels, and public services	**1,351**	**737**	**1,322**	**1,667**	**1,982**	**2,387**
Natural gas	116	60	91	137	186	242
Electricity	469	256	485	618	656	774
Fuel oil and other fuels	23	5	33	14	60	38
Telephone	646	385	607	783	933	1,109
Water and other public services	98	32	105	115	147	224

	complete income reporters under age 25	under $10,000	$10,000–$19,999	$20,000–$29,999	$30,000–$39,999	$40,000 or more
Household services	**$227**	**$91**	**$169**	**$371**	**$239**	**$553**
Personal services	126	32	98	261	102	326
Other household services	101	60	71	110	137	227
Housekeeping supplies	**244**	**131**	**231**	**280**	**271**	**393**
Laundry and cleaning supplies	88	42	95	101	90	130
Other household products	96	51	88	118	112	152
Postage and stationery	60	38	49	61	70	111
Household furnishings and equipment	**916**	**520**	**869**	**949**	**1,048**	**1,784**
Household textiles	72	17	45	210	72	79
Furniture	223	91	189	167	320	626
Floor coverings	8	4	6	12	24	7
Major appliances	84	27	76	106	118	194
Small appliances, misc. housewares	54	33	35	69	41	117
Miscellaneous household equipment	476	347	519	386	473	761
APPAREL AND RELATED SERVICES	**1,373**	**802**	**1,469**	**1,267**	**1,847**	**2,182**
Men and boys	**294**	**207**	**286**	**270**	**356**	**452**
Men, aged 16 or older	254	198	220	245	323	381
Boys, aged 2 to 15	39	9	66	25	32	70
Women and girls	**553**	**349**	**603**	**474**	**756**	**849**
Women, aged 16 or older	502	337	539	436	712	724
Girls, aged 2 to 15	51	14	63	38	44	125
Children under age 2	**107**	**46**	**130**	**126**	**152**	**148**
Footwear	**240**	**94**	**271**	**189**	**361**	**411**
Other apparel products and services	**179**	**105**	**180**	**209**	**222**	**322**
TRANSPORTATION	**5,084**	**2,323**	**4,866**	**6,482**	**7,256**	**10,297**
Vehicle purchases	**2,594**	**1,061**	**2,788**	**3,329**	**3,693**	**5,109**
Cars and trucks, new	723	175	716	955	1,283	1,664
Cars and trucks, used	1,828	884	1,997	2,374	2,351	3,314
Other vehicles	42	0	76	–	58	132
Gasoline and motor oil	**907**	**547**	**876**	**1,162**	**1,160**	**1,551**
Other vehicle expenses	**1,358**	**537**	**1,037**	**1,822**	**2,123**	**3,187**
Vehicle finance charges	229	51	156	278	420	665
Maintenance and repairs	401	219	330	607	639	652
Vehicle insurance	474	146	377	656	765	1,171
Vehicle rentals, leases, licenses, other charges	254	121	173	280	299	700
Public transportation	**225**	**179**	**167**	**169**	**281**	**451**
HEALTH CARE	**608**	**198**	**466**	**843**	**868**	**1,526**
Health insurance	266	55	190	383	459	736
Medical services	177	54	98	246	219	552
Drugs	127	63	152	169	143	172
Medical supplies	38	26	26	45	47	66
ENTERTAINMENT	**1,250**	**866**	**1,073**	**1,123**	**1,587**	**2,407**
Fees and admissions	317	282	282	250	374	493
Television, radio, sound equipment	499	343	478	545	709	778
Pets, toys, and playground equipment	201	76	158	154	292	543
Other entertainment products and services	232	166	155	174	212	593
PERSONAL CARE PRODUCTS AND SERVICES	**336**	**218**	**274**	**418**	**442**	**545**
READING	**61**	**48**	**61**	**62**	**71**	**91**
EDUCATION	**1,586**	**2,231**	**1,590**	**847**	**876**	**944**

	complete income reporters under age 25	under $10,000	$10,000–$19,999	$20,000–$29,999	$30,000–$39,999	$40,000 or more
TOBACCO PRODUCTS AND SMOKING SUPPLIES	$287	$180	$327	$341	$405	$389
MISCELLANEOUS	395	204	272	473	871	688
CASH CONTRIBUTIONS	262	130	165	273	369	703
PERSONAL INSURANCE AND PENSIONS	1,607	279	908	1,839	2,722	5,433
Life and other personal insurance	51	17	29	67	80	146
Pensions and Social Security	1,556	261	879	1,772	2,642	5,287
PERSONAL TAXES	503	–12	–29	711	879	2,336
Federal income taxes	361	–16	–82	534	596	1,791
State and local income taxes	131	4	49	165	251	504
Other taxes	12	1	3	12	33	41
GIFTS FOR NON–HOUSEHOLD MEMBERS	474	355	437	384	715	652
Food	30	31	15	23	77	26
Alcoholic beverages	15	15	13	18	7	18
Housing	117	80	108	128	137	170
Housekeeping supplies	24	7	27	14	57	32
Household textiles	4	–	2	7	9	6
Appliances and misc. housewares	14	4	10	17	3	41
Major appliances	1	–	0	5	–	1
Small appliances and misc. housewares	13	4	9	12	3	40
Miscellaneous household equipment	27	26	18	30	25	38
Other housing	49	43	52	60	43	53
Apparel and services	182	94	192	125	374	233
Males, aged 2 or older	60	38	52	41	114	88
Females, aged 2 or older	33	22	45	29	30	35
Children under age 2	37	12	35	26	98	57
Other apparel products and services	52	22	62	29	132	52
Jewelry and watches	20	22	25	16	7	21
All other apparel products and services	32	1	37	13	125	32
Transportation	10	3	23	7	4	12
Health care	3	4	1	6	4	5
Entertainment	43	28	36	33	33	109
Toys, games, hobbies, and tricycles	12	6	10	25	12	21
Other entertainment	30	23	26	8	20	88
Personal care products and services	16	28	2	28	23	4
Reading	–	0	1	–	–	–
Education	37	58	31	8	24	20
All other gifts	21	14	15	8	31	54

Note: Spending by category will not add to total spending because gift spending is also included in the preceding product and service categories and personal taxes are not included in the total. (–) means sample is too small to make a reliable estimate.
Source: Bureau of Labor Statistics, 2001 and 2002 Consumer Expenditure Surveys, Internet site http://www.bls.gov/cex/; calculations by New Strategist

Table 1.9 Under age 25: Indexed spending by income, 2001–02

(indexed average annual spending of consumer units (CU) headed by people under age 25 by product and service category and before-tax income of consumer unit, 2001–02; complete income reporters only; index definition: an index of 100 is the average for all consumer units; an index of 132 means that spending by consumer units in that group is 32 percent above the average for all consumer units; an index of 68 indicates spending that is 32 percent below the average for all consumer units)

	complete income reporters under age 25	under $10,000	$10,000–$19,999	$20,000–$29,999	$30,000–$39,999	$40,000 or more
Average spending of CU, total	$24,699	$14,803	$22,111	$26,937	$32,472	$46,419
Average spending of CU, index	100	60	90	109	131	188
FOOD	100	67	84	103	118	164
Food at home	100	58	91	116	119	154
Cereals and bakery products	100	58	97	114	114	149
Cereals and cereal products	100	64	97	115	111	137
Bakery products	100	54	97	113	116	157
Meats, poultry, fish, and eggs	100	48	89	124	123	167
Beef	100	45	88	113	127	181
Pork	100	53	85	143	120	144
Other meats	100	47	86	125	136	156
Poultry	100	49	95	129	116	160
Fish and seafood	100	46	94	115	117	181
Eggs	100	40	85	117	121	204
Dairy products	100	62	88	106	119	161
Fresh milk and cream	100	57	94	108	118	158
Other dairy products	100	65	83	104	119	163
Fruits and vegetables	100	54	88	113	126	164
Fresh fruits	100	51	95	104	121	170
Fresh vegetables	100	44	79	119	140	181
Processed fruits	100	69	84	114	113	154
Processed vegetables	100	51	101	123	133	138
Other food at home	100	66	94	116	114	141
Sugar and other sweets	100	67	95	115	123	131
Fats and oils	100	60	89	117	129	146
Miscellaneous foods	100	67	90	125	106	141
Nonalcoholic beverages	100	65	94	103	125	147
Food prepared by CU on trips	100	62	149	88	117	108
Food away from home	100	77	77	90	117	173
ALCOHOLIC BEVERAGES	100	67	97	99	133	146
HOUSING	100	59	92	113	133	188
Shelter	100	61	91	110	135	189
Owned dwellings	100	22	54	72	140	388
Mortgage interest and charges	100	12	28	66	150	457
Property taxes	100	41	103	56	105	294
Maintenance, repair, insurance, other expenses	100	13	39	142	190	338
Rented dwellings	100	62	99	123	143	159
Other lodging	100	146	88	53	38	76
Utilities, fuels, and public services	100	55	98	123	147	177
Natural gas	100	52	78	118	160	209
Electricity	100	54	103	132	140	165
Fuel oil and other fuels	100	20	146	61	261	165
Telephone	100	60	94	121	144	172
Water and other public services	100	32	107	117	150	229

	complete income reporters under age 25	under $10,000	$10,000– $19,999	$20,000– $29,999	$30,000– $39,999	$40,000 or more
Household services	100	40	75	163	105	244
Personal services	100	25	78	207	81	259
Other household services	100	59	70	109	136	225
Housekeeping supplies	100	54	95	115	111	161
Laundry and cleaning supplies	100	48	108	115	102	148
Other household products	100	53	92	123	117	158
Postage and stationery	100	64	81	102	117	185
Household furnishings and equipment	100	57	95	104	114	195
Household textiles	100	23	62	292	100	110
Furniture	100	41	85	75	143	281
Floor coverings	100	50	73	150	300	88
Major appliances	100	32	90	126	140	231
Small appliances, misc. housewares	100	61	64	128	76	217
Miscellaneous household equipment	100	73	109	81	99	160
APPAREL AND RELATED SERVICES	100	58	107	92	135	159
Men and boys	100	70	97	92	121	154
Men, aged 16 or older	100	78	87	96	127	150
Boys, aged 2 to 15	100	22	168	64	82	179
Women and girls	100	63	109	86	137	154
Women, aged 16 or older	100	67	107	87	142	144
Girls, aged 2 to 15	100	27	124	75	86	245
Children under age 2	100	43	122	118	142	138
Footwear	100	39	113	79	150	171
Other apparel products and services	100	59	100	117	124	180
TRANSPORTATION	100	46	96	127	143	203
Vehicle purchases	100	41	107	128	142	197
Cars and trucks, new	100	24	99	132	177	230
Cars and trucks, used	100	48	109	130	129	181
Other vehicles	100	1	180	–	138	314
Gasoline and motor oil	100	60	97	128	128	171
Other vehicle expenses	100	40	76	134	156	235
Vehicle finance charges	100	22	68	121	183	290
Maintenance and repairs	100	55	82	151	159	163
Vehicle insurance	100	31	80	138	161	247
Vehicle rentals, leases, licenses, other charges	100	48	68	110	118	276
Public transportation	100	80	74	75	125	200
HEALTH CARE	100	33	77	139	143	251
Health insurance	100	21	72	144	173	277
Medical services	100	30	55	139	124	312
Drugs	100	49	119	133	113	135
Medical supplies	100	69	67	118	124	174
ENTERTAINMENT	100	69	86	90	127	193
Fees and admissions	100	89	89	79	118	156
Television, radio, sound equipment	100	69	96	109	142	156
Pets, toys, and playground equipment	100	38	78	77	145	270
Other entertainment products and services	100	71	67	75	91	256
PERSONAL CARE PRODUCTS AND SERVICES	100	65	82	124	132	162
READING	100	79	100	102	116	149
EDUCATION	100	141	100	53	55	60

	complete income reporters under age 25	under $10,000	$10,000– $19,999	$20,000– $29,999	$30,000– $39,999	$40,000 or more
TOBACCO PRODUCTS AND SMOKING SUPPLIES	100	63	114	119	141	136
MISCELLANEOUS	100	52	69	120	221	174
CASH CONTRIBUTIONS	100	49	63	104	141	268
PERSONAL INSURANCE AND PENSIONS	100	17	57	114	169	338
Life and other personal insurance	100	33	58	131	157	286
Pensions and Social Security	100	17	56	114	170	340
PERSONAL TAXES	100	–	–	141	175	464
Federal income taxes	100	–	–	148	165	496
State and local income taxes	100	3	38	126	192	385
Other taxes	100	10	26	100	275	342
GIFTS FOR NON–HOUSEHOLD MEMBERS	100	75	92	81	151	138
Food	100	102	49	77	257	87
Alcoholic beverages	100	102	85	120	47	120
Housing	100	68	93	109	117	145
Housekeeping supplies	100	27	111	58	238	133
Household textiles	100	–	54	175	225	150
Appliances and misc. housewares	100	28	70	121	21	293
Major appliances	100	–	41	500	–	100
Small appliances and misc. housewares	100	30	72	92	23	308
Miscellaneous household equipment	100	95	67	111	93	141
Other housing	100	89	107	122	88	108
Apparel and services	100	52	106	69	205	128
Males, aged 2 or older	100	63	86	68	190	147
Females, aged 2 or older	100	66	136	88	91	106
Children under age 2	100	33	93	70	265	154
Other apparel products and services	100	43	119	56	254	100
Jewelry and watches	100	109	123	80	35	105
All other apparel products and services	100	2	116	41	391	100
Transportation	100	30	234	70	40	120
Health care	100	137	20	200	133	167
Entertainment	100	65	84	77	77	253
Toys, games, hobbies, and tricycles	100	46	85	208	100	175
Other entertainment	100	75	86	27	67	293
Personal care products and services	100	175	14	175	144	25
Reading	–	–	–	–	–	–
Education	100	158	84	22	65	54
All other gifts	100	67	72	38	148	257

Note: (–) means sample is too small to make a reliable estimate.
Source: Calculations by New Strategist based on the Bureau of Labor Statistics 2001 and 2002 Consumer Expenditure Surveys

Table 1.10 Aged 25 to 34: Average spending by income, 2001–02

(average annual spending of consumer units (CU) headed by people aged 25 to 34 by product and service category and before-tax income of consumer unit, 2001–02; complete income reporters only)

	complete income reporters aged 25 to 34	under $10,000	$10,000– $19,999	$20,000– $29,999	$30,000– $39,999	$40,000– $49,999	$50,000– $69,999	$70,000 or more
Number of consumer units (in thousands, add 000s)	15,569	1,102	1,986	2,321	2,141	1,880	2,772	3,367
Average number of persons per CU	2.8	2.5	2.8	2.7	2.7	2.8	3.0	3.0
Average income before taxes	$49,275	$5,320	$15,015	$24,691	$34,336	$44,236	$58,711	$105,369
Average annual spending	41,766	20,592	23,115	28,437	35,467	40,712	47,953	68,208
FOOD	**$5,659**	**$3,696**	**$3,931**	**$4,677**	**$5,026**	**$5,646**	**$6,129**	**$7,928**
Food at home	**3,155**	**2,450**	**2,559**	**2,784**	**2,995**	**3,309**	**3,262**	**3,884**
Cereals and bakery products	450	344	364	399	443	460	463	552
Cereals and cereal products	170	143	135	162	157	188	161	208
Bakery products	280	201	229	238	286	273	302	345
Meats, poultry, fish, and eggs	836	719	707	806	805	805	802	1,032
Beef	260	218	231	241	260	238	243	330
Pork	173	152	149	160	158	187	166	207
Other meats	93	81	88	105	85	95	83	103
Poultry	162	127	130	143	160	156	165	205
Fish and seafood	114	110	76	119	107	96	115	150
Eggs	34	31	34	37	35	33	31	37
Dairy products	342	254	279	292	309	404	345	420
Fresh milk and cream	142	115	127	135	125	164	143	160
Other dairy products	200	140	152	156	185	240	203	260
Fruits and vegetables	521	391	442	489	472	525	518	662
Fresh fruits	154	116	128	155	139	149	137	207
Fresh vegetables	162	123	145	160	148	144	157	212
Processed fruits	117	84	85	102	107	127	133	145
Processed vegetables	87	69	83	72	78	106	91	99
Other food at home	1,006	742	768	797	966	1,114	1,133	1,219
Sugar and other sweets	110	78	98	80	109	132	123	125
Fats and oils	83	77	71	72	81	88	92	91
Miscellaneous foods	517	366	365	396	488	573	587	659
Nonalcoholic beverages	264	208	220	232	261	287	290	292
Food prepared by CU on trips	32	14	14	19	27	34	41	52
Food away from home	**2,504**	**1,246**	**1,372**	**1,893**	**2,031**	**2,337**	**2,867**	**4,044**
ALCOHOLIC BEVERAGES	**439**	**250**	**246**	**299**	**379**	**447**	**512**	**671**
HOUSING	**13,895**	**7,587**	**8,096**	**9,879**	**11,235**	**12,809**	**15,508**	**23,092**
Shelter	**8,460**	**4,465**	**4,923**	**5,921**	**6,860**	**7,779**	**9,509**	**14,137**
Owned dwellings	4,552	1,091	1,019	1,521	3,008	3,613	5,854	10,292
Mortgage interest and charges	3,122	671	481	940	2,004	2,444	4,205	7,183
Property taxes	769	242	243	300	506	571	996	1,665
Maintenance, repair, insurance, other expenses	662	178	295	281	499	598	653	1,444
Rented dwellings	3,638	3,278	3,813	4,324	3,709	3,974	3,408	3,136
Other lodging	270	95	90	76	143	192	246	709
Utilities, fuels, and public services	**2,542**	**1,843**	**1,926**	**2,167**	**2,369**	**2,564**	**2,761**	**3,308**
Natural gas	318	209	195	289	307	305	346	439
Electricity	878	709	779	812	811	904	929	1,024
Fuel oil and other fuels	58	18	55	46	53	69	54	80
Telephone	1,024	746	748	833	964	1,012	1,126	1,368
Water and other public services	264	161	150	187	234	275	307	396

	complete income reporters aged 25 to 34	under $10,000	$10,000– $19,999	$20,000– $29,999	$30,000– $39,999	$40,000– $49,999	$50,000– $69,999	$70,000 or more
Household services	**$856**	**$361**	**$299**	**$629**	**$469**	**$687**	**$1,058**	**$1,676**
Personal services	612	201	201	504	299	487	760	1,210
Other household services	244	160	98	125	170	201	298	465
Housekeeping supplies	**452**	**298**	**290**	**330**	**390**	**413**	**527**	**669**
Laundry and cleaning supplies	138	142	105	110	140	133	152	166
Other household products	205	102	128	146	160	178	263	313
Postage and stationery	109	54	57	73	91	102	112	190
Household furnishings and equipment	**1,586**	**621**	**659**	**832**	**1,146**	**1,366**	**1,652**	**3,302**
Household textiles	115	34	47	75	85	102	151	200
Furniture	475	207	222	279	330	364	495	985
Floor coverings	27	10	14	15	13	29	25	59
Major appliances	188	51	79	80	168	155	213	381
Small appliances, misc. housewares	94	30	37	82	103	86	77	168
Miscellaneous household equipment	687	289	260	301	448	630	691	1,509
APPAREL AND RELATED SERVICES	**2,087**	**1,107**	**1,510**	**1,433**	**1,960**	**1,903**	**2,013**	**3,423**
Men and boys	**508**	**186**	**297**	**380**	**529**	**376**	**511**	**864**
Men, aged 16 or older	392	106	142	268	417	299	420	713
Boys, aged 2 to 15	115	80	155	112	112	78	91	151
Women and girls	**690**	**379**	**546**	**512**	**620**	**707**	**659**	**1,057**
Women, aged 16 or older	537	313	375	406	443	530	534	860
Girls, aged 2 to 15	153	65	171	107	178	178	125	197
Children under age 2	**189**	**70**	**163**	**104**	**179**	**172**	**204**	**304**
Footwear	**400**	**321**	**341**	**239**	**424**	**339**	**363**	**623**
Other apparel products and services	**301**	**152**	**164**	**198**	**208**	**309**	**276**	**576**
TRANSPORTATION	**8,617**	**4,153**	**4,645**	**5,693**	**7,790**	**9,148**	**10,502**	**13,116**
Vehicle purchases	**4,333**	**2,198**	**2,374**	**2,845**	**3,978**	**4,649**	**5,497**	**6,305**
Cars and trucks, new	1,716	557	551	716	1,304	1,820	2,363	3,144
Cars and trucks, used	2,544	1,588	1,822	2,127	2,594	2,768	3,069	2,980
Other vehicles	73	53	–	2	80	61	65	181
Gasoline and motor oil	**1,308**	**744**	**828**	**1,028**	**1,268**	**1,384**	**1,472**	**1,818**
Other vehicle expenses	**2,597**	**1,019**	**1,256**	**1,610**	**2,213**	**2,768**	**3,159**	**4,274**
Vehicle finance charges	504	114	168	338	429	551	676	823
Maintenance and repairs	638	394	401	426	600	675	717	943
Vehicle insurance	859	336	468	616	815	992	1,048	1,226
Vehicle rentals, leases, licenses, other charges	597	175	219	230	368	551	717	1,282
Public transportation	**378**	**192**	**186**	**210**	**331**	**347**	**374**	**719**
HEALTH CARE	**1,392**	**623**	**688**	**957**	**1,379**	**1,622**	**1,762**	**1,931**
Health insurance	742	262	303	472	783	923	936	1,058
Medical services	385	166	221	293	330	411	524	525
Drugs	206	157	136	150	213	225	235	263
Medical supplies	58	40	28	43	53	63	67	85
ENTERTAINMENT	**2,068**	**857**	**977**	**1,174**	**1,784**	**2,171**	**2,515**	**3,465**
Fees and admissions	504	175	205	209	347	488	494	1,109
Television, radio, sound equipment	749	427	468	569	702	730	858	1,092
Pets, toys, and playground equipment	394	208	203	248	331	416	504	598
Other entertainment products and services	421	46	100	148	404	537	659	665
PERSONAL CARE PRODUCTS AND SERVICES	**497**	**264**	**386**	**382**	**477**	**498**	**545**	**686**
READING	**113**	**51**	**56**	**72**	**96**	**100**	**122**	**205**
EDUCATION	**525**	**771**	**407**	**369**	**374**	**430**	**525**	**770**

	complete income reporters aged 25 to 34	under $10,000	$10,000– $19,999	$20,000– $29,999	$30,000– $39,999	$40,000– $49,999	$50,000– $69,999	$70,000 or more
TOBACCO PRODUCTS AND SMOKING SUPPLIES	$333	$300	$353	$317	$378	$410	$326	$276
MISCELLANEOUS	669	342	319	528	650	600	839	987
CASH CONTRIBUTIONS	807	268	348	540	714	801	846	1,467
PERSONAL INSURANCE AND PENSIONS	4,666	325	1,153	2,117	3,225	4,128	5,811	10,190
Life and other personal insurance	244	59	102	112	187	232	286	488
Pensions and Social Security	4,422	266	1,050	2,005	3,038	3,896	5,525	9,702
PERSONAL TAXES	2,589	–216	–175	432	1,239	1,879	2,831	7,681
Federal income taxes	1,948	–235	–269	221	864	1,324	2,126	6,052
State and local income taxes	577	7	76	189	337	513	632	1,472
Other taxes	64	11	17	22	38	42	74	158
GIFTS FOR NON–HOUSEHOLD MEMBERS	702	306	467	537	512	667	740	1,187
Food	36	17	18	26	45	19	40	61
Alcoholic beverages	15	6	0	8	15	13	15	30
Housing	224	105	108	217	146	190	251	381
Housekeeping supplies	41	7	28	34	21	28	39	84
Household textiles	13	18	1	22	9	10	24	7
Appliances and misc. housewares	19	2	6	19	11	39	18	27
Major appliances	5	2	1	1	–	15	3	11
Small appliances and misc. housewares	14	1	5	18	11	24	15	16
Miscellaneous household equipment	50	12	11	44	41	27	69	90
Other housing	102	66	62	98	63	87	101	174
Apparel and services	235	125	222	155	151	270	217	387
Males, aged 2 or older	50	6	39	42	25	53	48	92
Females, aged 2 or older	69	61	50	41	46	47	48	147
Children under age 2	61	35	85	29	42	54	64	95
Other apparel products and services	55	22	48	44	39	116	56	53
Jewelry and watches	34	16	7	23	14	109	40	27
All other apparel products and services	21	7	41	21	25	7	16	25
Transportation	29	3	58	4	10	22	56	32
Health care	10	3	2	5	8	12	3	27
Entertainment	67	20	28	50	56	76	69	117
Toys, games, hobbies, and tricycles	23	9	13	10	21	23	33	37
Other entertainment	44	10	15	41	34	53	36	80
Personal care products and services	15	5	4	13	28	10	11	20
Reading	1	–	–	–	1	2	–	1
Education	24	3	10	11	26	25	31	38
All other gifts	46	19	16	47	26	28	47	95

Note: Spending by category will not add to total spending because gift spending is also included in the preceding product and service categories and personal taxes are not included in the total. (–) means sample is too small to make a reliable estimate.
Source: Bureau of Labor Statistics, 2001 and 2002 Consumer Expenditure Surveys, Internet site http://www.bls.gov/cex/; calculations by New Strategist

Table 1.11 Aged 25 to 34: Indexed spending by income, 2001–02

(indexed average annual spending of consumer units (CU) headed by people aged 25 to 34 by product and service category and before-tax income of consumer unit, 2001–02; complete income reporters only; index definition: an index of 100 is the average for all consumer units; an index of 132 means that spending by consumer units in that group is 32 percent above the average for all consumer units; an index of 68 indicates spending that is 32 percent below the average for all consumer units)

	complete income reporters aged 25 to 34	under $10,000	$10,000–$19,999	$20,000–$29,999	$30,000–$39,999	$40,000–$49,999	$50,000–$69,999	$70,000 or more
Average spending of CU, total	$41,766	$20,592	$23,115	$28,437	$35,467	$40,712	$47,953	$68,208
Average spending of CU, index	100	49	55	68	85	97	115	163
FOOD	100	65	69	83	89	100	108	140
Food at home	100	78	81	88	95	105	103	123
Cereals and bakery products	100	76	81	89	98	102	103	123
Cereals and cereal products	100	84	79	95	92	111	95	122
Bakery products	100	72	82	85	102	98	108	123
Meats, poultry, fish, and eggs	100	86	85	96	96	96	96	123
Beef	100	84	89	93	100	92	93	127
Pork	100	88	86	92	91	108	96	120
Other meats	100	87	95	113	91	102	89	111
Poultry	100	79	80	88	99	96	102	127
Fish and seafood	100	96	67	104	94	84	101	132
Eggs	100	90	100	109	103	97	91	109
Dairy products	100	74	81	85	90	118	101	123
Fresh milk and cream	100	81	89	95	88	115	101	113
Other dairy products	100	70	76	78	93	120	102	130
Fruits and vegetables	100	75	85	94	91	101	99	127
Fresh fruits	100	75	83	101	90	97	89	134
Fresh vegetables	100	76	90	99	91	89	97	131
Processed fruits	100	72	72	87	91	109	114	124
Processed vegetables	100	79	96	83	90	122	105	114
Other food at home	100	74	76	79	96	111	113	121
Sugar and other sweets	100	71	89	73	99	120	112	114
Fats and oils	100	92	85	87	98	106	111	110
Miscellaneous foods	100	71	71	77	94	111	114	127
Nonalcoholic beverages	100	79	83	88	99	109	110	111
Food prepared by CU on trips	100	43	44	59	84	106	128	163
Food away from home	100	50	55	76	81	93	114	162
ALCOHOLIC BEVERAGES	100	57	56	68	86	102	117	153
HOUSING	100	55	58	71	81	92	112	166
Shelter	100	53	58	70	81	92	112	167
Owned dwellings	100	24	22	33	66	79	129	226
Mortgage interest and charges	100	21	15	30	64	78	135	230
Property taxes	100	31	32	39	66	74	130	217
Maintenance, repair, insurance, other expenses	100	27	45	42	75	90	99	218
Rented dwellings	100	90	105	119	102	109	94	86
Other lodging	100	35	33	28	53	71	91	263
Utilities, fuels, and public services	100	73	76	85	93	101	109	130
Natural gas	100	66	61	91	97	96	109	138
Electricity	100	81	89	92	92	103	106	117
Fuel oil and other fuels	100	30	95	79	91	119	93	138
Telephone	100	73	73	81	94	99	110	134
Water and other public services	100	61	57	71	89	104	116	150

	complete income reporters aged 25 to 34	under $10,000	$10,000– $19,999	$20,000– $29,999	$30,000– $39,999	$40,000– $49,999	$50,000– $69,999	$70,000 or more
Household services	100	42	35	73	55	80	124	196
Personal services	100	33	33	82	49	80	124	198
Other household services	100	66	40	51	70	82	122	191
Housekeeping supplies	100	66	64	73	86	91	117	148
Laundry and cleaning supplies	100	103	76	80	101	96	110	120
Other household products	100	50	62	71	78	87	128	153
Postage and stationery	100	49	53	67	83	94	103	174
Household furnishings and equipment	100	39	42	52	72	86	104	208
Household textiles	100	30	41	65	74	89	131	174
Furniture	100	44	47	59	69	77	104	207
Floor coverings	100	36	53	56	48	107	93	219
Major appliances	100	27	42	43	89	82	113	203
Small appliances, misc. housewares	100	32	39	87	110	91	82	179
Miscellaneous household equipment	100	42	38	44	65	92	101	220
APPAREL AND RELATED SERVICES	100	53	72	69	94	91	96	164
Men and boys	100	37	58	75	104	74	101	170
Men, aged 16 or older	100	27	36	68	106	76	107	182
Boys, aged 2 to 15	100	70	134	97	97	68	79	131
Women and girls	100	55	79	74	90	102	96	153
Women, aged 16 or older	100	58	70	76	82	99	99	160
Girls, aged 2 to 15	100	43	111	70	116	116	82	129
Children under age 2	100	37	86	55	95	91	108	161
Footwear	100	80	85	60	106	85	91	156
Other apparel products and services	100	51	55	66	69	103	92	191
TRANSPORTATION	100	48	54	66	90	106	122	152
Vehicle purchases	100	51	55	66	92	107	127	146
Cars and trucks, new	100	32	32	42	76	106	138	183
Cars and trucks, used	100	62	72	84	102	109	121	117
Other vehicles	100	73	–	3	110	84	89	248
Gasoline and motor oil	100	57	63	79	97	106	113	139
Other vehicle expenses	100	39	48	62	85	107	122	165
Vehicle finance charges	100	23	33	67	85	109	134	163
Maintenance and repairs	100	62	63	67	94	106	112	148
Vehicle insurance	100	39	55	72	95	115	122	143
Vehicle rentals, leases, licenses, other charges	100	29	37	39	62	92	120	215
Public transportation	100	51	49	56	88	92	99	190
HEALTH CARE	100	45	49	69	99	117	127	139
Health insurance	100	35	41	64	106	124	126	143
Medical services	100	43	57	76	86	107	136	136
Drugs	100	76	66	73	103	109	114	128
Medical supplies	100	69	48	74	91	109	116	147
ENTERTAINMENT	100	41	47	57	86	105	122	168
Fees and admissions	100	35	41	41	69	97	98	220
Television, radio, sound equipment	100	57	63	76	94	97	115	146
Pets, toys, and playground equipment	100	53	52	63	84	106	128	152
Other entertainment products and services	100	11	24	35	96	128	157	158
PERSONAL CARE PRODUCTS AND SERVICES	100	53	78	77	96	100	110	138
READING	100	45	49	64	85	88	108	181
EDUCATION	100	147	78	70	71	82	100	147

	complete income reporters aged 25 to 34	under $10,000	$10,000– $19,999	$20,000– $29,999	$30,000– $39,999	$40,000– $49,999	$50,000– $69,999	$70,000 or more
TOBACCO PRODUCTS AND SMOKING SUPPLIES	100	90	106	95	114	123	98	83
MISCELLANEOUS	100	51	48	79	97	90	125	148
CASH CONTRIBUTIONS	100	33	43	67	88	99	105	182
PERSONAL INSURANCE AND PENSIONS	100	7	25	45	69	88	125	218
Life and other personal insurance	100	24	42	46	77	95	117	200
Pensions and Social Security	100	6	24	45	69	88	125	219
PERSONAL TAXES	100	–	–	17	48	73	109	297
Federal income taxes	100	–	–	11	44	68	109	311
State and local income taxes	100	1	13	33	58	89	110	255
Other taxes	100	18	27	34	59	66	116	247
GIFTS FOR NON–HOUSEHOLD MEMBERS	100	44	66	76	73	95	105	169
Food	100	48	51	72	125	53	111	169
Alcoholic beverages	100	42	3	53	100	87	100	200
Housing	100	47	48	97	65	85	112	170
Housekeeping supplies	100	16	69	83	51	68	95	205
Household textiles	100	142	11	169	69	77	185	54
Appliances and misc. housewares	100	11	32	100	58	205	95	142
Major appliances	100	35	22	20	–	300	60	220
Small appliances and misc. housewares	100	7	35	129	79	171	107	114
Miscellaneous household equipment	100	24	22	88	82	54	138	180
Other housing	100	64	60	96	62	85	99	171
Apparel and services	100	53	94	66	64	115	92	165
Males, aged 2 or older	100	12	78	84	50	106	96	184
Females, aged 2 or older	100	88	73	59	67	68	70	213
Children under age 2	100	58	139	48	69	89	105	156
Other apparel products and services	100	40	87	80	71	211	102	96
Jewelry and watches	100	47	20	68	41	321	118	79
All other apparel products and services	100	33	194	100	119	33	76	119
Transportation	100	11	201	14	34	76	193	110
Health care	100	33	21	50	80	120	30	270
Entertainment	100	30	41	75	84	113	103	175
Toys, games, hobbies, and tricycles	100	40	55	43	91	100	143	161
Other entertainment	100	24	35	93	77	120	82	182
Personal care products and services	100	31	25	87	187	67	73	133
Reading	100	–	–	–	100	200	–	100
Education	100	12	41	46	108	104	129	158
All other gifts	100	41	34	102	57	61	102	207

Note: (–) means sample is too small to make a reliable estimate.
Source: Calculations by New Strategist based on the Bureau of Labor Statistics 2001 and 2002 Consumer Expenditure Surveys

Table 1.12 Aged 35 to 44: Average spending by income, 2001–02

(average annual spending of consumer units (CU) headed by people aged 35 to 44 by product and service category and before-tax income of consumer unit, 2001–02; complete income reporters only)

	complete income reporters aged 35 to 44	under $10,000	$10,000–$19,999	$20,000–$29,999	$30,000–$39,999	$40,000–$49,999	$50,000–$69,999	$70,000 or more
Number of consumer units (in thousands, add 000s)	19,847	1,255	1,971	2,222	2,320	2,231	3,641	6,208
Average number of persons per CU	3.2	2.6	3.0	2.8	3.0	3.2	3.4	3.6
Average income before taxes	$60,233	$4,080	$14,988	$24,698	$34,414	$44,680	$59,019	$114,611
Average annual spending	50,477	22,976	24,810	28,558	34,448	43,446	53,201	79,369
FOOD	**$6,728**	**$4,175**	**$4,770**	**$4,650**	**$4,910**	**$6,145**	**$7,440**	**$9,271**
Food at home	**3,827**	**2,553**	**3,303**	**2,996**	**3,068**	**3,655**	**4,048**	**4,842**
Cereals and bakery products	578	391	487	449	441	531	610	754
Cereals and cereal products	203	154	195	165	159	191	203	255
Bakery products	375	237	292	284	282	340	407	500
Meats, poultry, fish, and eggs	988	714	1,030	828	861	911	1,064	1,127
Beef	292	214	295	262	291	225	321	323
Pork	208	166	236	171	169	190	233	230
Other meats	133	93	129	117	115	117	136	161
Poultry	182	113	181	147	136	195	209	207
Fish and seafood	133	92	150	90	110	143	124	165
Eggs	40	36	39	42	39	42	42	40
Dairy products	423	279	323	333	340	398	438	556
Fresh milk and cream	169	122	145	150	150	165	176	200
Other dairy products	253	156	178	183	191	232	262	357
Fruits and vegetables	622	411	555	481	502	622	627	793
Fresh fruits	192	136	153	152	146	194	191	253
Fresh vegetables	190	115	173	155	158	200	187	237
Processed fruits	139	97	134	101	108	121	144	182
Processed vegetables	100	62	95	73	90	108	104	120
Other food at home	1,215	757	908	904	924	1,192	1,309	1,612
Sugar and other sweets	152	107	117	114	108	145	155	206
Fats and oils	98	65	101	89	85	103	103	106
Miscellaneous foods	588	348	420	443	429	594	629	796
Nonalcoholic beverages	329	219	259	234	268	317	376	417
Food prepared by CU on trips	48	18	9	24	34	34	47	87
Food away from home	**2,902**	**1,622**	**1,467**	**1,654**	**1,842**	**2,490**	**3,392**	**4,429**
ALCOHOLIC BEVERAGES	**445**	**272**	**225**	**294**	**279**	**474**	**401**	**696**
HOUSING	**16,452**	**8,617**	**8,722**	**9,959**	**11,396**	**13,848**	**16,610**	**25,617**
Shelter	**9,801**	**5,206**	**5,249**	**6,000**	**6,742**	**8,302**	**9,790**	**15,224**
Owned dwellings	6,967	2,489	1,733	2,562	3,728	5,432	7,369	12,636
Mortgage interest and charges	4,583	1,566	901	1,532	2,422	3,631	4,869	8,437
Property taxes	1,422	548	438	585	761	1,001	1,463	2,585
Maintenance, repair, insurance, other expenses	962	375	395	446	544	801	1,036	1,614
Rented dwellings	2,348	2,514	3,412	3,252	2,853	2,624	2,036	1,549
Other lodging	486	202	104	185	161	246	385	1,039
Utilities, fuels, and public services	**3,063**	**2,058**	**2,116**	**2,416**	**2,701**	**2,890**	**3,302**	**3,857**
Natural gas	409	268	258	295	348	390	434	542
Electricity	1,112	889	833	948	1,034	1,063	1,175	1,315
Fuel oil and other fuels	93	34	46	75	106	87	115	111
Telephone	1,080	657	767	848	928	993	1,166	1,385
Water and other public services	369	211	212	250	285	356	413	504

	complete income reporters aged 35 to 44	under $10,000	$10,000– $19,999	$20,000– $29,999	$30,000– $39,999	$40,000– $49,999	$50,000– $69,999	$70,000 or more
Household services	**$1,004**	**$317**	**$314**	**$330**	**$621**	**$561**	**$791**	**$2,030**
Personal services	578	79	152	164	387	287	425	1,227
Other household services	426	238	161	166	234	274	366	803
Housekeeping supplies	**660**	**347**	**397**	**386**	**424**	**600**	**837**	**942**
Laundry and cleaning supplies	166	100	148	116	133	171	203	195
Other household products	347	193	174	175	210	296	472	510
Postage and stationery	147	54	75	95	81	133	162	236
Household furnishings and equipment	**1,924**	**689**	**647**	**826**	**908**	**1,495**	**1,891**	**3,565**
Household textiles	158	65	82	65	100	136	118	295
Furniture	502	88	162	183	188	357	460	1,002
Floor coverings	49	9	11	10	17	25	45	104
Major appliances	238	127	86	124	123	189	261	396
Small appliances, misc. housewares	108	31	59	44	39	128	89	197
Miscellaneous household equipment	870	371	247	401	440	660	918	1,570
APPAREL AND RELATED SERVICES	**2,284**	**1,277**	**1,573**	**1,093**	**1,658**	**2,001**	**2,190**	**3,608**
Men and boys	**581**	**319**	**316**	**259**	**384**	**508**	**566**	**968**
Men, aged 16 or older	396	228	171	161	262	353	367	689
Boys, aged 2 to 15	186	91	145	98	122	155	199	279
Women and girls	**889**	**510**	**672**	**388**	**691**	**794**	**800**	**1,407**
Women, aged 16 or older	624	395	445	235	451	560	573	1,016
Girls, aged 2 to 15	264	115	227	153	240	234	227	391
Children under age 2	**105**	**25**	**67**	**56**	**97**	**71**	**98**	**171**
Footwear	**408**	**295**	**360**	**212**	**295**	**386**	**479**	**540**
Other apparel products and services	**301**	**127**	**157**	**177**	**190**	**242**	**247**	**522**
TRANSPORTATION	**9,711**	**4,434**	**4,431**	**5,417**	**6,745**	**9,152**	**10,872**	**14,643**
Vehicle purchases	**4,761**	**2,473**	**2,148**	**2,401**	**3,097**	**4,380**	**5,406**	**7,278**
Cars and trucks, new	2,318	890	816	711	1,120	2,202	2,548	4,013
Cars and trucks, used	2,365	1,584	1,332	1,689	1,962	2,103	2,732	3,122
Other vehicles	78	–	–	1	14	75	125	143
Gasoline and motor oil	**1,532**	**700**	**875**	**1,144**	**1,293**	**1,463**	**1,703**	**2,061**
Other vehicle expenses	**2,988**	**1,131**	**1,218**	**1,638**	**2,119**	**3,054**	**3,376**	**4,506**
Vehicle finance charges	503	154	138	263	398	509	622	744
Maintenance and repairs	900	385	404	513	577	1,073	985	1,332
Vehicle insurance	958	368	490	649	843	948	1,119	1,287
Vehicle rentals, leases, licenses, other charges	627	225	187	214	302	523	650	1,142
Public transportation	**430**	**129**	**191**	**234**	**236**	**255**	**387**	**799**
HEALTH CARE	**1,994**	**898**	**1,057**	**1,327**	**1,718**	**1,820**	**2,357**	**2,708**
Health insurance	984	440	460	632	878	983	1,181	1,312
Medical services	588	254	250	392	477	461	728	838
Drugs	326	171	282	261	276	295	342	416
Medical supplies	96	33	65	42	88	82	106	142
ENTERTAINMENT	**2,724**	**988**	**999**	**1,204**	**1,631**	**2,070**	**2,792**	**4,789**
Fees and admissions	746	181	147	214	327	468	685	1,533
Television, radio, sound equipment	828	451	422	513	658	833	908	1,162
Pets, toys, and playground equipment	484	155	215	294	303	396	527	784
Other entertainment products and services	665	200	215	183	343	373	672	1,310
PERSONAL CARE PRODUCTS AND SERVICES	**613**	**350**	**405**	**391**	**461**	**538**	**615**	**904**
READING	**142**	**37**	**48**	**64**	**89**	**113**	**160**	**240**
EDUCATION	**722**	**303**	**283**	**311**	**333**	**541**	**878**	**1,216**

	complete income reporters aged 35 to 44	under $10,000	$10,000– $19,999	$20,000– $29,999	$30,000– $39,999	$40,000– $49,999	$50,000– $69,999	$70,000 or more
TOBACCO PRODUCTS AND SMOKING SUPPLIES	$398	$403	$457	$489	$425	$439	$434	$301
MISCELLANEOUS	863	400	428	591	686	812	845	1,292
CASH CONTRIBUTIONS	1,324	347	278	610	785	1,084	1,394	2,356
PERSONAL INSURANCE AND PENSIONS	6,077	475	1,133	2,158	3,333	4,407	6,212	11,727
Life and other personal insurance	426	161	113	226	267	316	433	744
Pensions and Social Security	5,651	314	1,020	1,932	3,066	4,092	5,780	10,983
PERSONAL TAXES	3,322	–191	–261	317	1,134	2,076	2,916	7,750
Federal income taxes	2,514	–226	–325	120	737	1,379	2,111	6,134
State and local income taxes	674	8	44	149	322	540	676	1,375
Other taxes	134	27	20	48	76	157	129	240
GIFTS FOR NON–HOUSEHOLD MEMBERS	957	607	493	578	638	813	1,081	1,426
Food	59	38	36	24	18	25	89	95
Alcoholic beverages	18	23	7	11	5	10	16	33
Housing	248	159	78	156	139	250	284	377
Housekeeping supplies	48	22	14	36	22	51	72	67
Household textiles	10	8	0	2	2	17	6	21
Appliances and misc. housewares	22	9	6	15	8	38	18	36
Major appliances	6	1	2	4	4	17	6	5
Small appliances and misc. housewares	16	8	4	10	4	21	12	31
Miscellaneous household equipment	70	34	11	42	31	69	88	112
Other housing	97	86	48	61	76	75	99	142
Apparel and services	238	236	108	83	297	151	264	335
Males, aged 2 or older	61	93	32	25	62	41	65	81
Females, aged 2 or older	83	104	23	15	111	39	93	123
Children under age 2	45	22	19	33	52	35	48	63
Other apparel products and services	50	16	34	10	71	35	58	69
Jewelry and watches	21	6	10	7	26	14	10	38
All other apparel products and services	29	10	25	2	45	21	47	31
Transportation	73	55	87	119	25	189	74	32
Health care	28	4	91	47	14	18	14	22
Entertainment	81	28	39	42	66	63	102	122
Toys, games, hobbies, and tricycles	30	12	17	22	31	16	33	44
Other entertainment	51	15	23	20	35	47	69	78
Personal care products and services	25	36	17	22	8	19	21	36
Reading	1	–	–	–	–	–	1	2
Education	116	24	16	39	30	43	117	252
All other gifts	70	5	12	34	36	45	97	120

Note: Spending by category will not add to total spending because gift spending is also included in the preceding product and service categories and personal taxes are not included in the total. (–) means sample is too small to make a reliable estimate.
Source: Bureau of Labor Statistics, 2001 and 2002 Consumer Expenditure Surveys, Internet site http://www.bls.gov/cex/; calculations by New Strategist

Table 1.13 Aged 35 to 44: Indexed spending by income, 2001–02

(indexed average annual spending of consumer units (CU) headed by people aged 35 to 44 by product and service category and before-tax income of consumer unit, 2001–02; complete income reporters only; index definition: an index of 100 is the average for all consumer units; an index of 132 means that spending by consumer units in that group is 32 percent above the average for all consumer units; an index of 68 indicates spending that is 32 percent below the average for all consumer units)

	complete income reporters aged 35 to 44	under $10,000	$10,000– $19,999	$20,000– $29,999	$30,000– $39,999	$40,000– $49,999	$50,000– $69,999	$70,000 or more
Average spending of CU, total	$50,477	$22,976	$24,810	$28,558	$34,448	$43,446	$53,201	$79,369
Average spending of CU, index	100	46	49	57	68	86	105	157
FOOD	100	62	71	69	73	91	111	138
Food at home	100	67	86	78	80	96	106	127
Cereals and bakery products	100	68	84	78	76	92	106	130
Cereals and cereal products	100	76	96	81	78	94	100	126
Bakery products	100	63	78	76	75	91	109	133
Meats, poultry, fish, and eggs	100	72	104	84	87	92	108	114
Beef	100	73	101	90	100	77	110	111
Pork	100	80	114	82	81	91	112	111
Other meats	100	70	97	88	86	88	102	121
Poultry	100	62	99	81	75	107	115	114
Fish and seafood	100	69	113	68	83	108	93	124
Eggs	100	89	98	105	98	105	105	100
Dairy products	100	66	76	79	80	94	104	131
Fresh milk and cream	100	72	86	89	89	98	104	118
Other dairy products	100	62	70	72	75	92	104	141
Fruits and vegetables	100	66	89	77	81	100	101	127
Fresh fruits	100	71	80	79	76	101	99	132
Fresh vegetables	100	61	91	82	83	105	98	125
Processed fruits	100	70	96	73	78	87	104	131
Processed vegetables	100	62	95	73	90	108	104	120
Other food at home	100	62	75	74	76	98	108	133
Sugar and other sweets	100	70	77	75	71	95	102	136
Fats and oils	100	67	103	91	87	105	105	108
Miscellaneous foods	100	59	71	75	73	101	107	135
Nonalcoholic beverages	100	67	79	71	81	96	114	127
Food prepared by CU on trips	100	37	20	50	71	71	98	181
Food away from home	100	56	51	57	63	86	117	153
ALCOHOLIC BEVERAGES	100	61	51	66	63	107	90	156
HOUSING	100	52	53	61	69	84	101	156
Shelter	100	53	54	61	69	85	100	155
Owned dwellings	100	36	25	37	54	78	106	181
Mortgage interest and charges	100	34	20	33	53	79	106	184
Property taxes	100	39	31	41	54	70	103	182
Maintenance, repair, insurance, other expenses	100	39	41	46	57	83	108	168
Rented dwellings	100	107	145	139	122	112	87	66
Other lodging	100	42	21	38	33	51	79	214
Utilities, fuels, and public services	100	67	69	79	88	94	108	126
Natural gas	100	65	63	72	85	95	106	133
Electricity	100	80	75	85	93	96	106	118
Fuel oil and other fuels	100	36	49	81	114	94	124	119
Telephone	100	61	71	79	86	92	108	128
Water and other public services	100	57	57	68	77	96	112	137

	complete income reporters aged 35 to 44	under $10,000	$10,000– $19,999	$20,000– $29,999	$30,000– $39,999	$40,000– $49,999	$50,000– $69,999	$70,000 or more
Household services	**100**	**32**	**31**	**33**	**62**	**56**	**79**	**202**
Personal services	100	14	26	28	67	50	74	212
Other household services	100	56	38	39	55	64	86	188
Housekeeping supplies	**100**	**53**	**60**	**58**	**64**	**91**	**127**	**143**
Laundry and cleaning supplies	100	60	89	70	80	103	122	117
Other household products	100	56	50	50	61	85	136	147
Postage and stationery	100	37	51	65	55	90	110	161
Household furnishings and equipment	**100**	**36**	**34**	**43**	**47**	**78**	**98**	**185**
Household textiles	100	41	52	41	63	86	75	187
Furniture	100	17	32	36	37	71	92	200
Floor coverings	100	17	22	20	35	51	92	212
Major appliances	100	53	36	52	52	79	110	166
Small appliances, misc. housewares	100	28	55	41	36	119	82	182
Miscellaneous household equipment	100	43	28	46	51	76	106	180
APPAREL AND RELATED SERVICES	**100**	**56**	**69**	**48**	**73**	**88**	**96**	**158**
Men and boys	**100**	**55**	**54**	**45**	**66**	**87**	**97**	**167**
Men, aged 16 or older	100	58	43	41	66	89	93	174
Boys, aged 2 to 15	100	49	78	53	66	83	107	150
Women and girls	**100**	**57**	**76**	**44**	**78**	**89**	**90**	**158**
Women, aged 16 or older	100	63	71	38	72	90	92	163
Girls, aged 2 to 15	100	43	86	58	91	89	86	148
Children under age 2	**100**	**24**	**64**	**53**	**92**	**68**	**93**	**163**
Footwear	**100**	**72**	**88**	**52**	**72**	**95**	**117**	**132**
Other apparel products and services	**100**	**42**	**52**	**59**	**63**	**80**	**82**	**173**
TRANSPORTATION	**100**	**46**	**46**	**56**	**69**	**94**	**112**	**151**
Vehicle purchases	**100**	**52**	**45**	**50**	**65**	**92**	**114**	**153**
Cars and trucks, new	100	38	35	31	48	95	110	173
Cars and trucks, used	100	67	56	71	83	89	116	132
Other vehicles	100	–	–	1	18	96	160	183
Gasoline and motor oil	**100**	**46**	**57**	**75**	**84**	**95**	**111**	**135**
Other vehicle expenses	**100**	**38**	**41**	**55**	**71**	**102**	**113**	**151**
Vehicle finance charges	100	31	27	52	79	101	124	148
Maintenance and repairs	100	43	45	57	64	119	109	148
Vehicle insurance	100	38	51	68	88	99	117	134
Vehicle rentals, leases, licenses, other charges	100	36	30	34	48	83	104	182
Public transportation	**100**	**30**	**44**	**54**	**55**	**59**	**90**	**186**
HEALTH CARE	**100**	**45**	**53**	**67**	**86**	**91**	**118**	**136**
Health insurance	100	45	47	64	89	100	120	133
Medical services	100	43	43	67	81	78	124	143
Drugs	100	53	87	80	85	90	105	128
Medical supplies	100	34	68	44	92	85	110	148
ENTERTAINMENT	**100**	**36**	**37**	**44**	**60**	**76**	**102**	**176**
Fees and admissions	100	24	20	29	44	63	92	205
Television, radio, sound equipment	100	54	51	62	79	101	110	140
Pets, toys, and playground equipment	100	32	44	61	63	82	109	162
Other entertainment products and services	100	30	32	28	52	56	101	197
PERSONAL CARE PRODUCTS AND SERVICES	**100**	**57**	**66**	**64**	**75**	**88**	**100**	**147**
READING	**100**	**26**	**34**	**45**	**63**	**80**	**113**	**169**
EDUCATION	**100**	**42**	**39**	**43**	**46**	**75**	**122**	**168**

	complete income reporters aged 35 to 44	under $10,000	$10,000– $19,999	$20,000– $29,999	$30,000– $39,999	$40,000– $49,999	$50,000– $69,999	$70,000 or more
TOBACCO PRODUCTS AND SMOKING SUPPLIES	**100**	**101**	**115**	**123**	**107**	**110**	**109**	**76**
MISCELLANEOUS	**100**	**46**	**50**	**68**	**79**	**94**	**98**	**150**
CASH CONTRIBUTIONS	**100**	**26**	**21**	**46**	**59**	**82**	**105**	**178**
PERSONAL INSURANCE AND PENSIONS	**100**	**8**	**19**	**36**	**55**	**73**	**102**	**193**
Life and other personal insurance	100	38	26	53	63	74	102	175
Pensions and Social Security	100	6	18	34	54	72	102	194
PERSONAL TAXES	**100**	**–**	**–**	**10**	**34**	**62**	**88**	**233**
Federal income taxes	100	–	–	5	29	55	84	244
State and local income taxes	100	1	6	22	48	80	100	204
Other taxes	100	20	15	36	57	117	96	179
GIFTS FOR NON–HOUSEHOLD MEMBERS	**100**	**63**	**51**	**60**	**67**	**85**	**113**	**149**
Food	**100**	**64**	**61**	**41**	**31**	**42**	**151**	**161**
Alcoholic beverages	**100**	**128**	**40**	**61**	**28**	**56**	**89**	**183**
Housing	**100**	**64**	**32**	**63**	**56**	**101**	**115**	**152**
Housekeeping supplies	100	46	29	75	46	106	150	140
Household textiles	100	75	5	20	20	170	60	210
Appliances and misc. housewares	100	43	27	68	36	173	82	164
Major appliances	100	19	32	67	67	283	100	83
Small appliances and misc. housewares	100	51	25	63	25	131	75	194
Miscellaneous household equipment	100	49	15	60	44	99	126	160
Other housing	100	88	49	63	78	77	102	146
Apparel and services	**100**	**99**	**45**	**35**	**125**	**63**	**111**	**141**
Males, aged 2 or older	100	153	53	41	102	67	107	133
Females, aged 2 or older	100	125	27	18	134	47	112	148
Children under age 2	100	48	41	73	116	78	107	140
Other apparel products and services	100	32	68	20	142	70	116	138
Jewelry and watches	100	27	46	33	124	67	48	181
All other apparel products and services	100	36	86	7	155	72	162	107
Transportation	**100**	**76**	**119**	**163**	**34**	**259**	**101**	**44**
Health care	**100**	**13**	**324**	**168**	**50**	**64**	**50**	**79**
Entertainment	**100**	**35**	**49**	**52**	**81**	**78**	**126**	**151**
Toys, games, hobbies, and tricycles	100	41	57	73	103	53	110	147
Other entertainment	100	30	44	39	69	92	135	153
Personal care products and services	**100**	**144**	**70**	**88**	**32**	**76**	**84**	**144**
Reading	**100**	**–**	**–**	**–**	**–**	**–**	**100**	**200**
Education	**100**	**21**	**14**	**34**	**26**	**37**	**101**	**217**
All other gifts	**100**	**8**	**17**	**49**	**51**	**64**	**139**	**171**

Note: (–) means sample is too small to make a reliable estimate.
Source: Calculations by New Strategist based on the Bureau of Labor Statistics 2001 and 2002 Consumer Expenditure Surveys

Table 1.14 Aged 45 to 54: Average spending by income, 2001–02

(average annual spending of consumer units (CU) headed by people aged 45 to 54 by product and service category and before-tax income of consumer unit, 2001–02; complete income reporters only)

	complete income reporters aged 45 to 54	under $10,000	$10,000–$19,999	$20,000–$29,999	$30,000–$39,999	$40,000–$49,999	$50,000–$69,999	$70,000 or more
Number of consumer units (in thousands, add 000s)	17,889	1,290	1,721	1,881	2,024	1,881	3,109	5,984
Average number of persons per CU	2.7	1.9	2.2	2.4	2.4	2.4	2.8	3.1
Average income before taxes	$63,063	$4,995	$14,983	$24,579	$34,512	$44,070	$59,219	$119,121
Average annual spending	50,936	19,875	24,852	28,296	36,817	40,679	50,117	80,663
FOOD	**$6,637**	**$3,488**	**$3,603**	**$4,372**	**$5,586**	**$5,788**	**$6,881**	**$9,390**
Food at home	**3,752**	**2,423**	**2,520**	**2,852**	**3,622**	**3,456**	**3,854**	**4,763**
Cereals and bakery products	539	319	351	409	509	487	571	692
Cereals and cereal products	181	123	126	140	177	167	194	223
Bakery products	357	196	225	269	332	320	377	469
Meats, poultry, fish, and eggs	999	748	737	827	1,027	931	1,025	1,185
Beef	305	216	221	246	308	290	300	373
Pork	211	186	178	197	243	179	223	224
Other meats	126	100	87	98	116	125	141	146
Poultry	181	121	138	145	179	186	183	216
Fish and seafood	136	92	79	101	137	110	138	181
Eggs	41	33	34	39	43	42	41	46
Dairy products	399	266	273	299	350	365	416	515
Fresh milk and cream	156	119	123	133	154	142	151	188
Other dairy products	244	147	151	166	196	223	265	327
Fruits and vegetables	628	379	402	498	614	547	635	817
Fresh fruits	194	123	113	150	177	171	198	257
Fresh vegetables	204	126	127	166	201	177	208	262
Processed fruits	131	71	81	105	133	117	129	170
Processed vegetables	100	58	81	77	103	82	100	128
Other food at home	1,186	712	757	820	1,121	1,126	1,208	1,555
Sugar and other sweets	138	80	83	111	121	151	130	179
Fats and oils	106	73	73	91	103	92	111	130
Miscellaneous foods	567	307	352	361	540	547	602	747
Nonalcoholic beverages	324	232	237	233	319	302	318	410
Food prepared by CU on trips	51	21	12	24	38	34	48	89
Food away from home	**2,886**	**1,064**	**1,083**	**1,520**	**1,964**	**2,332**	**3,027**	**4,627**
ALCOHOLIC BEVERAGES	**462**	**277**	**167**	**210**	**293**	**323**	**450**	**769**
HOUSING	**15,475**	**7,707**	**8,566**	**9,559**	**11,395**	**12,058**	**14,548**	**23,938**
Shelter	**9,103**	**4,587**	**5,014**	**5,558**	**6,591**	**7,082**	**8,326**	**14,255**
Owned dwellings	6,694	2,435	2,155	3,062	3,978	4,696	6,119	11,904
Mortgage interest and charges	4,004	1,422	1,134	1,776	2,140	2,933	3,564	7,281
Property taxes	1,525	588	544	691	918	992	1,435	2,690
Maintenance, repair, insurance, other expenses	1,165	424	477	596	920	772	1,120	1,933
Rented dwellings	1,735	1,992	2,698	2,328	2,430	2,082	1,656	912
Other lodging	674	160	160	167	184	304	550	1,439
Utilities, fuels, and public services	**3,151**	**1,970**	**2,217**	**2,505**	**2,647**	**2,874**	**3,235**	**4,092**
Natural gas	414	221	256	298	348	386	398	577
Electricity	1,131	808	873	985	980	1,042	1,163	1,384
Fuel oil and other fuels	117	85	91	102	84	82	109	164
Telephone	1,106	649	762	833	929	1,020	1,158	1,450
Water and other public services	382	207	234	288	305	344	406	517

	complete income reporters aged 45 to 54	under $10,000	$10,000– $19,999	$20,000– $29,999	$30,000– $39,999	$40,000– $49,999	$50,000– $69,999	$70,000 or more
Household services	**$613**	**$170**	**$221**	**$266**	**$347**	**$410**	**$485**	**$1,151**
Personal services	158	21	19	47	89	122	125	314
Other household services	455	149	201	219	259	287	360	837
Housekeeping supplies	**679**	**379**	**359**	**410**	**566**	**518**	**761**	**962**
Laundry and cleaning supplies	164	127	115	127	133	142	177	207
Other household products	352	173	193	198	309	257	393	508
Postage and stationery	163	79	50	85	124	119	191	248
Household furnishings and equipment	**1,929**	**600**	**754**	**820**	**1,243**	**1,174**	**1,742**	**3,479**
Household textiles	161	76	93	85	103	114	141	267
Furniture	472	123	136	217	221	290	345	933
Floor coverings	64	25	4	18	29	28	38	141
Major appliances	230	71	74	115	154	156	242	388
Small appliances, misc. housewares	116	66	55	58	77	70	111	193
Miscellaneous household equipment	887	239	392	326	659	515	866	1,557
APPAREL AND RELATED SERVICES	**2,274**	**1,170**	**1,269**	**1,165**	**1,397**	**1,970**	**2,380**	**3,485**
Men and boys	**579**	**217**	**315**	**190**	**313**	**413**	**598**	**993**
Men, aged 16 or older	486	167	242	153	257	336	494	855
Boys, aged 2 to 15	93	51	74	36	56	77	104	139
Women and girls	**924**	**458**	**518**	**499**	**567**	**908**	**1,032**	**1,337**
Women, aged 16 or older	803	424	449	424	514	822	884	1,151
Girls, aged 2 to 15	120	33	69	75	53	86	148	187
Children under age 2	**65**	**39**	**25**	**40**	**65**	**65**	**69**	**87**
Footwear	**397**	**326**	**238**	**245**	**315**	**387**	**425**	**522**
Other apparel products and services	**309**	**130**	**172**	**191**	**137**	**197**	**257**	**546**
TRANSPORTATION	**9,614**	**2,844**	**5,551**	**5,425**	**8,083**	**8,339**	**9,597**	**14,488**
Vehicle purchases	**4,453**	**999**	**3,094**	**2,412**	**4,194**	**3,975**	**4,070**	**6,666**
Cars and trucks, new	2,001	464	616	371	1,349	1,258	1,845	3,776
Cars and trucks, used	2,366	498	2,478	1,924	2,778	2,639	2,086	2,795
Other vehicles	87	37	–	117	66	78	139	95
Gasoline and motor oil	**1,560**	**693**	**837**	**1,073**	**1,369**	**1,454**	**1,711**	**2,127**
Other vehicle expenses	**3,149**	**1,019**	**1,388**	**1,757**	**2,328**	**2,647**	**3,364**	**4,878**
Vehicle finance charges	462	136	176	236	326	429	554	694
Maintenance and repairs	907	336	534	591	728	779	926	1,330
Vehicle insurance	1,117	378	488	692	919	1,044	1,204	1,636
Vehicle rentals, leases, licenses, other charges	663	167	190	238	356	396	680	1,218
Public transportation	**452**	**133**	**231**	**183**	**191**	**262**	**451**	**817**
HEALTH CARE	**2,473**	**1,249**	**1,347**	**1,766**	**2,130**	**2,384**	**2,571**	**3,374**
Health insurance	1,125	630	584	750	930	1,167	1,193	1,521
Medical services	744	268	369	413	581	655	775	1,126
Drugs	478	297	331	529	497	441	492	539
Medical supplies	126	52	62	74	122	121	111	188
ENTERTAINMENT	**2,499**	**814**	**982**	**1,159**	**1,391**	**1,782**	**2,407**	**4,371**
Fees and admissions	676	164	209	207	266	374	554	1,364
Television, radio, sound equipment	815	394	449	533	643	688	875	1,166
Pets, toys, and playground equipment	463	174	256	310	302	381	501	695
Other entertainment products and services	546	82	68	108	180	338	477	1,147
PERSONAL CARE PRODUCTS AND SERVICES	**625**	**346**	**338**	**350**	**463**	**538**	**650**	**921**
READING	**179**	**60**	**80**	**88**	**114**	**143**	**183**	**294**
EDUCATION	**1,145**	**279**	**491**	**257**	**323**	**514**	**849**	**2,431**

	complete income reporters aged 45 to 54	under $10,000	$10,000– $19,999	$20,000– $29,999	$30,000– $39,999	$40,000– $49,999	$50,000– $69,999	$70,000 or more
TOBACCO PRODUCTS AND SMOKING SUPPLIES	$418	$411	$392	$478	$488	$452	$486	$338
MISCELLANEOUS	1,040	379	468	641	801	809	1,122	1,581
CASH CONTRIBUTIONS	1,686	403	413	647	950	1,170	1,734	3,040
PERSONAL INSURANCE AND PENSIONS	6,407	446	1,184	2,179	3,405	4,410	6,259	12,243
Life and other personal insurance	571	176	238	235	303	390	537	1,023
Pensions and Social Security	5,836	270	947	1,944	3,102	4,020	5,721	11,220
PERSONAL TAXES	4,318	228	236	645	1,376	2,171	3,297	9,728
Federal income taxes	3,291	140	123	430	883	1,583	2,474	7,557
State and local income taxes	841	59	70	165	363	466	668	1,812
Other taxes	186	29	42	50	130	121	155	359
GIFTS FOR NON–HOUSEHOLD MEMBERS	1,677	523	899	587	848	1,082	1,605	2,999
Food	161	27	44	48	100	82	132	320
Alcoholic beverages	15	23	3	2	8	11	12	25
Housing	387	169	171	190	280	227	419	628
Housekeeping supplies	52	32	17	27	53	26	63	76
Household textiles	20	7	19	8	24	17	8	33
Appliances and misc. housewares	31	20	21	8	22	22	25	53
Major appliances	10	1	3	1	12	3	8	20
Small appliances and misc. housewares	21	20	18	7	10	19	18	33
Miscellaneous household equipment	88	48	39	24	101	73	114	118
Other housing	195	61	75	122	80	90	208	347
Apparel and services	310	157	193	135	177	293	346	465
Males, aged 2 or older	86	19	79	31	34	100	82	138
Females, aged 2 or older	117	74	46	37	63	108	147	177
Children under age 2	52	28	19	33	45	47	53	75
Other apparel products and services	55	35	49	34	36	38	64	76
Jewelry and watches	20	6	6	14	9	19	27	29
All other apparel products and services	35	29	42	20	27	19	37	46
Transportation	90	11	84	57	28	168	55	135
Health care	46	7	21	33	24	25	49	76
Entertainment	111	28	49	53	87	72	108	188
Toys, games, hobbies, and tricycles	38	12	18	20	34	35	48	53
Other entertainment	73	17	31	33	53	37	60	135
Personal care products and services	31	15	52	7	5	13	47	44
Reading	1	1	0	1	1	1	3	2
Education	419	56	248	33	70	137	319	926
All other gifts	105	27	36	29	68	54	114	190

Note: Spending by category will not add to total spending because gift spending is also included in the preceding product and service categories and personal taxes are not included in the total. (–) means sample is too small to make a reliable estimate.
Source: Bureau of Labor Statistics, 2001 and 2002 Consumer Expenditure Surveys, Internet site http://www.bls.gov/cex/; calculations by New Strategist

Table 1.15 Aged 45 to 54: Indexed spending by income, 2001–02

(indexed average annual spending of consumer units (CU) headed by people aged 45 to 54 by product and service category and before-tax income of consumer unit, 2001–02; complete income reporters only; index definition: an index of 100 is the average for all consumer units; an index of 132 means that spending by consumer units in that group is 32 percent above the average for all consumer units; an index of 68 indicates spending that is 32 percent below the average for all consumer units)

	complete income reporters aged 45 to 54	under $10,000	$10,000– $19,999	$20,000– $29,999	$30,000– $39,999	$40,000– $49,999	$50,000– $69,999	$70,000 or more
Average spending of CU, total	$50,936	$19,875	$24,852	$28,296	$36,817	$40,679	$50,117	$80,663
Average spending of CU, index	100	39	49	56	72	80	98	158
FOOD	**100**	**53**	**54**	**66**	**84**	**87**	**104**	**141**
Food at home	**100**	**65**	**67**	**76**	**97**	**92**	**103**	**127**
Cereals and bakery products	100	59	65	76	94	90	106	128
Cereals and cereal products	100	68	70	77	98	92	107	123
Bakery products	100	55	63	75	93	90	106	131
Meats, poultry, fish, and eggs	100	75	74	83	103	93	103	119
Beef	100	71	72	81	101	95	98	122
Pork	100	88	84	93	115	85	106	106
Other meats	100	79	69	78	92	99	112	116
Poultry	100	67	76	80	99	103	101	119
Fish and seafood	100	68	58	74	101	81	101	133
Eggs	100	80	83	95	105	102	100	112
Dairy products	100	67	69	75	88	91	104	129
Fresh milk and cream	100	76	79	85	99	91	97	121
Other dairy products	100	60	62	68	80	91	109	134
Fruits and vegetables	100	60	64	79	98	87	101	130
Fresh fruits	100	63	58	77	91	88	102	132
Fresh vegetables	100	62	62	81	99	87	102	128
Processed fruits	100	54	62	80	102	89	98	130
Processed vegetables	100	58	81	77	103	82	100	128
Other food at home	100	60	64	69	95	95	102	131
Sugar and other sweets	100	58	60	80	88	109	94	130
Fats and oils	100	68	69	86	97	87	105	123
Miscellaneous foods	100	54	62	64	95	96	106	132
Nonalcoholic beverages	100	71	73	72	98	93	98	127
Food prepared by CU on trips	100	41	24	47	75	67	94	175
Food away from home	**100**	**37**	**38**	**53**	**68**	**81**	**105**	**160**
ALCOHOLIC BEVERAGES	**100**	**60**	**36**	**45**	**63**	**70**	**97**	**166**
HOUSING	**100**	**50**	**55**	**62**	**74**	**78**	**94**	**155**
Shelter	**100**	**50**	**55**	**61**	**72**	**78**	**91**	**157**
Owned dwellings	100	36	32	46	59	70	91	178
Mortgage interest and charges	100	36	28	44	53	73	89	182
Property taxes	100	39	36	45	60	65	94	176
Maintenance, repair, insurance, other expenses	100	36	41	51	79	66	96	166
Rented dwellings	100	115	156	134	140	120	95	53
Other lodging	100	24	24	25	27	45	82	214
Utilities, fuels, and public services	**100**	**63**	**70**	**79**	**84**	**91**	**103**	**130**
Natural gas	100	53	62	72	84	93	96	139
Electricity	100	71	77	87	87	92	103	122
Fuel oil and other fuels	100	73	78	87	72	70	93	140
Telephone	100	59	69	75	84	92	105	131
Water and other public services	100	54	61	75	80	90	106	135

	complete income reporters aged 45 to 54	under $10,000	$10,000– $19,999	$20,000– $29,999	$30,000– $39,999	$40,000– $49,999	$50,000– $69,999	$70,000 or more
Household services	100	28	36	43	57	67	79	188
Personal services	100	13	12	30	56	77	79	199
Other household services	100	33	44	48	57	63	79	184
Housekeeping supplies	100	56	53	60	83	76	112	142
Laundry and cleaning supplies	100	77	70	77	81	87	108	126
Other household products	100	49	55	56	88	73	112	144
Postage and stationery	100	49	31	52	76	73	117	152
Household furnishings and equipment	100	31	39	43	64	61	90	180
Household textiles	100	47	58	53	64	71	88	166
Furniture	100	26	29	46	47	61	73	198
Floor coverings	100	39	6	28	45	44	59	220
Major appliances	100	31	32	50	67	68	105	169
Small appliances, misc. housewares	100	56	47	50	66	60	96	166
Miscellaneous household equipment	100	27	44	37	74	58	98	176
APPAREL AND RELATED SERVICES	100	51	56	51	61	87	105	153
Men and boys	100	38	54	33	54	71	103	172
Men, aged 16 or older	100	34	50	31	53	69	102	176
Boys, aged 2 to 15	100	55	80	39	60	83	112	149
Women and girls	100	50	56	54	61	98	112	145
Women, aged 16 or older	100	53	56	53	64	102	110	143
Girls, aged 2 to 15	100	28	58	63	44	72	123	156
Children under age 2	100	60	38	62	100	100	106	134
Footwear	100	82	60	62	79	97	107	131
Other apparel products and services	100	42	56	62	44	64	83	177
TRANSPORTATION	100	30	58	56	84	87	100	151
Vehicle purchases	100	22	69	54	94	89	91	150
Cars and trucks, new	100	23	31	19	67	63	92	189
Cars and trucks, used	100	21	105	81	117	112	88	118
Other vehicles	100	42	–	134	76	90	160	109
Gasoline and motor oil	100	44	54	69	88	93	110	136
Other vehicle expenses	100	32	44	56	74	84	107	155
Vehicle finance charges	100	30	38	51	71	93	120	150
Maintenance and repairs	100	37	59	65	80	86	102	147
Vehicle insurance	100	34	44	62	82	93	108	146
Vehicle rentals, leases, licenses, other charges	100	25	29	36	54	60	103	184
Public transportation	100	29	51	40	42	58	100	181
HEALTH CARE	100	50	54	71	86	96	104	136
Health insurance	100	56	52	67	83	104	106	135
Medical services	100	36	50	56	78	88	104	151
Drugs	100	62	69	111	104	92	103	113
Medical supplies	100	42	49	59	97	96	88	149
ENTERTAINMENT	100	33	39	46	56	71	96	175
Fees and admissions	100	24	31	31	39	55	82	202
Television, radio, sound equipment	100	48	55	65	79	84	107	143
Pets, toys, and playground equipment	100	38	55	67	65	82	108	150
Other entertainment products and services	100	15	12	20	33	62	87	210
PERSONAL CARE PRODUCTS AND SERVICES	100	55	54	56	74	86	104	147
READING	100	34	44	49	64	80	102	164
EDUCATION	100	24	43	22	28	45	74	212

	complete income reporters aged 45 to 54	under $10,000	$10,000–$19,999	$20,000–$29,999	$30,000–$39,999	$40,000–$49,999	$50,000–$69,999	$70,000 or more
TOBACCO PRODUCTS AND SMOKING SUPPLIES	100	98	94	114	117	108	116	81
MISCELLANEOUS	100	36	45	62	77	78	108	152
CASH CONTRIBUTIONS	100	24	25	38	56	69	103	180
PERSONAL INSURANCE AND PENSIONS	100	7	18	34	53	69	98	191
Life and other personal insurance	100	31	42	41	53	68	94	179
Pensions and Social Security	100	5	16	33	53	69	98	192
PERSONAL TAXES	100	5	5	15	32	50	76	225
Federal income taxes	100	4	4	13	27	48	75	230
State and local income taxes	100	7	8	20	43	55	79	215
Other taxes	100	15	23	27	70	65	83	193
GIFTS FOR NON–HOUSEHOLD MEMBERS	100	31	54	35	51	65	96	179
Food	100	17	27	30	62	51	82	199
Alcoholic beverages	100	157	23	13	53	73	80	167
Housing	100	44	44	49	72	59	108	162
Housekeeping supplies	100	62	32	52	102	50	121	146
Household textiles	100	36	93	40	120	85	40	165
Appliances and misc. housewares	100	64	67	26	71	71	81	171
Major appliances	100	7	30	10	120	30	80	200
Small appliances and misc. housewares	100	93	85	33	48	90	86	157
Miscellaneous household equipment	100	54	44	27	115	83	130	134
Other housing	100	31	39	63	41	46	107	178
Apparel and services	100	51	62	44	57	95	112	150
Males, aged 2 or older	100	22	92	36	40	116	95	160
Females, aged 2 or older	100	64	40	32	54	92	126	151
Children under age 2	100	54	37	63	87	90	102	144
Other apparel products and services	100	63	88	62	65	69	116	138
Jewelry and watches	100	30	30	70	45	95	135	145
All other apparel products and services	100	82	120	57	77	54	106	131
Transportation	100	12	93	63	31	187	61	150
Health care	100	16	46	72	52	54	107	165
Entertainment	100	25	44	48	78	65	97	169
Toys, games, hobbies, and tricycles	100	30	48	53	89	92	126	139
Other entertainment	100	23	42	45	73	51	82	185
Personal care products and services	100	50	167	23	16	42	152	142
Reading	100	64	49	100	100	100	300	200
Education	100	13	59	8	17	33	76	221
All other gifts	100	26	34	28	65	51	109	181

Note: (–) means sample is too small to make a reliable estimate.
Source: Calculations by New Strategist based on the Bureau of Labor Statistics 2001 and 2002 Consumer Expenditure Surveys

Table 1.16 Aged 55 to 64: Average spending by income, 2001–02

(average annual spending of consumer units (CU) headed by people aged 55 to 64 by product and service category and before-tax income of consumer unit, 2001–02; complete income reporters only)

	complete income reporters aged 55 to 64	under $10,000	$10,000–$19,999	$20,000–$29,999	$30,000–$39,999	$40,000–$49,999	$50,000–$69,999	$70,000 or more
Number of consumer units (in thousands, add 000s)	12,087	1,274	1,686	1,452	1,526	1,295	1,950	2,904
Average number of persons per CU	2.1	1.6	1.8	2.0	2.0	2.2	2.3	2.5
Average income before taxes	$52,569	$5,958	$14,603	$24,699	$34,833	$44,447	$58,918	$117,653
Average annual spending	45,107	20,462	25,423	30,319	38,619	41,368	51,160	75,718
FOOD	**$5,715**	**$3,217**	**$3,591**	**$4,007**	**$5,111**	**$5,367**	**$6,316**	**$8,930**
Food at home	**3,258**	**2,228**	**2,384**	**2,762**	**3,248**	**3,155**	**3,489**	**4,360**
Cereals and bakery products	456	320	340	400	434	414	480	621
Cereals and cereal products	138	117	115	116	130	132	138	177
Bakery products	319	203	225	284	305	282	342	444
Meats, poultry, fish, and eggs	850	626	649	710	898	881	881	1,088
Beef	239	148	188	195	255	253	279	294
Pork	188	189	162	169	206	159	169	228
Other meats	102	60	87	94	120	77	112	128
Poultry	147	100	116	116	165	126	176	185
Fish and seafood	139	100	68	102	109	229	111	217
Eggs	34	30	30	34	42	36	34	36
Dairy products	343	221	243	312	345	332	381	448
Fresh milk and cream	131	104	110	131	138	120	138	150
Other dairy products	212	117	133	181	207	213	243	298
Fruits and vegetables	589	413	426	478	590	569	615	809
Fresh fruits	192	140	129	142	193	187	203	274
Fresh vegetables	195	132	142	155	188	175	219	267
Processed fruits	116	77	89	95	124	103	108	163
Processed vegetables	86	64	66	86	84	104	85	105
Other food at home	1,019	649	727	863	981	959	1,132	1,394
Sugar and other sweets	133	89	88	124	119	111	152	183
Fats and oils	93	69	81	74	98	83	96	119
Miscellaneous foods	459	272	298	397	446	486	510	629
Nonalcoholic beverages	277	194	225	229	261	244	314	363
Food prepared by CU on trips	57	24	35	39	57	36	61	100
Food away from home	**2,457**	**989**	**1,206**	**1,246**	**1,863**	**2,211**	**2,827**	**4,570**
ALCOHOLIC BEVERAGES	**410**	**199**	**160**	**208**	**330**	**386**	**349**	**833**
HOUSING	**13,629**	**7,450**	**8,504**	**9,364**	**11,576**	**12,219**	**15,702**	**21,798**
Shelter	**7,421**	**3,887**	**4,695**	**4,786**	**6,213**	**6,402**	**7,865**	**12,663**
Owned dwellings	5,339	2,172	2,769	2,790	4,295	4,508	5,774	10,122
Mortgage interest and charges	2,619	873	1,054	1,211	2,180	2,110	2,856	5,297
Property taxes	1,440	759	875	829	1,027	1,250	1,476	2,648
Maintenance, repair, insurance, other expenses	1,280	539	840	750	1,087	1,149	1,443	2,177
Rented dwellings	1,302	1,459	1,667	1,669	1,433	1,497	1,185	760
Other lodging	780	256	259	327	485	396	907	1,780
Utilities, fuels, and public services	**2,960**	**2,052**	**2,251**	**2,634**	**2,820**	**2,943**	**3,184**	**3,862**
Natural gas	397	255	281	355	375	397	438	532
Electricity	1,100	846	916	994	1,046	1,118	1,175	1,341
Fuel oil and other fuels	134	84	103	140	148	118	114	183
Telephone	955	629	673	824	919	962	1,017	1,301
Water and other public services	374	239	277	322	332	348	440	504

	complete income reporters aged 55 to 64	under $10,000	$10,000– $19,999	$20,000– $29,999	$30,000– $39,999	$40,000– $49,999	$50,000– $69,999	$70,000 or more
Household services	**$546**	**$280**	**$252**	**$298**	**$342**	**$447**	**$536**	**$1,114**
Personal services	92	83	31	66	46	75	68	192
Other household services	453	198	221	231	296	372	468	922
Housekeeping supplies	**842**	**358**	**375**	**523**	**650**	**709**	**2,028**	**902**
Laundry and cleaning supplies	161	112	115	137	214	144	168	197
Other household products	506	158	171	238	305	343	1,618	465
Postage and stationery	175	88	89	148	131	221	242	239
Household furnishings and equipment	**1,860**	**873**	**931**	**1,123**	**1,552**	**1,719**	**2,088**	**3,257**
Household textiles	191	43	122	101	124	188	179	368
Furniture	404	202	166	230	248	312	436	820
Floor coverings	54	23	58	29	18	9	38	128
Major appliances	216	71	164	142	152	284	242	331
Small appliances, misc. housewares	142	165	48	173	84	104	167	208
Miscellaneous household equipment	853	368	373	447	926	822	1,026	1,403
APPAREL AND RELATED SERVICES	**1,810**	**680**	**825**	**1,168**	**1,390**	**1,608**	**1,958**	**3,377**
Men and boys	**373**	**134**	**172**	**255**	**303**	**373**	**452**	**640**
Men, aged 16 or older	337	118	138	216	278	345	410	592
Boys, aged 2 to 15	36	16	34	39	25	28	42	48
Women and girls	**813**	**315**	**324**	**577**	**635**	**675**	**883**	**1,510**
Women, aged 16 or older	760	268	276	530	578	636	805	1,461
Girls, aged 2 to 15	53	46	48	47	57	39	78	50
Children under age 2	**54**	**25**	**21**	**31**	**53**	**61**	**62**	**92**
Footwear	**302**	**113**	**196**	**152**	**245**	**297**	**291**	**557**
Other apparel products and services	**267**	**93**	**112**	**154**	**153**	**202**	**270**	**577**
TRANSPORTATION	**8,457**	**4,085**	**4,742**	**6,406**	**8,256**	**8,556**	**10,134**	**12,481**
Vehicle purchases	**3,916**	**2,098**	**2,166**	**3,150**	**4,392**	**4,136**	**4,880**	**5,119**
Cars and trucks, new	2,101	833	1,099	1,480	2,762	2,128	2,297	3,057
Cars and trucks, used	1,759	1,265	1,067	1,670	1,586	1,978	2,545	1,886
Other vehicles	57	–	–	–	44	30	38	176
Gasoline and motor oil	**1,334**	**616**	**855**	**1,026**	**1,329**	**1,378**	**1,583**	**1,899**
Other vehicle expenses	**2,664**	**1,124**	**1,509**	**2,041**	**2,211**	**2,631**	**3,066**	**4,293**
Vehicle finance charges	367	149	202	325	363	361	406	559
Maintenance and repairs	780	399	421	659	642	805	907	1,178
Vehicle insurance	965	405	626	792	834	1,006	1,133	1,433
Vehicle rentals, leases, licenses, other charges	552	172	260	265	372	458	620	1,123
Public transportation	**542**	**246**	**213**	**190**	**324**	**411**	**605**	**1,171**
HEALTH CARE	**2,893**	**1,865**	**2,361**	**2,564**	**2,846**	**2,865**	**3,044**	**3,760**
Health insurance	1,281	790	1,055	1,251	1,373	1,154	1,363	1,595
Medical services	828	616	582	576	658	794	854	1,277
Drugs	635	346	639	661	635	773	610	708
Medical supplies	149	112	86	76	180	144	217	180
ENTERTAINMENT	**2,508**	**790**	**1,726**	**1,465**	**1,895**	**1,850**	**3,186**	**4,379**
Fees and admissions	610	184	178	198	351	405	654	1,452
Television, radio, sound equipment	699	360	467	571	649	705	756	1,030
Pets, toys, and playground equipment	438	146	235	274	400	524	546	689
Other entertainment products and services	760	99	846	422	494	215	1,230	1,209
PERSONAL CARE PRODUCTS AND SERVICES	**598**	**272**	**329**	**440**	**727**	**568**	**680**	**884**
READING	**190**	**96**	**96**	**109**	**145**	**186**	**226**	**329**
EDUCATION	**493**	**30**	**99**	**95**	**210**	**381**	**399**	**1,382**

	complete income reporters aged 55 to 64	under $10,000	$10,000–$19,999	$20,000–$29,999	$30,000–$39,999	$40,000–$49,999	$50,000–$69,999	$70,000 or more
TOBACCO PRODUCTS AND SMOKING SUPPLIES	$362	$282	$351	$365	$350	$459	$441	$312
MISCELLANEOUS	937	339	621	611	952	1,049	888	1,542
CASH CONTRIBUTIONS	1,575	578	542	908	1,414	1,068	1,925	3,022
PERSONAL INSURANCE AND PENSIONS	5,529	581	1,474	2,610	3,417	4,807	5,910	12,688
Life and other personal insurance	658	412	442	365	573	552	668	1,125
Pensions and Social Security	4,871	169	1,032	2,245	2,845	4,255	5,241	11,564
PERSONAL TAXES	3,179	213	292	744	1,374	2,269	2,843	8,951
Federal income taxes	2,378	95	122	442	919	1,623	2,137	6,921
State and local income taxes	586	28	44	147	246	476	505	1,646
Other taxes	215	91	125	154	209	170	202	384
GIFTS FOR NON–HOUSEHOLD MEMBERS	1,571	471	509	847	1,101	1,149	1,451	3,521
Food	141	21	24	42	67	74	120	395
Alcoholic beverages	13	9	5	12	6	3	27	16
Housing	384	174	114	302	253	377	379	747
Housekeeping supplies	67	26	25	46	32	72	86	119
Household textiles	28	3	8	2	3	18	52	62
Appliances and misc. housewares	55	40	9	75	23	50	53	97
Major appliances	23	–	4	34	7	9	22	52
Small appliances and misc. housewares	32	40	4	41	16	41	31	45
Miscellaneous household equipment	104	33	19	79	102	149	116	173
Other housing	131	71	52	100	94	89	72	296
Apparel and services	378	90	127	309	250	237	348	801
Males, aged 2 or older	87	19	22	110	69	57	108	147
Females, aged 2 or older	163	39	52	139	108	70	83	393
Children under age 2	48	21	18	18	35	58	61	86
Other apparel products and services	80	11	35	42	38	52	96	175
Jewelry and watches	29	4	13	6	15	9	25	79
All other apparel products and services	51	6	22	36	23	43	71	97
Transportation	93	39	1	6	43	19	151	233
Health care	62	14	3	15	22	58	38	179
Entertainment	99	47	40	83	83	102	104	169
Toys, games, hobbies, and tricycles	52	23	20	41	45	42	66	90
Other entertainment	47	25	20	42	37	60	39	79
Personal care products and services	40	20	20	34	154	8	32	34
Reading	2	2	–	1	2	2	3	3
Education	223	9	49	7	104	160	121	684
All other gifts	136	46	124	36	119	108	128	259

Note: Spending by category will not add to total spending because gift spending is also included in the preceding product and service categories and personal taxes are not included in the total. (–) means sample is too small to make a reliable estimate.
Source: Bureau of Labor Statistics, 2001 and 2002 Consumer Expenditure Surveys, Internet site http://www.bls.gov/cex/; calculations by New Strategist

Table 1.17 Aged 55 to 64: Indexed spending by income, 2001–02

(indexed average annual spending of consumer units (CU) headed by people aged 55 to 64 by product and service category and before-tax income of consumer unit, 2001–02; complete income reporters only; index definition: an index of 100 is the average for all consumer units; an index of 132 means that spending by consumer units in that group is 32 percent above the average for all consumer units; an index of 68 indicates spending that is 32 percent below the average for all consumer units)

	complete income reporters aged 55 to 64	under $10,000	$10,000– $19,999	$20,000– $29,999	$30,000– $39,999	$40,000– $49,999	$50,000– $69,999	$70,000 or more
Average spending of CU, total	$45,107	$20,462	$25,423	$30,319	$38,619	$41,368	$51,160	$75,718
Average spending of CU, index	100	45	56	67	86	92	113	168
FOOD	**100**	**56**	**63**	**70**	**89**	**94**	**111**	**156**
Food at home	**100**	**68**	**73**	**85**	**100**	**97**	**107**	**134**
Cereals and bakery products	100	70	75	88	95	91	105	136
Cereals and cereal products	100	85	83	84	94	96	100	128
Bakery products	100	64	71	89	96	88	107	139
Meats, poultry, fish, and eggs	100	74	76	84	106	104	104	128
Beef	100	62	79	82	107	106	117	123
Pork	100	101	86	90	110	85	90	121
Other meats	100	59	85	92	118	75	110	125
Poultry	100	68	79	79	112	86	120	126
Fish and seafood	100	72	49	73	78	165	80	156
Eggs	100	88	88	100	124	106	100	106
Dairy products	100	64	71	91	101	97	111	131
Fresh milk and cream	100	79	84	100	105	92	105	115
Other dairy products	100	55	63	85	98	100	115	141
Fruits and vegetables	100	70	72	81	100	97	104	137
Fresh fruits	100	73	67	74	101	97	106	143
Fresh vegetables	100	68	73	79	96	90	112	137
Processed fruits	100	66	77	82	107	89	93	141
Processed vegetables	100	74	77	100	98	121	99	122
Other food at home	100	64	71	85	96	94	111	137
Sugar and other sweets	100	67	66	93	89	83	114	138
Fats and oils	100	74	87	80	105	89	103	128
Miscellaneous foods	100	59	65	86	97	106	111	137
Nonalcoholic beverages	100	70	81	83	94	88	113	131
Food prepared by CU on trips	100	43	61	68	100	63	107	175
Food away from home	**100**	**40**	**49**	**51**	**76**	**90**	**115**	**186**
ALCOHOLIC BEVERAGES	**100**	**48**	**39**	**51**	**80**	**94**	**85**	**203**
HOUSING	**100**	**55**	**62**	**69**	**85**	**90**	**115**	**160**
Shelter	**100**	**52**	**63**	**64**	**84**	**86**	**106**	**171**
Owned dwellings	100	41	52	52	80	84	108	190
Mortgage interest and charges	100	33	40	46	83	81	109	202
Property taxes	100	53	61	58	71	87	103	184
Maintenance, repair, insurance, other expenses	100	42	66	59	85	90	113	170
Rented dwellings	100	112	128	128	110	115	91	58
Other lodging	100	33	33	42	62	51	116	228
Utilities, fuels, and public services	**100**	**69**	**76**	**89**	**95**	**99**	**108**	**130**
Natural gas	100	64	71	89	94	100	110	134
Electricity	100	77	83	90	95	102	107	122
Fuel oil and other fuels	100	62	77	104	110	88	85	137
Telephone	100	66	70	86	96	101	106	136

	complete income reporters aged 55 to 64	under $10,000	$10,000– $19,999	$20,000– $29,999	$30,000– $39,999	$40,000– $49,999	$50,000– $69,999	$70,000 or more
Water and other public services	**100**	**64**	**74**	**86**	**89**	**93**	**118**	**135**
Household services	100	51	46	55	63	82	98	204
Personal services	100	90	33	72	50	82	74	209
Other household services	**100**	**44**	**49**	**51**	**65**	**82**	**103**	**204**
Housekeeping supplies	100	43	45	62	77	84	241	107
Laundry and cleaning supplies	100	70	72	85	133	89	104	122
Other household products	100	31	34	47	60	68	320	92
Postage and stationery	100	50	51	85	75	126	138	137
Household furnishings and equipment	**100**	**47**	**50**	**60**	**83**	**92**	**112**	**175**
Household textiles	100	23	64	53	65	98	94	193
Furniture	100	50	41	57	61	77	108	203
Floor coverings	100	43	108	54	33	17	70	237
Major appliances	100	33	76	66	70	131	112	153
Small appliances, misc. housewares	100	116	34	122	59	73	118	146
Miscellaneous household equipment	100	43	44	52	109	96	120	164
APPAREL AND RELATED SERVICES	**100**	**38**	**46**	**65**	**77**	**89**	**108**	**187**
Men and boys	**100**	**36**	**46**	**68**	**81**	**100**	**121**	**172**
Men, aged 16 or older	100	35	41	64	82	102	122	176
Boys, aged 2 to 15	100	44	95	108	69	78	117	133
Women and girls	**100**	**39**	**40**	**71**	**78**	**83**	**109**	**186**
Women, aged 16 or older	100	35	36	70	76	84	106	192
Girls, aged 2 to 15	100	87	91	89	108	74	147	94
Children under age 2	**100**	**47**	**39**	**57**	**98**	**113**	**115**	**170**
Footwear	**100**	**37**	**65**	**50**	**81**	**98**	**96**	**184**
Other apparel products and services	**100**	**35**	**42**	**58**	**57**	**76**	**101**	**216**
TRANSPORTATION	**100**	**48**	**56**	**76**	**98**	**101**	**120**	**148**
Vehicle purchases	**100**	**54**	**55**	**80**	**112**	**106**	**125**	**131**
Cars and trucks, new	100	40	52	70	131	101	109	146
Cars and trucks, used	100	72	61	95	90	112	145	107
Other vehicles	100	–	–	–	77	53	67	309
Gasoline and motor oil	**100**	**46**	**64**	**77**	**100**	**103**	**119**	**142**
Other vehicle expenses	**100**	**42**	**57**	**77**	**83**	**99**	**115**	**161**
Vehicle finance charges	100	41	55	89	99	98	111	152
Maintenance and repairs	100	51	54	84	82	103	116	151
Vehicle insurance	100	42	65	82	86	104	117	148
Vehicle rentals, leases, licenses, other charges	100	31	47	48	67	83	112	203
Public transportation	**100**	**45**	**39**	**35**	**60**	**76**	**112**	**216**
HEALTH CARE	**100**	**64**	**82**	**89**	**98**	**99**	**105**	**130**
Health insurance	100	62	82	98	107	90	106	125
Medical services	100	74	70	70	79	96	103	154
Drugs	100	54	101	104	100	122	96	111
Medical supplies	100	75	58	51	121	97	146	121
ENTERTAINMENT	**100**	**31**	**69**	**58**	**76**	**74**	**127**	**175**
Fees and admissions	100	30	29	32	58	66	107	238
Television, radio, sound equipment	100	52	67	82	93	101	108	147
Pets, toys, and playground equipment	100	33	54	63	91	120	125	157
Other entertainment products and services	100	13	111	56	65	28	162	159
PERSONAL CARE PRODUCTS AND SERVICES	**100**	**46**	**55**	**74**	**122**	**95**	**114**	**148**
READING	**100**	**51**	**51**	**57**	**76**	**98**	**119**	**173**
EDUCATION	**100**	**6**	**20**	**19**	**43**	**77**	**81**	**280**

	complete income reporters aged 55 to 64	under $10,000	$10,000– $19,999	$20,000– $29,999	$30,000– $39,999	$40,000– $49,999	$50,000– $69,999	$70,000 or more
TOBACCO PRODUCTS AND SMOKING SUPPLIES	100	78	97	101	97	127	122	86
MISCELLANEOUS	100	36	66	65	102	112	95	165
CASH CONTRIBUTIONS	100	37	34	58	90	68	122	192
PERSONAL INSURANCE AND PENSIONS	100	11	27	47	62	87	107	229
Life and other personal insurance	100	63	67	55	87	84	102	171
Pensions and Social Security	100	3	21	46	58	87	108	237
PERSONAL TAXES	100	7	9	23	43	71	89	282
Federal income taxes	100	4	5	19	39	68	90	291
State and local income taxes	100	5	8	25	42	81	86	281
Other taxes	100	42	58	72	97	79	94	179
GIFTS FOR NON–HOUSEHOLD MEMBERS	100	30	32	54	70	73	92	224
Food	100	15	17	30	48	52	85	280
Alcoholic beverages	100	69	42	92	46	23	208	123
Housing	100	45	30	79	66	98	99	195
Housekeeping supplies	100	39	38	69	48	107	128	178
Household textiles	100	12	27	7	11	64	186	221
Appliances and misc. housewares	100	74	16	136	42	91	96	176
Major appliances	100	–	19	148	30	39	96	226
Small appliances and misc. housewares	100	126	13	128	50	128	97	141
Miscellaneous household equipment	100	32	18	76	98	143	112	166
Other housing	100	54	40	76	72	68	55	226
Apparel and services	100	24	34	82	66	63	92	212
Males, aged 2 or older	100	22	25	126	79	66	124	169
Females, aged 2 or older	100	24	32	85	66	43	51	241
Children under age 2	100	44	38	38	73	121	127	179
Other apparel products and services	100	14	43	53	48	65	120	219
Jewelry and watches	100	13	44	21	52	31	86	272
All other apparel products and services	100	13	43	71	45	84	139	190
Transportation	100	41	1	6	46	20	162	251
Health care	100	22	4	24	35	94	61	289
Entertainment	100	47	41	84	84	103	105	171
Toys, games, hobbies, and tricycles	100	44	39	79	87	81	127	173
Other entertainment	100	53	43	89	79	128	83	168
Personal care products and services	100	49	50	85	385	20	80	85
Reading	100	115	–	50	100	100	150	150
Education	100	4	22	3	47	72	54	307
All other gifts	100	34	91	26	88	79	94	190

Note: (–) means sample is too small to make a reliable estimate.
Source: Calculations by New Strategist based on the Bureau of Labor Statistics 2001 and 2002 Consumer Expenditure Surveys

Table 1.18 Aged 65 or older: Average spending by income, 2001–02

(average annual spending of consumer units (CU) headed by people aged 65 or older by product and service category and before-tax income of consumer unit, 2001–02; complete income reporters only)

	complete income reporters 65 or older	under $10,000	$10,000– $19,999	$20,000– $29,999	$30,000– $39,999	$40,000– $49,999	$50,000– $69,999	$70,000 or more
Number of consumer units (in thousands, add 000s)	18,013	3,174	6,070	3,381	1,924	1,130	1,127	1,208
Average number of persons per CU	1.7	1.2	1.5	1.8	2.0	2.0	2.2	2.4
Average income before taxes	$28,638	$6,879	$14,550	$24,259	$34,404	$44,719	$58,683	$116,596
Average annual spending	28,648	15,207	20,853	29,121	32,807	40,246	47,626	67,821
FOOD	**$4,037**	**$2,628**	**$3,044**	**$4,451**	**$4,437**	**$5,209**	**$6,113**	**$8,434**
Food at home	**2,626**	**1,973**	**2,158**	**2,980**	**2,815**	**3,166**	**3,447**	**4,383**
Cereals and bakery products	406	316	349	457	417	477	464	679
Cereals and cereal products	130	110	111	140	132	153	152	212
Bakery products	277	206	238	318	285	324	312	467
Meats, poultry, fish, and eggs	670	538	548	784	703	775	770	1,139
Beef	195	158	140	266	229	202	192	328
Pork	152	124	136	183	148	168	165	212
Other meats	85	65	73	93	86	103	109	138
Poultry	112	91	96	123	96	132	149	199
Fish and seafood	95	71	73	85	115	139	116	224
Eggs	31	28	29	35	29	32	39	38
Dairy products	281	199	230	321	321	340	383	445
Fresh milk and cream	115	89	101	131	125	132	149	160
Other dairy products	165	110	130	190	196	208	234	285
Fruits and vegetables	516	372	421	585	558	624	755	847
Fresh fruits	170	124	137	194	181	199	251	290
Fresh vegetables	159	113	131	175	182	204	219	265
Processed fruits	109	75	91	131	117	125	146	171
Processed vegetables	78	60	62	85	78	96	138	121
Other food at home	753	548	610	833	816	951	1,075	1,273
Sugar and other sweets	109	82	89	119	114	145	137	187
Fats and oils	79	72	63	86	78	90	134	112
Miscellaneous foods	345	235	286	375	399	425	500	580
Nonalcoholic beverages	186	147	158	210	189	212	254	286
Food prepared by CU on trips	34	12	14	43	36	80	50	108
Food away from home	**1,411**	**656**	**887**	**1,471**	**1,622**	**2,043**	**2,666**	**4,051**
ALCOHOLIC BEVERAGES	**243**	**103**	**149**	**175**	**313**	**357**	**556**	**859**
HOUSING	**9,222**	**5,839**	**7,248**	**9,439**	**10,531**	**11,891**	**13,266**	**19,262**
Shelter	**4,753**	**3,066**	**3,794**	**4,752**	**5,069**	**5,879**	**6,718**	**10,618**
Owned dwellings	3,132	1,454	2,246	3,358	3,343	4,326	5,123	8,050
Mortgage interest and charges	859	352	482	851	902	1,181	1,599	3,047
Property taxes	1,184	637	952	1,204	1,273	1,431	1,738	2,837
Maintenance, repair, insurance, other expenses	1,089	465	812	1,303	1,168	1,714	1,786	2,166
Rented dwellings	1,231	1,527	1,375	1,059	1,166	898	803	1,031
Other lodging	390	85	173	335	560	655	792	1,537
Utilities, fuels, and public services	**2,401**	**1,696**	**2,107**	**2,544**	**2,691**	**2,838**	**3,192**	**3,727**
Natural gas	370	235	349	389	444	424	445	527
Electricity	899	653	787	967	1,018	1,053	1,198	1,311
Fuel oil and other fuels	134	127	135	157	99	109	109	196
Telephone	671	482	555	676	769	846	1,000	1,116
Water and other public services	327	199	280	354	362	406	440	578

	complete income reporters 65 or older	under $10,000	$10,000– $19,999	$20,000– $29,999	$30,000– $39,999	$40,000– $49,999	$50,000– $69,999	$70,000 or more
Household services	**$633**	**$298**	**$427**	**$607**	**$1,002**	**$1,120**	**$767**	**$1,452**
Personal services	197	76	131	157	553	501	87	205
Other household services	436	222	296	450	449	618	680	1,247
Housekeeping supplies	**501**	**358**	**355**	**525**	**641**	**669**	**886**	**892**
Laundry and cleaning supplies	114	101	88	124	115	159	198	139
Other household products	236	161	166	223	334	300	429	484
Postage and stationery	150	96	100	178	192	210	259	270
Household furnishings and equipment	**933**	**422**	**565**	**1,011**	**1,127**	**1,385**	**1,704**	**2,572**
Household textiles	97	45	59	106	110	111	218	283
Furniture	186	66	107	234	240	282	268	514
Floor coverings	34	8	31	37	47	53	35	67
Major appliances	143	70	99	191	136	161	247	332
Small appliances, misc. housewares	70	35	55	55	108	79	115	175
Miscellaneous household equipment	404	198	214	387	486	700	820	1,201
APPAREL AND RELATED SERVICES	**990**	**708**	**653**	**838**	**1,129**	**1,253**	**1,705**	**2,962**
Men and boys	**219**	**147**	**139**	**185**	**239**	**284**	**486**	**629**
Men, aged 16 or older	193	136	119	157	214	255	445	553
Boys, aged 2 to 15	26	11	21	28	25	29	40	76
Women and girls	**450**	**322**	**298**	**374**	**545**	**619**	**704**	**1,328**
Women, aged 16 or older	417	298	277	343	465	598	668	1,268
Girls, aged 2 to 15	33	24	22	31	80	22	36	60
Children under age 2	**20**	**7**	**9**	**26**	**26**	**45**	**44**	**41**
Footwear	**162**	**163**	**117**	**130**	**164**	**129**	**289**	**450**
Other apparel products and services	**138**	**69**	**88**	**124**	**154**	**176**	**183**	**513**
TRANSPORTATION	**4,590**	**1,766**	**3,237**	**4,646**	**5,819**	**7,753**	**9,066**	**9,569**
Vehicle purchases	**1,923**	**666**	**1,421**	**1,910**	**2,532**	**3,840**	**3,892**	**3,178**
Cars and trucks, new	1,077	328	847	1,057	1,267	2,726	1,653	1,867
Cars and trucks, used	837	338	559	853	1,266	1,114	2,184	1,310
Other vehicles	9	–	15	–	–	–	55	–
Gasoline and motor oil	**765**	**349**	**552**	**851**	**1,015**	**1,093**	**1,351**	**1,438**
Other vehicle expenses	**1,574**	**622**	**1,084**	**1,594**	**1,949**	**2,390**	**3,011**	**3,775**
Vehicle finance charges	147	41	78	129	260	216	390	352
Maintenance and repairs	493	203	369	532	579	753	892	1,011
Vehicle insurance	659	302	494	716	836	1,041	1,091	1,224
Vehicle rentals, leases, licenses, other charges	275	76	143	217	274	380	638	1,187
Public transportation	**329**	**129**	**181**	**291**	**323**	**431**	**811**	**1,179**
HEALTH CARE	**3,617**	**2,016**	**3,154**	**4,058**	**4,263**	**4,735**	**5,156**	**5,423**
Health insurance	1,837	1,101	1,646	2,087	2,108	2,427	2,406	2,511
Medical services	667	267	442	635	977	1,033	1,373	1,435
Drugs	953	568	930	1,145	1,002	1,027	1,172	1,217
Medical supplies	160	80	136	191	176	248	205	261
ENTERTAINMENT	**1,099**	**476**	**729**	**1,100**	**1,308**	**1,727**	**2,092**	**2,761**
Fees and admissions	309	86	160	280	345	496	693	1,127
Television, radio, sound equipment	446	280	349	457	557	611	668	809
Pets, toys, and playground equipment	201	77	140	200	260	443	338	398
Other entertainment products and services	143	33	79	163	146	176	393	427
PERSONAL CARE PRODUCTS AND SERVICES	**442**	**274**	**327**	**480**	**504**	**657**	**758**	**780**
READING	**152**	**66**	**114**	**172**	**161**	**210**	**276**	**334**
EDUCATION	**201**	**48**	**63**	**172**	**242**	**422**	**210**	**1,118**

	complete income reporters 65 or older	under $10,000	$10,000– $19,999	$20,000– $29,999	$30,000– $39,999	$40,000– $49,999	$50,000– $69,999	$70,000 or more
TOBACCO PRODUCTS AND SMOKING SUPPLIES	**$161**	**$119**	**$132**	**$190**	**$184**	**$203**	**$154**	**$268**
MISCELLANEOUS	**713**	**355**	**439**	**819**	**599**	**824**	**1,335**	**2,267**
CASH CONTRIBUTIONS	**1,773**	**621**	**1,030**	**1,800**	**1,929**	**2,400**	**3,414**	**6,089**
PERSONAL INSURANCE AND PENSIONS	**1,408**	**189**	**533**	**780**	**1,389**	**2,605**	**3,525**	**7,694**
Life and other personal insurance	421	156	331	388	455	595	764	1,124
Pensions and Social Security	987	33	202	392	934	2,010	2,761	6,570
PERSONAL TAXES	**1,075**	**72**	**134**	**503**	**569**	**1,465**	**2,904**	**8,772**
Federal income taxes	773	1	57	289	265	1,025	2,188	7,013
State and local income taxes	143	3	11	49	91	177	345	1,292
Other taxes	159	67	66	165	213	263	371	468
GIFTS FOR NON–HOUSEHOLD MEMBERS	**905**	**387**	**462**	**890**	**1,023**	**1,521**	**1,762**	**3,087**
Food	**47**	**16**	**41**	**30**	**73**	**37**	**67**	**164**
Alcoholic beverages	**10**	**6**	**7**	**12**	**7**	**10**	**14**	**40**
Housing	**228**	**119**	**169**	**176**	**321**	**295**	**398**	**632**
Housekeeping supplies	42	24	26	44	65	49	126	60
Household textiles	17	0	5	15	21	13	41	114
Appliances and misc. housewares	23	9	18	19	43	24	36	60
Major appliances	5	–	2	5	6	7	11	31
Small appliances and misc. housewares	18	9	17	14	37	18	25	29
Miscellaneous household equipment	54	19	35	46	53	116	113	149
Other housing	92	67	84	51	139	92	84	251
Apparel and services	**205**	**114**	**124**	**260**	**176**	**252**	**295**	**658**
Males, aged 2 or older	76	48	45	89	78	127	100	196
Females, aged 2 or older	78	41	46	103	55	53	115	321
Children under age 2	19	7	9	25	21	44	39	40
Other apparel products and services	33	19	24	43	22	27	42	101
Jewelry and watches	11	2	8	8	11	24	20	33
All other apparel products and services	22	16	17	35	11	3	21	68
Transportation	**56**	**27**	**8**	**83**	**28**	**57**	**304**	**118**
Health care	**49**	**11**	**16**	**18**	**17**	**103**	**273**	**194**
Entertainment	**60**	**38**	**34**	**54**	**67**	**125**	**89**	**165**
Toys, games, hobbies, and tricycles	28	8	16	32	30	81	54	49
Other entertainment	32	30	18	22	37	44	35	116
Personal care products and services	**17**	**15**	**8**	**17**	**28**	**34**	**40**	**5**
Reading	**3**	**1**	**1**	**5**	**3**	**3**	**6**	**10**
Education	**124**	**9**	**17**	**142**	**147**	**380**	**95**	**670**
All other gifts	**106**	**31**	**37**	**94**	**154**	**224**	**182**	**432**

Note: Spending by category will not add to total spending because gift spending is also included in the preceding product and service categories and personal taxes are not included in the total. (–) means sample is too small to make a reliable estimate.
Source: Bureau of Labor Statistics, 2001 and 2002 Consumer Expenditure Surveys, Internet site http://www.bls.gov/cex/; calculations by New Strategist

Table 1.19 Aged 65 or older: Indexed spending by income, 2001–02

(indexed average annual spending of consumer units (CU) headed by people aged 65 or older by product and service category and before-tax income of consumer unit, 2001–02; index definition: an index of 100 is the average for all consumer units; an index of 132 means that spending by consumer units in that group is 32 percent above the average for all consumer units; an index of 68 indicates spending that is 32 percent below the average for all consumer units)

	complete income reporters 65 or older	under $10,000	$10,000–$19,999	$20,000–$29,999	$30,000–$39,999	$40,000–$49,999	$50,000–$69,999	$70,000 or more
Average spending of CU, total	$28,648	$15,207	$20,853	$29,121	$32,807	$40,246	$47,626	$67,821
Average spending of CU, index	100	53	73	102	115	140	166	237
FOOD	100	65	75	110	110	129	151	209
Food at home	100	75	82	113	107	121	131	167
Cereals and bakery products	100	78	86	113	103	117	114	167
Cereals and cereal products	100	85	85	108	102	118	117	163
Bakery products	100	74	86	115	103	117	113	169
Meats, poultry, fish, and eggs	100	80	82	117	105	116	115	170
Beef	100	81	72	136	117	104	98	168
Pork	100	81	90	120	97	111	109	139
Other meats	100	77	85	109	101	121	128	162
Poultry	100	82	86	110	86	118	133	178
Fish and seafood	100	75	77	89	121	146	122	236
Eggs	100	91	94	113	94	103	126	123
Dairy products	100	71	82	114	114	121	136	158
Fresh milk and cream	100	78	87	114	109	115	130	139
Other dairy products	100	67	79	115	119	126	142	173
Fruits and vegetables	100	72	82	113	108	121	146	164
Fresh fruits	100	73	81	114	106	117	148	171
Fresh vegetables	100	71	82	110	114	128	138	167
Processed fruits	100	69	84	120	107	115	134	157
Processed vegetables	100	76	79	109	100	123	177	155
Other food at home	100	73	81	111	108	126	143	169
Sugar and other sweets	100	75	82	109	105	133	126	172
Fats and oils	100	91	80	109	99	114	170	142
Miscellaneous foods	100	68	83	109	116	123	145	168
Nonalcoholic beverages	100	79	85	113	102	114	137	154
Food prepared by CU on trips	100	34	41	126	106	235	147	318
Food away from home	100	46	63	104	115	145	189	287
ALCOHOLIC BEVERAGES	100	42	61	72	129	147	229	353
HOUSING	100	63	79	102	114	129	144	209
Shelter	100	65	80	100	107	124	141	223
Owned dwellings	100	46	72	107	107	138	164	257
Mortgage interest and charges	100	41	56	99	105	137	186	355
Property taxes	100	54	80	102	108	121	147	240
Maintenance, repair, insurance, other expenses	100	43	75	120	107	157	164	199
Rented dwellings	100	124	112	86	95	73	65	84
Other lodging	100	22	44	86	144	168	203	394
Utilities, fuels, and public services	100	71	88	106	112	118	133	155
Natural gas	100	64	94	105	120	115	120	142
Electricity	100	73	88	108	113	117	133	146
Fuel oil and other fuels	100	94	101	117	74	81	81	146
Telephone	100	72	83	101	115	126	149	166
Water and other public services	100	61	86	108	111	124	135	177

	complete income reporters 65 or older	under $10,000	$10,000– $19,999	$20,000– $29,999	$30,000– $39,999	$40,000– $49,999	$50,000– $69,999	$70,000 or more
Household services	100	47	67	96	158	177	121	229
Personal services	100	39	67	80	281	254	44	104
Other household services	100	51	68	103	103	142	156	286
Housekeeping supplies	100	71	71	105	128	134	177	178
Laundry and cleaning supplies	100	88	77	109	101	139	174	122
Other household products	100	68	70	94	142	127	182	205
Postage and stationery	100	64	67	119	128	140	173	180
Household furnishings and equipment	100	45	61	108	121	148	183	276
Household textiles	100	46	61	109	113	114	225	292
Furniture	100	36	58	126	129	152	144	276
Floor coverings	100	23	92	109	138	156	103	197
Major appliances	100	49	69	134	95	113	173	232
Small appliances, misc. housewares	100	50	79	79	154	113	164	250
Miscellaneous household equipment	100	49	53	96	120	173	203	297
APPAREL AND RELATED SERVICES	100	71	66	85	114	127	172	299
Men and boys	100	67	64	84	109	130	222	287
Men, aged 16 or older	100	70	62	81	111	132	231	287
Boys, aged 2 to 15	100	41	79	108	96	112	154	292
Women and girls	100	71	66	83	121	138	156	295
Women, aged 16 or older	100	71	66	82	112	143	160	304
Girls, aged 2 to 15	100	72	66	94	242	67	109	182
Children under age 2	100	37	47	130	130	225	220	205
Footwear	100	101	72	80	101	80	178	278
Other apparel products and services	100	50	64	90	112	128	133	372
TRANSPORTATION	100	38	71	101	127	169	198	208
Vehicle purchases	100	35	74	99	132	200	202	165
Cars and trucks, new	100	31	79	98	118	253	153	173
Cars and trucks, used	100	40	67	102	151	133	261	157
Other vehicles	100	–	171	–	–	–	611	–
Gasoline and motor oil	100	46	72	111	133	143	177	188
Other vehicle expenses	100	39	69	101	124	152	191	240
Vehicle finance charges	100	28	53	88	177	147	265	239
Maintenance and repairs	100	41	75	108	117	153	181	205
Vehicle insurance	100	46	75	109	127	158	166	186
Vehicle rentals, leases, licenses, other charges	100	28	52	79	100	138	232	432
Public transportation	100	39	55	88	98	131	247	358
HEALTH CARE	100	56	87	112	118	131	143	150
Health insurance	100	60	90	114	115	132	131	137
Medical services	100	40	66	95	146	155	206	215
Drugs	100	60	98	120	105	108	123	128
Medical supplies	100	50	85	119	110	155	128	163
ENTERTAINMENT	100	43	66	100	119	157	190	251
Fees and admissions	100	28	52	91	112	161	224	365
Television, radio, sound equipment	100	63	78	102	125	137	150	181
Pets, toys, and playground equipment	100	38	70	100	129	220	168	198
Other entertainment products and services	100	23	55	114	102	123	275	299
PERSONAL CARE PRODUCTS AND SERVICES	100	62	74	109	114	149	171	176
READING	100	43	75	113	106	138	182	220
EDUCATION	100	24	31	86	120	210	104	556

	complete income reporters 65 or older	under $10,000	$10,000–$19,999	$20,000–$29,999	$30,000–$39,999	$40,000–$49,999	$50,000–$69,999	$70,000 or more
TOBACCO PRODUCTS AND SMOKING SUPPLIES	100	74	82	118	114	126	96	166
MISCELLANEOUS	100	50	62	115	84	116	187	318
CASH CONTRIBUTIONS	100	35	58	102	109	135	193	343
PERSONAL INSURANCE AND PENSIONS	100	13	38	55	99	185	250	546
Life and other personal insurance	100	37	79	92	108	141	181	267
Pensions and Social Security	100	3	20	40	95	204	280	666
PERSONAL TAXES	100	7	13	47	53	136	270	816
Federal income taxes	100	0	7	37	34	133	283	907
State and local income taxes	100	2	8	34	64	124	241	903
Other taxes	100	42	42	104	134	165	233	294
GIFTS FOR NON–HOUSEHOLD MEMBERS	100	43	51	98	113	168	195	341
Food	100	33	87	64	155	79	143	349
Alcoholic beverages	100	57	67	120	70	100	140	400
Housing	100	52	74	77	141	129	175	277
Housekeeping supplies	100	57	63	105	155	117	300	143
Household textiles	100	1	29	88	124	76	241	671
Appliances and misc. housewares	100	38	80	83	187	104	157	261
Major appliances	100	–	37	100	120	140	220	620
Small appliances and misc. housewares	100	49	92	78	206	100	139	161
Miscellaneous household equipment	100	36	65	85	98	215	209	276
Other housing	100	73	91	55	151	100	91	273
Apparel and services	100	56	60	127	86	123	144	321
Males, aged 2 or older	100	63	59	117	103	167	132	258
Females, aged 2 or older	100	52	58	132	71	68	147	412
Children under age 2	100	39	47	132	111	232	205	211
Other apparel products and services	100	57	73	130	67	82	127	306
Jewelry and watches	100	20	69	73	100	218	182	300
All other apparel products and services	100	72	77	159	50	14	95	309
Transportation	100	48	14	148	50	102	543	211
Health care	100	22	32	37	35	210	557	396
Entertainment	100	63	56	90	112	208	148	275
Toys, games, hobbies, and tricycles	100	27	59	114	107	289	193	175
Other entertainment	100	95	55	69	116	138	109	363
Personal care products and services	100	89	47	100	165	200	235	29
Reading	100	33	33	167	100	100	200	333
Education	100	7	14	115	119	306	77	540
All other gifts	100	29	35	89	145	211	172	408

Note: (–) means sample is too small to make a reliable estimate.
Source: Calculations by New Strategist based on the Bureau of Labor Statistics 2001 and 2002 Consumer Expenditure Surveys

Spending by Household Type, 2002

Married couples spent 29 percent more than the average household in 2002. Among married couples, those with children aged 18 or older living at home spend the most—$60,860 in 2002. Behind the higher spending levels of married couples are their higher incomes, stemming primarily from the greater number of earners in the household. Most married couples have at least two earners today, and couples with adult children at home often have three earners in the household. The more earners, the greater the spending—particularly on products and services needed by workers such as food away from home, men's and women's clothes, and transportation.

Married couples with younger children at home also have distinct spending patterns. Couples with school-aged children spend 43 percent more than the average household overall. They spend 57 percent more than the average household on milk and 61 percent more on cereal. They spend twice as much as the average household on fees and admissions to entertainment events and three times the average on children's clothes. The biggest spenders on household services (mostly day care) are married couples with preschoolers, while couples without children at home and those with adult children at home spend the most on alcohol, other lodging (mostly hotels and motels) and public transportation (e.g., airfare).

Single parents spend less than the average household on most items. Some of the exceptions are rent, children's clothes, and household personal services (mostly day care).

Table 1.20 Average spending by household type, 2002

(average annual spending of consumer units (CU) by product and service category and type of consumer unit, 2002)

	total married couples	married couples, no children	married couples with children				single parent, at least one child <18	single person
			total	oldest child under 6	oldest child 6 to 17	oldest child 18 or older		
Number of consumer units (in thousands, add 000s)	56,265	23,118	28,790	5,547	15,206	8,036	6,730	33,055
Average number of persons per CU	3.2	2.0	3.9	3.5	4.1	3.9	2.9	1.0
Average income before taxes	$67,155	$58,967	$73,918	$67,587	$72,720	$81,042	$26,966	$27,042
Average annual spending	52,334	45,557	57,835	52,779	58,104	60,860	30,185	24,190
FOOD	**$6,881**	**$5,676**	**$7,785**	**$6,348**	**$8,041**	**$8,324**	**$4,745**	**$2,913**
Food at home	**3,987**	**3,160**	**4,528**	**3,940**	**4,664**	**4,690**	**3,057**	**1,558**
Cereals and bakery products	579	442	676	560	708	697	461	225
Cereals and cereal products	197	140	235	206	248	229	180	74
Bakery products	383	302	441	354	460	468	281	151
Meats, poultry, fish, and eggs	1,025	813	1,146	942	1,163	1,263	832	359
Beef	303	227	350	275	355	397	225	93
Pork	215	182	229	193	240	234	195	73
Other meats	131	98	152	112	155	175	111	48
Poultry	183	136	212	180	214	233	146	65
Fish and seafood	152	134	158	143	156	174	117	64
Eggs	41	35	44	39	43	49	38	18
Dairy products	426	329	497	454	517	487	318	166
Fresh milk and cream	162	118	194	182	199	193	135	64
Other dairy products	264	211	303	272	319	294	183	102
Fruits and vegetables	714	602	779	711	789	808	498	292
Fresh fruits	233	202	252	211	259	270	152	97
Fresh vegetables	229	198	240	216	242	254	146	90
Processed fruits	147	115	170	172	172	166	116	62
Processed vegetables	106	87	116	112	116	118	84	43
Other food at home	1,242	974	1,431	1,274	1,487	1,434	948	515
Sugar and other sweets	153	126	172	132	190	164	106	64
Fats and oils	109	92	119	92	119	140	87	43
Miscellaneous foods	602	447	716	729	728	684	493	250
Nonalcoholic beverages	319	252	363	276	381	391	244	136
Food prepared by CU on trips	59	57	61	45	69	55	19	22
Food away from home	**2,894**	**2,516**	**3,257**	**2,408**	**3,376**	**3,634**	**1,688**	**1,356**
ALCOHOLIC BEVERAGES	**441**	**479**	**432**	**340**	**436**	**490**	**146**	**285**
HOUSING	**16,649**	**14,422**	**18,460**	**19,141**	**18,619**	**17,697**	**11,022**	**8,619**
Shelter	**9,578**	**8,110**	**10,795**	**11,269**	**10,912**	**10,247**	**6,513**	**5,465**
Owned dwellings	7,411	6,114	8,536	8,506	8,728	8,196	3,102	2,605
Mortgage interest and charges	4,376	3,053	5,472	5,950	5,739	4,635	1,872	1,260
Property taxes	1,722	1,670	1,786	1,545	1,822	1,883	623	755
Maintenance, repair, insurance, other expenses	1,313	1,391	1,279	1,011	1,166	1,677	607	590
Rented dwellings	1,451	1,157	1,611	2,384	1,600	1,097	3,280	2,538
Other lodging	715	840	648	379	584	954	131	322
Utilities, fuels, and public services	**3,271**	**2,915**	**3,478**	**2,979**	**3,491**	**3,797**	**2,471**	**1,712**
Natural gas	399	354	427	351	442	451	307	225
Electricity	1,199	1,088	1,262	1,041	1,285	1,371	961	600
Fuel oil and other fuels	111	114	107	78	106	131	50	63
Telephone	1,135	970	1,234	1,128	1,204	1,365	913	624
Water and other public services	426	389	448	381	455	480	240	201

	total married couples	married couples, no children	married couples with children				single parent, at least one child <18	single person
			total	oldest child under 6	oldest child 6 to 17	oldest child 18 or older		
Household services	**$943**	**$553**	**$1,264**	**$2,320**	**$1,221**	**$615**	**$814**	**$400**
Personal services	463	68	776	1,912	705	125	571	134
Other household services	480	485	488	408	515	490	243	266
Housekeeping supplies	**754**	**817**	**712**	**552**	**724**	**804**	**337**	**270**
Laundry and cleaning supplies	169	140	192	156	195	213	120	64
Other household products	414	495	357	252	378	392	147	118
Postage and stationery	171	182	163	145	151	199	70	88
Household furnishings and equipment	**2,104**	**2,027**	**2,212**	**2,021**	**2,271**	**2,234**	**886**	**772**
Household textiles	177	188	173	147	164	212	73	81
Furniture	574	590	578	540	620	526	232	179
Floor coverings	64	78	58	41	67	54	15	15
Major appliances	252	258	251	228	248	272	140	94
Small appliances, misc. housewares	134	134	141	158	128	153	56	57
Miscellaneous household equipment	903	779	1,010	907	1,044	1,017	371	346
APPAREL AND RELATED SERVICES	**2,218**	**1,633**	**2,643**	**2,630**	**2,689**	**2,565**	**1,885**	**921**
Men and boys	**567**	**374**	**713**	**579**	**769**	**702**	**392**	**176**
Men, aged 16 or older	442	353	511	452	469	634	178	162
Boys, aged 2 to 15	125	22	203	127	300	68	214	14
Women and girls	**849**	**702**	**951**	**758**	**1,020**	**961**	**878**	**413**
Women, aged 16 or older	690	677	685	594	627	866	566	397
Girls, aged 2 to 15	159	25	266	163	392	95	312	16
Children under age 2	**117**	**46**	**174**	**535**	**100**	**58**	**71**	**15**
Footwear	**392**	**228**	**500**	**471**	**508**	**507**	**391**	**149**
Other apparel products and services	**294**	**283**	**304**	**288**	**292**	**337**	**154**	**168**
TRANSPORTATION	**10,199**	**8,592**	**11,425**	**10,467**	**11,203**	**12,506**	**5,549**	**3,890**
Vehicle purchases	**4,795**	**3,898**	**5,513**	**5,391**	**5,512**	**5,600**	**2,833**	**1,662**
Cars and trucks, new	2,398	2,220	2,644	2,668	2,556	2,791	1,186	791
Cars and trucks, used	2,296	1,617	2,726	2,531	2,831	2,661	1,593	846
Other vehicles	101	60	144	191	125	148	54	25
Gasoline and motor oil	**1,621**	**1,345**	**1,807**	**1,494**	**1,761**	**2,112**	**912**	**646**
Other vehicle expenses	**3,287**	**2,818**	**3,649**	**3,176**	**3,491**	**4,274**	**1,645**	**1,306**
Vehicle finance charges	564	439	649	622	641	684	253	143
Maintenance and repairs	900	804	993	827	974	1,141	448	437
Vehicle insurance	1,157	1,015	1,247	993	1,140	1,623	643	486
Vehicle rentals, leases, licenses, other charges	667	560	761	733	736	825	301	240
Public transportation	**496**	**531**	**455**	**406**	**439**	**521**	**159**	**276**
HEALTH CARE	**3,110**	**3,614**	**2,716**	**2,233**	**2,676**	**3,127**	**1,252**	**1,522**
Health insurance	1,551	1,799	1,362	1,253	1,343	1,473	578	759
Medical services	808	828	806	633	815	909	411	330
Drugs	615	823	433	274	400	604	187	366
Medical supplies	136	164	115	73	118	140	77	68
ENTERTAINMENT	**2,762**	**2,265**	**3,213**	**2,425**	**3,593**	**3,037**	**1,362**	**1,193**
Fees and admissions	753	615	893	558	1,087	756	305	320
Television, radio, sound equipment	830	703	926	783	964	952	612	467
Pets, toys, and playground equipment	495	445	546	486	605	475	263	202
Other entertainment products and services	684	502	848	598	937	854	182	205
PERSONAL CARE PRODUCTS AND SERVICES	**662**	**608**	**711**	**549**	**757**	**736**	**428**	**310**
READING	**174**	**192**	**166**	**132**	**169**	**184**	**72**	**108**
EDUCATION	**952**	**490**	**1,366**	**336**	**1,246**	**2,303**	**454**	**562**
TOBACCO PRODUCTS AND SMOKING SUPPLIES	**$336**	**$286**	**$344**	**$275**	**$318**	**$440**	**$262**	**$210**

	total married couples	married couples, no children	married couples with children				single parent, at least one child <18	single person
			total	oldest child under 6	oldest child 6 to 17	oldest child 18 or older		
MISCELLANEOUS	$921	$865	$949	$913	$827	$1,205	$569	$602
CASH CONTRIBUTIONS	1,646	1,909	1,481	1,037	1,399	1,941	374	998
PERSONAL INSURANCE AND PENSIONS	5,384	4,524	6,144	5,952	6,129	6,304	2,066	2,055
Life and other personal insurance	605	634	592	424	609	675	182	183
Pensions and Social Security	4,779	3,891	5,552	5,528	5,520	5,629	1,883	1,872
PERSONAL TAXES	3,458	3,358	3,706	3,738	3,710	3,672	483	1,815
Federal income taxes	2,543	2,464	2,749	2,766	2,742	2,748	195	1,396
State and local income taxes	702	645	774	837	782	710	243	327
Other taxes	213	249	183	135	186	215	45	93
GIFTS FOR NON–HOUSEHOLD MEMBERS	1,338	1,479	1,286	773	1,253	1,710	513	744
Food	123	157	106	54	94	165	36	42
Alcoholic beverages	15	14	18	9	23	14	4	10
Housing	342	355	350	280	328	442	159	170
Housekeeping supplies	57	67	51	36	47	69	24	25
Household textiles	20	29	13	9	13	13	9	9
Appliances and misc. housewares	29	44	20	14	22	21	12	16
Major appliances	11	19	6	4	6	5	2	4
Small appliances and misc. housewares	18	25	14	10	15	15	10	12
Miscellaneous household equipment	83	97	76	59	65	112	49	46
Other housing	153	119	190	162	181	228	65	75
Apparel and services	273	319	244	231	212	314	185	187
Males, aged 2 or older	73	93	59	60	52	71	54	48
Females, aged 2 or older	99	124	82	52	72	124	49	64
Children under age 2	55	46	62	98	55	50	26	15
Other apparel products and services	46	56	41	21	33	69	55	61
Jewelry and watches	17	26	12	8	13	13	16	41
All other apparel products and services	29	30	29	14	21	56	39	20
Transportation	44	37	54	16	60	67	7	46
Health care	36	44	32	5	38	39	27	24
Entertainment	101	117	90	85	85	102	27	58
Toys, games, hobbies, and tricycles	39	54	27	33	19	38	7	22
Other entertainment	62	63	63	52	66	63	19	35
Personal care products and services	24	23	24	22	28	16	15	15
Reading	1	2	1	1	1	1	–	2
Education	279	270	307	34	329	454	35	111
All other gifts	100	141	61	35	54	94	18	80

Note: Spending by category will not add to total spending because gift spending is also included in the preceding product and service categories and personal taxes are not included in the total. (–) means sample is too small to make a reliable estimate.
Source: Bureau of Labor Statistics, 2002 Consumer Expenditure Survey, Internet site http://www.bls.gov/cex/

Table 1.21 Indexed spending by household type, 2002

(indexed average annual spending of consumer units (CU) by product and service category and type of consumer unit, 2002; index definition: an index of 100 is the average for all consumer units; an index of 132 means that spending by consumer units in that group is 32 percent above the average for all consumer units; an index of 68 indicates spending that is 32 percent below the average for all consumer units)

| | total married couples | married couples, no children | married couples with children | | | single parent, at least one child <18 | single person |
			total	oldest child under 6	oldest child 6 to 17	oldest child 18 or older		
Average spending of CU, total	$52,334	$45,557	$57,835	$52,779	$58,104	$60,860	$30,185	$24,190
Average spending of CU, index	129	112	142	130	143	150	74	59
FOOD	**128**	**106**	**145**	**118**	**150**	**155**	**88**	**54**
Food at home	**129**	**102**	**146**	**127**	**151**	**151**	**99**	**50**
Cereals and bakery products	129	98	150	124	157	155	102	50
Cereals and cereal products	128	91	153	134	161	149	117	48
Bakery products	129	102	149	120	155	158	95	51
Meats, poultry, fish, and eggs	128	102	144	118	146	158	104	45
Beef	131	98	152	119	154	172	97	40
Pork	129	109	137	116	144	140	117	44
Other meats	130	97	150	111	153	173	110	48
Poultry	127	94	147	125	149	162	101	45
Fish and seafood	126	111	131	118	129	144	97	53
Eggs	121	103	129	115	126	144	112	53
Dairy products	130	100	152	138	158	148	97	51
Fresh milk and cream	128	93	153	143	157	152	106	50
Other dairy products	131	105	151	135	159	146	91	51
Fruits and vegetables	129	109	141	129	143	146	90	53
Fresh fruits	131	113	142	119	146	152	85	54
Fresh vegetables	131	113	137	123	138	145	83	51
Processed fruits	127	99	147	148	148	143	100	53
Processed vegetables	128	105	140	135	140	142	101	52
Other food at home	128	100	148	131	153	148	98	53
Sugar and other sweets	131	108	147	113	162	140	91	55
Fats and oils	128	108	140	108	140	165	102	51
Miscellaneous foods	128	95	152	154	154	145	104	53
Nonalcoholic beverages	126	99	143	109	150	154	96	54
Food prepared by CU on trips	144	139	149	110	168	134	46	54
Food away from home	**127**	**111**	**143**	**106**	**148**	**160**	**74**	**60**
ALCOHOLIC BEVERAGES	**117**	**127**	**115**	**90**	**116**	**130**	**39**	**76**
HOUSING	**125**	**109**	**139**	**144**	**140**	**133**	**83**	**65**
Shelter	**122**	**104**	**138**	**144**	**139**	**131**	**83**	**70**
Owned dwellings	143	118	165	165	169	159	60	50
Mortgage interest and charges	148	103	185	201	194	156	63	43
Property taxes	139	134	144	124	147	152	50	61
Maintenance, repair, insurance, other expenses	137	145	133	105	121	175	63	61
Rented dwellings	67	54	75	110	74	51	152	118
Other lodging	142	166	128	75	116	189	26	64
Utilities, fuels, and public services	**122**	**109**	**130**	**111**	**130**	**141**	**92**	**64**
Natural gas	121	107	129	106	134	137	93	68
Electricity	122	111	129	106	131	140	98	61
Fuel oil and other fuels	126	130	122	89	120	149	57	72
Telephone	119	101	129	118	126	143	95	65
Water and other public services	130	119	137	116	139	146	73	61

	total married couples	married couples, no children	married couples with children				single parent, at least one child <18	single person
			total	oldest child under 6	oldest child 6 to 17	oldest child 18 or older		
Household services	**134**	**78**	**179**	**329**	**173**	**87**	**115**	**57**
Personal services	140	21	234	578	213	38	173	40
Other household services	128	129	130	109	137	131	65	71
Housekeeping supplies	**138**	**150**	**131**	**101**	**133**	**148**	**62**	**50**
Laundry and cleaning supplies	129	107	147	119	149	163	92	49
Other household products	146	175	126	89	134	139	52	42
Postage and stationery	131	139	124	111	115	152	53	67
Household furnishings and equipment	**139**	**134**	**146**	**133**	**150**	**147**	**58**	**51**
Household textiles	130	138	127	108	121	156	54	60
Furniture	143	147	144	135	155	131	58	45
Floor coverings	160	195	145	103	168	135	38	38
Major appliances	134	137	134	121	132	145	74	50
Small appliances, misc. housewares	134	134	141	158	128	153	56	57
Miscellaneous household equipment	138	119	155	139	160	156	57	53
APPAREL AND RELATED SERVICES	**127**	**93**	**151**	**150**	**154**	**147**	**108**	**53**
Men and boys	**139**	**91**	**174**	**142**	**188**	**172**	**96**	**43**
Men, aged 16 or older	139	111	160	142	147	199	56	51
Boys, aged 2 to 15	139	24	226	141	333	76	238	16
Women and girls	**121**	**100**	**135**	**108**	**145**	**137**	**125**	**59**
Women, aged 16 or older	118	115	117	101	107	148	96	68
Girls, aged 2 to 15	136	21	227	139	335	81	267	14
Children under age 2	**141**	**55**	**210**	**645**	**120**	**70**	**86**	**18**
Footwear	**125**	**73**	**160**	**150**	**162**	**162**	**125**	**48**
Other apparel products and services	**123**	**118**	**127**	**120**	**122**	**140**	**64**	**70**
TRANSPORTATION	**131**	**111**	**147**	**135**	**144**	**161**	**72**	**50**
Vehicle purchases	**131**	**106**	**150**	**147**	**150**	**153**	**77**	**45**
Cars and trucks, new	137	127	151	152	146	159	68	45
Cars and trucks, used	125	88	148	137	154	144	86	46
Other vehicles	144	86	206	273	179	211	77	36
Gasoline and motor oil	**131**	**109**	**146**	**121**	**143**	**171**	**74**	**52**
Other vehicle expenses	**133**	**114**	**148**	**129**	**141**	**173**	**67**	**53**
Vehicle finance charges	142	111	163	157	161	172	64	36
Maintenance and repairs	129	115	142	119	140	164	64	63
Vehicle insurance	129	114	139	111	128	182	72	54
Vehicle rentals, leases, licenses, other charges	138	116	158	152	152	171	62	50
Public transportation	**128**	**137**	**117**	**104**	**113**	**134**	**41**	**71**
HEALTH CARE	**132**	**154**	**116**	**95**	**114**	**133**	**53**	**65**
Health insurance	133	154	117	107	115	126	49	65
Medical services	137	140	137	107	138	154	70	56
Drugs	126	169	89	56	82	124	38	75
Medical supplies	130	156	110	70	112	133	73	65
ENTERTAINMENT	**133**	**109**	**155**	**117**	**173**	**146**	**66**	**57**
Fees and admissions	139	113	165	103	201	139	56	59
Television, radio, sound equipment	120	102	134	113	139	138	88	67
Pets, toys, and playground equipment	134	121	148	132	164	129	71	55
Other entertainment products and services	144	105	178	126	197	179	38	43
PERSONAL CARE PRODUCTS AND SERVICES	**126**	**116**	**135**	**104**	**144**	**140**	**81**	**59**
READING	**125**	**138**	**119**	**95**	**122**	**132**	**52**	**78**
EDUCATION	**127**	**65**	**182**	**45**	**166**	**306**	**60**	**75**

	total married couples	married couples, no children	married couples with children				single parent, at least one child <18	single person
			total	oldest child under 6	oldest child 6 to 17	oldest child 18 or older		
TOBACCO PRODUCTS AND SMOKING SUPPLIES	105	89	108	86	99	138	82	66
MISCELLANEOUS	116	109	120	115	104	152	72	76
CASH CONTRIBUTIONS	129	149	116	81	110	152	29	78
PERSONAL INSURANCE AND PENSIONS	138	116	158	153	157	162	53	53
Life and other personal insurance	149	156	146	104	150	166	45	45
Pensions and Social Security	137	111	159	158	158	161	54	54
PERSONAL TAXES	139	135	148	150	149	147	19	73
Federal income taxes	138	134	149	150	149	149	11	76
State and local income taxes	139	127	153	165	155	140	48	65
Other taxes	145	169	124	92	127	146	31	63
GIFTS FOR NON–HOUSEHOLD MEMBERS	129	143	124	75	121	165	50	72
Food	150	191	129	66	115	201	44	51
Alcoholic beverages	115	108	138	69	177	108	31	77
Housing	132	137	135	108	127	171	61	66
Housekeeping supplies	136	160	121	86	112	164	57	60
Household textiles	143	207	93	64	93	93	64	64
Appliances and misc. housewares	121	183	83	58	92	88	50	67
Major appliances	138	238	75	50	75	63	25	50
Small appliances and misc. housewares	113	156	88	63	94	94	63	75
Miscellaneous household equipment	128	149	117	91	100	172	75	71
Other housing	134	104	167	142	159	200	57	66
Apparel and services	115	135	103	97	89	132	78	79
Males, aged 2 or older	114	145	92	94	81	111	84	75
Females, aged 2 or older	121	151	100	63	88	151	60	78
Children under age 2	138	115	155	245	138	125	65	38
Other apparel products and services	88	108	79	40	63	133	106	117
Jewelry and watches	71	108	50	33	54	54	67	171
All other apparel products and services	104	107	104	50	75	200	139	71
Transportation	100	84	123	36	136	152	16	105
Health care	109	133	97	15	115	118	82	73
Entertainment	129	150	115	109	109	131	35	74
Toys, games, hobbies, and tricycles	130	180	90	110	63	127	23	73
Other entertainment	129	131	131	108	138	131	40	73
Personal care products and services	114	110	114	105	133	76	71	71
Reading	100	200	100	100	100	100	–	200
Education	152	147	167	18	179	247	19	60
All other gifts	119	168	73	42	64	112	21	95

Note: Spending index for total consumer units is 100. (–) means sample is too small to make a reliable estimate.
Source: Calculations by New Strategist based on the Bureau of Labor Statistics 2002 Consumer Expenditure Survey

Spending by Household Type and Age, 2001–02

Women who live alone spent an annual average of $22,209 in 2001–02, only 55 percent of the $40,102 spent by the average household during that time period. Forty-two percent of women who live alone are aged 65 or older, many of them widows with low incomes.

Among women who live alone, spending peaked in the 35-to-44 age group at $27,725 in 2001–02. Women under age 25 spend much more than the average household on education, with an index of 223. Women aged 25 to 34 spend fully 59 percent more than the average household on women's clothes—more than most other household types, despite their small household size. Women aged 65 or older spend less than their middle-aged counterparts, an average of $18,548 in 2001–02. But they spend more than the average household on household services, health care, cash contributions, and gifts of household textiles.

Men who live alone spent an annual average of $25,904 in 2001–02, only 64 percent of what the average household spent during the time period. Among men who live alone, those under age 25 spend much more than the average household on education, with an index of 293. Men aged 25 to 34 who live alone spend 4 percent more than the average household on food away from home despite their smaller household size. They spend 69 percent more than average on men's clothes and 54 percent more than average on alcoholic beverages. Men aged 25 to 34 who live alone spend more on alcoholic beverages than any other type of household. Those aged 25 to 34 spend more than six times the average on gifts of jewelry and watches, while those aged 35 to 44 spend four times the average on this item. Men aged 65 or older who live alone spend less than their middle-aged counterparts, an average of $21,389 in 2001–02. They spend more than the average household on drugs and cash contributions.

Table 1.22 Average spending of single-person consumer units headed by women, by age, 2001–02

(average annual spending of single-person consumer units (CU) headed by women by product and service category and age, 2001–02)

	total single-person consumer units headed by women	under 25	25 to 34	35 to 44	45 to 54	55 to 64	65 or older
Number of consumer units (in thousands, add 000s)	18,316	2,244	1,674	1,520	2,581	2,592	7,704
Average income before taxes	$22,936	$11,573	$31,432	$34,939	$33,864	$28,808	$16,437
Average annual spending	22,209	15,589	27,110	27,725	27,309	27,175	18,548
FOOD	$2,583	$2,088	$3,202	$2,856	$2,860	$2,903	$2,305
Food at home	1,598	860	1,562	1,530	1,805	1,827	1,672
Cereals and bakery products	234	140	235	207	242	246	259
Cereals and cereal products	77	61	82	69	79	79	81
Bakery products	157	80	153	139	164	167	178
Meats, poultry, fish, and eggs	360	133	313	380	400	452	384
Beef	92	36	75	95	118	105	97
Pork	74	23	58	68	72	97	85
Other meats	44	20	37	45	50	44	50
Poultry	68	27	61	67	70	82	75
Fish and seafood	63	18	65	83	67	104	55
Eggs	20	9	17	21	23	21	22
Dairy products	175	102	167	160	202	204	180
Fresh milk and cream	66	40	55	56	65	76	76
Other dairy products	108	62	112	104	138	128	104
Fruits and vegetables	319	165	299	277	326	378	354
Fresh fruits	104	56	96	90	103	119	118
Fresh vegetables	102	42	85	91	108	135	112
Processed fruits	65	43	67	55	61	76	72
Processed vegetables	48	24	51	40	54	48	53
Other food at home	509	320	547	506	635	547	496
Sugar and other sweets	68	36	55	68	63	91	75
Fats and oils	47	23	33	48	53	48	55
Miscellaneous foods	246	162	284	225	334	234	237
Nonalcoholic beverages	128	79	149	142	158	146	115
Food prepared by CU on trips	20	20	26	22	26	27	14
Food away from home	985	1,227	1,640	1,326	1,055	1,076	633
ALCOHOLIC BEVERAGES	173	256	355	222	191	141	100
HOUSING	8,434	5,262	10,218	10,855	10,703	9,703	7,292
Shelter	5,111	3,822	7,029	7,294	6,792	5,700	3,878
Owned dwellings	2,556	339	2,169	3,702	3,981	3,939	2,118
Mortgage interest and charges	1,085	112	1,417	2,374	2,258	1,785	413
Property taxes	801	204	438	731	923	1,123	918
Maintenance, repair, insurance, other expenses	671	23	314	596	799	1,032	787
Rented dwellings	2,287	2,977	4,605	3,415	2,448	1,461	1,585
Other lodging	267	506	256	177	363	299	175
Utilities, fuels, and public services	1,844	815	1,803	1,882	2,101	2,242	1,925
Natural gas	276	56	203	266	315	307	335
Electricity	648	253	537	616	738	812	708
Fuel oil and other fuels	68	2	21	28	64	85	101
Telephone	641	473	910	788	751	741	532
Water and other public services	211	31	133	183	234	297	249

	total single-person consumer units headed by women	under 25	25 to 34	35 to 44	45 to 54	55 to 64	65 or older
Household services	**$417**	**$69**	**$197**	**$247**	**$348**	**$430**	**$618**
Personal services	93	3	3	11	1	13	211
Other household services	324	66	195	236	348	417	406
Housekeeping supplies	**310**	**118**	**242**	**250**	**442**	**387**	**320**
Laundry and cleaning supplies	70	30	61	52	85	99	72
Other household products	148	51	102	112	254	168	148
Postage and stationery	93	37	79	87	103	120	100
Household furnishings and equipment	**751**	**439**	**946**	**1,182**	**1,020**	**944**	**552**
Household textiles	90	39	115	134	83	122	81
Furniture	168	134	270	302	244	203	92
Floor coverings	19	5	7	24	37	13	21
Major appliances	97	26	68	187	119	135	87
Small appliances, misc. housewares	59	30	80	84	74	77	45
Miscellaneous household equipment	318	204	406	451	463	394	226
APPAREL AND RELATED SERVICES	**1,030**	**1,249**	**1,536**	**1,103**	**1,327**	**1,134**	**705**
Men and boys	**56**	**66**	**94**	**39**	**51**	**63**	**47**
Men, aged 16 or older	41	58	84	23	32	47	32
Boys, aged 2 to 15	15	8	10	17	20	17	15
Women and girls	**656**	**918**	**946**	**675**	**759**	**702**	**463**
Women, aged 16 or older	637	908	934	666	721	671	448
Girls, aged 2 to 15	19	10	12	9	38	30	15
Children under age 2	**20**	**8**	**20**	**20**	**41**	**31**	**12**
Footwear	**156**	**151**	**265**	**109**	**249**	**194**	**98**
Other apparel products and services	**143**	**106**	**212**	**261**	**228**	**144**	**85**
TRANSPORTATION	**3,223**	**2,472**	**4,797**	**4,854**	**3,925**	**4,570**	**2,089**
Vehicle purchases	**1,292**	**1,057**	**1,964**	**2,311**	**1,451**	**2,108**	**685**
Cars and trucks, new	701	275	1,228	1,204	817	1,168	414
Cars and trucks, used	591	782	735	1,107	634	940	270
Other vehicles	–	–	–	–	–	–	–
Gasoline and motor oil	**528**	**554**	**706**	**657**	**681**	**652**	**363**
Other vehicle expenses	**1,117**	**631**	**1,696**	**1,542**	**1,483**	**1,466**	**809**
Vehicle finance charges	111	97	252	227	140	160	36
Maintenance and repairs	355	215	443	428	513	502	261
Vehicle insurance	420	186	567	529	489	534	374
Vehicle rentals, leases, licenses, other charges	230	134	434	358	341	270	138
Public transportation	**286**	**230**	**431**	**344**	**310**	**344**	**233**
HEALTH CARE	**1,772**	**331**	**875**	**1,173**	**1,509**	**1,782**	**2,589**
Health insurance	852	118	400	612	566	761	1,336
Medical services	353	109	223	262	517	429	390
Drugs	480	76	190	250	341	486	751
Medical supplies	87	28	61	48	85	106	111
ENTERTAINMENT	**986**	**714**	**1,221**	**1,359**	**1,362**	**1,356**	**685**
Fees and admissions	257	259	416	351	289	309	175
Television, radio, sound equipment	403	266	484	546	491	499	335
Pets, toys, and playground equipment	220	91	199	341	385	371	128
Other entertainment products and services	106	99	121	122	196	176	48
PERSONAL CARE PRODUCTS AND SERVICES	**388**	**322**	**441**	**448**	**439**	**433**	**350**
READING	**115**	**57**	**119**	**128**	**133**	**137**	**116**
EDUCATION	**370**	**1,677**	**665**	**196**	**309**	**120**	**64**

	total single-person consumer units headed by women	under 25	25 to 34	35 to 44	45 to 54	55 to 64	65 or older
TOBACCO PRODUCTS AND SMOKING SUPPLIES	$150	$149	$145	$227	$259	$210	$80
MISCELLANEOUS	478	318	509	570	555	826	359
CASH CONTRIBUTIONS	915	83	375	581	774	1,048	1,344
PERSONAL INSURANCE AND PENSIONS	1,592	612	2,653	3,153	2,962	2,812	470
Life and other personal insurance	182	27	77	175	182	264	223
Pensions and Social Security	1,410	584	2,575	2,979	2,781	2,548	246
PERSONAL TAXES	1,268	320	2,290	3,427	2,230	1,869	378
Federal income taxes	910	248	1,756	2,604	1,613	1,338	209
State and local income taxes	252	67	507	698	483	370	47
Other taxes	107	5	27	126	135	161	122
GIFTS FOR NON–HOUSEHOLD MEMBERS	699	382	545	753	1,118	885	607
Food	46	22	40	35	56	102	35
Alcoholic beverages	10	7	12	12	14	10	8
Housing	193	58	114	223	344	276	162
Housekeeping supplies	29	10	24	40	41	40	25
Household textiles	17	1	12	12	22	25	18
Appliances and misc. housewares	19	5	8	10	29	45	15
Major appliances	4	1	1	2	8	11	3
Small appliances and misc. housewares	15	5	7	7	21	33	12
Miscellaneous household equipment	55	16	44	87	111	71	37
Other housing	73	25	25	74	142	95	66
Apparel and services	185	171	212	191	232	254	142
Males, aged 2 or older	55	66	90	39	51	63	46
Females, aged 2 or older	76	57	73	90	104	100	60
Children under age 2	20	8	19	20	41	31	12
Other apparel products and services	35	40	30	42	37	60	24
Jewelry and watches	12	14	14	24	13	13	8
All other apparel products and services	23	26	16	18	24	47	16
Transportation	39	21	19	110	45	8	43
Health care	29	3	7	3	28	21	50
Entertainment	53	25	47	98	75	67	41
Toys, games, hobbies, and tricycles	23	9	16	32	26	37	22
Other entertainment	30	16	32	65	49	30	19
Personal care products and services	17	12	14	25	31	18	11
Reading	2	1	1	1	2	2	3
Education	64	50	19	20	224	36	43
All other gifts	61	13	61	35	68	89	68

Note: Spending by category will not add to total spending because gift spending is also included in the preceding product and service categories and personal taxes are not included in the total. (–) means sample is too small to make a reliable estimate.
Source: Bureau of Labor Statistics, 2001 and 2002 Consumer Expenditure Surveys, Internet site http://www.bls.gov/cex/

Table 1.23 Indexed spending of single-person consumer units headed by women, by age, 2001–02

(indexed average annual spending of single-person consumer units (CU) headed by women by product and service category and age, 2001–02; index definition: an index of 100 is the average for all consumer units; an index of 132 means that spending by consumer units in that group is 32 percent above the average for all consumer units; an index of 68 indicates spending that is 32 percent below the average for all consumer units)

	total single-person consumer units headed by women	under 25	25 to 34	35 to 44	45 to 54	55 to 64	65 or older
Average spending of CU, total	$22,209	$15,589	$27,110	$27,725	$27,309	$27,175	$18,548
Average spending of CU, index	55	38	67	68	67	67	46
FOOD	48	39	60	53	53	54	43
Food at home	52	28	50	49	58	59	54
Cereals and bakery products	52	31	52	46	54	55	58
Cereals and cereal products	50	40	53	45	51	51	53
Bakery products	53	27	52	47	55	56	60
Meats, poultry, fish, and eggs	45	17	39	48	50	57	48
Beef	40	16	32	41	51	45	42
Pork	44	14	35	41	43	58	51
Other meats	44	20	37	45	50	44	50
Poultry	47	19	42	47	49	57	52
Fish and seafood	52	15	54	69	55	86	45
Eggs	59	26	50	62	68	62	65
Dairy products	53	31	51	49	62	62	55
Fresh milk and cream	52	31	43	44	51	60	60
Other dairy products	54	31	56	52	69	64	52
Fruits and vegetables	58	30	54	50	59	68	64
Fresh fruits	58	31	54	51	58	67	66
Fresh vegetables	58	24	49	52	62	77	64
Processed fruits	56	37	58	47	53	66	62
Processed vegetables	58	29	61	48	65	58	64
Other food at home	52	33	56	52	65	56	51
Sugar and other sweets	58	31	47	58	54	78	64
Fats and oils	55	27	39	56	62	56	65
Miscellaneous foods	52	34	60	48	71	50	50
Nonalcoholic beverages	50	31	59	56	62	57	45
Food prepared by CU on trips	49	49	63	54	63	66	34
Food away from home	43	54	72	58	46	47	28
ALCOHOLIC BEVERAGES	46	68	94	59	51	38	27
HOUSING	63	40	77	82	81	73	55
Shelter	65	49	90	93	87	73	50
Owned dwellings	49	7	42	72	77	76	41
Mortgage interest and charges	37	4	48	80	76	60	14
Property taxes	64	16	35	59	74	90	74
Maintenance, repair, insurance, other expenses	70	2	33	62	83	108	82
Rented dwellings	106	138	213	158	113	68	73
Other lodging	53	100	51	35	72	59	35
Utilities, fuels, and public services	69	30	67	70	78	84	72
Natural gas	84	17	62	81	95	93	102
Electricity	66	26	55	63	75	83	72
Fuel oil and other fuels	77	2	24	32	73	97	115
Telephone	67	49	95	82	78	77	56
Water and other public services	64	9	41	56	71	91	76

	total single-person consumer units headed by women	under 25	25 to 34	35 to 44	45 to 54	55 to 64	65 or older
Household services	**59**	**10**	**28**	**35**	**49**	**61**	**88**
Personal services	28	1	1	3	0	4	64
Other household services	86	18	52	63	93	111	108
Housekeeping supplies	**57**	**22**	**44**	**46**	**81**	**71**	**59**
Laundry and cleaning supplies	53	23	47	40	65	76	55
Other household products	52	18	36	40	90	59	52
Postage and stationery	71	28	60	66	79	92	76
Household furnishings and equipment	**49**	**29**	**62**	**78**	**67**	**62**	**36**
Household textiles	66	29	85	99	61	90	60
Furniture	42	33	67	75	61	51	23
Floor coverings	48	13	18	60	93	33	53
Major appliances	52	14	36	99	63	72	46
Small appliances, misc. housewares	59	30	80	84	74	77	45
Miscellaneous household equipment	49	31	62	69	71	60	35
APPAREL AND RELATED SERVICES	**59**	**71**	**88**	**63**	**76**	**65**	**40**
Men and boys	**14**	**16**	**23**	**10**	**12**	**15**	**11**
Men, aged 16 or older	13	18	26	7	10	15	10
Boys, aged 2 to 15	17	9	11	19	22	19	17
Women and girls	**93**	**130**	**134**	**96**	**108**	**100**	**66**
Women, aged 16 or older	109	155	159	113	123	114	76
Girls, aged 2 to 15	16	9	10	8	32	26	13
Children under age 2	**24**	**10**	**24**	**24**	**49**	**37**	**14**
Footwear	**50**	**48**	**85**	**35**	**80**	**62**	**31**
Other apparel products and services	**60**	**44**	**88**	**109**	**95**	**60**	**35**
TRANSPORTATION	**42**	**32**	**62**	**63**	**51**	**59**	**27**
Vehicle purchases	**35**	**29**	**54**	**63**	**40**	**58**	**19**
Cars and trucks, new	40	16	70	69	47	67	24
Cars and trucks, used	32	42	40	60	34	51	15
Other vehicles	–	–	–	–	–	–	–
Gasoline and motor oil	**43**	**45**	**57**	**53**	**55**	**53**	**29**
Other vehicle expenses	**45**	**26**	**69**	**62**	**60**	**59**	**33**
Vehicle finance charges	28	24	63	57	35	40	9
Maintenance and repairs	51	31	64	61	74	72	37
Vehicle insurance	47	21	63	59	55	60	42
Vehicle rentals, leases, licenses, other charges	48	28	90	74	71	56	29
Public transportation	**74**	**59**	**111**	**88**	**80**	**88**	**60**
HEALTH CARE	**75**	**14**	**37**	**50**	**64**	**76**	**110**
Health insurance	73	10	34	52	48	65	114
Medical services	60	18	38	44	88	73	66
Drugs	99	16	39	51	70	100	154
Medical supplies	83	27	58	46	81	101	106
ENTERTAINMENT	**47**	**34**	**59**	**65**	**66**	**65**	**33**
Fees and admissions	47	48	77	65	53	57	32
Television, radio, sound equipment	58	38	70	79	71	72	48
Pets, toys, and playground equipment	60	25	54	92	104	101	35
Other entertainment products and services	22	21	25	26	41	37	10
PERSONAL CARE PRODUCTS AND SERVICES	**74**	**61**	**84**	**85**	**83**	**82**	**67**
READING	**83**	**41**	**86**	**92**	**96**	**99**	**83**
EDUCATION	**49**	**223**	**88**	**26**	**41**	**16**	**9**

	total single-person consumer units headed by women	under 25	25 to 34	35 to 44	45 to 54	55 to 64	65 or older
TOBACCO PRODUCTS AND SMOKING SUPPLIES	47	47	45	71	81	66	25
MISCELLANEOUS	60	40	64	72	70	104	45
CASH CONTRIBUTIONS	72	6	29	45	61	82	105
PERSONAL INSURANCE AND PENSIONS	41	16	68	81	76	72	12
Life and other personal insurance	45	7	19	43	45	65	55
Pensions and Social Security	40	17	74	85	80	73	7
PERSONAL TAXES	51	13	92	137	89	75	15
Federal income taxes	49	13	95	141	88	73	11
State and local income taxes	50	13	100	138	95	73	9
Other taxes	73	3	18	86	92	110	83
GIFTS FOR NON–HOUSEHOLD MEMBERS	67	37	53	73	108	85	59
Food	56	27	49	43	68	124	43
Alcoholic beverages	77	54	92	92	108	77	62
Housing	75	22	44	86	133	107	63
Housekeeping supplies	69	24	57	95	98	95	60
Household textiles	121	7	86	86	157	179	129
Appliances and misc. housewares	79	21	33	42	121	188	63
Major appliances	50	13	13	25	100	138	38
Small appliances and misc. housewares	94	31	44	44	131	206	75
Miscellaneous household equipment	85	25	68	134	171	109	57
Other housing	64	22	22	65	125	83	58
Apparel and services	78	72	89	81	98	107	60
Males, aged 2 or older	86	103	141	61	80	98	72
Females, aged 2 or older	93	70	89	110	127	122	73
Children under age 2	50	20	48	50	103	78	30
Other apparel products and services	67	77	58	81	71	115	46
Jewelry and watches	50	58	58	100	54	54	33
All other apparel products and services	82	93	57	64	86	168	57
Transportation	89	48	43	250	102	18	98
Health care	88	9	21	9	85	64	152
Entertainment	68	32	60	126	96	86	53
Toys, games, hobbies, and tricycles	77	30	53	107	87	123	73
Other entertainment	63	33	67	135	102	63	40
Personal care products and services	81	57	67	119	148	86	52
Reading	200	100	100	100	200	200	300
Education	35	27	10	11	122	20	23
All other gifts	73	15	73	42	81	106	81

Note: Spending index for total consumer units is 100. (–) means sample is too small to make a reliable estimate.
Source: Calculations by New Strategist based on the Bureau of Labor Statistics 2001 and 2002 Consumer Expenditure Surveys

Table 1.24 Average spending of single-person consumer units headed by men, by age, 2001–02

(average annual spending of single-person consumer units (CU) headed by men by product and service category and age, 2001–02)

	total single-person consumer units headed by men	under 25	25 to 34	35 to 44	45 to 54	55 to 64	65 or older
Number of consumer units (in thousands, add 000s)	14,603	2,514	2,612	2,551	2,634	1,672	2,620
Average income before taxes	$31,688	$12,557	$38,936	$40,670	$39,980	$36,148	$22,910
Average annual spending	25,904	17,516	29,736	30,412	29,201	27,326	21,389
FOOD	$3,230	$2,366	$3,831	$3,609	$3,483	$3,172	$2,750
Food at home	1,482	825	1,459	1,536	1,676	1,772	1,616
Cereals and bakery products	213	126	203	213	231	249	252
Cereals and cereal products	72	53	76	75	65	73	87
Bakery products	141	72	128	138	166	176	165
Meats, poultry, fish, and eggs	368	168	358	409	431	443	395
Beef	104	58	117	114	130	109	94
Pork	72	26	62	82	90	87	84
Other meats	52	20	41	59	65	60	62
Poultry	64	40	70	67	64	81	64
Fish and seafood	59	14	50	68	65	83	73
Eggs	17	9	18	18	17	24	19
Dairy products	159	92	150	163	183	200	170
Fresh milk and cream	66	42	63	65	72	78	74
Other dairy products	93	49	87	98	111	122	96
Fruits and vegetables	251	136	226	250	246	321	327
Fresh fruits	81	39	70	77	75	111	116
Fresh vegetables	71	36	66	67	78	94	90
Processed fruits	62	41	60	65	58	69	74
Processed vegetables	37	20	31	42	35	48	47
Other food at home	490	305	521	501	586	558	472
Sugar and other sweets	54	27	53	43	65	60	73
Fats and oils	37	19	38	39	36	50	39
Miscellaneous foods	232	152	238	236	290	251	222
Nonalcoholic beverages	144	82	169	154	171	176	119
Food prepared by CU on trips	24	25	23	30	24	21	20
Food away from home	1,749	1,540	2,372	2,073	1,807	1,400	1,134
ALCOHOLIC BEVERAGES	454	402	578	535	497	501	234
HOUSING	8,576	4,940	10,021	10,487	9,791	8,513	7,601
Shelter	5,671	3,231	7,078	7,224	6,565	5,285	4,445
Owned dwellings	2,539	283	2,647	3,646	3,515	2,894	2,308
Mortgage interest and charges	1,384	106	1,753	2,402	1,965	1,565	550
Property taxes	695	153	549	758	941	721	1,034
Maintenance, repair, insurance, other expenses	460	24	344	485	610	608	724
Rented dwellings	2,816	2,517	4,185	3,353	2,624	2,106	1,859
Other lodging	317	431	246	225	426	285	278
Utilities, fuels, and public services	1,645	733	1,727	1,840	1,938	1,806	1,850
Natural gas	218	56	195	249	286	244	279
Electricity	587	244	594	644	704	699	666
Fuel oil and other fuels	67	13	31	47	77	91	147
Telephone	598	376	754	717	645	584	504
Water and other public services	175	44	154	182	227	188	253

	total single-person consumer units headed by men	under 25	25 to 34	35 to 44	45 to 54	55 to 64	65 or older
Household services	**$329**	**$95**	**$312**	**$393**	**$232**	**$254**	**$656**
Personal services	123	10	126	155	19	19	370
Other household services	206	85	185	238	214	235	286
Housekeeping supplies	**194**	**79**	**172**	**199**	**232**	**280**	**217**
Laundry and cleaning supplies	52	21	59	51	57	84	48
Other household products	84	28	62	105	108	108	91
Postage and stationery	58	30	51	43	67	88	78
Household furnishings and equipment	**737**	**803**	**732**	**831**	**823**	**888**	**433**
Household textiles	45	14	28	62	64	107	20
Furniture	173	139	172	252	182	185	115
Floor coverings	9	3	8	9	18	7	8
Major appliances	79	29	70	99	105	90	83
Small appliances, misc. housewares	39	21	71	28	32	54	30
Miscellaneous household equipment	392	597	383	382	423	444	177
APPAREL AND RELATED SERVICES	**725**	**634**	**1,206**	**755**	**706**	**629**	**381**
Men and boys	**346**	**393**	**545**	**283**	**318**	**353**	**201**
Men, aged 16 or older	338	389	540	265	308	338	199
Boys, aged 2 to 15	9	4	5	17	10	15	2
Women and girls	**40**	**9**	**70**	**84**	**21**	**27**	**14**
Women, aged 16 or older	23	7	48	50	7	20	1
Girls, aged 2 to 15	16	2	22	34	14	7	13
Children under age 2	**7**	**2**	**20**	**9**	**2**	**5**	**4**
Footwear	**120**	**94**	**192**	**136**	**115**	**85**	**80**
Other apparel products and services	**212**	**135**	**380**	**244**	**250**	**158**	**82**
TRANSPORTATION	**4,863**	**3,890**	**6,061**	**5,943**	**4,654**	**5,193**	**3,519**
Vehicle purchases	**2,287**	**2,130**	**3,028**	**2,754**	**1,789**	**2,544**	**1,581**
Cars and trucks, new	950	570	1,527	1,206	425	1,152	892
Cars and trucks, used	1,264	1,484	1,478	1,480	1,186	1,295	689
Other vehicles	72	76	23	68	178	98	–
Gasoline and motor oil	**810**	**664**	**903**	**924**	**875**	**876**	**637**
Other vehicle expenses	**1,507**	**914**	**1,773**	**1,952**	**1,733**	**1,477**	**1,133**
Vehicle finance charges	182	131	261	244	194	138	107
Maintenance and repairs	518	313	569	800	503	460	406
Vehicle insurance	519	310	573	621	620	538	454
Vehicle rentals, leases, licenses, other charges	288	160	370	287	416	340	167
Public transportation	**260**	**182**	**357**	**314**	**256**	**296**	**168**
HEALTH CARE	**1,118**	**333**	**604**	**970**	**1,257**	**1,236**	**2,316**
Health insurance	563	107	379	529	614	630	1,122
Medical services	302	133	130	306	348	293	590
Drugs	209	68	69	103	242	238	534
Medical supplies	45	25	26	32	53	74	70
ENTERTAINMENT	**1,345**	**1,151**	**1,667**	**1,578**	**1,329**	**1,683**	**787**
Fees and admissions	371	343	501	431	397	348	202
Television, radio, sound equipment	529	516	698	593	549	452	339
Pets, toys, and playground equipment	166	72	176	224	166	270	117
Other entertainment products and services	278	220	292	331	218	612	129
PERSONAL CARE PRODUCTS AND SERVICES	**200**	**143**	**232**	**210**	**180**	**342**	**143**
READING	**102**	**54**	**108**	**105**	**132**	**128**	**92**
EDUCATION	**647**	**2,204**	**665**	**172**	**261**	**97**	**341**

	total single-person consumer units headed by men	under 25	25 to 34	35 to 44	45 to 54	55 to 64	65 or older
TOBACCO PRODUCTS AND SMOKING SUPPLIES	$278	$204	$255	$347	$386	$344	$153
MISCELLANEOUS	662	171	513	717	984	781	826
CASH CONTRIBUTIONS	1,175	191	875	1,448	2,052	964	1,406
PERSONAL INSURANCE AND PENSIONS	2,528	834	3,121	3,535	3,489	3,743	842
Life and other personal insurance	181	30	95	194	257	274	266
Pensions and Social Security	2,347	804	3,026	3,341	3,233	3,470	576
PERSONAL TAXES	2,508	489	3,606	2,661	4,566	2,301	1,288
Federal income taxes	2,006	377	2,855	1,988	3,853	1,840	1,010
State and local income taxes	427	103	694	575	651	365	147
Other taxes	74	8	57	98	62	97	130
GIFTS FOR NON–HOUSEHOLD MEMBERS	745	334	714	797	928	731	932
Food	29	15	24	13	48	40	37
Alcoholic beverages	12	14	4	11	22	10	12
Housing	140	94	99	125	190	126	198
Housekeeping supplies	14	13	15	11	13	13	20
Household textiles	2	3	–	–	7	1	1
Appliances and misc. housewares	8	4	5	8	9	12	12
Major appliances	5	1	3	6	2	9	8
Small appliances and misc. housewares	4	3	3	2	7	2	4
Miscellaneous household equipment	34	23	28	30	52	40	31
Other housing	82	50	51	77	109	61	135
Apparel and services	153	70	337	249	88	101	45
Males, aged 2 or older	33	21	59	41	24	37	14
Females, aged 2 or older	40	9	70	84	21	27	14
Children under age 2	7	2	20	9	2	5	4
Other apparel products and services	74	37	189	114	41	31	13
Jewelry and watches	62	33	160	96	33	26	12
All other apparel products and services	11	4	29	18	7	5	1
Transportation	63	6	16	117	108	148	14
Health care	41	4	7	17	47	10	148
Entertainment	68	44	109	84	73	43	43
Toys, games, hobbies, and tricycles	24	11	24	50	21	18	17
Other entertainment	44	32	85	34	52	24	26
Personal care products and services	24	14	14	10	16	114	11
Reading	1	–	1	1	–	1	1
Education	122	57	15	58	213	56	304
All other gifts	91	16	87	111	123	81	118

Note: Spending by category will not add to total spending because gift spending is also included in the preceding product and service categories and personal taxes are not included in the total. (–) means sample is too small to make a reliable estimate.
Source: Bureau of Labor Statistics, 2001 and 2002 Consumer Expenditure Surveys, Internet site http://www.bls.gov/cex/

Table 1.25 Indexed spending of single-person consumer units headed by men, by age, 2001–02

(indexed average annual spending of single-person consumer units (CU) headed by men by product and service category and age, 2001–02; index definition: an index of 100 is the average for all consumer units; an index of 132 means that spending by consumer units in that group is 32 percent above the average for all consumer units; an index of 68 indicates spending that is 32 percent below the average for all consumer units)

	total single-person consumer units headed by men	under 25	25 to 34	35 to 44	45 to 54	55 to 64	65 or older
Average spending of CU, total	$25,904	$17,516	$29,736	$30,412	$29,201	$27,326	$21,389
Average spending of CU, index	64	43	73	75	72	67	53
FOOD	**60**	**44**	**71**	**67**	**65**	**59**	**51**
Food at home	**48**	**27**	**47**	**50**	**54**	**57**	**52**
Cereals and bakery products	47	28	45	47	51	55	56
Cereals and cereal products	47	34	49	49	42	47	56
Bakery products	48	24	43	47	56	59	56
Meats, poultry, fish, and eggs	46	21	45	51	54	56	49
Beef	45	25	51	49	56	47	41
Pork	43	16	37	49	54	52	50
Other meats	51	20	41	58	64	59	61
Poultry	44	28	49	47	44	56	44
Fish and seafood	49	12	41	56	54	69	60
Eggs	50	26	53	53	50	71	56
Dairy products	48	28	46	50	56	61	52
Fresh milk and cream	52	33	50	51	57	61	58
Other dairy products	46	24	43	49	55	61	48
Fruits and vegetables	45	25	41	45	45	58	59
Fresh fruits	46	22	39	43	42	62	65
Fresh vegetables	41	21	38	38	45	54	51
Processed fruits	53	35	52	56	50	59	64
Processed vegetables	45	24	37	51	42	58	57
Other food at home	51	31	54	52	60	58	49
Sugar and other sweets	46	23	45	37	56	51	62
Fats and oils	44	22	45	46	42	59	46
Miscellaneous foods	49	32	50	50	61	53	47
Nonalcoholic beverages	57	32	67	61	67	69	47
Food prepared by CU on trips	59	61	56	73	59	51	49
Food away from home	**77**	**68**	**104**	**91**	**79**	**62**	**50**
ALCOHOLIC BEVERAGES	**121**	**107**	**154**	**142**	**132**	**133**	**62**
HOUSING	**65**	**37**	**75**	**79**	**74**	**64**	**57**
Shelter	**72**	**41**	**90**	**92**	**84**	**68**	**57**
Owned dwellings	49	5	51	71	68	56	45
Mortgage interest and charges	47	4	59	81	66	53	19
Property taxes	56	12	44	61	76	58	83
Maintenance, repair, insurance, other expenses	48	3	36	51	64	63	75
Rented dwellings	130	117	194	155	121	98	86
Other lodging	63	85	49	45	84	56	55
Utilities, fuels, and public services	**61**	**27**	**64**	**69**	**72**	**67**	**69**
Natural gas	66	17	59	75	87	74	85
Electricity	60	25	61	66	72	71	68
Fuel oil and other fuels	76	15	35	53	88	103	167
Telephone	62	39	79	75	67	61	53
Water and other public services	53	13	47	55	69	57	77

	total single-person consumer units headed by men	under 25	25 to 34	35 to 44	45 to 54	55 to 64	65 or older
Household services	**47**	**13**	**44**	**56**	**33**	**36**	**93**
Personal services	37	3	38	47	6	6	112
Other household services	55	23	49	63	57	63	76
Housekeeping supplies	**36**	**14**	**32**	**37**	**43**	**51**	**40**
Laundry and cleaning supplies	40	16	45	39	44	64	37
Other household products	30	10	22	37	38	38	32
Postage and stationery	44	23	39	33	51	67	60
Household furnishings and equipment	**49**	**53**	**48**	**55**	**54**	**58**	**29**
Household textiles	33	10	21	46	47	79	15
Furniture	43	35	43	63	45	46	29
Floor coverings	23	8	20	23	45	18	20
Major appliances	42	15	37	53	56	48	44
Small appliances, misc. housewares	39	21	71	28	32	54	30
Miscellaneous household equipment	60	92	59	59	65	68	27
APPAREL AND RELATED SERVICES	**41**	**36**	**69**	**43**	**40**	**36**	**22**
Men and boys	**85**	**96**	**133**	**69**	**78**	**86**	**49**
Men, aged 16 or older	106	122	169	83	97	106	62
Boys, aged 2 to 15	10	4	6	19	11	17	2
Women and girls	**6**	**1**	**10**	**12**	**3**	**4**	**2**
Women, aged 16 or older	4	1	8	9	1	3	0
Girls, aged 2 to 15	14	2	19	29	12	6	11
Children under age 2	**8**	**2**	**24**	**11**	**2**	**6**	**5**
Footwear	**38**	**30**	**61**	**43**	**37**	**27**	**26**
Other apparel products and services	**88**	**56**	**158**	**102**	**104**	**66**	**34**
TRANSPORTATION	**63**	**50**	**78**	**77**	**60**	**67**	**45**
Vehicle purchases	**62**	**58**	**83**	**75**	**49**	**69**	**43**
Cars and trucks, new	54	33	87	69	24	66	51
Cars and trucks, used	69	81	80	80	64	70	37
Other vehicles	103	109	33	97	254	140	–
Gasoline and motor oil	**66**	**54**	**73**	**75**	**71**	**71**	**52**
Other vehicle expenses	**61**	**37**	**72**	**79**	**70**	**60**	**46**
Vehicle finance charges	46	33	66	61	49	35	27
Maintenance and repairs	74	45	82	115	72	66	58
Vehicle insurance	58	35	64	69	69	60	51
Vehicle rentals, leases, licenses, other charges	60	33	77	59	86	70	35
Public transportation	**67**	**47**	**92**	**81**	**66**	**76**	**43**
HEALTH CARE	**48**	**14**	**26**	**41**	**53**	**53**	**99**
Health insurance	48	9	32	45	53	54	96
Medical services	51	23	22	52	59	50	100
Drugs	43	14	14	21	50	49	110
Medical supplies	43	24	25	30	50	70	67
ENTERTAINMENT	**65**	**55**	**80**	**76**	**64**	**81**	**38**
Fees and admissions	68	63	92	80	73	64	37
Television, radio, sound equipment	76	75	101	86	79	65	49
Pets, toys, and playground equipment	45	20	48	61	45	73	32
Other entertainment products and services	58	46	61	70	46	129	27
PERSONAL CARE PRODUCTS AND SERVICES	**38**	**27**	**44**	**40**	**34**	**65**	**27**
READING	**73**	**39**	**78**	**76**	**95**	**92**	**66**
EDUCATION	**86**	**293**	**88**	**23**	**35**	**13**	**45**

	total single-person consumer units headed by men	under 25	25 to 34	35 to 44	45 to 54	55 to 64	65 or older
TOBACCO PRODUCTS AND SMOKING SUPPLIES	87	64	80	108	121	108	48
MISCELLANEOUS	84	22	65	91	124	99	104
CASH CONTRIBUTIONS	92	15	69	113	161	75	110
PERSONAL INSURANCE AND PENSIONS	65	21	80	91	89	96	22
Life and other personal insurance	45	7	23	48	63	67	66
Pensions and Social Security	67	23	87	96	93	99	16
PERSONAL TAXES	100	20	144	107	183	92	52
Federal income taxes	109	20	155	108	209	100	55
State and local income taxes	84	20	137	114	129	72	29
Other taxes	50	5	39	67	42	66	88
GIFTS FOR NON–HOUSEHOLD MEMBERS	72	32	69	77	90	71	90
Food	35	18	29	16	59	49	45
Alcoholic beverages	92	108	31	85	169	77	92
Housing	54	36	38	48	73	49	76
Housekeeping supplies	33	31	36	26	31	31	48
Household textiles	14	21	–	–	50	7	7
Appliances and misc. housewares	33	17	21	33	38	50	50
Major appliances	63	13	38	75	25	113	100
Small appliances and misc. housewares	25	19	19	13	44	13	25
Miscellaneous household equipment	52	35	43	46	80	62	48
Other housing	72	44	45	68	96	54	118
Apparel and services	65	30	142	105	37	43	19
Males, aged 2 or older	52	33	92	64	38	58	22
Females, aged 2 or older	49	11	85	102	26	33	17
Children under age 2	18	5	50	23	5	13	10
Other apparel products and services	142	71	363	219	79	60	25
Jewelry and watches	258	138	667	400	138	108	50
All other apparel products and services	39	14	104	64	25	18	4
Transportation	143	14	36	266	245	336	32
Health care	124	12	21	52	142	30	448
Entertainment	87	56	140	108	94	55	55
Toys, games, hobbies, and tricycles	80	37	80	167	70	60	57
Other entertainment	92	67	177	71	108	50	54
Personal care products and services	114	67	67	48	76	543	52
Reading	100	–	100	100	–	100	100
Education	66	31	8	32	116	30	165
All other gifts	108	19	104	132	146	96	140

Note: Spending index for total consumer units is 100. (–) means sample is too small to make a reliable estimate.
Source: Calculations by New Strategist based on the Bureau of Labor Statistics 2001 and 2002 Consumer Expenditure Surveys

Spending by Region, 2002

Households in the Northeast have the highest incomes, but those in the West spend the most. With an average before-tax income of $52,016, Western households spent an average of $44,728 in 2002, 10 percent more than the average household. Households in the Northeast had even higher incomes, but they spent only $42,390 in 2002—just 4 percent more than the average household. Households in the South had the lowest incomes and spent 8 percent less than the average household, just $37,281 in 2002.

Households in the Northeast and West spend more than the average household on most products and services. Those in the Midwest spend close to the average, while households in the South spend less than average on most items. Households in the Northeast spend the most on property taxes. Those in the West spend the most on mortgage interest and rent. Households in the Midwest spend the most on tobacco. Not surprisingly, Midwestern households spend 25 percent less than the average household on fish and seafood. Households in the South spend 25 percent less than average on alcoholic beverages.

The biggest consumers of natural gas are households in the Midwest, spending 39 percent more than the average household on this item. The South spends the most on electricity, while the Northeast spends the most on fuel oil. Western households spend 24 percent more than the average household on water and other public services.

Households in the West spend the most on entertainment. Restaurant spending is highest in the Northeast. Spending on used cars and trucks is 26 percent above average in the Midwest. Households in the South spend the most on drugs and the least on education.

Table 1.26 Average spending by region, 2002

(average annual spending of consumer units (CU) by product and service category and region of residence, 2002)

	total	Northeast	Midwest	South	West
Number of consumer units (in thousands, add 000s)	112,108	21,313	25,883	40,004	24,907
Average number of persons per CU	2.5	2.5	2.5	2.5	2.6
Average income before taxes	$49,430	$53,983	$49,197	$45,641	$52,016
Average annual spending	40,677	42,390	40,601	37,281	44,728
FOOD	**$5,375**	**$5,813**	**$5,180**	**$5,102**	**$5,630**
Food at home	**3,099**	**3,296**	**2,932**	**2,961**	**3,317**
Cereals and bakery products	450	498	435	421	469
Cereals and cereal products	154	168	146	145	166
Bakery products	296	330	289	277	304
Meats, poultry, fish, and eggs	798	878	706	809	807
Beef	231	232	209	242	237
Pork	167	164	157	182	157
Other meats	101	120	100	96	94
Poultry	144	168	125	140	150
Fish and seafood	121	158	91	117	126
Eggs	34	35	26	33	42
Dairy products	328	348	320	300	365
Fresh milk and cream	127	128	129	119	138
Other dairy products	201	221	191	181	227
Fruits and vegetables	552	605	490	511	635
Fresh fruits	178	198	157	161	210
Fresh vegetables	175	196	145	159	213
Processed fruits	116	132	108	103	129
Processed vegetables	83	80	79	88	83
Other food at home	970	967	981	919	1,041
Sugar and other sweets	117	119	119	110	126
Fats and oils	85	93	80	83	88
Miscellaneous foods	472	451	482	457	503
Nonalcoholic beverages	254	261	264	233	270
Food prepared by CU on trips	41	43	36	35	54
Food away from home	**2,276**	**2,517**	**2,247**	**2,141**	**2,314**
ALCOHOLIC BEVERAGES	**376**	**458**	**410**	**282**	**420**
HOUSING	**13,283**	**14,558**	**12,641**	**11,766**	**15,297**
Shelter	**7,829**	**8,962**	**7,097**	**6,478**	**9,792**
Owned dwellings	5,165	5,793	4,944	4,322	6,211
Mortgage interest and charges	2,962	2,844	2,644	2,530	4,088
Property taxes	1,242	1,946	1,316	906	1,103
Maintenance, repair, insurance, other expenses	960	1,003	983	886	1,019
Rented dwellings	2,160	2,567	1,657	1,744	3,003
Other lodging	505	602	496	412	578
Utilities, fuels, and public services	**2,684**	**2,750**	**2,682**	**2,775**	**2,485**
Natural gas	330	450	458	203	298
Electricity	981	861	905	1,203	806
Fuel oil and other fuels	88	238	77	47	38
Telephone	957	952	934	987	936
Water and other public services	328	250	308	335	406

	total	Northeast	Midwest	South	West
Household services	**$706**	**$804**	**$570**	**$690**	**$787**
Personal services	331	432	260	337	310
Other household services	375	372	310	354	478
Housekeeping supplies	**545**	**498**	**709**	**489**	**506**
Laundry and cleaning supplies	131	118	136	137	125
Other household products	283	239	434	239	236
Postage and stationery	131	140	139	113	145
Household furnishings and equipment	**1,518**	**1,544**	**1,583**	**1,333**	**1,727**
Household textiles	136	122	129	115	186
Furniture	401	461	362	358	460
Floor coverings	40	48	45	37	34
Major appliances	188	189	196	163	222
Small appliances, misc. housewares	100	91	101	89	127
Miscellaneous household equipment	652	633	749	571	698
APPAREL AND RELATED SERVICES	**1,749**	**1,965**	**1,728**	**1,592**	**1,836**
Men and boys	**409**	**433**	**427**	**363**	**445**
Men, aged 16 or older	319	336	331	278	360
Boys, aged 2 to 15	90	97	96	85	85
Women and girls	**704**	**785**	**732**	**637**	**712**
Women, aged 16 or older	587	642	627	521	603
Girls, aged 2 to 15	117	142	105	116	110
Children under age 2	**83**	**79**	**88**	**80**	**84**
Footwear	**313**	**378**	**274**	**303**	**313**
Other apparel products and services	**240**	**289**	**207**	**209**	**282**
TRANSPORTATION	**7,759**	**7,185**	**8,133**	**7,393**	**8,449**
Vehicle purchases	**3,665**	**3,036**	**4,034**	**3,591**	**3,937**
Cars and trucks, new	1,753	1,603	1,612	1,796	1,959
Cars and trucks, used	1,842	1,372	2,314	1,742	1,917
Other vehicles	70	62	109	53	62
Gasoline and motor oil	**1,235**	**1,081**	**1,269**	**1,238**	**1,325**
Other vehicle expenses	**2,471**	**2,456**	**2,487**	**2,299**	**2,742**
Vehicle finance charges	397	298	396	452	393
Maintenance and repairs	697	593	687	644	883
Vehicle insurance	894	921	876	861	940
Vehicle rentals, leases, licenses, other charges	483	643	528	341	525
Public transportation	**389**	**612**	**342**	**265**	**445**
HEALTH CARE	**2,350**	**2,207**	**2,383**	**2,431**	**2,310**
Health insurance	1,168	1,178	1,185	1,196	1,096
Medical services	590	505	566	597	676
Drugs	487	418	519	546	421
Medical supplies	105	107	112	92	117
ENTERTAINMENT	**2,079**	**2,287**	**2,143**	**1,705**	**2,436**
Fees and admissions	542	657	538	419	644
Television, radio, sound equipment	692	725	688	643	747
Pets, toys, and playground equipment	369	363	403	341	384
Other entertainment products and services	476	542	514	302	660
PERSONAL CARE PRODUCTS AND SERVICES	**526**	**518**	**517**	**509**	**569**
READING	**139**	**165**	**149**	**103**	**162**
EDUCATION	**752**	**1,062**	**718**	**487**	**947**

	total	Northeast	Midwest	South	West
TOBACCO PRODUCTS AND SMOKING SUPPLIES	$320	$315	$396	$321	$247
MISCELLANEOUS	792	733	776	764	905
CASH CONTRIBUTIONS	1,277	1,199	1,363	1,193	1,389
PERSONAL INSURANCE AND PENSIONS	3,899	3,924	4,065	3,632	4,132
Life and other personal insurance	406	460	448	389	345
Pensions and Social Security	3,493	3,464	3,617	3,243	3,787
PERSONAL TAXES	2,496	2,405	2,827	2,024	3,008
Federal income taxes	1,843	1,710	1,945	1,605	2,238
State and local income taxes	506	520	684	313	629
Other taxes	147	175	197	106	140
GIFTS FOR NON–HOUSEHOLD MEMBERS	1,036	1,245	1,176	822	1,056
Food	82	126	101	57	65
Alcoholic beverages	13	12	17	10	17
Housing	259	259	299	244	240
Housekeeping supplies	42	48	44	36	46
Household textiles	14	17	16	11	13
Appliances and misc. housewares	24	28	26	22	22
Major appliances	8	9	13	5	9
Small appliances and misc. housewares	16	19	14	17	13
Miscellaneous household equipment	65	62	83	59	58
Other housing	114	104	130	116	102
Apparel and services	237	283	247	188	265
Males, aged 2 or older	64	68	72	52	70
Females, aged 2 or older	82	108	88	53	98
Children under age 2	40	44	45	34	41
Other apparel products and services	52	64	43	49	55
Jewelry and watches	24	31	20	19	30
All other apparel products and services	28	33	23	29	25
Transportation	44	49	41	34	58
Health care	33	31	39	25	41
Entertainment	78	80	96	69	73
Toys, games, hobbies, and tricycles	30	33	36	28	25
Other entertainment	48	47	60	41	49
Personal care products and services	21	25	22	19	19
Reading	1	1	2	1	2
Education	184	266	217	113	193
All other gifts	84	112	94	62	84

Note: Spending by category will not add to total spending because gift spending is also included in the preceding product and service categories and personal taxes are not included in the total.
Source: Bureau of Labor Statistics, 2002 Consumer Expenditure Survey, Internet site http://www.bls.gov/cex/

Table 1.27 Indexed spending by region, 2002

(indexed average annual spending of consumer units (CU) by product and service category and region of residence, 2002; index definition: an index of 100 is the average for all consumer units; an index of 132 means that spending by consumer units in that group is 32 percent above the average for all consumer units; an index of 68 indicates spending that is 32 percent below the average for all consumer units)

	total	Northeast	Midwest	South	West
Average spending of CU, total	$40,677	$42,390	$40,601	$37,281	$44,728
Average spending of CU, index	100	104	100	92	110
FOOD	**100**	**108**	**96**	**95**	**105**
Food at home	**100**	**106**	**95**	**96**	**107**
Cereals and bakery products	100	111	97	94	104
Cereals and cereal products	100	109	95	94	108
Bakery products	100	111	98	94	103
Meats, poultry, fish, and eggs	100	110	88	101	101
Beef	100	100	90	105	103
Pork	100	98	94	109	94
Other meats	100	119	99	95	93
Poultry	100	117	87	97	104
Fish and seafood	100	131	75	97	104
Eggs	100	103	76	97	124
Dairy products	100	106	98	91	111
Fresh milk and cream	100	101	102	94	109
Other dairy products	100	110	95	90	113
Fruits and vegetables	100	110	89	93	115
Fresh fruits	100	111	88	90	118
Fresh vegetables	100	112	83	91	122
Processed fruits	100	114	93	89	111
Processed vegetables	100	96	95	106	100
Other food at home	100	100	101	95	107
Sugar and other sweets	100	102	102	94	108
Fats and oils	100	109	94	98	104
Miscellaneous foods	100	96	102	97	107
Nonalcoholic beverages	100	103	104	92	106
Food prepared by CU on trips	100	105	88	85	132
Food away from home	**100**	**111**	**99**	**94**	**102**
ALCOHOLIC BEVERAGES	**100**	**122**	**109**	**75**	**112**
HOUSING	**100**	**110**	**95**	**89**	**115**
Shelter	**100**	**114**	**91**	**83**	**125**
Owned dwellings	100	112	96	84	120
Mortgage interest and charges	100	96	89	85	138
Property taxes	100	157	106	73	89
Maintenance, repair, insurance, other expenses	100	104	102	92	106
Rented dwellings	100	119	77	81	139
Other lodging	100	119	98	82	114
Utilities, fuels, and public services	**100**	**102**	**100**	**103**	**93**
Natural gas	100	136	139	62	90
Electricity	100	88	92	123	82
Fuel oil and other fuels	100	270	88	53	43
Telephone	100	99	98	103	98
Water and other public services	100	76	94	102	124

	total	Northeast	Midwest	South	West
Household services	**100**	**114**	**81**	**98**	**111**
Personal services	100	131	79	102	94
Other household services	100	99	83	94	127
Housekeeping supplies	**100**	**91**	**130**	**90**	**93**
Laundry and cleaning supplies	100	90	104	105	95
Other household products	100	84	153	84	83
Postage and stationery	100	107	106	86	111
Household furnishings and equipment	**100**	**102**	**104**	**88**	**114**
Household textiles	100	90	95	85	137
Furniture	100	115	90	89	115
Floor coverings	100	120	113	93	85
Major appliances	100	101	104	87	118
Small appliances, misc. housewares	100	91	101	89	127
Miscellaneous household equipment	100	97	115	88	107
APPAREL AND RELATED SERVICES	**100**	**112**	**99**	**91**	**105**
Men and boys	**100**	**106**	**104**	**89**	**109**
Men, aged 16 or older	100	105	104	87	113
Boys, aged 2 to 15	100	108	107	94	94
Women and girls	**100**	**112**	**104**	**90**	**101**
Women, aged 16 or older	100	109	107	89	103
Girls, aged 2 to 15	100	121	90	99	94
Children under age 2	**100**	**95**	**106**	**96**	**101**
Footwear	**100**	**121**	**88**	**97**	**100**
Other apparel products and services	**100**	**120**	**86**	**87**	**118**
TRANSPORTATION	**100**	**93**	**105**	**95**	**109**
Vehicle purchases	**100**	**83**	**110**	**98**	**107**
Cars and trucks, new	100	91	92	102	112
Cars and trucks, used	100	74	126	95	104
Other vehicles	100	89	156	76	89
Gasoline and motor oil	**100**	**88**	**103**	**100**	**107**
Other vehicle expenses	**100**	**99**	**101**	**93**	**111**
Vehicle finance charges	100	75	100	114	99
Maintenance and repairs	100	85	99	92	127
Vehicle insurance	100	103	98	96	105
Vehicle rentals, leases, licenses, other charges	100	133	109	71	109
Public transportation	**100**	**157**	**88**	**68**	**114**
HEALTH CARE	**100**	**94**	**101**	**103**	**98**
Health insurance	100	101	101	102	94
Medical services	100	86	96	101	115
Drugs	100	86	107	112	86
Medical supplies	100	102	107	88	111
ENTERTAINMENT	**100**	**110**	**103**	**82**	**117**
Fees and admissions	100	121	99	77	119
Television, radio, sound equipment	100	105	99	93	108
Pets, toys, and playground equipment	100	98	109	92	104
Other entertainment products and services	100	114	108	63	139
PERSONAL CARE PRODUCTS AND SERVICES	**100**	**98**	**98**	**97**	**108**
READING	**100**	**119**	**107**	**74**	**117**
EDUCATION	**100**	**141**	**95**	**65**	**126**

	total	Northeast	Midwest	South	West
TOBACCO PRODUCTS AND SMOKING SUPPLIES	100	98	124	100	77
MISCELLANEOUS	100	93	98	96	114
CASH CONTRIBUTIONS	100	94	107	93	109
PERSONAL INSURANCE AND PENSIONS	100	101	104	93	106
Life and other personal insurance	100	113	110	96	85
Pensions and Social Security	100	99	104	93	108
PERSONAL TAXES	100	96	113	81	121
Federal income taxes	100	93	106	87	121
State and local income taxes	100	103	135	62	124
Other taxes	100	119	134	72	95
GIFTS FOR NON–HOUSEHOLD MEMBERS	100	120	114	79	102
Food	100	154	123	70	79
Alcoholic beverages	100	92	131	77	131
Housing	100	100	115	94	93
Housekeeping supplies	100	114	105	86	110
Household textiles	100	121	114	79	93
Appliances and misc. housewares	100	117	108	92	92
Major appliances	100	113	163	63	113
Small appliances and misc. housewares	100	119	88	106	81
Miscellaneous household equipment	100	95	128	91	89
Other housing	100	91	114	102	89
Apparel and services	100	119	104	79	112
Males, aged 2 or older	100	106	113	81	109
Females, aged 2 or older	100	132	107	65	120
Children under age 2	100	110	113	85	103
Other apparel products and services	100	123	83	94	106
Jewelry and watches	100	129	83	79	125
All other apparel products and services	100	118	82	104	89
Transportation	100	111	93	77	132
Health care	100	94	118	76	124
Entertainment	100	103	123	88	94
Toys, games, hobbies, and tricycles	100	110	120	93	83
Other entertainment	100	98	125	85	102
Personal care products and services	100	119	105	90	90
Reading	100	100	200	100	200
Education	100	145	118	61	105
All other gifts	100	133	112	74	100

Source: Calculations by New Strategist based on the Bureau of Labor Statistics 2002 Consumer Expenditure Survey

Spending by Region and Income, 2001–02

Households with incomes of $70,000 or more are most commonly found in the Northeast and West, accounting for 25 and 24 percent of households, respectively. In the Midwest, 22 percent of households have incomes of $70,000 or more, while in the South the proportion is a smaller 19 percent.

In every region, spending rises with income. The most affluent households in the Northeast spend 78 percent more than the average Northeastern household, $77,308 versus $43,395 for complete income reporters in 2001–02. The spending gap is greatest for items such as mortgage interest, other lodging (a category that includes vacation homes and hotels and motels on out-of-town trips), household services, furniture, fees and admissions to entertainment events, and education.

In the Midwest, the most affluent households spent $75,224 in 2001–02, or 78 percent more than the $42,170 spent by the average Midwestern household. Households with incomes of $70,000 or more in the Midwest spend more than twice as much as the average household on such things as public transportation and fees and admissions to entertainment events.

The most affluent households in the South spend 88 percent more than the average Southern household, $72,755 versus $38,767 in 2001–02. The richest households in the South spend nearly three times as much as the average household on other lodging. They spend 9 percent less than the average household in the South on tobacco.

The most affluent households in the West spend 78 percent more than the average Western household, $81,448 versus $45,837 in 2001–02. The gap is greatest for items such as mortgage interest, other lodging, furniture, fees and admissions to entertainment events, and gifts.

Table 1.28 Average spending in the Northeast by income, 2001–02

(average annual spending of consumer units (CU) in the Northeast by product and service category and before-tax income of consumer unit, 2001–02; complete income reporters only)

	complete income reporters in Northeast	under $10,000	$10,000–$19,999	$20,000–$29,999	$30,000–$39,999	$40,000–$49,999	$50,000–$69,999	$70,000 or more
Number of consumer units (in thousands, add 000s)	17,081	2,062	2,725	2,153	1,819	1,484	2,563	4,274
Average number of persons per CU	2.4	1.6	1.9	2.2	2.3	2.5	2.8	3.2
Average income before taxes	$52,296	$5,457	$14,627	$24,467	$34,355	$44,506	$59,136	$119,170
Average annual spending	43,395	18,510	22,834	28,203	34,361	41,181	49,341	77,308
FOOD	**$6,021**	**$3,649**	**$3,516**	**$4,567**	**$5,385**	**$6,012**	**$6,747**	**$9,369**
Food at home	**3,494**	**2,381**	**2,407**	**3,142**	**3,185**	**3,597**	**3,663**	**4,898**
Cereals and bakery products	531	380	404	494	471	487	549	735
Cereals and cereal products	180	155	130	166	165	156	181	247
Bakery products	351	225	274	328	305	331	368	488
Meats, poultry, fish, and eggs	935	690	634	827	864	1,051	963	1,271
Beef	246	203	155	195	255	249	263	340
Pork	185	142	129	200	163	200	200	229
Other meats	126	94	92	111	115	136	136	168
Poultry	184	121	120	157	153	203	203	265
Fish and seafood	156	101	111	128	143	220	127	223
Eggs	37	31	29	36	36	43	36	47
Dairy products	380	244	260	362	352	389	389	533
Fresh milk and cream	141	102	112	142	136	144	144	176
Other dairy products	239	141	149	220	215	245	245	356
Fruits and vegetables	631	410	464	559	619	597	648	888
Fresh fruits	200	141	142	176	198	180	197	288
Fresh vegetables	198	111	145	169	193	202	213	278
Processed fruits	142	99	105	125	152	128	144	194
Processed vegetables	92	59	72	90	78	88	93	129
Other food at home	1,017	657	645	900	879	1,072	1,114	1,471
Sugar and other sweets	128	92	98	121	107	137	131	172
Fats and oils	97	83	64	89	92	97	111	125
Miscellaneous foods	475	269	291	428	390	512	508	716
Nonalcoholic beverages	275	197	174	230	246	289	322	382
Food prepared by CU on trips	42	15	18	32	44	37	42	75
Food away from home	**2,528**	**1,269**	**1,109**	**1,426**	**2,200**	**2,415**	**3,084**	**4,471**
ALCOHOLIC BEVERAGES	**477**	**343**	**219**	**194**	**468**	**530**	**531**	**814**
HOUSING	**14,569**	**6,516**	**8,701**	**10,144**	**11,812**	**13,471**	**15,929**	**25,193**
Shelter	**8,883**	**3,974**	**5,257**	**6,218**	**6,978**	**8,348**	**9,637**	**15,452**
Owned dwellings	5,664	1,177	2,291	2,709	3,664	4,832	6,325	12,212
Mortgage interest and charges	2,756	357	532	928	1,604	2,306	3,446	6,484
Property taxes	1,915	566	1,141	1,098	1,357	1,521	1,980	3,806
Maintenance, repair, insurance, other expenses	994	254	618	683	704	1,006	899	1,922
Rented dwellings	2,615	2,514	2,801	3,252	3,011	3,078	2,636	1,881
Other lodging	605	284	164	258	303	439	676	1,359
Utilities, fuels, and public services	**2,776**	**1,386**	**2,074**	**2,418**	**2,703**	**2,726**	**3,162**	**3,892**
Natural gas	468	234	372	478	523	476	526	577
Electricity	856	425	638	741	843	840	971	1,201
Fuel oil and other fuels	277	162	219	277	244	245	279	395
Telephone	932	494	663	729	895	928	1,086	1,343
Water and other public services	243	72	182	193	199	237	300	376

	complete income reporters in Northeast	under $10,000	$10,000–$19,999	$20,000–$29,999	$30,000–$39,999	$40,000–$49,999	$50,000–$69,999	$70,000 or more
Household services	**$762**	**$133**	**$364**	**$366**	**$487**	**$459**	**$612**	**$1,832**
Personal services	370	28	121	141	207	166	277	1,004
Other household services	392	104	242	225	281	293	334	827
Housekeeping supplies	**589**	**356**	**359**	**425**	**482**	**535**	**822**	**865**
Laundry and cleaning supplies	137	112	99	101	129	145	153	185
Other household products	299	165	142	199	245	250	472	458
Postage and stationery	153	78	119	125	108	139	197	222
Household furnishings and equipment	**1,558**	**667**	**646**	**718**	**1,162**	**1,403**	**1,696**	**3,153**
Household textiles	148	48	45	66	97	154	155	323
Furniture	396	97	156	187	226	338	371	905
Floor coverings	50	20	32	14	26	35	27	122
Major appliances	179	44	86	96	137	147	185	374
Small appliances, misc. housewares	96	46	40	60	108	106	105	161
Miscellaneous household equipment	689	412	287	295	568	622	853	1,268
APPAREL AND RELATED SERVICES	**2,173**	**1,258**	**1,233**	**1,155**	**1,851**	**2,147**	**2,195**	**3,894**
Men and boys	**526**	**318**	**284**	**297**	**510**	**510**	**609**	**864**
Men, aged 16 or older	427	278	224	231	433	410	505	687
Boys, aged 2 to 15	99	40	60	66	77	100	104	176
Women and girls	**865**	**473**	**547**	**430**	**664**	**887**	**850**	**1,576**
Women, aged 16 or older	718	418	451	332	570	805	702	1,278
Girls, aged 2 to 15	147	55	95	98	94	83	148	298
Children under age 2	**87**	**29**	**55**	**39**	**82**	**60**	**99**	**164**
Footwear	**401**	**326**	**191**	**222**	**381**	**413**	**393**	**682**
Other apparel products and services	**295**	**112**	**156**	**167**	**215**	**276**	**244**	**609**
TRANSPORTATION	**7,350**	**2,412**	**3,343**	**4,384**	**5,711**	**8,417**	**9,451**	**12,830**
Vehicle purchases	**3,174**	**1,059**	**1,386**	**1,723**	**2,297**	**3,747**	**4,484**	**5,452**
Cars and trucks, new	1,662	558	483	989	1,089	2,439	2,343	2,852
Cars and trucks, used	1,472	500	904	734	1,207	1,208	2,051	2,533
Other vehicles	39	1	–	–	–	99	90	67
Gasoline and motor oil	**1,082**	**395**	**527**	**787**	**990**	**1,098**	**1,391**	**1,765**
Other vehicle expenses	**2,481**	**700**	**1,116**	**1,510**	**1,947**	**3,024**	**2,949**	**4,441**
Vehicle finance charges	285	51	80	180	232	328	428	503
Maintenance and repairs	665	238	346	441	601	1,107	664	1,042
Vehicle insurance	890	288	487	619	727	1,004	1,091	1,485
Vehicle rentals, leases, licenses, other charges	641	123	202	270	386	585	766	1,411
Public transportation	**613**	**257**	**315**	**363**	**478**	**549**	**627**	**1,171**
HEALTH CARE	**2,180**	**1,003**	**2,041**	**2,173**	**2,082**	**1,897**	**2,173**	**2,984**
Health insurance	1,110	605	1,138	1,085	1,118	918	1,079	1,429
Medical services	539	131	330	441	481	457	608	930
Drugs	421	200	479	564	368	433	379	458
Medical supplies	111	66	94	83	115	89	107	167
ENTERTAINMENT	**2,133**	**719**	**904**	**1,223**	**1,477**	**1,854**	**2,562**	**4,172**
Fees and admissions	618	198	187	242	371	473	630	1,434
Television, radio, sound equipment	709	338	472	552	630	764	820	1,064
Pets, toys, and playground equipment	376	119	168	267	277	365	423	700
Other entertainment products and services	431	63	77	162	199	251	690	974
PERSONAL CARE PRODUCTS AND SERVICES	**525**	**370**	**302**	**412**	**432**	**544**	**590**	**799**
READING	**172**	**71**	**114**	**131**	**128**	**164**	**202**	**283**
EDUCATION	**894**	**1,105**	**252**	**536**	**371**	**353**	**653**	**1,938**

	complete income reporters in Northeast	under $10,000	$10,000–$19,999	$20,000–$29,999	$30,000–$39,999	$40,000–$49,999	$50,000–$69,999	$70,000 or more
TOBACCO PRODUCTS AND SMOKING SUPPLIES	$315	$227	$265	$277	$353	$331	$451	$304
MISCELLANEOUS	818	194	380	596	711	678	1,062	1,460
CASH CONTRIBUTIONS	1,185	284	587	806	810	978	1,202	2,414
PERSONAL INSURANCE AND PENSIONS	4,583	361	976	1,606	2,770	3,805	5,594	10,853
Life and other personal insurance	443	193	321	189	281	365	464	852
Pensions and Social Security	4,140	168	655	1,417	2,489	3,440	5,130	10,002
PERSONAL TAXES	2,466	67	102	574	1,205	1,755	2,989	6,552
Federal income taxes	1,769	6	4	315	721	1,109	2,063	4,976
State and local income taxes	534	9	21	145	331	492	725	1,297
Other taxes	163	53	77	114	152	155	202	280
GIFTS FOR NON–HOUSEHOLD MEMBERS	1,279	582	571	810	889	947	1,354	2,554
Food	114	28	48	53	104	43	89	275
Alcoholic beverages	16	40	5	12	5	4	18	25
Housing	291	127	109	220	300	242	336	509
Housekeeping supplies	56	23	27	57	53	54	69	83
Household textiles	23	7	5	32	16	28	10	46
Appliances and misc. housewares	31	9	5	10	30	57	21	64
Major appliances	8	–	1	5	8	24	2	13
Small appliances and misc. housewares	23	9	4	5	22	33	20	51
Miscellaneous household equipment	73	31	24	28	91	69	118	116
Other housing	109	56	48	93	110	34	118	201
Apparel and services	323	268	170	166	289	332	265	585
Males, aged 2 or older	93	98	65	62	75	125	68	139
Females, aged 2 or older	126	114	61	59	102	108	101	245
Children under age 2	47	18	26	19	40	44	61	86
Other apparel products and services	57	38	19	26	72	55	35	115
Jewelry and watches	24	10	5	7	22	34	10	58
All other apparel products and services	33	27	13	20	51	21	25	58
Transportation	59	7	67	4	5	21	244	32
Health care	40	6	6	13	10	55	23	109
Entertainment	77	29	44	56	49	74	87	141
Toys, games, hobbies, and tricycles	36	15	16	20	29	37	49	61
Other entertainment	42	13	27	36	20	37	38	80
Personal care products and services	21	26	12	42	10	11	17	24
Reading	1	1	1	1	2	2	2	2
Education	226	35	90	190	68	63	100	622
All other gifts	110	17	21	52	47	102	174	230

Note: Spending by category will not add to total spending because gift spending is also included in the preceding product and service categories and personal taxes are not included in the total. (–) means sample is too small to make a reliable estimate.
Source: Bureau of Labor Statistics, 2001 and 2002 Consumer Expenditure Surveys, Internet site http://www.bls.gov/cex/; calculations by New Strategist

Table 1.29 Indexed spending in the Northeast by income, 2001–02

(indexed average annual spending of consumer units (CU) in the Northeast by product and service category and before-tax income of consumer unit, 2001–02; complete income reporters only; index definition: an index of 100 is the average for all consumer units; an index of 132 means that spending by consumer units in that group is 32 percent above the average for all consumer units; an index of 68 indicates spending that is 32 percent below the average for all consumer units)

	complete income reporters in Northeast	under $10,000	$10,000– $19,999	$20,000– $29,999	$30,000– $39,999	$40,000– $49,999	$50,000– $69,999	$70,000 or more
Average spending of CU, total	$43,395	$18,510	$22,834	$28,203	$34,361	$41,181	$49,341	$77,308
Average spending of CU, index	100	43	53	65	79	95	114	178
FOOD	100	61	58	76	89	100	112	156
Food at home	100	68	69	90	91	103	105	140
Cereals and bakery products	100	72	76	93	89	92	103	138
Cereals and cereal products	100	86	72	92	92	87	101	137
Bakery products	100	64	78	93	87	94	105	139
Meats, poultry, fish, and eggs	100	74	68	88	92	112	103	136
Beef	100	82	63	79	104	101	107	138
Pork	100	77	70	108	88	108	108	124
Other meats	100	74	73	88	91	108	108	133
Poultry	100	66	65	85	83	110	110	144
Fish and seafood	100	65	71	82	92	141	81	143
Eggs	100	82	78	97	97	116	97	127
Dairy products	100	64	68	95	93	102	102	140
Fresh milk and cream	100	73	79	101	96	102	102	125
Other dairy products	100	59	62	92	90	103	103	149
Fruits and vegetables	100	65	74	89	98	95	103	141
Fresh fruits	100	71	71	88	99	90	99	144
Fresh vegetables	100	56	73	85	97	102	108	140
Processed fruits	100	70	74	88	107	90	101	137
Processed vegetables	100	64	78	98	85	96	101	140
Other food at home	100	65	63	88	86	105	110	145
Sugar and other sweets	100	72	76	95	84	107	102	134
Fats and oils	100	85	65	92	95	100	114	129
Miscellaneous foods	100	57	61	90	82	108	107	151
Nonalcoholic beverages	100	72	63	84	89	105	117	139
Food prepared by CU on trips	100	35	42	76	105	88	100	179
Food away from home	100	50	44	56	87	96	122	177
ALCOHOLIC BEVERAGES	100	72	46	41	98	111	111	171
HOUSING	100	45	60	70	81	92	109	173
Shelter	100	45	59	70	79	94	108	174
Owned dwellings	100	21	40	48	65	85	112	216
Mortgage interest and charges	100	13	19	34	58	84	125	235
Property taxes	100	30	60	57	71	79	103	199
Maintenance, repair, insurance, other expenses	100	26	62	69	71	101	90	193
Rented dwellings	100	96	107	124	115	118	101	72
Other lodging	100	47	27	43	50	73	112	225
Utilities, fuels, and public services	100	50	75	87	97	98	114	140
Natural gas	100	50	80	102	112	102	112	123
Electricity	100	50	75	87	98	98	113	140
Fuel oil and other fuels	100	58	79	100	88	88	101	143
Telephone	100	53	71	78	96	100	117	144
Water and other public services	100	29	75	79	82	98	123	155

	complete income reporters in Northeast	under $10,000	$10,000– $19,999	$20,000– $29,999	$30,000– $39,999	$40,000– $49,999	$50,000– $69,999	$70,000 or more
Household services	**100**	**17**	**48**	**48**	**64**	**60**	**80**	**240**
Personal services	100	8	33	38	56	45	75	271
Other household services	100	27	62	57	72	75	85	211
Housekeeping supplies	**100**	**60**	**61**	**72**	**82**	**91**	**140**	**147**
Laundry and cleaning supplies	100	82	72	74	94	106	112	135
Other household products	100	55	47	67	82	84	158	153
Postage and stationery	100	51	78	82	71	91	129	145
Household furnishings and equipment	**100**	**43**	**41**	**46**	**75**	**90**	**109**	**202**
Household textiles	100	33	30	45	66	104	105	218
Furniture	100	24	39	47	57	85	94	229
Floor coverings	100	40	64	28	52	70	54	244
Major appliances	100	25	48	54	77	82	103	209
Small appliances, misc. housewares	100	48	42	63	113	110	109	168
Miscellaneous household equipment	100	60	42	43	82	90	124	184
APPAREL AND RELATED SERVICES	**100**	**58**	**57**	**53**	**85**	**99**	**101**	**179**
Men and boys	**100**	**60**	**54**	**56**	**97**	**97**	**116**	**164**
Men, aged 16 or older	100	65	52	54	101	96	118	161
Boys, aged 2 to 15	100	40	61	67	78	101	105	178
Women and girls	**100**	**55**	**63**	**50**	**77**	**103**	**98**	**182**
Women, aged 16 or older	100	58	63	46	79	112	98	178
Girls, aged 2 to 15	100	37	65	67	64	56	101	203
Children under age 2	**100**	**33**	**64**	**45**	**94**	**69**	**114**	**189**
Footwear	**100**	**81**	**48**	**55**	**95**	**103**	**98**	**170**
Other apparel products and services	**100**	**38**	**53**	**57**	**73**	**94**	**83**	**206**
TRANSPORTATION	**100**	**33**	**45**	**60**	**78**	**115**	**129**	**175**
Vehicle purchases	**100**	**33**	**44**	**54**	**72**	**118**	**141**	**172**
Cars and trucks, new	100	34	29	60	66	147	141	172
Cars and trucks, used	100	34	61	50	82	82	139	172
Other vehicles	100	1	–	–	–	254	231	172
Gasoline and motor oil	**100**	**37**	**49**	**73**	**91**	**101**	**129**	**163**
Other vehicle expenses	**100**	**28**	**45**	**61**	**78**	**122**	**119**	**179**
Vehicle finance charges	100	18	28	63	81	115	150	176
Maintenance and repairs	100	36	52	66	90	166	100	157
Vehicle insurance	100	32	55	70	82	113	123	167
Vehicle rentals, leases, licenses, other charges	100	19	32	42	60	91	120	220
Public transportation	**100**	**42**	**51**	**59**	**78**	**90**	**102**	**191**
HEALTH CARE	**100**	**46**	**94**	**100**	**96**	**87**	**100**	**137**
Health insurance	100	54	103	98	101	83	97	129
Medical services	100	24	61	82	89	85	113	173
Drugs	100	48	114	134	87	103	90	109
Medical supplies	100	60	85	75	104	80	96	150
ENTERTAINMENT	**100**	**34**	**42**	**57**	**69**	**87**	**120**	**196**
Fees and admissions	100	32	30	39	60	77	102	232
Television, radio, sound equipment	100	48	67	78	89	108	116	150
Pets, toys, and playground equipment	100	32	45	71	74	97	113	186
Other entertainment products and services	100	15	18	38	46	58	160	226
PERSONAL CARE PRODUCTS AND SERVICES	**100**	**70**	**58**	**78**	**82**	**104**	**112**	**152**
READING	**100**	**41**	**66**	**76**	**74**	**95**	**117**	**165**
EDUCATION	**100**	**124**	**28**	**60**	**41**	**39**	**73**	**217**

	complete income reporters in Northeast	under $10,000	$10,000– $19,999	$20,000– $29,999	$30,000– $39,999	$40,000– $49,999	$50,000– $69,999	$70,000 or more
TOBACCO PRODUCTS AND SMOKING SUPPLIES	100	72	84	88	112	105	143	97
MISCELLANEOUS	100	24	46	73	87	83	130	178
CASH CONTRIBUTIONS	100	24	50	68	68	83	101	204
PERSONAL INSURANCE AND PENSIONS	100	8	21	35	60	83	122	237
Life and other personal insurance	100	44	73	43	63	82	105	192
Pensions and Social Security	100	4	16	34	60	83	124	242
PERSONAL TAXES	100	3	4	23	49	71	121	266
Federal income taxes	100	0	0	18	41	63	117	281
State and local income taxes	100	2	4	27	62	92	136	243
Other taxes	100	33	47	70	93	95	124	172
GIFTS FOR NON–HOUSEHOLD MEMBERS	100	46	45	63	70	74	106	200
Food	100	25	42	46	91	38	78	241
Alcoholic beverages	100	251	32	75	31	25	113	156
Housing	100	44	37	76	103	83	115	175
Housekeeping supplies	100	41	49	102	95	96	123	148
Household textiles	100	29	23	139	70	122	43	200
Appliances and misc. housewares	100	30	16	32	97	184	68	206
Major appliances	100	–	7	63	100	300	25	163
Small appliances and misc. housewares	100	41	17	22	96	143	87	222
Miscellaneous household equipment	100	43	32	38	125	95	162	159
Other housing	100	51	44	85	101	31	108	184
Apparel and services	100	83	53	51	89	103	82	181
Males, aged 2 or older	100	105	70	67	81	134	73	149
Females, aged 2 or older	100	90	48	47	81	86	80	194
Children under age 2	100	38	55	40	85	94	130	183
Other apparel products and services	100	67	33	46	126	96	61	202
Jewelry and watches	100	44	22	29	92	142	42	242
All other apparel products and services	100	80	41	61	155	64	76	176
Transportation	100	12	113	7	8	36	414	54
Health care	100	15	16	33	25	138	58	273
Entertainment	100	37	57	73	64	96	113	183
Toys, games, hobbies, and tricycles	100	43	45	56	81	103	136	169
Other entertainment	100	31	65	86	48	88	90	190
Personal care products and services	100	122	58	200	48	52	81	114
Reading	100	100	53	100	200	200	200	200
Education	100	15	40	84	30	28	44	275
All other gifts	100	16	19	47	43	93	158	209

Note: (–) means sample is too small to make a reliable estimate.
Source: Calculations by New Strategist based on the Bureau of Labor Statistics 2001 and 2002 Consumer Expenditure Surveys

Table 1.30 Average spending in the Midwest by income, 2001–02

(average annual spending of consumer units (CU) in the Midwest by product and service category and before-tax income of consumer unit, 2001–02; complete income reporters only)

	complete income reporters in Midwest	under $10,000	$10,000–$19,999	$20,000–$29,999	$30,000–$39,999	$40,000–$49,999	$50,000–$69,999	$70,000 or more
Number of consumer units (in thousands, add 000s)	20,713	2,247	3,443	2,680	2,487	2,214	3,121	4,521
Average number of persons per CU	2.4	1.6	1.8	2.1	2.4	2.5	2.8	3.2
Average income before taxes	$48,439	$5,344	$14,585	$24,612	$34,484	$44,217	$59,400	$111,939
Average annual spending	42,170	17,222	22,839	28,962	35,312	41,461	50,687	75,224
FOOD	**$5,438**	**$2,999**	**$3,354**	**$4,223**	**$4,848**	**$5,366**	**$6,377**	**$8,574**
Food at home	**3,069**	**1,753**	**2,203**	**2,657**	**3,005**	**3,108**	**3,377**	**4,365**
Cereals and bakery products	464	275	339	381	444	467	510	672
Cereals and cereal products	157	98	116	121	151	160	172	227
Bakery products	307	177	222	261	293	307	338	445
Meats, poultry, fish, and eggs	736	440	553	730	758	679	779	988
Beef	232	117	159	276	253	214	239	302
Pork	162	106	132	155	162	141	172	218
Other meats	100	70	68	97	96	95	115	134
Poultry	131	82	106	106	142	118	148	172
Fish and seafood	82	49	64	68	74	77	76	132
Eggs	28	19	24	28	32	33	27	30
Dairy products	348	183	251	286	334	369	392	499
Fresh milk and cream	143	80	114	119	145	158	157	190
Other dairy products	205	103	137	167	189	211	236	309
Fruits and vegetables	493	299	380	438	483	473	522	694
Fresh fruits	157	98	121	137	146	147	164	227
Fresh vegetables	144	82	110	134	142	135	147	208
Processed fruits	110	70	84	100	107	108	119	150
Processed vegetables	82	48	66	67	88	83	91	109
Other food at home	1,028	555	681	822	985	1,120	1,174	1,512
Sugar and other sweets	124	70	91	104	125	124	132	179
Fats and oils	81	47	67	71	86	83	84	108
Miscellaneous foods	504	267	323	400	487	559	587	736
Nonalcoholic beverages	281	155	189	226	259	316	324	407
Food prepared by CU on trips	39	16	12	21	28	38	49	83
Food away from home	**2,369**	**1,246**	**1,151**	**1,567**	**1,844**	**2,258**	**3,000**	**4,209**
ALCOHOLIC BEVERAGES	**419**	**222**	**205**	**282**	**329**	**524**	**445**	**741**
HOUSING	**12,692**	**5,929**	**7,384**	**9,144**	**10,322**	**12,427**	**15,306**	**21,793**
Shelter	**7,088**	**3,433**	**4,164**	**4,768**	**5,732**	**6,957**	**8,267**	**12,501**
Owned dwellings	4,915	1,333	1,833	2,502	3,456	4,718	6,269	10,437
Mortgage interest and charges	2,647	585	538	938	1,640	2,583	3,601	6,217
Property taxes	1,254	442	655	813	949	995	1,506	2,498
Maintenance, repair, insurance, other expenses	1,014	306	639	751	868	1,140	1,161	1,723
Rented dwellings	1,656	1,819	2,170	2,052	2,007	1,931	1,493	736
Other lodging	516	281	162	214	268	308	506	1,328
Utilities, fuels, and public services	**2,708**	**1,443**	**1,965**	**2,425**	**2,654**	**2,821**	**3,052**	**3,808**
Natural gas	511	241	378	462	495	535	528	762
Electricity	884	511	699	841	886	926	972	1,155
Fuel oil and other fuels	81	49	84	88	102	73	75	85
Telephone	929	509	606	786	881	971	1,111	1,350
Water and other public services	303	132	199	248	291	315	367	456

	complete income reporters in Midwest	under $10,000	$10,000– $19,999	$20,000– $29,999	$30,000– $39,999	$40,000– $49,999	$50,000– $69,999	$70,000 or more
Household services	**$592**	**$228**	**$262**	**$444**	**$380**	**$510**	**$721**	**$1,179**
Personal services	280	98	92	211	162	230	396	562
Other household services	312	130	170	233	218	279	325	617
Housekeeping supplies	**663**	**267**	**321**	**421**	**466**	**557**	**1,374**	**920**
Laundry and cleaning supplies	139	81	93	97	112	147	177	211
Other household products	377	113	154	200	236	260	1,009	475
Postage and stationery	146	72	73	123	117	150	187	235
Household furnishings and equipment	**1,641**	**559**	**672**	**1,086**	**1,091**	**1,583**	**1,891**	**3,384**
Household textiles	127	42	72	93	88	131	171	221
Furniture	361	112	118	227	210	378	366	821
Floor coverings	39	7	13	28	27	32	33	94
Major appliances	198	34	68	191	104	195	266	383
Small appliances, misc. housewares	98	75	46	116	67	128	105	138
Miscellaneous household equipment	818	289	354	432	594	718	950	1,727
APPAREL AND RELATED SERVICES	**1,856**	**904**	**997**	**1,148**	**1,400**	**1,676**	**2,164**	**3,527**
Men and boys	**461**	**220**	**174**	**206**	**280**	**422**	**576**	**992**
Men, aged 16 or older	367	183	102	160	215	340	466	811
Boys, aged 2 to 15	94	37	72	46	65	81	110	181
Women and girls	**786**	**374**	**459**	**570**	**633**	**654**	**877**	**1,448**
Women, aged 16 or older	665	323	385	512	516	527	741	1,229
Girls, aged 2 to 15	121	51	75	57	116	127	137	219
Children under age 2	**102**	**27**	**68**	**73**	**105**	**101**	**111**	**172**
Footwear	**289**	**177**	**187**	**163**	**221**	**277**	**358**	**497**
Other apparel products and services	**218**	**105**	**109**	**137**	**161**	**223**	**241**	**418**
TRANSPORTATION	**8,138**	**2,926**	**4,083**	**5,617**	**7,527**	**8,764**	**10,031**	**14,034**
Vehicle purchases	**3,915**	**1,432**	**2,068**	**2,700**	**3,886**	**4,263**	**4,622**	**6,633**
Cars and trucks, new	1,520	410	756	722	1,168	1,157	1,756	3,337
Cars and trucks, used	2,320	996	1,285	1,977	2,663	3,046	2,761	3,122
Other vehicles	74	26	27	1	55	60	105	174
Gasoline and motor oil	**1,324**	**566**	**692**	**1,044**	**1,271**	**1,419**	**1,630**	**2,120**
Other vehicle expenses	**2,541**	**795**	**1,178**	**1,655**	**2,182**	**2,787**	**3,375**	**4,473**
Vehicle finance charges	382	73	137	261	365	479	562	630
Maintenance and repairs	691	278	413	404	588	774	936	1,125
Vehicle insurance	869	255	441	689	860	1,006	1,154	1,346
Vehicle rentals, leases, licenses, other charges	599	188	187	301	368	528	723	1,371
Public transportation	**358**	**134**	**145**	**217**	**188**	**295**	**404**	**809**
HEALTH CARE	**2,397**	**1,160**	**2,217**	**2,298**	**2,566**	**2,572**	**2,569**	**2,909**
Health insurance	1,174	601	1,095	1,147	1,230	1,320	1,273	1,363
Medical services	588	211	382	444	737	617	679	862
Drugs	513	285	669	615	484	471	469	511
Medical supplies	122	63	71	92	116	165	149	173
ENTERTAINMENT	**2,313**	**799**	**1,284**	**1,239**	**1,818**	**1,962**	**2,733**	**4,633**
Fees and admissions	593	185	166	258	323	453	636	1,509
Television, radio, sound equipment	708	371	407	525	686	674	833	1,156
Pets, toys, and playground equipment	418	104	219	274	349	484	544	724
Other entertainment products and services	594	139	491	182	461	351	720	1,245
PERSONAL CARE PRODUCTS AND SERVICES	**535**	**258**	**406**	**398**	**543**	**504**	**570**	**838**
READING	**164**	**68**	**101**	**118**	**128**	**159**	**199**	**286**
EDUCATION	**731**	**676**	**311**	**206**	**391**	**661**	**774**	**1,585**

	complete income reporters in Midwest	under $10,000	$10,000–$19,999	$20,000–$29,999	$30,000–$39,999	$40,000–$49,999	$50,000–$69,999	$70,000 or more
TOBACCO PRODUCTS AND SMOKING SUPPLIES	$405	$273	$344	$449	$480	$548	$433	$363
MISCELLANEOUS	802	285	426	702	654	791	983	1,364
CASH CONTRIBUTIONS	1,508	402	779	1,282	1,295	1,333	1,677	2,834
PERSONAL INSURANCE AND PENSIONS	4,772	321	948	1,857	3,010	4,174	6,426	11,744
Life and other personal insurance	471	129	228	311	339	409	544	971
Pensions and Social Security	4,301	192	719	1,546	2,672	3,765	5,882	10,772
PERSONAL TAXES	3,135	5	200	854	1,140	2,430	3,374	9,555
Federal income taxes	2,212	–39	60	531	635	1,648	2,336	7,026
State and local income taxes	749	3	46	210	357	634	852	2,175
Other taxes	174	40	93	114	149	149	187	354
GIFTS FOR NON–HOUSEHOLD MEMBERS	1,216	408	593	802	1,012	1,050	1,289	2,469
Food	99	45	35	38	84	43	120	230
Alcoholic beverages	13	18	12	9	5	7	11	25
Housing	323	131	189	253	252	268	417	559
Housekeeping supplies	50	16	28	34	37	61	75	77
Household textiles	19	2	8	8	15	7	33	43
Appliances and misc. housewares	32	4	22	36	16	24	34	58
Major appliances	13	1	3	11	9	2	11	37
Small appliances and misc. housewares	18	4	20	25	7	21	23	21
Miscellaneous household equipment	87	39	43	82	78	101	114	126
Other housing	135	69	87	94	105	75	160	256
Apparel and services	275	57	189	257	196	247	239	533
Males, aged 2 or older	70	17	56	63	65	72	57	122
Females, aged 2 or older	106	11	50	105	55	72	94	242
Children under age 2	56	19	36	45	44	60	48	103
Other apparel products and services	44	10	45	45	32	44	39	66
Jewelry and watches	19	3	17	17	12	25	26	25
All other apparel products and services	25	6	28	28	20	19	14	41
Transportation	52	24	25	14	53	37	68	104
Health care	32	11	14	25	23	59	21	59
Entertainment	94	36	34	62	107	103	106	167
Toys, games, hobbies, and tricycles	40	8	18	38	42	41	53	62
Other entertainment	54	27	17	24	64	62	53	105
Personal care products and services	33	20	22	16	90	31	23	36
Reading	2	1	1	3	1	2	3	3
Education	216	48	50	44	153	175	192	598
All other gifts	78	17	24	80	49	79	89	155

Note: Spending by category will not add to total spending because gift spending is also included in the preceding product and service categories and personal taxes are not included in the total.
Source: Bureau of Labor Statistics, 2001 and 2002 Consumer Expenditure Surveys, Internet site http://www.bls.gov/cex/; calculations by New Strategist

Table 1.31 Indexed spending in the Midwest by income, 2001–02

(indexed average annual spending of consumer units (CU) in the Midwest by product and service category and before-tax income of consumer unit, 2001–02; complete income reporters only; index definition: an index of 100 is the average for all consumer units; an index of 132 means that spending by consumer units in that group is 32 percent above the average for all consumer units; an index of 68 indicates spending that is 32 percent below the average for all consumer units)

	complete income reporters in Midwest	under $10,000	$10,000–$19,999	$20,000–$29,999	$30,000–$39,999	$40,000–$49,999	$50,000–$69,999	$70,000 or more
Average spending of CU, total	$42,170	$17,222	$22,839	$28,962	$35,312	$41,461	$50,687	$75,224
Average spending of CU, index	100	41	54	69	84	98	120	178
FOOD	100	55	62	78	89	99	117	158
Food at home	100	57	72	87	98	101	110	142
Cereals and bakery products	100	59	73	82	96	101	110	145
Cereals and cereal products	100	62	74	77	96	102	110	145
Bakery products	100	58	72	85	95	100	110	145
Meats, poultry, fish, and eggs	100	60	75	99	103	92	106	134
Beef	100	50	69	119	109	92	103	130
Pork	100	65	81	96	100	87	106	135
Other meats	100	70	68	97	96	95	115	134
Poultry	100	62	81	81	108	90	113	131
Fish and seafood	100	60	78	83	90	94	93	161
Eggs	100	66	86	100	114	118	96	107
Dairy products	100	53	72	82	96	106	113	143
Fresh milk and cream	100	56	79	83	101	110	110	133
Other dairy products	100	50	67	81	92	103	115	151
Fruits and vegetables	100	61	77	89	98	96	106	141
Fresh fruits	100	62	77	87	93	94	104	145
Fresh vegetables	100	57	76	93	99	94	102	144
Processed fruits	100	64	76	91	97	98	108	136
Processed vegetables	100	59	80	82	107	101	111	133
Other food at home	100	54	66	80	96	109	114	147
Sugar and other sweets	100	56	73	84	101	100	106	144
Fats and oils	100	58	82	88	106	102	104	133
Miscellaneous foods	100	53	64	79	97	111	116	146
Nonalcoholic beverages	100	55	67	80	92	112	115	145
Food prepared by CU on trips	100	41	30	54	72	97	126	213
Food away from home	100	53	49	66	78	95	127	178
ALCOHOLIC BEVERAGES	100	53	49	67	79	125	106	177
HOUSING	100	47	58	72	81	98	121	172
Shelter	100	48	59	67	81	98	117	176
Owned dwellings	100	27	37	51	70	96	128	212
Mortgage interest and charges	100	22	20	35	62	98	136	235
Property taxes	100	35	52	65	76	79	120	199
Maintenance, repair, insurance, other expenses	100	30	63	74	86	112	114	170
Rented dwellings	100	110	131	124	121	117	90	44
Other lodging	100	54	31	41	52	60	98	257
Utilities, fuels, and public services	100	53	73	90	98	104	113	141
Natural gas	100	47	74	90	97	105	103	149
Electricity	100	58	79	95	100	105	110	131
Fuel oil and other fuels	100	60	104	109	126	90	93	105
Telephone	100	55	65	85	95	105	120	145
Water and other public services	100	44	66	82	96	104	121	150

	complete income reporters in Midwest	under $10,000	$10,000– $19,999	$20,000– $29,999	$30,000– $39,999	$40,000– $49,999	$50,000– $69,999	$70,000 or more
Household services	**100**	**39**	**44**	**75**	**64**	**86**	**122**	**199**
Personal services	100	35	33	75	58	82	141	201
Other household services	100	42	54	75	70	89	104	198
Housekeeping supplies	**100**	**40**	**48**	**63**	**70**	**84**	**207**	**139**
Laundry and cleaning supplies	100	59	67	70	81	106	127	152
Other household products	100	30	41	53	63	69	268	126
Postage and stationery	100	49	50	84	80	103	128	161
Household furnishings and equipment	**100**	**34**	**41**	**66**	**66**	**96**	**115**	**206**
Household textiles	100	33	56	73	69	103	135	174
Furniture	100	31	33	63	58	105	101	227
Floor coverings	100	18	33	72	69	82	85	241
Major appliances	100	17	34	96	53	98	134	193
Small appliances, misc. housewares	100	76	47	118	68	131	107	141
Miscellaneous household equipment	100	35	43	53	73	88	116	211
APPAREL AND RELATED SERVICES	**100**	**49**	**54**	**62**	**75**	**90**	**117**	**190**
Men and boys	**100**	**48**	**38**	**45**	**61**	**92**	**125**	**215**
Men, aged 16 or older	100	50	28	44	59	93	127	221
Boys, aged 2 to 15	100	39	77	49	69	86	117	193
Women and girls	**100**	**48**	**58**	**73**	**81**	**83**	**112**	**184**
Women, aged 16 or older	100	48	58	77	78	79	111	185
Girls, aged 2 to 15	100	42	62	47	96	105	113	181
Children under age 2	**100**	**27**	**67**	**72**	**103**	**99**	**109**	**169**
Footwear	**100**	**61**	**65**	**56**	**76**	**96**	**124**	**172**
Other apparel products and services	**100**	**48**	**50**	**63**	**74**	**102**	**111**	**192**
TRANSPORTATION	**100**	**36**	**50**	**69**	**92**	**108**	**123**	**172**
Vehicle purchases	**100**	**37**	**53**	**69**	**99**	**109**	**118**	**169**
Cars and trucks, new	100	27	50	48	77	76	116	220
Cars and trucks, used	100	43	55	85	115	131	119	135
Other vehicles	100	35	36	1	74	81	142	235
Gasoline and motor oil	**100**	**43**	**52**	**79**	**96**	**107**	**123**	**160**
Other vehicle expenses	**100**	**31**	**46**	**65**	**86**	**110**	**133**	**176**
Vehicle finance charges	100	19	36	68	96	125	147	165
Maintenance and repairs	100	40	60	58	85	112	135	163
Vehicle insurance	100	29	51	79	99	116	133	155
Vehicle rentals, leases, licenses, other charges	100	31	31	50	61	88	121	229
Public transportation	**100**	**37**	**41**	**61**	**53**	**82**	**113**	**226**
HEALTH CARE	**100**	**48**	**93**	**96**	**107**	**107**	**107**	**121**
Health insurance	100	51	93	98	105	112	108	116
Medical services	100	36	65	76	125	105	115	147
Drugs	100	56	130	120	94	92	91	100
Medical supplies	100	52	58	75	95	135	122	142
ENTERTAINMENT	**100**	**35**	**56**	**54**	**79**	**85**	**118**	**200**
Fees and admissions	100	31	28	44	54	76	107	254
Television, radio, sound equipment	100	52	57	74	97	95	118	163
Pets, toys, and playground equipment	100	25	52	66	83	116	130	173
Other entertainment products and services	100	23	83	31	78	59	121	210
PERSONAL CARE PRODUCTS AND SERVICES	**100**	**48**	**76**	**74**	**101**	**94**	**107**	**157**
READING	**100**	**41**	**62**	**72**	**78**	**97**	**121**	**174**
EDUCATION	**100**	**92**	**43**	**28**	**53**	**90**	**106**	**217**

	complete income reporters in Midwest	under $10,000	$10,000– $19,999	$20,000– $29,999	$30,000– $39,999	$40,000– $49,999	$50,000– $69,999	$70,000 or more
TOBACCO PRODUCTS AND SMOKING SUPPLIES	100	67	85	111	119	135	107	90
MISCELLANEOUS	100	36	53	88	82	99	123	170
CASH CONTRIBUTIONS	100	27	52	85	86	88	111	188
PERSONAL INSURANCE AND PENSIONS	100	7	20	39	63	87	135	246
Life and other personal insurance	100	27	48	66	72	87	115	206
Pensions and Social Security	100	4	17	36	62	88	137	250
PERSONAL TAXES	100	0	6	27	36	78	108	305
Federal income taxes	100	–	3	24	29	75	106	318
State and local income taxes	100	0	6	28	48	85	114	290
Other taxes	100	23	53	66	86	86	107	203
GIFTS FOR NON–HOUSEHOLD MEMBERS	100	34	49	66	83	86	106	203
Food	100	46	35	38	85	43	121	232
Alcoholic beverages	100	138	91	69	38	54	85	192
Housing	100	40	58	78	78	83	129	173
Housekeeping supplies	100	32	57	68	74	122	150	154
Household textiles	100	10	40	42	79	37	174	226
Appliances and misc. housewares	100	14	69	113	50	75	106	181
Major appliances	100	5	20	85	69	15	85	285
Small appliances and misc. housewares	100	21	109	139	39	117	128	117
Miscellaneous household equipment	100	45	49	94	90	116	131	145
Other housing	100	51	65	70	78	56	119	190
Apparel and services	100	21	69	93	71	90	87	194
Males, aged 2 or older	100	25	80	90	93	103	81	174
Females, aged 2 or older	100	10	48	99	52	68	89	228
Children under age 2	100	34	65	80	79	107	86	184
Other apparel products and services	100	22	103	102	73	100	89	150
Jewelry and watches	100	18	90	89	63	132	137	132
All other apparel products and services	100	25	113	112	80	76	56	164
Transportation	100	47	47	27	102	71	131	200
Health care	100	33	42	78	72	184	66	184
Entertainment	100	38	36	66	114	110	113	178
Toys, games, hobbies, and tricycles	100	21	45	95	105	103	133	155
Other entertainment	100	51	31	44	119	115	98	194
Personal care products and services	100	60	68	48	273	94	70	109
Reading	100	50	50	150	50	100	150	150
Education	100	22	23	20	71	81	89	277
All other gifts	100	22	31	103	63	101	114	199

Source: Calculations by New Strategist based on the Bureau of Labor Statistics 2001 and 2002 Consumer Expenditure Surveys

Table 1.32 Average spending in the South by income, 2001–02

(average annual spending of consumer units (CU) in the South by product and service category and before-tax income of consumer unit, 2001–02; complete income reporters only)

	complete income reporters in South	under $10,000	$10,000–$19,999	$20,000–$29,999	$30,000–$39,999	$40,000–$49,999	$50,000–$69,999	$70,000 or more
Number of consumer units (in thousands, add 000s)	32,528	4,242	5,707	4,760	3,894	3,130	4,526	6,270
Average number of persons per CU	2.5	1.8	2.1	2.4	2.5	2.6	2.9	3.0
Average income before taxes	$44,943	$5,703	$14,801	$24,447	$34,481	$44,531	$58,401	$111,478
Average annual spending	38,767	16,821	22,190	27,388	33,845	40,405	48,165	72,755
FOOD	**$5,433**	**$3,000**	**$3,590**	**$4,229**	**$4,795**	**$5,709**	**$6,796**	**$8,911**
Food at home	**3,140**	**2,069**	**2,464**	**2,687**	**2,913**	**3,329**	**3,661**	**4,467**
Cereals and bakery products	451	292	365	398	416	463	513	643
Cereals and cereal products	155	109	138	139	144	165	167	205
Bakery products	297	183	228	259	272	298	346	439
Meats, poultry, fish, and eggs	874	602	713	776	838	897	1,025	1,172
Beef	263	177	209	233	262	269	305	359
Pork	198	158	181	182	193	203	224	234
Other meats	103	66	89	100	96	105	117	136
Poultry	153	97	122	129	137	167	202	209
Fish and seafood	120	77	79	95	117	113	139	195
Eggs	35	27	33	36	33	41	37	39
Dairy products	317	207	239	273	291	346	363	464
Fresh milk and cream	129	97	110	121	121	137	137	167
Other dairy products	189	110	128	152	170	209	226	297
Fruits and vegetables	520	334	416	453	461	566	591	750
Fresh fruits	156	98	122	137	130	171	173	233
Fresh vegetables	162	107	128	143	141	167	182	241
Processed fruits	110	67	91	96	96	120	127	158
Processed vegetables	92	62	74	78	94	109	108	118
Other food at home	977	634	732	787	907	1,057	1,169	1,438
Sugar and other sweets	117	87	83	99	97	143	134	171
Fats and oils	90	67	77	77	82	87	109	117
Miscellaneous foods	481	295	344	378	447	537	581	730
Nonalcoholic beverages	255	173	209	208	257	253	307	346
Food prepared by CU on trips	35	13	19	26	24	37	39	73
Food away from home	**2,293**	**931**	**1,125**	**1,542**	**1,882**	**2,380**	**3,135**	**4,444**
ALCOHOLIC BEVERAGES	**315**	**172**	**183**	**226**	**263**	**299**	**364**	**607**
HOUSING	**11,834**	**6,178**	**7,151**	**8,857**	**10,376**	**11,779**	**13,771**	**21,713**
Shelter	**6,357**	**3,186**	**3,608**	**4,671**	**5,426**	**6,073**	**7,286**	**12,336**
Owned dwellings	4,179	1,370	1,623	2,285	2,917	3,691	5,308	10,059
Mortgage interest and charges	2,454	611	638	1,119	1,592	2,143	3,270	6,470
Property taxes	861	424	497	536	595	756	957	1,882
Maintenance, repair, insurance, other expenses	864	335	487	630	731	792	1,081	1,707
Rented dwellings	1,787	1,674	1,837	2,225	2,230	2,107	1,562	1,215
Other lodging	391	141	148	161	279	275	416	1,062
Utilities, fuels, and public services	**2,816**	**1,839**	**2,199**	**2,530**	**2,683**	**3,000**	**3,244**	**3,939**
Natural gas	232	148	181	194	201	246	246	367
Electricity	1,222	857	1,023	1,135	1,186	1,296	1,406	1,571
Fuel oil and other fuels	54	41	62	57	48	49	44	65
Telephone	970	590	675	835	950	1,059	1,148	1,439
Water and other public services	338	203	257	309	298	350	400	498

	complete income reporters in South	under $10,000	$10,000–$19,999	$20,000–$29,999	$30,000–$39,999	$40,000–$49,999	$50,000–$69,999	$70,000 or more
Household services	**$700**	**$289**	**$338**	**$476**	**$678**	**$750**	**$755**	**$1,429**
Personal services	327	98	138	228	435	451	331	596
Other household services	374	191	200	248	243	299	424	833
Housekeeping supplies	**546**	**311**	**338**	**393**	**526**	**534**	**719**	**905**
Laundry and cleaning supplies	152	109	114	129	160	153	196	195
Other household products	272	139	163	161	266	253	387	476
Postage and stationery	123	64	62	103	100	128	135	234
Household furnishings and equipment	**1,414**	**554**	**668**	**788**	**1,063**	**1,423**	**1,767**	**3,103**
Household textiles	118	34	74	61	103	115	134	252
Furniture	383	114	164	224	283	351	492	884
Floor coverings	35	10	19	22	20	15	35	97
Major appliances	173	85	103	110	132	179	247	316
Small appliances, misc. housewares	84	50	49	49	63	76	97	175
Miscellaneous household equipment	621	261	260	323	462	688	762	1,380
APPAREL AND RELATED SERVICES	**1,697**	**817**	**1,053**	**1,001**	**1,519**	**1,891**	**1,977**	**3,224**
Men and boys	**403**	**159**	**209**	**238**	**381**	**397**	**464**	**840**
Men, aged 16 or older	309	124	132	170	308	323	358	661
Boys, aged 2 to 15	94	35	77	69	72	74	106	178
Women and girls	**662**	**347**	**438**	**382**	**575**	**811**	**744**	**1,212**
Women, aged 16 or older	538	319	348	313	439	625	617	991
Girls, aged 2 to 15	124	28	89	69	135	186	126	221
Children under age 2	**82**	**38**	**52**	**51**	**79**	**113**	**105**	**134**
Footwear	**312**	**186**	**242**	**166**	**319**	**339**	**429**	**474**
Other apparel products and services	**239**	**87**	**112**	**164**	**166**	**231**	**235**	**565**
TRANSPORTATION	**7,697**	**2,798**	**4,611**	**5,542**	**7,310**	**8,457**	**10,210**	**13,499**
Vehicle purchases	**3,854**	**1,341**	**2,498**	**2,633**	**3,750**	**4,303**	**5,063**	**6,683**
Cars and trucks, new	1,820	445	1,039	956	1,476	1,997	2,246	3,937
Cars and trucks, used	1,977	896	1,437	1,677	2,210	2,275	2,705	2,608
Other vehicles	57	–	22	–	64	31	111	138
Gasoline and motor oil	**1,262**	**584**	**791**	**1,065**	**1,275**	**1,430**	**1,640**	**1,933**
Other vehicle expenses	**2,297**	**767**	**1,189**	**1,686**	**2,092**	**2,495**	**3,157**	**4,206**
Vehicle finance charges	437	109	149	268	395	510	669	870
Maintenance and repairs	644	262	375	557	576	650	849	1,100
Vehicle insurance	840	291	503	698	860	991	1,117	1,340
Vehicle rentals, leases, licenses, other charges	376	106	161	163	260	344	522	896
Public transportation	**285**	**105**	**134**	**159**	**194**	**228**	**351**	**677**
HEALTH CARE	**2,384**	**1,228**	**1,921**	**2,148**	**2,336**	**2,693**	**2,896**	**3,267**
Health insurance	1,148	571	885	1,070	1,161	1,364	1,352	1,575
Medical services	594	243	348	443	508	705	891	951
Drugs	546	367	610	567	556	521	537	602
Medical supplies	96	47	77	67	111	103	115	139
ENTERTAINMENT	**1,782**	**700**	**794**	**1,062**	**1,386**	**1,930**	**2,301**	**3,759**
Fees and admissions	440	131	163	166	266	402	492	1,199
Television, radio, sound equipment	653	330	399	512	622	771	827	1,044
Pets, toys, and playground equipment	346	132	158	203	321	377	536	638
Other entertainment products and services	343	106	73	181	176	380	447	877
PERSONAL CARE PRODUCTS AND SERVICES	**522**	**241**	**326**	**390**	**515**	**523**	**691**	**874**
READING	**110**	**45**	**59**	**83**	**92**	**100**	**131**	**219**
EDUCATION	**483**	**260**	**236**	**202**	**268**	**374**	**616**	**1,160**

	complete income reporters in South	under $10,000	$10,000– $19,999	$20,000– $29,999	$30,000– $39,999	$40,000– $49,999	$50,000– $69,999	$70,000 or more
TOBACCO PRODUCTS AND SMOKING SUPPLIES	$338	$266	$291	$355	$387	$419	$388	$309
MISCELLANEOUS	739	353	475	569	665	856	748	1,348
CASH CONTRIBUTIONS	1,290	431	582	782	969	1,218	1,761	2,797
PERSONAL INSURANCE AND PENSIONS	4,144	330	920	1,941	2,964	4,155	5,515	11,068
Life and other personal insurance	425	154	278	288	362	442	479	836
Pensions and Social Security	3,719	176	643	1,653	2,603	3,713	5,036	10,232
PERSONAL TAXES	2,125	–56	–96	298	844	1,704	2,277	7,904
Federal income taxes	1,727	–100	–182	143	547	1,251	1,840	6,791
State and local income taxes	297	11	29	86	191	347	331	913
Other taxes	101	32	57	69	106	106	106	201
GIFTS FOR NON–HOUSEHOLD MEMBERS	884	393	410	505	684	925	1,192	1,819
Food	58	11	23	17	34	37	88	153
Alcoholic beverages	9	3	3	6	6	12	16	18
Housing	236	150	110	167	192	272	275	446
Housekeeping supplies	38	26	18	31	34	29	51	71
Household textiles	10	3	3	4	5	17	21	19
Appliances and misc. housewares	24	24	9	25	19	37	21	39
Major appliances	6	1	2	8	1	13	6	10
Small appliances and misc. housewares	19	23	7	18	18	25	15	29
Miscellaneous household equipment	57	32	14	32	41	67	75	123
Other housing	106	66	67	74	93	122	107	194
Apparel and services	222	128	118	118	222	202	329	395
Males, aged 2 or older	60	34	31	40	52	55	88	108
Females, aged 2 or older	67	52	29	31	62	45	90	139
Children under age 2	38	17	19	21	48	53	47	62
Other apparel products and services	57	24	40	27	61	49	104	86
Jewelry and watches	23	12	6	13	16	38	34	43
All other apparel products and services	34	13	33	14	46	11	70	42
Transportation	50	23	24	52	13	120	38	89
Health care	36	7	10	28	17	22	91	67
Entertainment	74	31	34	48	53	83	90	156
Toys, games, hobbies, and tricycles	27	8	16	19	27	35	34	47
Other entertainment	47	23	18	29	26	48	56	109
Personal care products and services	21	18	13	10	20	10	36	36
Reading	1	–	–	1	1	1	2	2
Education	109	7	30	21	35	106	170	318
All other gifts	67	16	42	37	91	62	57	140

Note: Spending by category will not add to total spending because gift spending is also included in the preceding product and service categories and personal taxes are not included in the total. (–) means sample is too small to make a reliable estimate.
Source: Bureau of Labor Statistics, 2001 and 2002 Consumer Expenditure Surveys, Internet site http://www.bls.gov/cex/; calculations by New Strategist

Table 1.33 Indexed spending in the South by income, 2001–02

(indexed average annual spending of consumer units (CU) in the South by product and service category and before-tax income of consumer unit, 2001–02; complete income reporters only; index definition: an index of 100 is the average for all consumer units; an index of 132 means that spending by consumer units in that group is 32 percent above the average for all consumer units; an index of 68 indicates spending that is 32 percent below the average for all consumer units)

	complete income reporters in South	under $10,000	$10,000–$19,999	$20,000–$29,999	$30,000–$39,999	$40,000–$49,999	$50,000–$69,999	$70,000 or more
Average spending of CU, total	$38,767	$16,821	$22,190	$27,388	$33,845	$40,405	$48,165	$72,755
Average spending of CU, index	100	43	57	71	87	104	124	188
FOOD	100	55	66	78	88	105	125	164
Food at home	100	66	78	86	93	106	117	142
Cereals and bakery products	100	65	81	88	92	103	114	143
Cereals and cereal products	100	70	89	90	93	106	108	132
Bakery products	100	62	77	87	92	100	116	148
Meats, poultry, fish, and eggs	100	69	82	89	96	103	117	134
Beef	100	67	80	89	100	102	116	137
Pork	100	80	92	92	97	103	113	118
Other meats	100	64	86	97	93	102	114	132
Poultry	100	63	80	84	90	109	132	137
Fish and seafood	100	64	65	79	98	94	116	163
Eggs	100	78	95	103	94	117	106	111
Dairy products	100	65	75	86	92	109	115	146
Fresh milk and cream	100	75	86	94	94	106	106	129
Other dairy products	100	58	68	80	90	111	120	157
Fruits and vegetables	100	64	80	87	89	109	114	144
Fresh fruits	100	63	78	88	83	110	111	149
Fresh vegetables	100	66	79	88	87	103	112	149
Processed fruits	100	61	82	87	87	109	115	144
Processed vegetables	100	67	80	85	102	118	117	128
Other food at home	100	65	75	81	93	108	120	147
Sugar and other sweets	100	74	71	85	83	122	115	146
Fats and oils	100	74	86	86	91	97	121	130
Miscellaneous foods	100	61	72	79	93	112	121	152
Nonalcoholic beverages	100	68	82	82	101	99	120	136
Food prepared by CU on trips	100	38	54	74	69	106	111	209
Food away from home	100	41	49	67	82	104	137	194
ALCOHOLIC BEVERAGES	100	54	58	72	83	95	116	193
HOUSING	100	52	60	75	88	100	116	183
Shelter	100	50	57	73	85	96	115	194
Owned dwellings	100	33	39	55	70	88	127	241
Mortgage interest and charges	100	25	26	46	65	87	133	264
Property taxes	100	49	58	62	69	88	111	219
Maintenance, repair, insurance, other expenses	100	39	56	73	85	92	125	198
Rented dwellings	100	94	103	125	125	118	87	68
Other lodging	100	36	38	41	71	70	106	272
Utilities, fuels, and public services	100	65	78	90	95	107	115	140
Natural gas	100	64	78	84	87	106	106	158
Electricity	100	70	84	93	97	106	115	129
Fuel oil and other fuels	100	75	114	106	89	91	81	120
Telephone	100	61	70	86	98	109	118	148
Water and other public services	100	60	76	91	88	104	118	147

	complete income reporters in South	under $10,000	$10,000–$19,999	$20,000–$29,999	$30,000–$39,999	$40,000–$49,999	$50,000–$69,999	$70,000 or more
Household services	100	41	48	68	97	107	108	204
Personal services	100	30	42	70	133	138	101	182
Other household services	100	51	54	66	65	80	113	223
Housekeeping supplies	100	57	62	72	96	98	132	166
Laundry and cleaning supplies	100	71	75	85	105	101	129	128
Other household products	100	51	60	59	98	93	142	175
Postage and stationery	100	52	50	84	81	104	110	190
Household furnishings and equipment	100	39	47	56	75	101	125	219
Household textiles	100	29	63	52	87	97	114	214
Furniture	100	30	43	58	74	92	128	231
Floor coverings	100	28	53	63	57	43	100	277
Major appliances	100	49	60	64	76	103	143	183
Small appliances, misc. housewares	100	60	58	58	75	90	115	208
Miscellaneous household equipment	100	42	42	52	74	111	123	222
APPAREL AND RELATED SERVICES	100	48	62	59	90	111	116	190
Men and boys	100	39	52	59	95	99	115	208
Men, aged 16 or older	100	40	43	55	100	105	116	214
Boys, aged 2 to 15	100	37	82	73	77	79	113	189
Women and girls	100	52	66	58	87	123	112	183
Women, aged 16 or older	100	59	65	58	82	116	115	184
Girls, aged 2 to 15	100	23	72	56	109	150	102	178
Children under age 2	100	47	63	62	96	138	128	163
Footwear	100	60	77	53	102	109	138	152
Other apparel products and services	100	36	47	69	69	97	98	236
TRANSPORTATION	100	36	60	72	95	110	133	175
Vehicle purchases	100	35	65	68	97	112	131	173
Cars and trucks, new	100	24	57	53	81	110	123	216
Cars and trucks, used	100	45	73	85	112	115	137	132
Other vehicles	100	–	38	–	112	54	195	242
Gasoline and motor oil	100	46	63	84	101	113	130	153
Other vehicle expenses	100	33	52	73	91	109	137	183
Vehicle finance charges	100	25	34	61	90	117	153	199
Maintenance and repairs	100	41	58	86	89	101	132	171
Vehicle insurance	100	35	60	83	102	118	133	160
Vehicle rentals, leases, licenses, other charges	100	28	43	43	69	91	139	238
Public transportation	100	37	47	56	68	80	123	238
HEALTH CARE	100	52	81	90	98	113	121	137
Health insurance	100	50	77	93	101	119	118	137
Medical services	100	41	59	75	86	119	150	160
Drugs	100	67	112	104	102	95	98	110
Medical supplies	100	49	80	70	116	107	120	145
ENTERTAINMENT	100	39	45	60	78	108	129	211
Fees and admissions	100	30	37	38	60	91	112	273
Television, radio, sound equipment	100	51	61	78	95	118	127	160
Pets, toys, and playground equipment	100	38	46	59	93	109	155	184
Other entertainment products and services	100	31	21	53	51	111	130	256
PERSONAL CARE PRODUCTS AND SERVICES	100	46	62	75	99	100	132	167
READING	100	41	53	75	84	91	119	199
EDUCATION	100	54	49	42	55	77	128	240

	complete income reporters in South	under $10,000	$10,000– $19,999	$20,000– $29,999	$30,000– $39,999	$40,000– $49,999	$50,000– $69,999	$70,000 or more
TOBACCO PRODUCTS AND SMOKING SUPPLIES	**100**	79	86	105	114	124	115	91
MISCELLANEOUS	**100**	48	64	77	90	116	101	182
CASH CONTRIBUTIONS	**100**	33	45	61	75	94	137	217
PERSONAL INSURANCE AND PENSIONS	**100**	8	22	47	72	100	133	267
Life and other personal insurance	100	36	65	68	85	104	113	197
Pensions and Social Security	100	5	17	44	70	100	135	275
PERSONAL TAXES	**100**	–	–	14	40	80	107	372
Federal income taxes	100	–	–	8	32	72	107	393
State and local income taxes	100	4	10	29	64	117	111	307
Other taxes	100	32	56	68	105	105	105	199
GIFTS FOR NON–HOUSEHOLD MEMBERS	**100**	44	46	57	77	105	135	206
Food	**100**	19	40	29	59	64	152	264
Alcoholic beverages	**100**	34	37	67	67	133	178	200
Housing	**100**	63	47	71	81	115	117	189
Housekeeping supplies	100	67	46	82	89	76	134	187
Household textiles	100	26	29	40	50	170	210	190
Appliances and misc. housewares	100	100	37	104	79	154	88	163
Major appliances	100	17	32	133	17	217	100	167
Small appliances and misc. housewares	100	121	37	95	95	132	79	153
Miscellaneous household equipment	100	56	25	56	72	118	132	216
Other housing	100	62	63	70	88	115	101	183
Apparel and services	**100**	57	53	53	100	91	148	178
Males, aged 2 or older	100	56	51	67	87	92	147	180
Females, aged 2 or older	100	77	44	46	93	67	134	207
Children under age 2	100	46	49	55	126	139	124	163
Other apparel products and services	100	43	69	47	107	86	182	151
Jewelry and watches	100	53	28	57	70	165	148	187
All other apparel products and services	100	38	96	41	135	32	206	124
Transportation	**100**	45	49	104	26	240	76	178
Health care	**100**	18	28	78	47	61	253	186
Entertainment	**100**	42	46	65	72	112	122	211
Toys, games, hobbies, and tricycles	100	30	61	70	100	130	126	174
Other entertainment	100	49	38	62	55	102	119	232
Personal care products and services	**100**	87	63	48	95	48	171	171
Reading	**100**	–	–	100	100	100	200	200
Education	**100**	6	27	19	32	97	156	292
All other gifts	**100**	23	62	55	136	93	85	209

Note: (–) means sample is too small to make a reliable estimate.
Source: Calculations by New Strategist based on the Bureau of Labor Statistics 2001 and 2002 Consumer Expenditure Surveys

Table 1.34 Average spending in the West by income, 2001–02

(average annual spending of consumer units (CU) in the West by product and service category and before-tax income of consumer unit, 2001–02; complete income reporters only)

	complete income reporters in West	under $10,000	$10,000– $19,999	$20,000– $29,999	$30,000– $39,999	$40,000– $49,999	$50,000– $69,999	$70,000 or more
Number of consumer units (in thousands, add 000s)	20,238	2,385	3,214	2,601	2,417	1,978	2,788	4,854
Average number of persons per CU	2.6	1.6	2.1	2.5	2.5	2.8	2.9	3.2
Average income before taxes	$51,003	$5,274	$14,651	$24,487	$34,388	$44,455	$59,117	$118,044
Average annual spending	45,837	19,896	23,645	31,359	38,200	42,753	54,110	81,448
FOOD	**$5,872**	**$3,199**	**$3,606**	**$4,872**	**$5,111**	**$5,813**	**$6,878**	**$9,071**
Food at home	**3,360**	**1,902**	**2,360**	**3,052**	**3,317**	**3,518**	**3,931**	**4,526**
Cereals and bakery products	483	271	335	440	453	505	567	665
Cereals and cereal products	171	110	118	167	154	200	195	221
Bakery products	312	161	216	273	299	305	371	444
Meats, poultry, fish, and eggs	827	474	620	779	885	837	948	1,054
Beef	256	134	187	246	286	235	298	332
Pork	163	105	130	152	176	153	183	204
Other meats	95	46	78	88	104	91	106	127
Poultry	149	81	114	150	149	173	168	182
Fish and seafood	120	77	78	96	120	143	143	161
Eggs	44	30	34	47	48	43	50	48
Dairy products	375	227	254	334	350	416	447	506
Fresh milk and cream	154	98	109	161	150	165	183	187
Other dairy products	221	129	144	173	200	251	264	318
Fruits and vegetables	626	355	453	611	616	641	702	831
Fresh fruits	203	126	143	202	192	203	219	276
Fresh vegetables	211	113	157	207	227	218	243	264
Processed fruits	130	75	93	126	124	121	145	180
Processed vegetables	83	41	60	77	73	99	95	111
Other food at home	1,050	575	699	887	1,013	1,118	1,267	1,470
Sugar and other sweets	132	61	98	112	120	144	151	191
Fats and oils	88	54	62	92	87	103	105	101
Miscellaneous foods	494	266	318	408	481	542	621	685
Nonalcoholic beverages	277	173	198	232	266	281	326	383
Food prepared by CU on trips	58	22	23	42	60	47	64	110
Food away from home	**2,512**	**1,297**	**1,246**	**1,820**	**1,794**	**2,296**	**2,947**	**4,546**
ALCOHOLIC BEVERAGES	**460**	**213**	**237**	**306**	**364**	**418**	**498**	**866**
HOUSING	**15,224**	**7,221**	**8,707**	**10,776**	**12,638**	**13,906**	**17,216**	**26,555**
Shelter	**9,581**	**4,664**	**5,522**	**6,593**	**7,984**	**8,959**	**10,935**	**16,557**
Owned dwellings	5,975	1,716	1,972	2,882	4,238	5,101	7,323	12,826
Mortgage interest and charges	3,934	950	818	1,531	2,705	3,517	4,922	8,967
Property taxes	1,056	439	554	619	731	875	1,246	2,052
Maintenance, repair, insurance, other expenses	985	327	600	732	801	708	1,154	1,806
Rented dwellings	3,056	2,615	3,302	3,410	3,475	3,554	3,137	2,464
Other lodging	549	332	249	302	272	305	476	1,267
Utilities, fuels, and public services	**2,487**	**1,402**	**1,748**	**2,058**	**2,302**	**2,491**	**2,933**	**3,573**
Natural gas	328	185	228	252	314	308	393	482
Electricity	798	484	571	725	732	819	914	1,100
Fuel oil and other fuels	44	31	50	41	42	45	41	50
Telephone	924	521	646	752	868	916	1,104	1,325
Water and other public services	393	179	252	289	346	404	481	617

	complete income reporters in West	under $10,000	$10,000– $19,999	$20,000– $29,999	$30,000– $39,999	$40,000– $49,999	$50,000– $69,999	$70,000 or more
Household services	**$780**	**$237**	**$331**	**$492**	**$532**	**$637**	**$769**	**$1,683**
Personal services	328	38	95	209	184	236	324	801
Other household services	451	200	237	283	348	401	445	882
Housekeeping supplies	**565**	**314**	**363**	**476**	**476**	**586**	**690**	**837**
Laundry and cleaning supplies	141	87	114	144	137	151	168	164
Other household products	269	147	163	214	200	280	319	434
Postage and stationery	155	80	87	119	139	156	203	239
Household furnishings and equipment	**1,812**	**605**	**742**	**1,156**	**1,344**	**1,233**	**1,889**	**3,907**
Household textiles	167	66	87	194	111	108	128	331
Furniture	442	123	147	256	253	273	459	1,048
Floor coverings	52	9	37	23	27	34	51	121
Major appliances	234	76	125	144	213	187	261	446
Small appliances, misc. housewares	129	39	64	80	91	72	115	298
Miscellaneous household equipment	786	292	283	459	648	558	875	1,663
APPAREL AND RELATED SERVICES	**1,866**	**854**	**984**	**1,269**	**1,617**	**1,471**	**2,174**	**3,401**
Men and boys	**439**	**150**	**244**	**293**	**336**	**275**	**508**	**874**
Men, aged 16 or older	356	125	196	240	262	195	378	744
Boys, aged 2 to 15	83	26	48	53	74	80	130	131
Women and girls	**704**	**390**	**320**	**459**	**663**	**637**	**862**	**1,213**
Women, aged 16 or older	586	346	258	360	515	531	686	1,053
Girls, aged 2 to 15	119	44	60	98	148	106	176	161
Children under age 2	**87**	**23**	**39**	**67**	**124**	**80**	**111**	**133**
Footwear	**345**	**166**	**221**	**241**	**326**	**257**	**388**	**600**
Other apparel products and services	**290**	**124**	**160**	**209**	**168**	**222**	**307**	**581**
TRANSPORTATION	**8,687**	**3,273**	**4,260**	**6,032**	**8,214**	**9,025**	**11,235**	**14,345**
Vehicle purchases	**4,027**	**1,477**	**1,870**	**2,749**	**4,070**	**4,413**	**5,404**	**6,422**
Cars and trucks, new	1,946	405	652	748	2,075	2,466	2,417	3,654
Cars and trucks, used	2,015	1,052	1,218	1,916	1,971	1,896	2,907	2,627
Other vehicles	66	20	–	85	24	50	80	142
Gasoline and motor oil	**1,390**	**618**	**845**	**1,091**	**1,378**	**1,470**	**1,711**	**2,077**
Other vehicle expenses	**2,803**	**963**	**1,309**	**1,940**	**2,410**	**2,826**	**3,547**	**4,924**
Vehicle finance charges	387	94	134	236	402	411	543	672
Maintenance and repairs	922	375	457	729	753	879	1,080	1,620
Vehicle insurance	927	338	530	715	891	1,032	1,148	1,443
Vehicle rentals, leases, licenses, other charges	566	155	189	260	363	504	776	1,189
Public transportation	**468**	**214**	**235**	**252**	**356**	**315**	**572**	**922**
HEALTH CARE	**2,247**	**1,226**	**1,723**	**2,166**	**2,092**	**2,213**	**2,525**	**3,070**
Health insurance	1,040	540	832	1,013	1,011	1,056	1,227	1,341
Medical services	671	360	370	498	554	664	771	1,118
Drugs	413	260	408	509	417	391	405	453
Medical supplies	123	66	112	146	110	102	123	159
ENTERTAINMENT	**2,361**	**845**	**1,034**	**1,333**	**1,764**	**1,998**	**3,144**	**4,546**
Fees and admissions	631	235	243	315	405	487	708	1,380
Television, radio, sound equipment	728	393	395	507	663	709	889	1,181
Pets, toys, and playground equipment	398	126	198	291	280	449	484	712
Other entertainment products and services	604	91	199	221	415	353	1,064	1,272
PERSONAL CARE PRODUCTS AND SERVICES	**578**	**308**	**333**	**488**	**493**	**636**	**631**	**909**
READING	**165**	**66**	**92**	**108**	**129**	**157**	**193**	**299**
EDUCATION	**881**	**1,345**	**716**	**339**	**382**	**566**	**710**	**1,529**

	complete income reporters in West	under $10,000	$10,000– $19,999	$20,000– $29,999	$30,000– $39,999	$40,000– $49,999	$50,000– $69,999	$70,000 or more
TOBACCO PRODUCTS AND SMOKING SUPPLIES	$253	$170	$201	$278	$250	$291	$324	$261
MISCELLANEOUS	915	421	384	751	957	767	1,150	1,501
CASH CONTRIBUTIONS	1,403	421	557	995	1,211	1,107	1,559	2,791
PERSONAL INSURANCE AND PENSIONS	4,924	333	813	1,646	2,980	4,386	5,873	12,302
Life and other personal insurance	358	92	121	190	279	244	431	778
Pensions and Social Security	4,566	241	692	1,456	2,701	4,142	5,441	11,524
PERSONAL TAXES	3,396	156	119	548	1,467	2,147	3,589	10,042
Federal income taxes	2,577	92	86	356	1,093	1,598	2,783	7,658
State and local income taxes	677	32	61	128	286	401	661	2,011
Other taxes	142	32	–28	64	87	149	144	373
GIFTS FOR NON–HOUSEHOLD MEMBERS	1,123	433	586	718	644	909	1,051	2,407
Food	75	26	36	32	39	52	55	189
Alcoholic beverages	23	9	8	17	19	15	19	50
Housing	274	98	152	154	144	202	290	594
Housekeeping supplies	51	16	33	29	37	31	79	92
Household textiles	15	10	7	8	15	8	12	31
Appliances and misc. housewares	24	4	17	16	13	13	28	52
Major appliances	8	–	3	3	5	2	15	18
Small appliances and misc. housewares	16	3	15	14	8	11	13	34
Miscellaneous household equipment	61	13	26	39	42	68	82	114
Other housing	123	56	69	62	37	82	89	305
Apparel and services	247	120	139	221	204	176	268	433
Males, aged 2 or older	67	35	38	80	40	52	68	114
Females, aged 2 or older	93	54	48	73	84	32	95	182
Children under age 2	38	15	20	28	47	29	62	51
Other apparel products and services	49	17	33	40	33	63	42	86
Jewelry and watches	20	10	13	9	11	46	19	31
All other apparel products and services	29	6	20	31	22	17	23	55
Transportation	99	25	34	147	27	193	81	160
Health care	33	8	70	16	11	12	21	60
Entertainment	77	32	37	50	68	59	89	144
Toys, games, hobbies, and tricycles	27	11	13	24	24	25	39	41
Other entertainment	50	21	24	26	44	34	50	103
Personal care products and services	21	22	7	20	7	14	28	34
Reading	2	1	1	1	1	1	2	3
Education	172	44	41	17	34	115	82	549
All other gifts	100	48	62	43	89	70	115	192

Note: Spending by category will not add to total spending because gift spending is also included in the preceding product and service categories and personal taxes are not included in the total. (–) means sample is too small to make a reliable estimate.
Source: Bureau of Labor Statistics, 2001 and 2002 Consumer Expenditure Surveys, Internet site http://www.bls.gov/cex/; calculations by New Strategist

Table 1.35 Indexed spending in the West by income, 2001–02

(indexed average annual spending of consumer units (CU) in the West by product and service category and before-tax income of consumer unit, 2001–02; complete income reporters only; index definition: an index of 100 is the average for all consumer units; an index of 132 means that spending by consumer units in that group is 32 percent above the average for all consumer units; an index of 68 indicates spending that is 32 percent below the average for all consumer units)

	complete income reporters in West	under $10,000	$10,000–$19,999	$20,000–$29,999	$30,000–$39,999	$40,000–$49,999	$50,000–$69,999	$70,000 or more
Average spending of CU, total	$45,837	$19,896	$23,645	$31,359	$38,200	$42,753	$54,110	$81,448
Average spending of CU, index	100	43	52	68	83	93	118	178
FOOD	100	54	61	83	87	99	117	154
Food at home	100	57	70	91	99	105	117	135
Cereals and bakery products	100	56	69	91	94	105	117	138
Cereals and cereal products	100	64	69	98	90	117	114	129
Bakery products	100	52	69	88	96	98	119	142
Meats, poultry, fish, and eggs	100	57	75	94	107	101	115	127
Beef	100	52	73	96	112	92	116	130
Pork	100	64	80	93	108	94	112	125
Other meats	100	48	82	93	109	96	112	134
Poultry	100	54	76	101	100	116	113	122
Fish and seafood	100	64	65	80	100	119	119	134
Eggs	100	69	77	107	109	98	114	109
Dairy products	100	60	68	89	93	111	119	135
Fresh milk and cream	100	63	71	105	97	107	119	121
Other dairy products	100	59	65	78	90	114	119	144
Fruits and vegetables	100	57	72	98	98	102	112	133
Fresh fruits	100	62	70	100	95	100	108	136
Fresh vegetables	100	54	74	98	108	103	115	125
Processed fruits	100	57	72	97	95	93	112	138
Processed vegetables	100	50	73	93	88	119	114	134
Other food at home	100	55	67	84	96	106	121	140
Sugar and other sweets	100	46	74	85	91	109	114	145
Fats and oils	100	61	71	105	99	117	119	115
Miscellaneous foods	100	54	64	83	97	110	126	139
Nonalcoholic beverages	100	62	71	84	96	101	118	138
Food prepared by CU on trips	100	38	39	72	103	81	110	190
Food away from home	100	52	50	72	71	91	117	181
ALCOHOLIC BEVERAGES	100	46	51	67	79	91	108	188
HOUSING	100	47	57	71	83	91	113	174
Shelter	100	49	58	69	83	94	114	173
Owned dwellings	100	29	33	48	71	85	123	215
Mortgage interest and charges	100	24	21	39	69	89	125	228
Property taxes	100	42	52	59	69	83	118	194
Maintenance, repair, insurance, other expenses	100	33	61	74	81	72	117	183
Rented dwellings	100	86	108	112	114	116	103	81
Other lodging	100	61	45	55	50	56	87	231
Utilities, fuels, and public services	100	56	70	83	93	100	118	144
Natural gas	100	56	70	77	96	94	120	147
Electricity	100	61	72	91	92	103	115	138
Fuel oil and other fuels	100	71	114	93	95	102	93	114
Telephone	100	56	70	81	94	99	119	143
Water and other public services	100	46	64	74	88	103	122	157

	complete income reporters in West	under $10,000	$10,000–$19,999	$20,000–$29,999	$30,000–$39,999	$40,000–$49,999	$50,000–$69,999	$70,000 or more
Household services	100	30	42	63	68	82	99	216
Personal services	100	12	29	64	56	72	99	244
Other household services	100	44	52	63	77	89	99	196
Housekeeping supplies	100	56	64	84	84	104	122	148
Laundry and cleaning supplies	100	62	81	102	97	107	119	116
Other household products	100	55	60	80	74	104	119	161
Postage and stationery	100	51	56	77	90	101	131	154
Household furnishings and equipment	100	33	41	64	74	68	104	216
Household textiles	100	40	52	116	66	65	77	198
Furniture	100	28	33	58	57	62	104	237
Floor coverings	100	16	70	44	52	65	98	233
Major appliances	100	33	53	62	91	80	112	191
Small appliances, misc. housewares	100	30	50	62	71	56	89	231
Miscellaneous household equipment	100	37	36	58	82	71	111	212
APPAREL AND RELATED SERVICES	100	46	53	68	87	79	117	182
Men and boys	100	34	56	67	77	63	116	199
Men, aged 16 or older	100	35	55	67	74	55	106	209
Boys, aged 2 to 15	100	31	57	64	89	96	157	158
Women and girls	100	55	45	65	94	90	122	172
Women, aged 16 or older	100	59	44	61	88	91	117	180
Girls, aged 2 to 15	100	37	51	82	124	89	148	135
Children under age 2	100	26	45	77	143	92	128	153
Footwear	100	48	64	70	94	74	112	174
Other apparel products and services	100	43	55	72	58	77	106	200
TRANSPORTATION	100	38	49	69	95	104	129	165
Vehicle purchases	100	37	46	68	101	110	134	159
Cars and trucks, new	100	21	34	38	107	127	124	188
Cars and trucks, used	100	52	60	95	98	94	144	130
Other vehicles	100	30	–	129	36	76	121	215
Gasoline and motor oil	100	44	61	78	99	106	123	149
Other vehicle expenses	100	34	47	69	86	101	127	176
Vehicle finance charges	100	24	35	61	104	106	140	174
Maintenance and repairs	100	41	50	79	82	95	117	176
Vehicle insurance	100	36	57	77	96	111	124	156
Vehicle rentals, leases, licenses, other charges	100	27	33	46	64	89	137	210
Public transportation	100	46	50	54	76	67	122	197
HEALTH CARE	100	55	77	96	93	98	112	137
Health insurance	100	52	80	97	97	102	118	129
Medical services	100	54	55	74	83	99	115	167
Drugs	100	63	99	123	101	95	98	110
Medical supplies	100	53	91	119	89	83	100	129
ENTERTAINMENT	100	36	44	56	75	85	133	193
Fees and admissions	100	37	38	50	64	77	112	219
Television, radio, sound equipment	100	54	54	70	91	97	122	162
Pets, toys, and playground equipment	100	32	50	73	70	113	122	179
Other entertainment products and services	100	15	33	37	69	58	176	211
PERSONAL CARE PRODUCTS AND SERVICES	100	53	58	84	85	110	109	157
READING	100	40	56	65	78	95	117	181
EDUCATION	100	153	81	38	43	64	81	174

	complete income reporters in West	under $10,000	$10,000–$19,999	$20,000–$29,999	$30,000–$39,999	$40,000–$49,999	$50,000–$69,999	$70,000 or more
TOBACCO PRODUCTS AND SMOKING SUPPLIES	**100**	**67**	**79**	**110**	**99**	**115**	**128**	**103**
MISCELLANEOUS	**100**	**46**	**42**	**82**	**105**	**84**	**126**	**164**
CASH CONTRIBUTIONS	**100**	**30**	**40**	**71**	**86**	**79**	**111**	**199**
PERSONAL INSURANCE AND PENSIONS	**100**	**7**	**17**	**33**	**61**	**89**	**119**	**250**
Life and other personal insurance	100	26	34	53	78	68	120	217
Pensions and Social Security	100	5	15	32	59	91	119	252
PERSONAL TAXES	**100**	**5**	**4**	**16**	**43**	**63**	**106**	**296**
Federal income taxes	100	4	3	14	42	62	108	297
State and local income taxes	100	5	9	19	42	59	98	297
Other taxes	100	22	–	45	61	105	101	263
GIFTS FOR NON–HOUSEHOLD MEMBERS	**100**	**39**	**52**	**64**	**57**	**81**	**94**	**214**
Food	100	34	48	43	52	69	73	252
Alcoholic beverages	**100**	**41**	**35**	**74**	**83**	**65**	**83**	**217**
Housing	**100**	**36**	**55**	**56**	**53**	**74**	**106**	**217**
Housekeeping supplies	100	31	65	57	73	61	155	180
Household textiles	100	68	44	53	100	53	80	207
Appliances and misc. housewares	100	15	72	67	54	54	117	217
Major appliances	100	–	32	38	63	25	188	225
Small appliances and misc. housewares	100	19	93	88	50	69	81	213
Miscellaneous household equipment	100	21	42	64	69	111	134	187
Other housing	100	45	56	50	30	67	72	248
Apparel and services	**100**	**49**	**56**	**89**	**83**	**71**	**109**	**175**
Males, aged 2 or older	100	52	57	119	60	78	101	170
Females, aged 2 or older	100	58	51	78	90	34	102	196
Children under age 2	100	40	53	74	124	76	163	134
Other apparel products and services	100	34	68	82	67	129	86	176
Jewelry and watches	100	52	66	45	55	230	95	155
All other apparel products and services	100	22	70	107	76	59	79	190
Transportation	**100**	**25**	**35**	**148**	**27**	**195**	**82**	**162**
Health care	**100**	**23**	**211**	**48**	**33**	**36**	**64**	**182**
Entertainment	**100**	**42**	**48**	**65**	**88**	**77**	**116**	**187**
Toys, games, hobbies, and tricycles	100	41	46	89	89	93	144	152
Other entertainment	100	42	48	52	88	68	100	206
Personal care products and services	**100**	**103**	**34**	**95**	**33**	**67**	**133**	**162**
Reading	**100**	**50**	**53**	**50**	**50**	**50**	**100**	**150**
Education	**100**	**26**	**24**	**10**	**20**	**67**	**48**	**319**
All other gifts	**100**	**48**	**62**	**43**	**89**	**70**	**115**	**192**

Note: (–) means sample is too small to make a reliable estimate.
Source: Calculations by New Strategist based on the Bureau of Labor Statistics 2001 and 2002 Consumer Expenditure Surveys

Spending by Metropolitan Area, 2001–02

Within regions, spending levels vary considerably by metropolitan area. Among the four Northeastern metropolitan areas examined by the Consumer Expenditure Survey, average household spending ranged from $40,245 in Boston to $49,931 in New York in 2001–02. In the Midwest, spending ranged from $38,125 in Cleveland to $52,581 in Minneapolis–St. Paul. Among selected metropolitan areas in the South, spending was greatest in Dallas ($50,281) and least in Tampa ($38,167). In the West, Anchorage had the highest spending ($56,169)—not only for the region, but among all the metropolitan areas included in the survey. Among Western metropolitan areas, household spending was lowest in Phoenix ($41,615).

Spending levels by metropolitan area vary significantly by product and service category. Households in Boston spend much more on rent than the average household in Philadelphia or Pittsburgh, despite the higher overall spending in those metro areas. Households in Pittsburgh spend much more on entertainment than those in Boston, New York, or Philadelphia.

Households in Minneapolis–St. Paul spend more than twice as much as households in Cleveland on alcoholic beverages. But households in Cleveland spend more than those in Minneapolis–St. Paul on utilities, fuels, and public services.

In the South, households in Houston spend significantly more on alcoholic beverages than households in the other metropolitan areas. Households in Atlanta spend the least on entertainment.

In the West, spending on tobacco is 20 percent below average in Los Angeles, but more than twice the average in Anchorage. Spending on owned dwellings is 20 percent below the Western average in Honolulu and 19 percent lower in Phoenix.

Table 1.36 Average spending in selected Northeastern metros, 2001–02

(average annual spending of consumer units in selected Northeastern metropolitan areas by product and service category, 2001–02)

	total consumer units in the Northeast	Boston	New York	Philadelphia	Pittsburgh
Number of consumer units (in thousands, add 000s)	21,127	2,552	7,434	2,200	938
Average number of persons per consumer unit	2.5	2.4	2.7	2.7	2.3
Average income before taxes	$52,296	$56,680	$62,998	$56,687	$48,097
Average annual spending	41,785	40,245	49,931	40,346	41,626
FOOD	**$5,756**	**$5,659**	**$6,859**	**$5,168**	**$5,575**
Food at home	**3,347**	**3,378**	**3,855**	**2,831**	**3,224**
Cereals and bakery products	504	484	588	450	499
Meats, poultry, fish, and eggs	908	943	1,122	747	832
Dairy products	362	366	398	317	344
Fruits and vegetables	606	598	737	525	519
Other food at home	966	986	1,011	791	1,030
Food away from home	**2,409**	**2,281**	**3,004**	**2,338**	**2,351**
ALCOHOLIC BEVERAGES	**423**	**477**	**454**	**424**	**454**
HOUSING	**14,499**	**14,693**	**18,668**	**14,583**	**12,018**
Shelter	**8,952**	**9,685**	**12,203**	**8,713**	**6,363**
Owned dwellings	5,791	5,924	7,627	6,587	4,237
Rented dwellings	2,551	3,082	3,864	1,610	1,514
Other lodging	610	679	712	516	612
Utilities, fuels, and public services	**2,793**	**2,668**	**3,004**	**3,114**	**2,844**
Household services	**791**	**675**	**1,168**	**766**	**681**
Housekeeping supplies	**508**	**416**	**548**	**493**	**607**
Household furnishings and equipment	**1,455**	**1,249**	**1,745**	**1,497**	**1,523**
APPAREL AND RELATED SERVICES	**2,017**	**1,480**	**2,840**	**2,175**	**1,700**
TRANSPORTATION	**7,190**	**6,953**	**7,658**	**6,466**	**8,086**
Vehicle purchases	3,083	3,021	2,917	2,341	3,857
Gasoline and motor oil	1,084	1,134	1,051	1,146	1,117
Other vehicle expenses	2,429	2,363	2,618	2,672	2,721
Public transportation	593	435	1,071	308	392
HEALTH CARE	**2,146**	**2,056**	**2,277**	**2,068**	**2,339**
ENTERTAINMENT	**2,072**	**2,043**	**2,232**	**2,054**	**2,407**
PERSONAL CARE PRODUCTS AND SERVICES	**499**	**444**	**629**	**486**	**540**
READING	**167**	**187**	**177**	**140**	**168**
EDUCATION	**897**	**855**	**1,063**	**801**	**1,012**
TOBACCO PRODUCTS AND SMOKING SUPPLIES	**310**	**330**	**267**	**294**	**411**
MISCELLANEOUS	**858**	**496**	**1,313**	**747**	**996**
CASH CONTRIBUTIONS	**1,104**	**690**	**1,055**	**961**	**2,108**
PERSONAL INSURANCE AND PENSIONS	**3,848**	**3,880**	**4,439**	**3,977**	**3,812**
Life and other personal insurance	432	259	433	448	420
Pensions and Social Security	3,415	3,621	4,005	3,529	3,392

Source: Bureau of Labor Statistics, 2001 and 2002 Consumer Expenditure Surveys, Internet site http://www.bls.gov/cex/

Table 1.37 Indexed spending in selected Northeastern metros, 2001–02

(indexed average annual spending of consumer units in selected Northeastern metropolitan areas by product and service category, 2001–02; index definition: an index of 100 is the average for all consumer units; an index of 132 means that spending by consumer units in that group is 32 percent above the average for all consumer units; an index of 68 indicates spending that is 32 percent below the average for all consumer units)

	total consumer units in the Northeast	Boston	New York	Philadelphia	Pittsburgh
Average spending of consumer unit, total	$41,785	$40,245	$49,931	$40,346	$41,626
Average spending of consumer unit, index	100	96	119	97	100
FOOD	100	98	119	90	97
Food at home	100	101	115	85	96
Cereals and bakery products	100	96	117	89	99
Meats, poultry, fish, and eggs	100	104	124	82	92
Dairy products	100	101	110	88	95
Fruits and vegetables	100	99	122	87	86
Other food at home	100	102	105	82	107
Food away from home	100	95	125	97	98
ALCOHOLIC BEVERAGES	100	113	107	100	107
HOUSING	100	101	129	101	83
Shelter	100	108	136	97	71
Owned dwellings	100	102	132	114	73
Rented dwellings	100	121	151	63	59
Other lodging	100	111	117	85	100
Utilities, fuels, and public services	100	96	108	111	102
Huosehold services	100	85	148	97	86
Housekeeping supplies	100	82	108	97	119
Household furnishings and equipment	100	86	120	103	105
APPAREL AND RELATED SERVICES	100	73	141	108	84
TRANSPORTATION	100	97	107	90	112
Vehicle purchases	100	98	95	76	125
Gasoline and motor oil	100	105	97	106	103
Other vehicle expenses	100	97	108	110	112
Public transportation	100	73	181	52	66
HEALTH CARE	100	96	106	96	109
ENTERTAINMENT	100	99	108	99	116
PERSONAL CARE PRODUCTS AND SERVICES	100	89	126	97	108
READING	100	112	106	84	101
EDUCATION	100	95	119	89	113
TOBACCO PRODUCTS AND SMOKING SUPPLIES	100	106	86	95	133
MISCELLANEOUS	100	58	153	87	116
CASH CONTRIBUTIONS	100	63	96	87	191
PERSONAL INSURANCE AND PENSIONS	100	101	115	103	99
Life and other personal insurance	100	60	100	104	97
Pensions and Social Security	100	106	117	103	99

Source: Calculations by New Strategist based on the Bureau of Labor Statistics 2001 and 2002 Consumer Expenditure Surveys

Table 1.38 Average spending in selected Midwestern metros, 2001–02

(average annual spending of consumer units (CU) in selected Midwestern metropolitan areas by product and service category, 2001–02)

	total consumer units in the Midwest	Chicago	Cincinnati	Cleveland	Detroit	Kansas City	Milwaukee	Minneapolis–St. Paul	St. Louis
Number of consumer units (in thousands, add 000s)	25,863	3,072	911	1,225	2,072	774	711	1,261	1,004
Average number of persons per CU	2.5	2.8	2.4	2.4	2.6	2.6	2.5	2.3	2.4
Average income before taxes	$48,439	$61,853	$51,278	$49,660	$54,200	$59,689	$47,715	$64,159	$52,977
Average annual spending	40,074	47,861	40,421	38,125	44,491	43,201	40,341	52,581	43,034
FOOD	$5,116	$5,934	$5,547	$4,700	$5,422	$5,736	$5,280	$6,270	$5,951
Food at home	2,912	3,358	3,047	2,783	2,989	3,497	2,898	3,470	3,626
Cereals and bakery products	435	508	471	407	461	525	421	493	565
Meats, poultry, fish, and eggs	713	819	794	802	779	906	716	740	938
Dairy products	324	341	332	294	310	368	288	446	388
Fruits and vegetables	474	617	452	461	528	573	488	582	597
Other food at home	966	1,072	998	819	911	1,125	985	1,209	1,139
Food away from home	2,204	2,576	2,500	1,917	2,434	2,239	2,382	2,799	2,325
ALCOHOLIC BEVERAGES	378	510	410	279	421	322	565	575	391
HOUSING	12,549	17,239	12,912	12,698	14,663	13,962	13,968	16,668	13,220
Shelter	7,077	10,668	7,665	7,421	8,748	7,801	8,530	10,141	7,479
Owned dwellings	4,958	7,676	4,768	5,453	6,520	5,506	5,160	7,070	4,917
Rented dwellings	1,603	2,152	2,595	1,488	1,574	1,868	2,896	2,372	1,957
Other lodging	515	840	302	480	654	427	474	700	604
Utilities, fuels, and public services	2,752	3,206	2,609	3,024	2,904	3,406	2,462	2,648	2,948
Huosehold services	592	820	641	595	726	645	660	827	914
Housekeeping supplies	600	622	528	439	506	557	545	675	462
Household furnishings and equipment	1,528	1,922	1,469	1,219	1,779	1,553	1,772	2,377	1,417
APPAREL AND RELATED SERVICES	1,712	2,458	2,099	1,722	2,337	1,484	1,861	2,017	1,885
TRANSPORTATION	7,907	8,571	8,009	7,655	8,870	8,087	6,796	9,266	8,077
Vehicle purchases	3,765	4,061	3,932	3,470	3,376	3,579	3,007	4,104	4,023
Gasoline and motor oil	1,318	1,327	1,183	1,177	1,380	1,551	1,207	1,425	1,241
Other vehicle expenses	2,476	2,476	2,638	2,601	3,649	2,635	2,274	3,082	2,382
Public transportation	348	707	255	407	465	321	308	654	431
HEALTH CARE	2,338	2,255	2,034	1,929	2,155	2,528	2,175	2,297	2,184
ENTERTAINMENT	2,182	2,463	2,050	1,950	2,356	2,239	2,084	3,457	2,078
PERSONAL CARE PRODUCTS, SERVICES	499	585	582	393	651	511	491	568	759
READING	156	151	175	152	170	156	176	233	130
EDUCATION	703	948	725	809	694	541	643	793	646
TOBACCO PRODUCTS AND SMOKING SUPPLIES	385	313	389	367	394	287	385	303	303
MISCELLANEOUS	739	1,218	676	701	850	773	627	1,230	702
CASH CONTRIBUTIONS	1,452	1,116	1,187	863	1,613	1,598	1,499	2,533	1,598
PERSONAL INSURANCE AND PENSIONS	3,959	4,102	3,626	3,907	3,896	4,978	3,790	6,371	5,110
Life and other personal insurance	461	392	382	508	383	417	364	699	884
Pensions and Social Security	3,498	3,710	3,244	3,398	3,513	4,561	3,426	5,672	4,226

Source: Bureau of Labor Statistics, 2001 and 2002 Consumer Expenditure Surveys, Internet site http://www.bls.gov/cex/

Table 1.39 Indexed spending in selected Midwestern metros, 2001–02

(indexed average annual spending of consumer units (CU) in selected Midwestern metropolitan areas by product and service category, 2001–02; index definition: an index of 100 is the average for all consumer units; an index of 132 means that spending by consumer units in that group is 32 percent above the average for all consumer units; an index of 68 indicates spending that is 32 percent below the average for all consumer units)

	total consumer units in the Midwest	Chicago	Cincinnati	Cleveland	Detroit	Kansas City	Milwaukee	Minneapolis– St. Paul	St. Louis
Average spending of CU, total	$40,074	$47,861	$40,421	$38,125	$44,491	$43,201	$40,341	$52,581	$43,034
Average spending of CU, index	100	119	101	95	111	108	101	131	107
FOOD	100	116	108	92	106	112	103	123	116
Food at home	100	115	105	96	103	120	100	119	125
Cereals and bakery products	100	117	108	94	106	121	97	113	130
Meats, poultry, fish, and eggs	100	115	111	112	109	127	100	104	132
Dairy products	100	105	102	91	96	114	89	138	120
Fruits and vegetables	100	130	95	97	111	121	103	123	126
Other food at home	100	111	103	85	94	116	102	125	118
Food away from home	100	117	113	87	110	102	108	127	105
ALCOHOLIC BEVERAGES	100	135	108	74	111	85	149	152	103
HOUSING	100	137	103	101	117	111	111	133	105
Shelter	100	151	108	105	124	110	121	143	106
Owned dwellings	100	155	96	110	132	111	104	143	99
Rented dwellings	100	134	162	93	98	117	181	148	122
Other lodging	100	163	59	93	127	83	92	136	117
Utilities, fuels, and public services	100	116	95	110	106	124	89	96	107
Huosehold services	100	139	108	101	123	109	111	140	154
Housekeeping supplies	100	104	88	73	84	93	91	113	77
Household furnishings and equipment	100	126	96	80	116	102	116	156	93
APPAREL AND RELATED SERVICES	100	144	123	101	137	87	109	118	110
TRANSPORTATION	100	108	101	97	112	102	86	117	102
Vehicle purchases	100	108	104	92	90	95	80	109	107
Gasoline and motor oil	100	101	90	89	105	118	92	108	94
Other vehicle expenses	100	100	107	105	147	106	92	124	96
Public transportation	100	203	73	117	134	92	89	188	124
HEALTH CARE	100	96	87	83	92	108	93	98	93
ENTERTAINMENT	100	113	94	89	108	103	96	158	95
PERSONAL CARE PRODUCTS, SERVICES	100	117	117	79	130	102	98	114	152
READING	100	97	112	97	109	100	113	149	83
EDUCATION	100	135	103	115	99	77	91	113	92
TOBACCO PRODUCTS AND SMOKING SUPPLIES	100	81	101	95	102	75	100	79	79
MISCELLANEOUS	100	165	91	95	115	105	85	166	95
CASH CONTRIBUTIONS	100	77	82	59	111	110	103	174	110
PERSONAL INSURANCE AND PENSIONS	100	104	92	99	98	126	96	161	129
Life and other personal insurance	100	85	83	110	83	90	79	152	192
Pensions and Social Security	100	106	93	97	100	130	98	162	121

Source: Calculations by New Strategist based on the Bureau of Labor Statistics 2001 and 2002 Consumer Expenditure Surveys

Table 1.40 Average spending in selected Southern metros, 2001–02

(average annual spending of consumer units in selected Southern metropolitan areas by product and service category, 2001–02)

	total consumer units in the South	Atlanta	Baltimore	Dallas–Fort Worth	Houston	Miami	Tampa	Washington, D.C.
Number of consumer units (in thousands, add 000s)	39,591	1,766	996	2,071	1,758	1,564	1,020	1,924
Average number of persons per consumer unit	2.5	2.7	2.5	2.7	2.8	2.8	2.5	2.5
Average income before taxes	$44,943	$60,998	$56,830	$62,185	$54,804	$46,846	$53,091	$68,352
Average annual spending	36,788	40,492	38,628	50,281	47,523	41,850	38,167	47,775
FOOD	$5,127	$4,986	$5,737	$7,374	$6,373	$5,885	$3,888	$5,867
Food at home	2,972	2,658	3,322	4,077	3,164	3,394	2,298	3,114
Cereals and bakery products	426	349	478	580	448	475	313	469
Meats, poultry, fish, and eggs	828	801	1,016	1,152	848	996	657	748
Dairy products	300	253	299	411	338	375	247	339
Fruits and vegetables	497	514	559	672	535	663	429	609
Other food at home	921	742	970	1,262	994	885	652	949
Food away from home	2,155	2,328	2,415	3,298	3,210	2,490	1,589	2,753
ALCOHOLIC BEVERAGES	290	287	426	393	475	400	283	391
HOUSING	11,573	14,965	13,440	15,754	15,049	15,622	13,112	18,105
Shelter	6,291	8,998	8,202	9,047	8,127	9,823	7,752	11,545
Owned dwellings	4,159	6,397	5,546	5,849	4,951	6,321	5,228	8,252
Rented dwellings	1,749	2,175	2,056	2,689	2,726	3,228	2,023	2,537
Other lodging	383	427	601	509	451	274	501	756
Utilities, fuels, and public services	2,809	3,420	2,671	3,456	3,262	3,038	2,946	2,954
Huosehold services	655	859	641	902	1,198	975	826	977
Housekeeping supplies	492	378	626	583	582	647	374	578
Household furnishings and equipment	1,325	1,310	1,299	1,765	1,881	1,138	1,213	2,051
APPAREL AND RELATED SERVICES	1,597	1,548	2,007	2,528	2,112	1,720	1,057	2,032
TRANSPORTATION	7,420	7,458	5,108	10,051	9,536	7,617	8,850	7,543
Vehicle purchases	3,701	3,504	1,643	5,160	4,473	3,097	4,886	3,256
Gasoline and motor oil	1,241	1,276	1,182	1,506	1,525	1,315	1,219	1,242
Other vehicle expenses	2,206	2,392	1,970	3,033	3,044	2,781	2,518	2,331
Public transportation	273	286	313	352	494	424	227	714
HEALTH CARE	2,314	2,010	1,840	2,432	2,449	1,969	2,282	2,201
ENTERTAINMENT	1,678	1,401	1,760	2,201	2,516	1,579	1,591	2,711
PERSONAL CARE PRODUCTS AND SERVICES	489	359	646	648	674	611	387	640
READING	102	76	111	133	128	73	82	171
EDUCATION	485	412	714	385	528	982	469	690
TOBACCO PRODUCTS AND SMOKING SUPPLIES	318	204	332	256	363	291	357	190
MISCELLANEOUS	686	1,065	617	556	936	1,088	721	816
CASH CONTRIBUTIONS	1,200	1,253	815	1,446	1,677	738	981	1,242
PERSONAL INSURANCE AND PENSIONS	3,510	4,468	5,076	6,126	4,707	3,273	4,107	5,177
Life and other personal insurance	403	515	371	437	412	255	411	503
Pensions and Social Security	3,107	3,953	4,705	5,689	4,295	3,018	3,696	4,674

Source: Bureau of Labor Statistics, 2001 and 2002 Consumer Expenditure Surveys, Internet site http://www.bls.gov/cex/

Table 1.41 Indexed spending in selected Southern metros, 2001–02

(indexed average annual spending of consumer units (CU) in selected Southern metropolitan areas by product and service category, 2001–02; index definition: an index of 100 is the average for all consumer units; an index of 132 means that spending by consumer units in that group is 32 percent above the average for all consumer units; an index of 68 indicates spending that is 32 percent below the average for all consumer units)

	total consumer units in the South	Atlanta	Baltimore	Dallas–Fort Worth	Houston	Miami	Tampa	Washington, D.C.
Average spending of CU, total	$36,788	$40,492	$38,628	$50,281	$47,523	$41,850	$38,167	$47,775
Average spending of CU, index	100	110	105	137	129	114	104	130
FOOD	100	97	112	144	124	115	76	114
Food at home	100	89	112	137	106	114	77	105
Cereals and bakery products	100	82	112	136	105	112	73	110
Meats, poultry, fish, and eggs	100	97	123	139	102	120	79	90
Dairy products	100	84	100	137	113	125	82	113
Fruits and vegetables	100	103	112	135	108	133	86	123
Other food at home	100	81	105	137	108	96	71	103
Food away from home	100	108	112	153	149	116	74	128
ALCOHOLIC BEVERAGES	100	99	147	136	164	138	98	135
HOUSING	100	129	116	136	130	135	113	156
Shelter	100	143	130	144	129	156	123	184
Owned dwellings	100	154	133	141	119	152	126	198
Rented dwellings	100	124	118	154	156	185	116	145
Other lodging	100	111	157	133	118	72	131	197
Utilities, fuels, and public services	100	122	95	123	116	108	105	105
Huosehold services	100	131	98	138	183	149	126	149
Housekeeping supplies	100	77	127	118	118	132	76	117
Household furnishings and equipment	100	99	98	133	142	86	92	155
APPAREL AND RELATED SERVICES	100	97	126	158	132	108	66	127
TRANSPORTATION	100	101	69	135	129	103	119	102
Vehicle purchases	100	95	44	139	121	84	132	88
Gasoline and motor oil	100	103	95	121	123	106	98	100
Other vehicle expenses	100	108	89	137	138	126	114	106
Public transportation	100	105	115	129	181	155	83	262
HEALTH CARE	100	87	80	105	106	85	99	95
ENTERTAINMENT	100	83	105	131	150	94	95	162
PERSONAL CARE PRODUCTS AND SERVICES	100	73	132	133	138	125	79	131
READING	100	75	109	130	125	72	80	168
EDUCATION	100	85	147	79	109	202	97	142
TOBACCO PRODUCTS AND SMOKING SUPPLIES	100	64	104	81	114	92	112	60
MISCELLANEOUS	100	155	90	81	136	159	105	119
CASH CONTRIBUTIONS	100	104	68	121	140	62	82	104
PERSONAL INSURANCE AND PENSIONS	100	127	145	175	134	93	117	147
Life and other personal insurance	100	128	92	108	102	63	102	125
Pensions and Social Security	100	127	151	183	138	97	119	150

Source: Calculations by New Strategist based on the Bureau of Labor Statistics 2001 and 2002 Consumer Expenditure Surveys

Table 1.42 Average spending in selected Western metros, 2001–02

(average annual spending of consumer units (CU) in selected Western metropolitan areas by product and service category, 2001–02)

	total consumer units in the West	Anchorage	Denver	Honolulu	Los Angeles	Phoenix	Portland	San Diego	San Francisco	Seattle
Number of consumer units (in thousands, add 000s)	24,643	99	1,239	276	5,026	1,233	1,098	852	2,768	1,525
Average number of persons per CU	2.6	2.7	2.5	2.8	2.8	2.5	2.5	2.6	2.5	2.4
Average income before taxes	$51,003	$63,144	$60,983	$56,000	$55,543	$48,021	$52,021	$47,722	$75,270	$58,488
Average annual spending	44,002	56,169	49,014	43,458	47,459	41,615	43,358	42,588	55,346	48,348
FOOD	$5,590	$6,993	$5,819	$6,418	$5,883	$5,252	$5,203	$5,036	$6,453	$6,019
Food at home	3,250	4,056	3,442	3,879	3,215	3,029	2,971	2,734	3,423	4,143
Cereals and bakery products	462	547	514	542	438	456	414	367	498	574
Meats, poultry, fish, and eggs	811	1,016	789	1,182	862	721	671	721	826	1,028
Dairy products	356	431	401	336	347	337	344	307	359	430
Fruits and vegetables	606	709	606	750	633	542	485	510	733	722
Other food at home	1,015	1,352	1,132	1,069	936	974	1,058	829	1,007	1,390
Food away from home	2,340	2,937	2,377	2,539	2,668	2,222	2,232	2,301	3,029	1,875
ALCOHOLIC BEVERAGES	410	529	534	489	414	473	493	354	605	443
HOUSING	15,150	17,299	16,862	14,207	17,602	13,897	15,095	17,050	21,127	16,621
Shelter	9,618	10,628	10,590	9,470	11,675	8,116	9,476	11,465	14,592	10,685
Owned dwellings	6,043	6,323	6,708	4,810	7,021	4,912	6,180	6,883	8,960	6,991
Rented dwellings	3,011	3,699	3,410	4,030	4,065	2,657	2,681	4,138	4,932	3,047
Other lodging	564	607	472	630	589	548	614	443	700	647
Utilities, fuels, and public services	2,504	2,656	2,626	2,200	2,576	2,695	2,631	2,454	2,645	2,753
Huosehold services	766	950	829	569	1,012	699	808	935	1,326	800
Housekeeping supplies	525	592	584	567	478	550	377	429	514	572
Household furnishings, equipment	1,737	2,472	2,232	1,402	1,861	1,837	1,804	1,767	2,050	1,811
APPAREL, RELATED SERVICES	1,786	1,992	1,712	1,597	2,001	1,537	1,586	1,435	2,245	1,753
TRANSPORTATION	8,355	10,860	10,077	7,230	8,861	8,197	6,989	7,806	9,223	9,680
Vehicle purchases	3,808	5,242	4,676	3,040	3,923	3,632	2,673	3,424	3,962	4,424
Gasoline and motor oil	1,366	1,455	1,297	1,124	1,475	1,253	1,235	1,335	1,472	1,392
Other vehicle expenses	2,713	3,211	3,601	2,194	2,955	2,876	2,511	2,643	2,962	3,337
Public transportation	468	953	503	873	508	436	570	404	828	528
HEALTH CARE	2,221	2,484	2,393	2,365	2,031	2,241	2,353	1,884	2,349	2,326
ENTERTAINMENT	2,339	4,297	2,633	2,249	2,301	2,436	2,711	1,965	2,383	2,835
PERSONAL CARE PRODUCTS AND SERVICES	545	628	637	594	608	544	506	519	555	556
READING	160	290	141	161	158	142	218	145	270	172
EDUCATION	874	729	617	1,088	826	444	750	504	1,073	889
TOBACCO PRODUCTS AND SMOKING SUPPLIES	238	508	307	297	190	298	302	195	228	303
MISCELLANEOUS	869	1,387	1,075	759	1,037	785	1,107	869	997	848
CASH CONTRIBUTIONS	1,324	1,891	1,495	1,278	1,223	1,131	1,468	925	1,544	1,086
PERSONAL INSURANCE AND PENSIONS	4,141	6,280	4,713	4,727	4,325	4,238	4,577	3,903	6,294	4,816
Life and other personal insurance	340	543	447	641	318	387	326	377	357	392
Pensions and Social Security	3,801	5,737	4,265	4,086	4,007	3,851	4,251	3,526	5,936	4,424

Source: Bureau of Labor Statistics, 2001 and 2002 Consumer Expenditure Surveys, Internet site http://www.bls.gov/cex/

Table 1.43 Indexed spending in selected Western metros, 2001–02

(indexed average annual spending of consumer units (CU) in selected Western metropolitan areas by product and service category, 2001–02; index definition: an index of 100 is the average for all consumer units; an index of 132 means that spending by consumer units in that group is 32 percent above the average for all consumer units; an index of 68 indicates spending that is 32 percent below the average for all consumer units)

	total consumer units in the West	Anchorage	Denver	Honolulu	Los Angeles	Phoenix	Portland	San Diego	San Francisco	Seattle
Average spending of CU, total	$44,002	$56,169	$49,014	$43,458	$47,459	$41,615	$43,358	$42,588	$55,346	$48,348
Average spending of CU, index	100	128	111	99	108	95	99	97	126	110
FOOD	100	125	104	115	105	94	93	90	115	108
Food at home	100	125	106	119	99	93	91	84	105	127
Cereals and bakery products	100	118	111	117	95	99	90	79	108	124
Meats, poultry, fish, and eggs	100	125	97	146	106	89	83	89	102	127
Dairy products	100	121	113	94	97	95	97	86	101	121
Fruits and vegetables	100	117	100	124	104	89	80	84	121	119
Other food at home	100	133	112	105	92	96	104	82	99	137
Food away from home	100	126	102	109	114	95	95	98	129	80
ALCOHOLIC BEVERAGES	100	129	130	119	101	115	120	86	148	108
HOUSING	100	114	111	94	116	92	100	113	139	110
Shelter	100	111	110	98	121	84	99	119	152	111
Owned dwellings	100	105	111	80	116	81	102	114	148	116
Rented dwellings	100	123	113	134	135	88	89	137	164	101
Other lodging	100	108	84	112	104	97	109	79	124	115
Utilities, fuels, and public services	100	106	105	88	103	108	105	98	106	110
Huosehold services	100	124	108	74	132	91	105	122	173	104
Housekeeping supplies	100	113	111	108	91	105	72	82	98	109
Household furnishings, equipment	100	142	128	81	107	106	104	102	118	104
APPAREL, RELATED SERVICES	100	112	96	89	112	86	89	80	126	98
TRANSPORTATION	100	130	121	87	106	98	84	93	110	116
Vehicle purchases	100	138	123	80	103	95	70	90	104	116
Gasoline and motor oil	100	107	95	82	108	92	90	98	108	102
Other vehicle expenses	100	118	133	81	109	106	93	97	109	123
Public transportation	100	204	107	187	109	93	122	86	177	113
HEALTH CARE	100	112	108	106	91	101	106	85	106	105
ENTERTAINMENT	100	184	113	96	98	104	116	84	102	121
PERSONAL CARE PRODUCTS AND SERVICES	100	115	117	109	112	100	93	95	102	102
READING	100	181	88	101	99	89	136	91	169	108
EDUCATION	100	83	71	124	95	51	86	58	123	102
TOBACCO PRODUCTS AND SMOKING SUPPLIES	100	213	129	125	80	125	127	82	96	127
MISCELLANEOUS	100	160	124	87	119	90	127	100	115	98
CASH CONTRIBUTIONS	100	143	113	97	92	85	111	70	117	82
PERSONAL INSURANCE AND PENSIONS	100	152	114	114	104	102	111	94	152	116
Life and other personal insurance	100	160	131	189	94	114	96	111	105	115
Pensions and Social Security	100	151	112	107	105	101	112	93	156	116

Source: Calculations by New Strategist based on the Bureau of Labor Statistics 2001 and 2002 Consumer Expenditure Surveys

Spending by Race and Hispanic Origin, 2002

Hispanics and blacks spend less overall than non-Hispanic whites because their incomes are considerably lower. In 2002, whites and others (this category includes American Indians, Asians, and Pacific Islanders) spent an average of $42,135 versus the $30,136 spent by blacks. Non-Hispanics spent $41,295 versus the $34,742 spent by Hispanics.

Despite lower overall spending, Hispanic and black spending exceeds that of the average household in many categories. Because of their larger families, Hispanic households spend 18 percent more than average on food at home. They spend 32 percent more on meats, poultry, fish, and eggs, and 36 to 41 percent more on fresh fruits and vegetables. Hispanics spend 33 percent more than the average household on laundry and cleaning supplies and 20 percent more on apparel.

Blacks spend 25 percent more than average on pork and 17 percent more on poultry. They spend 10 percent more on telephone services, 38 percent more on boys' clothes, 19 percent more on girls' clothes, and 29 percent more on shoes.

Table 1.44 Average spending by race and Hispanic origin of householder, 2002

(average annual spending of consumer units (CU) by product and service category and by race and Hispanic origin of consumer unit reference person, 2002)

	total consumer units	race		Hispanic origin	
		black	white and other	Hispanic	non-Hispanic
Number of consumer units (in thousands, add 000s)	112,108	13,554	98,553	10,500	101,608
Average number of persons per CU	2.5	2.7	2.5	3.3	2.4
Average income before taxes	$49,430	$35,944	$51,177	$37,360	$50,742
Average annual spending	40,677	30,136	42,135	34,742	41,295
FOOD	**$5,375**	**$4,186**	**$5,542**	**$5,666**	**$5,349**
Food at home	**3,099**	**2,669**	**3,159**	**3,643**	**3,047**
Cereals and bakery products	450	390	459	498	446
Cereals and cereal products	154	152	154	191	151
Bakery products	296	238	304	308	295
Meats, poultry, fish, and eggs	798	862	789	1,057	774
Beef	231	220	233	334	221
Pork	167	208	162	216	163
Other meats	101	96	102	110	100
Poultry	144	168	141	202	139
Fish and seafood	121	133	119	137	119
Eggs	34	37	33	58	31
Dairy products	328	232	342	385	323
Fresh milk and cream	127	96	131	168	123
Other dairy products	201	135	211	217	200
Fruits and vegetables	552	460	565	720	536
Fresh fruits	178	136	184	242	172
Fresh vegetables	175	128	181	247	168
Processed fruits	116	114	116	138	113
Processed vegetables	83	82	84	92	83
Other food at home	970	725	1,004	982	968
Sugar and other sweets	117	91	121	110	118
Fats and oils	85	81	86	102	84
Miscellaneous foods	472	340	491	458	473
Nonalcoholic beverages	254	199	262	279	252
Food prepared by CU on trips	41	13	45	32	42
Food away from home	**2,276**	**1,517**	**2,383**	**2,023**	**2,302**
ALCOHOLIC BEVERAGES	**376**	**190**	**402**	**301**	**383**
HOUSING	**13,283**	**10,756**	**13,633**	**11,841**	**13,431**
Shelter	**7,829**	**6,279**	**8,043**	**7,372**	**7,877**
Owned dwellings	5,165	3,223	5,432	3,567	5,330
Mortgage interest and charges	2,962	2,000	3,095	2,232	3,038
Property taxes	1,242	669	1,321	696	1,299
Maintenance, repair, insurance, other expenses	960	554	1,016	639	994
Rented dwellings	2,160	2,852	2,065	3,645	2,006
Other lodging	505	204	546	161	540
Utilities, fuels, and public services	**2,684**	**2,768**	**2,673**	**2,413**	**2,712**
Natural gas	330	380	323	245	338
Electricity	981	1,034	974	808	999
Fuel oil and other fuels	88	30	96	46	93
Telephone	957	1,050	944	1,021	950
Water and other public services	328	274	336	292	332

	total consumer units	race		Hispanic origin	
		black	white and other	Hispanic	non-Hispanic
Household services	**$706**	**$509**	**$733**	**$407**	**$737**
Personal services	331	287	337	212	343
Other household services	375	222	396	195	393
Housekeeping supplies	**545**	**313**	**578**	**471**	**552**
Laundry and cleaning supplies	131	124	131	174	126
Other household products	283	124	306	225	289
Postage and stationery	131	65	141	72	137
Household furnishings and equipment	**1,518**	**887**	**1,606**	**1,179**	**1,553**
Household textiles	136	68	145	141	135
Furniture	401	293	416	345	407
Floor coverings	40	27	42	13	43
Major appliances	188	173	191	148	193
Small appliances, misc. housewares	100	51	107	91	101
Miscellaneous household equipment	652	276	705	441	673
APPAREL AND RELATED SERVICES	**1,749**	**1,704**	**1,756**	**2,097**	**1,716**
Men and boys	**409**	**363**	**416**	**551**	**396**
Men, aged 16 or older	319	239	331	413	311
Boys, aged 2 to 15	90	124	85	138	85
Women and girls	**704**	**649**	**712**	**638**	**710**
Women, aged 16 or older	587	510	598	479	597
Girls, aged 2 to 15	117	139	114	159	113
Children under age 2	**83**	**81**	**83**	**142**	**77**
Footwear	**313**	**404**	**300**	**521**	**294**
Other apparel products and services	**240**	**207**	**244**	**245**	**239**
TRANSPORTATION	**7,759**	**5,447**	**8,077**	**6,769**	**7,861**
Vehicle purchases	**3,665**	**2,420**	**3,836**	**3,130**	**3,720**
Cars and trucks, new	1,753	1,000	1,857	1,149	1,815
Cars and trucks, used	1,842	1,410	1,902	1,900	1,836
Other vehicles	70	11	78	81	68
Gasoline and motor oil	**1,235**	**925**	**1,278**	**1,261**	**1,232**
Other vehicle expenses	**2,471**	**1,875**	**2,553**	**2,062**	**2,513**
Vehicle finance charges	397	335	406	407	396
Maintenance and repairs	697	499	725	529	714
Vehicle insurance	894	692	921	799	903
Vehicle rentals, leases, licenses, other charges	483	349	501	327	499
Public transportation	**389**	**228**	**411**	**317**	**396**
HEALTH CARE	**2,350**	**1,339**	**2,490**	**1,366**	**2,452**
Health insurance	1,168	747	1,226	671	1,219
Medical services	590	247	637	358	614
Drugs	487	295	514	271	510
Medical supplies	105	50	113	66	109
ENTERTAINMENT	**2,079**	**1,124**	**2,211**	**1,409**	**2,148**
Fees and admissions	542	203	588	289	568
Television, radio, sound equipment	692	640	699	565	705
Pets, toys, and playground equipment	369	172	397	217	384
Other entertainment products and services	476	109	527	338	492
PERSONAL CARE PRODUCTS AND SERVICES	**526**	**488**	**531**	**492**	**529**
READING	**139**	**67**	**148**	**60**	**147**
EDUCATION	**752**	**463**	**792**	**488**	**779**

	total consumer units	race		Hispanic origin	
		black	white and other	Hispanic	non-Hispanic
TOBACCO PRODUCTS AND SMOKING SUPPLIES	$320	$210	$336	$186	$334
MISCELLANEOUS	792	606	818	628	809
CASH CONTRIBUTIONS	1,277	917	1,327	612	1,346
PERSONAL INSURANCE AND PENSIONS	3,899	2,640	4,072	2,827	4,009
Life and other personal insurance	406	312	419	196	428
Pensions and Social Security	3,493	2,328	3,653	2,631	3,581
PERSONAL TAXES	2,496	1,136	2,672	878	2,672
Federal income taxes	1,843	783	1,980	682	1,969
State and local income taxes	506	302	533	195	540
Other taxes	147	51	160	–	163
GIFTS FOR NON–HOUSEHOLD MEMBERS	1,036	587	1,099	635	1,077
Food	82	36	89	45	86
Alcoholic beverages	13	3	15	15	13
Housing	259	177	270	116	273
Housekeeping supplies	42	20	46	21	45
Household textiles	14	6	15	4	15
Appliances and misc. housewares	24	18	25	11	25
Major appliances	8	7	9	4	9
Small appliances and misc. housewares	16	11	16	6	16
Miscellaneous household equipment	65	19	71	36	68
Other housing	114	113	114	44	121
Apparel and services	237	154	249	224	239
Males, aged 2 or older	64	43	67	57	64
Females, aged 2 or older	82	30	89	63	84
Children under age 2	40	32	41	58	38
Other apparel products and services	52	49	52	46	52
Jewelry and watches	24	7	26	10	25
All other apparel products and services	28	41	26	36	27
Transportation	44	51	43	37	45
Health care	33	9	36	15	34
Entertainment	78	35	84	47	81
Toys, games, hobbies, and tricycles	30	17	32	21	31
Other entertainment	48	18	53	27	50
Personal care products and services	21	7	23	15	22
Reading	1	–	1	1	1
Education	184	82	198	56	197
All other gifts	84	33	91	65	86

Note: Other races include American Indians, Asians, and Pacific Islanders. Spending by category will not add to total spending because gift spending is also included in the preceding product and service categories and personal taxes are not included in the total. (–) means sample is too small to make a reliable estimate.

Source: Bureau of Labor Statistics, 2002 Consumer Expenditure Survey, Internet site http://www.bls.gov/cex/

Table 1.45 Indexed spending by race and Hispanic origin of householder, 2002

(indexed average annual spending of consumer units (CU) by product and service category and by race and Hispanic origin of consumer unit reference person, 2002; index definition: an index of 100 is the average for all consumer units; an index of 132 means that spending by consumer units in that group is 32 percent above the average for all consumer units; an index of 68 indicates spending that is 32 percent below the average for all consumer units)

	total consumer units	race		Hispanic origin	
		black	white and other	Hispanic	non-Hispanic
Average spending of CU, total	$40,677	$30,136	$42,135	$34,742	$41,295
Average spending of CU, index	100	74	104	85	102
FOOD	100	78	103	105	100
Food at home	100	86	102	118	98
Cereals and bakery products	100	87	102	111	99
Cereals and cereal products	100	99	100	124	98
Bakery products	100	80	103	104	100
Meats, poultry, fish, and eggs	100	108	99	132	97
Beef	100	95	101	145	96
Pork	100	125	97	129	98
Other meats	100	95	101	109	99
Poultry	100	117	98	140	97
Fish and seafood	100	110	98	113	98
Eggs	100	109	97	171	91
Dairy products	100	71	104	117	98
Fresh milk and cream	100	76	103	132	97
Other dairy products	100	67	105	108	100
Fruits and vegetables	100	83	102	130	97
Fresh fruits	100	76	103	136	97
Fresh vegetables	100	73	103	141	96
Processed fruits	100	98	100	119	97
Processed vegetables	100	99	101	111	100
Other food at home	100	75	104	101	100
Sugar and other sweets	100	78	103	94	101
Fats and oils	100	95	101	120	99
Miscellaneous foods	100	72	104	97	100
Nonalcoholic beverages	100	78	103	110	99
Food prepared by CU on trips	100	32	110	78	102
Food away from home	100	67	105	89	101
ALCOHOLIC BEVERAGES	100	51	107	80	102
HOUSING	100	81	103	89	101
Shelter	100	80	103	94	101
Owned dwellings	100	62	105	69	103
Mortgage interest and charges	100	68	104	75	103
Property taxes	100	54	106	56	105
Maintenance, repair, insurance, other expenses	100	58	106	67	104
Rented dwellings	100	132	96	169	93
Other lodging	100	40	108	32	107
Utilities, fuels, and public services	100	103	100	90	101
Natural gas	100	115	98	74	102
Electricity	100	105	99	82	102
Fuel oil and other fuels	100	34	109	52	106
Telephone	100	110	99	107	99
Water and other public services	100	84	102	89	101

	total consumer units	race		Hispanic origin	
		black	white and other	Hispanic	non-Hispanic
Household services	**100**	**72**	**104**	**58**	**104**
Personal services	100	87	102	64	104
Other household services	100	59	106	52	105
Housekeeping supplies	**100**	**57**	**106**	**86**	**101**
Laundry and cleaning supplies	100	95	100	133	96
Other household products	100	44	108	80	102
Postage and stationery	100	50	108	55	105
Household furnishings and equipment	**100**	**58**	**106**	**78**	**102**
Household textiles	100	50	107	104	99
Furniture	100	73	104	86	101
Floor coverings	100	68	105	33	108
Major appliances	100	92	102	79	103
Small appliances, misc. housewares	100	51	107	91	101
Miscellaneous household equipment	100	42	108	68	103
APPAREL AND RELATED SERVICES	**100**	**97**	**100**	**120**	**98**
Men and boys	**100**	**89**	**102**	**135**	**97**
Men, aged 16 or older	100	75	104	129	97
Boys, aged 2 to 15	100	138	94	153	94
Women and girls	**100**	**92**	**101**	**91**	**101**
Women, aged 16 or older	100	87	102	82	102
Girls, aged 2 to 15	100	119	97	136	97
Children under age 2	**100**	**98**	**100**	**171**	**93**
Footwear	**100**	**129**	**96**	**166**	**94**
Other apparel products and services	**100**	**86**	**102**	**102**	**100**
TRANSPORTATION	**100**	**70**	**104**	**87**	**101**
Vehicle purchases	**100**	**66**	**105**	**85**	**102**
Cars and trucks, new	100	57	106	66	104
Cars and trucks, used	100	77	103	103	100
Other vehicles	100	16	111	116	97
Gasoline and motor oil	**100**	**75**	**103**	**102**	**100**
Other vehicle expenses	**100**	**76**	**103**	**83**	**102**
Vehicle finance charges	100	84	102	103	100
Maintenance and repairs	100	72	104	76	102
Vehicle insurance	100	77	103	89	101
Vehicle rentals, leases, licenses, other charges	100	72	104	68	103
Public transportation	**100**	**59**	**106**	**81**	**102**
HEALTH CARE	**100**	**57**	**106**	**58**	**104**
Health insurance	100	64	105	57	104
Medical services	100	42	108	61	104
Drugs	100	61	106	56	105
Medical supplies	100	48	108	63	104
ENTERTAINMENT	**100**	**54**	**106**	**68**	**103**
Fees and admissions	100	37	108	53	105
Television, radio, sound equipment	100	92	101	82	102
Pets, toys, and playground equipment	100	47	108	59	104
Other entertainment products and services	100	23	111	71	103
PERSONAL CARE PRODUCTS AND SERVICES	**100**	**93**	**101**	**94**	**101**
READING	**100**	**48**	**106**	**43**	**106**
EDUCATION	**100**	**62**	**105**	**65**	**104**

	total consumer units	race		Hispanic origin	
		black	white and other	Hispanic	non-Hispanic
TOBACCO PRODUCTS AND SMOKING SUPPLIES	100	66	105	58	104
MISCELLANEOUS	100	77	103	79	102
CASH CONTRIBUTIONS	100	72	104	48	105
PERSONAL INSURANCE AND PENSIONS	100	68	104	73	103
Life and other personal insurance	100	77	103	48	105
Pensions and Social Security	100	67	105	75	103
PERSONAL TAXES	100	46	107	35	107
Federal income taxes	100	42	107	37	107
State and local income taxes	100	60	105	39	107
Other taxes	100	35	109	–	111
GIFTS FOR NON–HOUSEHOLD MEMBERS	100	57	106	61	104
Food	100	44	109	55	105
Alcoholic beverages	100	23	115	115	100
Housing	100	68	104	45	105
Housekeeping supplies	100	48	110	50	107
Household textiles	100	43	107	29	107
Appliances and misc. housewares	100	75	104	46	104
Major appliances	100	88	113	50	113
Small appliances and misc. housewares	100	69	100	38	100
Miscellaneous household equipment	100	29	109	55	105
Other housing	100	99	100	39	106
Apparel and services	100	65	105	95	101
Males, aged 2 or older	100	67	105	89	100
Females, aged 2 or older	100	37	109	77	102
Children under age 2	100	80	103	145	95
Other apparel products and services	100	94	100	88	100
Jewelry and watches	100	29	108	42	104
All other apparel products and services	100	146	93	129	96
Transportation	100	116	98	84	102
Health care	100	27	109	45	103
Entertainment	100	45	108	60	104
Toys, games, hobbies, and tricycles	100	57	107	70	103
Other entertainment	100	38	110	56	104
Personal care products and services	100	33	110	71	105
Reading	100	–	100	100	100
Education	100	45	108	30	107
All other gifts	100	39	108	77	102

Note: Other races include American Indians, Asians, and Pacific Islanders. (–) means sample is too small to make a reliable estimate.
Source: Calculations by New Strategist based on the Bureau of Labor Statistics 2002 Consumer Expenditure Survey

Spending by Education, 2002

Because college graduates have the highest incomes, their spending is well above average. The average household headed by a college graduate spent $57,384 in 2002, or 41 percent more than the average household. In contrast, households headed by people who did not graduate from high school spent only $24,930 in 2002, 39 percent less than average.

Households headed by the least educated—those without a high school diploma—spend more than average on only a few items. These include meat, eggs, rent, and tobacco.

High school graduates spent $33,708 in 2002, or 17 percent less than the average household. Their spending is also below average in most categories with some exceptions such as tobacco.

Householders with some college experience or an associate's degree make up the largest share of households (30 percent). Their spending is close to the average on most items.

College graduates, who account for 26 percent of householders, far outspend the average household on most items—particularly those favored by the affluent. These include food away from home (43 percent above average) and alcoholic beverages (49 percent). They spend twice the average on other lodging (which includes vacation homes and hotel and motel expenses) and public transportation (which includes airfares). They are also big spenders on fees and admissions to entertainment events and education.

Table 1.46 Average spending by education of householder, 2002

(average annual spending of consumer units (CU) by product and service category and educational attainment of consumer unit reference person, 2002)

	total consumer units	not a high school graduate	high school graduate	some college or associate's degree	college degree or more
Number of consumer units (in thousands, add 000s)	112,108	17,075	31,961	33,655	29,417
Average number of persons per CU	2.5	2.6	2.5	2.5	2.5
Average income before taxes	$49,430	$25,564	$39,618	$46,385	$77,820
Average annual spending	40,677	24,930	33,708	40,431	57,384
FOOD	**$5,375**	**$4,140**	**$4,708**	**$5,291**	**$6,779**
Food at home	**3,099**	**2,896**	**2,917**	**2,950**	**3,535**
Cereals and bakery products	450	405	422	435	516
Cereals and cereal products	154	153	144	145	174
Bakery products	296	252	278	290	342
Meats, poultry, fish, and eggs	798	843	800	755	819
Beef	231	237	242	228	221
Pork	167	206	179	157	147
Other meats	101	99	100	94	110
Poultry	144	143	143	134	157
Fish and seafood	121	117	102	111	153
Eggs	34	43	34	31	31
Dairy products	328	298	303	312	385
Fresh milk and cream	127	130	123	121	135
Other dairy products	201	168	180	190	250
Fruits and vegetables	552	523	487	496	690
Fresh fruits	178	166	152	153	236
Fresh vegetables	175	171	150	156	220
Processed fruits	116	100	102	106	146
Processed vegetables	83	86	82	79	87
Other food at home	970	827	905	952	1,126
Sugar and other sweets	117	103	110	113	136
Fats and oils	85	88	86	79	89
Miscellaneous foods	472	386	429	466	564
Nonalcoholic beverages	254	230	251	255	268
Food prepared by CU on trips	41	19	28	40	69
Food away from home	**2,276**	**1,245**	**1,791**	**2,340**	**3,244**
ALCOHOLIC BEVERAGES	**376**	**185**	**273**	**391**	**561**
HOUSING	**13,283**	**8,288**	**10,800**	**13,049**	**19,111**
Shelter	**7,829**	**4,597**	**6,180**	**7,566**	**11,800**
Owned dwellings	5,165	2,194	3,902	4,926	8,534
Mortgage interest and charges	2,962	1,016	2,098	2,915	5,085
Property taxes	1,242	666	1,000	1,078	2,029
Maintenance, repair, insurance, other expenses	960	512	804	934	1,421
Rented dwellings	2,160	2,279	1,987	2,185	2,250
Other lodging	505	124	290	455	1,015
Utilities, fuels, and public services	**2,684**	**2,211**	**2,597**	**2,635**	**3,111**
Natural gas	330	252	315	311	412
Electricity	981	885	997	957	1,047
Fuel oil and other fuels	88	93	97	82	85
Telephone	957	725	886	961	1,163
Water and other public services	328	256	302	324	404

	total consumer units	not a high school graduate	high school graduate	some college or associate's degree	college degree or more
Household services	**$706**	**$260**	**$427**	**$736**	**$1,232**
Personal services	331	126	195	378	543
Other household services	375	134	232	359	689
Housekeeping supplies	**545**	**402**	**440**	**617**	**653**
Laundry and cleaning supplies	131	130	128	128	136
Other household products	283	205	210	358	324
Postage and stationery	131	67	102	131	193
Household furnishings and equipment	**1,518**	**819**	**1,156**	**1,495**	**2,315**
Household textiles	136	84	104	135	196
Furniture	401	211	304	356	669
Floor coverings	40	25	32	29	72
Major appliances	188	112	141	223	244
Small appliances, misc. housewares	100	70	80	93	145
Miscellaneous household equipment	652	317	495	659	990
APPAREL AND RELATED SERVICES	**1,749**	**1,226**	**1,392**	**1,710**	**2,435**
Men and boys	**409**	**313**	**347**	**387**	**550**
Men, aged 16 or older	319	231	263	296	449
Boys, aged 2 to 15	90	82	84	89	101
Women and girls	**704**	**418**	**536**	**723**	**1,000**
Women, aged 16 or older	587	322	434	601	861
Girls, aged 2 to 15	117	96	102	122	139
Children under age 2	**83**	**78**	**70**	**79**	**103**
Footwear	**313**	**276**	**277**	**300**	**381**
Other apparel products and services	**240**	**142**	**163**	**222**	**401**
TRANSPORTATION	**7,759**	**4,826**	**6,983**	**7,991**	**10,035**
Vehicle purchases	**3,665**	**2,375**	**3,351**	**3,816**	**4,581**
Cars and trucks, new	1,753	891	1,457	1,781	2,543
Cars and trucks, used	1,842	1,466	1,817	1,939	1,977
Other vehicles	70	18	78	96	61
Gasoline and motor oil	**1,235**	**902**	**1,212**	**1,291**	**1,390**
Other vehicle expenses	**2,471**	**1,396**	**2,201**	**2,559**	**3,282**
Vehicle finance charges	397	226	395	444	446
Maintenance and repairs	697	396	573	727	970
Vehicle insurance	894	617	871	897	1,075
Vehicle rentals, leases, licenses, other charges	483	158	362	491	791
Public transportation	**389**	**154**	**218**	**325**	**782**
HEALTH CARE	**2,350**	**1,797**	**2,208**	**2,268**	**2,914**
Health insurance	1,168	914	1,133	1,112	1,417
Medical services	590	330	489	590	849
Drugs	487	489	496	464	500
Medical supplies	105	64	90	102	148
ENTERTAINMENT	**2,079**	**872**	**1,588**	**2,183**	**3,176**
Fees and admissions	542	119	311	511	1,072
Television, radio, sound equipment	692	448	633	718	866
Pets, toys, and playground equipment	369	181	312	396	505
Other entertainment products and services	476	124	332	558	732
PERSONAL CARE PRODUCTS AND SERVICES	**526**	**350**	**453**	**532**	**691**
READING	**139**	**55**	**96**	**130**	**242**
EDUCATION	**752**	**120**	**306**	**889**	**1,442**

	total consumer units	not a high school graduate	high school graduate	some college or associate's degree	college degree or more
TOBACCO PRODUCTS AND SMOKING SUPPLIES	$320	$354	$441	$324	$167
MISCELLANEOUS	792	495	624	868	1,060
CASH CONTRIBUTIONS	1,277	607	951	1,147	2,170
PERSONAL INSURANCE AND PENSIONS	3,899	1,614	2,886	3,657	6,600
Life and other personal insurance	406	204	336	390	618
Pensions and Social Security	3,493	1,410	2,551	3,268	5,982
PERSONAL TAXES	2,496	437	1,399	1,842	5,667
Federal income taxes	1,843	254	970	1,329	4,327
State and local income taxes	506	112	308	387	1,094
Other taxes	147	71	121	127	246
GIFTS FOR NON–HOUSEHOLD MEMBERS	1,036	445	704	977	1,785
Food	82	33	42	67	170
Alcoholic beverages	13	8	9	14	19
Housing	259	115	177	262	420
Housekeeping supplies	42	17	33	48	58
Household textiles	14	4	13	12	21
Appliances and misc. housewares	24	11	13	31	35
Major appliances	8	1	4	12	13
Small appliances and misc. housewares	16	10	9	19	22
Miscellaneous household equipment	65	30	46	62	104
Other housing	114	53	72	107	202
Apparel and services	237	132	192	225	350
Males, aged 2 or older	64	30	52	70	87
Females, aged 2 or older	82	41	69	74	122
Children under age 2	40	38	37	36	49
Other apparel products and services	52	24	34	46	93
Jewelry and watches	24	6	14	16	54
All other apparel products and services	28	18	20	30	38
Transportation	44	18	38	64	42
Health care	33	18	20	31	56
Entertainment	78	38	71	77	109
Toys, games, hobbies, and tricycles	30	18	34	30	32
Other entertainment	48	20	38	47	76
Personal care products and services	21	14	16	27	24
Reading	1	–	1	1	2
Education	184	20	75	133	455
All other gifts	84	48	61	75	138

Note: Spending by category will not add to total spending because gift spending is also included in the preceding product and service categories and personal taxes are not included in the total. (–) means sample is too small to make a reliable estimate.
Source: Bureau of Labor Statistics, 2002 Consumer Expenditure Survey, Internet site http://www.bls.gov/cex/

Table 1.47 Indexed spending by education of householder, 2002

(indexed average annual spending of consumer units (CU) by product and service category and educational attainment of consumer unit reference person, 2002; index definition: an index of 100 is the average for all consumer units; an index of 132 means that spending by consumer units in that group is 32 percent above the average for all consumer units; an index of 68 indicates spending that is 32 percent below the average for all consumer units)

	total consumer units	not a high school graduate	high school graduate	some college or associate's degree	college degree or more
Average spending of CU, total	$40,677	$24,930	$33,708	$40,431	$57,384
Average spending of CU, index	100	61	83	99	141
FOOD	**100**	**77**	**88**	**98**	**126**
Food at home	**100**	**93**	**94**	**95**	**114**
Cereals and bakery products	100	90	94	97	115
Cereals and cereal products	100	99	94	94	113
Bakery products	100	85	94	98	116
Meats, poultry, fish, and eggs	100	106	100	95	103
Beef	100	103	105	99	96
Pork	100	123	107	94	88
Other meats	100	98	99	93	109
Poultry	100	99	99	93	109
Fish and seafood	100	97	84	92	126
Eggs	100	126	100	92	91
Dairy products	100	91	92	95	117
Fresh milk and cream	100	102	97	96	106
Other dairy products	100	84	90	95	124
Fruits and vegetables	100	95	88	90	125
Fresh fruits	100	93	85	86	133
Fresh vegetables	100	98	86	89	126
Processed fruits	100	86	88	92	126
Processed vegetables	100	104	99	95	105
Other food at home	100	85	93	98	116
Sugar and other sweets	100	88	94	97	116
Fats and oils	100	104	101	93	105
Miscellaneous foods	100	82	91	99	119
Nonalcoholic beverages	100	91	99	100	106
Food prepared by CU on trips	100	46	68	98	168
Food away from home	**100**	**55**	**79**	**103**	**143**
ALCOHOLIC BEVERAGES	**100**	**49**	**73**	**104**	**149**
HOUSING	**100**	**62**	**81**	**98**	**144**
Shelter	**100**	**59**	**79**	**97**	**151**
Owned dwellings	100	42	76	95	165
Mortgage interest and charges	100	34	71	98	172
Property taxes	100	54	81	87	163
Maintenance, repair, insurance, other expenses	100	53	84	97	148
Rented dwellings	100	106	92	101	104
Other lodging	100	25	57	90	201
Utilities, fuels, and public services	**100**	**82**	**97**	**98**	**116**
Natural gas	100	76	95	94	125
Electricity	100	90	102	98	107
Fuel oil and other fuels	100	106	110	93	97
Telephone	100	76	93	100	122
Water and other public services	100	78	92	99	123

	total consumer units	not a high school graduate	high school graduate	some college or associate's degree	college degree or more
Household services	**100**	**37**	**60**	**104**	**175**
Personal services	100	38	59	114	164
Other household services	100	36	62	96	184
Housekeeping supplies	**100**	**74**	**81**	**113**	**120**
Laundry and cleaning supplies	100	99	98	98	104
Other household products	100	72	74	126	114
Postage and stationery	100	51	78	100	147
Household furnishings and equipment	**100**	**54**	**76**	**99**	**153**
Household textiles	100	62	76	99	144
Furniture	100	53	76	89	167
Floor coverings	100	63	80	73	180
Major appliances	100	60	75	119	130
Small appliances, misc. housewares	100	70	80	93	145
Miscellaneous household equipment	100	49	76	101	152
APPAREL AND RELATED SERVICES	**100**	**70**	**80**	**98**	**139**
Men and boys	**100**	**77**	**85**	**95**	**134**
Men, aged 16 or older	100	72	82	93	141
Boys, aged 2 to 15	100	91	93	99	112
Women and girls	**100**	**59**	**76**	**103**	**142**
Women, aged 16 or older	100	55	74	102	147
Girls, aged 2 to 15	100	82	87	104	119
Children under age 2	**100**	**94**	**84**	**95**	**124**
Footwear	**100**	**88**	**88**	**96**	**122**
Other apparel products and services	**100**	**59**	**68**	**92**	**167**
TRANSPORTATION	**100**	**62**	**90**	**103**	**129**
Vehicle purchases	**100**	**65**	**91**	**104**	**125**
Cars and trucks, new	100	51	83	102	145
Cars and trucks, used	100	80	99	105	107
Other vehicles	100	26	111	137	87
Gasoline and motor oil	**100**	**73**	**98**	**105**	**113**
Other vehicle expenses	**100**	**56**	**89**	**104**	**133**
Vehicle finance charges	100	57	99	112	112
Maintenance and repairs	100	57	82	104	139
Vehicle insurance	100	69	97	100	120
Vehicle rentals, leases, licenses, other charges	100	33	75	102	164
Public transportation	**100**	**40**	**56**	**84**	**201**
HEALTH CARE	**100**	**76**	**94**	**97**	**124**
Health insurance	100	78	97	95	121
Medical services	100	56	83	100	144
Drugs	100	100	102	95	103
Medical supplies	100	61	86	97	141
ENTERTAINMENT	**100**	**42**	**76**	**105**	**153**
Fees and admissions	100	22	57	94	198
Television, radio, sound equipment	100	65	91	104	125
Pets, toys, and playground equipment	100	49	85	107	137
Other entertainment products and services	100	26	70	117	154
PERSONAL CARE PRODUCTS AND SERVICES	**100**	**67**	**86**	**101**	**131**
READING	**100**	**40**	**69**	**94**	**174**
EDUCATION	**100**	**16**	**41**	**118**	**192**

	total consumer units	not a high school graduate	high school graduate	some college or associate's degree	college degree or more
TOBACCO PRODUCTS AND SMOKING SUPPLIES	100	111	138	101	52
MISCELLANEOUS	100	63	79	110	134
CASH CONTRIBUTIONS	100	48	74	90	170
PERSONAL INSURANCE AND PENSIONS	100	41	74	94	169
Life and other personal insurance	100	50	83	96	152
Pensions and Social Security	100	40	73	94	171
PERSONAL TAXES	100	18	56	74	227
Federal income taxes	100	14	53	72	235
State and local income taxes	100	22	61	76	216
Other taxes	100	48	82	86	167
GIFTS FOR NON–HOUSEHOLD MEMBERS	100	43	68	94	172
Food	100	40	51	82	207
Alcoholic beverages	100	62	69	107	146
Housing	100	44	68	101	162
Housekeeping supplies	100	40	79	114	138
Household textiles	100	29	93	89	150
Appliances and misc. housewares	100	46	54	131	146
Major appliances	100	13	50	155	163
Small appliances and misc. housewares	100	63	56	116	138
Miscellaneous household equipment	100	46	71	96	160
Other housing	100	46	63	94	177
Apparel and services	100	56	81	95	148
Males, aged 2 or older	100	47	81	109	136
Females, aged 2 or older	100	50	84	90	149
Children under age 2	100	95	93	89	123
Other apparel products and services	100	46	65	88	179
Jewelry and watches	100	25	58	67	225
All other apparel products and services	100	64	71	106	136
Transportation	100	41	86	145	95
Health care	100	55	61	93	170
Entertainment	100	49	91	99	140
Toys, games, hobbies, and tricycles	100	60	113	101	107
Other entertainment	100	42	79	97	158
Personal care products and services	100	67	76	128	114
Reading	100	–	100	100	200
Education	100	11	41	72	247
All other gifts	100	57	73	89	164

Note: (–) means sample is too small to make a reliable estimate.
Source: Calculations by New Strategist based on the Bureau of Labor Statistics 2002 Consumer Expenditure Survey

Spending by Household Size, 2002

Spending tends to increase with household size because larger households usually have more earners. Incomes peak for households with four people, at $67,755 in 2002. Spending is highest for this household size as well, at $54,033—33 percent above average. Only 14 percent of the nation's households are home to four people, however.

Two-person households are most common, accounting for 31 percent of the total. They spent an average of $41,797 in 2002—just 3 percent more than the average household. Households with two people (many of them older empty-nesters) spend the most on alcoholic beverages, other lodging (primarily hotel and motel expenses on trips), health care, and reading material.

Households with five or more people have slightly lower incomes and spending than those with just four people. They spend more than four-person households on many nondiscretionary items, however, such as food at home, laundry and cleaning supplies, telephone service, electricity, water, and children's clothing.

Single-person households are almost as numerous as two-person households, accounting for 29 percent of households in 2002. Single-person households spend less than the average household on almost every item.

Table 1.48 Average spending by size of household, 2002

(average annual spending of consumer units (CU) by product and service category, by number of people in consumer unit, 2002)

	total consumer units	one person	two or more people total	two people	three people	four people	five or more people
Number of consumer units (in thousands, add 000s)	112,108	33,055	79,053	34,849	17,308	15,822	11,074
Average number of persons per CU	2.5	1.0	3.1	2.0	3.0	4.0	5.6
Average income before taxes	$49,430	$27,042	$59,020	$52,694	$60,077	$67,755	$64,954
Average annual spending	40,677	24,190	47,508	41,797	48,098	54,033	55,501
FOOD	$5,375	$2,913	$6,367	$5,318	$6,361	$7,445	$8,302
Food at home	3,099	1,558	3,718	2,943	3,733	4,431	5,247
Cereals and bakery products	450	225	541	413	523	660	821
Cereals and cereal products	154	74	186	133	180	229	310
Bakery products	296	151	354	279	344	431	511
Meats, poultry, fish, and eggs	798	359	975	767	986	1,148	1,400
Beef	231	93	287	219	289	342	429
Pork	167	73	205	169	203	245	274
Other meats	101	48	123	93	128	147	178
Poultry	144	65	176	131	183	206	271
Fish and seafood	121	64	144	122	144	164	188
Eggs	34	18	40	32	39	44	60
Dairy products	328	166	394	307	398	480	552
Fresh milk and cream	127	64	152	112	152	191	235
Other dairy products	201	102	241	195	246	289	317
Fruits and vegetables	552	292	656	547	650	754	893
Fresh fruits	178	97	211	182	200	244	278
Fresh vegetables	175	90	209	181	204	234	276
Processed fruits	116	62	137	105	139	163	204
Processed vegetables	83	43	100	79	107	114	135
Other food at home	970	515	1,152	910	1,176	1,389	1,580
Sugar and other sweets	117	64	139	112	128	170	200
Fats and oils	85	43	102	85	101	117	139
Miscellaneous foods	472	250	561	421	599	685	788
Nonalcoholic beverages	254	136	301	246	306	357	397
Food prepared by CU on trips	41	22	49	46	43	59	56
Food away from home	2,276	1,356	2,649	2,375	2,628	3,014	3,055
ALCOHOLIC BEVERAGES	376	285	413	453	399	389	334
HOUSING	13,283	8,619	15,224	13,380	15,183	17,636	17,660
Shelter	7,829	5,465	8,818	7,728	8,847	10,299	10,088
Owned dwellings	5,165	2,605	6,235	5,225	6,121	7,809	7,344
Mortgage interest and charges	2,962	1,260	3,674	2,682	3,723	5,049	4,754
Property taxes	1,242	755	1,446	1,373	1,346	1,597	1,617
Maintenance, repair, insurance, other expenses	960	590	1,115	1,170	1,053	1,164	974
Rented dwellings	2,160	2,538	2,002	1,839	2,234	1,957	2,214
Other lodging	505	322	581	664	492	532	529
Utilities, fuels, and public services	2,684	1,712	3,091	2,736	3,114	3,418	3,702
Natural gas	330	225	374	321	368	425	476
Electricity	981	600	1,141	1,022	1,125	1,245	1,388
Fuel oil and other fuels	88	63	99	98	92	99	116
Telephone	957	624	1,096	955	1,160	1,219	1,262
Water and other public services	328	201	382	341	369	431	461

	total consumer units	one person	two or more people total	two people	three people	four people	five or more people
Household services	**$706**	**$400**	**$834**	**$513**	**$977**	**$1,267**	**$998**
Personal services	331	134	413	99	578	806	584
Other household services	375	266	420	415	399	461	413
Housekeeping supplies	**545**	**270**	**656**	**677**	**551**	**676**	**722**
Laundry and cleaning supplies	131	64	157	129	155	177	228
Other household products	283	118	350	394	252	355	347
Postage and stationery	131	88	149	154	143	144	147
Household furnishings and equipment	**1,518**	**772**	**1,826**	**1,725**	**1,695**	**1,976**	**2,151**
Household textiles	136	81	158	161	131	149	201
Furniture	401	179	494	487	407	548	576
Floor coverings	40	15	51	59	45	47	41
Major appliances	188	94	228	220	196	243	280
Small appliances, misc. housewares	100	57	118	118	128	97	137
Miscellaneous household equipment	652	346	778	680	787	892	916
APPAREL AND RELATED SERVICES	**1,749**	**921**	**2,086**	**1,559**	**2,247**	**2,380**	**3,150**
Men and boys	**409**	**176**	**505**	**341**	**522**	**635**	**829**
Men, aged 16 or older	319	162	383	309	411	414	544
Boys, aged 2 to 15	90	14	121	31	111	220	285
Women and girls	**704**	**413**	**822**	**673**	**887**	**882**	**1,124**
Women, aged 16 or older	587	397	663	634	730	632	703
Girls, aged 2 to 15	117	16	159	39	157	250	421
Children under age 2	**83**	**15**	**110**	**41**	**159**	**157**	**191**
Footwear	**313**	**149**	**379**	**250**	**390**	**436**	**718**
Other apparel products and services	**240**	**168**	**270**	**254**	**290**	**269**	**288**
TRANSPORTATION	**7,759**	**3,890**	**9,377**	**8,110**	**10,003**	**10,685**	**10,510**
Vehicle purchases	**3,665**	**1,662**	**4,502**	**3,805**	**4,994**	**5,177**	**4,966**
Cars and trucks, new	1,753	791	2,155	2,066	2,274	2,356	1,961
Cars and trucks, used	1,842	846	2,259	1,679	2,579	2,708	2,942
Other vehicles	70	25	88	59	141	114	63
Gasoline and motor oil	**1,235**	**646**	**1,481**	**1,257**	**1,512**	**1,713**	**1,809**
Other vehicle expenses	**2,471**	**1,306**	**2,957**	**2,591**	**3,099**	**3,318**	**3,366**
Vehicle finance charges	397	143	503	416	515	603	616
Maintenance and repairs	697	437	806	721	837	909	872
Vehicle insurance	894	486	1,064	951	1,090	1,156	1,246
Vehicle rentals, leases, licenses, other charges	483	240	584	503	657	650	631
Public transportation	**389**	**276**	**436**	**458**	**397**	**476**	**369**
HEALTH CARE	**2,350**	**1,522**	**2,696**	**3,010**	**2,496**	**2,472**	**2,340**
Health insurance	1,168	759	1,339	1,491	1,247	1,240	1,144
Medical services	590	330	699	700	648	740	715
Drugs	487	366	538	682	495	390	363
Medical supplies	105	68	121	137	106	102	119
ENTERTAINMENT	**2,079**	**1,193**	**2,448**	**2,115**	**2,308**	**2,928**	**3,038**
Fees and admissions	542	320	634	532	547	817	831
Television, radio, sound equipment	692	467	786	694	812	902	871
Pets, toys, and playground equipment	369	202	438	388	437	510	496
Other entertainment products and services	476	205	589	501	512	699	839
PERSONAL CARE PRODUCTS AND SERVICES	**526**	**310**	**614**	**557**	**611**	**682**	**706**
READING	**139**	**108**	**151**	**162**	**143**	**150**	**132**
EDUCATION	**752**	**562**	**831**	**491**	**935**	**1,156**	**1,279**

	total consumer units	one person	two or more people				
			total	two people	three people	four people	five or more people
TOBACCO PRODUCTS AND SMOKING SUPPLIES	$320	$210	$367	$327	$418	$352	$434
MISCELLANEOUS	792	602	872	797	859	926	1,049
CASH CONTRIBUTIONS	1,277	998	1,394	1,516	1,203	1,242	1,523
PERSONAL INSURANCE AND PENSIONS	3,899	2,055	4,670	4,002	4,932	5,590	5,043
Life and other personal insurance	406	183	499	492	499	520	493
Pensions and Social Security	3,493	1,872	4,170	3,510	4,433	5,071	4,550
PERSONAL TAXES	2,496	1,815	2,788	2,753	2,847	3,152	2,287
Federal income taxes	1,843	1,396	2,034	2,016	2,144	2,270	1,581
State and local income taxes	506	327	583	544	574	707	548
Other taxes	147	93	170	193	129	175	158
GIFTS FOR NON–HOUSEHOLD MEMBERS	1,036	744	1,156	1,210	1,225	998	1,105
Food	82	42	99	115	105	61	91
Alcoholic beverages	13	10	15	13	14	12	25
Housing	259	170	295	293	299	287	303
Housekeeping supplies	42	25	50	55	48	49	34
Household textiles	14	9	16	20	11	16	8
Appliances and misc. housewares	24	16	27	35	25	23	11
Major appliances	8	4	10	14	10	8	2
Small appliances and misc. housewares	16	12	17	21	16	15	9
Miscellaneous household equipment	65	46	72	78	66	70	68
Other housing	114	75	130	105	149	129	181
Apparel and services	237	187	257	282	231	227	261
Males, aged 2 or older	64	48	70	80	56	66	64
Females, aged 2 or older	82	64	89	109	69	62	95
Children under age 2	40	15	50	37	59	57	70
Other apparel products and services	52	61	48	56	46	42	32
Jewelry and watches	24	41	17	25	13	11	8
All other apparel products and services	28	20	31	31	33	31	25
Transportation	44	46	43	31	60	65	23
Health care	33	24	36	42	52	15	23
Entertainment	78	58	87	98	70	82	85
Toys, games, hobbies, and tricycles	30	22	33	43	30	24	19
Other entertainment	48	35	54	54	40	58	66
Personal care products and services	21	15	24	25	27	17	24
Reading	1	2	1	2	1	1	1
Education	184	111	214	197	302	183	179
All other gifts	84	80	85	111	63	49	91

Note: Spending by category will not add to total spending because gift spending is also included in the preceding product and service categories and personal taxes are not included in the total.
Source: Bureau of Labor Statistics, 2002 Consumer Expenditure Survey, Internet site http://www.bls.gov/cex/

Table 1.49 Indexed spending by size of household, 2002

(indexed annual spending of consumer units (CU) by product and service category and by number of people in consumer unit, 2002; index definition: an index of 100 is the average for all consumer units; an index of 132 means that spending by consumer units in that group is 32 percent above the average for all consumer units; an index of 68 indicates spending that is 32 percent below the average for all consumer units)

	total consumer units	one person	two or more people				
			total	two people	three people	four people	five or more people
Average spending of CU, total	$40,677	$24,190	$47,508	$41,797	$48,098	$54,033	$55,501
Average spending of CU, index	100	59	117	103	118	133	136
FOOD	100	54	118	99	118	139	154
Food at home	100	50	120	95	120	143	169
Cereals and bakery products	100	50	120	92	116	147	182
Cereals and cereal products	100	48	121	86	117	149	201
Bakery products	100	51	120	94	116	146	173
Meats, poultry, fish, and eggs	100	45	122	96	124	144	175
Beef	100	40	124	95	125	148	186
Pork	100	44	123	101	122	147	164
Other meats	100	48	122	92	127	146	176
Poultry	100	45	122	91	127	143	188
Fish and seafood	100	53	119	101	119	136	155
Eggs	100	53	118	94	115	129	176
Dairy products	100	51	120	94	121	146	168
Fresh milk and cream	100	50	120	88	120	150	185
Other dairy products	100	51	120	97	122	144	158
Fruits and vegetables	100	53	119	99	118	137	162
Fresh fruits	100	54	119	102	112	137	156
Fresh vegetables	100	51	119	103	117	134	158
Processed fruits	100	53	118	91	120	141	176
Processed vegetables	100	52	120	95	129	137	163
Other food at home	100	53	119	94	121	143	163
Sugar and other sweets	100	55	119	96	109	145	171
Fats and oils	100	51	120	100	119	138	164
Miscellaneous foods	100	53	119	89	127	145	167
Nonalcoholic beverages	100	54	119	97	120	141	156
Food prepared by CU on trips	100	54	120	112	105	144	137
Food away from home	100	60	116	104	115	132	134
ALCOHOLIC BEVERAGES	100	76	110	120	106	103	89
HOUSING	100	65	115	101	114	133	133
Shelter	100	70	113	99	113	132	129
Owned dwellings	100	50	121	101	119	151	142
Mortgage interest and charges	100	43	124	91	126	170	160
Property taxes	100	61	116	111	108	129	130
Maintenance, repair, insurance, other expenses	100	61	116	122	110	121	101
Rented dwellings	100	118	93	85	103	91	103
Other lodging	100	64	115	131	97	105	105
Utilities, fuels, and public services	100	64	115	102	116	127	138
Natural gas	100	68	113	97	112	129	144
Electricity	100	61	116	104	115	127	141
Fuel oil and other fuels	100	72	113	111	105	113	132
Telephone	100	65	115	100	121	127	132
Water and other public services	100	61	116	104	113	131	141

	total consumer units	one person	two or more people				
			total	two people	three people	four people	five or more people
Household services	100	57	118	73	138	179	141
Personal services	100	40	125	30	175	244	176
Other household services	100	71	112	111	106	123	110
Housekeeping supplies	100	50	120	124	101	124	132
Laundry and cleaning supplies	100	49	120	98	118	135	174
Other household products	100	42	124	139	89	125	123
Postage and stationery	100	67	114	118	109	110	112
Household furnishings and equipment	100	51	120	114	112	130	142
Household textiles	100	60	116	118	96	110	148
Furniture	100	45	123	121	101	137	144
Floor coverings	100	38	128	148	113	118	103
Major appliances	100	50	121	117	104	129	149
Small appliances, misc. housewares	100	57	118	118	128	97	137
Miscellaneous household equipment	100	53	119	104	121	137	140
APPAREL AND RELATED SERVICES	100	53	119	89	128	136	180
Men and boys	100	43	123	83	128	155	203
Men, aged 16 or older	100	51	120	97	129	130	171
Boys, aged 2 to 15	100	16	134	34	123	244	317
Women and girls	100	59	117	96	126	125	160
Women, aged 16 or older	100	68	113	108	124	108	120
Girls, aged 2 to 15	100	14	136	33	134	214	360
Children under age 2	100	18	133	49	192	189	230
Footwear	100	48	121	80	125	139	229
Other apparel products and services	100	70	113	106	121	112	120
TRANSPORTATION	100	50	121	105	129	138	135
Vehicle purchases	100	45	123	104	136	141	135
Cars and trucks, new	100	45	123	118	130	134	112
Cars and trucks, used	100	46	123	91	140	147	160
Other vehicles	100	36	126	84	201	163	90
Gasoline and motor oil	100	52	120	102	122	139	146
Other vehicle expenses	100	53	120	105	125	134	136
Vehicle finance charges	100	36	127	105	130	152	155
Maintenance and repairs	100	63	116	103	120	130	125
Vehicle insurance	100	54	119	106	122	129	139
Vehicle rentals, leases, licenses, other charges	100	50	121	104	136	135	131
Public transportation	100	71	112	118	102	122	95
HEALTH CARE	100	65	115	128	106	105	100
Health insurance	100	65	115	128	107	106	98
Medical services	100	56	118	119	110	125	121
Drugs	100	75	110	140	102	80	75
Medical supplies	100	65	115	130	101	97	113
ENTERTAINMENT	100	57	118	102	111	141	146
Fees and admissions	100	59	117	98	101	151	153
Television, radio, sound equipment	100	67	114	100	117	130	126
Pets, toys, and playground equipment	100	55	119	105	118	138	134
Other entertainment products and services	100	43	124	105	108	147	176
PERSONAL CARE PRODUCTS AND SERVICES	100	59	117	106	116	130	134
READING	100	78	109	117	103	108	95
EDUCATION	100	75	111	65	124	154	170

	total consumer units	one person	two or more people				
			total	two people	three people	four people	five or more people
TOBACCO PRODUCTS AND SMOKING SUPPLIES	100	66	115	102	131	110	136
MISCELLANEOUS	100	76	110	101	108	117	132
CASH CONTRIBUTIONS	100	78	109	119	94	97	119
PERSONAL INSURANCE AND PENSIONS	100	53	120	103	126	143	129
Life and other personal insurance	100	45	123	121	123	128	121
Pensions and Social Security	100	54	119	100	127	145	130
PERSONAL TAXES	100	73	112	110	114	126	92
Federal income taxes	100	76	110	109	116	123	86
State and local income taxes	100	65	115	108	113	140	108
Other taxes	100	63	116	131	88	119	107
GIFTS FOR NON–HOUSEHOLD MEMBERS	100	72	112	117	118	96	107
Food	100	51	121	140	128	74	111
Alcoholic beverages	100	77	115	100	108	92	192
Housing	100	66	114	113	115	111	117
Housekeeping supplies	100	60	119	131	114	117	81
Household textiles	100	64	114	143	79	114	57
Appliances and misc. housewares	100	67	113	146	104	96	46
Major appliances	100	50	125	175	125	100	25
Small appliances and misc. housewares	100	75	106	131	100	94	56
Miscellaneous household equipment	100	71	111	120	102	108	105
Other housing	100	66	114	92	131	113	159
Apparel and services	100	79	108	119	97	96	110
Males, aged 2 or older	100	75	109	125	88	103	100
Females, aged 2 or older	100	78	109	133	84	76	116
Children under age 2	100	38	125	93	148	143	175
Other apparel products and services	100	117	92	108	88	81	62
Jewelry and watches	100	171	71	104	54	46	33
All other apparel products and services	100	71	111	111	118	111	89
Transportation	100	105	98	70	136	148	52
Health care	100	73	109	127	158	45	70
Entertainment	100	74	112	126	90	105	109
Toys, games, hobbies, and tricycles	100	73	110	143	100	80	63
Other entertainment	100	73	113	113	83	121	138
Personal care products and services	100	71	114	119	129	81	114
Reading	100	200	100	200	100	100	100
Education	100	60	116	107	164	99	97
All other gifts	100	95	101	132	75	58	108

Source: Calculations by New Strategist based on the Bureau of Labor Statistics 2002 Consumer Expenditure Survey

Spending by Homeowners and Renters, 2002

Homeowners spend far more than renters because their incomes are higher. Homeowners had an average income of $59,345 in 2002, and they spent $46,908—15 percent more than the average household. In contrast, the average income of renters was just $30,386 and they spent $28,372—30 percent less than the average household.

Renters spend less than homeowners on nearly every product and service category. They spend an average amount on clothes for children under age two. They spend 8 percent more than average on tobacco.

Table 1.50 Average spending by homeowners and renters, 2002

(average annual spending of consumer units (CU) by product and service category and by homeownership status, 2002)

	total consumer units	homeowners	renters
Number of consumer units (in thousands, add 000s)	112,108	74,419	37,689
Average number of persons per CU	2.5	2.6	2.2
Average income before taxes	$49,430	$59,345	$30,386
Average annual spending	40,677	46,908	28,372
FOOD	**$5,375**	**$6,009**	**$4,123**
Food at home	**3,099**	**3,454**	**2,397**
Cereals and bakery products	450	501	350
Cereals and cereal products	154	166	131
Bakery products	296	335	219
Meats, poultry, fish, and eggs	798	881	636
Beef	231	253	189
Pork	167	185	133
Other meats	101	114	76
Poultry	144	158	118
Fish and seafood	121	136	91
Eggs	34	35	30
Dairy products	328	370	247
Fresh milk and cream	127	140	102
Other dairy products	201	230	145
Fruits and vegetables	552	613	432
Fresh fruits	178	199	136
Fresh vegetables	175	195	135
Processed fruits	116	127	93
Processed vegetables	83	92	67
Other food at home	970	1,090	732
Sugar and other sweets	117	136	81
Fats and oils	85	96	64
Miscellaneous foods	472	528	362
Nonalcoholic beverages	254	279	204
Food prepared by CU on trips	41	51	22
Food away from home	**2,276**	**2,555**	**1,725**
ALCOHOLIC BEVERAGES	**376**	**402**	**324**
HOUSING	**13,283**	**15,058**	**9,777**
Shelter	**7,829**	**8,458**	**6,588**
Owned dwellings	5,165	7,752	56
Mortgage interest and charges	2,962	4,449	26
Property taxes	1,242	1,865	12
Maintenance, repair, insurance, other expenses	960	1,438	18
Rented dwellings	2,160	67	6,293
Other lodging	505	639	239
Utilities, fuels, and public services	**2,684**	**3,155**	**1,755**
Natural gas	330	410	171
Electricity	981	1,158	633
Fuel oil and other fuels	88	118	30
Telephone	957	1,036	801
Water and other public services	328	434	120

	total consumer units	homeowners	renters
Household services	**$706**	**$876**	**$370**
Personal services	331	395	205
Other household services	375	481	165
Housekeeping supplies	**545**	**674**	**291**
Laundry and cleaning supplies	131	147	99
Other household products	283	366	120
Postage and stationery	131	161	73
Household furnishings and equipment	**1,518**	**1,896**	**773**
Household textiles	136	171	66
Furniture	401	495	216
Floor coverings	40	57	8
Major appliances	188	245	77
Small appliances, misc. housewares	100	115	71
Miscellaneous household equipment	652	813	336
APPAREL AND RELATED SERVICES	**1,749**	**1,942**	**1,369**
Men and boys	**409**	**460**	**310**
Men, aged 16 or older	319	360	239
Boys, aged 2 to 15	90	100	70
Women and girls	**704**	**808**	**498**
Women, aged 16 or older	587	673	416
Girls, aged 2 to 15	117	135	82
Children under age 2	**83**	**82**	**83**
Footwear	**313**	**341**	**259**
Other apparel products and services	**240**	**251**	**219**
TRANSPORTATION	**7,759**	**8,972**	**5,365**
Vehicle purchases	**3,665**	**4,238**	**2,533**
Cars and trucks, new	1,753	2,188	893
Cars and trucks, used	1,842	1,965	1,599
Other vehicles	70	84	41
Gasoline and motor oil	**1,235**	**1,413**	**883**
Other vehicle expenses	**2,471**	**2,886**	**1,651**
Vehicle finance charges	397	465	262
Maintenance and repairs	697	807	481
Vehicle insurance	894	1,033	619
Vehicle rentals, leases, licenses, other charges	483	581	289
Public transportation	**389**	**435**	**298**
HEALTH CARE	**2,350**	**2,921**	**1,223**
Health insurance	1,168	1,450	611
Medical services	590	737	300
Drugs	487	605	255
Medical supplies	105	130	57
ENTERTAINMENT	**2,079**	**2,501**	**1,246**
Fees and admissions	542	674	281
Television, radio, sound equipment	692	771	536
Pets, toys, and playground equipment	369	454	201
Other entertainment products and services	476	602	229
PERSONAL CARE PRODUCTS AND SERVICES	**526**	**598**	**384**
READING	**139**	**166**	**84**
EDUCATION	**752**	**774**	**708**

	total consumer units	homeowners	renters
TOBACCO PRODUCTS AND SMOKING SUPPLIES	$320	$307	$347
MISCELLANEOUS	792	895	589
CASH CONTRIBUTIONS	1,277	1,588	663
PERSONAL INSURANCE AND PENSIONS	3,899	4,773	2,171
Life and other personal insurance	406	524	173
Pensions and Social Security	3,493	4,249	1,998
PERSONAL TAXES	2,496	3,136	1,267
Federal income taxes	1,843	2,293	978
State and local income taxes	506	626	277
Other taxes	147	218	12
GIFTS FOR NON–HOUSEHOLD MEMBERS	1,036	1,276	564
Food	82	109	29
Alcoholic beverages	13	15	11
Housing	259	315	148
Housekeeping supplies	42	51	25
Household textiles	14	17	7
Appliances and misc. housewares	24	31	10
Major appliances	8	12	1
Small appliances and misc. housewares	16	19	9
Miscellaneous household equipment	65	80	34
Other housing	114	136	71
Apparel and services	237	262	188
Males, aged 2 or older	64	69	53
Females, aged 2 or older	82	97	51
Children under age 2	40	42	35
Other apparel products and services	52	53	48
Jewelry and watches	24	25	21
All other apparel products and services	28	28	27
Transportation	44	48	35
Health care	33	42	13
Entertainment	78	95	45
Toys, games, hobbies, and tricycles	30	37	17
Other entertainment	48	58	28
Personal care products and services	21	24	16
Reading	1	2	0
Education	184	255	43
All other gifts	84	109	35

Note: Spending by category will not add to total spending because gift spending is also included in the preceding product and service categories and personal taxes are not included in the total.
Source: Bureau of Labor Statistics, 2002 Consumer Expenditure Survey, Internet site http://www.bls.gov/cex/

Table 1.51 Indexed spending by homeowners and renters, 2002

(indexed annual spending of consumer units (CU) by product and service category and by homeownership status, 2002; index definition: an index of 100 is the average for all consumer units; an index of 132 means that spending by consumer units in that group is 32 percent above the average for all consumer units; an index of 68 indicates spending that is 32 percent below the average for all consumer units)

	total consumer units	homeowners	renters
Average spending of CU, total	$40,677	$46,908	$28,372
Average spending of CU, index	100	115	70
FOOD	100	112	77
Food at home	100	111	77
Cereals and bakery products	100	111	78
Cereals and cereal products	100	108	85
Bakery products	100	113	74
Meats, poultry, fish, and eggs	100	110	80
Beef	100	110	82
Pork	100	111	80
Other meats	100	113	75
Poultry	100	110	82
Fish and seafood	100	112	75
Eggs	100	103	88
Dairy products	100	113	75
Fresh milk and cream	100	110	80
Other dairy products	100	114	72
Fruits and vegetables	100	111	78
Fresh fruits	100	112	76
Fresh vegetables	100	111	77
Processed fruits	100	109	80
Processed vegetables	100	111	81
Other food at home	100	112	75
Sugar and other sweets	100	116	69
Fats and oils	100	113	75
Miscellaneous foods	100	112	77
Nonalcoholic beverages	100	110	80
Food prepared by CU on trips	100	124	54
Food away from home	100	112	76
ALCOHOLIC BEVERAGES	100	107	86
HOUSING	100	113	74
Shelter	100	108	84
Owned dwellings	100	150	1
Mortgage interest and charges	100	150	1
Property taxes	100	150	1
Maintenance, repair, insurance, other expenses	100	150	2
Rented dwellings	100	3	291
Other lodging	100	127	47
Utilities, fuels, and public services	100	118	65
Natural gas	100	124	52
Electricity	100	118	65
Fuel oil and other fuels	100	134	34
Telephone	100	108	84
Water and other public services	100	132	37

	total consumer units	homeowners	renters
Household services	**100**	**124**	**52**
Personal services	100	119	62
Other household services	100	128	44
Housekeeping supplies	**100**	**124**	**53**
Laundry and cleaning supplies	100	112	76
Other household products	100	129	42
Postage and stationery	100	123	56
Household furnishings and equipment	**100**	**125**	**51**
Household textiles	100	126	49
Furniture	100	123	54
Floor coverings	100	143	20
Major appliances	100	130	41
Small appliances, misc. housewares	100	115	71
Miscellaneous household equipment	100	125	52
APPAREL AND RELATED SERVICES	**100**	**111**	**78**
Men and boys	**100**	**112**	**76**
Men, aged 16 or older	100	113	75
Boys, aged 2 to 15	100	111	78
Women and girls	**100**	**115**	**71**
Women, aged 16 or older	100	115	71
Girls, aged 2 to 15	100	115	70
Children under age 2	**100**	**99**	**100**
Footwear	**100**	**109**	**83**
Other apparel products and services	**100**	**105**	**91**
TRANSPORTATION	**100**	**116**	**69**
Vehicle purchases	**100**	**116**	**69**
Cars and trucks, new	100	125	51
Cars and trucks, used	100	107	87
Other vehicles	100	120	59
Gasoline and motor oil	**100**	**114**	**71**
Other vehicle expenses	**100**	**117**	**67**
Vehicle finance charges	100	117	66
Maintenance and repairs	100	116	69
Vehicle insurance	100	116	69
Vehicle rentals, leases, licenses, other charges	100	120	60
Public transportation	**100**	**112**	**77**
HEALTH CARE	**100**	**124**	**52**
Health insurance	100	124	52
Medical services	100	125	51
Drugs	100	124	52
Medical supplies	100	124	54
ENTERTAINMENT	**100**	**120**	**60**
Fees and admissions	100	124	52
Television, radio, sound equipment	100	111	77
Pets, toys, and playground equipment	100	123	54
Other entertainment products and services	100	126	48
PERSONAL CARE PRODUCTS AND SERVICES	**100**	**114**	**73**
READING	**100**	**119**	**60**
EDUCATION	**100**	**103**	**94**

	total consumer units	homeowners	renters
TOBACCO PRODUCTS AND SMOKING SUPPLIES	100	96	108
MISCELLANEOUS	100	113	74
CASH CONTRIBUTIONS	100	124	52
PERSONAL INSURANCE AND PENSIONS	100	122	56
Life and other personal insurance	100	129	43
Pensions and Social Security	100	122	57
PERSONAL TAXES	100	126	51
Federal income taxes	100	124	53
State and local income taxes	100	124	55
Other taxes	100	148	8
GIFTS FOR NON–HOUSEHOLD MEMBERS	100	123	54
Food	100	133	35
Alcoholic beverages	100	115	85
Housing	100	122	57
Housekeeping supplies	100	121	60
Household textiles	100	121	50
Appliances and misc. housewares	100	129	42
Major appliances	100	150	13
Small appliances and misc. housewares	100	119	56
Miscellaneous household equipment	100	123	52
Other housing	100	119	62
Apparel and services	100	111	79
Males, aged 2 or older	100	108	83
Females, aged 2 or older	100	118	62
Children under age 2	100	105	88
Other apparel products and services	100	102	92
Jewelry and watches	100	104	88
All other apparel products and services	100	100	96
Transportation	100	109	80
Health care	100	127	39
Entertainment	100	122	58
Toys, games, hobbies, and tricycles	100	123	57
Other entertainment	100	121	58
Personal care products and services	100	114	76
Reading	100	200	0
Education	100	139	23
All other gifts	100	130	42

Source: Calculations by New Strategist based on the Bureau of Labor Statistics 2002 Consumer Expenditure Survey

Spending by Number of Earners in Household, 2002

Dual-earners account for 33 percent of the nation's households, and they outspend the average household by 30 percent. In 2002, the average dual-income household spent $52,991. Households with three or more earners spend even more ($60,844), but they account for a much smaller share of households—just 9 percent in 2002.

By category, spending does not always rise with the number of earners in a household. Single-person households with one earner (many of them young adults) spend more than other households on rent. Two-person households with no earners (many of them elderly) spend twice the average on drugs. In general, however, three-earner households outspend the others on many products and services because they are the largest households, averaging 4.4 people.

The needs of two-earner households are readily apparent in these tables. This household type spends 33 percent more than the average household on food away from home, 85 percent more than average on personal household services (primarily day care), 41 percent more on pets, toys, and playground equipment, and 35 percent more on new and used cars and trucks.

Table 1.52 Average spending by number of earners in household, 2002

(average annual spending of consumer units (CU) by product and service category, by CU size and number of earners in CU, 2002)

| | total CUs | single-person CUs | | CUs with two or more people | | | |
		no earner	one earner	no earner	one earner	two earners	three+ earners
Number of consumer units							
(in thousands, add 000s)	112,108	12,289	20,766	9,448	22,535	36,558	10,512
Average number of persons per CU	2.5	1.0	1.0	2.3	2.9	3.1	4.4
Average income before taxes	$49,430	$14,653	$33,475	$25,671	$44,393	$70,448	$79,070
Average annual spending	40,677	17,607	28,077	29,721	39,923	52,991	60,844
FOOD	$5,375	$2,383	$3,223	$4,542	$5,650	$6,729	$8,381
Food at home	3,099	1,620	1,521	2,959	3,546	3,704	4,884
Cereals and bakery products	450	240	216	460	525	525	711
Cereals and cereal products	154	75	74	155	183	181	242
Bakery products	296	166	142	305	342	344	469
Meats, poultry, fish, and eggs	798	387	344	738	931	967	1,328
Beef	231	93	93	202	270	287	403
Pork	167	88	63	184	198	202	253
Other meats	101	53	44	99	116	118	177
Poultry	144	69	62	118	165	179	245
Fish and seafood	121	64	64	99	142	143	198
Eggs	34	20	18	37	40	38	51
Dairy products	328	175	161	316	386	392	494
Fresh milk and cream	127	74	58	126	149	149	200
Other dairy products	201	101	102	190	237	243	294
Fruits and vegetables	552	314	279	563	641	635	859
Fresh fruits	178	105	91	188	207	201	279
Fresh vegetables	175	97	86	181	206	203	264
Processed fruits	116	66	60	108	130	136	186
Processed vegetables	83	46	42	86	98	96	130
Other food at home	970	504	522	882	1,063	1,184	1,493
Sugar and other sweets	117	80	55	117	134	139	172
Fats and oils	85	48	40	98	95	99	134
Miscellaneous foods	472	234	260	395	520	588	713
Nonalcoholic beverages	254	125	143	226	274	306	416
Food prepared by CU on trips	41	17	24	47	40	53	59
Food away from home	2,276	763	1,702	1,584	2,103	3,025	3,497
ALCOHOLIC BEVERAGES	376	113	385	208	320	491	528
HOUSING	13,283	7,030	9,559	9,825	13,324	17,101	17,640
Shelter	7,829	3,973	6,349	5,113	7,700	10,074	10,175
Owned dwellings	5,165	1,890	3,028	3,278	4,995	7,384	7,560
Mortgage interest and charges	2,962	417	1,759	958	2,812	4,661	4,531
Property taxes	1,242	799	730	1,219	1,243	1,576	1,633
Maintenance, repair, insurance, other expenses	960	674	540	1,101	939	1,147	1,396
Rented dwellings	2,160	1,903	2,914	1,293	2,229	2,084	1,864
Other lodging	505	180	406	542	476	606	752
Utilities, fuels, and public services	2,684	1,666	1,739	2,553	2,865	3,169	3,788
Natural gas	330	235	219	331	351	378	445
Electricity	981	622	587	1,019	1,093	1,146	1,333
Fuel oil and other fuels	88	91	46	116	85	96	125
Telephone	957	495	701	739	982	1,164	1,421
Water and other public services	328	224	187	348	354	384	464

		single-person CUs		CUs with two or more people			
	total CUs	no earner	one earner	no earner	one earner	two earners	three+ earners
Household services	**$706**	**$608**	**$277**	**$505**	**$681**	**$1,069**	**$636**
Personal services	331	329	19	162	291	614	204
Other household services	375	279	258	343	390	455	433
Housekeeping supplies	**545**	**272**	**268**	**541**	**551**	**710**	**798**
Laundry and cleaning supplies	131	65	63	130	150	155	210
Other household products	283	117	118	254	267	407	413
Postage and stationery	131	90	87	156	135	148	175
Household furnishings and equipment	**1,518**	**511**	**926**	**1,113**	**1,526**	**2,079**	**2,243**
Household textiles	136	66	90	127	113	175	224
Furniture	401	102	225	272	419	594	506
Floor coverings	40	16	15	48	46	57	46
Major appliances	188	84	100	138	199	256	271
Small appliances, misc. housewares	100	31	72	73	106	137	119
Miscellaneous household equipment	652	212	425	453	644	860	1,076
APPAREL AND RELATED SERVICES	**1,749**	**612**	**1,103**	**1,037**	**1,839**	**2,351**	**2,665**
Men and boys	**409**	**95**	**224**	**225**	**414**	**589**	**664**
Men, aged 16 or older	319	80	210	170	281	455	549
Boys, aged 2 to 15	90	14	14	55	133	133	115
Women and girls	**704**	**311**	**473**	**469**	**781**	**880**	**1,039**
Women, aged 16 or older	587	300	454	419	581	719	878
Girls, aged 2 to 15	117	11	19	50	201	161	161
Children under age 2	**83**	**13**	**17**	**34**	**115**	**131**	**96**
Footwear	**313**	**117**	**167**	**169**	**324**	**426**	**533**
Other apparel products and services	**240**	**76**	**223**	**140**	**205**	**325**	**333**
TRANSPORTATION	**7,759**	**2,173**	**4,906**	**5,330**	**7,576**	**10,384**	**13,372**
Vehicle purchases	**3,665**	**816**	**2,163**	**2,382**	**3,699**	**4,960**	**6,538**
Cars and trucks, new	1,753	417	1,013	1,300	1,898	2,369	2,729
Cars and trucks, used	1,842	399	1,110	1,041	1,760	2,489	3,624
Other vehicles	70	–	39	42	40	102	186
Gasoline and motor oil	**1,235**	**395**	**795**	**906**	**1,214**	**1,607**	**2,133**
Other vehicle expenses	**2,471**	**799**	**1,606**	**1,664**	**2,333**	**3,330**	**4,159**
Vehicle finance charges	397	48	199	151	360	618	727
Maintenance and repairs	697	267	537	550	642	902	1,054
Vehicle insurance	894	373	552	702	892	1,109	1,601
Vehicle rentals, leases, licenses, other charges	483	110	317	261	439	701	777
Public transportation	**389**	**164**	**342**	**377**	**330**	**487**	**541**
HEALTH CARE	**2,350**	**2,064**	**1,201**	**3,827**	**2,544**	**2,498**	**2,693**
Health insurance	1,168	1,108	552	1,990	1,242	1,248	1,277
Medical services	590	289	354	676	650	710	783
Drugs	487	597	229	972	538	433	510
Medical supplies	105	71	66	188	114	106	123
ENTERTAINMENT	**2,079**	**701**	**1,484**	**1,265**	**2,037**	**2,801**	**3,172**
Fees and admissions	542	159	415	358	528	734	762
Television, radio, sound equipment	692	335	544	516	710	847	981
Pets, toys, and playground equipment	369	134	241	199	384	520	488
Other entertainment products and services	476	73	283	192	415	701	941
PERSONAL CARE PRODUCTS AND SERVICES	**526**	**286**	**325**	**458**	**565**	**654**	**722**
READING	**139**	**97**	**114**	**140**	**133**	**162**	**164**
EDUCATION	**752**	**269**	**736**	**251**	**576**	**858**	**1,806**

		single-person CUs		CUs with two or more people			
	total CUs	no earner	one earner	no earner	one earner	two earners	three+ earners
TOBACCO PRODUCTS AND SMOKING SUPPLIES	$320	$142	$250	$210	$324	$387	$529
MISCELLANEOUS	792	439	698	608	731	975	1,052
CASH CONTRIBUTIONS	1,277	938	1,034	1,471	1,235	1,398	1,649
PERSONAL INSURANCE AND PENSIONS	3,899	361	3,058	550	3,070	6,202	6,470
Life and other personal insurance	406	171	190	415	452	534	556
Pensions and Social Security	3,493	189	2,868	135	2,618	5,668	5,914
PERSONAL TAXES	2,496	203	2,653	537	1,808	3,759	3,407
Federal income taxes	1,843	52	2,094	287	1,272	2,797	2,484
State and local income taxes	506	35	478	24	423	783	709
Other taxes	147	116	81	226	113	180	213
GIFTS FOR NON–HOUSEHOLD MEMBERS	1,036	542	863	645	862	1,359	1,546
Food	82	30	49	43	62	121	152
Alcoholic beverages	13	8	11	5	13	18	17
Housing	259	142	186	170	218	357	358
Housekeeping supplies	42	23	26	42	39	56	58
Household textiles	14	11	8	10	16	18	14
Appliances and misc. housewares	24	13	17	12	21	38	16
Major appliances	8	5	3	2	6	16	7
Small appliances and misc. housewares	16	8	14	10	15	22	9
Miscellaneous household equipment	65	36	51	45	62	76	107
Other housing	114	59	84	60	80	169	163
Apparel and services	237	116	229	146	224	308	250
Males, aged 2 or older	64	28	59	41	62	87	54
Females, aged 2 or older	82	56	68	56	75	105	94
Children under age 2	40	13	16	23	50	56	55
Other apparel products and services	52	19	85	26	37	60	47
Jewelry and watches	24	7	61	9	14	22	15
All other apparel products and services	28	12	25	17	24	38	32
Transportation	44	24	58	45	43	27	96
Health care	33	22	25	34	25	39	52
Entertainment	78	36	70	52	78	101	89
Toys, games, hobbies, and tricycles	30	17	26	29	30	38	28
Other entertainment	48	19	44	23	47	63	61
Personal care products and services	21	11	17	10	23	30	17
Reading	1	2	1	2	1	1	1
Education	184	100	117	61	110	251	450
All other gifts	84	51	97	77	66	106	64

Note: Spending by category will not add to total spending because gift spending is also included in the preceding product and service categories and personal taxes are not included in the total. (–) means sample is too small to make a reliable estimate.
Source: Bureau of Labor Statistics, 2002 Consumer Expenditure Surveys, Internet site http://www.bls.gov/cex/

Table 1.53 Indexed spending by number of earners in household, 2002

(indexed average annual spending of consumer units (CU) by product and service category, CU size, and number of earners in CU, 2002; index definition: an index of 100 is the average for all consumer units; an index of 132 means that spending by consumer units in that group is 32 percent above the average for all consumer units; an index of 68 indicates spending that is 32 percent below the average for all consumer units)

		single-person CUs		CUs with two or more people			
	total CUs	no earner	one earner	no earner	one earner	two earners	three+ earners
Average spending of CU, total	$40,677	$17,607	$28,077	$29,721	$39,923	$52,991	$60,844
Average spending of CU, index	100	43	69	73	98	130	150
FOOD	**100**	**44**	**60**	**85**	**105**	**125**	**156**
Food at home	**100**	**52**	**49**	**95**	**114**	**120**	**158**
Cereals and bakery products	100	53	48	102	117	117	158
Cereals and cereal products	100	49	48	101	119	118	157
Bakery products	100	56	48	103	116	116	158
Meats, poultry, fish, and eggs	100	48	43	92	117	121	166
Beef	100	40	40	87	117	124	174
Pork	100	53	38	110	119	121	151
Other meats	100	52	44	98	115	117	175
Poultry	100	48	43	82	115	124	170
Fish and seafood	100	53	53	82	117	118	164
Eggs	100	59	53	109	118	112	150
Dairy products	100	53	49	96	118	120	151
Fresh milk and cream	100	58	46	99	117	117	157
Other dairy products	100	50	51	95	118	121	146
Fruits and vegetables	100	57	51	102	116	115	156
Fresh fruits	100	59	51	106	116	113	157
Fresh vegetables	100	55	49	103	118	116	151
Processed fruits	100	57	52	93	112	117	160
Processed vegetables	100	55	51	104	118	116	157
Other food at home	100	52	54	91	110	122	154
Sugar and other sweets	100	68	47	100	115	119	147
Fats and oils	100	56	47	115	112	116	158
Miscellaneous foods	100	50	55	84	110	125	151
Nonalcoholic beverages	100	49	56	89	108	120	164
Food prepared by CU on trips	100	41	59	115	98	129	144
Food away from home	**100**	**34**	**75**	**70**	**92**	**133**	**154**
ALCOHOLIC BEVERAGES	**100**	**30**	**102**	**55**	**85**	**131**	**140**
HOUSING	**100**	**53**	**72**	**74**	**100**	**129**	**133**
Shelter	**100**	**51**	**81**	**65**	**98**	**129**	**130**
Owned dwellings	100	37	59	63	97	143	146
Mortgage interest and charges	100	14	59	32	95	157	153
Property taxes	100	64	59	98	100	127	131
Maintenance, repair, insurance, other expenses	100	70	56	115	98	119	145
Rented dwellings	100	88	135	60	103	96	86
Other lodging	100	36	80	107	94	120	149
Utilities, fuels, and public services	**100**	**62**	**65**	**95**	**107**	**118**	**141**
Natural gas	100	71	66	100	106	115	135
Electricity	100	63	60	104	111	117	136
Fuel oil and other fuels	100	103	52	132	97	109	142
Telephone	100	52	73	77	103	122	148
Water and other public services	100	68	57	106	108	117	141

	total CUs	single-person CUs		CUs with two or more people			
		no earner	one earner	no earner	one earner	two earners	three+ earners
Household services	**100**	**86**	**39**	**72**	**96**	**151**	**90**
Personal services	100	99	6	49	88	185	62
Other household services	100	74	69	91	104	121	115
Housekeeping supplies	**100**	**50**	**49**	**99**	**101**	**130**	**146**
Laundry and cleaning supplies	100	50	48	99	115	118	160
Other household products	100	41	42	90	94	144	146
Postage and stationery	100	69	66	119	103	113	134
Household furnishings and equipment	**100**	**34**	**61**	**73**	**101**	**137**	**148**
Household textiles	100	49	66	93	83	129	165
Furniture	100	25	56	68	104	148	126
Floor coverings	100	40	38	120	115	143	115
Major appliances	100	45	53	73	106	136	144
Small appliances, misc. housewares	100	31	72	73	106	137	119
Miscellaneous household equipment	100	33	65	69	99	132	165
APPAREL AND RELATED SERVICES	**100**	**35**	**63**	**59**	**105**	**134**	**152**
Men and boys	**100**	**23**	**55**	**55**	**101**	**144**	**162**
Men, aged 16 or older	100	25	66	53	88	143	172
Boys, aged 2 to 15	100	16	16	61	148	148	128
Women and girls	**100**	**44**	**67**	**67**	**111**	**125**	**148**
Women, aged 16 or older	100	51	77	71	99	122	150
Girls, aged 2 to 15	100	9	16	43	172	138	138
Children under age 2	**100**	**16**	**20**	**41**	**139**	**158**	**116**
Footwear	**100**	**37**	**53**	**54**	**104**	**136**	**170**
Other apparel products and services	**100**	**32**	**93**	**58**	**85**	**135**	**139**
TRANSPORTATION	**100**	**28**	**63**	**69**	**98**	**134**	**172**
Vehicle purchases	**100**	**22**	**59**	**65**	**101**	**135**	**178**
Cars and trucks, new	100	24	58	74	108	135	156
Cars and trucks, used	100	22	60	57	96	135	197
Other vehicles	100	–	56	60	57	146	266
Gasoline and motor oil	**100**	**32**	**64**	**73**	**98**	**130**	**173**
Other vehicle expenses	**100**	**32**	**65**	**67**	**94**	**135**	**168**
Vehicle finance charges	100	12	50	38	91	156	183
Maintenance and repairs	100	38	77	79	92	129	151
Vehicle insurance	100	42	62	79	100	124	179
Vehicle rentals, leases, licenses, other charges	100	23	66	54	91	145	161
Public transportation	**100**	**42**	**88**	**97**	**85**	**125**	**139**
HEALTH CARE	**100**	**88**	**51**	**163**	**108**	**106**	**115**
Health insurance	100	95	47	170	106	107	109
Medical services	100	49	60	115	110	120	133
Drugs	100	123	47	200	110	89	105
Medical supplies	100	68	63	179	109	101	117
ENTERTAINMENT	**100**	**34**	**71**	**61**	**98**	**135**	**153**
Fees and admissions	100	29	77	66	97	135	141
Television, radio, sound equipment	100	48	79	75	103	122	142
Pets, toys, and playground equipment	100	36	65	54	104	141	132
Other entertainment products and services	100	15	59	40	87	147	198
PERSONAL CARE PRODUCTS AND SERVICES	**100**	**54**	**62**	**87**	**107**	**124**	**137**
READING	**100**	**70**	**82**	**101**	**96**	**117**	**118**
EDUCATION	**100**	**36**	**98**	**33**	**77**	**114**	**240**

		single-person CUs		CUs with two or more people			
	total CUs	no earner	one earner	no earner	one earner	two earners	three+ earners
TOBACCO PRODUCTS AND SMOKING SUPPLIES	100	44	78	66	101	121	165
MISCELLANEOUS	100	55	88	77	92	123	133
CASH CONTRIBUTIONS	100	73	81	115	97	109	129
PERSONAL INSURANCE AND PENSIONS	100	9	78	14	79	159	166
Life and other personal insurance	100	42	47	102	111	132	137
Pensions and Social Security	100	5	82	4	75	162	169
PERSONAL TAXES	100	8	106	22	72	151	136
Federal income taxes	100	3	114	16	69	152	135
State and local income taxes	100	7	94	5	84	155	140
Other taxes	100	79	55	154	77	122	145
GIFTS FOR NON–HOUSEHOLD MEMBERS	100	52	83	62	83	131	149
Food	100	37	60	52	76	148	185
Alcoholic beverages	100	62	85	38	100	138	131
Housing	100	55	72	66	84	138	138
Housekeeping supplies	100	55	62	100	93	133	138
Household textiles	100	79	57	71	114	129	100
Appliances and misc. housewares	100	54	71	50	88	158	67
Major appliances	100	63	38	25	75	200	88
Small appliances and misc. housewares	100	50	88	63	94	138	56
Miscellaneous household equipment	100	55	78	69	95	117	165
Other housing	100	52	74	53	70	148	143
Apparel and services	100	49	97	62	95	130	105
Males, aged 2 or older	100	44	92	64	97	136	84
Females, aged 2 or older	100	68	83	68	91	128	115
Children under age 2	100	33	40	58	125	140	138
Other apparel products and services	100	37	163	50	71	115	90
Jewelry and watches	100	29	254	38	58	92	63
All other apparel products and services	100	43	89	61	86	136	114
Transportation	100	55	132	102	98	61	218
Health care	100	67	76	103	76	118	158
Entertainment	100	46	90	67	100	129	114
Toys, games, hobbies, and tricycles	100	57	87	97	100	127	93
Other entertainment	100	40	92	48	98	131	127
Personal care products and services	100	52	81	48	110	143	81
Reading	100	200	100	200	100	100	100
Education	100	54	64	33	60	136	245
All other gifts	100	61	115	92	79	126	76

Note: (–) means sample is too small to make a reliable estimate.
Source: Calculations by New Strategist based on the Bureau of Labor Statistics 2002 Consumer Expenditure Survey

Spending by Occupation of Householder, 2002

Households headed by managers and professionals spent $57,200 in 2002, 41 percent more than the average household. Behind the higher level of spending are their higher incomes, averaging $80,469 in 2002. Among all wage and salary workers, average household income was $57,422 with spending only 11 percent above average. Households headed by retirees spend 32 percent less than the average household, while the self-employed spend 15 percent more than average.

Households headed by managers and professionals spend more than average on many of the products and services associated with the income elite. They spend 44 percent more than the average household on food away from home, 47 percent more on alcoholic beverages, 64 percent more on other lodging (which includes vacation homes and hotel and motel expenses), 56 percent more on men's clothes, 49 percent more on women's clothes, 49 percent more on new cars and trucks, 78 percent more on fees and admissions to entertainment events, and 60 percent more on gifts for non–household members.

The self-employed are the biggest spenders on products and services needed by people who are likely to work at home. They spend more than managers and professionals on electricity and health insurance. Their spending is below that of managers and professionals on household personal services (mostly day care) and men's and women's clothes.

The retired spend more than the average household on postage and stationery, maintenance and repairs for owned homes, fuel oil, health care, and cash contributions.

Table 1.54 Average spending by occupation of householder, 2002

(average annual spending of consumer units (CU) by product and service category and by selected occupation of consumer unit reference person, 2002)

	total consumer units	self-employed	wage and salary workers total	managers and professionals	technical, sales, admin. support	service workers	construction workers, mechanics	operators, fabricators, laborers	retired
Number of consumer units (in thousands, add 000s)	112,108	5,106	74,695	27,104	20,964	10,704	4,885	11,038	19,204
Average number of persons per CU	2.5	2.5	2.7	2.6	2.6	2.7	2.8	2.9	1.7
Average income before taxes	$49,430	$54,787	$57,422	$80,469	$49,363	$35,108	$50,401	$40,214	$26,399
Average annual spending	40,677	46,880	45,296	57,200	42,069	34,515	40,711	34,601	27,535
FOOD	**$5,375**	**$5,906**	**$5,835**	**$6,797**	**$5,497**	**$5,114**	**$5,480**	**$4,939**	**$3,798**
Food at home	**3,099**	**3,063**	**3,244**	**3,526**	**3,035**	**3,127**	**3,261**	**3,038**	**2,519**
Cereals and bakery products	450	433	467	516	438	453	450	418	384
Cereals and cereal products	154	144	162	175	148	167	166	151	117
Bakery products	296	289	305	341	290	286	284	268	267
Meats, poultry, fish, and eggs	798	766	839	851	798	847	937	834	616
Beef	231	254	245	243	242	227	278	256	167
Pork	167	150	172	156	162	196	208	190	144
Other meats	101	91	105	105	95	104	122	114	82
Poultry	144	133	155	162	148	159	175	136	102
Fish and seafood	121	107	129	153	120	123	117	99	90
Eggs	34	31	34	32	32	37	38	39	30
Dairy products	328	322	340	377	318	315	335	316	277
Fresh milk and cream	127	129	130	133	120	129	141	135	108
Other dairy products	201	193	211	244	198	186	194	182	168
Fruits and vegetables	552	535	568	648	510	542	535	521	501
Fresh fruits	178	170	182	215	162	161	158	170	165
Fresh vegetables	175	163	180	206	160	172	178	162	160
Processed fruits	116	118	120	136	110	121	116	99	102
Processed vegetables	83	84	86	90	78	88	83	89	74
Other food at home	970	1,007	1,030	1,134	971	971	1,003	949	740
Sugar and other sweets	117	124	119	131	114	122	104	105	104
Fats and oils	85	77	87	88	80	88	104	87	79
Miscellaneous foods	472	495	508	565	484	471	487	460	341
Nonalcoholic beverages	254	253	272	291	255	258	276	267	179
Food prepared by CU on trips	41	58	43	59	38	32	33	30	37
Food away from home	**2,276**	**2,842**	**2,591**	**3,271**	**2,462**	**1,986**	**2,219**	**1,902**	**1,279**
ALCOHOLIC BEVERAGES	**376**	**500**	**436**	**554**	**374**	**323**	**428**	**369**	**208**
HOUSING	**13,283**	**15,193**	**14,621**	**18,644**	**13,717**	**11,053**	**12,640**	**10,782**	**9,307**
Shelter	**7,829**	**8,999**	**8,783**	**11,418**	**8,296**	**6,531**	**7,524**	**5,978**	**4,871**
Owned dwellings	5,165	6,597	5,830	8,268	5,303	3,364	5,198	3,515	3,217
Mortgage interest and charges	2,962	3,704	3,597	5,122	3,268	2,009	3,321	2,137	891
Property taxes	1,242	1,562	1,274	1,855	1,096	773	1,079	757	1,247
Maintenance, repair, insurance, other expenses	960	1,331	959	1,291	938	582	797	621	1,079
Rented dwellings	2,160	1,485	2,427	2,321	2,553	2,814	2,050	2,239	1,219
Other lodging	505	917	526	829	440	353	276	224	435
Utilities, fuels, and public services	**2,684**	**3,059**	**2,784**	**3,166**	**2,658**	**2,442**	**2,694**	**2,461**	**2,382**
Natural gas	330	386	333	393	315	274	298	291	340
Electricity	981	1,155	995	1,081	961	912	1,027	912	906
Fuel oil and other fuels	88	117	79	91	68	61	84	87	123
Telephone	957	996	1,048	1,208	1,006	917	967	898	678
Water and other public services	328	405	330	393	308	277	316	273	335

	total consumer units	self–employed	wage and salary workers						retired
			total	managers and professionals	technical, sales, admin. support	service workers	construction workers, mechanics	operators, fabricators, laborers	
Household services	**$706**	**$938**	**$758**	**$1,127**	**$700**	**$406**	**$531**	**$403**	**$616**
Personal services	331	309	380	547	359	202	349	199	244
Other household services	375	629	378	581	341	204	182	204	372
Housekeeping supplies	**545**	**539**	**578**	**644**	**511**	**452**	**452**	**716**	**477**
Laundry and cleaning supplies	131	148	135	140	134	139	140	120	108
Other household products	283	245	312	324	255	224	214	516	219
Postage and stationery	131	145	131	181	122	89	98	80	150
Household furnishings and equipment	**1,518**	**1,658**	**1,718**	**2,290**	**1,551**	**1,222**	**1,439**	**1,224**	**962**
Household textiles	136	182	148	191	144	127	87	95	99
Furniture	401	416	463	612	443	317	372	320	224
Floor coverings	40	44	44	61	36	32	52	24	31
Major appliances	188	188	212	264	181	167	239	175	144
Small appliances, misc. housewares	100	80	116	155	117	80	84	68	63
Miscellaneous household equipment	652	749	735	1,007	630	500	606	542	402
APPAREL AND RELATED SERVICES	**1,749**	**1,788**	**2,004**	**2,532**	**1,906**	**1,618**	**1,447**	**1,507**	**899**
Men and boys	**409**	**446**	**474**	**612**	**411**	**378**	**380**	**385**	**196**
Men, aged 16 or older	319	362	369	498	311	273	261	299	169
Boys, aged 2 to 15	90	83	105	114	100	105	119	87	26
Women and girls	**704**	**692**	**787**	**1,023**	**786**	**590**	**546**	**502**	**420**
Women, aged 16 or older	587	594	649	872	671	453	360	376	395
Girls, aged 2 to 15	117	99	138	151	116	137	186	126	25
Children under age 2	**83**	**71**	**98**	**106**	**99**	**94**	**89**	**88**	**22**
Footwear	**313**	**298**	**364**	**403**	**359**	**374**	**244**	**319**	**138**
Other apparel products and services	**240**	**282**	**281**	**388**	**251**	**183**	**189**	**213**	**123**
TRANSPORTATION	**7,759**	**7,102**	**8,959**	**10,494**	**8,491**	**7,507**	**9,025**	**7,458**	**4,468**
Vehicle purchases	**3,665**	**2,576**	**4,332**	**4,854**	**4,183**	**3,905**	**4,458**	**3,691**	**1,793**
Cars and trucks, new	1,753	839	2,048	2,617	1,999	1,683	1,313	1,426	1,068
Cars and trucks, used	1,842	1,686	2,196	2,144	2,128	2,112	2,952	2,203	714
Other vehicles	70	51	88	94	57	109	194	62	11
Gasoline and motor oil	**1,235**	**1,334**	**1,387**	**1,519**	**1,320**	**1,180**	**1,539**	**1,322**	**779**
Other vehicle expenses	**2,471**	**2,693**	**2,822**	**3,460**	**2,625**	**2,207**	**2,779**	**2,245**	**1,553**
Vehicle finance charges	397	323	487	549	482	361	552	438	149
Maintenance and repairs	697	799	782	971	724	636	650	626	481
Vehicle insurance	894	873	987	1,144	933	824	947	883	680
Vehicle rentals, leases, licenses, other charges	483	699	566	797	486	385	630	298	243
Public transportation	**389**	**498**	**418**	**661**	**362**	**215**	**247**	**200**	**343**
HEALTH CARE	**2,350**	**3,628**	**2,058**	**2,538**	**1,955**	**1,559**	**1,786**	**1,679**	**3,482**
Health insurance	1,168	1,760	1,012	1,251	998	728	810	815	1,815
Medical services	590	1,033	584	738	505	488	583	451	594
Drugs	487	669	369	420	369	285	319	347	925
Medical supplies	105	166	93	130	83	58	73	66	148
ENTERTAINMENT	**2,079**	**2,441**	**2,366**	**3,178**	**2,200**	**1,659**	**2,001**	**1,532**	**1,254**
Fees and admissions	542	740	613	963	516	344	428	280	330
Television, radio, sound equipment	692	704	766	912	740	626	666	636	490
Pets, toys, and playground equipment	369	444	421	532	386	356	357	303	212
Other entertainment products and services	476	554	567	771	559	332	549	314	221
PERSONAL CARE PRODUCTS AND SERVICES	**526**	**561**	**563**	**713**	**545**	**442**	**435**	**398**	**435**
READING	**139**	**177**	**142**	**211**	**127**	**83**	**90**	**82**	**146**
EDUCATION	**752**	**855**	**914**	**1,319**	**861**	**634**	**501**	**472**	**177**

			wage and salary workers					
	total consumer units	self– employed	total	managers and professionals	technical, sales, admin. support	service workers	construction workers, mechanics	operators, fabricators, laborers	retired
TOBACCO PRODUCTS AND SMOKING SUPPLIES	$320	$315	$354	$251	$354	$377	$582	$482	$163
MISCELLANEOUS	792	1,144	843	1,106	730	654	895	570	657
CASH CONTRIBUTIONS	1,277	1,750	1,278	1,792	1,069	742	1,298	928	1,546
PERSONAL INSURANCE AND PENSIONS	3,899	5,518	4,923	7,071	4,244	2,751	4,103	3,404	995
Life and other personal insurance	406	544	429	602	370	278	366	290	383
Pensions and Social Security	3,493	4,974	4,494	6,470	3,873	2,473	3,737	3,114	612
PERSONAL TAXES	2,496	2,672	3,141	5,475	2,251	991	2,443	1,424	826
Federal income taxes	1,843	2,112	2,346	4,195	1,664	624	1,765	976	534
State and local income taxes	506	328	656	1,088	476	257	542	360	93
Other taxes	147	232	139	193	111	110	136	88	199
GIFTS FOR NON–HOUSEHOLD MEMBERS	1,036	1,457	1,147	1,662	1,019	740	833	660	749
Food	82	84	98	154	88	51	52	45	49
Alcoholic beverages	13	19	16	21	14	12	15	9	8
Housing	259	282	290	406	274	211	199	151	191
Housekeeping supplies	42	53	44	54	46	40	26	26	46
Household textiles	14	10	14	15	17	16	4	7	13
Appliances and misc. housewares	24	12	28	41	28	14	15	17	20
Major appliances	8	2	10	15	9	2	10	9	8
Small appliances and misc. housewares	16	10	18	26	19	12	5	8	12
Miscellaneous household equipment	65	75	71	109	62	39	55	35	50
Other housing	114	132	133	188	121	102	99	66	62
Apparel and services	237	232	269	336	263	202	179	217	170
Males, aged 2 or older	64	71	70	87	74	50	41	50	56
Females, aged 2 or older	82	83	90	112	83	64	62	84	67
Children under age 2	40	32	46	53	47	38	42	39	20
Other apparel products and services	52	45	63	85	59	51	35	44	27
Jewelry and watches	24	22	31	52	22	15	25	15	8
All other apparel products and services	28	23	32	33	37	35	9	29	19
Transportation	44	85	39	62	22	56	13	10	32
Health care	33	89	30	51	19	13	33	18	30
Entertainment	78	109	85	107	80	54	82	70	58
Toys, games, hobbies, and tricycles	30	39	31	34	31	25	34	30	26
Other entertainment	48	69	54	73	49	29	48	40	31
Personal care products and services	21	12	25	35	23	18	20	17	11
Reading	1	2	1	2	1	–	–	1	2
Education	184	376	211	371	188	81	79	46	111
All other gifts	84	167	84	119	46	41	161	76	87

Note: Spending by category will not add to total spending because gift spending is also included in the preceding product and service categories and personal taxes are not included in the total. (–) means sample is too small to make a reliable estimate.
Source: Bureau of Labor Statistics, 2002 Consumer Expenditure Surveys, Internet site http://www.bls.gov/cex/

Table 1.55 Indexed spending by occupation of householder, 2002

(indexed average annual spending of consumer units (CU) by product and service category and selected occupation of consumer unit reference person, 2002; index definition: an index of 100 is the average for all consumer units; an index of 132 means that spending by consumer units in that group is 32 percent above the average for all consumer units; an index of 68 indicates spending that is 32 percent below the average for all consumer units)

| | total consumer units | self-employed | wage and salary workers | | | | | | retired |
			total	managers and professionals	technical, sales, admin. support	service workers	construction workers, mechanics	operators, fabricators, laborers	
Average spending of CU, total	$40,677	$46,880	$45,296	$57,200	$42,069	$34,515	$40,711	$34,601	$27,535
Average spending of CU, index	100	115	111	141	103	85	100	85	68
FOOD	100	110	109	126	102	95	102	92	71
Food at home	100	99	105	114	98	101	105	98	81
Cereals and bakery products	100	96	104	115	97	101	100	93	85
Cereals and cereal products	100	94	105	114	96	108	108	98	76
Bakery products	100	98	103	115	98	97	96	91	90
Meats, poultry, fish, and eggs	100	96	105	107	100	106	117	105	77
Beef	100	110	106	105	105	98	120	111	72
Pork	100	90	103	93	97	117	125	114	86
Other meats	100	90	104	104	94	103	121	113	81
Poultry	100	92	108	113	103	110	122	94	71
Fish and seafood	100	88	107	126	99	102	97	82	74
Eggs	100	91	100	94	94	109	112	115	88
Dairy products	100	98	104	115	97	96	102	96	84
Fresh milk and cream	100	102	102	105	94	102	111	106	85
Other dairy products	100	96	105	121	99	93	97	91	84
Fruits and vegetables	100	97	103	117	92	98	97	94	91
Fresh fruits	100	96	102	121	91	90	89	96	93
Fresh vegetables	100	93	103	118	91	98	102	93	91
Processed fruits	100	102	103	117	95	104	100	85	88
Processed vegetables	100	101	104	108	94	106	100	107	89
Other food at home	100	104	106	117	100	100	103	98	76
Sugar and other sweets	100	106	102	112	97	104	89	90	89
Fats and oils	100	91	102	104	94	104	122	102	93
Miscellaneous foods	100	105	108	120	103	100	103	97	72
Nonalcoholic beverages	100	100	107	115	100	102	109	105	70
Food prepared by CU on trips	100	141	105	144	93	78	80	73	90
Food away from home	100	125	114	144	108	87	97	84	56
ALCOHOLIC BEVERAGES	100	133	116	147	99	86	114	98	55
HOUSING	100	114	110	140	103	83	95	81	70
Shelter	100	115	112	146	106	83	96	76	62
Owned dwellings	100	128	113	160	103	65	101	68	62
Mortgage interest and charges	100	125	121	173	110	68	112	72	30
Property taxes	100	126	103	149	88	62	87	61	100
Maintenance, repair, insurance, other expenses	100	139	100	134	98	61	83	65	112
Rented dwellings	100	69	112	107	118	130	95	104	56
Other lodging	100	182	104	164	87	70	55	44	86
Utilities, fuels, and public services	100	114	104	118	99	91	100	92	89
Natural gas	100	117	101	119	95	83	90	88	103
Electricity	100	118	101	110	98	93	105	93	92
Fuel oil and other fuels	100	133	90	103	77	69	95	99	140
Telephone	100	104	110	126	105	96	101	94	71
Water and other public services	100	123	101	120	94	84	96	83	102

			wage and salary workers						
	total consumer units	self—employed	total	managers and professionals	technical, sales, admin. support	service workers	construction workers, mechanics	operators, fabricators, laborers	retired
Household services	100	133	107	160	99	58	75	57	87
Personal services	100	93	115	165	108	61	105	60	74
Other household services	100	168	101	155	91	54	49	54	99
Housekeeping supplies	100	99	106	118	94	83	83	131	88
Laundry and cleaning supplies	100	113	103	107	102	106	107	92	82
Other household products	100	87	110	114	90	79	76	182	77
Postage and stationery	100	111	100	138	93	68	75	61	115
Household furnishings and equipment	100	109	113	151	102	81	95	81	63
Household textiles	100	134	109	140	106	93	64	70	73
Furniture	100	104	115	153	110	79	93	80	56
Floor coverings	100	110	110	153	90	80	130	60	78
Major appliances	100	100	113	140	96	89	127	93	77
Small appliances, misc. housewares	100	80	116	155	117	80	84	68	63
Miscellaneous household equipment	100	115	113	154	97	77	93	83	62
APPAREL AND RELATED SERVICES	100	102	115	145	109	93	83	86	51
Men and boys	100	109	116	150	100	92	93	94	48
Men, aged 16 or older	100	113	116	156	97	86	82	94	53
Boys, aged 2 to 15	100	92	117	127	111	117	132	97	29
Women and girls	100	98	112	145	112	84	78	71	60
Women, aged 16 or older	100	101	111	149	114	77	61	64	67
Girls, aged 2 to 15	100	85	118	129	99	117	159	108	21
Children under age 2	100	86	118	128	119	113	107	106	27
Footwear	100	95	116	129	115	119	78	102	44
Other apparel products and services	100	118	117	162	105	76	79	89	51
TRANSPORTATION	100	92	115	135	109	97	116	96	58
Vehicle purchases	100	70	118	132	114	107	122	101	49
Cars and trucks, new	100	48	117	149	114	96	75	81	61
Cars and trucks, used	100	92	119	116	116	115	160	120	39
Other vehicles	100	73	126	134	81	156	277	89	16
Gasoline and motor oil	100	108	112	123	107	96	125	107	63
Other vehicle expenses	100	109	114	140	106	89	112	91	63
Vehicle finance charges	100	81	123	138	121	91	139	110	38
Maintenance and repairs	100	115	112	139	104	91	93	90	69
Vehicle insurance	100	98	110	128	104	92	106	99	76
Vehicle rentals, leases, licenses, other charges	100	145	117	165	101	80	130	62	50
Public transportation	100	128	107	170	93	55	63	51	88
HEALTH CARE	100	154	88	108	83	66	76	71	148
Health insurance	100	151	87	107	85	62	69	70	155
Medical services	100	175	99	125	86	83	99	76	101
Drugs	100	137	76	86	76	59	66	71	190
Medical supplies	100	158	89	124	79	55	70	63	141
ENTERTAINMENT	100	117	114	153	106	80	96	74	60
Fees and admissions	100	137	113	178	95	63	79	52	61
Television, radio, sound equipment	100	102	111	132	107	90	96	92	71
Pets, toys, and playground equipment	100	120	114	144	105	96	97	82	57
Other entertainment products and services	100	116	119	162	117	70	115	66	46
PERSONAL CARE PRODUCTS AND SERVICES	100	107	107	136	104	84	83	76	83
READING	100	127	102	152	91	60	65	59	105
EDUCATION	100	114	122	175	114	84	67	63	24

	total consumer units	self–employed	wage and salary workers						retired
			total	managers and professionals	technical, sales, admin. support	service workers	construction workers, mechanics	operators, fabricators, laborers	
TOBACCO PRODUCTS AND SMOKING SUPPLIES	100	98	111	78	111	118	182	151	51
MISCELLANEOUS	100	144	106	140	92	83	113	72	83
CASH CONTRIBUTIONS	100	137	100	140	84	58	102	73	121
PERSONAL INSURANCE AND PENSIONS	100	142	126	181	109	71	105	87	26
Life and other personal insurance	100	134	106	148	91	68	90	71	94
Pensions and Social Security	100	142	129	185	111	71	107	89	18
PERSONAL TAXES	100	107	126	219	90	40	98	57	33
Federal income taxes	100	115	127	228	90	34	96	53	29
State and local income taxes	100	65	130	215	94	51	107	71	18
Other taxes	100	158	95	131	76	75	93	60	135
GIFTS FOR NON–HOUSEHOLD MEMBERS	100	141	111	160	98	71	80	64	72
Food	100	102	120	188	107	62	63	55	60
Alcoholic beverages	100	146	123	162	108	92	115	69	62
Housing	100	109	112	157	106	81	77	58	74
Housekeeping supplies	100	126	105	129	110	95	62	62	110
Household textiles	100	71	100	107	121	114	29	50	93
Appliances and misc. housewares	100	50	117	171	117	58	63	71	83
Major appliances	100	25	125	188	113	25	125	113	100
Small appliances and misc. housewares	100	63	113	163	119	75	31	50	75
Miscellaneous household equipment	100	115	109	168	95	60	85	54	77
Other housing	100	116	117	165	106	89	87	58	54
Apparel and services	100	98	114	142	111	85	76	92	72
Males, aged 2 or older	100	111	109	136	116	78	64	78	88
Females, aged 2 or older	100	101	110	137	101	78	76	102	82
Children under age 2	100	80	115	133	118	95	105	98	50
Other apparel products and services	100	87	121	163	113	98	67	85	52
Jewelry and watches	100	92	129	217	92	63	104	63	33
All other apparel products and services	100	82	114	118	132	125	32	104	68
Transportation	100	193	89	141	50	127	30	23	73
Health care	100	270	91	155	58	39	100	55	91
Entertainment	100	140	109	137	103	69	105	90	74
Toys, games, hobbies, and tricycles	100	130	103	113	103	83	113	100	87
Other entertainment	100	144	113	152	102	60	100	83	65
Personal care products and services	100	57	119	167	110	86	95	81	52
Reading	100	200	100	200	100	–	–	100	200
Education	100	204	115	202	102	44	43	25	60
All other gifts	100	199	100	142	55	49	192	90	104

Note: (–) means sample is too small to make a reliable estimate.
Source: Calculations by New Strategist based on the Bureau of Labor Statistics 2002 Consumer Expenditure Survey

Spending on Apparel, 2002

Americans spend much less on apparel than they once did. In 2002, the average household spent $1,749 on clothes, shoes, and related items. This figure is 9 percent less than the $1,932 spent by the average household on apparel in 1997, after adjusting for inflation. Overall, Americans devoted 4.3 percent of their spending dollars to clothes, shoes, and related products and services in 2002, down from 5.0 percent in 1990.

Households headed by people aged 35 to 54 spend the most on apparel, more than $2,000 in 2002. Apparel spending patterns differ sharply by age. Householders aged 35 to 44 spend the most on boys' and girls' apparel. Those aged 25 to 34 spend the most on infants' apparel. Contrary to popular perception, householders aged 55 to 64 spend the most on women's clothes—34 percent more than the average household.

Affluent households spend much more on apparel, accessories, and related services than the average household. Households with incomes of $70,000 or more spent $3,469 on clothes in 2002, accounting for 42 percent of the market. Affluent households are particularly important consumers of men's coats and jackets (64 percent of the market), women's dresses (55 percent), watches (55 percent), and professional dry cleaning (61 percent).

Married couples with children under age 18 at home spend more on clothes and related products than any other household type, more than $2,600 in 2002. In part, this is because their households are larger than average. Married couples without children at home (most of them empty-nesters) spend more than any other household type on women's dresses.

Blacks spend almost as much as whites on apparel, and Hispanics outspend non-Hispanics. Black households spent just 3 percent less than the average household on apparel in 2002, while Hispanics spent 20 percent more. Blacks are the biggest spenders on boys' shoes, and professional laundry and dry cleaning. Hispanics are the biggest spenders on men's clothes, children's clothes, and men's and women's shoes. Both blacks and Hispanics spend much more than the average household on coin-operated laundries.

Spending on apparel is greatest in the Northeast, where households spent an average of $1,965 on clothes in 2002—12 percent more than the average household. In the Midwest, apparel spending is about average. Apparel spending is 9 percent below average in the South. Spending on boys' shoes is higher in the South than in any other region, however.

The most educated householders spend the most on clothes because they have the highest incomes. Householders with a college degree spent more than $2,000 on clothes in 2002—39 percent more than the average household. College graduates account for less than one-third of the market for children's clothes, but for fully 50 percent of the market for men's sports coats.

Table 2.1 Apparel: Average spending by age, 2002

(average annual spending of consumer units (CU) on apparel, accessories, and related services, by age of consumer unit reference person, 2002)

	total consumer units	under 25	25 to 34	35 to 44	45 to 54	55 to 64	65 to 74	75+
Number of consumer units (in thousands, add 000)	112,108	8,737	18,988	24,394	22,691	15,314	11,216	10,767
Average number of persons per CU	2.5	1.9	2.9	3.2	2.7	2.1	1.9	1.5
Average before-tax income of CU	$49,430.00	$20,773.00	$49,133.00	$61,532.00	$64,974.00	$53,162.00	$35,118.00	$23,890.00
Average spending of CU, total	40,676.60	24,229.46	40,318.29	48,330.48	48,748.24	44,330.04	32,242.52	23,758.89
Apparel, average spending	1,749.22	1,364.87	1,988.99	2,100.89	2,028.73	1,791.35	1,252.47	673.79
MEN'S APPAREL	**$319.48**	**$229.89**	**$367.05**	**$382.72**	**$391.28**	**$297.25**	**$251.65**	**$107.88**
Suits	32.96	20.73	33.93	38.73	43.59	36.72	20.93	12.91
Sport coats and tailored jackets	10.65	3.46	7.22	10.00	18.78	14.34	9.11	3.24
Coats and jackets	33.86	24.32	49.58	43.02	35.10	23.10	32.88	5.22
Underwear	15.27	7.25	14.40	21.16	18.49	13.58	14.26	6.36
Hosiery	12.22	9.79	11.33	18.14	14.48	9.94	9.54	3.17
Nightwear	2.98	1.60	2.53	3.77	3.25	3.85	3.20	1.08
Accessories	22.41	14.16	26.61	24.63	26.77	22.84	22.93	5.64
Sweaters and vests	15.68	14.82	15.12	17.05	20.50	16.35	14.09	4.80
Active sportswear	15.13	8.39	21.98	16.67	15.74	14.17	9.74	10.38
Shirts	78.89	55.67	94.94	95.35	100.01	70.41	57.26	19.37
Pants	57.64	57.94	62.43	67.69	66.83	49.70	45.86	28.88
Shorts and shorts sets	12.22	4.22	14.41	14.77	17.07	12.41	6.41	4.31
Uniforms	3.21	3.69	4.45	3.77	4.58	2.18	0.75	0.50
Costumes	6.35	3.84	8.13	7.96	6.09	7.67	4.68	2.02
BOYS' (AGED 2 TO 15) APPAREL	**89.98**	**36.21**	**119.07**	**179.14**	**85.49**	**40.19**	**33.25**	**17.63**
Coats and jackets	6.38	1.48	8.76	11.69	6.73	4.73	1.53	0.78
Sweaters	3.65	0.94	4.86	7.29	3.38	1.76	1.58	0.86
Shirts	19.50	11.61	25.27	41.07	16.09	6.09	7.35	4.63
Underwear	5.02	1.74	6.27	11.29	3.54	2.51	1.63	1.15
Nightwear	2.59	4.07	2.49	4.09	2.09	1.04	1.96	1.95
Hosiery	4.21	1.48	5.18	9.96	2.87	1.63	1.38	0.92
Accessories	4.12	2.87	7.18	6.57	3.63	1.27	2.58	0.66
Suits, sport coats, and vests	2.37	0.92	2.52	3.45	3.32	1.95	0.90	1.03
Pants	22.58	6.49	30.82	43.04	23.89	10.46	9.03	3.32
Shorts and shorts sets	8.66	1.86	12.82	17.05	9.26	3.38	2.17	0.82
Uniforms	3.35	0.68	3.40	7.50	3.62	1.44	1.33	0.23
Active sportswear	3.84	1.05	4.98	7.56	4.29	2.16	0.69	0.35
Costumes	3.72	1.03	4.52	8.58	2.78	1.77	1.12	0.94
WOMEN'S APPAREL	**586.91**	**558.81**	**511.05**	**540.45**	**731.65**	**787.66**	**522.93**	**318.30**
Coats and jackets	50.06	58.15	32.29	32.35	78.14	70.61	48.46	28.20
Dresses	56.40	39.90	31.91	38.73	54.42	156.05	41.51	31.04
Sport coats and tailored jackets	6.48	2.70	3.66	6.78	10.15	7.49	5.06	6.17
Sweaters and vests	50.47	44.92	41.37	55.20	67.02	55.41	36.34	32.60
Shirts, blouses, and tops	103.24	111.72	94.29	82.74	124.07	150.43	90.19	59.99
Skirts	17.48	16.60	20.76	20.17	18.43	19.37	14.14	4.39
Pants	96.29	138.15	93.63	89.05	111.24	106.92	94.77	35.76
Shorts and shorts sets	16.09	21.08	14.67	17.21	18.19	14.23	17.19	8.73
Active sportswear	30.07	21.07	32.21	28.68	44.82	25.92	20.53	21.24
Nightwear	27.63	16.96	22.55	32.20	32.85	27.06	29.40	22.94
Undergarments	33.55	32.51	33.08	35.37	39.79	37.33	28.12	17.57
Hosiery	21.22	13.04	15.94	22.99	26.58	23.56	27.67	11.76
Suits	29.01	17.88	23.75	28.83	42.29	35.12	22.77	17.56

	total consumer units	under 25	25 to 34	35 to 44	45 to 54	55 to 64	65 to 74	75+
Accessories	$33.37	$16.60	$28.92	$35.11	$43.11	$42.79	$34.38	$15.57
Uniforms	6.12	3.70	7.74	7.03	7.65	7.13	3.94	0.77
Costumes	9.42	3.83	14.26	8.02	12.88	8.23	8.47	4.01
GIRLS' (AGED 2 TO 15) APPAREL	**117.21**	**50.15**	**135.89**	**246.96**	**118.47**	**52.31**	**34.74**	**17.00**
Coats and jackets	6.49	1.92	7.97	13.02	6.74	2.81	2.92	1.22
Dresses and suits	12.41	1.96	9.89	23.32	21.02	5.73	2.57	1.77
Shirts, blouses, and sweaters	29.33	12.77	32.29	65.89	27.27	12.29	6.03	5.89
Skirts and pants	24.07	6.62	30.22	48.25	25.22	11.94	8.29	3.89
Shorts and shorts sets	8.28	2.10	11.16	18.27	7.31	2.31	4.08	0.55
Active sportswear	9.32	12.68	9.48	18.89	7.75	2.14	6.48	0.54
Underwear and nightwear	7.63	2.39	10.76	14.53	7.53	4.27	2.08	1.50
Hosiery	4.30	3.10	4.67	9.51	3.75	2.45	0.33	0.53
Accessories	5.81	2.07	5.59	14.58	3.36	5.31	0.68	0.22
Uniforms	4.77	1.79	6.90	10.95	3.86	1.60	0.55	0.20
Costumes	4.80	2.75	6.97	9.74	4.65	1.47	0.74	0.69
CHILDREN UNDER AGE 2	**82.60**	**101.63**	**188.24**	**97.16**	**51.26**	**48.56**	**26.80**	**15.27**
Coats, jackets, and snowsuits	2.43	2.26	4.68	2.88	1.34	2.49	1.75	0.50
Outerwear including dresses	23.71	28.55	39.47	25.32	20.27	22.80	14.91	6.05
Underwear	43.60	61.52	111.48	54.66	22.03	14.86	5.73	5.75
Nightwear and loungewear	4.07	3.01	7.06	4.12	3.40	5.26	2.55	0.86
Accessories	8.79	6.29	25.54	10.18	4.22	3.16	1.86	2.11
FOOTWEAR	**313.17**	**246.34**	**385.10**	**381.78**	**364.79**	**289.84**	**207.70**	**108.17**
Men's	102.90	88.10	121.04	108.10	142.36	72.84	98.92	31.88
Boys'	36.87	16.36	62.76	76.07	25.50	12.68	6.86	5.96
Women's	141.64	130.00	151.03	142.91	161.81	189.70	94.58	66.30
Girls'	31.76	11.88	50.27	54.70	35.11	14.61	7.34	4.04
OTHER APPAREL PRODUCTS AND SERVICES	**239.87**	**141.82**	**282.60**	**272.68**	**285.79**	**275.54**	**175.40**	**89.52**
Material for making clothes	5.11	0.85	2.22	4.50	5.23	7.31	13.65	2.95
Sewing patterns and notions	8.20	3.74	5.45	6.98	7.23	17.74	13.24	2.65
Watches	13.62	6.98	15.52	18.63	14.82	12.42	12.07	5.03
Jewelry	89.65	36.56	115.99	94.74	114.21	113.82	54.73	25.02
Shoe repair and other shoe services	1.44	0.35	1.00	1.51	2.00	1.98	1.30	1.20
Coin-operated apparel laundry and dry cleaning	37.58	62.85	63.56	42.71	29.58	22.09	19.22	17.67
Apparel alteration, repair, and tailoring services	5.86	2.59	5.35	6.09	8.13	6.68	5.35	3.53
Clothing rental	2.66	3.10	3.08	2.32	5.27	1.51	1.19	–
Watch and jewelry repair	5.49	0.79	2.65	5.10	5.17	11.20	7.40	5.82
Professional laundry, dry cleaning	69.69	23.61	67.70	89.19	93.88	80.24	45.60	25.52
Clothing storage	0.55	0.40	0.08	0.92	0.27	0.56	1.64	0.13

Note: (–) means sample is too small to make a reliable estimate.
Source: Bureau of Labor Statistics, unpublished data from the 2002 Consumer Expenditure Survey

Table 2.2 Apparel: Indexed spending by age, 2002

(indexed average annual spending of consumer units (CU) on apparel, accessories, and related services, by age of consumer unit reference person, 2002; index definition: an index of 100 is the average for all consumer units; an index of 132 means that spending by consumer units in that group is 32 percent above the average for all consumer units; an index of 68 indicates spending that is 32 percent below the average for all consumer units)

	total consumer units	under 25	25 to 34	35 to 44	45 to 54	55 to 64	65 to 74	75+
Average spending of CU, total	$40,677	$24,229	$40,318	$48,330	$48,748	$44,330	$32,243	$23,759
Average spending of CU, index	100	60	99	119	120	109	79	58
Apparel, spending index	100	78	114	120	116	102	72	39
MEN'S APPAREL	100	72	115	120	122	93	79	34
Suits	100	63	103	118	132	111	64	39
Sport coats and tailored jackets	100	32	68	94	176	135	86	30
Coats and jackets	100	72	146	127	104	68	97	15
Underwear	100	47	94	139	121	89	93	42
Hosiery	100	80	93	148	118	81	78	26
Nightwear	100	54	85	127	109	129	107	36
Accessories	100	63	119	110	119	102	102	25
Sweaters and vests	100	95	96	109	131	104	90	31
Active sportswear	100	55	145	110	104	94	64	69
Shirts	100	71	120	121	127	89	73	25
Pants	100	101	108	117	116	86	80	50
Shorts and shorts sets	100	35	118	121	140	102	52	35
Uniforms	100	115	139	117	143	68	23	16
Costumes	100	60	128	125	96	121	74	32
BOYS' (AGED 2 TO 15) APPAREL	100	40	132	199	95	45	37	20
Coats and jackets	100	23	137	183	105	74	24	12
Sweaters	100	26	133	200	93	48	43	24
Shirts	100	60	130	211	83	31	38	24
Underwear	100	35	125	225	71	50	32	23
Nightwear	100	157	96	158	81	40	76	75
Hosiery	100	35	123	237	68	39	33	22
Accessories	100	70	174	159	88	31	63	16
Suits, sport coats, and vests	100	39	106	146	140	82	38	43
Pants	100	29	136	191	106	46	40	15
Shorts and shorts sets	100	21	148	197	107	39	25	9
Uniforms	100	20	101	224	108	43	40	7
Active sportswear	100	27	130	197	112	56	18	9
Costumes	100	28	122	231	75	48	30	25
WOMEN'S APPAREL	100	95	87	92	125	134	89	54
Coats and jackets	100	116	65	65	156	141	97	56
Dresses	100	71	57	69	96	277	74	55
Sport coats and tailored jackets	100	42	56	105	157	116	78	95
Sweaters and vests	100	89	82	109	133	110	72	65
Shirts, blouses, and tops	100	108	91	80	120	146	87	58
Skirts	100	95	119	115	105	111	81	25
Pants	100	143	97	92	116	111	98	37
Shorts and shorts sets	100	131	91	107	113	88	107	54
Active sportswear	100	70	107	95	149	86	68	71
Nightwear	100	61	82	117	119	98	106	83
Undergarments	100	97	99	105	119	111	84	52
Hosiery	100	61	75	108	125	111	130	55
Suits	100	62	82	99	146	121	78	61

	total consumer units	under 25	25 to 34	35 to 44	45 to 54	55 to 64	65 to 74	75+
Accessories	100	50	87	105	129	128	103	47
Uniforms	100	60	126	115	125	117	64	13
Costumes	100	41	151	85	137	87	90	43
GIRLS' (AGED 2 TO 15) APPAREL	**100**	**43**	**116**	**211**	**101**	**45**	**30**	**15**
Coats and jackets	100	30	123	201	104	43	45	19
Dresses and suits	100	16	80	188	169	46	21	14
Shirts, blouses, and sweaters	100	44	110	225	93	42	21	20
Skirts and pants	100	28	126	200	105	50	34	16
Shorts and shorts sets	100	25	135	221	88	28	49	7
Active sportswear	100	136	102	203	83	23	70	6
Underwear and nightwear	100	31	141	190	99	56	27	20
Hosiery	100	72	109	221	87	57	8	12
Accessories	100	36	96	251	58	91	12	4
Uniforms	100	38	145	230	81	34	12	4
Costumes	100	57	145	203	97	31	15	14
CHILDREN UNDER AGE 2	**100**	**123**	**228**	**118**	**62**	**59**	**32**	**18**
Coats, jackets, and snowsuits	100	93	193	119	55	102	72	21
Outerwear including dresses	100	120	166	107	85	96	63	26
Underwear	100	141	256	125	51	34	13	13
Nightwear and loungewear	100	74	173	101	84	129	63	21
Accessories	100	72	291	116	48	36	21	24
FOOTWEAR	**100**	**79**	**123**	**122**	**116**	**93**	**66**	**35**
Men's	100	86	118	105	138	71	96	31
Boys'	100	44	170	206	69	34	19	16
Women's	100	92	107	101	114	134	67	47
Girls'	100	37	158	172	111	46	23	13
OTHER APPAREL PRODUCTS AND SERVICES	**100**	**59**	**118**	**114**	**119**	**115**	**73**	**37**
Material for making clothes	100	17	43	88	102	143	267	58
Sewing patterns and notions	100	46	66	85	88	216	161	32
Watches	100	51	114	137	109	91	89	37
Jewelry	100	41	129	106	127	127	61	28
Shoe repair and other shoe services	100	24	69	105	139	138	90	83
Coin-operated apparel laundry and dry cleaning	100	167	169	114	79	59	51	47
Apparel alteration, repair, and tailoring services	100	44	91	104	139	114	91	60
Clothing rental	100	117	116	87	198	57	45	–
Watch and jewelry repair	100	14	48	93	94	204	135	106
Professional laundry, dry cleaning	100	34	97	128	135	115	65	37
Clothing storage	100	73	15	167	49	102	298	24

Note: (–) means sample is too small to make a reliable estimate.
Source: Calculations by New Strategist based on the 2002 Consumer Expenditure Survey

Table 2.3 Apparel: Total spending by age, 2002

(total annual spending on apparel, accessories, and related services, by consumer unit (CU) age group, 2002; numbers in thousands)

	total consumer units	under 25	25 to 34	35 to 44	45 to 54	55 to 64	65 to 74	75+
Number of consumer units	112,108	8,737	18,988	24,394	22,691	15,314	11,216	10,767
Total spending of all CUs	$4,560,172,273	$211,692,792	$765,563,691	$1,178,973,729	$1,106,146,314	$678,870,233	$361,632,104	$255,811,969
Apparel, total spending	196,101,556	11,924,869	37,766,942	51,249,111	46,033,912	27,432,734	14,047,704	7,254,697
MEN'S APPAREL	**$35,816,264**	**$2,008,549**	**$6,969,545**	**$9,336,072**	**$8,878,534**	**$4,552,087**	**$2,822,506**	**$1,161,544**
Suits	3,695,080	181,118	644,263	944,780	989,101	562,330	234,751	139,002
Sport coats and tailored jackets	1,193,950	30,230	137,093	243,940	426,137	219,603	102,178	34,885
Coats and jackets	3,795,977	212,484	941,425	1,049,430	796,454	353,753	368,782	56,204
Underwear	1,711,889	63,343	273,427	516,177	419,557	207,964	159,940	68,478
Hosiery	1,369,960	85,535	215,134	442,507	328,566	152,221	107,001	34,131
Nightwear	334,082	13,979	48,040	91,965	73,746	58,959	35,891	11,628
Accessories	2,512,340	123,716	505,271	600,824	607,438	349,772	257,183	60,726
Sweaters and vests	1,757,853	129,482	287,099	415,918	465,166	250,384	158,033	51,682
Active sportswear	1,696,194	73,303	417,356	406,648	357,156	216,999	109,244	111,761
Shirts	8,844,200	486,389	1,802,721	2,325,968	2,269,327	1,078,259	642,228	208,557
Pants	6,461,905	506,222	1,185,421	1,651,230	1,516,440	761,106	514,366	310,951
Shorts and shorts sets	1,369,960	36,870	273,617	360,299	387,335	190,047	71,895	46,406
Uniforms	359,867	32,240	84,497	91,965	103,925	33,385	8,412	5,384
Costumes	711,886	33,550	154,372	194,176	138,188	117,458	52,491	21,749
BOYS' (AGED 2 TO 15) APPAREL	**10,087,478**	**316,367**	**2,260,901**	**4,369,941**	**1,939,854**	**615,470**	**372,932**	**189,822**
Coats and jackets	715,249	12,931	166,335	285,166	152,710	72,435	17,160	8,398
Sweaters	409,194	8,213	92,282	177,832	76,696	26,953	17,721	9,260
Shirts	2,186,106	101,437	479,827	1,001,862	365,098	93,262	82,438	49,851
Underwear	562,782	15,202	119,055	275,408	80,326	38,438	18,282	12,382
Nightwear	290,360	35,560	47,280	99,771	47,424	15,927	21,983	20,996
Hosiery	471,975	12,931	98,358	242,964	65,123	24,962	15,478	9,906
Accessories	461,885	25,075	136,334	160,269	82,368	19,449	28,937	7,106
Suits, sport coats, and vests	265,696	8,038	47,850	84,159	75,334	29,862	10,094	11,090
Pants	2,531,399	56,703	585,210	1,049,918	542,088	160,184	101,280	35,746
Shorts and shorts sets	970,855	16,251	243,426	415,918	210,119	51,761	24,339	8,829
Uniforms	375,562	5,941	64,559	182,955	82,141	22,052	14,917	2,476
Active sportswear	430,495	9,174	94,560	184,419	97,344	33,078	7,739	3,768
Costumes	417,042	8,999	85,826	209,301	63,081	27,106	12,562	10,121
WOMEN'S APPAREL	**65,797,306**	**4,882,323**	**9,703,817**	**13,183,737**	**16,601,870**	**12,062,225**	**5,865,183**	**3,427,136**
Coats and jackets	5,612,126	508,057	613,123	789,146	1,773,075	1,081,322	543,527	303,629
Dresses	6,322,891	348,606	605,907	944,780	1,234,844	2,389,750	465,576	334,208
Sport coats and tailored jackets	726,460	23,590	69,496	165,391	230,314	114,702	56,753	66,432
Sweaters and vests	5,658,091	392,466	785,534	1,346,549	1,520,751	848,549	407,589	351,004
Shirts, blouses, and tops	11,574,030	976,098	1,790,379	2,018,360	2,815,272	2,303,685	1,011,571	645,912
Skirts	1,959,648	145,034	394,191	492,027	418,195	296,632	158,594	47,267
Pants	10,794,879	1,207,017	1,777,846	2,172,286	2,524,147	1,637,373	1,062,940	385,028
Shorts and shorts sets	1,803,818	184,176	278,554	419,821	412,749	217,918	192,803	93,996
Active sportswear	3,371,088	184,089	611,603	699,620	1,017,011	396,939	230,264	228,691
Nightwear	3,097,544	148,180	428,179	785,487	745,399	414,397	329,750	246,995
Undergarments	3,761,223	284,040	628,123	862,816	902,875	571,672	315,394	189,176
Hosiery	2,378,932	113,930	302,669	560,818	603,127	360,798	310,347	126,620
Suits	3,252,253	156,218	450,965	703,279	959,602	537,828	255,388	189,069

	total consumer units	under 25	25 to 34	35 to 44	45 to 54	55 to 64	65 to 74	75+
Accessories	$3,741,044	$145,034	$549,133	$856,473	$978,209	$655,286	$385,606	$167,642
Uniforms	686,101	32,327	146,967	171,490	173,586	109,189	44,191	8,291
Costumes	1,056,057	33,463	270,769	195,640	292,260	126,034	95,000	43,176
GIRLS' (AGED 2 TO 15) APPAREL	**13,140,179**	**438,161**	**2,580,279**	**6,024,342**	**2,688,203**	**801,075**	**389,644**	**183,039**
Coats and jackets	727,581	16,775	151,334	317,610	152,937	43,032	32,751	13,136
Dresses and suits	1,391,260	17,125	187,791	568,868	476,965	87,749	28,825	19,058
Shirts, blouses, and sweaters	3,288,128	111,571	613,123	1,607,321	618,784	188,209	67,632	63,418
Skirts and pants	2,698,440	57,839	573,817	1,177,011	572,267	182,849	92,981	41,884
Shorts and shorts sets	928,254	18,348	211,906	445,678	165,871	35,375	45,761	5,922
Active sportswear	1,044,847	110,785	180,006	460,803	175,855	32,772	72,680	5,814
Underwear and nightwear	855,384	20,881	204,311	354,445	170,863	65,391	23,329	16,151
Hosiery	482,064	27,085	88,674	231,987	85,091	37,519	3,701	5,707
Accessories	651,347	18,086	106,143	355,665	76,242	81,317	7,627	2,369
Uniforms	534,755	15,639	131,017	267,114	87,587	24,502	6,169	2,153
Costumes	538,118	24,027	132,346	237,598	105,513	22,512	8,300	7,429
CHILDREN UNDER AGE 2	**9,260,121**	**887,941**	**3,574,301**	**2,370,121**	**1,163,141**	**743,648**	**300,589**	**164,412**
Coats, jackets, and snowsuits	272,422	19,746	88,864	70,255	30,406	38,132	19,628	5,384
Outerwear including dresses	2,658,081	249,441	749,456	617,656	459,947	349,159	167,231	65,140
Underwear	4,887,909	537,500	2,116,782	1,333,376	499,883	227,566	64,268	61,910
Nightwear and loungewear	456,280	26,298	134,055	100,503	77,149	80,552	28,601	9,260
Accessories	985,429	54,956	484,954	248,331	95,756	48,392	20,862	22,718
FOOTWEAR	**35,108,862**	**2,152,273**	**7,312,279**	**9,313,141**	**8,277,450**	**4,438,610**	**2,329,563**	**1,164,666**
Men's	11,535,913	769,730	2,298,308	2,636,991	3,230,291	1,115,472	1,109,487	343,252
Boys'	4,133,422	142,937	1,191,687	1,855,652	578,621	194,182	76,942	64,171
Women's	15,878,977	1,135,810	2,867,758	3,486,147	3,671,631	2,905,066	1,060,809	713,852
Girls'	3,560,550	103,796	954,527	1,334,352	796,681	223,738	82,325	43,499
OTHER APPAREL PRODUCTS AND SERVICES	**26,891,346**	**1,239,081**	**5,366,009**	**6,651,756**	**6,484,861**	**4,219,620**	**1,967,286**	**963,862**
Material for making clothes	572,872	7,426	42,153	109,773	118,674	111,945	153,098	31,763
Sewing patterns and notions	919,286	32,676	103,485	170,270	164,056	271,670	148,500	28,533
Watches	1,526,911	60,984	294,694	454,460	336,281	190,200	135,377	54,158
Jewelry	10,050,482	319,425	2,202,418	2,311,088	2,591,539	1,743,039	613,852	269,390
Shoe repair and other shoe services	161,436	3,058	18,988	36,835	45,382	30,322	14,581	12,920
Coin-operated apparel laundry, dry cleaning	4,213,019	549,120	1,206,877	1,041,868	671,200	338,286	215,572	190,253
Apparel alteration, repair, tailoring services	656,953	22,629	101,586	148,559	184,478	102,298	60,006	38,008
Clothing rental	298,207	27,085	58,483	56,594	119,582	23,124	13,347	–
Watch and jewelry repair	615,473	6,902	50,318	124,409	117,312	171,517	82,998	62,664
Professional laundry, dry cleaning	7,812,807	206,281	1,285,488	2,175,701	2,130,231	1,228,795	511,450	274,774
Clothing storage	61,659	3,495	1,519	22,442	6,127	8,576	18,394	1,400

Note: Numbers may not add to total because of rounding. (–) means sample is too small to make a reliable estimate.
Source: Calculations by New Strategist based on the 2002 Consumer Expenditure Survey

Table 2.4 Apparel: Market shares by age, 2002

(percentage of total annual spending on apparel, accessories, and related services accounted for by consumer unit age groups, 2002)

	total consumer units	under 25	25 to 34	35 to 44	45 to 54	55 to 64	65 to 74	75+
Share of total consumer units	100.0%	7.8%	16.9%	21.8%	20.2%	13.7%	10.0%	9.6%
Share of total before-tax income	100.0	3.3	16.8	27.1	26.6	14.7	7.1	4.6
Share of total spending	100.0	4.6	16.8	25.9	24.3	14.9	7.9	5.6
Share of apparel spending	100.0	6.1	19.3	26.1	23.5	14.0	7.2	3.7
MEN'S APPAREL	**100.0%**	**5.6%**	**19.5%**	**26.1%**	**24.8%**	**12.7%**	**7.9%**	**3.2%**
Suits	100.0	4.9	17.4	25.6	26.8	15.2	6.4	3.8
Sport coats and tailored jackets	100.0	2.5	11.5	20.4	35.7	18.4	8.6	2.9
Coats and jackets	100.0	5.6	24.8	27.6	21.0	9.3	9.7	1.5
Underwear	100.0	3.7	16.0	30.2	24.5	12.1	9.3	4.0
Hosiery	100.0	6.2	15.7	32.3	24.0	11.1	7.8	2.5
Nightwear	100.0	4.2	14.4	27.5	22.1	17.6	10.7	3.5
Accessories	100.0	4.9	20.1	23.9	24.2	13.9	10.2	2.4
Sweaters and vests	100.0	7.4	16.3	23.7	26.5	14.2	9.0	2.9
Active sportswear	100.0	4.3	24.6	24.0	21.1	12.8	6.4	6.6
Shirts	100.0	5.5	20.4	26.3	25.7	12.2	7.3	2.4
Pants	100.0	7.8	18.3	25.6	23.5	11.8	8.0	4.8
Shorts and shorts sets	100.0	2.7	20.0	26.3	28.3	13.9	5.2	3.4
Uniforms	100.0	9.0	23.5	25.6	28.9	9.3	2.3	1.5
Costumes	100.0	4.7	21.7	27.3	19.4	16.5	7.4	3.1
BOYS' (AGED 2 TO 15) APPAREL	**100.0**	**3.1**	**22.4**	**43.3**	**19.2**	**6.1**	**3.7**	**1.9**
Coats and jackets	100.0	1.8	23.3	39.9	21.4	10.1	2.4	1.2
Sweaters	100.0	2.0	22.6	43.5	18.7	6.6	4.3	2.3
Shirts	100.0	4.6	21.9	45.8	16.7	4.3	3.8	2.3
Underwear	100.0	2.7	21.2	48.9	14.3	6.8	3.2	2.2
Nightwear	100.0	12.2	16.3	34.4	16.3	5.5	7.6	7.2
Hosiery	100.0	2.7	20.8	51.5	13.8	5.3	3.3	2.1
Accessories	100.0	5.4	29.5	34.7	17.8	4.2	6.3	1.5
Suits, sport coats, and vests	100.0	3.0	18.0	31.7	28.4	11.2	3.8	4.2
Pants	100.0	2.2	23.1	41.5	21.4	6.3	4.0	1.4
Shorts and shorts sets	100.0	1.7	25.1	42.8	21.6	5.3	2.5	0.9
Uniforms	100.0	1.6	17.2	48.7	21.9	5.9	4.0	0.7
Active sportswear	100.0	2.1	22.0	42.8	22.6	7.7	1.8	0.9
Costumes	100.0	2.2	20.6	50.2	15.1	6.5	3.0	2.4
WOMEN'S APPAREL	**100.0**	**7.4**	**14.7**	**20.0**	**25.2**	**18.3**	**8.9**	**5.2**
Coats and jackets	100.0	9.1	10.9	14.1	31.6	19.3	9.7	5.4
Dresses	100.0	5.5	9.6	14.9	19.5	37.8	7.4	5.3
Sport coats and tailored jackets	100.0	3.2	9.6	22.8	31.7	15.8	7.8	9.1
Sweaters and vests	100.0	6.9	13.9	23.8	26.9	15.0	7.2	6.2
Shirts, blouses, and tops	100.0	8.4	15.5	17.4	24.3	19.9	8.7	5.6
Skirts	100.0	7.4	20.1	25.1	21.3	15.1	8.1	2.4
Pants	100.0	11.2	16.5	20.1	23.4	15.2	9.8	3.6
Shorts and shorts sets	100.0	10.2	15.4	23.3	22.9	12.1	10.7	5.2
Active sportswear	100.0	5.5	18.1	20.8	30.2	11.8	6.8	6.8
Nightwear	100.0	4.8	13.8	25.4	24.1	13.4	10.6	8.0
Undergarments	100.0	7.6	16.7	22.9	24.0	15.2	8.4	5.0
Hosiery	100.0	4.8	12.7	23.6	25.4	15.2	13.0	5.3
Suits	100.0	4.8	13.9	21.6	29.5	16.5	7.9	5.8

	total consumer units	under 25	25 to 34	35 to 44	45 to 54	55 to 64	65 to 74	75+
Accessories	100.0%	3.9%	14.7%	22.9%	26.1%	17.5%	10.3%	4.5%
Uniforms	100.0	4.7	21.4	25.0	25.3	15.9	6.4	1.2
Costumes	100.0	3.2	25.6	18.5	27.7	11.9	9.0	4.1
GIRLS' (AGED 2 TO 15) APPAREL	**100.0**	**3.3**	**19.6**	**45.8**	**20.5**	**6.1**	**3.0**	**1.4**
Coats and jackets	100.0	2.3	20.8	43.7	21.0	5.9	4.5	1.8
Dresses and suits	100.0	1.2	13.5	40.9	34.3	6.3	2.1	1.4
Shirts, blouses, and sweaters	100.0	3.4	18.6	48.9	18.8	5.7	2.1	1.9
Skirts and pants	100.0	2.1	21.3	43.6	21.2	6.8	3.4	1.6
Shorts and shorts sets	100.0	2.0	22.8	48.0	17.9	3.8	4.9	0.6
Active sportswear	100.0	10.6	17.2	44.1	16.8	3.1	7.0	0.6
Underwear and nightwear	100.0	2.4	23.9	41.4	20.0	7.6	2.7	1.9
Hosiery	100.0	5.6	18.4	48.1	17.7	7.8	0.8	1.2
Accessories	100.0	2.8	16.3	54.6	11.7	12.5	1.2	0.4
Uniforms	100.0	2.9	24.5	50.0	16.4	4.6	1.2	0.4
Costumes	100.0	4.5	24.6	44.2	19.6	4.2	1.5	1.4
CHILDREN UNDER AGE 2	**100.0**	**9.6**	**38.6**	**25.6**	**12.6**	**8.0**	**3.2**	**1.8**
Coats, jackets, and snowsuits	100.0	7.2	32.6	25.8	11.2	14.0	7.2	2.0
Outerwear including dresses	100.0	9.4	28.2	23.2	17.3	13.1	6.3	2.5
Underwear	100.0	11.0	43.3	27.3	10.2	4.7	1.3	1.3
Nightwear and loungewear	100.0	5.8	29.4	22.0	16.9	17.7	6.3	2.0
Accessories	100.0	5.6	49.2	25.2	9.7	4.9	2.1	2.3
FOOTWEAR	**100.0**	**6.1**	**20.8**	**26.5**	**23.6**	**12.6**	**6.6**	**3.3**
Men's	100.0	6.7	19.9	22.9	28.0	9.7	9.6	3.0
Boys'	100.0	3.5	28.8	44.9	14.0	4.7	1.9	1.6
Women's	100.0	7.2	18.1	22.0	23.1	18.3	6.7	4.5
Girls'	100.0	2.9	26.8	37.5	22.4	6.3	2.3	1.2
OTHER APPAREL PRODUCTS AND SERVICES	**100.0**	**4.6**	**20.0**	**24.7**	**24.1**	**15.7**	**7.3**	**3.6**
Material for making clothes	100.0	1.3	7.4	19.2	20.7	19.5	26.7	5.5
Sewing patterns and notions	100.0	3.6	11.3	18.5	17.8	29.6	16.2	3.1
Watches	100.0	4.0	19.3	29.8	22.0	12.5	8.9	3.5
Jewelry	100.0	3.2	21.9	23.0	25.8	17.3	6.1	2.7
Shoe repair and other shoe services	100.0	1.9	11.8	22.8	28.1	18.8	9.0	8.0
Coin-operated apparel laundry and dry cleaning	100.0	13.0	28.6	24.7	15.9	8.0	5.1	4.5
Apparel alteration, repair, and tailoring services	100.0	3.4	15.5	22.6	28.1	15.6	9.1	5.8
Clothing rental	100.0	9.1	19.6	19.0	40.1	7.8	4.5	–
Watch and jewelry repair	100.0	1.1	8.2	20.2	19.1	27.9	13.5	10.2
Professional laundry, dry cleaning	100.0	2.6	16.5	27.8	27.3	15.7	6.5	3.5
Clothing storage	100.0	5.7	2.5	36.4	9.9	13.9	29.8	2.3

Note: Numbers may not add to total because of rounding. (–) means sample is too small to make a reliable estimate.
Source: Calculations by New Strategist based on the 2002 Consumer Expenditure Survey

Table 2.5 Apparel: Average spending by income, 2002

(average annual spending on apparel, accessories, and related services, by before-tax income of consumer unit (CU), 2002; complete income reporters only)

	complete income reporters	under $10,000	$10,000– $19,999	$20,000– $29,999	$30,000– $39,999	$40,000– $49,999	$50,000– $69,999	$70,000 or more
Number of consumer units (in thousands, add 000)	92,388	10,933	15,075	12,312	10,727	8,873	13,521	20,947
Average number of persons per CU	2.5	1.7	1.9	2.3	2.5	2.6	2.8	3.1
Average before-tax income of CU	$49,430.00	$5,554.80	$14,724.33	$24,495.00	$34,423.00	$44,443.00	$58,933.00	$115,629.00
Average spending of CU, total	42,556.98	17,627.83	22,838.71	28,835.85	35,095.39	41,787.38	50,406.17	76,627.31
Apparel, average spending	1,871.96	939.00	1,058.22	1,176.48	1,496.86	1,691.94	2,043.40	3,469.49
MEN'S APPAREL	**$435.98**	**$188.00**	**$213.34**	**$235.84**	**$361.42**	**$386.81**	**$452.60**	**$879.56**
Suits	341.67	145.57	137.63	182.18	288.02	311.54	349.45	708.99
Sport coats and tailored jackets	33.67	9.06	9.80	10.81	22.07	22.66	32.53	88.48
Coats and jackets	10.77	2.33	2.18	4.29	7.59	7.41	7.21	30.52
Underwear	36.97	18.63	17.01	11.61	27.50	33.26	36.69	81.19
Hosiery	17.35	5.99	9.69	13.13	15.93	18.23	18.16	30.29
Nightwear	12.99	4.92	5.53	7.51	14.91	14.52	14.27	22.88
Accessories	2.96	0.72	1.23	2.23	2.63	3.21	3.71	5.37
Sweaters and vests	24.36	8.95	6.59	15.45	31.42	20.54	26.21	46.12
Active sportswear	15.13	10.63	7.15	7.88	9.68	10.58	13.08	33.53
Shirts	87.55	44.44	26.60	43.77	73.72	90.48	83.91	184.42
Pants	62.92	21.38	31.84	45.53	53.50	54.52	79.51	112.11
Shorts and shorts sets	12.45	4.73	11.14	10.34	11.46	13.53	7.40	21.28
Uniforms	3.22	0.59	0.99	3.10	3.34	3.01	4.45	5.51
Costumes	5.98	1.13	1.38	1.84	2.72	6.60	8.76	13.87
BOYS' (AGED 2 TO 15) APPAREL	**94.32**	**42.43**	**75.71**	**53.66**	**73.40**	**75.27**	**103.15**	**170.56**
Coats and jackets	6.36	2.85	3.49	3.56	7.25	5.95	6.98	11.23
Sweaters	3.67	1.94	3.83	1.87	2.65	3.45	4.24	5.78
Shirts	21.70	12.19	25.99	9.91	10.27	14.93	14.22	43.29
Underwear	5.85	3.62	3.94	2.37	2.16	2.57	6.70	12.99
Nightwear	3.00	1.41	5.14	2.26	2.86	0.97	4.94	2.39
Hosiery	4.75	1.80	2.42	2.35	3.72	1.17	6.37	10.17
Accessories	4.54	2.98	2.63	2.00	4.06	4.04	5.46	8.02
Suits, sport coats, and vests	2.56	0.40	1.10	0.69	1.29	3.09	3.49	5.68
Pants	22.85	9.82	17.21	15.48	23.90	23.30	27.03	34.60
Shorts and shorts sets	8.58	2.49	6.52	7.19	7.44	8.43	7.98	15.10
Uniforms	3.61	1.33	1.21	1.49	1.95	2.47	4.37	8.62
Active sportswear	3.39	1.40	0.88	2.38	3.96	3.04	4.08	6.25
Costumes	3.45	0.19	1.36	2.11	1.88	1.87	7.29	6.46
WOMEN'S APPAREL	**757.03**	**419.44**	**467.77**	**501.18**	**573.25**	**673.19**	**809.21**	**1,368.09**
Coats and jackets	627.95	384.88	383.62	413.68	473.38	528.88	659.88	1,140.92
Dresses	57.75	34.82	27.11	14.57	27.94	42.29	53.87	139.66
Sport coats and tailored jackets	6.88	3.17	2.22	2.47	3.19	2.63	6.06	19.00
Sweaters and vests	53.73	31.90	30.38	43.12	42.83	40.24	27.23	113.57
Shirts, blouses, and tops	115.60	61.43	57.58	91.52	102.26	110.51	137.99	190.59
Skirts	18.96	18.23	9.52	19.34	13.08	12.24	13.34	34.84
Pants	106.78	59.42	88.01	77.50	75.66	100.02	117.01	171.40
Shorts and shorts sets	17.91	27.34	14.13	12.44	7.56	22.76	16.83	23.52
Active sportswear	29.30	15.41	25.23	13.71	13.78	21.82	40.34	52.12
Nightwear	28.60	18.92	13.85	17.75	22.61	25.95	34.03	50.77
Undergarments	36.27	20.05	22.47	23.28	41.18	31.59	43.01	56.58
Hosiery	23.67	28.91	14.13	12.49	25.17	16.62	28.06	34.24
Suits	28.27	9.35	11.59	14.56	27.27	22.18	31.22	59.40

	complete income reporters	under $10,000	$10,000– $19,999	$20,000– $29,999	$30,000– $39,999	$40,000– $49,999	$50,000– $69,999	$70,000 or more
Accessories	$35.14	$21.10	$24.67	$21.36	$17.57	$32.63	$27.67	$71.61
Uniforms	6.40	1.75	4.02	3.29	9.45	4.40	8.67	10.19
Costumes	8.60	1.66	2.31	3.85	4.36	10.36	16.50	15.86
GIRLS' (AGED 2 TO 15) APPAREL	**129.08**	**34.56**	**84.15**	**87.50**	**99.87**	**144.32**	**149.32**	**227.17**
Coats and jackets	6.76	1.87	4.78	4.38	7.06	5.34	7.40	12.15
Dresses and suits	14.14	0.74	10.12	7.18	11.69	12.50	19.92	25.66
Shirts, blouses, and sweaters	35.73	12.41	25.06	25.46	30.29	43.04	36.94	59.01
Skirts and pants	24.96	8.27	17.31	18.21	24.03	25.16	30.10	40.20
Shorts and shorts sets	8.60	2.05	5.37	6.03	9.75	7.08	10.55	14.65
Active sportswear	10.48	2.65	2.96	11.27	0.95	22.63	5.55	21.67
Underwear and nightwear	7.68	2.84	5.45	4.62	5.76	6.47	10.96	12.98
Hosiery	4.96	1.26	2.04	4.72	3.25	6.26	8.00	7.30
Accessories	6.79	1.31	5.81	1.19	1.40	8.74	6.71	15.33
Uniforms	4.15	1.06	3.52	2.54	2.98	2.97	5.65	7.29
Costumes	4.85	0.11	1.77	1.89	2.72	4.12	7.53	10.94
CHILDREN UNDER AGE 2	**88.29**	**28.80**	**48.16**	**63.14**	**99.13**	**96.10**	**94.31**	**147.49**
Coats, jackets, and snowsuits	2.43	0.94	1.60	1.83	2.46	2.38	3.61	3.42
Outerwear including dresses	25.57	10.20	15.84	15.46	27.79	27.19	29.70	42.06
Underwear	46.86	12.86	24.99	37.43	58.08	54.34	48.57	73.60
Nightwear and loungewear	4.51	1.88	2.06	3.31	3.64	4.62	5.34	8.22
Accessories	8.92	2.92	3.67	5.12	7.17	7.57	7.09	20.19
FOOTWEAR	**338.31**	**196.75**	**205.73**	**199.47**	**296.13**	**303.98**	**425.92**	**562.15**
Men's	102.75	48.58	57.73	61.13	98.48	126.20	111.82	171.36
Boys'	41.20	32.50	25.03	20.06	51.43	26.42	60.48	58.59
Women's	157.35	98.51	97.77	96.05	112.58	113.56	199.67	277.87
Girls'	37.00	17.15	25.20	22.22	33.65	37.80	53.95	54.33
OTHER APPAREL PRODUCTS AND SERVICES	**252.34**	**106.01**	**123.21**	**176.84**	**166.92**	**231.85**	**261.37**	**512.21**
Material for making clothes	5.88	4.47	2.70	1.48	6.37	5.55	7.57	10.28
Sewing patterns and notions	8.95	3.04	5.73	9.12	5.16	6.91	13.30	13.83
Watches	15.24	6.69	5.03	6.84	8.29	10.77	15.97	36.96
Jewelry	95.01	26.11	23.21	69.84	48.55	110.02	108.47	206.20
Shoe repair and other shoe services	1.49	0.44	1.16	0.93	1.09	0.88	1.12	3.32
Coin-operated apparel laundry and dry cleaning	39.48	44.82	55.68	54.68	48.87	39.73	28.37	18.36
Apparel alteration, repair, and tailoring services	6.11	2.28	3.02	2.84	4.52	4.37	6.49	13.57
Clothing rental	3.05	0.12	1.46	1.60	2.95	2.20	4.13	6.29
Watch and jewelry repair	6.32	1.05	5.63	2.91	4.07	5.14	6.62	13.03
Professional laundry, dry cleaning	70.15	16.54	19.27	26.55	36.85	46.20	68.92	188.40
Clothing storage	0.65	0.44	0.34	0.03	0.22	0.07	0.43	1.97

Source: Bureau of Labor Statistics, unpublished data from the 2002 Consumer Expenditure Survey; calculations by New Strategist

Table 2.6 Apparel: Indexed spending by income, 2002

(indexed average annual spending of consumer units (CU) on apparel, accessories, and related services, by before-tax income of consumer unit, 2002; complete income reporters only; index definition: an index of 100 is the average for all consumer units; an index of 132 means that spending by consumer units in that group is 32 percent above the average for all consumer units; an index of 68 indicates spending that is 32 percent below the average for all consumer units)

	complete income reporters	under $10,000	$10,000–$19,999	$20,000–$29,999	$30,000–$39,999	$40,000–$49,999	$50,000–$69,999	$70,000 or more
Average spending of CU, total	$42,557	$17,628	$22,839	$28,836	$35,095	$41,787	$50,406	$76,627
Average spending of CU, index	100	41	54	68	82	98	118	180
Apparel, spending index	100	50	57	63	80	90	109	185
MEN'S APPAREL	100	43	49	54	83	89	104	202
Suits	100	43	40	53	84	91	102	208
Sport coats and tailored jackets	100	27	29	32	66	67	97	263
Coats and jackets	100	22	20	40	70	69	67	283
Underwear	100	50	46	31	74	90	99	220
Hosiery	100	35	56	76	92	105	105	175
Nightwear	100	38	43	58	115	112	110	176
Accessories	100	24	41	75	89	108	125	181
Sweaters and vests	100	37	27	63	129	84	108	189
Active sportswear	100	70	47	52	64	70	86	222
Shirts	100	51	30	50	84	103	96	211
Pants	100	34	51	72	85	87	126	178
Shorts and shorts sets	100	38	90	83	92	109	59	171
Uniforms	100	18	31	96	104	93	138	171
Costumes	100	19	23	31	45	110	146	232
BOYS' (AGED 2 TO 15) APPAREL	100	45	80	57	78	80	109	181
Coats and jackets	100	45	55	56	114	94	110	177
Sweaters	100	53	104	51	72	94	116	157
Shirts	100	56	120	46	47	69	66	199
Underwear	100	62	67	41	37	44	115	222
Nightwear	100	47	171	75	95	32	165	80
Hosiery	100	38	51	49	78	25	134	214
Accessories	100	66	58	44	89	89	120	177
Suits, sport coats, and vests	100	16	43	27	50	121	136	222
Pants	100	43	75	68	105	102	118	151
Shorts and shorts sets	100	29	76	84	87	98	93	176
Uniforms	100	37	33	41	54	68	121	239
Active sportswear	100	41	26	70	117	90	120	184
Costumes	100	6	39	61	54	54	211	187
WOMEN'S APPAREL	100	55	62	66	76	89	107	181
Coats and jackets	100	61	61	66	75	84	105	182
Dresses	100	60	47	25	48	73	93	242
Sport coats and tailored jackets	100	46	32	36	46	38	88	276
Sweaters and vests	100	59	57	80	80	75	51	211
Shirts, blouses, and tops	100	53	50	79	88	96	119	165
Skirts	100	96	50	102	69	65	70	184
Pants	100	56	82	73	71	94	110	161
Shorts and shorts sets	100	153	79	69	42	127	94	131
Active sportswear	100	53	86	47	47	74	138	178
Nightwear	100	66	48	62	79	91	119	178
Undergarments	100	55	62	64	114	87	119	156
Hosiery	100	122	60	53	106	70	119	145
Suits	100	33	41	52	96	78	110	210

	complete income reporters	under $10,000	$10,000–$19,999	$20,000–$29,999	$30,000–$39,999	$40,000–$49,999	$50,000–$69,999	$70,000 or more
Accessories	100	60	70	61	50	93	79	204
Uniforms	100	27	63	51	148	69	135	159
Costumes	100	19	27	45	51	120	192	184
GIRLS' (AGED 2 TO 15) APPAREL	**100**	**27**	**65**	**68**	**77**	**112**	**116**	**176**
Coats and jackets	100	28	71	65	104	79	109	180
Dresses and suits	100	5	72	51	83	88	141	181
Shirts, blouses, and sweaters	100	35	70	71	85	120	103	165
Skirts and pants	100	33	69	73	96	101	121	161
Shorts and shorts sets	100	24	62	70	113	82	123	170
Active sportswear	100	25	28	108	9	216	53	207
Underwear and nightwear	100	37	71	60	75	84	143	169
Hosiery	100	25	41	95	66	126	161	147
Accessories	100	19	86	18	21	129	99	226
Uniforms	100	26	85	61	72	72	136	176
Costumes	100	2	36	39	56	85	155	226
CHILDREN UNDER AGE 2	**100**	**33**	**55**	**72**	**112**	**109**	**107**	**167**
Coats, jackets, and snowsuits	100	39	66	75	101	98	149	141
Outerwear including dresses	100	40	62	60	109	106	116	164
Underwear	100	27	53	80	124	116	104	157
Nightwear and loungewear	100	42	46	73	81	102	118	182
Accessories	100	33	41	57	80	85	79	226
FOOTWEAR	**100**	**58**	**61**	**59**	**88**	**90**	**126**	**166**
Men's	100	47	56	59	96	123	109	167
Boys'	100	79	61	49	125	64	147	142
Women's	100	63	62	61	72	72	127	177
Girls'	100	46	68	60	91	102	146	147
OTHER APPAREL PRODUCTS AND SERVICES	**100**	**42**	**49**	**70**	**66**	**92**	**104**	**203**
Material for making clothes	100	76	46	25	108	94	129	175
Sewing patterns and notions	100	34	64	102	58	77	149	155
Watches	100	44	33	45	54	71	105	243
Jewelry	100	27	24	74	51	116	114	217
Shoe repair and other shoe services	100	29	78	62	73	59	75	223
Coin-operated apparel laundry and dry cleaning	100	114	141	139	124	101	72	47
Apparel alteration, repair, and tailoring services	100	37	49	46	74	72	106	222
Clothing rental	100	4	48	52	97	72	135	206
Watch and jewelry repair	100	17	89	46	64	81	105	206
Professional laundry, dry cleaning	100	24	27	38	53	66	98	269
Clothing storage	100	68	52	5	34	11	66	303

Source: Calculations by New Strategist based on the 2002 Consumer Expenditure Survey

Table 2.7 Apparel: Total spending by income, 2002

(total annual spending on apparel, accessories, and related services, by before-tax income group of consumer units (CU), 2002; complete income reporters only; numbers in thousands)

	complete income reporters	under $10,000	$10,000– $19,999	$20,000– $29,999	$30,000– $39,999	$40,000– $49,999	$50,000– $69,999	$70,000 or more
Number of consumer units	92,388	10,933	15,075	12,312	10,727	8,873	13,521	20,947
Total spending of all CUs	$3,931,754,268	$192,725,059	$344,293,530	$355,026,985	$376,468,249	$370,779,423	$681,541,825	$1,605,112,263
Apparel, total spending	172,946,640	10,266,097	15,952,599	14,484,822	16,056,817	15,012,584	27,628,811	72,675,407
MEN'S APPAREL	$40,279,320	$2,055,381	$3,216,123	$2,903,662	$3,876,952	$3,432,165	$6,119,605	$18,424,143
Suits	31,566,208	1,591,472	2,074,756	2,243,000	3,089,591	2,764,294	4,724,913	14,851,214
Sport coats and tailored jackets	3,110,704	99,101	147,686	133,093	236,745	201,062	439,838	1,853,391
Coats and jackets	995,019	25,431	32,887	52,818	81,418	65,749	97,486	639,302
Underwear	3,415,584	203,645	256,401	142,942	294,993	295,116	496,085	1,700,687
Hosiery	1,602,932	65,483	146,076	161,657	170,881	161,755	245,541	634,485
Nightwear	1,200,120	53,837	83,303	92,463	159,940	128,836	192,945	479,267
Accessories	273,468	7,819	18,478	27,456	28,212	28,482	50,163	112,485
Sweaters and vests	2,250,572	97,827	99,393	190,220	337,042	182,251	354,385	966,076
Active sportswear	1,397,830	116,216	107,759	97,019	103,837	93,876	176,855	702,353
Shirts	8,088,569	485,829	400,941	538,896	790,794	802,829	1,134,547	3,863,046
Pants	5,813,053	233,785	480,021	560,565	573,895	483,756	1,075,055	2,348,368
Shorts and shorts sets	1,150,231	51,712	168,001	127,306	122,931	120,052	100,055	445,752
Uniforms	297,489	6,445	14,891	38,167	35,828	26,708	60,168	115,418
Costumes	552,480	12,392	20,798	22,654	29,177	58,562	118,444	290,535
BOYS' (AGED 2 TO 15) APPAREL	8,714,036	463,910	1,141,367	660,662	787,362	667,871	1,394,691	3,572,720
Coats and jackets	587,588	31,126	52,540	43,831	77,771	52,794	94,377	235,235
Sweaters	339,064	21,255	57,763	23,023	28,427	30,612	57,329	121,074
Shirts	2,004,820	133,327	391,797	122,012	110,166	132,474	192,269	906,796
Underwear	540,470	39,533	59,354	29,179	23,170	22,804	90,591	272,102
Nightwear	277,164	15,364	77,495	27,825	30,679	8,607	66,794	50,063
Hosiery	438,843	19,643	36,441	28,933	39,904	10,381	86,129	213,031
Accessories	419,442	32,549	39,707	24,624	43,552	35,847	73,825	167,995
Suits, sport coats, and vests	236,513	4,349	16,544	8,495	13,838	27,418	47,188	118,979
Pants	2,111,066	107,407	259,375	190,590	256,375	206,741	365,473	724,766
Shorts and shorts sets	792,689	27,260	98,329	88,523	79,809	74,799	107,898	316,300
Uniforms	333,521	14,534	18,166	18,345	20,918	21,916	59,087	180,563
Active sportswear	313,195	15,257	13,320	29,303	42,479	26,974	55,166	130,919
Costumes	318,739	2,126	20,466	25,978	20,167	16,593	98,568	135,318
WOMEN'S APPAREL	69,940,488	4,585,743	7,051,702	6,170,528	6,149,253	5,973,215	10,941,328	28,657,381
Coats and jackets	58,015,045	4,207,901	5,783,110	5,093,228	5,077,947	4,692,752	8,922,237	23,898,851
Dresses	5,335,407	380,645	408,724	179,386	299,712	375,239	728,376	2,925,458
Sport coats and tailored jackets	635,629	34,608	33,414	30,411	34,219	23,336	81,937	397,993
Sweaters and vests	4,964,007	348,710	458,012	530,893	459,437	357,050	368,177	2,378,951
Shirts, blouses, and tops	10,680,053	671,589	868,060	1,126,794	1,096,943	980,555	1,865,763	3,992,289
Skirts	1,751,676	199,345	143,562	238,114	140,309	108,606	180,370	729,793
Pants	9,865,191	649,597	1,326,747	954,180	811,605	887,477	1,582,092	3,590,316
Shorts and shorts sets	1,654,669	298,878	213,012	153,161	81,096	201,949	227,558	492,673
Active sportswear	2,706,968	168,507	380,346	168,798	147,818	193,609	545,437	1,091,758
Nightwear	2,642,297	206,805	208,773	218,538	242,537	230,254	460,120	1,063,479
Undergarments	3,350,913	219,162	338,704	286,623	441,738	280,298	581,538	1,185,181
Hosiery	2,186,824	316,041	213,080	153,777	269,999	147,469	379,399	717,225
Suits	2,611,809	102,274	174,700	179,263	292,525	196,803	422,126	1,244,252

	complete income reporters	under $10,000	$10,000—$19,999	$20,000—$29,999	$30,000—$39,999	$40,000—$49,999	$50,000—$69,999	$70,000 or more
Accessories	$3,246,514	$230,636	$371,963	$262,984	$188,473	$289,526	$374,126	$1,500,015
Uniforms	591,283	19,176	60,603	40,506	101,370	39,041	117,227	213,450
Costumes	794,537	18,097	34,800	47,401	46,770	91,924	223,097	332,219
GIRLS' (AGED 2 TO 15) APPAREL	**11,925,443**	**377,842**	**1,268,592**	**1,077,300**	**1,071,305**	**1,280,551**	**2,018,956**	**4,758,530**
Coats and jackets	624,543	20,463	72,039	53,927	75,733	47,382	100,055	254,506
Dresses and suits	1,306,366	8,056	152,506	88,400	125,399	110,913	269,338	537,500
Shirts, blouses, and sweaters	3,301,023	135,721	377,706	313,464	324,921	381,894	499,466	1,236,082
Skirts and pants	2,306,004	90,388	260,914	224,202	257,770	223,245	406,982	842,069
Shorts and shorts sets	794,537	22,399	80,989	74,241	104,588	62,821	142,647	306,874
Active sportswear	968,226	28,949	44,550	138,756	10,191	200,796	75,042	453,921
Underwear and nightwear	709,540	31,009	82,146	56,881	61,788	57,408	148,190	271,892
Hosiery	458,244	13,814	30,700	58,113	34,863	55,545	108,168	152,913
Accessories	627,315	14,347	87,606	14,651	15,018	77,550	90,726	321,118
Uniforms	383,410	11,595	53,032	31,272	31,966	26,353	76,394	152,704
Costumes	448,082	1,241	26,624	23,270	29,177	36,557	101,813	229,160
CHILDREN UNDER AGE 2	**8,156,937**	**314,861**	**725,996**	**777,380**	**1,063,368**	**852,695**	**1,275,166**	**3,089,473**
Coats, jackets, and snowsuits	224,503	10,318	24,166	22,531	26,388	21,118	48,811	71,639
Outerwear including dresses	2,362,361	111,501	238,798	190,344	298,103	241,257	401,574	881,031
Underwear	4,329,302	140,561	376,726	460,838	623,024	482,159	656,715	1,541,699
Nightwear and loungewear	416,670	20,519	31,040	40,753	39,046	40,993	72,202	172,184
Accessories	824,101	31,962	55,265	63,037	76,913	67,169	95,864	422,920
FOOTWEAR	**31,255,784**	**2,151,084**	**3,101,335**	**2,455,875**	**3,176,587**	**2,697,215**	**5,758,864**	**11,775,356**
Men's	9,492,867	531,152	870,338	752,633	1,056,395	1,119,773	1,511,918	3,589,478
Boys'	3,806,386	355,356	377,301	246,979	551,690	234,425	817,750	1,227,285
Women's	14,537,252	1,076,988	1,473,842	1,182,568	1,207,646	1,007,618	2,699,738	5,820,543
Girls'	3,418,356	187,517	379,934	273,573	360,964	335,399	729,458	1,138,051
OTHER APPAREL PRODUCTS AND SERVICES	**23,313,188**	**1,158,988**	**1,857,381**	**2,177,254**	**1,790,551**	**2,057,205**	**3,533,984**	**10,729,263**
Material for making clothes	543,241	48,863	40,728	18,222	68,331	49,245	102,354	215,335
Sewing patterns and notions	826,873	33,208	86,326	112,285	55,351	61,312	179,829	289,697
Watches	1,407,993	73,160	75,791	84,214	88,927	95,562	215,930	774,201
Jewelry	8,777,784	285,493	349,934	859,870	520,796	976,207	1,466,623	4,319,271
Shoe repair and other shoe services	137,658	4,786	17,502	11,450	11,692	7,808	15,144	69,544
Coin-operated apparel laundry, dry cleaning	3,647,478	490,057	839,375	673,220	524,228	352,524	383,591	384,587
Apparel alteration, repair, tailoring services	564,491	24,906	45,529	34,966	48,486	38,775	87,751	284,251
Clothing rental	281,783	1,276	21,955	19,699	31,645	19,521	55,842	131,757
Watch and jewelry repair	583,892	11,498	84,894	35,828	43,659	45,607	89,509	272,939
Professional laundry, dry cleaning	6,481,018	180,808	290,490	326,884	395,290	409,933	931,867	3,946,415
Clothing storage	60,052	4,823	5,089	369	2,360	621	5,814	41,266

Note: Numbers may not add to total because of rounding.
Source: Calculations by New Strategist based on the 2002 Consumer Expenditure Survey

Table 2.8 Apparel: Market shares by income, 2002

(percentage of total annual spending on apparel, accessories, and related services accounted for by before-tax income group of consumer units, 2002; complete income reporters only)

	complete income reporters	under $10,000	$10,000–$19,999	$20,000–$29,999	$30,000–$39,999	$40,000–$49,999	$50,000–$69,999	$70,000 or more
Share of total consumer units	100.0%	11.8%	16.3%	13.3%	11.6%	9.6%	14.6%	22.7%
Share of total before-tax income	100.0	1.3	4.9	6.6	8.1	8.6	17.4	53.0
Share of total spending	100.0	4.9	8.8	9.0	9.6	9.4	17.3	40.8
Share of apparel spending	100.0	5.9	9.2	8.4	9.3	8.7	16.0	42.0
MEN'S APPAREL	**100.0%**	**5.1%**	**8.0%**	**7.2%**	**9.6%**	**8.5%**	**15.2%**	**45.7%**
Suits	100.0	5.0	6.6	7.1	9.8	8.8	15.0	47.0
Sport coats and tailored jackets	100.0	3.2	4.7	4.3	7.6	6.5	14.1	59.6
Coats and jackets	100.0	2.6	3.3	5.3	8.2	6.6	9.8	64.3
Underwear	100.0	6.0	7.5	4.2	8.6	8.6	14.5	49.8
Hosiery	100.0	4.1	9.1	10.1	10.7	10.1	15.3	39.6
Nightwear	100.0	4.5	6.9	7.7	13.3	10.7	16.1	39.9
Accessories	100.0	2.9	6.8	10.0	10.3	10.4	18.3	41.1
Sweaters and vests	100.0	4.3	4.4	8.5	15.0	8.1	15.7	42.9
Active sportswear	100.0	8.3	7.7	6.9	7.4	6.7	12.7	50.2
Shirts	100.0	6.0	5.0	6.7	9.8	9.9	14.0	47.8
Pants	100.0	4.0	8.3	9.6	9.9	8.3	18.5	40.4
Shorts and shorts sets	100.0	4.5	14.6	11.1	10.7	10.4	8.7	38.8
Uniforms	100.0	2.2	5.0	12.8	12.0	9.0	20.2	38.8
Costumes	100.0	2.2	3.8	4.1	5.3	10.6	21.4	52.6
BOYS' (AGED 2 TO 15) APPAREL	**100.0**	**5.3**	**13.1**	**7.6**	**9.0**	**7.7**	**16.0**	**41.0**
Coats and jackets	100.0	5.3	8.9	7.5	13.2	9.0	16.1	40.0
Sweaters	100.0	6.3	17.0	6.8	8.4	9.0	16.9	35.7
Shirts	100.0	6.7	19.5	6.1	5.5	6.6	9.6	45.2
Underwear	100.0	7.3	11.0	5.4	4.3	4.2	16.8	50.3
Nightwear	100.0	5.5	28.0	10.0	11.1	3.1	24.1	18.1
Hosiery	100.0	4.5	8.3	6.6	9.1	2.4	19.6	48.5
Accessories	100.0	7.8	9.5	5.9	10.4	8.5	17.6	40.1
Suits, sport coats, and vests	100.0	1.8	7.0	3.6	5.9	11.6	20.0	50.3
Pants	100.0	5.1	12.3	9.0	12.1	9.8	17.3	34.3
Shorts and shorts sets	100.0	3.4	12.4	11.2	10.1	9.4	13.6	39.9
Uniforms	100.0	4.4	5.4	5.5	6.3	6.6	17.7	54.1
Active sportswear	100.0	4.9	4.3	9.4	13.6	8.6	17.6	41.8
Costumes	100.0	0.7	6.4	8.2	6.3	5.2	30.9	42.5
WOMEN'S APPAREL	**100.0**	**6.6**	**10.1**	**8.8**	**8.8**	**8.5**	**15.6**	**41.0**
Coats and jackets	100.0	7.3	10.0	8.8	8.8	8.1	15.4	41.2
Dresses	100.0	7.1	7.7	3.4	5.6	7.0	13.7	54.8
Sport coats and tailored jackets	100.0	5.4	5.3	4.8	5.4	3.7	12.9	62.6
Sweaters and vests	100.0	7.0	9.2	10.7	9.3	7.2	7.4	47.9
Shirts, blouses, and tops	100.0	6.3	8.1	10.6	10.3	9.2	17.5	37.4
Skirts	100.0	11.4	8.2	13.6	8.0	6.2	10.3	41.7
Pants	100.0	6.6	13.4	9.7	8.2	9.0	16.0	36.4
Shorts and shorts sets	100.0	18.1	12.9	9.3	4.9	12.2	13.8	29.8
Active sportswear	100.0	6.2	14.1	6.2	5.5	7.2	20.1	40.3
Nightwear	100.0	7.8	7.9	8.3	9.2	8.7	17.4	40.2
Undergarments	100.0	6.5	10.1	8.6	13.2	8.4	17.4	35.4
Hosiery	100.0	14.5	9.7	7.0	12.3	6.7	17.3	32.8
Suits	100.0	3.9	6.7	6.9	11.2	7.5	16.2	47.6

	complete income reporters	under $10,000	$10,000— $19,999	$20,000— $29,999	$30,000— $39,999	$40,000— $49,999	$50,000— $69,999	$70,000 or more
Accessories	100.0%	7.1%	11.5%	8.1%	5.8%	8.9%	11.5%	46.2%
Uniforms	100.0	3.2	10.2	6.9	17.1	6.6	19.8	36.1
Costumes	100.0	2.3	4.4	6.0	5.9	11.6	28.1	41.8
GIRLS' (AGED 2 TO 15) APPAREL	**100.0**	**3.2**	**10.6**	**9.0**	**9.0**	**10.7**	**16.9**	**39.9**
Coats and jackets	100.0	3.3	11.5	8.6	12.1	7.6	16.0	40.8
Dresses and suits	100.0	0.6	11.7	6.8	9.6	8.5	20.6	41.1
Shirts, blouses, and sweaters	100.0	4.1	11.4	9.5	9.8	11.6	15.1	37.4
Skirts and pants	100.0	3.9	11.3	9.7	11.2	9.7	17.6	36.5
Shorts and shorts sets	100.0	2.8	10.2	9.3	13.2	7.9	18.0	38.6
Active sportswear	100.0	3.0	4.6	14.3	1.1	20.7	7.8	46.9
Underwear and nightwear	100.0	4.4	11.6	8.0	8.7	8.1	20.9	38.3
Hosiery	100.0	3.0	6.7	12.7	7.6	12.1	23.6	33.4
Accessories	100.0	2.3	14.0	2.3	2.4	12.4	14.5	51.2
Uniforms	100.0	3.0	13.8	8.2	8.3	6.9	19.9	39.8
Costumes	100.0	0.3	5.9	5.2	6.5	8.2	22.7	51.1
CHILDREN UNDER AGE 2	**100.0**	**3.9**	**8.9**	**9.5**	**13.0**	**10.5**	**15.6**	**37.9**
Coats, jackets, and snowsuits	100.0	4.6	10.8	10.0	11.8	9.4	21.7	31.9
Outerwear including dresses	100.0	4.7	10.1	8.1	12.6	10.2	17.0	37.3
Underwear	100.0	3.2	8.7	10.6	14.4	11.1	15.2	35.6
Nightwear and loungewear	100.0	4.9	7.4	9.8	9.4	9.8	17.3	41.3
Accessories	100.0	3.9	6.7	7.6	9.3	8.2	11.6	51.3
FOOTWEAR	**100.0**	**6.9**	**9.9**	**7.9**	**10.2**	**8.6**	**18.4**	**37.7**
Men's	100.0	5.6	9.2	7.9	11.1	11.8	15.9	37.8
Boys'	100.0	9.3	9.9	6.5	14.5	6.2	21.5	32.2
Women's	100.0	7.4	10.1	8.1	8.3	6.9	18.6	40.0
Girls'	100.0	5.5	11.1	8.0	10.6	9.8	21.3	33.3
OTHER APPAREL PRODUCTS AND SERVICES	**100.0**	**5.0**	**8.0**	**9.3**	**7.7**	**8.8**	**15.2**	**46.0**
Material for making clothes	100.0	9.0	7.5	3.4	12.6	9.1	18.8	39.6
Sewing patterns and notions	100.0	4.0	10.4	13.6	6.7	7.4	21.7	35.0
Watches	100.0	5.2	5.4	6.0	6.3	6.8	15.3	55.0
Jewelry	100.0	3.3	4.0	9.8	5.9	11.1	16.7	49.2
Shoe repair and other shoe services	100.0	3.5	12.7	8.3	8.5	5.7	11.0	50.5
Coin-operated apparel laundry and dry cleaning	100.0	13.4	23.0	18.5	14.4	9.7	10.5	10.5
Apparel alteration, repair, and tailoring services	100.0	4.4	8.1	6.2	8.6	6.9	15.5	50.4
Clothing rental	100.0	0.5	7.8	7.0	11.2	6.9	19.8	46.8
Watch and jewelry repair	100.0	2.0	14.5	6.1	7.5	7.8	15.3	46.7
Professional laundry, dry cleaning	100.0	2.8	4.5	5.0	6.1	6.3	14.4	60.9
Clothing storage	100.0	8.0	8.5	0.6	3.9	1.0	9.7	68.7

Note: Numbers may not add to total because of rounding.
Source: Calculations by New Strategist based on the 2002 Consumer Expenditure Survey

Table 2.9 Apparel: Average spending by household type, 2002

(average annual spending of consumer units (CU) on apparel, accessories, and related services, by type of consumer unit, 2002)

	total married couples	married couples, no children	married couples with children				single parent, at least one child <18	single person
			total	oldest child under 6	oldest child 6 to 17	oldest child 18 or older		
Number of consumer units (in thousands, add 000)	56,265	23,118	28,790	5,547	15,206	8,036	6,730	33,055
Average number of persons per CU	3.2	2.0	3.9	3.5	4.1	3.9	2.9	1.0
Average before-tax income of CU	$67,155.00	$58,967.00	$73,918.00	$67,587.00	$72,720.00	$81,042.00	$26,966.00	$27,042.00
Average spending of CU, total	52,333.70	45,557.33	57,835.01	52,778.62	58,103.75	60,859.78	30,185.38	24,189.90
Apparel, average spending	2,218.03	1,633.49	2,643.09	2,630.01	2,688.82	2,565.36	1,885.32	921.41
MEN'S APPAREL	**$566.77**	**$374.21**	**$713.46**	**$578.71**	**$768.83**	**$702.49**	**$392.27**	**$162.15**
Suits	46.73	40.98	52.06	34.70	41.68	83.69	6.36	17.18
Sport coats and tailored jackets	16.94	14.97	19.32	10.30	17.32	29.32	2.52	3.50
Coats and jackets	48.68	45.60	55.51	56.01	54.26	57.63	25.02	13.82
Underwear	21.01	16.37	22.96	16.06	23.59	26.76	13.11	7.44
Hosiery	16.50	12.65	18.36	14.00	20.67	16.95	5.24	6.65
Nightwear	4.13	4.07	4.22	3.72	4.11	4.77	1.07	1.80
Accessories	28.35	28.33	27.34	37.31	25.13	24.41	23.96	12.66
Sweaters and vests	21.45	20.02	22.73	14.96	20.60	32.12	5.80	8.91
Active sportswear	19.98	17.65	22.58	32.07	17.89	24.96	4.79	12.23
Shirts	107.57	72.65	134.32	122.23	115.66	180.46	34.81	41.76
Pants	79.54	54.60	96.66	90.68	90.99	112.37	46.63	28.67
Shorts and shorts sets	17.07	13.27	18.30	10.88	18.36	23.64	6.18	3.82
Uniforms	4.62	3.14	5.81	4.20	6.75	5.14	1.58	1.45
Costumes	9.49	8.27	10.58	4.67	11.94	12.09	1.08	2.28
BOYS' (AGED 2 TO 15) APPAREL	**124.70**	**21.65**	**202.73**	**126.93**	**299.87**	**68.19**	**214.12**	**13.96**
Coats and jackets	9.13	2.40	14.46	10.96	20.44	5.55	13.06	1.24
Sweaters	4.85	1.35	7.69	4.51	10.74	4.12	7.45	0.48
Shirts	24.66	2.35	39.56	26.59	61.18	5.97	46.76	3.51
Underwear	6.75	1.20	11.08	6.70	16.30	3.89	15.55	0.78
Nightwear	3.97	0.71	6.60	13.04	7.34	0.38	2.11	1.01
Hosiery	5.98	0.46	10.95	6.68	16.12	3.79	10.65	0.29
Accessories	5.39	1.09	8.73	9.07	12.12	1.70	11.15	1.59
Suits, sport coats, and vests	3.47	0.89	5.55	1.91	8.37	2.72	3.60	0.65
Pants	30.84	6.83	48.93	24.43	71.59	22.98	62.00	2.57
Shorts and shorts sets	12.67	1.66	20.61	11.16	30.13	9.12	20.28	0.84
Uniforms	5.39	0.97	9.04	2.87	14.85	2.31	5.42	0.42
Active sportswear	5.27	0.45	9.03	2.27	14.72	2.91	11.34	0.18
Costumes	6.31	1.29	10.50	6.73	15.97	2.76	4.74	0.40
WOMEN'S APPAREL	**848.64**	**702.43**	**951.46**	**757.80**	**1,019.63**	**961.27**	**878.03**	**397.13**
Coats and jackets	61.41	70.63	55.00	44.62	55.60	61.46	30.61	39.68
Dresses	74.78	100.45	51.37	35.76	41.95	81.69	70.14	25.23
Sport coats and tailored jackets	7.39	6.58	7.64	2.72	7.35	11.57	1.82	5.87
Sweaters and vests	64.13	53.72	69.32	59.53	63.91	87.33	37.18	30.78
Shirts, blouses, and tops	113.35	111.53	115.41	86.81	108.35	150.55	93.23	76.47
Skirts	18.12	13.43	23.62	29.99	24.64	16.88	18.07	14.02
Pants	108.89	90.07	114.72	94.34	98.56	161.96	92.80	63.76
Shorts and shorts sets	17.89	15.31	20.10	12.78	16.53	32.60	17.89	11.63
Active sportswear	38.02	37.35	40.45	38.76	37.37	47.85	36.39	18.25
Nightwear	32.56	31.34	32.92	37.41	30.38	34.67	23.20	18.39
Undergarments	38.94	36.99	36.05	31.62	32.89	45.62	45.90	18.96
Hosiery	24.99	23.60	25.86	16.60	26.44	31.51	22.90	15.25
Suits	31.51	31.64	29.97	36.00	21.38	42.08	20.57	24.78

	total married couples	married couples, no children	married couples with children				single parent, at least one child <18	single person
			total	oldest child under 6	oldest child 6 to 17	oldest child 18 or older		
Accessories	$39.04	$38.38	$41.43	$52.15	$38.41	$39.57	$36.42	$27.53
Uniforms	7.56	6.83	7.89	5.56	8.50	8.35	9.04	2.06
Costumes	11.43	9.33	13.29	9.83	15.12	12.23	9.42	4.47
GIRLS' (AGED 2 TO 15) APPAREL	**158.61**	**25.25**	**266.43**	**163.31**	**392.25**	**95.36**	**312.45**	**16.25**
Coats and jackets	8.64	1.52	14.24	7.74	21.79	4.46	16.65	1.07
Dresses and suits	17.69	1.05	32.39	16.17	42.51	24.12	28.95	1.26
Shirts, blouses, and sweaters	37.75	7.34	63.64	49.01	93.08	15.64	99.94	2.91
Skirts and pants	32.43	5.00	52.84	24.36	80.96	19.29	73.08	3.08
Shorts and shorts sets	11.96	2.03	19.42	14.53	28.57	5.48	23.69	0.40
Active sportswear	11.81	1.99	21.20	11.48	32.99	4.84	8.27	3.70
Underwear and nightwear	10.29	1.47	16.88	14.53	23.54	5.91	18.62	1.37
Hosiery	5.48	0.70	9.17	7.66	12.55	3.55	11.49	0.49
Accessories	8.39	3.32	12.15	6.02	18.95	3.08	14.65	0.97
Uniforms	6.87	0.17	12.02	3.18	18.94	5.04	10.33	0.56
Costumes	7.29	0.66	12.48	8.63	18.38	3.96	6.79	0.44
CHILDREN UNDER AGE 2	**117.27**	**45.90**	**173.93**	**535.02**	**99.78**	**57.92**	**70.64**	**15.21**
Coats, jackets, and snowsuits	3.21	1.77	4.21	11.98	2.86	1.40	2.52	0.80
Outerwear including dresses	32.94	24.75	38.76	100.98	25.02	21.80	19.51	7.21
Underwear	63.58	12.36	105.13	337.96	58.66	26.42	39.56	3.20
Nightwear and loungewear	5.56	3.98	6.53	17.68	3.80	3.98	2.42	1.48
Accessories	11.98	3.05	19.31	66.42	9.45	4.32	6.63	2.51
FOOTWEAR	**391.63**	**227.80**	**500.46**	**470.65**	**508.23**	**506.90**	**390.82**	**148.58**
Men's	136.37	67.94	181.53	223.90	139.48	234.26	37.83	48.12
Boys'	47.95	2.39	79.61	51.91	109.23	40.89	98.30	4.64
Women's	166.16	154.21	165.86	159.58	145.41	211.32	146.42	91.64
Girls'	41.14	3.27	73.46	35.27	114.12	20.43	108.26	4.18
OTHER APPAREL PRODUCTS AND SERVICES	**293.72**	**283.14**	**303.77**	**287.81**	**292.34**	**336.78**	**153.57**	**168.14**
Material for making clothes	7.72	8.83	7.34	10.53	4.03	11.60	0.65	3.32
Sewing patterns and notions	12.28	12.91	8.92	8.70	7.22	12.47	2.89	3.60
Watches	19.13	15.18	23.10	25.30	23.50	20.83	7.07	7.20
Jewelry	113.20	118.26	113.68	80.61	117.24	129.76	38.92	64.21
Shoe repair and other shoe services	1.91	1.96	1.79	1.68	2.17	1.17	0.31	1.31
Coin-operated apparel laundry and dry cleaning	26.48	17.45	29.06	43.03	27.48	22.42	65.65	35.98
Apparel alteration, repair, and tailoring services	7.49	7.92	7.64	7.02	7.29	8.73	2.92	4.20
Clothing rental	3.41	2.76	3.52	2.99	2.74	5.35	3.20	0.73
Watch and jewelry repair	8.09	10.93	6.10	3.72	7.39	5.31	1.16	3.13
Professional laundry, dry cleaning	93.41	86.29	101.97	103.20	92.44	119.14	30.79	43.94
Clothing storage	0.62	0.65	0.64	1.03	0.84	–	–	0.52

Note: Average spending figures for total consumer units can be found on Average Spending by Age and Average Spending by Region tables. (–) means sample is too small to make a reliable estimate.
Source: Bureau of Labor Statistics, unpublished data from the 2002 Consumer Expenditure Survey

Table 2.10 Apparel: Indexed spending by household type, 2002

(indexed average annual spending of consumer units (CU) on apparel, accessories, and related services, by type of consumer unit, 2002; index definition: an index of 100 is the average for all consumer units; an index of 132 means that spending by consumer units in that group is 32 percent above the average for all consumer units; an index of 68 indicates spending that is 32 percent below the average for all consumer units)

	total married couples	married couples, no children	married couples with children				single parent, at least one child <18	single person
			total	oldest child under 6	oldest child 6 to 17	oldest child 18 or older		
Average spending of CU, total	$52,334	$45,557	$57,835	$52,779	$58,104	$60,860	$30,185	$24,190
Average spending of CU, index	129	112	142	130	143	150	74	59
Apparel, spending index	127	93	151	150	154	147	108	53
MEN'S APPAREL	**177**	**117**	**223**	**181**	**241**	**220**	**123**	**51**
Suits	142	124	158	105	126	254	19	52
Sport coats and tailored jackets	159	141	181	97	163	275	24	33
Coats and jackets	144	135	164	165	160	170	74	41
Underwear	138	107	150	105	154	175	86	49
Hosiery	135	104	150	115	169	139	43	54
Nightwear	139	137	142	125	138	160	36	60
Accessories	127	126	122	166	112	109	107	56
Sweaters and vests	137	128	145	95	131	205	37	57
Active sportswear	132	117	149	212	118	165	32	81
Shirts	136	92	170	155	147	229	44	53
Pants	138	95	168	157	158	195	81	50
Shorts and shorts sets	140	109	150	89	150	193	51	31
Uniforms	144	98	181	131	210	160	49	45
Costumes	149	130	167	74	188	190	17	36
BOYS' (AGED 2 TO 15) APPAREL	**139**	**24**	**225**	**141**	**333**	**76**	**238**	**16**
Coats and jackets	143	38	227	172	320	87	205	19
Sweaters	133	37	211	124	294	113	204	13
Shirts	126	12	203	136	314	31	240	18
Underwear	134	24	221	133	325	77	310	16
Nightwear	153	27	255	503	283	15	81	39
Hosiery	142	11	260	159	383	90	253	7
Accessories	131	26	212	220	294	41	271	39
Suits, sport coats, and vests	146	38	234	81	353	115	152	27
Pants	137	30	217	108	317	102	275	11
Shorts and shorts sets	146	19	238	129	348	105	234	10
Uniforms	161	29	270	86	443	69	162	13
Active sportswear	137	12	235	59	383	76	295	5
Costumes	170	35	282	181	429	74	127	11
WOMEN'S APPAREL	**145**	**120**	**162**	**129**	**174**	**164**	**150**	**68**
Coats and jackets	123	141	110	89	111	123	61	79
Dresses	133	178	91	63	74	145	124	45
Sport coats and tailored jackets	114	102	118	42	113	179	28	91
Sweaters and vests	127	106	137	118	127	173	74	61
Shirts, blouses, and tops	110	108	112	84	105	146	90	74
Skirts	104	77	135	172	141	97	103	80
Pants	113	94	119	98	102	168	96	66
Shorts and shorts sets	111	95	125	79	103	203	111	72
Active sportswear	126	124	135	129	124	159	121	61
Nightwear	118	113	119	135	110	125	84	67
Undergarments	116	110	107	94	98	136	137	57
Hosiery	118	111	122	78	125	148	108	72
Suits	109	109	103	124	74	145	71	85

	total married couples	married couples, no children	married couples with children				single parent, at least one child <18	single person
			total	oldest child under 6	oldest child 6 to 17	oldest child 18 or older		
Accessories	117	115	124	156	115	119	109	82
Uniforms	124	112	129	91	139	136	148	34
Costumes	121	99	141	104	161	130	100	47
GIRLS' (AGED 2 TO 15) APPAREL	**135**	**22**	**227**	**139**	**335**	**81**	**267**	**14**
Coats and jackets	133	23	219	119	336	69	257	16
Dresses and suits	143	8	261	130	343	194	233	10
Shirts, blouses, and sweaters	129	25	217	167	317	53	341	10
Skirts and pants	135	21	220	101	336	80	304	13
Shorts and shorts sets	144	25	235	175	345	66	286	5
Active sportswear	127	21	227	123	354	52	89	40
Underwear and nightwear	135	19	221	190	309	77	244	18
Hosiery	127	16	213	178	292	83	267	11
Accessories	144	57	209	104	326	53	252	17
Uniforms	144	4	252	67	397	106	217	12
Costumes	152	14	260	180	383	83	141	9
CHILDREN UNDER AGE 2	**142**	**56**	**211**	**648**	**121**	**70**	**86**	**18**
Coats, jackets, and snowsuits	132	73	173	493	118	58	104	33
Outerwear including dresses	139	104	163	426	106	92	82	30
Underwear	146	28	241	775	135	61	91	7
Nightwear and loungewear	137	98	160	434	93	98	59	36
Accessories	136	35	220	756	108	49	75	29
FOOTWEAR	**125**	**73**	**160**	**150**	**162**	**162**	**125**	**47**
Men's	133	66	176	218	136	228	37	47
Boys'	130	6	216	141	296	111	267	13
Women's	117	109	117	113	103	149	103	65
Girls'	130	10	231	111	359	64	341	13
OTHER APPAREL PRODUCTS AND SERVICES	**122**	**118**	**127**	**120**	**122**	**140**	**64**	**70**
Material for making clothes	151	173	144	206	79	227	13	65
Sewing patterns and notions	150	157	109	106	88	152	35	44
Watches	140	111	170	186	173	153	52	53
Jewelry	126	132	127	90	131	145	43	72
Shoe repair and other shoe services	133	136	124	117	151	81	22	91
Coin-operated apparel laundry and dry cleaning	70	46	77	115	73	60	175	96
Apparel alteration, repair, and tailoring services	128	135	130	120	124	149	50	72
Clothing rental	128	104	132	112	103	201	120	27
Watch and jewelry repair	147	199	111	68	135	97	21	57
Professional laundry, dry cleaning	134	124	146	148	133	171	44	63
Clothing storage	113	118	116	187	153	–	–	95

Note: Spending index for total consumer units is 100. (–) means sample is too small to make a reliable estimate.
Source: Calculations by New Strategist based on the 2002 Consumer Expenditure Survey

Table 2.11 Apparel: Total spending by household type, 2002

(total annual spending on apparel, accessories, and related services, by consumer unit (CU) type, 2002; numbers in thousands)

	total married couples	married couples, no children	married couples with children total	oldest child under 6	oldest child 6 to 17	oldest child 18 or older	single parent, at least one child <18	single person
Number of consumer units	56,265	23,118	28,790	5,547	15,206	8,036	6,730	33,055
Total spending of all CUs	$2,944,555,631	$1,053,194,355	$1,665,069,938	$292,763,005	$883,525,623	$489,069,192	$203,147,607	$799,597,145
Apparel, total spending	124,797,458	37,763,022	76,094,561	14,588,665	40,886,197	20,615,233	12,688,204	30,457,208
MEN'S APPAREL	**$31,889,314**	**$8,650,987**	**$20,540,513**	**$3,210,104**	**$11,690,829**	**$5,645,210**	**$2,639,977**	**$5,359,868**
Suits	2,629,263	947,376	1,498,807	192,481	633,786	672,533	42,803	567,885
Sport coats and tailored jackets	953,129	346,076	556,223	57,134	263,368	235,616	16,960	115,693
Coats and jackets	2,738,980	1,054,181	1,598,133	310,687	825,078	463,115	168,385	456,820
Underwear	1,182,128	378,442	661,018	89,085	358,710	215,043	88,230	245,929
Hosiery	928,373	292,443	528,584	77,658	314,308	136,210	35,265	219,816
Nightwear	232,374	94,090	121,494	20,635	62,497	38,332	7,201	59,499
Accessories	1,595,113	654,933	787,119	206,959	382,127	196,159	161,251	418,476
Sweaters and vests	1,206,884	462,822	654,397	82,983	313,244	258,116	39,034	294,520
Active sportswear	1,124,175	408,033	650,078	177,892	272,035	200,579	32,237	404,263
Shirts	6,052,426	1,679,523	3,867,073	678,010	1,758,726	1,450,177	234,271	1,380,377
Pants	4,475,318	1,262,243	2,782,841	503,002	1,383,594	903,005	313,820	947,687
Shorts and shorts sets	960,444	306,776	526,857	60,351	279,182	189,971	41,591	126,270
Uniforms	259,944	72,591	167,270	23,297	102,641	41,305	10,633	47,930
Costumes	533,955	191,186	304,598	25,904	181,560	97,155	7,268	75,365
BOYS' (AGED 2 TO 15) APPAREL	**7,016,246**	**500,505**	**5,836,597**	**704,081**	**4,559,823**	**547,975**	**1,441,028**	**461,448**
Coats and jackets	513,699	55,483	416,303	60,795	310,811	44,600	87,894	40,988
Sweaters	272,885	31,209	221,395	25,017	163,312	33,108	50,139	15,866
Shirts	1,387,495	54,327	1,138,932	147,495	930,303	47,975	314,695	116,023
Underwear	379,789	27,742	318,993	37,165	247,858	31,260	104,652	25,783
Nightwear	223,372	16,414	190,014	72,333	111,612	3,054	14,200	33,386
Hosiery	336,465	10,634	315,251	37,054	245,121	30,456	71,675	9,586
Accessories	303,268	25,199	251,337	50,311	184,297	13,661	75,040	52,557
Suits, sport coats, and vests	195,240	20,575	159,785	10,595	127,274	21,858	24,228	21,486
Pants	1,735,213	157,896	1,408,695	135,513	1,088,598	184,667	417,260	84,951
Shorts and shorts sets	712,878	38,376	593,362	61,905	458,157	73,288	136,484	27,766
Uniforms	303,268	22,424	260,262	15,920	225,809	18,563	36,477	13,883
Active sportswear	296,517	10,403	259,974	12,592	223,832	23,385	76,318	5,950
Costumes	355,032	29,822	302,295	37,331	242,840	22,179	31,900	13,222
WOMEN'S APPAREL	**47,748,730**	**16,238,777**	**27,392,533**	**4,203,517**	**15,504,494**	**7,724,766**	**5,909,142**	**13,127,132**
Coats and jackets	3,455,234	1,632,824	1,583,450	247,507	845,454	493,893	206,005	1,311,622
Dresses	4,207,497	2,322,203	1,478,942	198,361	637,892	656,461	472,042	833,978
Sport coats and tailored jackets	415,798	152,116	219,956	15,088	111,764	92,977	12,249	194,033
Sweaters and vests	3,608,274	1,241,899	1,995,723	330,213	971,815	701,784	250,221	1,017,433
Shirts, blouses, and tops	6,377,638	2,578,351	3,322,654	481,535	1,647,570	1,209,820	627,438	2,527,716
Skirts	1,019,522	310,475	680,020	166,355	374,676	135,648	121,611	463,431
Pants	6,126,696	2,082,238	3,302,789	523,304	1,498,703	1,301,511	624,544	2,107,587
Shorts and shorts sets	1,006,581	353,937	578,679	70,891	251,355	261,974	120,400	384,430
Active sportswear	2,139,195	863,457	1,164,556	215,002	568,248	384,523	244,905	603,254
Nightwear	1,831,988	724,518	947,767	207,513	461,958	278,608	156,136	607,881
Undergarments	2,190,959	855,135	1,037,880	175,396	500,125	366,602	308,907	626,723
Hosiery	1,406,062	545,585	744,509	92,080	402,047	253,214	154,117	504,089
Suits	1,772,910	731,454	862,836	199,692	325,104	338,155	138,436	819,103

	total married couples	married couples, no children	married couples with children				single parent, at least one child <18	single person
			total	oldest child under 6	oldest child 6 to 17	oldest child 18 or older		
Accessories	$2,196,586	$887,269	$1,192,770	$289,276	$584,062	$317,985	$245,107	$910,004
Uniforms	425,363	157,896	227,153	30,841	129,251	67,101	60,839	68,093
Costumes	643,109	215,691	382,619	54,527	229,915	98,280	63,397	147,756
GIRLS' (AGED 2 TO 15) APPAREL	**8,924,192**	**583,730**	**7,670,520**	**905,881**	**5,964,554**	**766,313**	**2,102,789**	**537,144**
Coats and jackets	486,130	35,139	409,970	42,934	331,339	35,841	112,055	35,369
Dresses and suits	995,328	24,274	932,508	89,695	646,407	193,828	194,834	41,649
Shirts, blouses, and sweaters	2,124,004	169,686	1,832,196	271,858	1,415,374	125,683	672,596	96,190
Skirts and pants	1,824,674	115,590	1,521,264	135,125	1,231,078	155,014	491,828	101,809
Shorts and shorts sets	672,929	46,930	559,102	80,598	434,435	44,037	159,434	13,222
Active sportswear	664,490	46,005	610,348	63,680	501,646	38,894	55,657	122,304
Underwear and nightwear	578,967	33,983	485,975	80,598	357,949	47,493	125,313	45,285
Hosiery	308,332	16,183	264,004	42,490	190,835	28,528	77,328	16,197
Accessories	472,063	76,752	349,799	33,393	288,154	24,751	98,595	32,063
Uniforms	386,541	3,930	346,056	17,639	288,002	40,501	69,521	18,511
Costumes	410,172	15,258	359,299	47,871	279,486	31,823	45,697	14,544
CHILDREN UNDER AGE 2	**6,598,197**	**1,061,116**	**5,007,445**	**2,967,756**	**1,517,255**	**465,445**	**475,407**	**502,767**
Coats, jackets, and snowsuits	180,611	40,919	121,206	66,453	43,489	11,250	16,960	26,444
Outerwear including dresses	1,853,369	572,171	1,115,900	560,136	380,454	175,185	131,302	238,327
Underwear	3,577,329	285,738	3,026,693	1,874,664	891,984	212,311	266,239	105,776
Nightwear and loungewear	312,833	92,010	187,999	98,071	57,783	31,983	16,287	48,921
Accessories	674,055	70,510	555,935	368,432	143,697	34,716	44,620	82,968
FOOTWEAR	**22,035,062**	**5,266,280**	**14,408,243**	**2,610,696**	**7,728,145**	**4,073,448**	**2,630,219**	**4,911,312**
Men's	7,672,858	1,570,637	5,226,249	1,241,973	2,120,933	1,882,513	254,596	1,590,607
Boys'	2,697,907	55,252	2,291,972	287,945	1,660,951	328,592	661,559	153,375
Women's	9,348,992	3,565,027	4,775,109	885,190	2,211,104	1,698,168	985,407	3,029,160
Girls'	2,314,742	75,596	2,114,913	195,643	1,735,309	164,175	728,590	138,170
OTHER APPAREL PRODUCTS AND SERVICES	**16,526,156**	**6,545,631**	**8,745,538**	**1,596,482**	**4,445,322**	**2,706,364**	**1,033,526**	**5,557,868**
Material for making clothes	434,366	204,132	211,319	58,410	61,280	93,218	4,375	109,743
Sewing patterns and notions	690,934	298,453	256,807	48,259	109,787	100,209	19,450	118,998
Watches	1,076,349	350,931	665,049	140,339	357,341	167,390	47,581	237,996
Jewelry	6,369,198	2,733,935	3,272,847	447,144	1,782,751	1,042,751	261,932	2,122,462
Shoe repair and other shoe services	107,466	45,311	51,534	9,319	32,997	9,402	2,086	43,302
Coin-operated apparel laundry, dry cleaning	1,489,897	403,409	836,637	238,687	417,861	180,167	441,825	1,189,319
Apparel alteration, repair, tailoring services	421,425	183,095	219,956	38,940	110,852	70,154	19,652	138,831
Clothing rental	191,864	63,806	101,341	16,586	41,664	42,993	21,536	24,130
Watch and jewelry repair	455,184	252,680	175,619	20,635	112,372	42,671	7,807	103,462
Professional laundry, dry cleaning	5,255,714	1,994,852	2,935,716	572,450	1,405,643	957,409	207,217	1,452,437
Clothing storage	34,884	15,027	18,426	5,713	12,773	–	–	17,189

Note: Total spending figures for total consumer units can be found on Total Spending by Age and Total Spending by Region tables. Spending by type of consumer unit will not add to total because not all types of consumer units are shown. (–) means sample is too small to make a reliable estimate.
Source: Calculations by New Strategist based on the 2002 Consumer Expenditure Survey

Table 2.12 Apparel: Market shares by household type, 2002

(percentage of total annual spending on apparel, accessories, and related services accounted for by types of consumer units, 2002)

	total married couples	married couples, no children	married couples with children				single parent, at least one child <18	single person
			total	oldest child under 6	oldest child 6 to 17	oldest child 18 or older		
Share of total consumer units	50.2%	20.6%	25.7%	4.9%	13.6%	7.2%	6.0%	29.5%
Share of total before-tax income	68.2	24.6	38.4	6.8	20.0	11.8	3.3	16.1
Share of total spending	64.6	23.1	36.5	6.4	19.4	10.7	4.5	17.5
Share of apparel spending	63.6	19.3	38.8	7.4	20.8	10.5	6.5	15.5
MEN'S APPAREL	**89.0%**	**24.2%**	**57.3%**	**9.0%**	**32.6%**	**15.8%**	**7.4%**	**15.0%**
Suits	71.2	25.6	40.6	5.2	17.2	18.2	1.2	15.4
Sport coats and tailored jackets	79.8	29.0	46.6	4.8	22.1	19.7	1.4	9.7
Coats and jackets	72.2	27.8	42.1	8.2	21.7	12.2	4.4	12.0
Underwear	69.1	22.1	38.6	5.2	21.0	12.6	5.2	14.4
Hosiery	67.8	21.3	38.6	5.7	22.9	9.9	2.6	16.0
Nightwear	69.6	28.2	36.4	6.2	18.7	11.5	2.2	17.8
Accessories	63.5	26.1	31.3	8.2	15.2	7.8	6.4	16.7
Sweaters and vests	68.7	26.3	37.2	4.7	17.8	14.7	2.2	16.8
Active sportswear	66.3	24.1	38.3	10.5	16.0	11.8	1.9	23.8
Shirts	68.4	19.0	43.7	7.7	19.9	16.4	2.6	15.6
Pants	69.3	19.5	43.1	7.8	21.4	14.0	4.9	14.7
Shorts and shorts sets	70.1	22.4	38.5	4.4	20.4	13.9	3.0	9.2
Uniforms	72.2	20.2	46.5	6.5	28.5	11.5	3.0	13.3
Costumes	75.0	26.9	42.8	3.6	25.5	13.6	1.0	10.6
BOYS' (AGED 2 TO 15) APPAREL	**69.6**	**5.0**	**57.9**	**7.0**	**45.2**	**5.4**	**14.3**	**4.6**
Coats and jackets	71.8	7.8	58.2	8.5	43.5	6.2	12.3	5.7
Sweaters	66.7	7.6	54.1	6.1	39.9	8.1	12.3	3.9
Shirts	63.5	2.5	52.1	6.7	42.6	2.2	14.4	5.3
Underwear	67.5	4.9	56.7	6.6	44.0	5.6	18.6	4.6
Nightwear	76.9	5.7	65.4	24.9	38.4	1.1	4.9	11.5
Hosiery	71.3	2.3	66.8	7.9	51.9	6.5	15.2	2.0
Accessories	65.7	5.5	54.4	10.9	39.9	3.0	16.2	11.4
Suits, sport coats, and vests	73.5	7.7	60.1	4.0	47.9	8.2	9.1	8.1
Pants	68.5	6.2	55.6	5.4	43.0	7.3	16.5	3.4
Shorts and shorts sets	73.4	4.0	61.1	6.4	47.2	7.5	14.1	2.9
Uniforms	80.8	6.0	69.3	4.2	60.1	4.9	9.7	3.7
Active sportswear	68.9	2.4	60.4	2.9	52.0	5.4	17.7	1.4
Costumes	85.1	7.2	72.5	9.0	58.2	5.3	7.6	3.2
WOMEN'S APPAREL	**72.6**	**24.7**	**41.6**	**6.4**	**23.6**	**11.7**	**9.0**	**20.0**
Coats and jackets	61.6	29.1	28.2	4.4	15.1	8.8	3.7	23.4
Dresses	66.5	36.7	23.4	3.1	10.1	10.4	7.5	13.2
Sport coats and tailored jackets	57.2	20.9	30.3	2.1	15.4	12.8	1.7	26.7
Sweaters and vests	63.8	21.9	35.3	5.8	17.2	12.4	4.4	18.0
Shirts, blouses, and tops	55.1	22.3	28.7	4.2	14.2	10.5	5.4	21.8
Skirts	52.0	15.8	34.7	8.5	19.1	6.9	6.2	23.6
Pants	56.8	19.3	30.6	4.8	13.9	12.1	5.8	19.5
Shorts and shorts sets	55.8	19.6	32.1	3.9	13.9	14.5	6.7	21.3
Active sportswear	63.5	25.6	34.5	6.4	16.9	11.4	7.3	17.9
Nightwear	59.1	23.4	30.6	6.7	14.9	9.0	5.0	19.6
Undergarments	58.3	22.7	27.6	4.7	13.3	9.7	8.2	16.7
Hosiery	59.1	22.9	31.3	3.9	16.9	10.6	6.5	21.2
Suits	54.5	22.5	26.5	6.1	10.0	10.4	4.3	25.2

	total married couples	married couples, no children	married couples with children			single parent, at least one child <18	single person
			total	oldest child under 6	oldest child 6 to 17	oldest child 18 or older		
Accessories	58.7%	23.7%	31.9%	7.7%	15.6%	8.5%	6.6%	24.3%
Uniforms	62.0	23.0	33.1	4.5	18.8	9.8	8.9	9.9
Costumes	60.9	20.4	36.2	5.2	21.8	9.3	6.0	14.0
GIRLS' (AGED 2 TO 15) APPAREL	**67.9**	**4.4**	**58.4**	**6.9**	**45.4**	**5.8**	**16.0**	**4.1**
Coats and jackets	66.8	4.8	56.3	5.9	45.5	4.9	15.4	4.9
Dresses and suits	71.5	1.7	67.0	6.4	46.5	13.9	14.0	3.0
Shirts, blouses, and sweaters	64.6	5.2	55.7	8.3	43.0	3.8	20.5	2.9
Skirts and pants	67.6	4.3	56.4	5.0	45.6	5.7	18.2	3.8
Shorts and shorts sets	72.5	5.1	60.2	8.7	46.8	4.7	17.2	1.4
Active sportswear	63.6	4.4	58.4	6.1	48.0	3.7	5.3	11.7
Underwear and nightwear	67.7	4.0	56.8	9.4	41.8	5.6	14.6	5.3
Hosiery	64.0	3.4	54.8	8.8	39.6	5.9	16.0	3.4
Accessories	72.5	11.8	53.7	5.1	44.2	3.8	15.1	4.9
Uniforms	72.3	0.7	64.7	3.3	53.9	7.6	13.0	3.5
Costumes	76.2	2.8	66.8	8.9	51.9	5.9	8.5	2.7
CHILDREN UNDER AGE 2	**71.3**	**11.5**	**54.1**	**32.0**	**16.4**	**5.0**	**5.1**	**5.4**
Coats, jackets, and snowsuits	66.3	15.0	44.5	24.4	16.0	4.1	6.2	9.7
Outerwear including dresses	69.7	21.5	42.0	21.1	14.3	6.6	4.9	9.0
Underwear	73.2	5.8	61.9	38.4	18.2	4.3	5.4	2.2
Nightwear and loungewear	68.6	20.2	41.2	21.5	12.7	7.0	3.6	10.7
Accessories	68.4	7.2	56.4	37.4	14.6	3.5	4.5	8.4
FOOTWEAR	**62.8**	**15.0**	**41.0**	**7.4**	**22.0**	**11.6**	**7.5**	**14.0**
Men's	66.5	13.6	45.3	10.8	18.4	16.3	2.2	13.8
Boys'	65.3	1.3	55.4	7.0	40.2	7.9	16.0	3.7
Women's	58.9	22.5	30.1	5.6	13.9	10.7	6.2	19.1
Girls'	65.0	2.1	59.4	5.5	48.7	4.6	20.5	3.9
OTHER APPAREL PRODUCTS AND SERVICES	**61.5**	**24.3**	**32.5**	**5.9**	**16.5**	**10.1**	**3.8**	**20.7**
Material for making clothes	75.8	35.6	36.9	10.2	10.7	16.3	0.8	19.2
Sewing patterns and notions	75.2	32.5	27.9	5.2	11.9	10.9	2.1	12.9
Watches	70.5	23.0	43.6	9.2	23.4	11.0	3.1	15.6
Jewelry	63.4	27.2	32.6	4.4	17.7	10.4	2.6	21.1
Shoe repair and other shoe services	66.6	28.1	31.9	5.8	20.4	5.8	1.3	26.8
Coin-operated apparel laundry and dry cleaning	35.4	9.6	19.9	5.7	9.9	4.3	10.5	28.2
Apparel alteration, repair, and tailoring services	64.1	27.9	33.5	5.9	16.9	10.7	3.0	21.1
Clothing rental	64.3	21.4	34.0	5.6	14.0	14.4	7.2	8.1
Watch and jewelry repair	74.0	41.1	28.5	3.4	18.3	6.9	1.3	16.8
Professional laundry, dry cleaning	67.3	25.5	37.6	7.3	18.0	12.3	2.7	18.6
Clothing storage	56.6	24.4	29.9	9.3	20.7	–	–	27.9

Note: Market share for total consumer units is 100.0%. Market shares by type of consumer unit will not add to total because not all types of consumer units are shown. (–) means sample is too small to make a reliable estimate.
Source: Calculations by New Strategist based on the 2002 Consumer Expenditure Survey

Table 2.13 Apparel: Average spending by race and Hispanic origin, 2002

(average annual spending of consumer units (CU) on apparel, accessories, and related services, by race and Hispanic origin of consumer unit reference person, 2002)

	total consumer units	race black	race white and other	Hispanic origin Hispanic	Hispanic origin non-Hispanic
Number of consumer units (in thousands, add 000)	112,108	13,554	98,553	10,500	101,608
Average number of persons per CU	2.5	2.7	2.5	3.3	2.4
Average before-tax income of CU	$49,430.00	$35,944.00	$51,177.00	$37,360.00	$50,742.00
Average spending of CU, total	40,676.60	30,135.94	42,134.55	34,742.47	41,294.67
Apparel, average spending	1,749.22	1,704.40	1,755.67	2,097.50	1,716.05
MEN'S APPAREL	**$319.48**	**$239.15**	**$330.82**	**$412.67**	**$310.85**
Suits	32.96	33.01	32.95	21.74	34.12
Sport coats and tailored jackets	10.65	6.30	11.25	4.49	11.29
Coats and jackets	33.86	27.09	34.82	52.76	32.08
Underwear	15.27	13.82	15.48	23.70	14.48
Hosiery	12.22	8.37	12.76	18.91	11.59
Nightwear	2.98	1.71	3.16	2.25	3.06
Accessories	22.41	20.18	22.73	20.81	22.56
Sweaters and vests	15.68	12.51	16.12	15.31	15.72
Active sportswear	15.13	12.71	15.48	16.41	15.01
Shirts	78.89	40.27	84.36	111.10	75.85
Pants	57.64	46.09	59.28	91.37	54.46
Shorts and shorts sets	12.22	8.47	12.75	23.70	11.14
Uniforms	3.21	3.99	3.10	3.04	3.23
Costumes	6.35	4.64	6.59	7.07	6.28
BOYS' (AGED 2 TO 15) APPAREL	**89.98**	**124.20**	**85.21**	**138.29**	**85.14**
Coats and jackets	6.38	7.57	6.22	8.18	6.19
Sweaters	3.65	5.83	3.35	7.08	3.29
Shirts	19.50	26.38	18.53	27.97	18.70
Underwear	5.02	8.13	4.57	8.70	4.67
Nightwear	2.59	1.96	2.67	3.35	2.51
Hosiery	4.21	5.79	3.99	6.75	3.97
Accessories	4.12	7.14	3.70	5.38	4.01
Suits, sport coats, and vests	2.37	3.58	2.21	2.88	2.32
Pants	22.58	31.53	21.35	38.86	20.90
Shorts and shorts sets	8.66	9.35	8.56	13.44	8.17
Uniforms	3.35	5.83	3.00	3.01	3.38
Active sportswear	3.84	9.75	3.02	4.95	3.72
Costumes	3.72	1.36	4.04	7.74	3.30
WOMEN'S APPAREL	**586.91**	**509.83**	**597.88**	**479.07**	**597.22**
Coats and jackets	50.06	41.12	51.32	30.11	51.94
Dresses	56.40	68.21	54.73	46.40	57.35
Sport coats and tailored jackets	6.48	4.53	6.75	3.34	6.81
Sweaters and vests	50.47	33.32	52.90	43.28	51.15
Shirts, blouses, and tops	103.24	65.38	108.61	87.02	104.77
Skirts	17.48	28.80	15.87	13.16	17.88
Pants	96.29	66.70	100.48	102.11	95.74
Shorts and shorts sets	16.09	12.42	16.60	12.48	16.43
Active sportswear	30.07	19.68	31.54	14.18	31.57
Nightwear	27.63	25.21	27.97	22.42	28.12
Undergarments	33.55	29.06	34.18	33.35	33.57
Hosiery	21.22	22.60	21.03	17.85	21.54
Suits	29.01	40.24	27.47	17.11	30.24

	total consumer units	race		Hispanic origin	
		black	white and other	Hispanic	non-Hispanic
Accessories	$33.37	$32.39	$33.51	$21.36	$34.50
Uniforms	6.12	10.56	5.51	4.12	6.33
Costumes	9.42	9.62	9.40	10.77	9.28
GIRLS' (AGED 2 TO 15) APPAREL	**117.21**	**139.20**	**114.18**	**158.62**	**113.16**
Coats and jackets	6.49	8.85	6.17	8.21	6.31
Dresses and suits	12.41	13.87	12.20	25.01	11.22
Shirts, blouses, and sweaters	29.33	30.07	29.22	27.10	29.54
Skirts and pants	24.07	31.46	23.06	28.58	23.61
Shorts and shorts sets	8.28	12.11	7.76	11.17	7.99
Active sportswear	9.32	10.23	9.19	22.41	8.09
Underwear and nightwear	7.63	8.78	7.47	8.99	7.49
Hosiery	4.30	6.91	3.94	5.89	4.15
Accessories	5.81	2.77	6.24	5.94	5.80
Uniforms	4.77	10.97	3.91	8.94	4.33
Costumes	4.80	3.19	5.02	6.37	4.63
CHILDREN UNDER AGE 2	**82.60**	**80.70**	**82.88**	**142.29**	**76.91**
Coats, jackets, and snowsuits	2.43	3.40	2.30	2.79	2.39
Outerwear including dresses	23.71	26.69	23.30	30.20	23.04
Underwear	43.60	36.85	44.56	85.38	39.66
Nightwear and loungewear	4.07	3.64	4.13	4.17	4.06
Accessories	8.79	10.12	8.60	19.75	7.75
FOOTWEAR	**313.17**	**404.10**	**300.29**	**521.24**	**293.53**
Men's	102.90	105.67	102.51	226.65	91.23
Boys'	36.87	94.96	28.64	63.35	34.37
Women's	141.64	165.70	138.23	171.12	138.85
Girls'	31.76	37.77	30.90	60.12	29.08
OTHER APPAREL PRODUCTS AND SERVICES	**239.87**	**207.22**	**244.40**	**245.32**	**239.24**
Material for making clothes	5.11	0.91	5.71	1.68	5.44
Sewing patterns and notions	8.20	1.79	9.11	4.04	8.59
Watches	13.62	11.54	13.90	12.68	13.71
Jewelry	89.65	39.73	96.52	59.06	92.81
Shoe repair and other shoe services	1.44	0.86	1.52	1.41	1.45
Coin-operated apparel laundry and dry cleaning	37.58	57.87	34.79	110.04	30.09
Apparel alteration, repair, and tailoring services	5.86	3.26	6.22	4.88	5.97
Clothing rental	2.66	1.46	2.83	2.11	2.72
Watch and jewelry repair	5.49	1.39	6.06	1.61	5.90
Professional laundry, dry cleaning	69.69	88.05	67.17	47.26	72.01
Clothing storage	0.55	0.37	0.58	0.54	0.55

Note: Other races include American Indians, Asians, and Pacific Islanders.
Source: Bureau of Labor Statistics, unpublished data from the 2002 Consumer Expenditure Survey

Table 2.14 Apparel: Indexed spending by race and Hispanic origin, 2002

(indexed average annual spending of consumer units (CU) on apparel, accessories, and related services, by race and Hispanic origin of consumer unit reference person, 2002; index definition: an index of 100 is the average for all consumer units; an index of 132 means that spending by consumer units in that group is 32 percent above the average for all consumer units; an index of 68 indicates spending that is 32 percent below the average for all consumer units)

	total consumer units	race black	race white and other	Hispanic origin Hispanic	Hispanic origin non-Hispanic
Average spending of CU, total	$40,677	$30,136	$42,135	$34,742	$41,295
Average spending of CU, index	100	74	104	85	102
Apparel, spending index	100	97	100	120	98
MEN'S APPAREL	**100**	**75**	**104**	**129**	**97**
Suits	100	100	100	66	104
Sport coats and tailored jackets	100	59	106	42	106
Coats and jackets	100	80	103	156	95
Underwear	100	91	101	155	95
Hosiery	100	68	104	155	95
Nightwear	100	57	106	76	103
Accessories	100	90	101	93	101
Sweaters and vests	100	80	103	98	100
Active sportswear	100	84	102	108	99
Shirts	100	51	107	141	96
Pants	100	80	103	159	94
Shorts and shorts sets	100	69	104	194	91
Uniforms	100	124	97	95	101
Costumes	100	73	104	111	99
BOYS' (AGED 2 TO 15) APPAREL	**100**	**138**	**95**	**154**	**95**
Coats and jackets	100	119	97	128	97
Sweaters	100	160	92	194	90
Shirts	100	135	95	143	96
Underwear	100	162	91	173	93
Nightwear	100	76	103	129	97
Hosiery	100	138	95	160	94
Accessories	100	173	90	131	97
Suits, sport coats, and vests	100	151	93	122	98
Pants	100	140	95	172	93
Shorts and shorts sets	100	108	99	155	94
Uniforms	100	174	90	90	101
Active sportswear	100	254	79	129	97
Costumes	100	37	109	208	89
WOMEN'S APPAREL	**100**	**87**	**102**	**82**	**102**
Coats and jackets	100	82	103	60	104
Dresses	100	121	97	82	102
Sport coats and tailored jackets	100	70	104	52	105
Sweaters and vests	100	66	105	86	101
Shirts, blouses, and tops	100	63	105	84	101
Skirts	100	165	91	75	102
Pants	100	69	104	106	99
Shorts and shorts sets	100	77	103	78	102
Active sportswear	100	65	105	47	105
Nightwear	100	91	101	81	102
Undergarments	100	87	102	99	100
Hosiery	100	107	99	84	102
Suits	100	139	95	59	104

	total consumer units	race		Hispanic origin	
		black	white and other	Hispanic	non-Hispanic
Accessories	100	97	100	64	103
Uniforms	100	173	90	67	103
Costumes	100	102	100	114	99
GIRLS' (AGED 2 TO 15) APPAREL	**100**	**119**	**97**	**135**	**97**
Coats and jackets	100	136	95	127	97
Dresses and suits	100	112	98	202	90
Shirts, blouses, and sweaters	100	103	100	92	101
Skirts and pants	100	131	96	119	98
Shorts and shorts sets	100	146	94	135	96
Active sportswear	100	110	99	240	87
Underwear and nightwear	100	115	98	118	98
Hosiery	100	161	92	137	97
Accessories	100	48	107	102	100
Uniforms	100	230	82	187	91
Costumes	100	66	105	133	96
CHILDREN UNDER AGE 2	**100**	**98**	**100**	**172**	**93**
Coats, jackets, and snowsuits	100	140	95	115	98
Outerwear including dresses	100	113	98	127	97
Underwear	100	85	102	196	91
Nightwear and loungewear	100	89	101	102	100
Accessories	100	115	98	225	88
FOOTWEAR	**100**	**129**	**96**	**166**	**94**
Men's	100	103	100	220	89
Boys'	100	258	78	172	93
Women's	100	117	98	121	98
Girls'	100	119	97	189	92
OTHER APPAREL PRODUCTS AND SERVICES	**100**	**86**	**102**	**102**	**100**
Material for making clothes	100	18	112	33	106
Sewing patterns and notions	100	22	111	49	105
Watches	100	85	102	93	101
Jewelry	100	44	108	66	104
Shoe repair and other shoe services	100	60	106	98	101
Coin-operated apparel laundry and dry cleaning	100	154	93	293	80
Apparel alteration, repair, and tailoring services	100	56	106	83	102
Clothing rental	100	55	106	79	102
Watch and jewelry repair	100	25	110	29	107
Professional laundry, dry cleaning	100	126	96	68	103
Clothing storage	100	67	105	98	100

Note: Other races include American Indians, Asians, and Pacific Islanders.
Source: Calculations by New Strategist based on the 2002 Consumer Expenditure Survey

Table 2.15 Apparel: Total spending by race and Hispanic origin, 2002

(total annual spending on apparel, accessories, and related services, by race and Hispanic origin groups, 2002; numbers in thousands)

	total consumer units	race black	race white and other	Hispanic origin Hispanic	Hispanic origin non-Hispanic
Number of consumer units	112,108	13,554	98,553	10,500	101,608
Total spending of all consumer units	$4,560,172,273	$408,462,531	$4,152,486,306	$364,795,935	$4,195,868,829
Apparel, total spending	196,101,556	23,101,438	173,026,546	22,023,750	174,364,408
MEN'S APPAREL	**$35,816,264**	**$3,241,439**	**$32,603,303**	**$4,333,035**	**$31,584,847**
Suits	3,695,080	447,418	3,247,321	228,270	3,466,865
Sport coats and tailored jackets	1,193,950	85,390	1,108,721	47,145	1,147,154
Coats and jackets	3,795,977	367,178	3,431,615	553,980	3,259,585
Underwear	1,711,889	187,316	1,525,600	248,850	1,471,284
Hosiery	1,369,960	113,447	1,257,536	198,555	1,177,637
Nightwear	334,082	23,177	311,427	23,625	310,920
Accessories	2,512,340	273,520	2,240,110	218,505	2,292,276
Sweaters and vests	1,757,853	169,561	1,588,674	160,755	1,597,278
Active sportswear	1,696,194	172,271	1,525,600	172,305	1,525,136
Shirts	8,844,200	545,820	8,313,931	1,166,550	7,706,967
Pants	6,461,905	624,704	5,842,222	959,385	5,533,572
Shorts and shorts sets	1,369,960	114,802	1,256,551	248,850	1,131,913
Uniforms	359,867	54,080	305,514	31,920	328,194
Costumes	711,886	62,891	649,464	74,235	638,098
BOYS' (AGED 2 TO 15) APPAREL	**10,087,478**	**1,683,407**	**8,397,701**	**1,452,045**	**8,650,905**
Coats and jackets	715,249	102,604	613,000	85,890	628,954
Sweaters	409,194	79,020	330,153	74,340	334,290
Shirts	2,186,106	357,555	1,826,187	293,685	1,900,070
Underwear	562,782	110,194	450,387	91,350	474,509
Nightwear	290,360	26,566	263,137	35,175	255,036
Hosiery	471,975	78,478	393,226	70,875	403,384
Accessories	461,885	96,776	364,646	56,490	407,448
Suits, sport coats, and vests	265,696	48,523	217,802	30,240	235,731
Pants	2,531,399	427,358	2,104,107	408,030	2,123,607
Shorts and shorts sets	970,855	126,730	843,614	141,120	830,137
Uniforms	375,562	79,020	295,659	31,605	343,435
Active sportswear	430,495	132,152	297,630	51,975	377,982
Costumes	417,042	18,433	398,154	81,270	335,306
WOMEN'S APPAREL	**65,797,306**	**6,910,236**	**58,922,868**	**5,030,235**	**60,682,330**
Coats and jackets	5,612,126	557,340	5,057,740	316,155	5,277,520
Dresses	6,322,891	924,518	5,393,806	487,200	5,827,219
Sport coats and tailored jackets	726,460	61,400	665,233	35,070	691,950
Sweaters and vests	5,658,091	451,619	5,213,454	454,440	5,197,249
Shirts, blouses, and tops	11,574,030	886,161	10,703,841	913,710	10,645,470
Skirts	1,959,648	390,355	1,564,036	138,180	1,816,751
Pants	10,794,879	904,052	9,902,605	1,072,155	9,727,950
Shorts and shorts sets	1,803,818	168,341	1,635,980	131,040	1,669,419
Active sportswear	3,371,088	266,743	3,108,362	148,890	3,207,765
Nightwear	3,097,544	341,696	2,756,527	235,410	2,857,217
Undergarments	3,761,223	393,879	3,368,542	350,175	3,410,981
Hosiery	2,378,932	306,320	2,072,570	187,425	2,188,636
Suits	3,252,253	545,413	2,707,251	179,655	3,072,626

	total consumer units	race		Hispanic origin	
		black	white and other	Hispanic	non-Hispanic
Accessories	$3,741,044	$439,014	$3,302,511	$224,280	$3,505,476
Uniforms	686,101	143,130	543,027	43,260	643,179
Costumes	1,056,057	130,389	926,398	113,085	942,922
GIRLS' (AGED 2 TO 15) APPAREL	**13,140,179**	**1,886,717**	**11,252,782**	**1,665,510**	**11,497,961**
Coats and jackets	727,581	119,953	608,072	86,205	641,146
Dresses and suits	1,391,260	187,994	1,202,347	262,605	1,140,042
Shirts, blouses, and sweaters	3,288,128	407,569	2,879,719	284,550	3,001,500
Skirts and pants	2,698,440	426,409	2,272,632	300,090	2,398,965
Shorts and shorts sets	928,254	164,139	764,771	117,285	811,848
Active sportswear	1,044,847	138,657	905,702	235,305	822,009
Underwear and nightwear	855,384	119,004	736,191	94,395	761,044
Hosiery	482,064	93,658	388,299	61,845	421,673
Accessories	651,347	37,545	614,971	62,370	589,326
Uniforms	534,755	148,687	385,342	93,870	439,963
Costumes	538,118	43,237	494,736	66,885	470,445
CHILDREN UNDER AGE 2	**9,260,121**	**1,093,808**	**8,168,073**	**1,494,045**	**7,814,671**
Coats, jackets, and snowsuits	272,422	46,084	226,672	29,295	242,843
Outerwear including dresses	2,658,081	361,756	2,296,285	317,100	2,341,048
Underwear	4,887,909	499,465	4,391,522	896,490	4,029,773
Nightwear and loungewear	456,280	49,337	407,024	43,785	412,528
Accessories	985,429	137,166	847,556	207,375	787,462
FOOTWEAR	**35,108,862**	**5,477,171**	**29,594,480**	**5,473,020**	**29,824,996**
Men's	11,535,913	1,432,251	10,102,668	2,379,825	9,269,698
Boys'	4,133,422	1,287,088	2,822,558	665,175	3,492,267
Women's	15,878,977	2,245,898	13,622,981	1,796,760	14,108,271
Girls'	3,560,550	511,935	3,045,288	631,260	2,954,761
OTHER APPAREL PRODUCTS AND SERVICES	**26,891,346**	**2,808,660**	**24,086,353**	**2,575,860**	**24,308,698**
Material for making clothes	572,872	12,334	562,738	17,640	552,748
Sewing patterns and notions	919,286	24,262	897,818	42,420	872,813
Watches	1,526,911	156,413	1,369,887	133,140	1,393,046
Jewelry	10,050,482	538,500	9,512,336	620,130	9,430,238
Shoe repair and other shoe services	161,436	11,656	149,801	14,805	147,332
Coin-operated apparel laundry and dry cleaning	4,213,019	784,370	3,428,659	1,155,420	3,057,385
Apparel alteration, repair, and tailoring services	656,953	44,186	613,000	51,240	606,600
Clothing rental	298,207	19,789	278,905	22,155	276,374
Watch and jewelry repair	615,473	18,840	597,231	16,905	599,487
Professional laundry, dry cleaning	7,812,807	1,193,430	6,619,805	496,230	7,316,792
Clothing storage	61,659	5,015	57,161	5,670	55,884

Note: Other races include American Indians, Asians, and Pacific Islanders. Numbers may not add to total because of rounding.
Source: Calculations by New Strategist based on the 2002 Consumer Expenditure Survey

Table 2.16 Apparel: Market shares by race and Hispanic origin, 2002

(percentage of total annual spending on apparel, accessories, and related services accounted for by race and Hispanic origin groups, 2002)

	total consumer units	race		Hispanic origin	
		black	white and other	Hispanic	non-Hispanic
Share of total consumer units	100.0%	12.1%	87.9%	9.4%	90.6%
Share of total before-tax income	100.0	8.8	91.0	7.1	93.0
Share of total spending	100.0	9.0	91.1	8.0	92.0
Share of apparel spending	100.0	11.8	88.2	11.2	88.9
MEN'S APPAREL	**100.0%**	**9.1%**	**91.0%**	**12.1%**	**88.2%**
Suits	100.0	12.1	87.9	6.2	93.8
Sport coats and tailored jackets	100.0	7.2	92.9	3.9	96.1
Coats and jackets	100.0	9.7	90.4	14.6	85.9
Underwear	100.0	10.9	89.1	14.5	85.9
Hosiery	100.0	8.3	91.8	14.5	86.0
Nightwear	100.0	6.9	93.2	7.1	93.1
Accessories	100.0	10.9	89.2	8.7	91.2
Sweaters and vests	100.0	9.6	90.4	9.1	90.9
Active sportswear	100.0	10.2	89.9	10.2	89.9
Shirts	100.0	6.2	94.0	13.2	87.1
Pants	100.0	9.7	90.4	14.8	85.6
Shorts and shorts sets	100.0	8.4	91.7	18.2	82.6
Uniforms	100.0	15.0	84.9	8.9	91.2
Costumes	100.0	8.8	91.2	10.4	89.6
BOYS' (AGED 2 TO 15) APPAREL	**100.0**	**16.7**	**83.2**	**14.4**	**85.8**
Coats and jackets	100.0	14.3	85.7	12.0	87.9
Sweaters	100.0	19.3	80.7	18.2	81.7
Shirts	100.0	16.4	83.5	13.4	86.9
Underwear	100.0	19.6	80.0	16.2	84.3
Nightwear	100.0	9.1	90.6	12.1	87.8
Hosiery	100.0	16.6	83.3	15.0	85.5
Accessories	100.0	21.0	78.9	12.2	88.2
Suits, sport coats, and vests	100.0	18.3	82.0	11.4	88.7
Pants	100.0	16.9	83.1	16.1	83.9
Shorts and shorts sets	100.0	13.1	86.9	14.5	85.5
Uniforms	100.0	21.0	78.7	8.4	91.4
Active sportswear	100.0	30.7	69.1	12.1	87.8
Costumes	100.0	4.4	95.5	19.5	80.4
WOMEN'S APPAREL	**100.0**	**10.5**	**89.6**	**7.6**	**92.2**
Coats and jackets	100.0	9.9	90.1	5.6	94.0
Dresses	100.0	14.6	85.3	7.7	92.2
Sport coats and tailored jackets	100.0	8.5	91.6	4.8	95.2
Sweaters and vests	100.0	8.0	92.1	8.0	91.9
Shirts, blouses, and tops	100.0	7.7	92.5	7.9	92.0
Skirts	100.0	19.9	79.8	7.1	92.7
Pants	100.0	8.4	91.7	9.9	90.1
Shorts and shorts sets	100.0	9.3	90.7	7.3	92.5
Active sportswear	100.0	7.9	92.2	4.4	95.2
Nightwear	100.0	11.0	89.0	7.6	92.2
Undergarments	100.0	10.5	89.6	9.3	90.7
Hosiery	100.0	12.9	87.1	7.9	92.0
Suits	100.0	16.8	83.2	5.5	94.5

	total consumer units	race		Hispanic origin	
		black	white and other	Hispanic	non-Hispanic
Accessories	100.0%	11.7%	88.3%	6.0%	93.7%
Uniforms	100.0	20.9	79.1	6.3	93.7
Costumes	100.0	12.3	87.7	10.7	89.3
GIRLS' (AGED 2 TO 15) APPAREL	**100.0**	**14.4**	**85.6**	**12.7**	**87.5**
Coats and jackets	100.0	16.5	83.6	11.8	88.1
Dresses and suits	100.0	13.5	86.4	18.9	81.9
Shirts, blouses, and sweaters	100.0	12.4	87.6	8.7	91.3
Skirts and pants	100.0	15.8	84.2	11.1	88.9
Shorts and shorts sets	100.0	17.7	82.4	12.6	87.5
Active sportswear	100.0	13.3	86.7	22.5	78.7
Underwear and nightwear	100.0	13.9	86.1	11.0	89.0
Hosiery	100.0	19.4	80.5	12.8	87.5
Accessories	100.0	5.8	94.4	9.6	90.5
Uniforms	100.0	27.8	72.1	17.6	82.3
Costumes	100.0	8.0	91.9	12.4	87.4
CHILDREN UNDER AGE 2	**100.0**	**11.8**	**88.2**	**16.1**	**84.4**
Coats, jackets, and snowsuits	100.0	16.9	83.2	10.8	89.1
Outerwear including dresses	100.0	13.6	86.4	11.9	88.1
Underwear	100.0	10.2	89.8	18.3	82.4
Nightwear and loungewear	100.0	10.8	89.2	9.6	90.4
Accessories	100.0	13.9	86.0	21.0	79.9
FOOTWEAR	**100.0**	**15.6**	**84.3**	**15.6**	**85.0**
Men's	100.0	12.4	87.6	20.6	80.4
Boys'	100.0	31.1	68.3	16.1	84.5
Women's	100.0	14.1	85.8	11.3	88.8
Girls'	100.0	14.4	85.5	17.7	83.0
OTHER APPAREL PRODUCTS AND SERVICES	**100.0**	**10.4**	**89.6**	**9.6**	**90.4**
Material for making clothes	100.0	2.2	98.2	3.1	96.5
Sewing patterns and notions	100.0	2.6	97.7	4.6	94.9
Watches	100.0	10.2	89.7	8.7	91.2
Jewelry	100.0	5.4	94.6	6.2	93.8
Shoe repair and other shoe services	100.0	7.2	92.8	9.2	91.3
Coin-operated apparel laundry and dry cleaning	100.0	18.6	81.4	27.4	72.6
Apparel alteration, repair, and tailoring services	100.0	6.7	93.3	7.8	92.3
Clothing rental	100.0	6.6	93.5	7.4	92.7
Watch and jewelry repair	100.0	3.1	97.0	2.7	97.4
Professional laundry, dry cleaning	100.0	15.3	84.7	6.4	93.7
Clothing storage	100.0	8.1	92.7	9.2	90.6

Note: Other races include American Indians, Asians, and Pacific Islanders. Numbers may not add to total because of rounding.
Source: Calculations by New Strategist based on the 2002 Consumer Expenditure Survey

Table 2.17 Apparel: Average spending by region, 2002

(average annual spending of consumer units (CU) on apparel, accessories, and related services, by region in which consumer unit lives, 2002)

	total consumer units	Northeast	Midwest	South	West
Number of consumer units (in thousands, add 000)	112,108	21,313	25,883	40,004	24,907
Average number of persons per CU	2.5	2.5	2.5	2.5	2.6
Average before-tax income of CU	$49,430.00	$53,983.00	$49,197.00	$45,641.00	$52,016.00
Average spending of CU, total	40,676.60	42,390.20	40,601.14	37,280.55	44,728.34
Apparel, average spending	1,749.22	1,964.59	1,727.95	1,591.86	1,836.07
MEN'S APPAREL	**$319.48**	**$335.61**	**$330.93**	**$278.09**	**$360.11**
Suits	32.96	43.63	32.65	26.09	35.20
Sport coats and tailored jackets	10.65	19.96	8.12	9.10	7.80
Coats and jackets	33.86	30.14	27.94	34.83	41.69
Underwear	15.27	17.05	15.12	13.32	16.98
Hosiery	12.22	13.17	12.12	10.43	14.33
Nightwear	2.98	3.64	2.90	2.47	3.33
Accessories	22.41	18.61	24.92	19.60	27.61
Sweaters and vests	15.68	23.99	15.47	10.80	16.62
Active sportswear	15.13	17.13	16.32	9.18	21.63
Shirts	78.89	77.96	79.57	72.03	89.93
Pants	57.64	53.96	69.93	49.49	61.14
Shorts and shorts sets	12.22	11.62	14.91	12.56	9.42
Uniforms	3.21	1.57	2.90	4.19	3.36
Costumes	6.35	3.19	8.05	3.99	11.08
BOYS' (AGED 2 TO 15) APPAREL	**89.98**	**97.35**	**96.17**	**84.97**	**85.25**
Coats and jackets	6.38	9.47	6.83	5.14	5.26
Sweaters	3.65	5.70	3.26	2.75	3.73
Shirts	19.50	22.75	24.73	19.12	11.86
Underwear	5.02	3.86	6.17	5.17	4.59
Nightwear	2.59	3.15	3.06	1.74	2.95
Hosiery	4.21	3.86	4.67	4.16	4.14
Accessories	4.12	3.98	4.17	3.86	4.63
Suits, sport coats, and vests	2.37	2.25	2.33	2.42	2.45
Pants	22.58	23.30	21.17	22.28	23.91
Shorts and shorts sets	8.66	11.03	7.29	8.62	8.11
Uniforms	3.35	3.64	4.70	2.29	3.39
Active sportswear	3.84	2.32	3.27	5.20	3.54
Costumes	3.72	2.07	4.52	2.22	6.69
WOMEN'S APPAREL	**586.91**	**642.48**	**626.51**	**520.94**	**602.68**
Coats and jackets	50.06	85.11	51.43	34.36	42.94
Dresses	56.40	42.59	58.44	76.73	34.02
Sport coats and tailored jackets	6.48	9.32	8.16	4.18	6.01
Sweaters and vests	50.47	71.48	52.26	35.87	53.47
Shirts, blouses, and tops	103.24	88.68	99.57	99.09	126.41
Skirts	17.48	19.96	19.51	14.11	18.57
Pants	96.29	92.24	109.58	83.00	107.25
Shorts and shorts sets	16.09	15.78	21.32	14.71	13.13
Active sportswear	30.07	35.45	37.59	19.90	33.78
Nightwear	27.63	39.68	25.97	21.48	28.58
Undergarments	33.55	35.31	36.79	29.68	34.81
Hosiery	21.22	21.51	23.31	20.13	20.55
Suits	29.01	44.74	22.89	25.30	27.87

	total consumer units	Northeast	Midwest	South	West
Accessories	$33.37	$30.99	$41.89	$29.07	$33.47
Uniforms	6.12	4.59	6.12	7.77	4.77
Costumes	9.42	5.06	11.68	5.54	17.05
GIRLS' (AGED 2 TO 15) APPAREL	**117.21**	**142.14**	**105.31**	**116.02**	**109.72**
Coats and jackets	6.49	10.52	7.36	5.25	4.13
Dresses and suits	12.41	11.66	13.51	11.77	12.95
Shirts, blouses, and sweaters	29.33	34.26	23.44	32.00	26.85
Skirts and pants	24.07	24.75	24.75	24.56	22.00
Shorts and shorts sets	8.28	8.90	9.21	8.39	6.63
Active sportswear	9.32	18.46	4.07	7.90	9.00
Underwear and nightwear	7.63	7.73	8.81	6.42	8.26
Hosiery	4.30	6.86	3.03	3.56	4.57
Accessories	5.81	9.51	3.29	6.31	4.39
Uniforms	4.77	3.42	4.14	6.33	4.04
Costumes	4.80	6.06	3.70	3.52	6.90
CHILDREN UNDER AGE 2	**82.60**	**79.36**	**87.64**	**80.46**	**83.60**
Coats, jackets, and snowsuits	2.43	3.87	2.34	1.69	2.47
Outerwear including dresses	23.71	19.90	25.90	24.82	22.92
Underwear	43.60	41.79	48.07	41.68	43.61
Nightwear and loungewear	4.07	4.99	4.74	3.56	3.43
Accessories	8.79	8.82	6.59	8.70	11.17
FOOTWEAR	**313.17**	**378.27**	**274.39**	**302.58**	**313.10**
Men's	102.90	118.29	96.71	88.80	118.30
Boys'	36.87	39.09	30.91	45.25	27.76
Women's	141.64	177.96	125.73	136.66	134.19
Girls'	31.76	42.93	21.05	31.88	32.85
OTHER APPAREL PRODUCTS AND SERVICES	**239.87**	**289.37**	**207.01**	**208.80**	**281.60**
Material for making clothes	5.11	1.91	5.14	4.23	9.30
Sewing patterns and notions	8.20	7.24	6.61	6.17	13.92
Watches	13.62	16.85	11.99	12.46	14.39
Jewelry	89.65	103.05	86.64	71.68	110.18
Shoe repair and other shoe services	1.44	1.84	1.01	1.15	2.03
Coin-operated apparel laundry and dry cleaning	37.58	52.10	33.80	26.28	47.25
Apparel alteration, repair, and tailoring services	5.86	8.44	4.59	4.75	6.78
Clothing rental	2.66	2.53	3.35	2.29	2.66
Watch and jewelry repair	5.49	6.28	5.05	5.15	5.82
Professional laundry, dry cleaning	69.69	88.53	48.46	74.13	68.50
Clothing storage	0.55	0.61	0.36	0.51	0.77

Source: Bureau of Labor Statistics, unpublished data from the 2002 Consumer Expenditure Survey

Table 2.18 Apparel: Indexed spending by region, 2002

(indexed average annual spending of consumer units (CU) on apparel, accessories, and related services, by region in which consumer unit lives, 2002; index definition: an index of 100 is the average for all consumer units; an index of 132 means that spending by consumer units in that group is 32 percent above the average for all consumer units; an index of 68 indicates spending that is 32 percent below the average for all consumer units)

	total consumer units	Northeast	Midwest	South	West
Average spending of CU, total	$40,677	$42,390	$40,601	$37,281	$44,728
Average spending of CU, index	100	104	100	92	110
Apparel, spending index	100	112	99	91	105
MEN'S APPAREL	100	105	104	87	113
Suits	100	132	99	79	107
Sport coats and tailored jackets	100	187	76	85	73
Coats and jackets	100	89	83	103	123
Underwear	100	112	99	87	111
Hosiery	100	108	99	85	117
Nightwear	100	122	97	83	112
Accessories	100	83	111	87	123
Sweaters and vests	100	153	99	69	106
Active sportswear	100	113	108	61	143
Shirts	100	99	101	91	114
Pants	100	94	121	86	106
Shorts and shorts sets	100	95	122	103	77
Uniforms	100	49	90	131	105
Costumes	100	50	127	63	174
BOYS' (AGED 2 TO 15) APPAREL	100	108	107	94	95
Coats and jackets	100	148	107	81	82
Sweaters	100	156	89	75	102
Shirts	100	117	127	98	61
Underwear	100	77	123	103	91
Nightwear	100	122	118	67	114
Hosiery	100	92	111	99	98
Accessories	100	97	101	94	112
Suits, sport coats, and vests	100	95	98	102	103
Pants	100	103	94	99	106
Shorts and shorts sets	100	127	84	100	94
Uniforms	100	109	140	68	101
Active sportswear	100	60	85	135	92
Costumes	100	56	122	60	180
WOMEN'S APPAREL	100	109	107	89	103
Coats and jackets	100	170	103	69	86
Dresses	100	76	104	136	60
Sport coats and tailored jackets	100	144	126	65	93
Sweaters and vests	100	142	104	71	106
Shirts, blouses, and tops	100	86	96	96	122
Skirts	100	114	112	81	106
Pants	100	96	114	86	111
Shorts and shorts sets	100	98	133	91	82
Active sportswear	100	118	125	66	112
Nightwear	100	144	94	78	103
Undergarments	100	105	110	88	104
Hosiery	100	101	110	95	97
Suits	100	154	79	87	96

	total consumer units	Northeast	Midwest	South	West
Accessories	100	93	126	87	100
Uniforms	100	75	100	127	78
Costumes	100	54	124	59	181
GIRLS' (AGED 2 TO 15) APPAREL	**100**	**121**	**90**	**99**	**94**
Coats and jackets	100	162	113	81	64
Dresses and suits	100	94	109	95	104
Shirts, blouses, and sweaters	100	117	80	109	92
Skirts and pants	100	103	103	102	91
Shorts and shorts sets	100	107	111	101	80
Active sportswear	100	198	44	85	97
Underwear and nightwear	100	101	115	84	108
Hosiery	100	160	70	83	106
Accessories	100	164	57	109	76
Uniforms	100	72	87	133	85
Costumes	100	126	77	73	144
CHILDREN UNDER AGE 2	**100**	**96**	**106**	**97**	**101**
Coats, jackets, and snowsuits	100	159	96	70	102
Outerwear including dresses	100	84	109	105	97
Underwear	100	96	110	96	100
Nightwear and loungewear	100	123	116	87	84
Accessories	100	100	75	99	127
FOOTWEAR	**100**	**121**	**88**	**97**	**100**
Men's	100	115	94	86	115
Boys'	100	106	84	123	75
Women's	100	126	89	96	95
Girls'	100	135	66	100	103
OTHER APPAREL PRODUCTS AND SERVICES	**100**	**121**	**86**	**87**	**117**
Material for making clothes	100	37	101	83	182
Sewing patterns and notions	100	88	81	75	170
Watches	100	124	88	91	106
Jewelry	100	115	97	80	123
Shoe repair and other shoe services	100	128	70	80	141
Coin-operated apparel laundry and dry cleaning	100	139	90	70	126
Apparel alteration, repair, and tailoring services	100	144	78	81	116
Clothing rental	100	95	126	86	100
Watch and jewelry repair	100	114	92	94	106
Professional laundry, dry cleaning	100	127	70	106	98
Clothing storage	100	111	65	93	140

Source: Calculations by New Strategist based on the 2002 Consumer Expenditure Survey

Table 2.19 Apparel: Total spending by region, 2002

(total annual spending on apparel, accessories, and related services, by region in which consumer units live, 2002; numbers in thousands)

	total consumer units	Northeast	Midwest	South	West
Number of consumer units	112,108	21,313	25,883	40,004	24,907
Total spending of all consumer units	$4,560,172,273	$903,462,333	$1,050,879,307	$1,491,371,122	$1,114,048,764
Apparel, total spending	196,101,556	41,871,307	44,724,530	63,680,767	45,730,995
MEN'S APPAREL	**$35,816,264**	**$7,152,856**	**$8,565,461**	**$11,124,712**	**$8,969,260**
Suits	3,695,080	929,886	845,080	1,043,704	876,726
Sport coats and tailored jackets	1,193,950	425,407	210,170	364,036	194,275
Coats and jackets	3,795,977	642,374	723,171	1,393,339	1,038,373
Underwear	1,711,889	363,387	391,351	532,853	422,921
Hosiery	1,369,960	280,692	313,702	417,242	356,917
Nightwear	334,082	77,579	75,061	98,810	82,940
Accessories	2,512,340	396,635	645,004	784,078	687,682
Sweaters and vests	1,757,853	511,299	400,410	432,043	413,954
Active sportswear	1,696,194	365,092	422,411	367,237	538,738
Shirts	8,844,200	1,661,561	2,059,510	2,881,488	2,239,887
Pants	6,461,905	1,150,049	1,809,998	1,979,798	1,522,814
Shorts and shorts sets	1,369,960	247,657	385,916	502,450	234,624
Uniforms	359,867	33,461	75,061	167,617	83,688
Costumes	711,886	67,988	208,358	159,616	275,970
BOYS' (AGED 2 TO 15) APPAREL	**10,087,478**	**2,074,821**	**2,489,168**	**3,399,140**	**2,123,322**
Coats and jackets	715,249	201,834	176,781	205,621	131,011
Sweaters	409,194	121,484	84,379	110,011	92,903
Shirts	2,186,106	484,871	640,087	764,876	295,397
Underwear	562,782	82,268	159,698	206,821	114,323
Nightwear	290,360	67,136	79,202	69,607	73,476
Hosiery	471,975	82,268	120,874	166,417	103,115
Accessories	461,885	84,826	107,932	154,415	115,319
Suits, sport coats, and vests	265,696	47,954	60,307	96,810	61,022
Pants	2,531,399	496,593	547,943	891,289	595,526
Shorts and shorts sets	970,855	235,082	188,687	344,834	201,996
Uniforms	375,562	77,579	121,650	91,609	84,435
Active sportswear	430,495	49,446	84,637	208,021	88,171
Costumes	417,042	44,118	116,991	88,809	166,628
WOMEN'S APPAREL	**65,797,306**	**13,693,176**	**16,215,958**	**20,839,684**	**15,010,951**
Coats and jackets	5,612,126	1,813,949	1,331,163	1,374,537	1,069,507
Dresses	6,322,891	907,721	1,512,603	3,069,507	847,336
Sport coats and tailored jackets	726,460	198,637	211,205	167,217	149,691
Sweaters and vests	5,658,091	1,523,453	1,352,646	1,434,943	1,331,777
Shirts, blouses, and tops	11,574,030	1,890,037	2,577,170	3,963,996	3,148,494
Skirts	1,959,648	425,407	504,977	564,456	462,523
Pants	10,794,879	1,965,911	2,836,259	3,320,332	2,671,276
Shorts and shorts sets	1,803,818	336,319	551,826	588,459	327,029
Active sportswear	3,371,088	755,546	972,942	796,080	841,358
Nightwear	3,097,544	845,700	672,182	859,286	711,842
Undergarments	3,761,223	752,562	952,236	1,187,319	867,013
Hosiery	2,378,932	458,443	603,333	805,281	511,839
Suits	3,252,253	953,544	592,462	1,012,101	694,158

	total consumer units	Northeast	Midwest	South	West
Accessories	$3,741,044	$660,490	$1,084,239	$1,162,916	$833,637
Uniforms	686,101	97,827	158,404	310,831	118,806
Costumes	1,056,057	107,844	302,313	221,622	424,664
GIRLS' (AGED 2 TO 15) APPAREL	**13,140,179**	**3,029,430**	**2,725,739**	**4,641,264**	**2,732,796**
Coats and jackets	727,581	224,213	190,499	210,021	102,866
Dresses and suits	1,391,260	248,510	349,679	470,847	322,546
Shirts, blouses, and sweaters	3,288,128	730,183	606,698	1,280,128	668,753
Skirts and pants	2,698,440	527,497	640,604	982,498	547,954
Shorts and shorts sets	928,254	189,686	238,382	335,634	165,133
Active sportswear	1,044,847	393,438	105,344	316,032	224,163
Underwear and nightwear	855,384	164,749	228,029	256,826	205,732
Hosiery	482,064	146,207	78,425	142,414	113,825
Accessories	651,347	202,687	85,155	252,425	109,342
Uniforms	534,755	72,890	107,156	253,225	100,624
Costumes	538,118	129,157	95,767	140,814	171,858
CHILDREN UNDER AGE 2	**9,260,121**	**1,691,400**	**2,268,386**	**3,218,722**	**2,082,225**
Coats, jackets, and snowsuits	272,422	82,481	60,566	67,607	61,520
Outerwear including dresses	2,658,081	424,129	670,370	992,899	570,868
Underwear	4,887,909	890,670	1,244,196	1,667,367	1,086,194
Nightwear and loungewear	456,280	106,352	122,685	142,414	85,431
Accessories	985,429	187,981	170,569	348,035	278,211
FOOTWEAR	**35,108,862**	**8,062,069**	**7,102,036**	**12,104,410**	**7,798,382**
Men's	11,535,913	2,521,115	2,503,145	3,552,355	2,946,498
Boys'	4,133,422	833,125	800,044	1,810,181	691,418
Women's	15,878,977	3,792,861	3,254,270	5,466,947	3,342,270
Girls'	3,560,550	914,967	544,837	1,275,328	818,195
OTHER APPAREL PRODUCTS AND SERVICES	**26,891,346**	**6,167,343**	**5,358,040**	**8,352,835**	**7,013,811**
Material for making clothes	572,872	40,708	133,039	169,217	231,635
Sewing patterns and notions	919,286	154,306	171,087	246,825	346,705
Watches	1,526,911	359,124	310,337	498,450	358,412
Jewelry	10,050,482	2,196,305	2,242,503	2,867,487	2,744,253
Shoe repair and other shoe services	161,436	39,216	26,142	46,005	50,561
Coin-operated apparel laundry and dry cleaning	4,213,019	1,110,407	874,845	1,051,305	1,176,856
Apparel alteration, repair, and tailoring services	656,953	179,882	118,803	190,019	168,869
Clothing rental	298,207	53,922	86,708	91,609	66,253
Watch and jewelry repair	615,473	133,846	130,709	206,021	144,959
Professional laundry, dry cleaning	7,812,807	1,886,840	1,254,290	2,965,497	1,706,130
Clothing storage	61,659	13,001	9,318	20,402	19,178

Note: Numbers may not add to total because of rounding.
Source: Calculations by New Strategist based on the 2002 Consumer Expenditure Survey

Table 2.20 Apparel: Market shares by region, 2002

(percentage of total annual spending on apparel, accessories, and related services accounted for by consumer units by region, 2002)

	total consumer units	Northeast	Midwest	South	West
Share of total consumer units	100.0%	19.0%	23.1%	35.7%	22.2%
Share of total before-tax income	100.0	20.8	23.0	32.9	23.4
Share of total spending	100.0	19.8	23.0	32.7	24.4
Share of apparel spending	100.0	21.4	22.8	32.5	23.3
MEN'S APPAREL	**100.0%**	**20.0%**	**23.9%**	**31.1%**	**25.0%**
Suits	100.0	25.2	22.9	28.2	23.7
Sport coats and tailored jackets	100.0	35.6	17.6	30.5	16.3
Coats and jackets	100.0	16.9	19.1	36.7	27.4
Underwear	100.0	21.2	22.9	31.1	24.7
Hosiery	100.0	20.5	22.9	30.5	26.1
Nightwear	100.0	23.2	22.5	29.6	24.8
Accessories	100.0	15.8	25.7	31.2	27.4
Sweaters and vests	100.0	29.1	22.8	24.6	23.5
Active sportswear	100.0	21.5	24.9	21.7	31.8
Shirts	100.0	18.8	23.3	32.6	25.3
Pants	100.0	17.8	28.0	30.6	23.6
Shorts and shorts sets	100.0	18.1	28.2	36.7	17.1
Uniforms	100.0	9.3	20.9	46.6	23.3
Costumes	100.0	9.6	29.3	22.4	38.8
BOYS' (AGED 2 TO 15) APPAREL	**100.0**	**20.6**	**24.7**	**33.7**	**21.0**
Coats and jackets	100.0	28.2	24.7	28.7	18.3
Sweaters	100.0	29.7	20.6	26.9	22.7
Shirts	100.0	22.2	29.3	35.0	13.5
Underwear	100.0	14.6	28.4	36.7	20.3
Nightwear	100.0	23.1	27.3	24.0	25.3
Hosiery	100.0	17.4	25.6	35.3	21.8
Accessories	100.0	18.4	23.4	33.4	25.0
Suits, sport coats, and vests	100.0	18.0	22.7	36.4	23.0
Pants	100.0	19.6	21.6	35.2	23.5
Shorts and shorts sets	100.0	24.2	19.4	35.5	20.8
Uniforms	100.0	20.7	32.4	24.4	22.5
Active sportswear	100.0	11.5	19.7	48.3	20.5
Costumes	100.0	10.6	28.1	21.3	40.0
WOMEN'S APPAREL	**100.0**	**20.8**	**24.6**	**31.7**	**22.8**
Coats and jackets	100.0	32.3	23.7	24.5	19.1
Dresses	100.0	14.4	23.9	48.5	13.4
Sport coats and tailored jackets	100.0	27.3	29.1	23.0	20.6
Sweaters and vests	100.0	26.9	23.9	25.4	23.5
Shirts, blouses, and tops	100.0	16.3	22.3	34.2	27.2
Skirts	100.0	21.7	25.8	28.8	23.6
Pants	100.0	18.2	26.3	30.8	24.7
Shorts and shorts sets	100.0	18.6	30.6	32.6	18.1
Active sportswear	100.0	22.4	28.9	23.6	25.0
Nightwear	100.0	27.3	21.7	27.7	23.0
Undergarments	100.0	20.0	25.3	31.6	23.1
Hosiery	100.0	19.3	25.4	33.9	21.5
Suits	100.0	29.3	18.2	31.1	21.3

	total consumer units	Northeast	Midwest	South	West
Accessories	100.0%	17.7%	29.0%	31.1%	22.3%
Uniforms	100.0	14.3	23.1	45.3	17.3
Costumes	100.0	10.2	28.6	21.0	40.2
GIRLS' (AGED 2 TO 15) APPAREL	**100.0**	**23.1**	**20.7**	**35.3**	**20.8**
Coats and jackets	100.0	30.8	26.2	28.9	14.1
Dresses and suits	100.0	17.9	25.1	33.8	23.2
Shirts, blouses, and sweaters	100.0	22.2	18.5	38.9	20.3
Skirts and pants	100.0	19.5	23.7	36.4	20.3
Shorts and shorts sets	100.0	20.4	25.7	36.2	17.8
Active sportswear	100.0	37.7	10.1	30.2	21.5
Underwear and nightwear	100.0	19.3	26.7	30.0	24.1
Hosiery	100.0	30.3	16.3	29.5	23.6
Accessories	100.0	31.1	13.1	38.8	16.8
Uniforms	100.0	13.6	20.0	47.4	18.8
Costumes	100.0	24.0	17.8	26.2	31.9
CHILDREN UNDER AGE 2	**100.0**	**18.3**	**24.5**	**34.8**	**22.5**
Coats, jackets, and snowsuits	100.0	30.3	22.2	24.8	22.6
Outerwear including dresses	100.0	16.0	25.2	37.4	21.5
Underwear	100.0	18.2	25.5	34.1	22.2
Nightwear and loungewear	100.0	23.3	26.9	31.2	18.7
Accessories	100.0	19.1	17.3	35.3	28.2
FOOTWEAR	**100.0**	**23.0**	**20.2**	**34.5**	**22.2**
Men's	100.0	21.9	21.7	30.8	25.5
Boys'	100.0	20.2	19.4	43.8	16.7
Women's	100.0	23.9	20.5	34.4	21.0
Girls'	100.0	25.7	15.3	35.8	23.0
OTHER APPAREL PRODUCTS AND SERVICES	**100.0**	**22.9**	**19.9**	**31.1**	**26.1**
Material for making clothes	100.0	7.1	23.2	29.5	40.4
Sewing patterns and notions	100.0	16.8	18.6	26.8	37.7
Watches	100.0	23.5	20.3	32.6	23.5
Jewelry	100.0	21.9	22.3	28.5	27.3
Shoe repair and other shoe services	100.0	24.3	16.2	28.5	31.3
Coin-operated apparel laundry and dry cleaning	100.0	26.4	20.8	25.0	27.9
Apparel alteration, repair, and tailoring services	100.0	27.4	18.1	28.9	25.7
Clothing rental	100.0	18.1	29.1	30.7	22.2
Watch and jewelry repair	100.0	21.7	21.2	33.5	23.6
Professional laundry, dry cleaning	100.0	24.2	16.1	38.0	21.8
Clothing storage	100.0	21.1	15.1	33.1	31.1

Note: Numbers may not add to total because of rounding.
Source: Calculations by New Strategist based on the 2002 Consumer Expenditure Survey

Table 2.21 Apparel: Average spending by education, 2002

(average annual spending of consumer units (CU) on apparel, accessories, and related services, by education of consumer unit reference person, 2002)

	total consumer units	less than high school graduate	high school graduate	some college	associate's degree	college graduate total	bachelor's degree	master's, professional, doctorate
Number of consumer units (in thousands, add 000)	112,108	17,075	31,961	23,260	10,395	29,417	19,082	10,335
Average number of persons per CU	2.5	2.6	2.5	2.4	2.6	2.5	2.5	2.5
Average before-tax income of CU	$49,430.00	$25,564.00	$39,618.00	$42,598.00	$54,860.00	$77,820.00	$69,408.00	$92,783.00
Average spending of CU, total	40,676.60	24,930.40	33,707.63	38,653.57	44,405.79	57,384.01	53,731.57	64,118.48
Apparel, average spending	1,749.22	1,226.10	1,391.75	1,629.74	1,890.27	2,435.04	2,311.50	2,661.33
MEN'S APPAREL	**$319.48**	**$230.62**	**$262.83**	**$276.36**	**$342.02**	**$449.32**	**$425.99**	**$492.29**
Suits	32.96	13.68	23.05	29.80	28.59	58.96	47.14	80.80
Sport coats and tailored jackets	10.65	3.08	6.78	10.02	9.10	20.30	16.71	26.92
Coats and jackets	33.86	39.23	27.85	21.71	50.63	40.85	37.77	46.44
Underwear	15.27	15.67	11.91	11.85	15.29	20.90	21.78	19.29
Hosiery	12.22	12.16	9.21	11.76	12.72	15.48	14.72	16.86
Nightwear	2.98	2.02	2.79	2.85	3.36	3.72	3.59	3.95
Accessories	22.41	8.80	23.62	23.96	17.66	28.06	26.10	31.63
Sweaters and vests	15.68	7.96	11.11	16.47	13.67	25.21	22.47	30.28
Active sportswear	15.13	9.92	13.52	11.01	14.11	22.48	26.32	15.48
Shirts	78.89	52.26	53.05	70.31	93.53	119.61	120.10	118.71
Pants	57.64	52.22	57.46	47.14	66.48	65.11	66.70	62.23
Shorts and shorts sets	12.22	9.37	15.28	9.81	4.86	14.38	9.38	23.48
Uniforms	3.21	1.70	3.09	3.97	2.43	3.89	3.32	4.96
Costumes	6.35	2.57	4.11	5.68	9.59	10.37	9.88	11.27
BOYS' (AGED 2 TO 15) APPAREL	**89.98**	**81.93**	**84.15**	**83.15**	**103.89**	**100.82**	**104.50**	**94.13**
Coats and jackets	6.38	5.78	5.90	5.46	8.26	7.31	6.73	8.38
Sweaters	3.65	4.43	3.59	2.87	2.73	4.20	3.28	5.91
Shirts	19.50	14.32	18.50	21.37	21.00	21.25	25.04	14.35
Underwear	5.02	4.66	3.64	5.49	4.99	6.27	5.78	7.15
Nightwear	2.59	4.08	1.59	1.65	1.96	3.72	5.08	1.24
Hosiery	4.21	3.13	3.63	5.20	3.94	4.72	4.85	4.48
Accessories	4.12	3.89	2.62	4.02	4.40	5.76	5.05	7.07
Suits, sport coats, and vests	2.37	2.40	2.39	1.74	2.50	2.80	2.66	3.04
Pants	22.58	23.30	23.73	17.84	29.60	22.17	21.74	22.98
Shorts and shorts sets	8.66	8.12	7.81	7.76	9.35	10.36	10.53	10.04
Uniforms	3.35	2.25	3.87	2.80	3.47	3.80	4.22	3.02
Active sportswear	3.84	3.83	3.39	3.05	5.90	4.22	4.95	2.88
Costumes	3.72	1.73	3.50	3.89	5.80	4.24	4.59	3.59
WOMEN'S APPAREL	**586.91**	**322.12**	**433.54**	**560.02**	**692.38**	**861.23**	**800.45**	**972.28**
Coats and jackets	50.06	23.96	25.54	46.06	60.01	87.39	73.99	111.78
Dresses	56.40	35.72	43.73	41.28	142.42	63.86	53.38	82.92
Sport coats and tailored jackets	6.48	3.50	4.48	5.55	7.51	10.77	6.06	19.45
Sweaters and vests	50.47	26.87	36.00	40.76	52.09	82.86	82.70	83.16
Shirts, blouses, and tops	103.24	60.81	78.06	109.86	101.39	145.23	138.31	157.83
Skirts	17.48	8.35	10.66	10.06	15.62	34.56	35.54	32.79
Pants	96.29	57.80	76.89	105.08	101.53	126.83	129.96	121.13
Shorts and shorts sets	16.09	9.40	11.80	22.23	17.44	18.96	18.78	19.28
Active sportswear	30.07	6.21	25.03	27.90	31.53	47.76	48.89	45.70
Nightwear	27.63	17.99	22.01	24.58	24.58	41.06	37.36	47.78
Undergarments	33.55	22.20	23.90	33.09	30.43	50.11	48.18	53.62
Hosiery	21.22	16.09	16.39	18.16	26.54	29.15	26.22	34.47
Suits	29.01	11.32	23.00	26.37	24.71	49.43	38.45	69.69

	total consumer units	less than high school graduate	high school graduate	some college	associate's degree	college graduate total	college graduate bachelor's degree	college graduate master's, professional, doctorate
Accessories	$33.37	$16.05	$21.81	$32.12	$36.36	$53.44	$43.51	$71.52
Uniforms	6.12	2.76	5.96	6.97	7.99	6.91	7.18	6.41
Costumes	9.42	3.08	8.28	9.96	12.23	12.94	11.96	14.75
GIRLS' (AGED 2 TO 15) APPAREL	**117.21**	**95.88**	**102.00**	**120.42**	**126.18**	**138.88**	**139.86**	**137.14**
Coats and jackets	6.49	4.13	6.20	6.79	8.80	7.13	6.74	7.85
Dresses and suits	12.41	14.53	8.93	12.57	25.94	10.74	11.74	8.91
Shirts, blouses, and sweaters	29.33	25.51	20.92	30.50	17.27	42.55	44.96	38.17
Skirts and pants	24.07	19.08	24.63	24.32	28.26	24.69	23.72	26.48
Shorts and shorts sets	8.28	4.50	8.74	9.41	9.05	8.82	9.24	8.05
Active sportswear	9.32	7.17	9.95	11.78	5.65	9.10	9.96	7.56
Underwear and nightwear	7.63	5.81	6.36	8.56	9.66	8.62	8.36	9.10
Hosiery	4.30	4.08	3.91	4.88	3.41	4.68	5.02	4.08
Accessories	5.81	3.45	3.65	3.53	5.57	10.83	9.08	14.01
Uniforms	4.77	4.87	4.51	4.55	4.15	5.37	5.72	4.71
Costumes	4.80	2.76	4.21	3.52	8.42	6.35	5.33	8.23
CHILDREN UNDER AGE 2	**82.60**	**77.71**	**69.86**	**78.45**	**79.69**	**102.75**	**103.92**	**100.65**
Coats, jackets, and snowsuits	2.43	1.23	2.60	2.12	3.08	2.95	3.00	2.87
Outerwear including dresses	23.71	17.65	21.68	24.72	23.12	28.85	27.71	30.96
Underwear	43.60	49.97	36.40	41.46	43.41	49.44	52.74	43.44
Nightwear and loungewear	4.07	2.35	3.71	3.61	4.00	5.86	5.10	7.26
Accessories	8.79	6.51	5.48	6.54	6.09	15.64	15.39	16.11
FOOTWEAR	**313.17**	**276.10**	**276.60**	**286.04**	**332.35**	**381.45**	**349.26**	**440.03**
Men's	102.90	126.74	90.30	103.42	107.44	102.57	97.63	111.56
Boys'	36.87	26.39	44.23	45.44	30.15	30.45	32.25	27.16
Women's	141.64	91.08	114.42	105.48	165.75	211.69	184.32	261.52
Girls'	31.76	31.89	27.66	31.70	29.02	36.74	35.07	39.79
OTHER APPAREL PRODUCTS AND SERVICES	**239.87**	**141.73**	**162.77**	**225.31**	**213.74**	**400.60**	**387.51**	**424.82**
Material for making clothes	5.11	4.05	2.52	4.00	3.23	9.62	10.62	7.80
Sewing patterns and notions	8.20	5.48	3.81	12.84	5.92	11.42	12.15	10.11
Watches	13.62	6.97	8.45	13.94	13.92	22.72	22.88	22.44
Jewelry	89.65	34.07	64.12	83.50	84.27	156.42	155.48	158.16
Shoe repair and other shoe services	1.44	0.68	0.50	1.59	0.80	3.03	2.30	4.37
Coin-operated apparel laundry and dry cleaning	37.58	65.92	36.51	37.90	24.44	26.69	29.47	21.54
Apparel alteration, repair, and tailoring services	5.86	2.43	3.58	4.79	4.17	11.78	10.18	14.74
Clothing rental	2.66	1.29	1.99	1.73	5.30	3.99	3.78	4.36
Watch and jewelry repair	5.49	1.93	2.81	5.55	7.34	9.79	7.78	13.49
Professional laundry, dry cleaning	69.69	18.86	38.33	58.53	63.84	144.16	131.72	167.13
Clothing storage	0.55	0.06	0.15	0.94	0.52	0.98	1.14	0.68

Source: Bureau of Labor Statistics, unpublished data from the 2002 Consumer Expenditure Survey

Table 2.22 Apparel: Indexed spending by education, 2002

(indexed average annual spending of consumer units (CU) on apparel, accessories, and related services, by education of consumer unit reference person, 2002; index definition: an index of 100 is the average for all consumer units; an index of 132 means that spending by consumer units in that group is 32 percent above the average for all consumer units; an index of 68 indicates spending that is 32 percent below the average for all consumer units)

	total consumer units	less than high school graduate	high school graduate	some college	associate's degree	college graduate total	bachelor's degree	master's, professional, doctorate
Average spending of CU, total	$40,677	$24,930	$33,708	$38,654	$44,406	$57,384	$53,732	$64,118
Average spending of CU, index	100	61	83	95	109	141	132	158
Apparel, spending index	100	70	80	93	108	139	132	152
MEN'S APPAREL	100	72	82	87	107	141	133	154
Suits	100	42	70	90	87	179	143	245
Sport coats and tailored jackets	100	29	64	94	85	191	157	253
Coats and jackets	100	116	82	64	150	121	112	137
Underwear	100	103	78	78	100	137	143	126
Hosiery	100	100	75	96	104	127	120	138
Nightwear	100	68	94	96	113	125	120	133
Accessories	100	39	105	107	79	125	116	141
Sweaters and vests	100	51	71	105	87	161	143	193
Active sportswear	100	66	89	73	93	149	174	102
Shirts	100	66	67	89	119	152	152	150
Pants	100	91	100	82	115	113	116	108
Shorts and shorts sets	100	77	125	80	40	118	77	192
Uniforms	100	53	96	124	76	121	103	155
Costumes	100	40	65	89	151	163	156	177
BOYS' (AGED 2 TO 15) APPAREL	100	91	94	92	115	112	116	105
Coats and jackets	100	91	92	86	129	115	105	131
Sweaters	100	121	98	79	75	115	90	162
Shirts	100	73	95	110	108	109	128	74
Underwear	100	93	73	109	99	125	115	142
Nightwear	100	158	61	64	76	144	196	48
Hosiery	100	74	86	124	94	112	115	106
Accessories	100	94	64	98	107	140	123	172
Suits, sport coats, and vests	100	101	101	73	105	118	112	128
Pants	100	103	105	79	131	98	96	102
Shorts and shorts sets	100	94	90	90	108	120	122	116
Uniforms	100	67	116	84	104	113	126	90
Active sportswear	100	100	88	79	154	110	129	75
Costumes	100	47	94	105	156	114	123	97
WOMEN'S APPAREL	100	55	74	95	118	147	136	166
Coats and jackets	100	48	51	92	120	175	148	223
Dresses	100	63	78	73	253	113	95	147
Sport coats and tailored jackets	100	54	69	86	116	166	94	300
Sweaters and vests	100	53	71	81	103	164	164	165
Shirts, blouses, and tops	100	59	76	106	98	141	134	153
Skirts	100	48	61	58	89	198	203	188
Pants	100	60	80	109	105	132	135	126
Shorts and shorts sets	100	58	73	138	108	118	117	120
Active sportswear	100	21	83	93	105	159	163	152
Nightwear	100	65	80	89	89	149	135	173
Undergarments	100	66	71	99	91	149	144	160
Hosiery	100	76	77	86	125	137	124	162
Suits	100	39	79	91	85	170	133	240

	total consumer units	less than high school graduate	high school graduate	some college	associate's degree	college graduate total	bachelor's degree	master's, professional, doctorate
Accessories	100	48	65	96	109	160	130	214
Uniforms	100	45	97	114	131	113	117	105
Costumes	100	33	88	106	130	137	127	157
GIRLS' (AGED 2 TO 15) APPAREL	**100**	**82**	**87**	**103**	**108**	**118**	**119**	**117**
Coats and jackets	100	64	96	105	136	110	104	121
Dresses and suits	100	117	72	101	209	87	95	72
Shirts, blouses, and sweaters	100	87	71	104	59	145	153	130
Skirts and pants	100	79	102	101	117	103	99	110
Shorts and shorts sets	100	54	106	114	109	107	112	97
Active sportswear	100	77	107	126	61	98	107	81
Underwear and nightwear	100	76	83	112	127	113	110	119
Hosiery	100	95	91	113	79	109	117	95
Accessories	100	59	63	61	96	186	156	241
Uniforms	100	102	95	95	87	113	120	99
Costumes	100	58	88	73	175	132	111	171
CHILDREN UNDER AGE 2	**100**	**94**	**85**	**95**	**96**	**124**	**126**	**122**
Coats, jackets, and snowsuits	100	51	107	87	127	121	123	118
Outerwear including dresses	100	74	91	104	98	122	117	131
Underwear	100	115	83	95	100	113	121	100
Nightwear and loungewear	100	58	91	89	98	144	125	178
Accessories	100	74	62	74	69	178	175	183
FOOTWEAR	**100**	**88**	**88**	**91**	**106**	**122**	**112**	**141**
Men's	100	123	88	101	104	100	95	108
Boys'	100	72	120	123	82	83	87	74
Women's	100	64	81	74	117	149	130	185
Girls'	100	100	87	100	91	116	110	125
OTHER APPAREL PRODUCTS AND SERVICES	**100**	**59**	**68**	**94**	**89**	**167**	**162**	**177**
Material for making clothes	100	79	49	78	63	188	208	153
Sewing patterns and notions	100	67	46	157	72	139	148	123
Watches	100	51	62	102	102	167	168	165
Jewelry	100	38	72	93	94	174	173	176
Shoe repair and other shoe services	100	47	35	110	56	210	160	303
Coin-operated apparel laundry and dry cleaning	100	175	97	101	65	71	78	57
Apparel alteration, repair, and tailoring services	100	41	61	82	71	201	174	252
Clothing rental	100	48	75	65	199	150	142	164
Watch and jewelry repair	100	35	51	101	134	178	142	246
Professional laundry, dry cleaning	100	27	55	84	92	207	189	240
Clothing storage	100	11	27	171	95	178	207	124

Source: Calculations by New Strategist based on the 2002 Consumer Expenditure Survey

Table 2.23 Apparel: Total spending by education, 2002

(total annual spending on apparel, accessories, and related services, by consumer unit (CU) educational attainment group, 2002; numbers in thousands)

	total consumer units	less than high school graduate	high school graduate	some college	associate's degree	college graduate total	college graduate bachelor's degree	college graduate master's, professional, doctorate
Number of consumer units	112,108	17,075	31,961	23,260	10,395	29,417	19,082	10,335
Total spending of all CUs	$4,560,172,273	$425,686,580	$1,077,329,562	$899,082,038	$461,598,187	$1,688,065,422	$1,025,305,819	$662,664,491
Apparel, total spending	196,101,556	20,935,658	44,481,722	37,907,752	19,649,357	71,631,572	44,108,043	27,504,846
MEN'S APPAREL	**$35,816,264**	**$3,937,837**	**$8,400,310**	**$6,428,134**	**$3,555,298**	**$13,217,646**	**$8,128,741**	**$5,087,817**
Suits	3,695,080	233,586	736,701	693,148	297,193	1,734,426	899,525	835,068
Sport coats and tailored jackets	1,193,950	52,591	216,696	233,065	94,595	597,165	318,860	278,218
Coats and jackets	3,795,977	669,852	890,114	504,975	526,299	1,201,684	720,727	479,957
Underwear	1,711,889	267,565	380,656	275,631	158,940	614,815	415,606	199,362
Hosiery	1,369,960	207,632	294,361	273,538	132,224	455,375	280,887	174,248
Nightwear	334,082	34,492	89,171	66,291	34,927	109,431	68,504	40,823
Accessories	2,512,340	150,260	754,919	557,310	183,576	825,441	498,040	326,896
Sweaters and vests	1,757,853	135,917	355,087	383,092	142,100	741,603	428,773	312,944
Active sportswear	1,696,194	169,384	432,113	256,093	146,673	661,294	502,238	159,986
Shirts	8,844,200	892,340	1,695,531	1,635,411	972,244	3,518,567	2,291,748	1,226,868
Pants	6,461,905	891,657	1,836,479	1,096,476	691,060	1,915,341	1,272,769	643,147
Shorts and shorts sets	1,369,960	159,993	488,364	228,181	50,520	423,016	178,989	242,666
Uniforms	359,867	29,028	98,759	92,342	25,260	114,432	63,352	51,262
Costumes	711,886	43,883	131,360	132,117	99,688	305,054	188,530	116,475
BOYS' (AGED 2 TO 15) APPAREL	**10,087,478**	**1,398,955**	**2,689,518**	**1,934,069**	**1,079,937**	**2,965,822**	**1,994,069**	**972,834**
Coats and jackets	715,249	98,694	188,570	127,000	85,863	215,038	128,422	86,607
Sweaters	409,194	75,642	114,740	66,756	28,378	123,551	62,589	61,080
Shirts	2,186,106	244,514	591,279	497,066	218,295	625,111	477,813	148,307
Underwear	562,782	79,570	116,338	127,697	51,871	184,445	110,294	73,895
Nightwear	290,360	69,666	50,818	38,379	20,374	109,431	96,937	12,815
Hosiery	471,975	53,445	116,018	120,952	40,956	138,848	92,548	46,301
Accessories	461,885	66,422	83,738	93,505	45,738	169,442	96,364	73,068
Suits, sport coats, and vests	265,696	40,980	76,387	40,472	25,988	82,368	50,758	31,418
Pants	2,531,399	397,848	758,435	414,958	307,692	652,175	414,843	237,498
Shorts and shorts sets	970,855	138,649	249,615	180,498	97,193	304,760	200,933	103,763
Uniforms	375,562	38,419	123,689	65,128	36,071	111,785	80,526	31,212
Active sportswear	430,495	65,397	108,348	70,943	61,331	124,140	94,456	29,765
Costumes	417,042	29,540	111,864	90,481	60,291	124,728	87,586	37,103
WOMEN'S APPAREL	**65,797,306**	**5,500,199**	**13,856,372**	**13,026,065**	**7,197,290**	**25,334,803**	**15,274,187**	**10,048,514**
Coats and jackets	5,612,126	409,117	816,284	1,071,356	623,804	2,570,752	1,411,877	1,155,246
Dresses	6,322,891	609,919	1,397,655	960,173	1,480,456	1,878,570	1,018,597	856,978
Sport coats and tailored jackets	726,460	59,763	143,185	129,093	78,066	316,821	115,637	201,016
Sweaters and vests	5,658,091	458,805	1,150,596	948,078	541,476	2,437,493	1,578,081	859,459
Shirts, blouses, and tops	11,574,030	1,038,331	2,494,876	2,555,344	1,053,949	4,272,231	2,639,231	1,631,173
Skirts	1,959,648	142,576	340,704	233,996	162,370	1,016,652	678,174	338,885
Pants	10,794,879	986,935	2,457,481	2,444,161	1,055,404	3,730,958	2,479,897	1,251,879
Shorts and shorts sets	1,803,818	160,505	377,140	517,070	181,289	557,746	358,360	199,259
Active sportswear	3,371,088	106,036	799,984	648,954	327,754	1,404,956	932,919	472,310
Nightwear	3,097,544	307,179	703,462	571,731	255,509	1,207,862	712,904	493,806
Undergarments	3,761,223	379,065	763,868	769,673	316,320	1,474,086	919,371	554,163
Hosiery	2,378,932	274,737	523,841	422,402	275,883	857,506	500,330	356,247
Suits	3,252,253	193,289	735,103	613,366	256,860	1,454,082	733,703	720,246

	total consumer units	less than high school graduate	high school graduate	some college	associate's degree	college graduate total	bachelor's degree	master's, professional, doctorate
Accessories	$3,741,044	$274,054	$697,069	$747,111	$377,962	$1,572,044	$830,258	$739,159
Uniforms	686,101	47,127	190,488	162,122	83,056	203,271	137,009	66,247
Costumes	1,056,057	52,591	264,637	231,670	127,131	380,656	228,221	152,441
GIRLS' (AGED 2 TO 15) APPAREL	**13,140,179**	**1,637,151**	**3,260,022**	**2,800,969**	**1,311,641**	**4,085,433**	**2,668,809**	**1,417,342**
Coats and jackets	727,581	70,520	198,158	157,935	91,476	209,743	128,613	81,130
Dresses and suits	1,391,260	248,100	285,412	292,378	269,646	315,939	224,023	92,085
Shirts, blouses, and sweaters	3,288,128	435,583	668,624	709,430	179,522	1,251,693	857,927	394,487
Skirts and pants	2,698,440	325,791	787,199	565,683	293,763	726,306	452,625	273,671
Shorts and shorts sets	928,254	76,838	279,339	218,877	94,075	259,458	176,318	83,197
Active sportswear	1,044,847	122,428	318,012	274,003	58,732	267,695	190,057	78,133
Underwear and nightwear	855,384	99,206	203,272	199,106	100,416	253,575	159,526	94,049
Hosiery	482,064	69,666	124,968	113,509	35,447	137,672	95,792	42,167
Accessories	651,347	58,909	116,658	82,108	57,900	318,586	173,265	144,793
Uniforms	534,755	83,155	144,144	105,833	43,139	157,969	109,149	48,678
Costumes	538,118	47,127	134,556	81,875	87,526	186,798	101,707	85,057
CHILDREN UNDER AGE 2	**9,260,121**	**1,326,898**	**2,232,795**	**1,824,747**	**828,378**	**3,022,597**	**1,983,001**	**1,040,218**
Coats, jackets, and snowsuits	272,422	21,002	83,099	49,311	32,017	86,780	57,246	29,661
Outerwear including dresses	2,658,081	301,374	692,914	574,987	240,332	848,680	528,762	319,972
Underwear	4,887,909	853,238	1,163,380	964,360	451,247	1,454,376	1,006,385	448,952
Nightwear and loungewear	456,280	40,126	118,575	83,969	41,580	172,384	97,318	75,032
Accessories	985,429	111,158	175,146	152,120	63,306	460,082	293,672	166,497
FOOTWEAR	**35,108,862**	**4,714,408**	**8,840,413**	**6,653,290**	**3,454,778**	**11,221,115**	**6,664,579**	**4,547,710**
Men's	11,535,913	2,164,086	2,886,078	2,405,549	1,116,839	3,017,302	1,862,976	1,152,973
Boys'	4,133,422	450,609	1,413,635	1,056,934	313,409	895,748	615,395	280,699
Women's	15,878,977	1,555,191	3,656,978	2,453,465	1,722,971	6,227,285	3,517,194	2,702,809
Girls'	3,560,550	544,522	884,041	737,342	301,663	1,080,781	669,206	411,230
OTHER APPAREL PRODUCTS AND SERVICES	**26,891,346**	**2,420,040**	**5,202,292**	**5,240,711**	**2,221,827**	**11,784,450**	**7,394,466**	**4,390,515**
Material for making clothes	572,872	69,154	80,542	93,040	33,576	282,992	202,651	80,613
Sewing patterns and notions	919,286	93,571	121,771	298,658	61,538	335,942	231,846	104,487
Watches	1,526,911	119,013	270,070	324,244	144,698	668,354	436,596	231,917
Jewelry	10,050,482	581,745	2,049,339	1,942,210	875,987	4,601,407	2,966,869	1,634,584
Shoe repair and other shoe services	161,436	11,611	15,981	36,983	8,316	89,134	43,889	45,164
Coin-operated apparel laundry, dry cleaning	4,213,019	1,125,584	1,166,896	881,554	254,054	785,140	562,347	222,616
Apparel alteration, repair, tailoring services	656,953	41,492	114,420	111,415	43,347	346,532	194,255	152,338
Clothing rental	298,207	22,027	63,602	40,240	55,094	117,374	72,130	45,061
Watch and jewelry repair	615,473	32,955	89,810	129,093	76,299	287,992	148,458	139,419
Professional laundry, dry cleaning	7,812,807	322,035	1,225,065	1,361,408	663,617	4,240,755	2,513,481	1,727,289
Clothing storage	61,659	1,025	4,794	21,864	5,405	28,829	21,753	7,028

Note: Numbers may not add to total because of rounding.
Source: Calculations by New Strategist based on the 2002 Consumer Expenditure Survey

Table 2.24 Apparel: Market shares by education, 2002

(percentage of total annual spending on apparel, accessories, and related services accounted for by consumer unit educational attainment groups, 2002)

	total consumer units	less than high school graduate	high school graduate	some college	associate's degree	college graduate total	bachelor's degree	master's, professional, doctorate
Share of total consumer units	100.0%	15.2%	28.5%	20.7%	9.3%	26.2%	17.0%	9.2%
Share of total before-tax income	100.0	7.9	22.8	17.9	10.3	41.3	23.9	17.3
Share of total spending	100.0	9.3	23.6	19.7	10.1	37.0	22.5	14.5
Share of apparel spending	100.0	10.7	22.7	19.3	10.0	36.5	22.5	14.0
MEN'S APPAREL	**100.0%**	**11.0%**	**23.5%**	**17.9%**	**9.9%**	**36.9%**	**22.7%**	**14.2%**
Suits	100.0	6.3	19.9	18.8	8.0	46.9	24.3	22.6
Sport coats and tailored jackets	100.0	4.4	18.1	19.5	7.9	50.0	26.7	23.3
Coats and jackets	100.0	17.6	23.4	13.3	13.9	31.7	19.0	12.6
Underwear	100.0	15.6	22.2	16.1	9.3	35.9	24.3	11.6
Hosiery	100.0	15.2	21.5	20.0	9.7	33.2	20.5	12.7
Nightwear	100.0	10.3	26.7	19.8	10.5	32.8	20.5	12.2
Accessories	100.0	6.0	30.0	22.2	7.3	32.9	19.8	13.0
Sweaters and vests	100.0	7.7	20.2	21.8	8.1	42.2	24.4	17.8
Active sportswear	100.0	10.0	25.5	15.1	8.6	39.0	29.6	9.4
Shirts	100.0	10.1	19.2	18.5	11.0	39.8	25.9	13.9
Pants	100.0	13.8	28.4	17.0	10.7	29.6	19.7	10.0
Shorts and shorts sets	100.0	11.7	35.6	16.7	3.7	30.9	13.1	17.7
Uniforms	100.0	8.1	27.4	25.7	7.0	31.8	17.6	14.2
Costumes	100.0	6.2	18.5	18.6	14.0	42.9	26.5	16.4
BOYS' (AGED 2 TO 15) APPAREL	**100.0**	**13.9**	**26.7**	**19.2**	**10.7**	**29.4**	**19.8**	**9.6**
Coats and jackets	100.0	13.8	26.4	17.8	12.0	30.1	18.0	12.1
Sweaters	100.0	18.5	28.0	16.3	6.9	30.2	15.3	14.9
Shirts	100.0	11.2	27.0	22.7	10.0	28.6	21.9	6.8
Underwear	100.0	14.1	20.7	22.7	9.2	32.8	19.6	13.1
Nightwear	100.0	24.0	17.5	13.2	7.0	37.7	33.4	4.4
Hosiery	100.0	11.3	24.6	25.6	8.7	29.4	19.6	9.8
Accessories	100.0	14.4	18.1	20.2	9.9	36.7	20.9	15.8
Suits, sport coats, and vests	100.0	15.4	28.7	15.2	9.8	31.0	19.1	11.8
Pants	100.0	15.7	30.0	16.4	12.2	25.8	16.4	9.4
Shorts and shorts sets	100.0	14.3	25.7	18.6	10.0	31.4	20.7	10.7
Uniforms	100.0	10.2	32.9	17.3	9.6	29.8	21.4	8.3
Active sportswear	100.0	15.2	25.2	16.5	14.2	28.8	21.9	6.9
Costumes	100.0	7.1	26.8	21.7	14.5	29.9	21.0	8.9
WOMEN'S APPAREL	**100.0**	**8.4**	**21.1**	**19.8**	**10.9**	**38.5**	**23.2**	**15.3**
Coats and jackets	100.0	7.3	14.5	19.1	11.1	45.8	25.2	20.6
Dresses	100.0	9.6	22.1	15.2	23.4	29.7	16.1	13.6
Sport coats and tailored jackets	100.0	8.2	19.7	17.8	10.7	43.6	15.9	27.7
Sweaters and vests	100.0	8.1	20.3	16.8	9.6	43.1	27.9	15.2
Shirts, blouses, and tops	100.0	9.0	21.6	22.1	9.1	36.9	22.8	14.1
Skirts	100.0	7.3	17.4	11.9	8.3	51.9	34.6	17.3
Pants	100.0	9.1	22.8	22.6	9.8	34.6	23.0	11.6
Shorts and shorts sets	100.0	8.9	20.9	28.7	10.1	30.9	19.9	11.0
Active sportswear	100.0	3.1	23.7	19.3	9.7	41.7	27.7	14.0
Nightwear	100.0	9.9	22.7	18.5	8.2	39.0	23.0	15.9
Undergarments	100.0	10.1	20.3	20.5	8.4	39.2	24.4	14.7
Hosiery	100.0	11.5	22.0	17.8	11.6	36.0	21.0	15.0
Suits	100.0	5.9	22.6	18.9	7.9	44.7	22.6	22.1

	total consumer units	less than high school graduate	high school graduate	some college	associate's degree	college graduate		
						total	bachelor's degree	master's, professional, doctorate
Accessories	100.0%	7.3%	18.6%	20.0%	10.1%	42.0%	22.2%	19.8%
Uniforms	100.0	6.9	27.8	23.6	12.1	29.6	20.0	9.7
Costumes	100.0	5.0	25.1	21.9	12.0	36.0	21.6	14.4
GIRLS' (AGED 2 TO 15) APPAREL	**100.0**	**12.5**	**24.8**	**21.3**	**10.0**	**31.1**	**20.3**	**10.8**
Coats and jackets	100.0	9.7	27.2	21.7	12.6	28.8	17.7	11.2
Dresses and suits	100.0	17.8	20.5	21.0	19.4	22.7	16.1	6.6
Shirts, blouses, and sweaters	100.0	13.2	20.3	21.6	5.5	38.1	26.1	12.0
Skirts and pants	100.0	12.1	29.2	21.0	10.9	26.9	16.8	10.1
Shorts and shorts sets	100.0	8.3	30.1	23.6	10.1	28.0	19.0	9.0
Active sportswear	100.0	11.7	30.4	26.2	5.6	25.6	18.2	7.5
Underwear and nightwear	100.0	11.6	23.8	23.3	11.7	29.6	18.6	11.0
Hosiery	100.0	14.5	25.9	23.5	7.4	28.6	19.9	8.7
Accessories	100.0	9.0	17.9	12.6	8.9	48.9	26.6	22.2
Uniforms	100.0	15.6	27.0	19.8	8.1	29.5	20.4	9.1
Costumes	100.0	8.8	25.0	15.2	16.3	34.7	18.9	15.8
CHILDREN UNDER AGE 2	**100.0**	**14.3**	**24.1**	**19.7**	**8.9**	**32.6**	**21.4**	**11.2**
Coats, jackets, and snowsuits	100.0	7.7	30.5	18.1	11.8	31.9	21.0	10.9
Outerwear including dresses	100.0	11.3	26.1	21.6	9.0	31.9	19.9	12.0
Underwear	100.0	17.5	23.8	19.7	9.2	29.8	20.6	9.2
Nightwear and loungewear	100.0	8.8	26.0	18.4	9.1	37.8	21.3	16.4
Accessories	100.0	11.3	17.8	15.4	6.4	46.7	29.8	16.9
FOOTWEAR	**100.0**	**13.4**	**25.2**	**19.0**	**9.8**	**32.0**	**19.0**	**13.0**
Men's	100.0	18.8	25.0	20.9	9.7	26.2	16.1	10.0
Boys'	100.0	10.9	34.2	25.6	7.6	21.7	14.9	6.8
Women's	100.0	9.8	23.0	15.5	10.9	39.2	22.2	17.0
Girls'	100.0	15.3	24.8	20.7	8.5	30.4	18.8	11.5
OTHER APPAREL PRODUCTS AND SERVICES	**100.0**	**9.0**	**19.3**	**19.5**	**8.3**	**43.8**	**27.5**	**16.3**
Material for making clothes	100.0	12.1	14.1	16.2	5.9	49.4	35.4	14.1
Sewing patterns and notions	100.0	10.2	13.2	32.5	6.7	36.5	25.2	11.4
Watches	100.0	7.8	17.7	21.2	9.5	43.8	28.6	15.2
Jewelry	100.0	5.8	20.4	19.3	8.7	45.8	29.5	16.3
Shoe repair and other shoe services	100.0	7.2	9.9	22.9	5.2	55.2	27.2	28.0
Coin-operated apparel laundry and dry cleaning	100.0	26.7	27.7	20.9	6.0	18.6	13.3	5.3
Apparel alteration, repair, and tailoring services	100.0	6.3	17.4	17.0	6.6	52.7	29.6	23.2
Clothing rental	100.0	7.4	21.3	13.5	18.5	39.4	24.2	15.1
Watch and jewelry repair	100.0	5.4	14.6	21.0	12.4	46.8	24.1	22.7
Professional laundry, dry cleaning	100.0	4.1	15.7	17.4	8.5	54.3	32.2	22.1
Clothing storage	100.0	1.7	7.8	35.5	8.8	46.8	35.3	11.4

Note: Numbers may not add to total because of rounding.
Source: Calculations by New Strategist based on the 2002 Consumer Expenditure Survey

Spending on Entertainment, 2002

Entertainment spending has grown slightly since 1997, despite the recession of 2001 and the loss of discretionary income. The average household spent $2,079 on entertainment in 2002, up from $2,026 in 1997, a 3 percent rise after adjusting for inflation. Overall, Americans devoted 5.1 percent of their spending dollars to entertainment in 2002, down slightly from 5.2 percent in 1997. The average American household now spends substantially more on entertainment than it does on clothes.

Households headed by people aged 35 to 44 spend the most on entertainment, a total of $2,685 in 2002—29 percent more than the average household. Households headed by the youngest and oldest adults spend far less than average on entertainment. Interestingly, households headed by 55-to-64-year-olds spend significantly more on entertainment than those headed by 25-to-34-year-olds. They spend more than any other age group on social, recreation, and civic club memberships; pet food, supplies, and medicines; and hunting and fishing equipment.

Households with incomes of $70,000 or more spent $4,457 on entertainment in 2002, more than twice what the average household spends. High-income households spend far more than average on nearly every entertainment category. They account for 47 percent of all entertainment spending. They control an even larger 66 percent share of spending on fees for recreational lessons and 68 percent of spending on motorized recreational vehicles.

Married couples with school-aged children at home spend the most on entertainment among household types—73 percent more than the average household. They are especially big spenders on fees for recreational lessons, spending more than three times as much as the average household. They spend more than twice the average on video game hardware and software. Single parents spend 40 percent more than average on this item.

Blacks and Hispanics spend much less than the average household on entertainment. In some categories, however, they spend more. Blacks and Hispanics spend 13 percent more than the average household on portable color TVs, for example. Blacks spend more than twice the average on tape recorders and players.

Households in the South spend 18 percent less on entertainment than the average household, but they spend average amounts on cable TV service and on pets. Western households spend 41 percent more than average on bicycles.

College graduates spend 53 percent more than the average household on entertainment. They account for 59 percent of household spending on social, recreation, and civic club memberships. They also control 59 percent of household spending on fees for recreational lessons. Householders without a college degree account for 71 percent of spending on pet food.

Table 3.1 Entertainment: Average spending by age, 2002

(average annual spending of consumer units (CU) on entertainment, by age of consumer unit reference person, 2002)

	total consumer units	under 25	25 to 34	35 to 44	45 to 54	55 to 64	65 to 74	75+
Number of consumer units (in thousands, add 000)	112,108	8,737	18,988	24,394	22,691	15,314	11,216	10,767
Average number of persons per CU	2.5	1.9	2.9	3.2	2.7	2.1	1.9	1.5
Average before-tax income of CU	$49,430.00	$20,773.00	$49,133.00	$61,532.00	$64,974.00	$53,162.00	$35,118.00	$23,890.00
Average spending of CU, total	40,676.60	24,229.46	40,318.29	48,330.48	48,748.24	44,330.04	32,242.52	23,758.89
Entertainment, average spending	2,078.99	1,211.84	2,026.71	2,685.22	2,565.19	2,297.44	1,371.38	896.01
FEES AND ADMISSIONS	$541.67	$313.15	$489.59	$742.60	$662.18	$583.78	$382.28	$215.92
Recreation expenses on trips	25.64	14.91	22.60	30.60	32.27	32.02	21.50	9.68
Social, recreation, civic club membership	107.92	59.72	92.90	131.61	124.81	140.02	91.28	55.92
Fees for participant sports	75.05	35.77	72.67	91.61	81.96	78.97	75.41	53.07
Participant sports on trips	29.50	19.40	23.39	40.57	29.97	39.56	27.28	10.39
Movie, theater, opera, ballet	98.30	98.98	101.54	123.41	117.75	99.69	59.63	32.49
Movie, other admissions on trips	45.57	21.07	37.68	60.68	51.77	63.95	34.30	17.66
Admission to sports events	36.18	26.13	43.43	53.00	43.20	26.02	19.47	10.51
Admission to sports events on trips	15.19	7.02	12.56	20.23	17.26	21.31	11.43	5.89
Fees for recreational lessons	82.69	15.23	60.20	160.29	130.91	50.24	20.49	10.63
Other entertainment services on trips	25.64	14.91	22.60	30.60	32.27	32.02	21.50	9.68
TELEVISION, RADIO, SOUND EQUIPMENT	691.90	456.96	749.62	817.37	806.33	716.56	545.61	372.01
Television	543.66	305.98	559.56	625.16	621.56	600.70	473.50	351.58
Cable service and community antenna	382.28	169.76	358.63	425.26	436.45	439.91	380.23	305.13
Black-and-white TV	0.80	–	1.38	1.18	1.22	0.22	0.29	–
Color TV, console	38.63	17.47	45.95	50.00	41.93	55.92	16.11	9.06
Color TV, portable, table model	39.14	33.53	45.61	36.58	45.57	46.18	31.17	22.83
VCRs and video disc players	23.25	16.93	31.75	26.38	30.43	21.22	15.01	2.63
Video cassettes, tapes, and discs	33.13	41.06	43.74	40.34	38.13	22.98	23.45	5.61
Video game hardware and software	23.46	26.03	30.36	41.48	24.74	10.51	5.21	3.13
Repair of TV, radio, and sound equipment	2.50	0.15	1.65	3.06	2.95	3.30	1.95	3.14
Rental of television sets	0.46	1.05	0.49	0.89	0.14	0.45	0.09	0.06
Radio and sound equipment	148.25	150.97	190.07	192.21	184.77	115.86	72.12	20.43
Radios	3.98	–	3.19	1.96	8.88	3.60	7.22	–
Tape recorders and players	5.31	3.78	4.32	8.36	7.69	3.22	3.37	1.13
Sound components and component systems	20.19	17.03	20.90	23.95	26.72	23.79	10.95	3.76
Miscellaneous sound equipment	3.18	0.09	9.78	4.95	1.99	–	–	–
Sound equipment accessories	5.97	3.46	5.36	7.83	8.59	4.72	5.35	1.63
Satellite dishes	1.00	1.19	1.25	0.78	1.38	1.01	0.98	0.12
Compact disc, tape, record, video mail order clubs	6.53	6.94	7.82	8.11	6.86	6.42	3.83	2.65
Records, CDs, audio tapes, needles	36.47	50.20	43.17	45.11	47.07	27.71	15.38	5.98
Rental of VCR, radio, sound equipment	0.25	0.26	0.27	0.32	0.17	0.48	–	0.15
Musical instruments and accessories	24.82	20.05	37.97	30.46	28.97	20.39	14.45	1.06
Rental and repair of musical instruments	1.22	0.03	0.47	2.95	1.91	0.54	0.28	0.11
Rental of video cassettes, tapes, discs, films	39.33	47.94	55.56	57.42	44.54	23.99	10.31	3.84
PETS, TOYS, PLAYGROUND EQUIPMENT	369.12	192.62	367.76	462.79	465.65	419.90	262.42	135.19
Pets	248.25	119.31	197.97	288.01	347.92	315.36	184.88	109.12
Pet food	102.56	36.50	78.44	124.32	129.86	141.06	85.63	54.01
Pet purchase, supplies, and medicines	52.29	60.87	50.57	59.41	59.99	74.99	24.88	10.27
Pet services	21.95	5.45	15.24	23.74	38.88	21.96	20.03	9.37
Veterinarian services	71.44	16.49	53.72	80.54	119.18	77.36	54.35	35.47
Toys, games, hobbies, and tricycles	117.34	72.83	163.50	169.49	112.26	103.92	76.79	25.90
Playground equipment	3.54	0.48	6.28	5.29	5.48	0.62	0.75	0.17

	total consumer units	under 25	25 to 34	35 to 44	45 to 54	55 to 64	65 to 74	75+
OTHER ENTERTAINMENT SUPPLIES, EQUIPMENT, SERVICES	**$476.30**	**$249.11**	**$419.74**	**$662.46**	**$631.04**	**$577.20**	**$181.07**	**$172.89**
Unmotored recreational vehicles	**47.14**	**40.27**	**75.36**	**42.86**	**39.49**	**86.74**	**16.50**	**4.39**
Boat without motor and boat trailers	16.15	0.61	29.25	11.76	4.45	49.41	8.30	1.15
Trailer and other attachable campers	30.99	39.66	46.11	31.10	35.05	37.33	8.21	3.24
Motorized recreational vehicles	**170.19**	**68.57**	**86.28**	**251.86**	**277.23**	**174.98**	**46.65**	**111.93**
Motorized camper	40.05	–	–	93.26	51.08	67.34	2.22	–
Other vehicle	35.47	27.61	42.29	39.93	24.06	46.31	29.47	34.62
Motorboats	94.67	40.96	43.99	118.66	202.09	61.32	14.96	77.31
Rental of recreational vehicles	**1.99**	**0.81**	**1.81**	**2.96**	**1.53**	**4.10**	**1.04**	**–**
Outboard motors	**0.71**	**0.31**	**0.30**	**0.33**	**0.25**	**3.61**	**0.18**	**–**
Docking and landing fees	**6.66**	**1.27**	**2.73**	**5.32**	**12.65**	**12.04**	**5.31**	**2.10**
Sports, recreation, exercise equipment	**150.33**	**79.80**	**133.14**	**221.28**	**177.14**	**209.54**	**58.75**	**28.39**
Athletic gear, game tables, exercise equipment	60.51	36.71	59.03	79.11	81.53	60.80	35.51	20.00
Bicycles	13.45	7.59	19.46	25.96	14.74	3.75	2.89	1.34
Camping equipment	9.59	8.40	6.54	14.71	17.11	6.11	2.08	0.97
Hunting and fishing equipment	35.68	8.80	26.66	51.51	16.32	105.82	12.62	1.23
Winter sports equipment	5.45	7.56	3.92	7.32	10.66	2.10	0.91	0.67
Water sports equipment	8.95	1.65	4.77	11.39	16.33	15.92	0.56	0.02
Other sports equipment	14.62	8.32	12.23	27.13	17.27	14.03	3.86	2.07
Rental and repair of misc. sports equipment	2.07	0.76	0.54	4.15	3.19	1.01	0.33	2.11
Photographic equipment and supplies	**90.48**	**55.54**	**109.61**	**121.38**	**112.02**	**82.82**	**50.98**	**21.80**
Film	17.74	13.63	18.99	23.38	21.05	17.56	12.18	5.15
Other photographic supplies	2.27	–	2.22	0.01	6.82	1.75	0.96	1.84
Film processing	26.60	20.11	29.22	34.48	31.88	25.69	18.98	7.44
Repair and rental of photographic equipment	0.12	0.03	–	0.13	0.20	0.11	0.01	0.31
Photographic equipment	23.34	13.35	26.89	30.55	28.96	25.00	14.41	3.97
Photographer fees	20.42	8.41	32.29	32.82	23.11	12.71	4.44	3.08
Fireworks	**1.52**	**–**	**4.45**	**1.86**	**0.53**	**1.75**	**–**	**–**
Souvenirs	**1.25**	**–**	**2.21**	**2.59**	**1.10**	**0.16**	**0.61**	**–**
Visual goods	**1.19**	**–**	**1.23**	**2.62**	**1.02**	**1.23**	**0.03**	**0.29**
Pinball, electronic video games	**4.84**	**2.55**	**2.62**	**9.40**	**8.07**	**0.23**	**1.02**	**3.98**

Note: (–) means sample is too small to make a reliable estimate.
Source: Bureau of Labor Statistics, unpublished data from the 2002 Consumer Expenditure Survey

Table 3.2 Entertainment: Indexed spending by age, 2002

(indexed average annual spending of consumer units (CU) on entertainment by age of consumer unit reference person, 2002; index definition: an index of 100 is the average for all consumer units; an index of 132 means that spending by consumer units in that group is 32 percent above the average for all consumer units; an index of 68 indicates spending that is 32 percent below the average for all consumer units)

	total consumer units	under 25	25 to 34	35 to 44	45 to 54	55 to 64	65 to 74	75+
Average spending of CU, total	$40,677	$24,229	$40,318	$48,330	$48,748	$44,330	$32,243	$23,759
Average spending of CU, index	100	60	99	119	120	109	79	58
Entertainment, spending index	100	58	97	129	123	111	66	43
FEES AND ADMISSIONS	100	58	90	137	122	108	71	40
Recreation expenses on trips	100	58	88	119	126	125	84	38
Social, recreation, civic club membership	100	55	86	122	116	130	85	52
Fees for participant sports	100	48	97	122	109	105	100	71
Participant sports on trips	100	66	79	138	102	134	92	35
Movie, theater, opera, ballet	100	101	103	126	120	101	61	33
Movie, other admissions on trips	100	46	83	133	114	140	75	39
Admission to sports events	100	72	120	146	119	72	54	29
Admission to sports events on trips	100	46	83	133	114	140	75	39
Fees for recreational lessons	100	18	73	194	158	61	25	13
Other entertainment services on trips	100	58	88	119	126	125	84	38
TELEVISION, RADIO, SOUND EQUIPMENT	100	66	108	118	117	104	79	54
Television	100	56	103	115	114	110	87	65
Cable service and community antenna	100	44	94	111	114	115	99	80
Black-and-white TV	100	–	173	148	153	28	36	–
Color TV, console	100	45	119	129	109	145	42	23
Color TV, portable, table model	100	86	117	93	116	118	80	58
VCRs and video disc players	100	73	137	113	131	91	65	11
Video cassettes, tapes, and discs	100	124	132	122	115	69	71	17
Video game hardware and software	100	111	129	177	105	45	22	13
Repair of TV, radio, and sound equipment	100	6	66	122	118	132	78	126
Rental of television sets	100	228	107	193	30	98	20	13
Radio and sound equipment	100	102	128	130	125	78	49	14
Radios	100	–	80	49	223	90	181	–
Tape recorders and players	100	71	81	157	145	61	63	21
Sound components and component systems	100	84	104	119	132	118	54	19
Miscellaneous sound equipment	100	3	308	156	63	–	–	–
Sound equipment accessories	100	58	90	131	144	79	90	27
Satellite dishes	100	119	125	78	138	101	98	12
Compact disc, tape, record, video mail order clubs	100	106	120	124	105	98	59	41
Records, CDs, audio tapes, needles	100	138	118	124	129	76	42	16
Rental of VCR, radio, sound equipment	100	104	108	128	68	192	–	60
Musical instruments and accessories	100	81	153	123	117	82	58	4
Rental and repair of musical instruments	100	2	39	242	157	44	23	9
Rental of video cassettes, tapes, discs, films	100	122	141	146	113	61	26	10
PETS, TOYS, PLAYGROUND EQUIPMENT	100	52	100	125	126	114	71	37
Pets	100	48	80	116	140	127	74	44
Pet food	100	36	76	121	127	138	83	53
Pet purchase, supplies, and medicines	100	116	97	114	115	143	48	20
Pet services	100	25	69	108	177	100	91	43
Veterinarian services	100	23	75	113	167	108	76	50
Toys, games, hobbies, and tricycles	100	62	139	144	96	89	65	22
Playground equipment	100	14	177	149	155	18	21	5

OTHER ENTERTAINMENT SUPPLIES, EQUIPMENT, SERVICES	total consumer units	under 25	25 to 34	35 to 44	45 to 54	55 to 64	65 to 74	75+
OTHER ENTERTAINMENT SUPPLIES, EQUIPMENT, SERVICES	**100**	**52**	**88**	**139**	**132**	**121**	**38**	**36**
Unmotored recreational vehicles	**100**	**85**	**160**	**91**	**84**	**184**	**35**	**9**
Boat without motor and boat trailers	100	4	181	73	28	306	51	7
Trailer and other attachable campers	100	128	149	100	113	120	26	10
Motorized recreational vehicles	**100**	**40**	**51**	**148**	**163**	**103**	**27**	**66**
Motorized camper	100	–	–	233	128	168	6	–
Other vehicle	100	78	119	113	68	131	83	98
Motorboats	100	43	46	125	213	65	16	82
Rental of recreational vehicles	**100**	**41**	**91**	**149**	**77**	**206**	**52**	**–**
Outboard motors	**100**	**44**	**42**	**46**	**35**	**508**	**25**	**–**
Docking and landing fees	**100**	**19**	**41**	**80**	**190**	**181**	**80**	**32**
Sports, recreation, exercise equipment	**100**	**53**	**89**	**147**	**118**	**139**	**39**	**19**
Athletic gear, game tables, exercise equipment	100	61	98	131	135	100	59	33
Bicycles	100	56	145	193	110	28	21	10
Camping equipment	100	88	68	153	178	64	22	10
Hunting and fishing equipment	100	25	75	144	46	297	35	3
Winter sports equipment	100	139	72	134	196	39	17	12
Water sports equipment	100	18	53	127	182	178	6	0
Other sports equipment	100	57	84	186	118	96	26	14
Rental and repair of misc. sports equipment	100	37	26	200	154	49	16	102
Photographic equipment and supplies	**100**	**61**	**121**	**134**	**124**	**92**	**56**	**24**
Film	100	77	107	132	119	99	69	29
Other photographic supplies	100	–	98	0	300	77	42	81
Film processing	100	76	110	130	120	97	71	28
Repair and rental of photographic equipment	100	25	–	108	167	92	8	258
Photographic equipment	100	57	115	131	124	107	62	17
Photographer fees	100	41	158	161	113	62	22	15
Fireworks	**100**	**–**	**293**	**122**	**35**	**115**	**–**	**–**
Souvenirs	**100**	**–**	**177**	**207**	**88**	**13**	**49**	**–**
Visual goods	**100**	**–**	**103**	**220**	**86**	**103**	**3**	**24**
Pinball, electronic video games	**100**	**53**	**54**	**194**	**167**	**5**	**21**	**82**

Note: (–) means sample is too small to make a reliable estimate.
Source: Calculations by New Strategist based on the 2002 Consumer Expenditure Survey

Table 3.3 Entertainment: Total spending by age, 2002

(total annual spending on entertainment, by consumer unit (CU) age groups, 2002; numbers in thousands)

	total consumer units	under 25	25 to 34	35 to 44	45 to 54	55 to 64	65 to 74	75+
Number of consumer units	112,108	8,737	18,988	24,394	22,691	15,314	11,216	10,767
Total spending of all CUs	$4,560,172,273	$211,692,792	$765,563,691	$1,178,973,729	$1,106,146,314	$678,870,233	$361,632,104	$255,811,969
Entertainment, total spending	233,071,411	10,587,846	38,483,169	65,503,257	58,206,726	35,182,996	15,381,398	9,647,340
FEES AND ADMISSIONS	**$60,725,540**	**$2,735,992**	**$9,296,335**	**$18,114,984**	**$15,025,526**	**$8,940,007**	**$4,287,652**	**$2,324,811**
Recreation expenses on trips	2,874,449	130,269	429,129	746,456	732,239	490,354	241,144	104,225
Social, recreation, civic club membership	12,098,695	521,774	1,763,985	3,210,494	2,832,064	2,144,266	1,023,796	602,091
Fees for participant sports	8,413,705	312,522	1,379,858	2,234,734	1,859,754	1,209,347	845,799	571,405
Participant sports on trips	3,307,186	169,498	444,129	989,665	680,049	605,822	305,972	111,869
Movie, theater, opera, ballet	11,020,216	864,788	1,928,042	3,010,464	2,671,865	1,526,653	668,810	349,820
Movie, other admissions on trips	5,108,762	184,089	715,468	1,480,228	1,174,713	979,330	384,709	190,145
Admission to sports events	4,056,067	228,298	824,649	1,292,882	980,251	398,470	218,376	113,161
Admission to sports events on trips	1,702,921	61,334	238,489	493,491	391,647	326,341	128,199	63,418
Fees for recreational lessons	9,270,211	133,065	1,143,078	3,910,114	2,970,479	769,375	229,816	114,453
Other entertainment services on trips	2,874,449	130,269	429,129	746,456	732,239	490,354	241,144	104,225
TELEVISION, RADIO, SOUND EQUIPMENT	**77,567,525**	**3,992,460**	**14,233,785**	**19,938,924**	**18,296,434**	**10,973,400**	**6,119,562**	**4,005,432**
Television	**60,948,635**	**2,673,347**	**10,624,925**	**15,250,153**	**14,103,818**	**9,199,120**	**5,310,776**	**3,785,462**
Cable service and community antenna	42,856,646	1,483,193	6,809,666	10,373,792	9,903,487	6,736,782	4,264,660	3,285,335
Black-and-white TV	89,686	–	26,203	28,785	27,683	3,369	3,253	–
Color TV, console	4,330,732	152,635	872,499	1,219,700	951,434	856,359	180,690	97,549
Color TV, portable, table model	4,387,907	292,952	866,043	892,333	1,034,029	707,201	349,603	245,811
VCRs and video disc players	2,606,511	147,917	602,869	643,514	690,487	324,963	168,352	28,317
Video cassettes, tapes, and discs	3,714,138	358,741	830,535	984,054	865,208	351,916	263,015	60,403
Video game hardware and software	2,630,054	227,424	576,476	1,011,863	561,375	160,950	58,435	33,701
Repair of TV, radio, and sound equipment	280,270	1,311	31,330	74,646	66,938	50,536	21,871	33,808
Rental of television sets	51,570	9,174	9,304	21,711	3,177	6,891	1,009	646
Radio and sound equipment	**16,620,011**	**1,319,025**	**3,609,049**	**4,688,771**	**4,192,616**	**1,774,280**	**808,898**	**219,970**
Radios	446,190	–	60,572	47,812	201,496	55,130	80,980	–
Tape recorders and players	595,293	33,026	82,028	203,934	174,494	49,311	37,798	12,167
Sound components and component systems	2,263,461	148,791	396,849	584,236	606,304	364,320	122,815	40,484
Miscellaneous sound equipment	356,503	786	185,703	120,750	45,155	–	–	–
Sound equipment accessories	669,285	30,230	101,776	191,005	194,916	72,282	60,006	17,550
Satellite dishes	112,108	10,397	23,735	19,027	31,314	15,467	10,992	1,292
Compact disc, tape, record, video mail order clubs	732,065	60,635	148,486	197,835	155,660	98,316	42,957	28,533
Records, CDs, audio tapes, needles	4,088,579	438,597	819,712	1,100,413	1,068,065	424,351	172,502	64,387
Rental of VCR, radio, sound equipment	28,027	2,272	5,127	7,806	3,857	7,351	–	1,615
Musical instruments and accessories	2,782,521	175,177	720,974	743,041	657,358	312,252	162,071	11,413
Rental and repair of musical instruments	136,772	262	8,924	71,962	43,340	8,270	3,140	1,184
Rental of video cassettes, tapes, discs, films	4,409,208	418,852	1,054,973	1,400,703	1,010,657	367,383	115,637	41,345
PETS, TOYS, PLAYGROUND EQUIPMENT	**41,381,305**	**1,682,921**	**6,983,027**	**11,289,299**	**10,566,064**	**6,430,349**	**2,943,303**	**1,455,591**
Pets	**27,830,811**	**1,042,411**	**3,759,054**	**7,025,716**	**7,894,653**	**4,829,423**	**2,073,614**	**1,174,895**
Pet food	11,497,796	318,901	1,489,419	3,032,662	2,946,653	2,160,193	960,426	581,526
Pet purchase, supplies, and medicines	5,862,127	531,821	960,223	1,449,248	1,361,233	1,148,397	279,054	110,577
Pet services	2,460,771	47,617	289,377	579,114	882,226	336,295	224,656	100,887
Veterinarian services	8,008,996	144,073	1,020,035	1,964,693	2,704,313	1,184,691	609,590	381,905
Toys, games, hobbies, and tricycles	**13,154,753**	**636,316**	**3,104,538**	**4,134,539**	**2,547,292**	**1,591,431**	**861,277**	**278,865**
Playground equipment	**396,862**	**4,194**	**119,245**	**129,044**	**124,347**	**9,495**	**8,412**	**1,830**

	total consumer units	under 25	25 to 34	35 to 44	45 to 54	55 to 64	65 to 74	75+
OTHER ENTERTAINMENT SUPPLIES, EQUIPMENT, SERVICES	$53,397,040	$2,176,474	$7,970,023	$16,160,049	$14,318,929	$8,839,241	$2,030,881	$1,861,507
Unmotored recreational vehicles	5,284,771	351,839	1,430,936	1,045,527	896,068	1,328,336	185,064	47,267
Boat without motor and boat trailers	1,810,544	5,330	555,399	286,873	100,975	756,665	93,093	12,382
Trailer and other attachable campers	3,474,227	346,509	875,537	758,653	795,320	571,672	92,083	34,885
Motorized recreational vehicles	19,079,661	599,096	1,638,285	6,143,873	6,290,626	2,679,644	523,226	1,205,150
Motorized camper	4,489,925	–	–	2,274,984	1,159,056	1,031,245	24,900	–
Other vehicle	3,976,471	241,229	803,003	974,052	545,945	709,191	24,900	–
Motorboats	10,613,264	357,868	835,282	2,894,592	4,585,624	939,054	330,536	372,754
Rental of recreational vehicles	223,095	7,077	34,368	72,206	34,717	62,787	11,665	–
Outboard motors	79,597	2,708	5,696	8,050	5,673	55,284	2,019	–
Docking and landing fees	746,639	11,096	51,837	129,776	287,041	184,381	59,557	22,611
Sports, recreation, exercise equipment	16,853,196	697,213	2,528,062	5,397,904	4,019,484	3,208,896	658,940	305,675
Athletic gear, game tables, exercise equipment	6,783,655	320,735	1,120,862	1,929,809	1,849,997	931,091	398,280	215,340
Bicycles	1,507,853	66,314	369,506	633,268	334,465	57,428	32,414	14,428
Camping equipment	1,075,116	73,391	124,182	358,836	388,243	93,569	23,329	10,444
Hunting and fishing equipment	4,000,013	76,886	506,220	1,256,535	370,317	1,620,527	141,546	13,243
Winter sports equipment	610,989	66,052	74,433	178,564	241,886	32,159	10,207	7,214
Water sports equipment	1,003,367	14,416	90,573	277,848	370,544	243,799	6,281	215
Other sports equipment	1,639,019	72,692	232,223	661,809	391,874	214,855	43,294	22,288
Rental and repair of misc. sports equipment	232,064	6,640	10,254	101,235	72,384	15,467	3,701	22,718
Photographic equipment and supplies	10,143,532	485,253	2,081,275	2,960,944	2,541,846	1,268,305	571,792	234,721
Film	1,988,796	119,085	360,582	570,332	477,646	268,914	136,611	55,450
Other photographic supplies	254,485	–	42,153	244	154,753	26,800	10,767	19,811
Film processing	2,982,073	175,701	554,829	841,105	723,389	393,417	212,880	80,106
Repair and rental of photographic equipment	13,453	262	–	3,171	4,538	1,685	112	3,338
Photographic equipment	2,616,601	116,639	510,587	745,237	657,131	382,850	161,623	42,745
Photographer fees	2,289,245	73,478	613,123	800,611	524,389	194,641	49,799	33,162
Fireworks	170,404	–	84,497	45,373	12,026	26,800	–	–
Souvenirs	140,135	–	41,963	63,180	24,960	2,450	6,842	–
Visual goods	133,409	–	23,355	63,912	23,145	18,836	336	3,122
Pinball, electronic video games	542,603	22,279	49,749	229,304	183,116	3,522	11,440	42,853

Note: Numbers may not add to total because of rounding. (–) means sample is too small to make a reliable estimate.
Source: Calculations by New Strategist based on the 2002 Consumer Expenditure Survey

Table 3.4 Entertainment: Market shares by age, 2002

(percentage of total annual spending on entertainment accounted for by consumer unit age groups, 2002)

	total consumer units	under 25	25 to 34	35 to 44	45 to 54	55 to 64	65 to 74	75+
						13.7%	10.0%	9.6%
Share of total consumer units	100.0%	7.8%	16.9%	21.8%	20.2%	14.7	7.1	4.6
Share of total before-tax income	100.0	3.3	16.8	27.1	26.6	14.9	7.9	5.6
Share of total spending	100.0	4.6	16.8	25.9	24.3	15.1	6.6	4.1
Share of entertainment spending	100.0	4.5	16.5	28.1	25.0			
FEES AND ADMISSIONS	**100.0%**	**4.5%**	**15.3%**	**29.8%**	**24.7%**	**14.7%**	**7.1%**	**3.8%**
Recreation expenses on trips	100.0	4.5	14.9	26.0	25.5	17.1	8.4	3.6
Social, recreation, civic club membership	100.0	4.3	14.6	26.5	23.4	17.7	8.5	5.0
Fees for participant sports	100.0	3.7	16.4	26.6	22.1	14.4	10.1	6.8
Participant sports on trips	100.0	5.1	13.4	29.9	20.6	18.3	9.3	3.4
Movie, theater, opera, ballet	100.0	7.8	17.5	27.3	24.2	13.9	6.1	3.2
Movie, other admissions on trips	100.0	3.6	14.0	29.0	23.0	19.2	7.5	3.7
Admission to sports events	100.0	5.6	20.3	31.9	24.2	9.8	5.4	2.8
Admission to sports events on trips	100.0	3.6	14.0	29.0	23.0	19.2	7.5	3.7
Fees for recreational lessons	100.0	1.4	12.3	42.2	32.0	8.3	2.5	1.2
Other entertainment services on trips	100.0	4.5	14.9	26.0	25.5	17.1	8.4	3.6
TELEVISION, RADIO, SOUND EQUIPMENT	**100.0**	**5.1**	**18.4**	**25.7**	**23.6**	**14.1**	**7.9**	**5.2**
Television	**100.0**	**4.4**	**17.4**	**25.0**	**23.1**	**15.1**	**8.7**	**6.2**
Cable service and community antenna	100.0	3.5	15.9	24.2	23.1	15.7	10.0	7.7
Black-and-white TV	100.0	–	29.2	32.1	30.9	3.8	3.6	–
Color TV, console	100.0	3.5	20.1	28.2	22.0	19.8	4.2	2.3
Color TV, portable, table model	100.0	6.7	19.7	20.3	23.6	16.1	8.0	5.6
VCRs and video disc players	100.0	5.7	23.1	24.7	26.5	12.5	6.5	1.1
Video cassettes, tapes, and discs	100.0	9.7	22.4	26.5	23.3	9.5	7.1	1.6
Video game hardware and software	100.0	8.6	21.9	38.5	21.3	6.1	2.2	1.3
Repair of TV, radio, and sound equipment	100.0	0.5	11.2	26.6	23.9	18.0	7.8	12.1
Rental of television sets	100.0	17.8	18.0	42.1	6.2	13.4	2.0	1.3
Radio and sound equipment	**100.0**	**7.9**	**21.7**	**28.2**	**25.2**	**10.7**	**4.9**	**1.3**
Radios	100.0	–	13.6	10.7	45.2	12.4	18.1	–
Tape recorders and players	100.0	5.5	13.8	34.3	29.3	8.3	6.3	2.0
Sound components and component systems	100.0	6.6	17.5	25.8	26.8	16.1	5.4	1.8
Miscellaneous sound equipment	100.0	0.2	52.1	33.9	12.7	–	–	–
Sound equipment accessories	100.0	4.5	15.2	28.5	29.1	10.8	9.0	2.6
Satellite dishes	100.0	9.3	21.2	17.0	27.9	13.8	9.8	1.2
Compact disc, tape, record, video mail order clubs	100.0	8.3	20.3	27.0	21.3	13.4	5.9	3.9
Records, CDs, audio tapes, needles	100.0	10.7	20.0	26.9	26.1	10.4	4.2	1.6
Rental of VCR, radio, sound equipment	100.0	8.1	18.3	27.9	13.8	26.2	–	5.8
Musical instruments and accessories	100.0	6.3	25.9	26.7	23.6	11.2	5.8	0.4
Rental and repair of musical instruments	100.0	0.2	6.5	52.6	31.7	6.0	2.3	0.9
Rental of video cassettes, tapes, discs, films	100.0	9.5	23.9	31.8	22.9	8.3	2.6	0.9
PETS, TOYS, PLAYGROUND EQUIPMENT	**100.0**	**4.1**	**16.9**	**27.3**	**25.5**	**15.5**	**7.1**	**3.5**
Pets	**100.0**	**3.7**	**13.5**	**25.2**	**28.4**	**17.4**	**7.5**	**4.2**
Pet food	100.0	2.8	13.0	26.4	25.6	18.8	8.4	5.1
Pet purchase, supplies, and medicines	100.0	9.1	16.4	24.7	23.2	19.6	4.8	1.9
Pet services	100.0	1.9	11.8	23.5	35.9	13.7	9.1	4.1
Veterinarian services	100.0	1.8	12.7	24.5	33.8	14.8	7.6	4.8
Toys, games, hobbies, and tricycles	**100.0**	**4.8**	**23.6**	**31.4**	**19.4**	**12.1**	**6.5**	**2.1**
Playground equipment	**100.0**	**1.1**	**30.0**	**32.5**	**31.3**	**2.4**	**2.1**	**0.5**

OTHER ENTERTAINMENT SUPPLIES, EQUIPMENT, SERVICES	total consumer units	under 25	25 to 34	35 to 44	45 to 54	55 to 64	65 to 74	75+
	100.0%	4.1%	14.9%	30.3%	26.8%	16.6%	3.8%	3.5%
Unmotored recreational vehicles	100.0	6.7	27.1	19.8	17.0	25.1	3.5	0.9
Boat without motor and boat trailers	100.0	0.3	30.7	15.8	5.6	41.8	5.1	0.7
Trailer and other attachable campers	100.0	10.0	25.2	21.8	22.9	16.5	2.7	1.0
Motorized recreational vehicles	100.0	3.1	8.6	32.2	33.0	14.0	2.7	6.3
Motorized camper	100.0	–	–	50.7	25.8	23.0	0.6	–
Other vehicle	100.0	6.1	20.2	24.5	13.7	17.8	8.3	9.4
Motorboats	100.0	3.4	7.9	27.3	43.2	8.8	1.6	7.8
Rental of recreational vehicles	100.0	3.2	15.4	32.4	15.6	28.1	5.2	–
Outboard motors	100.0	3.4	7.2	10.1	7.1	69.5	2.5	–
Docking and landing fees	100.0	1.5	6.9	17.4	38.4	24.7	8.0	3.0
Sports, recreation, exercise equipment	100.0	4.1	15.0	32.0	23.8	19.0	3.9	1.8
Athletic gear, game tables, exercise equipment	100.0	4.7	16.5	28.4	27.3	13.7	5.9	3.2
Bicycles	100.0	4.4	24.5	42.0	22.2	3.8	2.1	1.0
Camping equipment	100.0	6.8	11.6	33.4	36.1	8.7	2.2	1.0
Hunting and fishing equipment	100.0	1.9	12.7	31.4	9.3	40.5	3.5	0.3
Winter sports equipment	100.0	10.8	12.2	29.2	39.6	5.3	1.7	1.2
Water sports equipment	100.0	1.4	9.0	27.7	36.9	24.3	0.6	0.0
Other sports equipment	100.0	4.4	14.2	40.4	23.9	13.1	2.6	1.4
Rental and repair of misc. sports equipment	100.0	2.9	4.4	43.6	31.2	6.7	1.6	9.8
Photographic equipment and supplies	100.0	4.8	20.5	29.2	25.1	12.5	5.6	2.3
Film	100.0	6.0	18.1	28.7	24.0	13.5	6.9	2.8
Other photographic supplies	100.0	–	16.6	0.1	60.8	10.5	4.2	7.8
Film processing	100.0	5.9	18.6	28.2	24.3	13.2	7.1	2.7
Repair and rental of photographic equipment	100.0	1.9	–	23.6	33.7	12.5	0.8	24.8
Photographic equipment	100.0	4.5	19.5	28.5	25.1	14.6	6.2	1.6
Photographer fees	100.0	3.2	26.8	35.0	22.9	8.5	2.2	1.4
Fireworks	100.0	–	49.6	26.6	7.1	15.7	–	–
Souvenirs	100.0	–	29.9	45.1	17.8	1.7	4.9	–
Visual goods	100.0	–	17.5	47.9	17.3	14.1	0.3	2.3
Pinball, electronic video games	100.0	4.1	9.2	42.3	33.7	0.6	2.1	7.9

Note: Numbers may not add to total because of rounding. (–) means sample is too small to make a reliable estimate.
Source: Calculations by New Strategist based on the 2002 Consumer Expenditure Survey

Table 3.5 Entertainment: Average spending by income, 2002

(average annual spending on entertainment, by before-tax income of consumer units (CU), 2002; complete income reporters only)

	complete income reporters	under $10,000	$10,000– $19,999	$20,000– $29,999	$30,000– $39,999	$40,000– $49,999	$50,000– $69,999	$70,000 or more
Number of consumer units (in thousands, add 000)	92,388	10,933	15,075	12,312	10,727	8,873	13,521	20,947
Average number of persons per CU	2.5	1.7	1.9	2.3	2.5	2.6	2.8	3.1
Average before-tax income of CU	$49,430.00	$5,554.80	$14,724.33	$24,495.00	$34,423.00	$44,443.00	$58,933.00	$115,629.00
Average spending of CU, total	42,556.98	17,627.83	22,838.71	28,835.85	35,095.39	41,787.38	50,406.17	76,627.31
Entertainment, average spending	2,166.55	772.98	925.71	1,187.34	1,561.33	1,923.82	2,640.54	4,457.01
FEES AND ADMISSIONS	**$561.57**	**$189.03**	**$191.61**	**$233.13**	**$303.09**	**$476.55**	**$592.39**	**$1,363.78**
Recreation expenses on trips	27.08	9.24	9.83	14.25	12.16	28.79	32.99	59.46
Social, recreation, civic club membership	108.90	39.61	35.81	45.77	50.08	93.88	99.68	277.21
Fees for participant sports	78.20	21.29	36.26	35.62	46.53	76.15	85.13	175.73
Participant sports on trips	30.90	10.29	10.08	9.39	10.64	19.55	31.10	84.36
Movie, theater, opera, ballet	101.87	52.43	39.74	51.18	82.06	90.95	116.00	207.81
Movie, other admissions on trips	48.24	12.91	12.44	21.98	29.49	42.89	55.56	115.02
Admission to sports events	38.36	12.60	15.96	10.72	15.92	25.70	41.72	98.84
Admission to sports events on trips	16.08	4.30	4.15	7.33	9.83	14.29	18.52	38.34
Fees for recreational lessons	84.86	17.13	17.53	22.65	34.22	55.56	78.68	247.56
Other entertainment services on trips	27.08	9.24	9.83	14.25	12.16	28.79	32.99	59.46
TELEVISION, RADIO, SOUND EQUIPMENT	**710.24**	**356.94**	**431.92**	**531.62**	**650.65**	**740.17**	**876.47**	**1,110.49**
Television	**556.13**	**277.58**	**356.54**	**438.58**	**524.94**	**582.63**	**669.68**	**845.72**
Cable service and community antenna	384.29	205.66	272.13	319.02	372.94	410.88	474.96	532.65
Black-and-white TV	0.83	0.48	0.03	0.86	1.00	1.39	0.21	1.63
Color TV, console	41.87	9.93	14.11	18.05	37.85	33.34	33.17	103.81
Color TV, portable, table model	41.17	22.60	22.78	43.84	33.98	56.26	43.14	58.55
VCRs and video disc players	24.58	8.41	12.77	17.69	16.54	24.02	31.16	45.68
Video cassettes, tapes, and discs	35.56	15.97	20.96	24.80	35.83	33.58	50.00	54.02
Video game hardware and software	24.78	13.44	12.13	12.19	21.16	20.88	34.36	44.51
Repair of TV, radio, and sound equipment	2.57	0.98	1.02	1.44	3.98	2.28	2.11	4.87
Rental of television sets	0.48	0.10	0.62	0.68	1.65	–	0.56	–
Radio and sound equipment	**154.11**	**79.37**	**75.39**	**93.04**	**125.71**	**157.54**	**206.79**	**264.77**
Radios	3.83	0.26	2.02	4.80	1.76	–	7.84	6.27
Tape recorders and players	5.26	–	9.03	1.51	4.06	8.10	9.65	4.05
Sound components and component systems	20.83	8.85	12.42	13.49	16.32	18.69	19.39	41.57
Miscellaneous sound equipment	3.15	0.58	–	–	–	0.68	20.00	0.73
Sound equipment accessories	6.88	2.45	1.71	2.66	9.63	10.71	11.21	9.52
Satellite dishes	1.14	1.08	0.90	0.58	0.50	1.13	0.58	2.35
Compact disc, tape, record, video mail order clubs	7.08	3.54	3.35	6.23	7.23	8.48	9.60	9.83
Records, CDs, audio tapes, needles	37.90	20.09	18.28	25.84	31.44	37.20	47.06	66.09
Rental of VCR, radio, sound equipment	0.30	0.01	0.39	0.64	–	0.16	0.16	0.50
Musical instruments and accessories	25.03	22.45	4.68	6.49	17.02	26.70	27.19	53.93
Rental and repair of musical instruments	1.26	0.31	0.39	0.28	0.40	1.47	1.56	3.13
Rental of video cassettes, tapes, discs, films	41.45	19.76	22.19	30.52	37.36	44.21	52.56	66.79
PETS, TOYS, PLAYGROUND EQUIPMENT	**396.84**	**129.82**	**190.02**	**249.26**	**318.85**	**412.84**	**551.80**	**701.13**
Pets	**269.24**	**96.56**	**128.80**	**170.90**	**209.80**	**274.43**	**371.42**	**476.73**
Pet food	116.30	53.53	65.85	89.00	95.66	133.72	168.13	168.35
Pet purchase, supplies, and medicines	57.05	24.04	28.33	22.49	52.91	56.89	87.83	96.57
Pet services	23.48	2.65	5.75	16.50	10.31	16.90	20.04	62.95
Veterinarian services	72.42	16.34	28.86	42.90	50.92	66.93	95.42	148.87
Toys, games, hobbies, and tricycles	**123.56**	**32.73**	**60.53**	**77.06**	**107.28**	**135.37**	**173.45**	**214.78**
Playground equipment	**4.04**	**0.53**	**0.69**	**1.30**	**1.77**	**3.04**	**6.93**	**9.63**

	complete income reporters	under $10,000	$10,000–$19,999	$20,000–$29,999	$30,000–$39,999	$40,000–$49,999	$50,000–$69,999	$70,000 or more
OTHER ENTERTAINMENT SUPPLIES, EQUIPMENT, SERVICES	**$497.90**	**$97.18**	**$112.15**	**$173.33**	**$288.74**	**$294.26**	**$619.88**	**$1,281.60**
Unmotored recreational vehicles	**51.55**	–	**0.68**	**13.13**	**60.38**	**9.00**	**115.13**	**109.87**
Boat without motor and boat trailers	16.77	–	0.68	13.13	2.94	6.06	55.50	25.58
Trailer and other attachable campers	34.79	–	–	–	57.44	2.95	59.63	84.29
Motorized recreational vehicles	**163.21**	**28.31**	**17.20**	**55.12**	**40.60**	**71.05**	**183.09**	**491.22**
Motorized camper	30.56	–	–	2.02	–	–	59.75	95.02
Other vehicle	38.73	2.52	5.59	51.42	18.11	44.82	55.09	71.45
Motorboats	93.92	25.78	11.61	1.68	22.49	26.23	68.24	324.75
Rental of recreational vehicles	**2.19**	**1.70**	**0.27**	**0.51**	**0.14**	**0.08**	**2.69**	**6.41**
Outboard motors	**0.86**	–	**0.10**	**0.16**	**0.02**	**0.30**	**4.41**	**0.64**
Docking and landing fees	**7.35**	**1.29**	**3.01**	**2.87**	**0.61**	**0.99**	**7.48**	**22.33**
Sports, recreation, exercise equipment	**166.44**	**29.32**	**56.65**	**49.97**	**115.87**	**121.81**	**175.46**	**416.55**
Athletic gear, game tables, exercise equipment	64.76	10.29	13.12	19.12	57.43	33.26	79.86	160.68
Bicycles	15.07	3.37	5.19	3.94	14.20	19.61	13.18	34.56
Camping equipment	10.80	3.40	2.44	1.68	14.36	5.42	14.86	23.49
Hunting and fishing equipment	44.10	4.54	28.70	16.76	13.16	29.68	25.04	122.47
Winter sports equipment	5.62	3.16	2.66	1.78	3.24	3.69	5.74	13.24
Water sports equipment	8.47	1.73	0.67	0.41	4.41	12.10	18.64	16.30
Other sports equipment	15.21	2.74	2.22	5.63	8.81	17.11	14.12	39.87
Rental and repair of misc. sports equipment	2.42	0.08	1.65	0.64	0.26	0.94	4.01	5.95
Photographic equipment and supplies	**96.39**	**35.35**	**31.88**	**48.86**	**59.16**	**78.27**	**118.74**	**214.76**
Film	18.91	8.82	8.36	11.69	13.80	18.02	23.33	36.16
Other photographic supplies	2.65	0.22	0.13	–	1.46	0.02	3.99	7.97
Film processing	28.21	12.44	12.28	16.51	19.21	24.91	35.69	55.94
Repair and rental of photographic equipment	0.12	0.06	0.05	–	0.13	0.06	0.13	0.30
Photographic equipment	25.94	9.14	6.57	12.71	13.47	18.60	30.68	62.88
Photographer fees	20.56	4.67	4.49	7.94	11.09	16.66	24.92	51.51
Fireworks	**1.31**	–	–	–	**4.03**	**1.01**	**0.60**	**2.82**
Souvenirs	**1.56**	–	–	**0.49**	**3.59**	**1.86**	**3.89**	**1.46**
Visual goods	**1.36**	–	**0.23**	–	**0.74**	**1.58**	**0.49**	**4.37**
Pinball, electronic video games	**5.68**	**0.72**	**2.12**	**2.21**	**3.60**	**8.29**	**7.90**	**11.16**

Note: (–) means sample is too small to make a reliable estimate.
Source: Bureau of Labor Statistics, unpublished data from the 2002 Consumer Expenditure Survey; calculations by New Strategist

Table 3.6 Entertainment: Indexed spending by income, 2002

(indexed average annual spending of consumer units (CU) on entertainment by before-tax income of consumer unit, 2002; complete income reporters only; index definition: an index of 100 is the average for all consumer units; an index of 132 means that spending by consumer units in that group is 32 percent above the average for all consumer units; an index of 68 indicates spending that is 32 percent below the average for all consumer units)

	complete income reporters	under $10,000	$10,000– $19,999	$20,000– $29,999	$30,000– $39,999	$40,000– $49,999	$50,000– $69,999	$70,000 or more
Average spending of CU, total	$42,557	$17,628	$22,839	$28,836	$35,095	$41,787	$50,406	$76,627
Average spending of CU, index	100	41	54	68	82	98	118	180
Entertainment, spending index	100	36	43	55	72	89	122	206
FEES AND ADMISSIONS	**100**	**34**	**34**	**42**	**54**	**85**	**105**	**243**
Recreation expenses on trips	100	34	36	53	45	106	122	220
Social, recreation, civic club membership	100	36	33	42	46	86	92	255
Fees for participant sports	100	27	46	46	60	97	109	225
Participant sports on trips	100	33	33	30	34	63	101	273
Movie, theater, opera, ballet	100	51	39	50	81	89	114	204
Movie, other admissions on trips	100	27	26	46	61	89	115	238
Admission to sports events	100	33	42	28	42	67	109	258
Admission to sports events on trips	100	27	26	46	61	89	115	238
Fees for recreational lessons	100	20	21	27	40	65	93	292
Other entertainment services on trips	100	34	36	53	45	106	122	220
TELEVISION, RADIO, SOUND EQUIPMENT	**100**	**50**	**61**	**75**	**92**	**104**	**123**	**156**
Television	**100**	**50**	**64**	**79**	**94**	**105**	**120**	**152**
Cable service and community antenna	100	54	71	83	97	107	124	139
Black-and-white TV	100	57	3	104	120	167	25	196
Color TV, console	100	24	34	43	90	80	79	248
Color TV, portable, table model	100	55	55	106	83	137	105	142
VCRs and video disc players	100	34	52	72	67	98	127	186
Video cassettes, tapes, and discs	100	45	59	70	101	94	141	152
Video game hardware and software	100	54	49	49	85	84	139	180
Repair of TV, radio, and sound equipment	100	38	40	56	155	89	82	189
Rental of television sets	100	21	128	142	344	–	117	–
Radio and sound equipment	**100**	**51**	**49**	**60**	**82**	**102**	**134**	**172**
Radios	100	7	53	125	46	–	205	164
Tape recorders and players	100	–	172	29	77	154	183	77
Sound components and component systems	100	42	60	65	78	90	93	200
Miscellaneous sound equipment	100	18	–	–	–	22	635	23
Sound equipment accessories	100	36	25	39	140	156	163	138
Satellite dishes	100	94	79	51	44	99	51	206
Compact disc, tape, record, video mail order clubs	100	50	47	88	102	120	136	139
Records, CDs, audio tapes, needles	100	53	48	68	83	98	124	174
Rental of VCR, radio, sound equipment	100	4	132	213	–	53	53	167
Musical instruments and accessories	100	90	19	26	68	107	109	215
Rental and repair of musical instruments	100	25	31	22	32	117	124	248
Rental of video cassettes, tapes, discs, films	100	48	54	74	90	107	127	161
PETS, TOYS, PLAYGROUND EQUIPMENT	**100**	**33**	**48**	**63**	**80**	**104**	**139**	**177**
Pets	**100**	**36**	**48**	**63**	**78**	**102**	**138**	**177**
Pet food	100	46	57	77	82	115	145	145
Pet purchase, supplies, and medicines	100	42	50	39	93	100	154	169
Pet services	100	11	25	70	44	72	85	268
Veterinarian services	100	23	40	59	70	92	132	206
Toys, games, hobbies, and tricycles	**100**	**26**	**49**	**62**	**87**	**110**	**140**	**174**
Playground equipment	**100**	**13**	**17**	**32**	**44**	**75**	**172**	**238**

	complete income reporters	under $10,000	$10,000–$19,999	$20,000–$29,999	$30,000–$39,999	$40,000–$49,999	$50,000–$69,999	$70,000 or more
OTHER ENTERTAINMENT SUPPLIES, EQUIPMENT, SERVICES	**100**	**20**	**23**	**35**	**58**	**59**	**124**	**257**
Unmotored recreational vehicles	**100**	**–**	**1**	**25**	**117**	**17**	**223**	**213**
Boat without motor and boat trailers	100	–	4	78	18	36	331	153
Trailer and other attachable campers	100	–	–	–	165	8	171	242
Motorized recreational vehicles	**100**	**17**	**11**	**34**	**25**	**44**	**112**	**301**
Motorized camper	100	–	–	7	–	–	196	311
Other vehicle	100	7	14	133	47	116	142	184
Motorboats	100	27	12	2	24	28	73	346
Rental of recreational vehicles	**100**	**78**	**12**	**23**	**6**	**4**	**123**	**293**
Outboard motors	**100**	**–**	**11**	**19**	**2**	**35**	**513**	**74**
Docking and landing fees	**100**	**17**	**41**	**39**	**8**	**13**	**102**	**304**
Sports, recreation, exercise equipment	**100**	**18**	**34**	**30**	**70**	**73**	**105**	**250**
Athletic gear, game tables, exercise equipment	100	16	20	30	89	51	123	248
Bicycles	100	22	34	26	94	130	87	229
Camping equipment	100	32	23	16	133	50	138	218
Hunting and fishing equipment	100	10	65	38	30	67	57	278
Winter sports equipment	100	56	47	32	58	66	102	236
Water sports equipment	100	20	8	5	52	143	220	192
Other sports equipment	100	18	15	37	58	112	93	262
Rental and repair of misc. sports equipment	100	3	68	26	11	39	166	246
Photographic equipment and supplies	**100**	**37**	**33**	**51**	**61**	**81**	**123**	**223**
Film	100	47	44	62	73	95	123	191
Other photographic supplies	100	8	5	–	55	1	151	301
Film processing	100	44	44	59	68	88	127	198
Repair and rental of photographic equipment	100	54	43	–	108	50	108	250
Photographic equipment	100	35	25	49	52	72	118	242
Photographer fees	100	23	22	39	54	81	121	251
Fireworks	**100**	**–**	**–**	**–**	**308**	**77**	**46**	**215**
Souvenirs	**100**	**–**	**–**	**31**	**230**	**119**	**249**	**94**
Visual goods	**100**	**–**	**17**	**–**	**54**	**116**	**36**	**321**
Pinball, electronic video games	**100**	**13**	**37**	**39**	**63**	**146**	**139**	**196**

Note: (–) means sample is too small to make a reliable estimate.
Source: Calculations by New Strategist based on the 2002 Consumer Expenditure Survey

Table 3.7 Entertainment: Total spending by income, 2002

(total annual spending on entertainment, by before-tax income group of consumer units (CU), 2002; complete income reporters only; numbers in thousands)

	complete income reporters	under $10,000	$10,000–$19,999	$20,000–$29,999	$30,000–$39,999	$40,000–$49,999	$50,000–$69,999	$70,000 or more
Number of consumer units	92,388	10,933	15,075	12,312	10,727	8,873	13,521	20,947
Total spending of all CUs	$3,931,754,268	$192,725,059	$344,293,530	$355,026,985	$376,468,249	$370,779,423	$681,541,825	$1,605,112,263
Entertainment, total spending	200,163,221	8,450,996	13,955,019	14,618,530	16,748,387	17,070,055	35,702,741	93,360,988
FEES AND ADMISSIONS	**$51,882,329**	**$2,066,636**	**$2,888,586**	**$2,870,297**	**$3,251,246**	**$4,228,428**	**$8,009,705**	**$28,567,100**
Recreation expenses on trips	2,501,867	100,976	148,163	175,446	130,440	255,454	446,058	1,245,509
Social, recreation, civic club membership	10,061,053	433,053	539,831	563,520	537,208	832,997	1,347,773	5,806,718
Fees for participant sports	7,224,742	232,794	546,552	438,553	499,127	675,679	1,151,043	3,681,016
Participant sports on trips	2,854,789	112,554	151,917	115,610	114,135	173,467	420,503	1,767,089
Movie, theater, opera, ballet	9,411,566	573,265	599,152	630,128	880,258	806,999	1,568,436	4,352,996
Movie, other admissions on trips	4,456,797	141,097	187,500	270,618	316,339	380,563	751,227	2,409,324
Admission to sports events	3,544,004	137,751	240,542	131,985	170,774	228,036	564,096	2,070,401
Admission to sports events on trips	1,485,599	47,045	62,524	90,247	105,446	126,795	250,409	803,108
Fees for recreational lessons	7,840,046	187,235	264,331	278,867	367,078	492,984	1,063,832	5,185,639
Other entertainment services on trips	2,501,867	100,976	148,163	175,446	130,440	255,454	446,058	1,245,509
TELEVISION, RADIO, SOUND EQUIPMENT	**65,617,653**	**3,902,480**	**6,511,248**	**6,545,305**	**6,979,523**	**6,567,528**	**11,850,751**	**23,261,434**
Television	**51,379,738**	**3,034,767**	**5,374,855**	**5,399,797**	**5,631,031**	**5,169,676**	**9,054,743**	**17,715,297**
Cable service and community antenna	35,503,785	2,248,514	4,102,350	3,927,774	4,000,527	3,645,738	6,421,934	11,157,420
Black-and-white TV	76,682	5,218	391	10,588	10,727	12,333	2,839	34,144
Color TV, console	3,868,286	108,546	212,715	222,232	406,017	295,826	448,492	2,174,508
Color TV, portable, table model	3,803,614	247,120	343,414	539,758	364,503	499,195	583,296	1,226,447
VCRs and video disc players	2,270,897	91,908	192,488	217,799	177,425	213,129	421,314	956,859
Video cassettes, tapes, and discs	3,285,317	174,593	315,906	305,338	384,348	297,955	676,050	1,131,557
Video game hardware and software	2,289,375	146,993	182,829	150,083	226,983	185,268	464,582	932,351
Repair of TV, radio, and sound equipment	237,437	10,748	15,415	17,729	42,693	20,230	28,529	102,012
Rental of television sets	44,346	1,128	9,277	8,372	17,700	–	7,572	–
Radio and sound equipment	**14,237,915**	**867,712**	**1,136,464**	**1,145,508**	**1,348,491**	**1,397,852**	**2,796,008**	**5,546,137**
Radios	353,846	2,820	30,427	59,098	18,880	–	106,005	131,338
Tape recorders and players	485,961	–	136,170	18,591	43,552	71,871	130,478	84,835
Sound components and component systems	1,924,442	96,721	187,294	166,089	175,065	165,836	262,172	870,767
Miscellaneous sound equipment	291,022	6,366	–	–	–	6,034	270,420	15,291
Sound equipment accessories	635,629	26,821	25,745	32,750	103,301	95,030	151,570	199,415
Satellite dishes	105,322	11,757	13,592	7,141	5,364	10,026	7,842	49,225
Compact disc, tape, record, video mail order clubs	654,107	38,689	50,571	76,704	77,556	75,243	129,802	205,909
Records, CDs, audio tapes, needles	3,501,505	219,668	275,531	318,142	337,257	330,076	636,298	1,384,387
Rental of VCR, radio, sound equipment	27,716	141	5,949	7,880	–	1,420	2,163	10,474
Musical instruments and accessories	2,312,472	245,433	70,492	79,905	182,574	236,909	367,636	1,129,672
Rental and repair of musical instruments	116,409	3,382	5,912	3,447	4,291	13,043	21,093	65,564
Rental of video cassettes, tapes, discs, films	3,829,483	215,992	334,549	375,762	400,761	392,275	710,664	1,399,050
PETS, TOYS, PLAYGROUND EQUIPMENT	**36,663,254**	**1,419,342**	**2,864,566**	**3,068,889**	**3,420,304**	**3,663,129**	**7,460,888**	**14,686,570**
Pets	**24,874,545**	**1,055,728**	**1,941,726**	**2,104,121**	**2,250,525**	**2,435,017**	**5,021,970**	**9,986,063**
Pet food	10,744,724	585,220	992,745	1,095,768	1,026,145	1,186,498	2,273,286	3,526,427
Pet purchase, supplies, and medicines	5,270,735	262,832	427,079	276,897	567,566	504,785	1,187,549	2,022,852
Pet services	2,169,270	29,026	86,754	203,148	110,595	149,954	270,961	1,318,614
Veterinarian services	6,690,739	178,611	435,077	528,185	546,219	593,870	1,290,174	3,118,380
Toys, games, hobbies, and tricycles	**11,415,461**	**357,862**	**912,471**	**948,763**	**1,150,793**	**1,201,138**	**2,345,217**	**4,498,997**
Playground equipment	**373,248**	**5,823**	**10,360**	**16,006**	**18,987**	**26,974**	**93,701**	**201,720**

	complete income reporters	under $10,000	$10,000– $19,999	$20,000– $29,999	$30,000– $39,999	$40,000– $49,999	$50,000– $69,999	$70,000 or more
OTHER ENTERTAINMENT SUPPLIES, EQUIPMENT, SERVICES	**$45,999,985**	**$1,062,429**	**$1,690,619**	**$2,134,039**	**$3,097,314**	**$2,610,969**	**$8,381,397**	**$26,845,675**
Unmotored recreational vehicles	**4,762,601**	–	**10,249**	**161,657**	**647,696**	**79,857**	**1,556,673**	**2,301,447**
Boat without motor and boat trailers	1,549,347	–	10,249	161,657	31,537	53,770	750,416	535,824
Trailer and other attachable campers	3,214,179	–	–	–	616,159	26,175	806,257	1,765,623
Motorized recreational vehicles	**15,078,645**	**309,500**	**259,336**	**678,637**	**435,516**	**630,427**	**2,475,560**	**10,289,585**
Motorized camper	2,823,377	–	–	24,870	–	–	807,880	1,990,384
Other vehicle	3,578,187	27,601	84,262	633,083	194,266	397,688	744,872	1,496,663
Motorboats	8,677,081	281,899	175,074	20,684	241,250	232,739	922,673	6,802,538
Rental of recreational vehicles	**202,330**	**18,591**	**4,118**	**6,279**	**1,502**	**710**	**36,371**	**134,270**
Outboard motors	**79,454**	–	**1,484**	**1,970**	**215**	**2,662**	**59,628**	**13,406**
Docking and landing fees	**679,052**	**14,054**	**45,411**	**35,335**	**6,543**	**8,784**	**101,137**	**467,747**
Sports, recreation, exercise equipment	**15,377,059**	**320,506**	**853,937**	**615,231**	**1,242,937**	**1,080,820**	**2,372,395**	**8,725,473**
Athletic gear, game tables, exercise equip.	5,983,047	112,546	197,826	235,405	616,052	295,116	1,079,787	3,365,764
Bicycles	1,392,287	36,866	78,277	48,509	152,323	174,000	178,207	723,928
Camping equipment	997,790	37,227	36,857	20,684	154,040	48,092	200,922	492,045
Hunting and fishing equipment	4,074,311	49,672	432,629	206,349	141,167	263,351	338,566	2,565,379
Winter sports equipment	519,221	34,599	40,071	21,915	34,755	32,741	77,611	277,338
Water sports equipment	782,526	18,895	10,139	5,048	47,306	107,363	252,031	341,436
Other sports equipment	1,405,221	29,911	33,429	69,317	94,505	151,817	190,917	835,157
Rental and repair of misc. sports equipment	223,579	860	24,860	7,880	2,789	8,341	54,219	124,635
Photographic equipment and supplies	**8,905,279**	**386,495**	**480,606**	**601,564**	**634,609**	**694,490**	**1,605,484**	**4,498,578**
Film	1,747,057	96,381	126,014	143,927	148,033	159,891	315,445	757,444
Other photographic supplies	244,828	2,446	1,979	–	15,661	177	53,949	166,948
Film processing	2,606,265	136,034	185,145	203,271	206,066	221,026	482,564	1,171,775
Repair and rental of photographic equipment	11,087	705	777	–	1,395	532	1,758	6,284
Photographic equipment	2,396,545	99,955	99,031	156,486	144,493	165,038	414,824	1,317,147
Photographer fees	1,899,497	51,045	67,730	97,757	118,962	147,824	336,943	1,078,980
Fireworks	**121,028**	–	–	–	**43,230**	**8,962**	**8,113**	**59,071**
Souvenirs	**144,125**	–	–	**6,033**	**38,510**	**16,504**	**52,597**	**30,583**
Visual goods	**125,648**	–	**3,448**	–	**7,938**	**14,019**	**6,625**	**91,538**
Pinball, electronic video games	**524,764**	**7,926**	**31,968**	**27,210**	**38,617**	**73,557**	**106,816**	**233,769**

Note: Numbers may not add to total because of rounding. (–) means sample is too small to make a reliable estimate.
Source: Calculations by New Strategist based on the 2002 Consumer Expenditure Survey

Table 3.08 Entertainment: Market shares by income, 2002

(percentage of total annual spending on entertainment accounted for by before-tax income group of consumer units, 2002; complete income reporters only)

	complete income reporters	under $10,000	$10,000–$19,999	$20,000–$29,999	$30,000–$39,999	$40,000–$49,999	$50,000–$69,999	$70,000 or more
Share of total consumer units	100.0%	11.8%	16.3%	13.3%	11.6%	9.6%	14.6%	22.7%
Share of total before-tax income	100.0	1.3	4.9	6.6	8.1	9.4	17.3	53.0
Share of total spending	100.0	4.9	8.8	9.0	9.6	9.4	17.8	40.8
Share of entertainment spending	100.0	4.2	7.0	7.3	8.4	8.5	17.8	46.6
FEES AND ADMISSIONS	**100.0%**	**4.0%**	**5.6%**	**5.5%**	**6.3%**	**8.2%**	**15.4%**	**55.1%**
Recreation expenses on trips	100.0	4.0	5.9	7.0	5.2	10.2	17.8	49.8
Social, recreation, civic club membership	100.0	4.3	5.4	5.6	5.3	8.3	13.4	57.7
Fees for participant sports	100.0	3.2	7.6	6.1	6.9	9.4	15.9	51.0
Participant sports on trips	100.0	3.9	5.3	4.0	4.0	6.1	14.7	61.9
Movie, theater, opera, ballet	100.0	6.1	6.4	6.7	9.4	8.6	16.7	46.3
Movie, other admissions on trips	100.0	3.2	4.2	6.1	7.1	8.5	16.9	54.1
Admission to sports events	100.0	3.9	6.8	3.7	4.8	6.4	15.9	58.4
Admission to sports events on trips	100.0	3.2	4.2	6.1	7.1	8.5	16.9	54.1
Fees for recreational lessons	100.0	2.4	3.4	3.6	4.7	6.3	13.6	66.1
Other entertainment services on trips	100.0	4.0	5.9	7.0	5.2	10.2	17.8	49.8
TELEVISION, RADIO, SOUND EQUIPMENT	**100.0**	**5.9**	**9.9**	**10.0**	**10.6**	**10.0**	**18.1**	**35.4**
Television	**100.0**	**5.9**	**10.5**	**10.5**	**11.0**	**10.1**	**17.6**	**34.5**
Cable service and community antenna	100.0	6.3	11.6	11.1	11.3	10.3	18.1	31.4
Black-and-white TV	100.0	6.8	0.5	13.8	14.0	16.1	3.7	44.5
Color TV, console	100.0	2.8	5.5	5.7	10.5	7.6	11.6	56.2
Color TV, portable, table model	100.0	6.5	9.0	14.2	9.6	13.1	15.3	32.2
VCRs and video disc players	100.0	4.0	8.5	9.6	7.8	9.4	18.6	42.1
Video cassettes, tapes, and discs	100.0	5.3	9.6	9.3	11.7	9.1	20.6	34.4
Video game hardware and software	100.0	6.4	8.0	6.6	9.9	8.1	20.3	40.7
Repair of TV, radio, and sound equipment	100.0	4.5	6.5	7.5	18.0	8.5	12.0	43.0
Rental of television sets	100.0	2.5	20.9	18.9	39.9	–	17.1	–
Radio and sound equipment	**100.0**	**6.1**	**8.0**	**8.0**	**9.5**	**9.8**	**19.6**	**39.0**
Radios	100.0	0.8	8.6	16.7	5.3	–	30.0	37.1
Tape recorders and players	100.0	–	28.0	3.8	9.0	14.8	26.8	17.5
Sound components and component systems	100.0	5.0	9.7	8.6	9.1	8.6	13.6	45.2
Miscellaneous sound equipment	100.0	2.2	–	–	–	2.1	92.9	5.3
Sound equipment accessories	100.0	4.2	4.1	5.2	16.3	15.0	23.8	31.4
Satellite dishes	100.0	11.2	12.9	6.8	5.1	9.5	7.4	46.7
Compact disc, tape, record, video mail order clubs	100.0	5.9	7.7	11.7	11.9	11.5	19.8	31.5
Records, CDs, audio tapes, needles	100.0	6.3	7.9	9.1	9.6	9.4	18.2	39.5
Rental of VCR, radio, sound equipment	100.0	0.5	21.5	28.4	–	5.1	7.8	37.8
Musical instruments and accessories	100.0	10.6	3.0	3.5	7.9	10.2	15.9	48.9
Rental and repair of musical instruments	100.0	2.9	5.1	3.0	3.7	11.2	18.1	56.3
Rental of video cassettes, tapes, discs, films	100.0	5.6	8.7	9.8	10.5	10.2	18.6	36.5
PETS, TOYS, PLAYGROUND EQUIPMENT	**100.0**	**3.9**	**7.8**	**8.4**	**9.3**	**10.0**	**20.3**	**40.1**
Pets	**100.0**	**4.2**	**7.8**	**8.5**	**9.0**	**9.8**	**20.2**	**40.1**
Pet food	100.0	5.4	9.2	10.2	9.6	11.0	21.2	32.8
Pet purchase, supplies, and medicines	100.0	5.0	8.1	5.3	10.8	9.6	22.5	38.4
Pet services	100.0	1.3	4.0	9.4	5.1	6.9	12.5	60.8
Veterinarian services	100.0	2.7	6.5	7.9	8.2	8.9	19.3	46.6
Toys, games, hobbies, and tricycles	**100.0**	**3.1**	**8.0**	**8.3**	**10.1**	**10.5**	**20.5**	**39.4**
Playground equipment	**100.0**	**1.6**	**2.8**	**4.3**	**5.1**	**7.2**	**25.1**	**54.0**

	complete income reporters	under $10,000	$10,000–$19,999	$20,000–$29,999	$30,000–$39,999	$40,000–$49,999	$50,000–$69,999	$70,000 or more
OTHER ENTERTAINMENT SUPPLIES, EQUIPMENT, SERVICES	100.0%	2.3%	3.7%	4.6%	6.7%	5.7%	18.2%	58.4%
Unmotored recreational vehicles	100.0	–	0.2	3.4	13.6	1.7	32.7	48.3
Boat without motor and boat trailers	100.0	–	0.7	10.4	2.0	3.5	48.4	34.6
Trailer and other attachable campers	100.0	–	–	–	19.2	0.8	25.1	54.9
Motorized recreational vehicles	100.0	2.1	1.7	4.5	2.9	4.2	16.4	68.2
Motorized camper	100.0	–	–	0.9	–	–	28.6	70.5
Other vehicle	100.0	0.8	2.4	17.7	5.4	11.1	20.8	41.8
Motorboats	100.0	3.2	2.0	0.2	2.8	2.7	10.6	78.4
Rental of recreational vehicles	100.0	9.2	2.0	3.1	0.7	0.4	18.0	66.4
Outboard motors	100.0	–	1.9	2.5	0.3	3.4	75.0	16.9
Docking and landing fees	100.0	2.1	6.7	5.2	1.0	1.3	14.9	68.9
Sports, recreation, exercise equipment	100.0	2.1	5.6	4.0	8.1	7.0	15.4	56.7
Athletic gear, game tables, exercise equipment	100.0	1.9	3.3	3.9	10.3	4.9	18.0	56.3
Bicycles	100.0	2.6	5.6	3.5	10.9	12.5	12.8	52.0
Camping equipment	100.0	3.7	3.7	2.1	15.4	4.8	20.1	49.3
Hunting and fishing equipment	100.0	1.2	10.6	5.1	3.5	6.5	8.3	63.0
Winter sports equipment	100.0	6.7	7.7	4.2	6.7	6.3	14.9	53.4
Water sports equipment	100.0	2.4	1.3	0.6	6.0	13.7	32.2	43.6
Other sports equipment	100.0	2.1	2.4	4.9	6.7	10.8	13.6	59.4
Rental and repair of miscellaneous sports equipment	100.0	0.4	11.1	3.5	1.2	3.7	24.3	55.7
Photographic equipment and supplies	100.0	4.3	5.4	6.8	7.1	7.8	18.0	50.5
Film	100.0	5.5	7.2	8.2	8.5	9.2	18.1	43.4
Other photographic supplies	100.0	1.0	0.8	–	6.4	0.1	22.0	68.2
Film processing	100.0	5.2	7.1	7.8	7.9	8.5	18.5	45.0
Repair and rental of photographic equipment	100.0	6.4	7.0	–	12.6	4.8	15.9	56.7
Photographic equipment	100.0	4.2	4.1	6.5	6.0	6.9	17.3	55.0
Photographer fees	100.0	2.7	3.6	5.1	6.3	7.8	17.7	56.8
Fireworks	100.0	–	–	–	35.7	7.4	6.7	48.8
Souvenirs	100.0	–	–	4.2	26.7	11.5	36.5	21.2
Visual goods	100.0	–	2.7	–	6.3	11.2	5.3	72.9
Pinball, electronic video games	100.0	1.5	6.1	5.2	7.4	14.0	20.4	44.5

Note: Numbers may not add to total because of rounding. (–) means sample is too small to make a reliable estimate.
Source: Calculations by New Strategist based on the 2002 Consumer Expenditure Survey

Table 3.9 Entertainment: Average spending by household type, 2002

(average annual spending of consumer units (CU) on entertainment, by type of consumer unit, 2002)

	total married couples	married couples, no children	married couples with children total	oldest child under 6	oldest child 6 to 17	oldest child 18 or older	single parent, at least one child <18	single person
Number of consumer units (in thousands, add 000)	56,265	23,118	28,790	5,547	15,206	8,036	6,730	33,055
Average number of persons per CU	3.2	2.0	3.9	3.5	4.1	3.9	2.9	1.0
Average before-tax income of CU	$67,155.00	$58,967.00	$73,918.00	$67,587.00	$72,720.00	$81,042.00	$26,966.00	$27,042.00
Average spending of CU, total	52,333.70	45,557.33	57,835.01	52,778.62	58,103.75	60,859.78	30,185.38	24,189.90
Entertainment, average spending	2,761.66	2,264.89	3,212.67	2,425.05	3,593.09	3,037.50	1,361.52	1,193.11
FEES AND ADMISSIONS	**$752.82**	**$615.18**	**$892.59**	**$558.03**	**$1,086.77**	**$756.12**	**$304.98**	**$320.09**
Recreation expenses on trips	34.92	33.92	33.85	25.56	33.78	39.69	11.08	16.26
Social, recreation, civic club membership	152.07	140.09	175.76	127.22	205.25	153.47	35.70	65.19
Fees for participant sports	99.58	106.11	100.23	71.38	120.19	82.37	38.82	54.70
Participant sports on trips	42.39	45.72	41.31	30.74	46.67	38.45	7.19	20.29
Movie, theater, opera, ballet	117.99	96.59	136.36	77.69	153.88	143.70	69.16	75.07
Movie, other admissions on trips	66.85	66.80	70.42	48.82	79.15	68.82	17.54	24.16
Admission to sports events	49.56	36.74	64.65	40.98	74.38	62.60	17.49	21.89
Admission to sports events on trips	22.28	22.27	23.47	16.26	26.38	22.94	5.84	8.05
Fees for recreational lessons	132.27	33.03	212.71	93.84	313.33	104.37	91.09	18.21
Other entertainment services on trips	34.92	33.92	33.85	25.56	33.78	39.69	11.08	16.26
TELEVISION, RADIO, SOUND EQUIPMENT	**829.66**	**703.47**	**925.85**	**782.92**	**964.47**	**951.96**	**612.01**	**466.51**
Television	**649.21**	**596.43**	**688.08**	**619.22**	**697.67**	**717.46**	**475.67**	**371.98**
Cable service and community antenna	445.94	435.43	451.43	398.89	450.62	489.26	341.01	277.12
Black-and-white TV	1.34	0.36	2.07	0.95	2.48	2.06	0.01	0.20
Color TV, console	51.76	50.93	52.35	46.48	53.42	54.39	22.37	19.18
Color TV, portable, table model	49.01	44.81	52.72	59.23	45.61	61.66	32.34	26.06
VCRs and video disc players	30.26	24.42	34.64	30.20	38.82	29.79	13.66	13.56
Video cassettes, tapes, and discs	37.97	24.74	48.40	57.10	48.54	42.12	30.65	24.32
Video game hardware and software	28.76	12.06	42.16	23.01	53.18	34.55	32.95	10.19
Repair of TV, radio, and sound equipment	3.77	3.66	3.73	3.25	4.09	3.39	1.09	1.20
Rental of television sets	0.41	–	0.57	0.10	0.91	0.23	1.59	0.15
Radio and sound equipment	**180.44**	**107.04**	**237.77**	**163.70**	**266.81**	**234.49**	**136.34**	**94.52**
Radios	6.35	7.18	4.75	4.39	3.22	8.05	1.46	1.17
Tape recorders and players	4.10	1.66	6.80	4.83	3.10	15.62	7.72	7.18
Sound components and component systems	27.41	24.20	31.29	26.02	34.87	28.16	14.52	10.59
Miscellaneous sound equipment	2.75	0.76	4.89	1.41	8.53	0.18	0.57	5.54
Sound equipment accessories	9.01	4.88	13.18	13.05	12.44	14.76	2.97	2.50
Satellite dishes	1.53	0.51	1.86	2.16	2.06	1.27	–	0.17
Compact disc, tape, record, video mail order clubs	6.64	5.77	6.87	6.48	7.08	6.76	6.58	4.78
Records, CDs, audio tapes, needles	40.12	25.98	51.79	35.43	52.75	61.26	36.84	28.55
Rental of VCR, radio, sound equipment	0.26	0.39	0.11	–	0.16	0.09	0.65	–
Musical instruments and accessories	32.54	11.64	46.06	16.73	62.94	34.35	19.75	12.33
Rental and repair of musical instruments	1.92	0.58	3.14	0.42	5.11	1.30	2.71	0.11
Rental of video cassettes, tapes, discs, films	47.81	23.50	67.04	52.79	74.54	62.68	42.58	21.61
PETS, TOYS, PLAYGROUND EQUIPMENT	**495.18**	**444.65**	**546.03**	**486.25**	**605.11**	**475.20**	**262.61**	**201.55**
Pets	**324.45**	**341.25**	**324.48**	**177.35**	**366.54**	**346.13**	**142.11**	**157.21**
Pet food	128.66	136.90	125.49	85.82	135.35	135.02	63.27	72.46
Pet purchase, supplies, and medicines	70.73	74.02	70.23	22.48	102.18	41.61	30.97	27.11
Pet services	29.32	30.18	31.46	19.57	31.86	38.91	10.30	14.30
Veterinarian services	95.74	100.14	97.30	49.48	97.15	130.59	37.56	43.35
Toys, games, hobbies, and tricycles	**164.74**	**102.71**	**210.78**	**282.08**	**231.04**	**123.23**	**119.21**	**44.20**
Playground equipment	**5.99**	**0.69**	**10.78**	**26.83**	**7.53**	**5.84**	**1.29**	**0.14**

	total married couples	married couples, no children	married couples with children				single parent, at least one child <18	single person
			total	oldest child under 6	oldest child 6 to 17	oldest child 18 or older		
OTHER ENTERTAINMENT SUPPLIES, EQUIPMENT, SERVICES	**$684.00**	**$501.59**	**$848.19**	**$597.84**	**$936.73**	**$854.22**	**$181.90**	**$204.96**
Unmotored recreational vehicles	**66.90**	**72.63**	**61.66**	**90.20**	**52.35**	**59.56**	**13.02**	**20.02**
Boat without motor and boat trailers	24.94	37.28	18.80	8.62	28.34	7.77	–	11.54
Trailer and other attachable campers	41.96	35.35	42.86	81.58	24.01	51.79	13.02	8.48
Motorized recreational vehicles	**256.81**	**199.59**	**310.64**	**172.51**	**346.97**	**337.25**	**52.83**	**31.54**
Motorized camper	77.50	79.17	87.89	–	79.20	165.00	–	–
Other vehicle	42.06	45.08	36.08	63.27	45.24	–	52.83	15.06
Motorboats	137.25	75.34	186.66	109.24	222.53	172.25	–	16.48
Rental of recreational vehicles	**2.98**	**3.71**	**2.36**	**1.27**	**2.84**	**2.20**	**0.03**	**1.16**
Outboard motors	**1.35**	**2.59**	**0.56**	**1.26**	**0.35**	**0.46**	**0.22**	**0.01**
Docking and landing fees	**10.92**	**11.07**	**11.79**	**4.89**	**8.79**	**22.22**	**1.08**	**2.28**
Sports, recreation, exercise equipment	**206.96**	**106.64**	**293.94**	**141.26**	**356.94**	**281.20**	**52.52**	**103.10**
Athletic gear, game tables, exercise equipment	90.47	40.57	134.19	39.59	174.71	122.98	18.41	27.56
Bicycles	17.65	7.45	24.41	32.40	26.67	14.60	7.69	9.39
Camping equipment	12.89	7.54	17.88	1.43	26.26	13.28	8.95	4.76
Hunting and fishing equipment	39.26	16.18	57.80	40.13	55.84	74.74	5.15	49.69
Winter sports equipment	7.89	3.72	11.22	0.46	15.95	9.68	4.35	3.02
Water sports equipment	13.71	13.79	15.27	2.31	23.92	7.87	3.09	2.98
Other sports equipment	22.32	15.50	29.63	24.00	28.50	35.66	4.69	4.58
Rental and repair of misc. sports equipment	2.77	1.90	3.54	0.94	5.09	2.41	0.20	1.11
Photographic equipment and supplies	**127.16**	**102.30**	**150.10**	**177.88**	**143.99**	**142.53**	**53.89**	**41.45**
Film	24.07	17.64	29.33	31.44	28.20	30.01	12.45	9.31
Other photographic supplies	4.17	7.75	1.65	2.85	0.65	2.74	–	0.01
Film processing	37.33	27.26	45.42	55.93	43.69	41.45	16.07	13.86
Repair and rental of photographic equipment	0.15	0.26	0.09	–	0.12	0.10	0.08	0.10
Photographic equipment	31.66	28.66	34.87	46.73	30.20	35.51	11.85	15.16
Photographer fees	29.78	20.72	38.74	40.93	41.12	32.71	13.45	3.02
Fireworks	**1.68**	**0.13**	**3.27**	**0.73**	**5.27**	**1.15**	**0.40**	**1.37**
Souvenirs	**1.56**	**0.59**	**2.38**	**4.25**	**1.57**	**2.62**	**3.84**	**0.46**
Visual goods	**2.11**	**1.58**	**1.35**	**–**	**2.29**	**0.45**	**–**	**0.10**
Pinball, electronic video games	**5.57**	**0.75**	**10.15**	**3.58**	**15.37**	**4.59**	**4.08**	**3.48**

Note: Average spending figures for total consumer units can be found on Average Spending by Age and Average Spending by Region tables. (–) means sample is too small to make a reliable estimate.
Source: Bureau of Labor Statistics, unpublished data from the 2002 Consumer Expenditure Survey

Table 3.10 Entertainment: Indexed spending by household type, 2002

(indexed average annual spending of consumer units (CU) on entertainment by type of consumer unit, 2002; index definition: an index of 100 is the average for all consumer units; an index of 132 means that spending by consumer units in that group is 32 percent above the average for all consumer units; an index of 68 indicates spending that is 32 percent below the average for all consumer units)

	total married couples	married couples, no children	married couples with children total	oldest child under 6	oldest child 6 to 17	oldest child 18 or older	single parent, at least one child <18	single person
Average spending of CU, total	$52,334	$45,557	$57,835	$52,779	$58,104	$60,860	$30,185	$24,190
Average spending of CU, index	129	112	142	130	143	150	74	59
Entertainment, spending index	133	109	155	117	173	146	65	57
FEES AND ADMISSIONS	**139**	**114**	**165**	**103**	**201**	**140**	**56**	**59**
Recreation expenses on trips	136	132	132	100	132	155	43	63
Social, recreation, civic club membership	141	130	163	118	190	142	33	60
Fees for participant sports	133	141	134	95	160	110	52	73
Participant sports on trips	144	155	140	104	158	130	24	69
Movie, theater, opera, ballet	120	98	139	79	157	146	70	76
Movie, other admissions on trips	147	147	155	107	174	151	38	53
Admission to sports events	137	102	179	113	206	173	48	61
Admission to sports events on trips	147	147	155	107	174	151	38	53
Fees for recreational lessons	160	40	257	113	379	126	110	22
Other entertainment services on trips	136	132	132	100	132	155	43	63
TELEVISION, RADIO, SOUND EQUIPMENT	**120**	**102**	**134**	**113**	**139**	**138**	**88**	**67**
Television	**119**	**110**	**127**	**114**	**128**	**132**	**87**	**68**
Cable service and community antenna	117	114	118	104	118	128	89	72
Black-and-white TV	168	45	259	119	310	258	1	25
Color TV, console	134	132	136	120	138	141	58	50
Color TV, portable, table model	125	114	135	151	117	158	83	67
VCRs and video disc players	130	105	149	130	167	128	59	58
Video cassettes, tapes, and discs	115	75	146	172	147	127	93	73
Video game hardware and software	123	51	180	98	227	147	140	43
Repair of TV, radio, and sound equipment	151	146	149	130	164	136	44	48
Rental of television sets	89	–	124	22	198	50	346	33
Radio and sound equipment	**122**	**72**	**160**	**110**	**180**	**158**	**92**	**64**
Radios	160	180	119	110	81	202	37	29
Tape recorders and players	77	31	128	91	58	294	145	135
Sound components and component systems	136	120	155	129	173	139	72	52
Miscellaneous sound equipment	86	24	154	44	268	6	18	174
Sound equipment accessories	151	82	221	219	208	247	50	42
Satellite dishes	153	51	186	216	206	127	–	17
Compact disc, tape, record, video mail order clubs	102	88	105	99	108	104	101	73
Records, CDs, audio tapes, needles	110	71	142	97	145	168	101	78
Rental of VCR, radio, sound equipment	104	156	44	–	64	36	260	–
Musical instruments and accessories	131	47	186	67	254	138	80	50
Rental and repair of musical instruments	157	48	257	34	419	107	222	9
Rental of video cassettes, tapes, discs, films	122	60	170	134	190	159	108	55
PETS, TOYS, PLAYGROUND EQUIPMENT	**134**	**120**	**148**	**132**	**164**	**129**	**71**	**55**
Pets	**131**	**137**	**131**	**71**	**148**	**139**	**57**	**63**
Pet food	125	133	122	84	132	132	62	71
Pet purchase, supplies, and medicines	135	142	134	43	195	80	59	52
Pet services	134	137	143	89	145	177	47	65
Veterinarian services	134	140	136	69	136	183	53	61
Toys, games, hobbies, and tricycles	**140**	**88**	**180**	**240**	**197**	**105**	**102**	**38**
Playground equipment	**169**	**19**	**305**	**758**	**213**	**165**	**36**	**4**

	total married couples	married couples, no children	married couples with children				single parent, at least one child <18	single person
			total	oldest child under 6	oldest child 6 to 17	oldest child 18 or older		
OTHER ENTERTAINMENT SUPPLIES, EQUIPMENT, SERVICES	**144**	**105**	**178**	**126**	**197**	**179**	**38**	**43**
Unmotored recreational vehicles	**142**	**154**	**131**	**191**	**111**	**126**	**28**	**42**
Boat without motor and boat trailers	154	231	116	53	175	48	–	71
Trailer and other attachable campers	135	114	138	263	77	167	42	27
Motorized recreational vehicles	**151**	**117**	**183**	**101**	**204**	**198**	**31**	**19**
Motorized camper	194	198	219	–	198	412	–	–
Other vehicle	119	127	102	178	128	–	149	42
Motorboats	145	80	197	115	235	182	–	17
Rental of recreational vehicles	**150**	**186**	**119**	**64**	**143**	**111**	**2**	**58**
Outboard motors	**190**	**365**	**79**	**177**	**49**	**65**	**31**	**1**
Docking and landing fees	**164**	**166**	**177**	**73**	**132**	**334**	**16**	**34**
Sports, recreation, exercise equipment	**138**	**71**	**196**	**94**	**237**	**187**	**35**	**69**
Athletic gear, game tables, exercise equipment	150	67	222	65	289	203	30	46
Bicycles	131	55	181	241	198	109	57	70
Camping equipment	134	79	186	15	274	138	93	50
Hunting and fishing equipment	110	45	162	112	157	209	14	139
Winter sports equipment	145	68	206	8	293	178	80	55
Water sports equipment	153	154	171	26	267	88	35	33
Other sports equipment	153	106	203	164	195	244	32	31
Rental and repair of misc. sports equipment	134	92	171	45	246	116	10	54
Photographic equipment and supplies	**141**	**113**	**166**	**197**	**159**	**158**	**60**	**46**
Film	136	99	165	177	159	169	70	52
Other photographic supplies	184	341	73	126	29	121	–	0
Film processing	140	102	171	210	164	156	60	52
Repair and rental of photographic equipment	125	217	75	–	100	83	67	83
Photographic equipment	136	123	149	200	129	152	51	65
Photographer fees	146	101	190	200	201	160	66	15
Fireworks	**111**	**9**	**215**	**48**	**347**	**76**	**26**	**90**
Souvenirs	**125**	**47**	**190**	**340**	**126**	**210**	**307**	**37**
Visual goods	**177**	**133**	**113**	**–**	**192**	**38**	**–**	**8**
Pinball, electronic video games	**115**	**15**	**210**	**74**	**318**	**95**	**84**	**72**

Note: Spending index for total consumer units is 100. (–) means sample is too small to make a reliable estimate.
Source: Calculations by New Strategist based on the 2002 Consumer Expenditure Survey

Table 3.11 Entertainment: Total spending by household type, 2002

(total annual spending on entertainment, by consumer unit (CU) type, 2002; numbers in thousands)

	total married couples	married couples, no children	married couples with children				single parent, at least one child <18	single person
			total	oldest child under 6	oldest child 6 to 17	oldest child 18 or older		
Number of consumer units	56,265	23,118	28,790	5,547	15,206	8,036	6,730	33,055
Total spending of all CUs	$2,944,555,631	$1,053,194,355	$1,665,069,938	$292,763,005	$883,525,623	$489,069,192	$203,147,607	$799,597,145
Entertainment, total spending	155,384,800	52,359,727	92,492,769	13,451,752	54,636,527	24,409,350	9,163,030	39,438,251
FEES AND ADMISSIONS	$42,357,417	$14,221,731	$25,697,666	$3,095,392	$16,525,425	$6,076,180	$2,052,515	$10,580,575
Recreation expenses on trips	1,964,774	784,163	974,542	141,781	513,659	318,949	74,568	537,474
Social, recreation, civic club membership	8,556,219	3,238,601	5,060,130	705,689	3,121,032	1,233,285	240,261	2,154,855
Fees for participant sports	5,602,869	2,453,051	2,885,622	395,945	1,827,609	661,925	261,259	1,808,109
Participant sports on trips	2,385,073	1,056,955	1,189,315	170,515	709,664	308,984	48,389	670,686
Movie, theater, opera, ballet	6,638,707	2,232,968	3,925,804	430,946	2,339,899	1,154,773	465,447	2,481,439
Movie, other admissions on trips	3,761,315	1,544,282	2,027,392	270,805	1,203,555	553,038	118,044	798,609
Admission to sports events	2,788,493	849,355	1,861,274	227,316	1,131,022	503,054	117,708	723,574
Admission to sports events on trips	1,253,584	514,838	675,701	90,194	401,134	184,346	39,303	266,093
Fees for recreational lessons	7,442,172	763,588	6,123,921	520,530	4,764,496	838,717	613,036	601,932
Other entertainment services on trips	1,964,774	784,163	974,542	141,781	513,659	318,949	74,568	537,474
TELEVISION, RADIO, SOUND EQUIPMENT	46,680,820	16,262,819	26,655,222	4,342,857	14,665,731	7,649,951	4,118,827	15,420,488
Television	36,527,801	13,788,269	19,809,823	3,434,813	10,608,770	5,765,509	3,201,259	12,295,799
Cable service and community antenna	25,090,814	10,066,271	12,996,670	2,212,643	6,852,128	3,931,693	2,294,997	9,160,202
Black-and-white TV	75,395	8,322	59,595	5,270	37,711	16,554	67	6,611
Color TV, console	2,912,276	1,177,400	1,507,157	257,825	812,305	437,078	150,550	633,995
Color TV, portable, table model	2,757,548	1,035,918	1,517,809	328,549	693,546	495,500	217,648	861,413
VCRs and video disc players	1,702,579	564,542	997,286	167,519	590,297	239,392	91,932	448,226
Video cassettes, tapes, and discs	2,136,382	571,939	1,393,436	316,734	738,099	338,476	206,275	803,898
Video game hardware and software	1,618,181	278,803	1,213,786	127,636	808,655	277,644	221,754	336,830
Repair of TV, radio, and sound equipment	212,119	84,612	107,387	18,028	62,193	27,242	7,336	39,666
Rental of television sets	23,069	–	16,410	555	13,837	1,848	10,701	4,958
Radio and sound equipment	10,152,457	2,474,551	6,845,398	908,044	4,057,113	1,884,362	917,568	3,124,359
Radios	357,283	165,987	136,753	24,351	48,963	64,690	9,826	38,674
Tape recorders and players	230,687	38,376	195,772	26,792	47,139	125,522	51,956	237,335
Sound components and component systems	1,542,224	559,456	900,839	144,333	530,233	226,294	97,720	350,052
Miscellaneous sound equipment	154,729	17,570	140,783	7,821	129,707	1,446	3,836	183,125
Sound equipment accessories	506,948	112,816	379,452	72,388	189,163	118,611	19,988	82,638
Satellite dishes	86,085	11,790	53,549	11,982	31,324	10,206	–	5,619
Compact disc, tape, record, video mail order clubs	373,600	133,391	197,787	35,945	107,658	54,323	44,283	158,003
Records, CDs, audio tapes, needles	2,257,352	600,606	1,491,034	196,530	802,117	492,285	247,933	943,720
Rental of VCR, radio, sound equipment	14,629	9,016	3,167	–	2,433	723	4,375	–
Musical instruments and accessories	1,830,863	269,094	1,326,067	92,801	957,066	276,037	132,918	407,568
Rental and repair of musical instruments	108,029	13,408	90,401	2,330	77,703	10,447	18,238	3,636
Rental of video cassettes, tapes, discs, films	2,690,030	543,273	1,930,082	292,826	1,133,455	503,696	286,563	714,319
PETS, TOYS, PLAYGROUND EQUIPMENT	27,861,303	10,279,419	15,720,204	2,697,229	9,201,303	3,818,707	1,767,365	6,662,235
Pets	18,255,179	7,889,018	9,341,779	983,760	5,573,607	2,781,501	956,400	5,196,577
Pet food	7,239,055	3,164,854	3,612,857	476,044	2,058,132	1,085,021	425,807	2,395,165
Pet purchase, supplies, and medicines	3,979,623	1,711,194	2,021,922	124,697	1,553,749	334,378	208,428	896,121
Pet services	1,649,690	697,701	905,733	108,555	484,463	312,681	69,319	472,687
Veterinarian services	5,386,811	2,315,037	2,801,267	274,466	1,477,263	1,049,421	252,779	1,432,934
Toys, games, hobbies, and tricycles	9,269,096	2,374,450	6,068,356	1,564,698	3,513,194	990,276	802,283	1,461,031
Playground equipment	337,027	15,951	310,356	148,826	114,501	46,930	8,682	4,628

	total married couples	married couples, no children	married couples with children				single parent, at least one child <18	single person
			total	oldest child under 6	oldest child 6 to 17	oldest child 18 or older		
OTHER ENTERTAINMENT SUPPLIES, EQUIPMENT, SERVICES	**$38,485,260**	**$11,595,758**	**$24,419,390**	**$3,316,218**	**$14,243,916**	**$6,864,512**	**$1,224,187**	**$6,774,953**
Unmotored recreational vehicles	**3,764,129**	**1,679,060**	**1,775,191**	**500,339**	**796,034**	**478,624**	**87,625**	**661,761**
Boat without motor and boat trailers	1,403,249	861,839	541,252	47,815	430,938	62,440	–	381,455
Trailer and other attachable campers	2,360,879	817,221	1,233,939	452,524	365,096	416,184	87,625	280,306
Motorized recreational vehicles	14,449,415	4,614,122	8,943,326	956,913	5,276,026	2,710,141	355,546	1,042,555
Motorized camper	**4,360,538**	**1,830,252**	**2,530,353**	**–**	**1,204,315**	**1,325,940**		
Other vehicle	2,366,506	1,042,159	1,038,743	350,959	687,919	–	355,546	497,808
Motorboats	7,722,371	1,741,710	5,373,941	605,954	3,383,791	1,384,201	–	544,746
Rental of recreational vehicles	**167,670**	**85,768**	**67,944**	**7,045**	**43,185**	**17,679**	**202**	**38,344**
Outboard motors	**75,958**	**59,876**	**16,122**	**6,989**	**5,322**	**3,697**	**1,481**	**331**
Docking and landing fees	**614,414**	**255,916**	**339,434**	**27,125**	**133,661**	**178,560**	**7,268**	**75,365**
Sports, recreation, exercise equipment	**11,644,604**	**2,465,304**	**8,462,533**	**783,569**	**5,427,630**	**2,259,723**	**353,460**	**3,407,971**
Athletic gear, game tables, exercise equip.	5,090,295	937,897	3,863,330	219,606	2,656,640	988,267	123,899	910,996
Bicycles	993,077	172,229	702,764	179,723	405,544	117,326	51,754	310,386
Camping equipment	725,256	174,310	514,765	7,932	399,310	106,718	60,234	157,342
Hunting and fishing equipment	2,208,964	374,049	1,664,062	222,601	849,103	600,611	34,660	1,642,503
Winter sports equipment	443,931	85,999	323,024	2,552	242,536	77,788	29,276	99,826
Water sports equipment	771,393	318,797	439,623	12,814	363,728	63,243	20,796	98,504
Other sports equipment	1,255,835	358,329	853,048	133,128	433,371	286,564	31,564	151,392
Rental and repair of misc. sports equipment	155,854	43,924	101,917	5,214	77,399	19,367	1,346	36,691
Photographic equipment and supplies	**7,154,657**	**2,364,971**	**4,321,379**	**986,700**	**2,189,512**	**1,145,371**	**362,680**	**1,370,130**
Film	1,354,299	407,802	844,411	174,398	428,809	241,160	83,789	307,742
Other photographic supplies	234,625	179,165	47,504	15,809	9,884	22,019	–	331
Film processing	2,100,372	630,197	1,307,642	310,244	664,350	333,092	108,151	458,142
Repair and rental of photographic equipment	8,440	6,011	2,591	–	1,825	804	538	3,306
Photographic equipment	1,781,350	662,562	1,003,907	259,211	459,221	285,358	79,751	501,114
Photographer fees	1,675,572	479,005	1,115,325	227,039	625,271	262,858	90,519	99,826
Fireworks	**94,525**	**3,005**	**94,143**	**4,049**	**80,136**	**9,241**	**2,692**	**45,285**
Souvenirs	**87,773**	**13,640**	**68,520**	**23,575**	**23,873**	**21,054**	**25,843**	**15,205**
Visual goods	**118,719**	**36,526**	**38,867**	**–**	**34,822**	**3,616**	**–**	**3,306**
Pinball, electronic video games	**313,396**	**17,339**	**292,219**	**19,858**	**233,716**	**36,885**	**27,458**	**115,031**

Note: Total spending figures for total consumer units can be found on Total Spending by Age and Total Spending by Region tables. Spending by type of consumer unit will not add to total because not all types of consumer units are shown. (–) means sample is too small to make a reliable estimate.
Source: Calculations by New Strategist based on the 2002 Consumer Expenditure Survey

Table 3.12 Entertainment: Market shares by household type, 2002

(percentage of total annual spending on entertainment accounted for by types of consumer units, 2002)

	total married couples	married couples, no children	married couples with children				single parent, at least one child <18	single person
			total	oldest child under 6	oldest child 6 to 17	oldest child 18 or older		
Share of total consumer units	50.2%	20.6%	25.7%	4.9%	13.6%	7.2%	6.0%	29.5%
Share of total before-tax income	68.2	24.6	38.4	6.8	20.0	11.8	3.3	16.1
Share of total spending	64.6	23.1	36.5	6.4	19.4	10.7	4.5	17.5
Share of entertainment spending	66.7	22.5	39.7	5.8	23.4	10.5	3.9	16.9
FEES AND ADMISSIONS	**69.8%**	**23.4%**	**42.3%**	**5.1%**	**27.2%**	**10.0%**	**3.4%**	**17.4%**
Recreation expenses on trips	68.4	27.3	33.9	4.9	17.9	11.1	2.6	18.7
Social, recreation, civic club membership	70.7	26.8	41.8	5.8	25.8	10.2	2.0	17.8
Fees for participant sports	66.6	29.2	34.3	4.7	21.7	7.9	3.1	21.5
Participant sports on trips	72.1	32.0	36.0	5.2	21.5	9.3	1.5	20.3
Movie, theater, opera, ballet	60.2	20.3	35.6	3.9	21.2	10.5	4.2	22.5
Movie, other admissions on trips	73.6	30.2	39.7	5.3	23.6	10.8	2.3	15.6
Admission to sports events	68.7	20.9	45.9	5.6	27.9	12.4	2.9	17.8
Admission to sports events on trips	73.6	30.2	39.7	5.3	23.6	10.8	2.3	15.6
Fees for recreational lessons	80.3	8.2	66.1	5.6	51.4	9.0	6.6	6.5
Other entertainment services on trips	68.4	27.3	33.9	4.9	17.9	11.1	2.6	18.7
TELEVISION, RADIO, SOUND EQUIPMENT	**60.2**	**21.0**	**34.4**	**5.6**	**18.9**	**9.9**	**5.3**	**19.9**
Television	**59.9**	**22.6**	**32.5**	**5.6**	**17.4**	**9.5**	**5.3**	**20.2**
Cable service and community antenna	58.5	23.5	30.3	5.2	16.0	9.2	5.4	21.4
Black-and-white TV	84.1	9.3	66.4	5.9	42.0	18.5	0.1	7.4
Color TV, console	67.2	27.2	34.8	6.0	18.8	10.1	3.5	14.6
Color TV, portable, table model	62.8	23.6	34.6	7.5	15.8	11.3	5.0	19.6
VCRs and video disc players	65.3	21.7	38.3	6.4	22.6	9.2	3.5	17.2
Video cassettes, tapes, and discs	57.5	15.4	37.5	8.5	19.9	9.1	5.6	21.6
Video game hardware and software	61.5	10.6	46.2	4.9	30.7	10.6	8.4	12.8
Repair of TV, radio, and sound equipment	75.7	30.2	38.3	6.4	22.2	9.7	2.6	14.2
Rental of television sets	44.7	–	31.8	1.1	26.8	3.6	20.7	9.6
Radio and sound equipment	**61.1**	**14.9**	**41.2**	**5.5**	**24.4**	**11.3**	**5.5**	**18.8**
Radios	80.1	37.2	30.6	5.5	11.0	14.5	2.2	8.7
Tape recorders and players	38.8	6.4	32.9	4.5	7.9	21.1	8.7	39.9
Sound components and component systems	68.1	24.7	39.8	6.4	23.4	10.0	4.3	15.5
Miscellaneous sound equipment	43.4	4.9	39.5	2.2	36.4	0.4	1.1	51.4
Sound equipment accessories	75.7	16.9	56.7	10.8	28.3	17.7	3.0	12.3
Satellite dishes	76.8	10.5	47.8	10.7	27.9	9.1	–	5.0
Compact disc, tape, record, video mail order clubs	51.0	18.2	27.0	4.9	14.7	7.4	6.0	21.6
Records, CDs, audio tapes, needles	55.2	14.7	36.5	4.8	19.6	12.0	6.1	23.1
Rental of VCR, radio, sound equipment	52.2	32.2	11.3	–	8.7	2.6	15.6	–
Musical instruments and accessories	65.8	9.7	47.7	3.3	34.4	9.9	4.8	14.6
Rental and repair of musical instruments	79.0	9.8	66.1	1.7	56.8	7.6	13.3	2.7
Rental of video cassettes, tapes, discs, films	61.0	12.3	43.8	6.6	25.7	11.4	6.5	16.2
PETS, TOYS, PLAYGROUND EQUIPMENT	**67.3**	**24.8**	**38.0**	**6.5**	**22.2**	**9.2**	**4.3**	**16.1**
Pets	**65.6**	**28.3**	**33.6**	**3.5**	**20.0**	**10.0**	**3.4**	**18.7**
Pet food	63.0	27.5	31.4	4.1	17.9	9.4	3.7	20.8
Pet purchase, supplies, and medicines	67.9	29.2	34.5	2.1	26.5	5.7	3.6	15.3
Pet services	67.0	28.4	36.8	4.4	19.7	12.7	2.8	19.2
Veterinarian services	67.3	28.9	35.0	3.4	18.4	13.1	3.2	17.9
Toys, games, hobbies, and tricycles	**70.5**	**18.1**	**46.1**	**11.9**	**26.7**	**7.5**	**6.1**	**11.1**
Playground equipment	**84.9**	**4.0**	**78.2**	**37.5**	**28.9**	**11.8**	**2.2**	**1.2**

	total married couples	married couples, no children	married couples with children				single parent, at least one child <18	single person
			total	oldest child under 6	oldest child 6 to 17	oldest child 18 or older		
OTHER ENTERTAINMENT SUPPLIES, EQUIPMENT, SERVICES	**72.1%**	**21.7%**	**45.7%**	**6.2%**	**26.7%**	**12.9%**	**2.3%**	**12.7%**
Unmotored recreational vehicles	**71.2**	**31.8**	**33.6**	**9.5**	**15.1**	**9.1**	**1.7**	**12.5**
Boat without motor and boat trailers	77.5	47.6	29.9	2.6	23.8	3.4	–	21.1
Trailer and other attachable campers	68.0	23.5	35.5	13.0	10.5	12.0	2.5	8.1
Motorized recreational vehicles	**75.7**	**24.2**	**46.9**	**5.0**	**27.7**	**14.2**	**1.9**	**5.5**
Motorized camper	97.1	40.8	56.4	–	26.8	29.5	–	–
Other vehicle	59.5	26.2	26.1	8.8	17.3	–	8.9	12.5
Motorboats	72.8	16.4	50.6	5.7	31.9	13.0	–	5.1
Rental of recreational vehicles	**75.2**	**38.4**	**30.5**	**3.2**	**19.4**	**7.9**	**0.1**	**17.2**
Outboard motors	**95.4**	**75.2**	**20.3**	**8.8**	**6.7**	**4.6**	**1.9**	**0.4**
Docking and landing fees	**82.3**	**34.3**	**45.5**	**3.6**	**17.9**	**23.9**	**1.0**	**10.1**
Sports, recreation, exercise equipment	**69.1**	**14.6**	**50.2**	**4.6**	**32.2**	**13.4**	**2.1**	**20.2**
Athletic gear, game tables, exercise equipment	75.0	13.8	57.0	3.2	39.2	14.6	1.8	13.4
Bicycles	65.9	11.4	46.6	11.9	26.9	7.8	3.4	20.6
Camping equipment	67.5	16.2	47.9	0.7	37.1	9.9	5.6	14.6
Hunting and fishing equipment	55.2	9.4	41.6	5.6	21.2	15.0	0.9	41.1
Winter sports equipment	72.7	14.1	52.9	0.4	39.7	12.7	4.8	16.3
Water sports equipment	76.9	31.8	43.8	1.3	36.3	6.3	2.1	9.8
Other sports equipment	76.6	21.9	52.0	8.1	26.4	17.5	1.9	9.2
Rental and repair of misc. sports equipment	67.2	18.9	43.9	2.2	33.4	8.3	0.6	15.8
Photographic equipment and supplies	**70.5**	**23.3**	**42.6**	**9.7**	**21.6**	**11.3**	**3.6**	**13.5**
Film	68.1	20.5	42.5	8.8	21.6	12.1	4.2	15.5
Other photographic supplies	92.2	70.4	18.7	6.2	3.9	8.7	–	0.1
Film processing	70.4	21.1	43.9	10.4	22.3	11.2	3.6	15.4
Repair and rental of photographic equipment	62.7	44.7	19.3	–	13.6	6.0	4.0	24.6
Photographic equipment	68.1	25.3	38.4	9.9	17.6	10.9	3.0	19.2
Photographer fees	73.2	20.9	48.7	9.9	27.3	11.5	4.0	4.4
Fireworks	**55.5**	**1.8**	**55.2**	**2.4**	**47.0**	**5.4**	**1.6**	**26.6**
Souvenirs	**62.6**	**9.7**	**48.9**	**16.8**	**17.0**	**15.0**	**18.4**	**10.9**
Visual goods	**89.0**	**27.4**	**29.1**	**–**	**26.1**	**2.7**	**–**	**2.5**
Pinball, electronic video games	**57.8**	**3.2**	**53.9**	**3.7**	**43.1**	**6.8**	**5.1**	**21.2**

Note: Market share for total consumer units is 100.0%. Market shares by type of consumer unit will not add to total because not all types of consumer units are shown. (–) means sample is too small to make a reliable estimate.
Source: Calculations by New Strategist based on the 2002 Consumer Expenditure Survey

Table 3.13 Entertainment: Average spending by race and Hispanic origin, 2002

(average annual spending of consumer units (CU) on entertainment, by race and Hispanic origin of consumer unit reference person, 2002)

	total consumer units	race		Hispanic origin	
		black	white and other	Hispanic	non-Hispanic
Number of consumer units (in thousands, add 000)	112,108	13,554	98,553	10,500	101,608
Average number of persons per CU	2.5	2.7	2.5	3.3	2.4
Average before-tax income of CU	$49,430.00	$35,944.00	$51,177.00	$37,360.00	$50,742.00
Average spending of CU, total	40,676.60	30,135.94	42,134.55	34,742.47	41,294.67
Entertainment, average spending	2,078.99	1,123.57	2,210.93	1,409.49	2,148.49
FEES AND ADMISSIONS	**$541.67**	**$202.89**	**$588.27**	**$289.33**	**$567.75**
Recreation expenses on trips	25.64	9.19	27.90	21.42	26.07
Social, recreation, civic club membership	107.92	34.12	118.07	39.64	114.97
Fees for participant sports	75.05	20.58	82.54	28.26	79.88
Participant sports on trips	29.50	5.19	32.84	10.93	31.42
Movie, theater, opera, ballet	98.30	56.53	104.05	76.66	100.54
Movie, other admissions on trips	45.57	16.20	49.61	27.34	47.46
Admission to sports events	36.18	16.83	38.84	10.40	38.84
Admission to sports events on trips	15.19	5.40	16.53	9.11	15.82
Fees for recreational lessons	82.69	29.65	89.99	44.14	86.67
Other entertainment services on trips	25.64	9.19	27.90	21.42	26.07
TELEVISION, RADIO, SOUND EQUIPMENT	**691.90**	**639.70**	**699.04**	**564.70**	**704.94**
Television	**543.66**	**533.11**	**545.11**	**437.63**	**554.61**
Cable service and community antenna	382.28	404.73	379.20	297.63	391.03
Black-and-white TV	0.80	1.34	0.72	0.68	0.81
Color TV, console	38.63	14.27	41.98	19.98	40.56
Color TV, portable, table model	39.14	44.23	38.44	44.31	38.61
VCRs and video disc players	23.25	16.52	24.18	24.05	23.17
Video cassettes, tapes, and discs	33.13	24.71	34.29	26.83	33.78
Video game hardware and software	23.46	25.53	23.18	21.82	23.63
Repair of TV, radio, and sound equipment	2.50	1.10	2.69	1.90	2.56
Rental of television sets	0.46	0.68	0.43	0.44	0.46
Radio and sound equipment	**148.25**	**106.59**	**153.93**	**127.07**	**150.33**
Radios	3.98	0.74	4.44	0.32	4.32
Tape recorders and players	5.31	13.68	4.12	4.35	5.40
Sound components and component systems	20.19	9.83	21.62	25.36	19.66
Miscellaneous sound equipment	3.18	11.58	1.99	–	3.48
Sound equipment accessories	5.97	2.70	6.43	1.77	6.36
Satellite dishes	1.00	0.77	1.03	0.85	1.02
Compact disc, tape, record, video mail order clubs	6.53	5.66	6.65	8.26	6.36
Records, CDs, audio tapes, needles	36.47	31.07	37.21	33.70	36.75
Rental of VCR, radio, sound equipment	0.25	0.07	0.27	–	0.28
Musical instruments and accessories	24.82	2.34	27.91	11.66	26.18
Rental and repair of musical instruments	1.22	0.67	1.30	0.67	1.28
Rental of video cassettes, tapes, discs, films	39.33	27.47	40.96	40.12	39.25
PETS, TOYS, PLAYGROUND EQUIPMENT	**369.12**	**172.00**	**396.53**	**217.05**	**384.27**
Pets	**248.25**	**97.68**	**269.25**	**134.15**	**259.47**
Pet food	102.56	38.45	111.64	63.47	106.25
Pet purchase, supplies, and medicines	52.29	42.86	53.63	28.83	54.51
Pet services	21.95	5.05	24.27	9.66	23.22
Veterinarian services	71.44	11.32	79.71	32.19	75.50
Toys, games, hobbies, and tricycles	**117.34**	**73.94**	**123.30**	**80.62**	**121.13**
Playground equipment	**3.54**	**0.38**	**3.97**	**2.28**	**3.67**

	total consumer units	race		Hispanic origin	
		black	white and other	Hispanic	non-Hispanic
OTHER ENTERTAINMENT SUPPLIES, EQUIPMENT, SERVICES	$476.30	$108.99	$527.09	$338.41	$491.52
Unmotored recreational vehicles	47.14	–	53.63	5.51	51.45
Boat without motor and boat trailers	16.15	–	18.37	2.90	17.52
Trailer and other attachable campers	30.99	–	35.26	2.61	33.93
Motorized recreational vehicles	170.19	3.12	193.17	32.64	184.41
Motorized camper	40.05	–	45.56	–	44.19
Other vehicle	35.47	3.12	39.92	22.16	36.85
Motorboats	94.67	–	107.69	10.48	103.37
Rental of recreational vehicles	1.99	0.16	2.24	1.66	2.02
Outboard motors	0.71	–	0.81	–	0.78
Docking and landing fees	6.66	0.30	7.53	0.82	7.26
Sports, recreation, exercise equipment	150.33	66.64	162.08	230.25	143.02
Athletic gear, game tables, exercise equipment	60.51	34.79	64.16	57.19	60.83
Bicycles	13.45	8.76	14.10	8.09	14.00
Camping equipment	9.59	9.03	9.67	7.21	9.82
Hunting and fishing equipment	35.68	2.22	40.41	147.27	25.15
Winter sports equipment	5.45	0.28	6.16	3.50	5.65
Water sports equipment	8.95	0.19	10.16	2.85	9.58
Other sports equipment	14.62	11.01	15.11	3.79	15.74
Rental and repair of misc. sports equipment	2.07	0.36	2.31	0.35	2.25
Photographic equipment and supplies	90.48	35.19	98.09	55.17	94.13
Film	17.74	8.30	19.04	12.42	18.29
Other photographic supplies	2.27	0.87	2.46	1.48	2.34
Film processing	26.60	9.41	28.96	16.87	27.60
Repair and rental of photographic equipment	0.12	0.06	0.13	0.06	0.12
Photographic equipment	23.34	11.24	25.01	12.58	24.45
Photographer fees	20.42	5.31	22.50	11.76	21.32
Fireworks	1.52	1.13	1.57	6.79	1.02
Souvenirs	1.25	–	1.43	0.79	1.29
Visual goods	1.19	–	1.36	0.82	1.23
Pinball, electronic video games	4.84	2.45	5.18	3.96	4.92

Note: Other races include Asians, Native Americans, and Pacific Islanders. (–) means sample is too small to make a reliable estimate.
Source: Bureau of Labor Statistics, unpublished data from the 2002 Consumer Expenditure Survey

Table 3.14 Entertainment: Indexed spending by race and Hispanic origin, 2002

(indexed average annual spending of consumer units (CU) on entertainment by race and Hispanic origin of consumer unit reference person, 2002; index definition: an index of 100 is the average for all consumer units; an index of 132 means that spending by consumer units in that group is 32 percent above the average for all consumer units; an index of 68 indicates spending that is 32 percent below the average for all consumer units)

	total consumer units	race black	race white and other	Hispanic origin Hispanic	Hispanic origin non-Hispanic
Average spending of CU, total	$40,677	$30,136	$42,135	$34,742	$41,295
Average spending of CU, index	100	74	104	85	102
Entertainment, spending index	100	54	106	68	103
FEES AND ADMISSIONS	100	37	109	53	105
Recreation expenses on trips	100	36	109	84	102
Social, recreation, civic club membership	100	32	109	37	107
Fees for participant sports	100	27	110	38	106
Participant sports on trips	100	18	111	37	107
Movie, theater, opera, ballet	100	58	106	78	102
Movie, other admissions on trips	100	36	109	60	104
Admission to sports events	100	47	107	29	107
Admission to sports events on trips	100	36	109	60	104
Fees for recreational lessons	100	36	109	53	105
Other entertainment services on trips	100	36	109	84	102
TELEVISION, RADIO, SOUND EQUIPMENT	100	92	101	82	102
Television	100	98	100	80	102
Cable service and community antenna	100	106	99	78	102
Black-and-white TV	100	168	90	85	101
Color TV, console	100	37	109	52	105
Color TV, portable, table model	100	113	98	113	99
VCRs and video disc players	100	71	104	103	100
Video cassettes, tapes, and discs	100	75	104	81	102
Video game hardware and software	100	109	99	93	101
Repair of TV, radio, and sound equipment	100	44	108	76	102
Rental of television sets	100	148	93	96	100
Radio and sound equipment	100	72	104	86	101
Radios	100	19	112	8	109
Tape recorders and players	100	258	78	82	102
Sound components and component systems	100	49	107	126	97
Miscellaneous sound equipment	100	364	63	–	109
Sound equipment accessories	100	45	108	30	107
Satellite dishes	100	77	103	85	102
Compact disc, tape, record, video mail order clubs	100	87	102	126	97
Records, CDs, audio tapes, needles	100	85	102	92	101
Rental of VCR, radio, sound equipment	100	28	108	–	112
Musical instruments and accessories	100	9	112	47	105
Rental and repair of musical instruments	100	55	107	55	105
Rental of video cassettes, tapes, discs, films	100	70	104	102	100
PETS, TOYS, PLAYGROUND EQUIPMENT	100	47	107	59	104
Pets	100	39	108	54	105
Pet food	100	37	109	62	104
Pet purchase, supplies, and medicines	100	82	103	55	104
Pet services	100	23	111	44	106
Veterinarian services	100	16	112	45	106
Toys, games, hobbies, and tricycles	100	63	105	69	103
Playground equipment	100	11	112	64	104

	total consumer units	race		Hispanic origin	
		black	white and other	Hispanic	non-Hispanic
OTHER ENTERTAINMENT SUPPLIES, EQUIPMENT, SERVICES	100	23	111	71	103
Unmotored recreational vehicles	100	–	114	12	109
Boat without motor and boat trailers	100	–	114	18	108
Trailer and other attachable campers	100	–	114	8	109
Motorized recreational vehicles	100	2	114	19	108
Motorized camper	100	–	114	–	110
Other vehicle	100	9	113	62	104
Motorboats	100	–	114	11	109
Rental of recreational vehicles	100	8	113	83	102
Outboard motors	100	–	114	–	110
Docking and landing fees	100	5	113	12	109
Sports, recreation, exercise equipment	100	44	108	153	95
Athletic gear, game tables, exercise equipment	100	57	106	95	101
Bicycles	100	65	105	60	104
Camping equipment	100	94	101	75	102
Hunting and fishing equipment	100	6	113	413	70
Winter sports equipment	100	5	113	64	104
Water sports equipment	100	2	114	32	107
Other sports equipment	100	75	103	26	108
Rental and repair of misc. sports equipment	100	17	112	17	109
Photographic equipment and supplies	100	39	108	61	104
Film	100	47	107	70	103
Other photographic supplies	100	38	108	65	103
Film processing	100	35	109	63	104
Repair and rental of photographic equipment	100	50	108	50	100
Photographic equipment	100	48	107	54	105
Photographer fees	100	26	110	58	104
Fireworks	100	74	103	447	67
Souvenirs	100	–	114	63	103
Visual goods	100	–	114	69	103
Pinball, electronic video games	100	51	107	82	102

Note: Other races include Asians, Native Americans, and Pacific Islanders. (–) means sample is too small to make a reliable estimate.
Source: Calculations by New Strategist based on the 2002 Consumer Expenditure Survey

Table 3.15 Entertainment: Total spending by race and Hispanic origin, 2002

(total annual spending on entertainment, by consumer unit race and Hispanic origin groups, 2002; numbers in thousands)

	total consumer units	race black	race white and other	Hispanic origin Hispanic	Hispanic origin non-Hispanic
Number of consumer units	112,108	13,554	98,553	10,500	101,608
Total spending of all consumer units	$4,560,172,273	$408,462,531	$4,152,486,306	$364,795,935	$4,195,868,829
Entertainment, total spending	233,071,411	15,228,868	217,893,784	14,799,645	218,303,772
FEES AND ADMISSIONS	**$60,725,540**	**$2,749,971**	**$57,975,773**	**$3,037,965**	**$57,687,942**
Recreation expenses on trips	2,874,449	124,561	2,749,629	224,910	2,648,921
Social, recreation, civic club membership	12,098,695	462,462	11,636,153	416,220	11,681,872
Fees for participant sports	8,413,705	278,941	8,134,565	296,730	8,116,447
Participant sports on trips	3,307,186	70,345	3,236,481	114,765	3,192,523
Movie, theater, opera, ballet	11,020,216	766,208	10,254,440	804,930	10,215,668
Movie, other admissions on trips	5,108,762	219,575	4,889,214	287,070	4,822,316
Admission to sports events	4,056,067	228,114	3,827,799	109,200	3,946,455
Admission to sports events on trips	1,702,921	73,192	1,629,081	95,655	1,607,439
Fees for recreational lessons	9,270,211	401,876	8,868,784	463,470	8,806,365
Other entertainment services on trips	2,874,449	124,561	2,749,629	224,910	2,648,921
TELEVISION, RADIO, SOUND EQUIPMENT	**77,567,525**	**8,670,494**	**68,892,489**	**5,929,350**	**71,627,544**
Television	**60,948,635**	**7,225,773**	**53,722,226**	**4,595,115**	**56,352,813**
Cable service and community antenna	42,856,646	5,485,710	37,371,298	3,125,115	39,731,776
Black-and-white TV	89,686	18,162	70,958	7,140	82,302
Color TV, console	4,330,732	193,416	4,137,255	209,790	4,121,220
Color TV, portable, table model	4,387,907	599,493	3,788,377	465,255	3,923,085
VCRs and video disc players	2,606,511	223,912	2,383,012	252,525	2,354,257
Video cassettes, tapes, and discs	3,714,138	334,919	3,379,382	281,715	3,432,318
Video game hardware and software	2,630,054	346,034	2,284,459	229,110	2,400,997
Repair of TV, radio, and sound equipment	280,270	14,909	265,108	19,950	260,116
Rental of television sets	51,570	9,217	42,378	4,620	46,740
Radio and sound equipment	**16,620,011**	**1,444,721**	**15,170,263**	**1,334,235**	**15,274,731**
Radios	446,190	10,030	437,575	3,360	438,947
Tape recorders and players	595,293	185,419	406,038	45,675	548,683
Sound components and component systems	2,263,461	133,236	2,130,716	266,280	1,997,613
Miscellaneous sound equipment	356,503	156,955	196,120	–	353,596
Sound equipment accessories	669,285	36,596	633,696	18,585	646,227
Satellite dishes	112,108	10,437	101,510	8,925	103,640
Compact disc, tape, record, video mail order clubs	732,065	76,716	655,377	86,730	646,227
Records, CDs, audio tapes, needles	4,088,579	421,123	3,667,157	353,850	3,734,094
Rental of VCR, radio, sound equipment	28,027	949	26,609	–	28,450
Musical instruments and accessories	2,782,521	31,716	2,750,614	122,430	2,660,097
Rental and repair of musical instruments	136,772	9,081	128,119	7,035	130,058
Rental of video cassettes, tapes, discs, films	4,409,208	372,328	4,036,731	421,260	3,988,114
PETS, TOYS, PLAYGROUND EQUIPMENT	**41,381,305**	**2,331,288**	**39,079,221**	**2,279,025**	**39,044,906**
Pets	**27,830,811**	**1,323,955**	**26,535,395**	**1,408,575**	**26,364,228**
Pet food	11,497,796	521,151	11,002,457	666,435	10,795,850
Pet purchase, supplies, and medicines	5,862,127	580,924	5,285,397	302,715	5,538,652
Pet services	2,460,771	68,448	2,391,881	101,430	2,359,338
Veterinarian services	8,008,996	153,431	7,855,660	337,995	7,671,404
Toys, games, hobbies, and tricycles	**13,154,753**	**1,002,183**	**12,151,585**	**846,510**	**12,307,777**
Playground equipment	**396,862**	**5,151**	**391,255**	**23,940**	**372,901**

	total consumer units	race		Hispanic origin	
		black	white and other	Hispanic	non-Hispanic
OTHER ENTERTAINMENT SUPPLIES, EQUIPMENT, SERVICES	**$53,397,040**	**$1,477,250**	**$51,946,301**	**$3,553,305**	**$49,942,364**
Unmotored recreational vehicles	**5,284,771**	–	**5,285,397**	**57,855**	**5,227,732**
Boat without motor and boat trailers	1,810,544	–	1,810,419	30,450	1,780,172
Trailer and other attachable campers	3,474,227	–	3,474,979	27,405	3,447,559
Motorized recreational vehicles	**19,079,661**	**42,288**	**19,037,483**	**342,720**	**18,737,531**
Motorized camper	4,489,925	–	4,490,075	–	4,490,058
Other vehicle	3,976,471	42,288	3,934,236	232,680	3,744,255
Motorboats	10,613,264	–	10,613,173	110,040	10,503,219
Rental of recreational vehicles	**223,095**	**2,169**	**220,759**	**17,430**	**205,248**
Outboard motors	**79,597**	–	**79,828**	–	**79,254**
Docking and landing fees	**746,639**	**4,066**	**742,104**	**8,610**	**737,674**
Sports, recreation, exercise equipment	**16,853,196**	**903,239**	**15,973,470**	**2,417,625**	**14,531,976**
Athletic gear, game tables, exercise equipment	6,783,655	471,544	6,323,160	600,495	6,180,815
Bicycles	1,507,853	118,733	1,389,597	84,945	1,422,512
Camping equipment	1,075,116	122,393	953,008	75,705	997,791
Hunting and fishing equipment	4,000,013	30,090	3,982,527	1,546,335	2,555,441
Winter sports equipment	610,989	3,795	607,086	36,750	574,085
Water sports equipment	1,003,367	2,575	1,001,298	29,925	973,405
Other sports equipment	1,639,019	149,230	1,489,136	39,795	1,599,310
Rental and repair of misc. sports equipment	232,064	4,879	227,657	3,675	228,618
Photographic equipment and supplies	**10,143,532**	**476,965**	**9,667,064**	**579,285**	**9,564,361**
Film	1,988,796	112,498	1,876,449	130,410	1,858,410
Other photographic supplies	254,485	11,792	242,440	15,540	237,763
Film processing	2,982,073	127,543	2,854,095	177,135	2,804,381
Repair and rental of photographic equipment	13,453	813	12,812	630	12,193
Photographic equipment	2,616,601	152,347	2,464,811	132,090	2,484,316
Photographer fees	2,289,245	71,972	2,217,443	123,480	2,166,283
Fireworks	**170,404**	**15,316**	**154,728**	**71,295**	**103,640**
Souvenirs	**140,135**	–	**140,931**	**8,295**	**131,074**
Visual goods	**133,409**	–	**134,032**	**8,610**	**124,978**
Pinball, electronic video games	**542,603**	**33,207**	**510,505**	**41,580**	**499,911**

Note: Other races include Asians, Native Americans, and Pacific Islanders. Numbers may not add to total because of rounding. (–) means sample is too small to make a reliable estimate.
Source: Calculations by New Strategist based on the 2002 Consumer Expenditure Survey

Table 3.16 Entertainment: Market shares by race and Hispanic origin, 2002

(percentage of total annual spending on entertainment accounted for by consumer unit race and Hispanic origin groups, 2002)

	total consumer units	race black	race white and other	Hispanic origin Hispanic	Hispanic origin non-Hispanic
Share of total consumer units	100.0%	12.1%	87.9%	9.4%	90.6%
Share of total before-tax income	100.0	8.8	91.0	7.1	93.0
Share of total spending	100.0	9.0	91.1	8.0	92.0
Share of entertainment spending	100.0	6.5	93.5	6.3	93.7
FEES AND ADMISSIONS	100.0%	4.5%	95.5%	5.0%	95.0%
Recreation expenses on trips	100.0	4.3	95.7	7.8	92.2
Social, recreation, civic club membership	100.0	3.8	96.2	3.4	96.6
Fees for participant sports	100.0	3.3	96.7	3.5	96.5
Participant sports on trips	100.0	2.1	97.9	3.5	96.5
Movie, theater, opera, ballet	100.0	7.0	93.1	7.3	92.7
Movie, other admissions on trips	100.0	4.3	95.7	5.6	94.4
Admission to sports events	100.0	5.6	94.4	2.7	97.3
Admission to sports events on trips	100.0	4.3	95.7	5.6	94.4
Fees for recreational lessons	100.0	4.3	95.7	5.0	95.0
Other entertainment services on trips	100.0	4.3	95.7	7.8	92.2
TELEVISION, RADIO, SOUND EQUIPMENT	100.0	11.2	88.8	7.6	92.3
Television	100.0	11.9	88.1	7.5	92.5
Cable service and community antenna	100.0	12.8	87.2	7.3	92.7
Black-and-white TV	100.0	20.3	79.1	8.0	91.8
Color TV, console	100.0	4.5	95.5	4.8	95.2
Color TV, portable, table model	100.0	13.7	86.3	10.6	89.4
VCRs and video disc players	100.0	8.6	91.4	9.7	90.3
Video cassettes, tapes, and discs	100.0	9.0	91.0	7.6	92.4
Video game hardware and software	100.0	13.2	86.9	8.7	91.3
Repair of TV, radio, and sound equipment	100.0	5.3	94.6	7.1	92.8
Rental of television sets	100.0	17.9	82.2	9.0	90.6
Radio and sound equipment	100.0	8.7	91.3	8.0	91.9
Radios	100.0	2.2	98.1	0.8	98.4
Tape recorders and players	100.0	31.1	68.2	7.7	92.2
Sound components and component systems	100.0	5.9	94.1	11.8	88.3
Miscellaneous sound equipment	100.0	44.0	55.0	–	99.2
Sound equipment accessories	100.0	5.5	94.7	2.8	96.6
Satellite dishes	100.0	9.3	90.5	8.0	92.4
Compact disc, tape, record, video mail order clubs	100.0	10.5	89.5	11.8	88.3
Records, CDs, audio tapes, needles	100.0	10.3	89.7	8.7	91.3
Rental of VCR, radio, sound equipment	100.0	3.4	94.9	–	100.0
Musical instruments and accessories	100.0	1.1	98.9	4.4	95.6
Rental and repair of musical instruments	100.0	6.6	93.7	5.1	95.1
Rental of video cassettes, tapes, discs, films	100.0	8.4	91.6	9.6	90.4
PETS, TOYS, PLAYGROUND EQUIPMENT	100.0	5.6	94.4	5.5	94.4
Pets	100.0	4.8	95.3	5.1	94.7
Pet food	100.0	4.5	95.7	5.8	93.9
Pet purchase, supplies, and medicines	100.0	9.9	90.2	5.2	94.5
Pet services	100.0	2.8	97.2	4.1	95.9
Veterinarian services	100.0	1.9	98.1	4.2	95.8
Toys, games, hobbies, and tricycles	100.0	7.6	92.4	6.4	93.6
Playground equipment	100.0	1.3	98.6	6.0	94.0

	total consumer units	race		Hispanic origin	
		black	white and other	Hispanic	non-Hispanic
OTHER ENTERTAINMENT SUPPLIES, EQUIPMENT, SERVICES	**100.0%**	**2.8%**	**97.3%**	**6.7%**	**93.5%**
Unmotored recreational vehicles	**100.0**	**–**	**100.0**	**1.1**	**98.9**
Boat without motor and boat trailers	100.0	–	100.0	1.7	98.3
Trailer and other attachable campers	100.0	–	100.0	0.8	99.2
Motorized recreational vehicles	**100.0**	**0.2**	**99.8**	**1.8**	**98.2**
Motorized camper	100.0	–	100.0	–	100.0
Other vehicle	100.0	1.1	98.9	5.9	94.2
Motorboats	100.0	–	100.0	1.0	99.0
Rental of recreational vehicles	**100.0**	**1.0**	**99.0**	**7.8**	**92.0**
Outboard motors	**100.0**	**–**	**100.0**	**–**	**99.6**
Docking and landing fees	**100.0**	**0.5**	**99.4**	**1.2**	**98.8**
Sports, recreation, exercise equipment	**100.0**	**5.4**	**94.8**	**14.3**	**86.2**
Athletic gear, game tables, exercise equipment	100.0	7.0	93.2	8.9	91.1
Bicycles	100.0	7.9	92.2	5.6	94.3
Camping equipment	100.0	11.4	88.6	7.0	92.8
Hunting and fishing equipment	100.0	0.8	99.6	38.7	63.9
Winter sports equipment	100.0	0.6	99.4	6.0	94.0
Water sports equipment	100.0	0.3	99.8	3.0	97.0
Other sports equipment	100.0	9.1	90.9	2.4	97.6
Rental and repair of misc. sports equipment	100.0	2.1	98.1	1.6	98.5
Photographic equipment and supplies	**100.0**	**4.7**	**95.3**	**5.7**	**94.3**
Film	100.0	5.7	94.4	6.6	93.4
Other photographic supplies	100.0	4.6	95.3	6.1	93.4
Film processing	100.0	4.3	95.7	5.9	94.0
Repair and rental of photographic equipment	100.0	6.0	95.2	4.7	90.6
Photographic equipment	100.0	5.8	94.2	5.0	94.9
Photographer fees	100.0	3.1	96.9	5.4	94.6
Fireworks	**100.0**	**9.0**	**90.8**	**41.8**	**60.8**
Souvenirs	**100.0**	**–**	**100.0**	**5.9**	**93.5**
Visual goods	**100.0**	**–**	**100.0**	**6.5**	**93.7**
Pinball, electronic video games	**100.0**	**6.1**	**94.1**	**7.7**	**92.1**

Note: Other races include Asians, Native Americans, and Pacific Islanders. Numbers may not add to total because of rounding. (–) means sample is too small to make a reliable estimate.
Source: Calculations by New Strategist based on the 2002 Consumer Expenditure Survey

Table 3.17 Entertainment: Average spending by region, 2002

(average annual spending of consumer units (CU) on entertainment, by region in which consumer unit lives, 2002)

	total consumer units	Northeast	Midwest	South	West
Number of consumer units (in thousands, add 000)	112,108	21,313	25,883	40,004	24,907
Average number of persons per CU	2.5	2.5	2.5	2.5	2.6
Average before-tax income of CU	$49,430.00	$53,983.00	$49,197.00	$45,641.00	$52,016.00
Average spending of CU, total	40,676.60	42,390.20	40,601.14	37,280.55	44,728.34
Entertainment, average spending	2,078.99	2,287.23	2,143.41	1,704.58	2,435.58
FEES AND ADMISSIONS	**$541.67**	**$657.22**	**$538.13**	**$418.90**	**$643.67**
Recreation expenses on trips	25.64	27.90	27.31	21.27	28.96
Social, recreation, civic club membership	107.92	134.39	107.54	91.45	112.11
Fees for participant sports	75.05	82.70	77.68	57.83	93.42
Participant sports on trips	29.50	32.84	28.44	21.85	40.02
Movie, theater, opera, ballet	98.30	121.95	95.03	67.49	130.96
Movie, other admissions on trips	45.57	55.04	45.61	36.45	52.07
Admission to sports events	36.18	36.63	40.14	31.24	39.61
Admission to sports events on trips	15.19	18.34	15.20	12.15	17.36
Fees for recreational lessons	82.69	119.52	73.86	57.89	100.19
Other entertainment services on trips	25.64	27.90	27.31	21.27	28.96
TELEVISION, RADIO, SOUND EQUIPMENT	**691.90**	**725.01**	**687.55**	**642.54**	**747.35**
Television	**543.66**	**592.17**	**545.07**	**529.75**	**523.00**
Cable service and community antenna	382.28	445.89	367.94	383.63	340.60
Black-and-white TV	0.80	0.98	0.88	1.03	0.18
Color TV, console	38.63	30.58	49.36	35.39	39.57
Color TV, portable, table model	39.14	38.22	37.91	37.69	43.54
VCRs and video disc players	23.25	23.19	26.53	19.08	26.60
Video cassettes, tapes, and discs	33.13	24.88	36.22	27.59	45.87
Video game hardware and software	23.46	24.78	23.55	22.40	23.95
Repair of TV, radio, and sound equipment	2.50	2.27	2.43	2.60	2.62
Rental of television sets	0.46	1.39	0.25	0.35	0.06
Radio and sound equipment	**148.25**	**132.83**	**142.48**	**112.79**	**224.35**
Radios	3.98	3.89	4.84	1.66	6.85
Tape recorders and players	5.31	3.22	7.97	5.07	4.75
Sound components and component systems	20.19	26.53	18.60	12.71	28.44
Miscellaneous sound equipment	3.18	7.44	2.19	1.70	2.81
Sound equipment accessories	5.97	3.35	7.46	6.44	5.96
Satellite dishes	1.00	0.43	0.83	1.01	1.65
Compact disc, tape, record, video mail order clubs	6.53	5.77	5.53	5.22	10.34
Records, CDs, audio tapes, needles	36.47	34.68	38.05	29.58	47.40
Rental of VCR, radio, sound equipment	0.25	–	0.81	0.06	0.19
Musical instruments and accessories	24.82	15.39	14.22	13.56	61.99
Rental and repair of musical instruments	1.22	1.03	2.01	0.68	1.44
Rental of video cassettes, tapes, discs, films	39.33	31.10	39.97	35.10	52.52
PETS, TOYS, PLAYGROUND EQUIPMENT	**369.12**	**362.78**	**403.47**	**340.93**	**384.50**
Pets	**248.25**	**237.02**	**252.71**	**238.25**	**269.64**
Pet food	102.56	100.65	99.58	100.73	110.24
Pet purchase, supplies, and medicines	52.29	37.84	64.11	54.52	49.20
Pet services	21.95	23.86	19.05	17.40	30.62
Veterinarian services	71.44	74.67	69.97	65.61	79.58
Toys, games, hobbies, and tricycles	**117.34**	**122.33**	**147.31**	**98.62**	**111.97**
Playground equipment	**3.54**	**3.43**	**3.45**	**4.05**	**2.89**

	total consumer units	Northeast	Midwest	South	West
OTHER ENTERTAINMENT SUPPLIES, EQUIPMENT, SERVICES	**$476.30**	**$542.22**	**$514.26**	**$302.20**	**$660.06**
Unmotored recreational vehicles	**47.14**	**29.34**	**98.19**	**12.84**	**64.43**
Boat without motor and boat trailers	16.15	17.69	26.41	5.18	21.79
Trailer and other attachable campers	30.99	11.65	71.79	7.66	42.64
Motorized recreational vehicles	170.19	265.79	185.44	88.30	204.07
Motorized camper	**40.05**	**20.31**	**69.77**	**2.64**	**86.16**
Other vehicle	35.47	49.24	52.10	23.59	25.50
Motorboats	94.67	196.24	63.58	62.07	92.41
Rental of recreational vehicles	**1.99**	**3.83**	**1.36**	**1.66**	**1.59**
Outboard motors	**0.71**	**0.27**	**2.36**	**0.07**	**0.39**
Docking and landing fees	**6.66**	**7.09**	**4.35**	**3.89**	**13.13**
Sports, recreation, exercise equipment	**150.33**	**128.29**	**112.33**	**116.12**	**263.65**
Athletic gear, game tables, exercise equipment	60.51	62.31	51.86	51.06	82.93
Bicycles	13.45	10.84	9.88	13.73	18.94
Camping equipment	9.59	6.90	6.42	6.28	20.53
Hunting and fishing equipment	35.68	9.80	21.27	23.88	92.01
Winter sports equipment	5.45	12.64	2.95	1.14	8.80
Water sports equipment	8.95	6.88	4.67	5.52	20.70
Other sports equipment	14.62	17.60	12.83	12.87	16.73
Rental and repair of misc. sports equipment	2.07	1.32	2.45	1.65	3.01
Photographic equipment and supplies	**90.48**	**98.31**	**101.05**	**73.60**	**99.92**
Film	17.74	19.57	18.70	14.85	19.81
Other photographic supplies	2.27	0.82	1.11	0.63	7.32
Film processing	26.60	29.31	29.60	21.00	30.13
Repair and rental of photographic equipment	0.12	0.01	0.03	0.12	0.29
Photographic equipment	23.34	25.95	23.87	19.40	26.89
Photographer fees	20.42	22.65	27.73	17.59	15.47
Fireworks	**1.52**	**0.31**	**1.88**	**1.14**	**2.80**
Souvenirs	**1.25**	**1.05**	**2.07**	**0.39**	**1.94**
Visual goods	**1.19**	**1.45**	**2.47**	**0.86**	**0.17**
Pinball, electronic video games	**4.84**	**6.47**	**2.77**	**3.33**	**7.97**

Note: (–) means sample is too small to make a reliable estimate.
Source: Bureau of Labor Statistics, unpublished data from the 2002 Consumer Expenditure Survey

Table 3.18 Entertainment: Indexed spending by region, 2002

(indexed average annual spending of consumer units (CU) on entertainment by region in which consumer unit lives, 2002; index definition: an index of 100 is the average for all consumer units; an index of 132 means that spending by consumer units in that group is 32 percent above the average for all consumer units; an index of 68 indicates spending that is 32 percent below the average for all consumer units)

	total consumer units	Northeast	Midwest	South	West
Average spending of CU, total	$40,677	$42,390	$40,601	$37,281	$44,728
Average spending of CU, index	100	104	100	92	110
Entertainment, spending index	100	110	103	82	117
FEES AND ADMISSIONS	100	121	99	77	119
Recreation expenses on trips	100	109	107	83	113
Social, recreation, civic club membership	100	125	100	85	104
Fees for participant sports	100	110	104	77	124
Participant sports on trips	100	111	96	74	136
Movie, theater, opera, ballet	100	124	97	69	133
Movie, other admissions on trips	100	121	100	80	114
Admission to sports events	100	101	111	86	109
Admission to sports events on trips	100	121	100	80	114
Fees for recreational lessons	100	145	89	70	121
Other entertainment services on trips	100	109	107	83	113
TELEVISION, RADIO, SOUND EQUIPMENT	100	105	99	93	108
Television	100	109	100	97	96
Cable service and community antenna	100	117	96	100	89
Black-and-white TV	100	123	110	129	23
Color TV, console	100	79	128	92	102
Color TV, portable, table model	100	98	97	96	111
VCRs and video disc players	100	100	114	82	114
Video cassettes, tapes, and discs	100	75	109	83	138
Video game hardware and software	100	106	100	95	102
Repair of TV, radio, and sound equipment	100	91	97	104	105
Rental of television sets	100	302	54	76	13
Radio and sound equipment	100	90	96	76	151
Radios	100	98	122	42	172
Tape recorders and players	100	61	150	95	89
Sound components and component systems	100	131	92	63	141
Miscellaneous sound equipment	100	234	69	53	88
Sound equipment accessories	100	56	125	108	100
Satellite dishes	100	43	83	101	165
Compact disc, tape, record, video mail order clubs	100	88	85	80	158
Records, CDs, audio tapes, needles	100	95	104	81	130
Rental of VCR, radio, sound equipment	100	–	324	24	76
Musical instruments and accessories	100	62	57	55	250
Rental and repair of musical instruments	100	84	165	56	118
Rental of video cassettes, tapes, discs, films	100	79	102	89	134
PETS, TOYS, PLAYGROUND EQUIPMENT	100	98	109	92	104
Pets	100	95	102	96	109
Pet food	100	98	97	98	107
Pet purchase, supplies, and medicines	100	72	123	104	94
Pet services	100	109	87	79	139
Veterinarian services	100	105	98	92	111
Toys, games, hobbies, and tricycles	100	104	126	84	95
Playground equipment	100	97	97	114	82

	total consumer units	Northeast	Midwest	South	West
OTHER ENTERTAINMENT SUPPLIES, EQUIPMENT, SERVICES	**100**	**114**	**108**	**63**	**139**
Unmotored recreational vehicles	**100**	**62**	**208**	**27**	**137**
Boat without motor and boat trailers	100	110	164	32	135
Trailer and other attachable campers	100	38	232	25	138
Motorized recreational vehicles	**100**	**156**	**109**	**52**	**120**
Motorized camper	100	51	174	7	215
Other vehicle	100	139	147	67	72
Motorboats	100	207	67	66	98
Rental of recreational vehicles	**100**	**192**	**68**	**83**	**80**
Outboard motors	**100**	**38**	**332**	**10**	**55**
Docking and landing fees	**100**	**106**	**65**	**58**	**197**
Sports, recreation, exercise equipment	**100**	**85**	**75**	**77**	**175**
Athletic gear, game tables, exercise equipment	100	103	86	84	137
Bicycles	100	81	73	102	141
Camping equipment	100	72	67	65	214
Hunting and fishing equipment	100	27	60	67	258
Winter sports equipment	100	232	54	21	161
Water sports equipment	100	77	52	62	231
Other sports equipment	100	120	88	88	114
Rental and repair of misc. sports equipment	100	64	118	80	145
Photographic equipment and supplies	**100**	**109**	**112**	**81**	**110**
Film	100	110	105	84	112
Other photographic supplies	100	36	49	28	322
Film processing	100	110	111	79	113
Repair and rental of photographic equipment	100	8	25	100	242
Photographic equipment	100	111	102	83	115
Photographer fees	100	111	136	86	76
Fireworks	**100**	**20**	**124**	**75**	**184**
Souvenirs	**100**	**84**	**166**	**31**	**155**
Visual goods	**100**	**122**	**208**	**72**	**14**
Pinball, electronic video games	**100**	**134**	**57**	**69**	**165**

Note: (–) means sample is too small to make a reliable estimate.
Source: Calculations by New Strategist based on the 2002 Consumer Expenditure Survey

Table 3.19 Entertainment: Total spending by region, 2002

(total annual spending on entertainment, by region in which consumer units live, 2002; numbers in thousands)

	total consumer units	Northeast	Midwest	South	West
Number of consumer units	112,108	21,313	25,883	40,004	24,907
Total spending of all consumer units	$4,560,172,273	$903,462,333	$1,050,879,307	$1,491,371,122	$1,114,048,764
Entertainment, total spending	233,071,411	48,747,733	55,477,881	68,190,018	60,662,991
FEES AND ADMISSIONS	**$60,725,540**	**$14,007,330**	**$13,928,419**	**$16,757,676**	**$16,031,889**
Recreation expenses on trips	2,874,449	594,633	706,865	850,885	721,307
Social, recreation, civic club membership	12,098,695	2,864,254	2,783,458	3,658,366	2,792,324
Fees for participant sports	8,413,705	1,762,585	2,010,591	2,313,431	2,326,812
Participant sports on trips	3,307,186	699,919	736,113	874,087	996,778
Movie, theater, opera, ballet	11,020,216	2,599,120	2,459,661	2,699,870	3,261,821
Movie, other admissions on trips	5,108,762	1,173,068	1,180,524	1,458,146	1,296,907
Admission to sports events	4,056,067	780,695	1,038,944	1,249,725	986,566
Admission to sports events on trips	1,702,921	390,880	393,422	486,049	432,386
Fees for recreational lessons	9,270,211	2,547,330	1,911,718	2,315,832	2,495,432
Other entertainment services on trips	2,874,449	594,633	706,865	850,885	721,307
TELEVISION, RADIO, SOUND EQUIPMENT	**77,567,525**	**15,452,138**	**17,795,857**	**25,704,170**	**18,614,246**
Television	**60,948,635**	**12,620,919**	**14,108,047**	**21,192,119**	**13,026,361**
Cable service and community antenna	42,856,646	9,503,254	9,523,391	15,346,735	8,483,324
Black-and-white TV	89,686	20,887	22,777	41,204	4,483
Color TV, console	4,330,732	651,752	1,277,585	1,415,742	985,570
Color TV, portable, table model	4,387,907	814,583	981,225	1,507,751	1,084,451
VCRs and video disc players	2,606,511	494,248	686,676	763,276	662,526
Video cassettes, tapes, and discs	3,714,138	530,267	937,482	1,103,710	1,142,484
Video game hardware and software	2,630,054	528,136	609,545	896,090	596,523
Repair of TV, radio, and sound equipment	280,270	48,381	62,896	104,010	65,256
Rental of television sets	51,570	29,625	6,471	14,001	1,494
Radio and sound equipment	**16,620,011**	**2,831,006**	**3,687,810**	**4,512,051**	**5,587,885**
Radios	446,190	82,908	125,274	66,407	170,613
Tape recorders and players	595,293	68,628	206,288	202,820	118,308
Sound components and component systems	2,263,461	565,434	481,424	508,451	708,355
Miscellaneous sound equipment	356,503	158,569	56,684	68,007	69,989
Sound equipment accessories	669,285	71,399	193,087	257,626	148,446
Satellite dishes	112,108	9,165	21,483	40,404	41,097
Compact disc, tape, record, video mail order clubs	732,065	122,976	143,133	208,821	257,538
Records, CDs, audio tapes, needles	4,088,579	739,135	984,848	1,183,318	1,180,592
Rental of VCR, radio, sound equipment	28,027	–	20,965	2,400	4,732
Musical instruments and accessories	2,782,521	328,007	368,056	542,454	1,543,985
Rental and repair of musical instruments	136,772	21,952	52,025	27,203	35,866
Rental of video cassettes, tapes, discs, films	4,409,208	662,834	1,034,544	1,404,140	1,308,116
PETS, TOYS, PLAYGROUND EQUIPMENT	**41,381,305**	**7,731,930**	**10,443,014**	**13,638,564**	**9,576,742**
Pets	**27,830,811**	**5,051,607**	**6,540,893**	**9,530,953**	**6,715,923**
Pet food	11,497,796	2,145,153	2,577,429	4,029,603	2,745,748
Pet purchase, supplies, and medicines	5,862,127	806,484	1,659,359	2,181,018	1,225,424
Pet services	2,460,771	508,528	493,071	696,070	762,652
Veterinarian services	8,008,996	1,591,442	1,811,034	2,624,662	1,982,099
Toys, games, hobbies, and tricycles	**13,154,753**	**2,607,219**	**3,812,825**	**3,945,194**	**2,788,837**
Playground equipment	**396,862**	**73,104**	**89,296**	**162,016**	**71,981**

	total consumer units	Northeast	Midwest	South	West
OTHER ENTERTAINMENT SUPPLIES, EQUIPMENT, SERVICES	**$53,397,040**	**$11,556,335**	**$13,310,592**	**$12,089,209**	**$16,440,114**
Unmotored recreational vehicles	**5,284,771**	**625,323**	**2,541,452**	**513,651**	**1,604,758**
Boat without motor and boat trailers	1,810,544	377,027	683,570	207,221	542,724
Trailer and other attachable campers	3,474,227	248,296	1,858,141	306,431	1,062,034
Motorized recreational vehicles	19,079,661	5,664,782	4,799,744	3,532,353	5,082,771
Motorized camper	**4,489,925**	**432,867**	**1,805,857**	**105,611**	**2,145,987**
Other vehicle	3,976,471	1,049,452	1,348,504	943,694	635,129
Motorboats	10,613,264	4,182,463	1,645,641	2,483,048	2,301,656
Rental of recreational vehicles	**223,095**	**81,629**	**35,201**	**66,407**	**39,602**
Outboard motors	**79,597**	**5,755**	**61,084**	**2,800**	**9,714**
Docking and landing fees	**746,639**	**151,109**	**112,591**	**155,616**	**327,029**
Sports, recreation, exercise equipment	**16,853,196**	**2,734,245**	**2,907,437**	**4,645,264**	**6,566,731**
Athletic gear, game tables, exercise equipment	6,783,655	1,328,013	1,342,292	2,042,604	2,065,538
Bicycles	1,507,853	231,033	255,724	549,255	471,739
Camping equipment	1,075,116	147,060	166,169	251,225	511,341
Hunting and fishing equipment	4,000,013	208,867	550,531	955,296	2,291,693
Winter sports equipment	610,989	269,396	76,355	45,605	219,182
Water sports equipment	1,003,367	146,633	120,874	220,822	515,575
Other sports equipment	1,639,019	375,109	332,079	514,851	416,694
Rental and repair of misc. sports equipment	232,064	28,133	63,413	66,007	74,970
Photographic equipment and supplies	**10,143,532**	**2,095,281**	**2,615,477**	**2,944,294**	**2,488,707**
Film	1,988,796	417,095	484,012	594,059	493,408
Other photographic supplies	254,485	17,477	28,730	25,203	182,319
Film processing	2,982,073	624,684	766,137	840,084	750,448
Repair and rental of photographic equipment	13,453	213	776	4,800	7,223
Photographic equipment	2,616,601	553,072	617,827	776,078	669,749
Photographer fees	2,289,245	482,739	717,736	703,670	385,311
Fireworks	**170,404**	**6,607**	**48,660**	**45,605**	**69,740**
Souvenirs	**140,135**	**22,379**	**53,578**	**15,602**	**48,320**
Visual goods	**133,409**	**30,904**	**63,931**	**34,403**	**4,234**
Pinball, electronic video games	**542,603**	**137,895**	**71,696**	**133,213**	**198,509**

Note: Numbers may not add to total because of rounding. (–) means sample is too small to make a reliable estimate.
Source: Calculations by New Strategist based on the 2002 Consumer Expenditure Survey

Table 3.20 Entertainment: Market shares by region, 2002

(percentage of total annual spending on entertainment accounted for by consumer units by region, 2002)

	total consumer units	Northeast	Midwest	South	West
Share of total consumer units	100.0%	19.0%	23.1%	35.7%	22.2%
Share of total before-tax income	100.0	20.8	23.0	32.9	23.4
Share of total spending	100.0	19.8	23.0	32.7	24.4
Share of entertainment spending	100.0	20.9	23.8	29.3	26.0
FEES AND ADMISSIONS	**100.0%**	**23.1%**	**22.9%**	**27.6%**	**26.4%**
Recreation expenses on trips	100.0	20.7	24.6	29.6	25.1
Social, recreation, civic club membership	100.0	23.7	23.0	30.2	23.1
Fees for participant sports	100.0	20.9	23.9	27.5	27.7
Participant sports on trips	100.0	21.2	22.3	26.4	30.1
Movie, theater, opera, ballet	100.0	23.6	22.3	24.5	29.6
Movie, other admissions on trips	100.0	23.0	23.1	28.5	25.4
Admission to sports events	100.0	19.2	25.6	30.8	24.3
Admission to sports events on trips	100.0	23.0	23.1	28.5	25.4
Fees for recreational lessons	100.0	27.5	20.6	25.0	26.9
Other entertainment services on trips	100.0	20.7	24.6	29.6	25.1
TELEVISION, RADIO, SOUND EQUIPMENT	**100.0**	**19.9**	**22.9**	**33.1**	**24.0**
Television	**100.0**	**20.7**	**23.1**	**34.8**	**21.4**
Cable service and community antenna	100.0	22.2	22.2	35.8	19.8
Black-and-white TV	100.0	23.3	25.4	45.9	5.0
Color TV, console	100.0	15.0	29.5	32.7	22.8
Color TV, portable, table model	100.0	18.6	22.4	34.4	24.7
VCRs and video disc players	100.0	19.0	26.3	29.3	25.4
Video cassettes, tapes, and discs	100.0	14.3	25.2	29.7	30.8
Video game hardware and software	100.0	20.1	23.2	34.1	22.7
Repair of TV, radio, and sound equipment	100.0	17.3	22.4	37.1	23.3
Rental of television sets	100.0	57.4	12.5	27.2	2.9
Radio and sound equipment	**100.0**	**17.0**	**22.2**	**27.1**	**33.6**
Radios	100.0	18.6	28.1	14.9	38.2
Tape recorders and players	100.0	11.5	34.7	34.1	19.9
Sound components and component systems	100.0	25.0	21.3	22.5	31.3
Miscellaneous sound equipment	100.0	44.5	15.9	19.1	19.6
Sound equipment accessories	100.0	10.7	28.8	38.5	22.2
Satellite dishes	100.0	8.2	19.2	36.0	36.7
Compact disc, tape, record, video mail order clubs	100.0	16.8	19.6	28.5	35.2
Records, CDs, audio tapes, needles	100.0	18.1	24.1	28.9	28.9
Rental of VCR, radio, sound equipment	100.0	–	74.8	8.6	16.9
Musical instruments and accessories	100.0	11.8	13.2	19.5	55.5
Rental and repair of musical instruments	100.0	16.1	38.0	19.9	26.2
Rental of video cassettes, tapes, discs, films	100.0	15.0	23.5	31.8	29.7
PETS, TOYS, PLAYGROUND EQUIPMENT	**100.0**	**18.7**	**25.2**	**33.0**	**23.1**
Pets	**100.0**	**18.2**	**23.5**	**34.2**	**24.1**
Pet food	100.0	18.7	22.4	35.0	23.9
Pet purchase, supplies, and medicines	100.0	13.8	28.3	37.2	20.9
Pet services	100.0	20.7	20.0	28.3	31.0
Veterinarian services	100.0	19.9	22.6	32.8	24.7
Toys, games, hobbies, and tricycles	**100.0**	**19.8**	**29.0**	**30.0**	**21.2**
Playground equipment	**100.0**	**18.4**	**22.5**	**40.8**	**18.1**

	total consumer units	Northeast	Midwest	South	West
OTHER ENTERTAINMENT SUPPLIES, EQUIPMENT, SERVICES	**100.0%**	**21.6%**	**24.9%**	**22.6%**	**30.8%**
Unmotored recreational vehicles	**100.0**	**11.8**	**48.1**	**9.7**	**30.4**
Boat without motor and boat trailers	100.0	20.8	37.8	11.4	30.0
Trailer and other attachable campers	100.0	7.1	53.5	8.8	30.6
Motorized recreational vehicles	**100.0**	**29.7**	**25.2**	**18.5**	**26.6**
Motorized camper	100.0	9.6	40.2	2.4	47.8
Other vehicle	100.0	26.4	33.9	23.7	16.0
Motorboats	100.0	39.4	15.5	23.4	21.7
Rental of recreational vehicles	**100.0**	**36.6**	**15.8**	**29.8**	**17.8**
Outboard motors	**100.0**	**7.2**	**76.7**	**3.5**	**12.2**
Docking and landing fees	**100.0**	**20.2**	**15.1**	**20.8**	**43.8**
Sports, recreation, exercise equipment	**100.0**	**16.2**	**17.3**	**27.6**	**39.0**
Athletic gear, game tables, exercise equipment	100.0	19.6	19.8	30.1	30.4
Bicycles	100.0	15.3	17.0	36.4	31.3
Camping equipment	100.0	13.7	15.5	23.4	47.6
Hunting and fishing equipment	100.0	5.2	13.8	23.9	57.3
Winter sports equipment	100.0	44.1	12.5	7.5	35.9
Water sports equipment	100.0	14.6	12.0	22.0	51.4
Other sports equipment	100.0	22.9	20.3	31.4	25.4
Rental and repair of misc. sports equipment	100.0	12.1	27.3	28.4	32.3
Photographic equipment and supplies	**100.0**	**20.7**	**25.8**	**29.0**	**24.5**
Film	100.0	21.0	24.3	29.9	24.8
Other photographic supplies	100.0	6.9	11.3	9.9	71.6
Film processing	100.0	20.9	25.7	28.2	25.2
Repair and rental of photographic equipment	100.0	1.6	5.8	35.7	53.7
Photographic equipment	100.0	21.1	23.6	29.7	25.6
Photographer fees	100.0	21.1	31.4	30.7	16.8
Fireworks	**100.0**	**3.9**	**28.6**	**26.8**	**40.9**
Souvenirs	**100.0**	**16.0**	**38.2**	**11.1**	**34.5**
Visual goods	**100.0**	**23.2**	**47.9**	**25.8**	**3.2**
Pinball, electronic video games	**100.0**	**25.4**	**13.2**	**24.6**	**36.6**

Note: Numbers may not add to total because of rounding. (-) means sample is too small to make a reliable estimate.
Source: Calculations by New Strategist based on the 2002 Consumer Expenditure Survey

Table 3.21 Entertainment: Average spending by education, 2002

(average annual spending of consumer units (CU) on entertainment, by education of consumer unit reference person, 2002)

	total consumer units	less than high school graduate	high school graduate	some college	associate's degree	college graduate total	bachelor's degree	master's, professional, doctorate
Number of consumer units (in thousands, add 000)	112,108	17,075	31,961	23,260	10,395	29,417	19,082	10,335
Average number of persons per CU	2.5	2.6	2.5	2.4	2.6	2.5	2.5	2.5
Average before-tax income of CU	$49,430.00	$25,564.00	$39,618.00	$42,598.00	$54,860.00	$77,820.00	$69,408.00	$92,783.00
Average spending of CU, total	40,676.60	24,930.40	33,707.63	38,653.57	44,405.79	57,384.01	53,731.57	64,118.48
Entertainment, average spending	2,078.99	872.11	1,588.12	2,070.66	2,433.14	3,176.02	3,020.56	3,462.08
FEES AND ADMISSIONS	**$541.67**	**$119.43**	**$310.75**	**$459.98**	**$626.49**	**$1,072.28**	**$950.59**	**$1,296.98**
Recreation expenses on trips	25.64	7.97	17.39	23.91	26.99	45.74	42.76	51.22
Social, recreation, civic club membership	107.92	15.67	48.40	79.30	121.47	243.97	214.41	298.55
Fees for participant sports	75.05	19.56	49.04	62.00	83.28	142.92	135.37	156.87
Participant sports on trips	29.50	4.21	14.04	27.31	29.22	62.80	55.83	75.66
Movie, theater, opera, ballet	98.30	28.91	60.87	98.66	112.88	173.83	143.40	230.01
Movie, other admissions on trips	45.57	10.18	29.29	40.67	56.48	83.82	75.37	99.43
Admission to sports events	36.18	7.32	29.29	30.62	49.64	60.05	61.07	58.18
Admission to sports events on trips	15.19	3.39	9.76	13.55	18.82	27.94	25.12	33.14
Fees for recreational lessons	82.69	14.24	35.28	60.04	100.72	185.47	154.48	242.69
Other entertainment services on trips	25.64	7.97	17.39	23.91	26.99	45.74	42.76	51.22
TELEVISION, RADIO, SOUND EQUIPMENT	**691.90**	**447.97**	**632.57**	**688.66**	**783.08**	**866.49**	**849.59**	**897.69**
Television	**543.66**	**385.74**	**523.52**	**530.28**	**610.08**	**644.30**	**630.96**	**668.94**
Cable service and community antenna	382.28	296.07	395.21	349.74	431.17	426.74	411.41	455.04
Black-and-white TV	0.80	1.65	0.55	0.49	0.89	0.78	0.78	0.79
Color TV, console	38.63	17.00	29.15	25.70	52.41	66.84	70.33	60.41
Color TV, portable, table model	39.14	32.51	30.95	49.63	31.93	46.15	44.09	49.96
VCRs and video disc players	23.25	9.61	18.44	30.33	23.93	30.56	31.47	28.86
Video cassettes, tapes, and discs	33.13	14.61	28.07	43.00	36.91	40.23	39.60	41.40
Video game hardware and software	23.46	11.40	17.90	28.60	31.57	29.59	30.08	28.68
Repair of TV, radio, and sound equipment	2.50	2.20	2.21	2.60	1.27	3.35	3.15	3.71
Rental of television sets	0.46	0.68	1.06	0.20	–	0.06	0.04	0.10
Radio and sound equipment	**148.25**	**62.23**	**109.04**	**158.38**	**173.00**	**222.19**	**218.63**	**228.75**
Radios	3.98	1.81	2.71	3.01	3.09	7.26	5.37	10.70
Tape recorders and players	5.31	3.19	5.54	8.71	3.95	4.11	5.46	1.65
Sound components and component systems	20.19	11.29	14.15	21.29	16.07	32.51	28.71	39.53
Miscellaneous sound equipment	3.18	0.09	0.84	0.49	1.67	9.38	11.19	6.09
Sound equipment accessories	5.97	3.16	5.28	4.49	2.60	10.07	8.20	13.47
Satellite dishes	1.00	0.66	0.48	1.46	0.50	1.58	1.90	0.98
Compact disc, tape, record, video mail order clubs	6.53	3.68	5.15	8.79	8.89	7.07	6.94	7.32
Records, CDs, audio tapes, needles	36.47	15.21	25.82	41.42	41.73	54.59	54.18	55.36
Rental of VCR, radio, sound equipment	0.25	0.61	0.15	0.03	0.16	0.35	0.16	0.71
Musical instruments and accessories	24.82	2.95	15.85	21.23	44.78	43.04	44.31	40.71
Rental and repair of musical instruments	1.22	0.16	0.48	1.03	2.87	2.22	1.76	3.06
Rental of video cassettes, tapes, discs, films	39.33	19.42	32.60	46.43	46.69	50.00	50.43	49.19
PETS, TOYS, PLAYGROUND EQUIPMENT	**369.12**	**181.15**	**312.38**	**365.14**	**464.81**	**505.01**	**486.06**	**540.12**
Pets	**248.25**	**120.43**	**202.53**	**242.38**	**319.50**	**347.37**	**331.87**	**376.13**
Pet food	102.56	68.46	94.13	107.15	137.77	113.69	115.77	109.90
Pet purchase, supplies, and medicines	52.29	25.94	42.96	47.59	76.66	70.41	73.28	65.20
Pet services	21.95	5.47	12.36	16.39	21.70	46.41	36.34	64.99
Veterinarian services	71.44	20.57	53.08	71.25	83.37	116.87	106.48	136.04
Toys, games, hobbies, and tricycles	**117.34**	**59.80**	**108.09**	**120.66**	**140.57**	**149.94**	**146.49**	**156.32**
Playground equipment	**3.54**	**0.91**	**1.77**	**2.10**	**4.74**	**7.69**	**7.70**	**7.67**

	total consumer units	less than high school graduate	high school graduate	some college	associate's degree	college graduate total	bachelor's degree	master's, professional, doctorate
OTHER ENTERTAINMENT SUPPLIES, EQUIPMENT, SERVICES	$476.30	$123.55	$332.42	$556.88	$558.77	$732.24	$734.33	$727.29
Unmotored recreational vehicles	47.14	6.07	48.74	50.73	73.23	57.20	71.78	30.28
Boat without motor and boat trailers	16.15	4.46	9.16	28.29	17.24	20.54	29.95	3.17
Trailer and other attachable campers	30.99	1.60	39.58	22.44	55.99	36.66	41.83	27.12
Motorized recreational vehicles	170.19	34.53	120.60	235.51	251.76	222.35	258.60	155.42
Motorized camper	40.05	14.95	67.95	57.01	70.92	–	–	–
Other vehicle	35.47	4.67	34.00	51.50	68.32	30.67	21.92	46.84
Motorboats	94.67	14.90	18.66	127.01	112.52	191.67	236.67	108.58
Rental of recreational vehicles	1.99	0.51	0.64	1.90	5.28	3.21	2.69	4.16
Outboard motors	0.71	0.09	1.76	0.17	0.12	0.56	0.45	0.76
Docking and landing fees	6.66	0.62	3.16	12.94	9.82	7.88	4.98	13.22
Sports, recreation, exercise equipment	150.33	49.32	89.70	162.95	104.30	269.66	228.88	343.93
Athletic gear, game tables, exercise equipment	60.51	26.11	43.46	55.77	32.79	106.12	103.01	111.79
Bicycles	13.45	5.02	5.41	12.43	17.00	26.64	30.48	19.54
Camping equipment	9.59	6.21	4.42	11.69	6.99	15.82	16.32	14.91
Hunting and fishing equipment	35.68	5.33	19.08	45.75	13.08	66.96	30.83	132.71
Winter sports equipment	5.45	0.54	2.28	5.42	5.38	11.77	10.02	15.01
Water sports equipment	8.95	3.38	4.88	14.00	10.23	12.18	9.33	17.45
Other sports equipment	14.62	2.66	7.93	16.24	15.81	27.12	25.62	29.90
Rental and repair of misc. sports equipment	2.07	0.07	2.24	1.65	3.03	3.05	3.29	2.61
Photographic equipment and supplies	90.48	27.90	63.39	81.52	104.66	157.96	151.36	170.03
Film	17.74	6.96	13.24	18.56	19.21	27.72	25.55	31.71
Other photographic supplies	2.27	1.28	0.38	1.02	1.85	5.66	1.04	14.07
Film processing	26.60	8.97	18.01	27.57	28.13	44.84	40.59	52.70
Repair and rental of photographic equipment	0.12	–	0.07	0.13	0.10	0.23	0.11	0.46
Photographic equipment	23.34	5.63	17.79	18.39	30.32	41.11	43.74	36.24
Photographer fees	20.42	5.06	13.90	15.86	25.06	38.40	40.32	34.84
Fireworks	1.52	1.74	0.35	2.40	4.01	1.24	1.72	0.36
Souvenirs	1.25	0.63	0.22	1.17	1.23	2.66	3.25	1.57
Visual goods	1.19	0.52	0.25	0.37	0.07	3.38	3.90	2.44
Pinball, electronic video games	4.84	1.64	3.60	7.22	4.29	6.15	6.72	5.12

Note: (–) means sample is too small to make a reliable estimate.
Source: Bureau of Labor Statistics, unpublished data from the 2002 Consumer Expenditure Survey

Table 3.22 Entertainment: Indexed spending by education, 2002

(indexed average annual spending of consumer units (CU) on entertainment by education of consumer unit reference person, 2002; index definition: an index of 100 is the average for all consumer units; an index of 132 means that spending by consumer units in that group is 32 percent above the average for all consumer units; an index of 68 indicates spending that is 32 percent below the average for all consumer units)

	total consumer units	less than high school graduate	high school graduate	some college	associate's degree	college graduate total	bachelor's degree	master's, professional, doctorate
Average spending of CU, total	$40,677	$24,930	$33,708	$38,654	$44,406	$57,384	$53,732	$64,118
Average spending of CU, index	100	61	83	95	109	141	132	158
Entertainment, spending index	100	42	76	100	117	153	145	167
FEES AND ADMISSIONS	**100**	**22**	**57**	**85**	**116**	**198**	**175**	**239**
Recreation expenses on trips	100	31	68	93	105	178	167	200
Social, recreation, civic club membership	100	15	45	73	113	226	199	277
Fees for participant sports	100	26	65	83	111	190	180	209
Participant sports on trips	100	14	48	93	99	213	189	256
Movie, theater, opera, ballet	100	29	62	100	115	177	146	234
Movie, other admissions on trips	100	22	64	89	124	184	165	218
Admission to sports events	100	20	81	85	137	166	169	161
Admission to sports events on trips	100	22	64	89	124	184	165	218
Fees for recreational lessons	100	17	43	73	122	224	187	293
Other entertainment services on trips	100	31	68	93	105	178	167	200
TELEVISION, RADIO, SOUND EQUIPMENT	**100**	**65**	**91**	**100**	**113**	**125**	**123**	**130**
Television	**100**	**71**	**96**	**98**	**112**	**119**	**116**	**123**
Cable service and community antenna	100	77	103	91	113	112	108	119
Black-and-white TV	100	206	69	61	111	98	98	99
Color TV, console	100	44	75	67	136	173	182	156
Color TV, portable, table model	100	83	79	127	82	118	113	128
VCRs and video disc players	100	41	79	130	103	131	135	124
Video cassettes, tapes, and discs	100	44	85	130	111	121	120	125
Video game hardware and software	100	49	76	122	135	126	128	122
Repair of TV, radio, and sound equipment	100	88	88	104	51	134	126	148
Rental of television sets	100	148	230	43	–	13	9	22
Radio and sound equipment	**100**	**42**	**74**	**107**	**117**	**150**	**147**	**154**
Radios	100	45	68	76	78	182	135	269
Tape recorders and players	100	60	104	164	74	77	103	31
Sound components and component systems	100	56	70	105	80	161	142	196
Miscellaneous sound equipment	100	3	26	15	53	295	352	192
Sound equipment accessories	100	53	88	75	44	169	137	226
Satellite dishes	100	66	48	146	50	158	190	98
Compact disc, tape, record, video mail order clubs	100	56	79	135	136	108	106	112
Records, CDs, audio tapes, needles	100	42	71	114	114	150	149	152
Rental of VCR, radio, sound equipment	100	244	60	12	64	140	64	284
Musical instruments and accessories	100	12	64	86	180	173	179	164
Rental and repair of musical instruments	100	13	39	84	235	182	144	251
Rental of video cassettes, tapes, discs, films	100	49	83	118	119	127	128	125
PETS, TOYS, PLAYGROUND EQUIPMENT	**100**	**49**	**85**	**99**	**126**	**137**	**132**	**146**
Pets	**100**	**49**	**82**	**98**	**129**	**140**	**134**	**152**
Pet food	100	67	92	104	134	111	113	107
Pet purchase, supplies, and medicines	100	50	82	91	147	135	140	125
Pet services	100	25	56	75	99	211	166	296
Veterinarian services	100	29	74	100	117	164	149	190
Toys, games, hobbies, and tricycles	**100**	**51**	**92**	**103**	**120**	**128**	**125**	**133**
Playground equipment	**100**	**26**	**50**	**59**	**134**	**217**	**218**	**217**

	total consumer units	less than high school graduate	high school graduate	some college	associate's degree	college graduate total	bachelor's degree	master's, professional, doctorate
OTHER ENTERTAINMENT SUPPLIES, EQUIPMENT, SERVICES	**100**	**26**	**70**	**117**	**117**	**154**	**154**	**153**
Unmotored recreational vehicles	**100**	**13**	**103**	**108**	**155**	**121**	**152**	**64**
Boat without motor and boat trailers	100	28	57	175	107	127	185	20
Trailer and other attachable campers	100	5	128	72	181	118	135	88
Motorized recreational vehicles	100	20	71	138	148	131	152	91
Motorized camper	**100**	**37**	**170**	**142**	**177**	**–**	**–**	**–**
Other vehicle	100	13	96	145	193	86	62	132
Motorboats	100	16	20	134	119	202	250	115
Rental of recreational vehicles	**100**	**26**	**32**	**95**	**265**	**161**	**135**	**209**
Outboard motors	**100**	**13**	**248**	**24**	**17**	**79**	**63**	**107**
Docking and landing fees	**100**	**9**	**47**	**194**	**147**	**118**	**75**	**198**
Sports, recreation, exercise equipment	**100**	**33**	**60**	**108**	**69**	**179**	**152**	**229**
Athletic gear, game tables, exercise equipment	100	43	72	92	54	175	170	185
Bicycles	100	37	40	92	126	198	227	145
Camping equipment	100	65	46	122	73	165	170	155
Hunting and fishing equipment	100	15	53	128	37	188	86	372
Winter sports equipment	100	10	42	99	99	216	184	275
Water sports equipment	100	38	55	156	114	136	104	195
Other sports equipment	100	18	54	111	108	185	175	205
Rental and repair of misc. sports equipment	100	3	108	80	146	147	159	126
Photographic equipment and supplies	**100**	**31**	**70**	**90**	**116**	**175**	**167**	**188**
Film	100	39	75	105	108	156	144	179
Other photographic supplies	100	56	17	45	81	249	46	620
Film processing	100	34	68	104	106	169	153	198
Repair and rental of photographic equipment	100	–	58	108	83	192	92	383
Photographic equipment	100	24	76	79	130	176	187	155
Photographer fees	100	25	68	78	123	188	197	171
Fireworks	**100**	**114**	**23**	**158**	**264**	**82**	**113**	**24**
Souvenirs	**100**	**50**	**18**	**94**	**98**	**213**	**260**	**126**
Visual goods	**100**	**44**	**21**	**31**	**6**	**284**	**328**	**205**
Pinball, electronic video games	**100**	**34**	**74**	**149**	**89**	**127**	**139**	**106**

Note: (–) means sample is too small to make a reliable estimate.
Source: Calculations by New Strategist based on the 2002 Consumer Expenditure Survey

Table 3.23 Entertainment: Total spending by education, 2002

(total annual spending on entertainment, by consumer unit (CU) educational attainment group, 2002; numbers in thousands)

	total consumer units	less than high school graduate	high school graduate	some college	associate's degree	college graduate total	bachelor's degree	master's, professional, doctorate
Number of consumer units	112,108	17,075	31,961	23,260	10,395	29,417	19,082	10,335
Total spending of all CUs	$4,560,172,273	$425,686,580	$1,077,329,562	$899,082,038	$461,598,187	$1,688,065,422	$1,025,305,819	$662,664,491
Entertainment, total spending	233,071,411	14,891,278	50,757,903	48,163,552	25,292,490	93,428,980	57,638,326	35,780,597
FEES AND ADMISSIONS	**$60,725,540**	**$2,039,267**	**$9,931,881**	**$10,699,135**	**$6,512,364**	**$31,543,261**	**$18,139,158**	**$13,404,288**
Recreation expenses on trips	2,874,449	136,088	555,802	556,147	280,561	1,345,534	815,946	529,359
Social, recreation, civic club membership	12,098,695	267,565	1,546,912	1,844,518	1,262,681	7,176,865	4,091,372	3,085,514
Fees for participant sports	8,413,705	333,987	1,567,367	1,442,120	865,696	4,204,278	2,583,130	1,621,251
Participant sports on trips	3,307,186	71,886	448,732	635,231	303,742	1,847,388	1,065,348	781,946
Movie, theater, opera, ballet	11,020,216	493,638	1,945,466	2,294,832	1,173,388	5,113,557	2,736,359	2,377,153
Movie, other admissions on trips	5,108,762	173,824	936,138	945,984	587,110	2,465,733	1,438,210	1,027,609
Admission to sports events	4,056,067	124,989	936,138	712,221	516,008	1,766,491	1,165,338	601,290
Admission to sports events on trips	1,702,921	57,884	311,939	315,173	195,634	821,911	479,340	342,502
Fees for recreational lessons	9,270,211	243,148	1,127,584	1,396,530	1,046,984	5,455,971	2,947,787	2,508,201
Other entertainment services on trips	2,874,449	136,088	555,802	556,147	280,561	1,345,534	815,946	529,359
TELEVISION, RADIO, SOUND EQUIPMENT	**77,567,525**	**7,649,088**	**20,217,570**	**16,018,232**	**8,140,117**	**25,489,536**	**16,211,876**	**9,277,626**
Television	**60,948,635**	**6,586,511**	**16,732,223**	**12,334,313**	**6,341,782**	**18,953,373**	**12,039,979**	**6,913,495**
Cable service and community antenna	42,856,646	5,055,395	12,631,307	8,134,952	4,482,012	12,553,411	7,850,526	4,702,838
Black-and-white TV	89,686	28,174	17,579	11,397	9,252	22,945	14,884	8,165
Color TV, console	4,330,732	290,275	931,663	597,782	544,802	1,966,232	1,342,037	624,337
Color TV, portable, table model	4,387,907	555,108	989,193	1,154,394	331,912	1,357,595	841,325	516,337
VCRs and video disc players	2,606,511	164,091	589,361	705,476	248,752	898,984	600,511	298,268
Video cassettes, tapes, and discs	3,714,138	249,466	897,145	1,000,180	383,679	1,183,446	755,647	427,869
Video game hardware and software	2,630,054	194,655	572,102	665,236	328,170	870,449	573,987	296,408
Repair of TV, radio, and sound equipment	280,270	37,565	70,634	60,476	13,202	98,547	60,108	38,343
Rental of television sets	51,570	11,611	33,879	4,652	–	1,765	763	1,034
Radio and sound equipment	**16,620,011**	**1,062,577**	**3,485,027**	**3,683,919**	**1,798,335**	**6,536,163**	**4,171,898**	**2,364,131**
Radios	446,190	30,906	86,614	70,013	32,121	213,567	102,470	110,585
Tape recorders and players	595,293	54,469	177,064	202,595	41,060	120,904	104,188	17,053
Sound components and component systems	2,263,461	192,777	452,248	495,205	167,048	956,347	547,844	408,543
Miscellaneous sound equipment	356,503	1,537	26,847	11,397	17,360	275,931	213,528	62,940
Sound equipment accessories	669,285	53,957	168,754	104,437	27,027	296,229	156,472	139,212
Satellite dishes	112,108	11,270	15,341	33,960	5,198	46,479	36,256	10,128
Compact disc, tape, record, video mail order clubs	732,065	62,836	164,599	204,455	92,412	207,978	132,429	75,652
Records, CDs, audio tapes, needles	4,088,579	259,711	825,233	963,429	433,783	1,605,874	1,033,863	572,146
Rental of VCR, radio, sound equipment	28,027	10,416	4,794	698	1,663	10,296	3,053	7,338
Musical instruments and accessories	2,782,521	50,371	506,582	493,810	465,488	1,266,108	845,523	420,738
Rental and repair of musical instruments	136,772	2,732	15,341	23,958	29,834	65,306	33,584	31,625
Rental of video cassettes, tapes, discs, films	4,409,208	331,597	1,041,929	1,079,962	485,343	1,470,850	962,305	508,379
PETS, TOYS, PLAYGROUND EQUIPMENT	**41,381,305**	**3,093,136**	**9,983,977**	**8,493,156**	**4,831,700**	**14,855,879**	**9,274,997**	**5,582,140**
Pets	**27,830,811**	**2,056,342**	**6,473,061**	**5,637,759**	**3,321,203**	**10,218,583**	**6,332,743**	**3,887,304**
Pet food	11,497,796	1,168,955	3,008,489	2,492,309	1,432,119	3,344,419	2,209,123	1,135,817
Pet purchase, supplies, and medicines	5,862,127	442,926	1,373,045	1,106,943	796,881	2,071,251	1,398,329	673,842
Pet services	2,460,771	93,400	395,038	381,231	225,572	1,365,243	693,440	671,672
Veterinarian services	8,008,996	351,233	1,696,490	1,657,275	866,631	3,437,965	2,031,851	1,405,973
Toys, games, hobbies, and tricycles	**13,154,753**	**1,021,085**	**3,454,664**	**2,806,552**	**1,461,225**	**4,410,785**	**2,795,322**	**1,615,567**
Playground equipment	**396,862**	**15,538**	**56,571**	**48,846**	**49,272**	**226,217**	**146,931**	**79,269**

	total consumer units	less than high school graduate	high school graduate	some college	associate's degree	college graduate total	bachelor's degree	master's, professional, doctorate
OTHER ENTERTAINMENT SUPPLIES, EQUIPMENT, SERVICES	**$53,397,040**	**$2,109,616**	**$10,624,476**	**$12,953,029**	**$5,808,414**	**$21,540,304**	**$14,012,485**	**$7,516,542**
Unmotored recreational vehicles	**5,284,771**	**103,645**	**1,557,779**	**1,179,980**	**761,226**	**1,682,652**	**1,369,706**	**312,944**
Boat without motor and boat trailers	1,810,544	76,155	292,763	658,025	179,210	604,225	571,506	32,762
Trailer and other attachable campers	3,474,227	27,320	1,265,016	521,954	582,016	1,078,427	798,200	280,285
Motorized recreational vehicles	19,079,661	589,600	3,854,497	5,477,963	2,617,045	6,540,870	4,934,605	1,606,266
Motorized camper	**4,489,925**	**255,271**	**2,171,750**	**1,326,053**	**737,213**	**–**	**–**	**–**
Other vehicle	3,976,471	79,740	1,086,674	1,197,890	710,186	902,219	418,277	484,091
Motorboats	10,613,264	254,418	596,392	2,954,253	1,169,645	5,638,356	4,516,137	1,122,174
Rental of recreational vehicles	**223,095**	**8,708**	**20,455**	**44,194**	**54,886**	**94,429**	**51,331**	**42,994**
Outboard motors	**79,597**	**1,537**	**56,251**	**3,954**	**1,247**	**16,474**	**8,587**	**7,855**
Docking and landing fees	**746,639**	**10,587**	**100,997**	**300,984**	**102,079**	**231,806**	**95,028**	**136,629**
Sports, recreation, exercise equipment	**16,853,196**	**842,139**	**2,866,902**	**3,790,217**	**1,084,199**	**7,932,588**	**4,367,488**	**3,554,517**
Athletic gear, game tables, exercise equip.	6,783,655	445,828	1,389,025	1,297,210	340,852	3,121,732	1,965,637	1,155,350
Bicycles	1,507,853	85,717	172,909	289,122	176,715	783,669	581,619	201,946
Camping equipment	1,075,116	106,036	141,268	271,909	72,661	465,377	311,418	154,095
Hunting and fishing equipment	4,000,013	91,010	609,816	1,064,145	135,967	1,969,762	588,298	1,371,558
Winter sports equipment	610,989	9,221	72,871	126,069	55,925	346,238	191,202	155,128
Water sports equipment	1,003,367	57,714	155,970	325,640	106,341	358,299	178,035	180,346
Other sports equipment	1,639,019	45,420	253,451	377,742	164,345	797,789	488,881	309,017
Rental and repair of misc. sports equipment	232,064	1,195	71,593	38,379	31,497	89,722	62,780	26,974
Photographic equipment and supplies	**10,143,532**	**476,393**	**2,026,008**	**1,896,155**	**1,087,941**	**4,646,709**	**2,888,252**	**1,757,260**
Film	1,988,796	118,842	423,164	431,706	199,688	815,439	487,545	327,723
Other photographic supplies	254,485	21,856	12,145	23,725	19,231	166,500	19,845	145,413
Film processing	2,982,073	153,163	575,618	641,278	292,411	1,319,058	774,538	544,655
Repair and rental of photographic equipment	13,453	–	2,237	3,024	1,040	6,766	2,099	4,754
Photographic equipment	2,616,601	96,132	568,586	427,751	315,176	1,209,333	834,647	374,540
Photographer fees	2,289,245	86,400	444,258	368,904	260,499	1,129,613	769,386	360,071
Fireworks	**170,404**	**29,711**	**11,186**	**55,824**	**41,684**	**36,477**	**32,821**	**3,721**
Souvenirs	**140,135**	**10,757**	**7,031**	**27,214**	**12,786**	**78,249**	**62,017**	**16,226**
Visual goods	**133,409**	**8,879**	**7,990**	**8,606**	**728**	**99,429**	**74,420**	**25,217**
Pinball, electronic video games	**542,603**	**28,003**	**115,060**	**167,937**	**44,595**	**180,915**	**128,231**	**52,915**

Note: Numbers may not add to total because of rounding. (–) means sample is too small to make a reliable estimate.
Source: Calculations by New Strategist based on the 2002 Consumer Expenditure Survey

Table 3.24 Entertainment: Market shares by education, 2002

(percentage of total annual spending on entertainment accounted for by consumer unit educational attainment groups, 2002)

	total consumer units	less than high school graduate	high school graduate	some college	associate's degree	college graduate total	bachelor's degree	master's, professional, doctorate
Share of total consumer units	100.0%	15.2%	28.5%	20.7%	9.3%	26.2%	17.0%	9.2%
Share of total before-tax income	100.0	7.9	22.8	17.9	10.3	41.3	23.9	17.3
Share of total spending	100.0	9.3	23.6	19.7	10.1	37.0	22.5	14.5
Share of entertainment spending	100.0	6.4	21.8	20.7	10.9	40.1	24.7	15.4
FEES AND ADMISSIONS	100.0%	3.4%	16.4%	17.6%	10.7%	51.9%	29.9%	22.1%
Recreation expenses on trips	100.0	4.7	19.3	19.3	9.8	46.8	28.4	18.4
Social, recreation, civic club membership	100.0	2.2	12.8	15.2	10.4	59.3	33.8	25.5
Fees for participant sports	100.0	4.0	18.6	17.1	10.3	50.0	30.7	19.3
Participant sports on trips	100.0	2.2	13.6	19.2	9.2	55.9	32.2	23.6
Movie, theater, opera, ballet	100.0	4.5	17.7	20.8	10.6	46.4	24.8	21.6
Movie, other admissions on trips	100.0	3.4	18.3	18.5	11.5	48.3	28.2	20.1
Admission to sports events	100.0	3.1	23.1	17.6	12.7	43.6	28.7	14.8
Admission to sports events on trips	100.0	3.4	18.3	18.5	11.5	48.3	28.1	20.1
Fees for recreational lessons	100.0	2.6	12.2	15.1	11.3	58.9	31.8	27.1
Other entertainment services on trips	100.0	4.7	19.3	19.3	9.8	46.8	28.4	18.4
TELEVISION, RADIO, SOUND EQUIPMENT	100.0	9.9	26.1	20.7	10.5	32.9	20.9	12.0
Television	100.0	10.8	27.5	20.2	10.4	31.1	19.8	11.3
Cable service and community antenna	100.0	11.8	29.5	19.0	10.5	29.3	18.3	11.0
Black-and-white TV	100.0	31.4	19.6	12.7	10.3	25.6	16.6	9.1
Color TV, console	100.0	6.7	21.5	13.8	12.6	45.4	31.0	14.4
Color TV, portable, table model	100.0	12.7	22.5	26.3	7.6	30.9	19.2	11.8
VCRs and video disc players	100.0	6.3	22.6	27.1	9.5	34.5	23.0	11.4
Video cassettes, tapes, and discs	100.0	6.7	24.2	26.9	10.3	31.9	20.3	11.5
Video game hardware and software	100.0	7.4	21.8	25.3	12.5	33.1	21.8	11.3
Repair of TV, radio, and sound equipment	100.0	13.4	25.2	21.6	4.7	35.2	21.4	13.7
Rental of television sets	100.0	22.5	65.7	9.0	–	3.4	1.5	2.0
Radio and sound equipment	100.0	6.4	21.0	22.2	10.8	39.3	25.1	14.2
Radios	100.0	6.9	19.4	15.7	7.2	47.9	23.0	24.8
Tape recorders and players	100.0	9.1	29.7	34.0	6.9	20.3	17.5	2.9
Sound components and component systems	100.0	8.5	20.0	21.9	7.4	42.3	24.2	18.0
Miscellaneous sound equipment	100.0	0.4	7.5	3.2	4.9	77.4	59.9	17.7
Sound equipment accessories	100.0	8.1	25.2	15.6	4.0	44.3	23.4	20.8
Satellite dishes	100.0	10.1	13.7	30.3	4.6	41.5	32.3	9.0
Compact disc, tape, record, video mail order clubs	100.0	8.6	22.5	27.9	12.6	28.4	18.1	10.3
Records, CDs, audio tapes, needles	100.0	6.4	20.2	23.6	10.6	39.3	25.3	14.0
Rental of VCR, radio, sound equipment	100.0	37.2	17.1	2.5	5.9	36.7	10.9	26.2
Musical instruments and accessories	100.0	1.8	18.2	17.7	16.7	45.5	30.4	15.1
Rental and repair of musical instruments	100.0	2.0	11.2	17.5	21.8	47.7	24.6	23.1
Rental of video cassettes, tapes, discs, films	100.0	7.5	23.6	24.5	11.0	33.4	21.8	11.5
PETS, TOYS, PLAYGROUND EQUIPMENT	100.0	7.5	24.1	20.5	11.7	35.9	22.4	13.5
Pets	100.0	7.4	23.3	20.3	11.9	36.7	22.8	14.0
Pet food	100.0	10.2	26.2	21.7	12.5	29.1	19.2	9.9
Pet purchase, supplies, and medicines	100.0	7.6	23.4	18.9	13.6	35.3	23.9	11.5
Pet services	100.0	3.8	16.1	15.5	9.2	55.5	28.2	27.3
Veterinarian services	100.0	4.4	21.2	20.7	10.8	42.9	25.4	17.6
Toys, games, hobbies, and tricycles	100.0	7.8	26.3	21.3	11.1	33.5	21.2	12.3
Playground equipment	100.0	3.9	14.3	12.3	12.4	57.0	37.0	20.0

	total consumer units	less than high school graduate	high school graduate	some college	associate's degree	college graduate		
						total	bachelor's degree	master's, professional, doctorate
OTHER ENTERTAINMENT SUPPLIES, EQUIPMENT, SERVICES	100.0%	4.0%	19.9%	24.3%	10.9%	40.3%	26.2%	14.1%
Unmotored recreational vehicles	100.0	2.0	29.5	22.3	14.4	31.8	25.9	5.9
Boat without motor and boat trailers	100.0	4.2	16.2	36.3	9.9	33.4	31.6	1.8
Trailer and other attachable campers	100.0	0.8	36.4	15.0	16.8	31.0	23.0	8.1
Motorized recreational vehicles	100.0	3.1	20.2	28.7	13.7	34.3	25.9	8.4
Motorized camper	100.0	5.7	48.4	29.5	16.4	–	–	–
Other vehicle	100.0	2.0	27.3	30.1	17.9	22.7	10.5	12.2
Motorboats	100.0	2.4	5.6	27.8	11.0	53.1	42.6	10.6
Rental of recreational vehicles	100.0	3.9	9.2	19.8	24.6	42.3	23.0	19.3
Outboard motors	100.0	1.9	70.7	5.0	1.6	20.7	10.8	9.9
Docking and landing fees	100.0	1.4	13.5	40.3	13.7	31.0	12.7	18.3
Sports, recreation, exercise equipment	100.0	5.0	17.0	22.5	6.4	47.1	25.9	21.1
Athletic gear, game tables, exercise equipment	100.0	6.6	20.5	19.1	5.0	46.0	29.0	17.0
Bicycles	100.0	5.7	11.5	19.2	11.7	52.0	38.6	13.4
Camping equipment	100.0	9.9	13.1	25.3	6.8	43.3	29.0	14.3
Hunting and fishing equipment	100.0	2.3	15.2	26.6	3.4	49.2	14.7	34.3
Winter sports equipment	100.0	1.5	11.9	20.6	9.2	56.7	31.3	25.4
Water sports equipment	100.0	5.8	15.5	32.5	10.6	35.7	17.7	18.0
Other sports equipment	100.0	2.8	15.5	23.0	10.0	48.7	29.8	18.9
Rental and repair of misc. sports equipment	100.0	0.5	30.9	16.5	13.6	38.7	27.1	11.6
Photographic equipment and supplies	100.0	4.7	20.0	18.7	10.7	45.8	28.5	17.3
Film	100.0	6.0	21.3	21.7	10.0	41.0	24.5	16.5
Other photographic supplies	100.0	8.6	4.8	9.3	7.6	65.4	7.8	57.1
Film processing	100.0	5.1	19.3	21.5	9.8	44.2	26.0	18.3
Repair and rental of photographic equipment	100.0	–	16.6	22.5	7.7	50.3	15.6	35.3
Photographic equipment	100.0	3.7	21.7	16.3	12.0	46.2	31.9	14.3
Photographer fees	100.0	3.8	19.4	16.1	11.4	49.3	33.6	15.7
Fireworks	100.0	17.4	6.6	32.8	24.5	21.4	19.3	2.2
Souvenirs	100.0	7.7	5.0	19.4	9.1	55.8	44.3	11.6
Visual goods	100.0	6.7	6.0	6.5	0.5	74.5	55.8	18.9
Pinball, electronic video games	100.0	5.2	21.2	31.0	8.2	33.3	23.6	9.8

Note: Numbers may not add to total because of rounding. (–) means sample is too small to make a reliable estimate.
Source: Calculations by New Strategist based on the 2002 Consumer Expenditure Survey

Spending on Financial Products and Services, 2002

Trends in spending on financial products and services have been mixed since 1997. Spending on miscellaneous financial services (such as bank fees, accounting fees, credit card fees, and legal fees) fell 16 percent between 1997 and 2002, after adjusting for inflation. During the same time, spending on cash contributions (a category that includes child support as well as gifts to charities) rose 14 percent. Spending on pensions and Social Security rose 10 percent, while spending on life and other personal insurance fell 4 percent. Households spent less on federal and state taxes, but other taxes rose 2 percent. Overall, Americans devoted 14.7 percent of their spending in 2002 to miscellaneous financial services, cash contributions, life insurance, and pensions—slightly more than the 14.6 percent of 1997.

Households headed by 45-to-54-year-olds spend more than other age groups on financial products and services, including lottery and gambling losses and credit card memberships. Householders aged 55 to 64 spend the most on life and other personal insurance—47 percent more than the average household. The biggest spenders on cash contributions are householders aged 65 to 74, although those aged 35 to 44 spend the most on child support.

Households with incomes of $70,000 or more represent just 23 percent of consumer units but account for 56 percent of spending on personal insurance and pensions. This high-income group accounts for 59 percent of household contributions to educational institutions and 69 percent of contributions to political organizations.

Married couples with children at home spend more than other household types on most financial categories because their households are larger and more likely to have two or more wage earners. Married couples without children at home spend the most on cash gifts. They are also the biggest spenders on gifts to charities.

Blacks and Hispanics spend less than average on nearly every financial product and service. They spend more than the average household on finance charges.

Households in the West spend more than the average household on most financial products and services. They spend 20 percent more than average on legal fees and 31 percent more on accounting fees. Households in the Midwest spend the most on lottery and gambling losses.

Households headed by college graduates account for 26 percent of households, but they account for 63 percent of cash gifts to charities. Because college graduates dominate high-income households, they also account for 74 percent of cash contributions to educational institutions and 70 percent of cash gifts to political organizations.

Table 4.1 Financial: Average spending by age, 2002

(average annual spending of consumer units (CU) on financial products and services, cash contributions, and miscellaneous items, by age of consumer unit reference person, 2002)

	total consumer units	under 25	25 to 34	35 to 44	45 to 54	55 to 64	65 to 74	75+
Number of consumer units (in thousands, add 000)	112,108	8,737	18,988	24,394	22,691	15,314	11,216	10,767
Average number of persons per CU	2.5	1.9	2.9	3.2	2.7	2.1	1.9	1.5
Average before-tax income of CU	$49,430.00	$20,773.00	$49,133.00	$61,532.00	$64,974.00	$53,162.00	$35,118.00	$23,890.00
Average spending of CU, total	40,676.60	24,229.46	40,318.29	48,330.48	48,748.24	44,330.04	32,242.52	23,758.89
FINANCIAL PRODUCTS AND SERVICES	**$788.12**	**$422.38**	**$678.16**	**$824.99**	**$985.42**	**$929.71**	**$793.67**	**$572.27**
Miscellaneous fees	2.25	–	3.40	2.76	2.57	2.72	1.63	0.15
Lottery and gambling losses	46.94	8.15	31.75	24.44	87.53	39.85	80.94	47.16
Legal fees	132.99	50.82	87.10	137.59	175.74	206.21	102.31	107.92
Funeral expenses	77.91	26.65	20.58	50.45	81.06	112.44	154.91	146.89
Safe deposit box rental	3.84	1.14	1.71	2.70	3.55	5.50	7.70	6.64
Checking accounts, other bank service charges	25.91	27.85	32.41	33.38	28.96	20.90	15.36	7.66
Cemetery lots, vaults, and maintenance fees	16.05	0.39	5.40	3.36	15.92	19.71	30.82	55.95
Accounting fees	57.85	11.33	41.73	55.67	64.95	83.41	75.96	58.82
Miscellaneous personal services	39.77	73.51	44.16	46.49	32.79	28.59	50.81	6.66
Finance charges, except mortgage and vehicles	271.37	199.07	342.72	305.62	338.54	267.17	195.92	69.58
Occupational expenses	38.46	14.05	36.88	59.00	52.80	45.76	9.70	3.88
Expenses for other properties	65.99	6.72	23.46	92.94	89.09	86.16	59.75	57.15
Credit card memberships	2.82	1.25	2.77	3.23	3.84	3.40	2.35	0.74
Shopping club membership fees	5.97	1.45	4.09	7.36	8.08	7.89	5.51	3.07
CASH CONTRIBUTIONS	**1,277.10**	**318.97**	**743.28**	**1,247.46**	**1,571.36**	**1,520.18**	**1,620.48**	**1,739.54**
Support for college students	75.94	5.11	7.17	44.56	178.91	148.53	65.10	16.87
Alimony expenditures	21.18	0.60	2.94	15.68	34.39	47.14	12.76	26.51
Child support expenditures	190.75	60.96	219.43	376.22	247.34	65.31	63.44	17.01
Gifts to non–CU members of stocks, bonds, and mutual funds	24.23	6.38	2.33	1.36	4.18	32.85	52.18	130.02
Cash contributions to charities and other organizations	137.62	20.24	45.31	105.76	180.63	186.43	227.83	213.82
Cash contributions to church, religious organizations	557.29	142.53	344.32	542.84	699.35	710.09	751.56	583.11
Cash contributions to educational institutions	33.42	1.75	8.07	29.31	40.39	43.72	86.83	28.15
Cash contributions to political organizations	10.90	1.28	4.32	4.08	10.89	13.17	7.22	46.44
Other cash gifts	225.76	80.13	109.38	127.66	175.28	272.94	353.57	677.61
PERSONAL INSURANCE, PENSIONS	**3,898.62**	**1,382.11**	**3,971.75**	**5,182.53**	**5,322.82**	**4,837.93**	**1,852.78**	**696.41**
Life and other personal insurance	406.11	51.26	230.07	408.79	559.25	594.98	521.11	287.31
Life, endowment, annuity, other personal insurance	391.65	49.29	220.85	396.24	537.89	577.35	505.50	269.38
Other nonhealth insurance	14.46	1.97	9.22	12.55	21.36	17.63	15.62	17.93
Pensions and Social Security	3,492.51	1,330.85	3,741.68	4,773.74	4,763.57	4,242.95	1,331.66	409.09
Deductions for government retirement	69.48	6.03	44.54	92.65	134.23	96.39	8.95	0.82
Deductions for private pensions	390.38	46.63	361.40	576.38	621.57	453.85	112.18	11.27
Nonpayroll deposit to retirement plans	426.12	57.22	303.49	429.68	484.29	1,022.10	284.88	110.50
Deductions for Social Security	2,604.32	1,220.97	3,032.02	3,668.54	3,521.05	2,668.69	925.65	286.50
PERSONAL TAXES	**2,496.26**	**566.64**	**2,258.58**	**3,074.86**	**4,050.63**	**2,855.85**	**1,556.12**	**478.66**
Federal income taxes	1,842.57	401.66	1,642.07	2,258.45	3,052.10	2,136.26	1,110.82	309.57
State and local income taxes	506.45	148.58	545.80	679.93	797.79	492.51	229.85	51.09
Other taxes	147.24	16.41	70.71	136.49	200.74	227.08	215.45	117.99

Note: (–) means sample is too small to make a reliable estimate.
Source: Bureau of Labor Statistics, unpublished tables from the 2002 Consumer Expenditure Survey

Table 4.2 Financial: Indexed spending by age, 2002

(indexed average annual spending of consumer units (CU) on financial products and services, cash contributions, and miscellaneous items, by age of consumer unit reference person, 2002; index definition: an index of 100 is the average for all consumer units; an index of 132 means that spending by consumer units in that group is 32 percent above the average for all consumer units; an index of 68 indicates spending that is 32 percent below the average for all consumer units)

	total consumer units	under 25	25 to 34	35 to 44	45 to 54	55 to 64	65 to 74	75+
Average spending of CU, total	$40,677	$24,229	$40,318	$48,330	$48,748	$44,330	$32,243	$23,759
Average spending of CU, index	100	60	99	119	120	109	79	58
FINANCIAL PRODUCTS AND SERVICES	**100**	**54**	**86**	**105**	**125**	**118**	**101**	**73**
Miscellaneous fees	100	–	151	123	114	121	72	7
Lottery and gambling losses	100	17	68	52	186	85	172	100
Legal fees	100	38	65	103	132	155	77	81
Funeral expenses	100	34	26	65	104	144	199	189
Safe deposit box rental	100	30	45	70	92	143	201	173
Checking accounts, other bank service charges	100	107	125	129	112	81	59	30
Cemetery lots, vaults, and maintenance fees	100	2	34	21	99	123	192	349
Accounting fees	100	20	72	96	112	144	131	102
Miscellaneous personal services	100	185	111	117	82	72	128	17
Finance charges, except mortgage and vehicles	100	73	126	113	125	98	72	26
Occupational expenses	100	37	96	153	137	119	25	10
Expenses for other properties	100	10	36	141	135	131	91	87
Credit card memberships	100	44	98	115	136	121	83	26
Shopping club membership fees	100	24	69	123	135	132	92	51
CASH CONTRIBUTIONS	**100**	**25**	**58**	**98**	**123**	**119**	**127**	**136**
Support for college students	100	7	9	59	236	196	86	22
Alimony expenditures	100	3	14	74	162	223	60	125
Child support expenditures	100	32	115	197	130	34	33	9
Gifts to non–CU members of stocks, bonds, and mutual funds	100	26	10	6	17	136	215	537
Cash contributions to charities and other organizations	100	15	33	77	131	135	166	155
Cash contributions to church, religious organizations	100	26	62	97	125	127	135	105
Cash contributions to educational institutions	100	5	24	88	121	131	260	84
Cash contributions to political organizations	100	12	40	37	100	121	66	426
Other cash gifts	100	35	48	57	78	121	157	300
PERSONAL INSURANCE AND PENSIONS	**100**	**35**	**102**	**133**	**137**	**124**	**48**	**18**
Life and other personal insurance	100	13	57	101	138	147	128	71
Life, endowment, annuity, other personal insurance	100	13	56	101	137	147	129	69
Other nonhealth insurance	100	14	64	87	148	122	108	124
Pensions and Social Security	100	38	107	137	136	121	38	12
Deductions for government retirement	100	9	64	133	193	139	13	1
Deductions for private pensions	100	12	93	148	159	116	29	3
Nonpayroll deposit to retirement plans	100	13	71	101	114	240	67	26
Deductions for Social Security	100	47	116	141	135	102	36	11
PERSONAL TAXES	**100**	**23**	**90**	**123**	**162**	**114**	**62**	**19**
Federal income taxes	100	22	89	123	166	116	60	17
State and local income taxes	100	29	108	134	158	97	45	10
Other taxes	100	11	48	93	136	154	146	80

Note: (–) means sample is too small to make a reliable estimate.
Source: Calculations by New Strategist based on the 2002 Consumer Expenditure Survey

Table 4.3 Financial: Total spending by age, 2002

(total annual spending on financial products and services, cash contributions, and miscellaneous items, by consumer unit (CU) age groups, 2002; numbers in thousands)

	total consumer units	under 25	25 to 34	35 to 44	45 to 54	55 to 64	65 to 74	75+
Number of consumer units	112,108	8,737	18,988	24,394	22,691	15,314	11,216	10,767
Total spending of all CUs	$4,560,172,273	$211,692,792	$765,563,691	$1,178,973,729	$1,106,146,314	$678,870,233	$361,632,104	$255,811,969
FINANCIAL PRODUCTS AND SERVICES	**$88,354,557**	**$3,690,334**	**$12,876,902**	**$20,124,806**	**$22,360,165**	**$14,237,579**	**$8,901,803**	**$6,161,631**
Miscellaneous fees	252,243	–	64,559	67,327	58,316	41,654	18,282	1,615
Lottery and gambling losses	5,262,350	71,207	602,869	596,189	1,986,143	610,263	907,823	507,772
Legal fees	14,909,243	444,014	1,653,855	3,356,370	3,987,716	3,157,900	1,147,509	1,161,975
Funeral expenses	8,734,334	232,841	390,773	1,230,677	1,839,332	1,721,906	1,737,471	1,581,565
Safe deposit box rental	430,495	9,960	32,469	65,864	80,553	84,227	86,363	71,493
Checking accounts, other bank service charges	2,904,718	243,325	615,401	814,272	657,131	320,063	172,278	82,475
Cemetery lots, vaults, and maintenance fees	1,799,333	3,407	102,535	81,964	361,241	301,839	345,677	602,414
Accounting fees	6,485,448	98,990	792,369	1,358,014	1,473,780	1,277,341	851,967	633,315
Miscellaneous personal services	4,458,535	642,257	838,510	1,134,077	744,038	437,827	569,885	71,708
Finance charges, except mortgage, vehicles	30,422,748	1,739,275	6,507,567	7,455,294	7,681,811	4,091,441	2,197,439	749,168
Occupational expenses	4,311,674	122,755	700,277	1,439,246	1,198,085	700,769	108,795	41,776
Expenses for other properties	7,398,007	58,713	445,458	2,267,178	2,021,541	1,319,454	670,156	615,334
Credit card memberships	316,145	10,921	52,597	78,793	87,133	52,068	26,358	7,968
Shopping club membership fees	669,285	12,669	77,661	179,540	183,343	120,827	61,800	33,055
CASH CONTRIBUTIONS	**143,173,127**	**2,786,841**	**14,113,401**	**30,430,539**	**35,655,730**	**23,280,037**	**18,175,304**	**18,729,627**
Support for college students	8,513,482	44,646	136,144	1,086,997	4,059,647	2,274,588	730,162	181,639
Alimony expenditures	2,374,447	5,242	55,825	382,498	780,343	721,902	143,116	285,433
Child support expenditures	21,384,601	532,608	4,166,537	9,177,511	5,612,392	1,000,157	711,543	183,147
Gifts to non–CU members of stocks, bonds, and mutual funds	2,716,377	55,742	44,242	33,176	94,848	503,065	585,251	1,399,925
Cash contributions to charities and other organizations	15,428,303	176,837	860,346	2,579,909	4,098,675	2,854,989	2,555,341	2,302,200
Cash contributions to church, religious organizations	62,476,667	1,245,285	6,537,948	13,242,039	15,868,951	10,874,318	8,429,497	6,278,345
Cash contributions to educational institutions	3,746,649	15,290	153,233	714,988	916,489	669,528	973,885	303,091
Cash contributions to political organizations	1,221,977	11,183	82,028	99,528	247,105	201,685	80,980	500,019
Other cash gifts	25,309,502	700,096	2,076,907	3,114,138	3,977,278	4,179,803	3,965,641	7,295,827
PERSONAL INSURANCE AND PENSIONS	**437,066,491**	**12,075,495**	**75,415,589**	**126,422,637**	**120,780,109**	**74,088,060**	**20,780,780**	**7,498,246**
Life and other personal insurance	45,528,180	447,859	4,368,569	9,972,023	12,689,942	9,111,524	5,844,770	3,093,467
Life, endowment, annuity, other personal insurance	43,907,098	430,647	4,193,500	9,665,879	12,205,262	8,841,538	5,669,688	2,900,414
Other nonhealth insurance	1,621,082	17,212	175,069	306,145	484,680	269,986	175,194	193,052
Pensions and Social Security	391,538,311	11,627,636	71,047,020	116,450,614	108,090,167	64,976,536	14,935,899	4,404,672
Deductions for government retirement	7,789,264	52,684	845,726	2,260,104	3,045,813	1,476,116	100,383	8,829
Deductions for private pensions	43,764,721	407,406	6,862,263	14,060,214	14,104,045	6,950,259	1,258,211	121,344
Nonpayroll deposit to retirement plans	47,771,461	499,931	5,762,668	10,481,614	10,989,024	15,652,439	3,195,214	1,189,754
Deductions for Social Security	291,965,107	10,667,615	57,571,996	89,490,365	79,896,146	40,868,319	10,382,090	3,084,746
PERSONAL TAXES	**279,850,716**	**4,950,734**	**42,885,917**	**75,008,135**	**91,912,845**	**43,734,487**	**17,453,442**	**5,153,732**
Federal income taxes	206,566,838	3,509,303	31,179,625	55,092,629	69,255,201	32,714,686	12,458,957	3,333,140
State and local income taxes	56,777,097	1,298,143	10,363,650	16,586,212	18,102,653	7,542,298	2,577,998	550,086
Other taxes	16,506,782	143,374	1,342,641	3,329,537	4,554,991	3,477,503	2,416,487	1,270,398

Note: Numbers may not add to total because of rounding. (–) means sample is too small to make a reliable estimate.
Source: Calculations by New Strategist based on the 2002 Consumer Expenditure Survey

Table 4.4 Financial: Market shares by age, 2002

(percentage of total annual spending on financial products and services, cash contributions, and miscellaneous items accounted for by consumer unit (CU) age groups, 2002)

	total consumer units	under 25	25 to 34	35 to 44	45 to 54	55 to 64	65 to 74	75+
Share of total consumer units	100.0%	7.8%	16.9%	21.8%	20.2%	13.7%	10.0%	9.6%
Share of total before-tax income	100.0	3.3	16.8	27.1	26.6	14.7	7.1	4.6
Share of total spending	100.0	4.6	16.8	25.9	24.3	14.9	7.9	5.6
FINANCIAL PRODUCTS AND SERVICES	**100.0%**	**4.2%**	**14.6%**	**22.8%**	**25.3%**	**16.1%**	**10.1%**	**7.0%**
Miscellaneous fees	100.0	–	25.6	26.7	23.1	16.5	7.2	0.6
Lottery and gambling losses	100.0	1.4	11.5	11.3	37.7	11.6	17.3	9.6
Legal fees	100.0	3.0	11.1	22.5	26.7	21.2	7.7	7.8
Funeral expenses	100.0	2.7	4.5	14.1	21.1	19.7	19.9	18.1
Safe deposit box rental	100.0	2.3	7.5	15.3	18.7	19.6	20.1	16.6
Checking accounts, other bank service charges	100.0	8.4	21.2	28.0	22.6	11.0	5.9	2.8
Cemetery lots, vaults, and maintenance fees	100.0	0.2	5.7	4.6	20.1	16.8	19.2	33.5
Accounting fees	100.0	1.5	12.2	20.9	22.7	19.7	13.1	9.8
Miscellaneous personal services	100.0	14.4	18.8	25.4	16.7	9.8	12.8	1.6
Finance charges, except mortgage and vehicles	100.0	5.7	21.4	24.5	25.3	13.4	7.2	2.5
Occupational expenses	100.0	2.8	16.2	33.4	27.8	16.3	2.5	1.0
Expenses for other properties	100.0	0.8	6.0	30.6	27.3	17.8	9.1	8.3
Credit card memberships	100.0	3.5	16.6	24.9	27.6	16.5	8.3	2.5
Shopping club membership fees	100.0	1.9	11.6	26.8	27.4	18.1	9.2	4.9
CASH CONTRIBUTIONS	**100.0**	**1.9**	**9.9**	**21.3**	**24.9**	**16.3**	**12.7**	**13.1**
Support for college students	100.0	0.5	1.6	12.8	47.7	26.7	8.6	2.1
Alimony expenditures	100.0	0.2	2.4	16.1	32.9	30.4	6.0	12.0
Child support expenditures	100.0	2.5	19.5	42.9	26.2	4.7	3.3	0.9
Gifts to non–CU members of stocks, bonds, and mutual funds	100.0	2.1	1.6	1.2	3.5	18.5	21.5	51.5
Cash contributions to charities and other organizations	100.0	1.1	5.6	16.7	26.6	18.5	16.6	14.9
Cash contributions to church, religious organizations	100.0	2.0	10.5	21.2	25.4	17.4	13.5	10.0
Cash contributions to educational institutions	100.0	0.4	4.1	19.1	24.5	17.9	26.0	8.1
Cash contributions to political organizations	100.0	0.9	6.7	8.1	20.2	16.5	6.6	40.9
Other cash gifts	100.0	2.8	8.2	12.3	15.7	16.5	15.7	28.8
PERSONAL INSURANCE AND PENSIONS	**100.0**	**2.8**	**17.3**	**28.9**	**27.6**	**17.0**	**4.8**	**1.7**
Life and other personal insurance	100.0	1.0	9.6	21.9	27.9	20.0	12.8	6.8
Life, endowment, annuity, other personal insurance	100.0	1.0	9.6	22.0	27.8	20.1	12.9	6.6
Other nonhealth insurance	100.0	1.1	10.8	18.9	29.9	16.7	10.8	11.9
Pensions and Social Security	100.0	3.0	18.1	29.7	27.6	16.6	3.8	1.1
Deductions for government retirement	100.0	0.7	10.9	29.0	39.1	19.0	1.3	0.1
Deductions for private pensions	100.0	0.9	15.7	32.1	32.2	15.9	2.9	0.3
Nonpayroll deposit to retirement plans	100.0	1.0	12.1	21.9	23.0	32.8	6.7	2.5
Deductions for Social Security	100.0	3.7	19.7	30.7	27.4	14.0	3.6	1.1
PERSONAL TAXES	**100.0**	**1.8**	**15.3**	**26.8**	**32.8**	**15.6**	**6.2**	**1.8**
Federal income taxes	100.0	1.7	15.1	26.7	33.5	15.8	6.0	1.6
State and local income taxes	100.0	2.3	18.3	29.2	31.9	13.3	4.5	1.0
Other taxes	100.0	0.9	8.1	20.2	27.6	21.1	14.6	7.7

Note: Numbers may not add to total because of rounding. (–) means sample is too small to make a reliable estimate.
Source: Calculations by New Strategist based on the 2002 Consumer Expenditure Survey

Table 4.5 Financial: Average spending by income, 2002

(average annual spending on financial products and services, cash contributions, and miscellaneous items, by before-tax income of consumer units (CU), 2002; complete income reporters only)

	complete income reporters	under $10,000	$10,000–$19,999	$20,000–$29,999	$30,000–$39,999	$40,000–$49,999	$50,000–$69,999	$70,000 or more
Number of consumer units (in thousands, add 000)	92,388	10,933	15,075	12,312	10,727	8,873	13,521	20,947
Average number of persons per CU	2.5	1.7	1.9	2.3	2.5	2.6	2.8	3.1
Average before-tax income of CU	$49,430.00	$5,554.80	$14,724.33	$24,495.00	$34,423.00	$44,443.00	$58,933.00	$115,629.00
Average spending of CU, total	42,556.98	17,627.83	22,838.71	28,835.85	35,095.39	41,787.38	50,406.17	76,627.31
FINANCIAL PRODUCTS AND SERVICES	**$846.40**	**$343.79**	**$451.35**	**$675.16**	**$808.05**	**$777.96**	**$1,035.05**	**$1,416.84**
Miscellaneous fees	2.49	–	0.61	2.87	5.60	–	3.63	3.48
Lottery and gambling losses	54.94	30.24	30.68	43.87	28.37	38.04	120.41	70.11
Legal fees	143.91	34.56	55.66	89.40	150.29	108.46	170.94	290.83
Funeral expenses	78.55	71.03	74.12	107.16	72.03	32.57	48.80	110.87
Safe deposit box rental	4.07	1.28	2.83	3.88	4.23	4.42	4.29	6.16
Checking accounts, other bank service charges	27.76	14.07	14.08	22.13	29.48	36.83	34.22	39.17
Cemetery lots, vaults, and maintenance fees	15.94	3.92	17.77	18.41	17.33	18.66	17.42	16.62
Accounting fees	60.79	19.05	42.49	50.61	47.22	51.33	54.83	116.53
Miscellaneous personal services	46.30	15.77	11.17	45.76	95.50	28.69	25.29	80.27
Finance charges, except mortgage and vehicles	291.36	134.97	156.29	233.94	260.47	359.15	440.29	394.92
Occupational expenses	42.05	5.33	7.96	15.49	33.90	38.73	50.29	101.64
Expenses for other properties	65.60	10.97	33.59	35.46	55.13	51.02	53.70	154.08
Credit card memberships	3.11	–	–	–	–	–	–	–
Shopping club membership fees	6.43	1.44	2.16	3.50	5.82	6.98	7.70	13.09
CASH CONTRIBUTIONS	**1,365.74**	**406.16**	**644.80**	**980.86**	**1,092.70**	**1,182.35**	**1,560.39**	**2,703.53**
Support for college students	78.38	18.06	8.48	26.05	30.63	81.65	72.81	217.61
Alimony expenditures	21.64	0.15	1.58	10.30	35.08	8.32	27.22	49.10
Child support expenditures	206.98	36.76	52.91	137.96	222.36	210.38	288.01	385.67
Gifts to non–CU members of stocks, bonds, and mutual funds	27.82	36.44	1.65	57.23	104.60	6.10	7.39	7.94
Cash contributions to charities and other organizations	140.44	42.96	52.84	68.82	70.34	90.75	126.66	362.29
Cash contributions to church, religious organizations	590.37	180.51	278.52	381.71	414.10	548.68	755.41	1,152.76
Cash contributions to educational institutions	36.64	21.62	6.34	6.25	7.82	11.14	58.89	95.37
Cash contributions to political organizations	12.08	2.88	1.67	4.40	5.21	5.33	9.89	36.68
Other cash gifts	251.39	66.76	240.80	288.14	202.57	220.00	214.12	396.11
PERSONAL INSURANCE AND PENSIONS	**4,593.39**	**333.19**	**886.28**	**1,821.81**	**2,898.27**	**4,238.75**	**5,755.90**	**11,381.92**
Life and other personal insurance	424.56	131.03	212.46	259.16	324.31	384.99	468.64	867.29
Life, endowment, annuity, other personal insurance	408.66	128.30	208.05	244.77	313.68	367.47	449.70	835.28
Other nonhealth insurance	15.91	2.73	4.41	14.39	10.62	17.52	18.94	32.01
Pensions and Social Security	4,168.83	202.17	673.82	1,562.65	2,573.96	3,853.77	5,287.26	10,514.63
Deductions for government retirement	83.60	0.14	2.15	17.58	58.93	93.07	127.61	204.79
Deductions for private pensions	470.43	2.10	10.02	61.86	174.06	300.33	603.05	1,424.59
Nonpayroll deposit to retirement plans	498.11	28.67	134.74	245.27	253.80	501.67	438.04	1,315.66
Deductions for Social Security	3,114.01	171.27	526.90	1,237.93	2,087.18	2,955.52	4,112.95	7,562.77
PERSONAL TAXES	**2,496.26**	**1.01**	**19.84**	**475.56**	**831.06**	**1,934.30**	**2,584.68**	**7,802.32**
Federal income taxes	1,842.57	−46.43	−58.58	250.52	481.27	1,333.19	1,879.50	6,021.57
State and local income taxes	506.45	9.57	36.53	132.27	223.92	466.14	540.18	1,463.91
Other taxes	147.24	37.87	41.89	92.77	125.87	134.98	164.99	316.85

Note: (–) means sample is too small to make a reliable estimate.
Source: Bureau of Labor Statistics, unpublished tables from the 2002 Consumer Expenditure Survey; calculations by New Strategist

Table 4.6 Financial: Indexed spending by income, 2002

(indexed average annual spending of consumer units (CU) on financial products and services, cash contributions, and miscellaneous items, by before-tax income of consumer unit, 2002; complete income reporters only; index definition: an index of 100 is the average for all consumer units; an index of 132 means that spending by consumer units in that group is 32 percent above the average for all consumer units; an index of 68 indicates spending that is 32 percent below the average for all consumer units)

	complete income reporters	under $10,000	$10,000–$19,999	$20,000–$29,999	$30,000–$39,999	$40,000–$49,999	$50,000–$69,999	$70,000 or more
Average spending of CU, total	$42,557	$17,628	$22,839	$28,836	$35,095	$41,787	$50,406	$76,627
Average spending of CU, index	100	41	54	68	82	98	118	180
FINANCIAL PRODUCTS AND SERVICES	**100**	**41**	**53**	**80**	**95**	**92**	**122**	**167**
Miscellaneous fees	100	–	24	115	225	–	146	140
Lottery and gambling losses	100	55	56	80	52	69	219	128
Legal fees	100	24	39	62	104	75	119	202
Funeral expenses	100	90	94	136	92	41	62	141
Safe deposit box rental	100	31	70	95	104	109	105	151
Checking accounts, other bank service charges	100	51	51	80	106	133	123	141
Cemetery lots, vaults, and maintenance fees	100	25	111	115	109	117	109	104
Accounting fees	100	31	70	83	78	84	90	192
Miscellaneous personal services	100	34	24	99	206	62	55	173
Finance charges, except mortgage and vehicles	100	46	54	80	89	123	151	136
Occupational expenses	100	13	19	37	81	92	120	242
Expenses for other properties	100	17	51	54	84	78	82	235
Credit card memberships	100	–	–	–	–	–	–	–
Shopping club membership fees	100	22	34	54	91	109	120	204
CASH CONTRIBUTIONS	**100**	**30**	**47**	**72**	**80**	**87**	**114**	**198**
Support for college students	100	23	11	33	39	104	93	278
Alimony expenditures	100	1	7	48	162	38	126	227
Child support expenditures	100	18	26	67	107	102	139	186
Gifts to non–CU members of stocks, bonds, and mutual funds	100	131	6	206	376	22	27	29
Cash contributions to charities and other organizations	100	31	38	49	50	65	90	258
Cash contributions to church, religious organizations	100	31	47	65	70	93	128	195
Cash contributions to educational institutions	100	59	17	17	21	30	161	260
Cash contributions to political organizations	100	24	14	36	43	44	82	304
Other cash gifts	100	27	96	115	81	88	85	158
PERSONAL INSURANCE AND PENSIONS	**100**	**7**	**19**	**40**	**63**	**92**	**125**	**248**
Life and other personal insurance	100	31	50	61	76	91	110	204
Life, endowment, annuity, other personal insurance	100	31	51	60	77	90	110	204
Other nonhealth insurance	100	17	28	90	67	110	119	201
Pensions and Social Security	100	5	16	37	62	92	127	252
Deductions for government retirement	100	0	3	21	70	111	153	245
Deductions for private pensions	100	0	2	13	37	64	128	303
Nonpayroll deposit to retirement plans	100	6	27	49	51	101	88	264
Deductions for Social Security	100	5	17	40	67	95	132	243
PERSONAL TAXES	**100**	**0**	**1**	**19**	**33**	**77**	**104**	**313**
Federal income taxes	100	-3	–3	14	26	72	102	327
State and local income taxes	100	2	7	26	44	92	107	289
Other taxes	100	26	28	63	85	92	112	215

Note: (–) means sample is too small to make a reliable estimate.
Source: Calculations by New Strategist based on the 2002 Consumer Expenditure Survey

Table 4.7 Financial: Total spending by income, 2002

(total annual spending on financial products and services, cash contributions, and miscellaneous items, by before-tax income group of consumer units (CU), 2002; complete income reporters only; numbers in thousands)

	complete income reporters	under $10,000	$10,000–$19,999	$20,000–$29,999	$30,000–$39,999	$40,000–$49,999	$50,000–$69,999	$70,000 or more
Number of consumer units	92,388	10,933	15,075	12,312	10,727	8,873	13,521	20,947
Total spending of all CUs	$3,931,754,268	$192,725,059	$344,293,530	$355,026,985	$376,468,249	$370,779,423	$681,541,825	$1,605,112,263
FINANCIAL PRODUCTS AND SERVICES	**$78,197,203**	**$3,758,620**	**$6,804,147**	**$8,312,570**	**$8,667,952**	**$6,902,839**	**$13,994,911**	**$29,678,547**
Miscellaneous fees	230,046	–	9,183	35,335	60,071	–	49,081	72,896
Lottery and gambling losses	5,075,797	330,589	462,508	540,127	304,325	337,529	1,628,064	1,468,594
Legal fees	13,295,557	377,878	839,135	1,100,693	1,612,161	962,366	2,311,280	6,092,016
Funeral expenses	7,257,077	776,520	1,117,306	1,319,354	772,666	288,994	659,825	2,322,394
Safe deposit box rental	376,019	13,996	42,672	47,771	45,375	39,219	58,005	129,034
Checking accounts, other bank service charges	2,564,691	153,805	212,244	272,465	316,232	326,793	462,689	820,494
Cemetery lots, vaults, and maintenance fees	1,472,665	42,842	267,844	226,664	185,899	165,570	235,536	348,139
Accounting fees	5,616,267	208,307	640,504	623,110	506,529	455,451	741,356	2,440,954
Miscellaneous personal services	4,277,564	172,428	168,448	563,397	1,024,429	254,566	341,946	1,681,416
Finance charges, except mortgage, vehicles	26,918,168	1,475,597	2,356,138	2,880,269	2,794,062	3,186,738	5,953,161	8,272,389
Occupational expenses	3,884,915	58,274	120,001	190,713	363,645	343,651	679,971	2,129,053
Expenses for other properties	6,060,653	119,941	506,298	436,584	591,380	452,700	726,078	3,227,514
Credit card memberships	287,327	–	–	–	–	–	–	274,196
Shopping club membership fees	594,055	15,723	32,596	43,092	62,431	61,934	104,112	274,196
CASH CONTRIBUTIONS	**126,177,987**	**4,440,538**	**9,720,375**	**12,076,348**	**11,721,393**	**10,490,992**	**21,098,033**	**56,630,843**
Support for college students	7,241,371	197,460	127,878	320,728	328,568	724,480	984,464	4,558,277
Alimony expenditures	1,999,276	1,692	23,847	126,814	376,303	73,823	368,042	1,028,498
Child support expenditures	19,122,468	401,922	797,598	1,698,564	2,385,256	1,866,702	3,894,183	8,078,629
Gifts to non–CU members of stocks, bonds, and mutual funds	2,570,234	398,451	24,833	704,616	1,122,044	54,125	99,920	166,319
Cash contributions to charities and other organizations	12,974,971	469,675	796,610	847,312	754,537	805,225	1,712,570	7,588,889
Cash contributions to church, religious organizations	54,543,104	1,973,554	4,198,750	4,699,614	4,442,051	4,868,438	10,213,899	24,146,864
Cash contributions to educational institutions	3,385,096	236,374	95,633	76,950	83,885	98,845	796,252	1,997,715
Cash contributions to political organizations	1,116,047	31,491	25,174	54,173	55,888	47,293	133,723	768,336
Other cash gifts	23,225,419	729,887	3,630,061	3,547,580	2,172,968	1,952,060	2,895,117	8,297,316
PERSONAL INSURANCE AND PENSIONS	**424,374,115**	**3,642,782**	**13,360,654**	**22,430,125**	**31,089,742**	**37,610,429**	**77,825,524**	**238,417,078**
Life and other personal insurance	39,224,249	1,432,510	3,202,873	3,190,778	3,478,873	3,416,016	6,336,481	18,167,124
Life, endowment, annuity, other personal insurance	37,755,280	1,402,664	3,136,376	3,013,608	3,364,845	3,260,561	6,080,394	17,496,610
Other nonhealth insurance	1,469,893	29,846	66,497	177,170	113,921	155,455	256,088	670,513
Pensions and Social Security	385,149,866	2,210,311	10,157,781	19,239,347	27,610,869	34,194,501	71,489,042	220,249,955
Deductions for government retirement	7,723,637	1,485	32,437	216,445	632,142	825,810	1,725,415	4,289,736
Deductions for private pensions	43,462,087	22,908	151,124	761,620	1,867,142	2,664,828	8,153,839	29,840,887
Nonpayroll deposit to retirement plans	46,019,387	313,406	2,031,245	3,019,764	2,722,513	4,451,318	5,922,739	27,559,130
Deductions for Social Security	287,697,156	1,872,473	7,943,046	15,241,394	22,389,180	26,224,329	55,611,197	158,417,343
PERSONAL TAXES	**230,624,469**	**11,038**	**299,090**	**5,855,095**	**8,914,781**	**17,163,044**	**34,947,458**	**163,435,197**
Federal income taxes	170,231,357	–507,666	–883,046	3,084,402	5,162,583	11,829,395	25,412,720	126,133,827
State and local income taxes	46,789,903	104,622	550,756	1,628,508	2,401,990	4,136,060	7,303,774	30,664,523
Other taxes	13,603,209	414,082	631,461	1,142,184	1,350,207	1,197,678	2,230,830	6,637,057

Note: Numbers may not add to total because of rounding. (–) means sample is too small to make a reliable estimate.
Source: Calculations by New Strategist based on the 2002 Consumer Expenditure Survey

Table 4.8 Financial: Market shares by income, 2002

(percentage of total annual spending on financial products and services, cash contributions, and miscellaneous items accounted for by before-tax income group of consumer units (CU), 2002; complete income reporters only)

	complete income reporters	under $10,000	$10,000–$19,999	$20,000–$29,999	$30,000–$39,999	$40,000–$49,999	$50,000–$69,999	$70,000 or more
Share of total consumer units	100.0%	11.8%	16.3%	13.3%	11.6%	9.6%	14.6%	22.7%
Share of total before-tax income	100.0	1.3	4.9	6.6	8.1	8.6	17.4	53.0
Share of total spending	100.0	4.9	8.8	9.0	9.6	9.4	17.3	40.8
FINANCIAL PRODUCTS AND SERVICES	**100.0%**	**4.8%**	**8.7%**	**10.6%**	**11.1%**	**8.8%**	**17.9%**	**38.0%**
Miscellaneous fees	100.0	–	4.0	15.4	26.1	–	21.3	31.7
Lottery and gambling losses	100.0	6.5	9.1	10.6	6.0	6.6	32.1	28.9
Legal fees	100.0	2.8	6.3	8.3	12.1	7.2	17.4	45.8
Funeral expenses	100.0	10.7	15.4	18.2	10.6	4.0	9.1	32.0
Safe deposit box rental	100.0	3.7	11.3	12.7	12.1	10.4	15.4	34.3
Checking accounts, other bank service charges	100.0	6.0	8.3	10.6	12.3	12.7	18.0	32.0
Cemetery lots, vaults, and maintenance fees	100.0	2.9	18.2	15.4	12.6	11.2	16.0	23.6
Accounting fees	100.0	3.7	11.4	11.1	9.0	8.1	13.2	43.5
Miscellaneous personal services	100.0	4.0	3.9	13.2	23.9	6.0	8.0	39.3
Finance charges, except mortgage and vehicles	100.0	5.5	8.8	10.7	10.4	11.8	22.1	30.7
Occupational expenses	100.0	1.5	3.1	4.9	9.4	8.8	17.5	54.8
Expenses for other properties	100.0	2.0	8.4	7.2	9.8	7.5	12.0	53.3
Credit card memberships	100.0	–	–	–	–	–	–	–
Shopping club membership fees	100.0	2.6	5.5	7.3	10.5	10.4	17.5	46.2
CASH CONTRIBUTIONS	**100.0**	**3.5**	**7.7**	**9.6**	**9.3**	**8.3**	**16.7**	**44.9**
Support for college students	100.0	2.7	1.8	4.4	4.5	10.0	13.6	62.9
Alimony expenditures	100.0	0.1	1.2	6.3	18.8	3.7	18.4	51.4
Child support expenditures	100.0	2.1	4.2	8.9	12.5	9.8	20.4	42.2
Gifts to non–CU members of stocks, bonds, and mutual funds	100.0	15.5	1.0	27.4	43.7	2.1	3.9	6.5
Cash contributions to charities and other organizations	100.0	3.6	6.1	6.5	5.8	6.2	13.2	58.5
Cash contributions to church, religious organizations	100.0	3.6	7.7	8.6	8.1	8.9	18.7	44.3
Cash contributions to educational institutions	100.0	7.0	2.8	2.3	2.5	2.9	23.5	59.0
Cash contributions to political organizations	100.0	2.8	2.3	4.9	5.0	4.2	12.0	68.8
Other cash gifts	100.0	3.1	15.6	15.3	9.4	8.4	12.5	35.7
PERSONAL INSURANCE AND PENSIONS	**100.0**	**0.9**	**3.1**	**5.3**	**7.3**	**8.9**	**18.3**	**56.2**
Life and other personal insurance	100.0	3.7	8.2	8.1	8.9	8.7	16.2	46.3
Life, endowment, annuity, other personal insurance	100.0	3.7	8.3	8.0	8.9	8.6	16.1	46.3
Other nonhealth insurance	100.0	2.0	4.5	12.1	7.8	10.6	17.4	45.6
Pensions and Social Security	100.0	0.6	2.6	5.0	7.2	8.9	18.6	57.2
Deductions for government retirement	100.0	0.0	0.4	2.8	8.2	10.7	22.3	55.5
Deductions for private pensions	100.0	0.1	0.3	1.8	4.3	6.1	18.8	68.7
Nonpayroll deposit to retirement plans	100.0	0.7	4.4	6.6	5.9	9.7	12.9	59.9
Deductions for Social Security	100.0	0.7	2.8	5.3	7.8	9.1	19.3	55.1
PERSONAL TAXES	**100.0**	**0.0**	**0.1**	**2.5**	**3.9**	**7.4**	**15.2**	**70.9**
Federal income taxes	100.0	–0.3	–0.5	1.8	3.0	6.9	14.9	74.1
State and local income taxes	100.0	0.2	1.2	3.5	5.1	8.8	15.6	65.5
Other taxes	100.0	3.0	4.6	8.4	9.9	8.8	16.4	48.8

Note: Numbers may not add to total because of rounding. (–) means sample is too small to make a reliable estimate.
Source: Calculations by New Strategist based on the 2002 Consumer Expenditure Survey

Table 4.9 Financial: Average spending by household type, 2002

(average annual spending of consumer units (CU) on financial products and services, cash contributions, and miscellaneous items, by type of consumer unit, 2002)

	total married couples	married couples, no children	married couples with children			single parent, at least one child <18	single person
			total	oldest child under 6	oldest child 6 to 17	oldest child 18 or older	
Number of consumer units (in thousands, add 000)	56,265	23,118	28,790	5,547	15,206	8,036	6,730	33,055
Average number of persons per CU	3.2	2.0	3.9	3.5	4.1	3.9	2.9	1.0
Average before-tax income of CU	$67,155.00	$58,967.00	$73,918.00	$67,587.00	$72,720.00	$81,042.00	$26,966.00	$27,042.00
Average spending of CU, total	52,333.70	45,557.33	57,835.01	52,778.62	58,103.75	60,859.78	30,185.38	24,189.90
FINANCIAL PRODUCTS AND SERVICES	$921.41	$865.39	$948.96	$912.54	$827.03	$1,204.54	$569.46	$601.90
Miscellaneous fees	$3.26	$3.73	$3.11	$1.84	$2.62	$5.01	–	$1.31
Lottery and gambling losses	52.23	73.38	37.48	34.33	30.77	53.17	11.64	44.30
Legal fees	136.58	89.45	176.56	69.31	130.04	338.63	130.68	103.42
Funeral expenses	74.93	82.54	43.03	20.07	36.45	71.31	30.76	73.84
Safe deposit box rental	4.85	7.12	3.34	2.65	3.14	4.19	0.92	3.43
Checking accounts, other bank service charges	28.69	22.29	33.36	35.16	34.71	29.57	22.92	20.10
Cemetery lots, vaults, and maintenance fees	21.10	39.72	5.09	0.65	5.61	7.18	5.14	8.51
Accounting fees	74.91	82.48	72.11	56.40	74.08	79.22	30.32	44.04
Miscellaneous personal services	41.01	34.90	51.52	123.02	31.29	39.24	54.58	33.22
Finance charges, except mortgage and vehicles	320.91	293.23	330.99	366.76	312.23	341.78	249.10	200.56
Occupational expenses	47.61	41.40	54.97	52.84	50.55	64.79	15.28	30.05
Expenses for other properties	94.59	82.16	108.73	130.24	76.57	154.73	12.07	34.73
Credit card memberships	3.26	3.68	3.09	4.39	2.42	3.47	2.82	2.02
Shopping club membership fees	8.96	9.21	9.03	6.71	10.17	8.48	3.22	2.37
CASH CONTRIBUTIONS	1,645.53	1,909.28	1,480.79	1,037.24	1,399.31	1,941.15	374.03	998.23
Support for college students	120.21	148.08	102.33	17.70	63.91	233.46	15.90	37.52
Alimony expenditures	24.13	34.59	15.45	14.83	20.84	5.69	9.18	20.72
Child support expenditures	141.24	109.05	171.23	186.54	196.54	112.75	78.24	212.20
Gifts to non–CU members of stocks, bonds, and mutual funds	17.11	36.25	3.41	3.59	1.77	6.39	0.13	50.92
Cash contributions to charities and other organizations	193.33	263.86	151.34	78.90	136.93	228.60	23.64	97.55
Cash contributions to church, religious organizations	835.08	827.94	849.34	633.22	798.46	1,094.80	187.72	301.58
Cash contributions to educational institutions	45.50	63.41	35.27	29.37	43.08	24.58	8.30	30.49
Cash contributions to political organizations	18.22	19.23	19.47	3.06	7.77	52.95	1.05	4.08
Other cash gifts	250.70	406.86	132.95	70.03	130.02	181.93	49.86	243.17
PERSONAL INSURANCE AND PENSIONS	5,383.71	4,524.22	6,144.01	5,952.38	6,129.29	6,304.13	2,065.57	2,054.94
Life and other personal insurance	604.90	633.61	591.85	424.39	608.98	675.03	182.38	182.88
Life, endowment, annuity, other personal insurance	585.15	610.15	573.57	413.72	589.30	654.14	177.22	173.52
Other nonhealth insurance	19.76	23.47	18.28	10.67	19.68	20.89	5.16	9.36
Pensions and Social Security	4,778.80	3,890.60	5,552.16	5,527.98	5,520.31	5,629.10	1,883.20	1,872.06
Deductions for government retirement	93.85	85.41	103.93	57.85	108.54	127.02	70.53	43.16
Deductions for private pensions	566.47	473.50	681.87	669.11	710.65	636.21	151.94	211.04
Nonpayroll deposit to retirement plans	516.93	553.47	509.41	604.84	434.83	584.66	137.05	372.12
Deductions for Social Security	3,597.77	2,776.96	4,251.28	4,195.35	4,256.09	4,280.78	1,523.68	1,244.90
PERSONAL TAXES	3,457.82	3,358.28	3,705.74	3,738.11	3,710.32	3,672.37	483.10	1,815.47
Federal income taxes	2,542.71	2,463.71	2,748.53	2,766.02	2,742.21	2,747.76	195.06	1,395.87
State and local income taxes	702.40	645.25	773.86	837.48	781.91	710.11	243.00	326.58
Other taxes	212.71	249.32	183.35	134.61	186.20	214.50	45.04	93.02

Note: Average spending figures for total consumer units can be found on Average Spending by Age and Average Spending by Region tables. (–) means sample is too small to make a reliable estimate.
Source: Bureau of Labor Statistics, unpublished tables from the 2002 Consumer Expenditure Survey

Table 4.10 Financial: Indexed spending by household type, 2002

(indexed average annual spending of consumer units (CU) on financial products and services, cash contributions, and miscellaneous items, by type of consumer unit, 2002; index definition: an index of 100 is the average for all consumer units; an index of 132 means that spending by consumer units in that group is 32 percent above the average for all consumer units; an index of 68 indicates spending that is 32 percent below the average for all consumer units)

	total married couples	married couples, no children	married couples with children — total	oldest child under 6	oldest child 6 to 17	oldest child 18 or older	single parent, at least one child <18	single person
Average spending of CU, total	$52,334	$45,557	$57,835	$52,779	$58,104	$60,860	$30,185	$24,190
Average spending of CU, index	129	112	142	130	143	150	74	59
FINANCIAL PRODUCTS AND SERVICES	**117**	**110**	**120**	**116**	**105**	**153**	**72**	**76**
Miscellaneous fees	145	166	138	82	116	223	–	58
Lottery and gambling losses	111	156	80	73	66	113	25	94
Legal fees	103	67	133	52	98	255	98	78
Funeral expenses	96	106	55	26	47	92	39	95
Safe deposit box rental	126	185	87	69	82	109	24	89
Checking accounts, other bank service charges	111	86	129	136	134	114	88	78
Cemetery lots, vaults, and maintenance fees	131	247	32	4	35	45	32	53
Accounting fees	129	143	125	97	128	137	52	76
Miscellaneous personal services	103	88	130	309	79	99	137	84
Finance charges, except mortgage and vehicles	118	108	122	135	115	126	92	74
Occupational expenses	124	108	143	137	131	168	40	78
Expenses for other properties	143	125	165	197	116	234	18	53
Credit card memberships	116	130	110	156	86	123	100	72
Shopping club membership fees	150	154	151	112	170	142	54	40
CASH CONTRIBUTIONS	**129**	**150**	**116**	**81**	**110**	**152**	**29**	**78**
Support for college students	158	195	135	23	84	307	21	49
Alimony expenditures	114	163	73	70	98	27	43	98
Child support expenditures	74	57	90	98	103	59	41	111
Gifts to non–CU members of stocks, bonds, and mutual funds	71	150	14	15	7	26	1	210
Cash contributions to charities and other organizations	140	192	110	57	99	166	17	71
Cash contributions to church, religious organizations	150	149	152	114	143	196	34	54
Cash contributions to educational institutions	136	190	106	88	129	74	25	91
Cash contributions to political organizations	167	176	179	28	71	486	10	37
Other cash gifts	111	180	59	31	58	81	22	108
PERSONAL INSURANCE AND PENSIONS	**138**	**116**	**158**	**153**	**157**	**162**	**53**	**53**
Life and other personal insurance	149	156	146	105	150	166	45	45
Life, endowment, annuity, other personal insurance	149	156	146	106	150	167	45	44
Other nonhealth insurance	137	162	126	74	136	144	36	65
Pensions and Social Security	137	111	159	158	158	161	54	54
Deductions for government retirement	135	123	150	83	156	183	102	62
Deductions for private pensions	145	121	175	171	182	163	39	54
Nonpayroll deposit to retirement plans	121	130	120	142	102	137	32	87
Deductions for Social Security	138	107	163	161	163	164	59	48
PERSONAL TAXES	**139**	**135**	**148**	**150**	**149**	**147**	**19**	**73**
Federal income taxes	138	134	149	150	149	149	11	76
State and local income taxes	139	127	153	165	154	140	48	64
Other taxes	144	169	125	91	126	146	31	63

Note: Spending index for total consumer units is 100. (–) means sample is too small to make a reliable estimate.
Source: Calculations by New Strategist based on the 2002 Consumer Expenditure Survey

Table 4.11 Financial: Total spending by household type, 2002

(total annual spending on financial products and services, cash contributions, and miscellaneous items, by consumer unit (CU) type, 2002; numbers in thousands)

	total married couples	married couples, no children	married couples with children: total	oldest child under 6	oldest child 6 to 17	oldest child 18 or older	single parent, at least one child <18	single person
Number of consumer units	56,265	23,118	28,790	5,547	15,206	8,036	6,730	33,055
Total spending of all CUs	$2,944,555,631	$1,053,194,355	$1,665,069,938	$292,763,005	$883,525,623	$489,069,192	$203,147,607	$799,597,145
FINANCIAL PRODUCTS AND SERVICES	**$51,843,134**	**$20,006,086**	**$27,320,558**	**$5,061,859**	**$12,575,818**	**$9,679,683**	**$3,832,466**	**$19,895,805**
Miscellaneous fees	183,424	86,230	89,537	10,206	39,840	40,260	–	43,302
Lottery and gambling losses	2,938,721	1,696,399	1,079,049	190,429	467,889	427,274	78,337	1,464,337
Legal fees	7,684,674	2,067,905	5,083,162	384,463	1,977,388	2,721,231	879,476	3,418,548
Funeral expenses	4,215,936	1,908,160	1,238,834	111,328	554,259	573,047	207,015	2,440,781
Safe deposit box rental	272,885	164,600	96,159	14,700	47,747	33,671	6,192	113,379
Checking accounts, other bank service charges	1,614,243	515,300	960,434	195,033	527,800	237,625	154,252	664,406
Cemetery lots, vaults, and maintenance fees	1,187,192	918,247	146,541	3,606	85,306	57,698	34,592	281,298
Accounting fees	4,214,811	1,906,773	2,076,047	312,851	1,126,460	636,612	204,054	1,455,742
Miscellaneous personal services	2,307,428	806,818	1,483,261	682,392	475,796	315,333	367,323	1,098,087
Finance charges, except mortgage, vehicles	18,056,001	6,778,891	9,529,202	2,034,418	4,747,769	2,746,544	1,676,443	6,629,511
Occupational expenses	2,678,777	957,085	1,582,586	293,103	768,663	520,652	102,834	993,303
Expenses for other properties	5,322,106	1,899,375	3,130,337	722,441	1,164,323	1,243,410	81,231	1,148,000
Credit card memberships	183,424	85,074	88,961	24,351	36,799	27,885	18,979	66,771
Shopping club membership fees	504,134	212,917	259,974	37,220	154,645	68,145	21,671	78,340
CASH CONTRIBUTIONS	**92,585,745**	**44,138,735**	**42,631,944**	**5,753,570**	**21,277,908**	**15,599,081**	**2,517,222**	**32,996,493**
Support for college students	6,763,616	3,423,313	2,946,081	98,182	971,815	1,876,085	107,007	1,240,224
Alimony expenditures	1,357,674	799,652	444,806	82,262	316,893	45,725	61,781	684,900
Child support expenditures	7,946,869	2,521,018	4,929,712	1,034,737	2,988,587	906,059	526,555	7,014,271
Gifts to non–CU members of stocks, bonds, and mutual funds	962,694	838,028	98,174	19,914	26,915	51,350	875	1,683,161
Cash contributions to charities and other organizations	10,877,712	6,099,915	4,357,079	437,658	2,082,158	1,837,030	159,097	3,224,515
Cash contributions to church, religious organizations	46,985,776	19,140,317	24,452,499	3,512,471	12,141,383	8,797,813	1,263,356	9,968,727
Cash contributions to educational institutions	2,560,058	1,465,912	1,015,423	162,915	655,074	197,525	55,859	1,007,847
Cash contributions to political organizations	1,025,148	444,559	560,541	16,974	118,151	425,506	7,067	134,864
Other cash gifts	14,105,636	9,405,789	3,827,631	388,456	1,977,084	1,461,989	335,558	8,037,984
PERSONAL INSURANCE AND PENSIONS	**302,914,443**	**104,590,918**	**176,886,048**	**33,017,852**	**93,201,984**	**50,659,989**	**13,901,286**	**67,926,042**
Life and other personal insurance	34,034,699	14,647,796	17,039,362	2,354,091	9,260,150	5,424,541	1,227,417	6,045,098
Life, endowment, annuity, other personal insurance	32,923,465	14,105,448	16,513,080	2,294,905	8,960,896	5,256,669	1,192,691	5,735,704
Other nonhealth insurance	1,111,796	542,579	526,281	59,186	299,254	167,872	34,727	309,395
Pensions and Social Security	268,879,182	89,942,891	159,846,686	30,663,705	83,941,834	45,235,448	12,673,936	61,880,943
Deductions for government retirement	5,280,470	1,974,508	2,992,145	320,894	1,650,459	1,020,733	474,667	1,426,654
Deductions for private pensions	31,872,435	10,946,373	19,631,037	3,711,553	10,806,144	5,112,584	1,022,556	6,975,927
Nonpayroll deposit to retirement plans	29,085,066	12,795,119	14,665,914	3,355,047	6,612,025	4,698,328	922,347	12,300,427
Deductions for Social Security	202,428,529	64,197,761	122,394,351	23,271,606	64,718,105	34,400,348	10,254,366	41,150,170
PERSONAL TAXES	**194,554,242**	**77,636,717**	**106,688,255**	**20,735,296**	**56,419,126**	**29,511,165**	**3,251,263**	**60,010,361**
Federal income taxes	143,065,578	56,956,048	79,130,179	15,343,113	41,698,045	22,080,999	1,312,754	46,140,483
State and local income taxes	39,520,536	14,916,890	22,279,429	4,645,502	11,889,723	5,706,444	1,635,390	10,795,102
Other taxes	11968128.15	5763779.76	5278646.5	746681.67	2831357.2	1723722	303119.2	3074776.1

Note: Total spending figures for total consumer units can be found on Total Spending by Age and Total Spending by Region tables. Spending by type of consumer unit will not add to total because not all types of consumer units are shown. (–) means sample is too small to make a reliable estimate.
Source: Calculations by New Strategist based on the 2002 Consumer Expenditure Survey

Table 4.12 Financial: Market shares by household type, 2002

(percentage of total annual spending on financial products and services, cash contributions, and miscellaneous items accounted for by types of consumer units (CU), 2002)

	total married couples	married couples, no children	married couples with children				single parent, at least one child <18	single person
			total	oldest child under 6	oldest child 6 to 17	oldest child 18 or older		
Share of total consumer units	**50.2%**	**20.6%**	**25.7%**	**4.9%**	**13.6%**	**7.2%**	**6.0%**	**29.5%**
Share of total before-tax income	**68.2**	**24.6**	**38.4**	**6.8**	**20.0**	**11.8**	**3.3**	**16.1**
Share of total spending	**64.6**	**23.1**	**36.5**	**6.4**	**19.4**	**10.7**	**4.5**	**17.5**
FINANCIAL PRODUCTS AND SERVICES	**58.7%**	**22.6%**	**30.9%**	**5.7%**	**14.2%**	**11.0%**	**4.3%**	**22.5%**
Miscellaneous fees	72.7	34.2	35.5	4.0	15.8	16.0	–	17.2
Lottery and gambling losses	55.8	32.2	20.5	3.6	8.9	8.1	1.5	27.8
Legal fees	51.5	13.9	34.1	2.6	13.3	18.3	5.9	22.9
Funeral expenses	48.3	21.8	14.2	1.3	6.3	6.6	2.4	27.9
Safe deposit box rental	63.4	38.2	22.3	3.4	11.1	7.8	1.4	26.3
Checking accounts, other bank service charges	55.6	17.7	33.1	6.7	18.2	8.2	5.3	22.9
Cemetery lots, vaults, and maintenance fees	66.0	51.0	8.1	0.2	4.7	3.2	1.9	15.6
Accounting fees	65.0	29.4	32.0	4.8	17.4	9.8	3.1	22.4
Miscellaneous personal services	51.8	18.1	33.3	15.3	10.7	7.1	8.2	24.6
Finance charges, except mortgage and vehicles	59.4	22.3	31.3	6.7	15.6	9.0	5.5	21.8
Occupational expenses	62.1	22.2	36.7	6.8	17.8	12.1	2.4	23.0
Expenses for other properties	71.9	25.7	42.3	9.8	15.7	16.8	1.1	15.5
Credit card memberships	58.0	26.9	28.1	7.7	11.6	8.8	6.0	21.1
Shopping club membership fees	75.3	31.8	38.8	5.6	23.1	10.2	3.2	11.7
CASH CONTRIBUTIONS	**64.7**	**30.8**	**29.8**	**4.0**	**14.9**	**10.9**	**1.8**	**23.0**
Support for college students	79.4	40.2	34.6	1.2	11.4	22.0	1.3	14.6
Alimony expenditures	57.2	33.7	18.7	3.5	13.3	1.9	2.6	28.8
Child support expenditures	37.2	11.8	23.1	4.8	14.0	4.2	2.5	32.8
Gifts to non–CU members of stocks, bonds, and mutual funds	35.4	30.9	3.6	0.7	1.0	1.9	0.0	62.0
Cash contributions to charities and other organizations	70.5	39.5	28.2	2.8	13.5	11.9	1.0	20.9
Cash contributions to church, religious organizations	75.2	30.6	39.1	5.6	19.4	14.1	2.0	16.0
Cash contributions to educational institutions	68.3	39.1	27.1	4.3	17.5	5.3	1.5	26.9
Cash contributions to political organizations	83.9	36.4	45.9	1.4	9.7	34.8	0.6	11.0
Other cash gifts	55.7	37.2	15.1	1.5	7.8	5.8	1.3	31.8
PERSONAL INSURANCE AND PENSIONS	**69.3**	**23.9**	**40.5**	**7.6**	**21.3**	**11.6**	**3.2**	**15.5**
Life and other personal insurance	74.8	32.2	37.4	5.2	20.3	11.9	2.7	13.3
Life, endowment, annuity, other personal insurance	75.0	32.1	37.6	5.2	20.4	12.0	2.7	13.1
Other nonhealth insurance	68.6	33.5	32.5	3.7	18.5	10.4	2.1	19.1
Pensions and Social Security	68.7	23.0	40.8	7.8	21.4	11.6	3.2	15.8
Deductions for government retirement	67.8	25.3	38.4	4.1	21.2	13.1	6.1	18.3
Deductions for private pensions	72.8	25.0	44.9	8.5	24.7	11.7	2.3	15.9
Nonpayroll deposit to retirement plans	60.9	26.8	30.7	7.0	13.8	9.8	1.9	25.7
Deductions for Social Security	69.3	22.0	41.9	8.0	22.2	11.8	3.5	14.1
PERSONAL TAXES	**69.5**	**27.7**	**38.1**	**7.4**	**20.2**	**10.5**	**1.2**	**21.4**
Federal income taxes	69.3	27.6	38.3	7.4	20.2	10.7	0.6	22.3
State and local income taxes	69.6	26.3	39.2	8.2	20.9	10.1	2.9	19.0
Other taxes	72.5	34.9	32.0	4.5	17.2	10.4	1.8	18.6

Note: Market share for total consumer units is 100.0%. Market shares by type of consumer unit will not add to total because not all types of consumer units are shown. (–) means sample is too small to make a reliable estimate.
Source: Calculations by New Strategist based on the 2002 Consumer Expenditure Survey

Table 4.13 Financial: Average spending by race and Hispanic origin, 2002

(average annual spending of consumer units (CU) on financial products and services, cash contributions, and miscellaneous items, by race and Hispanic origin of consumer unit reference person, 2002)

	total consumer units	race black	race white and other	Hispanic origin Hispanic	Hispanic origin non-Hispanic
Number of consumer units (in thousands, add 000)	112,108	13,554	98,553	10,500	101,608
Average number of persons per CU	2.5	2.7	2.5	3.3	2.4
Average before-tax income of CU	$49,430.00	$35,944.00	$51,177.00	$37,360.00	$50,742.00
Average spending of CU, total	40,676.60	30,135.94	42,134.55	34,742.47	41,294.67
FINANCIAL PRODUCTS AND SERVICES	**$792.40**	**$605.66**	**$818.18**	**$628.13**	**$809.11**
Miscellaneous fees	2.25	–	2.57	–	2.47
Lottery and gambling losses	46.94	21.97	50.47	25.04	49.00
Legal fees	132.99	38.66	145.97	67.94	139.72
Funeral expenses	77.91	51.85	81.50	61.75	79.58
Safe deposit box rental	3.84	1.07	4.22	1.38	4.10
Checking accounts, other bank service charges	25.91	24.34	26.13	23.59	26.16
Cemetery lots, vaults, and maintenance fees	16.05	10.56	16.80	10.77	16.59
Accounting fees	57.85	20.86	62.94	24.11	61.34
Miscellaneous personal services	39.77	42.63	39.37	35.40	40.18
Finance charges, except mortgage and vehicles	271.37	337.54	262.27	307.20	267.66
Occupational expenses	38.46	18.76	41.17	18.59	40.51
Expenses for other properties	65.99	31.46	70.74	45.22	68.14
Credit card memberships	2.82	2.20	2.90	2.03	2.90
Shopping club membership fees	5.97	3.76	6.27	5.11	6.05
CASH CONTRIBUTIONS	**1,277.10**	**917.34**	**1,326.58**	**611.53**	**1,345.88**
Support for college students	75.94	52.55	79.16	24.44	81.27
Alimony expenditures	21.18	3.66	23.59	8.74	22.47
Child support expenditures	190.75	186.13	191.38	155.33	194.41
Gifts to non–CU members of stocks, bonds, and mutual funds	24.23	1.77	27.32	5.55	26.16
Cash contributions to charities and other organizations	137.62	57.19	148.68	30.03	148.74
Cash contributions to church, religious organizations	557.29	550.16	558.27	201.34	594.08
Cash contributions to educational institutions	33.42	8.70	36.82	2.19	36.64
Cash contributions to political organizations	10.90	1.04	12.26	2.34	11.79
Other cash gifts	225.76	56.13	249.09	181.59	230.33
PERSONAL INSURANCE AND PENSIONS	**3,898.62**	**2,639.59**	**4,071.78**	**2,827.11**	**4,009.35**
Life and other personal insurance	406.11	311.64	419.11	195.74	427.85
Life, endowment, annuity, other personal insurance	391.65	305.08	403.56	193.05	412.17
Other nonhealth insurance	14.46	6.56	15.55	2.68	15.68
Pensions and Social Security	3,492.51	2,327.95	3,652.67	2,631.37	3,581.50
Deductions for government retirement	69.48	50.98	72.03	47.31	71.78
Deductions for private pensions	390.38	212.60	414.83	185.67	411.53
Nonpayroll deposit to retirement plans	426.12	220.67	454.37	124.51	457.29
Deductions for Social Security	2,604.32	1,843.35	2,708.98	2,273.89	2,638.47
PERSONAL TAXES	**2,496.26**	**1,135.92**	**2,672.41**	**877.91**	**2,672.16**
Federal income taxes	1,842.57	783.35	1,979.72	682.31	1,968.68
State and local income taxes	506.45	301.77	532.95	195.17	540.28
Other taxes	147.24	50.80	159.73	0.43	163.20

Note: Other races include Asians, Native Americans, and Pacific Islanders. (–) means sample is too small to make a reliable estimate.
Source: Bureau of Labor Statistics, unpublished tables from the 2002 Consumer Expenditure Survey

Table 4.14 Financial: Indexed spending by race and Hispanic origin, 2002

(indexed average annual spending of consumer units (CU) on financial products and services, cash contributions, and miscellaneous items, by race and Hispanic origin of consumer unit reference person, 2002; index definition: an index of 100 is the average for all consumer units; an index of 132 means that spending by consumer units in that group is 32 percent above the average for all consumer units; an index of 68 indicates spending that is 32 percent below the average for all consumer units)

	total consumer units	race		Hispanic origin	
		black	white and other	Hispanic	non-Hispanic
Average spending of CU, total	$40,677	$30,136	$42,135	$34,742	$41,295
Average spending of CU, index	100	74	104	85	102
FINANCIAL PRODUCTS AND SERVICES	100	76	103	79	102
Miscellaneous fees	100	–	114	–	110
Lottery and gambling losses	100	47	108	53	104
Legal fees	100	29	110	51	105
Funeral expenses	100	67	105	79	102
Safe deposit box rental	100	28	110	36	107
Checking accounts, other bank service charges	100	94	101	91	101
Cemetery lots, vaults, and maintenance fees	100	66	105	67	103
Accounting fees	100	36	109	42	106
Miscellaneous personal services	100	107	99	89	101
Finance charges, except mortgage and vehicles	100	124	97	113	99
Occupational expenses	100	49	107	48	105
Expenses for other properties	100	48	107	69	103
Credit card memberships	100	78	103	72	103
Shopping club membership fees	100	63	105	86	101
CASH CONTRIBUTIONS	100	72	104	48	105
Support for college students	100	69	104	32	107
Alimony expenditures	100	17	111	41	106
Child support expenditures	100	98	100	81	102
Gifts to non–CU members of stocks, bonds, and mutual funds	100	7	113	23	108
Cash contributions to charities and other organizations	100	42	108	22	108
Cash contributions to church, religious organizations	100	99	100	36	107
Cash contributions to educational institutions	100	26	110	7	110
Cash contributions to political organizations	100	10	112	21	108
Other cash gifts	100	25	110	80	102
PERSONAL INSURANCE AND PENSIONS	100	68	104	73	103
Life and other personal insurance	100	77	103	48	105
Life, endowment, annuity, other personal insurance	100	78	103	49	105
Other nonhealth insurance	100	45	108	19	108
Pensions and Social Security	100	67	105	75	103
Deductions for government retirement	100	73	104	68	103
Deductions for private pensions	100	54	106	48	105
Nonpayroll deposit to retirement plans	100	52	107	29	107
Deductions for Social Security	100	71	104	87	101
PERSONAL TAXES	100	46	107	35	107
Federal income taxes	100	43	107	37	107
State and local income taxes	100	60	105	39	107
Other taxes	100	35	108	0	111

Note: Other races include Asians, Native Americans, and Pacific Islanders. (–) means sample is too small to make a reliable estimate.
Source: Calculations by New Strategist based on the 2002 Consumer Expenditure Survey

Table 4.15 Financial: Total spending by race and Hispanic origin, 2002

(total annual spending on financial products and services, cash contributions, and miscellaneous items, by consumer unit (CU) race and Hispanic origin groups, 2002; numbers in thousands)

	total consumer units	race		Hispanic origin	
		black	white and other	Hispanic	non-Hispanic
Number of consumer units	112,108	13,554	98,553	10,500	101,608
Total spending of all consumer units	$4,560,172,273	$408,462,531	$4,152,486,306	$364,795,935	$4,195,868,829
FINANCIAL PRODUCTS AND SERVICES	**$88,834,379**	**$8,209,116**	**$80,634,094**	**$6,595,365**	**$82,212,049**
Miscellaneous fees	252,243	–	252,243	–	250,972
Lottery and gambling losses	5,262,350	297,781	4,973,970	262,920	4,978,792
Legal fees	14,909,243	523,998	14,385,781	713,370	14,196,670
Funeral expenses	8,734,334	702,775	8,032,070	648,375	8,085,965
Safe deposit box rental	430,495	14,503	415,894	14,490	416,593
Checking accounts, other bank service charges	2,904,718	329,904	2,575,190	247,695	2,658,065
Cemetery lots, vaults, and maintenance fees	1,799,333	143,130	1,655,690	113,085	1,685,677
Accounting fees	6,485,448	282,736	6,202,926	253,155	6,232,635
Miscellaneous personal services	4,458,535	577,807	3,880,032	371,700	4,082,609
Finance charges, except mortgage and vehicles	30,422,748	4,575,017	25,847,495	3,225,600	27,196,397
Occupational expenses	4,311,674	254,273	4,057,427	195,195	4,116,140
Expenses for other properties	7,398,007	426,409	6,971,639	474,810	6,923,569
Credit card memberships	316,145	29,819	285,804	21,315	294,663
Shopping club membership fees	669,285	50,963	617,927	53,655	614,728
CASH CONTRIBUTIONS	**143,173,127**	**12,433,626**	**130,738,439**	**6,421,065**	**136,752,175**
Support for college students	8,513,482	712,263	7,801,455	256,620	8,257,682
Alimony expenditures	2,374,447	49,608	2,324,865	91,770	2,283,132
Child support expenditures	21,384,601	2,522,806	18,861,073	1,630,965	19,753,611
Gifts to non–CU members of stocks, bonds, and mutual funds	2,716,377	23,991	2,692,468	58,275	2,658,065
Cash contributions to charities and other organizations	15,428,303	775,153	14,652,860	315,315	15,113,174
Cash contributions to church, religious organizations	62,476,667	7,456,869	55,019,183	2,114,070	60,363,281
Cash contributions to educational institutions	3,746,649	117,920	3,628,721	22,995	3,722,917
Cash contributions to political organizations	1,221,977	14,096	1,208,260	24,570	1,197,958
Other cash gifts	25,309,502	760,786	24,548,567	1,906,695	23,403,371
PERSONAL INSURANCE AND PENSIONS	**437,066,491**	**35,777,003**	**401,286,134**	**29,684,655**	**407,382,035**
Life and other personal insurance	45,528,180	4,223,969	41,304,548	2,055,270	43,472,983
Life, endowment, annuity, other personal insurance	43,907,098	4,135,054	39,772,049	2,027,025	41,879,769
Other nonhealth insurance	1,621,082	88,914	1,532,499	28,140	1,593,213
Pensions and Social Security	391,538,311	31,553,034	359,981,587	27,629,385	363,909,052
Deductions for government retirement	7,789,264	690,983	7,098,773	496,755	7,293,422
Deductions for private pensions	43,764,721	2,881,580	40,882,741	1,949,535	41,814,740
Nonpayroll deposit to retirement plans	47,771,461	2,990,961	44,779,527	1,307,355	46,464,322
Deductions for Social Security	291,965,107	24,984,766	266,978,106	23,875,845	268,089,660
PERSONAL TAXES	**279,850,716**	**15,396,260**	**263,374,023**	**9,218,055**	**271,512,833**
Federal income taxes	206,566,838	10,617,526	195,107,345	7,164,255	200,033,637
State and local income taxes	56,777,097	4,090,191	52,523,821	2,049,285	54,896,770
Other taxes	16,506,782	688,543	15,741,871	4,515	16,582,426

Note: Other races include Asians, Native Americans, and Pacific Islanders. Numbers may not add to total because of rounding. (–) means sample is too small to make a reliable estimate.
Source: Calculations by New Strategist based on the 2002 Consumer Expenditure Survey

Table 4.16 Financial: Market shares by race and Hispanic origin, 2002

(percentage of total annual spending on financial products and services, cash contributions, and miscellaneous items accounted for by consumer unit (CU) race and Hispanic origin groups, 2002)

	total consumer units	race black	race white and other	Hispanic origin Hispanic	Hispanic origin non-Hispanic
Share of total consumer units	100.0%	12.1%	87.9%	9.4%	90.6%
Share of total before-tax income	100.0	8.8	91.0	7.1	93.0
Share of total spending	100.0	9.0	91.1	8.0	92.0
FINANCIAL PRODUCTS AND SERVICES	**100.0%**	**9.2%**	**90.8%**	**7.4%**	**92.5%**
Miscellaneous fees	100.0	–	100.0	–	99.5
Lottery and gambling losses	100.0	5.7	94.5	5.0	94.6
Legal fees	100.0	3.5	96.5	4.8	95.2
Funeral expenses	100.0	8.0	92.0	7.4	92.6
Safe deposit box rental	100.0	3.4	96.6	3.4	96.8
Checking accounts, other bank service charges	100.0	11.4	88.7	8.5	91.5
Cemetery lots, vaults, and maintenance fees	100.0	8.0	92.0	6.3	93.7
Accounting fees	100.0	4.4	95.6	3.9	96.1
Miscellaneous personal services	100.0	13.0	87.0	8.3	91.6
Finance charges, except mortgage and vehicles	100.0	15.0	85.0	10.6	89.4
Occupational expenses	100.0	5.9	94.1	4.5	95.5
Expenses for other properties	100.0	5.8	94.2	6.4	93.6
Credit card memberships	100.0	9.4	90.4	6.7	93.2
Shopping club membership fees	100.0	7.6	92.3	8.0	91.8
CASH CONTRIBUTIONS	**100.0**	**8.7**	**91.3**	**4.5**	**95.5**
Support for college students	100.0	8.4	91.6	3.0	97.0
Alimony expenditures	100.0	2.1	97.9	3.9	96.2
Child support expenditures	100.0	11.8	88.2	7.6	92.4
Gifts to non–CU members of stocks, bonds, and mutual funds	100.0	0.9	99.1	2.1	97.9
Cash contributions to charities and other organizations	100.0	5.0	95.0	2.0	98.0
Cash contributions to church, religious organizations	100.0	11.9	88.1	3.4	96.6
Cash contributions to educational institutions	100.0	3.1	96.9	0.6	99.4
Cash contributions to political organizations	100.0	1.2	98.9	2.0	98.0
Other cash gifts	100.0	3.0	97.0	7.5	92.5
PERSONAL INSURANCE AND PENSIONS	**100.0**	**8.2**	**91.8**	**6.8**	**93.2**
Life and other personal insurance	100.0	9.3	90.7	4.5	95.5
Life, endowment, annuity, other personal insurance	100.0	9.4	90.6	4.6	95.4
Other nonhealth insurance	100.0	5.5	94.5	1.7	98.3
Pensions and Social Security	100.0	8.1	91.9	7.1	92.9
Deductions for government retirement	100.0	8.9	91.1	6.4	93.6
Deductions for private pensions	100.0	6.6	93.4	4.5	95.5
Nonpayroll deposit to retirement plans	100.0	6.3	93.7	2.7	97.3
Deductions for Social Security	100.0	8.6	91.4	8.2	91.8
PERSONAL TAXES	**100.0**	**5.5**	**94.1**	**3.3**	**97.0**
Federal income taxes	100.0	5.1	94.5	3.5	96.8
State and local income taxes	100.0	7.2	92.5	3.6	96.7
Other taxes	100.0	4.2	95.4	–	100.0

Note: Other races include Asians, Native Americans, and Pacific Islanders. Numbers may not add to total because of rounding. (–) means sample is too small to make a reliable estimate.

Source: Calculations by New Strategist based on the 2002 Consumer Expenditure Survey

Table 4.17 Financial: Average spending by region, 2002

(average annual spending of consumer units (CU) on financial products and services, cash contributions, and miscellaneous items, by region in which consumer unit lives, 2002)

	total consumer units	Northeast	Midwest	South	West
Number of consumer units (in thousands, add 000)	112,108	21,313	25,883	40,004	24,907
Average number of persons per CU	2.5	2.5	2.5	2.5	2.6
Average before-tax income of CU	$49,430.00	$53,983.00	$49,197.00	$45,641.00	$52,016.00
Average spending of CU, total	40,676.60	42,390.20	40,601.14	37,280.55	44,728.34
FINANCIAL PRODUCTS AND SERVICES	**$792.40**	**$732.94**	**$776.28**	**$764.29**	**$904.75**
Miscellaneous fees	2.25	1.38	3.55	0.67	4.20
Lottery and gambling losses	46.94	67.90	76.26	26.80	30.32
Legal fees	132.99	103.86	123.76	137.66	160.03
Funeral expenses	77.91	108.39	63.42	89.45	48.35
Safe deposit box rental	3.84	4.53	4.24	3.25	3.80
Checking accounts, other bank service charges	25.91	20.46	24.66	24.92	33.48
Cemetery lots, vaults, and maintenance fees	16.05	13.51	13.48	20.39	13.90
Accounting fees	57.85	63.07	57.76	44.09	75.59
Miscellaneous personal services	39.77	28.32	63.02	25.71	48.14
Finance charges, except mortgage and vehicles	271.37	243.26	209.69	294.45	322.43
Occupational expenses	38.46	31.51	56.30	14.57	64.24
Expenses for other properties	65.99	39.25	70.11	74.45	71.00
Credit card memberships	2.82	2.49	2.65	2.58	3.64
Shopping club membership fees	5.97	4.70	5.01	4.88	9.78
CASH CONTRIBUTIONS	**1,277.10**	**1,199.05**	**1,363.46**	**1,193.28**	**1,388.76**
Support for college students	75.94	74.64	79.71	81.75	63.82
Alimony expenditures	21.18	20.81	17.44	17.39	31.48
Child support expenditures	190.75	235.02	193.45	188.29	154.00
Gifts to non–CU members of stocks, bonds, and mutual funds	24.23	3.01	22.38	5.47	74.44
Cash contributions to charities and other organizations	137.62	164.95	145.87	91.24	180.15
Cash contributions to church, religious organizations	557.29	368.98	602.95	603.20	597.25
Cash contributions to educational institutions	33.42	56.01	37.11	19.51	32.58
Cash contributions to political organizations	10.90	4.65	8.45	7.31	24.58
Other cash gifts	225.76	270.98	256.09	179.11	230.48
PERSONAL INSURANCE AND PENSIONS	**3,898.62**	**3,923.94**	**4,064.52**	**3,632.38**	**4,132.18**
Life and other personal insurance	406.11	459.53	447.58	388.94	344.90
Life, endowment, annuity, other personal insurance	391.65	444.11	431.11	377.25	328.89
Other nonhealth insurance	14.46	15.42	16.47	11.70	16.01
Pensions and Social Security	3,492.51	3,464.40	3,616.95	3,243.44	3,787.28
Deductions for government retirement	69.48	41.69	93.60	72.18	63.88
Deductions for private pensions	390.38	295.63	474.48	373.17	411.69
Nonpayroll deposit to retirement plans	426.12	354.68	507.49	351.16	523.08
Deductions for Social Security	2,604.32	2,771.88	2,541.37	2,446.38	2,780.03
PERSONAL TAXES	**2,496.26**	**2,405.24**	**2,826.58**	**2,024.34**	**3,007.78**
Federal income taxes	1,842.57	1,709.63	1,945.28	1,605.08	2,238.25
State and local income taxes	506.45	520.15	683.97	313.49	629.37
Other taxes	147.24	175.45	197.33	105.77	140.16

Note: (–) means sample is too small to make a reliable estimate.
Source: Bureau of Labor Statistics, unpublished tables from the 2002 Consumer Expenditure Survey

Table 4.18 Financial: Indexed spending by region, 2002

(indexed average annual spending of consumer units (CU) on financial products and services, cash contributions, and miscellaneous items, by region in which consumer unit lives, 2002; index definition: an index of 100 is the average for all consumer units; an index of 132 means that spending by consumer units in that group is 32 percent above the average for all consumer units; an index of 68 indicates spending that is 32 percent below the average for all consumer units)

	total consumer units	Northeast	Midwest	South	West
Average spending of CU, total	$40,677	$42,390	$40,601	$37,281	$44,728
Average spending of CU, index	100	104	100	92	110
FINANCIAL PRODUCTS AND SERVICES	**100**	**92**	**98**	**96**	**114**
Miscellaneous fees	100	61	158	30	187
Lottery and gambling losses	100	145	162	57	65
Legal fees	100	78	93	104	120
Funeral expenses	100	139	81	115	62
Safe deposit box rental	100	118	110	85	99
Checking accounts, other bank service charges	100	79	95	96	129
Cemetery lots, vaults, and maintenance fees	100	84	84	127	87
Accounting fees	100	109	100	76	131
Miscellaneous personal services	100	71	158	65	121
Finance charges, except mortgage and vehicles	100	90	77	109	119
Occupational expenses	100	82	146	38	167
Expenses for other properties	100	59	106	113	108
Credit card memberships	100	88	94	91	129
Shopping club membership fees	100	79	84	82	164
CASH CONTRIBUTIONS	**100**	**94**	**107**	**93**	**109**
Support for college students	100	98	105	108	84
Alimony expenditures	100	98	82	82	149
Child support expenditures	100	123	101	99	81
Gifts to non–CU members of stocks, bonds, and mutual funds	100	12	92	23	307
Cash contributions to charities and other organizations	100	120	106	66	131
Cash contributions to church, religious organizations	100	66	108	108	107
Cash contributions to educational institutions	100	168	111	58	97
Cash contributions to political organizations	100	43	78	67	226
Other cash gifts	100	120	113	79	102
PERSONAL INSURANCE AND PENSIONS	**100**	**101**	**104**	**93**	**106**
Life and other personal insurance	100	113	110	96	85
Life, endowment, annuity, other personal insurance	100	113	110	96	84
Other nonhealth insurance	100	107	114	81	111
Pensions and Social Security	100	99	104	93	108
Deductions for government retirement	100	60	135	104	92
Deductions for private pensions	100	76	122	96	105
Nonpayroll deposit to retirement plans	100	83	119	82	123
Deductions for Social Security	100	106	98	94	107
PERSONAL TAXES	**100**	**96**	**113**	**81**	**120**
Federal income taxes	100	93	106	87	121
State and local income taxes	100	103	135	62	124
Other taxes	100	119	134	72	95

Note: (–) means sample is too small to make a reliable estimate.
Source: Calculations by New Strategist based on the 2002 Consumer Expenditure Survey

Table 4.19 Financial: Total spending by region, 2002

(total annual spending on financial products and services, cash contributions, and miscellaneous items, by region in which consumer units (CU) live, 2002; numbers in thousands)

	total consumer units	Northeast	Midwest	South	West
Number of consumer units	112,108	21,313	25,883	40,004	24,907
Total spending of all consumer units	$4,560,172,273	$903,462,333	$1,050,879,307	$1,491,371,122	$1,114,048,764
FINANCIAL PRODUCTS AND SERVICES	**$88,834,379**	**$15,621,150**	**$20,092,455**	**$30,574,657**	**$22,534,608**
Miscellaneous fees	252,243	29,412	91,885	26,803	104,609
Lottery and gambling losses	5,262,350	1,447,153	1,973,838	1,072,107	755,180
Legal fees	14,909,243	2,213,568	3,203,280	5,506,951	3,985,867
Funeral expenses	8,734,334	2,310,116	1,641,500	3,578,358	1,204,253
Safe deposit box rental	430,495	96,548	109,744	130,013	94,647
Checking accounts, other bank service charges	2,904,718	436,064	638,275	996,900	833,886
Cemetery lots, vaults, and maintenance fees	1,799,333	287,939	348,903	815,682	346,207
Accounting fees	6,485,448	1,344,211	1,495,002	1,763,776	1,882,720
Miscellaneous personal services	4,458,535	603,584	1,631,147	1,028,503	1,199,023
Finance charges, except mortgage and vehicles	30,422,748	5,184,600	5,427,406	11,779,178	8,030,764
Occupational expenses	4,311,674	671,573	1,457,213	582,858	1,600,026
Expenses for other properties	7,398,007	836,535	1,814,657	2,978,298	1,768,397
Credit card memberships	316,145	53,069	68,590	103,210	90,661
Shopping club membership fees	669,285	100,171	129,674	195,220	243,590
CASH CONTRIBUTIONS	**143,173,127**	**25,555,353**	**35,290,435**	**47,735,973**	**34,589,845**
Support for college students	8,513,482	1,590,802	2,063,134	3,270,327	1,589,565
Alimony expenditures	2,374,447	443,524	451,400	695,670	784,072
Child support expenditures	21,384,601	5,008,981	5,007,066	7,532,353	3,835,678
Gifts to non–CU members of stocks, bonds, and mutual funds	2,716,377	64,152	579,262	218,822	1,854,077
Cash contributions to charities and other organizations	15,428,303	3,515,579	3,775,553	3,649,965	4,486,996
Cash contributions to church, religious organizations	62,476,667	7,864,071	15,606,155	24,130,413	14,875,706
Cash contributions to educational institutions	3,746,649	1,193,741	960,518	780,478	811,470
Cash contributions to political organizations	1,221,977	99,105	218,711	292,429	612,214
Other cash gifts	25,309,502	5,775,397	6,628,377	7,165,116	5,740,565
PERSONAL INSURANCE AND PENSIONS	**437,066,491**	**83,630,933**	**105,201,971**	**145,309,730**	**102,920,207**
Life and other personal insurance	45,528,180	9,793,963	11,584,713	15,559,156	8,590,424
Life, endowment, annuity, other personal insurance	43,907,098	9,465,316	11,158,420	15,091,509	8,191,663
Other nonhealth insurance	1,621,082	328,646	426,293	468,047	398,761
Pensions and Social Security	391,538,311	73,836,757	93,617,517	129,750,574	94,329,783
Deductions for government retirement	7,789,264	888,539	2,422,649	2,887,489	1,591,059
Deductions for private pensions	43,764,721	6,300,762	12,280,966	14,928,293	10,253,963
Nonpayroll deposit to retirement plans	47,771,461	7,559,295	13,135,364	14,047,805	13,028,354
Deductions for Social Security	291,965,107	59,077,078	65,778,280	97,864,986	69,242,207
PERSONAL TAXES	**279,850,716**	**51,262,880**	**73,160,370**	**80,981,697**	**74,914,776**
Federal income taxes	206,566,838	36,437,344	50,349,682	64,209,620	55,748,093
State and local income taxes	56,777,097	11,085,957	17,703,196	12,540,854	15,675,719
Other taxes	16,506,782	3,739,366	5,107,492	4,231,223	3,490,965

Note: Numbers may not add to total because of rounding. (–) means sample is too small to make a reliable estimate.
Source: Calculations by New Strategist based on the 2002 Consumer Expenditure Survey

Table 4.20   Financial: Market shares by region, 2002

(percentage of total annual spending on financial products and services, cash contributions, and miscellaneous items accounted for by consumer units (CU) by region, 2002)

	total consumer units	Northeast	Midwest	South	West
Share of total consumer units	100.0%	19.0%	23.1%	35.7%	22.2%
Share of total before-tax income	100.0	20.8	23.0	32.9	23.4
Share of total spending	100.0	19.8	23.0	32.7	24.4
FINANCIAL PRODUCTS AND SERVICES	100.0%	17.6%	22.6%	34.4%	25.4%
Miscellaneous fees	100.0	11.7	36.4	10.6	41.5
Lottery and gambling losses	100.0	27.5	37.5	20.4	14.4
Legal fees	100.0	14.8	21.5	36.9	26.7
Funeral expenses	100.0	26.4	18.8	41.0	13.8
Safe deposit box rental	100.0	22.4	25.5	30.2	22.0
Checking accounts, other bank service charges	100.0	15.0	22.0	34.3	28.7
Cemetery lots, vaults, and maintenance fees	100.0	16.0	19.4	45.3	19.2
Accounting fees	100.0	20.7	23.1	27.2	29.0
Miscellaneous personal services	100.0	13.5	36.6	23.1	26.9
Finance charges, except mortgage and vehicles	100.0	17.0	17.8	38.7	26.4
Occupational expenses	100.0	15.6	33.8	13.5	37.1
Expenses for other properties	100.0	11.3	24.5	40.3	23.9
Credit card memberships	100.0	16.8	21.7	32.6	28.7
Shopping club membership fees	100.0	15.0	19.4	29.2	36.4
CASH CONTRIBUTIONS	100.0	17.8	24.6	33.3	24.2
Support for college students	100.0	18.7	24.2	38.4	18.7
Alimony expenditures	100.0	18.7	19.0	29.3	33.0
Child support expenditures	100.0	23.4	23.4	35.2	17.9
Gifts to non–CU members of stocks, bonds, and mutual funds	100.0	2.4	21.3	8.1	68.3
Cash contributions to charities and other organizations	100.0	22.8	24.5	23.7	29.1
Cash contributions to church, religious organizations	100.0	12.6	25.0	38.6	23.8
Cash contributions to educational institutions	100.0	31.9	25.6	20.8	21.7
Cash contributions to political organizations	100.0	8.1	17.9	23.9	50.1
Other cash gifts	100.0	22.8	26.2	28.3	22.7
PERSONAL INSURANCE AND PENSIONS	100.0	19.1	24.1	33.2	23.5
Life and other personal insurance	100.0	21.5	25.4	34.2	18.9
Life, endowment, annuity, other personal insurance	100.0	21.6	25.4	34.4	18.7
Other nonhealth insurance	100.0	20.3	26.3	28.9	24.6
Pensions and Social Security	100.0	18.9	23.9	33.1	24.1
Deductions for government retirement	100.0	11.4	31.1	37.1	20.4
Deductions for private pensions	100.0	14.4	28.1	34.1	23.4
Nonpayroll deposit to retirement plans	100.0	15.8	27.5	29.4	27.3
Deductions for Social Security	100.0	20.2	22.5	33.5	23.7
PERSONAL TAXES	100.0	18.3	26.1	28.9	26.8
Federal income taxes	100.0	17.6	24.4	31.1	27.0
State and local income taxes	100.0	19.5	31.2	22.1	27.6
Other taxes	100.0	22.7	30.9	25.6	21.1

Note: Numbers may not add to total because of rounding. (–) means sample is too small to make a reliable estimate.
Source: Calculations by New Strategist based on the 2002 Consumer Expenditure Survey

Table 4.21 Financial: Average spending by education, 2002

(average annual spending of consumer units (CU) on financial products and services, cash contributions, and miscellaneous items, by education of consumer unit reference person, 2002)

	total consumer units	less than high school graduate	high school graduate	some college	associate's degree	college graduate total	college graduate bachelor's degree	master's, professional, doctorate
Number of consumer units (in thousands, add 000)	112,108	17,075	31,961	23,260	10,395	29,417	19,082	10,335
Average number of persons per CU	2.5	2.6	2.5	2.4	2.6	2.5	2.5	2.5
Average before-tax income of CU	$49,430.00	$25,564.00	$39,618.00	$42,598.00	$54,860.00	$77,820.00	$69,408.00	$92,783.00
Average spending of CU, total	40,676.60	24,930.40	33,707.63	38,653.57	44,405.79	57,384.01	53,731.57	64,118.48
FINANCIAL PRODUCTS AND SERVICES	**$792.40**	**$494.80**	**$623.57**	**$881.08**	**$838.94**	**$1,059.68**	**$932.06**	**$1,295.18**
Miscellaneous fees	2.25	1.76	1.08	2.49	5.61	2.51	3.89	–
Lottery and gambling losses	46.94	29.24	54.85	57.58	80.14	29.90	22.29	43.76
Legal fees	132.99	40.46	73.04	153.57	143.72	231.79	218.03	257.19
Funeral expenses	77.91	120.58	85.87	63.45	46.24	67.13	55.34	88.91
Safe deposit box rental	3.84	1.85	2.70	3.77	3.52	6.41	5.48	8.11
Checking accounts, other bank service charges	25.91	13.51	21.87	30.74	32.56	31.34	31.09	31.81
Cemetery lots, vaults, and maintenance fees	16.05	22.45	16.27	12.04	15.83	15.34	13.76	18.25
Accounting fees	57.85	22.15	38.21	64.08	54.85	96.06	79.43	126.78
Miscellaneous personal services	39.77	24.96	14.13	34.35	37.60	77.48	78.36	75.88
Finance charges, except mortgage and vehicles	271.37	161.19	219.53	328.34	305.74	334.43	304.77	389.20
Occupational expenses	38.46	11.52	26.87	30.56	45.49	70.46	49.12	109.88
Expenses for other properties	65.99	41.97	62.65	73.87	55.90	80.90	56.89	125.22
Credit card memberships	2.82	1.07	1.41	2.81	3.62	5.08	4.45	6.24
Shopping club membership fees	5.97	2.10	4.41	6.47	8.12	8.74	8.29	9.58
CASH CONTRIBUTIONS	**1,277.10**	**606.89**	**950.53**	**1,045.57**	**1,373.38**	**2,169.96**	**2,011.76**	**2,462.07**
Support for college students	75.94	17.34	39.89	60.42	55.08	168.78	138.83	224.08
Alimony expenditures	21.18	2.01	10.79	31.88	6.77	40.23	39.53	41.53
Child support expenditures	190.75	112.32	208.97	190.38	267.92	189.48	179.27	208.33
Gifts to non–CU members of stocks, bonds, and mutual funds	24.23	2.85	16.45	7.34	10.73	63.21	90.11	13.55
Cash contributions to charities and other organizations	137.62	26.75	71.23	79.87	113.85	328.17	288.25	401.87
Cash contributions to church, religious organizations	557.29	266.82	389.62	484.93	655.83	930.47	903.11	980.98
Cash contributions to educational institutions	33.42	1.08	17.35	6.43	25.94	93.62	57.00	161.25
Cash contributions to political organizations	10.90	6.09	2.88	3.67	7.82	29.22	30.74	26.42
Other cash gifts	225.76	171.64	193.35	180.65	229.44	326.77	284.91	404.06
PERSONAL INSURANCE AND PENSIONS	**3,898.62**	**1,614.16**	**2,886.07**	**3,364.07**	**4,314.32**	**6,600.50**	**5,833.56**	**8,016.56**
Life and other personal insurance	406.11	204.42	335.56	365.55	444.13	618.48	532.07	778.05
Life, endowment, annuity, other personal insurance	391.65	198.60	324.06	354.50	425.75	594.47	507.64	754.81
Other nonhealth insurance	14.46	5.82	11.50	11.06	18.38	24.01	24.43	23.24
Pensions and Social Security	3,492.51	1,409.74	2,550.52	2,998.52	3,870.19	5,982.01	5,301.50	7,238.51
Deductions for government retirement	69.48	7.26	37.32	57.06	69.65	150.31	95.89	250.79
Deductions for private pensions	390.38	57.29	215.31	361.64	452.11	774.83	677.28	954.95
Nonpayroll deposit to retirement plans	426.12	180.84	221.05	241.15	374.60	955.75	779.08	1,281.94
Deductions for Social Security	2,604.32	1,164.36	2,073.20	2,334.70	2,973.83	4,099.81	3,747.21	4,750.83
PERSONAL TAXES	**2,496.26**	**436.79**	**1,399.32**	**1,648.56**	**2,274.16**	**5,667.00**	**5,099.57**	**6,676.45**
Federal income taxes	1,842.57	253.61	970.41	1,194.01	1,629.67	4,326.92	3,852.20	5,171.44
State and local income taxes	506.45	112.03	308.30	345.80	478.80	1,094.25	1,010.05	1,244.03
Other taxes	147.24	71.15	120.61	108.74	165.69	245.83	237.32	260.98

Note: (–) means sample is too small to make a reliable estimate.
Source: Bureau of Labor Statistics, unpublished tables from the 2002 Consumer Expenditure Survey

Table 4.2 Financial: Indexed spending by education, 2002

(indexed average annual spending of consumer units (CU) on financial products and services, cash contributions, and miscellaneous items, by education of consumer unit reference person, 2002; index definition: an index of 100 is the average for all consumer units; an index of 132 means that spending by consumer units in that group is 32 percent above the average for all consumer units; an index of 68 indicates spending that is 32 percent below the average for all consumer units)

	total consumer units	less than high school graduate	high school graduate	some college	associate's degree	college graduate total	college graduate bachelor's degree	college graduate master's, professional, doctorate
Average spending of CU, total	$40,677	$24,930	$33,708	$38,654	$44,406	$57,384	$53,732	$64,118
Average spending of CU, index	100	61	83	95	109	141	132	158
FINANCIAL PRODUCTS AND SERVICES	**100**	**62**	**79**	**111**	**106**	**134**	**118**	**163**
Miscellaneous fees	100	78	48	111	249	112	173	–
Lottery and gambling losses	100	62	117	123	171	64	47	93
Legal fees	100	30	55	115	108	174	164	193
Funeral expenses	100	155	110	81	59	86	71	114
Safe deposit box rental	100	48	70	98	92	167	143	211
Checking accounts, other bank service charges	100	52	84	119	126	121	120	123
Cemetery lots, vaults, and maintenance fees	100	140	101	75	99	96	86	114
Accounting fees	100	38	66	111	95	166	137	219
Miscellaneous personal services	100	63	36	86	95	195	197	191
Finance charges, except mortgage and vehicles	100	59	81	121	113	123	112	143
Occupational expenses	100	30	70	79	118	183	128	286
Expenses for other properties	100	64	95	112	85	123	86	190
Credit card memberships	100	38	50	100	128	180	158	221
Shopping club membership fees	100	35	74	108	136	146	139	160
CASH CONTRIBUTIONS	**100**	**48**	**74**	**82**	**108**	**170**	**158**	**193**
Support for college students	100	23	53	80	73	222	183	295
Alimony expenditures	100	9	51	151	32	190	187	196
Child support expenditures	100	59	110	100	140	99	94	109
Gifts to non–CU members of stocks, bonds, and mutual funds	100	12	68	30	44	261	372	56
Cash contributions to charities and other organizations	100	19	52	58	83	238	209	292
Cash contributions to church, religious organizations	100	48	70	87	118	167	162	176
Cash contributions to educational institutions	100	3	52	19	78	280	171	482
Cash contributions to political organizations	100	56	26	34	72	268	282	242
Other cash gifts	100	76	86	80	102	145	126	179
PERSONAL INSURANCE AND PENSIONS	**100**	**41**	**74**	**86**	**111**	**169**	**150**	**206**
Life and other personal insurance	100	50	83	90	109	152	131	192
Life, endowment, annuity, other personal insurance	100	51	83	91	109	152	130	193
Other nonhealth insurance	100	40	80	76	127	166	169	161
Pensions and Social Security	100	40	73	86	111	171	152	207
Deductions for government retirement	100	10	54	82	100	216	138	361
Deductions for private pensions	100	15	55	93	116	198	173	245
Nonpayroll deposit to retirement plans	100	42	52	57	88	224	183	301
Deductions for Social Security	100	45	80	90	114	157	144	182
PERSONAL TAXES	**100**	**17**	**56**	**66**	**91**	**227**	**204**	**267**
Federal income taxes	100	14	53	65	88	235	209	281
State and local income taxes	100	22	61	68	95	216	199	246
Other taxes	100	48	82	74	113	167	161	177

Note: (–) means sample is too small to make a reliable estimate.
Source: Calculations by New Strategist based on the 2002 Consumer Expenditure Survey

Table 4.23 Financial: Total spending by education, 2002

(total annual spending on financial products and services, cash contributions, and miscellaneous items, by consumer unit (CU) educational attainment group, 2002; numbers in thousands)

	total consumer units	less than high school graduate	high school graduate	some college	associate's degree	college graduate total	bachelor's degree	master's, professional, doctorate
Number of consumer units	112,108	17,075	31,961	23,260	10,395	29,417	19,082	10,335
Total spending of all CUs	$4,560,172,273	$425,686,580	$1,077,329,562	$899,082,038	$461,598,187	$1,688,065,422	$1,025,305,819	$662,664,491
FINANCIAL PRODUCTS AND SERVICES	**$88,834,379**	**$8,448,710**	**$19,929,921**	**$20,493,921**	**$8,720,781**	**$31,172,607**	**$17,785,569**	**$13,385,685**
Miscellaneous fees	252,243	30,052	34,518	57,917	58,316	73,837	74,229	–
Lottery and gambling losses	5,262,350	499,273	1,753,061	1,339,311	833,055	879,568	425,338	452,260
Legal fees	14,909,243	690,855	2,334,431	3,572,038	1,493,969	6,818,566	4,160,448	2,658,059
Funeral expenses	8,734,334	2,058,904	2,744,491	1,475,847	480,665	1,974,763	1,055,998	918,885
Safe deposit box rental	430,495	31,589	86,295	87,690	36,590	188,563	104,569	83,817
Checking accounts, other bank service charges	2,904,718	230,683	698,987	715,012	338,461	921,929	593,259	328,756
Cemetery lots, vaults, and maintenance fees	1,799,333	383,334	520,005	280,050	164,553	451,257	262,568	188,614
Accounting fees	6,485,448	378,211	1,221,230	1,490,501	570,166	2,825,797	1,515,683	1,310,271
Miscellaneous personal services	4,458,535	426,192	451,609	798,981	390,852	2,279,229	1,495,266	784,220
Finance charges, except mortgage, vehicles	30,422,748	2,752,319	7,016,398	7,637,188	3,178,167	9,837,927	5,815,621	4,022,382
Occupational expenses	4,311,674	196,704	858,792	710,826	472,869	2,072,722	937,308	1,135,610
Expenses for other properties	7,398,007	716,638	2,002,357	1,718,216	581,081	2,379,835	1,085,575	1,294,149
Credit card memberships	316,145	18,270	45,065	65,361	37,630	149,438	84,915	64,490
Shopping club membership fees	669,285	35,858	140,948	150,492	84,407	257,105	158,190	99,009
CASH CONTRIBUTIONS	**143,173,127**	**10,362,647**	**30,379,889**	**24,319,958**	**14,276,285**	**63,833,713**	**38,388,404**	**25,445,493**
Support for college students	8,513,482	296,081	1,274,924	1,405,369	572,557	4,965,001	2,649,154	2,315,867
Alimony expenditures	2,374,447	34,321	344,859	741,529	70,374	1,183,446	754,311	429,213
Child support expenditures	21,384,601	1,917,864	6,678,890	4,428,239	2,785,028	5,573,933	3,420,830	2,153,091
Gifts to non–CU members of stocks, bonds, and mutual funds	2,716,377	48,664	525,758	170,728	111,538	1,859,449	1,719,479	140,039
Cash contributions to charities and other organizations	15,428,303	456,756	2,276,582	1,857,776	1,183,471	9,653,777	5,500,387	4,153,326
Cash contributions to church, religious organizations	62,476,667	4,555,952	12,452,645	11,279,472	6,817,353	27,371,636	17,233,145	10,138,428
Cash contributions to educational institutions	3,746,649	18,441	554,523	149,562	269,646	2,754,020	1,087,674	1,666,519
Cash contributions to political organizations	1,221,977	103,987	92,048	85,364	81,289	859,565	586,581	273,051
Other cash gifts	25,309,502	2,930,753	6,179,659	4,201,919	2,385,029	9,612,593	5,436,653	4,175,960
PERSONAL INSURANCE AND PENSIONS	**437,066,491**	**27,561,782**	**92,241,683**	**78,248,268**	**44,847,356**	**194,166,909**	**111,315,992**	**82,851,148**
Life and other personal insurance	45,528,180	3,490,472	10,724,833	8,502,693	4,616,731	18,193,826	10,152,960	8,041,147
Life, endowment, annuity, other personal insurance	43,907,098	3,391,095	10,357,282	8,245,670	4,425,671	17,487,524	9,686,786	7,800,961
Other nonhealth insurance	1,621,082	99,377	367,552	257,256	191,060	706,302	466,173	240,185
Pensions and Social Security	391,538,311	24,071,311	81,517,170	69,745,575	40,230,625	175,972,788	101,163,223	74,810,001
Deductions for government retirement	7,789,264	123,965	1,192,785	1,327,216	724,012	4,421,669	1,829,773	2,591,915
Deductions for private pensions	43,764,721	978,227	6,881,523	8,411,746	4,699,683	22,793,174	12,923,857	9,869,408
Nonpayroll deposit to retirement plans	47,771,461	3,087,843	7,064,979	5,609,149	3,893,967	28,115,298	14,866,405	13,248,850
Deductions for Social Security	291,965,107	19,881,447	66,261,545	54,305,122	30,912,963	120,604,111	71,504,261	49,099,828
PERSONAL TAXES	**279,850,716**	**7,458,189**	**44,723,667**	**38,345,506**	**23,639,893**	**166,706,139**	**97,309,995**	**69,001,111**
Federal income taxes	206,566,838	4,330,391	31,015,274	27,772,673	16,940,420	127,285,006	73,507,680	53,446,832
State and local income taxes	56,777,097	1,912,912	9,853,576	8,043,308	4,977,126	32,189,552	19,273,774	12,857,050
Other taxes	16,506,782	1,214,886	3,854,816	2,529,292	1,722,348	7,231,581	4,528,540	2,697,228

Note: Numbers may not add to total because of rounding. (–) means sample is too small to make a reliable estimate.
Source: Calculations by New Strategist based on the 2002 Consumer Expenditure Survey

Table 4.24 Financial: Market shares by education, 2002

(percentage of total annual spending on financial products and services, cash contributions, and miscellaneous items accounted for by consumer unit (CU) educational attainment groups, 2002)

	total consumer units	less than high school graduate	high school graduate	some college	associate's degree	college graduate total	bachelor's degree	master's, professional, doctorate
Share of total consumer units	100.0%	15.2%	28.5%	20.7%	9.3%	26.2%	17.0%	9.2%
Share of total before-tax income	100.0	7.9	22.8	17.9	10.3	41.3	23.9	17.3
Share of total spending	100.0	9.3	23.6	19.7	10.1	37.0	22.5	14.5
FINANCIAL PRODUCTS AND SERVICES	**100.0%**	**9.5%**	**22.4%**	**23.1%**	**9.8%**	**35.1%**	**20.0%**	**15.1%**
Miscellaneous fees	100.0	11.9	13.7	23.0	23.1	29.3	29.4	–
Lottery and gambling losses	100.0	9.5	33.3	25.5	15.8	16.7	8.1	8.6
Legal fees	100.0	4.6	15.7	24.0	10.0	45.7	27.9	17.8
Funeral expenses	100.0	23.6	31.4	16.9	5.5	22.6	12.1	10.5
Safe deposit box rental	100.0	7.3	20.0	20.4	8.5	43.8	24.3	19.5
Checking accounts, other bank service charges	100.0	7.9	24.1	24.6	11.7	31.7	20.4	11.3
Cemetery lots, vaults, and maintenance fees	100.0	21.3	28.9	15.6	9.1	25.1	14.6	10.5
Accounting fees	100.0	5.8	18.8	23.0	8.8	43.6	23.4	20.2
Miscellaneous personal services	100.0	9.6	10.1	17.9	8.8	51.1	33.5	17.6
Finance charges, except mortgage and vehicles	100.0	9.0	23.1	25.1	10.4	32.3	19.1	13.2
Occupational expenses	100.0	4.6	19.9	16.5	11.0	48.1	21.7	26.3
Expenses for other properties	100.0	9.7	27.1	23.2	7.9	32.2	14.7	17.5
Credit card memberships	100.0	5.8	14.3	20.7	11.9	47.3	26.9	20.4
Shopping club membership fees	100.0	5.4	21.1	22.5	12.6	38.4	23.6	14.8
CASH CONTRIBUTIONS	**100.0**	**7.2**	**21.2**	**17.0**	**10.0**	**44.6**	**26.8**	**17.8**
Support for college students	100.0	3.5	15.0	16.5	6.7	58.3	31.1	27.2
Alimony expenditures	100.0	1.4	14.5	31.2	3.0	49.8	31.8	18.1
Child support expenditures	100.0	9.0	31.2	20.7	13.0	26.1	16.0	10.1
Gifts to non–CU members of stocks, bonds, and mutual funds	100.0	1.8	19.4	6.3	4.1	68.5	63.3	5.2
Cash contributions to charities and other organizations	100.0	3.0	14.8	12.0	7.7	62.6	35.7	26.9
Cash contributions to church, religious organizations	100.0	7.3	19.9	18.1	10.9	43.8	27.6	16.2
Cash contributions to educational institutions	100.0	0.5	14.8	4.0	7.2	73.5	29.0	44.5
Cash contributions to political organizations	100.0	8.5	7.5	7.0	6.7	70.3	48.0	22.3
Other cash gifts	100.0	11.6	24.4	16.6	9.4	38.0	21.5	16.5
PERSONAL INSURANCE AND PENSIONS	**100.0**	**6.3**	**21.1**	**17.9**	**10.3**	**44.4**	**25.5**	**19.0**
Life and other personal insurance	100.0	7.7	23.6	18.7	10.1	40.0	22.3	17.7
Life, endowment, annuity, other personal insurance	100.0	7.7	23.6	18.8	10.1	39.8	22.1	17.8
Other nonhealth insurance	100.0	6.1	22.7	15.9	11.8	43.6	28.8	14.8
Pensions and Social Security	100.0	6.1	20.8	17.8	10.3	44.9	25.8	19.1
Deductions for government retirement	100.0	1.6	15.3	17.0	9.3	56.8	23.5	33.3
Deductions for private pensions	100.0	2.2	15.7	19.2	10.7	52.1	29.5	22.6
Nonpayroll deposit to retirement plans	100.0	6.5	14.8	11.7	8.2	58.9	31.1	27.7
Deductions for Social Security	100.0	6.8	22.7	18.6	10.6	41.3	24.5	16.8
PERSONAL TAXES	**100.0**	**2.7**	**16.0**	**13.7**	**8.4**	**59.6**	**34.8**	**24.7**
Federal income taxes	100.0	2.1	15.0	13.4	8.2	61.6	35.6	25.9
State and local income taxes	100.0	3.4	17.4	14.2	8.8	56.7	33.9	22.6
Other taxes	100.0	7.4	23.4	15.3	10.4	43.8	27.4	16.3

Note: Numbers may not add to total because of rounding. (–) means sample is too small to make a reliable estimate.
Source: Calculations by New Strategist based on the 2002 Consumer Expenditure Survey

Spending on Food and Alcoholic Beverages, 2002

The average household spent 6 percent more on food away from home (primarily sit-down meals and take-outs from restaurants) in 2002 than in 1997, after adjusting for inflation. Spending on food at home (groceries) fell 4 percent during those years as busy families increasingly turned to others to prepare their meals. Overall, Americans devoted 13.2 percent of their expenditures to food in 2002, down from 13.8 percent in 1997. Spending on alcoholic beverages rose 9 percent between 1997 and 2002, after adjusting for inflation.

Householders aged 35 to 44 spend the most on food at home because they have the largest households. In 2002, they spent an average of $3,601 on food at home, 16 percent more than the average household. When eating out, householders aged 35 to 44 spend the most on lunch and dinner at fast-food restaurants. Householders aged 55 to 64 are the biggest spenders on lunch and dinner at full-service restaurants. Householders aged 45 to 54 spend the most on alcoholic beverages.

Households with incomes of $70,000 or more spend 41 percent more than the average household on food at home. They spend 82 percent more than the average household on food away from home and 88 percent more on alcoholic beverages. The most affluent households account for 45 percent of spending on dinners in full-service restaurants. They account for 56 percent of spending on wine consumed at home.

Married couples with adult children at home spend more on food than any other household type—$8,324 in 2002. These households are not only larger than average, but they also have the highest incomes. Married couples without children at home (most of them empty-nesters) and couples with adult children at home are the best customers of full-service restaurants. Married couples with school-aged children spend 52 percent more than the average household on fast-food lunches and 59 percent more on fast-food dinners. Spending on alcoholic beverages is highest among married couples without children at home and couples with adult children at home, while it is lowest for single parents.

Hispanic households spend more on food at home than non-Hispanics—18 percent more than the average household in 2002. Behind the higher spending of Hispanics is their larger household size, with 3.3 people on average versus 2.5 in the average household. Hispanics spend more than twice the average on flour and 80 percent more than average on rice. They spend more than three times the average on dried beans. Blacks spend 24 percent more than average on pork and 19 percent more on fresh fish and seafood.

Spending on food at home is slightly above average in the Northeast and West and slightly below average in the Midwest and South. Households in the Northeast spend more than those in other regions on food away from home (11 percent more than the average household) and on alcoholic beverages (22 percent above average). Spending on wine consumed at home is 37 percent above average in the Northeast and 30 percent above average in the West. Spending on beer consumed at home is highest in the Midwest, at 16 percent above average. Spending on alcoholic beverages is 25 percent below average in the South.

Because college graduates dominate the affluent, they account for a large share of the food away from home market. College graduates control 42 percent of spending on dinners at full-service restaurants, for example, much greater than their 26 percent share of all households. They account for 50 percent of household spending on wine consumed at home, but for only 24 percent of spending on beer consumed at home.

Table 5.1 Food and Alcohol: Average spending by age, 2002

(average annual spending of consumer units (CU) on food and alcoholic beverages, by age of consumer unit reference person, 2002)

	total consumer units	under 25	25 to 34	35 to 44	45 to 54	55 to 64	65 to 74	75+
Number of consumer units (in thousands, add 000)	112,108	8,737	18,988	24,394	22,691	15,314	11,216	10,767
Average number of persons per CU	2.5	1.9	2.9	3.2	2.7	2.1	1.9	1.5
Average before-tax income of CU	$49,430.00	$20,773.00	$49,133.00	$61,532.00	$64,974.00	$53,162.00	$35,118.00	$23,890.00
Average spending of CU, total	40,676.60	24,229.46	40,318.29	48,330.48	48,748.24	44,330.04	32,242.52	23,758.89
Food, average spending	5,374.80	3,621.39	5,470.74	6,313.58	6,228.49	5,559.05	4,479.05	3,302.10
Alcoholic beverages, average spending	375.95	394.21	394.69	366.91	465.38	419.57	323.56	144.05
FOOD AT HOME	**$3,098.52**	**$1,925.70**	**$3,092.85**	**$3,601.44**	**$3,528.31**	**$3,114.21**	**$2,877.08**	**$2,195.04**
Cereals and bakery products	**450.13**	**287.26**	**441.68**	**542.20**	**500.16**	**422.98**	**418.14**	**351.99**
Cereals and cereal products	154.07	112.99	163.18	191.07	168.52	133.10	128.14	111.74
Flour	8.65	5.83	8.88	10.43	8.82	7.06	9.25	7.74
Prepared flour mixes	12.40	7.27	10.73	15.09	14.27	12.28	12.16	9.87
Ready-to-eat and cooked cereals	87.66	69.04	94.35	109.94	92.14	72.70	71.24	68.16
Rice	17.82	11.47	20.74	20.52	22.16	15.39	14.45	9.20
Pasta, cornmeal, and other cereal products	27.54	19.38	28.48	35.09	31.13	25.67	21.04	16.77
Bakery products	296.06	174.27	278.50	351.13	331.65	289.88	290.00	240.26
Bread	83.83	53.84	77.80	95.06	90.66	83.24	93.10	70.05
White bread	35.21	24.88	36.01	42.40	37.01	31.99	34.89	26.62
Bread, other than white	48.62	28.96	41.79	52.66	53.65	51.26	58.21	43.43
Crackers and cookies	70.67	41.94	63.82	87.55	77.96	69.12	64.77	60.67
Cookies	46.31	29.89	42.80	58.71	50.16	42.01	43.12	38.87
Crackers	24.36	12.05	21.02	28.84	27.80	27.11	21.65	21.81
Frozen and refrigerated bakery products	25.64	12.78	25.12	34.47	28.86	22.75	21.79	18.05
Other bakery products	115.92	65.72	111.76	134.05	134.16	114.76	110.34	91.49
Biscuits and rolls	41.04	23.25	36.88	48.87	49.00	42.71	37.70	29.11
Cakes and cupcakes	35.73	21.69	39.40	41.34	42.17	32.10	31.62	23.25
Bread and cracker products	3.50	2.04	3.62	3.51	3.84	3.48	4.23	2.98
Sweetrolls, coffee cakes, doughnuts	25.84	12.03	23.79	32.30	27.58	24.56	24.61	25.60
Pies, tarts, turnovers	9.82	6.70	8.08	8.02	11.58	11.91	12.17	10.54
Meats, poultry, fish, and eggs	**798.42**	**460.36**	**817.05**	**918.33**	**928.61**	**807.14**	**744.65**	**528.87**
Beef	231.17	130.85	252.70	270.97	273.25	215.90	207.53	138.46
Ground beef	86.29	54.18	94.03	103.14	102.04	75.01	75.09	53.65
Roast	40.99	18.55	41.35	48.90	44.81	45.74	37.77	28.92
Chuck roast	11.71	5.09	12.27	13.13	13.50	13.53	11.00	7.06
Round roast	10.23	7.68	7.94	13.32	9.09	12.16	10.94	8.29
Other roast	19.05	5.77	21.14	22.45	22.22	20.04	15.83	13.57
Steak	84.47	46.96	98.77	97.02	101.81	77.11	75.76	42.52
Round steak	13.29	10.09	17.34	14.25	16.01	11.63	9.03	7.26
Sirloin steak	26.62	15.12	33.57	29.50	33.18	25.89	19.33	11.21
Other steak	44.56	21.74	47.86	53.26	52.61	39.59	47.40	24.05
Pork	167.34	95.36	162.42	197.85	188.03	168.63	168.57	117.25
Bacon	28.45	17.75	24.97	33.69	32.26	27.29	29.51	23.90
Pork chops	38.43	24.70	40.11	46.04	42.95	36.20	33.47	27.73
Ham	37.16	21.17	35.05	41.55	41.96	41.79	42.66	21.13
Ham, not canned	35.66	20.23	33.77	39.58	40.29	40.08	41.32	20.39
Canned ham	1.50	0.94	1.28	1.96	1.67	1.71	1.33	0.74
Sausage	26.17	13.13	26.07	32.79	26.81	27.31	24.94	20.08
Other pork	37.13	18.61	36.23	43.78	44.05	36.04	38.00	24.40
Other meats	101.08	52.49	96.36	121.81	116.63	102.59	97.26	70.15
Frankfurters	20.95	10.39	20.61	27.75	22.89	21.82	15.84	14.46

	total consumer units	under 25	25 to 34	35 to 44	45 to 54	55 to 64	65 to 74	75+
Lunch meats (cold cuts)	$68.99	$36.11	$66.61	$85.17	$78.06	$71.42	$65.02	$44.03
Bologna, liverwurst, salami	21.11	9.92	20.36	25.83	23.02	23.30	17.70	17.17
Lamb, organ meats, and others	11.14	5.98	9.14	8.90	15.68	9.35	16.41	11.67
Lamb and organ meats	7.99	5.25	6.56	7.51	8.78	6.16	11.91	10.90
Mutton, goat, and game	3.15	0.73	2.57	1.38	6.90	3.19	4.50	0.77
Poultry	144.13	96.39	158.75	164.14	167.98	133.57	123.44	95.92
Fresh and frozen chicken	113.25	74.71	124.45	131.29	131.89	104.65	93.34	75.90
Fresh and frozen whole chicken	32.08	21.73	34.65	34.89	38.88	29.66	26.95	23.67
Fresh and frozen chicken parts	81.17	52.98	89.80	96.41	93.00	74.99	66.38	52.23
Other poultry	30.88	21.68	34.30	32.84	36.09	28.92	30.10	20.02
Fish and seafood	120.97	61.49	112.79	125.71	145.60	154.23	114.93	79.34
Canned fish and seafood	16.13	8.94	13.20	16.69	19.35	17.87	19.56	13.07
Fresh fish and shellfish	69.31	36.68	68.48	66.56	84.25	89.43	66.48	45.95
Frozen fish and shellfish	35.53	15.86	31.10	42.46	42.00	46.93	28.90	20.32
Eggs	33.75	23.79	34.03	37.85	37.12	32.23	32.92	27.74
Dairy products	**328.34**	**199.73**	**324.24**	**391.66**	**367.32**	**325.44**	**301.03**	**244.24**
Fresh milk and cream	127.15	86.53	129.72	153.21	135.52	121.47	111.56	102.08
Fresh milk, all types	114.63	79.42	117.64	139.97	121.34	108.08	98.49	91.35
Cream	12.52	7.11	12.08	13.24	14.18	13.40	13.07	10.73
Other dairy products	201.19	113.20	194.52	238.45	231.80	203.96	189.47	142.16
Butter	18.48	9.10	16.06	20.60	22.58	19.33	19.64	14.57
Cheese	95.64	50.60	95.60	111.55	111.76	98.20	92.71	60.65
Ice cream and related products	58.74	32.84	55.86	72.27	63.39	59.50	53.45	48.63
Miscellaneous dairy products	28.33	20.66	27.01	34.04	34.06	26.94	23.67	18.31
Fruits and vegetables	**552.01**	**337.94**	**521.81**	**596.57**	**626.67**	**591.26**	**555.66**	**460.80**
Fresh fruits	178.20	104.78	153.54	190.56	204.23	206.58	184.83	151.74
Apples	32.59	21.65	30.32	38.01	36.54	36.07	30.50	21.74
Bananas	31.24	20.39	28.12	32.38	34.89	32.49	32.29	32.72
Oranges	20.34	14.22	19.16	21.07	25.72	20.25	17.19	17.78
Citrus fruits, excl. oranges	14.29	8.70	11.91	15.85	14.33	17.56	17.24	11.76
Other fresh fruits	79.74	39.82	64.03	83.25	92.75	100.22	87.61	67.73
Fresh vegetables	174.88	99.97	162.41	184.83	204.85	190.74	175.87	148.64
Potatoes	33.35	18.91	30.85	35.73	35.94	36.65	35.16	32.27
Lettuce	22.22	12.53	20.16	23.55	26.93	25.02	21.48	17.56
Tomatoes	33.71	24.27	32.71	35.13	39.17	35.41	32.82	26.81
Other fresh vegetables	85.60	44.26	78.70	90.42	102.81	93.65	86.41	71.99
Processed fruits	115.50	80.55	118.03	128.34	126.53	113.38	108.04	97.34
Frozen fruits and fruit juices	12.45	13.24	13.41	13.54	12.08	11.55	10.49	11.63
Frozen orange juice	6.31	6.72	6.42	7.50	5.52	5.00	5.76	7.17
Frozen fruits	2.79	1.36	3.20	2.19	3.12	3.60	2.68	2.83
Frozen fruit juices, excl. orange	3.35	5.15	3.79	3.85	3.43	2.95	2.05	1.63
Canned fruits	15.06	8.71	14.06	15.36	16.06	15.87	17.71	15.42
Dried fruits	6.06	3.10	5.56	5.19	5.50	7.23	8.65	8.33
Fresh fruit juice	22.20	9.60	21.87	22.74	26.80	22.93	23.10	20.22
Canned and bottled fruit juice	59.74	45.91	63.14	71.51	66.09	55.79	48.08	41.73
Processed vegetables	83.43	52.64	87.83	92.84	91.06	80.56	86.93	63.09
Frozen vegetables	27.85	18.77	26.88	31.19	29.99	28.38	27.60	24.28
Canned and dried vegetables and juices	55.58	33.87	60.94	61.65	61.07	52.18	59.33	38.81
Canned beans	12.47	7.19	13.06	15.10	13.92	10.93	12.03	9.20
Canned corn	7.34	4.00	8.87	8.97	7.34	6.56	6.90	5.15
Canned miscellaneous vegetables	17.85	9.23	17.17	18.63	20.96	18.28	21.39	13.38
Dried peas	0.36	0.34	0.36	0.31	0.32	0.47	0.54	0.23
Dried beans	2.55	2.51	2.64	2.50	3.19	2.33	2.52	1.51

	total consumer units	under 25	25 to 34	35 to 44	45 to 54	55 to 64	65 to 74	75+
Dried miscellaneous vegetables	$7.38	$6.83	$9.91	$7.81	$6.83	$6.89	$6.46	$5.03
Dried processed vegetables	0.34	0.14	0.08	0.37	0.59	0.57	0.36	–
Fresh and canned vegetable juices	7.23	3.54	8.86	7.83	7.81	6.13	9.08	4.33
Sugar and other sweets	**117.39**	**64.28**	**103.74**	**138.80**	**130.49**	**124.70**	**124.81**	**90.11**
Candy and chewing gum	75.44	40.61	66.60	90.09	83.53	83.45	81.00	51.48
Sugar	15.56	10.14	15.16	17.46	17.59	15.33	13.76	14.31
Artificial sweeteners	4.33	1.70	2.44	4.59	4.81	5.53	5.54	5.34
Jams, preserves, other sweets	22.06	11.83	19.55	26.66	24.56	20.39	24.51	18.97
Fats and oils	85.16	47.46	81.00	92.79	98.64	89.59	89.60	66.36
Margarine	9.86	4.23	7.87	9.83	11.34	12.35	12.00	9.29
Fats and oils	**26.08**	**15.43**	**24.65**	**29.45**	**29.32**	**25.22**	**30.18**	**19.61**
Salad dressings	27.01	15.52	26.28	30.53	32.76	28.43	24.11	18.26
Nondairy cream and imitation milk	9.33	3.43	8.24	9.33	11.40	11.46	10.07	7.91
Peanut butter	12.89	8.85	13.94	13.65	13.83	12.13	13.24	11.28
Miscellaneous foods	**471.92**	**344.32**	**511.81**	**571.58**	**530.73**	**434.23**	**392.08**	**283.09**
Frozen prepared foods	98.09	65.01	103.86	126.43	112.12	81.91	76.30	65.07
Frozen meals	29.88	21.29	29.79	32.02	36.56	25.65	28.10	25.85
Other frozen prepared foods	68.22	43.72	74.07	94.41	75.56	56.26	48.20	39.22
Canned and packaged soups	35.82	21.18	30.72	39.06	42.54	35.16	38.54	33.54
Potato chips, nuts, and other snacks	100.53	60.15	94.89	127.06	124.25	92.05	88.47	56.26
Potato chips and other snacks	76.37	51.89	77.66	104.44	93.79	62.05	54.45	34.94
Nuts	24.16	8.26	17.23	22.62	30.46	30.00	34.02	21.32
Condiments and seasonings	86.81	56.60	88.96	100.70	101.88	86.78	81.28	48.73
Salt, spices, and other seasonings	21.14	14.39	21.42	25.15	24.34	20.70	19.86	11.96
Olives, pickles, relishes	9.70	4.95	8.45	11.28	11.28	10.78	10.38	6.55
Sauces and gravies	37.78	28.14	40.03	43.90	47.10	34.60	32.28	17.56
Baking needs and miscellaneous products	18.19	9.12	19.06	20.37	19.17	20.72	18.76	12.66
Other canned/packaged prepared foods	150.67	141.38	193.39	178.33	149.94	138.32	107.49	79.49
Prepared salads	21.46	9.20	15.92	24.08	25.28	29.88	20.43	16.35
Prepared desserts	10.32	4.76	9.25	13.45	10.41	11.46	10.06	8.09
Baby food	31.57	56.69	73.65	33.87	17.59	17.39	6.26	4.78
Miscellaneous prepared foods	87.24	70.74	94.55	106.60	96.62	79.58	70.74	50.27
Nonalcoholic beverages	**253.94**	**159.59**	**260.44**	**303.16**	**296.27**	**264.79**	**206.59**	**148.00**
Cola	81.11	54.00	87.45	99.86	93.51	83.10	62.25	38.18
Other carbonated drinks	43.93	33.93	52.75	52.53	50.06	39.16	34.06	19.94
Coffee	41.59	12.74	27.73	43.62	53.42	55.69	43.85	38.14
Roasted coffee	27.38	8.64	18.72	29.89	35.72	38.44	25.57	20.92
Instant and freeze-dried coffee	14.21	4.09	9.02	13.73	17.70	17.25	18.28	17.22
Noncarbonated fruit-flavored drinks, incl. nonfrozen lemonade	18.95	14.05	23.40	27.30	20.04	14.24	11.71	7.38
Tea	15.86	7.88	12.96	18.02	17.28	19.50	17.42	12.81
Nonalcoholic beer	0.64	–	0.49	0.98	1.00	0.67	0.53	–
Other nonalcoholic beverages and ice	51.85	36.99	55.66	60.85	60.96	52.43	36.77	31.55
Food prepared by CU on trips	**41.20**	**24.76**	**31.08**	**46.35**	**49.41**	**54.09**	**44.53**	**21.58**
FOOD AWAY FROM HOME	**2,276.29**	**1,695.69**	**2,377.89**	**2,712.13**	**2,700.17**	**2,444.84**	**1,601.98**	**1,107.06**
Meals at restaurants, carry-outs, other	**1,866.42**	**1,390.49**	**2,040.46**	**2,225.31**	**2,179.95**	**1,869.18**	**1,328.81**	**984.79**
Lunch	685.79	511.07	761.52	863.61	812.62	624.10	444.48	344.96
• At fast food, take-out, delivery, concession stands, buffet, and cafeteria (other than employer and school cafeteria)	377.71	338.28	460.31	505.45	424.62	299.43	193.16	165.44
• At full-service restaurants	224.82	118.97	217.71	212.35	272.37	283.36	223.40	169.29
• At vending machines, mobile vendors	5.50	4.85	6.67	9.17	5.06	4.17	2.88	0.93
• At employer and school cafeterias	77.76	48.97	76.84	136.64	110.57	37.14	25.05	9.31

	total consumer units	under 25	25 to 34	35 to 44	45 to 54	55 to 64	65 to 74	75+
Dinner	$736.54	$460.76	$799.06	$827.67	$837.82	$836.79	$599.46	$417.25
• At fast food, take-out, delivery, concession stands, buffet, and cafeteria (other than employer and school cafeteria)	213.33	193.43	276.20	289.37	227.49	170.82	97.81	88.54
• At full-service restaurants	518.02	252.60	517.09	532.04	607.76	659.86	500.24	326.88
• At vending machines, mobile vendors	1.87	0.46	2.27	2.95	0.34	4.09	0.55	1.28
• At employer and school cafeterias	3.32	14.27	3.50	3.31	2.23	2.03	0.86	0.55
Snacks and nonalcoholic beverages	262.67	252.11	292.48	342.30	312.97	224.31	142.83	102.47
• At fast food, take-out, delivery, concession stands, buffet, and cafeteria (other than employer and school cafeteria)	185.69	175.82	202.22	242.55	226.78	160.95	98.43	68.68
• At full-service restaurants	30.17	21.77	29.28	30.28	37.08	30.00	29.47	24.68
• At vending machines, mobile vendors	36.71	43.68	50.26	53.08	36.68	26.26	12.45	8.14
• At employer and school cafeterias	10.11	10.84	10.72	16.39	12.43	7.10	2.47	0.96
Breakfast and brunch	181.42	166.55	187.39	191.74	216.55	183.98	142.05	120.11
• At fast food, take-out, delivery, concession stands, buffet, and cafeteria (other than employer and school cafeteria)	87.83	97.87	106.62	105.75	102.52	66.27	50.91	41.03
• At full-service restaurants	87.08	56.03	75.01	77.98	105.51	113.04	88.93	77.07
• At vending machines, mobile vendors	1.40	1.86	1.53	1.08	1.66	1.89	0.72	0.95
• At employer and school cafeterias	5.11	10.79	4.22	6.94	6.85	2.77	1.48	1.06
Board (including at school)	**46.54**	**108.35**	**9.54**	**31.31**	**99.42**	**50.44**	**18.15**	**8.72**
Catered affairs	**69.00**	**39.50**	**71.86**	**56.73**	**61.92**	**184.76**	**20.77**	**16.13**
Food on trips	**211.49**	**117.19**	**168.38**	**232.03**	**250.52**	**303.24**	**223.38**	**92.30**
School lunches	**60.00**	**6.67**	**51.71**	**142.04**	**83.11**	**16.13**	**6.24**	**1.66**
Meals as pay	**22.86**	**33.49**	**35.93**	**24.71**	**25.24**	**21.09**	**4.63**	**3.46**
ALCOHOLIC BEVERAGES	**375.95**	**394.21**	**394.69**	**366.91**	**465.38**	**419.57**	**323.56**	**144.05**
At home	**228.08**	**230.11**	**226.96**	**221.68**	**287.17**	**242.66**	**223.83**	**97.37**
Beer and ale	112.34	156.18	141.39	125.07	137.00	84.48	69.76	23.37
Whiskey	13.90	13.17	7.47	12.42	16.35	11.94	26.10	14.46
Wine	77.75	28.08	56.18	58.55	111.92	119.39	98.31	47.69
Other alcoholic beverages	24.09	32.68	21.92	25.65	21.89	26.85	29.66	11.85
Away from home	**147.87**	**164.10**	**167.73**	**145.23**	**178.21**	**176.91**	**99.73**	**46.68**
Beer and ale	52.86	61.51	60.13	53.57	62.33	59.40	35.93	17.96
• At fast food, take-out, delivery, concession stands, buffet, and cafeteria	7.99	14.70	12.94	6.79	7.70	7.41	3.98	1.65
• At full-service restaurants	41.95	45.90	46.85	39.06	49.95	51.82	30.69	16.29
• At vending machines, mobile vendors	0.32	0.63	0.17	0.14	0.85	0.16	0.16	0.02
• At catered affairs	2.59	0.29	0.16	7.58	3.84	–	1.10	–
Wine	25.85	27.17	30.37	22.70	30.51	34.36	16.62	10.91
• At fast food, take-out, delivery, concession stands, buffet and cafeteria	4.41	5.24	6.06	4.13	5.94	3.96	1.97	1.23
• At full-service restaurants	20.36	21.90	24.30	17.77	20.20	30.40	14.43	9.68
• At catered affairs	1.09	0.03	0.02	0.80	4.37	–	0.22	–
Other alcoholic beverages	69.16	75.42	77.23	68.96	85.37	83.16	47.18	17.81
• At fast food, take-out, delivery, concession stands, buffet, and cafeteria	3.50	7.73	6.32	3.16	3.49	1.71	0.81	1.00
• At full-service restaurants	28.94	29.24	34.73	26.26	32.76	41.74	20.61	5.92
• At catered affairs	3.94	0.13	0.07	3.34	15.54	–	0.49	–
Alcoholic beverages purchased on trips	32.78	38.31	36.11	36.20	33.58	39.70	25.27	10.89

Note: (–) means sample is too small to make a reliable estimate.
Source: Bureau of Labor Statistics, unpublished tables from the 2002 Consumer Expenditure Survey

Table 5.2 Food and Alcohol: Indexed spending by age, 2002

(indexed average annual spending of consumer units (CU) on food and alcoholic beverages, by age of consumer unit reference person, 2002; index definition: an index of 100 is the average for all consumer units; an index of 132 means that spending by consumer units in that group is 32 percent above the average for all consumer units; an index of 68 indicates spending that is 32 percent below the average for all consumer units)

	total consumer units	under 25	25 to 34	35 to 44	45 to 54	55 to 64	65 to 74	75+
Average spending of CU, total	$40,677	$24,229	$40,318	$48,330	$48,748	$44,330	$32,243	$23,759
Average spending of CU, index	100	60	99	119	120	109	79	58
Food, spending index	100	67	102	117	116	103	83	61
Alcoholic beverages, spending index	100	105	105	98	124	112	86	38
FOOD AT HOME	**100**	**62**	**100**	**116**	**114**	**101**	**93**	**71**
Cereals and bakery products	**100**	**64**	**98**	**120**	**111**	**94**	**93**	**78**
Cereals and cereal products	100	73	106	124	109	86	83	73
Flour	100	67	103	121	102	82	107	89
Prepared flour mixes	100	59	87	122	115	99	98	80
Ready-to-eat and cooked cereals	100	79	108	125	105	83	81	78
Rice	100	64	116	115	124	86	81	52
Pasta, cornmeal, and other cereal products	100	70	103	127	113	93	76	61
Bakery products	100	59	94	119	112	98	98	81
Bread	100	64	93	113	108	99	111	84
White bread	100	71	102	120	105	91	99	76
Bread, other than white	100	60	86	108	110	105	120	89
Crackers and cookies	100	59	90	124	110	98	92	86
Cookies	100	65	92	127	108	91	93	84
Crackers	100	49	86	118	114	111	89	90
Frozen and refrigerated bakery products	100	50	98	134	113	89	85	70
Other bakery products	100	57	96	116	116	99	95	79
Biscuits and rolls	100	57	90	119	119	104	92	71
Cakes and cupcakes	100	61	110	116	118	90	88	65
Bread and cracker products	100	58	103	100	110	99	121	85
Sweetrolls, coffee cakes, doughnuts	100	47	92	125	107	95	95	99
Pies, tarts, turnovers	100	68	82	82	118	121	124	107
Meats, poultry, fish, and eggs	**100**	**58**	**102**	**115**	**116**	**101**	**93**	**66**
Beef	100	57	109	117	118	93	90	60
Ground beef	100	63	109	120	118	87	87	62
Roast	100	45	101	119	109	112	92	71
Chuck roast	100	43	105	112	115	116	94	60
Round roast	100	75	78	130	89	119	107	81
Other roast	100	30	111	118	117	105	83	71
Steak	100	56	117	115	121	91	90	50
Round steak	100	76	130	107	120	88	68	55
Sirloin steak	100	57	126	111	125	97	73	42
Other steak	100	49	107	120	118	89	106	54
Pork	100	57	97	118	112	101	101	70
Bacon	100	62	88	118	113	96	104	84
Pork chops	100	64	104	120	112	94	87	72
Ham	100	57	94	112	113	112	115	57
Ham, not canned	100	57	95	111	113	112	116	57
Canned ham	100	63	85	131	111	114	89	49
Sausage	100	50	100	125	102	104	95	77
Other pork	100	50	98	118	119	97	102	66
Other meats	100	52	95	121	115	101	96	69
Frankfurters	100	50	98	132	109	104	76	69

	total consumer units	under 25	25 to 34	35 to 44	45 to 54	55 to 64	65 to 74	75+
Lunch meats (cold cuts)	100	52	97	123	113	104	94	64
Bologna, liverwurst, salami	100	47	96	122	109	110	84	81
Lamb, organ meats, and others	100	54	82	80	141	84	147	105
Lamb and organ meats	100	66	82	94	110	77	149	136
Mutton, goat, and game	100	23	82	44	219	101	143	24
Poultry	100	67	110	114	117	93	86	67
Fresh and frozen chicken	100	66	110	116	116	92	82	67
Fresh and frozen whole chicken	100	68	108	109	121	92	84	74
Fresh and frozen chicken parts	100	65	111	119	115	92	82	64
Other poultry	100	70	111	106	117	94	97	65
Fish and seafood	100	51	93	104	120	127	95	66
Canned fish and seafood	100	55	82	103	120	111	121	81
Fresh fish and shellfish	100	53	99	96	122	129	96	66
Frozen fish and shellfish	100	45	88	120	118	132	81	57
Eggs	100	70	101	112	110	95	98	82
Dairy products	**100**	**61**	**99**	**119**	**112**	**99**	**92**	**74**
Fresh milk and cream	100	68	102	120	107	96	88	80
Fresh milk, all types	100	69	103	122	106	94	86	80
Cream	100	57	96	106	113	107	104	86
Other dairy products	100	56	97	119	115	101	94	71
Butter	100	49	87	111	122	105	106	79
Cheese	100	53	100	117	117	103	97	63
Ice cream and related products	100	56	95	123	108	101	91	83
Miscellaneous dairy products	100	73	95	120	120	95	84	65
Fruits and vegetables	**100**	**61**	**95**	**108**	**114**	**107**	**101**	**83**
Fresh fruits	100	59	86	107	115	116	104	85
Apples	100	66	93	117	112	111	94	67
Bananas	100	65	90	104	112	104	103	105
Oranges	100	70	94	104	126	100	85	87
Citrus fruits, excl. oranges	100	61	83	111	100	123	121	82
Other fresh fruits	100	50	80	104	116	126	110	85
Fresh vegetables	100	57	93	106	117	109	101	85
Potatoes	100	57	93	107	108	110	105	97
Lettuce	100	56	91	106	121	113	97	79
Tomatoes	100	72	97	104	116	105	97	80
Other fresh vegetables	100	52	92	106	120	109	101	84
Processed fruits	100	70	102	111	110	98	94	84
Frozen fruits and fruit juices	100	106	108	109	97	93	84	93
Frozen orange juice	100	106	102	119	87	79	91	114
Frozen fruits	100	49	115	78	112	129	96	101
Frozen fruit juices, excl. orange	100	154	113	115	102	88	61	49
Canned fruits	100	58	93	102	107	105	118	102
Dried fruits	100	51	92	86	91	119	143	137
Fresh fruit juice	100	43	99	102	121	103	104	91
Canned and bottled fruit juice	100	77	106	120	111	93	80	70
Processed vegetables	100	63	105	111	109	97	104	76
Frozen vegetables	100	67	97	112	108	102	99	87
Canned and dried vegetables and juices	100	61	110	111	110	94	107	70
Canned beans	100	58	105	121	112	88	96	74
Canned corn	100	54	121	122	100	89	94	70
Canned miscellaneous vegetables	100	52	96	104	117	102	120	75
Dried peas	100	94	100	86	89	131	150	64
Dried beans	100	98	104	98	125	91	99	59

	total consumer units	under 25	25 to 34	35 to 44	45 to 54	55 to 64	65 to 74	75+
Dried miscellaneous vegetables	100	93	134	106	93	93	88	68
Dried processed vegetables	100	41	24	109	174	168	106	–
Fresh and canned vegetable juices	100	49	123	108	108	85	126	60
Sugar and other sweets	**100**	**55**	**88**	**118**	**111**	**106**	**106**	**77**
Candy and chewing gum	100	54	88	119	111	111	107	68
Sugar	100	65	97	112	113	99	88	92
Artificial sweeteners	100	39	56	106	111	128	128	123
Jams, preserves, other sweets	100	54	89	121	111	92	111	86
Fats and oils	**100**	**56**	**95**	**109**	**116**	**105**	**105**	**78**
Margarine	100	43	80	100	115	125	122	94
Fats and oils	100	59	95	113	112	97	116	75
Salad dressings	100	57	97	113	121	105	89	68
Nondairy cream and imitation milk	100	37	88	100	122	123	108	85
Peanut butter	100	69	108	106	107	94	103	88
Miscellaneous foods	**100**	**73**	**108**	**121**	**112**	**92**	**83**	**60**
Frozen prepared foods	100	66	106	129	114	84	78	66
Frozen meals	100	71	100	107	122	86	94	87
Other frozen prepared foods	100	64	109	138	111	82	71	57
Canned and packaged soups	100	59	86	109	119	98	108	94
Potato chips, nuts, and other snacks	100	60	94	126	124	92	88	56
Potato chips and other snacks	100	68	102	137	123	81	71	46
Nuts	100	34	71	94	126	124	141	88
Condiments and seasonings	100	65	102	116	117	100	94	56
Salt, spices, and other seasonings	100	68	101	119	115	98	94	57
Olives, pickles, relishes	100	51	87	116	116	111	107	68
Sauces and gravies	100	74	106	116	125	92	85	46
Baking needs and miscellaneous products	100	50	105	112	105	114	103	70
Other canned/packaged prepared foods	100	94	128	118	100	92	71	53
Prepared salads	100	43	74	112	118	139	95	76
Prepared desserts	100	46	90	130	101	111	97	78
Baby food	100	180	233	107	56	55	20	15
Miscellaneous prepared foods	100	81	108	122	111	91	81	58
Nonalcoholic beverages	**100**	**63**	**103**	**119**	**117**	**104**	**81**	**58**
Cola	100	67	108	123	115	102	77	47
Other carbonated drinks	100	77	120	120	114	89	78	45
Coffee	100	31	67	105	128	134	105	92
Roasted coffee	100	32	68	109	130	140	93	76
Instant and freeze-dried coffee	100	29	63	97	125	121	129	121
Noncarbonated fruit-flavored drinks, incl. nonfrozen lemonade	100	74	123	144	106	75	62	39
Tea	100	50	82	114	109	123	110	81
Nonalcoholic beer	100	–	77	153	156	105	83	–
Other nonalcoholic beverages and ice	100	71	107	117	118	101	71	61
Food prepared by CU on trips	**100**	**60**	**75**	**113**	**120**	**131**	**108**	**52**
FOOD AWAY FROM HOME	**100**	**74**	**104**	**119**	**119**	**107**	**70**	**49**
Meals at restaurants, carry-outs, other	**100**	**75**	**109**	**119**	**117**	**100**	**71**	**53**
Lunch	100	75	111	126	118	91	65	50
• At fast food, take-out, delivery, concession stands, buffet, and cafeteria (other than employer and school cafeteria)	100	90	122	134	112	79	51	44
• At full-service restaurants	100	53	97	94	121	126	99	75
• At vending machines, mobile vendors	100	88	121	167	92	76	52	17
• At employer and school cafeterias	100	63	99	176	142	48	32	12

	total consumer units	under 25	25 to 34	35 to 44	45 to 54	55 to 64	65 to 74	75+
Dinner	100	63	108	112	114	114	81	57
• At fast food, take-out, delivery, concession stands, buffet, and cafeteria (other than employer and school cafeteria)	100	91	129	136	107	80	46	42
• At full-service restaurants	100	49	100	103	117	127	97	63
• At vending machines, mobile vendors	100	25	121	158	18	219	29	68
• At employer and school cafeterias	100	430	105	100	67	61	26	17
Snacks and nonalcoholic beverages	100	96	111	130	119	85	54	39
• At fast food, take-out, delivery, concession stands, buffet, and cafeteria (other than employer and school cafeteria)	100	95	109	131	122	87	53	37
• At full-service restaurants	100	72	97	100	123	99	98	82
• At vending machines, mobile vendors	100	119	137	145	100	72	34	22
• At employer and school cafeterias	100	107	106	162	123	70	24	9
Breakfast and brunch	100	92	103	106	119	101	78	66
• At fast food, take-out, delivery, concession stands, buffet, and cafeteria (other than employer and school cafeteria)	100	111	121	120	117	75	58	47
• At full-service restaurants	100	64	86	90	121	130	102	89
• At vending machines, mobile vendors	100	133	109	77	119	135	51	68
• At employer and school cafeterias	100	211	83	136	134	54	29	21
Board (including at school)	**100**	**233**	**20**	**67**	**214**	**108**	**39**	**19**
Catered affairs	**100**	**57**	**104**	**82**	**90**	**268**	**30**	**23**
Food on trips	**100**	**55**	**80**	**110**	**118**	**143**	**106**	**44**
School lunches	**100**	**11**	**86**	**237**	**139**	**27**	**10**	**3**
Meals as pay	**100**	**147**	**157**	**108**	**110**	**92**	**20**	**15**
ALCOHOLIC BEVERAGES	**100**	**105**	**105**	**98**	**124**	**112**	**86**	**38**
At home	**100**	**101**	**100**	**97**	**126**	**106**	**98**	**43**
Beer and ale	100	139	126	111	122	75	62	21
Whiskey	100	95	54	89	118	86	188	104
Wine	100	36	72	75	144	154	126	61
Other alcoholic beverages	100	136	91	106	91	111	123	49
Away from home	**100**	**111**	**113**	**98**	**121**	**120**	**67**	**32**
Beer and ale	100	116	114	101	118	112	68	34
• At fast food, take-out, delivery, concession stands, buffet, and cafeteria	100	184	162	85	96	93	50	21
• At full-service restaurants	100	109	112	93	119	124	73	39
• At vending machines, mobile vendors	100	197	53	44	266	50	50	6
• At catered affairs	100	11	6	293	148	–	42	–
Wine	100	105	117	88	118	133	64	42
• At fast food, take-out, delivery, concession stands, buffet and cafeteria	100	119	137	94	135	90	45	28
• At full-service restaurants	100	108	119	87	99	149	71	48
• At catered affairs	100	3	2	73	401	–	20	–
Other alcoholic beverages	100	109	112	100	123	120	68	26
• At fast food, take-out, delivery, concession stands, buffet, and cafeteria	100	221	181	90	100	49	23	29
• At full-service restaurants	100	101	120	91	113	144	71	20
• At catered affairs	100	3	2	85	394	–	12	–
Alcoholic beverages purchased on trips	100	117	110	110	102	121	77	33

Note: (–) means sample is too small to make a reliable estimate.
Source: Calculations by New Strategist based on the 2002 Consumer Expenditure Survey

Table 5.3 Food and Alcohol: Total spending by age, 2002

(total annual spending on food and alcoholic beverages, by consumer unit (CU) age groups, 2002; numbers in thousands)

	total consumer units	under 25	25 to 34	35 to 44	45 to 54	55 to 64	65 to 74	75+
Number of consumer units	112,108	8,737	18,988	24,394	22,691	15,314	11,216	10,767
Total spending of all CUs	$4,560,172,273	$211,692,792	$765,563,691	$1,178,973,729	$1,106,146,314	$678,870,233	$361,632,104	$255,811,969
Food, total spending	602,558,078	31,640,084	103,878,411	154,013,471	141,330,667	85,131,292	50,237,025	35,553,711
Alcoholic beverages, total spending	42,147,003	3,444,213	7,494,374	8,950,403	10,559,938	6,425,295	3,629,049	1,550,986
FOOD AT HOME	**$347,368,880**	**$16,824,841**	**$58,727,036**	**$87,853,527**	**$80,060,882**	**$47,691,012**	**$32,269,329**	**$23,633,996**
Cereals and bakery products	**50,463,174**	**2,509,791**	**8,386,620**	**13,226,427**	**11,349,131**	**6,477,516**	**4,689,858**	**3,789,876**
Cereals and cereal products	17,272,480	987,194	3,098,462	4,660,962	3,823,887	2,038,293	1,437,218	1,203,105
Flour	969,734	50,937	168,613	254,429	200,135	108,117	103,748	83,337
Prepared flour mixes	1,390,139	63,518	203,741	368,105	323,801	188,056	136,387	106,270
Ready-to-eat and cooked cereals	9,827,387	603,202	1,791,518	2,681,876	2,090,749	1,113,328	799,028	733,879
Rice	1,997,765	100,213	393,811	500,565	502,833	235,682	162,071	99,056
Pasta, cornmeal, and other cereal products	3,087,454	169,323	540,778	855,985	706,371	393,110	235,985	180,563
Bakery products	33,190,694	1,522,597	5,288,158	8,565,465	7,525,470	4,439,222	3,252,640	2,586,879
Bread	9,398,014	470,400	1,477,266	2,318,894	2,057,166	1,274,737	1,044,210	754,228
White bread	3,947,323	217,377	683,758	1,034,306	839,794	489,895	391,326	286,618
Bread, other than white	5,450,691	253,024	793,509	1,284,588	1,217,372	784,996	652,883	467,611
Crackers and cookies	7,922,672	366,430	1,211,814	2,135,695	1,768,990	1,058,504	726,460	653,234
Cookies	5,191,721	261,149	812,686	1,432,172	1,138,181	643,341	483,634	418,513
Crackers	2,730,951	105,281	399,128	703,523	630,810	415,163	242,826	234,828
Frozen and refrigerated bakery products	2,874,449	111,659	476,979	840,861	654,862	348,394	244,397	194,344
Other bakery products	12,995,559	574,196	2,122,099	3,270,016	3,044,225	1,757,435	1,237,573	985,073
Biscuits and rolls	4,600,912	203,135	700,277	1,192,135	1,111,859	654,061	422,843	313,427
Cakes and cupcakes	4,005,619	189,506	748,127	1,008,448	956,879	491,579	354,650	250,333
Bread and cracker products	392,378	17,823	68,737	85,623	87,133	53,293	47,444	32,086
Sweetrolls, coffee cakes, doughnuts	2,896,871	105,106	451,725	787,926	625,818	376,112	276,026	275,635
Pies, tarts, turnovers	1,100,901	58,538	153,423	195,640	262,762	182,390	136,499	113,484
Meats, poultry, fish, and eggs	**89,509,269**	**4,022,165**	**15,514,145**	**22,401,742**	**21,071,090**	**12,360,542**	**8,351,994**	**5,694,343**
Beef	25,916,006	1,143,236	4,798,268	6,610,042	6,200,316	3,306,293	2,327,656	1,490,799
Ground beef	9,673,799	473,371	1,785,442	2,515,997	2,315,390	1,148,703	842,209	577,650
Roast	4,595,307	162,071	785,154	1,192,867	1,016,784	700,462	423,628	311,382
Chuck roast	1,312,785	44,471	232,983	320,293	306,329	207,198	123,376	76,015
Round roast	1,146,865	67,100	150,765	324,928	206,261	186,218	122,703	89,258
Other roast	2,135,657	50,412	401,406	547,645	504,194	306,893	177,549	146,108
Steak	9,469,763	410,290	1,875,445	2,366,706	2,310,171	1,180,863	849,724	457,813
Round steak	1,489,915	88,156	329,252	347,615	363,283	178,102	101,280	78,168
Sirloin steak	2,984,315	132,103	637,427	719,623	752,887	396,479	216,805	120,698
Other steak	4,995,532	189,942	908,766	1,299,224	1,193,774	606,281	531,638	258,946
Pork	18,760,153	833,160	3,084,031	4,826,353	4,266,589	2,582,400	1,890,681	1,262,431
Bacon	3,189,473	155,082	474,130	821,834	732,012	417,919	330,984	257,331
Pork chops	4,308,310	215,804	761,609	1,123,100	974,578	554,367	375,400	298,569
Ham	4,165,933	184,962	665,529	1,013,571	952,114	639,972	478,475	227,507
Ham, not canned	3,997,771	176,750	641,225	965,515	914,220	613,785	463,445	219,539
Canned ham	168,162	8,213	24,305	47,812	37,894	26,187	14,917	7,968
Sausage	2,933,866	114,717	495,017	799,879	608,346	418,225	279,727	216,201
Other pork	4,162,570	162,596	687,935	1,067,969	999,539	551,917	426,208	262,715
Other meats	11,331,877	458,605	1,829,684	2,971,433	2,646,451	1,571,063	1,090,868	755,305
Frankfurters	2,348,663	90,777	391,343	676,934	519,397	334,151	177,661	155,691

	total consumer units	under 25	25 to 34	35 to 44	45 to 54	55 to 64	65 to 74	75+
Lunch meats (cold cuts)	$7,734,331	$315,493	$1,264,791	$2,077,637	$1,771,259	$1,093,726	$729,264	$474,071
Bologna, liverwurst, salami	2,366,600	86,671	386,596	630,097	522,347	356,816	198,523	184,869
Lamb, organ meats, and others	1,248,883	52,247	173,550	217,107	355,795	143,186	184,055	125,651
Lamb and organ meats	895,743	45,869	124,561	183,199	199,227	94,334	133,583	117,360
Mutton, goat, and game	353,140	6,378	48,799	33,664	156,568	48,852	50,472	8,291
Poultry	16,158,126	842,159	3,014,345	4,004,031	3,811,634	2,045,491	1,384,503	1,032,771
Fresh and frozen chicken	12,696,231	652,741	2,363,057	3,202,688	2,992,716	1,602,610	1,046,901	817,215
Fresh and frozen whole chicken	3,596,425	189,855	657,934	851,107	882,226	454,213	302,271	254,855
Fresh and frozen chicken parts	9,099,806	462,886	1,705,122	2,351,826	2,110,263	1,148,397	744,518	562,360
Other poultry	3,461,895	189,418	651,288	801,099	818,918	442,881	337,602	215,555
Fish and seafood	13,561,705	537,238	2,141,657	3,066,570	3,303,810	2,361,878	1,289,055	854,254
Canned fish and seafood	1,808,302	78,109	250,642	407,136	439,071	273,661	219,385	140,725
Fresh fish and shellfish	7,770,205	320,473	1,300,298	1,623,665	1,911,717	1,369,531	745,640	494,744
Frozen fish and shellfish	3,983,197	138,569	590,527	1,035,769	953,022	718,686	324,142	218,785
Eggs	3,783,645	207,853	646,162	923,313	842,290	493,570	369,231	298,677
Dairy products	**36,809,541**	**1,745,041**	**6,156,669**	**9,554,154**	**8,334,858**	**4,983,788**	**3,376,352**	**2,629,732**
Fresh milk and cream	14,254,532	756,013	2,463,123	3,737,405	3,075,084	1,860,192	1,251,257	1,099,095
Fresh milk, all types	12,850,940	693,893	2,233,748	3,414,428	2,753,326	1,655,137	1,104,664	983,565
Cream	1,403,592	62,120	229,375	322,977	321,758	205,208	146,593	115,530
Other dairy products	22,555,009	989,028	3,693,546	5,816,749	5,259,774	3,123,443	2,125,096	1,530,637
Butter	2,071,756	79,507	304,947	502,516	512,363	296,020	220,282	156,875
Cheese	10,722,009	442,092	1,815,253	2,721,151	2,535,946	1,503,835	1,039,835	653,019
Ice cream and related products	6,585,224	286,923	1,060,670	1,762,954	1,438,382	911,183	599,495	523,599
Miscellaneous dairy products	3,176,020	180,506	512,866	830,372	772,855	412,559	265,483	197,144
Fruits and vegetables	**61,884,737**	**2,952,582**	**9,908,128**	**14,552,729**	**14,219,769**	**9,054,556**	**6,232,283**	**4,961,434**
Fresh fruits	19,977,646	915,463	2,915,418	4,648,521	4,634,183	3,163,566	2,073,053	1,633,785
Apples	3,653,600	189,156	575,716	927,216	829,129	552,376	342,088	234,075
Bananas	3,502,254	178,147	533,943	789,878	791,689	497,552	362,165	352,296
Oranges	2,280,277	124,240	363,810	513,982	583,613	310,109	192,803	191,437
Citrus fruits, excl. oranges	1,602,023	76,012	226,147	386,645	325,162	268,914	193,364	126,620
Other fresh fruits	8,939,492	347,907	1,215,802	2,030,801	2,104,590	1,534,769	982,634	729,249
Fresh vegetables	19,605,447	873,438	3,083,841	4,508,743	4,648,251	2,920,992	1,972,558	1,600,407
Potatoes	3,738,802	165,217	585,780	871,598	815,515	561,258	394,355	347,451
Lettuce	2,491,040	109,475	382,798	574,479	611,069	383,156	240,920	189,069
Tomatoes	3,779,161	212,047	621,097	856,961	888,806	542,269	368,109	288,663
Other fresh vegetables	9,596,445	386,700	1,494,356	2,205,705	2,332,862	1,434,156	969,175	775,116
Processed fruits	12,948,474	703,765	2,241,154	3,130,726	2,871,092	1,736,301	1,211,777	1,048,060
Frozen fruits and fruit juices	1,395,745	115,678	254,629	330,295	274,107	176,877	117,656	125,220
Frozen orange juice	707,401	58,713	121,903	182,955	125,254	76,570	64,604	77,199
Frozen fruits	312,781	11,882	60,762	53,423	70,796	55,130	30,059	30,471
Frozen fruit juices, excl. orange	375,562	44,996	71,965	93,917	77,830	45,176	22,993	17,550
Canned fruits	1,688,346	76,099	266,971	374,692	364,417	243,033	198,635	166,027
Dried fruits	679,374	27,085	105,573	126,605	124,801	110,720	97,018	89,689
Fresh fruit juice	2,488,798	83,875	415,268	554,720	608,119	351,150	259,090	217,709
Canned and bottled fruit juice	6,697,332	401,116	1,198,902	1,744,415	1,499,648	854,368	539,265	449,307
Processed vegetables	9,353,170	459,916	1,667,716	2,264,739	2,066,242	1,233,696	975,007	679,290
Frozen vegetables	3,122,208	163,993	510,397	760,849	680,503	434,611	309,562	261,423
Canned and dried vegetables and juices	6,230,963	295,922	1,157,129	1,503,890	1,385,739	799,085	665,445	417,867
Canned beans	1,397,987	62,819	247,983	368,349	315,859	167,382	134,928	99,056
Canned corn	822,873	34,948	168,424	218,814	166,552	100,460	77,390	55,450
Canned miscellaneous vegetables	2,001,128	80,643	326,024	454,460	475,603	279,940	239,910	144,062
Dried peas	40,359	2,971	6,836	7,562	7,261	7,198	6,057	2,476
Dried beans	285,875	21,930	50,128	60,985	72,384	35,682	28,264	16,258

	total consumer units	under 25	25 to 34	35 to 44	45 to 54	55 to 64	65 to 74	75+
Dried miscellaneous vegetables	$827,357	$59,674	$188,171	$190,517	$154,980	$105,513	$72,455	$54,158
Dried processed vegetables	38,117	1,223	1,519	9,026	13,388	8,729	4,038	–
Fresh and canned vegetable juices	810,541	30,929	168,234	191,005	177,217	93,875	101,841	46,621
Sugar and other sweets	**13,160,358**	**561,614**	**1,969,815**	**3,385,887**	**2,960,949**	**1,909,656**	**1,399,869**	**970,214**
Candy and chewing gum	8,457,428	354,810	1,264,601	2,197,655	1,895,379	1,277,953	908,496	554,285
Sugar	1,744,400	88,593	287,858	425,919	399,135	234,764	154,332	154,076
Artificial sweeteners	485,428	14,853	46,331	111,968	109,144	84,686	62,137	57,496
Jams, preserves, other sweets	2,473,102	103,359	371,215	650,344	557,291	312,252	274,904	204,250
Fats and oils	**9,547,117**	**414,658**	**1,538,028**	**2,263,519**	**2,238,240**	**1,371,981**	**1,004,954**	**714,498**
Margarine	1,105,385	36,958	149,436	239,793	257,316	189,128	134,592	100,025
Fats and oils	2,923,777	134,812	468,054	718,403	665,300	386,219	338,499	211,141
Salad dressings	3,028,037	135,598	499,005	744,749	743,357	435,377	270,418	196,605
Nondairy cream and imitation milk	1,045,968	29,968	156,461	227,596	258,677	175,498	112,945	85,167
Peanut butter	1,445,072	77,322	264,693	332,978	313,817	185,759	148,500	121,452
Miscellaneous foods	**52,906,007**	**3,008,324**	**9,718,248**	**13,943,123**	**12,042,794**	**6,649,798**	**4,397,569**	**3,048,030**
Frozen prepared foods	10,996,674	567,992	1,972,094	3,084,133	2,544,115	1,254,370	855,781	700,609
Frozen meals	3,349,787	186,011	565,653	781,096	829,583	392,804	315,170	278,327
Other frozen prepared foods	7,648,008	381,982	1,406,441	2,303,038	1,714,532	861,566	540,611	422,282
Canned and packaged soups	4,015,709	185,050	583,311	952,830	965,275	538,440	432,265	361,125
Potato chips, nuts, and other snacks	11,270,217	525,531	1,801,771	3,099,502	2,819,357	1,409,654	992,280	605,751
Potato chips and other snacks	8,561,688	453,363	1,474,608	2,547,709	2,128,189	950,234	610,711	376,199
Nuts	2,708,529	72,168	327,163	551,792	691,168	459,420	381,568	229,552
Condiments and seasonings	9,732,095	494,514	1,689,172	2,456,476	2,311,759	1,328,949	911,636	524,676
Salt, spices, and other seasonings	2,369,963	125,725	406,723	613,509	552,299	317,000	222,750	128,773
Olives, pickles, relishes	1,087,448	43,248	160,449	275,164	255,954	165,085	116,422	70,524
Sauces and gravies	4,235,440	245,859	760,090	1,070,897	1,068,746	529,864	362,052	189,069
Baking needs and miscellaneous products	2,039,245	79,681	361,911	496,906	434,986	317,306	210,412	136,310
Other canned/packaged prepared foods	16,891,312	1,235,237	3,672,089	4,350,182	3,402,289	2,118,232	1,205,608	855,869
Prepared salads	2,405,838	80,380	302,289	587,408	573,628	457,582	229,143	176,040
Prepared desserts	1,156,955	41,588	175,639	328,099	236,213	175,498	112,833	87,105
Baby food	3,539,250	495,301	1,398,466	826,225	399,135	266,310	70,212	51,466
Miscellaneous prepared foods	9,780,302	618,055	1,795,315	2,600,400	2,192,404	1,218,688	793,420	541,257
Nonalcoholic beverages	**28,468,706**	**1,394,338**	**4,945,235**	**7,395,285**	**6,722,663**	**4,054,994**	**2,317,113**	**1,593,516**
Cola	9,093,080	471,798	1,660,501	2,435,985	2,121,835	1,272,593	698,196	411,084
Other carbonated drinks	4,924,904	296,446	1,001,617	1,281,417	1,135,911	599,696	382,017	214,694
Coffee	4,662,572	111,309	526,537	1,064,066	1,212,153	852,837	491,822	410,653
Roasted coffee	3,069,517	75,488	355,455	729,137	810,523	588,670	286,793	225,246
Instant and freeze-dried coffee	1,593,055	35,734	171,272	334,930	401,631	264,167	205,028	185,408
Noncarbonated fruit-flavored drinks, incl. nonfrozen lemonade	2,124,447	122,755	444,319	665,956	454,728	218,071	131,339	79,460
Tea	1,778,033	68,848	246,084	439,580	392,100	298,623	195,383	137,925
Nonalcoholic beer	71,749	–	9,304	23,906	22,691	10,260	5,944	–
Other nonalcoholic beverages and ice	5,812,800	323,182	1,056,872	1,484,375	1,383,243	802,913	412,412	339,699
Food prepared by CU on trips	**4,618,850**	**216,328**	**590,147**	**1,130,662**	**1,121,162**	**828,334**	**499,448**	**232,352**
FOOD AWAY FROM HOME	**255,190,319**	**14,815,244**	**45,151,375**	**66,159,699**	**61,269,557**	**37,440,280**	**17,967,808**	**11,919,715**
Meals at restaurants, carry-outs, other	**209,240,613**	**12,148,711**	**38,744,254**	**54,284,212**	**49,465,245**	**28,624,623**	**14,903,933**	**10,603,234**
Lunch	76,882,545	4,465,219	14,459,742	21,066,902	18,439,160	9,557,467	4,985,288	3,714,184
• At fast food, take-out, delivery, concession stands, buffet, and cafeteria (other than employer and school cafeteria)	42,344,313	2,955,552	8,740,366	12,329,947	9,635,052	4,585,471	2,166,483	1,781,292
• At full-service restaurants	25,204,121	1,039,441	4,133,877	5,180,066	6,180,348	4,339,375	2,505,654	1,822,745
• At vending machines, mobile vendors	616,594	42,374	126,650	223,693	114,816	63,859	32,302	10,013
• At employer and school cafeterias	8,717,518	427,851	1,459,038	3,333,196	2,508,944	568,762	280,961	100,241

	total consumer units	under 25	25 to 34	35 to 44	45 to 54	55 to 64	65 to 74	75+
Dinner	$82,572,026	$4,025,660	$15,172,551	$20,190,182	$19,010,974	$12,814,602	$6,723,543	$4,492,531
• At fast food, take-out, delivery, concession stands, buffet, and cafeteria (other than employer and school cafeteria)	23,916,000	1,689,998	5,244,486	7,058,892	5,161,976	2,615,937	1,097,037	953,310
• At full-service restaurants	58,074,186	2,206,966	9,818,505	12,978,584	13,790,682	10,105,096	5,610,692	3,519,517
• At vending machines, mobile vendors	209,642	4,019	43,103	71,962	7,715	62,634	6,169	13,782
• At employer and school cafeterias	372,199	124,677	66,458	80,744	50,601	31,087	9,646	5,922
Snacks and nonalcoholic beverages	29,447,408	2,202,685	5,553,610	8,350,066	7,101,602	3,435,083	1,601,981	1,103,294
• At fast food, take-out, delivery, concession stands, buffet, and cafeteria (other than employer and school cafeteria)	20,817,335	1,536,139	3,839,753	5,916,765	5,145,865	2,464,788	1,103,991	739,478
• At full-service restaurants	3,382,298	190,204	555,969	738,650	841,382	459,420	330,536	265,730
• At vending machines, mobile vendors	4,115,485	381,632	954,337	1,294,834	832,306	402,146	139,639	87,643
• At employer and school cafeterias	1,133,412	94,709	203,551	399,818	282,049	108,729	27,704	10,336
Breakfast and brunch	20,338,633	1,455,147	3,558,161	4,677,306	4,913,736	2,817,470	1,593,233	1,293,224
• At fast food, take-out, delivery, concession stands, buffet, and cafeteria (other than employer and school cafeteria)	9,846,446	855,090	2,024,501	2,579,666	2,326,281	1,014,859	571,007	441,770
• At full-service restaurants	9,762,365	489,534	1,424,290	1,902,244	2,394,127	1,731,095	997,439	829,813
• At vending machines, mobile vendors	156,951	16,251	29,052	26,346	37,667	28,943	8,076	10,229
• At employer and school cafeterias	572,872	94,272	80,129	169,294	155,433	42,420	16,600	11,413
Board (including at school)	**5,217,506**	**946,654**	**181,146**	**763,776**	**2,255,939**	**772,438**	**203,570**	**93,888**
Catered affairs	**7,735,452**	**345,112**	**1,364,478**	**1,383,872**	**1,405,027**	**2,829,415**	**232,956**	**173,672**
Food on trips	**23,709,721**	**1,023,889**	**3,197,199**	**5,660,140**	**5,684,549**	**4,643,817**	**2,505,430**	**993,794**
School lunches	**6,726,480**	**58,276**	**981,869**	**3,464,924**	**1,885,849**	**247,015**	**69,988**	**17,873**
Meals as pay	**2,562,789**	**292,602**	**682,239**	**602,776**	**572,721**	**322,972**	**51,930**	**37,254**
ALCOHOLIC BEVERAGES	**42,147,003**	**3,444,213**	**7,494,374**	**8,950,403**	**10,559,938**	**6,425,295**	**3,629,049**	**1,550,986**
At home	**25,569,593**	**2,010,471**	**4,309,516**	**5,407,662**	**6,516,174**	**3,716,095**	**2,510,477**	**1,048,383**
Beer and ale	12,594,213	1,364,545	2,684,713	3,050,958	3,108,667	1,293,727	782,428	251,625
Whiskey	1,558,301	115,066	141,840	302,973	370,998	182,849	292,738	155,691
Wine	8,716,397	245,335	1,066,746	1,428,269	2,539,577	1,828,338	1,102,645	513,478
Other alcoholic beverages	2,700,682	285,525	416,217	625,706	496,706	411,181	332,667	127,589
Away from home	**16,577,410**	**1,433,742**	**3,184,857**	**3,542,741**	**4,043,763**	**2,709,200**	**1,118,572**	**502,604**
Beer and ale	5,926,029	537,413	1,141,748	1,306,787	1,414,330	909,652	402,991	193,375
• At fast food, take-out, delivery, concession stands, buffet, and cafeteria	895,743	128,434	245,705	165,635	174,721	113,477	44,640	17,766
• At full-service restaurants	4,702,931	401,028	889,588	952,830	1,133,415	793,571	344,219	175,394
• At vending machines, mobile vendors	35,875	5,504	3,228	3,415	19,287	2,450	1,795	215
• At catered affairs	290,360	2,534	3,038	184,907	87,133	–	12,338	–
Wine	2,897,992	237,384	576,666	553,744	692,302	526,189	186,410	117,468
• At fast food, take-out, delivery, concession stands, buffet and cafeteria	494,396	45,782	115,067	100,747	134,785	60,643	22,096	13,243
• At full-service restaurants	2,282,519	191,340	461,408	433,481	458,358	465,546	161,847	104,225
• At catered affairs	122,198	262	380	19,515	99,160	–	2,468	–
Other alcoholic beverages	7,753,389	658,945	1,466,443	1,682,210	1,937,131	1,273,512	529,171	191,760
• At fast food, take-out, delivery, concession stands, buffet, and cafeteria	392,378	67,537	120,004	77,085	79,192	26,187	9,085	10,767
• At full-service restaurants	3,244,406	255,470	659,453	640,586	743,357	639,206	231,162	63,741
• At catered affairs	441,706	1,136	1,329	81,476	352,618	–	5,496	–
Alcoholic beverages purchased on trips	3,674,900	334,714	685,657	883,063	761,964	607,966	283,428	117,253

Note: Numbers may not add to total because of rounding. (–) means sample is too small to make a reliable estimate.
Source: Calculations by New Strategist based on the 2002 Consumer Expenditure Survey

Table 5.4 Food and Alcohol: Market shares by age, 2002

(percentage of total annual spending on food and alcoholic beverages accounted for by consumer unit age groups, 2002)

	total consumer units	under 25	25 to 34	35 to 44	45 to 54	55 to 64	65 to 74	75+
Share of total consumer units	100.0%	7.8%	16.9%	21.8%	20.2%	13.7%	10.0%	9.6%
Share of total before-tax income	100.0	3.3	16.8	27.1	26.6	14.7	7.1	4.6
Share of total spending	100.0	4.6	16.8	25.9	24.3	14.9	7.9	5.6
Share of food spending	100.0	5.3	17.2	25.6	23.5	14.1	8.3	5.9
Share of alcoholic beverages spending	100.0	8.2	17.8	21.2	25.1	15.2	8.6	3.7
FOOD AT HOME	100.0%	4.8%	16.9%	25.3%	23.0%	13.7%	9.3%	6.8%
Cereals and bakery products	100.0	5.0	16.6	26.2	22.5	12.8	9.3	7.5
Cereals and cereal products	100.0	5.7	17.9	27.0	22.1	11.8	8.3	7.0
Flour	100.0	5.3	17.4	26.2	20.6	11.1	10.7	8.6
Prepared flour mixes	100.0	4.6	14.7	26.5	23.3	13.5	9.8	7.6
Ready-to-eat and cooked cereals	100.0	6.1	18.2	27.3	21.3	11.3	8.1	7.5
Rice	100.0	5.0	19.7	25.1	25.2	11.8	8.1	5.0
Pasta, cornmeal, and other cereal products	100.0	5.5	17.5	27.7	22.9	12.7	7.6	5.8
Bakery products	100.0	4.6	15.9	25.8	22.7	13.4	9.8	7.8
Bread	100.0	5.0	15.7	24.7	21.9	13.6	11.1	8.0
White bread	100.0	5.5	17.3	26.2	21.3	12.4	9.9	7.3
Bread, other than white	100.0	4.6	14.6	23.6	22.3	14.4	12.0	8.6
Crackers and cookies	100.0	4.6	15.3	27.0	22.3	13.4	9.2	8.2
Cookies	100.0	5.0	15.7	27.6	21.9	12.4	9.3	8.1
Crackers	100.0	3.9	14.6	25.8	23.1	15.2	8.9	8.6
Frozen and refrigerated bakery products	100.0	3.9	16.6	29.3	22.8	12.1	8.5	6.8
Other bakery products	100.0	4.4	16.3	25.2	23.4	13.5	9.5	7.6
Biscuits and rolls	100.0	4.4	15.2	25.9	24.2	14.2	9.2	6.8
Cakes and cupcakes	100.0	4.7	18.7	25.2	23.9	12.3	8.9	6.2
Bread and cracker products	100.0	4.5	17.5	21.8	22.2	13.6	12.1	8.2
Sweetrolls, coffee cakes, doughnuts	100.0	3.6	15.6	27.2	21.6	13.0	9.5	9.5
Pies, tarts, turnovers	100.0	5.3	13.9	17.8	23.9	16.6	12.4	10.3
Meats, poultry, fish, and eggs	100.0	4.5	17.3	25.0	23.5	13.8	9.3	6.4
Beef	100.0	4.4	18.5	25.5	23.9	12.8	9.0	5.8
Ground beef	100.0	4.9	18.5	26.0	23.9	11.9	8.7	6.0
Roast	100.0	3.5	17.1	26.0	22.1	15.2	9.2	6.8
Chuck roast	100.0	3.4	17.7	24.4	23.3	15.8	9.4	5.8
Round roast	100.0	5.9	13.1	28.3	18.0	16.2	10.7	7.8
Other roast	100.0	2.4	18.8	25.6	23.6	14.4	8.3	6.8
Steak	100.0	4.3	19.8	25.0	24.4	12.5	9.0	4.8
Round steak	100.0	5.9	22.1	23.3	24.4	12.0	6.8	5.2
Sirloin steak	100.0	4.4	21.4	24.1	25.2	13.3	7.3	4.0
Other steak	100.0	3.8	18.2	26.0	23.9	12.1	10.6	5.2
Pork	100.0	4.4	16.4	25.7	22.7	13.8	10.1	6.7
Bacon	100.0	4.9	14.9	25.8	23.0	13.1	10.4	8.1
Pork chops	100.0	5.0	17.7	26.1	22.6	12.9	8.7	6.9
Ham	100.0	4.4	16.0	24.3	22.9	15.4	11.5	5.5
Ham, not canned	100.0	4.4	16.0	24.2	22.9	15.4	11.6	5.5
Canned ham	100.0	4.9	14.5	28.4	22.5	15.6	8.9	4.7
Sausage	100.0	3.9	16.9	27.3	20.7	14.3	9.5	7.4
Other pork	100.0	3.9	16.5	25.7	24.0	13.3	10.2	6.3
Other meats	100.0	4.0	16.1	26.2	23.4	13.9	9.6	6.7
Frankfurters	100.0	3.9	16.7	28.8	22.1	14.2	7.6	6.6

	total consumer units	under 25	25 to 34	35 to 44	45 to 54	55 to 64	65 to 74	75+
Lunch meats (cold cuts)	100.0%	4.1%	16.4%	26.9%	22.9%	14.1%	9.4%	6.1%
Bologna, liverwurst, salami	100.0	3.7	16.3	26.6	22.1	15.1	8.4	7.8
Lamb, organ meats, and others	100.0	4.2	13.9	17.4	28.5	11.5	14.7	10.1
Lamb and organ meats	100.0	5.1	13.9	20.5	22.2	10.5	14.9	13.1
Mutton, goat, and game	100.0	1.8	13.8	9.5	44.3	13.8	14.3	2.3
Poultry	100.0	5.2	18.7	24.8	23.6	12.7	8.6	6.4
Fresh and frozen chicken	100.0	5.1	18.6	25.2	23.6	12.6	8.2	6.4
Fresh and frozen whole chicken	100.0	5.3	18.3	23.7	24.5	12.6	8.4	7.1
Fresh and frozen chicken parts	100.0	5.1	18.7	25.8	23.2	12.6	8.2	6.2
Other poultry	100.0	5.5	18.8	23.1	23.7	12.8	9.8	6.2
Fish and seafood	100.0	4.0	15.8	22.6	24.4	17.4	9.5	6.3
Canned fish and seafood	100.0	4.3	13.9	22.5	24.3	15.1	12.1	7.8
Fresh fish and shellfish	100.0	4.1	16.7	20.9	24.6	17.6	9.6	6.4
Frozen fish and shellfish	100.0	3.5	14.8	26.0	23.9	18.0	8.1	5.5
Eggs	100.0	5.5	17.1	24.4	22.3	13.0	9.8	7.9
Dairy products	**100.0**	**4.7**	**16.7**	**26.0**	**22.6**	**13.5**	**9.2**	**7.1**
Fresh milk and cream	100.0	5.3	17.3	26.2	21.6	13.0	8.8	7.7
Fresh milk, all types	100.0	5.4	17.4	26.6	21.4	12.9	8.6	7.7
Cream	100.0	4.4	16.3	23.0	22.9	14.6	10.4	8.2
Other dairy products	100.0	4.4	16.4	25.8	23.3	13.8	9.4	6.8
Butter	100.0	3.8	14.7	24.3	24.7	14.3	10.6	7.6
Cheese	100.0	4.1	16.9	25.4	23.7	14.0	9.7	6.1
Ice cream and related products	100.0	4.4	16.1	26.8	21.8	13.8	9.1	8.0
Miscellaneous dairy products	100.0	5.7	16.1	26.1	24.3	13.0	8.4	6.2
Fruits and vegetables	**100.0**	**4.8**	**16.0**	**23.5**	**23.0**	**14.6**	**10.1**	**8.0**
Fresh fruits	100.0	4.6	14.6	23.3	23.2	15.8	10.4	8.2
Apples	100.0	5.2	15.8	25.4	22.7	15.1	9.4	6.4
Bananas	100.0	5.1	15.2	22.6	22.6	14.2	10.3	10.1
Oranges	100.0	5.4	16.0	22.5	25.6	13.6	8.5	8.4
Citrus fruits, excl. oranges	100.0	4.7	14.1	24.1	20.3	16.8	12.1	7.9
Other fresh fruits	100.0	3.9	13.6	22.7	23.5	17.2	11.0	8.2
Fresh vegetables	100.0	4.5	15.7	23.0	23.7	14.9	10.1	8.2
Potatoes	100.0	4.4	15.7	23.3	21.8	15.0	10.5	9.3
Lettuce	100.0	4.4	15.4	23.1	24.5	15.4	9.7	7.6
Tomatoes	100.0	5.6	16.4	22.7	23.5	14.3	9.7	7.6
Other fresh vegetables	100.0	4.0	15.6	23.0	24.3	14.9	10.1	8.1
Processed fruits	100.0	5.4	17.3	24.2	22.2	13.4	9.4	8.1
Frozen fruits and fruit juices	100.0	8.3	18.2	23.7	19.6	12.7	8.4	9.0
Frozen orange juice	100.0	8.3	17.2	25.9	17.7	10.8	9.1	10.9
Frozen fruits	100.0	3.8	19.4	17.1	22.6	17.6	9.6	9.7
Frozen fruit juices, excl. orange	100.0	12.0	19.2	25.0	20.7	12.0	6.1	4.7
Canned fruits	100.0	4.5	15.8	22.2	21.6	14.4	11.8	9.8
Dried fruits	100.0	4.0	15.5	18.6	18.4	16.3	14.3	13.2
Fresh fruit juice	100.0	3.4	16.7	22.3	24.4	14.1	10.4	8.7
Canned and bottled fruit juice	100.0	6.0	17.9	26.0	22.4	12.8	8.1	6.7
Processed vegetables	100.0	4.9	17.8	24.2	22.1	13.2	10.4	7.3
Frozen vegetables	100.0	5.3	16.3	24.4	21.8	13.9	9.9	8.4
Canned and dried vegetables and juices	100.0	4.7	18.6	24.1	22.2	12.8	10.7	6.7
Canned beans	100.0	4.5	17.7	26.3	22.6	12.0	9.7	7.1
Canned corn	100.0	4.2	20.5	26.6	20.2	12.2	9.4	6.7
Canned miscellaneous vegetables	100.0	4.0	16.3	22.7	23.8	14.0	12.0	7.2
Dried peas	100.0	7.4	16.9	18.7	18.0	17.8	15.0	6.1
Dried beans	100.0	7.7	17.5	21.3	25.3	12.5	9.9	5.7

	total consumer units	under 25	25 to 34	35 to 44	45 to 54	55 to 64	65 to 74	75+
Dried miscellaneous vegetables	100.0%	7.2%	22.7%	23.0%	18.7%	12.8%	8.8%	6.5%
Dried processed vegetables	100.0	3.2	4.0	23.7	35.1	22.9	10.6	–
Fresh and canned vegetable juices	100.0	3.8	20.8	23.6	21.9	11.6	12.6	5.8
Sugar and other sweets	**100.0**	**4.3**	**15.0**	**25.7**	**22.5**	**14.5**	**10.6**	**7.4**
Candy and chewing gum	100.0	4.2	15.0	26.0	22.4	15.1	10.7	6.6
Sugar	100.0	5.1	16.5	24.4	22.9	13.5	8.8	8.8
Artificial sweeteners	100.0	3.1	9.5	23.1	22.5	17.4	12.8	11.8
Jams, preserves, other sweets	100.0	4.2	15.0	26.3	22.5	12.6	11.1	8.3
Fats and oils	**100.0**	**4.3**	**16.1**	**23.7**	**23.4**	**14.4**	**10.5**	**7.5**
Margarine	100.0	3.3	13.5	21.7	23.3	17.1	12.2	9.0
Fats and oils	100.0	4.6	16.0	24.6	22.8	13.2	11.6	7.2
Salad dressings	100.0	4.5	16.5	24.6	24.5	14.4	8.9	6.5
Nondairy cream and imitation milk	100.0	2.9	15.0	21.8	24.7	16.8	10.8	8.1
Peanut butter	100.0	5.4	18.3	23.0	21.7	12.9	10.3	8.4
Miscellaneous foods	**100.0**	**5.7**	**18.4**	**26.4**	**22.8**	**12.6**	**8.3**	**5.8**
Frozen prepared foods	100.0	5.2	17.9	28.0	23.1	11.4	7.8	6.4
Frozen meals	100.0	5.6	16.9	23.3	24.8	11.7	9.4	8.3
Other frozen prepared foods	100.0	5.0	18.4	30.1	22.4	11.3	7.1	5.5
Canned and packaged soups	100.0	4.6	14.5	23.7	24.0	13.4	10.8	9.0
Potato chips, nuts, and other snacks	100.0	4.7	16.0	27.5	25.0	12.5	8.8	5.4
Potato chips and other snacks	100.0	5.3	17.2	29.8	24.9	11.1	7.1	4.4
Nuts	100.0	2.7	12.1	20.4	25.5	17.0	14.1	8.5
Condiments and seasonings	100.0	5.1	17.4	25.2	23.8	13.7	9.4	5.4
Salt, spices, and other seasonings	100.0	5.3	17.2	25.9	23.3	13.4	9.4	5.4
Olives, pickles, relishes	100.0	4.0	14.8	25.3	23.5	15.2	10.7	6.5
Sauces and gravies	100.0	5.8	17.9	25.3	25.2	12.5	8.5	4.5
Baking needs and miscellaneous products	100.0	3.9	17.7	24.4	21.3	15.6	10.3	6.7
Other canned/packaged prepared foods	100.0	7.3	21.7	25.8	20.1	12.5	7.1	5.1
Prepared salads	100.0	3.3	12.6	24.4	23.8	19.0	9.5	7.3
Prepared desserts	100.0	3.6	15.2	28.4	20.4	15.2	9.8	7.5
Baby food	100.0	14.0	39.5	23.3	11.3	7.5	2.0	1.5
Miscellaneous prepared foods	100.0	6.3	18.4	26.6	22.4	12.5	8.1	5.5
Nonalcoholic beverages	**100.0**	**4.9**	**17.4**	**26.0**	**23.6**	**14.2**	**8.1**	**5.6**
Cola	100.0	5.2	18.3	26.8	23.3	14.0	7.7	4.5
Other carbonated drinks	100.0	6.0	20.3	26.0	23.1	12.2	7.8	4.4
Coffee	100.0	2.4	11.3	22.8	26.0	18.3	10.5	8.8
Roasted coffee	100.0	2.5	11.6	23.8	26.4	19.2	9.3	7.3
Instant and freeze-dried coffee	100.0	2.2	10.8	21.0	25.2	16.6	12.9	11.6
Noncarbonated fruit-flavored drinks, incl. nonfrozen lemonade	100.0	5.8	20.9	31.3	21.4	10.3	6.2	3.7
Tea	100.0	3.9	13.8	24.7	22.1	16.8	11.0	7.8
Nonalcoholic beer	100.0	–	13.0	33.3	31.6	14.3	8.3	–
Other nonalcoholic beverages and ice	100.0	5.6	18.2	25.5	23.8	13.8	7.1	5.8
Food prepared by CU on trips	**100.0**	**4.7**	**12.8**	**24.5**	**24.3**	**17.9**	**10.8**	**5.0**
FOOD AWAY FROM HOME	**100.0**	**5.8**	**17.7**	**25.9**	**24.0**	**14.7**	**7.0**	**4.7**
Meals at restaurants, carry-outs, other	**100.0**	**5.8**	**18.5**	**25.9**	**23.6**	**13.7**	**7.1**	**5.1**
Lunch	100.0	5.8	18.8	27.4	24.0	12.4	6.5	4.8
• At fast food, take-out, delivery, concession stands, buffet, and cafeteria (other than employer and school cafeteria)	100.0	7.0	20.6	29.1	22.8	10.8	5.1	4.2
• At full-service restaurants	100.0	4.1	16.4	20.6	24.5	17.2	9.9	7.2
• At vending machines, mobile vendors	100.0	6.9	20.5	36.3	18.6	10.4	5.2	1.6
• At employer and school cafeterias	100.0	4.9	16.7	38.2	28.8	6.5	3.2	1.1

	total consumer units	under 25	25 to 34	35 to 44	45 to 54	55 to 64	65 to 74	75+
Dinner	100.0%	4.9%	18.4%	24.5%	23.0%	15.5%	8.1%	5.4%
• At fast food, take-out, delivery, concession stands, buffet, and cafeteria (other than employer and school cafeteria)	100.0	7.1	21.9	29.5	21.6	10.9	4.6	4.0
• At full-service restaurants	100.0	3.8	16.9	22.3	23.7	17.4	9.7	6.1
• At vending machines, mobile vendors	100.0	1.9	20.6	34.3	3.7	29.9	2.9	6.6
• At employer and school cafeterias	100.0	33.5	17.9	21.7	13.6	8.4	2.6	1.6
Snacks and nonalcoholic beverages	100.0	7.5	18.9	28.4	24.1	11.7	5.4	3.7
• At fast food, take-out, delivery, concession stands, buffet, and cafeteria (other than employer and school cafeteria)	100.0	7.4	18.4	28.4	24.7	11.8	5.3	3.6
• At full-service restaurants	100.0	5.6	16.4	21.8	24.9	13.6	9.8	7.9
• At vending machines, mobile vendors	100.0	9.3	23.2	31.5	20.2	9.8	3.4	2.1
• At employer and school cafeterias	100.0	8.4	18.0	35.3	24.9	9.6	2.4	0.9
Breakfast and brunch	100.0	7.2	17.5	23.0	24.2	13.9	7.8	6.4
• At fast food, take-out, delivery, concession stands, buffet, and cafeteria (other than employer and school cafeteria)	100.0	8.7	20.6	26.2	23.6	10.3	5.8	4.5
• At full-service restaurants	100.0	5.0	14.6	19.5	24.5	17.7	10.2	8.5
• At vending machines, mobile vendors	100.0	10.4	18.5	16.8	24.0	18.4	5.1	6.5
• At employer and school cafeterias	100.0	16.5	14.0	29.6	27.1	7.4	2.9	2.0
Board (including at school)	**100.0**	**18.1**	**3.5**	**14.6**	**43.2**	**14.8**	**3.9**	**1.8**
Catered affairs	**100.0**	**4.5**	**17.6**	**17.9**	**18.2**	**36.6**	**3.0**	**2.2**
Food on trips	**100.0**	**4.3**	**13.5**	**23.9**	**24.0**	**19.6**	**10.6**	**4.2**
School lunches	**100.0**	**0.9**	**14.6**	**51.5**	**28.0**	**3.7**	**1.0**	**0.3**
Meals as pay	**100.0**	**11.4**	**26.6**	**23.5**	**22.3**	**12.6**	**2.0**	**1.5**
ALCOHOLIC BEVERAGES	**100.0**	**8.2**	**17.8**	**21.2**	**25.1**	**15.2**	**8.6**	**3.7**
At home	**100.0**	**7.9**	**16.9**	**21.1**	**25.5**	**14.5**	**9.8**	**4.1**
Beer and ale	100.0	10.8	21.3	24.2	24.7	10.3	6.2	2.0
Whiskey	100.0	7.4	9.1	19.4	23.8	11.7	18.8	10.0
Wine	100.0	2.8	12.2	16.4	29.1	21.0	12.7	5.9
Other alcoholic beverages	100.0	10.6	15.4	23.2	18.4	15.2	12.3	4.7
Away from home	**100.0**	**8.6**	**19.2**	**21.4**	**24.4**	**16.3**	**6.7**	**3.0**
Beer and ale	100.0	9.1	19.3	22.1	23.9	15.4	6.8	3.3
• At fast food, take-out, delivery, concession stands, buffet, and cafeteria	100.0	14.3	27.4	18.5	19.5	12.7	5.0	2.0
• At full-service restaurants	100.0	8.5	18.9	20.3	24.1	16.9	7.3	3.7
• At vending machines, mobile vendors	100.0	15.3	9.0	9.5	53.8	6.8	5.0	0.6
• At catered affairs	100.0	0.9	1.0	63.7	30.0	–	4.2	–
Wine	100.0	8.2	19.9	19.1	23.9	18.2	6.4	4.1
• At fast food, take-out, delivery, concession stands, buffet and cafeteria	100.0	9.3	23.3	20.4	27.3	12.3	4.5	2.7
• At full-service restaurants	100.0	8.4	20.2	19.0	20.1	20.4	7.1	4.6
• At catered affairs	100.0	0.2	0.3	16.0	81.1	–	2.0	–
Other alcoholic beverages	100.0	8.5	18.9	21.7	25.0	16.4	6.8	2.5
• At fast food, take-out, delivery, concession stands, buffet, and cafeteria	100.0	17.2	30.6	19.6	20.2	6.7	2.3	2.7
• At full-service restaurants	100.0	7.9	20.3	19.7	22.9	19.7	7.1	2.0
• At catered affairs	100.0	0.3	0.3	18.4	79.8	–	1.2	–
Alcoholic beverages purchased on trips	100.0	9.1	18.7	24.0	20.7	16.5	7.7	3.2

Note: Numbers may not add to total because of rounding. (–) means sample is too small to make a reliable estimate.
Source: Calculations by New Strategist based on the 2002 Consumer Expenditure Survey

Table 5.5 Food and Alcohol: Average spending by income, 2002

(average annual spending on food and alcoholic beverages, by before-tax income of consumer units (CU), 2002; complete income reporters only)

	complete income reporters	under $10,000	$10,000–$19,999	$20,000–$29,999	$30,000–$39,999	$40,000–$49,999	$50,000–$69,999	$70,000 or more
Number of consumer units								
(in thousands, add 000)	92,388	10,933	15,075	12,312	10,727	8,873	13,521	20,947
Average number of persons per CU	2.5	1.7	1.9	2.3	2.5	2.6	2.8	3.1
Average before-tax income of CU	$49,430.00	$5,554.80	$14,724.33	$24,495.00	$34,423.00	$44,443.00	$58,933.00	$115,629.00
Average spending of CU, total	42,556.98	17,627.83	22,838.71	28,835.85	35,095.39	41,787.38	50,406.17	76,627.31
Food, average spending	5,611.89	3,085.09	3,486.84	4,348.64	4,880.78	5,501.98	6,548.22	8,873.86
Alcoholic beverages, average spending	414.74	182.06	172.07	274.95	346.16	433.45	453.36	779.70
FOOD AT HOME	**$3,216.91**	**$1,968.91**	**$2,394.57**	**$2,767.99**	**$3,005.86**	**$3,240.92**	**$3,554.69**	**$4,523.94**
Cereals and bakery products	**470.59**	**289.49**	**363.56**	**403.46**	**430.83**	**453.71**	**518.87**	**665.86**
Cereals and cereal products	160.52	113.09	127.29	139.61	146.87	155.92	173.67	218.76
Flour	8.55	6.51	7.98	10.68	9.02	6.57	10.69	7.83
Prepared flour mixes	13.11	7.43	10.60	8.61	11.13	18.31	15.42	17.66
Ready-to-eat and cooked cereals	91.75	62.24	73.20	79.02	80.42	87.80	96.18	130.46
Rice	18.37	11.88	14.70	18.19	20.91	17.19	19.93	22.26
Pasta, cornmeal, and other cereal products	28.74	25.01	20.82	23.11	25.39	26.06	31.45	40.55
Bakery products	310.07	176.40	236.27	263.85	283.97	297.78	345.20	447.09
Bread	87.65	56.47	76.50	76.90	82.84	88.81	93.97	114.23
White bread	36.75	25.50	35.02	34.28	35.92	36.32	40.60	42.82
Bread, other than white	50.90	30.97	41.48	42.62	46.92	52.49	53.37	71.41
Crackers and cookies	74.71	41.92	54.58	64.06	63.46	68.90	81.74	113.85
Cookies	49.13	26.52	36.65	41.60	39.76	43.22	55.30	76.03
Crackers	25.58	15.40	17.93	22.46	23.70	25.68	26.44	37.82
Frozen and refrigerated bakery products	26.29	14.34	18.69	23.23	20.11	21.65	30.14	41.52
Other bakery products	121.42	63.69	86.50	99.66	117.55	118.42	139.35	177.49
Biscuits and rolls	42.81	20.89	28.71	30.70	39.26	39.20	49.24	69.31
Cakes and cupcakes	37.23	23.19	26.47	27.39	35.14	37.04	45.74	53.05
Bread and cracker products	3.58	1.55	2.34	3.44	3.27	3.36	3.59	5.71
Sweetrolls, coffee cakes, doughnuts	27.60	13.89	20.12	26.93	28.27	28.52	31.77	36.21
Pies, tarts, turnovers	10.19	4.16	8.86	11.20	11.61	10.30	9.01	13.21
Meats, poultry, fish, and eggs	**814.78**	**525.70**	**628.56**	**728.52**	**781.66**	**807.25**	**895.84**	**1,099.04**
Beef	238.35	147.84	174.95	212.56	250.54	220.50	263.43	325.31
Ground beef	88.74	57.09	70.65	82.01	92.70	89.81	105.45	107.22
Roast	42.31	25.92	30.42	36.47	46.15	36.13	43.17	61.66
Chuck roast	11.69	6.90	8.24	12.26	11.12	13.08	13.95	14.26
Round roast	10.55	6.81	12.15	9.07	9.14	10.15	10.40	13.00
Other roast	20.07	12.20	10.03	15.15	25.88	12.90	18.82	34.41
Steak	86.72	52.41	56.97	74.79	94.33	78.06	96.12	124.37
Round steak	13.71	8.88	9.34	11.60	14.84	12.06	16.86	18.43
Sirloin steak	27.35	14.62	19.83	23.02	26.07	26.85	30.52	39.93
Other steak	45.66	28.92	27.80	40.17	53.42	39.15	48.74	66.01
Pork	171.55	126.09	141.49	165.49	164.20	167.51	191.21	210.24
Bacon	28.58	24.31	24.00	28.15	25.28	26.77	32.81	33.82
Pork chops	39.23	28.06	33.36	37.44	38.12	44.13	40.67	47.19
Ham	38.79	25.02	27.28	38.37	36.03	41.37	47.50	48.38
Ham, not canned	37.11	23.23	26.81	36.88	34.48	39.84	43.27	47.18
Canned ham	1.69	1.79	0.46	1.49	1.55	1.53	4.23	1.20
Sausage	27.53	21.05	23.55	27.39	29.13	23.94	32.69	30.84
Other pork	37.41	27.65	33.29	34.15	35.64	31.31	37.53	50.01
Other meats	103.06	62.86	90.34	95.02	87.06	102.76	115.36	135.70
Frankfurters	21.37	12.37	21.59	20.18	20.22	22.02	22.78	25.47

	complete income reporters	under $10,000	$10,000–$19,999	$20,000–$29,999	$30,000–$39,999	$40,000–$49,999	$50,000–$69,999	$70,000 or more
Lunch meats (cold cuts)	$70.38	$43.61	$60.85	$59.53	$57.60	$72.88	$74.82	$98.50
Bologna, liverwurst, salami	21.06	17.58	21.27	20.55	19.14	18.35	17.26	27.19
Lamb, organ meats, and others	11.30	6.89	7.90	15.31	9.24	7.85	17.75	11.73
Lamb and organ meats	8.32	6.77	7.03	12.75	7.91	5.84	5.35	10.24
Mutton, goat, and game	2.98	0.12	0.87	2.56	1.33	2.01	12.41	1.49
Poultry	146.14	86.84	108.50	130.17	137.17	155.23	163.19	199.56
Fresh and frozen chicken	113.68	69.03	86.11	100.39	111.42	125.71	125.43	150.43
Fresh and frozen whole chicken	31.96	18.18	28.76	32.51	31.70	32.62	33.72	38.92
Fresh and frozen chicken parts	81.72	50.84	57.35	67.88	79.72	93.10	91.71	111.51
Other poultry	32.46	17.81	22.39	29.77	25.75	29.52	37.76	49.13
Fish and seafood	120.93	76.87	82.23	89.04	108.26	125.91	126.75	188.26
Canned fish and seafood	16.34	10.11	13.43	14.18	15.82	16.97	17.29	21.97
Fresh fish and shellfish	70.72	48.31	45.97	48.03	64.86	77.58	71.87	111.51
Frozen fish and shellfish	33.87	18.46	22.83	26.83	27.58	31.36	37.59	54.78
Eggs	34.75	25.19	31.05	36.25	34.42	35.35	35.90	39.98
Dairy products	**344.57**	**219.30**	**252.96**	**293.75**	**315.25**	**371.22**	**376.93**	**480.52**
Fresh milk and cream	134.19	90.54	108.79	129.47	126.54	136.48	144.64	171.12
Fresh milk, all types	121.29	83.59	100.44	119.15	114.10	121.52	131.06	151.80
Cream	12.89	6.95	8.35	10.32	12.44	14.96	13.58	19.32
Other dairy products	210.38	128.76	144.17	164.28	188.71	234.74	232.29	309.41
Butter	18.50	12.42	15.78	12.27	16.04	21.38	20.63	25.71
Cheese	101.06	56.46	69.11	75.95	94.61	106.27	111.22	153.88
Ice cream and related products	60.71	40.79	41.10	51.83	52.48	74.39	66.16	84.10
Miscellaneous dairy products	30.11	19.11	18.17	24.24	25.57	32.70	34.27	45.72
Fruits and vegetables	**568.48**	**337.52**	**431.88**	**501.92**	**527.49**	**558.71**	**612.29**	**807.12**
Fresh fruits	180.62	109.15	133.52	161.09	167.62	176.31	184.24	263.92
Apples	32.72	18.76	21.99	30.42	31.67	33.43	34.35	47.19
Bananas	31.72	22.86	28.88	32.48	28.16	30.83	32.92	38.64
Oranges	19.58	11.60	16.09	19.96	16.62	16.53	20.09	27.82
Citrus fruits, excl. oranges	14.95	8.57	12.33	12.28	13.76	14.87	13.40	22.87
Other fresh fruits	81.65	47.36	54.22	65.94	77.40	80.65	83.48	127.40
Fresh vegetables	181.38	105.04	137.11	165.50	164.39	174.82	200.25	256.29
Potatoes	33.75	22.54	28.36	34.15	32.20	31.12	37.80	41.76
Lettuce	22.82	13.77	16.25	17.82	19.56	24.69	24.82	34.21
Tomatoes	33.90	17.84	28.18	32.20	34.32	34.18	35.69	44.81
Other fresh vegetables	90.90	50.89	64.33	81.33	78.31	84.82	101.94	135.52
Processed fruits	119.34	70.79	91.01	103.74	111.54	114.26	130.74	169.72
Frozen fruits and fruit juices	12.52	4.88	8.78	11.43	11.08	15.48	11.47	19.44
Frozen orange juice	6.40	3.10	4.54	5.57	6.02	6.68	6.17	9.89
Frozen fruits	2.79	0.60	1.60	3.06	1.97	4.29	3.00	4.13
Frozen fruit juices, excl. orange	3.34	1.18	2.63	2.80	3.09	4.50	2.30	5.42
Canned fruits	15.78	8.87	13.69	14.65	12.76	16.35	16.88	21.65
Dried fruits	6.28	2.99	5.03	6.61	5.31	5.60	6.26	9.21
Fresh fruit juice	22.34	14.12	14.58	16.91	21.36	22.48	25.80	33.12
Canned and bottled fruit juice	62.43	39.93	48.93	54.14	61.04	54.34	70.34	86.31
Processed vegetables	87.14	52.53	70.25	71.58	83.94	93.31	97.05	117.18
Frozen vegetables	28.61	15.29	19.42	22.07	25.48	34.89	32.74	41.57
Canned and dried vegetables and juices	58.53	37.25	50.83	49.51	58.46	58.42	64.31	75.60
Canned beans	13.14	8.53	11.87	11.06	13.00	17.12	14.44	15.02
Canned corn	7.65	5.19	7.31	7.96	7.51	7.76	8.76	8.15
Canned miscellaneous vegetables	18.76	9.26	16.32	14.73	17.44	16.76	21.46	27.07
Dried peas	0.35	0.23	0.31	0.42	0.35	0.32	0.23	0.47
Dried beans	2.46	1.94	2.31	3.00	3.28	2.17	2.03	2.42

	complete income reporters	under $10,000	$10,000– $19,999	$20,000– $29,999	$30,000– $39,999	$40,000– $49,999	$50,000– $69,999	$70,000 or more
Dried miscellaneous vegetables	$7.97	$6.54	$6.10	$6.63	$9.39	$7.30	$8.30	$10.09
Dried processed vegetables	0.36	–	0.16	0.10	0.18	0.55	0.32	0.86
Fresh and canned vegetable juices	7.79	5.56	6.32	5.56	7.31	6.40	8.65	11.50
Sugar and other sweets	125.49	73.56	95.90	105.43	116.53	133.86	131.71	179.26
Candy and chewing gum	82.08	43.05	59.12	63.80	76.77	85.26	88.68	124.33
Sugar	15.70	14.01	15.90	14.53	17.86	17.10	17.04	14.56
Artificial sweeteners	4.34	2.15	2.82	6.39	2.05	3.43	4.80	6.39
Jams, preserves, other sweets	23.37	14.35	18.06	20.71	19.85	28.08	21.19	33.98
Fats and oils	**87.76**	**58.50**	**70.67**	**82.56**	**82.07**	**84.22**	**100.46**	**112.70**
Margarine	10.17	6.42	8.35	10.42	11.82	10.87	11.25	11.24
Fats and oils	26.56	20.71	23.58	24.30	25.05	20.80	32.63	32.06
Salad dressings	28.30	15.39	20.87	27.43	24.01	29.02	32.38	39.24
Nondairy cream and imitation milk	9.67	6.33	6.84	8.80	10.16	10.13	9.95	13.10
Peanut butter	13.06	9.66	11.02	11.61	11.02	13.41	14.24	17.06
Miscellaneous foods	**494.75**	**278.43**	**339.14**	**402.83**	**456.02**	**522.44**	**570.90**	**719.40**
Frozen prepared foods	102.82	64.79	71.66	78.68	95.34	116.80	120.01	144.14
Frozen meals	30.77	23.33	25.71	29.04	29.64	31.02	31.36	38.81
Other frozen prepared foods	72.05	41.46	45.94	49.64	65.71	85.78	88.65	105.33
Canned and packaged soups	37.58	23.14	30.57	33.76	35.19	36.08	42.37	50.24
Potato chips, nuts, and other snacks	106.42	57.29	70.90	84.09	96.92	116.76	131.16	152.63
Potato chips and other snacks	81.52	46.33	55.43	63.30	75.75	89.98	99.52	115.32
Nuts	24.90	10.95	15.47	20.79	21.17	26.77	31.64	37.32
Condiments and seasonings	91.06	50.71	60.40	73.40	84.33	90.57	106.49	135.74
Salt, spices, and other seasonings	22.44	14.48	14.76	18.65	20.37	21.65	26.79	32.44
Olives, pickles, relishes	10.11	4.96	7.86	8.60	9.08	7.67	9.81	16.61
Sauces and gravies	39.39	19.89	25.21	30.39	37.16	42.13	48.78	57.92
Baking needs and miscellaneous products	19.12	11.38	12.57	15.75	17.72	19.12	21.10	28.78
Other canned/packaged prepared foods	156.87	82.50	105.61	132.91	144.24	162.24	170.88	236.64
Prepared salads	21.33	12.84	14.95	15.49	16.77	15.33	22.63	37.15
Prepared desserts	11.22	4.43	7.43	10.96	12.14	13.05	10.98	16.05
Baby food	29.61	13.40	19.29	36.43	26.41	26.54	30.05	42.54
Miscellaneous prepared foods	94.59	51.76	63.89	70.03	88.93	106.34	107.21	140.84
Nonalcoholic beverages	**266.44**	**169.54**	**193.50**	**219.69**	**254.47**	**268.85**	**302.34**	**373.09**
Cola	85.88	54.73	64.09	76.47	93.00	86.52	101.70	107.50
Other carbonated drinks	46.50	25.28	34.90	39.41	48.01	49.40	56.64	60.44
Coffee	41.90	29.71	31.93	31.00	33.74	34.37	45.11	66.24
Roasted coffee	26.97	16.40	19.54	18.52	23.81	23.01	28.23	44.52
Instant and freeze-dried coffee	14.93	13.31	12.38	12.48	9.92	11.35	16.88	21.72
Noncarbonated fruit-flavored drinks, incl. nonfrozen lemonade	20.57	13.94	15.98	17.05	18.60	20.34	22.52	28.83
Tea	16.43	9.26	12.85	14.38	14.24	16.91	18.07	23.33
Nonalcoholic beer	0.76	–	0.27	0.15	1.07	1.51	0.40	1.58
Other nonalcoholic beverages and ice	54.41	36.61	33.48	41.23	45.82	59.81	57.90	85.17
Food prepared by CU on trips	**44.05**	**16.86**	**18.41**	**29.82**	**41.55**	**40.65**	**45.36**	**86.95**
FOOD AWAY FROM HOME	**2,394.98**	**1,116.18**	**1,092.27**	**1,580.65**	**1,874.92**	**2,261.06**	**2,993.53**	**4,349.93**
Meals at restaurants, carry-outs, other	**1,980.74**	**940.70**	**949.94**	**1,401.59**	**1,609.22**	**1,925.64**	**2,507.75**	**3,413.85**
Lunch	740.53	390.97	349.06	535.77	580.35	733.73	966.21	1,243.21
• At fast food, take-out, delivery, concession stands, buffet, and cafeteria (other than employer and school cafeteria)	412.71	239.90	223.51	336.87	352.45	424.42	542.18	616.07
• At full-service restaurants	234.59	110.24	97.78	143.59	170.70	213.12	261.56	466.50
• At vending machines, mobile vendors	5.98	0.67	2.35	6.64	8.66	6.85	10.64	5.99
• At employer and school cafeterias	87.25	40.17	25.43	48.67	48.53	89.33	151.82	154.65

	complete income reporters	under $10,000	$10,000– $19,999	$20,000– $29,999	$30,000– $39,999	$40,000– $49,999	$50,000– $69,999	$70,000 or more
Dinner	$757.67	$287.08	$338.45	$482.77	$592.32	$725.19	$887.51	$1,448.80
• At fast food, take-out, delivery, concession stands, buffet, and cafeteria (other than employer and school cafeteria)	231.75	120.14	118.09	165.17	205.29	234.12	308.51	367.91
• At full-service restaurants	519.54	153.59	216.71	313.73	380.66	487.33	573.30	1,072.71
• At vending machines, mobile vendors	2.27	0.19	1.37	1.28	4.29	2.85	1.32	3.77
• At employer and school cafeterias	4.11	13.14	2.28	2.59	2.09	0.89	4.37	4.41
Snacks and nonalcoholic beverages	290.43	162.41	157.37	244.86	262.69	279.54	391.61	426.07
• At fast food, take-out, delivery, concession stands, buffet, and cafeteria (other than employer and school cafeteria)	205.92	121.96	111.57	168.68	177.82	193.87	261.07	318.09
• At full-service restaurants	31.78	14.71	18.46	31.51	37.07	29.61	39.88	42.25
• At vending machines, mobile vendors	41.31	16.22	21.27	36.42	40.07	46.68	75.99	46.99
• At employer and school cafeterias	11.43	9.52	6.07	8.25	7.72	9.38	14.67	18.73
Breakfast and brunch	192.11	100.24	105.06	138.19	173.86	187.19	262.42	295.76
• At fast food, take-out, delivery, concession stands, buffet, and cafeteria (other than employer and school cafeteria)	93.93	58.98	63.91	70.33	101.88	95.51	138.41	113.41
• At full-service restaurants	90.33	31.07	38.72	62.63	67.01	83.31	112.63	171.09
• At vending machines, mobile vendors	1.46	1.16	0.21	1.59	2.15	2.86	1.57	1.40
• At employer and school cafeterias	6.39	9.02	2.22	3.64	2.81	5.52	9.82	9.86
Board (including at school)	**44.02**	**68.38**	**19.35**	**8.22**	**6.51**	**12.29**	**40.76**	**104.85**
Catered affairs	**62.64**	**2.82**	**5.79**	**11.38**	**35.71**	**32.92**	**79.46**	**180.43**
Food on trips	**220.35**	**71.39**	**80.01**	**111.02**	**146.68**	**201.79**	**249.04**	**490.43**
School lunches	**62.34**	**14.49**	**16.14**	**23.29**	**48.72**	**70.11**	**86.12**	**131.86**
Meals as pay	**24.90**	**18.41**	**21.04**	**25.16**	**28.08**	**18.30**	**30.41**	**28.51**
ALCOHOLIC BEVERAGES	**414.74**	**182.06**	**172.07**	**274.95**	**346.16**	**433.45**	**453.36**	**779.70**
At home	**255.24**	**120.90**	**123.22**	**192.59**	**232.49**	**278.59**	**274.15**	**437.09**
Beer and ale	125.22	75.54	77.07	111.19	133.18	167.00	147.72	155.24
Whiskey	16.17	5.46	8.36	10.21	15.01	19.05	18.43	28.16
Wine	85.35	26.86	25.33	45.63	56.84	62.99	69.64	211.09
Other alcoholic beverages	28.50	13.05	12.45	25.55	27.46	29.55	38.37	42.60
Away from home	**159.50**	**61.16**	**48.86**	**82.37**	**113.67**	**154.87**	**179.20**	**342.61**
Beer and ale	56.80	22.00	18.16	35.01	46.96	62.99	71.43	106.38
• At fast food, take-out, delivery, concession stands, buffet, and cafeteria	9.43	6.42	3.27	7.33	15.64	8.82	10.86	12.63
• At full-service restaurants	43.37	13.94	14.45	26.87	31.05	34.12	51.79	91.79
• At vending machines, mobile vendors	0.41	0.06	0.33	0.76	0.27	0.16	0.35	0.61
• At catered affairs	3.60	1.59	0.11	0.05	–	19.89	8.43	1.36
Wine	27.66	9.78	8.33	13.87	19.68	24.08	28.75	62.48
• At fast food, take-out, delivery, concession stands, buffet and cafeteria	5.23	2.64	2.14	4.63	5.63	5.51	4.23	9.22
• At full-service restaurants	20.91	6.66	6.18	9.23	14.05	16.46	23.40	48.52
• At catered affairs	1.52	0.48	0.01	0.01	–	2.11	1.12	4.73
Other alcoholic beverages	75.03	29.36	22.37	33.49	47.03	67.79	79.02	173.74
• At fast food, take-out, delivery, concession stands, buffet, and cafeteria	4.16	1.94	2.14	2.62	6.75	5.43	2.87	6.49
• At full-service restaurants	30.34	8.58	5.51	16.68	20.33	19.97	36.95	71.09
• At catered affairs	5.51	0.70	0.05	0.02	–	8.76	3.71	17.39
Alcoholic beverages purchased on trips	35.03	18.15	14.66	14.16	19.96	33.63	35.48	78.77

Note: (–) means sample is too small to make a reliable estimate.
Source: Bureau of Labor Statistics, unpublished tables from the 2002 Consumer Expenditure Survey; calculations by New Strategist

Table 5.6 Food and Alcohol: Indexed spending by income, 2002

(indexed average annual spending of consumer units (CU) on food and beverages, by before-tax income of consumer unit, 2002; complete income reporters only; index definition: an index of 100 is the average for all consumer units; an index of 132 means that spending by consumer units in that group is 32 percent above the average for all consumer units; an index of 68 indicates spending that is 32 percent below the average for all consumer units)

	complete income reporters	under $10,000	$10,000–$19,999	$20,000–$29,999	$30,000–$39,999	$40,000–$49,999	$50,000–$69,999	$70,000 or more
Average spending of CU, total	$42,557	$17,628	$22,839	$28,836	$35,095	$41,787	$50,406	$76,627
Average spending of CU, index	100	41	54	68	82	98	118	180
Food, spending index	100	55	62	77	87	98	117	158
Alcoholic beverages, spending index	100	44	41	66	83	105	109	188
FOOD AT HOME	**100**	**61**	**74**	**86**	**93**	**101**	**111**	**141**
Cereals and bakery products	**100**	**62**	**77**	**86**	**92**	**96**	**110**	**141**
Cereals and cereal products	100	70	79	87	91	97	108	136
Flour	100	76	93	125	105	77	125	92
Prepared flour mixes	100	57	81	66	85	140	118	135
Ready-to-eat and cooked cereals	100	68	80	86	88	96	105	142
Rice	100	65	80	99	114	94	108	121
Pasta, cornmeal, and other cereal products	100	87	72	80	88	91	109	141
Bakery products	100	57	76	85	92	96	111	144
Bread	100	64	87	88	95	101	107	130
White bread	100	69	95	93	98	99	110	117
Bread, other than white	100	61	81	84	92	103	105	140
Crackers and cookies	100	56	73	86	85	92	109	152
Cookies	100	54	75	85	81	88	113	155
Crackers	100	60	70	88	93	100	103	148
Frozen and refrigerated bakery products	100	55	71	88	76	82	115	158
Other bakery products	100	52	71	82	97	98	115	146
Biscuits and rolls	100	49	67	72	92	92	115	162
Cakes and cupcakes	100	62	71	74	94	99	123	142
Bread and cracker products	100	43	65	96	91	94	100	159
Sweetrolls, coffee cakes, doughnuts	100	50	73	98	102	103	115	131
Pies, tarts, turnovers	100	41	87	110	114	101	88	130
Meats, poultry, fish, and eggs	**100**	**65**	**77**	**89**	**96**	**99**	**110**	**135**
Beef	100	62	73	89	105	93	111	136
Ground beef	100	64	80	92	104	101	119	121
Roast	100	61	72	86	109	85	102	146
Chuck roast	100	59	70	105	95	112	119	122
Round roast	100	65	115	86	87	96	99	123
Other roast	100	61	50	75	129	64	94	171
Steak	100	60	66	86	109	90	111	143
Round steak	100	65	68	85	108	88	123	134
Sirloin steak	100	53	73	84	95	98	112	146
Other steak	100	63	61	88	117	86	107	145
Pork	100	74	82	96	96	98	111	123
Bacon	100	85	84	98	88	94	115	118
Pork chops	100	72	85	95	97	112	104	120
Ham	100	65	70	99	93	107	122	125
Ham, not canned	100	63	72	99	93	107	117	127
Canned ham	100	106	27	88	92	91	250	71
Sausage	100	76	86	99	106	87	119	112
Other pork	100	74	89	91	95	84	100	134
Other meats	100	61	88	92	84	100	112	132
Frankfurters	100	58	101	94	95	103	107	119

	complete income reporters	under $10,000	$10,000– $19,999	$20,000– $29,999	$30,000– $39,999	$40,000– $49,999	$50,000– $69,999	$70,000 or more
Lunch meats (cold cuts)	100	62	86	85	82	104	106	140
Bologna, liverwurst, salami	100	83	101	98	91	87	82	129
Lamb, organ meats, and others	100	61	70	135	82	69	157	104
Lamb and organ meats	100	81	84	153	95	70	64	123
Mutton, goat, and game	100	4	29	86	45	67	416	50
Poultry	100	59	74	89	94	106	112	137
Fresh and frozen chicken	100	61	76	88	98	111	110	132
Fresh and frozen whole chicken	100	57	90	102	99	102	106	122
Fresh and frozen chicken parts	100	62	70	83	98	114	112	136
Other poultry	100	55	69	92	79	91	116	151
Fish and seafood	100	64	68	74	90	104	105	156
Canned fish and seafood	100	62	82	87	97	104	106	134
Fresh fish and shellfish	100	68	65	68	92	110	102	158
Frozen fish and shellfish	100	54	67	79	81	93	111	162
Eggs	100	72	89	104	99	102	103	115
Dairy products	**100**	**64**	**73**	**85**	**91**	**108**	**109**	**139**
Fresh milk and cream	100	67	81	96	94	102	108	128
Fresh milk, all types	100	69	83	98	94	100	108	125
Cream	100	54	65	80	97	116	105	150
Other dairy products	100	61	69	78	90	112	110	147
Butter	100	67	85	66	87	116	112	139
Cheese	100	56	68	75	94	105	110	152
Ice cream and related products	100	67	68	85	86	123	109	139
Miscellaneous dairy products	100	63	60	81	85	109	114	152
Fruits and vegetables	**100**	**59**	**76**	**88**	**93**	**98**	**108**	**142**
Fresh fruits	100	60	74	89	93	98	102	146
Apples	100	57	67	93	97	102	105	144
Bananas	100	72	91	102	89	97	104	122
Oranges	100	59	82	102	85	84	103	142
Citrus fruits, excl. oranges	100	57	82	82	92	99	90	153
Other fresh fruits	100	58	66	81	95	99	102	156
Fresh vegetables	100	58	76	91	91	96	110	141
Potatoes	100	67	84	101	95	92	112	124
Lettuce	100	60	71	78	86	108	109	150
Tomatoes	100	53	83	95	101	101	105	132
Other fresh vegetables	100	56	71	89	86	93	112	149
Processed fruits	100	59	76	87	93	96	110	142
Frozen fruits and fruit juices	100	39	70	91	88	124	92	155
Frozen orange juice	100	48	71	87	94	104	96	155
Frozen fruits	100	21	57	110	71	154	108	148
Frozen fruit juices, excl. orange	100	35	79	84	93	135	69	162
Canned fruits	100	56	87	93	81	104	107	137
Dried fruits	100	48	80	105	85	89	100	147
Fresh fruit juice	100	63	65	76	96	101	115	148
Canned and bottled fruit juice	100	64	78	87	98	87	113	138
Processed vegetables	100	60	81	82	96	107	111	134
Frozen vegetables	100	53	68	77	89	122	114	145
Canned and dried vegetables and juices	100	64	87	85	100	100	110	129
Canned beans	100	65	90	84	99	130	110	114
Canned corn	100	68	96	104	98	101	115	107
Canned miscellaneous vegetables	100	49	87	79	93	89	114	144
Dried peas	100	65	90	120	100	91	66	134
Dried beans	100	79	94	122	133	88	83	98

	complete income reporters	under $10,000	$10,000– $19,999	$20,000– $29,999	$30,000– $39,999	$40,000– $49,999	$50,000– $69,999	$70,000 or more
Dried miscellaneous vegetables	100	82	76	83	118	92	104	127
Dried processed vegetables	100	–	44	28	50	153	89	239
Fresh and canned vegetable juices	100	71	81	71	94	82	111	148
Sugar and other sweets	**100**	**59**	**76**	**84**	**93**	**107**	**105**	**143**
Candy and chewing gum	100	52	72	78	94	104	108	151
Sugar	100	89	101	93	114	109	109	93
Artificial sweeteners	100	50	65	147	47	79	111	147
Jams, preserves, other sweets	100	61	77	89	85	120	91	145
Fats and oils	**100**	**67**	**81**	**94**	**94**	**96**	**114**	**128**
Margarine	100	63	82	102	116	107	111	111
Fats and oils	100	78	89	91	94	78	123	121
Salad dressings	100	54	74	97	85	103	114	139
Nondairy cream and imitation milk	100	65	71	91	105	105	103	135
Peanut butter	100	74	84	89	84	103	109	131
Miscellaneous foods	**100**	**56**	**69**	**81**	**92**	**106**	**115**	**145**
Frozen prepared foods	100	63	70	77	93	114	117	140
Frozen meals	100	76	84	94	96	101	102	126
Other frozen prepared foods	100	58	64	69	91	119	123	146
Canned and packaged soups	100	62	81	90	94	96	113	134
Potato chips, nuts, and other snacks	100	54	67	79	91	110	123	143
Potato chips and other snacks	100	57	68	78	93	110	122	141
Nuts	100	44	62	83	85	108	127	150
Condiments and seasonings	100	56	66	81	93	99	117	149
Salt, spices, and other seasonings	100	65	66	83	91	96	119	145
Olives, pickles, relishes	100	49	78	85	90	76	97	164
Sauces and gravies	100	50	64	77	94	107	124	147
Baking needs and miscellaneous products	100	60	66	82	93	100	110	151
Other canned/packaged prepared foods	100	53	67	85	92	103	109	151
Prepared salads	100	60	70	73	79	72	106	174
Prepared desserts	100	39	66	98	108	116	98	143
Baby food	100	45	65	123	89	90	101	144
Miscellaneous prepared foods	100	55	68	74	94	112	113	149
Nonalcoholic beverages	**100**	**64**	**73**	**82**	**96**	**101**	**113**	**140**
Cola	100	64	75	89	108	101	118	125
Other carbonated drinks	100	54	75	85	103	106	122	130
Coffee	100	71	76	74	81	82	108	158
Roasted coffee	100	61	72	69	88	85	105	165
Instant and freeze-dried coffee	100	89	83	84	66	76	113	145
Noncarbonated fruit-flavored drinks, incl. nonfrozen lemonade	100	68	78	83	90	99	109	140
Tea	100	56	78	88	87	103	110	142
Nonalcoholic beer	100	–	35	20	141	199	53	208
Other nonalcoholic beverages and ice	100	67	62	76	84	110	106	157
Food prepared by CU on trips	**100**	**38**	**42**	**68**	**94**	**92**	**103**	**197**
FOOD AWAY FROM HOME	**100**	**47**	**46**	**66**	**78**	**94**	**125**	**182**
Meals at restaurants, carry-outs, other	**100**	**47**	**48**	**71**	**81**	**97**	**127**	**172**
Lunch	100	53	47	72	78	99	130	168
• At fast food, take-out, delivery, concession stands, buffet, and cafeteria (other than employer and school cafeteria)	100	58	54	82	85	103	131	149
• At full-service restaurants	100	47	42	61	73	91	111	199
• At vending machines, mobile vendors	100	11	39	111	145	115	178	100
• At employer and school cafeterias	100	46	29	56	56	102	174	177

	complete income reporters	under $10,000	$10,000–$19,999	$20,000–$29,999	$30,000–$39,999	$40,000–$49,999	$50,000–$69,999	$70,000 or more
Dinner	100	38	45	64	78	96	117	191
• At fast food, take-out, delivery, concession stands, buffet, and cafeteria (other than employer and school cafeteria)	100	52	51	71	89	101	133	159
• At full-service restaurants	100	30	42	60	73	94	110	206
• At vending machines, mobile vendors	100	9	61	56	189	126	58	166
• At employer and school cafeterias	100	320	55	63	51	22	106	107
Snacks and nonalcoholic beverages	100	56	54	84	90	96	135	147
• At fast food, take-out, delivery, concession stands, buffet, and cafeteria (other than employer and school cafeteria)	100	59	54	82	86	94	127	154
• At full-service restaurants	100	46	58	99	117	93	125	133
• At vending machines, mobile vendors	100	39	51	88	97	113	184	114
• At employer and school cafeterias	100	83	53	72	68	82	128	164
Breakfast and brunch	100	52	55	72	91	97	137	154
• At fast food, take-out, delivery, concession stands, buffet, and cafeteria (other than employer and school cafeteria)	100	63	68	75	108	102	147	121
• At full-service restaurants	100	34	43	69	74	92	125	189
• At vending machines, mobile vendors	100	79	14	109	147	196	108	96
• At employer and school cafeterias	100	141	35	57	44	86	154	154
Board (including at school)	**100**	**155**	**44**	**19**	**15**	**28**	**93**	**238**
Catered affairs	**100**	**4**	**9**	**18**	**57**	**53**	**127**	**288**
Food on trips	**100**	**32**	**36**	**50**	**67**	**92**	**113**	**223**
School lunches	**100**	**23**	**26**	**37**	**78**	**112**	**138**	**212**
Meals as pay	**100**	**74**	**84**	**101**	**113**	**73**	**122**	**114**
ALCOHOLIC BEVERAGES	**100**	**44**	**41**	**66**	**83**	**105**	**109**	**188**
At home	**100**	**47**	**48**	**75**	**91**	**109**	**107**	**171**
Beer and ale	100	60	62	89	106	133	118	124
Whiskey	100	34	52	63	93	118	114	174
Wine	100	31	30	53	67	74	82	247
Other alcoholic beverages	100	46	44	90	96	104	135	149
Away from home	**100**	**38**	**31**	**52**	**71**	**97**	**112**	**215**
Beer and ale	100	39	32	62	83	111	126	187
• At fast food, take-out, delivery, concession stands, buffet, and cafeteria	100	68	35	78	166	94	115	134
• At full-service restaurants	100	32	33	62	72	79	119	212
• At vending machines, mobile vendors	100	14	80	185	66	39	85	149
• At catered affairs	100	44	3	1	–	553	234	38
Wine	100	35	30	50	71	87	104	226
• At fast food, take-out, delivery, concession stands, buffet and cafeteria	100	51	41	89	108	105	81	176
• At full-service restaurants	100	32	30	44	67	79	112	232
• At catered affairs	100	31	1	1	–	139	74	311
Other alcoholic beverages	100	39	30	45	63	90	105	232
• At fast food, take-out, delivery, concession stands, buffet, and cafeteria	100	47	52	63	162	131	69	156
• At full-service restaurants	100	28	18	55	67	66	122	234
• At catered affairs	100	13	1	0	–	159	67	316
Alcoholic beverages purchased on trips	100	52	42	40	57	96	101	225

Note: (–) means sample is too small to make a reliable estimate.
Source: Calculations by New Strategist based on the 2002 Consumer Expenditure Survey

Table 5.7 Food and Alcohol: Total spending by income, 2002

(total annual spending on food and alcoholic beverages, by before-tax income group of consumer units (CU), 2002; complete income reporters only; numbers in thousands)

	complete income reporters	under $10,000	$10,000–$19,999	$20,000–$29,999	$30,000–$39,999	$40,000–$49,999	$50,000–$69,999	$70,000 or more
Number of consumer units	92,388	10,933	15,075	12,312	10,727	8,873	13,521	20,947
Total spending of all CUs	$3,931,754,268	$192,725,059	$344,293,530	$355,026,985	$376,468,249	$370,779,423	$681,541,825	$1,605,112,263
Food, total spending	518,471,293	33,729,274	52,564,157	53,540,456	52,356,127	48,819,069	88,538,483	185,880,745
Alcoholic beverages, total spending	38,316,999	1,990,439	2,594,014	3,385,184	3,713,258	3,846,002	6,129,881	16,332,376
FOOD AT HOME	**$297,203,881**	**$21,526,147**	**$36,098,139**	**$34,079,493**	**$32,243,860**	**$28,756,683**	**$48,062,963**	**$94,762,971**
Cereals and bakery products	**43,476,869**	**3,164,961**	**5,480,607**	**4,967,400**	**4,621,513**	**4,025,769**	**7,015,641**	**13,947,769**
Cereals and cereal products	14,830,122	1,236,360	1,918,888	1,718,878	1,575,474	1,383,478	2,348,192	4,582,366
Flour	789,917	71,198	120,293	131,492	96,758	58,296	144,539	164,015
Prepared flour mixes	1,211,207	81,283	159,804	106,006	119,392	162,465	208,494	369,924
Ready-to-eat and cooked cereals	8,476,599	680,461	1,103,418	972,894	862,665	779,049	1,300,450	2,732,746
Rice	1,697,168	129,900	221,573	223,955	224,302	152,527	269,474	466,280
Pasta, cornmeal, and other cereal products	2,655,231	273,409	313,800	284,530	272,359	231,230	425,235	849,401
Bakery products	28,646,747	1,928,633	3,561,799	3,248,521	3,046,146	2,642,202	4,667,449	9,365,194
Bread	8,097,808	617,344	1,153,173	946,793	888,625	788,011	1,270,568	2,392,776
White bread	3,395,259	278,776	527,879	422,055	385,314	322,267	548,953	896,951
Bread, other than white	4,702,549	338,568	625,294	524,737	503,311	465,744	721,616	1,495,825
Crackers and cookies	6,902,307	458,324	822,796	788,707	680,735	611,350	1,105,207	2,384,816
Cookies	4,539,022	289,994	552,556	512,179	426,506	383,491	747,711	1,592,600
Crackers	2,363,285	168,330	270,240	276,528	254,230	227,859	357,495	792,216
Frozen and refrigerated bakery products	2,428,881	156,750	281,697	286,008	215,720	192,100	407,523	869,719
Other bakery products	11,217,751	696,286	1,303,982	1,227,014	1,260,959	1,050,741	1,884,151	3,717,883
Biscuits and rolls	3,955,130	228,427	432,817	377,978	421,142	347,822	665,774	1,451,837
Cakes and cupcakes	3,439,605	253,534	398,974	337,226	376,947	328,656	618,451	1,111,238
Bread and cracker products	330,749	16,928	35,328	42,353	35,077	29,813	48,540	119,607
Sweetrolls, coffee cakes, doughnuts	2,549,909	151,813	303,268	331,562	303,252	253,058	429,562	758,491
Pies, tarts, turnovers	941,434	45,514	133,596	137,894	124,540	91,392	121,824	276,710
Meats, poultry, fish, and eggs	**75,275,895**	**5,747,443**	**9,475,545**	**8,969,538**	**8,384,867**	**7,162,729**	**12,112,653**	**23,021,591**
Beef	22,020,680	1,616,389	2,637,398	2,617,039	2,687,543	1,956,497	3,561,837	6,814,269
Ground beef	8,198,511	624,163	1,065,099	1,009,707	994,393	796,884	1,425,789	2,245,937
Roast	3,908,936	283,337	458,552	449,019	495,051	320,581	583,702	1,291,592
Chuck roast	1,080,016	75,425	124,212	150,945	119,284	116,059	188,618	298,704
Round roast	974,693	74,442	183,122	111,670	98,045	90,061	140,618	272,311
Other roast	1,854,227	133,361	151,218	186,527	277,615	114,462	254,465	720,786
Steak	8,011,887	573,012	858,804	920,814	1,011,878	692,626	1,299,639	2,605,178
Round steak	1,266,639	97,037	140,773	142,819	159,189	107,008	227,964	386,053
Sirloin steak	2,526,812	159,794	299,011	283,422	279,653	238,240	412,661	836,414
Other steak	4,218,436	316,180	419,019	494,573	573,036	347,378	659,014	1,382,711
Pork	15,849,161	1,378,553	2,132,918	2,037,513	1,761,373	1,486,316	2,585,350	4,403,897
Bacon	2,640,449	265,831	361,777	346,583	271,179	237,530	443,624	708,428
Pork chops	3,624,381	306,786	502,972	460,961	408,913	391,565	549,899	988,489
Ham	3,583,731	273,550	411,276	472,411	386,494	367,076	642,248	1,013,416
Ham, not canned	3,428,519	254,027	404,224	454,067	369,867	353,500	585,054	988,279
Canned ham	156,136	19,523	6,973	18,345	16,627	13,576	57,194	25,136
Sausage	2,543,442	230,134	355,064	337,226	312,478	212,420	442,001	646,005
Other pork	3,456,235	302,251	501,909	420,455	382,310	277,814	507,443	1,047,559
Other meats	9,521,507	687,221	1,361,924	1,169,886	933,893	911,789	1,559,783	2,842,508
Frankfurters	1,974,332	135,194	325,532	248,456	216,900	195,383	308,008	533,520

	complete income reporters	under $10,000	$10,000–$19,999	$20,000–$29,999	$30,000–$39,999	$40,000–$49,999	$50,000–$69,999	$70,000 or more
Lunch meats (cold cuts)	$6,502,267	$476,742	$917,348	$732,933	$617,875	$646,664	$1,011,641	$2,063,280
Bologna, liverwurst, salami	1,945,691	192,220	320,632	253,012	205,315	162,820	233,372	569,549
Lamb, organ meats, and others	1,043,984	75,355	119,044	188,497	99,117	69,653	233,372	569,549
Lamb and organ meats	768,668	74,035	105,907	156,978	99,117	69,653	239,998	245,708
Mutton, goat, and game	275,316	1,320	13,056	31,519	84,851	51,818	72,337	214,497
Poultry	13,501,582	949,399	1,635,645	1,602,653	14,267	17,835	167,796	31,211
Fresh and frozen chicken	10,502,668	754,683	1,298,079	1,236,002	1,471,423	1,377,356	2,206,492	4,180,183
Fresh and frozen whole chicken	2,952,720	198,759	433,594	400,263	1,195,202	1,115,425	1,695,939	3,151,057
Fresh and frozen chicken parts	7,549,947	555,884	864,486	835,739	340,046	289,437	455,928	815,257
Other poultry	2,998,914	194,717	337,566	366,528	855,156	826,076	1,240,011	2,335,800
Fish and seafood	11,172,481	840,474	1,239,624	1,096,260	276,220	261,931	510,553	1,029,126
Canned fish and seafood	1,509,620	110,546	202,486	174,584	1,161,305	1,117,199	1,713,787	3,943,482
Fresh fish and shellfish	6,533,679	528,194	693,013	591,345	169,701	150,575	233,778	460,206
Frozen fish and shellfish	3,129,182	201,773	344,125	330,331	695,753	688,367	971,754	2,335,800
Eggs	3,210,483	275,367	468,035	446,310	295,851	278,257	508,254	1,147,477
Dairy products	**31,834,133**	**2,397,656**	**3,813,331**	**3,616,650**	369,223	313,661	485,404	837,461
Fresh milk and cream	12,397,546	989,875	1,639,947	1,594,035	**3,381,687**	**3,293,835**	**5,096,471**	**10,065,452**
Fresh milk, all types	11,205,741	913,857	1,514,134	1,466,975	1,357,395	1,210,987	1,955,677	3,584,451
Cream	1,190,881	76,018	125,884	127,060	1,223,951	1,078,247	1,772,062	3,179,755
Other dairy products	19,436,587	1,407,781	2,173,313	2,022,615	133,444	132,740	183,615	404,696
Butter	1,709,178	135,738	237,949	151,068	2,024,292	2,082,848	3,140,793	6,481,211
Cheese	9,336,731	617,270	1,041,893	935,096	172,061	189,705	278,938	538,547
Ice cream and related products	5,608,875	445,917	619,539	638,131	1,014,881	942,934	1,503,806	3,223,324
Miscellaneous dairy products	2,781,803	208,965	273,932	298,443	562,953	660,062	894,549	1,761,643
Fruits and vegetables	**52,520,730**	**3,690,159**	**6,510,624**	**6,179,639**	274,289	290,147	463,365	957,697
Fresh fruits	16,687,121	1,193,362	2,012,806	1,983,340	**5,658,385**	**4,957,434**	**8,278,773**	**16,906,743**
Apples	3,022,935	205,156	331,559	374,531	1,798,060	1,564,399	2,491,109	5,528,332
Bananas	2,930,547	249,892	435,415	399,894	339,724	296,624	464,446	988,489
Oranges	1,808,957	126,825	242,516	245,748	302,072	273,555	445,111	809,392
Citrus fruits, excl. oranges	1,381,201	93,700	185,824	151,191	178,283	146,671	271,637	582,746
Other fresh fruits	7,543,480	517,789	817,421	811,853	147,604	131,942	181,181	479,058
Fresh vegetables	16,757,335	1,148,435	2,066,937	2,037,636	830,270	715,607	1,128,733	2,668,648
Potatoes	3,118,095	246,388	427,452	420,455	1,763,412	1,551,178	2,707,580	5,368,507
Lettuce	2,108,294	150,570	244,975	219,400	345,409	276,128	511,094	874,747
Tomatoes	3,131,953	195,047	424,838	396,446	209,820	219,074	335,591	716,597
Other fresh vegetables	8,398,069	556,391	969,743	1,001,335	368,151	303,279	482,564	938,635
Processed fruits	11,025,584	773,950	1,371,928	1,277,247	840,031	752,608	1,378,331	2,838,737
Frozen fruits and fruit juices	1,156,698	53,401	132,326	140,726	1,196,490	1,013,829	1,767,736	3,555,125
Frozen orange juice	591,283	33,936	68,491	68,578	118,855	137,354	155,086	407,210
Frozen fruits	257,763	6,553	24,148	37,675	64,577	59,272	83,425	207,166
Frozen fruit juices, excl. orange	308,576	12,912	39,607	34,474	21,132	38,065	40,563	86,511
Canned fruits	1,457,883	96,964	206,390	180,371	33,146	39,929	31,098	113,533
Dried fruits	580,197	32,652	75,774	81,382	136,877	145,074	228,234	453,503
Fresh fruit juice	2,063,948	154,387	219,806	208,196	56,960	49,689	84,641	192,922
Canned and bottled fruit juice	5,767,783	436,547	737,622	666,572	229,129	199,465	348,842	693,765
Processed vegetables	8,050,690	574,341	1,058,961	881,293	654,776	482,159	951,067	1,807,936
Frozen vegetables	2,643,221	167,129	292,731	271,726	900,424	827,940	1,312,213	2,454,569
Canned and dried vegetables and juices	5,407,470	407,283	766,301	609,567	273,324	309,579	442,678	870,767
Canned beans	1,213,978	93,220	179,003	136,171	627,100	518,361	869,536	1,583,593
Canned corn	706,768	56,745	110,143	98,004	139,451	151,906	195,243	314,624
Canned miscellaneous vegetables	1,733,199	101,232	246,036	181,356	80,560	68,854	118,444	170,718
Dried peas	32,336	2,494	4,734	5,171	187,079	148,711	290,161	567,035
Dried beans	227,274	21,176	34,858	36,936	3,754	2,839	3,110	9,845
					35,185	19,254	27,448	50,692

	complete income reporters	under $10,000	$10,000– $19,999	$20,000– $29,999	$30,000– $39,999	$40,000– $49,999	$50,000– $69,999	$70,000 or more
Dried miscellaneous vegetables	$736,332	$71,513	$91,908	$81,629	$100,727	$64,773	$112,224	$211,355
Dried processed vegetables	33,260	–	2,402	1,231	1,931	4,880	4,327	18,014
Fresh and canned vegetable juices	719,703	60,793	95,229	68,455	78,414	56,787	116,957	240,891
Sugar and other sweets	**11,593,770**	**804,195**	**1,445,763**	**1,298,054**	**1,250,017**	**1,187,740**	**1,780,851**	**3,754,959**
Candy and chewing gum	7,583,207	470,643	891,164	785,506	823,512	756,512	1,199,042	2,604,341
Sugar	1,450,492	153,205	239,648	178,893	191,584	151,728	230,398	304,988
Artificial sweeteners	400,964	23,512	42,582	78,674	21,990	30,434	64,901	133,851
Jams, preserves, other sweets	2,159,108	156,906	272,299	254,982	212,931	249,154	286,510	711,779
Fats and oils	**8,107,971**	**639,619**	**1,065,334**	**1,016,479**	**880,365**	**747,284**	**1,358,320**	**2,360,727**
Margarine	939,586	70,176	125,870	128,291	126,793	96,450	152,111	235,444
Fats and oils	2,453,825	226,417	355,498	299,182	268,711	184,558	441,190	671,561
Salad dressings	2,614,580	168,211	314,614	337,718	257,555	257,494	437,810	821,960
Nondairy cream and imitation milk	893,392	69,194	103,091	108,346	108,986	89,883	134,534	274,406
Peanut butter	1,206,587	105,621	166,189	142,942	118,212	118,987	192,539	357,356
Miscellaneous foods	**45,708,963**	**3,044,099**	**5,112,471**	**4,959,643**	**4,891,727**	**4,635,610**	**7,719,139**	**15,069,272**
Frozen prepared foods	9,499,334	708,321	1,080,227	968,708	1,022,712	1,036,366	1,622,655	3,019,301
Frozen meals	2,842,779	255,024	387,641	357,540	317,948	275,240	424,019	812,953
Other frozen prepared foods	6,656,555	453,296	692,587	611,168	704,871	761,126	1,198,637	2,206,348
Canned and packaged soups	3,471,941	252,997	460,860	415,653	377,483	320,138	572,885	1,052,377
Potato chips, nuts, and other snacks	9,831,931	626,324	1,068,769	1,035,316	1,039,661	1,036,011	1,773,414	3,197,141
Potato chips and other snacks	7,531,470	506,518	835,541	779,350	812,570	798,393	1,345,610	2,415,608
Nuts	2,300,461	119,767	233,219	255,966	227,091	237,530	427,804	781,742
Condiments and seasonings	8,412,851	554,416	910,579	903,701	904,608	803,628	1,439,851	2,843,346
Salt, spices, and other seasonings	2,073,187	158,277	222,498	229,619	218,509	192,100	362,228	679,521
Olives, pickles, relishes	934,043	54,248	118,448	105,883	97,401	68,056	132,641	347,930
Sauces and gravies	3,639,163	217,445	380,046	374,162	398,615	373,819	659,554	1,213,250
Baking needs and miscellaneous products	1,766,459	124,446	189,517	193,914	190,082	169,652	285,293	602,855
Other canned/packaged prepared foods	14,492,906	902,002	1,592,035	1,636,388	1,547,262	1,439,556	2,310,468	4,956,898
Prepared salads	1,970,636	140,383	225,393	190,713	179,892	136,023	305,980	778,181
Prepared desserts	1,036,593	48,424	111,958	134,940	130,226	115,793	148,461	336,199
Baby food	2,735,609	146,517	290,785	448,526	283,300	235,489	406,306	891,085
Miscellaneous prepared foods	8,738,981	565,947	963,192	862,209	953,952	943,555	1,449,586	2,950,175
Nonalcoholic beverages	**24,615,859**	**1,853,612**	**2,916,995**	**2,704,823**	**2,729,700**	**2,385,506**	**4,087,939**	**7,815,116**
Cola	7,934,281	598,401	966,213	941,499	997,611	767,692	1,375,086	2,251,803
Other carbonated drinks	4,296,042	276,429	526,047	485,216	515,003	438,326	765,829	1,266,037
Coffee	3,871,057	324,849	481,274	381,672	361,929	304,965	609,932	1,387,529
Roasted coffee	2,491,704	179,293	294,538	228,018	255,410	204,168	381,698	932,560
Instant and freeze-dried coffee	1,379,353	145,555	186,665	153,654	106,412	100,709	228,234	454,969
Noncarbonated fruit-flavored drinks, incl. nonfrozen lemonade	1,900,421	152,419	240,901	209,920	199,522	180,477	304,493	603,902
Tea	1,517,935	101,198	193,683	177,047	152,752	150,042	244,324	488,694
Nonalcoholic beer	70,215	–	4,060	1,847	11,478	13,398	5,408	33,096
Other nonalcoholic beverages and ice	5,026,831	400,207	504,667	507,624	491,511	530,694	782,866	1,784,056
Food prepared by CU on trips	**4,069,691**	**184,292**	**277,540**	**367,144**	**445,707**	**360,687**	**613,313**	**1,821,342**
FOOD AWAY FROM HOME	**221,267,412**	**12,203,166**	**16,465,947**	**19,460,963**	**20,112,267**	**20,062,385**	**40,475,519**	**91,117,984**
Meals at restaurants, carry-outs, other	**182,996,607**	**10,284,649**	**14,320,324**	**17,256,376**	**17,262,103**	**17,086,204**	**33,907,288**	**71,509,916**
Lunch	68,416,086	4,274,466	5,262,092	6,596,400	6,225,414	6,510,386	13,064,125	26,041,520
• At fast food, take-out, delivery, concession stands, buffet, and cafeteria (other than employer and school cafeteria)	38,129,451	2,622,837	3,369,402	4,147,543	3,780,731	3,765,879	7,330,816	12,904,818
• At full-service restaurants	21,673,301	1,205,248	1,473,983	1,767,880	1,831,099	1,891,014	3,536,553	9,771,776
• At vending machines, mobile vendors	552,480	7,283	35,409	81,752	92,896	60,780	143,863	125,473
• At employer and school cafeterias	8,060,853	439,137	383,297	599,225	520,581	792,625	2,052,758	3,239,454

	complete income reporters	under $10,000	$10,000– $19,999	$20,000– $29,999	$30,000– $39,999	$40,000– $49,999	$50,000– $69,999	$70,000 or more
Dinner	$69,999,616	$3,138,604	$5,102,192	$5,943,864	$6,353,817	$6,434,611	$12,000,023	$30,348,014
• At fast food, take-out, delivery, concession stands, buffet, and cafeteria (other than employer and school cafeteria)	21,410,919	1,313,491	1,780,234	2,033,573	2,202,146	2,077,347	4,171,364	7,706,611
• At full-service restaurants	47,999,262	1,679,225	3,266,842	3,862,644	4,083,340	4,324,079	7,751,589	22,470,056
• At vending machines, mobile vendors	209,721	2,127	20,712	15,759	46,019	25,288	17,848	78,970
• At employer and school cafeterias	379,715	143,691	34,325	31,888	22,419	7,897	59,087	92,376
Snacks and nonalcoholic beverages	26,832,247	1,775,648	2,372,361	3,014,716	2,817,876	2,480,358	5,294,959	8,924,888
• At fast food, take-out, delivery, concession stands, buffet, and cafeteria (other than employer and school cafeteria)	19,024,537	1,333,388	1,681,846	2,076,788	1,907,475	1,720,209	3,529,927	6,663,031
• At full-service restaurants	2,936,091	160,827	278,335	387,951	397,650	262,730	539,217	885,011
• At vending machines, mobile vendors	3,816,548	177,297	320,600	448,403	429,831	414,192	1,027,461	984,300
• At employer and school cafeterias	1,055,995	104,097	91,570	101,574	82,812	83,229	198,353	392,337
Breakfast and brunch	17,748,659	1,095,962	1,583,760	1,701,395	1,864,996	1,660,937	3,548,181	6,195,285
• At fast food, take-out, delivery, concession stands, buffet, and cafeteria (other than employer and school cafeteria)	8,678,005	644,881	963,411	865,903	1,092,867	847,460	1,871,442	2,375,599
• At full-service restaurants	8,345,408	339,712	583,678	771,101	718,816	739,210	1,522,870	3,583,822
• At vending machines, mobile vendors	134,886	12,686	3,118	19,576	23,063	25,377	21,228	29,326
• At employer and school cafeterias	590,359	98,612	33,482	44,816	30,143	48,979	132,776	206,537
Board (including at school)	**4,066,920**	**747,579**	**291,726**	**101,205**	**69,833**	**109,049**	**551,116**	**2,196,293**
Catered affairs	**5,787,184**	**30,806**	**87,334**	**140,111**	**383,061**	**292,099**	**1,074,379**	**3,779,467**
Food on trips	**20,357,696**	**780,487**	**1,206,154**	**1,366,878**	**1,573,436**	**1,790,483**	**3,367,270**	**10,273,037**
School lunches	**5,759,468**	**158,414**	**243,238**	**286,746**	**522,619**	**622,086**	**1,164,429**	**2,762,071**
Meals as pay	**2,300,461**	**201,233**	**317,172**	**309,770**	**301,214**	**162,376**	**411,174**	**597,199**
ALCOHOLIC BEVERAGES	**38,316,999**	**1,990,439**	**2,594,014**	**3,385,184**	**3,713,258**	**3,846,002**	**6,129,881**	**16,332,376**
At home	**23,581,113**	**1,321,815**	**1,857,513**	**2,371,168**	**2,493,920**	**2,471,929**	**3,706,782**	**9,155,724**
Beer and ale	11,568,825	825,857	1,161,837	1,368,971	1,428,622	1,481,791	1,997,322	3,251,812
Whiskey	1,493,914	59,746	126,077	125,706	161,012	169,031	249,192	589,868
Wine	7,885,316	293,616	381,918	561,797	609,723	558,910	941,602	4,421,702
Other alcoholic beverages	2,633,058	142,667	187,682	314,572	294,563	262,197	518,801	892,342
Away from home	**14,735,886**	**668,623**	**736,581**	**1,014,139**	**1,219,338**	**1,374,162**	**2,422,963**	**7,176,652**
Beer and ale	5,247,638	240,576	273,790	431,043	503,740	558,910	965,805	2,228,342
• At fast food, take-out, delivery, concession stands, buffet, and cafeteria	871,219	70,227	49,327	90,247	167,770	78,260	146,838	264,561
• At full-service restaurants	4,006,868	152,389	217,848	330,823	333,073	302,747	700,253	1,922,725
• At vending machines, mobile vendors	37,879	607	4,919	9,357	2,896	1,420	4,732	12,778
• At catered affairs	332,597	17,353	1,696	616	–	176,484	113,982	28,488
Wine	2,555,452	106,956	125,575	170,767	211,107	213,662	388,729	1,308,769
• At fast food, take-out, delivery, concession stands, buffet and cafeteria	483,189	28,899	32,249	57,005	60,393	48,890	57,194	193,131
• At full-service restaurants	1,931,833	72,849	93,105	113,640	150,714	146,050	316,391	1,016,348
• At catered affairs	140,430	5,209	141	123	–	18,722	15,144	99,079
Other alcoholic beverages	6,931,872	320,982	337,215	412,329	504,491	601,501	1,068,429	3,639,332
• At fast food, take-out, delivery, concession stands, buffet, and cafeteria	384,334	21,166	32,325	32,257	72,407	48,180	38,805	135,946
• At full-service restaurants	2,803,052	93,794	82,998	205,364	218,080	177,194	499,601	1,489,122
• At catered affairs	509,058	7,648	707	246	–	77,727	50,163	364,268
Alcoholic beverages purchased on trips	3,236,352	198,444	221,034	174,338	214,111	298,399	479,725	1,649,995

Note: Numbers may not add to total because of rounding. (–) means sample is too small to make a reliable estimate.
Source: Calculations by New Strategist based on the 2002 Consumer Expenditure Survey

Table 5.8 Food and Alcohol: Market shares by income, 2002

(percentage of total annual spending on food and alcoholic beverages accounted for by before-tax income group of consumer units, 2002; complete income reporters only)

	complete income reporters	under $10,000	$10,000– $19,999	$20,000– $29,999	$30,000– $39,999	$40,000– $49,999	$50,000– $69,999	$70,000 or more
Share of total consumer units	100.0%	11.8%	16.3%	13.3%	11.6%	9.6%	14.6%	22.7%
Share of total before-tax income	100.0	1.3	4.9	6.6	8.1	8.6	17.4	53.0
Share of total spending	100.0	4.9	8.8	9.0	9.6	9.4	17.3	40.8
Share of food spending	100.0	6.5	10.1	10.3	10.1	9.4	17.1	35.9
Share of alcoholic beverages spending	100.0	5.2	6.8	8.8	9.7	10.0	16.0	42.6
FOOD AT HOME	100.0%	7.2%	12.1%	11.5%	10.8%	9.7%	16.2%	31.9%
Cereals and bakery products	100.0	7.3	12.6	11.4	10.6	9.3	16.1	32.1
Cereals and cereal products	100.0	8.3	12.9	11.6	10.6	9.3	15.8	30.9
Flour	100.0	9.0	15.2	16.6	12.2	7.4	18.3	20.8
Prepared flour mixes	100.0	6.7	13.2	8.8	9.9	13.4	17.2	30.5
Ready-to-eat and cooked cereals	100.0	8.0	13.0	11.5	10.2	9.2	15.3	32.2
Rice	100.0	7.7	13.1	13.2	13.2	9.0	15.9	27.5
Pasta, cornmeal, and other cereal products	100.0	10.3	11.8	10.7	10.3	8.7	16.0	32.0
Bakery products	100.0	6.7	12.4	11.3	10.6	9.2	16.3	32.7
Bread	100.0	7.6	14.2	11.7	11.0	9.7	15.7	29.5
White bread	100.0	8.2	15.5	12.4	11.3	9.5	16.2	26.4
Bread, other than white	100.0	7.2	13.3	11.2	10.7	9.9	15.3	31.8
Crackers and cookies	100.0	6.6	11.9	11.4	9.9	8.9	16.0	34.6
Cookies	100.0	6.4	12.2	11.3	9.4	8.4	16.5	35.1
Crackers	100.0	7.1	11.4	11.7	10.8	9.6	15.1	33.5
Frozen and refrigerated bakery products	100.0	6.5	11.6	11.8	8.9	7.9	16.8	35.8
Other bakery products	100.0	6.2	11.6	10.9	11.2	9.4	16.8	33.1
Biscuits and rolls	100.0	5.8	10.9	9.6	10.6	8.8	16.8	36.7
Cakes and cupcakes	100.0	7.4	11.6	9.8	11.0	9.6	18.0	32.3
Bread and cracker products	100.0	5.1	10.7	12.8	10.6	9.0	14.7	36.2
Sweetrolls, coffee cakes, doughnuts	100.0	6.0	11.9	13.0	11.9	9.9	16.8	29.7
Pies, tarts, turnovers	100.0	4.8	14.2	14.6	13.2	9.7	12.9	29.4
Meats, poultry, fish, and eggs	100.0	7.6	12.6	11.9	11.1	9.5	16.1	30.6
Beef	100.0	7.3	12.0	11.9	12.2	8.9	16.2	30.9
Ground beef	100.0	7.6	13.0	12.3	12.1	9.7	17.4	27.4
Roast	100.0	7.2	11.7	11.5	12.7	8.2	14.9	33.0
Chuck roast	100.0	7.0	11.5	14.0	11.0	10.7	17.5	27.7
Round roast	100.0	7.6	18.8	11.5	10.1	9.2	14.4	27.9
Other roast	100.0	7.2	8.2	10.1	15.0	6.2	13.7	38.9
Steak	100.0	7.2	10.7	11.5	12.6	8.6	16.2	32.5
Round steak	100.0	7.7	11.1	11.3	12.6	8.4	18.0	30.5
Sirloin steak	100.0	6.3	11.8	11.2	11.1	9.4	16.3	33.1
Other steak	100.0	7.5	9.9	11.7	13.6	8.2	15.6	32.8
Pork	100.0	8.7	13.5	12.9	11.1	9.4	16.3	27.8
Bacon	100.0	10.1	13.7	13.1	10.3	9.0	16.8	26.8
Pork chops	100.0	8.5	13.9	12.7	11.3	10.8	15.2	27.3
Ham	100.0	7.6	11.5	13.2	10.8	10.2	17.9	28.3
Ham, not canned	100.0	7.4	11.8	13.2	10.8	10.3	17.1	28.8
Canned ham	100.0	12.5	4.5	11.7	10.6	8.7	36.6	16.1
Sausage	100.0	9.0	14.0	13.3	12.3	8.4	17.4	25.4
Other pork	100.0	8.7	14.5	12.2	11.1	8.0	14.7	30.3
Other meats	100.0	7.2	14.3	12.3	9.8	9.6	16.4	29.9
Frankfurters	100.0	6.8	16.5	12.6	11.0	9.9	15.6	27.0

	complete income reporters	under $10,000	$10,000—$19,999	$20,000—$29,999	$30,000—$39,999	$40,000—$49,999	$50,000—$69,999	$70,000 or more
Lunch meats (cold cuts)	100.0%	7.3%	14.1%	11.3%	9.5%	9.9%	15.6%	31.7%
Bologna, liverwurst, salami	100.0	9.9	16.5	13.0	10.6	8.4	12.0	29.3
Lamb, organ meats, and others	100.0	7.2	11.4	18.1	9.5	6.7	23.0	23.5
Lamb and organ meats	100.0	9.6	13.8	20.4	11.0	6.7	9.4	27.9
Mutton, goat, and game	100.0	0.5	4.7	11.4	5.2	6.5	60.9	11.3
Poultry	100.0	7.0	12.1	11.9	10.9	10.2	16.3	31.0
Fresh and frozen chicken	100.0	7.2	12.4	11.8	11.4	10.6	16.1	30.0
Fresh and frozen whole chicken	100.0	6.7	14.7	13.6	11.5	9.8	15.4	27.6
Fresh and frozen chicken parts	100.0	7.4	11.5	11.1	11.3	10.9	16.4	30.9
Other poultry	100.0	6.5	11.3	12.2	9.2	8.7	17.0	34.3
Fish and seafood	100.0	7.5	11.1	9.8	10.4	10.0	15.3	35.3
Canned fish and seafood	100.0	7.3	13.4	11.6	11.2	10.0	15.5	30.5
Fresh fish and shellfish	100.0	8.1	10.6	9.1	10.6	10.5	14.9	35.8
Frozen fish and shellfish	100.0	6.4	11.0	10.6	9.5	8.9	16.2	36.7
Eggs	100.0	8.6	14.6	13.9	11.5	9.8	15.1	26.1
Dairy products	**100.0**	**7.5**	**12.0**	**11.4**	**10.6**	**10.3**	**16.0**	**31.6**
Fresh milk and cream	100.0	8.0	13.2	12.9	10.9	9.8	15.8	28.9
Fresh milk, all types	100.0	8.2	13.5	13.1	10.9	9.6	15.8	28.4
Cream	100.0	6.4	10.6	10.7	11.2	11.1	15.4	34.0
Other dairy products	100.0	7.2	11.2	10.4	10.4	10.7	16.2	33.3
Butter	100.0	7.9	13.9	8.8	10.1	11.1	16.3	31.5
Cheese	100.0	6.6	11.2	10.0	10.9	10.1	16.1	34.5
Ice cream and related products	100.0	8.0	11.0	11.4	10.0	11.8	15.9	31.4
Miscellaneous dairy products	100.0	7.5	9.8	10.7	9.9	10.4	16.7	34.4
Fruits and vegetables	**100.0**	**7.0**	**12.4**	**11.8**	**10.8**	**9.4**	**15.8**	**32.2**
Fresh fruits	100.0	7.2	12.1	11.9	10.8	9.4	14.9	33.1
Apples	100.0	6.8	11.0	12.4	11.2	9.8	15.4	32.7
Bananas	100.0	8.5	14.9	13.6	10.3	9.3	15.2	27.6
Oranges	100.0	7.0	13.4	13.6	9.9	8.1	15.0	32.2
Citrus fruits, excl. oranges	100.0	6.8	13.5	10.9	10.7	9.6	13.1	34.7
Other fresh fruits	100.0	6.9	10.8	10.8	11.0	9.5	15.0	35.4
Fresh vegetables	100.0	6.9	12.3	12.2	10.5	9.3	16.2	32.0
Potatoes	100.0	7.9	13.7	13.5	11.1	8.9	16.4	28.1
Lettuce	100.0	7.1	11.6	10.4	10.0	10.4	15.9	34.0
Tomatoes	100.0	6.2	13.6	12.7	11.8	9.7	15.4	30.0
Other fresh vegetables	100.0	6.6	11.5	11.9	10.0	9.0	16.4	33.8
Processed fruits	100.0	7.0	12.4	11.6	10.9	9.2	16.0	32.2
Frozen fruits and fruit juices	100.0	4.6	11.4	12.2	10.3	11.9	13.4	35.2
Frozen orange juice	100.0	5.7	11.6	11.6	10.9	10.0	14.1	35.0
Frozen fruits	100.0	2.5	9.4	14.6	8.2	14.8	15.7	33.6
Frozen fruit juices, excl. orange	100.0	4.2	12.8	11.2	10.7	12.9	10.1	36.8
Canned fruits	100.0	6.7	14.2	12.4	9.4	10.0	15.7	31.1
Dried fruits	100.0	5.6	13.1	14.0	9.8	8.6	14.6	33.3
Fresh fruit juice	100.0	7.5	10.6	10.1	11.1	9.7	16.9	33.6
Canned and bottled fruit juice	100.0	7.6	12.8	11.6	11.4	8.4	16.5	31.3
Processed vegetables	100.0	7.1	13.2	10.9	11.2	10.3	16.3	30.5
Frozen vegetables	100.0	6.3	11.1	10.3	10.3	11.7	16.7	32.9
Canned and dried vegetables and juices	100.0	7.5	14.2	11.3	11.6	9.6	16.1	29.3
Canned beans	100.0	7.7	14.7	11.2	11.5	12.5	16.1	25.9
Canned corn	100.0	8.0	15.6	13.9	11.4	9.7	16.8	24.2
Canned miscellaneous vegetables	100.0	5.8	14.2	10.5	10.8	8.6	16.7	32.7
Dried peas	100.0	7.7	14.6	16.0	11.6	8.8	9.6	30.4
Dried beans	100.0	9.3	15.3	16.3	15.5	8.5	12.1	22.3

	complete income reporters	under $10,000	$10,000–$19,999	$20,000–$29,999	$30,000–$39,999	$40,000–$49,999	$50,000–$69,999	$70,000 or more
Dried miscellaneous vegetables	100.0%	9.7%	12.5%	11.1%	13.7%	8.8%	15.2%	28.7%
Dried processed vegetables	100.0	–	7.2	3.7	5.8	14.7	13.0	54.2
Fresh and canned vegetable juices	100.0	8.4	13.2	9.5	10.9	7.9	16.3	33.5
Sugar and other sweets	**100.0**	**6.9**	**12.5**	**11.2**	**10.8**	**10.2**	**15.4**	**32.4**
Candy and chewing gum	100.0	6.2	11.8	10.4	10.9	10.0	15.8	34.3
Sugar	100.0	10.6	16.5	12.3	13.2	10.5	15.9	21.0
Artificial sweeteners	100.0	5.9	10.6	19.6	5.5	7.6	16.2	33.4
Jams, preserves, other sweets	100.0	7.3	12.6	11.8	9.9	11.5	13.3	33.0
Fats and oils	**100.0**	**7.9**	**13.1**	**12.5**	**10.9**	**9.2**	**16.8**	**29.1**
Margarine	100.0	7.5	13.4	13.7	13.5	10.3	16.2	25.1
Fats and oils	100.0	9.2	14.5	12.2	11.0	7.5	18.0	27.4
Salad dressings	100.0	6.4	12.0	12.9	9.9	9.8	16.7	31.4
Nondairy cream and imitation milk	100.0	7.7	11.5	12.1	12.2	10.1	15.1	30.7
Peanut butter	100.0	8.8	13.8	11.8	9.8	9.9	16.0	29.6
Miscellaneous foods	**100.0**	**6.7**	**11.2**	**10.9**	**10.7**	**10.1**	**16.9**	**33.0**
Frozen prepared foods	100.0	7.5	11.4	10.2	10.8	10.9	17.1	31.8
Frozen meals	100.0	9.0	13.6	12.6	11.2	9.7	14.9	28.6
Other frozen prepared foods	100.0	6.8	10.4	9.2	10.6	11.4	18.0	33.1
Canned and packaged soups	100.0	7.3	13.3	12.0	10.9	9.2	16.5	30.3
Potato chips, nuts, and other snacks	100.0	6.4	10.9	10.5	10.6	10.5	18.0	32.5
Potato chips and other snacks	100.0	6.7	11.1	10.3	10.8	10.6	17.9	32.1
Nuts	100.0	5.2	10.1	11.1	9.9	10.3	18.6	34.0
Condiments and seasonings	100.0	6.6	10.8	10.7	10.8	9.6	17.1	33.8
Salt, spices, and other seasonings	100.0	7.6	10.7	11.1	10.5	9.3	17.5	32.8
Olives, pickles, relishes	100.0	5.8	12.7	11.3	10.4	7.3	14.2	37.2
Sauces and gravies	100.0	6.0	10.4	10.3	11.0	10.3	18.1	33.3
Baking needs and miscellaneous products	100.0	7.0	10.7	11.0	10.8	9.6	16.2	34.1
Other canned/packaged prepared foods	100.0	6.2	11.0	11.3	10.7	9.9	15.9	34.2
Prepared salads	100.0	7.1	11.4	9.7	9.1	6.9	15.5	39.5
Prepared desserts	100.0	4.7	10.8	13.0	12.6	11.2	14.3	32.4
Baby food	100.0	5.4	10.6	16.4	10.4	8.6	14.9	32.6
Miscellaneous prepared foods	100.0	6.5	11.0	9.9	10.9	10.8	16.6	33.8
Nonalcoholic beverages	**100.0**	**7.5**	**11.9**	**11.0**	**11.1**	**9.7**	**16.6**	**31.7**
Cola	100.0	7.5	12.2	11.9	12.6	9.7	17.3	28.4
Other carbonated drinks	100.0	6.4	12.2	11.3	12.0	10.2	17.8	29.5
Coffee	100.0	8.4	12.4	9.9	9.3	7.9	15.8	35.8
Roasted coffee	100.0	7.2	11.8	9.2	10.3	8.2	15.3	37.4
Instant and freeze-dried coffee	100.0	10.6	13.5	11.1	7.7	7.3	16.5	33.0
Noncarbonated fruit-flavored drinks, incl. nonfrozen lemonade	100.0	8.0	12.7	11.0	10.5	9.5	16.0	31.8
Tea	100.0	6.7	12.8	11.7	10.1	9.9	16.1	32.2
Nonalcoholic beer	100.0	–	5.8	2.6	16.3	19.1	7.7	47.1
Other nonalcoholic beverages and ice	100.0	8.0	10.0	10.1	9.8	10.6	15.6	35.5
Food prepared by CU on trips	**100.0**	**4.5**	**6.8**	**9.0**	**11.0**	**8.9**	**15.1**	**44.8**
FOOD AWAY FROM HOME	**100.0**	**5.5**	**7.4**	**8.8**	**9.1**	**9.1**	**18.3**	**41.2**
Meals at restaurants, carry-outs, other	**100.0**	**5.6**	**7.8**	**9.4**	**9.4**	**9.3**	**18.5**	**39.1**
Lunch	100.0	6.2	7.7	9.6	9.1	9.5	19.1	38.1
• At fast food, take-out, delivery, concession stands, buffet, and cafeteria (other than employer and school cafeteria)	100.0	6.9	8.8	10.9	9.9	9.9	19.2	33.8
• At full-service restaurants	100.0	5.6	6.8	8.2	8.4	8.7	16.3	45.1
• At vending machines, mobile vendors	100.0	1.3	6.4	14.8	16.8	11.0	26.0	22.7
• At employer and school cafeterias	100.0	5.4	4.8	7.4	6.5	9.8	25.5	40.2

	complete income reporters	under $10,000	$10,000–$19,999	$20,000–$29,999	$30,000–$39,999	$40,000–$49,999	$50,000–$69,999	$70,000 or more
Dinner	100.0%	4.5%	7.3%	8.5%	9.1%	9.2%	17.1%	43.4%
• At fast food, take-out, delivery, concession stands, buffet, and cafeteria (other than employer and school cafeteria)	100.0	6.1	8.3	9.5	10.3	9.7	19.5	36.0
• At full-service restaurants	100.0	3.5	6.8	8.0	8.5	9.0	16.1	46.8
• At vending machines, mobile vendors	100.0	1.0	9.9	7.5	21.9	12.1	8.5	37.7
• At employer and school cafeterias	100.0	37.8	9.0	8.4	5.9	2.1	15.6	24.3
Snacks and nonalcoholic beverages	100.0	6.6	8.8	11.2	10.5	9.2	19.7	33.3
• At fast food, take-out, delivery, concession stands, buffet, and cafeteria (other than employer and school cafeteria)	100.0	7.0	8.8	10.9	10.0	9.0	18.6	35.0
• At full-service restaurants	100.0	5.5	9.5	13.2	13.5	8.9	18.4	30.1
• At vending machines, mobile vendors	100.0	4.6	8.4	11.7	11.3	10.9	26.9	25.8
• At employer and school cafeterias	100.0	9.9	8.7	9.6	7.8	7.9	18.8	37.2
Breakfast and brunch	100.0	6.2	8.9	9.6	10.5	9.4	20.0	34.9
• At fast food, take-out, delivery, concession stands, buffet, and cafeteria (other than employer and school cafeteria)	100.0	7.4	11.1	10.0	12.6	9.8	21.6	27.4
• At full-service restaurants	100.0	4.1	7.0	9.2	8.6	8.9	18.2	42.9
• At vending machines, mobile vendors	100.0	9.4	2.3	14.5	17.1	18.8	15.7	21.7
• At employer and school cafeterias	100.0	16.7	5.7	7.6	5.1	8.3	22.5	35.0
Board (including at school)	**100.0**	**18.4**	**7.2**	**2.5**	**1.7**	**2.7**	**13.6**	**54.0**
Catered affairs	**100.0**	**0.5**	**1.5**	**2.4**	**6.6**	**5.0**	**18.6**	**65.3**
Food on trips	**100.0**	**3.8**	**5.9**	**6.7**	**7.7**	**8.8**	**16.5**	**50.5**
School lunches	**100.0**	**2.8**	**4.2**	**5.0**	**9.1**	**10.8**	**20.2**	**48.0**
Meals as pay	**100.0**	**8.7**	**13.8**	**13.5**	**13.1**	**7.1**	**17.9**	**26.0**
ALCOHOLIC BEVERAGES	**100.0**	**5.2**	**6.8**	**8.8**	**9.7**	**10.0**	**16.0**	**42.6**
At home	**100.0**	**5.6**	**7.9**	**10.1**	**10.6**	**10.5**	**15.7**	**38.8**
Beer and ale	100.0	7.1	10.0	11.8	12.3	12.8	17.3	28.1
Whiskey	100.0	4.0	8.4	8.4	10.8	11.3	16.7	39.5
Wine	100.0	3.7	4.8	7.1	7.7	7.1	11.9	56.1
Other alcoholic beverages	100.0	5.4	7.1	11.9	11.2	10.0	19.7	33.9
Away from home	**100.0**	**4.5**	**5.0**	**6.9**	**8.3**	**9.3**	**16.4**	**48.7**
Beer and ale	100.0	4.6	5.2	8.2	9.6	10.7	18.4	42.5
• At fast food, take-out, delivery, concession stands, buffet, and cafeteria	100.0	8.1	5.7	10.4	19.3	9.0	16.9	30.4
• At full-service restaurants	100.0	3.8	5.4	8.3	8.3	7.6	17.5	48.0
• At vending machines, mobile vendors	100.0	1.6	13.0	24.7	7.6	3.7	12.5	33.7
• At catered affairs	100.0	5.2	0.5	0.2	–	53.1	34.3	8.6
Wine	100.0	4.2	4.9	6.7	8.3	8.4	15.2	51.2
• At fast food, take-out, delivery, concession stands, buffet and cafeteria	100.0	6.0	6.7	11.8	12.5	10.1	11.8	40.0
• At full-service restaurants	100.0	3.8	4.8	5.9	7.8	7.6	16.4	52.6
• At catered affairs	100.0	3.7	0.1	0.1	–	13.3	10.8	70.6
Other alcoholic beverages	100.0	4.6	4.9	5.9	7.3	8.7	15.4	52.5
• At fast food, take-out, delivery, concession stands, buffet, and cafeteria	100.0	5.5	8.4	8.4	18.8	12.5	10.1	35.4
• At full-service restaurants	100.0	3.3	3.0	7.3	7.8	6.3	17.8	53.1
• At catered affairs	100.0	1.5	0.1	0.0	–	15.3	9.9	71.6
Alcoholic beverages purchased on trips	100.0	6.1	6.8	5.4	6.6	9.2	14.8	51.0

Note: Numbers may not add to total because of rounding. (–) means sample is too small to make a reliable estimate.
Source: Calculations by New Strategist based on the 2002 Consumer Expenditure Survey

Table 5.9 Food and Alcohol: Average spending by household type, 2002

(average annual spending of consumer units (CU) on food and alcoholic beverages, by type of consumer unit, 2002)

	total married couples	married couples, no children	married couples with children				single parent, at least one child <18	single person
			total	oldest child under 6	oldest child 6 to 17	oldest child 18 or older		
Number of consumer units (in thousands, add 000)	56,265	23,118	28,790	5,547	15,206	8,036	6,730	33,055
Average number of persons per CU	3.2	2.0	3.9	3.5	4.1	3.9	2.9	1.0
Average before-tax income of CU	$67,155.00	$58,967.00	$73,918.00	$67,587.00	$72,720.00	$81,042.00	$26,966.00	$27,042.00
Average spending of CU, total	52,333.70	45,557.33	57,835.01	52,778.62	58,103.75	60,859.78	30,185.38	24,189.90
Food, average spending	6,881.01	5,675.98	7,785.00	6,348.00	8,040.63	8,323.52	4,745.12	2,913.45
Alcoholic beverages, average spending	441.06	479.14	431.98	340.43	436.46	490.20	146.08	284.95
FOOD AT HOME	**$3,986.74**	**$3,160.44**	**$4,528.07**	**$3,939.52**	**$4,664.31**	**$4,689.75**	**$3,057.19**	**$1,557.57**
Cereals and bakery products	**579.43**	**442.35**	**675.87**	**559.51**	**708.07**	**697.30**	**461.25**	**224.94**
Cereals and cereal products	196.56	140.47	234.75	205.90	248.13	229.29	180.08	74.38
Flour	12.17	8.83	13.43	10.66	15.05	12.24	7.89	3.07
Prepared flour mixes	17.25	14.85	19.09	14.41	20.01	20.71	11.82	4.74
Ready-to-eat and cooked cereals	109.59	78.58	134.21	117.27	145.43	124.29	107.49	46.24
Rice	22.73	14.12	25.96	26.50	23.59	30.27	23.19	6.93
Pasta, cornmeal, and other cereal products	34.83	24.10	42.06	37.04	44.05	41.78	29.69	13.40
Bakery products	382.87	301.88	441.12	353.61	459.94	468.00	281.17	150.56
Bread	103.32	86.18	113.63	97.04	117.02	119.08	78.85	46.67
White bread	43.06	31.81	50.15	42.22	54.31	47.68	39.61	17.89
Bread, other than white	60.26	54.36	63.48	54.82	62.71	71.40	39.24	28.78
Crackers and cookies	93.27	72.80	109.22	87.39	118.69	106.39	67.33	35.82
Cookies	60.80	45.77	72.00	56.75	78.19	70.88	44.62	23.20
Crackers	32.47	27.03	37.22	30.64	40.49	35.52	22.71	12.62
Frozen and refrigerated bakery products	34.38	23.71	41.41	34.57	45.39	38.53	26.19	10.97
Other bakery products	151.90	119.20	176.86	134.62	178.85	204.00	108.79	57.09
Biscuits and rolls	54.35	44.13	62.01	46.31	65.53	66.54	34.51	22.13
Cakes and cupcakes	45.75	32.17	56.19	43.16	55.42	67.32	37.78	16.08
Bread and cracker products	4.78	4.37	4.94	3.71	5.59	4.56	2.93	1.36
Sweetrolls, coffee cakes, doughnuts	34.30	26.53	41.11	32.28	41.13	47.58	26.33	12.16
Pies, tarts, turnovers	12.73	12.00	12.61	9.17	11.17	18.00	7.24	5.36
Meats, poultry, fish, and eggs	**1,025.35**	**812.99**	**1,146.22**	**941.52**	**1,163.09**	**1,263.29**	**832.32**	**359.44**
Beef	303.30	227.09	350.39	274.80	354.75	397.34	225.03	92.89
Ground beef	110.40	77.63	131.58	98.51	137.99	143.14	103.32	34.70
Roast	55.22	43.36	60.35	48.15	57.90	74.24	36.11	15.09
Chuck roast	16.02	12.59	17.59	13.21	16.07	23.86	8.98	3.88
Round roast	14.49	11.56	16.62	18.02	13.77	21.28	10.39	3.19
Other roast	24.71	19.21	26.14	16.93	28.06	29.10	16.74	8.01
Steak	111.12	87.57	127.35	106.97	122.90	151.26	70.06	36.38
Round steak	17.39	13.20	20.81	16.55	20.32	24.92	11.87	5.52
Sirloin steak	34.73	26.35	41.11	43.58	39.73	42.04	23.63	10.65
Other steak	58.99	48.02	65.43	46.84	62.84	84.30	34.56	20.22
Pork	214.86	182.44	229.25	193.26	240.14	234.01	194.64	72.52
Bacon	35.17	31.88	37.34	27.30	39.20	41.01	38.17	13.88
Pork chops	47.76	38.18	52.60	44.03	55.76	52.63	48.76	16.67
Ham	49.86	42.85	51.99	45.42	51.31	58.20	41.20	15.45
Ham, not canned	48.04	41.59	49.91	44.31	48.41	57.01	39.82	14.81
Canned ham	1.82	1.26	2.09	1.11	2.90	1.19	1.38	0.64
Sausage	33.55	26.72	38.22	34.67	38.90	39.48	27.93	12.11
Other pork	48.53	42.81	49.09	41.84	54.98	42.68	38.57	14.40
Other meats	130.52	98.16	152.09	111.63	155.29	175.48	111.39	47.52
Frankfurters	26.13	17.90	32.14	25.81	33.29	34.50	30.44	9.48

	total married couples	married couples, no children	married couples with children				single parent, at least one child <18	single person
			total	oldest child under 6	oldest child 6 to 17	oldest child 18 or older		
Lunch meats (cold cuts)	$88.34	$70.69	$102.19	$78.75	$109.34	$105.18	$71.87	$34.50
Bologna, liverwurst, salami	25.95	20.14	29.74	22.79	30.09	34.16	27.14	11.11
Lamb, organ meats, and others	16.04	9.57	17.76	7.06	12.66	35.80	9.08	3.54
Lamb and organ meats	10.49	8.21	10.70	5.64	9.13	17.58	7.89	3.28
Mutton, goat, and game	5.55	1.36	7.05	1.43	3.53	18.22	1.19	0.26
Poultry	183.07	135.99	212.19	179.78	213.74	232.96	146.41	64.50
Fresh and frozen chicken	143.28	107.32	165.17	138.02	168.34	178.84	109.15	51.64
Fresh and frozen whole chicken	40.38	30.36	44.51	38.87	43.14	51.38	29.16	13.51
Fresh and frozen chicken parts	102.90	76.97	120.67	99.14	125.20	127.47	79.99	38.13
Other poultry	39.79	28.67	47.02	41.76	45.40	54.11	37.27	12.86
Fish and seafood	152.36	134.45	158.26	143.00	155.94	174.14	117.19	63.53
Canned fish and seafood	19.68	17.69	20.31	16.42	20.03	23.73	12.19	11.05
Fresh fish and shellfish	85.92	75.68	86.95	81.93	84.83	94.86	63.32	37.21
Frozen fish and shellfish	46.76	41.08	51.01	44.65	51.08	55.55	41.68	15.27
Eggs	41.24	34.86	44.04	39.05	43.23	49.35	37.66	18.47
Dairy products	**426.04**	**328.91**	**496.51**	**453.53**	**517.24**	**486.79**	**317.54**	**165.84**
Fresh milk and cream	162.42	117.56	193.62	181.84	198.50	192.56	134.85	64.02
Fresh milk, all types	146.02	104.06	175.74	165.54	180.76	173.22	125.61	57.40
Cream	16.40	13.49	17.88	16.31	17.74	19.34	9.24	6.62
Other dairy products	263.62	211.35	302.89	271.69	318.73	294.23	182.70	101.82
Butter	23.86	20.49	26.11	20.34	28.64	25.31	15.70	9.96
Cheese	125.77	102.64	143.56	135.38	147.32	142.08	86.06	47.80
Ice cream and related products	76.46	60.69	88.30	64.64	96.30	89.77	53.63	29.26
Miscellaneous dairy products	37.53	27.55	44.91	51.33	46.48	37.06	27.31	14.80
Fruits and vegetables	**714.27**	**602.09**	**778.53**	**710.61**	**788.75**	**808.16**	**497.70**	**292.02**
Fresh fruits	232.78	201.87	252.29	210.52	259.05	269.57	151.69	96.53
Apples	42.40	35.47	46.52	38.55	51.74	41.99	32.25	17.50
Bananas	38.36	31.71	42.17	36.06	40.21	50.58	28.82	19.04
Oranges	26.94	21.46	30.77	26.06	30.68	34.41	18.75	9.90
Citrus fruits, excl. oranges	18.81	17.78	18.61	17.11	19.32	18.31	11.17	7.67
Other fresh fruits	106.28	95.45	114.22	92.74	117.10	124.28	60.71	42.42
Fresh vegetables	228.71	198.09	240.50	216.17	242.47	254.47	146.12	90.06
Potatoes	41.75	37.41	43.52	37.14	45.61	44.05	33.72	18.63
Lettuce	29.53	25.23	31.97	27.84	31.60	35.74	18.07	11.25
Tomatoes	43.93	35.81	46.63	43.23	43.42	55.52	31.16	15.17
Other fresh vegetables	113.50	99.64	118.38	107.96	121.84	119.15	63.17	45.00
Processed fruits	147.05	114.99	170.18	172.12	171.50	166.12	115.77	62.24
Frozen fruits and fruit juices	15.68	12.19	18.32	18.66	17.99	18.74	11.88	5.93
Frozen orange juice	7.75	5.86	9.16	9.89	9.15	8.64	7.30	2.85
Frozen fruits	3.92	3.78	3.88	2.02	3.92	5.18	1.90	1.43
Frozen fruit juices, excl. orange	4.01	2.54	5.28	6.75	4.92	4.92	2.68	1.65
Canned fruits	20.20	17.63	21.79	23.40	20.00	24.19	13.95	7.78
Dried fruits	7.88	8.26	7.29	8.71	6.18	8.45	4.86	3.28
Fresh fruit juice	27.93	23.77	30.43	23.57	30.45	35.44	18.54	13.45
Canned and bottled fruit juice	75.37	53.14	92.35	97.77	96.88	79.29	66.55	31.81
Processed vegetables	105.73	87.14	115.56	111.80	115.73	118.00	84.12	43.19
Frozen vegetables	35.24	28.95	39.00	33.74	39.77	41.34	24.85	15.30
Canned and dried vegetables and juices	70.49	58.20	76.56	78.06	75.96	76.66	59.27	27.89
Canned beans	15.73	12.55	17.95	20.49	17.65	16.68	14.32	6.36
Canned corn	8.89	6.59	10.35	8.58	10.59	11.18	10.67	3.23
Canned miscellaneous vegetables	23.47	21.41	24.50	24.37	24.18	25.25	16.35	9.03
Dried peas	0.43	0.40	0.45	0.57	0.46	0.34	0.34	0.29
Dried beans	3.15	2.25	3.44	4.72	3.03	3.31	2.70	1.12

	total married couples	married couples, no children	married couples with children				single parent, at least one child <18	single person
			total	oldest child under 6	oldest child 6 to 17	oldest child 18 or older		
Dried miscellaneous vegetables	$9.58	$6.96	$10.24	$11.05	$10.87	$8.37	$7.74	$2.98
Dried processed vegetables	0.44	0.12	0.42	0.19	–	1.43	0.42	0.21
Fresh and canned vegetable juices	8.74	7.85	9.17	8.08	9.09	10.11	6.65	4.64
Sugar and other sweets	**152.73**	**126.11**	**171.66**	**132.03**	**190.19**	**163.85**	**105.78**	**64.04**
Candy and chewing gum	97.78	81.65	110.90	79.39	126.11	103.74	62.72	43.94
Sugar	19.59	14.92	22.05	17.80	22.77	23.73	19.65	6.94
Artificial sweeteners	5.84	5.86	5.59	2.46	6.49	6.10	2.28	2.16
Jams, preserves, other sweets	29.51	23.68	33.12	32.38	34.82	30.28	21.14	11.01
Fats and oils	**109.28**	**92.34**	**119.08**	**91.77**	**118.78**	**139.81**	**86.64**	**43.17**
Margarine	12.64	12.10	11.96	7.60	11.63	15.85	10.45	4.71
Fats and oils	34.41	28.17	37.67	29.38	38.46	42.21	24.94	11.70
Salad dressings	34.00	29.10	37.74	28.18	37.19	45.89	29.03	14.33
Nondairy cream and imitation milk	12.36	10.86	13.33	10.44	12.98	16.17	8.35	4.85
Peanut butter	15.86	12.11	18.37	16.16	18.52	19.69	13.87	7.58
Miscellaneous foods	**601.55**	**446.52**	**716.50**	**729.34**	**727.83**	**684.42**	**493.07**	**250.25**
Frozen prepared foods	118.63	83.96	145.56	112.18	159.55	142.23	112.39	61.57
Frozen meals	31.66	23.67	36.83	36.20	37.46	36.05	29.54	27.68
Other frozen prepared foods	86.96	60.30	108.73	75.97	122.09	106.18	82.85	33.89
Canned and packaged soups	44.37	40.00	47.68	39.56	49.79	49.45	32.81	22.74
Potato chips, nuts, and other snacks	130.92	98.98	158.65	115.27	173.20	161.54	103.73	50.49
Potato chips and other snacks	98.69	63.69	128.45	92.77	141.54	128.61	88.02	35.83
Nuts	32.23	35.29	30.20	22.50	31.66	32.94	15.71	14.67
Condiments and seasonings	113.01	95.43	125.42	107.62	129.51	130.38	78.64	40.28
Salt, spices, and other seasonings	27.71	22.83	30.09	27.13	30.76	30.94	18.07	9.93
Olives, pickles, relishes	12.94	12.38	13.54	9.25	15.10	13.60	7.47	4.78
Sauces and gravies	48.56	36.90	57.42	49.15	58.29	61.78	37.58	16.19
Baking needs and miscellaneous products	23.79	23.32	24.37	22.09	25.36	24.05	15.51	9.39
Other canned/packaged prepared foods	194.63	128.15	239.19	354.72	215.78	200.82	165.50	75.15
Prepared salads	26.47	26.56	26.37	22.50	25.35	31.26	17.97	14.54
Prepared desserts	14.08	11.10	15.59	13.78	16.59	14.93	10.69	4.91
Baby food	44.22	9.46	71.76	222.38	36.05	32.12	37.70	5.15
Miscellaneous prepared foods	109.84	81.03	125.42	96.05	137.71	122.51	98.07	50.54
Nonalcoholic beverages	**318.74**	**252.19**	**363.10**	**275.98**	**381.11**	**391.32**	**244.34**	**136.12**
Cola	99.05	75.06	114.42	91.29	118.75	122.83	77.34	43.02
Other carbonated drinks	55.44	43.45	63.24	46.30	70.23	61.75	45.02	21.26
Coffee	55.19	58.01	54.12	31.22	52.65	73.93	31.09	24.73
Roasted coffee	36.82	37.76	36.99	20.09	35.87	51.69	21.55	15.81
Instant and freeze-dried coffee	18.37	20.25	17.13	11.13	16.78	22.24	9.54	8.92
Noncarbonated fruit-flavored drinks, incl. nonfrozen lemonade	23.07	11.95	30.53	26.21	35.48	23.82	26.55	7.83
Tea	19.96	17.81	19.62	12.24	20.20	23.90	13.83	9.10
Nonalcoholic beer	1.00	0.89	1.01	0.49	1.31	0.80	1.11	0.11
Other nonalcoholic beverages and ice	65.02	45.02	80.16	68.24	82.49	84.29	49.40	30.07
Food prepared by CU on trips	**59.36**	**56.94**	**60.60**	**45.23**	**69.25**	**54.82**	**18.55**	**21.75**
FOOD AWAY FROM HOME	**2,894.27**	**2,515.54**	**3,256.93**	**2,408.48**	**3,376.32**	**3,633.77**	**1,687.93**	**1,355.88**
Meals at restaurants, carry-outs, other	**2,331.17**	**1,993.00**	**2,638.80**	**2,128.46**	**2,701.35**	**2,889.78**	**1,426.85**	**1,153.75**
Lunch	852.03	641.67	1,044.02	805.57	1,088.53	1,130.79	611.20	415.34
• At fast food, take-out, delivery, concession stands, buffet, and cafeteria (other than employer and school cafeteria)	449.71	307.74	572.58	475.79	574.96	639.08	359.40	231.91
• At full-service restaurants	294.00	306.31	293.79	269.95	280.02	338.84	113.74	148.27
• At vending machines, mobile vendors	6.26	2.69	8.43	8.03	9.08	7.43	3.38	4.36
• At employer and school cafeterias	102.07	24.92	169.23	51.80	224.47	145.43	134.68	30.80

	total married couples	married couples, no children	married couples with children				single parent, at least one child <18	single person
			total	oldest child under 6	oldest child 6 to 17	oldest child 18 or older		
Dinner	$959.86	$922.73	$1,000.77	$824.54	$1,016.40	$1,099.33	$429.51	$436.90
• At fast food, take-out, delivery, concession stands, buffet, and cafeteria (other than employer and school cafeteria)	259.76	171.10	330.75	304.57	339.18	333.22	198.12	116.43
• At full-service restaurants	694.91	748.40	663.11	513.44	670.06	759.47	230.37	313.28
• At vending machines, mobile vendors	2.99	2.36	3.51	5.19	2.93	3.43	0.19	0.64
• At employer and school cafeterias	2.21	0.87	3.39	1.34	4.24	3.20	0.83	6.55
Snacks and nonalcoholic beverages	306.00	233.43	364.66	305.90	377.27	382.75	259.90	175.39
• At fast food, take-out, delivery, concession stands, buffet, and cafeteria (other than employer and school cafeteria)	219.41	161.45	268.26	222.43	279.32	279.94	178.78	120.89
• At full-service restaurants	34.72	33.17	33.05	27.47	31.36	40.52	25.71	22.37
• At vending machines, mobile vendors	39.80	32.16	46.83	45.87	44.59	52.03	42.41	25.51
• At employer and school cafeterias	12.08	6.64	16.52	10.14	22.01	10.26	12.99	6.63
Breakfast and brunch	213.27	195.18	229.35	192.45	219.14	276.91	126.24	126.13
• At fast food, take-out, delivery, concession stands, buffet, and cafeteria (other than employer and school cafeteria)	97.83	70.70	119.63	103.57	117.39	135.94	86.90	58.77
• At full-service restaurants	108.52	121.87	99.66	84.20	88.67	132.97	34.88	61.47
• At vending machines, mobile vendors	1.40	0.61	1.95	2.05	1.91	1.97	0.28	1.66
• At employer and school cafeterias	5.51	2.00	8.11	2.63	11.17	6.03	4.18	4.23
Board (including at school)	**60.40**	**29.08**	**93.06**	**14.18**	**55.51**	**218.57**	**32.48**	**37.00**
Catered affairs	**90.20**	**151.46**	**48.52**	**28.17**	**45.03**	**69.17**	**8.43**	**11.78**
Food on trips	297.29	324.25	283.65	203.72	290.42	326.01	78.41	125.11
School lunches	95.42	–	173.64	13.75	266.19	108.89	129.21	–
Meals as pay	**19.80**	**17.75**	**19.26**	**20.20**	**17.81**	**21.35**	**12.55**	**28.24**
ALCOHOLIC BEVERAGES	**441.06**	**479.14**	**431.98**	**340.43**	**436.46**	**490.20**	**146.08**	**284.95**
At home	**267.74**	**276.29**	**270.54**	**215.29**	**283.86**	**284.64**	**96.88**	**165.60**
Beer and ale	119.15	103.45	132.29	112.03	142.61	126.60	54.70	83.48
Whiskey	15.93	17.60	14.77	12.02	15.93	14.47	2.14	10.59
Wine	107.43	125.95	99.73	80.63	96.79	119.69	26.20	50.28
Other alcoholic beverages	25.24	29.29	23.75	10.61	28.54	23.88	13.84	21.25
Away from home	**173.32**	**202.85**	**161.44**	**125.14**	**152.60**	**205.56**	**49.20**	**119.35**
Beer and ale	61.27	73.06	56.26	50.09	58.95	55.43	19.15	43.17
• At fast food, take-out, delivery, concession stands, buffet, and cafeteria	8.10	8.79	7.91	8.90	7.57	7.88	5.44	6.51
• At full-service restaurants	48.70	60.90	42.24	41.13	41.29	44.95	11.60	36.04
• At vending machines, mobile vendors	0.14	0.11	0.19	0.05	0.22	0.22	0.24	0.38
• At catered affairs	4.32	3.26	5.92	–	9.88	2.37	1.88	0.24
Wine	30.30	36.99	27.21	19.25	24.22	39.05	8.12	19.39
• At fast food, take-out, delivery, concession stands, buffet and cafeteria	4.69	4.96	4.38	3.26	4.37	5.24	3.32	3.10
• At full-service restaurants	23.60	31.58	19.15	15.99	18.71	22.35	4.60	16.27
• At catered affairs	2.02	0.45	3.68	–	1.14	11.46	0.20	0.03
Other alcoholic beverages	81.75	92.80	77.97	55.80	69.43	111.08	21.92	56.79
• At fast food, take-out, delivery, concession stands, buffet, and cafeteria	3.29	3.30	2.95	2.76	3.18	2.65	2.22	2.72
• At full-service restaurants	33.35	42.64	28.22	24.72	28.82	29.61	9.60	22.08
• At catered affairs	7.36	1.44	13.59	–	4.35	42.03	0.83	0.10
Alcoholic beverages purchased on trips	37.75	45.43	33.20	28.32	33.09	36.79	9.27	31.88

Note: Average spending figures for total consumer units can be found on Average Spending by Age and Average Spending by Region tables. (–) means sample is too small to make a reliable estimate.

Source: Bureau of Labor Statistics, unpublished tables from the 2002 Consumer Expenditure Survey

Table 5.10 Food and Alcohol: Indexed spending by household type, 2002

(indexed average annual spending of consumer units (CU) on food and alcoholic beverages, by type of consumer unit, 2002; index definition: an index of 100 is the average for all consumer units; an index of 132 means that spending by consumer units in that group is 32 percent above the average for all consumer units; an index of 68 indicates spending that is 32 percent below the average for all consumer units)

| | total married couples | married couples, no children | married couples with children | | | | single parent, at least one child <18 | single person |
			total	oldest child under 6	oldest child 6 to 17	oldest child 18 or older		
Average spending of CU, total	$52,334	$45,557	$57,835	$52,779	$58,104	$60,860	$30,185	$24,190
Average spending of CU, index	129	112	142	130	143	150	74	59
Food, spending index	128	106	145	118	150	155	88	54
Alcoholic beverages, spending index	117	127	115	91	116	130	39	76
FOOD AT HOME	**129**	**102**	**146**	**127**	**151**	**151**	**99**	**50**
Cereals and bakery products	**129**	**98**	**150**	**124**	**157**	**155**	**102**	**50**
Cereals and cereal products	128	91	152	134	161	149	117	48
Flour	141	102	155	123	174	142	91	35
Prepared flour mixes	139	120	154	116	161	167	95	38
Ready-to-eat and cooked cereals	125	90	153	134	166	142	123	53
Rice	128	79	146	149	132	170	130	39
Pasta, cornmeal, and other cereal products	126	88	153	134	160	152	108	49
Bakery products	129	102	149	119	155	158	95	51
Bread	123	103	136	116	140	142	94	56
White bread	122	90	142	120	154	135	112	51
Bread, other than white	124	112	131	113	129	147	81	59
Crackers and cookies	132	103	155	124	168	151	95	51
Cookies	131	99	155	123	169	153	96	50
Crackers	133	111	153	126	166	146	93	52
Frozen and refrigerated bakery products	134	92	162	135	177	150	102	43
Other bakery products	131	103	153	116	154	176	94	49
Biscuits and rolls	132	108	151	113	160	162	84	54
Cakes and cupcakes	128	90	157	121	155	188	106	45
Bread and cracker products	137	125	141	106	160	130	84	39
Sweetrolls, coffee cakes, doughnuts	133	103	159	125	159	184	102	47
Pies, tarts, turnovers	130	122	128	93	114	183	74	55
Meats, poultry, fish, and eggs	**128**	**102**	**144**	**118**	**146**	**158**	**104**	**45**
Beef	131	98	152	119	153	172	97	40
Ground beef	128	90	152	114	160	166	120	40
Roast	135	106	147	117	141	181	88	37
Chuck roast	137	108	150	113	137	204	77	33
Round roast	142	113	162	176	135	208	102	31
Other roast	130	101	137	89	147	153	88	42
Steak	132	104	151	127	145	179	83	43
Round steak	131	99	157	125	153	188	89	42
Sirloin steak	130	99	154	164	149	158	89	40
Other steak	132	108	147	105	141	189	78	45
Pork	128	109	137	115	144	140	116	43
Bacon	124	112	131	96	138	144	134	49
Pork chops	124	99	137	115	145	137	127	43
Ham	134	115	140	122	138	157	111	42
Ham, not canned	135	117	140	124	136	160	112	42
Canned ham	121	84	139	74	193	79	92	43
Sausage	128	102	146	132	149	151	107	46
Other pork	131	115	132	113	148	115	104	39
Other meats	129	97	150	110	154	174	110	47
Frankfurters	125	85	153	123	159	165	145	45

	total married couples	married couples, no children	married couples with children				single parent, at least one child <18	single person
			total	oldest child under 6	oldest child 6 to 17	oldest child 18 or older		
Lunch meats (cold cuts)	128	102	148	114	158	152	104	50
Bologna, liverwurst, salami	123	95	141	108	143	162	129	53
Lamb, organ meats, and others	144	86	159	63	114	321	82	32
Lamb and organ meats	131	103	134	71	114	220	99	41
Mutton, goat, and game	176	43	224	45	112	578	38	8
Poultry	127	94	147	125	148	162	102	45
Fresh and frozen chicken	127	95	146	122	149	158	96	46
Fresh and frozen whole chicken	126	95	139	121	134	160	91	42
Fresh and frozen chicken parts	127	95	149	122	154	157	99	47
Other poultry	129	93	152	135	147	175	121	42
Fish and seafood	126	111	131	118	129	144	97	53
Canned fish and seafood	122	110	126	102	124	147	76	69
Fresh fish and shellfish	124	109	125	118	122	137	91	54
Frozen fish and shellfish	132	116	144	126	144	156	117	43
Eggs	122	103	130	116	128	146	112	55
Dairy products	**130**	**100**	**151**	**138**	**158**	**148**	**97**	**51**
Fresh milk and cream	128	92	152	143	156	151	106	50
Fresh milk, all types	127	91	153	144	158	151	110	50
Cream	131	108	143	130	142	154	74	53
Other dairy products	131	105	151	135	158	146	91	51
Butter	129	111	141	110	155	137	85	54
Cheese	132	107	150	142	154	149	90	50
Ice cream and related products	130	103	150	110	164	153	91	50
Miscellaneous dairy products	132	97	159	181	164	131	96	52
Fruits and vegetables	**129**	**109**	**141**	**129**	**143**	**146**	**90**	**53**
Fresh fruits	131	113	142	118	145	151	85	54
Apples	130	109	143	118	159	129	99	54
Bananas	123	102	135	115	129	162	92	61
Oranges	132	106	151	128	151	169	92	49
Citrus fruits, excl. oranges	132	124	130	120	135	128	78	54
Other fresh fruits	133	120	143	116	147	156	76	53
Fresh vegetables	131	113	138	124	139	146	84	51
Potatoes	125	112	130	111	137	132	101	56
Lettuce	133	114	144	125	142	161	81	51
Tomatoes	130	106	138	128	129	165	92	45
Other fresh vegetables	133	116	138	126	142	139	74	53
Processed fruits	127	100	147	149	148	144	100	54
Frozen fruits and fruit juices	126	98	147	150	144	151	95	48
Frozen orange juice	123	93	145	157	145	137	116	45
Frozen fruits	141	135	139	72	141	186	68	51
Frozen fruit juices, excl. orange	120	76	158	201	147	147	80	49
Canned fruits	134	117	145	155	133	161	93	52
Dried fruits	130	136	120	144	102	139	80	54
Fresh fruit juice	126	107	137	106	137	160	84	61
Canned and bottled fruit juice	126	89	155	164	162	133	111	53
Processed vegetables	127	104	139	134	139	141	101	52
Frozen vegetables	127	104	140	121	143	148	89	55
Canned and dried vegetables and juices	127	105	138	140	137	138	107	50
Canned beans	126	101	144	164	142	134	115	51
Canned corn	121	90	141	117	144	152	145	44
Canned miscellaneous vegetables	131	120	137	137	135	141	92	51
Dried peas	119	111	125	158	128	94	94	81
Dried beans	124	88	135	185	119	130	106	44

	total married couples	married couples, no children	married couples with children				single parent, at least one child <18	single person
			total	oldest child under 6	oldest child 6 to 17	oldest child 18 or older		
Dried miscellaneous vegetables	130	94	139	150	147	113	105	40
Dried processed vegetables	129	35	124	56	–	421	124	62
Fresh and canned vegetable juices	121	109	127	112	126	140	92	64
Sugar and other sweets	**130**	**107**	**146**	**112**	**162**	**140**	**90**	**55**
Candy and chewing gum	130	108	147	105	167	138	83	58
Sugar	126	96	142	114	146	153	126	45
Artificial sweeteners	135	135	129	57	150	141	53	50
Jams, preserves, other sweets	134	107	150	147	158	137	96	50
Fats and oils	**128**	**108**	**140**	**108**	**139**	**164**	**102**	**51**
Margarine	128	123	121	77	118	161	106	48
Fats and oils	132	108	144	113	147	162	96	45
Salad dressings	126	108	140	104	138	170	107	53
Nondairy cream and imitation milk	132	116	143	112	139	173	89	52
Peanut butter	123	94	143	125	144	153	108	59
Miscellaneous foods	**127**	**95**	**152**	**155**	**154**	**145**	**104**	**53**
Frozen prepared foods	121	86	148	114	163	145	115	63
Frozen meals	106	79	123	121	125	121	99	93
Other frozen prepared foods	127	88	159	111	179	156	121	50
Canned and packaged soups	124	112	133	110	139	138	92	63
Potato chips, nuts, and other snacks	130	98	158	115	172	161	103	50
Potato chips and other snacks	129	83	168	121	185	168	115	47
Nuts	133	146	125	93	131	136	65	61
Condiments and seasonings	130	110	144	124	149	150	91	46
Salt, spices, and other seasonings	131	108	142	128	146	146	85	47
Olives, pickles, relishes	133	128	140	95	156	140	77	49
Sauces and gravies	129	98	152	130	154	164	99	43
Baking needs and miscellaneous products	131	128	134	121	139	132	85	52
Other canned/packaged prepared foods	129	85	159	235	143	133	110	50
Prepared salads	123	124	123	105	118	146	84	68
Prepared desserts	136	108	151	134	161	145	104	48
Baby food	140	30	227	704	114	102	119	16
Miscellaneous prepared foods	126	93	144	110	158	140	112	58
Nonalcoholic beverages	**126**	**99**	**143**	**109**	**150**	**154**	**96**	**54**
Cola	122	93	141	113	146	151	95	53
Other carbonated drinks	126	99	144	105	160	141	102	48
Coffee	133	139	130	75	127	178	75	59
Roasted coffee	134	138	135	73	131	189	79	58
Instant and freeze-dried coffee	129	143	121	78	118	157	67	63
Noncarbonated fruit-flavored drinks, incl. nonfrozen lemonade	122	63	161	138	187	126	140	41
Tea	126	112	124	77	127	151	87	57
Nonalcoholic beer	156	139	158	77	205	125	173	17
Other nonalcoholic beverages and ice	125	87	155	132	159	163	95	58
Food prepared by CU on trips	**144**	**138**	**147**	**110**	**168**	**133**	**45**	**53**
FOOD AWAY FROM HOME	**127**	**111**	**143**	**106**	**148**	**160**	**74**	**60**
Meals at restaurants, carry-outs, other	**125**	**107**	**141**	**114**	**145**	**155**	**76**	**62**
Lunch	124	94	152	117	159	165	89	61
• At fast food, take-out, delivery, concession stands, buffet, and cafeteria (other than employer and school cafeteria)	119	81	152	126	152	169	95	61
• At full-service restaurants	131	136	131	120	125	151	51	66
• At vending machines, mobile vendors	114	49	153	146	165	135	61	79
• At employer and school cafeterias	131	32	218	67	289	187	173	40

	total married couples	married couples, no children	married couples with children				single parent, at least one child <18	single person
			total	oldest child under 6	oldest child 6 to 17	oldest child 18 or older		
Dinner	130	125	136	112	138	149	58	59
• At fast food, take-out, delivery, concession stands, buffet, and cafeteria (other than employer and school cafeteria)	122	80	155	143	159	156	93	55
• At full-service restaurants	134	144	128	99	129	147	44	60
• At vending machines, mobile vendors	160	126	188	278	157	183	10	34
• At employer and school cafeterias	67	26	102	40	128	96	25	197
Snacks and nonalcoholic beverages	116	89	139	116	144	146	99	67
• At fast food, take-out, delivery, concession stands, buffet, and cafeteria (other than employer and school cafeteria)	118	87	144	120	150	151	96	65
• At full-service restaurants	115	110	110	91	104	134	85	74
• At vending machines, mobile vendors	108	88	128	125	121	142	116	69
• At employer and school cafeterias	119	66	163	100	218	101	128	66
Breakfast and brunch	118	108	126	106	121	153	70	70
• At fast food, take-out, delivery, concession stands, buffet, and cafeteria (other than employer and school cafeteria)	111	80	136	118	134	155	99	67
• At full-service restaurants	125	140	114	97	102	153	40	71
• At vending machines, mobile vendors	100	44	139	146	136	141	20	119
• At employer and school cafeterias	108	39	159	51	219	118	82	83
Board (including at school)	**130**	**62**	**200**	**30**	**119**	**470**	**70**	**80**
Catered affairs	**131**	**220**	**70**	**41**	**65**	**100**	**12**	**17**
Food on trips	**141**	**153**	**134**	**96**	**137**	**154**	**37**	**59**
School lunches	**159**	**–**	**289**	**23**	**444**	**181**	**215**	**–**
Meals as pay	**87**	**78**	**84**	**88**	**78**	**93**	**55**	**124**
ALCOHOLIC BEVERAGES	**117**	**127**	**115**	**91**	**116**	**130**	**39**	**76**
At home	**117**	**121**	**119**	**94**	**124**	**125**	**42**	**73**
Beer and ale	106	92	118	100	127	113	49	74
Whiskey	115	127	106	86	115	104	15	76
Wine	138	162	128	104	124	154	34	65
Other alcoholic beverages	105	122	99	44	118	99	57	88
Away from home	**117**	**137**	**109**	**85**	**103**	**139**	**33**	**81**
Beer and ale	116	138	106	95	112	105	36	82
• At fast food, take-out, delivery, concession stands, buffet, and cafeteria	101	110	99	111	95	99	68	81
• At full-service restaurants	116	145	101	98	98	107	28	86
• At vending machines, mobile vendors	44	34	59	16	69	69	75	119
• At catered affairs	167	126	229	–	381	92	73	9
Wine	117	143	105	74	94	151	31	75
• At fast food, take-out, delivery, concession stands, buffet and cafeteria	106	112	99	74	99	119	75	70
• At full-service restaurants	116	155	94	79	92	110	23	80
• At catered affairs	185	41	338	–	105	1,051	18	3
Other alcoholic beverages	118	134	113	81	100	161	32	82
• At fast food, take-out, delivery, concession stands, buffet, and cafeteria	94	94	84	79	91	76	63	78
• At full-service restaurants	115	147	98	85	100	102	33	76
• At catered affairs	187	37	345	–	110	1,067	21	3
Alcoholic beverages purchased on trips	115	139	101	86	101	112	28	97

Note: Spending index for total consumer units is 100. (–) means sample is too small to make a reliable estimate.
Source: Calculations by New Strategist based on the 2002 Consumer Expenditure Survey

Table 5.11 Food and Alcohol: Total spending by household type, 2002

(total annual spending on food and alcoholic beverages, by consumer unit (CU) type, 2002; numbers in thousands)

	total married couples	married couples, no children	married couples with children total	oldest child under 6	oldest child 6 to 17	oldest child 18 or older	single parent, at least one child <18	single person
Number of consumer units	56,265	23,118	28,790	5,547	15,206	8,036	6,730	33,055
Total spending of all CUs	$2,944,555,631	$1,053,194,355	$1,665,069,938	$292,763,005	$883,525,623	$489,069,192	$203,147,607	$799,597,145
Food, total spending	387,160,028	131,217,306	224,130,150	35,212,356	122,265,820	66,887,807	31,934,658	96,304,090
Alcoholic beverages, total spending	24,816,241	11,076,759	12,436,704	1,888,365	6,636,811	3,939,247	983,118	9,419,022
FOOD AT HOME	**$224,313,926**	**$73,063,052**	**$130,363,135**	**$21,852,517**	**$70,925,498**	**$37,686,831**	**$20,574,889**	**$51,485,476**
Cereals and bakery products	32,601,629	10,226,247	19,458,297	3,103,602	10,766,912	5,603,503	3,104,213	7,435,392
Cereals and cereal products	11,059,448	3,247,385	6,758,453	1,142,127	3,773,065	1,842,574	1,211,938	2,458,631
Flour	684,745	204,132	386,650	59,131	228,850	98,361	53,100	101,479
Prepared flour mixes	970,571	343,302	549,601	79,932	304,272	166,426	79,549	156,681
Ready-to-eat and cooked cereals	6,166,081	1,816,612	3,863,906	650,497	2,211,409	998,794	723,408	1,528,463
Rice	1,278,903	326,426	747,388	146,996	358,710	243,250	156,069	229,071
Pasta, cornmeal, and other cereal products	1,959,710	557,144	1,210,907	205,461	669,824	335,744	199,814	442,937
Bakery products	21,542,181	6,978,862	12,699,845	1,961,475	6,993,848	3,760,848	1,892,274	4,976,761
Bread	5,813,300	1,992,309	3,271,408	538,281	1,779,406	956,927	530,661	1,542,677
White bread	2,422,771	735,384	1,443,819	234,194	825,838	383,156	266,575	591,354
Bread, other than white	3,390,529	1,256,694	1,827,589	304,087	953,568	573,770	264,085	951,323
Crackers and cookies	5,247,837	1,682,990	3,144,444	484,752	1,804,800	854,950	453,131	1,184,030
Cookies	3,420,912	1,058,111	2,072,880	314,792	1,188,957	569,592	300,293	766,876
Crackers	1,826,925	624,880	1,071,564	169,960	615,691	285,439	152,838	417,154
Frozen and refrigerated bakery products	1,934,391	548,128	1,192,194	191,760	690,200	309,627	176,259	362,613
Other bakery products	8,546,654	2,755,666	5,091,799	746,737	2,719,593	1,639,344	732,157	1,887,110
Biscuits and rolls	3,058,003	1,020,197	1,785,268	256,882	996,449	534,715	232,252	731,507
Cakes and cupcakes	2,574,124	743,706	1,617,710	239,409	842,717	540,984	254,259	531,524
Bread and cracker products	268,947	101,026	142,223	20,579	85,002	36,644	19,719	44,955
Sweetrolls, coffee cakes, doughnuts	1,929,890	613,321	1,183,557	179,057	625,423	382,353	177,201	401,949
Pies, tarts, turnovers	716,253	277,416	363,042	50,866	169,851	144,648	48,725	177,175
Meats, poultry, fish, and eggs	**57,691,318**	**18,794,703**	**32,999,674**	**5,222,611**	**17,685,947**	**10,151,798**	**5,601,514**	**11,881,289**
Beef	17,065,175	5,249,867	10,087,728	1,524,316	5,394,329	3,193,024	1,514,452	3,070,479
Ground beef	6,211,656	1,794,650	3,788,188	546,435	2,098,276	1,150,273	695,344	1,147,009
Roast	3,106,953	1,002,396	1,737,477	267,088	880,427	596,593	243,020	498,800
Chuck roast	901,365	291,056	506,416	73,276	244,360	191,739	60,435	128,253
Round roast	815,280	267,244	478,490	99,957	209,387	171,006	69,925	105,445
Other roast	1,390,308	444,097	752,571	93,911	426,680	233,848	112,660	264,771
Steak	6,252,167	2,024,443	3,666,407	593,363	1,868,817	1,215,525	471,504	1,202,541
Round steak	978,448	305,158	599,120	91,803	308,986	200,257	79,885	182,464
Sirloin steak	1,954,083	609,159	1,183,557	241,738	604,134	337,833	159,030	352,036
Other steak	3,319,072	1,110,126	1,883,730	259,821	955,545	677,435	232,589	668,372
Pork	12,089,098	4,217,648	6,600,108	1,072,013	3,651,569	1,880,504	1,309,927	2,397,149
Bacon	1,978,840	737,002	1,075,019	151,433	596,075	329,556	256,884	458,803
Pork chops	2,687,216	882,645	1,514,354	244,234	847,887	422,935	328,155	551,027
Ham	2,805,373	990,606	1,496,792	251,945	780,220	467,695	277,276	510,700
Ham, not canned	2,702,971	961,478	1,436,909	245,788	736,122	458,132	267,989	489,545
Canned ham	102,402	29,129	60,171	6,157	44,097	9,563	9,287	21,155
Sausage	1,887,691	617,713	1,100,354	192,314	591,513	317,261	187,969	400,296
Other pork	2,730,540	989,682	1,413,301	232,086	836,026	342,976	259,576	475,992
Other meats	7,343,708	2,269,263	4,378,671	619,212	2,361,340	1,410,157	749,655	1,570,774
Frankfurters	1,470,204	413,812	925,311	143,168	506,208	277,242	204,861	313,361

	total married couples	married couples, no children	married couples with children			single parent, at least one child <18	single person
			total	oldest child under 6	oldest child 6 to 17	oldest child 18 or older	
Lunch meats (cold cuts)	$4,970,450	$1,634,211	$2,942,050	$436,826	$1,662,624	$845,226	$483,685	$1,140,398
Bologna, liverwurst, salami	1,460,077	465,597	856,215	126,416	457,549	274,510	182,652	367,241
Lamb, organ meats, and others	902,491	221,239	511,310	39,162	192,508	287,689	61,108	117,015
Lamb and organ meats	590,220	189,799	308,053	31,285	138,831	141,273	53,100	108,420
Mutton, goat, and game	312,271	31,440	202,970	7,932	53,677	146,416	8,009	8,594
Poultry	10,300,434	3,143,817	6,108,950	997,240	3,250,130	1,872,067	985,339	2,132,048
Fresh and frozen chicken	8,061,649	2,481,024	4,755,244	765,597	2,559,778	1,437,158	734,580	1,706,960
Fresh and frozen whole chicken	2,271,981	701,862	1,281,443	215,612	655,987	412,890	196,247	446,573
Fresh and frozen chicken parts	5,789,669	1,779,392	3,474,089	549,930	1,903,791	1,024,349	538,333	1,260,387
Other poultry	2,238,784	662,793	1,353,706	231,643	690,352	434,828	250,827	425,087
Fish and seafood	8,572,535	3,108,215	4,556,305	793,221	2,371,224	1,399,389	788,689	2,099,984
Canned fish and seafood	1,107,295	408,957	584,725	91,082	304,576	190,694	82,039	365,258
Fresh fish and shellfish	4,834,289	1,749,570	2,503,291	454,466	1,289,925	762,295	426,144	1,229,977
Frozen fish and shellfish	2,630,951	949,687	1,468,578	247,674	776,722	446,400	280,506	504,750
Eggs	2,320,369	805,893	1,267,912	216,610	657,355	396,577	253,452	610,526
Dairy products	**23,971,141**	**7,603,741**	**14,294,523**	**2,515,731**	**7,865,151**	**3,911,844**	**2,137,044**	**5,481,841**
Fresh milk and cream	9,138,561	2,717,752	5,574,320	1,008,666	3,018,391	1,547,412	907,541	2,116,181
Fresh milk, all types	8,215,815	2,405,659	5,059,555	918,250	2,748,637	1,391,996	845,355	1,897,357
Cream	922,746	311,862	514,765	90,472	269,754	155,416	62,185	218,824
Other dairy products	14,832,579	4,885,989	8,720,203	1,507,064	4,846,608	2,364,432	1,229,571	3,365,660
Butter	1,342,483	473,688	751,707	112,826	435,500	203,391	105,661	329,228
Cheese	7,076,449	2,372,832	4,133,092	750,953	2,240,148	1,141,755	579,184	1,580,029
Ice cream and related products	4,302,022	1,403,031	2,542,157	358,558	1,464,338	721,392	360,930	967,189
Miscellaneous dairy products	2,111,625	636,901	1,292,959	284,728	706,775	297,814	183,796	489,214
Fruits and vegetables	**40,188,402**	**13,919,117**	**22,413,879**	**3,941,754**	**11,993,733**	**6,494,374**	**3,349,521**	**9,652,721**
Fresh fruits	13,097,367	4,666,831	7,263,429	1,167,754	3,939,114	2,166,265	1,020,874	3,190,799
Apples	2,385,636	819,995	1,339,311	213,837	786,758	337,432	217,043	578,463
Bananas	2,158,325	733,072	1,214,074	200,025	611,433	406,461	193,959	629,367
Oranges	1,515,779	496,112	885,868	144,555	466,520	276,519	126,188	327,245
Citrus fruits, excl. oranges	1,058,345	411,038	535,782	94,909	293,780	147,139	75,174	253,532
Other fresh fruits	5,979,844	2,206,613	3,288,394	514,429	1,780,623	998,714	408,578	1,402,193
Fresh vegetables	12,868,368	4,579,445	6,923,995	1,199,095	3,686,999	2,044,921	983,388	2,976,933
Potatoes	2,349,064	864,844	1,252,941	206,016	693,546	353,986	226,936	615,815
Lettuce	1,661,505	583,267	920,416	154,428	480,510	287,207	121,611	371,869
Tomatoes	2,471,721	827,856	1,342,478	239,797	660,245	446,159	209,707	501,444
Other fresh vegetables	6,386,078	2,303,478	3,408,160	598,854	1,852,699	957,489	425,134	1,487,475
Processed fruits	8,273,768	2,658,339	4,899,482	954,750	2,607,829	1,334,940	779,132	2,057,343
Frozen fruits and fruit juices	882,235	281,808	527,433	103,507	273,556	150,595	79,952	196,016
Frozen orange juice	436,054	135,471	263,716	54,860	139,135	69,431	49,129	94,207
Frozen fruits	220,559	87,386	111,705	11,205	59,608	41,626	12,787	47,269
Frozen fruit juices, excl. orange	225,623	58,720	152,011	37,442	74,814	39,537	18,036	54,541
Canned fruits	1,136,553	407,570	627,334	129,800	304,120	194,391	93,884	257,168
Dried fruits	443,368	190,955	209,879	48,314	93,973	67,904	32,708	108,420
Fresh fruit juice	1,571,481	549,515	876,080	130,743	463,023	284,796	124,774	444,590
Canned and bottled fruit juice	4,240,693	1,228,491	2,658,757	542,330	1,473,157	637,174	447,882	1,051,480
Processed vegetables	5,948,898	2,014,503	3,326,972	620,155	1,759,790	948,248	566,128	1,427,645
Frozen vegetables	1,982,779	669,266	1,122,810	187,156	604,743	332,208	167,241	505,742
Canned and dried vegetables and juices	3,966,120	1,345,468	2,204,162	432,999	1,155,048	616,040	398,887	921,904
Canned beans	885,048	290,131	516,781	113,658	268,386	134,040	96,374	210,230
Canned corn	500,196	152,348	297,977	47,593	161,032	89,842	71,809	106,768
Canned miscellaneous vegetables	1,320,540	494,956	705,355	135,180	367,681	202,909	110,036	298,487
Dried peas	24,194	9,247	12,956	3,162	6,995	2,732	2,288	9,586
Dried beans	177,235	52,016	99,038	26,182	46,074	26,599	18,171	37,022

	total married couples	married couples, no children	married couples with children				single parent, at least one child <18	single person
			total	oldest child under 6	oldest child 6 to 17	oldest child 18 or older		
Dried miscellaneous vegetables	$539,019	$160,901	$294,810	$61,294	$165,289	$67,261	$52,090	$98,504
Dried processed vegetables	24,757	2,774	12,092	1,054	–	11,491	2,827	6,942
Fresh and canned vegetable juices	491,756	181,476	264,004	44,820	138,223	81,244	44,755	153,375
Sugar and other sweets	**8,593,353**	**2,915,411**	**4,942,091**	**732,370**	**2,892,029**	**1,316,699**	**711,899**	**2,116,842**
Candy and chewing gum	5,501,592	1,887,585	3,192,811	440,376	1,917,629	833,655	422,106	1,452,437
Sugar	1,102,231	344,921	634,820	98,737	346,241	190,694	132,245	229,402
Artificial sweeteners	328,588	135,471	160,936	13,646	98,687	49,020	15,344	71,399
Jams, preserves, other sweets	1,660,380	547,434	953,525	179,612	529,473	243,330	142,272	363,936
Fats and oils	**6,148,639**	**2,134,716**	**3,428,313**	**509,048**	**1,806,169**	**1,123,513**	**583,087**	**1,426,984**
Margarine	711,190	279,728	344,328	42,157	176,846	127,371	70,329	155,689
Fats and oils	1,936,079	651,234	1,084,519	162,971	584,823	339,200	167,846	386,744
Salad dressings	1,913,010	672,734	1,086,535	156,314	565,511	368,772	195,372	473,678
Nondairy cream and imitation milk	695,435	251,061	383,771	57,911	197,374	129,942	56,196	160,317
Peanut butter	892,363	279,959	528,872	89,640	281,615	158,229	93,345	250,557
Miscellaneous foods	**33,846,211**	**10,322,649**	**20,628,035**	**4,045,649**	**11,067,383**	**5,499,999**	**3,318,361**	**8,272,014**
Frozen prepared foods	6,674,717	1,940,987	4,190,672	622,262	2,426,117	1,142,960	756,385	2,035,196
Frozen meals	1,781,350	547,203	1,060,336	200,801	569,617	289,698	198,804	914,962
Other frozen prepared foods	4,892,804	1,394,015	3,130,337	421,406	1,856,501	853,262	557,581	1,120,234
Canned and packaged soups	2,496,478	924,720	1,372,707	219,439	757,107	397,380	220,811	751,671
Potato chips, nuts, and other snacks	7,366,214	2,288,220	4,567,534	639,403	2,633,679	1,298,135	698,103	1,668,947
Potato chips and other snacks	5,552,793	1,472,385	3,698,076	514,595	2,152,257	1,033,510	592,375	1,184,361
Nuts	1,813,421	815,834	869,458	124,808	481,422	264,706	105,728	484,917
Condiments and seasonings	6,358,508	2,206,151	3,610,842	596,968	1,969,329	1,047,734	529,247	1,331,455
Salt, spices, and other seasonings	1,559,103	527,784	866,291	150,490	467,737	248,634	121,611	328,236
Olives, pickles, relishes	728,069	286,201	389,817	51,310	229,611	109,290	50,273	158,003
Sauces and gravies	2,732,228	853,054	1,653,122	272,635	886,358	496,464	252,913	535,160
Baking needs and miscellaneous products	1,338,544	539,112	701,612	122,533	385,624	193,266	104,382	310,386
Other canned/packaged prepared foods	10,950,857	2,962,572	6,886,280	1,967,632	3,281,151	1,613,790	1,113,815	2,484,083
Prepared salads	1,489,335	614,014	759,192	124,808	385,472	251,205	120,938	480,620
Prepared desserts	792,211	256,610	448,836	76,438	252,268	119,977	71,944	162,300
Baby food	2,488,038	218,696	2,065,970	1,233,542	548,176	258,116	253,721	170,233
Miscellaneous prepared foods	6,180,148	1,873,252	3,610,842	532,789	2,094,018	984,490	660,011	1,670,600
Nonalcoholic beverages	**17,933,906**	**5,830,128**	**10,453,649**	**1,530,861**	**5,795,159**	**3,144,648**	**1,644,408**	**4,499,447**
Cola	5,573,048	1,735,237	3,294,152	506,386	1,805,713	987,062	520,498	1,422,026
Other carbonated drinks	3,119,332	1,004,477	1,820,680	256,826	1,067,917	496,223	302,985	702,749
Coffee	3,105,265	1,341,075	1,558,115	173,177	800,596	594,101	209,236	817,450
Roasted coffee	2,071,677	872,936	1,064,942	111,439	545,439	415,381	145,032	522,600
Instant and freeze-dried coffee	1,033,588	468,140	493,173	61,738	255,157	178,721	64,204	294,851
Noncarbonated fruit-flavored drinks, incl. nonfrozen lemonade	1,298,034	276,260	878,959	145,387	539,509	191,418	178,682	258,821
Tea	1,123,049	411,732	564,860	67,895	307,161	192,060	93,076	300,801
Nonalcoholic beer	56,265	20,575	29,078	2,718	19,920	6,429	7,470	3,636
Other nonalcoholic beverages and ice	3,658,350	1,040,772	2,307,806	378,527	1,254,343	677,354	332,462	993,964
Food prepared by CU on trips	**3,339,890**	**1,316,339**	**1,744,674**	**250,891**	**1,053,016**	**440,534**	**124,842**	**718,946**
FOOD AWAY FROM HOME	**162,846,102**	**58,154,254**	**93,767,015**	**13,359,839**	**51,340,322**	**29,200,976**	**11,359,769**	**44,818,613**
Meals at restaurants, carry-outs, other	**131,163,280**	**46,074,174**	**75,971,052**	**11,806,568**	**41,076,728**	**23,222,272**	**9,602,701**	**38,137,206**
Lunch	47,939,468	14,834,127	30,057,336	4,468,497	16,552,187	9,087,028	4,113,376	13,729,064
• At fast food, take-out, delivery, concession stands, buffet, and cafeteria (other than employer and school cafeteria)	25,302,933	7,114,333	16,484,578	2,639,207	8,742,842	5,135,647	2,418,762	7,665,785
• At full-service restaurants	16,541,910	7,081,275	8,458,214	1,497,413	4,257,984	2,722,918	765,470	4,901,065
• At vending machines, mobile vendors	352,219	62,187	242,700	44,542	138,070	59,707	22,747	144,120
• At employer and school cafeterias	5,742,969	576,101	4,872,132	287,335	3,413,291	1,168,675	906,396	1,018,094

	total married couples	married couples, no children	married couples with children				single parent, at least one child <18	single person
			total	oldest child under 6	oldest child 6 to 17	oldest child 18 or older		
Dinner	$54,006,523	$21,331,672	$28,812,168	$4,573,723	$15,455,378	$8,834,216	$2,890,602	$14,441,730
• At fast food, take-out, delivery, concession stands, buffet, and cafeteria (other than employer and school cafeteria)	14,615,396	3,955,490	9,522,293	1,689,450	5,157,571	2,677,756	1,333,348	3,848,594
• At full-service restaurants	39,099,111	17,301,511	19,090,937	2,848,052	10,188,932	6,103,101	1,550,390	10,355,470
• At vending machines, mobile vendors	168,232	54,558	101,053	28,789	44,554	27,563	1,279	21,155
• At employer and school cafeterias	124,346	20,113	97,598	7,433	64,473	25,715	5,586	216,510
Snacks and nonalcoholic beverages	17,217,090	5,396,435	10,498,561	1,696,827	5,736,768	3,075,779	1,749,127	5,797,516
• At fast food, take-out, delivery, concession stands, buffet, and cafeteria (other than employer and school cafeteria)	12,345,104	3,732,401	7,723,205	1,233,819	4,247,340	2,249,598	1,203,189	3,996,019
• At full-service restaurants	1,953,521	766,824	951,510	152,376	476,860	325,619	173,028	739,440
• At vending machines, mobile vendors	2,239,347	743,475	1,348,236	254,441	678,036	418,113	285,419	843,233
• At employer and school cafeterias	679,681	153,504	475,611	56,247	334,684	82,449	87,423	219,155
Breakfast and brunch	11,999,637	4,512,171	6,602,987	1,067,520	3,332,243	2,225,249	849,595	4,169,227
• At fast food, take-out, delivery, concession stands, buffet, and cafeteria (other than employer and school cafeteria)	5,504,405	1,634,443	3,444,148	574,503	1,785,032	1,092,414	584,837	1,942,642
• At full-service restaurants	6,105,878	2,817,391	2,869,211	467,057	1,348,316	1,068,547	234,742	2,031,891
• At vending machines, mobile vendors	78,771	14,102	56,141	11,371	29,043	15,831	1,884	54,871
• At employer and school cafeterias	310,020	46,236	233,487	14,589	169,851	48,457	28,131	139,823
Board (including at school)	**3,398,406**	**672,271**	**2,679,197**	**78,656**	**844,085**	**1,756,429**	**218,590**	**1,223,035**
Catered affairs	**5,075,103**	**3,501,452**	**1,396,891**	**156,259**	**684,726**	**555,850**	**56,734**	**389,388**
Food on trips	**16,727,022**	**7,496,012**	**8,166,284**	**1,130,035**	**4,416,127**	**2,619,816**	**527,699**	**4,135,511**
School lunches	**5,368,806**	**–**	**4,999,096**	**76,271**	**4,047,685**	**875,040**	**869,583**	**–**
Meals as pay	**1,114,047**	**410,345**	**554,495**	**112,049**	**270,819**	**171,569**	**84,462**	**933,473**
ALCOHOLIC BEVERAGES	**24,816,241**	**11,076,759**	**12,436,704**	**1,888,365**	**6,636,811**	**3,939,247**	**983,118**	**9,419,022**
At home	**15,064,391**	**6,387,272**	**7,788,847**	**1,194,214**	**4,316,375**	**2,287,367**	**652,002**	**5,473,908**
Beer and ale	6,703,975	2,391,557	3,808,629	621,430	2,168,528	1,017,358	368,131	2,759,431
Whiskey	896,301	406,877	425,228	66,675	242,232	116,281	14,402	350,052
Wine	6,044,549	2,911,712	2,871,227	447,255	1,471,789	961,829	176,326	1,662,005
Other alcoholic beverages	1,420,129	677,126	683,763	58,854	433,979	191,900	93,143	702,419
Away from home	**9,751,850**	**4,689,486**	**4,647,858**	**694,152**	**2,320,436**	**1,651,880**	**331,116**	**3,945,114**
Beer and ale	3,447,357	1,689,001	1,619,725	277,849	896,394	445,435	128,880	1,426,984
• At fast food, take-out, delivery, concession stands, buffet, and cafeteria	455,747	203,207	227,729	49,368	115,109	63,324	36,611	215,188
• At full-service restaurants	2,740,106	1,407,886	1,216,090	228,148	627,856	361,218	78,068	1,191,302
• At vending machines, mobile vendors	7,877	2,543	5,470	277	3,345	1,768	1,615	12,561
• At catered affairs	243,065	75,365	170,437	–	150,235	19,045	12,652	7,933
Wine	1,704,830	855,135	783,376	106,780	368,289	313,806	54,648	640,936
• At fast food, take-out, delivery, concession stands, buffet and cafeteria	263,883	114,665	126,100	18,083	66,450	42,109	22,344	102,471
• At full-service restaurants	1,327,854	730,066	551,329	88,697	284,504	179,605	30,958	537,805
• At catered affairs	113,655	10,403	105,947	–	17,335	92,093	1,346	992
Other alcoholic beverages	4,599,664	2,145,350	2,244,756	309,523	1,055,753	892,639	147,522	1,877,193
• At fast food, take-out, delivery, concession stands, buffet, and cafeteria	185,112	76,289	84,931	15,310	48,355	21,295	14,941	89,910
• At full-service restaurants	1,876,438	985,752	812,454	137,122	438,237	237,946	64,608	729,854
• At catered affairs	414,110	33,290	391,256	–	66,146	337,753	5,586	3,306
Alcoholic beverages purchased on trips	2,124,004	1,050,251	955,828	157,091	503,167	295,644	62,387	1,053,793

Note: Total spending figures for total consumer units can be found on Total Spending by Age and Total Spending by Region tables. Spending by type of consumer unit will not add to total because not all types of consumer units are shown. (–) means sample is too small to make a reliable estimate.
Source: Calculations by New Strategist based on the 2002 Consumer Expenditure Survey

Table 5.12 Food and Alcohol: Market shares by household type, 2002

(percentage of total annual spending on food and alcoholic beverages accounted for by types of consumer units, 2002)

	total married couples	married couples, no children	married couples with children				single parent, at least one child <18	single person
			total	oldest child under 6	oldest child 6 to 17	oldest child 18 or older		
Share of total consumer units	50.2%	20.6%	25.7%	4.9%	13.6%	7.2%	6.0%	29.5%
Share of total before-tax income	68.2	24.6	38.4	6.8	20.0	11.8	3.3	16.1
Share of total spending	64.6	23.1	36.5	6.4	19.4	10.7	4.5	17.5
Share of food spending	64.3	21.8	37.2	5.8	20.3	11.1	5.3	16.0
Share of alcoholic beverages spending	58.9	26.3	29.5	4.5	15.7	9.3	2.3	22.3
FOOD AT HOME	**64.6%**	**21.0%**	**37.5%**	**6.3%**	**20.4%**	**10.8%**	**5.9%**	**14.8%**
Cereals and bakery products	**64.6**	**20.3**	**38.6**	**6.2**	**21.3**	**11.1**	**6.2**	**14.7**
Cereals and cereal products	64.0	18.8	39.1	6.6	21.8	10.7	7.0	14.2
Flour	70.6	21.1	39.9	6.1	23.6	10.1	5.5	10.5
Prepared flour mixes	69.8	24.7	39.5	5.7	21.9	12.0	5.7	11.3
Ready-to-eat and cooked cereals	62.7	18.5	39.3	6.6	22.5	10.2	7.4	15.6
Rice	64.0	16.3	37.4	7.4	18.0	12.2	7.8	11.5
Pasta, cornmeal, and other cereal products	63.5	18.0	39.2	6.7	21.7	10.9	6.5	14.3
Bakery products	64.9	21.0	38.3	5.9	21.1	11.3	5.7	15.0
Bread	61.9	21.2	34.8	5.7	18.9	10.2	5.6	16.4
White bread	61.4	18.6	36.6	5.9	20.9	9.7	6.8	15.0
Bread, other than white	62.2	23.1	33.5	5.6	17.5	10.5	4.8	17.5
Crackers and cookies	66.2	21.2	39.7	6.1	22.8	10.8	5.7	14.9
Cookies	65.9	20.4	39.9	6.1	22.9	11.0	5.8	14.8
Crackers	66.9	22.9	39.2	6.2	22.5	10.5	5.6	15.3
Frozen and refrigerated bakery products	67.3	19.1	41.5	6.7	24.0	10.8	6.1	12.6
Other bakery products	65.8	21.2	39.2	5.7	20.9	12.6	5.6	14.5
Biscuits and rolls	66.5	22.2	38.8	5.6	21.7	11.6	5.0	15.9
Cakes and cupcakes	64.3	18.6	40.4	6.0	21.0	13.5	6.3	13.3
Bread and cracker products	68.5	25.7	36.2	5.2	21.7	9.3	5.0	11.5
Sweetrolls, coffee cakes, doughnuts	66.6	21.2	40.9	6.2	21.6	13.2	6.1	13.9
Pies, tarts, turnovers	65.1	25.2	33.0	4.6	15.4	13.1	4.4	16.1
Meats, poultry, fish, and eggs	**64.5**	**21.0**	**36.9**	**5.8**	**19.8**	**11.3**	**6.3**	**13.3**
Beef	65.8	20.3	38.9	5.9	20.8	12.3	5.8	11.8
Ground beef	64.2	18.6	39.2	5.6	21.7	11.9	7.2	11.9
Roast	67.6	21.8	37.8	5.8	19.2	13.0	5.3	10.9
Chuck roast	68.7	22.2	38.6	5.6	18.6	14.6	4.6	9.8
Round roast	71.1	23.3	41.7	8.7	18.3	14.9	6.1	9.2
Other roast	65.1	20.8	35.2	4.4	20.0	10.9	5.3	12.4
Steak	66.0	21.4	38.7	6.3	19.7	12.8	5.0	12.7
Round steak	65.7	20.5	40.2	6.2	20.7	13.4	5.4	12.2
Sirloin steak	65.5	20.4	39.7	8.1	20.2	11.3	5.3	11.8
Other steak	66.4	22.2	37.7	5.2	19.1	13.6	4.7	13.4
Pork	64.4	22.5	35.2	5.7	19.5	10.0	7.0	12.8
Bacon	62.0	23.1	33.7	4.7	18.7	10.3	8.1	14.4
Pork chops	62.4	20.5	35.1	5.7	19.7	9.8	7.6	12.8
Ham	67.3	23.8	35.9	6.0	18.7	11.2	6.7	12.3
Ham, not canned	67.6	24.1	35.9	6.1	18.4	11.5	6.7	12.2
Canned ham	60.9	17.3	35.8	3.7	26.2	5.7	5.5	12.6
Sausage	64.3	21.1	37.5	6.6	20.2	10.8	6.4	13.6
Other pork	65.6	23.8	34.0	5.6	20.1	8.2	6.2	11.4
Other meats	64.8	20.0	38.6	5.5	20.8	12.4	6.6	13.9
Frankfurters	62.6	17.6	39.4	6.1	21.6	11.8	8.7	13.3

	total married couples	married couples, no children	married couples with children				single parent, at least one child <18	single person
			total	oldest child under 6	oldest child 6 to 17	oldest child 18 or older		
Lunch meats (cold cuts)	64.3%	21.1%	38.0%	5.6%	21.5%	10.9%	6.3%	14.7%
Bologna, liverwurst, salami	61.7	19.7	36.2	5.3	19.3	11.6	7.7	15.5
Lamb, organ meats, and others	72.3	17.7	40.9	3.1	15.4	23.0	4.9	9.4
Lamb and organ meats	65.9	21.2	34.4	3.5	15.5	15.8	5.9	12.1
Mutton, goat, and game	88.4	8.9	57.5	2.2	15.2	41.5	2.3	2.4
Poultry	63.7	19.5	37.8	6.2	20.1	11.6	6.1	13.2
Fresh and frozen chicken	63.5	19.5	37.5	6.0	20.2	11.3	5.8	13.4
Fresh and frozen whole chicken	63.2	19.5	35.6	6.0	18.2	11.5	5.5	12.4
Fresh and frozen chicken parts	63.6	19.6	38.2	6.0	20.9	11.3	5.9	13.9
Other poultry	64.7	19.1	39.1	6.7	19.9	12.6	7.2	12.3
Fish and seafood	63.2	22.9	33.6	5.8	17.5	10.3	5.8	15.5
Canned fish and seafood	61.2	22.6	32.3	5.0	16.8	10.5	4.5	20.2
Fresh fish and shellfish	62.2	22.5	32.2	5.8	16.6	9.8	5.5	15.8
Frozen fish and shellfish	66.1	23.8	36.9	6.2	19.5	11.2	7.0	12.7
Eggs	61.3	21.3	33.5	5.7	17.4	10.5	6.7	16.1
Dairy products	**65.1**	**20.7**	**38.8**	**6.8**	**21.4**	**10.6**	**5.8**	**14.9**
Fresh milk and cream	64.1	19.1	39.1	7.1	21.2	10.9	6.4	14.8
Fresh milk, all types	63.9	18.7	39.4	7.1	21.4	10.8	6.6	14.8
Cream	65.7	22.2	36.7	6.4	19.2	11.1	4.4	15.6
Other dairy products	65.8	21.7	38.7	6.7	21.5	10.5	5.5	14.9
Butter	64.8	22.9	36.3	5.4	21.0	9.8	5.1	15.9
Cheese	66.0	22.1	38.5	7.0	20.9	10.6	5.4	14.7
Ice cream and related products	65.3	21.3	38.6	5.4	22.2	11.0	5.5	14.7
Miscellaneous dairy products	66.5	20.1	40.7	9.0	22.3	9.4	5.8	15.4
Fruits and vegetables	**64.9**	**22.5**	**36.2**	**6.4**	**19.4**	**10.5**	**5.4**	**15.6**
Fresh fruits	65.6	23.4	36.4	5.8	19.7	10.8	5.1	16.0
Apples	65.3	22.4	36.7	5.9	21.5	9.2	5.9	15.8
Bananas	61.6	20.9	34.7	5.7	17.5	11.6	5.5	18.0
Oranges	66.5	21.8	38.8	6.3	20.5	12.1	5.5	14.4
Citrus fruits, excl. oranges	66.1	25.7	33.4	5.9	18.3	9.2	4.7	15.8
Other fresh fruits	66.9	24.7	36.8	5.8	19.9	11.2	4.6	15.7
Fresh vegetables	65.6	23.4	35.3	6.1	18.8	10.4	5.0	15.2
Potatoes	62.8	23.1	33.5	5.5	18.5	9.5	6.1	16.5
Lettuce	66.7	23.4	36.9	6.2	19.3	11.5	4.9	14.9
Tomatoes	65.4	21.9	35.5	6.3	17.5	11.8	5.5	13.3
Other fresh vegetables	66.5	24.0	35.5	6.2	19.3	10.0	4.4	15.5
Processed fruits	63.9	20.5	37.8	7.4	20.1	10.3	6.0	15.9
Frozen fruits and fruit juices	63.2	20.2	37.8	7.4	19.6	10.8	5.7	14.0
Frozen orange juice	61.6	19.2	37.3	7.8	19.7	9.8	6.9	13.3
Frozen fruits	70.5	27.9	35.7	3.6	19.1	13.3	4.1	15.1
Frozen fruit juices, excl. orange	60.1	15.6	40.5	10.0	19.9	10.5	4.8	14.5
Canned fruits	67.3	24.1	37.2	7.7	18.0	11.5	5.6	15.2
Dried fruits	65.3	28.1	30.9	7.1	13.8	10.0	4.8	16.0
Fresh fruit juice	63.1	22.1	35.2	5.3	18.6	11.4	5.0	17.9
Canned and bottled fruit juice	63.3	18.3	39.7	8.1	22.0	9.5	6.7	15.7
Processed vegetables	63.6	21.5	35.6	6.6	18.8	10.1	6.1	15.3
Frozen vegetables	63.5	21.4	36.0	6.0	19.4	10.6	5.4	16.2
Canned and dried vegetables and juices	63.7	21.6	35.4	6.9	18.5	9.9	6.4	14.8
Canned beans	63.3	20.8	37.0	8.1	19.2	9.6	6.9	15.0
Canned corn	60.8	18.5	36.2	5.8	19.6	10.9	8.7	13.0
Canned miscellaneous vegetables	66.0	24.7	35.2	6.8	18.4	10.1	5.5	14.9
Dried peas	59.9	22.9	32.1	7.8	17.3	6.8	5.7	23.8
Dried beans	62.0	18.2	34.6	9.2	16.1	9.3	6.4	13.0

	total married couples	married couples, no children	married couples with children			single parent, at least one child <18	single person
			total	oldest child under 6	oldest child 6 to 17	oldest child 18 or older		
Dried miscellaneous vegetables	65.1%	19.4%	35.6%	7.4%	20.0%	8.1%	6.3%	11.9%
Dried processed vegetables	64.9	7.3	31.7	2.8	–	30.1	7.4	18.2
Fresh and canned vegetable juices	60.7	22.4	32.6	5.5	17.1	10.0	5.5	18.9
Sugar and other sweets	65.3	22.2	37.6	5.6	22.0	10.0	5.4	16.1
Candy and chewing gum	65.1	22.3	37.8	5.2	22.7	9.9	5.0	17.2
Sugar	**63.2**	**19.8**	**36.4**	**5.7**	**19.8**	**10.9**	**7.6**	**13.2**
Artificial sweeteners	67.7	27.9	33.2	2.8	20.3	10.1	3.2	14.7
Jams, preserves, other sweets	67.1	22.1	38.6	7.3	21.4	9.8	5.8	14.7
Fats and oils	**64.4**	**22.4**	**35.9**	**5.3**	**18.9**	**11.8**	**6.1**	**14.9**
Margarine	64.3	25.3	31.2	3.8	16.0	11.5	6.4	14.1
Fats and oils	66.2	22.3	37.1	5.6	20.0	11.6	5.7	13.2
Salad dressings	63.2	22.2	35.9	5.2	18.7	12.2	6.5	15.6
Nondairy cream and imitation milk	66.5	24.0	36.7	5.5	18.9	12.4	5.4	15.3
Peanut butter	61.8	19.4	36.6	6.2	19.5	10.9	6.5	17.3
Miscellaneous foods	**64.0**	**19.5**	**39.0**	**7.6**	**20.9**	**10.4**	**6.3**	**15.6**
Frozen prepared foods	60.7	17.7	38.1	5.7	22.1	10.4	6.9	18.5
Frozen meals	53.2	16.3	31.7	6.0	17.0	8.6	5.9	27.3
Other frozen prepared foods	64.0	18.2	40.9	5.5	24.3	11.2	7.3	14.6
Canned and packaged soups	62.2	23.0	34.2	5.5	18.9	9.9	5.5	18.7
Potato chips, nuts, and other snacks	65.4	20.3	40.5	5.7	23.4	11.5	6.2	14.8
Potato chips and other snacks	64.9	17.2	43.2	6.0	25.1	12.1	6.9	13.8
Nuts	67.0	30.1	32.1	4.6	17.8	9.8	3.9	17.9
Condiments and seasonings	65.3	22.7	37.1	6.1	20.2	10.8	5.4	13.7
Salt, spices, and other seasonings	65.8	22.3	36.6	6.3	19.7	10.5	5.1	13.8
Olives, pickles, relishes	67.0	26.3	35.8	4.7	21.1	10.1	4.6	14.5
Sauces and gravies	64.5	20.1	39.0	6.4	20.9	11.7	6.0	12.6
Baking needs and miscellaneous products	65.6	26.4	34.4	6.0	18.9	9.5	5.1	15.2
Other canned/packaged prepared foods	64.8	17.5	40.8	11.6	19.4	9.6	6.6	14.7
Prepared salads	61.9	25.5	31.6	5.2	16.0	10.4	5.0	20.0
Prepared desserts	68.5	22.2	38.8	6.6	21.8	10.4	6.2	14.0
Baby food	70.3	6.2	58.4	34.9	15.5	7.3	7.2	4.8
Miscellaneous prepared foods	63.2	19.2	36.9	5.4	21.4	10.1	6.7	17.1
Nonalcoholic beverages	**63.0**	**20.5**	**36.7**	**5.4**	**20.4**	**11.0**	**5.8**	**15.8**
Cola	61.3	19.1	36.2	5.6	19.9	10.9	5.7	15.6
Other carbonated drinks	63.3	20.4	37.0	5.2	21.7	10.1	6.2	14.3
Coffee	66.6	28.8	33.4	3.7	17.2	12.7	4.5	17.5
Roasted coffee	67.5	28.4	34.7	3.6	17.8	13.5	4.7	17.0
Instant and freeze-dried coffee	64.9	29.4	31.0	3.9	16.0	11.2	4.0	18.5
Noncarbonated fruit-flavored drinks, incl. nonfrozen lemonade	61.1	13.0	41.4	6.8	25.4	9.0	8.4	12.2
Tea	63.2	23.2	31.8	3.8	17.3	10.8	5.2	16.9
Nonalcoholic beer	78.4	28.7	40.5	3.8	27.8	9.0	10.4	5.1
Other nonalcoholic beverages and ice	62.9	17.9	39.7	6.5	21.6	11.7	5.7	17.1
Food prepared by CU on trips	**72.3**	**28.5**	**37.8**	**5.4**	**22.8**	**9.5**	**2.7**	**15.6**
FOOD AWAY FROM HOME	**63.8**	**22.8**	**36.7**	**5.2**	**20.1**	**11.4**	**4.5**	**17.6**
Meals at restaurants, carry-outs, other	**62.7**	**22.0**	**36.3**	**5.6**	**19.6**	**11.1**	**4.6**	**18.2**
Lunch	62.4	19.3	39.1	5.8	21.5	11.8	5.4	17.9
• At fast food, take-out, delivery, concession stands, buffet, and cafeteria (other than employer and school cafeteria)	59.8	16.8	38.9	6.2	20.6	12.1	5.7	18.1
• At full-service restaurants	65.6	28.1	33.6	5.9	16.9	10.8	3.0	19.4
• At vending machines, mobile vendors	57.1	10.1	39.4	7.2	22.4	9.7	3.7	23.4
• At employer and school cafeterias	65.9	6.6	55.9	3.3	39.2	13.4	10.4	11.7

	total married couples	married couples, no children	married couples with children				single parent, at least one child <18	single person
			total	oldest child under 6	oldest child 6 to 17	oldest child 18 or older		
Dinner	65.4%	25.8%	34.9%	5.5%	18.7%	10.7%	3.5%	17.5%
• At fast food, take-out, delivery, concession stands, buffet, and cafeteria (other than employer and school cafeteria)	61.1	16.5	39.8	7.1	21.6	11.2	5.6	16.1
• At full-service restaurants	67.3	29.8	32.9	4.9	17.5	10.5	2.7	17.8
• At vending machines, mobile vendors	80.2	26.0	48.2	13.7	21.3	13.1	0.6	10.1
• At employer and school cafeterias	33.4	5.4	26.2	2.0	17.3	6.9	1.5	58.2
Snacks and nonalcoholic beverages	58.5	18.3	35.7	5.8	19.5	10.4	5.9	19.7
• At fast food, take-out, delivery, concession stands, buffet, and cafeteria (other than employer and school cafeteria)	59.3	17.9	37.1	5.9	20.4	10.8	5.8	19.2
• At full-service restaurants	57.8	22.7	28.1	4.5	14.1	9.6	5.1	21.9
• At vending machines, mobile vendors	54.4	18.1	32.8	6.2	16.5	10.2	6.9	20.5
• At employer and school cafeterias	60.0	13.5	42.0	5.0	29.5	7.3	7.7	19.3
Breakfast and brunch	59.0	22.2	32.5	5.2	16.4	10.9	4.2	20.5
• At fast food, take-out, delivery, concession stands, buffet, and cafeteria (other than employer and school cafeteria)	55.9	16.6	35.0	5.8	18.1	11.1	5.9	19.7
• At full-service restaurants	62.5	28.9	29.4	4.8	13.8	10.9	2.4	20.8
• At vending machines, mobile vendors	50.2	9.0	35.8	7.2	18.5	10.1	1.2	35.0
• At employer and school cafeterias	54.1	8.1	40.8	2.5	29.6	8.5	4.9	24.4
Board (including at school)	**65.1**	**12.9**	**51.4**	**1.5**	**16.2**	**33.7**	**4.2**	**23.4**
Catered affairs	**65.6**	**45.3**	**18.1**	**2.0**	**8.9**	**7.2**	**0.7**	**5.0**
Food on trips	**70.5**	**31.6**	**34.4**	**4.8**	**18.6**	**11.0**	**2.2**	**17.4**
School lunches	**79.8**	**–**	**74.3**	**1.1**	**60.2**	**13.0**	**12.9**	**–**
Meals as pay	**43.5**	**16.0**	**21.6**	**4.4**	**10.6**	**6.7**	**3.3**	**36.4**
ALCOHOLIC BEVERAGES	**58.9**	**26.3**	**29.5**	**4.5**	**15.7**	**9.3**	**2.3**	**22.3**
At home	**58.9**	**25.0**	**30.5**	**4.7**	**16.9**	**8.9**	**2.5**	**21.4**
Beer and ale	53.2	19.0	30.2	4.9	17.2	8.1	2.9	21.9
Whiskey	57.5	26.1	27.3	4.3	15.5	7.5	0.9	22.5
Wine	69.3	33.4	32.9	5.1	16.9	11.0	2.0	19.1
Other alcoholic beverages	52.6	25.1	25.3	2.2	16.1	7.1	3.4	26.0
Away from home	**58.8**	**28.3**	**28.0**	**4.2**	**14.0**	**10.0**	**2.0**	**23.8**
Beer and ale	58.2	28.5	27.3	4.7	15.1	7.5	2.2	24.1
• At fast food, take-out, delivery, concession stands, buffet, and cafeteria	50.9	22.7	25.4	5.5	12.9	7.1	4.1	24.0
• At full-service restaurants	58.3	29.9	25.9	4.9	13.4	7.7	1.7	25.3
• At vending machines, mobile vendors	22.0	7.1	15.2	0.8	9.3	4.9	4.5	35.0
• At catered affairs	83.7	26.0	58.7	–	51.7	6.6	4.4	2.7
Wine	58.8	29.5	27.0	3.7	12.7	10.8	1.9	22.1
• At fast food, take-out, delivery, concession stands, buffet and cafeteria	53.4	23.2	25.5	3.7	13.4	8.5	4.5	20.7
• At full-service restaurants	58.2	32.0	24.2	3.9	12.5	7.9	1.4	23.6
• At catered affairs	93.0	8.5	86.7	–	14.2	75.4	1.1	0.8
Other alcoholic beverages	59.3	27.7	29.0	4.0	13.6	11.5	1.9	24.2
• At fast food, take-out, delivery, concession stands, buffet, and cafeteria	47.2	19.4	21.6	3.9	12.3	5.4	3.8	22.9
• At full-service restaurants	57.8	30.4	25.0	4.2	13.5	7.3	2.0	22.5
• At catered affairs	93.8	7.5	88.6	–	15.0	76.5	1.3	0.7
Alcoholic beverages purchased on trips	57.8	28.6	26.0	4.3	13.7	8.0	1.7	28.7

Note: Market share for total consumer units is 100.0%. Market shares by type of consumer unit will not add to total because not all types of consumer units are shown. (–) means sample is too small to make a reliable estimate.
Source: Calculations by New Strategist based on the 2002 Consumer Expenditure Survey

Table 5.13 Food and Alcohol: Average spending by race and Hispanic origin, 2002

(average annual spending of consumer units (CU) on food and alcoholic beverages, by race and Hispanic origin of consumer unit reference person, 2002)

	total consumer units	race		Hispanic origin	
		black	white and other	Hispanic	non-Hispanic
Number of consumer units					
(in thousands, add 000)	**112,108**	**13,554**	**98,553**	**10,500**	**101,608**
Average number of persons per CU	2.5	2.7	2.5	3.3	2.4
Average before-tax income of CU	$49,430.00	$35,944.00	$51,177.00	$37,360.00	$50,742.00
Average spending of CU, total	40,676.60	30,135.94	42,134.55	34,742.47	41,294.67
Food, average spending	5,374.80	4,185.81	5,542.10	5,665.63	5,348.83
Alcoholic beverages, average spending	375.95	189.73	402.24	301.40	383.12
FOOD AT HOME	**$3,098.52**	**$2,668.70**	**$3,159.28**	**$3,642.73**	**$3,047.25**
Cereals and bakery products	**450.13**	**389.85**	**458.67**	**498.17**	**445.60**
Cereals and cereal products	154.07	151.92	154.38	190.64	150.62
Flour	8.65	12.76	8.07	19.78	7.60
Prepared flour mixes	12.40	11.38	12.55	9.97	12.63
Ready-to-eat and cooked cereals	87.66	79.29	88.84	90.87	87.35
Rice	17.82	22.18	17.21	32.01	16.49
Pasta, cornmeal, and other cereal products	27.54	26.30	27.72	38.00	26.56
Bakery products	296.06	237.93	304.29	307.53	294.98
Bread	83.83	72.79	85.39	102.53	82.06
White bread	35.21	34.27	35.34	49.56	33.85
Bread, other than white	48.62	38.51	50.05	52.98	48.21
Crackers and cookies	70.67	54.85	72.91	67.88	70.93
Cookies	46.31	39.83	47.23	47.61	46.19
Crackers	24.36	15.01	25.68	20.27	24.75
Frozen and refrigerated bakery products	25.64	20.42	26.38	20.63	26.11
Other bakery products	115.92	89.87	119.61	116.49	115.87
Biscuits and rolls	41.04	25.56	43.23	30.80	42.00
Cakes and cupcakes	35.73	37.64	35.46	38.40	35.47
Bread and cracker products	3.50	2.12	3.69	2.19	3.62
Sweetrolls, coffee cakes, doughnuts	25.84	16.15	27.21	30.43	25.41
Pies, tarts, turnovers	9.82	8.40	10.02	14.67	9.36
Meats, poultry, fish, and eggs	**798.42**	**862.35**	**789.37**	**1,057.26**	**774.00**
Beef	231.17	220.38	232.70	334.10	221.46
Ground beef	86.29	94.34	85.15	114.38	83.64
Roast	40.99	42.52	40.78	64.65	38.76
Chuck roast	11.71	14.92	11.25	18.38	11.08
Round roast	10.23	11.93	9.99	14.62	9.82
Other roast	19.05	15.67	19.53	31.65	17.87
Steak	84.47	68.37	86.75	120.21	81.10
Round steak	13.29	10.03	13.75	26.06	12.08
Sirloin steak	26.62	23.45	27.07	42.26	25.14
Other steak	44.56	34.89	45.93	51.90	43.87
Pork	167.34	207.66	161.63	216.31	162.72
Bacon	28.45	35.02	27.52	33.59	27.96
Pork chops	38.43	55.08	36.07	55.99	36.77
Ham	37.16	35.28	37.43	52.18	35.74
Ham, not canned	35.66	33.96	35.91	50.02	34.31
Canned ham	1.50	1.32	1.52	2.16	1.43
Sausage	26.17	35.66	24.83	24.54	26.32
Other pork	37.13	46.62	35.78	50.00	35.91
Other meats	101.08	95.95	101.81	109.63	100.27
Frankfurters	20.95	24.24	20.49	26.71	20.41

	total consumer units	race		Hispanic origin	
		black	white and other	Hispanic	non-Hispanic
Lunch meats (cold cuts)	$68.99	$60.88	$70.14	$72.02	$68.70
Bologna, liverwurst, salami	21.11	24.62	20.61	26.86	20.57
Lamb, organ meats, and others	11.14	10.83	11.18	10.90	11.16
Lamb and organ meats	7.99	9.13	7.83	10.26	7.78
Mutton, goat, and game	3.15	1.69	3.35	0.64	3.38
Poultry	144.13	168.14	140.72	202.22	138.64
Fresh and frozen chicken	113.25	128.24	111.13	170.75	107.82
Fresh and frozen whole chicken	32.08	38.84	31.12	61.21	29.33
Fresh and frozen chicken parts	81.17	89.40	80.01	109.54	78.50
Other poultry	30.88	39.91	29.60	31.47	30.82
Fish and seafood	120.97	133.25	119.23	136.95	119.46
Canned fish and seafood	16.13	14.45	16.36	17.38	16.01
Fresh fish and shellfish	69.31	82.49	67.44	93.68	67.01
Frozen fish and shellfish	35.53	36.31	35.42	25.89	36.44
Eggs	33.75	36.97	33.29	58.04	31.45
Dairy products	**328.34**	**231.70**	**342.03**	**385.35**	**322.96**
Fresh milk and cream	127.15	96.41	131.50	168.18	123.27
Fresh milk, all types	114.63	89.32	118.21	154.61	110.86
Cream	12.52	7.09	13.29	13.57	12.42
Other dairy products	201.19	135.29	210.53	217.17	199.69
Butter	18.48	17.03	18.69	17.55	18.57
Cheese	95.64	55.38	101.34	104.20	94.83
Ice cream and related products	58.74	44.04	60.83	61.63	58.47
Miscellaneous dairy products	28.33	18.85	29.67	33.79	27.81
Fruits and vegetables	**552.01**	**460.21**	**565.02**	**719.70**	**536.19**
Fresh fruits	178.20	136.20	184.15	242.12	172.17
Apples	32.59	26.29	33.48	43.10	31.60
Bananas	31.24	26.64	31.89	49.02	29.57
Oranges	20.34	18.63	20.58	29.75	19.45
Citrus fruits, excl. oranges	14.29	9.92	14.91	25.33	13.25
Other fresh fruits	79.74	54.73	83.28	94.92	78.31
Fresh vegetables	174.88	128.44	181.46	247.31	168.04
Potatoes	33.35	29.70	33.87	41.19	32.61
Lettuce	22.22	13.80	23.41	30.92	21.40
Tomatoes	33.71	25.93	34.81	63.80	30.87
Other fresh vegetables	85.60	59.01	89.36	111.40	83.16
Processed fruits	115.50	113.88	115.73	138.45	113.34
Frozen fruits and fruit juices	12.45	12.15	12.49	11.10	12.58
Frozen orange juice	6.31	6.84	6.23	5.38	6.40
Frozen fruits	2.79	1.58	2.96	1.93	2.87
Frozen fruit juices, excl. orange	3.35	3.72	3.30	3.78	3.31
Canned fruits	15.06	11.41	15.58	13.49	15.21
Dried fruits	6.06	3.30	6.46	4.44	6.22
Fresh fruit juice	22.20	19.86	22.53	23.46	22.08
Canned and bottled fruit juice	59.74	67.16	58.68	85.96	57.26
Processed vegetables	83.43	81.69	83.68	91.83	82.64
Frozen vegetables	27.85	26.19	28.08	21.21	28.47
Canned and dried vegetables and juices	55.58	55.50	55.60	70.62	54.17
Canned beans	12.47	15.87	11.99	15.89	12.14
Canned corn	7.34	8.94	7.12	11.22	6.98
Canned miscellaneous vegetables	17.85	13.06	18.52	14.04	18.21
Dried peas	0.36	0.25	0.38	0.40	0.36
Dried beans	2.55	3.14	2.47	9.42	1.90

	total consumer units	race		Hispanic origin	
		black	white and other	Hispanic	non-Hispanic
Dried miscellaneous vegetables	$7.38	$7.14	$7.42	$12.03	$6.94
Dried processed vegetables	0.34	0.08	0.38	0.49	0.32
Fresh and canned vegetable juices	7.23	6.87	7.28	7.13	7.24
Sugar and other sweets	**117.39**	**90.91**	**121.14**	**109.85**	**118.10**
Candy and chewing gum	75.44	47.83	79.35	58.71	77.02
Sugar	15.56	21.45	14.73	22.77	14.88
Artificial sweeteners	4.33	3.08	4.50	5.27	4.24
Jams, preserves, other sweets	22.06	18.55	22.56	23.11	21.96
Fats and oils	**85.16**	**80.86**	**85.77**	**102.04**	**83.57**
Margarine	9.86	9.79	9.87	9.67	9.88
Fats and oils	26.08	32.55	25.16	47.37	24.07
Salad dressings	27.01	20.73	27.89	25.33	27.16
Nondairy cream and imitation milk	9.33	5.75	9.83	7.47	9.50
Peanut butter	12.89	12.03	13.01	12.20	12.96
Miscellaneous foods	**471.92**	**340.11**	**490.59**	**458.46**	**473.19**
Frozen prepared foods	98.09	59.97	103.49	69.54	100.79
Frozen meals	29.88	17.80	31.59	19.76	30.83
Other frozen prepared foods	68.22	42.17	71.91	49.77	69.96
Canned and packaged soups	35.82	26.40	37.15	30.98	36.28
Potato chips, nuts, and other snacks	100.53	68.22	105.10	83.59	102.13
Potato chips and other snacks	76.37	53.04	79.68	68.73	77.09
Nuts	24.16	15.18	25.43	14.87	25.03
Condiments and seasonings	86.81	67.17	89.59	89.23	86.58
Salt, spices, and other seasonings	21.14	22.25	20.99	27.43	20.55
Olives, pickles, relishes	9.70	6.04	10.21	8.26	9.83
Sauces and gravies	37.78	29.08	39.01	38.58	37.71
Baking needs and miscellaneous products	18.19	9.80	19.37	14.95	18.49
Other canned/packaged prepared foods	150.67	118.35	155.25	185.13	147.42
Prepared salads	21.46	14.60	22.43	12.41	22.31
Prepared desserts	10.32	6.21	10.91	10.34	10.32
Baby food	31.57	34.72	31.12	44.89	30.31
Miscellaneous prepared foods	87.24	62.30	90.77	117.50	84.38
Nonalcoholic beverages	**253.94**	**199.33**	**261.67**	**279.43**	**251.53**
Cola	81.11	62.78	83.71	102.17	79.12
Other carbonated drinks	43.93	33.53	45.41	41.56	44.16
Coffee	41.59	24.34	44.03	32.35	42.46
Roasted coffee	27.38	15.35	29.08	20.19	28.05
Instant and freeze-dried coffee	14.21	8.99	14.95	12.17	14.40
Noncarbonated fruit-flavored drinks, incl. nonfrozen lemonade	18.95	26.17	17.93	31.38	17.78
Tea	15.86	11.48	16.48	13.96	16.04
Nonalcoholic beer	0.64	–	0.74	–	0.70
Other nonalcoholic beverages and ice	51.85	41.02	53.39	58.00	51.27
Food prepared by CU on trips	**41.20**	**13.38**	**45.02**	**32.47**	**42.10**
FOOD AWAY FROM HOME	**2,276.29**	**1,517.10**	**2,382.82**	**2,022.90**	**2,301.58**
Meals at restaurants, carry-outs, other	**1,866.42**	**1,348.07**	**1,939.83**	**1,767.56**	**1,875.74**
Lunch	685.79	529.35	707.94	711.00	683.41
• At fast food, take-out, delivery, concession stands, buffet, and cafeteria (other than employer and school cafeteria)	377.71	350.70	381.53	446.95	371.17
• At full-service restaurants	224.82	89.28	244.01	176.94	229.34
• At vending machines, mobile vendors	5.50	4.70	5.61	16.81	4.43
• At employer and school cafeterias	77.76	84.67	76.78	70.31	78.46

	total consumer units	race		Hispanic origin	
		black	white and other	Hispanic	non-Hispanic
Dinner	$736.54	$457.85	$776.01	$585.41	$750.80
• At fast food, take-out, delivery, concession stands, buffet, and cafeteria (other than employer and school cafeteria)	213.33	192.42	216.29	243.66	210.47
• At full-service restaurants	518.02	257.80	554.87	333.94	535.39
• At vending machines, mobile vendors	1.87	1.58	1.91	4.76	1.60
• At employer and school cafeterias	3.32	6.05	2.93	3.05	3.34
Snacks and nonalcoholic beverages	262.67	219.23	268.83	261.66	262.77
• At fast food, take-out, delivery, concession stands, buffet, and cafeteria (other than employer and school cafeteria)	185.69	155.97	189.90	170.92	187.08
• At full-service restaurants	30.17	20.36	31.56	38.83	29.35
• At vending machines, mobile vendors	36.71	32.58	37.29	42.55	36.16
• At employer and school cafeterias	10.11	10.31	10.08	9.36	10.18
Breakfast and brunch	181.42	141.65	187.05	209.49	178.77
• At fast food, take-out, delivery, concession stands, buffet, and cafeteria (other than employer and school cafeteria)	87.83	95.98	86.68	129.03	83.94
• At full-service restaurants	87.08	39.59	93.80	72.07	88.49
• At vending machines, mobile vendors	1.40	0.59	1.52	2.07	1.34
• At employer and school cafeterias	5.11	5.49	5.05	6.31	4.99
Board (including at school)	**46.54**	**18.39**	**50.41**	**21.77**	**49.10**
Catered affairs	**69.00**	**11.21**	**76.94**	**21.95**	**73.86**
Food on trips	**211.49**	**85.74**	**228.78**	**125.39**	**220.38**
School lunches	**60**	**40.7**	**62.65**	**51.75**	**60.85**
Meals as pay	**22.86**	**12.99**	**24.21**	**34.49**	**21.66**
ALCOHOLIC BEVERAGES	**375.95**	**189.73**	**402.24**	**301.4**	**383.12**
At home	**228.08**	**133.21**	**241.52**	**210.49**	**229.74**
Beer and ale	112.34	79.21	117.04	145.11	109.25
Whiskey	13.9	9.46	14.53	10.31	14.24
Wine	77.75	28.65	84.7	42.07	81.11
Other alcoholic beverages	24.09	15.9	25.25	13	25.14
Away from home	**147.87**	**56.52**	**160.72**	**90.91**	**153.38**
Beer and ale	52.86	22.15	57.21	33.65	54.67
• At fast food, take-out, delivery, concession stands, buffet, and cafeteria	7.99	4.2	8.53	9.86	7.81
• At full-service restaurants	41.95	17.62	45.4	23.64	43.68
• At vending machines, mobile vendors	0.32	0.33	0.32	0.14	0.34
• At catered affairs	2.59	–	2.96	–	2.84
Wine	25.85	13.09	27.66	18.17	26.58
• At fast food, take-out, delivery, concession stands, buffet and cafeteria	4.41	4.03	4.46	5.41	4.32
• At full-service restaurants	20.36	9.06	21.96	12.49	21.1
• At catered affairs	1.09	–	1.24	0.27	1.16
Other alcoholic beverages	69.16	21.28	75.85	39.09	72.13
• At fast food, take-out, delivery, concession stands, buffet, and cafeteria	3.5	1.06	3.85	4.63	3.39
• At full-service restaurants	28.94	8.91	31.78	16.92	30.08
• At catered affairs	3.94	–	4.5	–	4.31
Alcoholic beverages purchased on trips	32.78	11.31	35.73	17.55	34.35

Note: Other races include Asians, Native Americans, and Pacific Islanders. (–) means sample is too small to make a reliable estimate.
Source: Bureau of Labor Statistics, unpublished tables from the 2002 Consumer Expenditure Survey

Table 5.14 Food and Alcohol: Indexed spending by race and Hispanic origin, 2002

(indexed average annual spending of consumer units (CU) on food and alcoholic beverages, by race and Hispanic origin of consumer unit reference person, 2002; index definition: an index of 100 is the average for all consumer units; an index of 132 means that spending by consumer units in that group is 32 percent above the average for all consumer units; an index of 68 indicates spending that is 32 percent below the average for all consumer units)

	total consumer units	race black	race white and other	Hispanic origin Hispanic	Hispanic origin non-Hispanic
Average spending of CU, total	$40,677	$30,136	$42,135	$34,742	$41,295
Average spending of CU, index	100	74	104	85	102
Food, spending index	100	78	103	105	100
Alcoholic beverages, spending index	100	50	107	80	102
FOOD AT HOME	100	86	102	118	98
Cereals and bakery products	100	87	102	111	99
Cereals and cereal products	100	99	100	124	98
Flour	100	148	93	229	88
Prepared flour mixes	100	92	101	80	102
Ready-to-eat and cooked cereals	100	90	101	104	100
Rice	100	124	97	180	93
Pasta, cornmeal, and other cereal products	100	95	101	138	96
Bakery products	100	80	103	104	100
Bread	100	87	102	122	98
White bread	100	97	100	141	96
Bread, other than white	100	79	103	109	99
Crackers and cookies	100	78	103	96	100
Cookies	100	86	102	103	100
Crackers	100	62	105	83	102
Frozen and refrigerated bakery products	100	80	103	80	102
Other bakery products	100	78	103	100	100
Biscuits and rolls	100	62	105	75	102
Cakes and cupcakes	100	105	99	107	99
Bread and cracker products	100	61	105	63	103
Sweetrolls, coffee cakes, doughnuts	100	63	105	118	98
Pies, tarts, turnovers	100	86	102	149	95
Meats, poultry, fish, and eggs	100	108	99	132	97
Beef	100	95	101	145	96
Ground beef	100	109	99	133	97
Roast	100	104	99	158	95
Chuck roast	100	127	96	157	95
Round roast	100	117	98	143	96
Other roast	100	82	103	166	94
Steak	100	81	103	142	96
Round steak	100	75	103	196	91
Sirloin steak	100	88	102	159	94
Other steak	100	78	103	116	98
Pork	100	124	97	129	97
Bacon	100	123	97	118	98
Pork chops	100	143	94	146	96
Ham	100	95	101	140	96
Ham, not canned	100	95	101	140	96
Canned ham	100	88	101	144	95
Sausage	100	136	95	94	101
Other pork	100	126	96	135	97
Other meats	100	95	101	108	99
Frankfurters	100	116	98	127	97

	total consumer units	race		Hispanic origin	
		black	white and other	Hispanic	non-Hispanic
Lunch meats (cold cuts)	100	88	102	104	100
Bologna, liverwurst, salami	100	117	98	127	97
Lamb, organ meats, and others	100	97	100	98	100
Lamb and organ meats	100	114	98	128	97
Mutton, goat, and game	100	54	106	20	107
Poultry	100	117	98	140	96
Fresh and frozen chicken	100	113	98	151	95
Fresh and frozen whole chicken	100	121	97	191	91
Fresh and frozen chicken parts	100	110	99	135	97
Other poultry	100	129	96	102	100
Fish and seafood	100	110	99	113	99
Canned fish and seafood	100	90	101	108	99
Fresh fish and shellfish	100	119	97	135	97
Frozen fish and shellfish	100	102	100	73	103
Eggs	100	110	99	172	93
Dairy products	**100**	**71**	**104**	**117**	**98**
Fresh milk and cream	100	76	103	132	97
Fresh milk, all types	100	78	103	135	97
Cream	100	57	106	108	99
Other dairy products	100	67	105	108	99
Butter	100	92	101	95	100
Cheese	100	58	106	109	99
Ice cream and related products	100	75	104	105	100
Miscellaneous dairy products	100	67	105	119	98
Fruits and vegetables	**100**	**83**	**102**	**130**	**97**
Fresh fruits	100	76	103	136	97
Apples	100	81	103	132	97
Bananas	100	85	102	157	95
Oranges	100	92	101	146	96
Citrus fruits, excl. oranges	100	69	104	177	93
Other fresh fruits	100	69	104	119	98
Fresh vegetables	100	73	104	141	96
Potatoes	100	89	102	124	98
Lettuce	100	62	105	139	96
Tomatoes	100	77	103	189	92
Other fresh vegetables	100	69	104	130	97
Processed fruits	100	99	100	120	98
Frozen fruits and fruit juices	100	98	100	89	101
Frozen orange juice	100	108	99	85	101
Frozen fruits	100	57	106	69	103
Frozen fruit juices, excl. orange	100	111	99	113	99
Canned fruits	100	76	103	90	101
Dried fruits	100	54	107	73	103
Fresh fruit juice	100	89	101	106	99
Canned and bottled fruit juice	100	112	98	144	96
Processed vegetables	100	98	100	110	99
Frozen vegetables	100	94	101	76	102
Canned and dried vegetables and juices	100	100	100	127	97
Canned beans	100	127	96	127	97
Canned corn	100	122	97	153	95
Canned miscellaneous vegetables	100	73	104	79	102
Dried peas	100	69	106	111	100
Dried beans	100	123	97	369	75

	total consumer units	race		Hispanic origin	
		black	white and other	Hispanic	non-Hispanic
Dried miscellaneous vegetables	100	97	101	163	94
Dried processed vegetables	100	24	112	144	94
Fresh and canned vegetable juices	100	95	101	99	100
Sugar and other sweets	**100**	**77**	**103**	**94**	**101**
Candy and chewing gum	100	63	105	78	102
Sugar	100	138	95	146	96
Artificial sweeteners	100	71	104	122	98
Jams, preserves, other sweets	100	84	102	105	100
Fats and oils	**100**	**95**	**101**	**120**	**98**
Margarine	100	99	100	98	100
Fats and oils	100	125	96	182	92
Salad dressings	100	77	103	94	101
Nondairy cream and imitation milk	100	62	105	80	102
Peanut butter	100	93	101	95	101
Miscellaneous foods	**100**	**72**	**104**	**97**	**100**
Frozen prepared foods	100	61	106	71	103
Frozen meals	100	60	106	66	103
Other frozen prepared foods	100	62	105	73	103
Canned and packaged soups	100	74	104	86	101
Potato chips, nuts, and other snacks	100	68	105	83	102
Potato chips and other snacks	100	69	104	90	101
Nuts	100	63	105	62	104
Condiments and seasonings	100	77	103	103	100
Salt, spices, and other seasonings	100	105	99	130	97
Olives, pickles, relishes	100	62	105	85	101
Sauces and gravies	100	77	103	102	100
Baking needs and miscellaneous products	100	54	106	82	102
Other canned/packaged prepared foods	100	79	103	123	98
Prepared salads	100	68	105	58	104
Prepared desserts	100	60	106	100	100
Baby food	100	110	99	142	96
Miscellaneous prepared foods	100	71	104	135	97
Nonalcoholic beverages	**100**	**78**	**103**	**110**	**99**
Cola	100	77	103	126	98
Other carbonated drinks	100	76	103	95	101
Coffee	100	59	106	78	102
Roasted coffee	100	56	106	74	102
Instant and freeze-dried coffee	100	63	105	86	101
Noncarbonated fruit-flavored drinks, incl. nonfrozen lemonade	100	138	95	166	94
Tea	100	72	104	88	101
Nonalcoholic beer	100	–	116	–	109
Other nonalcoholic beverages and ice	100	79	103	112	99
Food prepared by CU on trips	**100**	**32**	**109**	**79**	**102**
FOOD AWAY FROM HOME	**100**	**67**	**105**	**89**	**101**
Meals at restaurants, carry-outs, other	**100**	**72**	**104**	**95**	**100**
Lunch	100	77	103	104	100
• At fast food, take-out, delivery, concession stands, buffet, and cafeteria (other than employer and school cafeteria)	100	93	101	118	98
• At full-service restaurants	100	40	109	79	102
• At vending machines, mobile vendors	100	85	102	306	81
• At employer and school cafeterias	100	109	99	90	101

	total consumer units	race		Hispanic origin	
		black	white and other	Hispanic	non-Hispanic
Dinner	100	62	105	79	102
• At fast food, take-out, delivery, concession stands, buffet, and cafeteria (other than employer and school cafeteria)	100	90	101	114	99
• At full-service restaurants	100	50	107	64	103
• At vending machines, mobile vendors	100	84	102	255	86
• At employer and school cafeterias	100	182	88	92	101
Snacks and nonalcoholic beverages	100	83	102	100	100
• At fast food, take-out, delivery, concession stands, buffet, and cafeteria (other than employer and school cafeteria)	100	84	102	92	101
• At full-service restaurants	100	67	105	129	97
• At vending machines, mobile vendors	100	89	102	116	99
• At employer and school cafeterias	100	102	100	93	101
Breakfast and brunch	100	78	103	115	99
• At fast food, take-out, delivery, concession stands, buffet, and cafeteria (other than employer and school cafeteria)	100	109	99	147	96
• At full-service restaurants	100	45	108	83	102
• At vending machines, mobile vendors	100	42	109	148	96
• At employer and school cafeterias	100	107	99	123	98
Board (including at school)	**100**	**40**	**108**	**47**	**106**
Catered affairs	**100**	**16**	**112**	**32**	**107**
Food on trips	**100**	**41**	**108**	**59**	**104**
School lunches	**100**	**68**	**104**	**86**	**101**
Meals as pay	**100**	**57**	**106**	**151**	**95**
ALCOHOLIC BEVERAGES	**100**	**50**	**107**	**80**	**102**
At home	**100**	**58**	**106**	**92**	**101**
Beer and ale	100	71	104	129	97
Whiskey	100	68	105	74	102
Wine	100	37	109	54	104
Other alcoholic beverages	100	66	105	54	104
Away from home	**100**	**38**	**109**	**61**	**104**
Beer and ale	100	42	108	64	103
• At fast food, take-out, delivery, concession stands, buffet, and cafeteria	100	53	107	123	98
• At full-service restaurants	100	42	108	56	104
• At vending machines, mobile vendors	100	103	100	44	106
• At catered affairs	100	–	114	–	110
Wine	100	51	107	70	103
• At fast food, take-out, delivery, concession stands, buffet and cafeteria	100	91	101	123	98
• At full-service restaurants	100	44	108	61	104
• At catered affairs	100	–	114	25	106
Other alcoholic beverages	100	31	110	57	104
• At fast food, take-out, delivery, concession stands, buffet, and cafeteria	100	30	110	132	97
• At full-service restaurants	100	31	110	58	104
• At catered affairs	100	–	114	–	109
Alcoholic beverages purchased on trips	100	35	109	54	105

Note: Other races include Asians, Native Americans, and Pacific Islanders. (–) means sample is too small to make a reliable estimate.
Source: Calculations by New Strategist based on the 2002 Consumer Expenditure Survey

Table 5.15 Food and Alcohol: Total spending by race and Hispanic origin, 2002

(total annual spending on food and alcoholic beverages, by consumer unit race and Hispanic origin groups, 2002; numbers in thousands)

	total consumer units	race black	race white and other	Hispanic origin Hispanic	Hispanic origin non-Hispanic
Number of consumer units	112,108	13,554	98,553	10,500	101,608
Total spending of all consumer units	$4,560,172,273	$408,462,531	$4,152,486,306	$364,795,935	$4,195,868,829
Food, total spending	602,558,078	56,734,469	546,190,581	59,489,115	543,483,919
Alcoholic beverages, total spending	42,147,003	2,571,600	39,641,959	3,164,700	38,928,057
FOOD AT HOME	**$347,368,880**	**$36,171,560**	**$311,356,522**	**$38,248,665**	**$309,624,978**
Cereals and bakery products	**50,463,174**	**5,284,027**	**45,203,305**	**5,230,785**	**45,276,525**
Cereals and cereal products	17,272,480	2,059,124	15,214,612	2,001,720	15,304,197
Flour	969,734	172,949	795,323	207,690	772,221
Prepared flour mixes	1,390,139	154,245	1,236,840	104,685	1,283,309
Ready-to-eat and cooked cereals	9,827,387	1,074,697	8,755,449	954,135	8,875,459
Rice	1,997,765	300,628	1,696,097	336,105	1,675,516
Pasta, cornmeal, and other cereal products	3,087,454	356,470	2,731,889	399,000	2,698,708
Bakery products	33,190,694	3,224,903	29,988,692	3,229,065	29,972,328
Bread	9,398,014	986,596	8,415,441	1,076,565	8,337,952
White bread	3,947,323	464,496	3,482,863	520,380	3,439,431
Bread, other than white	5,450,691	521,965	4,932,578	556,290	4,898,522
Crackers and cookies	7,922,672	743,437	7,185,499	712,740	7,207,055
Cookies	5,191,721	539,856	4,654,658	499,905	4,693,274
Crackers	2,730,951	203,446	2,530,841	212,835	2,514,798
Frozen and refrigerated bakery products	2,874,449	276,773	2,599,828	216,615	2,652,985
Other bakery products	12,995,559	1,218,098	11,787,924	1,223,145	11,773,319
Biscuits and rolls	4,600,912	346,440	4,260,446	323,400	4,267,536
Cakes and cupcakes	4,005,619	510,173	3,494,689	403,200	3,604,036
Bread and cracker products	392,378	28,734	363,661	22,995	367,821
Sweetrolls, coffee cakes, doughnuts	2,896,871	218,897	2,681,627	319,515	2,581,859
Pies, tarts, turnovers	1,100,901	113,854	987,501	154,035	951,051
Meats, poultry, fish, and eggs	**89,509,269**	**11,688,292**	**77,794,782**	**11,101,230**	**78,644,592**
Beef	25,916,006	2,987,031	22,933,283	3,508,050	22,502,108
Ground beef	9,673,799	1,278,684	8,391,788	1,200,990	8,498,493
Roast	4,595,307	576,316	4,018,991	678,825	3,938,326
Chuck roast	1,312,785	202,226	1,108,721	192,990	1,125,817
Round roast	1,146,865	161,699	984,544	153,510	997,791
Other roast	2,135,657	212,391	1,924,740	332,325	1,815,735
Steak	9,469,763	926,687	8,549,473	1,262,205	8,240,409
Round steak	1,489,915	135,947	1,355,104	273,630	1,227,425
Sirloin steak	2,984,315	317,841	2,667,830	443,730	2,554,425
Other steak	4,995,532	472,899	4,526,539	544,950	4,457,543
Pork	18,760,153	2,814,624	15,929,121	2,271,255	16,533,654
Bacon	3,189,473	474,661	2,712,179	352,695	2,840,960
Pork chops	4,308,310	746,554	3,554,807	587,895	3,736,126
Ham	4,165,933	478,185	3,688,839	547,890	3,631,470
Ham, not canned	3,997,771	460,294	3,539,038	525,210	3,486,170
Canned ham	168,162	17,891	149,801	22,680	145,299
Sausage	2,933,866	483,336	2,447,071	257,670	2,674,323
Other pork	4,162,570	631,887	3,526,226	525,000	3,648,743
Other meats	11,331,877	1,300,506	10,033,681	1,151,115	10,188,234
Frankfurters	2,348,663	328,549	2,019,351	280,455	2,073,819

	total consumer units	race		Hispanic origin	
		black	white and other	Hispanic	non-Hispanic
Lunch meats (cold cuts)	$7,734,331	$825,168	$6,912,507	$756,210	$6,980,470
Bologna, liverwurst, salami	2,366,600	333,699	2,031,177	282,030	2,090,077
Lamb, organ meats, and others	1,248,883	146,790	1,101,823	114,450	1,133,945
Lamb and organ meats	895,743	123,748	771,670	107,730	790,510
Mutton, goat, and game	353,140	22,906	330,153	6,720	343,435
Poultry	16,158,126	2,278,970	13,868,378	2,123,310	14,086,933
Fresh and frozen chicken	12,696,231	1,738,165	10,952,195	1,792,875	10,955,375
Fresh and frozen whole chicken	3,596,425	526,437	3,066,969	642,705	2,980,163
Fresh and frozen chicken parts	9,099,806	1,211,728	7,885,226	1,150,170	7,976,228
Other poultry	3,461,895	540,940	2,917,169	330,435	3,131,559
Fish and seafood	13,561,705	1,806,071	11,750,474	1,437,975	12,138,092
Canned fish and seafood	1,808,302	195,855	1,612,327	182,490	1,626,744
Fresh fish and shellfish	7,770,205	1,118,069	6,646,414	983,640	6,808,752
Frozen fish and shellfish	3,983,197	492,146	3,490,747	271,845	3,702,596
Eggs	3,783,645	501,091	3,280,829	609,420	3,195,572
Dairy products	**36,809,541**	**3,140,462**	**33,708,083**	**4,046,175**	**32,815,320**
Fresh milk and cream	14,254,532	1,306,741	12,959,720	1,765,890	12,525,218
Fresh milk, all types	12,850,940	1,210,643	11,649,950	1,623,405	11,264,263
Cream	1,403,592	96,098	1,309,769	142,485	1,261,971
Other dairy products	22,555,009	1,833,721	20,748,363	2,280,285	20,290,102
Butter	2,071,756	230,825	1,841,956	184,275	1,886,861
Cheese	10,722,009	750,621	9,987,361	1,094,100	9,635,487
Ice cream and related products	6,585,224	596,918	5,994,979	647,115	5,941,020
Miscellaneous dairy products	3,176,020	255,493	2,924,068	354,795	2,825,718
Fruits and vegetables	**61,884,737**	**6,237,686**	**55,684,416**	**7,556,850**	**54,481,194**
Fresh fruits	19,977,646	1,846,055	18,148,535	2,542,260	17,493,849
Apples	3,653,600	356,335	3,299,554	452,550	3,210,813
Bananas	3,502,254	361,079	3,142,855	514,710	3,004,549
Oranges	2,280,277	252,511	2,028,221	312,375	1,976,276
Citrus fruits, excl. oranges	1,602,023	134,456	1,469,425	265,965	1,346,306
Other fresh fruits	8,939,492	741,810	8,207,494	996,660	7,956,922
Fresh vegetables	19,605,447	1,740,876	17,883,427	2,596,755	17,074,208
Potatoes	3,738,802	402,554	3,337,990	432,495	3,313,437
Lettuce	2,491,040	187,045	2,307,126	324,660	2,174,411
Tomatoes	3,779,161	351,455	3,430,630	669,900	3,136,639
Other fresh vegetables	9,596,445	799,822	8,806,696	1,169,700	8,449,721
Processed fruits	12,948,474	1,543,530	11,405,539	1,453,725	11,516,251
Frozen fruits and fruit juices	1,395,745	164,681	1,230,927	116,550	1,278,229
Frozen orange juice	707,401	92,709	613,985	56,490	650,291
Frozen fruits	312,781	21,415	291,717	20,265	291,615
Frozen fruit juices, excl. orange	375,562	50,421	325,225	39,690	336,322
Canned fruits	1,688,346	154,651	1,535,456	141,645	1,545,458
Dried fruits	679,374	44,728	636,652	46,620	632,002
Fresh fruit juice	2,488,798	269,182	2,220,399	246,330	2,243,505
Canned and bottled fruit juice	6,697,332	910,287	5,783,090	902,580	5,818,074
Processed vegetables	9,353,170	1,107,226	8,246,915	964,215	8,396,885
Frozen vegetables	3,122,208	354,979	2,767,368	222,705	2,892,780
Canned and dried vegetables and juices	6,230,963	752,247	5,479,547	741,510	5,504,105
Canned beans	1,397,987	215,102	1,181,650	166,845	1,233,521
Canned corn	822,873	121,173	701,697	117,810	709,224
Canned miscellaneous vegetables	2,001,128	177,015	1,825,202	147,420	1,850,282
Dried peas	40,359	3,389	37,450	4,200	36,579
Dried beans	285,875	42,560	243,426	98,910	193,055

	total consumer units	race		Hispanic origin	
		black	white and other	Hispanic	non-Hispanic
Dried miscellaneous vegetables	$827,357	$96,776	$731,263	$126,315	$705,160
Dried processed vegetables	38,117	1,084	37,450	5,145	32,515
Fresh and canned vegetable juices	810,541	93,116	717,466	74,865	735,642
Sugar and other sweets	**13,160,358**	**1,232,194**	**11,938,710**	**1,153,425**	**11,999,905**
Candy and chewing gum	8,457,428	648,288	7,820,181	616,455	7,825,848
Sugar	1,744,400	290,733	1,451,686	239,085	1,511,927
Artificial sweeteners	485,428	41,746	443,489	55,335	430,818
Jams, preserves, other sweets	2,473,102	251,427	2,223,356	242,655	2,231,312
Fats and oils	**9,547,117**	**1,095,976**	**8,452,891**	**1,071,420**	**8,491,381**
Margarine	1,105,385	132,694	972,718	101,535	1,003,887
Fats and oils	2,923,777	441,183	2,479,593	497,385	2,445,705
Salad dressings	3,028,037	280,974	2,748,643	265,965	2,759,673
Nondairy cream and imitation milk	1,045,968	77,936	968,776	78,435	965,276
Peanut butter	1,445,072	163,055	1,282,175	128,100	1,316,840
Miscellaneous foods	**52,906,007**	**4,609,851**	**48,349,116**	**4,813,830**	**48,079,890**
Frozen prepared foods	10,996,674	812,833	10,199,250	730,170	10,241,070
Frozen meals	3,349,787	241,261	3,113,289	207,480	3,132,575
Other frozen prepared foods	7,648,008	571,572	7,086,946	522,585	7,108,496
Canned and packaged soups	4,015,709	357,826	3,661,244	325,290	3,686,338
Potato chips, nuts, and other snacks	11,270,217	924,654	10,357,920	877,695	10,377,225
Potato chips and other snacks	8,561,688	718,904	7,852,703	721,665	7,832,961
Nuts	2,708,529	205,750	2,506,203	156,135	2,543,248
Condiments and seasonings	9,732,095	910,422	8,829,363	936,915	8,797,221
Salt, spices, and other seasonings	2,369,963	301,577	2,068,627	288,015	2,088,044
Olives, pickles, relishes	1,087,448	81,866	1,006,226	86,730	998,807
Sauces and gravies	4,235,440	394,150	3,844,553	405,090	3,831,638
Baking needs and miscellaneous products	2,039,245	132,829	1,908,972	156,975	1,878,732
Other canned/packaged prepared foods	16,891,312	1,604,116	15,300,353	1,943,865	14,979,051
Prepared salads	2,405,838	197,888	2,210,544	130,305	2,266,874
Prepared desserts	1,156,955	84,170	1,075,213	108,570	1,048,595
Baby food	3,539,250	470,595	3,066,969	471,345	3,079,738
Miscellaneous prepared foods	9,780,302	844,414	8,945,656	1,233,750	8,573,683
Nonalcoholic beverages	**28,468,706**	**2,701,719**	**25,788,364**	**2,934,015**	**25,557,460**
Cola	9,093,080	850,920	8,249,872	1,072,785	8,039,225
Other carbonated drinks	4,924,904	454,466	4,475,292	436,380	4,487,009
Coffee	4,662,572	329,904	4,339,289	339,675	4,314,276
Roasted coffee	3,069,517	208,054	2,865,921	211,995	2,850,104
Instant and freeze-dried coffee	1,593,055	121,850	1,473,367	127,785	1,463,155
Noncarbonated fruit-flavored drinks, incl. nonfrozen lemonade	2,124,447	354,708	1,767,055	329,490	1,806,590
Tea	1,778,033	155,600	1,624,153	146,580	1,629,792
Nonalcoholic beer	71,749	–	71,749	–	71,126
Other nonalcoholic beverages and ice	5,812,800	555,985	5,261,745	609,000	5,209,442
Food prepared by CU on trips	**4,618,850**	**181,353**	**4,436,856**	**340,935**	**4,277,697**
FOOD AWAY FROM HOME	**255,190,319**	**20,562,773**	**234,834,059**	**21,240,450**	**233,858,941**
Meals at restaurants, carry-outs, other	**209,240,613**	**18,271,741**	**191,176,066**	**18,559,380**	**190,590,190**
Lunch	76,882,545	7,174,810	69,769,611	7,465,500	69,439,923
• At fast food, take-out, delivery, concession stands, buffet, and cafeteria (other than employer and school cafeteria)	42,344,313	4,753,388	37,600,926	4,692,975	37,713,841
• At full-service restaurants	25,204,121	1,210,101	24,047,918	1,857,870	23,302,779
• At vending machines, mobile vendors	616,594	63,704	552,882	176,505	450,123
• At employer and school cafeterias	8,717,518	1,147,617	7,566,899	738,255	7,972,164

	total consumer units	race		Hispanic origin	
		black	white and other	Hispanic	non-Hispanic
Dinner	$82,572,026	$6,205,699	$76,478,114	$6,146,805	$76,287,286
• At fast food, take-out, delivery, concession stands, buffet, and cafeteria (other than employer and school cafeteria)	23,916,000	2,608,061	21,316,028	2,558,430	21,385,436
• At full-service restaurants	58,074,186	3,494,221	54,684,103	3,506,370	54,399,907
• At vending machines, mobile vendors	209,642	21,415	188,236	49,980	162,573
• At employer and school cafeterias	372,199	82,002	288,760	32,025	339,371
Snacks and nonalcoholic beverages	29,447,408	2,971,443	26,494,003	2,747,430	26,699,534
• At fast food, take-out, delivery, concession stands, buffet, and cafeteria (other than employer and school cafeteria)	20,817,335	2,114,017	18,715,215	1,794,660	19,008,825
• At full-service restaurants	3,382,298	275,959	3,110,333	407,715	2,982,195
• At vending machines, mobile vendors	4,115,485	441,589	3,675,041	446,775	3,674,145
• At employer and school cafeterias	1,133,412	139,742	993,414	98,280	1,034,369
Breakfast and brunch	20,338,633	1,919,924	18,434,339	2,199,645	18,164,462
• At fast food, take-out, delivery, concession stands, buffet, and cafeteria (other than employer and school cafeteria)	9,846,446	1,300,913	8,542,574	1,354,815	8,528,976
• At full-service restaurants	9,762,365	536,603	9,244,271	756,735	8,991,292
• At vending machines, mobile vendors	156,951	7,997	149,801	21,735	136,155
• At employer and school cafeterias	572,872	74,411	497,693	66,255	507,024
Board (including at school)	**5,217,506**	**249,258**	**4,968,057**	**228,585**	**4,988,953**
Catered affairs	**7,735,452**	**151,940**	**7,582,668**	**230,475**	**7,504,767**
Food on trips	**23,709,721**	**1,162,120**	**22,546,955**	**1,316,595**	**22,392,371**
School lunches	**6,726,480**	**551,648**	**6,174,345**	**543,375**	**6,182,847**
Meals as pay	**2,562,789**	**176,066**	**2,385,968**	**362,145**	**2,200,829**
ALCOHOLIC BEVERAGES	**42,147,003**	**2,571,600**	**39,641,959**	**3,164,700**	**38,928,057**
At home	**25,569,593**	**1,805,528**	**23,802,521**	**2,210,145**	**23,343,422**
Beer and ale	12,594,213	1,073,612	11,534,643	1,523,655	11,100,674
Whiskey	1,558,301	128,221	1,431,975	108,255	1,446,898
Wine	8,716,397	388,322	8,347,439	441,735	8,241,425
Other alcoholic beverages	2,700,682	215,509	2,488,463	136,500	2,554,425
Away from home	**16,577,410**	**766,072**	**15,839,438**	**954,555**	**15,584,635**
Beer and ale	5,926,029	300,221	5,638,217	353,325	5,554,909
• At fast food, take-out, delivery, concession stands, buffet, and cafeteria	895,743	56,927	840,657	103,530	793,558
• At full-service restaurants	4,702,931	238,821	4,474,306	248,220	4,438,237
• At vending machines, mobile vendors	35,875	4,473	31,537	1,470	34,547
• At catered affairs	290,360	–	290,360	–	288,567
Wine	2,897,992	177,422	2,725,976	190,785	2,700,741
• At fast food, take-out, delivery, concession stands, buffet and cafeteria	494,396	54,623	439,546	56,805	438,947
• At full-service restaurants	2,282,519	122,799	2,164,224	131,145	2,143,929
• At catered affairs	122,198	–	122,198	2,835	117,865
Other alcoholic beverages	7,753,389	288,429	7,475,245	410,445	7,328,985
• At fast food, take-out, delivery, concession stands, buffet, and cafeteria	392,378	14,367	379,429	48,615	344,451
• At full-service restaurants	3,244,406	120,766	3,132,014	177,660	3,056,369
• At catered affairs	441,706	–	441,706	–	437,930
Alcoholic beverages purchased on trips	3,674,900	153,296	3,521,299	184,275	3,490,235

Note: Other races include Asians, Native Americans, and Pacific Islanders. Numbers may not add to total because of rounding. (–) means sample is too small to make a reliable estimate.
Source: Calculations by New Strategist based on the 2002 Consumer Expenditure Survey

(percentage of total annual spending on food and alcoholic beverages accounted for by consumer unit race and Hispanic origin groups, 2002)

	total consumer units	race		Hispanic origin	
		black	white and other	Hispanic	non-Hispanic
Share of total consumer units	100.0%	12.1%	87.9%	9.4%	90.6%
Share of total before-tax income	100.0	8.8	91.0	7.1	93.0
Share of total spending	100.0	9.0	91.1	8.0	92.0
Share of food spending	100.0	9.4	90.6	9.9	90.2
Share of alcoholic beverages spending	100.0	6.1	94.1	7.5	92.4
FOOD AT HOME	100.0%	10.4%	89.6%	11.0%	89.1%
Cereals and bakery products	100.0	10.5	89.6	10.4	89.7
Cereals and cereal products	100.0	11.9	88.1	11.6	88.6
Flour	100.0	17.8	82.0	21.4	79.6
Prepared flour mixes	100.0	11.1	89.0	7.5	92.3
Ready-to-eat and cooked cereals	100.0	10.9	89.1	9.7	90.3
Rice	100.0	15.0	84.9	16.8	83.9
Pasta, cornmeal, and other cereal products	100.0	11.5	88.5	12.9	87.4
Bakery products	100.0	9.7	90.4	9.7	90.3
Bread	100.0	10.5	89.5	11.5	88.7
White bread	100.0	11.8	88.2	13.2	87.1
Bread, other than white	100.0	9.6	90.5	10.2	89.9
Crackers and cookies	100.0	9.4	90.7	9.0	91.0
Cookies	100.0	10.4	89.7	9.6	90.4
Crackers	100.0	7.4	92.7	7.8	92.1
Frozen and refrigerated bakery products	100.0	9.6	90.4	7.5	92.3
Other bakery products	100.0	9.4	90.7	9.4	90.6
Biscuits and rolls	100.0	7.5	92.6	7.0	92.8
Cakes and cupcakes	100.0	12.7	87.2	10.1	90.0
Bread and cracker products	100.0	7.3	92.7	5.9	93.7
Sweetrolls, coffee cakes, doughnuts	100.0	7.6	92.6	11.0	89.1
Pies, tarts, turnovers	100.0	10.3	89.7	14.0	86.4
Meats, poultry, fish, and eggs	100.0	13.1	86.9	12.4	87.9
Beef	100.0	11.5	88.5	13.5	86.8
Ground beef	100.0	13.2	86.7	12.4	87.9
Roast	100.0	12.5	87.5	14.8	85.7
Chuck roast	100.0	15.4	84.5	14.7	85.8
Round roast	100.0	14.1	85.8	13.4	87.0
Other roast	100.0	9.9	90.1	15.6	85.0
Steak	100.0	9.8	90.3	13.3	87.0
Round steak	100.0	9.1	91.0	18.4	82.4
Sirloin steak	100.0	10.7	89.4	14.9	85.6
Other steak	100.0	9.5	90.6	10.9	89.2
Pork	100.0	15.0	84.9	12.1	88.1
Bacon	100.0	14.9	85.0	11.1	89.1
Pork chops	100.0	17.3	82.5	13.6	86.7
Ham	100.0	11.5	88.5	13.2	87.2
Ham, not canned	100.0	11.5	88.5	13.1	87.2
Canned ham	100.0	10.6	89.1	13.5	86.4
Sausage	100.0	16.5	83.4	8.8	91.2
Other pork	100.0	15.2	84.7	12.6	87.7
Other meats	100.0	11.5	88.5	10.2	89.9
Frankfurters	100.0	14.0	86.0	11.9	88.3

	total consumer units	race		Hispanic origin	
		black	white and other	Hispanic	non-Hispanic
Lunch meats (cold cuts)	100.0%	10.7%	89.4%	9.8%	90.3%
Bologna, liverwurst, salami	100.0	14.1	85.8	11.9	88.3
Lamb, organ meats, and others	100.0	11.8	88.2	9.2	90.8
Lamb and organ meats	100.0	13.8	86.1	12.0	88.3
Mutton, goat, and game	100.0	6.5	93.5	1.9	97.3
Poultry	100.0	14.1	85.8	13.1	87.2
Fresh and frozen chicken	100.0	13.7	86.3	14.1	86.3
Fresh and frozen whole chicken	100.0	14.6	85.3	17.9	82.9
Fresh and frozen chicken parts	100.0	13.3	86.7	12.6	87.7
Other poultry	100.0	15.6	84.3	9.5	90.5
Fish and seafood	100.0	13.3	86.6	10.6	89.5
Canned fish and seafood	100.0	10.8	89.2	10.1	90.0
Fresh fish and shellfish	100.0	14.4	85.5	12.7	87.6
Frozen fish and shellfish	100.0	12.4	87.6	6.8	93.0
Eggs	100.0	13.2	86.7	16.1	84.5
Dairy products	**100.0**	**8.5**	**91.6**	**11.0**	**89.1**
Fresh milk and cream	100.0	9.2	90.9	12.4	87.9
Fresh milk, all types	100.0	9.4	90.7	12.6	87.7
Cream	100.0	6.8	93.3	10.2	89.9
Other dairy products	100.0	8.1	92.0	10.1	90.0
Butter	100.0	11.1	88.9	8.9	91.1
Cheese	100.0	7.0	93.1	10.2	89.9
Ice cream and related products	100.0	9.1	91.0	9.8	90.2
Miscellaneous dairy products	100.0	8.0	92.1	11.2	89.0
Fruits and vegetables	**100.0**	**10.1**	**90.0**	**12.2**	**88.0**
Fresh fruits	100.0	9.2	90.8	12.7	87.6
Apples	100.0	9.8	90.3	12.4	87.9
Bananas	100.0	10.3	89.7	14.7	85.8
Oranges	100.0	11.1	88.9	13.7	86.7
Citrus fruits, excl. oranges	100.0	8.4	91.7	16.6	84.0
Other fresh fruits	100.0	8.3	91.8	11.1	89.0
Fresh vegetables	100.0	8.9	91.2	13.2	87.1
Potatoes	100.0	10.8	89.3	11.6	88.6
Lettuce	100.0	7.5	92.6	13.0	87.3
Tomatoes	100.0	9.3	90.8	17.7	83.0
Other fresh vegetables	100.0	8.3	91.8	12.2	88.1
Processed fruits	100.0	11.9	88.1	11.2	88.9
Frozen fruits and fruit juices	100.0	11.8	88.2	8.4	91.6
Frozen orange juice	100.0	13.1	86.8	8.0	91.9
Frozen fruits	100.0	6.8	93.3	6.5	93.2
Frozen fruit juices, excl. orange	100.0	13.4	86.6	10.6	89.6
Canned fruits	100.0	9.2	90.9	8.4	91.5
Dried fruits	100.0	6.6	93.7	6.9	93.0
Fresh fruit juice	100.0	10.8	89.2	9.9	90.1
Canned and bottled fruit juice	100.0	13.6	86.3	13.5	86.9
Processed vegetables	100.0	11.8	88.2	10.3	89.8
Frozen vegetables	100.0	11.4	88.6	7.1	92.7
Canned and dried vegetables and juices	100.0	12.1	87.9	11.9	88.3
Canned beans	100.0	15.4	84.5	11.9	88.2
Canned corn	100.0	14.7	85.3	14.3	86.2
Canned miscellaneous vegetables	100.0	8.8	91.2	7.4	92.5
Dried peas	100.0	8.4	92.8	10.4	90.6
Dried beans	100.0	14.9	85.2	34.6	67.5

	total consumer units	race		Hispanic origin	
		black	white and other	Hispanic	non-Hispanic
Dried miscellaneous vegetables	100.0%	11.7%	88.4%	15.3%	85.2%
Dried processed vegetables	100.0	2.8	98.3	13.5	85.3
Fresh and canned vegetable juices	100.0	11.5	88.5	9.2	90.8
Sugar and other sweets	**100.0**	**9.4**	**90.7**	**8.8**	**91.2**
Candy and chewing gum	100.0	7.7	92.5	7.3	92.5
Sugar	100.0	16.7	83.2	13.7	86.7
Artificial sweeteners	100.0	8.6	91.4	11.4	88.8
Jams, preserves, other sweets	100.0	10.2	89.9	9.8	90.2
Fats and oils	**100.0**	**11.5**	**88.5**	**11.2**	**88.9**
Margarine	100.0	12.0	88.0	9.2	90.8
Fats and oils	100.0	15.1	84.8	17.0	83.6
Salad dressings	100.0	9.3	90.8	8.8	91.1
Nondairy cream and imitation milk	100.0	7.5	92.6	7.5	92.3
Peanut butter	100.0	11.3	88.7	8.9	91.1
Miscellaneous foods	**100.0**	**8.7**	**91.4**	**9.1**	**90.9**
Frozen prepared foods	100.0	7.4	92.7	6.6	93.1
Frozen meals	100.0	7.2	92.9	6.2	93.5
Other frozen prepared foods	100.0	7.5	92.7	6.8	92.9
Canned and packaged soups	100.0	8.9	91.2	8.1	91.8
Potato chips, nuts, and other snacks	100.0	8.2	91.9	7.8	92.1
Potato chips and other snacks	100.0	8.4	91.7	8.4	91.5
Nuts	100.0	7.6	92.5	5.8	93.9
Condiments and seasonings	100.0	9.4	90.7	9.6	90.4
Salt, spices, and other seasonings	100.0	12.7	87.3	12.2	88.1
Olives, pickles, relishes	100.0	7.5	92.5	8.0	91.8
Sauces and gravies	100.0	9.3	90.8	9.6	90.5
Baking needs and miscellaneous products	100.0	6.5	93.6	7.7	92.1
Other canned/packaged prepared foods	100.0	9.5	90.6	11.5	88.7
Prepared salads	100.0	8.2	91.9	5.4	94.2
Prepared desserts	100.0	7.3	92.9	9.4	90.6
Baby food	100.0	13.3	86.7	13.3	87.0
Miscellaneous prepared foods	100.0	8.6	91.5	12.6	87.7
Nonalcoholic beverages	**100.0**	**9.5**	**90.6**	**10.3**	**89.8**
Cola	100.0	9.4	90.7	11.8	88.4
Other carbonated drinks	100.0	9.2	90.9	8.9	91.1
Coffee	100.0	7.1	93.1	7.3	92.5
Roasted coffee	100.0	6.8	93.4	6.9	92.9
Instant and freeze-dried coffee	100.0	7.6	92.5	8.0	91.8
Noncarbonated fruit-flavored drinks, incl. nonfrozen lemonade	100.0	16.7	83.2	15.5	85.0
Tea	100.0	8.8	91.3	8.2	91.7
Nonalcoholic beer	100.0	–	100.0	–	99.1
Other nonalcoholic beverages and ice	100.0	9.6	90.5	10.5	89.6
Food prepared by CU on trips	**100.0**	**3.9**	**96.1**	**7.4**	**92.6**
FOOD AWAY FROM HOME	**100.0**	**8.1**	**92.0**	**8.3**	**91.6**
Meals at restaurants, carry-outs, other	**100.0**	**8.7**	**91.4**	**8.9**	**91.1**
Lunch	100.0	9.3	90.7	9.7	90.3
• At fast food, take-out, delivery, concession stands, buffet, and cafeteria (other than employer and school cafeteria)	100.0	11.2	88.8	11.1	89.1
• At full-service restaurants	100.0	4.8	95.4	7.4	92.5
• At vending machines, mobile vendors	100.0	10.3	89.7	28.6	73.0
• At employer and school cafeterias	100.0	13.2	86.8	8.5	91.4

	total consumer units	race		Hispanic origin	
		black	white and other	Hispanic	non-Hispanic
Dinner	100.0%	7.5%	92.6%	7.4%	92.4%
• At fast food, take-out, delivery, concession stands, buffet, and cafeteria (other than employer and school cafeteria)	100.0	10.9	89.1	10.7	89.4
• At full-service restaurants	100.0	6.0	94.2	6.0	93.7
• At vending machines, mobile vendors	100.0	10.2	89.8	23.8	77.5
• At employer and school cafeterias	100.0	22.0	77.6	8.6	91.2
Snacks and nonalcoholic beverages	100.0	10.1	90.0	9.3	90.7
• At fast food, take-out, delivery, concession stands, buffet, and cafeteria (other than employer and school cafeteria)	100.0	10.2	89.9	8.6	91.3
• At full-service restaurants	100.0	8.2	92.0	12.1	88.2
• At vending machines, mobile vendors	100.0	10.7	89.3	10.9	89.3
• At employer and school cafeterias	100.0	12.3	87.6	8.7	91.3
Breakfast and brunch	100.0	9.4	90.6	10.8	89.3
• At fast food, take-out, delivery, concession stands, buffet, and cafeteria (other than employer and school cafeteria)	100.0	13.2	86.8	13.8	86.6
• At full-service restaurants	100.0	5.5	94.7	7.8	92.1
• At vending machines, mobile vendors	100.0	5.1	95.4	13.8	86.7
• At employer and school cafeterias	100.0	13.0	86.9	11.6	88.5
Board (including at school)	**100.0**	**4.8**	**95.2**	**4.4**	**95.6**
Catered affairs	**100.0**	**2.0**	**98.0**	**3.0**	**97.0**
Food on trips	**100.0**	**4.9**	**95.1**	**5.6**	**94.4**
School lunches	**100.0**	**8.2**	**91.8**	**8.1**	**91.9**
Meals as pay	**100.0**	**6.9**	**93.1**	**14.1**	**85.9**
ALCOHOLIC BEVERAGES	**100.0**	**6.1**	**94.1**	**7.5**	**92.4**
At home	**100.0**	**7.1**	**93.1**	**8.6**	**91.3**
Beer and ale	100.0	8.5	91.6	12.1	88.1
Whiskey	100.0	8.2	91.9	6.9	92.9
Wine	100.0	4.5	95.8	5.1	94.6
Other alcoholic beverages	100.0	8.0	92.1	5.1	94.6
Away from home	**100.0**	**4.6**	**95.5**	**5.8**	**94.0**
Beer and ale	100.0	5.1	95.1	6.0	93.7
• At fast food, take-out, delivery, concession stands, buffet, and cafeteria	100.0	6.4	93.9	11.6	88.6
• At full-service restaurants	100.0	5.1	95.1	5.3	94.4
• At vending machines, mobile vendors	100.0	12.5	87.9	4.1	96.3
• At catered affairs	100.0	–	100.0	–	99.4
Wine	100.0	6.1	94.1	6.6	93.2
• At fast food, take-out, delivery, concession stands, buffet and cafeteria	100.0	11.0	88.9	11.5	88.8
• At full-service restaurants	100.0	5.4	94.8	5.7	93.9
• At catered affairs	100.0	–	100.0	2.3	96.5
Other alcoholic beverages	100.0	3.7	96.4	5.3	94.5
• At fast food, take-out, delivery, concession stands, buffet, and cafeteria	100.0	3.7	96.7	12.4	87.8
• At full-service restaurants	100.0	3.7	96.5	5.5	94.2
• At catered affairs	100.0	–	100.0	–	99.1
Alcoholic beverages purchased on trips	100.0	4.2	95.8	5.0	95.0

Note: Other races include Asians, Native Americans, and Pacific Islanders. Numbers may not add to total because of rounding. (–) means sample is too small to make a reliable estimate.
Source: Calculations by New Strategist based on the 2002 Consumer Expenditure Survey

Table 5.17 Food and Alcohol: Average spending by region, 2002

(average annual spending of consumer units (CU) on food and alcoholic beverages, by region in which consumer unit lives, 2002)

	total consumer units	Northeast	Midwest	South	West
Number of consumer units (in thousands, add 000)	112,108	21,313	25,883	40,004	24,907
Average number of persons per CU	2.5	2.5	2.5	2.5	2.6
Average before-tax income of CU	$49,430.00	$53,983.00	$49,197.00	$45,641.00	$52,016.00
Average spending of CU, total	40,676.60	42,390.20	40,601.14	37,280.55	44,728.34
Food, average spending	5,374.80	5,813.35	5,179.70	5,101.68	5,630.33
Alcoholic beverages, average spending	375.95	457.77	409.75	281.76	419.55
FOOD AT HOME	**$3,098.52**	**$3,296.41**	**$2,932.25**	**$2,960.68**	**$3,316.74**
Cereals and bakery products	**450.13**	**498.21**	**435.06**	**421.44**	**469.28**
Cereals and cereal products	154.07	167.89	145.58	144.74	165.60
Flour	8.65	7.45	6.60	9.07	11.15
Prepared flour mixes	12.40	12.65	12.48	11.87	12.94
Ready-to-eat and cooked cereals	87.66	94.85	88.00	80.97	91.64
Rice	17.82	20.92	11.86	17.73	21.44
Pasta, cornmeal, and other cereal products	27.54	32.02	26.64	25.11	28.43
Bakery products	296.06	330.32	289.49	276.69	303.68
Bread	83.83	92.48	79.46	75.51	94.00
White bread	35.21	38.44	34.97	33.12	35.93
Bread, other than white	48.62	54.04	44.49	42.39	58.07
Crackers and cookies	70.67	75.05	71.05	67.74	71.11
Cookies	46.31	51.69	45.47	44.31	45.65
Crackers	24.36	23.36	25.58	23.43	25.46
Frozen and refrigerated bakery products	25.64	25.00	24.78	27.89	23.52
Other bakery products	115.92	137.80	114.20	105.55	115.05
Biscuits and rolls	41.04	51.04	39.29	36.87	40.71
Cakes and cupcakes	35.73	44.80	33.67	34.44	31.95
Bread and cracker products	3.50	4.57	3.33	2.91	3.67
Sweetrolls, coffee cakes, doughnuts	25.84	26.77	28.91	22.34	27.43
Pies, tarts, turnovers	9.82	10.61	9.01	8.99	11.28
Meats, poultry, fish, and eggs	**798.42**	**877.90**	**706.32**	**809.28**	**806.79**
Beef	231.17	231.67	208.71	242.06	236.61
Ground beef	86.29	80.67	86.71	89.91	85.02
Roast	40.99	37.10	38.74	43.66	42.50
Chuck roast	11.71	9.49	10.71	12.19	13.90
Round roast	10.23	9.72	9.16	11.88	9.18
Other roast	19.05	17.89	18.87	19.59	19.42
Steak	84.47	94.63	67.31	89.59	85.19
Round steak	13.29	15.22	9.14	13.59	15.41
Sirloin steak	26.62	29.67	18.52	29.21	28.19
Other steak	44.56	49.74	39.64	46.78	41.59
Pork	167.34	164.33	156.55	182.19	157.49
Bacon	28.45	25.76	26.32	31.00	28.94
Pork chops	38.43	42.20	34.04	42.56	33.09
Ham	37.16	36.88	36.66	40.15	33.16
Ham, not canned	35.66	35.99	35.78	38.22	31.19
Canned ham	1.50	0.89	0.88	1.93	1.97
Sausage	26.17	23.92	23.68	30.28	24.19
Other pork	37.13	35.56	35.85	38.20	38.11
Other meats	101.08	119.81	99.94	95.78	94.29
Frankfurters	20.95	24.41	19.04	21.73	18.66

	total consumer units	Northeast	Midwest	South	West
Lunch meats (cold cuts)	$68.99	$81.44	$68.45	$66.09	$63.26
Bologna, liverwurst, salami	21.11	25.02	20.66	21.07	18.23
Lamb, organ meats, and others	11.14	13.97	12.44	7.96	12.37
Lamb and organ meats	7.99	8.59	6.30	7.28	10.35
Mutton, goat, and game	3.15	5.38	6.14	0.69	2.02
Poultry	144.13	168.42	124.56	139.70	150.11
Fresh and frozen chicken	113.25	134.80	95.78	108.06	120.70
Fresh and frozen whole chicken	32.08	39.99	23.17	30.06	37.57
Fresh and frozen chicken parts	81.17	94.81	72.61	78.00	83.13
Other poultry	30.88	33.62	28.78	31.65	29.41
Fish and seafood	120.97	158.24	90.78	117.02	125.82
Canned fish and seafood	16.13	19.88	13.33	14.22	18.76
Fresh fish and shellfish	69.31	100.23	38.46	71.06	71.36
Frozen fish and shellfish	35.53	38.14	38.99	31.74	35.70
Eggs	33.75	35.42	25.78	32.52	42.47
Dairy products	**328.34**	**348.30**	**320.12**	**299.96**	**364.54**
Fresh milk and cream	127.15	127.53	128.64	119.17	137.96
Fresh milk, all types	114.63	113.86	117.02	108.14	123.15
Cream	12.52	13.67	11.62	11.03	14.81
Other dairy products	201.19	220.77	191.49	180.79	226.57
Butter	18.48	22.66	17.97	14.78	21.25
Cheese	95.64	104.43	93.88	86.12	104.91
Ice cream and related products	58.74	62.36	55.75	54.57	65.31
Miscellaneous dairy products	28.33	31.32	23.88	25.32	35.10
Fruits and vegetables	**552.01**	**605.20**	**489.78**	**510.87**	**635.29**
Fresh fruits	178.20	197.50	157.38	161.25	209.82
Apples	32.59	36.51	29.24	29.28	37.88
Bananas	31.24	33.29	26.43	29.06	37.90
Oranges	20.34	21.10	17.67	18.67	25.08
Citrus fruits, excl. oranges	14.29	15.62	12.09	12.39	18.43
Other fresh fruits	79.74	90.98	71.95	71.84	90.53
Fresh vegetables	174.88	195.60	145.26	158.79	212.98
Potatoes	33.35	36.33	29.92	33.70	33.74
Lettuce	22.22	25.99	19.28	18.90	27.24
Tomatoes	33.71	35.28	24.64	31.12	45.82
Other fresh vegetables	85.60	97.99	71.42	75.06	106.18
Processed fruits	115.50	131.71	107.76	103.00	129.22
Frozen fruits and fruit juices	12.45	10.19	14.20	9.39	17.49
Frozen orange juice	6.31	4.54	7.30	4.83	9.18
Frozen fruits	2.79	2.92	2.95	2.36	3.17
Frozen fruit juices, excl. orange	3.35	2.72	3.94	2.20	5.14
Canned fruits	15.06	14.86	16.63	13.75	15.69
Dried fruits	6.06	6.37	6.18	5.34	6.84
Fresh fruit juice	22.20	26.75	20.41	19.20	24.84
Canned and bottled fruit juice	59.74	73.56	50.35	55.32	64.37
Processed vegetables	83.43	80.38	79.38	87.84	83.27
Frozen vegetables	27.85	30.53	25.50	27.28	28.84
Canned and dried vegetables and juices	55.58	49.86	53.88	60.56	54.43
Canned beans	12.47	9.23	12.95	15.18	10.48
Canned corn	7.34	6.84	7.60	7.87	6.68
Canned miscellaneous vegetables	17.85	17.61	16.77	19.47	16.58
Dried peas	0.36	0.40	0.22	0.46	0.32
Dried beans	2.55	1.67	1.40	2.98	3.83

	total consumer units	Northeast	Midwest	South	West
Dried miscellaneous vegetables	$7.38	$6.84	$7.67	$7.33	$7.63
Dried processed vegetables	0.34	0.47	0.03	0.44	0.38
Fresh and canned vegetable juices	7.23	6.69	7.12	6.80	8.51
Sugar and other sweets	**117.39**	**118.67**	**119.09**	**110.46**	**125.53**
Candy and chewing gum	75.44	74.82	81.64	66.52	83.78
Sugar	15.56	14.17	13.33	18.97	13.68
Artificial sweeteners	4.33	4.29	3.18	4.52	5.24
Jams, preserves, other sweets	22.06	25.39	20.94	20.46	22.84
Fats and oils	**85.16**	**92.97**	**79.71**	**82.80**	**87.73**
Margarine	9.86	9.44	10.61	9.51	10.03
Fats and oils	26.08	31.93	19.39	27.50	25.59
Salad dressings	27.01	28.73	26.76	24.90	29.11
Nondairy cream and imitation milk	9.33	9.18	10.51	8.15	10.10
Peanut butter	12.89	13.69	12.45	12.73	12.90
Miscellaneous foods	**471.92**	**451.25**	**481.67**	**457.31**	**503.19**
Frozen prepared foods	98.09	96.06	108.06	94.55	95.20
Frozen meals	29.88	29.81	32.69	28.37	29.42
Other frozen prepared foods	68.22	66.25	75.37	66.18	65.78
Canned and packaged soups	35.82	36.57	37.27	32.92	38.28
Potato chips, nuts, and other snacks	100.53	99.44	110.37	96.66	97.46
Potato chips and other snacks	76.37	72.75	87.33	75.62	69.41
Nuts	24.16	26.69	23.05	21.04	28.05
Condiments and seasonings	86.81	84.41	83.11	82.51	99.58
Salt, spices, and other seasonings	21.14	19.07	18.08	21.59	25.40
Olives, pickles, relishes	9.70	10.22	8.55	9.07	11.42
Sauces and gravies	37.78	37.48	37.23	34.82	43.34
Baking needs and miscellaneous products	18.19	17.64	19.25	17.03	19.42
Other canned/packaged prepared foods	150.67	134.77	142.85	150.68	172.67
Prepared salads	21.46	25.60	19.35	19.78	22.69
Prepared desserts	10.32	8.09	11.04	10.27	11.63
Baby food	31.57	29.78	34.11	32.55	28.92
Miscellaneous prepared foods	87.24	71.26	78.05	88.08	109.39
Nonalcoholic beverages	**253.94**	**260.98**	**264.03**	**233.44**	**269.98**
Cola	81.11	70.95	96.79	76.64	80.90
Other carbonated drinks	43.93	39.94	52.74	41.69	41.89
Coffee	41.59	50.43	42.02	34.48	44.71
Roasted coffee	27.38	31.73	28.88	23.22	28.63
Instant and freeze-dried coffee	14.21	18.70	13.15	11.26	16.08
Noncarbonated fruit-flavored drinks, incl. nonfrozen lemonade	18.95	18.61	15.77	19.01	22.44
Tea	15.86	22.67	14.20	13.78	14.93
Nonalcoholic beer	0.64	0.03	0.76	0.57	1.17
Other nonalcoholic beverages and ice	51.85	58.34	41.75	47.26	63.93
Food prepared by CU on trips	**41.20**	**42.93**	**36.46**	**35.12**	**54.40**
FOOD AWAY FROM HOME	**2,276.29**	**2,516.94**	**2,247.45**	**2,141.01**	**2,313.60**
Meals at restaurants, carry-outs, other	**1,866.42**	**2,015.71**	**1,822.55**	**1,810.30**	**1,870.37**
Lunch	685.79	675.32	668.73	701.83	687.06
• At fast food, take-out, delivery, concession stands, buffet, and cafeteria (other than employer and school cafeteria)	377.71	353.78	371.00	383.96	395.63
• At full-service restaurants	224.82	230.62	204.40	237.14	221.22
• At vending machines, mobile vendors	5.50	4.01	5.49	4.76	7.99
• At employer and school cafeterias	77.76	86.90	87.83	75.96	62.21

	total consumer units	Northeast	Midwest	South	West
Dinner	$736.54	$887.32	$708.79	$677.15	$727.75
• At fast food, take-out, delivery, concession stands, buffet, and cafeteria (other than employer and school cafeteria)	213.33	219.68	204.40	213.32	217.02
• At full-service restaurants	518.02	663.15	496.82	459.22	506.46
• At vending machines, mobile vendors	1.87	1.79	2.85	1.25	1.94
• At employer and school cafeterias	3.32	2.70	4.72	3.36	2.34
Snacks and nonalcoholic beverages	262.67	283.98	265.48	245.49	268.46
• At fast food, take-out, delivery, concession stands, buffet, and cafeteria (other than employer and school cafeteria)	185.69	207.06	178.09	169.58	200.47
• At full-service restaurants	30.17	32.83	30.58	27.86	31.10
• At vending machines, mobile vendors	36.71	33.90	43.99	39.22	27.65
• At employer and school cafeterias	10.11	10.19	12.83	8.84	9.24
Breakfast and brunch	181.42	169.09	179.55	185.83	187.10
• At fast food, take-out, delivery, concession stands, buffet, and cafeteria (other than employer and school cafeteria)	87.83	76.38	81.18	96.97	90.19
• At full-service restaurants	87.08	86.58	90.64	82.48	91.14
• At vending machines, mobile vendors	1.40	0.88	1.40	1.49	1.70
• At employer and school cafeterias	5.11	5.25	6.33	4.88	4.07
Board (including at school)	**46.54**	**48.61**	**57.84**	**37.02**	**48.31**
Catered affairs	**69.00**	**138.44**	**56.56**	**48.62**	**55.22**
Food on trips	**211.49**	**228.66**	**212.99**	**177.83**	**249.28**
School lunches	**60.00**	**61.71**	**75.86**	**52.45**	**54.16**
Meals as pay	**22.86**	**23.81**	**21.64**	**14.80**	**36.25**
ALCOHOLIC BEVERAGES	**375.95**	**457.77**	**409.75**	**281.76**	**419.55**
At home	**228.08**	**247.80**	**242.68**	**185.97**	**262.77**
Beer and ale	112.34	109.73	130.31	99.68	116.22
Whiskey	13.90	15.77	14.45	12.26	14.30
Wine	77.75	106.74	66.68	54.47	100.86
Other alcoholic beverages	24.09	15.55	31.23	19.57	31.39
Away from home	**147.87**	**209.98**	**167.07**	**95.78**	**156.78**
Beer and ale	52.86	84.10	56.37	34.41	51.24
• At fast food, take-out, delivery, concession stands, buffet, and cafeteria	7.99	10.88	9.65	5.15	8.26
• At full-service restaurants	41.95	64.77	42.19	28.86	42.56
• At vending machines, mobile vendors	0.32	0.55	0.35	0.30	0.11
• At catered affairs	2.59	7.89	4.18	0.09	0.30
Wine	25.85	36.44	29.19	16.39	28.20
• At fast food, take-out, delivery, concession stands, buffet and cafeteria	4.41	4.20	5.34	4.04	4.22
• At full-service restaurants	20.36	31.35	20.02	12.27	23.95
• At catered affairs	1.09	0.89	3.83	0.08	0.03
Other alcoholic beverages	69.16	89.44	81.52	44.99	77.35
• At fast food, take-out, delivery, concession stands, buffet, and cafeteria	3.50	3.72	6.26	2.21	2.50
• At full-service restaurants	28.94	42.73	28.10	17.97	35.21
• At catered affairs	3.94	3.48	14.01	0.04	0.13
Alcoholic beverages purchased on trips	32.78	39.51	33.15	24.76	39.50

Source: Bureau of Labor Statistics, unpublished tables from the 2002 Consumer Expenditure Survey

Table 5.18 Food and Alcohol: Indexed spending by region, 2002

(indexed average annual spending of consumer units (CU) on food and alcoholic beverages, by region in which consumer unit lives, 2002; index definition: an index of 100 is the average for all consumer units; an index of 132 means that spending by consumer units in that group is 32 percent above the average for all consumer units; an index of 68 indicates spending that is 32 percent below the average for all consumer units)

	total consumer units	Northeast	Midwest	South	West
Average spending of CU, total	$40,677	$42,390	$40,601	$37,281	$44,728
Average spending of CU, index	100	104	100	92	110
Food, spending index	100	108	96	95	105
Alcoholic beverages, spending index	100	122	109	75	112
FOOD AT HOME	**100**	**106**	**95**	**96**	**107**
Cereals and bakery products	**100**	**111**	**97**	**94**	**104**
Cereals and cereal products	100	109	94	94	107
Flour	100	86	76	105	129
Prepared flour mixes	100	102	101	96	104
Ready-to-eat and cooked cereals	100	108	100	92	105
Rice	100	117	67	99	120
Pasta, cornmeal, and other cereal products	100	116	97	91	103
Bakery products	100	112	98	93	103
Bread	100	110	95	90	112
White bread	100	109	99	94	102
Bread, other than white	100	111	92	87	119
Crackers and cookies	100	106	101	96	101
Cookies	100	112	98	96	99
Crackers	100	96	105	96	105
Frozen and refrigerated bakery products	100	98	97	109	92
Other bakery products	100	119	99	91	99
Biscuits and rolls	100	124	96	90	99
Cakes and cupcakes	100	125	94	96	89
Bread and cracker products	100	131	95	83	105
Sweetrolls, coffee cakes, doughnuts	100	104	112	86	106
Pies, tarts, turnovers	100	108	92	92	115
Meats, poultry, fish, and eggs	**100**	**110**	**88**	**101**	**101**
Beef	100	100	90	105	102
Ground beef	100	93	100	104	99
Roast	100	91	95	107	104
Chuck roast	100	81	91	104	119
Round roast	100	95	90	116	90
Other roast	100	94	99	103	102
Steak	100	112	80	106	101
Round steak	100	115	69	102	116
Sirloin steak	100	111	70	110	106
Other steak	100	112	89	105	93
Pork	100	98	94	109	94
Bacon	100	91	93	109	102
Pork chops	100	110	89	111	86
Ham	100	99	99	108	89
Ham, not canned	100	101	100	107	87
Canned ham	100	59	59	129	131
Sausage	100	91	90	116	92
Other pork	100	96	97	103	103
Other meats	100	119	99	95	93
Frankfurters	100	117	91	104	89

	total consumer units	Northeast	Midwest	South	West
Lunch meats (cold cuts)	100	118	99	96	92
Bologna, liverwurst, salami	100	119	98	100	86
Lamb, organ meats, and others	100	125	112	71	111
Lamb and organ meats	100	108	79	91	130
Mutton, goat, and game	100	171	195	22	64
Poultry	100	117	86	97	104
Fresh and frozen chicken	100	119	85	95	107
Fresh and frozen whole chicken	100	125	72	94	117
Fresh and frozen chicken parts	100	117	89	96	102
Other poultry	100	109	93	102	95
Fish and seafood	100	131	75	97	104
Canned fish and seafood	100	123	83	88	116
Fresh fish and shellfish	100	145	55	103	103
Frozen fish and shellfish	100	107	110	89	100
Eggs	100	105	76	96	126
Dairy products	**100**	**106**	**97**	**91**	**111**
Fresh milk and cream	100	100	101	94	109
Fresh milk, all types	100	99	102	94	107
Cream	100	109	93	88	118
Other dairy products	100	110	95	90	113
Butter	100	123	97	80	115
Cheese	100	109	98	90	110
Ice cream and related products	100	106	95	93	111
Miscellaneous dairy products	100	111	84	89	124
Fruits and vegetables	**100**	**110**	**89**	**93**	**115**
Fresh fruits	100	111	88	90	118
Apples	100	112	90	90	116
Bananas	100	107	85	93	121
Oranges	100	104	87	92	123
Citrus fruits, excl. oranges	100	109	85	87	129
Other fresh fruits	100	114	90	90	114
Fresh vegetables	100	112	83	91	122
Potatoes	100	109	90	101	101
Lettuce	100	117	87	85	123
Tomatoes	100	105	73	92	136
Other fresh vegetables	100	114	83	88	124
Processed fruits	100	114	93	89	112
Frozen fruits and fruit juices	100	82	114	75	140
Frozen orange juice	100	72	116	77	145
Frozen fruits	100	105	106	85	114
Frozen fruit juices, excl. orange	100	81	118	66	153
Canned fruits	100	99	110	91	104
Dried fruits	100	105	102	88	113
Fresh fruit juice	100	120	92	86	112
Canned and bottled fruit juice	100	123	84	93	108
Processed vegetables	100	96	95	105	100
Frozen vegetables	100	110	92	98	104
Canned and dried vegetables and juices	100	90	97	109	98
Canned beans	100	74	104	122	84
Canned corn	100	93	104	107	91
Canned miscellaneous vegetables	100	99	94	109	93
Dried peas	100	111	61	128	89
Dried beans	100	65	55	117	150

	total consumer units	Northeast	Midwest	South	West
Dried miscellaneous vegetables	100	93	104	99	103
Dried processed vegetables	100	138	9	129	112
Fresh and canned vegetable juices	100	93	98	94	118
Sugar and other sweets	**100**	**101**	**101**	**94**	**107**
Candy and chewing gum	100	99	108	88	111
Sugar	100	91	86	122	88
Artificial sweeteners	100	99	73	104	121
Jams, preserves, other sweets	100	115	95	93	104
Fats and oils	**100**	**109**	**94**	**97**	**103**
Margarine	100	96	108	96	102
Fats and oils	100	122	74	105	98
Salad dressings	100	106	99	92	108
Nondairy cream and imitation milk	100	98	113	87	108
Peanut butter	100	106	97	99	100
Miscellaneous foods	**100**	**96**	**102**	**97**	**107**
Frozen prepared foods	100	98	110	96	97
Frozen meals	100	100	109	95	98
Other frozen prepared foods	100	97	110	97	96
Canned and packaged soups	100	102	104	92	107
Potato chips, nuts, and other snacks	100	99	110	96	97
Potato chips and other snacks	100	95	114	99	91
Nuts	100	110	95	87	116
Condiments and seasonings	100	97	96	95	115
Salt, spices, and other seasonings	100	90	86	102	120
Olives, pickles, relishes	100	105	88	94	118
Sauces and gravies	100	99	99	92	115
Baking needs and miscellaneous products	100	97	106	94	107
Other canned/packaged prepared foods	100	89	95	100	115
Prepared salads	100	119	90	92	106
Prepared desserts	100	78	107	100	113
Baby food	100	94	108	103	92
Miscellaneous prepared foods	100	82	89	101	125
Nonalcoholic beverages	**100**	**103**	**104**	**92**	**106**
Cola	100	87	119	94	100
Other carbonated drinks	100	91	120	95	95
Coffee	100	121	101	83	108
Roasted coffee	100	116	105	85	105
Instant and freeze-dried coffee	100	132	93	79	113
Noncarbonated fruit-flavored drinks, incl. nonfrozen lemonade	100	98	83	100	118
Tea	100	143	90	87	94
Nonalcoholic beer	100	5	119	89	183
Other nonalcoholic beverages and ice	100	113	81	91	123
Food prepared by CU on trips	**100**	**104**	**88**	**85**	**132**
FOOD AWAY FROM HOME	**100**	**111**	**99**	**94**	**102**
Meals at restaurants, carry-outs, other	**100**	**108**	**98**	**97**	**100**
Lunch	100	98	98	102	100
• At fast food, take-out, delivery, concession stands, buffet, and cafeteria (other than employer and school cafeteria)	100	94	98	102	105
• At full-service restaurants	100	103	91	105	98
• At vending machines, mobile vendors	100	73	100	87	145
• At employer and school cafeterias	100	112	113	98	80

	total consumer units	Northeast	Midwest	South	West
Dinner	100	120	96	92	99
• At fast food, take-out, delivery, concession stands, buffet, and cafeteria (other than employer and school cafeteria)	100	103	96	100	102
• At full-service restaurants	100	128	96	89	98
• At vending machines, mobile vendors	100	96	152	67	104
• At employer and school cafeterias	100	81	142	101	70
Snacks and nonalcoholic beverages	100	108	101	93	102
• At fast food, take-out, delivery, concession stands, buffet, and cafeteria (other than employer and school cafeteria)	100	112	96	91	108
• At full-service restaurants	100	109	101	92	103
• At vending machines, mobile vendors	100	92	120	107	75
• At employer and school cafeterias	100	101	127	87	91
Breakfast and brunch	100	93	99	102	103
• At fast food, take-out, delivery, concession stands, buffet, and cafeteria (other than employer and school cafeteria)	100	87	92	110	103
• At full-service restaurants	100	99	104	95	105
• At vending machines, mobile vendors	100	63	100	106	121
• At employer and school cafeterias	100	103	124	95	80
Board (including at school)	**100**	**104**	**124**	**80**	**104**
Catered affairs	**100**	**201**	**82**	**70**	**80**
Food on trips	**100**	**108**	**101**	**84**	**118**
School lunches	**100**	**103**	**126**	**87**	**90**
Meals as pay	**100**	**104**	**95**	**65**	**159**
ALCOHOLIC BEVERAGES	**100**	**122**	**109**	**75**	**112**
At home	**100**	**109**	**106**	**82**	**115**
Beer and ale	100	98	116	89	103
Whiskey	100	113	104	88	103
Wine	100	137	86	70	130
Other alcoholic beverages	100	65	130	81	130
Away from home	**100**	**142**	**113**	**65**	**106**
Beer and ale	100	159	107	65	97
• At fast food, take-out, delivery, concession stands, buffet, and cafeteria	100	136	121	64	103
• At full-service restaurants	100	154	101	69	101
• At vending machines, mobile vendors	100	172	109	94	34
• At catered affairs	100	305	161	3	12
Wine	100	141	113	63	109
• At fast food, take-out, delivery, concession stands, buffet and cafeteria	100	95	121	92	96
• At full-service restaurants	100	154	98	60	118
• At catered affairs	100	82	351	7	3
Other alcoholic beverages	100	129	118	65	112
• At fast food, take-out, delivery, concession stands, buffet, and cafeteria	100	106	179	63	71
• At full-service restaurants	100	148	97	62	122
• At catered affairs	100	88	356	1	3
Alcoholic beverages purchased on trips	100	121	101	76	121

Source: Calculations by New Strategist based on the 2002 Consumer Expenditure Survey

Table 5.19 Food and Alcohol: Total spending by region, 2002

(total annual spending on food and alcoholic beverages, by region in which consumer units live, 2002; numbers in thousands)

	total consumer units	Northeast	Midwest	South	West
Number of consumer units	112,108	21,313	25,883	40,004	24,907
Total spending of all consumer units	$4,560,172,273	$903,462,333	$1,050,879,307	$1,491,371,122	$1,114,048,764
Food, total spending	602,558,078	123,899,929	134,066,175	204,087,607	140,234,629
Alcoholic beverages, total spending	42,147,003	9,756,452	10,605,559	11,271,527	10,449,732
FOOD AT HOME	$347,368,880	$70,256,386	$75,895,427	$118,439,043	$82,610,043
Cereals and bakery products	50,463,174	10,618,350	11,260,658	16,859,286	11,688,357
Cereals and cereal products	17,272,480	3,578,240	3,768,047	5,790,179	4,124,599
Flour	969,734	158,782	170,828	362,836	277,713
Prepared flour mixes	1,390,139	269,609	323,020	474,847	322,297
Ready-to-eat and cooked cereals	9,827,387	2,021,538	2,277,704	3,239,124	2,282,477
Rice	1,997,765	445,868	306,972	709,271	534,006
Pasta, cornmeal, and other cereal products	3,087,454	682,442	689,523	1,004,500	708,106
Bakery products	33,190,694	7,040,110	7,492,870	11,068,707	7,563,758
Bread	9,398,014	1,971,026	2,056,663	3,020,702	2,341,258
White bread	3,947,323	819,272	905,129	1,324,932	894,909
Bread, other than white	5,450,691	1,151,755	1,151,535	1,695,770	1,446,349
Crackers and cookies	7,922,672	1,599,541	1,838,987	2,709,871	1,771,137
Cookies	5,191,721	1,101,669	1,176,900	1,772,577	1,137,005
Crackers	2,730,951	497,872	662,087	937,294	634,132
Frozen and refrigerated bakery products	2,874,449	532,825	641,381	1,115,712	585,813
Other bakery products	12,995,559	2,936,931	2,955,839	4,222,422	2,865,550
Biscuits and rolls	4,600,912	1,087,816	1,016,943	1,474,947	1,013,964
Cakes and cupcakes	4,005,619	954,822	871,481	1,377,738	795,779
Bread and cracker products	392,378	97,400	86,190	116,412	91,409
Sweetrolls, coffee cakes, doughnuts	2,896,871	570,549	748,278	893,689	683,199
Pies, tarts, turnovers	1,100,901	226,131	233,206	359,636	280,951
Meats, poultry, fish, and eggs	89,509,269	18,710,683	18,281,681	32,374,437	20,094,719
Beef	25,916,006	4,937,583	5,402,041	9,683,368	5,893,245
Ground beef	9,673,799	1,719,320	2,244,315	3,596,760	2,117,593
Roast	4,595,307	790,712	1,002,707	1,746,575	1,058,548
Chuck roast	1,312,785	202,260	277,207	487,649	346,207
Round roast	1,146,865	207,162	237,088	475,248	228,646
Other roast	2,135,657	381,290	488,412	783,678	483,694
Steak	9,469,763	2,016,849	1,742,185	3,583,958	2,121,827
Round steak	1,489,915	324,384	236,571	543,654	383,817
Sirloin steak	2,984,315	632,357	479,353	1,168,517	702,128
Other steak	4,995,532	1,060,109	1,026,002	1,871,387	1,035,882
Pork	18,760,153	3,502,365	4,051,984	7,288,329	3,922,603
Bacon	3,189,473	549,023	681,241	1,240,124	720,809
Pork chops	4,308,310	899,409	881,057	1,702,570	824,173
Ham	4,165,933	786,023	948,871	1,606,161	825,916
Ham, not canned	3,997,771	767,055	926,094	1,528,953	776,849
Canned ham	168,162	18,969	22,777	77,208	49,067
Sausage	2,933,866	509,807	612,909	1,211,321	602,500
Other pork	4,162,570	757,890	927,906	1,528,153	949,206
Other meats	11,331,877	2,553,511	2,586,747	3,831,583	2,348,481
Frankfurters	2,348,663	520,250	492,812	869,287	464,765

	total consumer units	Northeast	Midwest	South	West
Lunch meats (cold cuts)	$7,734,331	$1,735,731	$1,771,691	$2,643,864	$1,575,617
Bologna, liverwurst, salami	2,366,600	533,251	534,743	842,884	454,055
Lamb, organ meats, and others	1,248,883	297,743	321,985	318,432	308,100
Lamb and organ meats	895,743	183,079	163,063	291,229	257,787
Mutton, goat, and game	353,140	114,664	158,922	27,603	50,312
Poultry	16,158,126	3,589,535	3,223,986	5,588,559	3,738,790
Fresh and frozen chicken	12,696,231	2,872,992	2,479,074	4,322,832	3,006,275
Fresh and frozen whole chicken	3,596,425	852,307	599,709	1,202,520	935,756
Fresh and frozen chicken parts	9,099,806	2,020,686	1,879,365	3,120,312	2,070,519
Other poultry	3,461,895	716,543	744,913	1,266,127	732,515
Fish and seafood	13,561,705	3,372,569	2,349,659	4,681,268	3,133,799
Canned fish and seafood	1,808,302	423,702	345,020	568,857	467,255
Fresh fish and shellfish	7,770,205	2,136,202	995,460	2,842,684	1,777,364
Frozen fish and shellfish	3,983,197	812,878	1,009,178	1,269,727	889,180
Eggs	3,783,645	754,906	667,264	1,300,930	1,057,800
Dairy products	**36,809,541**	**7,423,318**	**8,285,666**	**11,999,600**	**9,079,598**
Fresh milk and cream	14,254,532	2,718,047	3,329,589	4,767,277	3,436,170
Fresh milk, all types	12,850,940	2,426,698	3,028,829	4,326,033	3,067,297
Cream	1,403,592	291,349	300,760	441,244	368,873
Other dairy products	22,555,009	4,705,271	4,956,336	7,232,323	5,643,179
Butter	2,071,756	482,953	465,118	591,259	529,274
Cheese	10,722,009	2,225,717	2,429,896	3,445,144	2,612,993
Ice cream and related products	6,585,224	1,329,079	1,442,977	2,183,018	1,626,676
Miscellaneous dairy products	3,176,020	667,523	618,086	1,012,901	874,236
Fruits and vegetables	**61,884,737**	**12,898,628**	**12,676,976**	**20,436,843**	**15,823,168**
Fresh fruits	19,977,646	4,209,318	4,073,467	6,450,645	5,225,987
Apples	3,653,600	778,138	756,819	1,171,317	943,477
Bananas	3,502,254	709,510	684,088	1,162,516	943,975
Oranges	2,280,277	449,704	457,353	746,875	624,668
Citrus fruits, excl. oranges	1,602,023	332,909	312,925	495,650	459,036
Other fresh fruits	8,939,492	1,939,057	1,862,282	2,873,887	2,254,831
Fresh vegetables	19,605,447	4,168,823	3,759,765	6,352,235	5,304,693
Potatoes	3,738,802	774,301	774,419	1,348,135	840,362
Lettuce	2,491,040	553,925	499,024	756,076	678,467
Tomatoes	3,779,161	751,923	637,757	1,244,924	1,141,239
Other fresh vegetables	9,596,445	2,088,461	1,848,564	3,002,700	2,644,625
Processed fruits	12,948,474	2,807,135	2,789,152	4,120,412	3,218,483
Frozen fruits and fruit juices	1,395,745	217,179	367,539	375,638	435,623
Frozen orange juice	707,401	96,761	188,946	193,219	228,646
Frozen fruits	312,781	62,234	76,355	94,409	78,955
Frozen fruit juices, excl. orange	375,562	57,971	101,979	88,009	128,022
Canned fruits	1,688,346	316,711	430,434	550,055	390,791
Dried fruits	679,374	135,764	159,957	213,621	170,364
Fresh fruit juice	2,488,798	570,123	528,272	768,077	618,690
Canned and bottled fruit juice	6,697,332	1,567,784	1,303,209	2,213,021	1,603,264
Processed vegetables	9,353,170	1,713,139	2,054,593	3,513,951	2,074,006
Frozen vegetables	3,122,208	650,686	660,017	1,091,309	718,318
Canned and dried vegetables and juices	6,230,963	1,062,666	1,394,576	2,422,642	1,355,688
Canned beans	1,397,987	196,719	335,185	607,261	261,025
Canned corn	822,873	145,781	196,711	314,831	166,379
Canned miscellaneous vegetables	2,001,128	375,322	434,058	778,878	412,958
Dried peas	40,359	8,525	5,694	18,402	7,970
Dried beans	285,875	35,593	36,236	119,212	95,394

	total consumer units	Northeast	Midwest	South	West
Dried miscellaneous vegetables	$827,357	$145,781	$198,523	$293,229	$190,040
Dried processed vegetables	38,117	10,017	776	17,602	9,465
Fresh and canned vegetable juices	810,541	142,584	184,287	272,027	211,959
Sugar and other sweets	**13,160,358**	**2,529,214**	**3,082,406**	**4,418,842**	**3,126,576**
Candy and chewing gum	8,457,428	1,594,639	2,113,088	2,661,066	2,086,708
Sugar	1,744,400	302,005	345,020	758,876	340,728
Artificial sweeteners	485,428	91,433	82,308	180,818	130,513
Jams, preserves, other sweets	2,473,102	541,137	541,990	818,482	568,876
Fats and oils	**9,547,117**	**1,981,470**	**2,063,134**	**3,312,331**	**2,185,091**
Margarine	1,105,385	201,195	274,619	380,438	249,817
Fats and oils	2,923,777	680,524	501,871	1,100,110	637,370
Salad dressings	3,028,037	612,322	692,629	996,100	725,043
Nondairy cream and imitation milk	1,045,968	195,653	272,030	326,033	251,561
Peanut butter	1,445,072	291,775	322,243	509,251	321,300
Miscellaneous foods	**52,906,007**	**9,617,491**	**12,467,065**	**18,294,229**	**12,532,953**
Frozen prepared foods	10,996,674	2,047,327	2,796,917	3,782,378	2,371,146
Frozen meals	3,349,787	635,341	846,115	1,134,913	732,764
Other frozen prepared foods	7,648,008	1,411,986	1,950,802	2,647,465	1,638,382
Canned and packaged soups	4,015,709	779,416	964,659	1,316,932	953,440
Potato chips, nuts, and other snacks	11,270,217	2,119,365	2,856,707	3,866,787	2,427,436
Potato chips and other snacks	8,561,688	1,550,521	2,260,362	3,025,102	1,728,795
Nuts	2,708,529	568,844	596,603	841,684	698,641
Condiments and seasonings	9,732,095	1,799,030	2,151,136	3,300,730	2,480,239
Salt, spices, and other seasonings	2,369,963	406,439	467,965	863,686	632,638
Olives, pickles, relishes	1,087,448	217,819	221,300	362,836	284,438
Sauces and gravies	4,235,440	798,811	963,624	1,392,939	1,079,469
Baking needs and miscellaneous products	2,039,245	375,961	498,248	681,268	483,694
Other canned/packaged prepared foods	16,891,312	2,872,353	3,697,387	6,027,803	4,300,692
Prepared salads	2,405,838	545,613	500,836	791,279	565,140
Prepared desserts	1,156,955	172,422	285,748	410,841	289,668
Baby food	3,539,250	634,701	882,869	1,302,130	720,310
Miscellaneous prepared foods	9,780,302	1,518,764	2,020,168	3,523,552	2,724,577
Nonalcoholic beverages	**28,468,706**	**5,562,267**	**6,833,888**	**9,338,534**	**6,724,392**
Cola	9,093,080	1,512,157	2,505,216	3,065,907	2,014,976
Other carbonated drinks	4,924,904	851,241	1,365,069	1,667,767	1,043,354
Coffee	4,662,572	1,074,815	1,087,604	1,379,338	1,113,592
Roasted coffee	3,069,517	676,261	747,501	928,893	713,087
Instant and freeze-dried coffee	1,593,055	398,553	340,361	450,445	400,505
Noncarbonated fruit-flavored drinks, incl. nonfrozen lemonade	2,124,447	396,635	408,175	760,476	558,913
Tea	1,778,033	483,166	367,539	551,255	371,862
Nonalcoholic beer	71,749	639	19,671	22,802	29,141
Other nonalcoholic beverages and ice	5,812,800	1,243,400	1,080,615	1,890,589	1,592,305
Food prepared by CU on trips	**4,618,850**	**914,967**	**943,694**	**1,404,940**	**1,354,941**
FOOD AWAY FROM HOME	**255,190,319**	**53,643,542**	**58,170,748**	**85,648,964**	**57,624,835**
Meals at restaurants, carry-outs, other	**209,240,613**	**42,960,827**	**47,173,062**	**72,419,241**	**46,585,306**
Lunch	76,882,545	14,393,095	17,308,739	28,076,007	17,112,603
• At fast food, take-out, delivery, concession stands, buffet, and cafeteria (other than employer and school cafeteria)	42,344,313	7,540,113	9,602,593	15,359,936	9,853,956
• At full-service restaurants	25,204,121	4,915,204	5,290,485	9,486,549	5,509,927
• At vending machines, mobile vendors	616,594	85,465	142,098	190,419	199,007
• At employer and school cafeterias	8,717,518	1,852,100	2,273,304	3,038,704	1,549,464

	total consumer units	Northeast	Midwest	South	West
Dinner	$82,572,026	$18,911,451	$18,345,612	$27,088,709	$18,126,069
• At fast food, take-out, delivery, concession stands, buffet, and cafeteria (other than employer and school cafeteria)	23,916,000	4,682,040	5,290,485	8,533,653	5,405,317
• At full-service restaurants	58,074,186	14,133,716	12,859,192	18,370,637	12,614,399
• At vending machines, mobile vendors	209,642	38,150	73,767	50,005	48,320
• At employer and school cafeterias	372,199	57,545	122,168	134,413	58,282
Snacks and nonalcoholic beverages	29,447,408	6,052,466	6,871,419	9,820,582	6,686,533
• At fast food, take-out, delivery, concession stands, buffet, and cafeteria (other than employer and school cafeteria)	20,817,335	4,413,070	4,609,503	6,783,878	4,993,106
• At full-service restaurants	3,382,298	699,706	791,502	1,114,511	774,608
• At vending machines, mobile vendors	4,115,485	722,511	1,138,593	1,568,957	688,679
• At employer and school cafeterias	1,133,412	217,179	332,079	353,635	230,141
Breakfast and brunch	20,338,633	3,603,815	4,647,293	7,433,943	4,660,100
• At fast food, take-out, delivery, concession stands, buffet, and cafeteria (other than employer and school cafeteria)	9,846,446	1,627,887	2,101,182	3,879,188	2,246,362
• At full-service restaurants	9,762,365	1,845,280	2,346,035	3,299,530	2,270,024
• At vending machines, mobile vendors	156,951	18,755	36,236	59,606	42,342
• At employer and school cafeterias	572,872	111,893	163,839	195,220	101,371
Board (including at school)	**5,217,506**	**1,036,025**	**1,497,073**	**1,480,948**	**1,203,257**
Catered affairs	**7,735,452**	**2,950,572**	**1,463,942**	**1,944,994**	**1,375,365**
Food on trips	**23,709,721**	**4,873,431**	**5,512,820**	**7,113,911**	**6,208,817**
School lunches	**6,726,480**	**1,315,225**	**1,963,484**	**2,098,210**	**1,348,963**
Meals as pay	**2,562,789**	**507,463**	**560,108**	**592,059**	**902,879**
ALCOHOLIC BEVERAGES	**42,147,003**	**9,756,452**	**10,605,559**	**11,271,527**	**10,449,732**
At home	**25,569,593**	**5,281,361**	**6,281,286**	**7,439,544**	**6,544,812**
Beer and ale	12,594,213	2,338,675	3,372,814	3,987,599	2,894,692
Whiskey	1,558,301	336,106	374,009	490,449	356,170
Wine	8,716,397	2,274,950	1,725,878	2,179,018	2,512,120
Other alcoholic beverages	2,700,682	331,417	808,326	782,878	781,831
Away from home	**16,577,410**	**4,475,304**	**4,324,273**	**3,831,583**	**3,904,919**
Beer and ale	5,926,029	1,792,423	1,459,025	1,376,538	1,276,235
• At fast food, take-out, delivery, concession stands, buffet, and cafeteria	895,743	231,885	249,771	206,021	205,732
• At full-service restaurants	4,702,931	1,380,443	1,092,004	1,154,515	1,060,042
• At vending machines, mobile vendors	35,875	11,722	9,059	12,001	2,740
• At catered affairs	290,360	168,160	108,191	3,600	7,472
Wine	2,897,992	776,646	755,525	655,666	702,377
• At fast food, take-out, delivery, concession stands, buffet and cafeteria	494,396	89,515	138,215	161,616	105,108
• At full-service restaurants	2,282,519	668,163	518,178	490,849	596,523
• At catered affairs	122,198	18,969	99,132	3,200	747
Other alcoholic beverages	7,753,389	1,906,235	2,109,982	1,799,780	1,926,556
• At fast food, take-out, delivery, concession stands, buffet, and cafeteria	392,378	79,284	162,028	88,409	62,268
• At full-service restaurants	3,244,406	910,704	727,312	718,872	876,975
• At catered affairs	441,706	74,169	362,621	1,600	3,238
Alcoholic beverages purchased on trips	3,674,900	842,077	858,021	990,499	983,827

Note: Numbers may not add to total because of rounding.
Source: Calculations by New Strategist based on the 2002 Consumer Expenditure Survey

Table 5.20 Food and Alcohol: Market shares by region, 2002

(percentage of total annual spending on food and alcoholic beverages accounted for by consumer units by region, 2002)

	total consumer units	Northeast	Midwest	South	West
Share of total consumer units	100.0%	19.0%	23.1%	35.7%	22.2%
Share of total before-tax income	100.0	20.8	23.0	32.9	23.4
Share of total spending	100.0	19.8	23.0	32.7	24.4
Share of food spending	100.0	20.6	22.2	33.9	23.3
Share of alcoholic beverages spending	100.0	23.1	25.2	26.7	24.8
FOOD AT HOME	**100.0%**	**20.2%**	**21.8%**	**34.1%**	**23.8%**
Cereals and bakery products	**100.0**	**21.0**	**22.3**	**33.4**	**23.2**
Cereals and cereal products	100.0	20.7	21.8	33.5	23.9
Flour	100.0	16.4	17.6	37.4	28.6
Prepared flour mixes	100.0	19.4	23.2	34.2	23.2
Ready-to-eat and cooked cereals	100.0	20.6	23.2	33.0	23.2
Rice	100.0	22.3	15.4	35.5	26.7
Pasta, cornmeal, and other cereal products	100.0	22.1	22.3	32.5	22.9
Bakery products	100.0	21.2	22.6	33.3	22.8
Bread	100.0	21.0	21.9	32.1	24.9
White bread	100.0	20.8	22.9	33.6	22.7
Bread, other than white	100.0	21.1	21.1	31.1	26.5
Crackers and cookies	100.0	20.2	23.2	34.2	22.4
Cookies	100.0	21.2	22.7	34.1	21.9
Crackers	100.0	18.2	24.2	34.3	23.2
Frozen and refrigerated bakery products	100.0	18.5	22.3	38.8	20.4
Other bakery products	100.0	22.6	22.7	32.5	22.1
Biscuits and rolls	100.0	23.6	22.1	32.1	22.0
Cakes and cupcakes	100.0	23.8	21.8	34.4	19.9
Bread and cracker products	100.0	24.8	22.0	29.7	23.3
Sweetrolls, coffee cakes, doughnuts	100.0	19.7	25.8	30.9	23.6
Pies, tarts, turnovers	100.0	20.5	21.2	32.7	25.5
Meats, poultry, fish, and eggs	**100.0**	**20.9**	**20.4**	**36.2**	**22.4**
Beef	100.0	19.1	20.8	37.4	22.7
Ground beef	100.0	17.8	23.2	37.2	21.9
Roast	100.0	17.2	21.8	38.0	23.0
Chuck roast	100.0	15.4	21.1	37.1	26.4
Round roast	100.0	18.1	20.7	41.4	19.9
Other roast	100.0	17.9	22.9	36.7	22.6
Steak	100.0	21.3	18.4	37.8	22.4
Round steak	100.0	21.8	15.9	36.5	25.8
Sirloin steak	100.0	21.2	16.1	39.2	23.5
Other steak	100.0	21.2	20.5	37.5	20.7
Pork	100.0	18.7	21.6	38.9	20.9
Bacon	100.0	17.2	21.4	38.9	22.6
Pork chops	100.0	20.9	20.5	39.5	19.1
Ham	100.0	18.9	22.8	38.6	19.8
Ham, not canned	100.0	19.2	23.2	38.2	19.4
Canned ham	100.0	11.3	13.5	45.9	29.2
Sausage	100.0	17.4	20.9	41.3	20.5
Other pork	100.0	18.2	22.3	36.7	22.8
Other meats	100.0	22.5	22.8	33.8	20.7
Frankfurters	100.0	22.2	21.0	37.0	19.8

	total consumer units	Northeast	Midwest	South	West
Lunch meats (cold cuts)	100.0%	22.4%	22.9%	34.2%	20.4%
Bologna, liverwurst, salami	100.0	22.5	22.6	35.6	19.2
Lamb, organ meats, and others	100.0	23.8	25.8	25.5	24.7
Lamb and organ meats	100.0	20.4	18.2	32.5	28.8
Mutton, goat, and game	100.0	32.5	45.0	7.8	14.2
Poultry	100.0	22.2	20.0	34.6	23.1
Fresh and frozen chicken	100.0	22.6	19.5	34.0	23.7
Fresh and frozen whole chicken	100.0	23.7	16.7	33.4	26.0
Fresh and frozen chicken parts	100.0	22.2	20.7	34.3	22.8
Other poultry	100.0	20.7	21.5	36.6	21.2
Fish and seafood	100.0	24.9	17.3	34.5	23.1
Canned fish and seafood	100.0	23.4	19.1	31.5	25.8
Fresh fish and shellfish	100.0	27.5	12.8	36.6	22.9
Frozen fish and shellfish	100.0	20.4	25.3	31.9	22.3
Eggs	100.0	20.0	17.6	34.4	28.0
Dairy products	**100.0**	**20.2**	**22.5**	**32.6**	**24.7**
Fresh milk and cream	100.0	19.1	23.4	33.4	24.1
Fresh milk, all types	100.0	18.9	23.6	33.7	23.9
Cream	100.0	20.8	21.4	31.4	26.3
Other dairy products	100.0	20.9	22.0	32.1	25.0
Butter	100.0	23.3	22.5	28.5	25.5
Cheese	100.0	20.8	22.7	32.1	24.4
Ice cream and related products	100.0	20.2	21.9	33.2	24.7
Miscellaneous dairy products	100.0	21.0	19.5	31.9	27.5
Fruits and vegetables	**100.0**	**20.8**	**20.5**	**33.0**	**25.6**
Fresh fruits	100.0	21.1	20.4	32.3	26.2
Apples	100.0	21.3	20.7	32.1	25.8
Bananas	100.0	20.3	19.5	33.2	27.0
Oranges	100.0	19.7	20.1	32.8	27.4
Citrus fruits, excl. oranges	100.0	20.8	19.5	30.9	28.7
Other fresh fruits	100.0	21.7	20.8	32.1	25.2
Fresh vegetables	100.0	21.3	19.2	32.4	27.1
Potatoes	100.0	20.7	20.7	36.1	22.5
Lettuce	100.0	22.2	20.0	30.4	27.2
Tomatoes	100.0	19.9	16.9	32.9	30.2
Other fresh vegetables	100.0	21.8	19.3	31.3	27.6
Processed fruits	100.0	21.7	21.5	31.8	24.9
Frozen fruits and fruit juices	100.0	15.6	26.3	26.9	31.2
Frozen orange juice	100.0	13.7	26.7	27.3	32.3
Frozen fruits	100.0	19.9	24.4	30.2	25.2
Frozen fruit juices, excl. orange	100.0	15.4	27.2	23.4	34.1
Canned fruits	100.0	18.8	25.5	32.6	23.1
Dried fruits	100.0	20.0	23.5	31.4	25.1
Fresh fruit juice	100.0	22.9	21.2	30.9	24.9
Canned and bottled fruit juice	100.0	23.4	19.5	33.0	23.9
Processed vegetables	100.0	18.3	22.0	37.6	22.2
Frozen vegetables	100.0	20.8	21.1	35.0	23.0
Canned and dried vegetables and juices	100.0	17.1	22.4	38.9	21.8
Canned beans	100.0	14.1	24.0	43.4	18.7
Canned corn	100.0	17.7	23.9	38.3	20.2
Canned miscellaneous vegetables	100.0	18.8	21.7	38.9	20.6
Dried peas	100.0	21.1	14.1	45.6	19.7
Dried beans	100.0	12.5	12.7	41.7	33.4

	total consumer units	Northeast	Midwest	South	West
Dried miscellaneous vegetables	100.0%	17.6%	24.0%	35.4%	23.0%
Dried processed vegetables	100.0	26.3	2.0	46.2	24.8
Fresh and canned vegetable juices	100.0	17.6	22.7	33.6	26.2
Sugar and other sweets	**100.0**	**19.2**	**23.4**	**33.6**	**23.8**
Candy and chewing gum	100.0	18.9	25.0	31.5	24.7
Sugar	100.0	17.3	19.8	43.5	19.5
Artificial sweeteners	100.0	18.8	17.0	37.2	26.9
Jams, preserves, other sweets	100.0	21.9	21.9	33.1	23.0
Fats and oils	**100.0**	**20.8**	**21.6**	**34.7**	**22.9**
Margarine	100.0	18.2	24.8	34.4	22.6
Fats and oils	100.0	23.3	17.2	37.6	21.8
Salad dressings	100.0	20.2	22.9	32.9	23.9
Nondairy cream and imitation milk	100.0	18.7	26.0	31.2	24.1
Peanut butter	100.0	20.2	22.3	35.2	22.2
Miscellaneous foods	**100.0**	**18.2**	**23.6**	**34.6**	**23.7**
Frozen prepared foods	100.0	18.6	25.4	34.4	21.6
Frozen meals	100.0	19.0	25.3	33.9	21.9
Other frozen prepared foods	100.0	18.5	25.5	34.6	21.4
Canned and packaged soups	100.0	19.4	24.0	32.8	23.7
Potato chips, nuts, and other snacks	100.0	18.8	25.3	34.3	21.5
Potato chips and other snacks	100.0	18.1	26.4	35.3	20.2
Nuts	100.0	21.0	22.0	31.1	25.8
Condiments and seasonings	100.0	18.5	22.1	33.9	25.5
Salt, spices, and other seasonings	100.0	17.1	19.7	36.4	26.7
Olives, pickles, relishes	100.0	20.0	20.4	33.4	26.2
Sauces and gravies	100.0	18.9	22.8	32.9	25.5
Baking needs and miscellaneous products	100.0	18.4	24.4	33.4	23.7
Other canned/packaged prepared foods	100.0	17.0	21.9	35.7	25.5
Prepared salads	100.0	22.7	20.8	32.9	23.5
Prepared desserts	100.0	14.9	24.7	35.5	25.0
Baby food	100.0	17.9	24.9	36.8	20.4
Miscellaneous prepared foods	100.0	15.5	20.7	36.0	27.9
Nonalcoholic beverages	**100.0**	**19.5**	**24.0**	**32.8**	**23.6**
Cola	100.0	16.6	27.6	33.7	22.2
Other carbonated drinks	100.0	17.3	27.7	33.9	21.2
Coffee	100.0	23.1	23.3	29.6	23.9
Roasted coffee	100.0	22.0	24.4	30.3	23.2
Instant and freeze-dried coffee	100.0	25.0	21.4	28.3	25.1
Noncarbonated fruit-flavored drinks, incl. nonfrozen lemonade	100.0	18.7	19.2	35.8	26.3
Tea	100.0	27.2	20.7	31.0	20.9
Nonalcoholic beer	100.0	0.9	27.4	31.8	40.6
Other nonalcoholic beverages and ice	100.0	21.4	18.6	32.5	27.4
Food prepared by CU on trips	**100.0**	**19.8**	**20.4**	**30.4**	**29.3**
FOOD AWAY FROM HOME	**100.0**	**21.0**	**22.8**	**33.6**	**22.6**
Meals at restaurants, carry-outs, other	**100.0**	**20.5**	**22.5**	**34.6**	**22.3**
Lunch	100.0	18.7	22.5	36.5	22.3
• At fast food, take-out, delivery, concession stands, buffet, and cafeteria (other than employer and school cafeteria)	100.0	17.8	22.7	36.3	23.3
• At full-service restaurants	100.0	19.5	21.0	37.6	21.9
• At vending machines, mobile vendors	100.0	13.9	23.0	30.9	32.3
• At employer and school cafeterias	100.0	21.2	26.1	34.9	17.8
Dinner	100.0%	22.9%	22.2%	32.8%	22.0%

	total consumer units	Northeast	Midwest	South	West
• At fast food, take-out, delivery, concession stands, buffet, and cafeteria (other than employer and school cafeteria)	100.0%	19.6%	22.1%	35.7%	22.6%
• At full-service restaurants	100.0	24.3	22.1	31.6	21.7
• At vending machines, mobile vendors	100.0	18.2	35.2	23.9	23.0
• At employer and school cafeterias	100.0	15.5	32.8	36.1	15.7
Snacks and nonalcoholic beverages	100.0	20.6	23.3	33.3	22.7
• At fast food, take-out, delivery, concession stands, buffet, and cafeteria (other than employer and school cafeteria)	100.0	21.2	22.1	32.6	24.0
• At full-service restaurants	100.0	20.7	23.4	33.0	22.9
• At vending machines, mobile vendors	100.0	17.6	27.7	38.1	16.7
• At employer and school cafeterias	100.0	19.2	29.3	31.2	20.3
Breakfast and brunch	100.0	17.7	22.8	36.6	22.9
• At fast food, take-out, delivery, concession stands, buffet, and cafeteria (other than employer and school cafeteria)	100.0	16.5	21.3	39.4	22.8
• At full-service restaurants	100.0	18.9	24.0	33.8	23.3
• At vending machines, mobile vendors	100.0	11.9	23.1	38.0	27.0
• At employer and school cafeterias	100.0	19.5	28.6	34.1	17.7
Board (including at school)	**100.0**	**19.9**	**28.7**	**28.4**	**23.1**
Catered affairs	**100.0**	**38.1**	**18.9**	**25.1**	**17.8**
Food on trips	**100.0**	**20.6**	**23.3**	**30.0**	**26.2**
School lunches	**100.0**	**19.6**	**29.2**	**31.2**	**20.1**
Meals as pay	**100.0**	**19.8**	**21.9**	**23.1**	**35.2**
ALCOHOLIC BEVERAGES	**100.0**	**23.1**	**25.2**	**26.7**	**24.8**
At home	**100.0**	**20.7**	**24.6**	**29.1**	**25.6**
Beer and ale	100.0	18.6	26.8	31.7	23.0
Whiskey	100.0	21.6	24.0	31.5	22.9
Wine	100.0	26.1	19.8	25.0	28.8
Other alcoholic beverages	100.0	12.3	29.9	29.0	28.9
Away from home	**100.0**	**27.0**	**26.1**	**23.1**	**23.6**
Beer and ale	100.0	30.2	24.6	23.2	21.5
• At fast food, take-out, delivery, concession stands, buffet, and cafeteria	100.0	25.9	27.9	23.0	23.0
• At full-service restaurants	100.0	29.4	23.2	24.5	22.5
• At vending machines, mobile vendors	100.0	32.7	25.3	33.5	7.6
• At catered affairs	100.0	57.9	37.3	1.2	2.6
Wine	100.0	26.8	26.1	22.6	24.2
• At fast food, take-out, delivery, concession stands, buffet and cafeteria	100.0	18.1	28.0	32.7	21.3
• At full-service restaurants	100.0	29.3	22.7	21.5	26.1
• At catered affairs	100.0	15.5	81.1	2.6	0.6
Other alcoholic beverages	100.0	24.6	27.2	23.2	24.8
• At fast food, take-out, delivery, concession stands, buffet, and cafeteria	100.0	20.2	41.3	22.5	15.9
• At full-service restaurants	100.0	28.1	22.4	22.2	27.0
• At catered affairs	100.0	16.8	82.1	0.4	0.7
Alcoholic beverages purchased on trips	100.0	22.9	23.3	27.0	26.8

Note: Numbers may not add to total because of rounding.

Source: Calculations by New Strategist based on the 2002 Consumer Expenditure Survey

Table 5.21 Food and Alcohol: Average spending by education, 2002

(average annual spending of consumer units (CU) on food and alcoholic beverages, by education of consumer unit reference person, 2002)

	total consumer units	less than high school graduate	high school graduate	some college	associate's degree	college graduate total	bachelor's degree	master's, professional, doctorate
Number of consumer units (in thousands, add 000)	112,108	17,075	31,961	23,260	10,395	29,417	19,082	10,335
Average number of persons per CU	2.5	2.6	2.5	2.4	2.6	2.5	2.5	2.5
Average before-tax income of CU	$49,430.00	$25,564.00	$39,618.00	$42,598.00	$54,860.00	$77,820.00	$69,408.00	$92,783.00
Average spending of CU, total	40,676.60	24,930.40	33,707.63	38,653.57	44,405.79	57,384.01	53,731.57	64,118.48
Food, average spending	5,374.80	4,140.16	4,707.57	5,111.93	5,690.50	6,779.12	6,564.97	7,171.16
Alcoholic beverages, average spending	375.95	185.42	272.79	372.33	432.75	561.45	538.26	603.77
FOOD AT HOME	**$3,098.52**	**$2,895.61**	**$2,916.80**	**$2,868.09**	**$3,134.04**	**$3,534.96**	**$3,439.17**	**$3,709.46**
Cereals and bakery products	**450.13**	**404.68**	**422.15**	**422.88**	**462.11**	**515.94**	**499.38**	**546.09**
Cereals and cereal products	154.07	152.57	144.10	146.68	141.32	173.99	170.14	181.00
Flour	8.65	15.35	8.23	6.75	5.72	8.07	8.09	8.04
Prepared flour mixes	12.40	10.14	13.12	11.05	13.61	13.34	12.30	15.21
Ready-to-eat and cooked cereals	87.66	77.43	81.45	85.70	82.68	101.76	98.41	107.87
Rice	17.82	22.11	16.07	15.59	16.28	19.59	20.32	18.25
Pasta, cornmeal, and other cereal products	27.54	27.55	25.23	27.58	23.02	31.24	31.02	31.63
Bakery products	296.06	252.11	278.05	276.20	320.79	341.95	329.24	365.09
Bread	83.83	80.42	83.94	76.42	80.62	91.50	87.41	98.94
White bread	35.21	40.10	37.92	33.32	32.40	32.25	31.92	32.86
Bread, other than white	48.62	40.32	46.02	43.10	48.21	59.25	55.49	66.08
Crackers and cookies	70.67	55.01	64.99	67.46	72.04	85.81	83.69	89.67
Cookies	46.31	37.37	43.25	45.14	46.70	54.42	53.62	55.90
Crackers	24.36	17.64	21.74	22.32	25.34	31.39	30.08	33.77
Frozen and refrigerated bakery products	25.64	21.38	23.98	22.13	30.11	30.50	30.58	30.36
Other bakery products	115.92	95.30	105.14	110.20	138.03	134.14	127.56	146.12
Biscuits and rolls	41.04	28.54	35.17	38.55	42.99	54.17	50.65	60.58
Cakes and cupcakes	35.73	30.18	31.31	34.86	49.88	39.22	38.64	40.27
Bread and cracker products	3.50	2.20	3.15	2.93	4.75	4.49	4.57	4.35
Sweetrolls, coffee cakes, doughnuts	25.84	24.41	26.06	22.73	30.98	26.94	25.36	29.82
Pies, tarts, turnovers	9.82	9.97	9.45	11.14	9.43	9.32	8.34	11.11
Meats, poultry, fish, and eggs	**798.42**	**843.30**	**800.13**	**731.86**	**808.30**	**818.71**	**807.99**	**838.24**
Beef	231.17	236.77	242.46	213.79	258.29	220.93	220.60	221.55
Ground beef	86.29	96.26	96.92	80.99	85.57	74.59	78.82	66.90
Roast	40.99	41.40	43.04	39.42	46.77	38.07	38.89	36.57
Chuck roast	11.71	14.94	12.82	10.14	13.13	9.68	9.85	9.36
Round roast	10.23	9.12	10.71	9.82	8.98	10.96	10.58	11.65
Other roast	19.05	17.34	19.51	19.46	24.66	17.43	18.47	15.55
Steak	84.47	79.34	85.50	75.83	106.45	85.30	79.15	96.49
Round steak	13.29	15.15	14.34	11.03	14.46	12.55	12.53	12.58
Sirloin steak	26.62	24.22	26.59	22.52	37.83	27.29	28.28	25.48
Other steak	44.56	39.97	44.57	42.28	54.17	45.46	38.34	58.43
Pork	167.34	205.60	179.11	156.57	158.39	147.18	150.21	141.67
Bacon	28.45	36.39	28.93	27.03	30.73	24.45	23.84	25.56
Pork chops	38.43	49.40	42.67	37.04	38.88	29.67	31.76	25.86
Ham	37.16	38.10	43.94	32.72	30.65	34.87	33.99	36.48
Ham, not canned	35.66	35.91	42.58	31.39	28.93	33.51	32.20	35.91
Canned ham	1.50	2.18	1.35	1.33	1.72	1.36	1.80	0.57
Sausage	26.17	33.97	26.68	26.56	21.11	23.16	25.04	19.74
Other pork	37.13	47.75	36.89	33.22	37.02	35.03	35.58	34.04
Other meats	101.08	98.70	100.15	92.24	99.02	109.97	115.13	100.58
Frankfurters	20.95	21.51	21.94	20.62	21.25	19.81	20.59	18.39

	total consumer units	less than high school graduate	high school graduate	some college	associate's degree	college graduate total	bachelor's degree	master's, professional, doctorate
Lunch meats (cold cuts)	$68.99	$68.40	$68.78	$63.37	$65.03	$74.62	$75.97	$72.16
Bologna, liverwurst, salami	21.11	26.71	23.33	17.87	18.17	19.32	19.51	18.96
Lamb, organ meats, and others	11.14	8.79	9.43	8.25	12.74	15.54	18.57	10.03
Lamb and organ meats	7.99	7.54	8.09	6.74	8.80	8.74	8.37	9.40
Mutton, goat, and game	3.15	1.25	1.35	1.51	3.94	6.81	10.20	0.63
Poultry	144.13	142.57	142.55	129.84	143.54	156.65	160.40	149.82
Fresh and frozen chicken	113.25	118.15	109.29	104.94	108.71	122.11	125.35	116.22
Fresh and frozen whole chicken	32.08	43.66	31.55	27.21	29.48	31.24	32.70	28.59
Fresh and frozen chicken parts	81.17	74.49	77.75	77.73	79.23	90.87	92.65	87.64
Other poultry	30.88	24.42	33.26	24.89	34.83	34.54	35.06	33.60
Fish and seafood	120.97	116.70	101.88	107.95	116.76	152.86	130.71	193.15
Canned fish and seafood	16.13	17.18	13.50	15.79	15.87	18.61	16.48	22.49
Fresh fish and shellfish	69.31	75.65	56.89	60.58	61.21	87.49	73.82	112.38
Frozen fish and shellfish	35.53	23.88	31.49	31.58	39.69	46.76	40.42	58.29
Eggs	33.75	42.96	33.97	31.47	32.30	31.12	30.93	31.46
Dairy products	**328.34**	**297.65**	**303.37**	**305.25**	**326.81**	**385.16**	**374.84**	**403.95**
Fresh milk and cream	127.15	129.83	123.37	119.34	126.81	135.27	134.09	137.42
Fresh milk, all types	114.63	120.60	111.67	108.41	113.40	119.50	118.98	120.43
Cream	12.52	9.23	11.70	10.93	13.40	15.78	15.11	16.99
Other dairy products	201.19	167.82	180.00	185.90	200.00	249.89	240.74	266.53
Butter	18.48	17.14	18.21	16.46	22.58	19.59	19.27	20.18
Cheese	95.64	74.83	84.80	88.87	91.78	122.59	120.91	125.65
Ice cream and related products	58.74	53.69	53.70	57.20	57.34	67.82	65.14	72.69
Miscellaneous dairy products	28.33	22.16	23.30	23.37	28.30	39.89	35.43	48.01
Fruits and vegetables	**552.01**	**522.99**	**486.60**	**479.83**	**531.05**	**689.50**	**646.28**	**768.17**
Fresh fruits	178.20	166.13	152.13	147.11	167.06	235.71	218.82	266.44
Apples	32.59	31.50	29.11	28.72	28.96	40.46	38.23	44.53
Bananas	31.24	34.96	28.53	25.60	27.87	37.19	36.59	38.28
Oranges	20.34	18.99	18.05	17.16	20.43	25.51	23.70	28.79
Citrus fruits, excl. oranges	14.29	14.72	10.85	11.40	14.14	19.67	17.00	24.54
Other fresh fruits	79.74	65.97	65.59	64.22	75.67	112.88	103.31	130.30
Fresh vegetables	174.88	171.02	150.50	153.29	164.13	219.95	201.44	253.64
Potatoes	33.35	38.28	31.98	29.91	30.77	35.57	33.28	39.74
Lettuce	22.22	20.10	19.59	19.65	22.76	27.56	26.01	30.38
Tomatoes	33.71	37.29	30.23	29.20	29.31	40.03	36.87	45.77
Other fresh vegetables	85.60	75.35	68.70	74.53	81.30	116.79	105.27	137.74
Processed fruits	115.50	100.12	101.57	103.11	113.54	146.37	137.31	162.85
Frozen fruits and fruit juices	12.45	8.84	10.11	13.62	9.86	16.52	15.46	18.44
Frozen orange juice	6.31	4.44	5.62	6.92	5.39	7.76	6.71	9.68
Frozen fruits	2.79	1.63	2.30	2.85	2.41	3.91	4.17	3.45
Frozen fruit juices, excl. orange	3.35	2.78	2.20	3.85	2.07	4.84	4.58	5.32
Canned fruits	15.06	15.10	13.09	14.22	14.97	17.66	15.92	20.81
Dried fruits	6.06	5.29	5.58	5.21	5.42	7.72	7.07	8.91
Fresh fruit juice	22.20	17.80	20.65	18.66	21.38	28.62	25.94	33.48
Canned and bottled fruit juice	59.74	53.09	52.14	51.40	61.91	75.85	72.91	81.20
Processed vegetables	83.43	85.71	82.41	76.33	86.31	87.48	88.70	85.24
Frozen vegetables	27.85	23.20	27.12	26.32	30.52	31.08	31.25	30.78
Canned and dried vegetables and juices	55.58	62.51	55.29	50.01	55.79	56.39	57.46	54.46
Canned beans	12.47	14.25	12.20	10.10	13.77	13.14	13.94	11.68
Canned corn	7.34	10.06	8.36	6.65	6.98	5.59	6.11	4.64
Canned miscellaneous vegetables	17.85	17.08	17.74	16.26	19.62	18.90	19.25	18.28
Dried peas	0.36	0.43	0.34	0.25	0.40	0.42	0.35	0.56
Dried beans	2.55	4.64	2.03	3.01	1.97	1.94	2.01	1.80

	total consumer units	less than high school graduate	high school graduate	some college	associate's degree	college graduate total	bachelor's degree	master's, professional, doctorate
Dried miscellaneous vegetables	$7.38	$9.97	$7.20	$6.86	$5.43	$7.28	$7.33	$7.18
Dried processed vegetables	0.34	0.14	0.44	0.05	0.88	0.36	0.46	0.20
Fresh and canned vegetable juices	7.23	5.93	6.86	6.79	6.75	8.69	7.94	10.06
Sugar and other sweets	**117.39**	**103.34**	**110.04**	**108.96**	**122.24**	**136.07**	**137.66**	**133.16**
Candy and chewing gum	75.44	59.13	67.39	71.66	82.83	91.90	92.67	90.50
Sugar	15.56	22.13	16.70	13.78	13.68	13.07	13.29	12.67
Artificial sweeteners	4.33	4.67	4.80	3.70	3.76	4.29	4.56	3.79
Jams, preserves, other sweets	22.06	17.40	21.15	19.82	21.97	26.81	27.15	26.20
Fats and oils	**85.16**	**88.32**	**86.06**	**75.81**	**85.77**	**89.09**	**88.03**	**91.03**
Margarine	9.86	9.70	10.53	9.21	10.41	9.56	9.20	10.23
Fats and oils	26.08	36.21	26.15	18.52	23.18	27.29	26.73	28.31
Salad dressings	27.01	20.88	27.72	26.47	28.73	29.08	29.17	28.91
Nondairy cream and imitation milk	9.33	8.29	9.57	9.55	10.43	9.08	8.18	10.73
Peanut butter	12.89	13.25	12.08	12.06	13.02	14.08	14.75	12.86
Miscellaneous foods	**471.92**	**385.75**	**429.04**	**453.56**	**491.67**	**563.92**	**559.70**	**571.61**
Frozen prepared foods	98.09	79.57	88.23	97.03	110.59	114.01	113.33	115.25
Frozen meals	29.88	25.66	26.42	28.50	32.12	35.72	34.60	37.74
Other frozen prepared foods	68.22	53.92	61.81	68.53	78.47	78.30	78.73	77.51
Canned and packaged soups	35.82	26.83	34.19	33.20	34.82	43.94	42.76	46.08
Potato chips, nuts, and other snacks	100.53	72.98	90.36	96.82	108.72	124.25	125.23	122.46
Potato chips and other snacks	76.37	58.84	69.43	75.25	83.35	90.54	93.17	85.77
Nuts	24.16	14.14	20.93	21.57	25.37	33.70	32.06	36.69
Condiments and seasonings	86.81	71.61	78.11	81.92	90.40	105.32	101.90	111.55
Salt, spices, and other seasonings	21.14	19.41	19.50	19.06	23.12	24.51	23.20	26.90
Olives, pickles, relishes	9.70	8.26	9.01	8.43	9.98	11.89	10.95	13.60
Sauces and gravies	37.78	29.99	34.14	38.45	39.10	44.37	43.47	46.02
Baking needs and miscellaneous products	18.19	13.95	15.47	15.98	18.19	24.54	24.27	25.03
Other canned/packaged prepared foods	150.67	134.75	138.15	144.58	147.14	176.41	176.48	176.28
Prepared salads	21.46	14.44	17.86	16.78	23.97	31.02	30.13	32.63
Prepared desserts	10.32	8.72	9.28	10.39	11.26	11.83	10.76	13.77
Baby food	31.57	28.71	34.28	32.53	22.65	32.19	34.90	27.24
Miscellaneous prepared foods	87.24	82.85	76.50	84.85	89.27	101.34	100.64	102.61
Nonalcoholic beverages	**253.94**	**230.15**	**251.13**	**248.97**	**266.94**	**267.78**	**263.00**	**276.47**
Cola	81.11	80.77	85.34	82.17	85.49	74.89	76.88	71.28
Other carbonated drinks	43.93	40.65	45.29	45.89	47.27	41.75	43.62	38.35
Coffee	41.59	36.34	38.02	38.76	39.60	50.32	45.12	59.79
Roasted coffee	27.38	20.97	24.64	24.91	28.41	34.65	30.70	41.83
Instant and freeze-dried coffee	14.21	15.37	13.38	13.85	11.19	15.67	14.42	17.95
Noncarbonated fruit-flavored drinks, incl. nonfrozen lemonade	18.95	19.13	19.52	18.47	19.22	18.54	18.39	18.81
Tea	15.86	15.71	15.27	15.24	16.87	16.66	16.46	17.04
Nonalcoholic beer	0.64	0.11	0.79	0.93	0.19	0.69	0.81	0.48
Other nonalcoholic beverages and ice	51.85	37.44	46.90	47.52	58.30	64.92	61.73	70.72
Food prepared by CU on trips	**41.20**	**19.43**	**28.27**	**40.97**	**39.14**	**68.78**	**62.30**	**80.74**
FOOD AWAY FROM HOME	**2,276.29**	**1,244.55**	**1,790.77**	**2,243.83**	**2,556.46**	**3,244.16**	**3,125.80**	**3,461.70**
Meals at restaurants, carry-outs, other	**1,866.42**	**1,117.32**	**1,542.36**	**1,864.43**	**2,093.17**	**2,489.60**	**2,452.36**	**2,557.36**
Lunch	685.79	451.86	576.19	697.99	749.85	882.01	886.27	874.27
• At fast food, take-out, delivery, concession stands, buffet, and cafeteria (other than employer and school cafeteria)	377.71	285.15	342.75	398.89	401.24	435.89	463.11	386.35
• At full-service restaurants	224.82	112.16	153.40	213.21	249.36	352.47	329.14	394.93
• At vending machines, mobile vendors	5.50	12.07	5.69	5.41	4.99	2.37	2.61	1.92
• At employer and school cafeterias	77.76	42.49	74.35	80.49	94.26	91.29	91.41	91.07

	total consumer units	less than high school graduate	high school graduate	some college	associate's degree	college graduate total	college graduate bachelor's degree	college graduate master's, professional, doctorate
Dinner	$736.54	$359.09	$560.01	$700.27	$851.07	$1,088.65	$1,040.46	$1,176.35
• At fast food, take-out, delivery, concession stands, buffet, and cafeteria (other than employer and school cafeteria)	213.33	153.75	179.13	224.26	282.41	248.30	251.57	242.35
• At full-service restaurants	518.02	202.00	377.18	467.52	564.29	834.80	783.78	927.65
• At vending machines, mobile vendors	1.87	1.96	1.39	1.43	0.90	2.92	2.27	4.11
• At employer and school cafeterias	3.32	1.38	2.31	7.05	3.48	2.62	2.83	2.24
Snacks and nonalcoholic beverages	262.67	185.08	239.96	276.40	294.42	303.92	310.90	291.22
• At fast food, take-out, delivery, concession stands, buffet, and cafeteria (other than employer and school cafeteria)	185.69	125.07	160.82	194.42	213.53	225.64	228.07	221.22
• At full-service restaurants	30.17	26.36	28.79	29.51	28.13	34.49	33.58	36.13
• At vending machines, mobile vendors	36.71	26.11	41.23	42.08	41.76	31.90	36.49	23.54
• At employer and school cafeterias	10.11	7.54	9.10	10.39	11.01	11.89	12.75	10.32
Breakfast and brunch	181.42	121.27	166.20	189.77	197.83	215.02	214.74	215.52
• At fast food, take-out, delivery, concession stands, buffet, and cafeteria (other than employer and school cafeteria)	87.83	73.87	92.58	89.84	101.70	84.10	92.67	68.51
• At full-service restaurants	87.08	41.20	67.74	91.50	89.20	125.10	115.27	142.99
• At vending machines, mobile vendors	1.40	3.18	1.20	1.47	1.63	0.63	0.77	0.38
• At employer and school cafeterias	5.11	3.02	4.69	6.96	5.30	5.18	6.03	3.64
Board (including at school)	**46.54**	**6.55**	**20.98**	**68.94**	**23.20**	**88.05**	**67.63**	**125.74**
Catered affairs	**69.00**	**14.41**	**21.43**	**30.78**	**89.70**	**175.25**	**156.93**	**209.09**
Food on trips	**211.49**	**56.35**	**132.95**	**186.79**	**238.58**	**396.81**	**352.68**	**478.29**
School lunches	**60.00**	**32.09**	**52.87**	**61.99**	**90.89**	**71.45**	**76.15**	**62.75**
Meals as pay	**22.86**	**17.83**	**20.18**	**30.90**	**20.92**	**23.01**	**20.05**	**28.48**
ALCOHOLIC BEVERAGES	**375.95**	**185.42**	**272.79**	**372.33**	**432.75**	**561.45**	**538.26**	**603.77**
At home	**228.08**	**147.30**	**185.48**	**234.52**	**235.76**	**303.52**	**297.15**	**315.10**
Beer and ale	112.34	101.32	113.72	129.39	120.76	101.77	116.79	74.42
Whiskey	13.90	5.69	8.18	15.96	21.43	19.96	18.15	23.25
Wine	77.75	28.51	44.77	67.68	60.06	147.41	123.65	190.66
Other alcoholic beverages	24.09	11.77	18.81	21.48	33.52	34.38	38.56	26.77
Away from home	**147.87**	**38.12**	**87.32**	**137.81**	**196.98**	**257.94**	**241.11**	**288.68**
Beer and ale	52.86	14.95	35.27	49.29	58.62	89.76	85.45	97.60
• At fast food, take-out, delivery, concession stands, buffet, and cafeteria	7.99	2.89	6.47	7.80	9.68	11.62	11.26	12.26
• At full-service restaurants	41.95	11.51	23.64	39.29	48.64	75.09	73.36	78.25
• At vending machines, mobile vendors	0.32	0.56	0.21	0.51	0.17	0.23	0.22	0.23
• At catered affairs	2.59	–	4.95	1.69	0.12	2.82	0.60	6.86
Wine	25.85	8.33	14.82	23.83	34.88	44.22	40.49	51.00
• At fast food, take-out, delivery, concession stands, buffet and cafeteria	4.41	2.12	3.04	4.64	5.44	6.43	6.34	6.60
• At full-service restaurants	20.36	6.21	11.22	19.01	20.57	37.36	33.89	43.68
• At catered affairs	1.09	–	0.56	0.18	8.87	0.43	0.26	0.73
Other alcoholic beverages	69.16	14.85	37.23	64.70	103.49	123.96	115.17	140.07
• At fast food, take-out, delivery, concession stands, buffet, and cafeteria	3.50	0.29	2.46	4.45	4.29	5.20	6.46	2.91
• At full-service restaurants	28.94	7.82	13.83	26.79	31.15	55.34	50.84	63.53
• At catered affairs	3.94	–	2.18	0.75	32.44	1.24	0.26	3.02
Alcoholic beverages purchased on trips	32.78	6.73	18.75	32.71	35.61	62.18	57.62	70.60

Note: (–) means sample is too small to make a reliable estimate.
Source: Bureau of Labor Statistics, unpublished tables from the 2002 Consumer Expenditure Survey

Table 5.22 Food and Alcohol: Indexed spending by education, 2002

(indexed average annual spending of consumer units (CU) on food and alcoholic beverages, by education of consumer unit reference person, 2002; index definition: an index of 100 is the average for all consumer units; an index of 132 means that spending by consumer units in that group is 32 percent above the average for all consumer units; an index of 68 indicates spending that is 32 percent below the average for all consumer units)

	total consumer units	less than high school graduate	high school graduate	some college	associate's degree	college graduate total	bachelor's degree	master's, professional, doctorate
Average spending of CU, total	$40,677	$24,930	$33,708	$38,654	$44,406	$57,384	$53,732	$64,118
Average spending of CU, index	100	61	83	95	109	141	132	158
Food, spending index	100	77	88	95	106	126	122	133
Alcoholic beverages, spending index	100	49	73	99	115	149	143	161
FOOD AT HOME	100	93	94	93	101	114	111	120
Cereals and bakery products	100	90	94	94	103	115	111	121
Cereals and cereal products	100	99	94	95	92	113	110	117
Flour	100	177	95	78	66	93	94	93
Prepared flour mixes	100	82	106	89	110	108	99	123
Ready-to-eat and cooked cereals	100	88	93	98	94	116	112	123
Rice	100	124	90	87	91	110	114	102
Pasta, cornmeal, and other cereal products	100	100	92	100	84	113	113	115
Bakery products	100	85	94	93	108	116	111	123
Bread	100	96	100	91	96	109	104	118
White bread	100	114	108	95	92	92	91	93
Bread, other than white	100	83	95	89	99	122	114	136
Crackers and cookies	100	78	92	95	102	121	118	127
Cookies	100	81	93	97	101	118	116	121
Crackers	100	72	89	92	104	129	123	139
Frozen and refrigerated bakery products	100	83	94	86	117	119	119	118
Other bakery products	100	82	91	95	119	116	110	126
Biscuits and rolls	100	70	86	94	105	132	123	148
Cakes and cupcakes	100	84	88	98	140	110	108	113
Bread and cracker products	100	63	90	84	136	128	131	124
Sweetrolls, coffee cakes, doughnuts	100	94	101	88	120	104	98	115
Pies, tarts, turnovers	100	102	96	113	96	95	85	113
Meats, poultry, fish, and eggs	100	106	100	92	101	103	101	105
Beef	100	102	105	92	112	96	95	96
Ground beef	100	112	112	94	99	86	91	78
Roast	100	101	105	96	114	93	95	89
Chuck roast	100	128	109	87	112	83	84	80
Round roast	100	89	105	96	88	107	103	114
Other roast	100	91	102	102	129	91	97	82
Steak	100	94	101	90	126	101	94	114
Round steak	100	114	108	83	109	94	94	95
Sirloin steak	100	91	100	85	142	103	106	96
Other steak	100	90	100	95	122	102	86	131
Pork	100	123	107	94	95	88	90	85
Bacon	100	128	102	95	108	86	84	90
Pork chops	100	129	111	96	101	77	83	67
Ham	100	103	118	88	82	94	91	98
Ham, not canned	100	101	119	88	81	94	90	101
Canned ham	100	145	90	89	115	91	120	38
Sausage	100	130	102	101	81	88	96	75
Other pork	100	129	99	89	100	94	96	92
Other meats	100	98	99	91	98	109	114	100
Frankfurters	100	103	105	98	101	95	98	88

	total consumer units	less than high school graduate	high school graduate	some college	associate's degree	college graduate total	bachelor's degree	master's, professional, doctorate
Lunch meats (cold cuts)	100	99	100	92	94	108	110	105
Bologna, liverwurst, salami	100	127	111	85	86	92	92	90
Lamb, organ meats, and others	100	79	85	74	114	139	167	90
Lamb and organ meats	100	94	101	84	110	109	105	118
Mutton, goat, and game	100	40	43	48	125	216	324	20
Poultry	100	99	99	90	100	109	111	104
Fresh and frozen chicken	100	104	97	93	96	108	111	103
Fresh and frozen whole chicken	100	136	98	85	92	97	102	89
Fresh and frozen chicken parts	100	92	96	96	98	112	114	108
Other poultry	100	79	108	81	113	112	114	109
Fish and seafood	100	96	84	89	97	126	108	160
Canned fish and seafood	100	107	84	98	98	115	102	139
Fresh fish and shellfish	100	109	82	87	88	126	107	162
Frozen fish and shellfish	100	67	89	89	112	132	114	164
Eggs	100	127	101	93	96	92	92	93
Dairy products	**100**	**91**	**92**	**93**	**100**	**117**	**114**	**123**
Fresh milk and cream	100	102	97	94	100	106	105	108
Fresh milk, all types	100	105	97	95	99	104	104	105
Cream	100	74	93	87	107	126	121	136
Other dairy products	100	83	89	92	99	124	120	132
Butter	100	93	99	89	122	106	104	109
Cheese	100	78	89	93	96	128	126	131
Ice cream and related products	100	91	91	97	98	115	111	124
Miscellaneous dairy products	100	78	82	82	100	141	125	169
Fruits and vegetables	**100**	**95**	**88**	**87**	**96**	**125**	**117**	**139**
Fresh fruits	100	93	85	83	94	132	123	150
Apples	100	97	89	88	89	124	117	137
Bananas	100	112	91	82	89	119	117	123
Oranges	100	93	89	84	100	125	117	142
Citrus fruits, excl. oranges	100	103	76	80	99	138	119	172
Other fresh fruits	100	83	82	81	95	142	130	163
Fresh vegetables	100	98	86	88	94	126	115	145
Potatoes	100	115	96	90	92	107	100	119
Lettuce	100	90	88	88	102	124	117	137
Tomatoes	100	111	90	87	87	119	109	136
Other fresh vegetables	100	88	80	87	95	136	123	161
Processed fruits	100	87	88	89	98	127	119	141
Frozen fruits and fruit juices	100	71	81	109	79	133	124	148
Frozen orange juice	100	70	89	110	85	123	106	153
Frozen fruits	100	58	82	102	86	140	149	124
Frozen fruit juices, excl. orange	100	83	66	115	62	144	137	159
Canned fruits	100	100	87	94	99	117	106	138
Dried fruits	100	87	92	86	89	127	117	147
Fresh fruit juice	100	80	93	84	96	129	117	151
Canned and bottled fruit juice	100	89	87	86	104	127	122	136
Processed vegetables	100	103	99	91	103	105	106	102
Frozen vegetables	100	83	97	95	110	112	112	111
Canned and dried vegetables and juices	100	112	99	90	100	101	103	98
Canned beans	100	114	98	81	110	105	112	94
Canned corn	100	137	114	91	95	76	83	63
Canned miscellaneous vegetables	100	96	99	91	110	106	108	102
Dried peas	100	119	94	69	111	117	97	156
Dried beans	100	182	80	118	77	76	79	71

	total consumer units	less than high school graduate	high school graduate	some college	associate's degree	college graduate total	college graduate bachelor's degree	college graduate master's, professional, doctorate
Dried miscellaneous vegetables	100	135	98	93	74	99	99	97
Dried processed vegetables	100	41	129	15	259	106	135	59
Fresh and canned vegetable juices	100	82	95	94	93	120	110	139
Sugar and other sweets	100	88	94	93	104	116	117	113
Candy and chewing gum	**100**	**78**	**89**	**95**	**110**	**122**	**123**	**120**
Sugar	100	142	107	89	88	84	85	81
Artificial sweeteners	100	108	111	85	87	99	105	88
Jams, preserves, other sweets	100	79	96	90	100	122	123	119
Fats and oils	**100**	**104**	**101**	**89**	**101**	**105**	**103**	**107**
Margarine	100	98	107	93	106	97	93	104
Fats and oils	100	139	100	71	89	105	102	109
Salad dressings	100	77	103	98	106	108	108	107
Nondairy cream and imitation milk	100	89	103	102	112	97	88	115
Peanut butter	100	103	94	94	101	109	114	100
Miscellaneous foods	**100**	**82**	**91**	**96**	**104**	**119**	**119**	**121**
Frozen prepared foods	100	81	90	99	113	116	116	117
Frozen meals	100	86	88	95	107	120	116	126
Other frozen prepared foods	100	79	91	100	115	115	115	114
Canned and packaged soups	100	75	95	93	97	123	119	129
Potato chips, nuts, and other snacks	100	73	90	96	108	124	125	122
Potato chips and other snacks	100	77	91	99	109	119	122	112
Nuts	100	59	87	89	105	139	133	152
Condiments and seasonings	100	82	90	94	104	121	117	128
Salt, spices, and other seasonings	100	92	92	90	109	116	110	127
Olives, pickles, relishes	100	85	93	87	103	123	113	140
Sauces and gravies	100	79	90	102	103	117	115	122
Baking needs and miscellaneous products	100	77	85	88	100	135	133	138
Other canned/packaged prepared foods	100	89	92	96	98	117	117	117
Prepared salads	100	67	83	78	112	145	140	152
Prepared desserts	100	84	90	101	109	115	104	133
Baby food	100	91	109	103	72	102	111	86
Miscellaneous prepared foods	100	95	88	97	102	116	115	118
Nonalcoholic beverages	**100**	**91**	**99**	**98**	**105**	**105**	**104**	**109**
Cola	100	100	105	101	105	92	95	88
Other carbonated drinks	100	93	103	104	108	95	99	87
Coffee	100	87	91	93	95	121	108	144
Roasted coffee	100	77	90	91	104	127	112	153
Instant and freeze-dried coffee	100	108	94	97	79	110	101	126
Noncarbonated fruit-flavored drinks, incl. nonfrozen lemonade	100	101	103	97	101	98	97	99
Tea	100	99	96	96	106	105	104	107
Nonalcoholic beer	100	17	123	145	30	108	127	75
Other nonalcoholic beverages and ice	100	72	90	92	112	125	119	136
Food prepared by CU on trips	**100**	**47**	**69**	**99**	**95**	**167**	**151**	**196**
FOOD AWAY FROM HOME	**100**	**55**	**79**	**99**	**112**	**143**	**137**	**152**
Meals at restaurants, carry-outs, other	**100**	**60**	**83**	**100**	**112**	**133**	**131**	**137**
Lunch	100	66	84	102	109	129	129	127
• At fast food, take-out, delivery, concession stands, buffet, and cafeteria (other than employer and school cafeteria)	100	75	91	106	106	115	123	102
• At full-service restaurants	100	50	68	95	111	157	146	176
• At vending machines, mobile vendors	100	219	103	98	91	43	47	35
• At employer and school cafeterias	100	55	96	104	121	117	118	117

	total consumer units	less than high school graduate	high school graduate	some college	associate's degree	college graduate		
						total	bachelor's degree	master's, professional, doctorate
Dinner	100	49	76	95	116	148	141	160
• At fast food, take-out, delivery, concession stands, buffet, and cafeteria (other than employer and school cafeteria)	100	72	84	105	132	116	118	114
• At full-service restaurants	100	39	73	90	109	161	151	179
• At vending machines, mobile vendors	100	105	74	76	48	156	121	220
• At employer and school cafeterias	100	42	70	212	105	79	85	67
Snacks and nonalcoholic beverages	100	70	91	105	112	116	118	111
• At fast food, take-out, delivery, concession stands, buffet, and cafeteria (other than employer and school cafeteria)	100	67	87	105	115	122	123	119
• At full-service restaurants	100	87	95	98	93	114	111	120
• At vending machines, mobile vendors	100	71	112	115	114	87	99	64
• At employer and school cafeterias	100	75	90	103	109	118	126	102
Breakfast and brunch	100	67	92	105	109	119	118	119
• At fast food, take-out, delivery, concession stands, buffet, and cafeteria (other than employer and school cafeteria)	100	84	105	102	116	96	106	78
• At full-service restaurants	100	47	78	105	102	144	132	164
• At vending machines, mobile vendors	100	227	86	105	116	45	55	27
• At employer and school cafeterias	100	59	92	136	104	101	118	71
Board (including at school)	**100**	**14**	**45**	**148**	**50**	**189**	**145**	**270**
Catered affairs	**100**	**21**	**31**	**45**	**130**	**254**	**227**	**303**
Food on trips	**100**	**27**	**63**	**88**	**113**	**188**	**167**	**226**
School lunches	**100**	**53**	**88**	**103**	**151**	**119**	**127**	**105**
Meals as pay	**100**	**78**	**88**	**135**	**92**	**101**	**88**	**125**
ALCOHOLIC BEVERAGES	**100**	**49**	**73**	**99**	**115**	**149**	**143**	**161**
At home	**100**	**65**	**81**	**103**	**103**	**133**	**130**	**138**
Beer and ale	100	90	101	115	107	91	104	66
Whiskey	100	41	59	115	154	144	131	167
Wine	100	37	58	87	77	190	159	245
Other alcoholic beverages	100	49	78	89	139	143	160	111
Away from home	**100**	**26**	**59**	**93**	**133**	**174**	**163**	**195**
Beer and ale	100	28	67	93	111	170	162	185
• At fast food, take-out, delivery, concession stands, buffet, and cafeteria	100	36	81	98	121	145	141	153
• At full-service restaurants	100	27	56	94	116	179	175	187
• At vending machines, mobile vendors	100	175	66	159	53	72	69	72
• At catered affairs	100	–	191	65	5	109	23	265
Wine	100	32	57	92	135	171	157	197
• At fast food, take-out, delivery, concession stands, buffet and cafeteria	100	48	69	105	123	146	144	150
• At full-service restaurants	100	31	55	93	101	183	166	215
• At catered affairs	100	–	51	17	814	39	24	67
Other alcoholic beverages	100	21	54	94	150	179	167	203
• At fast food, take-out, delivery, concession stands, buffet, and cafeteria	100	8	70	127	123	149	185	83
• At full-service restaurants	100	27	48	93	108	191	176	220
• At catered affairs	100	–	55	19	823	31	7	77
Alcoholic beverages purchased on trips	100	21	57	100	109	190	176	215

Note: (–) means sample is too small to make a reliable estimate.
Source: Calculations by New Strategist based on the 2002 Consumer Expenditure Survey

Table 5.23 Food and Alcohol: Total spending by education, 2002

(total annual spending on food and alcoholic beverages, by consumer unit (CU) educational attainment group, 2002; numbers in thousands)

	total consumer units	less than high school graduate	high school graduate	some college	associate's degree	college graduate total	bachelor's degree	master's, professional, doctorate
Number of consumer units	112,108	17,075	31,961	23,260	10,395	29,417	19,082	10,335
Total spending of all CUs	$4,560,172,273	$425,686,580	$1,077,329,562	$899,082,038	$461,598,187	$1,688,065,422	$1,025,305,819	$662,664,491
Food, total spending	602,558,078	70,693,232	150,458,645	118,903,492	59,152,748	199,421,373	125,272,758	74,113,939
Alcoholic beverages, total spending	42,147,003	3,166,047	8,718,641	8,660,396	4,498,436	16,516,175	10,271,077	6,239,963
FOOD AT HOME	**$347,368,880**	**$49,442,541**	**$93,223,845**	**$66,711,773**	**$32,578,346**	**$103,987,918**	**$65,626,242**	**$38,337,269**
Cereals and bakery products	**50,463,174**	**6,909,911**	**13,492,336**	**9,836,189**	**4,803,633**	**15,177,407**	**9,529,169**	**5,643,840**
Cereals and cereal products	17,272,480	2,605,133	4,605,580	3,411,777	1,469,021	5,118,264	3,246,611	1,870,635
Flour	969,734	262,101	263,039	157,005	59,459	237,395	154,373	83,093
Prepared flour mixes	1,390,139	173,141	419,328	257,023	141,476	392,423	234,709	157,195
Ready-to-eat and cooked cereals	9,827,387	1,322,117	2,603,223	1,993,382	859,459	2,993,474	1,877,860	1,114,836
Rice	1,997,765	377,528	513,613	362,623	169,231	576,279	387,746	188,614
Pasta, cornmeal, and other cereal products	3,087,454	470,416	806,376	641,511	239,293	918,987	591,924	326,896
Bakery products	33,190,694	4,304,778	8,886,756	6,424,412	3,334,612	10,059,143	6,282,558	3,773,205
Bread	9,398,014	1,373,172	2,682,806	1,777,529	838,045	2,691,656	1,667,958	1,022,545
White bread	3,947,323	684,708	1,211,961	775,023	336,798	948,698	609,097	339,608
Bread, other than white	5,450,691	688,464	1,470,845	1,002,506	501,143	1,742,957	1,058,860	682,937
Crackers and cookies	7,922,672	939,296	2,077,145	1,569,120	748,856	2,524,273	1,596,973	926,739
Cookies	5,191,721	638,093	1,382,313	1,049,956	485,447	1,600,873	1,023,177	577,727
Crackers	2,730,951	301,203	694,832	519,163	263,409	923,400	573,987	349,013
Frozen and refrigerated bakery products	2,874,449	365,064	766,425	514,744	312,993	897,219	583,528	313,771
Other bakery products	12,995,559	1,627,248	3,360,380	2,563,252	1,434,822	3,945,996	2,434,100	1,510,150
Biscuits and rolls	4,600,912	487,321	1,124,068	896,673	446,881	1,593,519	966,503	626,094
Cakes and cupcakes	4,005,619	515,324	1,000,699	810,844	518,503	1,153,735	737,328	416,190
Bread and cracker products	392,378	37,565	100,677	68,152	49,376	132,082	87,205	44,957
Sweetrolls, coffee cakes, doughnuts	2,896,871	416,801	832,904	528,700	322,037	792,494	483,920	308,190
Pies, tarts, turnovers	1,100,901	170,238	302,031	259,116	98,025	274,166	159,144	114,822
Meats, poultry, fish, and eggs	**89,509,269**	**14,399,348**	**25,572,955**	**17,023,064**	**8,402,279**	**24,083,992**	**15,418,065**	**8,663,210**
Beef	25,916,006	4,042,848	7,749,264	4,972,755	2,684,925	6,499,098	4,209,489	2,289,719
Ground beef	9,673,799	1,643,640	3,097,660	1,883,827	889,500	2,194,214	1,504,043	691,412
Roast	4,595,307	706,905	1,375,601	916,909	486,174	1,119,905	742,099	377,951
Chuck roast	1,312,785	255,101	409,740	235,856	136,486	284,757	187,958	96,736
Round roast	1,146,865	155,724	342,302	228,413	93,347	322,410	201,888	120,403
Other roast	2,135,657	296,081	623,559	452,640	256,341	512,738	352,445	160,709
Steak	9,469,763	1,354,731	2,732,666	1,763,806	1,106,548	2,509,270	1,510,340	997,224
Round steak	1,489,915	258,686	458,321	256,558	150,312	369,183	239,097	130,014
Sirloin steak	2,984,315	413,557	849,843	523,815	393,243	802,790	539,639	263,336
Other steak	4,995,532	682,488	1,424,502	983,433	563,097	1,337,297	731,604	603,874
Pork	18,760,153	3,510,620	5,724,535	3,641,818	1,646,464	4,329,594	2,866,307	1,464,159
Bacon	3,189,473	621,359	924,632	628,718	319,438	719,246	454,915	264,163
Pork chops	4,308,310	843,505	1,363,776	861,550	404,158	872,802	606,044	267,263
Ham	4,165,933	650,558	1,404,366	761,067	318,607	1,025,771	648,597	377,021
Ham, not canned	3,997,771	613,163	1,360,899	730,131	300,727	985,764	614,440	371,130
Canned ham	168,162	37,224	43,147	30,936	17,879	40,007	34,348	5,891
Sausage	2,933,866	580,038	852,719	617,786	219,438	681,298	477,813	204,013
Other pork	4,162,570	815,331	1,179,041	772,697	384,823	1,030,478	678,938	351,803
Other meats	11,331,877	1,685,303	3,200,894	2,145,502	1,029,313	3,234,987	2,196,911	1,039,494
Frankfurters	2,348,663	367,283	701,224	479,621	220,894	582,751	392,898	190,061

	total consumer units	less than high school graduate	high school graduate	some college	associate's degree	college graduate total	college graduate bachelor's degree	master's, professional, doctorate
Lunch meats (cold cuts)	$7,734,331	$1,167,930	$2,198,278	$1,473,986	$675,987	$2,195,097	$1,449,660	$745,774
Bologna, liverwurst, salami	2,366,600	456,073	745,650	415,656	188,877	568,336	372,290	195,952
Lamb, organ meats, and others	1,248,883	150,089	301,392	191,895	132,432	457,140	354,353	103,660
Lamb and organ meats	895,743	128,746	258,564	156,772	91,476	257,105	159,716	103,660
Mutton, goat, and game	353,140	21,344	43,147	35,123	40,956	200,330	194,636	6,511
Poultry	16,158,126	2,434,383	4,556,041	3,020,078	1,492,098	4,608,173	3,060,753	1,548,390
Fresh and frozen chicken	12,696,231	2,017,411	3,493,018	2,440,904	1,130,040	3,592,110	2,391,929	1,201,134
Fresh and frozen whole chicken	3,596,425	745,495	1,008,370	632,905	306,445	918,987	623,981	295,478
Fresh and frozen chicken parts	9,099,806	1,271,917	2,484,968	1,808,000	823,596	2,673,123	1,767,947	905,759
Other poultry	3,461,895	416,972	1,063,023	578,941	362,058	1,016,063	669,015	347,256
Fish and seafood	13,561,705	1,992,653	3,256,187	2,510,917	1,213,720	4,496,683	2,494,208	1,996,205
Canned fish and seafood	1,808,302	293,349	431,474	367,275	164,969	547,450	314,471	232,434
Fresh fish and shellfish	7,770,205	1,291,724	1,818,261	1,409,091	636,278	2,573,693	1,408,633	1,161,447
Frozen fish and shellfish	3,983,197	407,751	1,006,452	734,551	412,578	1,375,539	771,294	602,427
Eggs	3,783,645	733,542	1,085,715	731,992	335,759	915,457	590,206	325,139
Dairy products	**36,809,541**	**5,082,374**	**9,696,009**	**7,100,115**	**3,397,190**	**11,330,252**	**7,152,697**	**4,174,823**
Fresh milk and cream	14,254,532	2,216,847	3,943,029	2,775,848	1,318,190	3,979,238	2,558,705	1,420,236
Fresh milk, all types	12,850,940	2,059,245	3,569,085	2,521,617	1,178,793	3,515,332	2,270,376	1,244,644
Cream	1,403,592	157,602	373,944	254,232	139,293	464,200	288,329	175,592
Other dairy products	22,555,009	2,865,527	5,752,980	4,324,034	2,079,000	7,351,014	4,593,801	2,754,588
Butter	2,071,756	292,666	582,010	382,860	234,719	576,279	367,710	208,560
Cheese	10,722,009	1,277,722	2,710,293	2,067,116	954,053	3,606,230	2,307,205	1,298,593
Ice cream and related products	6,585,224	916,757	1,716,306	1,330,472	596,049	1,995,061	1,243,001	751,251
Miscellaneous dairy products	3,176,020	378,382	744,691	543,586	294,179	1,173,444	676,075	496,183
Fruits and vegetables	**61,884,737**	**8,930,054**	**15,552,223**	**11,160,846**	**5,520,265**	**20,283,022**	**12,332,315**	**7,939,037**
Fresh fruits	19,977,646	2,836,670	4,862,227	3,421,779	1,736,589	6,933,881	4,175,523	2,753,657
Apples	3,653,600	537,863	930,385	668,027	301,039	1,190,212	729,505	460,218
Bananas	3,502,254	596,942	911,847	595,456	289,709	1,094,018	698,210	395,624
Oranges	2,280,277	324,254	576,896	399,142	212,370	750,428	452,243	297,545
Citrus fruits, excl. oranges	1,602,023	251,344	346,777	265,164	146,985	578,632	324,394	253,621
Other fresh fruits	8,939,492	1,126,438	2,096,322	1,493,757	786,590	3,320,591	1,971,361	1,346,651
Fresh vegetables	19,605,447	2,920,167	4,810,131	3,565,525	1,706,131	6,470,269	3,843,878	2,621,369
Potatoes	3,738,802	653,631	1,022,113	695,707	319,854	1,046,363	635,049	410,713
Lettuce	2,491,040	343,208	626,116	457,059	236,590	810,733	496,323	313,977
Tomatoes	3,779,161	636,727	966,181	679,192	304,677	1,177,563	703,553	473,033
Other fresh vegetables	9,596,445	1,286,601	2,195,721	1,733,568	845,114	3,435,611	2,008,762	1,423,543
Processed fruits	12,948,474	1,709,549	3,246,279	2,398,339	1,180,248	4,305,766	2,620,149	1,683,055
Frozen fruits and fruit juices	1,395,745	150,943	323,126	316,801	102,495	485,969	295,008	190,577
Frozen orange juice	707,401	75,813	179,621	160,959	56,029	228,276	128,040	100,043
Frozen fruits	312,781	27,832	73,510	66,291	25,052	115,020	79,572	35,656
Frozen fruit juices, excl. orange	375,562	47,469	70,314	89,551	21,518	142,378	87,396	54,982
Canned fruits	1,688,346	257,833	418,369	330,757	155,613	519,504	303,785	215,071
Dried fruits	679,374	90,327	178,342	121,185	56,341	227,099	134,910	92,085
Fresh fruit juice	2,488,798	303,935	659,995	434,032	222,245	841,915	494,987	346,016
Canned and bottled fruit juice	6,697,332	906,512	1,666,447	1,195,564	643,554	2,231,279	1,391,269	839,202
Processed vegetables	9,353,170	1,463,498	2,633,906	1,775,436	897,192	2,573,399	1,692,573	880,955
Frozen vegetables	3,122,208	396,140	866,782	612,203	317,255	914,280	596,313	318,111
Canned and dried vegetables and juices	6,230,963	1,067,358	1,767,124	1,163,233	579,937	1,658,825	1,096,452	562,844
Canned beans	1,397,987	243,319	389,924	234,926	143,139	386,539	266,003	120,713
Canned corn	822,873	171,775	267,194	154,679	72,557	164,441	116,591	47,954
Canned miscellaneous vegetables	2,001,128	291,641	566,988	378,208	203,950	555,981	367,329	188,924
Dried peas	40,359	7,342	10,867	5,815	4,158	12,355	6,679	5,788
Dried beans	285,875	79,228	64,881	70,013	20,478	57,069	38,355	18,603

	total consumer units	less than high school graduate	high school graduate	some college	associate's degree	college graduate total	college graduate bachelor's degree	master's, professional, doctorate
Dried miscellaneous vegetables	$827,357	$170,238	$230,119	$159,564	$56,445	$214,156	$139,871	$74,205
Dried processed vegetables	38,117	2,391	14,063	1,163	9,148	10,590	8,778	2,067
Fresh and canned vegetable juices	810,541	101,255	219,252	157,935	70,166	255,634	151,511	103,970
Sugar and other sweets	**13,160,358**	**1,764,531**	**3,516,988**	**2,534,410**	**1,270,685**	**4,002,771**	**2,626,828**	**1,376,209**
Candy and chewing gum	8,457,428	1,009,645	2,153,852	1,666,812	861,018	2,703,422	1,768,329	935,318
Sugar	1,744,400	377,870	533,749	320,523	142,204	384,480	253,600	130,944
Artificial sweeteners	485,428	79,740	153,413	86,062	39,085	126,199	87,014	39,170
Jams, preserves, other sweets	2,473,102	297,105	675,975	461,013	228,378	788,670	518,076	270,777
Fats and oils	**9,547,117**	**1,508,064**	**2,750,564**	**1,763,341**	**891,579**	**2,620,761**	**1,679,788**	**940,795**
Margarine	1,105,385	165,628	336,549	214,225	108,212	281,227	175,554	105,727
Fats and oils	2,923,777	618,286	835,780	430,775	240,956	802,790	510,062	292,584
Salad dressings	3,028,037	356,526	885,959	615,692	298,648	855,446	556,622	298,785
Nondairy cream and imitation milk	1,045,968	141,552	305,867	222,133	108,420	267,106	156,091	110,895
Peanut butter	1,445,072	226,244	386,089	280,516	135,343	414,191	281,460	132,908
Miscellaneous foods	**52,906,007**	**6,586,681**	**13,712,547**	**10,549,806**	**5,110,910**	**16,588,835**	**10,680,195**	**5,907,589**
Frozen prepared foods	10,996,674	1,358,658	2,819,919	2,256,918	1,149,583	3,353,832	2,162,563	1,191,109
Frozen meals	3,349,787	438,145	844,410	662,910	333,887	1,050,775	660,237	390,043
Other frozen prepared foods	7,648,008	920,684	1,975,509	1,594,008	815,696	2,303,351	1,502,326	801,066
Canned and packaged soups	4,015,709	458,122	1,092,747	772,232	361,954	1,292,583	815,946	476,237
Potato chips, nuts, and other snacks	11,270,217	1,246,134	2,887,996	2,252,033	1,130,144	3,655,062	2,389,639	1,265,624
Potato chips and other snacks	8,561,688	1,004,693	2,219,052	1,750,315	866,423	2,663,415	1,777,870	886,433
Nuts	2,708,529	241,441	668,944	501,718	263,721	991,353	611,769	379,191
Condiments and seasonings	9,732,095	1,222,741	2,496,474	1,905,459	939,708	3,098,198	1,944,456	1,152,869
Salt, spices, and other seasonings	2,369,963	331,426	623,240	443,336	240,332	721,011	442,702	278,012
Olives, pickles, relishes	1,087,448	141,040	287,969	196,082	103,742	349,768	208,948	140,556
Sauces and gravies	4,235,440	512,079	1,091,149	894,347	406,445	1,305,232	829,495	475,617
Baking needs and miscellaneous products	2,039,245	238,196	494,437	371,695	189,085	721,893	463,120	258,685
Other canned/packaged prepared foods	16,891,312	2,300,856	4,415,412	3,362,931	1,529,520	5,189,453	3,367,591	1,821,854
Prepared salads	2,405,838	246,563	570,823	390,303	249,168	912,515	574,941	337,231
Prepared desserts	1,156,955	148,894	296,598	241,671	117,048	348,003	205,322	142,313
Baby food	3,539,250	490,223	1,095,623	756,648	235,447	946,933	665,962	281,525
Miscellaneous prepared foods	9,780,302	1,414,664	2,445,017	1,973,611	927,962	2,981,119	1,920,412	1,060,474
Nonalcoholic beverages	**28,468,706**	**3,929,811**	**8,026,366**	**5,791,042**	**2,774,841**	**7,877,284**	**5,018,566**	**2,857,317**
Cola	9,093,080	1,379,148	2,727,552	1,911,274	888,669	2,203,039	1,467,024	736,679
Other carbonated drinks	4,924,904	694,099	1,447,514	1,067,401	491,372	1,228,160	832,357	396,347
Coffee	4,662,572	620,506	1,215,157	901,558	411,642	1,480,263	860,980	617,930
Roasted coffee	3,069,517	358,063	787,519	579,407	295,322	1,019,299	585,817	432,313
Instant and freeze-dried coffee	1,593,055	262,443	427,638	322,151	116,320	460,964	275,162	185,513
Noncarbonated fruit-flavored drinks, incl. nonfrozen lemonade	2,124,447	326,645	623,879	429,612	199,792	545,391	350,918	194,401
Tea	1,778,033	268,248	488,044	354,482	175,364	490,087	314,090	176,108
Nonalcoholic beer	71,749	1,878	25,249	21,632	1,975	20,298	15,456	4,961
Other nonalcoholic beverages and ice	5,812,800	639,288	1,498,971	1,105,315	606,029	1,909,752	1,177,932	730,891
Food prepared by CU on trips	**4,618,850**	**331,767**	**903,537**	**952,962**	**406,860**	**2,023,301**	**1,188,809**	**834,448**
FOOD AWAY FROM HOME	**255,190,319**	**21,250,691**	**57,234,800**	**52,191,486**	**26,574,402**	**95,433,455**	**59,646,516**	**35,776,670**
Meals at restaurants, carry-outs, other	**209,240,613**	**19,078,239**	**49,295,368**	**43,366,642**	**21,758,502**	**73,236,563**	**46,795,934**	**26,430,316**
Lunch	76,882,545	7,715,510	18,415,609	16,235,247	7,794,691	25,946,088	16,911,804	9,035,580
• At fast food, take-out, delivery, concession stands, buffet, and cafeteria (other than employer and school cafeteria)	42,344,313	4,868,936	10,954,633	9,278,181	4,170,890	12,822,576	8,837,065	3,992,927
• At full-service restaurants	25,204,121	1,915,132	4,902,817	4,959,265	2,592,097	10,368,610	6,280,649	4,081,602
• At vending machines, mobile vendors	616,594	206,095	181,858	125,837	51,871	69,718	49,804	19,843
• At employer and school cafeterias	8,717,518	725,517	2,376,300	1,872,197	979,833	2,685,478	1,744,286	941,208

	total consumer units	less than high school graduate	high school graduate	some college	associate's degree	college graduate total	college graduate bachelor's degree	college graduate master's, professional, doctorate
Dinner	$82,572,026	$6,131,462	$17,898,480	$16,288,280	$8,846,873	$32,024,817	$19,854,058	$12,157,577
• At fast food, take-out, delivery, concession stands, buffet, and cafeteria (other than employer and school cafeteria)	23,916,000	2,625,281	5,725,174	5,216,288	2,935,652	7,304,241	4,800,459	2,504,687
• At full-service restaurants	58,074,186	3,449,150	12,055,050	10,874,515	5,865,795	24,557,312	14,956,090	9,587,263
• At vending machines, mobile vendors	209,642	33,467	44,426	33,262	9,356	85,898	43,316	42,477
• At employer and school cafeterias	372,199	23,564	73,830	163,983	36,175	77,073	54,002	23,150
Snacks and nonalcoholic beverages	29,447,408	3,160,241	7,669,362	6,429,064	3,060,496	8,940,415	5,932,594	3,009,759
• At fast food, take-out, delivery, concession stands, buffet, and cafeteria (other than employer and school cafeteria)	20,817,335	2,135,570	5,139,968	4,522,209	2,219,644	6,637,652	4,352,032	2,286,309
• At full-service restaurants	3,382,298	450,097	920,157	686,403	292,411	1,014,592	640,774	373,404
• At vending machines, mobile vendors	4,115,485	445,828	1,317,752	978,781	434,095	938,402	696,302	243,286
• At employer and school cafeterias	1,133,412	128,746	290,845	241,671	114,449	349,768	243,296	106,657
Breakfast and brunch	20,338,633	2,070,685	5,311,918	4,414,050	2,056,443	6,325,243	4,097,669	2,227,399
• At fast food, take-out, delivery, concession stands, buffet, and cafeteria (other than employer and school cafeteria)	9,846,446	1,261,330	2,958,949	2,089,678	1,057,172	2,473,970	1,768,329	708,051
• At full-service restaurants	9,762,365	703,490	2,165,038	2,128,290	927,234	3,680,067	2,199,582	1,477,802
• At vending machines, mobile vendors	156,951	54,299	38,353	34,192	16,944	18,533	14,693	3,927
• At employer and school cafeterias	572,872	51,567	149,897	161,890	55,094	152,380	115,064	37,619
Board (including at school)	**5,217,506**	**111,841**	**670,542**	**1,603,544**	**241,164**	**2,590,167**	**1,290,516**	**1,299,523**
Catered affairs	**7,735,452**	**246,051**	**684,924**	**715,943**	**932,432**	**5,155,329**	**2,994,538**	**2,160,945**
Food on trips	**23,709,721**	**962,176**	**4,249,215**	**4,344,735**	**2,480,039**	**11,672,960**	**6,729,840**	**4,943,127**
School lunches	**6,726,480**	**547,937**	**1,689,778**	**1,441,887**	**944,802**	**2,101,845**	**1,453,094**	**648,521**
Meals as pay	**2,562,789**	**304,447**	**644,973**	**718,734**	**217,463**	**676,885**	**382,594**	**294,341**
ALCOHOLIC BEVERAGES	**42,147,003**	**3,166,047**	**8,718,641**	**8,660,396**	**4,498,436**	**16,516,175**	**10,271,077**	**6,239,963**
At home	**25,569,593**	**2,515,148**	**5,928,126**	**5,454,935**	**2,450,725**	**8,928,648**	**5,670,216**	**3,256,559**
Beer and ale	12,594,213	1,730,039	3,634,605	3,009,611	1,255,300	2,993,768	2,228,587	769,131
Whiskey	1,558,301	97,157	261,441	371,230	222,765	587,163	346,338	240,289
Wine	8,716,397	486,808	1,430,894	1,574,237	624,324	4,336,360	2,359,489	1,970,471
Other alcoholic beverages	2,700,682	200,973	601,186	499,625	348,440	1,011,356	735,802	276,668
Away from home	**16,577,410**	**650,899**	**2,790,835**	**3,205,461**	**2,047,607**	**7,587,821**	**4,600,861**	**2,983,508**
Beer and ale	5,926,029	255,271	1,127,264	1,146,485	609,355	2,640,470	1,630,557	1,008,696
• At fast food, take-out, delivery, concession stands, buffet, and cafeteria	895,743	49,347	206,788	181,428	100,624	341,826	214,863	126,707
• At full-service restaurants	4,702,931	196,533	755,558	913,885	505,613	2,208,923	1,399,856	808,714
• At vending machines, mobile vendors	35,875	9,562	6,712	11,863	1,767	6,766	4,198	2,377
• At catered affairs	290,360	–	158,207	39,309	1,247	82,956	11,449	70,898
Wine	2,897,992	142,235	473,662	554,286	362,578	1,300,820	772,630	527,085
• At fast food, take-out, delivery, concession stands, buffet and cafeteria	494,396	36,199	97,161	107,926	56,549	189,151	120,980	68,211
• At full-service restaurants	2,282,519	106,036	358,602	442,173	213,825	1,099,019	646,689	451,433
• At catered affairs	122,198	–	17,898	4,187	92,204	12,649	4,961	7,545
Other alcoholic beverages	7,753,389	253,564	1,189,908	1,504,922	1,075,779	3,646,531	2,197,674	1,447,623
• At fast food, take-out, delivery, concession stands, buffet, and cafeteria	392,378	4,952	78,624	103,507	44,595	152,968	123,270	30,075
• At full-service restaurants	3,244,406	133,527	442,021	623,135	323,804	1,627,937	970,129	656,583
• At catered affairs	441,706	–	69,675	17,445	337,214	36,477	4,961	31,212
Alcoholic beverages purchased on trips	3,674,900	114,915	599,269	760,835	370,166	1,829,149	1,099,505	729,651

Note: Numbers may not add to total because of rounding. (–) means sample is too small to make a reliable estimate.
Source: Calculations by New Strategist based on the 2002 Consumer Expenditure Survey

Table 5.24 Food and Alcohol: Market shares by education, 2002

(percentage of total annual spending on food and alcoholic beverages accounted for by consumer unit educational attainment groups, 2002)

	total consumer units	less than high school graduate	high school graduate	some college	associate's degree	college graduate total	bachelor's degree	master's, professional, doctorate
Share of total consumer units	**100.0%**	**15.2%**	**28.5%**	**20.7%**	**9.3%**	**26.2%**	**17.0%**	**9.2%**
Share of total before-tax income	**100.0**	**7.9**	**22.8**	**17.9**	**10.3**	**41.3**	**23.9**	**17.3**
Share of total spending	**100.0**	**9.3**	**23.6**	**19.7**	**10.1**	**37.0**	**22.5**	**14.5**
Share of food spending	**100.0**	**11.7**	**25.0**	**19.7**	**9.8**	**33.1**	**20.8**	**12.3**
Share of alcoholic beverages spending	**100.0**	**7.5**	**20.7**	**20.5**	**10.7**	**39.2**	**24.4**	**14.8**
FOOD AT HOME	**100.0%**	**14.2%**	**26.8%**	**19.2%**	**9.4%**	**29.9%**	**18.9%**	**11.0%**
Cereals and bakery products	**100.0**	**13.7**	**26.7**	**19.5**	**9.5**	**30.1**	**18.9**	**11.2**
Cereals and cereal products	100.0	15.1	26.7	19.8	8.5	29.6	18.8	10.8
Flour	100.0	27.0	27.1	16.2	6.1	24.5	15.9	8.6
Prepared flour mixes	100.0	12.5	30.2	18.5	10.2	28.2	16.9	11.3
Ready-to-eat and cooked cereals	100.0	13.5	26.5	20.3	8.7	30.5	19.1	11.3
Rice	100.0	18.9	25.7	18.2	8.5	28.8	19.4	9.4
Pasta, cornmeal, and other cereal products	100.0	15.2	26.1	20.8	7.8	29.8	19.2	10.6
Bakery products	100.0	13.0	26.8	19.4	10.0	30.3	18.9	11.4
Bread	100.0	14.6	28.5	18.9	8.9	28.6	17.7	10.9
White bread	100.0	17.3	30.7	19.6	8.5	24.0	15.4	8.6
Bread, other than white	100.0	12.6	27.0	18.4	9.2	32.0	19.4	12.5
Crackers and cookies	100.0	11.9	26.2	19.8	9.5	31.9	20.2	11.7
Cookies	100.0	12.3	26.6	20.2	9.4	30.8	19.7	11.1
Crackers	100.0	11.0	25.4	19.0	9.6	33.8	21.0	12.8
Frozen and refrigerated bakery products	100.0	12.7	26.7	17.9	10.9	31.2	20.3	10.9
Other bakery products	100.0	12.5	25.9	19.7	11.0	30.4	18.7	11.6
Biscuits and rolls	100.0	10.6	24.4	19.5	9.7	34.6	21.0	13.6
Cakes and cupcakes	100.0	12.9	25.0	20.2	12.9	28.8	18.4	10.4
Bread and cracker products	100.0	9.6	25.7	17.4	12.6	33.7	22.2	11.5
Sweetrolls, coffee cakes, doughnuts	100.0	14.4	28.8	18.3	11.1	27.4	16.7	10.6
Pies, tarts, turnovers	100.0	15.5	27.4	23.5	8.9	24.9	14.5	10.4
Meats, poultry, fish, and eggs	**100.0**	**16.1**	**28.6**	**19.0**	**9.4**	**26.9**	**17.2**	**9.7**
Beef	100.0	15.6	29.9	19.2	10.4	25.1	16.2	8.8
Ground beef	100.0	17.0	32.0	19.5	9.2	22.7	15.5	7.1
Roast	100.0	15.4	29.9	20.0	10.6	24.4	16.1	8.2
Chuck roast	100.0	19.4	31.2	18.0	10.4	21.7	14.3	7.4
Round roast	100.0	13.6	29.8	19.9	8.1	28.1	17.6	10.5
Other roast	100.0	13.9	29.2	21.2	12.0	24.0	16.5	7.5
Steak	100.0	14.3	28.9	18.6	11.7	26.5	15.9	10.5
Round steak	100.0	17.4	30.8	17.2	10.1	24.8	16.0	8.7
Sirloin steak	100.0	13.9	28.5	17.6	13.2	26.9	18.1	8.8
Other steak	100.0	13.7	28.5	19.7	11.3	26.8	14.6	12.1
Pork	100.0	18.7	30.5	19.4	8.8	23.1	15.3	7.8
Bacon	100.0	19.5	29.0	19.7	10.0	22.6	14.3	8.3
Pork chops	100.0	19.6	31.7	20.0	9.4	20.3	14.1	6.2
Ham	100.0	15.6	33.7	18.3	7.6	24.6	15.6	9.1
Ham, not canned	100.0	15.3	34.0	18.3	7.5	24.7	15.4	9.3
Canned ham	100.0	22.1	25.7	18.4	10.6	23.8	20.4	3.5
Sausage	100.0	19.8	29.1	21.1	7.5	23.2	16.3	7.0
Other pork	100.0	19.6	28.3	18.6	9.2	24.8	16.3	8.5
Other meats	100.0	14.9	28.2	18.9	9.1	28.5	19.4	9.2
Frankfurters	100.0	15.6	29.9	20.4	9.4	24.8	16.7	8.1

	total consumer units	less than high school graduate	high school graduate	some college	associate's degree	college graduate		
						total	bachelor's degree	master's, professional, doctorate
Lunch meats (cold cuts)	100.0%	15.1%	28.4%	19.1%	8.7%	28.4%	18.7%	9.6%
Bologna, liverwurst, salami	100.0	19.3	31.5	17.6	8.0	24.0	15.7	8.3
Lamb, organ meats, and others	100.0	12.0	24.1	15.4	10.6	36.6	28.4	8.3
Lamb and organ meats	100.0	14.4	28.9	17.5	10.2	28.7	17.8	10.8
Mutton, goat, and game	100.0	6.0	12.2	9.9	11.6	56.7	55.1	1.8
Poultry	100.0	15.1	28.2	18.7	9.2	28.5	18.9	9.6
Fresh and frozen chicken	100.0	15.9	27.5	19.2	8.9	28.3	18.8	9.5
Fresh and frozen whole chicken	100.0	20.7	28.0	17.6	8.5	25.6	17.4	8.2
Fresh and frozen chicken parts	100.0	14.0	27.3	19.9	9.1	29.4	19.4	10.0
Other poultry	100.0	12.0	30.7	16.7	10.5	29.3	19.3	10.0
Fish and seafood	100.0	14.7	24.0	18.5	8.9	33.2	18.4	14.7
Canned fish and seafood	100.0	16.2	23.9	20.3	9.1	30.3	17.4	12.9
Fresh fish and shellfish	100.0	16.6	23.4	18.1	8.2	33.1	18.1	14.9
Frozen fish and shellfish	100.0	10.2	25.3	18.4	10.4	34.5	19.4	15.1
Eggs	100.0	19.4	28.7	19.3	8.9	24.2	15.6	8.6
Dairy products	**100.0**	**13.8**	**26.3**	**19.3**	**9.2**	**30.8**	**19.4**	**11.3**
Fresh milk and cream	100.0	15.6	27.7	19.5	9.2	27.9	18.0	10.0
Fresh milk, all types	100.0	16.0	27.8	19.6	9.2	27.4	17.7	9.7
Cream	100.0	11.2	26.6	18.1	9.9	33.1	20.5	12.5
Other dairy products	100.0	12.7	25.5	19.2	9.2	32.6	20.4	12.2
Butter	100.0	14.1	28.1	18.5	11.3	27.8	17.7	10.1
Cheese	100.0	11.9	25.3	19.3	8.9	33.6	21.5	12.1
Ice cream and related products	100.0	13.9	26.1	20.2	9.1	30.3	18.9	11.4
Miscellaneous dairy products	100.0	11.9	23.4	17.1	9.3	36.9	21.3	15.6
Fruits and vegetables	**100.0**	**14.4**	**25.1**	**18.0**	**8.9**	**32.8**	**19.9**	**12.8**
Fresh fruits	100.0	14.2	24.3	17.1	8.7	34.7	20.9	13.8
Apples	100.0	14.7	25.5	18.3	8.2	32.6	20.0	12.6
Bananas	100.0	17.0	26.0	17.0	8.3	31.2	19.9	11.3
Oranges	100.0	14.2	25.3	17.5	9.3	32.9	19.8	13.0
Citrus fruits, excl. oranges	100.0	15.7	21.6	16.6	9.2	36.1	20.2	15.8
Other fresh fruits	100.0	12.6	23.5	16.7	8.8	37.1	22.1	15.1
Fresh vegetables	100.0	14.9	24.5	18.2	8.7	33.0	19.6	13.4
Potatoes	100.0	17.5	27.3	18.6	8.6	28.0	17.0	11.0
Lettuce	100.0	13.8	25.1	18.3	9.5	32.5	19.9	12.6
Tomatoes	100.0	16.8	25.6	18.0	8.1	31.2	18.6	12.5
Other fresh vegetables	100.0	13.4	22.9	18.1	8.8	35.8	20.9	14.8
Processed fruits	100.0	13.2	25.1	18.5	9.1	33.3	20.2	13.0
Frozen fruits and fruit juices	100.0	10.8	23.2	22.7	7.3	34.8	21.1	13.7
Frozen orange juice	100.0	10.7	25.4	22.8	7.9	32.3	18.1	14.1
Frozen fruits	100.0	8.9	23.5	21.2	8.0	36.8	25.4	11.4
Frozen fruit juices, excl. orange	100.0	12.6	18.7	23.8	5.7	37.9	23.3	14.6
Canned fruits	100.0	15.3	24.8	19.6	9.2	30.8	18.0	12.7
Dried fruits	100.0	13.3	26.3	17.8	8.3	33.4	19.9	13.6
Fresh fruit juice	100.0	12.2	26.5	17.4	8.9	33.8	19.9	13.9
Canned and bottled fruit juice	100.0	13.5	24.9	17.9	9.6	33.3	20.8	12.5
Processed vegetables	100.0	15.6	28.2	19.0	9.6	27.5	18.1	9.4
Frozen vegetables	100.0	12.7	27.8	19.6	10.2	29.3	19.1	10.2
Canned and dried vegetables and juices	100.0	17.1	28.4	18.7	9.3	26.6	17.6	9.0
Canned beans	100.0	17.4	27.9	16.8	10.2	27.6	19.0	8.6
Canned corn	100.0	20.9	32.5	18.8	8.8	20.0	14.2	5.8
Canned miscellaneous vegetables	100.0	14.6	28.3	18.9	10.2	27.8	18.4	9.4
Dried peas	100.0	18.2	26.9	14.4	10.3	30.6	16.5	14.3
Dried beans	100.0	27.7	22.7	24.5	7.2	20.0	13.4	6.5

	total consumer units	less than high school graduate	high school graduate	some college	associate's degree	college graduate total	college graduate bachelor's degree	master's, professional, doctorate
Dried miscellaneous vegetables	100.0%	20.6%	27.8%	19.3%	6.8%	25.9%	16.9%	9.0%
Dried processed vegetables	100.0	6.3	36.9	3.1	24.0	27.8	23.0	5.4
Fresh and canned vegetable juices	100.0	12.5	27.1	19.5	8.7	31.5	18.7	12.8
Sugar and other sweets	**100.0**	**13.4**	**26.7**	**19.3**	**9.7**	**30.4**	**20.0**	**10.5**
Candy and chewing gum	100.0	11.9	25.5	19.7	10.2	32.0	20.9	11.1
Sugar	100.0	21.7	30.6	18.4	8.2	22.0	14.5	7.5
Artificial sweeteners	100.0	16.4	31.6	17.7	8.1	26.0	17.9	8.1
Jams, preserves, other sweets	100.0	12.0	27.3	18.6	9.2	31.9	20.9	10.9
Fats and oils	**100.0**	**15.8**	**28.8**	**18.5**	**9.3**	**27.5**	**17.6**	**9.9**
Margarine	100.0	15.0	30.4	19.4	9.8	25.4	15.9	9.6
Fats and oils	100.0	21.1	28.6	14.7	8.2	27.5	17.4	10.0
Salad dressings	100.0	11.8	29.3	20.3	9.9	28.3	18.4	9.9
Nondairy cream and imitation milk	100.0	13.5	29.2	21.2	10.4	25.5	14.9	10.6
Peanut butter	100.0	15.7	26.7	19.4	9.4	28.7	19.5	9.2
Miscellaneous foods	**100.0**	**12.4**	**25.9**	**19.9**	**9.7**	**31.4**	**20.2**	**11.2**
Frozen prepared foods	100.0	12.4	25.6	20.5	10.5	30.5	19.7	10.8
Frozen meals	100.0	13.1	25.2	19.8	10.0	31.4	19.7	11.6
Other frozen prepared foods	100.0	12.0	25.8	20.8	10.7	30.1	19.6	10.5
Canned and packaged soups	100.0	11.4	27.2	19.2	9.0	32.2	20.3	11.9
Potato chips, nuts, and other snacks	100.0	11.1	25.6	20.0	10.0	32.4	21.2	11.2
Potato chips and other snacks	100.0	11.7	25.9	20.4	10.1	31.1	20.8	10.4
Nuts	100.0	8.9	24.7	18.5	9.7	36.6	22.6	14.0
Condiments and seasonings	100.0	12.6	25.7	19.6	9.7	31.8	20.0	11.8
Salt, spices, and other seasonings	100.0	14.0	26.3	18.7	10.1	30.4	18.7	11.7
Olives, pickles, relishes	100.0	13.0	26.5	18.0	9.5	32.2	19.2	12.9
Sauces and gravies	100.0	12.1	25.8	21.1	9.6	30.8	19.6	11.2
Baking needs and miscellaneous products	100.0	11.7	24.2	18.2	9.3	35.4	22.7	12.7
Other canned/packaged prepared foods	100.0	13.6	26.1	19.9	9.1	30.7	19.9	10.8
Prepared salads	100.0	10.2	23.7	16.2	10.4	37.9	23.9	14.0
Prepared desserts	100.0	12.9	25.6	20.9	10.1	30.1	17.7	12.3
Baby food	100.0	13.9	31.0	21.4	6.7	26.8	18.8	8.0
Miscellaneous prepared foods	100.0	14.5	25.0	20.2	9.5	30.5	19.6	10.8
Nonalcoholic beverages	**100.0**	**13.8**	**28.2**	**20.3**	**9.7**	**27.7**	**17.6**	**10.0**
Cola	100.0	15.2	30.0	21.0	9.8	24.2	16.1	8.1
Other carbonated drinks	100.0	14.1	29.4	21.7	10.0	24.9	16.9	8.0
Coffee	100.0	13.3	26.1	19.3	8.8	31.7	18.5	13.3
Roasted coffee	100.0	11.7	25.7	18.9	9.6	33.2	19.1	14.1
Instant and freeze-dried coffee	100.0	16.5	26.8	20.2	7.3	28.9	17.3	11.6
Noncarbonated fruit-flavored drinks, incl. nonfrozen lemonade	100.0	15.4	29.4	20.2	9.4	25.7	16.5	9.2
Tea	100.0	15.1	27.4	19.9	9.9	27.6	17.7	9.9
Nonalcoholic beer	100.0	2.6	35.2	30.1	2.8	28.3	21.5	6.9
Other nonalcoholic beverages and ice	100.0	11.0	25.8	19.0	10.4	32.9	20.3	12.6
Food prepared by CU on trips	**100.0**	**7.2**	**19.6**	**20.6**	**8.8**	**43.8**	**25.7**	**18.1**
FOOD AWAY FROM HOME	**100.0**	**8.3**	**22.4**	**20.5**	**10.4**	**37.4**	**23.4**	**14.0**
Meals at restaurants, carry-outs, other	**100.0**	**9.1**	**23.6**	**20.7**	**10.4**	**35.0**	**22.4**	**12.6**
Lunch	100.0	10.0	24.0	21.1	10.1	33.7	22.0	11.8
• At fast food, take-out, delivery, concession stands, buffet, and cafeteria (other than employer and school cafeteria)	100.0	11.5	25.9	21.9	9.8	30.3	20.9	9.4
• At full-service restaurants	100.0	7.6	19.5	19.7	10.3	41.1	24.9	16.2
• At vending machines, mobile vendors	100.0	33.4	29.5	20.4	8.4	11.3	8.1	3.2
• At employer and school cafeterias	100.0	8.3	27.3	21.5	11.2	30.8	20.0	10.8

	total consumer units	less than high school graduate	high school graduate	some college	associate's degree	college graduate		
						total	bachelor's degree	master's, professional, doctorate
Dinner	100.0%	7.4%	21.7%	19.7%	10.7%	38.8%	24.0%	14.7%
• At fast food, take-out, delivery, concession stands, buffet, and cafeteria (other than employer and school cafeteria)	100.0	11.0	23.9	21.8	12.3	30.5	20.1	10.5
• At full-service restaurants	100.0	5.9	20.8	18.7	10.1	42.3	25.8	16.5
• At vending machines, mobile vendors	100.0	16.0	21.2	15.9	4.5	41.0	20.7	20.3
• At employer and school cafeterias	100.0	6.3	19.8	44.1	9.7	20.7	14.5	6.2
Snacks and nonalcoholic beverages	100.0	10.7	26.0	21.8	10.4	30.4	20.1	10.2
• At fast food, take-out, delivery, concession stands, buffet, and cafeteria (other than employer and school cafeteria)	100.0	10.3	24.7	21.7	10.7	31.9	20.9	11.0
• At full-service restaurants	100.0	13.3	27.2	20.3	8.6	30.0	18.9	11.0
• At vending machines, mobile vendors	100.0	10.8	32.0	23.8	10.5	22.8	16.9	5.9
• At employer and school cafeterias	100.0	11.4	25.7	21.3	10.1	30.9	21.5	9.4
Breakfast and brunch	100.0	10.2	26.1	21.7	10.1	31.1	20.1	11.0
• At fast food, take-out, delivery, concession stands, buffet, and cafeteria (other than employer and school cafeteria)	100.0	12.8	30.1	21.2	10.7	25.1	18.0	7.2
• At full-service restaurants	100.0	7.2	22.2	21.8	9.5	37.7	22.5	15.1
• At vending machines, mobile vendors	100.0	34.6	24.4	21.8	10.8	11.8	9.4	2.5
• At employer and school cafeterias	100.0	9.0	26.2	28.3	9.6	26.6	20.1	6.6
Board (including at school)	**100.0**	**2.1**	**12.9**	**30.7**	**4.6**	**49.6**	**24.7**	**24.9**
Catered affairs	**100.0**	**3.2**	**8.9**	**9.3**	**12.1**	**66.6**	**38.7**	**27.9**
Food on trips	**100.0**	**4.1**	**17.9**	**18.3**	**10.5**	**49.2**	**28.4**	**20.8**
School lunches	**100.0**	**8.1**	**25.1**	**21.4**	**14.0**	**31.2**	**21.6**	**9.6**
Meals as pay	**100.0**	**11.9**	**25.2**	**28.0**	**8.5**	**26.4**	**14.9**	**11.5**
ALCOHOLIC BEVERAGES	**100.0**	**7.5**	**20.7**	**20.5**	**10.7**	**39.2**	**24.4**	**14.8**
At home	**100.0**	**9.8**	**23.2**	**21.3**	**9.6**	**34.9**	**22.2**	**12.7**
Beer and ale	100.0	13.7	28.9	23.9	10.0	23.8	17.7	6.1
Whiskey	100.0	6.2	16.8	23.8	14.3	37.7	22.2	15.4
Wine	100.0	5.6	16.4	18.1	7.2	49.7	27.1	22.6
Other alcoholic beverages	100.0	7.4	22.3	18.5	12.9	37.4	27.2	10.2
Away from home	**100.0**	**3.9**	**16.8**	**19.3**	**12.4**	**45.8**	**27.8**	**18.0**
Beer and ale	100.0	4.3	19.0	19.3	10.3	44.6	27.5	17.0
• At fast food, take-out, delivery, concession stands, buffet, and cafeteria	100.0	5.5	23.1	20.3	11.2	38.2	24.0	14.1
• At full-service restaurants	100.0	4.2	16.1	19.4	10.8	47.0	29.8	17.2
• At vending machines, mobile vendors	100.0	26.7	18.7	33.1	4.9	18.9	11.7	6.6
• At catered affairs	100.0	–	54.5	13.5	0.4	28.6	3.9	24.4
Wine	100.0	4.9	16.3	19.1	12.5	44.9	26.7	18.2
• At fast food, take-out, delivery, concession stands, buffet and cafeteria	100.0	7.3	19.7	21.8	11.4	38.3	24.5	13.8
• At full-service restaurants	100.0	4.6	15.7	19.4	9.4	48.1	28.3	19.8
• At catered affairs	100.0	–	14.6	3.4	75.5	10.4	4.1	6.2
Other alcoholic beverages	100.0	3.3	15.3	19.4	13.9	47.0	28.3	18.7
• At fast food, take-out, delivery, concession stands, buffet, and cafeteria	100.0	1.3	20.0	26.4	11.4	39.0	31.4	7.7
• At full-service restaurants	100.0	4.1	13.6	19.2	10.0	50.2	29.9	20.2
• At catered affairs	100.0	–	15.8	3.9	76.3	8.3	1.1	7.1
Alcoholic beverages purchased on trips	100.0	3.1	16.3	20.7	10.1	49.8	29.9	19.9

Note: Numbers may not add to total because of rounding. (–) means sample is too small to make a reliable estimate.
Source: Calculations by New Strategist based on the 2002 Consumer Expenditure Survey

Spending on Gifts for Non–Household, 2002

Spending on gifts for non–household members fell a steep 12 percent between 1997 and 2002, to $1,036 after adjusting for inflation. Many gift categories fell sharply, and few increased during those years. Gifts of food were one of the gainers, up 8 percent between 1997 and 2002. Spending on gifts of apparel fell 16 percent, of small appliances 32 percent, and of jewelry and watches 56 percent. In addition to food, the gift categories that saw spending increases were housekeeping supplies, household textiles, major appliances, infants' apparel, and educational expenses.

Households headed by 45-to-54-year-olds spend the most on gifts for non–household members, a total of $1,604 in 2002—55 percent more than the average household. This age group, the most affluent, accounts for 31 percent of all spending on gifts for people in other households—much greater than its 20 percent share of households. Householders aged 55 to 64 spend 48 percent more than the average household on gifts for non–household members, or $1,531 in 2002. Householders aged 65 to 74 spend 5 percent more than average on this item. All other age groups spend less than average on gifts for non–household members.

Households with incomes of $70,000 or more spent $2,267 on gifts for non-household members in 2002, more than twice as much as the average household. While overall spending on gifts is less in lower-income households, gift spending by category varies by household income. Lower-income households spend more than average on practical gifts such as helping a relative pay utility bills.

Among household types, married couples with adult children at home, many of whom also have children living away from home, spend the most on gifts for non–household members—65 percent more than the average household. Married couples without children at home, many of whom are empty-nesters, spend 43 percent more than average on this item. Spending on gifts for non–household members is well below average for married couples with preschoolers, for single parents, and for people living alone.

Black and Hispanic households spend less than the average household on gifts for non–household members. But they spend more than average on a variety of individual gift categories. Black households spend more than average on gifts of footwear. Hispanics spend 46 percent more than average on gifts of infant clothing.

Households in the Northeast spend the most on gifts for non–household members, 20 percent more than the average household. In the South, spending on gifts is 21 percent below average.

Because college graduates dominate the nation's affluent households, they spend the most on gifts for non–household members. In 2002, households headed by college graduates spent $1,785 on gifts for non–household members, 72 percent more than the average household. College graduates spend more than twice the average on gifts of food and educational expenses. They account for 60 percent of the market for gifts of jewelry for non–household members.

Table 6.1 Gifts for Non—Household Members: Average spending by age, 2002

(average annual spending of consumer units (CU) on selected gifts of products and services for non—household members by age of consumer unit reference person, 2002)

	total consumer units	under 25	25 to 34	35 to 44	45 to 54	55 to 64	65 to 74	75+
Number of consumer units (in thousands, add 000)	112,108	8,737	18,988	24,394	22,691	15,314	11,216	10,767
Average number of persons per CU	2.5	1.9	2.9	3.2	2.7	2.1	1.9	1.5
Average before-tax income of CU	$49,430.00	$20,773.00	$49,133.00	$61,532.00	$64,974.00	$53,162.00	$35,118.00	$23,890.00
Average spending of CU, total	40,676.60	24,229.46	40,318.29	48,330.48	48,748.24	44,330.04	32,242.52	23,758.89
Gifts, average spending	1,036.24	436.63	687.66	868.25	1,604.45	1,530.65	1,089.07	559.82
FOOD	**$82.18**	**$26.83**	**$34.26**	**$59.93**	**$152.65**	**$152.00**	**$60.51**	**$36.79**
Cakes and cupcakes	2.41	0.53	2.34	2.14	4.83	2.45	0.74	1.25
Fresh fruit other than apples, bananas, and citrus	2.26	2.26	1.51	2.38	1.96	4.10	3.04	0.49
Candy and chewing gum	11.69	3.22	8.38	8.50	12.88	19.00	18.71	11.71
Board (including at school)	21.90	2.43	2.57	15.68	67.07	18.59	14.57	3.02
Catered affairs	26.19	12.22	2.04	13.25	40.84	89.36	2.19	13.67
ALCOHOLIC BEVERAGES	**13.42**	**14.93**	**13.13**	**15.68**	**13.98**	**13.22**	**16.95**	**2.56**
Beer and ale	4.73	11.50	4.14	4.52	4.65	4.80	4.93	0.37
Wine	5.84	1.55	5.32	6.46	7.46	6.02	9.31	1.46
HOUSING	**258.69**	**104.49**	**213.45**	**231.02**	**386.63**	**334.28**	**268.07**	**138.96**
Housekeeping supplies	**42.48**	**24.34**	**32.04**	**41.42**	**50.91**	**54.87**	**55.87**	**28.86**
Laundry and cleaning supplies	2.93	5.70	1.70	2.90	4.04	2.07	3.34	1.29
Other household products	11.69	6.36	10.28	12.21	11.81	20.59	8.60	7.53
Miscellaneous household products	5.85	5.22	3.54	6.92	7.22	8.28	3.08	4.52
Lawn and garden supplies	4.20	0.01	5.70	3.64	2.89	9.95	3.96	0.99
Postage and stationery	27.86	12.28	20.06	26.30	35.05	32.21	43.93	20.05
Stationery, stationery supplies, giftwrap	21.13	8.97	16.78	20.59	27.02	25.41	27.10	15.34
Postage	6.14	2.91	3.03	5.45	7.05	5.43	16.34	4.44
Household textiles	**13.72**	**1.55**	**13.35**	**10.68**	**13.89**	**28.81**	**17.55**	**5.25**
Bathroom linens	2.59	0.50	2.31	2.93	1.74	3.79	5.12	1.50
Bedroom linens	6.10	0.88	3.84	3.52	7.92	17.26	5.65	0.95
Appliances and miscellaneous housewares	**23.98**	**12.75**	**12.21**	**16.51**	**28.18**	**54.41**	**31.56**	**10.88**
Major appliances	8.41	0.23	2.01	7.05	8.65	27.23	8.23	2.37
Small appliances and miscellaneous housewares	15.57	12.52	10.19	9.46	19.53	27.18	23.34	8.51
China and other dinnerware	2.46	1.18	2.84	0.96	2.26	4.55	4.07	2.06
Nonelectric cookware	3.53	8.50	1.54	0.47	5.77	4.01	6.58	1.43
Tableware, nonelectric kitchenware	2.63	0.61	1.24	3.29	3.82	4.63	1.79	0.73
Small electric kitchen appliances	2.71	1.45	1.56	1.99	3.35	4.44	3.72	2.56
Miscellaneous household equipment	**64.70**	**23.55**	**45.22**	**64.81**	**94.41**	**84.91**	**75.43**	**29.16**
Infants' equipment	3.82	0.15	2.11	1.31	13.93	0.70	2.44	0.14
Outdoor equipment	2.07	–	1.50	2.23	5.11	1.33	1.03	0.12
Other household decorative items	25.76	8.86	21.23	28.88	31.34	37.24	31.35	6.09
Power tools	2.80	–	4.75	3.57	2.06	4.07	2.29	–
Indoor plants, fresh flowers	13.43	8.71	7.55	11.24	18.12	17.47	17.73	12.47
Computers and computer hardware	6.59	0.18	1.49	7.46	10.31	12.59	5.31	3.81
Miscellaneous household equipment	2.19	2.11	2.42	1.96	2.39	1.29	3.04	2.34
Other housing	**113.80**	**42.31**	**110.63**	**97.62**	**199.24**	**111.29**	**87.66**	**64.81**
Repair or maintenance services	4.51	1.47	8.34	0.42	8.96	1.87	7.24	1.02
Housing while attending school	39.93	3.42	3.32	15.55	125.05	54.26	22.28	8.03
Natural gas (renter)	3.62	1.13	3.46	3.98	3.69	3.72	2.12	6.33
Electricity (renter)	14.67	13.95	11.20	20.07	10.82	15.55	13.29	17.43
Water, sewer maintenance (renter)	3.04	2.11	2.22	3.66	2.56	4.18	4.24	1.96
Day-care centers, nurseries, and preschools	23.81	5.69	64.45	32.80	15.00	6.03	8.00	6.80

	total consumer units	under 25	25 to 34	35 to 44	45 to 54	55 to 64	65 to 74	75+
APPAREL AND SERVICES	$237.13	$169.74	$248.95	$208.27	$256.52	$341.33	$250.78	$131.60
Men and boys, aged 2 or older	63.74	55.08	55.55	63.44	68.63	74.00	89.13	33.93
Men's coats and jackets	5.09	3.65	3.48	8.45	7.00	4.34	2.76	0.78
Men's accessories	4.45	3.27	4.55	2.62	9.67	2.43	4.40	1.25
Men's sweaters and vests	3.06	2.45	2.66	3.11	3.30	4.28	3.65	1.30
Men's active sportswear	2.76	–	2.17	2.73	3.37	1.69	1.80	7.58
Men's shirts	16.79	24.70	19.16	15.89	11.93	21.28	22.87	5.21
Men's pants	6.93	9.53	6.94	6.08	5.41	7.08	15.72	0.42
Boys' shirts	3.71	1.09	1.40	5.26	3.57	3.75	6.05	4.34
Boys' pants	3.76	0.70	2.25	3.55	4.17	5.69	7.04	2.33
Women and girls, aged 2 or older	81.76	36.73	71.82	55.82	88.86	157.95	88.37	65.12
Women's coats and jackets	5.62	1.11	5.77	0.63	9.29	13.86	4.71	1.81
Women's dresses	7.66	1.95	5.07	2.32	7.19	22.61	4.95	11.89
Women's vests and sweaters	8.50	3.87	10.18	3.35	11.37	17.06	7.89	3.29
Women's shirts, tops, blouses	9.06	10.48	7.33	3.84	10.39	14.27	11.38	10.34
Women's pants	6.62	3.82	7.13	2.01	4.82	18.39	11.81	–
Women's active sportswear	4.33	0.60	8.83	2.09	4.23	2.72	4.30	7.12
Women's sleepwear	6.45	1.75	6.71	9.05	4.42	7.58	5.60	7.45
Women's accessories	5.71	1.49	5.53	4.23	3.36	16.67	4.70	3.18
Girls' dresses and suits	2.98	0.05	0.02	1.92	8.28	4.12	2.53	0.66
Girls' shirts, blouses, sweaters	4.48	0.37	2.76	3.17	6.37	8.71	5.42	2.89
Girls' skirts and pants	3.32	1.12	2.96	3.76	2.88	5.14	3.99	2.41
Girls' accessories	2.38	0.25	1.77	5.86	1.22	3.22	0.68	0.22
Children under age 2	39.99	33.56	56.75	45.31	40.33	41.40	25.68	14.54
Infant dresses, outerwear	15.28	11.38	15.39	14.55	18.31	21.48	14.23	5.75
Infant underwear	16.91	19.22	27.64	23.53	15.09	9.99	5.73	5.41
Infant nightwear, loungewear	2.55	1.06	2.72	2.06	2.85	5.04	2.12	0.83
Infant accessories	3.93	1.48	9.87	3.51	3.04	2.59	1.86	2.11
Other apparel products and services	51.63	44.37	64.82	43.70	58.70	67.99	47.60	18.02
Jewelry and watches	24.01	12.79	43.98	20.36	22.58	32.97	14.54	6.31
Watches	2.16	1.45	1.89	2.18	2.20	2.72	3.61	0.77
Jewelry	21.85	11.33	42.09	18.19	20.38	30.25	10.93	5.54
Men's footwear	8.37	18.78	8.48	4.41	10.70	8.57	11.44	–
Boys' footwear	4.46	2.30	1.82	6.75	6.39	3.70	1.52	5.88
Women's footwear	8.82	7.39	5.20	7.98	14.62	11.99	6.79	3.61
Girls' footwear	3.30	1.23	3.96	2.60	2.71	5.40	6.34	0.44
TRANSPORTATION	43.87	15.09	21.83	44.93	80.43	69.71	11.17	23.96
Used cars	12.21	8.81	–	12.17	27.47	20.40	–	5.50
Airline fares	6.78	1.81	4.39	6.36	12.64	6.41	5.45	5.55
Ship fares	2.74	0.88	2.91	1.91	2.68	4.53	2.29	3.91
HEALTH CARE	32.59	1.12	10.74	20.64	54.82	55.16	39.97	37.24
Physician's services	3.07	–	0.58	1.03	6.25	9.96	1.00	0.16
Dental services	4.03	–	0.87	3.85	5.96	6.44	4.50	5.35
Care in convalescent or nursing home	5.19	–	–	0.08	3.31	13.12	10.47	17.30
Nonprescription vitamins	3.93	–	0.92	1.50	13.35	2.63	3.90	–
Prescription drugs	2.38	–	0.30	1.32	3.37	3.71	5.30	3.37
ENTERTAINMENT	78.24	29.87	60.10	85.78	105.68	107.30	73.48	37.66
Toys, games, hobbies, and tricycles	29.98	10.55	20.33	29.00	36.31	49.82	38.33	14.78
Other entertainment	48.26	19.33	39.77	56.78	69.37	57.48	35.15	22.88
Fees for recreational lessons	7.88	1.05	3.11	10.19	15.02	10.88	2.21	3.23
Community antenna or cable TV	6.37	7.18	4.22	8.35	5.13	6.81	6.11	7.31

	total consumer units	under 25	25 to 34	35 to 44	45 to 54	55 to 64	65 to 74	75+
VCRs and videodisc players	$2.26	$1.11	$2.32	$2.14	$3.37	$3.14	$1.44	$0.64
Video game hardware and software	2.13	1.18	1.78	2.13	2.45	3.34	2.19	1.07
Athletic gear, game tables, exercise equipment	6.60	0.87	3.48	8.85	9.12	9.28	7.42	1.66
Hunting and fishing equipment	3.06	1.40	12.25	2.18	0.81	0.24	1.68	0.04
Photographer fees	3.19	–	1.04	1.79	7.76	6.66	0.90	0.63
PERSONAL CARE PRODUCTS AND SERVICES	**21.15**	**13.16**	**15.81**	**27.07**	**25.79**	**16.94**	**30.81**	**9.68**
Cosmetics, perfume, bath preparation	12.53	11.50	12.03	13.53	14.84	9.48	18.80	4.73
Electric personal care appliances	3.31	–	0.77	6.17	4.48	3.19	3.68	1.33
EDUCATION	**183.88**	**43.25**	**27.05**	**107.53**	**414.52**	**292.98**	**194.24**	**95.65**
College tuition	127.83	23.90	13.14	56.74	298.28	244.04	96.43	83.73
Elementary and high school tuition	25.95	0.20	1.59	32.89	54.39	10.32	58.60	2.33
Other school tuition	4.44	0.49	2.72	1.85	8.36	10.41	4.25	0.03
Other school expenses including rentals	3.99	1.06	1.61	3.73	11.03	1.27	1.88	2.36
College books and supplies	11.93	15.29	1.99	4.24	28.86	15.56	10.29	5.00
Miscellaneous school supplies	7.38	1.81	3.09	5.02	10.00	9.62	21.00	2.06
ALL OTHER GIFTS	**83.76**	**17.94**	**41.82**	**66.84**	**112.22**	**145.43**	**140.28**	**42.97**
Gifts of trip expenses	44.40	11.39	30.29	32.28	56.10	75.41	70.78	27.27
Lotteries and gambling losses	2.86	0.46	0.44	0.03	11.23	1.37	2.07	0.90
Legal fees	5.82	1.75	0.16	2.20	6.05	6.41	30.79	–
Funeral expenses	25.25	2.10	8.81	24.28	32.98	54.67	28.88	13.27
Miscellaneous personal services	2.16	1.55	0.47	2.98	3.46	1.00	4.55	0.25

Note: (–) means sample is too small to make a reliable estimate. Expenditures for items in a given category may not add to category total because categories with annual spending of less than $2.00 for the average household are omitted. Spending on gifts is also included in the product and service categories in other chapters.
Source: Bureau of Labor Statistics, unpublished tables from the 2002 Consumer Expenditure Survey

Table 6.2 Gifts for Non–Household Members: Indexed spending by age, 2002

(indexed average annual spending of consumer units (CU) on selected gifts of products and services for non–household members by age of consumer unit reference person, 2002; index definition: an index of 100 is the average for all consumer units; an index of 132 means that spending by consumer units in that group is 32 percent above the average for all consumer units; an index of 68 indicates spending that is 32 percent below the average for all consumer units)

	total consumer units	under 25	25 to 34	35 to 44	45 to 54	55 to 64	65 to 74	75+
Average spending of CU, total	$40,677	$24,229	$40,318	$48,330	$48,748	$44,330	$32,243	$23,759
Average spending of CU, index	100	60	99	119	120	109	79	58
Gifts, spending index	100	42	66	84	155	148	105	54
FOOD	**100**	**33**	**42**	**73**	**186**	**185**	**74**	**45**
Cakes and cupcakes	100	22	97	89	200	102	31	52
Fresh fruit other than apples, bananas, and citrus	100	100	67	105	87	181	135	22
Candy and chewing gum	100	28	72	73	110	163	160	100
Board (including at school)	100	11	12	72	306	85	67	14
Catered affairs	100	47	8	51	156	341	8	52
ALCOHOLIC BEVERAGES	**100**	**111**	**98**	**117**	**104**	**99**	**126**	**19**
Beer and ale	100	243	88	96	98	101	104	8
Wine	100	27	91	111	128	103	159	25
HOUSING	**100**	**40**	**83**	**89**	**149**	**129**	**104**	**54**
Housekeeping supplies	**100**	**57**	**75**	**98**	**120**	**129**	**132**	**68**
Laundry and cleaning supplies	100	195	58	99	138	71	114	44
Other household products	100	54	88	104	101	176	74	64
Miscellaneous household products	100	89	61	118	123	142	53	77
Lawn and garden supplies	100	0	136	87	69	237	94	24
Postage and stationery	100	44	72	94	126	116	158	72
Stationery, stationery supplies, giftwrap	100	42	79	97	128	120	128	73
Postage	100	47	49	89	115	88	266	72
Household textiles	**100**	**11**	**97**	**78**	**101**	**210**	**128**	**38**
Bathroom linens	100	19	89	113	67	146	198	58
Bedroom linens	100	14	63	58	130	283	93	16
Appliances and miscellaneous housewares	**100**	**53**	**51**	**69**	**118**	**227**	**132**	**45**
Major appliances	100	3	24	84	103	324	98	28
Small appliances and miscellaneous housewares	100	80	65	61	125	175	150	55
China and other dinnerware	100	48	115	39	92	185	165	84
Nonelectric cookware	100	241	44	13	163	114	186	41
Tableware, nonelectric kitchenware	100	23	47	125	145	176	68	28
Small electric kitchen appliances	100	54	58	73	124	164	137	94
Miscellaneous household equipment	**100**	**36**	**70**	**100**	**146**	**131**	**117**	**45**
Infants' equipment	100	4	55	34	365	18	64	4
Outdoor equipment	100	–	72	108	247	64	50	6
Other household decorative items	100	34	82	112	122	145	122	24
Power tools	100	–	170	128	74	145	82	–
Indoor plants, fresh flowers	100	65	56	84	135	130	132	93
Computers and computer hardware	100	3	23	113	156	191	81	58
Miscellaneous household equipment	100	96	111	89	109	59	139	107
Other housing	**100**	**37**	**97**	**86**	**175**	**98**	**77**	**57**
Repair or maintenance services	100	33	185	9	199	41	161	23
Housing while attending school	100	9	8	39	313	136	56	20
Natural gas (renter)	100	31	96	110	102	103	59	175
Electricity (renter)	100	95	76	137	74	106	91	119
Water, sewer maintenance (renter)	100	69	73	120	84	138	139	64
Day-care centers, nurseries, and preschools	100	24	271	138	63	25	34	29

	total consumer units	under 25	25 to 34	35 to 44	45 to 54	55 to 64	65 to 74	75+
APPAREL AND SERVICES	**100**	**72**	**105**	**88**	**108**	**144**	**106**	**55**
Men and boys, aged 2 or older	**100**	**86**	**87**	**100**	**108**	**116**	**140**	**53**
Men's coats and jackets	100	72	68	166	138	85	54	15
Men's accessories	100	73	102	59	217	55	99	28
Men's sweaters and vests	100	80	87	102	108	140	119	42
Men's active sportswear	100	–	79	99	122	61	65	275
Men's shirts	100	147	114	95	71	127	136	31
Men's pants	100	138	100	88	78	102	227	6
Boys' shirts	100	29	38	142	96	101	163	117
Boys' pants	100	19	60	94	111	151	187	62
Women and girls, aged 2 or older	**100**	**45**	**88**	**68**	**109**	**193**	**108**	**80**
Women's coats and jackets	100	20	103	11	165	247	84	32
Women's dresses	100	25	66	30	94	295	65	155
Women's vests and sweaters	100	46	120	39	134	201	93	39
Women's shirts, tops, blouses	100	116	81	42	115	158	126	114
Women's pants	100	58	108	30	73	278	178	–
Women's active sportswear	100	14	204	48	98	63	99	164
Women's sleepwear	100	27	104	140	69	118	87	116
Women's accessories	100	26	97	74	59	292	82	56
Girls' dresses and suits	100	2	1	64	278	138	85	22
Girls' shirts, blouses, sweaters	100	8	62	71	142	194	121	65
Girls' skirts and pants	100	34	89	113	87	155	120	73
Girls' accessories	100	11	74	246	51	135	29	9
Children under age 2	**100**	**84**	**142**	**113**	**101**	**104**	**64**	**36**
Infant dresses, outerwear	100	74	101	95	120	141	93	38
Infant underwear	100	114	163	139	89	59	34	32
Infant nightwear, loungewear	100	42	107	81	112	198	83	33
Infant accessories	100	38	251	89	77	66	47	54
Other apparel products and services	**100**	**86**	**126**	**85**	**114**	**132**	**92**	**35**
Jewelry and watches	100	53	183	85	94	137	61	26
Watches	100	67	88	101	102	126	167	36
Jewelry	100	52	193	83	93	138	50	25
Men's footwear	100	224	101	53	128	102	137	–
Boys' footwear	100	52	41	151	143	83	34	132
Women's footwear	100	84	59	90	166	136	77	41
Girls' footwear	100	37	120	79	82	164	192	13
TRANSPORTATION	**100**	**34**	**50**	**102**	**183**	**159**	**25**	**55**
Used cars	100	72	–	100	225	167	–	45
Airline fares	100	27	65	94	186	95	80	82
Ship fares	100	32	106	70	98	165	84	143
HEALTH CARE	**100**	**3**	**33**	**63**	**168**	**169**	**123**	**114**
Physician's services	100	–	19	34	204	324	33	5
Dental services	100	–	22	96	148	160	112	133
Care in convalescent or nursing home	100	–	–	2	64	253	202	333
Nonprescription vitamins	100	–	23	38	340	67	99	–
Prescription drugs	100	–	13	55	142	156	223	142
ENTERTAINMENT	**100**	**38**	**77**	**110**	**135**	**137**	**94**	**48**
Toys, games, hobbies, and tricycles	100	35	68	97	121	166	128	49
Other entertainment	100	40	82	118	144	119	73	47
Fees for recreational lessons	100	13	39	129	191	138	28	41
Community antenna or cable TV	100	113	66	131	81	107	96	115

	total consumer units	under 25	25 to 34	35 to 44	45 to 54	55 to 64	65 to 74	75+
VCRs and videodisc players	100	49	103	95	149	139	64	28
Video game hardware and software	100	55	84	100	115	157	103	50
Athletic gear, game tables, exercise equipment	100	13	53	134	138	141	112	25
Hunting and fishing equipment	100	46	400	71	26	8	55	1
Photographer fees	100	–	33	56	243	209	28	20
PERSONAL CARE PRODUCTS AND SERVICES	**100**	**62**	**75**	**128**	**122**	**80**	**146**	**46**
Cosmetics, perfume, bath preparation	100	92	96	108	118	76	150	38
Electric personal care appliances	100	–	23	186	135	96	111	40
EDUCATION	**100**	**24**	**15**	**58**	**225**	**159**	**106**	**52**
College tuition	100	19	10	44	233	191	75	66
Elementary and high school tuition	100	1	6	127	210	40	226	9
Other school tuition	100	11	61	42	188	234	96	1
Other school expenses including rentals	100	27	40	93	276	32	47	59
College books and supplies	100	128	17	36	242	130	86	42
Miscellaneous school supplies	100	25	42	68	136	130	285	28
ALL OTHER GIFTS	**100**	**21**	**50**	**80**	**134**	**174**	**167**	**51**
Gifts of trip expenses	100	26	68	73	126	170	159	61
Lotteries and gambling losses	100	16	15	1	393	48	72	31
Legal fees	100	30	3	38	104	110	529	–
Funeral expenses	100	8	35	96	131	217	114	53
Miscellaneous personal services	100	72	22	138	160	46	211	12

Note: (–) means sample is too small to make a reliable estimate. Categories with annual spending of less than $2.00 for the average household are omitted.
Spending on gifts is also included in the product and service categories in other chapters.
Source: Calculations by New Strategist based on the 2002 Consumer Expenditure Survey

Table 6.3 Gifts for Non—Household Members: Total spending by age, 2002

(total annual spending on selected gifts of products and services for non—household members by consumer unit (CU) age groups, 2002; numbers in thousands)

	total consumer units	under 25	25 to 34	35 to 44	45 to 54	55 to 64	65 to 74	75+
Number of consumer units	112,108	8,737	18,988	24,394	22,691	15,314	11,216	10,767
Total spending of all CUs	$4,560,172,273	$211,692,792	$765,563,691	$1,178,973,729	$1,106,146,314	$678,870,233	$361,632,104	$255,811,969
Gifts, total spending	116,170,794	3,814,836	13,057,288	21,180,091	36,406,575	23,440,374	12,215,009	6,027,582
FOOD	**$9,213,035**	**$234,414**	**$650,529**	**$1,461,932**	**$3,463,781**	**$2,327,728**	**$678,680**	**$396,118**
Cakes and cupcakes	270,180	4,631	44,432	52,203	109,598	37,519	8,300	13,459
Fresh fruit other than apples, bananas, and citrus	253,364	19,746	28,672	58,058	44,474	62,787	34,097	5,276
Candy and chewing gum	1,310,543	28,133	159,119	207,349	292,260	290,966	209,851	126,082
Board (including at school)	2,455,165	21,231	48,799	382,498	1,521,885	284,687	163,417	32,516
Catered affairs	2,936,109	106,766	38,736	323,221	926,700	1,368,459	24,563	147,185
ALCOHOLIC BEVERAGES	**1,504,489**	**130,443**	**249,312**	**382,498**	**317,220**	**202,451**	**190,111**	**27,564**
Beer and ale	530,271	100,476	78,610	110,261	105,513	73,507	55,295	3,984
Wine	654,711	13,542	101,016	157,585	169,275	92,190	104,421	15,720
HOUSING	**29,001,219**	**912,929**	**4,052,989**	**5,635,502**	**8,773,021**	**5,119,164**	**3,006,673**	**1,496,182**
Housekeeping supplies	**4,762,348**	**212,659**	**608,376**	**1,010,399**	**1,155,199**	**840,279**	**626,638**	**310,736**
Laundry and cleaning supplies	328,476	49,801	32,280	70,743	91,672	31,700	37,461	13,889
Other household products	1,310,543	55,567	195,197	297,851	267,981	315,315	96,458	81,076
Miscellaneous household products	655,832	45,607	67,218	168,806	163,829	126,800	34,545	48,667
Lawn and garden supplies	470,854	87	108,232	88,794	65,577	152,374	44,415	10,659
Postage and stationery	3,123,329	107,290	380,899	641,562	795,320	493,264	492,719	215,878
Stationery, stationery supplies, giftwrap	2,368,842	78,371	318,619	502,272	613,111	389,129	303,954	165,166
Postage	688,343	25,425	57,534	132,947	159,972	83,155	183,269	47,805
Household textiles	**1,538,122**	**13,542**	**253,490**	**260,528**	**315,178**	**441,196**	**196,841**	**56,527**
Bathroom linens	290,360	4,369	43,862	71,474	39,482	58,040	57,426	16,151
Bedroom linens	683,859	7,689	72,914	85,867	179,713	264,320	63,370	10,229
Appliances and miscellaneous housewares	**2,688,350**	**111,397**	**231,843**	**402,745**	**639,432**	**833,235**	**353,977**	**117,145**
Major appliances	942,828	2,010	38,166	171,978	196,277	417,000	92,308	25,518
Small appliances and miscellaneous housewares	1,745,522	109,387	193,488	230,767	443,155	416,235	261,781	91,627
China and other dinnerware	275,786	10,310	53,926	23,418	51,282	69,679	45,649	22,180
Nonelectric cookware	395,741	74,265	29,242	11,465	130,927	61,409	73,801	15,397
Tableware, nonelectric kitchenware	294,844	5,330	23,545	80,256	86,680	70,904	20,077	7,860
Small electric kitchen appliances	303,813	12,669	29,621	48,544	76,015	67,994	41,724	27,564
Miscellaneous household equipment	**7,253,388**	**205,756**	**858,637**	**1,580,975**	**2,142,257**	**1,300,312**	**846,023**	**313,966**
Infants' equipment	428,253	1,311	40,065	31,956	316,086	10,720	27,367	1,507
Outdoor equipment	232,064	–	28,482	54,399	115,951	20,368	11,552	1,292
Other household decorative items	2,887,902	77,410	403,115	704,499	711,136	570,293	351,622	65,571
Power tools	313,902	–	90,193	87,087	46,743	62,328	25,685	–
Indoor plants, fresh flowers	1,505,610	76,099	143,359	274,189	411,161	267,536	198,860	134,264
Computers and computer hardware	738,792	1,573	28,292	181,979	233,944	192,803	59,557	41,022
Miscellaneous household equipment	245,517	18,435	45,951	47,812	54,231	19,755	34,097	25,195
Other housing	**12,757,890**	**369,662**	**2,100,642**	**2,381,342**	**4,520,955**	**1,704,295**	**983,195**	**697,809**
Repair or maintenance services	505,607	12,843	158,360	10,245	203,311	28,637	81,204	10,982
Housing while attending school	4,476,472	29,881	63,040	379,327	2,837,510	830,938	249,892	86,459
Natural gas (renter)	405,831	9,873	65,698	97,088	83,730	56,968	23,778	68,155
Electricity (renter)	1,644,624	121,881	212,666	489,588	245,517	238,133	149,061	187,669
Water, sewer maintenance (renter)	340,808	18,435	42,153	89,282	58,089	64,013	47,556	21,103
Day-care centers, nurseries, and preschools	2,669,291	49,714	1,223,777	800,123	340,365	92,343	89,728	73,216

	total consumer units	under 25	25 to 34	35 to 44	45 to 54	55 to 64	65 to 74	75+
APPAREL AND SERVICES	**$26,584,170**	**$1,483,018**	**$4,727,063**	**$5,080,538**	**$5,820,695**	**$5,227,128**	**$2,812,748**	**$1,416,937**
Men and boys, aged 2 or older	**7,145,764**	**481,234**	**1,054,783**	**1,547,555**	**1,557,283**	**1,133,236**	**999,682**	**365,324**
Men's coats and jackets	570,630	31,890	66,078	206,129	158,837	66,463	30,956	8,398
Men's accessories	498,881	28,570	86,395	63,912	219,422	37,213	49,350	13,459
Men's sweaters and vests	343,050	21,406	50,508	75,865	74,880	65,544	40,938	13,997
Men's active sportswear	309,418	–	41,204	66,596	76,469	25,881	20,189	81,614
Men's shirts	1,882,293	215,804	363,810	387,621	270,704	325,882	256,510	56,096
Men's pants	776,908	83,264	131,777	148,316	122,758	108,423	176,316	4,522
Boys' shirts	415,921	9,523	26,583	128,312	81,007	57,428	67,857	46,729
Boys' pants	421,526	6,116	42,723	86,599	94,621	87,137	78,961	25,087
Women and girls, aged 2 or older	**9,165,950**	**320,910**	**1,363,718**	**1,361,673**	**2,016,322**	**2,418,846**	**991,158**	**701,147**
Women's coats and jackets	630,047	9,698	109,561	15,368	210,799	212,252	52,827	19,488
Women's dresses	858,747	17,037	96,269	56,594	163,148	346,250	55,519	128,020
Women's vests and sweaters	952,918	33,812	193,298	81,720	257,997	261,257	88,494	35,423
Women's shirts, tops, blouses	1,015,698	91,564	139,182	93,673	235,759	218,531	127,638	111,331
Women's pants	742,155	33,375	135,384	49,032	109,371	281,624	132,461	–
Women's active sportswear	485,428	5,242	167,664	50,983	95,983	41,654	48,229	76,661
Women's sleepwear	723,097	15,290	127,409	220,766	100,294	116,080	62,810	80,214
Women's accessories	640,137	13,018	105,004	103,187	76,242	255,284	52,715	34,239
Girls' dresses and suits	334,082	437	380	46,836	187,881	63,094	28,376	7,106
Girls' shirts, blouses, sweaters	502,244	3,233	52,407	77,329	144,542	133,385	60,791	31,117
Girls' skirts and pants	372,199	9,785	56,204	91,721	65,350	78,714	44,752	25,948
Girls' accessories	266,817	2,184	33,609	142,949	27,683	49,311	7,627	2,369
Children under age 2	**4,483,199**	**293,214**	**1,077,569**	**1,105,292**	**915,128**	**634,000**	**288,027**	**156,552**
Infant dresses, outerwear	1,713,010	99,427	292,225	354,933	415,472	328,945	159,604	61,910
Infant underwear	1,895,746	167,925	524,828	573,991	342,407	152,987	64,268	58,249
Infant nightwear, loungewear	285,875	9,261	51,647	50,252	64,669	77,183	23,778	8,937
Infant accessories	440,584	12,931	187,412	85,623	68,981	39,663	20,862	22,718
Other apparel products and services	**5,788,136**	**387,661**	**1,230,802**	**1,066,018**	**1,331,962**	**1,041,199**	**533,882**	**194,021**
Jewelry and watches	2,691,713	111,746	835,092	496,662	512,363	504,903	163,081	67,940
Watches	242,153	12,669	35,887	53,179	49,920	41,654	40,490	8,291
Jewelry	2,449,560	98,990	799,205	443,727	462,443	463,249	122,591	59,649
Men's footwear	938,344	164,081	161,018	107,578	242,794	131,241	128,311	–
Boys' footwear	500,002	20,095	34,558	164,660	144,995	56,662	17,048	63,310
Women's footwear	988,793	64,566	98,738	194,664	331,742	183,615	76,157	38,869
Girls' footwear	369,956	10,747	75,192	63,424	61,493	82,696	71,109	4,737
TRANSPORTATION	**4,918,178**	**131,841**	**414,508**	**1,096,022**	**1,825,037**	**1,067,539**	**125,283**	**257,977**
Used cars	1,368,839	76,973	–	296,875	623,322	312,406	–	59,219
Airline fares	760,092	15,814	83,357	155,146	286,814	98,163	61,127	59,757
Ship fares	307,176	7,689	55,255	46,593	60,812	69,372	25,685	42,099
HEALTH CARE	**3,653,600**	**9,785**	**203,931**	**503,492**	**1,243,921**	**844,720**	**448,304**	**400,963**
Physician's services	344,172	–	11,013	25,126	141,819	152,527	11,216	1,723
Dental services	451,795	–	16,520	93,917	135,238	98,622	50,472	57,603
Care in convalescent or nursing home	581,841	–	–	1,952	75,107	200,920	117,432	186,269
Nonprescription vitamins	440,584	–	17,469	36,591	302,925	40,276	43,742	–
Prescription drugs	266,817	–	5,696	32,200	76,469	56,815	59,445	36,285
ENTERTAINMENT	**8,771,330**	**260,974**	**1,141,179**	**2,092,517**	**2,397,985**	**1,643,192**	**824,152**	**405,485**
Toys, games, hobbies, and tricycles	3,360,998	92,175	386,026	707,426	823,910	762,943	429,909	159,136
Other entertainment	5,410,332	168,886	755,153	1,385,091	1,574,075	880,249	394,242	246,349
Fees for recreational lessons	883,411	9,174	59,053	248,575	340,819	166,616	24,787	34,777
Community antenna or cable TV	714,128	62,732	80,129	203,690	116,405	104,288	68,530	78,707

	total consumer units	under 25	25 to 34	35 to 44	45 to 54	55 to 64	65 to 74	75+
VCRs and videodisc players	$253,364	$9,698	$44,052	$52,203	$76,469	$48,086	$16,151	$6,891
Video game hardware and software	238,790	10,310	33,799	51,959	55,593	51,149	24,563	11,521
Athletic gear, game tables, exercise equipment	739,913	7,601	66,078	215,887	206,942	142,114	83,223	17,873
Hunting and fishing equipment	343,050	12,232	232,603	53,179	18,380	3,675	18,843	431
Photographer fees	357,625	–	19,748	43,665	176,082	101,991	10,094	6,783
PERSONAL CARE PRODUCTS AND SERVICES	**2,371,084**	**114,979**	**300,200**	**660,346**	**585,201**	**259,419**	**345,565**	**104,225**
Cosmetics, perfume, bath preparation	1,404,713	100,476	228,426	330,051	336,734	145,177	210,861	50,928
Electric personal care appliances	371,077	–	14,621	150,511	101,656	48,852	41,275	14,320
EDUCATION	**20,614,419**	**377,875**	**513,625**	**2,623,087**	**9,405,873**	**4,486,696**	**2,178,596**	**1,029,864**
College tuition	14,330,766	208,814	249,502	1,384,116	6,768,271	3,737,229	1,081,559	901,521
Elementary and high school tuition	2,909,203	1,747	30,191	802,319	1,234,163	158,040	657,258	25,087
Other school tuition	497,760	4,281	51,647	45,129	189,697	159,419	47,668	323
Other school expenses including rentals	447,311	9,261	30,571	90,990	250,282	19,449	21,086	25,410
College books and supplies	1,337,448	133,589	37,786	103,431	654,862	238,286	115,413	53,835
Miscellaneous school supplies	827,357	15,814	58,673	122,458	226,910	147,321	235,536	22,180
ALL OTHER GIFTS	**9,390,166**	**156,742**	**794,078**	**1,630,495**	**2,546,384**	**2,227,115**	**1,573,380**	**462,658**
Gifts of trip expenses	4,977,595	99,514	575,147	787,438	1,272,965	1,154,829	793,868	293,616
Lotteries and gambling losses	320,629	4,019	8,355	732	254,820	20,980	23,217	9,690
Legal fees	652,469	15,290	3,038	53,667	137,281	98,163	345,341	–
Funeral expenses	2,830,727	18,348	167,284	592,286	748,349	837,216	323,918	142,878
Miscellaneous personal services	242,153	13,542	8,924	72,694	78,511	15,314	51,033	2,692

Note: Numbers may not add to total because of rounding. (–) means sample is too small to make a reliable estimate. Expenditures for items in a given category may not add to category total because categories with annual spending of less than $2.00 for the average household are omitted. Spending on gifts is also included in the product and service categories in other chapters.
Source: Calculations by New Strategist based on the 2002 Consumer Expenditure Survey

Table 6.4 Gifts for Non—Household Members: Market shares by age, 2002

(percentage of total annual spending on selected gifts of products and services for non–household members accounted for by consumer unit age groups, 2002)

	total consumer units	under 25	25 to 34	35 to 44	45 to 54	55 to 64	65 to 74	75+
Share of total consumer units	100.0%	7.8%	16.9%	21.8%	20.2%	13.7%	10.0%	9.6%
Share of total before-tax income	100.0	3.3	16.8	27.1	26.6	14.7	7.1	4.6
Share of total spending	100.0	4.6	16.8	25.9	24.3	14.9	7.9	5.6
Share of gifts spending	100.0	3.3	11.2	18.2	31.3	20.2	10.5	5.2
FOOD	100.0%	2.5%	7.1%	15.9%	37.6%	25.3%	7.4%	4.3%
Cakes and cupcakes	100.0	1.7	16.4	19.3	40.6	13.9	3.1	5.0
Fresh fruit other than apples, bananas, and citrus	100.0	7.8	11.3	22.9	17.6	24.8	13.5	2.1
Candy and chewing gum	100.0	2.1	12.1	15.8	22.3	22.2	16.0	9.6
Board (including at school)	100.0	0.9	2.0	15.6	62.0	11.6	6.7	1.3
Catered affairs	100.0	3.6	1.3	11.0	31.6	46.6	0.8	5.0
ALCOHOLIC BEVERAGES	100.0	8.7	16.6	25.4	21.1	13.5	12.6	1.8
Beer and ale	100.0	18.9	14.8	20.8	19.9	13.9	10.4	0.8
Wine	100.0	2.1	15.4	24.1	25.9	14.1	15.9	2.4
HOUSING	100.0	3.1	14.0	19.4	30.3	17.7	10.4	5.2
Housekeeping supplies	100.0	4.5	12.8	21.2	24.3	17.6	13.2	6.5
Laundry and cleaning supplies	100.0	15.2	9.8	21.5	27.9	9.7	11.4	4.2
Other household products	100.0	4.2	14.9	22.7	20.4	24.1	7.4	6.2
Miscellaneous household products	100.0	7.0	10.2	25.7	25.0	19.3	5.3	7.4
Lawn and garden supplies	100.0	0.0	23.0	18.9	13.9	32.4	9.4	2.3
Postage and stationery	100.0	3.4	12.2	20.5	25.5	15.8	15.8	6.9
Stationery, stationery supplies, giftwrap	100.0	3.3	13.5	21.2	25.9	16.4	12.8	7.0
Postage	100.0	3.7	8.4	19.3	23.2	12.1	26.6	6.9
Household textiles	100.0	0.9	16.5	16.9	20.5	28.7	12.8	3.7
Bathroom linens	100.0	1.5	15.1	24.6	13.6	20.0	19.8	5.6
Bedroom linens	100.0	1.1	10.7	12.6	26.3	38.7	9.3	1.5
Appliances and miscellaneous housewares	100.0	4.1	8.6	15.0	23.8	31.0	13.2	4.4
Major appliances	100.0	0.2	4.0	18.2	20.8	44.2	9.8	2.7
Small appliances and miscellaneous housewares	100.0	6.3	11.1	13.2	25.4	23.8	15.0	5.2
China and other dinnerware	100.0	3.7	19.6	8.5	18.6	25.3	16.6	8.0
Nonelectric cookware	100.0	18.8	7.4	2.9	33.1	15.5	18.6	3.9
Tableware, nonelectric kitchenware	100.0	1.8	8.0	27.2	29.4	24.0	6.8	2.7
Small electric kitchen appliances	100.0	4.2	9.7	16.0	25.0	22.4	13.7	9.1
Miscellaneous household equipment	100.0	2.8	11.8	21.8	29.5	17.9	11.7	4.3
Infants' equipment	100.0	0.3	9.4	7.5	73.8	2.5	6.4	0.4
Outdoor equipment	100.0	–	12.3	23.4	50.0	8.8	5.0	0.6
Other household decorative items	100.0	2.7	14.0	24.4	24.6	19.7	12.2	2.3
Power tools	100.0	–	28.7	27.7	14.9	19.9	8.2	–
Indoor plants, fresh flowers	100.0	5.1	9.5	18.2	27.3	17.8	13.2	8.9
Computers and computer hardware	100.0	0.2	3.8	24.6	31.7	26.1	8.1	5.6
Miscellaneous household equipment	100.0	7.5	18.7	19.5	22.1	8.0	13.9	10.3
Other housing	100.0	2.9	16.5	18.7	35.4	13.4	7.7	5.5
Repair or maintenance services	100.0	2.5	31.3	2.0	40.2	5.7	16.1	2.2
Housing while attending school	100.0	0.7	1.4	8.5	63.4	18.6	5.6	1.9
Natural gas (renter)	100.0	2.4	16.2	23.9	20.6	14.0	5.9	16.8
Electricity (renter)	100.0	7.4	12.9	29.8	14.9	14.5	9.1	11.4
Water, sewer maintenance (renter)	100.0	5.4	12.4	26.2	17.0	18.8	14.0	6.2
Day-care centers, nurseries, and preschools	100.0	1.9	45.8	30.0	12.8	3.5	3.4	2.7

	total consumer units	under 25	25 to 34	35 to 44	45 to 54	55 to 64	65 to 74	75+
APPAREL AND SERVICES	100.0%	5.6%	17.8%	19.1%	21.9%	19.7%	10.6%	5.3%
Men and boys, aged 2 or older	100.0	6.7	14.8	21.7	21.8	15.9	14.0	5.1
Men's coats and jackets	100.0	5.6	11.6	36.1	27.8	11.6	5.4	1.5
Men's accessories	100.0	5.7	17.3	12.8	44.0	7.5	9.9	2.7
Men's sweaters and vests	100.0	6.2	14.7	22.1	21.8	19.1	11.9	4.1
Men's active sportswear	100.0	–	13.3	21.5	24.7	8.4	6.5	26.4
Men's shirts	100.0	11.5	19.3	20.6	14.4	17.3	13.6	3.0
Men's pants	100.0	10.7	17.0	19.1	15.8	14.0	22.7	0.6
Boys' shirts	100.0	2.3	6.4	30.9	19.5	13.8	16.3	11.2
Boys' pants	100.0	1.5	10.1	20.5	22.4	20.7	18.7	6.0
Women and girls, aged 2 or older	100.0	3.5	14.9	14.9	22.0	26.4	10.8	7.6
Women's coats and jackets	100.0	1.5	17.4	2.4	33.5	33.7	8.4	3.1
Women's dresses	100.0	2.0	11.2	6.6	19.0	40.3	6.5	14.9
Women's vests and sweaters	100.0	3.5	20.3	8.6	27.1	27.4	9.3	3.7
Women's shirts, tops, blouses	100.0	9.0	13.7	9.2	23.2	21.5	12.6	11.0
Women's pants	100.0	4.5	18.2	6.6	14.7	37.9	17.8	–
Women's active sportswear	100.0	1.1	34.5	10.5	19.8	8.6	9.9	15.8
Women's sleepwear	100.0	2.1	17.6	30.5	13.9	16.1	8.7	11.1
Women's accessories	100.0	2.0	16.4	16.1	11.9	39.9	8.2	5.3
Girls' dresses and suits	100.0	0.1	0.1	14.0	56.2	18.9	8.5	2.1
Girls' shirts, blouses, sweaters	100.0	0.6	10.4	15.4	28.8	26.6	12.1	6.2
Girls' skirts and pants	100.0	2.6	15.1	24.6	17.6	21.1	12.0	7.0
Girls' accessories	100.0	0.8	12.6	53.6	10.4	18.5	2.9	0.9
Children under age 2	100.0	6.5	24.0	24.7	20.4	14.1	6.4	3.5
Infant dresses, outerwear	100.0	5.8	17.1	20.7	24.3	19.2	9.3	3.6
Infant underwear	100.0	8.9	27.7	30.3	18.1	8.1	3.4	3.1
Infant nightwear, loungewear	100.0	3.2	18.1	17.6	22.6	27.0	8.3	3.1
Infant accessories	100.0	2.9	42.5	19.4	15.7	9.0	4.7	5.2
Other apparel products and services	100.0	6.7	21.3	18.4	23.0	18.0	9.2	3.4
Jewelry and watches	100.0	4.2	31.0	18.5	19.0	18.8	6.1	2.5
Watches	100.0	5.2	14.8	22.0	20.6	17.2	16.7	3.4
Jewelry	100.0	4.0	32.6	18.1	18.9	18.9	5.0	2.4
Men's footwear	100.0	17.5	17.2	11.5	25.9	14.0	13.7	–
Boys' footwear	100.0	4.0	6.9	32.9	29.0	11.3	3.4	12.7
Women's footwear	100.0	6.5	10.0	19.7	33.6	18.6	7.7	3.9
Girls' footwear	100.0	2.9	20.3	17.1	16.6	22.4	19.2	1.3
TRANSPORTATION	100.0	2.7	8.4	22.3	37.1	21.7	2.5	5.2
Used cars	100.0	5.6	–	21.7	45.5	22.8	–	4.3
Airline fares	100.0	2.1	11.0	20.4	37.7	12.9	8.0	7.9
Ship fares	100.0	2.5	18.0	15.2	19.8	22.6	8.4	13.7
HEALTH CARE	100.0	0.3	5.6	13.8	34.0	23.1	12.3	11.0
Physician's services	100.0	–	3.2	7.3	41.2	44.3	3.3	0.5
Dental services	100.0	–	3.7	20.8	29.9	21.8	11.2	12.7
Care in convalescent or nursing home	100.0	–	–	0.3	12.9	34.5	20.2	32.0
Nonprescription vitamins	100.0	–	4.0	8.3	68.8	9.1	9.9	–
Prescription drugs	100.0	–	2.1	12.1	28.7	21.3	22.3	13.6
ENTERTAINMENT	100.0	3.0	13.0	23.9	27.3	18.7	9.4	4.6
Toys, games, hobbies, and tricycles	100.0	2.7	11.5	21.0	24.5	22.7	12.8	4.7
Other entertainment	100.0	3.1	14.0	25.6	29.1	16.3	7.3	4.6
Fees for recreational lessons	100.0	1.0	6.7	28.1	38.6	18.9	2.8	3.9
Community antenna or cable TV	100.0	8.8	11.2	28.5	16.3	14.6	9.6	11.0

	total consumer units	under 25	25 to 34	35 to 44	45 to 54	55 to 64	65 to 74	75+
VCRs and videodisc players	100.0%	3.8%	17.4%	20.6%	30.2%	19.0%	6.4%	2.7%
Video game hardware and software	100.0	4.3	14.2	21.8	23.3	21.4	10.3	4.8
Athletic gear, game tables, exercise equipment	100.0	1.0	8.9	29.2	28.0	19.2	11.2	2.4
Hunting and fishing equipment	100.0	3.6	67.8	15.5	5.4	1.1	5.5	0.1
Photographer fees	100.0	–	5.5	12.2	49.2	28.5	2.8	1.9
PERSONAL CARE PRODUCTS AND SERVICES	**100.0**	**4.8**	**12.7**	**27.8**	**24.7**	**10.9**	**14.6**	**4.4**
Cosmetics, perfume, bath preparation	100.0	7.2	16.3	23.5	24.0	10.3	15.0	3.6
Electric personal care appliances	100.0	–	3.9	40.6	27.4	13.2	11.1	3.9
EDUCATION	**100.0**	**1.8**	**2.5**	**12.7**	**45.6**	**21.8**	**10.6**	**5.0**
College tuition	100.0	1.5	1.7	9.7	47.2	26.1	7.5	6.3
Elementary and high school tuition	100.0	0.1	1.0	27.6	42.4	5.4	22.6	0.9
Other school tuition	100.0	0.9	10.4	9.1	38.1	32.0	9.6	0.1
Other school expenses including rentals	100.0	2.1	6.8	20.3	56.0	4.3	4.7	5.7
College books and supplies	100.0	10.0	2.8	7.7	49.0	17.8	8.6	4.0
Miscellaneous school supplies	100.0	1.9	7.1	14.8	27.4	17.8	28.5	2.7
ALL OTHER GIFTS	**100.0**	**1.7**	**8.5**	**17.4**	**27.1**	**23.7**	**16.8**	**4.9**
Gifts of trip expenses	100.0	2.0	11.6	15.8	25.6	23.2	15.9	5.9
Lotteries and gambling losses	100.0	1.3	2.6	0.2	79.5	6.5	7.2	3.0
Legal fees	100.0	2.3	0.5	8.2	21.0	15.0	52.9	–
Funeral expenses	100.0	0.6	5.9	20.9	26.4	29.6	11.4	5.0
Miscellaneous personal services	100.0	5.6	3.7	30.0	32.4	6.3	21.1	1.1

Note: Numbers may not add to total because of rounding. (–) means sample is too small to make a reliable estimate. Expenditures for items in a given category may not add to category total because categories with annual spending of less than $2.00 for the average household are omitted. Spending on gifts is also included in the product and service categories in other chapters.
Source: Calculations by New Strategist based on the 2002 Consumer Expenditure Survey

Table 6.5 Gifts for Non–Household Members: Average spending by income, 2002

(average annual spending on selected gifts of products and services for non–household members by before-tax income of consumer units (CU), 2002; complete income reporters only)

	complete income reporters	under $10,000	$10,000–$19,999	$20,000–$29,999	$30,000–$39,999	$40,000–$49,999	$50,000–$69,999	$70,000 or more
Number of consumer units								
(in thousands, add 000)	92,388	10,933	15,075	12,312	10,727	8,873	13,521	20,947
Average number of persons per CU	2.5	1.7	1.9	2.3	2.5	2.6	2.8	3.1
Average before-tax income of CU	$49,430.00	$5,554.80	$14,724.33	$24,495.00	$34,423.00	$44,443.00	$58,933.00	$115,629.00
Average spending of CU, total	42,556.98	17,627.83	22,838.71	28,835.85	35,095.39	41,787.38	50,406.17	76,627.31
Gifts, average spending	1,095.23	402.43	515.94	652.13	779.92	952.31	1,206.83	2,267.31
FOOD	**$87.10**	**$28.23**	**$33.11**	**$36.46**	**$66.71**	**$44.16**	**$92.17**	**$210.23**
Cakes and cupcakes	3.19	2.19	0.38	3.25	4.17	0.76	0.52	7.71
Fresh fruit other than apples, bananas, and citrus	2.47	2.30	1.32	1.88	2.44	1.94	1.25	4.68
Candy and chewing gum	13.92	3.04	14.22	12.50	14.75	7.72	16.71	19.90
Board (including at school)	18.94	7.73	3.47	1.52	1.78	7.37	30.03	52.68
Catered affairs	29.05	1.61	1.58	5.04	26.41	14.05	22.96	88.91
ALCOHOLIC BEVERAGES	**14.13**	**9.40**	**4.35**	**15.51**	**4.95**	**6.46**	**22.02**	**25.18**
Beer and ale	5.38	6.85	1.81	9.33	1.80	1.71	7.44	6.84
Wine	5.81	2.45	1.25	5.34	1.74	4.46	8.00	12.06
HOUSING	**275.48**	**128.11**	**122.30**	**196.52**	**212.41**	**284.82**	**313.07**	**509.47**
Housekeeping supplies	**48.11**	**21.82**	**25.90**	**39.84**	**35.63**	**43.92**	**71.14**	**74.54**
Laundry and cleaning supplies	3.67	2.79	4.60	2.26	2.22	3.74	4.16	4.70
Other household products	12.82	4.04	5.74	9.98	10.12	10.64	16.41	23.55
Miscellaneous household products	6.24	1.62	1.41	7.37	4.72	5.88	5.80	12.19
Lawn and garden supplies	4.66	0.84	2.70	1.26	4.16	2.41	7.97	8.98
Postage and stationery	31.61	14.99	15.56	27.60	23.29	29.54	50.57	46.28
Stationery, stationery supplies, giftwrap	23.38	11.55	12.18	15.86	19.07	24.23	31.80	37.85
Postage	7.65	3.05	2.56	11.03	4.02	4.68	17.25	8.38
Household textiles	**16.54**	**8.93**	**6.81**	**13.39**	**16.62**	**21.65**	**23.41**	**22.51**
Bathroom linens	3.26	0.92	1.95	1.58	1.58	3.36	5.79	5.53
Bedroom linens	6.99	1.19	3.54	1.53	10.58	14.45	10.04	8.67
Appliances and miscellaneous housewares	**28.56**	**13.23**	**10.40**	**23.29**	**25.44**	**42.54**	**20.23**	**53.11**
Major appliances	9.64	0.76	1.23	6.79	8.23	9.64	6.81	24.19
Small appliances and miscellaneous housewares	18.92	12.46	9.17	16.50	17.21	32.91	13.41	28.92
China and other dinnerware	2.96	5.41	0.51	5.21	1.58	8.22	0.03	2.54
Nonelectric cookware	4.54	–	2.29	1.70	9.18	13.54	1.33	5.88
Tableware, nonelectric kitchenware	3.17	3.13	0.70	2.30	0.95	5.46	1.61	6.60
Small electric kitchen appliances	3.09	0.65	1.32	2.38	3.74	2.36	3.93	5.49
Miscellaneous household equipment	**70.53**	**32.79**	**24.98**	**44.05**	**46.94**	**83.45**	**87.51**	**132.89**
Infants' equipment	2.63	0.74	0.82	0.33	8.26	2.00	3.02	3.35
Outdoor equipment	2.15	0.86	0.31	1.32	1.37	4.46	2.28	3.93
Other household decorative items	29.29	11.04	10.66	17.80	13.17	38.10	28.80	62.44
Power tools	3.92	–	1.04	–	1.92	5.25	7.09	8.65
Indoor plants, fresh flowers	14.08	7.96	7.18	12.48	10.22	13.33	17.20	23.45
Computers and computer hardware	6.98	–	1.09	2.00	0.57	2.99	18.24	15.51
Miscellaneous household equipment	2.40	0.75	0.67	3.90	5.80	3.66	1.12	2.03
Other housing	**111.74**	**51.34**	**54.20**	**75.94**	**87.77**	**93.26**	**110.79**	**226.43**
Repair or maintenance services	5.06	0.36	4.81	2.11	16.92	2.07	4.44	5.01
Housing while attending school	36.86	10.20	2.46	12.80	10.86	25.50	35.76	108.50
Natural gas (renter)	3.48	3.59	4.81	5.77	3.94	2.86	2.18	1.98
Electricity (renter)	13.50	18.58	18.67	20.90	13.65	7.60	11.96	6.19
Water, sewer maintenance (renter)	2.82	2.93	4.02	5.14	2.58	1.21	2.13	1.80
Day-care centers, nurseries, and preschools	24.47	3.47	4.22	12.28	16.44	23.38	28.58	59.10

	complete income reporters	under $10,000	$10,000–$19,999	$20,000–$29,999	$30,000–$39,999	$40,000–$49,999	$50,000–$69,999	$70,000 or more
APPAREL AND SERVICES	**$258.46**	**$125.12**	**$135.97**	**$204.34**	**$185.55**	**$219.79**	**$277.71**	**$480.74**
Men and boys, aged 2 or older	**71.42**	**34.86**	**47.39**	**58.54**	**49.29**	**61.32**	**70.08**	**129.62**
Men's coats and jackets	6.21	–	3.09	1.54	–	5.50	18.79	9.80
Men's accessories	4.98	2.86	1.09	4.27	3.86	0.90	4.67	11.51
Men's sweaters and vests	3.00	0.95	1.06	1.93	2.57	2.10	3.14	6.61
Men's active sportswear	3.50	1.34	4.86	2.28	–	6.93	–	6.78
Men's shirts	18.72	12.44	4.19	15.76	12.64	13.91	12.77	42.16
Men's pants	8.63	3.35	1.21	10.56	7.65	11.47	8.29	14.61
Boys' shirts	4.10	4.71	8.66	2.25	2.10	0.97	2.95	4.77
Boys' pants	4.03	1.47	3.24	3.72	4.83	4.96	4.59	4.97
Women and girls, aged 2 or older	**88.23**	**50.54**	**36.99**	**75.10**	**46.42**	**51.72**	**87.60**	**185.67**
Women's coats and jackets	6.98	4.81	0.88	5.74	3.47	4.96	6.51	15.88
Women's dresses	8.13	–	0.60	13.00	–	3.58	4.99	21.95
Women's vests and sweaters	10.10	8.29	2.34	10.55	4.07	2.51	3.18	26.39
Women's shirts, tops, blouses	10.25	12.45	3.81	9.34	4.96	3.74	14.62	16.97
Women's pants	7.55	1.98	1.31	3.60	2.24	3.55	2.25	24.37
Women's active sportswear	3.75	0.89	0.60	–	1.79	3.58	3.70	10.63
Women's sleepwear	5.96	3.27	5.35	4.51	1.16	12.14	3.57	9.84
Women's accessories	5.87	4.20	2.11	5.43	4.87	0.92	2.04	14.37
Girls' dresses and suits	3.48	0.74	1.43	1.96	2.54	0.27	13.10	2.99
Girls' shirts, blouses, sweaters	4.60	4.63	4.49	3.02	4.13	1.79	5.59	6.40
Girls' skirts and pants	3.56	0.94	2.67	3.73	3.66	4.69	4.96	4.03
Girls' accessories	2.12	0.54	1.34	5.38	0.40	–	1.20	3.68
Children under age 2	**43.30**	**19.43**	**22.77**	**27.24**	**45.48**	**47.58**	**44.80**	**75.27**
Infant dresses, outerwear	16.39	6.66	8.70	9.43	17.16	19.96	18.07	28.13
Infant underwear	18.68	9.67	11.60	11.80	21.97	19.75	19.90	29.09
Infant nightwear, loungewear	2.85	1.15	1.04	2.12	2.25	2.87	3.04	5.66
Infant accessories	3.98	1.29	0.72	2.74	2.51	4.23	1.73	10.23
Other apparel products and services	**55.52**	**20.29**	**28.82**	**43.46**	**44.36**	**59.17**	**75.23**	**90.18**
Jewelry and watches	24.52	9.93	9.64	15.25	10.02	52.85	30.20	40.04
Watches	2.45	1.31	1.20	1.14	2.14	2.90	2.53	4.65
Jewelry	22.06	8.62	8.44	14.11	7.88	49.95	27.67	35.39
Men's footwear	8.78	–	9.04	7.41	22.21	0.98	6.67	11.12
Boys' footwear	4.63	1.30	2.38	5.66	5.27	0.18	7.73	6.66
Women's footwear	10.74	3.54	6.01	8.64	2.74	0.81	20.54	20.68
Girls' footwear	3.52	3.84	0.26	2.99	2.28	1.00	4.32	7.12
TRANSPORTATION	**42.79**	**4.53**	**54.28**	**9.05**	**24.63**	**35.68**	**101.06**	**48.99**
Used cars	14.60	–	40.66	0.83	7.23	20.05	30.87	2.52
Airline fares	7.42	1.66	2.73	4.15	5.51	8.66	9.05	15.13
Ship fares	2.74	0.54	0.14	0.74	5.84	2.35	4.14	4.60
HEALTH CARE	**33.63**	**8.45**	**14.78**	**19.66**	**16.29**	**45.13**	**34.60**	**71.81**
Physician's services	3.60	0.25	0.58	1.40	2.66	2.70	3.46	9.76
Dental services	4.54	0.44	0.19	1.55	3.56	3.60	8.67	9.80
Care in convalescent or nursing home	6.08	3.05	0.91	–	–	11.69	5.19	16.28
Nonprescription vitamins	2.32	0.87	2.44	0.54	3.77	1.82	1.78	3.79
Prescription drugs	2.71	0.76	1.06	1.59	1.64	3.49	3.52	5.28
ENTERTAINMENT	**80.48**	**27.35**	**37.74**	**52.04**	**66.70**	**81.63**	**101.83**	**147.74**
Toys, games, hobbies, and tricycles	31.42	9.19	17.17	26.12	28.74	31.98	44.58	49.02
Other entertainment	49.06	18.16	20.57	25.93	37.96	49.65	57.25	98.72
Fees for recreational lessons	6.69	0.99	1.86	0.74	3.77	5.92	3.29	20.65
Community antenna or cable TV	6.06	8.59	7.84	8.61	5.31	2.96	6.28	3.50

	complete income reporters	under $10,000	$10,000– $19,999	$20,000– $29,999	$30,000– $39,999	$40,000– $49,999	$50,000– $69,999	$70,000 or more
VCRs and videodisc players	$2.16	$0.79	$0.36	–	$2.27	$2.20	$2.96	$4.83
Video game hardware and software	2.48	0.45	0.86	$2.02	2.60	3.02	3.99	3.69
Athletic gear, game tables, exercise equipment	6.80	0.47	1.15	1.56	2.93	1.26	5.32	21.90
Hunting and fishing equipment	3.00	2.72	0.61	5.42	2.27	10.26	1.23	1.80
Photographer fees	2.83	1.66	0.31	1.03	1.95	1.26	2.17	7.86
PERSONAL CARE PRODUCTS AND SERVICES	**23.99**	**12.98**	**19.81**	**18.64**	**20.04**	**19.62**	**25.02**	**38.29**
Cosmetics, perfume, bath preparation	13.33	6.23	10.45	6.27	17.95	11.02	11.34	22.71
Electric personal care appliances	4.32	4.24	3.50	7.73	0.16	–	6.30	5.47
EDUCATION	**189.38**	**33.89**	**52.34**	**49.16**	**95.79**	**149.98**	**142.03**	**546.15**
College tuition	132.86	18.14	39.25	29.84	70.37	93.20	92.71	395.36
Elementary and high school tuition	23.43	1.74	2.72	9.30	6.90	35.85	19.62	63.63
Other school tuition	5.06	0.33	1.51	0.19	2.52	2.82	1.76	17.35
Other school expenses including rentals	3.96	0.53	1.09	1.39	3.16	5.05	5.35	8.36
College books and supplies	12.54	9.75	2.23	4.92	4.12	6.87	15.26	30.85
Miscellaneous school supplies	8.88	2.62	4.66	2.40	4.27	3.64	5.54	25.12
ALL OTHER GIFTS	**88.28**	**23.52**	**40.70**	**48.83**	**85.87**	**63.68**	**95.29**	**186.46**
Gifts of trip expenses	50.00	12.73	13.40	25.89	47.44	39.23	57.57	110.94
Lotteries and gambling losses	0.99	0.52	1.02	1.87	0.27	0.84	0.22	1.56
Legal fees	5.97	2.19	–	0.96	19.78	13.37	5.14	5.50
Funeral expenses	25.65	5.69	24.09	19.30	14.63	7.05	25.02	54.86
Miscellaneous personal services	2.35	0.35	0.23	0.22	1.28	0.41	4.46	6.08

Note: (–) means sample is too small to make a reliable estimate. Expenditures for items in a given category may not add to category total because categories with annual spending of less than $2.00 for the average household are omitted. Spending on gifts is also included in the product and service categories in other chapters.
Source: Bureau of Labor Statistics, unpublished tables from the 2002 Consumer Expenditure Survey; calculations by New Strategist

Table 6.6 Gifts for Non–Household Members: Indexed spending by income, 2002

(indexed average annual spending of consumer units (CU) on selected gifts of products and services for non–household members by before-tax income of consumer unit, 2002; complete income reporters only; index definition: an index of 100 is the average for all consumer units; an index of 132 means that spending by consumer units in that group is 32 percent above the average for all consumer units; an index of 68 indicates spending that is 32 percent below the average for all consumer units)

	complete income reporters	under $10,000	$10,000– $19,999	$20,000– $29,999	$30,000– $39,999	$40,000– $49,999	$50,000– $69,999	$70,000 or more
Average spending of CU, total	$42,557	$17,628	$22,839	$28,836	$35,095	$41,787	$50,406	$76,627
Average spending of CU, index	100	41	54	68	82	98	118	180
Gifts, spending index	100	37	47	60	71	87	110	207
FOOD	**100**	**32**	**38**	**42**	**77**	**51**	**106**	**241**
Cakes and cupcakes	100	69	12	102	131	24	16	242
Fresh fruit other than apples, bananas, and citrus	100	93	54	76	99	79	51	189
Candy and chewing gum	100	22	102	90	106	55	120	143
Board (including at school)	100	41	18	8	9	39	159	278
Catered affairs	100	6	5	17	91	48	79	306
ALCOHOLIC BEVERAGES	**100**	**67**	**31**	**110**	**35**	**46**	**156**	**178**
Beer and ale	100	127	34	173	33	32	138	127
Wine	100	42	22	92	30	77	138	208
HOUSING	**100**	**47**	**44**	**71**	**77**	**103**	**114**	**185**
Housekeeping supplies	**100**	**45**	**54**	**83**	**74**	**91**	**148**	**155**
Laundry and cleaning supplies	100	76	125	62	60	102	113	128
Other household products	100	32	45	78	79	83	128	184
Miscellaneous household products	100	26	23	118	76	94	93	195
Lawn and garden supplies	100	18	58	27	89	52	171	193
Postage and stationery	100	47	49	87	74	93	160	146
Stationery, stationery supplies, giftwrap	100	49	52	68	82	104	136	162
Postage	100	40	33	144	53	61	225	110
Household textiles	**100**	**54**	**41**	**81**	**100**	**131**	**142**	**136**
Bathroom linens	100	28	60	48	48	103	178	170
Bedroom linens	100	17	51	22	151	207	144	124
Appliances and miscellaneous housewares	**100**	**46**	**36**	**82**	**89**	**149**	**71**	**186**
Major appliances	100	8	13	70	85	100	71	251
Small appliances and miscellaneous housewares	100	66	48	87	91	174	71	153
China and other dinnerware	100	183	17	176	53	278	1	86
Nonelectric cookware	100	–	51	37	202	298	29	130
Tableware, nonelectric kitchenware	100	99	22	73	30	172	51	208
Small electric kitchen appliances	100	21	43	77	121	76	127	178
Miscellaneous household equipment	**100**	**46**	**35**	**62**	**67**	**118**	**124**	**188**
Infants' equipment	100	28	31	13	314	76	115	127
Outdoor equipment	100	40	14	61	64	207	106	183
Other household decorative items	100	38	36	61	45	130	98	213
Power tools	100	–	27	–	49	134	181	221
Indoor plants, fresh flowers	100	57	51	89	73	95	122	167
Computers and computer hardware	100	–	16	29	8	43	261	222
Miscellaneous household equipment	100	31	28	163	242	153	47	85
Other housing	**100**	**46**	**49**	**68**	**79**	**83**	**99**	**203**
Repair or maintenance services	100	7	95	42	334	41	88	99
Housing while attending school	100	28	7	35	29	69	97	294
Natural gas (renter)	100	103	138	166	113	82	63	57
Electricity (renter)	100	138	138	155	101	56	89	46
Water, sewer maintenance (renter)	100	104	143	182	91	43	76	64
Day-care centers, nurseries, and preschools	100	14	17	50	67	96	117	242

	complete income reporters	under $10,000	$10,000– $19,999	$20,000– $29,999	$30,000– $39,999	$40,000– $49,999	$50,000– $69,999	$70,000 or more
APPAREL AND SERVICES	**100**	**48**	**53**	**79**	**72**	**85**	**107**	**186**
Men and boys, aged 2 or older	**100**	**49**	**66**	**82**	**69**	**86**	**98**	**181**
Men's coats and jackets	100	–	50	25	–	89	303	158
Men's accessories	100	57	22	86	78	18	94	231
Men's sweaters and vests	100	32	35	64	86	70	105	220
Men's active sportswear	100	38	139	65	–	198	–	194
Men's shirts	100	66	22	84	68	74	68	225
Men's pants	100	39	14	122	89	133	96	169
Boys' shirts	100	115	211	55	51	24	72	116
Boys' pants	100	37	80	92	120	123	114	123
Women and girls, aged 2 or older	**100**	**57**	**42**	**85**	**53**	**59**	**99**	**210**
Women's coats and jackets	100	69	13	82	50	71	93	228
Women's dresses	100	–	7	160	–	44	61	270
Women's vests and sweaters	100	82	23	104	40	25	31	261
Women's shirts, tops, blouses	100	122	37	91	48	36	143	166
Women's pants	100	26	17	48	30	47	30	323
Women's active sportswear	100	24	16	–	48	95	99	283
Women's sleepwear	100	55	90	76	19	204	60	165
Women's accessories	100	71	36	93	83	16	35	245
Girls' dresses and suits	100	21	41	56	73	8	376	86
Girls' shirts, blouses, sweaters	100	101	98	66	90	39	122	139
Girls' skirts and pants	100	26	75	105	103	132	139	113
Girls' accessories	100	26	63	254	19	–	57	174
Children under age 2	**100**	**45**	**53**	**63**	**105**	**110**	**103**	**174**
Infant dresses, outerwear	100	41	53	58	105	122	110	172
Infant underwear	100	52	62	63	118	106	107	156
Infant nightwear, loungewear	100	40	37	74	79	101	107	199
Infant accessories	100	33	18	69	63	106	43	257
Other apparel products and services	**100**	**37**	**52**	**78**	**80**	**107**	**136**	**162**
Jewelry and watches	100	40	39	62	41	216	123	163
Watches	100	53	49	47	87	118	103	190
Jewelry	100	39	38	64	36	226	125	160
Men's footwear	100	–	103	84	253	11	76	127
Boys' footwear	100	28	51	122	114	4	167	144
Women's footwear	100	33	56	80	26	8	191	193
Girls' footwear	100	109	7	85	65	28	123	202
TRANSPORTATION	**100**	**11**	**127**	**21**	**58**	**83**	**236**	**114**
Used cars	100	–	278	6	50	137	211	17
Airline fares	100	22	37	56	74	117	122	204
Ship fares	100	20	5	27	213	86	151	168
HEALTH CARE	**100**	**25**	**44**	**58**	**48**	**134**	**103**	**214**
Physician's services	100	7	16	39	74	75	96	271
Dental services	100	10	4	34	78	79	191	216
Care in convalescent or nursing home	100	50	15	–	–	192	85	268
Nonprescription vitamins	100	37	105	23	163	78	77	163
Prescription drugs	100	28	39	59	61	129	130	195
ENTERTAINMENT	**100**	**34**	**47**	**65**	**83**	**101**	**127**	**184**
Toys, games, hobbies, and tricycles	100	29	55	83	91	102	142	156
Other entertainment	100	37	42	53	77	101	117	201
Fees for recreational lessons	100	15	28	11	56	88	49	309
Community antenna or cable TV	100	142	129	142	88	49	104	58

	complete income reporters	under $10,000	$10,000– $19,999	$20,000– $29,999	$30,000– $39,999	$40,000– $49,999	$50,000– $69,999	$70,000 or more
VCRs and videodisc players	100	37	16	–	105	102	137	224
Video game hardware and software	100	18	35	81	105	122	161	149
Athletic gear, game tables, exercise equipment	100	7	17	23	43	19	78	322
Hunting and fishing equipment	100	91	20	181	76	342	41	60
Photographer fees	100	59	11	36	69	45	77	278
PERSONAL CARE PRODUCTS AND SERVICES	**100**	**54**	**83**	**78**	**84**	**82**	**104**	**160**
Cosmetics, perfume, bath preparation	100	47	78	47	135	83	85	170
Electric personal care appliances	100	98	81	179	4	–	146	127
EDUCATION	**100**	**18**	**28**	**26**	**51**	**79**	**75**	**288**
College tuition	100	14	30	22	53	70	70	298
Elementary and high school tuition	100	7	12	40	29	153	84	272
Other school tuition	100	6	30	4	50	56	35	343
Other school expenses including rentals	100	13	28	35	80	128	135	211
College books and supplies	100	78	18	39	33	55	122	246
Miscellaneous school supplies	100	29	52	27	48	41	62	283
ALL OTHER GIFTS	**100**	**27**	**46**	**55**	**97**	**72**	**108**	**211**
Gifts of trip expenses	100	25	27	52	95	78	115	222
Lotteries and gambling losses	100	52	103	189	27	85	22	158
Legal fees	100	37	–	16	331	224	86	92
Funeral expenses	100	22	94	75	57	27	98	214
Miscellaneous personal services	100	15	10	9	54	17	190	259

Note: (–) means sample is too small to make a reliable estimate. Categories with annual spending of less than $2.00 for the average household are omitted. Spending on gifts is also included in the product and service categories in other chapters.
Source: Calculations by New Strategist based on the 2002 Consumer Expenditure Survey

Table 6.7 Gifts for Non–Household Members: Total spending by income, 2002

(total annual spending on selected gifts of products and services for non–household members by before-tax income group of consumer units (CU), 2002; complete income reporters only; numbers in thousands)

	complete income reporters	under $10,000	$10,000–$19,999	$20,000–$29,999	$30,000–$39,999	$40,000–$49,999	$50,000–$69,999	$70,000 or more
Number of consumer units	92,388	10,933	15,075	12,312	10,727	8,873	13,521	20,947
Total spending of all CUs	$3,931,754,268	$192,725,059	$344,293,530	$355,026,985	$376,468,249	$370,779,423	$681,541,825	$1,605,112,263
Gifts, total spending	101,186,109	4,399,787	7,777,797	8,029,025	8,366,202	8,449,847	16,317,548	47,493,343
FOOD	**$8,046,995**	**$308,629**	**$499,123**	**$448,896**	**$715,598**	**$391,832**	**$1,246,231**	**$4,403,688**
Cakes and cupcakes	294,718	23,904	5,765	40,014	44,732	6,743	7,031	161,501
Fresh fruit other than apples, bananas, and citrus	228,198	25,170	19,971	23,147	26,174	17,214	16,901	98,032
Candy and chewing gum	1,286,041	33,289	214,398	153,900	158,223	68,500	225,936	416,845
Board (including at school)	1,749,829	84,546	52,333	18,714	19,094	65,394	406,036	1,103,488
Catered affairs	2,683,871	17,627	23,783	62,052	283,300	124,666	310,442	1,862,398
ALCOHOLIC BEVERAGES	**1,305,442**	**102,769**	**65,526**	**190,959**	**53,099**	**57,320**	**297,732**	**527,445**
Beer and ale	497,047	74,904	27,230	114,871	19,309	15,173	100,596	143,277
Wine	536,774	26,793	18,862	65,746	18,665	39,574	108,168	252,621
HOUSING	**25,451,046**	**1,400,616**	**1,843,658**	**2,419,554**	**2,278,522**	**2,527,208**	**4,233,019**	**10,671,868**
Housekeeping supplies	**4,444,787**	**238,605**	**390,495**	**490,510**	**382,203**	**389,702**	**961,884**	**1,561,389**
Laundry and cleaning supplies	339,064	30,492	69,279	27,825	23,814	33,185	56,247	98,451
Other household products	1,184,414	44,191	86,602	122,874	108,557	94,409	221,880	493,302
Miscellaneous household products	576,501	17,665	21,260	90,739	50,631	52,173	78,422	255,344
Lawn and garden supplies	430,528	9,237	40,730	15,513	44,624	21,384	107,762	188,104
Postage and stationery	2,920,385	163,922	234,614	339,811	249,832	262,108	683,757	969,427
Stationery, stationery supplies, giftwrap	2,160,031	126,256	183,572	195,268	204,564	214,993	429,968	792,844
Postage	706,768	33,365	38,551	135,801	43,123	41,526	233,237	175,536
Household textiles	**1,528,098**	**97,598**	**102,679**	**164,858**	**178,283**	**192,100**	**316,527**	**471,517**
Bathroom linens	301,185	10,016	29,376	19,453	16,949	29,813	78,287	115,837
Bedroom linens	645,792	13,044	53,410	18,837	113,492	128,215	135,751	181,610
Appliances and miscellaneous housewares	**2,638,601**	**144,611**	**156,828**	**286,746**	**272,895**	**377,457**	**273,530**	**1,112,495**
Major appliances	890,620	8,329	18,529	83,598	88,283	85,536	92,078	506,708
Small appliances and misc. housewares	1,747,981	136,251	138,227	203,148	184,612	292,010	181,317	605,787
China and other dinnerware	273,468	59,161	7,687	64,146	16,949	72,936	406	53,205
Nonelectric cookware	419,442	–	34,581	20,930	98,474	120,140	17,983	123,168
Tableware, nonelectric kitchenware	292,870	34,215	10,568	28,318	10,191	48,447	21,769	138,250
Small electric kitchen appliances	285,479	7,137	19,913	29,303	40,119	20,940	53,138	114,999
Miscellaneous household equipment	**6,516,126**	**358,542**	**376,633**	**542,344**	**503,525**	**740,452**	**1,183,223**	**2,783,647**
Infants' equipment	242,980	8,038	12,329	4,063	88,605	17,746	40,833	70,172
Outdoor equipment	198,634	9,410	4,616	16,252	14,696	39,574	30,828	82,322
Other household decorative items	2,706,045	120,696	160,671	219,154	141,275	338,061	389,405	1,307,931
Power tools	362,161	–	15,694	–	20,596	46,583	95,864	181,192
Indoor plants, fresh flowers	1,300,823	86,993	108,213	153,654	109,630	118,277	232,561	491,207
Computers and computer hardware	644,868	–	16,405	24,624	6,114	26,530	246,623	324,888
Miscellaneous household equipment	221,731	8,152	10,037	48,017	62,217	32,475	15,144	42,522
Other housing	**10,323,435**	**561,293**	**817,023**	**934,973**	**941,509**	**827,496**	**1,497,992**	**4,743,029**
Repair or maintenance services	467,483	3,907	72,499	25,978	181,501	18,367	60,033	104,944
Housing while attending school	3,405,422	111,569	37,046	157,594	116,495	226,262	483,511	2,272,750
Natural gas (renter)	321,510	39,291	72,540	71,040	42,264	25,377	29,476	41,475
Electricity (renter)	1,247,238	203,180	281,499	257,321	146,424	67,435	161,711	129,662
Water, sewer maintenance (renter)	260,534	31,997	60,594	63,284	27,676	10,736	28,800	37,705
Day-care centers, nurseries, and preschools	2,260,734	37,904	63,624	151,191	176,352	207,451	386,430	1,237,968

APPAREL AND SERVICES	complete income reporters	under $10,000	$10,000– $19,999	$20,000– $29,999	$30,000– $39,999	$40,000– $49,999	$50,000– $69,999	$70,000 or more
APPAREL AND SERVICES	**$23,878,602**	**$1,367,972**	**$2,049,792**	**$2,515,834**	**$1,990,395**	**$1,950,197**	**$3,754,917**	**$10,070,061**
Men and boys, aged 2 or older	**6,598,351**	**381,108**	**714,380**	**720,744**	**528,734**	**544,092**	**947,552**	**2,715,150**
Men's coats and jackets	573,729	–	46,649	18,960	–	48,802	254,060	205,281
Men's accessories	460,092	31,236	16,430	52,572	41,406	7,986	63,143	241,100
Men's sweaters and vests	277,164	10,393	15,918	23,762	27,568	18,633	42,456	138,460
Men's active sportswear	323,358	14,596	73,308	28,071	–	61,490	–	142,021
Men's shirts	1,729,503	136,048	63,189	194,037	135,589	123,423	172,663	883,126
Men's pants	797,308	36,607	18,176	130,015	82,062	101,773	112,089	306,036
Boys' shirts	378,791	51,464	130,490	27,702	22,527	8,607	39,887	99,917
Boys' pants	372,324	16,097	48,840	45,801	51,811	44,010	62,061	104,107
Women and girls, aged 2 or older	**8,151,393**	**552,588**	**557,610**	**924,631**	**497,947**	**458,912**	**1,184,440**	**3,889,229**
Women's coats and jackets	644,868	52,640	13,288	70,671	37,223	44,010	88,022	332,638
Women's dresses	751,114	–	8,976	160,056	–	31,765	67,470	459,787
Women's vests and sweaters	933,119	90,671	35,212	129,892	43,659	22,271	42,997	552,791
Women's shirts, tops, blouses	946,977	136,166	57,446	114,994	53,206	33,185	197,677	355,471
Women's pants	697,529	21,659	19,790	44,323	24,028	31,499	30,422	510,478
Women's active sportswear	346,455	9,699	9,036	–	19,201	31,765	50,028	222,667
Women's sleepwear	550,632	35,792	80,599	55,527	12,443	107,718	48,270	206,118
Women's accessories	542,318	45,866	31,846	66,854	52,240	8,163	27,583	301,008
Girls' dresses and suits	321,510	8,056	21,487	24,132	27,247	2,396	177,125	62,632
Girls' shirts, blouses, sweaters	424,985	50,674	67,636	37,182	44,303	15,883	75,582	134,061
Girls' skirts and pants	328,901	10,295	40,213	45,924	39,261	41,614	67,064	84,416
Girls' accessories	195,863	5,923	20,128	66,239	4,291	–	16,225	77,085
Children under age 2	**4,000,400**	**212,403**	**343,269**	**335,379**	**487,864**	**422,177**	**605,741**	**1,576,681**
Infant dresses, outerwear	1,514,239	72,776	131,169	116,102	184,075	177,105	244,324	589,239
Infant underwear	1,725,808	105,754	174,825	145,282	235,672	175,242	269,068	609,348
Infant nightwear, loungewear	263,306	12,567	15,693	26,101	24,136	25,466	41,104	118,560
Infant accessories	367,704	14,143	10,808	33,735	26,925	37,533	23,391	214,288
Other apparel products and services	**5,129,382**	**221,873**	**434,533**	**535,080**	**475,850**	**525,015**	**1,017,185**	**1,889,000**
Jewelry and watches	2,265,354	108,555	145,367	187,758	107,485	468,938	408,334	838,718
Watches	226,351	14,294	18,112	14,036	22,956	25,732	34,208	97,404
Jewelry	2,038,079	94,261	127,246	173,722	84,529	443,206	374,126	741,314
Men's footwear	811,167	–	136,271	91,232	238,247	8,696	90,185	232,931
Boys' footwear	427,756	14,243	35,806	69,686	56,531	1,597	104,517	139,507
Women's footwear	992,247	38,665	90,649	106,376	29,392	7,187	277,721	433,184
Girls' footwear	325,206	42,024	3,923	36,813	24,458	8,873	58,411	149,143
TRANSPORTATION	**3,953,283**	**49,508**	**818,298**	**111,424**	**264,206**	**316,589**	**1,366,432**	**1,026,194**
Used cars	1,348,865	–	612,950	10,219	77,556	177,904	417,393	52,786
Airline fares	685,519	18,184	41,220	51,095	59,106	76,840	122,365	316,928
Ship fares	253,143	5,871	2,124	9,111	62,646	20,852	55,977	96,356
HEALTH CARE	**3,107,008**	**92,403**	**222,763**	**242,054**	**174,743**	**400,438**	**467,827**	**1,504,204**
Physician's services	332,597	2,705	8,715	17,237	28,534	23,957	46,783	204,443
Dental services	419,442	4,795	2,898	19,084	38,188	31,943	117,227	205,281
Care in convalescent or nursing home	561,719	33,351	13,772	–	–	103,725	70,174	341,017
Nonprescription vitamins	214,340	9,471	36,844	6,648	40,441	16,149	24,067	79,389
Prescription drugs	250,371	8,304	16,017	19,576	17,592	30,967	47,594	110,600
ENTERTAINMENT	**7,435,386**	**298,983**	**568,895**	**640,716**	**715,491**	**724,303**	**1,376,843**	**3,094,710**
Toys, games, hobbies, and tricycles	2,902,831	100,453	258,774	321,589	308,294	283,759	602,766	1,026,822
Other entertainment	4,532,555	198,531	310,042	319,250	407,197	440,544	774,077	2,067,888
Fees for recreational lessons	618,076	10,859	28,084	9,111	40,441	52,528	44,484	432,556
Community antenna or cable TV	559,871	93,897	118,223	106,006	56,960	26,264	84,912	73,315

	complete income reporters	under $10,000	$10,000– $19,999	$20,000– $29,999	$30,000– $39,999	$40,000– $49,999	$50,000– $69,999	$70,000 or more
VCRs and videodisc players	$199,558	$8,622	$5,365	–	$24,350	$19,521	$40,022	$101,174
Video game hardware and software	229,122	4,970	13,027	$24,870	27,890	26,796	53,949	77,294
Athletic gear, game tables, exercise equipment	628,238	5,147	17,374	19,207	31,430	11,180	71,932	458,739
Hunting and fishing equipment	277,164	29,685	9,164	66,731	24,350	91,037	16,631	37,705
Photographer fees	261,458	18,164	4,660	12,681	20,918	11,180	29,341	164,643
PERSONAL CARE PRODUCTS								
AND SERVICES	**2,216,388**	**141,907**	**298,682**	**229,496**	**214,969**	**174,088**	**338,295**	**802,061**
Cosmetics, perfume, bath preparation	1,231,532	68,083	157,519	77,196	192,550	97,780	153,328	475,706
Electric personal care appliances	399,116	46,344	52,700	95,172	1,716	–	85,182	114,580
EDUCATION	**17,496,439**	**370,490**	**788,951**	**605,258**	**1,027,539**	**1,330,773**	**1,920,388**	**11,440,204**
College tuition	12,274,670	198,292	591,643	367,390	754,859	826,964	1,253,532	8,281,606
Elementary and high school tuition	2,164,651	18,982	40,998	114,502	74,016	318,097	265,282	1,332,858
Other school tuition	467,483	3,570	22,773	2,339	27,032	25,022	23,797	363,430
Other school expenses including rentals	365,856	5,814	16,479	17,114	33,897	44,809	72,337	175,117
College books and supplies	1,158,546	106,544	33,677	60,575	44,195	60,958	206,330	646,215
Miscellaneous school supplies	820,405	28,609	70,219	29,549	45,804	32,298	74,906	526,189
ALL OTHER GIFTS	**8,156,013**	**257,121**	**613,557**	**601,195**	**921,127**	**565,033**	**1,288,416**	**3,905,778**
Gifts of trip expenses	4,619,400	139,214	201,989	318,758	508,889	348,088	778,404	2,323,860
Lotteries and gambling losses	91,464	5,643	15,311	23,023	2,896	7,453	2,975	32,677
Legal fees	551,556	23,944	–	11,820	212,180	118,632	69,498	115,209
Funeral expenses	2,369,752	62,187	363,092	237,622	156,936	62,555	338,295	1,149,152
Miscellaneous personal services	217,112	3,832	3,457	2,709	13,731	3,638	60,304	127,358

Note: Numbers may not add to total because of rounding. (–) means sample is too small to make a reliable estimate. Expenditures for items in a given category may not add to category total because categories with annual spending of less than $2.00 for the average household are omitted. Spending on gifts is also included in the product and service categories in other chapters.
Source: Calculations by New Strategist based on the 2002 Consumer Expenditure Survey

Table 6.8 Gifts for Non—Household Members: Market shares by income, 2002

(percentage of total annual spending on selected gifts of products and services for non–household members accounted for by before-tax income group of consumer units, 2002; complete income reporters only)

	complete income reporters	under $10,000	$10,000–$19,999	$20,000–$29,999	$30,000–$39,999	$40,000–$49,999	$50,000–$69,999	$70,000 or more
Share of total consumer units	100.0%	11.8%	16.3%	13.3%	11.6%	9.6%	14.6%	22.7%
Share of total before-tax income	100.0	1.3	4.9	6.6	8.1	8.6	17.4	53.0
Share of total spending	100.0	4.9	8.8	9.0	9.6	9.4	17.3	40.8
Share of gifts spending	100.0	4.3	7.7	7.9	8.3	8.4	16.1	46.9
FOOD	100.0%	3.8%	6.2%	5.6%	8.9%	4.9%	15.5%	54.7%
Cakes and cupcakes	100.0	8.1	2.0	13.6	15.2	2.3	2.4	54.8
Fresh fruit other than apples, bananas, and citrus	100.0	11.0	8.8	10.1	11.5	7.5	7.4	43.0
Candy and chewing gum	100.0	2.6	16.7	12.0	12.3	5.3	17.6	32.4
Board (including at school)	100.0	4.8	3.0	1.1	1.1	3.7	23.2	63.1
Catered affairs	100.0	0.7	0.9	2.3	10.6	4.6	11.6	69.4
ALCOHOLIC BEVERAGES	100.0	7.9	5.0	14.6	4.1	4.4	22.8	40.4
Beer and ale	100.0	15.1	5.5	23.1	3.9	3.1	20.2	28.8
Wine	100.0	5.0	3.5	12.2	3.5	7.4	20.2	47.1
HOUSING	100.0	5.5	7.2	9.5	9.0	9.9	16.6	41.9
Housekeeping supplies	100.0	5.4	8.8	11.0	8.6	8.8	21.6	35.1
Laundry and cleaning supplies	100.0	9.0	20.4	8.2	7.0	9.8	16.6	29.0
Other household products	100.0	3.7	7.3	10.4	9.2	8.0	18.7	41.6
Miscellaneous household products	100.0	3.1	3.7	15.7	8.8	9.0	13.6	44.3
Lawn and garden supplies	100.0	2.1	9.5	3.6	10.4	5.0	25.0	43.7
Postage and stationery	100.0	5.6	8.0	11.6	8.6	9.0	23.4	33.2
Stationery, stationery supplies, giftwrap	100.0	5.8	8.5	9.0	9.5	10.0	19.9	36.7
Postage	100.0	4.7	5.5	19.2	6.1	5.9	33.0	24.8
Household textiles	100.0	6.4	6.7	10.8	11.7	12.6	20.7	30.9
Bathroom linens	100.0	3.3	9.8	6.5	5.6	9.9	26.0	38.5
Bedroom linens	100.0	2.0	8.3	2.9	17.6	19.9	21.0	28.1
Appliances and miscellaneous housewares	100.0	5.5	5.9	10.9	10.3	14.3	10.4	42.2
Major appliances	100.0	0.9	2.1	9.4	9.9	9.6	10.3	56.9
Small appliances and miscellaneous housewares	100.0	7.8	7.9	11.6	10.6	16.7	10.4	34.7
China and other dinnerware	100.0	21.6	2.8	23.5	6.2	26.7	0.1	19.5
Nonelectric cookware	100.0	–	8.2	5.0	23.5	28.6	4.3	29.4
Tableware, nonelectric kitchenware	100.0	11.7	3.6	9.7	3.5	16.5	7.4	47.2
Small electric kitchen appliances	100.0	2.5	7.0	10.3	14.1	7.3	18.6	40.3
Miscellaneous household equipment	100.0	5.5	5.8	8.3	7.7	11.4	18.2	42.7
Infants' equipment	100.0	3.3	5.1	1.7	36.5	7.3	16.8	28.9
Outdoor equipment	100.0	4.7	2.3	8.2	7.4	19.9	15.5	41.4
Other household decorative items	100.0	4.5	5.9	8.1	5.2	12.5	14.4	48.3
Power tools	100.0	–	4.3	–	5.7	12.9	26.5	50.0
Indoor plants, fresh flowers	100.0	6.7	8.3	11.8	8.4	9.1	17.9	37.8
Computers and computer hardware	100.0	–	2.5	3.8	0.9	4.1	38.2	50.4
Miscellaneous household equipment	100.0	3.7	4.5	21.7	28.1	14.6	6.8	19.2
Other housing	100.0	5.4	7.9	9.1	9.1	8.0	14.5	45.9
Repair or maintenance services	100.0	0.8	15.5	5.6	38.8	3.9	12.8	22.4
Housing while attending school	100.0	3.3	1.1	4.6	3.4	6.6	14.2	66.7
Natural gas (renter)	100.0	12.2	22.6	22.1	13.1	7.9	9.2	12.9
Electricity (renter)	100.0	16.3	22.6	20.6	11.7	5.4	13.0	10.4
Water, sewer maintenance (renter)	100.0	12.3	23.3	24.3	10.6	4.1	11.1	14.5
Day-care centers, nurseries, and preschools	100.0	1.7	2.8	6.7	7.8	9.2	17.1	54.8

	complete income reporters	under $10,000	$10,000– $19,999	$20,000– $29,999	$30,000– $39,999	$40,000– $49,999	$50,000– $69,999	$70,000 or more
APPAREL AND SERVICES	**100.0%**	**5.7%**	**8.6%**	**10.5%**	**8.3%**	**8.2%**	**15.7%**	**42.2%**
Men and boys, aged 2 or older	**100.0**	**5.8**	**10.8**	**10.9**	**8.0**	**8.2**	**14.4**	**41.1**
Men's coats and jackets	100.0	–	8.1	3.3	–	8.5	44.3	35.8
Men's accessories	100.0	6.8	3.6	11.4	9.0	1.7	13.7	52.4
Men's sweaters and vests	100.0	3.7	5.7	8.6	9.9	6.7	15.3	50.0
Men's active sportswear	100.0	4.5	22.7	8.7	–	19.0	–	43.9
Men's shirts	100.0	7.9	3.7	11.2	7.8	7.1	10.0	51.1
Men's pants	100.0	4.6	2.3	16.3	10.3	12.8	14.1	38.4
Boys' shirts	100.0	13.6	34.4	7.3	5.9	2.3	10.5	26.4
Boys' pants	100.0	4.3	13.1	12.3	13.9	11.8	16.7	28.0
Women and girls, aged 2 or older	**100.0**	**6.8**	**6.8**	**11.3**	**6.1**	**5.6**	**14.5**	**47.7**
Women's coats and jackets	100.0	8.2	2.1	11.0	5.8	6.8	13.6	51.6
Women's dresses	100.0	–	1.2	21.3	–	4.2	9.0	61.2
Women's vests and sweaters	100.0	9.7	3.8	13.9	4.7	2.4	4.6	59.2
Women's shirts, tops, blouses	100.0	14.4	6.1	12.1	5.6	3.5	20.9	37.5
Women's pants	100.0	3.1	2.8	6.4	3.4	4.5	4.4	73.2
Women's active sportswear	100.0	2.8	2.6	–	5.5	9.2	14.4	64.3
Women's sleepwear	100.0	6.5	14.6	10.1	2.3	19.6	8.8	37.4
Women's accessories	100.0	8.5	5.9	12.3	9.6	1.5	5.1	55.5
Girls' dresses and suits	100.0	2.5	6.7	7.5	8.5	0.7	55.1	19.5
Girls' shirts, blouses, sweaters	100.0	11.9	15.9	8.7	10.4	3.7	17.8	31.5
Girls' skirts and pants	100.0	3.1	12.2	14.0	11.9	12.7	20.4	25.7
Girls' accessories	100.0	3.0	10.3	33.8	2.2	–	8.3	39.4
Children under age 2	**100.0**	**5.3**	**8.6**	**8.4**	**12.2**	**10.6**	**15.1**	**39.4**
Infant dresses, outerwear	100.0	4.8	8.7	7.7	12.2	11.7	16.1	38.9
Infant underwear	100.0	6.1	10.1	8.4	13.7	10.2	15.6	35.3
Infant nightwear, loungewear	100.0	4.8	6.0	9.9	9.2	9.7	15.6	45.0
Infant accessories	100.0	3.8	2.9	9.2	7.3	10.2	6.4	58.3
Other apparel products and services	**100.0**	**4.3**	**8.5**	**10.4**	**9.3**	**10.2**	**19.8**	**36.8**
Jewelry and watches	100.0	4.8	6.4	8.3	4.7	20.7	18.0	37.0
Watches	100.0	6.3	8.0	6.2	10.1	11.4	15.1	43.0
Jewelry	100.0	4.6	6.2	8.5	4.1	21.7	18.4	36.4
Men's footwear	100.0	–	16.8	11.2	29.4	1.1	11.1	28.7
Boys' footwear	100.0	3.3	8.4	16.3	13.2	0.4	24.4	32.6
Women's footwear	100.0	3.9	9.1	10.7	3.0	0.7	28.0	43.7
Girls' footwear	100.0	12.9	1.2	11.3	7.5	2.7	18.0	45.9
TRANSPORTATION	**100.0**	**1.3**	**20.7**	**2.8**	**6.7**	**8.0**	**34.6**	**26.0**
Used cars	100.0	–	45.4	0.8	5.7	13.2	30.9	3.9
Airline fares	100.0	2.7	6.0	7.5	8.6	11.2	17.8	46.2
Ship fares	100.0	2.3	0.8	3.6	24.7	8.2	22.1	38.1
HEALTH CARE	**100.0**	**3.0**	**7.2**	**7.8**	**5.6**	**12.9**	**15.1**	**48.4**
Physician's services	100.0	0.8	2.6	5.2	8.6	7.2	14.1	61.5
Dental services	100.0	1.1	0.7	4.5	9.1	7.6	27.9	48.9
Care in convalescent or nursing home	100.0	5.9	2.5	–	–	18.5	12.5	60.7
Nonprescription vitamins	100.0	4.4	17.2	3.1	18.9	7.5	11.2	37.0
Prescription drugs	100.0	3.3	6.4	7.8	7.0	12.4	19.0	44.2
ENTERTAINMENT	**100.0**	**4.0**	**7.7**	**8.6**	**9.6**	**9.7**	**18.5**	**41.6**
Toys, games, hobbies, and tricycles	100.0	3.5	8.9	11.1	10.6	9.8	20.8	35.4
Other entertainment	100.0	4.4	6.8	7.0	9.0	9.7	17.1	45.6
Fees for recreational lessons	100.0	1.8	4.5	1.5	6.5	8.5	7.2	70.0
Community antenna or cable TV	100.0	16.8	21.1	18.9	10.2	4.7	15.2	13.1

	complete income reporters	under $10,000	$10,000– $19,999	$20,000– $29,999	$30,000– $39,999	$40,000– $49,999	$50,000– $69,999	$70,000 or more
VCRs and videodisc players	100.0%	4.3%	2.7%	–	12.2%	9.8%	20.1%	50.7%
Video game hardware and software	100.0	2.2	5.7	10.9%	12.2	11.7	23.5	33.7
Athletic gear, game tables, exercise equipment	100.0	0.8	2.8	3.1	5.0	1.8	11.4	73.0
Hunting and fishing equipment	100.0	10.7	3.3	24.1	8.8	32.8	6.0	13.6
Photographer fees	100.0	6.9	1.8	4.9	8.0	4.3	11.2	63.0
PERSONAL CARE PRODUCTS AND SERVICES	**100.0**	**6.4**	**13.5**	**10.4**	**9.7**	**7.9**	**15.3**	**36.2**
Cosmetics, perfume, bath preparation	100.0	5.5	12.8	6.3	15.6	7.9	12.5	38.6
Electric personal care appliances	100.0	11.6	13.2	23.8	0.4	–	21.3	28.7
EDUCATION	**100.0**	**2.1**	**4.5**	**3.5**	**5.9**	**7.6**	**11.0**	**65.4**
College tuition	100.0	1.6	4.8	3.0	6.1	6.7	10.2	67.5
Elementary and high school tuition	100.0	0.9	1.9	5.3	3.4	14.7	12.3	61.6
Other school tuition	100.0	0.8	4.9	0.5	5.8	5.4	5.1	77.7
Other school expenses including rentals	100.0	1.6	4.5	4.7	9.3	12.2	19.8	47.9
College books and supplies	100.0	9.2	2.9	5.2	3.8	5.3	17.8	55.8
Miscellaneous school supplies	100.0	3.5	8.6	3.6	5.6	3.9	9.1	64.1
ALL OTHER GIFTS	**100.0**	**3.2**	**7.5**	**7.4**	**11.3**	**6.9**	**15.8**	**47.9**
Gifts of trip expenses	100.0	3.0	4.4	6.9	11.0	7.5	16.9	50.3
Lotteries and gambling losses	100.0	6.2	16.7	25.2	3.2	8.1	3.3	35.7
Legal fees	100.0	4.3	–	2.1	38.5	21.5	12.6	20.9
Funeral expenses	100.0	2.6	15.3	10.0	6.6	2.6	14.3	48.5
Miscellaneous personal services	100.0	1.8	1.6	1.2	6.3	1.7	27.8	58.7

Note: Numbers may not add to total because of rounding. (–) means sample is too small to make a reliable estimate.
Expenditures for items in a given category may not add to category total because categories with annual spending of less than $2.00 for the average household are omitted. Spending on gifts is also included in the product and service categories in other chapters.
Source: Calculations by New Strategist based on the 2002 Consumer Expenditure Survey

Table 6.9 Gifts for Non–Household Members: Average spending by household type, 2002

(average annual spending of consumer units (CU) on selected gifts of products and services for non–household members by type of consumer unit, 2002)

	total married couples	married couples, no children	married couples with children				single parent, at least one child <18	single person
			total	oldest child under 6	oldest child 6 to 17	oldest child 18 or older		
Number of consumer units (in thousands, add 000)	56,265	23,118	28,790	5,547	15,206	8,036	6,730	33,055
Average number of persons per CU	3.2	2.0	3.9	3.5	4.1	3.9	2.9	1.0
Average before-tax income of CU	$67,155.00	$58,967.00	$73,918.00	$67,587.00	$72,720.00	$81,042.00	$26,966.00	$27,042.00
Average spending of CU, total	52,333.70	45,557.33	57,835.01	52,778.62	58,103.75	60,859.78	30,185.38	24,189.90
Gifts, average spending	1,337.98	1,478.71	1,286.20	773.24	1,252.89	1,709.75	512.74	744.02
FOOD	$122.81	$157.19	$106.00	$54.18	$93.83	$165.33	$35.84	$42.18
Cakes and cupcakes	2.32	1.27	3.04	–	3.37	4.63	0.26	2.28
Fresh fruit other than apples, bananas, and citrus	2.15	2.35	2.21	1.67	1.96	3.10	2.87	1.15
Candy and chewing gum	14.13	15.29	12.98	15.45	10.56	15.99	4.00	9.70
Board (including at school)	36.25	24.58	50.35	10.25	41.17	95.39	5.01	7.93
Catered affairs	45.58	90.99	15.04	7.64	15.14	19.95	1.27	6.76
ALCOHOLIC BEVERAGES	15.19	13.77	18.14	9.29	23.32	14.31	4.23	10.08
Beer and ale	4.05	4.27	4.36	1.42	6.21	2.81	2.65	4.07
Wine	7.51	6.42	9.63	4.01	12.41	8.23	0.83	4.25
HOUSING	342.09	355.08	350.25	280.41	328.15	442.36	158.55	169.98
Housekeeping supplies	56.75	67.31	50.78	36.07	47.32	68.53	23.67	24.72
Laundry and cleaning supplies	2.49	3.06	2.02	2.03	0.93	4.19	1.67	1.53
Other household products	14.98	18.17	12.74	2.09	16.14	13.79	9.40	5.61
Miscellaneous household products	6.85	7.54	6.14	1.90	7.12	7.30	6.42	3.95
Lawn and garden supplies	6.12	8.87	4.57	0.01	7.68	1.71	1.60	0.69
Postage and stationery	37.89	44.82	34.41	30.75	29.00	47.91	10.34	17.58
Stationery, stationery supplies, giftwrap	27.73	29.81	27.48	28.13	24.58	32.81	8.52	14.52
Postage	9.28	13.75	6.23	2.63	3.89	13.56	0.88	2.78
Household textiles	19.64	28.69	12.62	9.49	13.44	13.14	8.88	9.17
Bathroom linens	4.08	5.48	2.86	3.59	1.95	4.12	2.12	1.20
Bedroom linens	8.61	14.62	3.85	5.01	3.70	3.27	4.35	4.05
Appliances and miscellaneous housewares	29.43	43.56	20.01	13.92	21.71	20.93	11.96	15.64
Major appliances	11.18	18.96	5.52	3.65	6.21	5.45	1.58	3.84
Small appliances and miscellaneous housewares	18.25	24.60	14.50	10.27	15.50	15.47	10.38	11.80
China and other dinnerware	3.75	4.38	3.31	0.31	6.07	–	–	1.64
Nonelectric cookware	3.42	5.70	1.77	1.34	2.08	1.48	0.67	3.10
Tableware, nonelectric kitchenware	3.50	4.28	3.31	2.64	3.51	3.41	5.10	1.27
Small electric kitchen appliances	3.07	3.94	2.66	2.49	1.77	4.47	2.32	1.95
Miscellaneous household equipment	82.91	96.63	76.40	58.88	64.80	111.65	49.39	45.70
Infants' equipment	6.00	4.12	6.96	2.09	2.17	20.09	2.60	1.32
Outdoor equipment	3.59	5.23	2.75	2.12	4.28	0.15	0.56	0.60
Other household decorative items	32.83	39.38	29.87	33.24	23.39	40.34	20.85	18.93
Power tools	2.62	5.29	0.51	–	0.95	–	7.14	0.99
Indoor plants, fresh flowers	15.65	18.95	13.68	10.62	13.28	16.56	4.19	14.31
Computers and computer hardware	9.17	8.25	10.73	3.38	9.75	17.64	6.04	3.90
Miscellaneous household equipment	3.06	3.31	3.08	3.46	2.97	3.03	1.28	1.34
Other housing	153.37	118.89	190.44	162.05	180.89	228.11	64.65	74.76
Repair or maintenance services	4.05	2.36	2.66	0.26	3.82	2.11	–	7.78
Housing while attending school	66.36	54.26	82.04	12.33	62.96	166.28	3.51	18.04
Natural gas (renter)	2.74	2.17	2.91	1.24	3.82	2.34	5.71	4.66
Electricity (renter)	11.34	8.95	12.19	8.73	14.31	10.55	19.65	14.48
Water, sewer maintenance (renter)	2.40	1.89	2.84	1.75	3.67	2.03	4.70	2.43
Day-care centers, nurseries, and preschools	36.78	7.68	65.06	126.75	65.05	22.50	20.76	7.09

	total married couples	married couples, no children	married couples with children				single parent, at least one child <18	single person
			total	oldest child under 6	oldest child 6 to 17	oldest child 18 or older		
APPAREL AND SERVICES	$273.08	$318.66	$243.62	$231.27	$212.16	$314.49	$184.89	$187.50
Men and boys, aged 2 or older	73.42	92.68	58.92	60.48	52.01	71.10	54.43	48.04
Men's coats and jackets	6.70	8.57	6.17	–	3.31	16.42	0.06	2.48
Men's accessories	3.36	3.28	3.87	8.53	1.13	5.90	18.62	3.07
Men's sweaters and vests	3.66	4.33	3.36	2.27	2.15	6.40	1.29	2.24
Men's active sportswear	3.45	5.47	2.27	8.91	0.55	0.81	–	3.21
Men's shirts	19.03	25.51	14.62	18.02	17.64	6.10	8.78	11.68
Men's pants	8.68	12.80	5.99	3.41	3.23	13.41	5.36	6.53
Boys' shirts	3.65	2.28	3.06	0.17	5.22	0.89	5.21	3.23
Boys' pants	4.61	6.83	3.06	2.14	2.68	4.41	2.39	2.57
Women and girls, aged 2 or older	98.56	124.34	81.86	51.58	71.71	124.28	49.39	63.73
Women's coats and jackets	7.67	12.91	4.40	1.47	3.08	9.21	–	2.35
Women's dresses	11.02	15.25	5.89	1.68	5.73	9.31	–	4.43
Women's vests and sweaters	9.26	9.56	10.27	8.32	10.21	11.84	4.20	6.99
Women's shirts, tops, blouses	10.33	12.65	9.25	5.87	6.74	16.76	9.29	7.31
Women's pants	8.79	13.16	5.34	1.12	3.35	12.43	2.27	2.50
Women's active sportswear	5.36	9.15	2.96	6.58	1.04	4.14	1.01	5.25
Women's sleepwear	7.38	7.75	8.08	6.71	9.65	5.95	2.48	6.79
Women's accessories	2.42	3.56	1.61	–	0.75	4.52	–	5.14
Girls' dresses and suits	2.27	3.06	1.51	0.49	1.07	3.15	0.84	1.26
Girls' shirts, blouses, sweaters	5.76	7.44	4.94	6.24	4.81	4.26	9.37	2.85
Girls' skirts and pants	4.66	1.05	7.57	0.08	2.79	22.64	1.74	3.08
Girls' accessories	5.56	7.19	4.11	7.32	2.78	4.38	6.68	0.97
Children under age 2	55.03	45.90	62.32	97.76	55.11	50.32	26.17	15.09
Infant dresses, outerwear	20.08	24.75	16.71	17.99	13.67	21.57	8.50	7.21
Infant underwear	25.03	12.36	34.73	63.41	31.85	19.36	14.65	3.14
Infant nightwear, loungewear	3.29	3.98	2.77	3.34	2.05	3.72	0.91	1.48
Infant accessories	4.97	3.05	6.57	10.16	6.38	4.32	1.60	2.47
Other apparel products and services	46.07	55.74	40.52	21.46	33.33	68.78	54.90	60.63
Jewelry and watches	17.03	25.76	11.78	7.72	12.55	13.11	15.62	40.57
Watches	2.52	3.12	2.32	1.78	2.45	2.44	1.25	1.88
Jewelry	14.51	22.64	9.46	5.94	10.10	10.67	14.36	38.69
Men's footwear	29.03	29.98	28.74	13.74	20.78	55.66	39.29	3.36
Boys' footwear	3.83	2.19	5.84	2.79	1.87	16.00	7.48	4.64
Women's footwear	9.97	9.97	10.64	0.47	9.79	19.84	21.08	5.47
Girls' footwear	2.87	3.01	1.83	–	1.65	3.52	5.58	4.18
TRANSPORTATION	43.94	37.12	53.83	16.29	60.43	67.15	7.10	45.63
Used cars	7.12	9.33	6.42	–	–	23.01	–	18.31
Airline fares	3.37	3.88	3.30	–	1.79	8.44	–	6.33
Ship fares	3.34	2.97	3.36	5.84	2.55	3.17	1.36	2.29
HEALTH CARE	35.78	44.09	31.91	5.18	37.75	39.13	27.06	24.11
Physician's services	4.61	6.08	3.86	0.08	4.42	5.42	0.38	1.57
Dental services	5.45	8.53	2.97	0.78	3.12	4.21	0.69	1.36
Care in convalescent or nursing home	2.61	6.14	0.17	–	–	0.60	6.45	6.05
Nonprescription vitamins	2.53	3.29	2.13	0.28	1.45	4.85	0.61	0.81
Prescription drugs	6.29	1.84	11.09	0.23	19.94	1.43	–	2.65
ENTERTAINMENT	100.97	117.00	89.70	85.01	85.22	101.52	26.84	57.54
Toys, games, hobbies, and tricycles	38.68	54.43	27.12	33.14	19.16	38.03	7.48	22.44
Other entertainment	62.29	62.57	62.58	51.86	66.07	63.48	19.36	35.10
Fees for recreational lessons	11.76	9.03	12.87	2.68	19.81	6.77	2.54	4.17
Community antenna or cable TV	5.20	3.69	6.29	3.71	8.98	2.99	3.93	7.27

	total married couples	married couples, no children	married couples with children				single parent, at least one child <18	single person
			total	oldest child under 6	oldest child 6 to 17	oldest child 18 or older		
VCRs and videodisc players	$2.93	$3.18	$3.08	$5.30	$1.92	$3.73	$0.87	$1.55
Video game hardware and software	2.50	3.68	1.53	1.76	1.01	2.35	0.49	1.76
Athletic gear, game tables, exercise equipment	9.54	7.78	10.51	6.24	8.29	18.10	1.51	3.35
Hunting and fishing equipment	4.15	1.86	6.35	16.12	5.93	–	2.12	2.80
Photographer fees	2.93	5.67	0.90	0.26	1.02	1.13	0.10	0.64
PERSONAL CARE PRODUCTS AND SERVICES	**23.68**	**22.60**	**23.78**	**22.23**	**28.27**	**15.96**	**14.87**	**14.74**
Cosmetics, perfume, bath preparation	14.58	14.42	15.13	11.97	20.24	7.27	7.13	8.51
Electric personal care appliances	2.52	2.09	2.75	2.64	3.51	1.33	1.69	2.73
EDUCATION	**278.98**	**269.72**	**306.91**	**33.69**	**329.38**	**454.11**	**34.89**	**110.67**
College tuition	199.30	209.28	208.03	19.98	205.85	341.97	21.99	70.57
Elementary and high school tuition	35.34	21.01	48.67	0.06	77.90	26.92	1.57	23.40
Other school tuition	7.32	8.84	6.12	7.33	5.54	6.39	1.05	2.00
Other school expenses including rentals	5.61	3.30	7.77	0.28	6.47	15.41	3.83	2.42
College books and supplies	16.46	17.51	15.94	2.24	14.64	27.85	4.73	7.95
Miscellaneous school supplies	11.45	8.60	15.04	1.52	10.26	34.53	0.49	3.50
ALL OTHER GIFTS	**99.98**	**141.06**	**61.18**	**34.95**	**53.54**	**94.28**	**18.40**	**80.07**
Gifts of trip expenses	54.43	81.15	29.51	22.65	23.14	46.28	8.84	44.42
Lotteries and gambling losses	4.81	9.72	1.38	–	2.18	0.79	–	0.67
Legal fees	6.60	12.13	1.78	3.45	0.16	3.69	–	7.13
Funeral expenses	27.14	31.42	20.87	7.28	22.49	27.20	5.55	24.50
Miscellaneous personal services	3.12	3.20	3.51	–	0.23	12.67	1.54	1.42

Note: Average spending figures for total consumer units can be found on Average Spending by Age and Average Spending by Region tables. (–) means sample is too small to make a reliable estimate. Expenditures for items in a given category may not add to category total because categories with annual spending of less than $2.00 for the average household are omitted. Spending on gifts is also included in the product and service categories in other chapters.
Source: Bureau of Labor Statistics, unpublished tables from the 2002 Consumer Expenditure Survey

Table 6.10 Gifts for Non—Household Members: Indexed spending by household type, 2002

(indexed average annual spending of consumer units (CU) on selected gifts of products and services for non—household members by type of consumer unit, 2002; index definition: an index of 100 is the average for all consumer units; an index of 132 means that spending by consumer units in that group is 32 percent above the average for all consumer units; an index of 68 indicates spending that is 32 percent below the average for all consumer units)

	total married couples	married couples, no children	married couples with children				single parent, at least one child <18	single person
			total	oldest child under 6	oldest child 6 to 17	oldest child 18 or older		
Average spending of CU, total	$52,334	$45,557	$57,835	$52,779	$58,104	$60,860	$30,185	$24,190
Average spending of CU, index	129	112	142	130	143	150	74	59
Gifts, spending index	129	143	124	75	121	165	49	72
FOOD	**149**	**191**	**129**	**66**	**114**	**201**	**44**	**51**
Cakes and cupcakes	96	53	126	–	140	192	11	95
Fresh fruit other than apples, bananas, and citrus	95	104	98	74	87	137	127	51
Candy and chewing gum	121	131	111	132	90	137	34	83
Board (including at school)	166	112	230	47	188	436	23	36
Catered affairs	174	347	57	29	58	76	5	26
ALCOHOLIC BEVERAGES	**113**	**103**	**135**	**69**	**174**	**107**	**32**	**75**
Beer and ale	86	90	92	30	131	59	56	86
Wine	129	110	165	69	213	141	14	73
HOUSING	**132**	**137**	**135**	**108**	**127**	**171**	**61**	**66**
Housekeeping supplies	**134**	**158**	**120**	**85**	**111**	**161**	**56**	**58**
Laundry and cleaning supplies	85	104	69	69	32	143	57	52
Other household products	128	155	109	18	138	118	80	48
Miscellaneous household products	117	129	105	32	122	125	110	68
Lawn and garden supplies	146	211	109	0	183	41	38	16
Postage and stationery	136	161	124	110	104	172	37	63
Stationery, stationery supplies, giftwrap	131	141	130	133	116	155	40	69
Postage	151	224	101	43	63	221	14	45
Household textiles	**143**	**209**	**92**	**69**	**98**	**96**	**65**	**67**
Bathroom linens	158	212	110	139	75	159	82	46
Bedroom linens	141	240	63	82	61	54	71	66
Appliances and miscellaneous housewares	**123**	**182**	**83**	**58**	**91**	**87**	**50**	**65**
Major appliances	133	225	66	43	74	65	19	46
Small appliances and miscellaneous housewares	117	158	93	66	100	99	67	76
China and other dinnerware	152	178	135	13	247	–	–	67
Nonelectric cookware	97	161	50	38	59	42	19	88
Tableware, nonelectric kitchenware	133	163	126	100	133	130	194	48
Small electric kitchen appliances	113	145	98	92	65	165	86	72
Miscellaneous household equipment	**128**	**149**	**118**	**91**	**100**	**173**	**76**	**71**
Infants' equipment	157	108	182	55	57	526	68	35
Outdoor equipment	173	253	133	102	207	7	27	29
Other household decorative items	127	153	116	129	91	157	81	73
Power tools	94	189	18	–	34	–	255	35
Indoor plants, fresh flowers	117	141	102	79	99	123	31	107
Computers and computer hardware	139	125	163	51	148	268	92	59
Miscellaneous household equipment	140	151	141	158	136	138	58	61
Other housing	**135**	**104**	**167**	**142**	**159**	**200**	**57**	**66**
Repair or maintenance services	90	52	59	6	85	47	–	173
Housing while attending school	166	136	205	31	158	416	9	45
Natural gas (renter)	76	60	80	34	106	65	158	129
Electricity (renter)	77	61	83	60	98	72	134	99
Water, sewer maintenance (renter)	79	62	93	58	121	67	155	80
Day-care centers, nurseries, and preschools	154	32	273	532	273	94	87	30

	total married couples	married couples, no children	married couples with children				single parent, at least one child <18	single person
			total	oldest child under 6	oldest child 6 to 17	oldest child 18 or older		
APPAREL AND SERVICES	**115**	**134**	**103**	**98**	**89**	**133**	**78**	**79**
Men and boys, aged 2 or older	**115**	**145**	**92**	**95**	**82**	**112**	**85**	**75**
Men's coats and jackets	132	168	121	–	65	323	1	49
Men's accessories	76	74	87	192	25	133	418	69
Men's sweaters and vests	120	142	110	74	70	209	42	73
Men's active sportswear	125	198	82	323	20	29	–	116
Men's shirts	113	152	87	107	105	36	52	70
Men's pants	125	185	86	49	47	194	77	94
Boys' shirts	98	61	82	5	141	24	140	87
Boys' pants	123	182	81	57	71	117	64	68
Women and girls, aged 2 or older	**121**	**152**	**100**	**63**	**88**	**152**	**60**	**78**
Women's coats and jackets	136	230	78	26	55	164	–	42
Women's dresses	144	199	77	22	75	122	–	58
Women's vests and sweaters	109	112	121	98	120	139	49	82
Women's shirts, tops, blouses	114	140	102	65	74	185	103	81
Women's pants	133	199	81	17	51	188	34	38
Women's active sportswear	124	211	68	152	24	96	23	121
Women's sleepwear	114	120	125	104	150	92	38	105
Women's accessories	42	62	28	–	13	79	–	90
Girls' dresses and suits	76	103	51	16	36	106	28	42
Girls' shirts, blouses, sweaters	129	166	110	139	107	95	209	64
Girls' skirts and pants	140	32	228	2	84	682	52	93
Girls' accessories	234	302	173	308	117	184	281	41
Children under age 2	**138**	**115**	**156**	**244**	**138**	**126**	**65**	**38**
Infant dresses, outerwear	131	162	109	118	89	141	56	47
Infant underwear	148	73	205	375	188	114	87	19
Infant nightwear, loungewear	129	156	109	131	80	146	36	58
Infant accessories	126	78	167	259	162	110	41	63
Other apparel products and services	**89**	**108**	**78**	**42**	**65**	**133**	**106**	**117**
Jewelry and watches	71	107	49	32	52	55	65	169
Watches	117	144	107	82	113	113	58	87
Jewelry	66	104	43	27	46	49	66	177
Men's footwear	347	358	343	164	248	665	469	40
Boys' footwear	86	49	131	63	42	359	168	104
Women's footwear	113	113	121	5	111	225	239	62
Girls' footwear	87	91	55	–	50	107	169	127
TRANSPORTATION	**100**	**85**	**123**	**37**	**138**	**153**	**16**	**104**
Used cars	58	76	53	–	–	188	–	150
Airline fares	50	57	49	–	26	124	–	93
Ship fares	122	108	123	213	93	116	50	84
HEALTH CARE	**110**	**135**	**98**	**16**	**116**	**120**	**83**	**74**
Physician's services	150	198	126	3	144	177	12	51
Dental services	135	212	74	19	77	104	17	34
Care in convalescent or nursing home	50	118	3	–	–	12	124	117
Nonprescription vitamins	64	84	54	7	37	123	16	21
Prescription drugs	264	77	466	10	838	60	–	111
ENTERTAINMENT	**129**	**150**	**115**	**109**	**109**	**130**	**34**	**74**
Toys, games, hobbies, and tricycles	129	182	90	111	64	127	25	75
Other entertainment	129	130	130	107	137	132	40	73
Fees for recreational lessons	149	115	163	34	251	86	32	53
Community antenna or cable TV	82	58	99	58	141	47	62	114

	total married couples	married couples, no children	married couples with children				single parent, at least one child <18	single person
			total	oldest child under 6	oldest child 6 to 17	oldest child 18 or older		
VCRs and videodisc players	130	141	136	235	85	165	38	69
Video game hardware and software	117	173	72	83	47	110	23	83
Athletic gear, game tables, exercise equipment	145	118	159	95	126	274	23	51
Hunting and fishing equipment	136	61	208	527	194	–	69	92
Photographer fees	92	178	28	8	32	35	3	20
PERSONAL CARE PRODUCTS AND SERVICES	**112**	**107**	**112**	**105**	**134**	**75**	**70**	**70**
Cosmetics, perfume, bath preparation	116	115	121	96	162	58	57	68
Electric personal care appliances	76	63	83	80	106	40	51	82
EDUCATION	**152**	**147**	**167**	**18**	**179**	**247**	**19**	**60**
College tuition	156	164	163	16	161	268	17	55
Elementary and high school tuition	136	81	188	0	300	104	6	90
Other school tuition	165	199	138	165	125	144	24	45
Other school expenses including rentals	141	83	195	7	162	386	96	61
College books and supplies	138	147	134	19	123	233	40	67
Miscellaneous school supplies	155	117	204	21	139	468	7	47
ALL OTHER GIFTS	**119**	**168**	**73**	**42**	**64**	**113**	**22**	**96**
Gifts of trip expenses	123	183	66	51	52	104	20	100
Lotteries and gambling losses	168	340	48	–	76	28	–	23
Legal fees	113	208	31	59	3	63	–	123
Funeral expenses	107	124	83	29	89	108	22	97
Miscellaneous personal services	144	148	163	–	11	587	71	66

Note: Spending index for total consumer units is 100. (–) means sample is too small to make a reliable estimate. Categories with annual spending of less than $2.00 for the average household are omitted. Spending on gifts is also included in the product and service categories in other chapters.
Source: Calculations by New Strategist based on the 2002 Consumer Expenditure Survey

Table 6.11 Gifts for Non—Household Members: Total spending by household type, 2002

(total annual spending on selected gifts of products and services for non–household members by consumer unit (CU) type, 2002; numbers in thousands)

	total married couples	married couples, no children	married couples with children total	oldest child under 6	oldest child 6 to 17	oldest child 18 or older	single parent, at least one child <18	single person
Number of consumer units	56,265	23,118	28,790	5,547	15,206	8,036	6,730	33,055
Total spending of all CUs	$2,944,555,631	$1,053,194,355	$1,665,069,938	$292,763,005	$883,525,623	$489,069,192	$203,147,607	$799,597,145
Gifts, total spending	75,281,445	34,184,818	37,029,698	4,289,162	19,051,445	13,739,551	3,450,740	24,593,581
FOOD	**$6,909,905**	**$3,633,918**	**$3,051,740**	**$300,536**	**$1,426,779**	**$1,328,592**	**$241,203**	**$1,394,260**
Cakes and cupcakes	130,535	29,360	87,522	–	51,244	37,207	1,750	75,365
Fresh fruit other than apples, bananas, and citrus	120,970	54,327	63,626	9,263	29,804	24,912	19,315	38,013
Candy and chewing gum	795,024	353,474	373,694	85,701	160,575	128,496	26,920	320,634
Board (including at school)	2,039,606	568,240	1,449,577	56,857	626,031	766,554	33,717	262,126
Catered affairs	2,564,559	2,103,507	433,002	42,379	230,219	160,318	8,547	223,452
ALCOHOLIC BEVERAGES	**854,665**	**318,335**	**522,251**	**51,532**	**354,604**	**114,995**	**28,468**	**333,194**
Beer and ale	227,873	98,714	125,524	7,877	94,429	22,581	17,835	134,534
Wine	422,550	148,418	277,248	22,243	188,706	66,136	5,586	140,484
HOUSING	**19,247,694**	**8,208,739**	**10,083,698**	**1,555,434**	**4,989,849**	**3,554,805**	**1,067,042**	**5,618,689**
Housekeeping supplies	**3,193,039**	**1,556,073**	**1,461,956**	**200,080**	**719,548**	**550,707**	**159,299**	**817,120**
Laundry and cleaning supplies	140,100	70,741	58,156	11,260	14,142	33,671	11,239	50,574
Other household products	842,850	420,054	366,785	11,593	245,425	110,816	63,262	185,439
Miscellaneous household products	385,415	174,310	176,771	10,539	108,267	58,663	43,207	130,567
Lawn and garden supplies	344,342	205,057	131,570	55	116,782	13,742	10,768	22,808
Postage and stationery	2,131,881	1,036,149	990,664	170,570	440,974	385,005	69,588	581,107
Stationery, stationery supplies, giftwrap	1,560,228	689,148	791,149	156,037	373,763	263,661	57,340	479,959
Postage	522,139	317,873	179,362	14,589	59,151	108,968	5,922	91,893
Household textiles	**1,105,045**	**663,255**	**363,330**	**52,641**	**204,369**	**105,593**	**59,762**	**303,114**
Bathroom linens	229,561	126,687	82,339	19,914	29,652	33,108	14,268	39,666
Bedroom linens	484,442	337,985	110,842	27,790	56,262	26,278	29,276	133,873
Appliances and miscellaneous housewares	**1,655,879**	**1,007,020**	**576,088**	**77,214**	**330,122**	**168,193**	**80,491**	**516,980**
Major appliances	629,043	438,317	158,921	20,247	94,429	43,796	10,633	126,931
Small appliances and misc. housewares	1,026,836	568,703	417,455	56,968	235,693	124,317	69,857	390,049
China and other dinnerware	210,994	101,257	95,295	1,720	92,300	–	–	54,210
Nonelectric cookware	192,426	131,773	50,958	7,433	31,628	11,893	4,509	102,471
Tableware, nonelectric kitchenware	196,928	98,945	95,295	14,644	53,373	27,403	34,323	41,980
Small electric kitchen appliances	172,734	91,085	76,581	13,812	26,915	35,921	15,614	64,457
Miscellaneous household equipment	**4,664,931**	**2,233,892**	**2,199,556**	**326,607**	**985,349**	**897,219**	**332,395**	**1,510,614**
Infants' equipment	337,590	95,246	200,378	11,593	32,997	161,443	17,498	43,633
Outdoor equipment	201,991	120,907	79,173	11,760	65,082	1,205	3,769	19,833
Other household decorative items	1,847,180	910,387	859,957	184,382	355,668	324,172	140,321	625,731
Power tools	147,414	122,294	14,683	–	14,446	–	48,052	32,724
Indoor plants, fresh flowers	880,547	438,086	393,847	58,909	201,936	133,076	28,199	473,017
Computers and computer hardware	515,950	190,724	308,917	18,749	148,259	141,755	40,649	128,915
Miscellaneous household equipment	172,171	76,521	88,673	19,193	45,162	24,349	8,614	44,294
Other housing	**8,629,363**	**2,748,499**	**5,482,768**	**898,891**	**2,750,613**	**1,833,092**	**435,095**	**2,471,192**
Repair or maintenance services	227,873	54,558	76,581	1,442	58,087	16,956	–	257,168
Housing while attending school	3,733,745	1,254,383	2,361,932	68,395	957,370	1,336,226	23,622	596,312
Natural gas (renter)	154,166	50,166	83,779	6,878	58,087	18,804	38,428	154,036
Electricity (renter)	638,045	206,906	350,950	48,425	217,598	84,780	132,245	478,636
Water, sewer maintenance (renter)	135,036	43,693	81,764	9,707	55,806	16,313	31,631	80,324
Day-care centers, nurseries, and preschools	2,069,427	177,546	1,873,077	703,082	989,150	180,810	139,715	234,360

	total married couples	married couples, no children	married couples with children			single parent, at least one child <18	single person
			total	oldest child under 6	oldest child 6 to 17	oldest child 18 or older		
APPAREL AND SERVICES	**$15,364,846**	**$7,366,782**	**$7,013,820**	**$1,282,855**	**$3,226,105**	**$2,527,242**	**$1,244,310**	**$6,197,813**
Men and boys, aged 2 or older	**4,130,976**	**2,142,576**	**1,696,307**	**335,483**	**790,864**	**571,360**	**366,314**	**1,587,962**
Men's coats and jackets	376,976	198,121	177,634	–	50,332	131,951	404	81,976
Men's accessories	189,050	75,827	111,417	47,316	17,183	47,412	125,313	101,479
Men's sweaters and vests	205,930	100,101	96,734	12,592	32,693	51,430	8,682	74,043
Men's active sportswear	194,114	126,455	65,353	49,424	8,363	6,509	–	106,107
Men's shirts	1,070,723	589,740	420,910	99,957	268,234	49,020	59,089	386,082
Men's pants	488,380	295,910	172,452	18,915	49,115	107,763	36,073	215,849
Boys' shirts	205,367	52,709	88,097	943	79,375	7,152	35,063	106,768
Boys' pants	259,382	157,896	88,097	11,871	40,752	35,439	16,085	84,951
Women and girls, aged 2 or older	**5,545,478**	**2,874,492**	**2,356,749**	**286,114**	**1,090,422**	**998,714**	**332,395**	**2,106,595**
Women's coats and jackets	431,553	298,453	126,676	8,154	46,834	74,012	–	77,679
Women's dresses	620,040	352,550	169,573	9,319	87,130	74,815	–	146,434
Women's vests and sweaters	521,014	221,008	295,673	46,151	155,253	95,146	28,266	231,054
Women's shirts, tops, blouses	581,217	292,443	266,308	32,561	102,488	134,683	62,522	241,632
Women's pants	494,569	304,233	153,739	6,213	50,940	99,887	15,277	82,638
Women's active sportswear	301,580	211,530	85,218	36,499	15,814	33,269	6,797	173,539
Women's sleepwear	415,236	179,165	232,623	37,220	146,738	47,814	16,690	224,443
Women's accessories	136,161	82,300	46,352	–	11,405	36,323	–	169,903
Girls' dresses and suits	127,722	70,741	43,473	2,718	16,270	25,313	5,653	41,649
Girls' shirts, blouses, sweaters	324,086	171,998	142,223	34,613	73,141	34,233	63,060	94,207
Girls' skirts and pants	262,195	24,274	217,940	444	42,425	181,935	11,710	101,809
Girls' accessories	312,833	166,218	118,327	40,604	42,273	35,198	44,956	32,063
Children under age 2	**3,096,263**	**1,061,116**	**1,794,193**	**542,275**	**838,003**	**404,372**	**176,124**	**498,800**
Infant dresses, outerwear	1,129,801	572,171	481,081	99,791	207,866	173,337	57,205	238,327
Infant underwear	1,408,313	285,738	999,877	351,735	484,311	155,577	98,595	103,793
Infant nightwear, loungewear	185,112	92,010	79,748	18,527	31,172	29,894	6,124	48,921
Infant accessories	279,637	70,510	189,150	56,358	97,014	34,716	10,768	81,646
Other apparel products and services	**2,592,129**	**1,288,597**	**1,166,571**	**119,039**	**506,816**	**552,716**	**369,477**	**2,004,125**
Jewelry and watches	958,193	595,520	339,146	42,823	190,835	105,352	105,123	1,341,041
Watches	141,788	72,128	66,793	9,874	37,255	19,608	8,413	62,143
Jewelry	816,405	523,392	272,353	32,949	153,581	85,744	96,643	1,278,898
Men's footwear	1,633,373	693,078	827,425	76,216	315,981	447,284	264,422	111,065
Boys' footwear	215,495	50,628	168,134	15,476	28,435	128,576	50,340	153,375
Women's footwear	560,962	230,486	306,326	2,607	148,867	159,434	141,868	180,811
Girls' footwear	161,481	69,585	52,686	–	25,090	28,287	37,553	138,170
TRANSPORTATION	**2,472,284**	**858,140**	**1,549,766**	**90,361**	**918,899**	**539,617**	**47,783**	**1,508,300**
Used cars	400,607	215,691	184,832	–	–	184,908	–	605,237
Airline fares	189,613	89,698	95,007	–	27,219	67,824	–	209,238
Ship fares	187,925	68,660	96,734	32,394	38,775	25,474	9,153	75,696
HEALTH CARE	**2,013,162**	**1,019,273**	**918,689**	**28,733**	**574,027**	**314,449**	**182,114**	**796,956**
Physician's services	259,382	140,557	111,129	444	67,211	43,555	2,557	51,896
Dental services	306,644	197,197	85,506	4,327	47,443	33,832	4,644	44,955
Care in convalescent or nursing home	146,852	141,945	4,894	–	–	4,822	43,409	199,983
Nonprescription vitamins	142,350	76,058	61,323	1,553	22,049	38,975	4,105	26,775
Prescription drugs	353,907	42,537	319,281	1,276	303,208	11,491	–	87,596
ENTERTAINMENT	**5,681,077**	**2,704,806**	**2,582,463**	**471,550**	**1,295,855**	**815,815**	**180,633**	**1,901,985**
Toys, games, hobbies, and tricycles	2,176,330	1,258,313	780,785	183,828	291,347	305,609	50,340	741,754
Other entertainment	3,504,747	1,446,493	1,801,678	287,667	1,004,660	510,125	130,293	1,160,231
Fees for recreational lessons	661,676	208,756	370,527	14,866	301,231	54,404	17,094	137,839
Community antenna or cable TV	292,578	85,305	181,089	20,579	136,550	24,028	26,449	240,310

	total married couples	married couples, no children	married couples with children				single parent, at least one child <18	single person
			total	oldest child under 6	oldest child 6 to 17	oldest child 18 or older		
VCRs and videodisc players	$164,856	$73,515	$88,673	$29,399	$29,196	$29,974	$5,855	$51,235
Video game hardware and software	140,663	85,074	44,049	9,763	15,358	18,885	3,298	58,177
Athletic gear, game tables, exercise equipment	536,768	179,858	302,583	34,613	126,058	145,452	10,162	110,734
Hunting and fishing equipment	233,500	42,999	182,817	89,418	90,172	–	14,268	92,554
Photographer fees	164,856	131,079	25,911	1,442	15,510	9,081	673	21,155
PERSONAL CARE PRODUCTS AND SERVICES	**1,332,355**	**522,467**	**684,626**	**123,310**	**429,874**	**128,255**	**100,075**	**487,231**
Cosmetics, perfume, bath preparation	820,344	333,362	435,593	66,398	307,769	58,422	47,985	281,298
Electric personal care appliances	141,788	48,317	79,173	14,644	53,373	10,688	11,374	90,240
EDUCATION	**15,696,810**	**6,235,387**	**8,835,939**	**186,878**	**5,008,552**	**3,649,228**	**234,810**	**3,658,197**
College tuition	11,213,615	4,838,135	5,989,184	110,829	3,130,155	2,748,071	147,993	2,332,691
Elementary and high school tuition	1,988,405	485,709	1,401,209	333	1,184,547	216,329	10,566	773,487
Other school tuition	411,860	204,363	176,195	40,660	84,241	51,350	7,067	66,110
Other school expenses including rentals	315,647	76,289	223,698	1,553	98,383	123,835	25,776	79,993
College books and supplies	926,122	404,796	458,913	12,425	222,616	223,803	31,833	262,787
Miscellaneous school supplies	644,234	198,815	433,002	8,431	156,014	277,483	3,298	115,693
ALL OTHER GIFTS	**5,625,375**	**3,261,025**	**1,761,372**	**193,868**	**814,129**	**757,634**	**123,832**	**2,646,714**
Gifts of trip expenses	3,062,504	1,876,026	849,593	125,640	351,867	371,906	59,493	1,468,303
Lotteries and gambling losses	270,635	224,707	39,730	–	33,149	6,348	–	22,147
Legal fees	371,349	280,421	51,246	19,137	2,433	29,653	–	235,682
Funeral expenses	1,527,032	726,368	600,847	40,382	341,983	218,579	37,352	809,848
Miscellaneous personal services	175,547	73,978	101,053	–	3,497	101,816	10,364	46,938

Note: Total spending figures for total consumer units can be found on Total Spending by Age and Total Spending by Region tables. Spending by type of consumer unit will not add to total because not all types of consumer units are shown. (–) means sample is too small to make a reliable estimate. Expenditures for items in a given category may not add to category total because categories with annual spending of less than $2.00 for the average household are omitted. Spending on gifts is also included in the product and service categories in other chapters.
Source: Calculations by New Strategist based on the 2002 Consumer Expenditure Survey

Table 6.12 Gifts for Non—Household Members: Market shares by household type, 2002

(percentage of total annual spending on selected gifts of products and services for non–household members accounted for by types of consumer units, 2002)

	total married couples	married couples, no children	married couples with children				single parent, at least one child <18	single person
			total	oldest child under 6	oldest child 6 to 17	oldest child 18 or older		
Share of total consumer units	50.2%	20.6%	25.7%	4.9%	13.6%	7.2%	6.0%	29.5%
Share of total before-tax income	68.2	24.6	38.4	6.8	20.0	11.8	3.3	16.1
Share of total spending	64.6	23.1	36.5	6.4	19.4	10.7	4.5	17.5
Share of gifts spending	64.8	29.4	31.9	3.7	16.4	11.8	3.0	21.2
FOOD	**75.0%**	**39.4%**	**33.1%**	**3.3%**	**15.5%**	**14.4%**	**2.6%**	**15.1%**
Cakes and cupcakes	48.3	10.9	32.4	–	19.0	13.8	0.6	27.9
Fresh fruit other than apples, bananas, and citrus	47.7	21.4	25.1	3.7	11.8	9.8	7.6	15.0
Candy and chewing gum	60.7	27.0	28.5	6.5	12.3	9.8	2.1	24.5
Board (including at school)	83.1	23.1	59.0	2.3	25.5	31.2	1.4	10.7
Catered affairs	87.3	71.6	14.7	1.4	7.8	5.5	0.3	7.6
ALCOHOLIC BEVERAGES	**56.8**	**21.2**	**34.7**	**3.4**	**23.6**	**7.6**	**1.9**	**22.1**
Beer and ale	43.0	18.6	23.7	1.5	17.8	4.3	3.4	25.4
Wine	64.5	22.7	42.3	3.4	28.8	10.1	0.9	21.5
HOUSING	**66.4**	**28.3**	**34.8**	**5.4**	**17.2**	**12.3**	**3.7**	**19.4**
Housekeeping supplies	**67.0**	**32.7**	**30.7**	**4.2**	**15.1**	**11.6**	**3.3**	**17.2**
Laundry and cleaning supplies	42.7	21.5	17.7	3.4	4.3	10.3	3.4	15.4
Other household products	64.3	32.1	28.0	0.9	18.7	8.5	4.8	14.1
Miscellaneous household products	58.8	26.6	27.0	1.6	16.5	8.9	6.6	19.9
Lawn and garden supplies	73.1	43.5	27.9	0.0	24.8	2.9	2.3	4.8
Postage and stationery	68.3	33.2	31.7	5.5	14.1	12.3	2.2	18.6
Stationery, stationery supplies, giftwrap	65.9	29.1	33.4	6.6	15.8	11.1	2.4	20.3
Postage	75.9	46.2	26.1	2.1	8.6	15.8	0.9	13.3
Household textiles	**71.8**	**43.1**	**23.6**	**3.4**	**13.3**	**6.9**	**3.9**	**19.7**
Bathroom linens	79.1	43.6	28.4	6.9	10.2	11.4	4.9	13.7
Bedroom linens	70.8	49.4	16.2	4.1	8.2	3.8	4.3	19.6
Appliances and miscellaneous housewares	**61.6**	**37.5**	**21.4**	**2.9**	**12.3**	**6.3**	**3.0**	**19.2**
Major appliances	66.7	46.5	16.9	2.1	10.0	4.6	1.1	13.5
Small appliances and miscellaneous housewares	58.8	32.6	23.9	3.3	13.5	7.1	4.0	22.3
China and other dinnerware	76.5	36.7	34.6	0.6	33.5	–	–	19.7
Nonelectric cookware	48.6	33.3	12.9	1.9	8.0	3.0	1.1	25.9
Tableware, nonelectric kitchenware	66.8	33.6	32.3	5.0	18.1	9.3	11.6	14.2
Small electric kitchen appliances	56.9	30.0	25.2	4.5	8.9	11.8	5.1	21.2
Miscellaneous household equipment	**64.3**	**30.8**	**30.3**	**4.5**	**13.6**	**12.4**	**4.6**	**20.8**
Infants' equipment	78.8	22.2	46.8	2.7	7.7	37.7	4.1	10.2
Outdoor equipment	87.0	52.1	34.1	5.1	28.0	0.5	1.6	8.5
Other household decorative items	64.0	31.5	29.8	6.4	12.3	11.2	4.9	21.7
Power tools	47.0	39.0	4.7	–	4.6	–	15.3	10.4
Indoor plants, fresh flowers	58.5	29.1	26.2	3.9	13.4	8.8	1.9	31.4
Computers and computer hardware	69.8	25.8	41.8	2.5	20.1	19.2	5.5	17.4
Miscellaneous household equipment	70.1	31.2	36.1	7.8	18.4	9.9	3.5	18.0
Other housing	**67.6**	**21.5**	**43.0**	**7.0**	**21.6**	**14.4**	**3.4**	**19.4**
Repair or maintenance services	45.1	10.8	15.1	0.3	11.5	3.4	–	50.9
Housing while attending school	83.4	28.0	52.8	1.5	21.4	29.8	0.5	13.3
Natural gas (renter)	38.0	12.4	20.6	1.7	14.3	4.6	9.5	38.0
Electricity (renter)	38.8	12.6	21.3	2.9	13.2	5.2	8.0	29.1
Water, sewer maintenance (renter)	39.6	12.8	24.0	2.8	16.4	4.8	9.3	23.6
Day-care centers, nurseries, and preschools	77.5	6.7	70.2	26.3	37.1	6.8	5.2	8.8

	total married couples	married couples, no children	married couples with children			single parent, at least one child <18	single person
			total	oldest child under 6	oldest child 6 to 17	oldest child 18 or older	
APPAREL AND SERVICES	**57.8%**	**27.7%**	**26.4%**	**4.8%**	**12.1%**	**9.5%**	**4.7%**	**23.3%**
Men and boys, aged 2 or older	**57.8**	**30.0**	**23.7**	**4.7**	**11.1**	**8.0**	**5.1**	**22.2**
Men's coats and jackets	66.1	34.7	31.1	–	8.8	23.1	0.1	14.4
Men's accessories	37.9	15.2	22.3	9.5	3.4	9.5	25.1	20.3
Men's sweaters and vests	60.0	29.2	28.2	3.7	9.5	15.0	2.5	21.6
Men's active sportswear	62.7	40.9	21.1	16.0	2.7	2.1	–	34.3
Men's shirts	56.9	31.3	22.4	5.3	14.3	2.6	3.1	20.5
Men's pants	62.9	38.1	22.2	2.4	6.3	13.9	4.6	27.8
Boys' shirts	49.4	12.7	21.2	0.2	19.1	1.7	8.4	25.7
Boys' pants	61.5	37.5	20.9	2.8	9.7	8.4	3.8	20.2
Women and girls, aged 2 or older	**60.5**	**31.4**	**25.7**	**3.1**	**11.9**	**10.9**	**3.6**	**23.0**
Women's coats and jackets	68.5	47.4	20.1	1.3	7.4	11.7	–	12.3
Women's dresses	72.2	41.1	19.7	1.1	10.1	8.7	–	17.1
Women's vests and sweaters	54.7	23.2	31.0	4.8	16.3	10.0	3.0	24.2
Women's shirts, tops, blouses	57.2	28.8	26.2	3.2	10.1	13.3	6.2	23.8
Women's pants	66.6	41.0	20.7	0.8	6.9	13.5	2.1	11.1
Women's active sportswear	62.1	43.6	17.6	7.5	3.3	6.9	1.4	35.7
Women's sleepwear	57.4	24.8	32.2	5.1	20.3	6.6	2.3	31.0
Women's accessories	21.3	12.9	7.2	–	1.8	5.7	–	26.5
Girls' dresses and suits	38.2	21.2	13.0	0.8	4.9	7.6	1.7	12.5
Girls' shirts, blouses, sweaters	64.5	34.2	28.3	6.9	14.6	6.8	12.6	18.8
Girls' skirts and pants	70.4	6.5	58.6	0.1	11.4	48.9	3.1	27.4
Girls' accessories	117.2	62.3	44.3	15.2	15.8	13.2	16.8	12.0
Children under age 2	**69.1**	**23.7**	**40.0**	**12.1**	**18.7**	**9.0**	**3.9**	**11.1**
Infant dresses, outerwear	66.0	33.4	28.1	5.8	12.1	10.1	3.3	13.9
Infant underwear	74.3	15.1	52.7	18.6	25.5	8.2	5.2	5.5
Infant nightwear, loungewear	64.8	32.2	27.9	6.5	10.9	10.5	2.1	17.1
Infant accessories	63.5	16.0	42.9	12.8	22.0	7.9	2.4	18.5
Other apparel products and services	**44.8**	**22.3**	**20.2**	**2.1**	**8.8**	**9.5**	**6.4**	**34.6**
Jewelry and watches	35.6	22.1	12.6	1.6	7.1	3.9	3.9	49.8
Watches	58.6	29.8	27.6	4.1	15.4	8.1	3.5	25.7
Jewelry	33.3	21.4	11.1	1.3	6.3	3.5	3.9	52.2
Men's footwear	174.1	73.9	88.2	8.1	33.7	47.7	28.2	11.8
Boys' footwear	43.1	10.1	33.6	3.1	5.7	25.7	10.1	30.7
Women's footwear	56.7	23.3	31.0	0.3	15.1	16.1	14.3	18.3
Girls' footwear	43.6	18.8	14.2	–	6.8	7.6	10.2	37.3
TRANSPORTATION	**50.3**	**17.4**	**31.5**	**1.8**	**18.7**	**11.0**	**1.0**	**30.7**
Used cars	29.3	15.8	13.5	–	–	13.5	–	44.2
Airline fares	24.9	11.8	12.5	–	3.6	8.9	–	27.5
Ship fares	61.2	22.4	31.5	10.5	12.6	8.3	3.0	24.6
HEALTH CARE	**55.1**	**27.9**	**25.1**	**0.8**	**15.7**	**8.6**	**5.0**	**21.8**
Physician's services	75.4	40.8	32.3	0.1	19.5	12.7	0.7	15.1
Dental services	67.9	43.6	18.9	1.0	10.5	7.5	1.0	10.0
Care in convalescent or nursing home	25.2	24.4	0.8	–	–	0.8	7.5	34.4
Nonprescription vitamins	32.3	17.3	13.9	0.4	5.0	8.8	0.9	6.1
Prescription drugs	132.6	15.9	119.7	0.5	113.6	4.3	–	32.8
ENTERTAINMENT	**64.8**	**30.8**	**29.4**	**5.4**	**14.8**	**9.3**	**2.1**	**21.7**
Toys, games, hobbies, and tricycles	64.8	37.4	23.2	5.5	8.7	9.1	1.5	22.1
Other entertainment	64.8	26.7	33.3	5.3	18.6	9.4	2.4	21.4
Fees for recreational lessons	74.9	23.6	41.9	1.7	34.1	6.2	1.9	15.6
Community antenna or cable TV	41.0	11.9	25.4	2.9	19.1	3.4	3.7	33.7

	total married couples	married couples, no children	married couples with children				single parent, at least one child <18	single person
			total	oldest child under 6	oldest child 6 to 17	oldest child 18 or older		
VCRs and videodisc players	65.1%	29.0%	35.0%	11.6%	11.5%	11.8%	2.3%	20.2%
Video game hardware and software	58.9	35.6	18.4	4.1	6.4	7.9	1.4	24.4
Athletic gear, game tables, exercise equipment	72.5	24.3	40.9	4.7	17.0	19.7	1.4	15.0
Hunting and fishing equipment	68.1	12.5	53.3	26.1	26.3	–	4.2	27.0
Photographer fees	46.1	36.7	7.2	0.4	4.3	2.5	0.2	5.9
PERSONAL CARE PRODUCTS AND SERVICES	**56.2**	**22.0**	**28.9**	**5.2**	**18.1**	**5.4**	**4.2**	**20.5**
Cosmetics, perfume, bath preparation	58.4	23.7	31.0	4.7	21.9	4.2	3.4	20.0
Electric personal care appliances	38.2	13.0	21.3	3.9	14.4	2.9	3.1	24.3
EDUCATION	**76.1**	**30.2**	**42.9**	**0.9**	**24.3**	**17.7**	**1.1**	**17.7**
College tuition	78.2	33.8	41.8	0.8	21.8	19.2	1.0	16.3
Elementary and high school tuition	68.3	16.7	48.2	0.0	40.7	7.4	0.4	26.6
Other school tuition	82.7	41.1	35.4	8.2	16.9	10.3	1.4	13.3
Other school expenses including rentals	70.6	17.1	50.0	0.3	22.0	27.7	5.8	17.9
College books and supplies	69.2	30.3	34.3	0.9	16.6	16.7	2.4	19.6
Miscellaneous school supplies	77.9	24.0	52.3	1.0	18.9	33.5	0.4	14.0
ALL OTHER GIFTS	**59.9**	**34.7**	**18.8**	**2.1**	**8.7**	**8.1**	**1.3**	**28.2**
Gifts of trip expenses	61.5	37.7	17.1	2.5	7.1	7.5	1.2	29.5
Lotteries and gambling losses	84.4	70.1	12.4	–	10.3	2.0	–	6.9
Legal fees	56.9	43.0	7.9	2.9	0.4	4.5	–	36.1
Funeral expenses	53.9	25.7	21.2	1.4	12.1	7.7	1.3	28.6
Miscellaneous personal services	72.5	30.5	41.7	–	1.4	42.0	4.3	19.4

Note: Market share for total consumer units is 100.0%. Market shares by type of consumer unit will not add to total because not all types of consumer units are shown. (–) means sample is too small to make a reliable estimate.
Source: Calculations by New Strategist based on the 2002 Consumer Expenditure Survey

Table 6.13 Gifts for Non—Household Members: Average spending by race and Hispanic origin, 2002

(average annual spending of consumer units (CU) on selected gifts of products and services for non–household members by race and Hispanic origin of consumer unit reference person, 2002)

	total consumer units	race		Hispanic origin	
		black	white and other	Hispanic	non-Hispanic
Number of consumer units (in thousands, add 000)	112,108	13,554	98,553	10,500	101,608
Average number of persons per CU	2.5	2.7	2.5	3.3	2.4
Average before-tax income of CU	$49,430.00	$35,944.00	$51,177.00	$37,360.00	$50,742.00
Average spending of CU, total	40,676.60	30,135.94	42,134.55	34,742.47	41,294.67
Gifts, average spending	1,036.24	586.82	1,098.81	635.27	1,076.95
FOOD	**$82.18**	**$35.92**	**$88.58**	**$45.44**	**$85.91**
Cakes and cupcakes	2.41	0.66	2.66	1.32	2.51
Fresh fruit other than apples, bananas, and citrus	2.26	4.15	2.00	1.57	2.33
Candy and chewing gum	11.69	8.53	12.13	7.12	12.12
Board (including at school)	21.90	8.77	23.71	13.74	22.74
Catered affairs	26.19	1.10	29.64	4.77	28.40
ALCOHOLIC BEVERAGES	**13.42**	**2.75**	**14.93**	**15.00**	**13.27**
Beer and ale	4.73	0.76	5.29	8.37	4.39
Wine	5.84	1.16	6.50	4.46	5.97
HOUSING	**258.69**	**177.13**	**270.16**	**115.84**	**272.95**
Housekeeping supplies	**42.48**	**20.02**	**45.66**	**20.98**	**44.51**
Laundry and cleaning supplies	2.93	2.67	2.96	6.34	2.60
Other household products	11.69	3.54	12.85	5.07	12.32
Miscellaneous household products	5.85	1.05	6.53	2.75	6.14
Lawn and garden supplies	4.20	0.72	4.70	0.52	4.55
Postage and stationery	27.86	13.81	29.85	9.57	29.59
Stationery, stationery supplies, giftwrap	21.13	6.62	23.19	4.42	22.71
Postage	6.14	7.19	5.99	3.19	6.42
Household textiles	**13.72**	**6.12**	**14.79**	**4.41**	**14.62**
Bathroom linens	2.59	1.22	2.78	2.05	2.64
Bedroom linens	6.10	3.87	6.42	1.86	6.51
Appliances and miscellaneous housewares	**23.98**	**18.23**	**24.80**	**10.56**	**25.28**
Major appliances	8.41	7.46	8.55	4.22	8.81
Small appliances and miscellaneous housewares	15.57	10.77	16.24	6.34	16.47
China and other dinnerware	2.46	0.40	2.76	1.30	2.57
Nonelectric cookware	3.53	8.24	2.87	0.84	3.79
Tableware, nonelectric kitchenware	2.63	0.71	2.90	2.10	2.68
Small electric kitchen appliances	2.71	0.55	3.01	1.05	2.88
Miscellaneous household equipment	**64.70**	**19.49**	**71.04**	**35.76**	**67.54**
Infants' equipment	3.82	1.27	4.18	2.23	3.97
Outdoor equipment	2.07	–	2.36	–	2.27
Other household decorative items	25.76	4.39	28.79	15.22	26.76
Power tools	2.80	0.51	3.12	–	3.06
Indoor plants, fresh flowers	13.43	4.63	14.64	5.85	14.21
Computers and computer hardware	6.59	1.63	7.28	4.34	6.83
Miscellaneous household equipment	2.19	–	2.50	2.03	2.20
Other housing	**113.80**	**113.27**	**113.87**	**44.13**	**121.00**
Repair or maintenance services	4.51	12.68	3.39	0.09	4.97
Housing while attending school	39.93	27.69	41.62	12.27	42.79
Natural gas (renter)	3.62	5.16	3.40	2.63	3.72
Electricity (renter)	14.67	13.13	14.88	8.54	15.30
Water, sewer maintenance (renter)	3.04	2.01	3.18	3.30	3.01
Day-care centers, nurseries, and preschools	23.81	38.72	21.76	6.17	25.63

		race		Hispanic origin	
	total consumer units	black	white and other	Hispanic	non-Hispanic
APPAREL AND SERVICES	**$237.13**	**$153.55**	**$248.89**	**$223.89**	**$238.55**
Men and boys, aged 2 or older	**63.74**	**43.11**	**66.65**	**56.52**	**64.41**
Men's coats and jackets	5.09	0.18	5.78	5.22	5.08
Men's accessories	4.45	9.84	3.69	1.74	4.71
Men's sweaters and vests	3.06	0.89	3.36	3.41	3.02
Men's active sportswear	2.76	–	3.15	5.19	2.53
Men's shirts	16.79	5.34	18.42	14.18	17.04
Men's pants	6.93	6.96	6.93	–	7.59
Boys' shirts	3.71	2.20	3.93	5.59	3.54
Boys' pants	3.76	3.29	3.82	5.48	3.58
Women and girls, aged 2 or older	**81.76**	**30.07**	**89.09**	**62.59**	**83.60**
Women's coats and jackets	5.62	1.86	6.15	8.41	5.36
Women's dresses	7.66	1.05	8.60	5.01	7.91
Women's vests and sweaters	8.50	1.35	9.51	5.31	8.80
Women's shirts, tops, blouses	9.06	0.99	10.20	3.93	9.54
Women's pants	6.62	1.56	7.34	3.29	6.94
Women's active sportswear	4.33	–	4.95	0.72	4.68
Women's sleepwear	6.45	0.74	7.25	2.89	6.78
Women's accessories	5.71	1.57	6.30	4.68	5.81
Girls' dresses and suits	2.98	2.43	3.05	15.50	1.79
Girls' shirts, blouses, sweaters	4.48	2.00	4.83	1.03	4.80
Girls' skirts and pants	3.32	2.80	3.40	2.20	3.44
Girls' accessories	2.38	0.14	2.70	0.54	2.56
Children under age 2	**39.99**	**31.78**	**41.15**	**58.34**	**38.28**
Infant dresses, outerwear	15.28	15.53	15.24	14.30	15.38
Infant underwear	16.91	10.69	17.79	32.61	15.43
Infant nightwear, loungewear	2.55	2.22	2.59	1.86	2.62
Infant accessories	3.93	2.08	4.19	8.79	3.47
Other apparel products and services	**51.63**	**48.59**	**52.00**	**46.44**	**52.25**
Jewelry and watches	24.01	7.20	26.32	10.12	25.45
Watches	2.16	2.10	2.17	1.75	2.20
Jewelry	21.85	5.11	24.16	8.37	23.25
Men's footwear	8.37	11.10	7.99	17.64	7.50
Boys' footwear	4.46	12.33	3.35	7.99	4.13
Women's footwear	8.82	13.23	8.20	5.55	9.13
Girls' footwear	3.30	4.11	3.18	5.10	3.13
TRANSPORTATION	**43.87**	**50.77**	**42.93**	**36.83**	**44.60**
Used cars	12.21	39.83	8.41	1.42	13.33
Airline fares	6.78	5.54	6.95	6.76	6.78
Ship fares	2.74	2.44	2.79	3.70	2.64
HEALTH CARE	**32.59**	**8.59**	**35.92**	**14.74**	**34.44**
Physician's services	3.07	0.70	3.39	0.58	3.32
Dental services	4.03	2.52	4.24	2.51	4.19
Care in convalescent or nursing home	5.19	–	5.90	–	5.73
Nonprescription vitamins	3.93	0.10	4.47	2.97	4.02
Prescription drugs	2.38	2.16	2.41	1.31	2.49
ENTERTAINMENT	**78.24**	**34.96**	**84.26**	**47.26**	**81.36**
Toys, games, hobbies, and tricycles	29.98	17.43	31.71	20.64	30.95
Other entertainment	48.26	17.52	52.55	26.62	50.41
Fees for recreational lessons	7.88	4.48	8.35	4.02	8.28
Community antenna or cable TV	6.37	3.96	6.70	5.23	6.49

	total consumer units	race		Hispanic origin	
		black	white and other	Hispanic	non-Hispanic
VCRs and videodisc players	$2.26	$0.80	$2.46	$0.70	$2.42
Video game hardware and software	2.13	1.47	2.22	1.72	2.17
Athletic gear, game tables, exercise equipment	6.60	–	7.54	4.41	6.81
Hunting and fishing equipment	3.06	–	3.50	0.86	3.27
Photographer fees	3.19	0.08	3.62	0.51	3.47
PERSONAL CARE PRODUCTS AND SERVICES	**21.15**	**7.44**	**23.10**	**15.15**	**21.72**
Cosmetics, perfume, bath preparation	12.53	4.92	13.61	8.48	12.92
Electric personal care appliances	3.31	–	3.78	3.55	3.29
EDUCATION	**183.88**	**82.42**	**197.82**	**55.86**	**197.05**
College tuition	127.83	49.11	138.66	32.43	137.69
Elementary and high school tuition	25.95	7.18	28.53	13.90	27.19
Other school tuition	4.44	4.29	4.47	0.34	4.87
Other school expenses including rentals	3.99	1.94	4.27	4.90	3.89
College books and supplies	11.93	9.27	12.29	2.29	12.92
Miscellaneous school supplies	7.38	8.44	7.23	1.43	7.94
ALL OTHER GIFTS	**83.76**	**32.81**	**90.78**	**64.58**	**85.70**
Gifts of trip expenses	44.40	8.36	49.36	25.32	46.37
Lotteries and gambling losses	2.86	0.30	3.22	0.21	3.11
Legal fees	5.82	1.07	6.48	3.44	6.07
Funeral expenses	25.25	21.65	25.74	31.56	24.59
Miscellaneous personal services	2.16	0.90	2.34	1.12	2.26

Note: Other races include Asians, Native Americans, and Pacific Islanders. (–) means sample is too small to make a reliable estimate. Expenditures for items in a given category may not add to category total because categories with annual spending of less than $2.00 for the average household are omitted. Spending on gifts is also included in the product and service categories in other chapters.
Source: Bureau of Labor Statistics, unpublished tables from the 2002 Consumer Expenditure Survey

Table 6.14 Gifts for Non—Household Members: Indexed spending by race and Hispanic origin, 2002

(indexed average annual spending of consumer units (CU) on selected gifts of products and services for non—household members by race and Hispanic origin of consumer unit reference person, 2002; index definition: an index of 100 is the average for all consumer units; an index of 132 means that spending by consumer units in that group is 32 percent above the average for all consumer units; an index of 68 indicates spending that is 32 percent below the average for all consumer units)

	total consumer units	race		Hispanic origin	
		black	white and other	Hispanic	non-Hispanic
Average spending of CU, total	$40,677	$30,136	$42,135	$34,742	$41,295
Average spending of CU, index	100	74	104	85	102
Gifts, spending index	100	57	106	61	104
FOOD	100	44	108	55	105
Cakes and cupcakes	100	27	110	55	104
Fresh fruit other than apples, bananas, and citrus	100	184	88	69	103
Candy and chewing gum	100	73	104	61	104
Board (including at school)	100	40	108	63	104
Catered affairs	100	4	113	18	108
ALCOHOLIC BEVERAGES	100	20	111	112	99
Beer and ale	100	16	112	177	93
Wine	100	20	111	76	102
HOUSING	100	68	104	45	106
Housekeeping supplies	100	47	107	49	105
Laundry and cleaning supplies	100	91	101	216	89
Other household products	100	30	110	43	105
Miscellaneous household products	100	18	112	47	105
Lawn and garden supplies	100	17	112	12	108
Postage and stationery	100	50	107	34	106
Stationery, stationery supplies, giftwrap	100	31	110	21	107
Postage	100	117	98	52	105
Household textiles	100	45	108	32	107
Bathroom linens	100	47	107	79	102
Bedroom linens	100	63	105	30	107
Appliances and miscellaneous housewares	100	76	103	44	105
Major appliances	100	89	102	50	105
Small appliances and miscellaneous housewares	100	69	104	41	106
China and other dinnerware	100	16	112	53	104
Nonelectric cookware	100	233	81	24	107
Tableware, nonelectric kitchenware	100	27	110	80	102
Small electric kitchen appliances	100	20	111	39	106
Miscellaneous household equipment	100	30	110	55	104
Infants' equipment	100	33	109	58	104
Outdoor equipment	100	–	114	–	110
Other household decorative items	100	17	112	59	104
Power tools	100	18	111	–	109
Indoor plants, fresh flowers	100	34	109	44	106
Computers and computer hardware	100	25	110	66	104
Miscellaneous household equipment	100	–	114	93	100
Other housing	100	100	100	39	106
Repair or maintenance services	100	281	75	2	110
Housing while attending school	100	69	104	31	107
Natural gas (renter)	100	143	94	73	103
Electricity (renter)	100	90	101	58	104
Water, sewer maintenance (renter)	100	66	105	109	99
Day-care centers, nurseries, and preschools	100	163	91	26	108

	total consumer units	race		Hispanic origin	
		black	white and other	Hispanic	non-Hispanic
APPAREL AND SERVICES	**100**	**65**	**105**	**94**	**101**
Men and boys, aged 2 or older	**100**	**68**	**105**	**89**	**101**
Men's coats and jackets	100	4	114	103	100
Men's accessories	100	221	83	39	106
Men's sweaters and vests	100	29	110	111	99
Men's active sportswear	100	–	114	188	92
Men's shirts	100	32	110	84	101
Men's pants	100	100	100	–	110
Boys' shirts	100	59	106	151	95
Boys' pants	100	88	102	146	95
Women and girls, aged 2 or older	**100**	**37**	**109**	**77**	**102**
Women's coats and jackets	100	33	109	150	95
Women's dresses	100	14	112	65	103
Women's vests and sweaters	100	16	112	62	104
Women's shirts, tops, blouses	100	11	113	43	105
Women's pants	100	24	111	50	105
Women's active sportswear	100	–	114	17	108
Women's sleepwear	100	11	112	45	105
Women's accessories	100	27	110	82	102
Girls' dresses and suits	100	82	102	520	60
Girls' shirts, blouses, sweaters	100	45	108	23	107
Girls' skirts and pants	100	84	102	66	104
Girls' accessories	100	6	113	23	108
Children under age 2	**100**	**79**	**103**	**146**	**96**
Infant dresses, outerwear	100	102	100	94	101
Infant underwear	100	63	105	193	91
Infant nightwear, loungewear	100	87	102	73	103
Infant accessories	100	53	107	224	88
Other apparel products and services	**100**	**94**	**101**	**90**	**101**
Jewelry and watches	100	30	110	42	106
Watches	100	97	100	81	102
Jewelry	100	23	111	38	106
Men's footwear	100	133	95	211	90
Boys' footwear	100	276	75	179	93
Women's footwear	100	150	93	63	104
Girls' footwear	100	125	96	155	95
TRANSPORTATION	**100**	**116**	**98**	**84**	**102**
Used cars	100	326	69	12	109
Airline fares	100	82	103	100	100
Ship fares	100	89	102	135	96
HEALTH CARE	**100**	**26**	**110**	**45**	**106**
Physician's services	100	23	110	19	108
Dental services	100	63	105	62	104
Care in convalescent or nursing home	100	–	114	–	110
Nonprescription vitamins	100	3	114	76	102
Prescription drugs	100	91	101	55	105
ENTERTAINMENT	**100**	**45**	**108**	**60**	**104**
Toys, games, hobbies, and tricycles	100	58	106	69	103
Other entertainment	100	36	109	55	104
Fees for recreational lessons	100	57	106	51	105
Community antenna or cable TV	100	62	105	82	102

	total consumer units	race		Hispanic origin	
		black	white and other	Hispanic	non-Hispanic
VCRs and videodisc players	100	35	109	31	107
Video game hardware and software	100	69	104	81	102
Athletic gear, game tables, exercise equipment	100	–	114	67	103
Hunting and fishing equipment	100	–	114	28	107
Photographer fees	100	3	113	16	109
PERSONAL CARE PRODUCTS AND SERVICES	**100**	**35**	**109**	**72**	**103**
Cosmetics, perfume, bath preparation	100	39	109	68	103
Electric personal care appliances	100	–	114	107	99
EDUCATION	**100**	**45**	**108**	**30**	**107**
College tuition	100	38	108	25	108
Elementary and high school tuition	100	28	110	54	105
Other school tuition	100	97	101	8	110
Other school expenses including rentals	100	49	107	123	97
College books and supplies	100	78	103	19	108
Miscellaneous school supplies	100	114	98	19	108
ALL OTHER GIFTS	**100**	**39**	**108**	**77**	**102**
Gifts of trip expenses	100	19	111	57	104
Lotteries and gambling losses	100	10	113	7	109
Legal fees	100	18	111	59	104
Funeral expenses	100	86	102	125	97
Miscellaneous personal services	100	42	108	52	105

Note: Other races include Asians, Native Americans, and Pacific Islanders. (–) means sample is too small to make a reliable estimate. Categories with annual spending of less than $2.00 for the average household are omitted. Spending on gifts is also included in the product and service categories in other chapters.
Source: Calculations by New Strategist based on the 2002 Consumer Expenditure Survey

Table 6.15 Gifts for Non—Household Members: Total spending by race and Hispanic origin, 2002

(total annual spending on selected gifts of products and services for non—household members by consumer unit race and Hispanic origin groups, 2002; numbers in thousands)

	total consumer units	race black	race white and other	Hispanic origin Hispanic	Hispanic origin non-Hispanic
Number of consumer units	112,108	13,554	98,553	10,500	101,608
Total spending of all consumer units	$4,560,172,273	$408,462,531	$4,152,486,306	$364,795,935	$4,195,868,829
Gifts, total spending	116,170,794	7,953,758	108,291,022	6,670,335	109,426,736
FOOD	**$9,213,035**	**$486,860**	**$8,729,825**	**$477,120**	**$8,729,143**
Cakes and cupcakes	270,180	8,946	262,151	13,860	255,036
Fresh fruit other than apples, bananas, and citrus	253,364	56,249	197,106	16,485	236,747
Candy and chewing gum	1,310,543	115,616	1,195,448	74,760	1,231,489
Board (including at school)	2,455,165	118,869	2,336,692	144,270	2,310,566
Catered affairs	2,936,109	14,909	2,921,111	50,085	2,885,667
ALCOHOLIC BEVERAGES	**1,504,489**	**37,274**	**1,471,396**	**157,500**	**1,348,338**
Beer and ale	530,271	10,301	521,345	87,885	446,059
Wine	654,711	15,723	640,595	46,830	606,600
HOUSING	**29,001,219**	**2,400,820**	**26,625,078**	**1,216,320**	**27,733,904**
Housekeeping supplies	**4,762,348**	**271,351**	**4,499,930**	**220,290**	**4,522,572**
Laundry and cleaning supplies	328,476	36,189	291,717	66,570	264,181
Other household products	1,310,543	47,981	1,266,406	53,235	1,251,811
Miscellaneous household products	655,832	14,232	643,551	28,875	623,873
Lawn and garden supplies	470,854	9,759	463,199	5,460	462,316
Postage and stationery	3,123,329	187,181	2,941,807	100,485	3,006,581
Stationery, stationery supplies, giftwrap	2,368,842	89,727	2,285,444	46,410	2,307,518
Postage	688,343	97,453	590,332	33,495	652,323
Household textiles	**1,538,122**	**82,950**	**1,457,599**	**46,305**	**1,485,509**
Bathroom linens	290,360	16,536	273,977	21,525	268,245
Bedroom linens	683,859	52,454	632,710	19,530	661,468
Appliances and miscellaneous housewares	**2,688,350**	**247,089**	**2,444,114**	**110,880**	**2,568,650**
Major appliances	942,828	101,113	842,628	44,310	895,166
Small appliances and miscellaneous housewares	1,745,522	145,977	1,600,501	66,570	1,673,484
China and other dinnerware	275,786	5,422	272,006	13,650	261,133
Nonelectric cookware	395,741	111,685	282,847	8,820	385,094
Tableware, nonelectric kitchenware	294,844	9,623	285,804	22,050	272,309
Small electric kitchen appliances	303,813	7,455	296,645	11,025	292,631
Miscellaneous household equipment	**7,253,388**	**264,167**	**7,001,205**	**375,480**	**6,862,604**
Infants' equipment	428,253	17,214	411,952	23,415	403,384
Outdoor equipment	232,064	–	232,064	–	230,650
Other household decorative items	2,887,902	59,502	2,837,341	159,810	2,719,030
Power tools	313,902	6,913	307,485	–	310,920
Indoor plants, fresh flowers	1,505,610	62,755	1,442,816	61,425	1,443,850
Computers and computer hardware	738,792	22,093	717,466	45,570	693,983
Miscellaneous household equipment	245,517	–	245,517	21,315	223,538
Other housing	**12,757,890**	**1,535,262**	**11,222,230**	**463,365**	**12,294,568**
Repair or maintenance services	505,607	171,865	334,095	945	504,992
Housing while attending school	4,476,472	375,310	4,101,776	128,835	4,347,806
Natural gas (renter)	405,831	69,939	335,080	27,615	377,982
Electricity (renter)	1,644,624	177,964	1,466,469	89,670	1,554,602
Water, sewer maintenance (renter)	340,808	27,244	313,399	34,650	305,840
Day-care centers, nurseries, and preschools	2,669,291	524,811	2,144,513	64,785	2,604,213

	total consumer units	race		Hispanic origin	
		black	white and other	Hispanic	non-Hispanic
APPAREL AND SERVICES	$26,584,170	$2,081,217	$24,528,856	$2,350,845	$24,238,588
Men and boys, aged 2 or older	7,145,764	584,313	6,568,557	593,460	6,544,571
Men's coats and jackets	570,630	2,440	569,636	54,810	516,169
Men's accessories	498,881	133,371	363,661	18,270	478,574
Men's sweaters and vests	343,050	12,063	331,138	35,805	306,856
Men's active sportswear	309,418	–	309,418	54,495	257,068
Men's shirts	1,882,293	72,378	1,815,346	148,890	1,731,400
Men's pants	776,908	94,336	682,972	–	771,205
Boys' shirts	415,921	29,819	387,313	58,695	359,692
Boys' pants	421,526	44,593	376,472	57,540	363,757
Women and girls, aged 2 or older	9,165,950	407,569	8,780,087	657,195	8,494,429
Women's coats and jackets	630,047	25,210	606,101	88,305	544,619
Women's dresses	858,747	14,232	847,556	52,605	803,719
Women's vests and sweaters	952,918	18,298	937,239	55,755	894,150
Women's shirts, tops, blouses	1,015,698	13,418	1,005,241	41,265	969,340
Women's pants	742,155	21,144	723,379	34,545	705,160
Women's active sportswear	485,428	–	485,428	7,560	475,525
Women's sleepwear	723,097	10,030	714,509	30,345	688,902
Women's accessories	640,137	21,280	620,884	49,140	590,342
Girls' dresses and suits	334,082	32,936	300,587	162,750	181,878
Girls' shirts, blouses, sweaters	502,244	27,108	476,011	10,815	487,718
Girls' skirts and pants	372,199	37,951	335,080	23,100	349,532
Girls' accessories	266,817	1,898	266,093	5,670	260,116
Children under age 2	4,483,199	430,746	4,055,456	612,570	3,889,554
Infant dresses, outerwear	1,713,010	210,494	1,501,948	150,150	1,562,731
Infant underwear	1,895,746	144,892	1,753,258	342,405	1,567,811
Infant nightwear, loungewear	285,875	30,090	255,252	19,530	266,213
Infant accessories	440,584	28,192	412,937	92,295	352,580
Other apparel products and services	5,788,136	658,589	5,124,756	487,620	5,309,018
Jewelry and watches	2,691,713	97,589	2,593,915	106,260	2,585,924
Watches	242,153	28,463	213,860	18,375	223,538
Jewelry	2,449,560	69,261	2,381,040	87,885	2,362,386
Men's footwear	938,344	150,449	787,438	185,220	762,060
Boys' footwear	500,002	167,121	330,153	83,895	419,641
Women's footwear	988,793	179,319	808,135	58,275	927,681
Girls' footwear	369,956	55,707	313,399	53,550	318,033
TRANSPORTATION	4,918,178	688,137	4,230,880	386,715	4,531,717
Used cars	1,368,839	539,856	828,831	14,910	1,354,435
Airline fares	760,092	75,089	684,943	70,980	688,902
Ship fares	307,176	33,072	274,963	38,850	268,245
HEALTH CARE	3,653,600	116,429	3,540,024	154,770	3,499,380
Physician's services	344,172	9,488	334,095	6,090	337,339
Dental services	451,795	34,156	417,865	26,355	425,738
Care in convalescent or nursing home	581,841	–	581,463	–	581,841
Nonprescription vitamins	440,584	1,355	440,532	31,185	408,464
Prescription drugs	266,817	29,277	237,513	13,755	253,004
ENTERTAINMENT	8,771,330	473,848	8,304,076	496,230	8,266,827
Toys, games, hobbies, and tricycles	3,360,998	236,246	3,125,116	216,720	3,144,768
Other entertainment	5,410,332	237,466	5,178,960	279,510	5,122,059
Fees for recreational lessons	883,411	60,722	822,918	42,210	841,314
Community antenna or cable TV	714,128	53,674	660,305	54,915	659,436

	total consumer units	race		Hispanic origin	
		black	white and other	Hispanic	non-Hispanic
VCRs and videodisc players	$253,364	$10,843	$242,440	$7,350	$245,891
Video game hardware and software	238,790	19,924	218,788	18,060	220,489
Athletic gear, game tables, exercise equipment	739,913	–	739,913	46,305	691,950
Hunting and fishing equipment	343,050	–	343,050	9,030	332,258
Photographer fees	357,625	1,084	356,762	5,355	352,580
PERSONAL CARE PRODUCTS AND SERVICES	**2,371,084**	**100,842**	**2,276,574**	**159,075**	**2,206,926**
Cosmetics, perfume, bath preparation	1,404,713	66,686	1,341,306	89,040	1,312,775
Electric personal care appliances	371,077	–	371,077	37,275	334,290
EDUCATION	**20,614,419**	**1,117,121**	**19,495,754**	**586,530**	**20,021,856**
College tuition	14,330,766	665,637	13,665,359	340,515	13,990,406
Elementary and high school tuition	2,909,203	97,318	2,811,717	145,950	2,762,722
Other school tuition	497,760	58,147	440,532	3,570	494,831
Other school expenses including rentals	447,311	26,295	420,821	51,450	395,255
College books and supplies	1,337,448	125,646	1,211,216	24,045	1,312,775
Miscellaneous school supplies	827,357	114,396	712,538	15,015	806,768
ALL OTHER GIFTS	**9,390,166**	**444,707**	**8,946,641**	**678,090**	**8,707,806**
Gifts of trip expenses	4,977,595	113,311	4,864,576	265,860	4,711,563
Lotteries and gambling losses	320,629	4,066	317,341	2,205	316,001
Legal fees	652,469	14,503	638,623	36,120	616,761
Funeral expenses	2,830,727	293,444	2,536,754	331,380	2,498,541
Miscellaneous personal services	242,153	12,199	230,614	11,760	229,634

Note: Other races include Asians, Native Americans, and Pacific Islanders. Numbers may not add to total because of rounding. (–) means sample is too small to make a reliable estimate. Expenditures for items in a given category may not add to category total because categories with annual spending of less than $2.00 for the average household are omitted. Spending on gifts is also included in the product and service categories in other chapters.
Source: Calculations by New Strategist based on the 2002 Consumer Expenditure Survey

Table 6.16 Gifts for Non—Household Members: Market shares by race and Hispanic origin, 2002

(percentage of total annual spending on selected gifts of products and services for non—household members accounted for by consumer unit race and Hispanic origin groups, 2002)

	total consumer units	race		Hispanic origin	
		black	white and other	Hispanic	non-Hispanic
Share of total consumer units	**100.0%**	**12.1%**	**87.9%**	**9.4%**	**90.6%**
Share of total before-tax income	**100.0**	**8.8**	**91.0**	**7.1**	**93.0**
Share of total spending	**100.0**	**9.0**	**91.1**	**8.0**	**92.0**
Share of gifts spending	**100.0**	**6.8**	**93.2**	**5.7**	**94.2**
FOOD	**100.0%**	**5.3%**	**94.8%**	**5.2%**	**94.7%**
Cakes and cupcakes	100.0	3.3	97.0	5.1	94.4
Fresh fruit other than apples, bananas, and citrus	100.0	22.2	77.8	6.5	93.4
Candy and chewing gum	100.0	8.8	91.2	5.7	94.0
Board (including at school)	100.0	4.8	95.2	5.9	94.1
Catered affairs	100.0	0.5	99.5	1.7	98.3
ALCOHOLIC BEVERAGES	**100.0**	**2.5**	**97.8**	**10.5**	**89.6**
Beer and ale	100.0	1.9	98.3	16.6	84.1
Wine	100.0	2.4	97.8	7.2	92.7
HOUSING	**100.0**	**8.3**	**91.8**	**4.2**	**95.6**
Housekeeping supplies	**100.0**	**5.7**	**94.5**	**4.6**	**95.0**
Laundry and cleaning supplies	100.0	11.0	88.8	20.3	80.4
Other household products	100.0	3.7	96.6	4.1	95.5
Miscellaneous household products	100.0	2.2	98.1	4.4	95.1
Lawn and garden supplies	100.0	2.1	98.4	1.2	98.2
Postage and stationery	100.0	6.0	94.2	3.2	96.3
Stationery, stationery supplies, giftwrap	100.0	3.8	96.5	2.0	97.4
Postage	100.0	14.2	85.8	4.9	94.8
Household textiles	**100.0**	**5.4**	**94.8**	**3.0**	**96.6**
Bathroom linens	100.0	5.7	94.4	7.4	92.4
Bedroom linens	100.0	7.7	92.5	2.9	96.7
Appliances and miscellaneous housewares	**100.0**	**9.2**	**90.9**	**4.1**	**95.5**
Major appliances	100.0	10.7	89.4	4.7	94.9
Small appliances and miscellaneous housewares	100.0	8.4	91.7	3.8	95.9
China and other dinnerware	100.0	2.0	98.6	4.9	94.7
Nonelectric cookware	100.0	28.2	71.5	2.2	97.3
Tableware, nonelectric kitchenware	100.0	3.3	96.9	7.5	92.4
Small electric kitchen appliances	100.0	2.5	97.6	3.6	96.3
Miscellaneous household equipment	**100.0**	**3.6**	**96.5**	**5.2**	**94.6**
Infants' equipment	100.0	4.0	96.2	5.5	94.2
Outdoor equipment	100.0	–	100.0	–	99.4
Other household decorative items	100.0	2.1	98.2	5.5	94.2
Power tools	100.0	2.2	98.0	–	99.1
Indoor plants, fresh flowers	100.0	4.2	95.8	4.1	95.9
Computers and computer hardware	100.0	3.0	97.1	6.2	93.9
Miscellaneous household equipment	100.0	–	100.0	8.7	91.0
Other housing	**100.0**	**12.0**	**88.0**	**3.6**	**96.4**
Repair or maintenance services	100.0	34.0	66.1	0.2	99.9
Housing while attending school	100.0	8.4	91.6	2.9	97.1
Natural gas (renter)	100.0	17.2	82.6	6.8	93.1
Electricity (renter)	100.0	10.8	89.2	5.5	94.5
Water, sewer maintenance (renter)	100.0	8.0	92.0	10.2	89.7
Day-care centers, nurseries, and preschools	100.0	19.7	80.3	2.4	97.6

	total consumer units	race		Hispanic origin	
		black	white and other	Hispanic	non-Hispanic
APPAREL AND SERVICES	**100.0%**	**7.8%**	**92.3%**	**8.8%**	**91.2%**
Men and boys, aged 2 or older	**100.0**	**8.2**	**91.9**	**8.3**	**91.6**
Men's coats and jackets	100.0	0.4	99.8	9.6	90.5
Men's accessories	100.0	26.7	72.9	3.7	95.9
Men's sweaters and vests	100.0	3.5	96.5	10.4	89.4
Men's active sportswear	100.0	–	100.0	17.6	83.1
Men's shirts	100.0	3.8	96.4	7.9	92.0
Men's pants	100.0	12.1	87.9	–	99.3
Boys' shirts	100.0	7.2	93.1	14.1	86.5
Boys' pants	100.0	10.6	89.3	13.7	86.3
Women and girls, aged 2 or older	**100.0**	**4.4**	**95.8**	**7.2**	**92.7**
Women's coats and jackets	100.0	4.0	96.2	14.0	86.4
Women's dresses	100.0	1.7	98.7	6.1	93.6
Women's vests and sweaters	100.0	1.9	98.4	5.9	93.8
Women's shirts, tops, blouses	100.0	1.3	99.0	4.1	95.4
Women's pants	100.0	2.8	97.5	4.7	95.0
Women's active sportswear	100.0	–	100.0	1.6	98.0
Women's sleepwear	100.0	1.4	98.8	4.2	95.3
Women's accessories	100.0	3.3	97.0	7.7	92.2
Girls' dresses and suits	100.0	9.9	90.0	48.7	54.4
Girls' shirts, blouses, sweaters	100.0	5.4	94.8	2.2	97.1
Girls' skirts and pants	100.0	10.2	90.0	6.2	93.9
Girls' accessories	100.0	0.7	99.7	2.1	97.5
Children under age 2	**100.0**	**9.6**	**90.5**	**13.7**	**86.8**
Infant dresses, outerwear	100.0	12.3	87.7	8.8	91.2
Infant underwear	100.0	7.6	92.5	18.1	82.7
Infant nightwear, loungewear	100.0	10.5	89.3	6.8	93.1
Infant accessories	100.0	6.4	93.7	20.9	80.0
Other apparel products and services	**100.0**	**11.4**	**88.5**	**8.4**	**91.7**
Jewelry and watches	100.0	3.6	96.4	3.9	96.1
Watches	100.0	11.8	88.3	7.6	92.3
Jewelry	100.0	2.8	97.2	3.6	96.4
Men's footwear	100.0	16.0	83.9	19.7	81.2
Boys' footwear	100.0	33.4	66.0	16.8	83.9
Women's footwear	100.0	18.1	81.7	5.9	93.8
Girls' footwear	100.0	15.1	84.7	14.5	86.0
TRANSPORTATION	**100.0**	**14.0**	**86.0**	**7.9**	**92.1**
Used cars	100.0	39.4	60.5	1.1	98.9
Airline fares	100.0	9.9	90.1	9.3	90.6
Ship fares	100.0	10.8	89.5	12.6	87.3
HEALTH CARE	**100.0**	**3.2**	**96.9**	**4.2**	**95.8**
Physician's services	100.0	2.8	97.1	1.8	98.0
Dental services	100.0	7.6	92.5	5.8	94.2
Care in convalescent or nursing home	100.0	–	99.9	–	100.0
Nonprescription vitamins	100.0	0.3	100.0	7.1	92.7
Prescription drugs	100.0	11.0	89.0	5.2	94.8
ENTERTAINMENT	**100.0**	**5.4**	**94.7**	**5.7**	**94.2**
Toys, games, hobbies, and tricycles	100.0	7.0	93.0	6.4	93.6
Other entertainment	100.0	4.4	95.7	5.2	94.7
Fees for recreational lessons	100.0	6.9	93.2	4.8	95.2
Community antenna or cable TV	100.0	7.5	92.5	7.7	92.3

	total consumer units	race		Hispanic origin	
		black	white and other	Hispanic	non-Hispanic
VCRs and videodisc players	100.0%	4.3%	95.7%	2.9%	97.1%
Video game hardware and software	100.0	8.3	91.6	7.6	92.3
Athletic gear, game tables, exercise equipment	100.0	–	100.0	6.3	93.5
Hunting and fishing equipment	100.0	–	100.0	2.6	96.9
Photographer fees	100.0	0.3	99.8	1.5	98.6
PERSONAL CARE PRODUCTS AND SERVICES	**100.0**	**4.3**	**96.0**	**6.7**	**93.1**
Cosmetics, perfume, bath preparation	100.0	4.7	95.5	6.3	93.5
Electric personal care appliances	100.0	–	100.0	10.0	90.1
EDUCATION	**100.0**	**5.4**	**94.6**	**2.8**	**97.1**
College tuition	100.0	4.6	95.4	2.4	97.6
Elementary and high school tuition	100.0	3.3	96.6	5.0	95.0
Other school tuition	100.0	11.7	88.5	0.7	99.4
Other school expenses including rentals	100.0	5.9	94.1	11.5	88.4
College books and supplies	100.0	9.4	90.6	1.8	98.2
Miscellaneous school supplies	100.0	13.8	86.1	1.8	97.5
ALL OTHER GIFTS	**100.0**	**4.7**	**95.3**	**7.2**	**92.7**
Gifts of trip expenses	100.0	2.3	97.7	5.3	94.7
Lotteries and gambling losses	100.0	1.3	99.0	0.7	98.6
Legal fees	100.0	2.2	97.9	5.5	94.5
Funeral expenses	100.0	10.4	89.6	11.7	88.3
Miscellaneous personal services	100.0	5.0	95.2	4.9	94.8

Note: Other races include Asians, Native Americans, and Pacific Islanders. Numbers may not add to total because of rounding. (–) means sample is too small to make a reliable estimate. Expenditures for items in a given category may not add to category total because categories with annual spending of less than $2.00 for the average household are omitted. Spending on gifts is also included in the product and service categories in other chapters.
Source: Calculations by New Strategist based on the 2002 Consumer Expenditure Survey

Table 6.17 Gifts for Non—Household Members: Average spending by region, 2002

(average annual spending of consumer units (CU) on selected gifts of products and services for non–household members by region in which consumer unit lives, 2002)

	total consumer units	Northeast	Midwest	South	West
Number of consumer units					
(in thousands, add 000)	112,108	21,313	25,883	40,004	24,907
Average number of persons per CU	2.5	2.5	2.5	2.5	2.6
Average before-tax income of CU	$49,430.00	$53,983.00	$49,197.00	$45,641.00	$52,016.00
Average spending of CU, total	40,676.60	42,390.20	40,601.14	37,280.55	44,728.34
Gifts, average spending	1,036.24	1,244.56	1,175.80	821.55	1,056.44
FOOD	$82.18	$125.72	$101.38	$57.11	$65.08
Cakes and cupcakes	2.41	2.54	2.80	1.37	3.55
Fresh fruit other than apples, bananas, and citrus	2.26	4.73	2.38	1.71	0.86
Candy and chewing gum	11.69	14.08	12.61	8.29	14.04
Board (including at school)	21.90	16.97	32.15	21.35	16.36
Catered affairs	26.19	71.13	31.60	9.07	9.61
ALCOHOLIC BEVERAGES	13.42	11.56	17.16	9.51	17.40
Beer and ale	4.73	3.85	6.01	4.12	5.14
Wine	5.84	5.42	6.50	3.52	9.21
HOUSING	258.69	258.60	299.17	243.98	240.04
Housekeeping supplies	42.48	48.06	44.46	35.89	46.03
Laundry and cleaning supplies	2.93	1.46	2.52	3.10	4.36
Other household products	11.69	11.32	13.97	10.09	12.21
Miscellaneous household products	5.85	4.65	7.22	6.06	5.13
Lawn and garden supplies	4.20	5.23	5.16	2.54	4.96
Postage and stationery	27.86	35.28	27.97	22.70	29.46
Stationery, stationery supplies, giftwrap	21.13	26.84	24.39	16.82	19.63
Postage	6.14	7.74	3.44	5.11	9.17
Household textiles	13.72	16.80	15.78	11.37	12.61
Bathroom linens	2.59	2.34	2.31	2.30	3.57
Bedroom linens	6.10	6.07	8.28	5.72	4.50
Appliances and miscellaneous housewares	23.98	27.73	26.37	21.67	21.97
Major appliances	8.41	9.06	12.62	5.15	8.69
Small appliances and miscellaneous housewares	15.57	18.67	13.75	16.52	13.28
China and other dinnerware	2.46	1.58	1.39	4.69	0.80
Nonelectric cookware	3.53	6.07	3.76	3.57	1.02
Tableware, nonelectric kitchenware	2.63	1.92	3.43	2.51	2.63
Small electric kitchen appliances	2.71	3.45	3.24	1.76	3.07
Miscellaneous household equipment	64.70	61.79	82.81	59.05	57.55
Infants' equipment	3.82	1.87	3.99	6.29	1.44
Outdoor equipment	2.07	2.62	2.38	1.74	1.78
Other household decorative items	25.76	21.26	37.77	24.57	19.17
Power tools	2.80	7.51	1.47	0.08	4.36
Indoor plants, fresh flowers	13.43	14.40	15.99	12.43	11.55
Computers and computer hardware	6.59	5.02	9.06	4.36	8.96
Miscellaneous household equipment	2.19	2.31	2.77	1.83	2.06
Other housing	113.80	104.22	129.75	116.00	101.89
Repair or maintenance services	4.51	1.34	2.94	7.42	4.19
Housing while attending school	39.93	29.05	59.08	32.39	41.47
Natural gas (renter)	3.62	5.73	4.25	2.75	2.54
Electricity (renter)	14.67	11.20	13.57	20.09	10.08
Water, sewer maintenance (renter)	3.04	2.20	2.51	4.24	2.39
Day-care centers, nurseries, and preschools	23.81	20.50	22.74	25.74	24.65

	total consumer units	Northeast	Midwest	South	West
APPAREL AND SERVICES	**$237.13**	**$283.16**	**$247.08**	**$188.23**	**$264.77**
Men and boys, aged 2 or older	**63.74**	**68.16**	**71.64**	**52.25**	**70.15**
Men's coats and jackets	5.09	5.78	7.15	2.90	5.84
Men's accessories	4.45	3.13	2.47	5.97	5.23
Men's sweaters and vests	3.06	5.31	3.32	1.76	2.95
Men's active sportswear	2.76	4.47	1.95	2.00	3.31
Men's shirts	16.79	15.82	19.02	13.71	20.27
Men's pants	6.93	7.04	11.12	4.24	6.80
Boys' shirts	3.71	3.56	5.35	3.32	2.78
Boys' pants	3.76	3.73	3.63	3.69	4.02
Women and girls, aged 2 or older	**81.76**	**107.86**	**87.58**	**53.35**	**98.14**
Women's coats and jackets	5.62	12.73	2.95	2.12	7.73
Women's dresses	7.66	4.76	10.28	8.12	6.76
Women's vests and sweaters	8.50	13.28	12.07	2.64	9.96
Women's shirts, tops, blouses	9.06	7.96	10.27	8.38	9.85
Women's pants	6.62	6.64	8.66	2.82	10.54
Women's active sportswear	4.33	8.49	5.58	0.91	4.87
Women's sleepwear	6.45	12.71	5.48	2.84	7.71
Women's accessories	5.71	3.88	5.76	6.46	6.08
Girls' dresses and suits	2.98	2.78	1.04	1.84	6.96
Girls' shirts, blouses, sweaters	4.48	6.44	3.69	2.75	6.33
Girls' skirts and pants	3.32	3.36	3.94	2.94	3.27
Girls' accessories	2.38	6.09	1.18	1.38	1.98
Children under age 2	**39.99**	**43.58**	**44.73**	**34.10**	**41.35**
Infant dresses, outerwear	15.28	14.40	17.40	15.20	13.95
Infant underwear	16.91	18.58	20.62	13.32	17.33
Infant nightwear, loungewear	2.55	3.29	3.12	2.10	2.05
Infant accessories	3.93	4.95	2.24	2.61	6.88
Other apparel products and services	**51.63**	**63.56**	**43.14**	**48.54**	**55.12**
Jewelry and watches	24.01	30.63	19.87	19.35	30.14
Watches	2.16	2.76	2.49	1.95	1.64
Jewelry	21.85	27.87	17.37	17.41	28.50
Men's footwear	8.37	11.07	7.21	7.39	8.77
Boys' footwear	4.46	6.49	4.69	5.35	1.03
Women's footwear	8.82	6.73	5.09	12.44	8.75
Girls' footwear	3.30	7.51	2.96	1.38	3.01
TRANSPORTATION	**43.87**	**49.29**	**41.29**	**33.94**	**57.86**
Used cars	12.21	13.90	6.10	6.35	26.53
Airline fares	6.78	5.60	6.72	6.05	9.01
Ship fares	2.74	3.16	3.63	2.16	2.41
HEALTH CARE	**32.59**	**30.78**	**38.53**	**24.79**	**40.54**
Physician's services	3.07	1.25	3.57	2.87	4.41
Dental services	4.03	4.66	4.05	4.12	3.34
Care in convalescent or nursing home	5.19	6.29	10.52	2.15	3.59
Nonprescription vitamins	3.93	0.83	2.48	1.73	11.64
Prescription drugs	2.38	1.49	3.58	3.08	0.77
ENTERTAINMENT	**78.24**	**80.45**	**96.44**	**68.57**	**73.19**
Toys, games, hobbies, and tricycles	29.98	33.07	36.26	27.59	24.67
Other entertainment	48.26	47.38	60.17	40.98	48.53
Fees for recreational lessons	7.88	10.34	7.73	4.74	10.99
Community antenna or cable TV	6.37	8.18	5.70	6.34	5.57

	total consumer units	Northeast	Midwest	South	West
VCRs and videodisc players	$2.26	$1.51	$2.68	$1.93	$3.02
Video game hardware and software	2.13	2.63	2.30	1.72	2.18
Athletic gear, game tables, exercise equipment	6.60	3.25	10.49	6.83	5.15
Hunting and fishing equipment	3.06	1.23	4.89	2.37	3.88
Photographer fees	3.19	5.25	5.25	2.47	0.47
PERSONAL CARE PRODUCTS AND SERVICES	**21.15**	**25.45**	**22.27**	**19.47**	**18.93**
Cosmetics, perfume, bath preparation	12.53	13.87	13.33	12.35	10.83
Electric personal care appliances	3.31	4.12	3.33	2.56	3.78
EDUCATION	**183.88**	**265.77**	**217.13**	**113.32**	**192.63**
College tuition	127.83	189.85	170.64	62.40	135.38
Elementary and high school tuition	25.95	50.90	11.09	24.44	22.45
Other school tuition	4.44	4.84	2.38	4.85	5.60
Other school expenses including rentals	3.99	2.37	3.24	5.16	4.26
College books and supplies	11.93	10.20	13.31	8.74	17.09
Miscellaneous school supplies	7.38	5.06	14.75	5.17	5.30
ALL OTHER GIFTS	**83.76**	**112.33**	**93.68**	**61.70**	**84.47**
Gifts of trip expenses	44.40	61.04	44.99	27.65	56.46
Lotteries and gambling losses	2.86	0.70	10.75	0.21	0.81
Legal fees	5.82	0.92	11.12	6.79	2.96
Funeral expenses	25.25	47.28	16.83	22.73	19.18
Miscellaneous personal services	2.16	0.62	5.26	0.82	2.46

Note: (–) means sample is too small to make a reliable estimate. Expenditures for items in a given category may not add to category total because categories with annual spending of less than $2.00 for the average household are omitted. Spending on gifts is also included in the product and service categories in other chapters.
Source: Bureau of Labor Statistics, unpublished tables from the 2002 Consumer Expenditure Survey

Table 6.18 Gifts for Non—Household Members: Indexed spending by region, 2002

(indexed average annual spending of consumer units (CU) on selected gifts of products and services for non–household members by region in which consumer unit lives, 2002; index definition: an index of 100 is the average for all consumer units; an index of 132 means that spending by consumer units in that group is 32 percent above the average for all consumer units; an index of 68 indicates spending that is 32 percent below the average for all consumer units)

	total consumer units	Northeast	Midwest	South	West
Average spending of CU, total	$40,677	$42,390	$40,601	$37,281	$44,728
Average spending of CU, index	100	104	100	92	110
Gifts, spending index	100	120	113	79	102
FOOD	**100**	**153**	**123**	**69**	**79**
Cakes and cupcakes	100	105	116	57	147
Fresh fruit other than apples, bananas, and citrus	100	209	105	76	38
Candy and chewing gum	100	120	108	71	120
Board (including at school)	100	77	147	97	75
Catered affairs	100	272	121	35	37
ALCOHOLIC BEVERAGES	**100**	**86**	**128**	**71**	**130**
Beer and ale	100	81	127	87	109
Wine	100	93	111	60	158
HOUSING	**100**	**100**	**116**	**94**	**93**
Housekeeping supplies	**100**	**113**	**105**	**84**	**108**
Laundry and cleaning supplies	100	50	86	106	149
Other household products	100	97	120	86	104
Miscellaneous household products	100	79	123	104	88
Lawn and garden supplies	100	125	123	60	118
Postage and stationery	100	127	100	81	106
Stationery, stationery supplies, giftwrap	100	127	115	80	93
Postage	100	126	56	83	149
Household textiles	**100**	**122**	**115**	**83**	**92**
Bathroom linens	100	90	89	89	138
Bedroom linens	100	100	136	94	74
Appliances and miscellaneous housewares	**100**	**116**	**110**	**90**	**92**
Major appliances	100	108	150	61	103
Small appliances and miscellaneous housewares	100	120	88	106	85
China and other dinnerware	100	64	57	191	33
Nonelectric cookware	100	172	107	101	29
Tableware, nonelectric kitchenware	100	73	130	95	100
Small electric kitchen appliances	100	127	120	65	113
Miscellaneous household equipment	**100**	**96**	**128**	**91**	**89**
Infants' equipment	100	49	104	165	38
Outdoor equipment	100	127	115	84	86
Other household decorative items	100	83	147	95	74
Power tools	100	268	53	3	156
Indoor plants, fresh flowers	100	107	119	93	86
Computers and computer hardware	100	76	137	66	136
Miscellaneous household equipment	100	105	126	84	94
Other housing	**100**	**92**	**114**	**102**	**90**
Repair or maintenance services	100	30	65	165	93
Housing while attending school	100	73	148	81	104
Natural gas (renter)	100	158	117	76	70
Electricity (renter)	100	76	93	137	69
Water, sewer maintenance (renter)	100	72	83	139	79
Day-care centers, nurseries, and preschools	100	86	96	108	104

	total consumer units	Northeast	Midwest	South	West
APPAREL AND SERVICES	**100**	**119**	**104**	**79**	**112**
Men and boys, aged 2 or older	**100**	**107**	**112**	**82**	**110**
Men's coats and jackets	100	114	140	57	115
Men's accessories	100	70	56	134	118
Men's sweaters and vests	100	174	108	58	96
Men's active sportswear	100	162	71	72	120
Men's shirts	100	94	113	82	121
Men's pants	100	102	160	61	98
Boys' shirts	100	96	144	89	75
Boys' pants	100	99	97	98	107
Women and girls, aged 2 or older	**100**	**132**	**107**	**65**	**120**
Women's coats and jackets	100	227	52	38	138
Women's dresses	100	62	134	106	88
Women's vests and sweaters	100	156	142	31	117
Women's shirts, tops, blouses	100	88	113	92	109
Women's pants	100	100	131	43	159
Women's active sportswear	100	196	129	21	112
Women's sleepwear	100	197	85	44	120
Women's accessories	100	68	101	113	106
Girls' dresses and suits	100	93	35	62	234
Girls' shirts, blouses, sweaters	100	144	82	61	141
Girls' skirts and pants	100	101	119	89	98
Girls' accessories	100	256	50	58	83
Children under age 2	**100**	**109**	**112**	**85**	**103**
Infant dresses, outerwear	100	94	114	99	91
Infant underwear	100	110	122	79	102
Infant nightwear, loungewear	100	129	122	82	80
Infant accessories	100	126	57	66	175
Other apparel products and services	**100**	**123**	**84**	**94**	**107**
Jewelry and watches	100	128	83	81	126
Watches	100	128	115	90	76
Jewelry	100	128	79	80	130
Men's footwear	100	132	86	88	105
Boys' footwear	100	146	105	120	23
Women's footwear	100	76	58	141	99
Girls' footwear	100	228	90	42	91
TRANSPORTATION	**100**	**112**	**94**	**77**	**132**
Used cars	100	114	50	52	217
Airline fares	100	83	99	89	133
Ship fares	100	115	132	79	88
HEALTH CARE	**100**	**94**	**118**	**76**	**124**
Physician's services	100	41	116	93	144
Dental services	100	116	100	102	83
Care in convalescent or nursing home	100	121	203	41	69
Nonprescription vitamins	100	21	63	44	296
Prescription drugs	100	63	150	129	32
ENTERTAINMENT	**100**	**103**	**123**	**88**	**94**
Toys, games, hobbies, and tricycles	100	110	121	92	82
Other entertainment	100	98	125	85	101
Fees for recreational lessons	100	131	98	60	139
Community antenna or cable TV	100	128	89	100	87

	total consumer units	Northeast	Midwest	South	West
VCRs and videodisc players	100	67	119	85	134
Video game hardware and software	100	123	108	81	102
Athletic gear, game tables, exercise equipment	100	49	159	103	78
Hunting and fishing equipment	100	40	160	77	127
Photographer fees	100	165	165	77	15
PERSONAL CARE PRODUCTS AND SERVICES	**100**	**120**	**105**	**92**	**90**
Cosmetics, perfume, bath preparation	100	111	106	99	86
Electric personal care appliances	100	124	101	77	114
EDUCATION	**100**	**145**	**118**	**62**	**105**
College tuition	100	149	133	49	106
Elementary and high school tuition	100	196	43	94	87
Other school tuition	100	109	54	109	126
Other school expenses including rentals	100	59	81	129	107
College books and supplies	100	85	112	73	143
Miscellaneous school supplies	100	69	200	70	72
ALL OTHER GIFTS	**100**	**134**	**112**	**74**	**101**
Gifts of trip expenses	100	137	101	62	127
Lotteries and gambling losses	100	24	376	7	28
Legal fees	100	16	191	117	51
Funeral expenses	100	187	67	90	76
Miscellaneous personal services	100	29	244	38	114

Note: (–) means sample is too small to make a reliable estimate. Categories with annual spending of less than $2.00 for the average household are omitted. Spending on gifts is also included in the product and service categories in other chapters.
Source: Calculations by New Strategist based on the 2002 Consumer Expenditure Survey

Table 6.19 Gifts for Non–Household Members: Total spending by region, 2002

(total annual spending on selected gifts of products and services for non–household members by region in which consumer units live, 2002; numbers in thousands)

	total consumer units	Northeast	Midwest	South	West
Number of consumer units	112,108	21,313	25,883	40,004	24,907
Total spending of all consumer units	$4,560,172,273	$903,462,333	$1,050,879,307	$1,491,371,122	$1,114,048,764
Gifts, total spending	116,170,794	26,525,307	30,433,231	32,865,286	26,312,751
FOOD	**$9,213,035**	**$2,679,470**	**$2,624,019**	**$2,284,628**	**$1,620,948**
Cakes and cupcakes	270,180	54,135	72,472	54,805	88,420
Fresh fruit other than apples, bananas, and citrus	253,364	100,810	61,602	68,407	21,420
Candy and chewing gum	1,310,543	300,087	326,385	331,633	349,694
Board (including at school)	2,455,165	361,682	832,138	854,085	407,479
Catered affairs	2,936,109	1,515,994	817,903	362,836	239,356
ALCOHOLIC BEVERAGES	**1,504,489**	**246,378**	**444,152**	**380,438**	**433,382**
Beer and ale	530,271	82,055	155,557	164,816	128,022
Wine	654,711	115,516	168,240	140,814	229,393
HOUSING	**29,001,219**	**5,511,542**	**7,743,417**	**9,760,176**	**5,978,676**
Housekeeping supplies	**4,762,348**	**1,024,303**	**1,150,758**	**1,435,744**	**1,146,469**
Laundry and cleaning supplies	328,476	31,117	65,225	124,012	108,595
Other household products	1,310,543	241,263	361,586	403,640	304,114
Miscellaneous household products	655,832	99,105	186,875	242,424	127,773
Lawn and garden supplies	470,854	111,467	133,556	101,610	123,539
Postage and stationery	3,123,329	751,923	723,948	908,091	733,760
Stationery, stationery supplies, giftwrap	2,368,842	572,041	631,286	672,867	488,924
Postage	688,343	164,963	89,038	204,420	228,397
Household textiles	**1,538,122**	**358,058**	**408,434**	**454,845**	**314,077**
Bathroom linens	290,360	49,872	59,790	92,009	88,918
Bedroom linens	683,859	129,370	214,311	228,823	112,082
Appliances and miscellaneous housewares	**2,688,350**	**591,009**	**682,535**	**866,887**	**547,207**
Major appliances	942,828	193,096	326,643	206,021	216,442
Small appliances and miscellaneous housewares	1,745,522	397,914	355,891	660,866	330,765
China and other dinnerware	275,786	33,675	35,977	187,619	19,926
Nonelectric cookware	395,741	129,370	97,320	142,814	25,405
Tableware, nonelectric kitchenware	294,844	40,921	88,779	100,410	65,505
Small electric kitchen appliances	303,813	73,530	83,861	70,407	76,464
Miscellaneous household equipment	**7,253,388**	**1,316,930**	**2,143,371**	**2,362,236**	**1,433,398**
Infants' equipment	428,253	39,855	103,273	251,625	35,866
Outdoor equipment	232,064	55,840	61,602	69,607	44,334
Other household decorative items	2,887,902	453,114	977,601	982,898	477,467
Power tools	313,902	160,061	38,048	3,200	108,595
Indoor plants, fresh flowers	1,505,610	306,907	413,869	497,250	287,676
Computers and computer hardware	738,792	106,991	234,500	174,417	223,167
Miscellaneous household equipment	245,517	49,233	71,696	73,207	51,308
Other housing	**12,757,890**	**2,221,241**	**3,358,319**	**4,640,464**	**2,537,774**
Repair or maintenance services	505,607	28,559	76,096	296,830	104,360
Housing while attending school	4,476,472	619,143	1,529,168	1,295,730	1,032,893
Natural gas (renter)	405,831	122,123	110,003	110,011	63,264
Electricity (renter)	1,644,624	238,706	351,232	803,680	251,063
Water, sewer maintenance (renter)	340,808	46,889	64,966	169,617	59,528
Day-care centers, nurseries, and preschools	2,669,291	436,917	588,579	1,029,703	613,958

	total consumer units	Northeast	Midwest	South	West
APPAREL AND SERVICES	**$26,584,170**	**$6,034,989**	**$6,395,172**	**$7,529,953**	**$6,594,626**
Men and boys, aged 2 or older	**7,145,764**	**1,452,694**	**1,854,258**	**2,090,209**	**1,747,226**
Men's coats and jackets	570,630	123,189	185,063	116,012	145,457
Men's accessories	498,881	66,710	63,931	238,824	130,264
Men's sweaters and vests	343,050	113,172	85,932	70,407	73,476
Men's active sportswear	309,418	95,269	50,472	80,008	82,442
Men's shirts	1,882,293	337,172	492,295	548,455	504,865
Men's pants	776,908	150,044	287,819	169,617	169,368
Boys' shirts	415,921	75,874	138,474	132,813	69,241
Boys' pants	421,526	79,497	93,955	147,615	100,126
Women and girls, aged 2 or older	**9,165,950**	**2,298,820**	**2,266,833**	**2,134,213**	**2,444,373**
Women's coats and jackets	630,047	271,314	76,355	84,808	192,531
Women's dresses	858,747	101,450	266,077	324,832	168,371
Women's vests and sweaters	952,918	283,037	312,408	105,611	248,074
Women's shirts, tops, blouses	1,015,698	169,651	265,818	335,234	245,334
Women's pants	742,155	141,518	224,147	112,811	262,520
Women's active sportswear	485,428	180,947	144,427	36,404	121,297
Women's sleepwear	723,097	270,888	141,839	113,611	192,033
Women's accessories	640,137	82,694	149,086	258,426	151,435
Girls' dresses and suits	334,082	59,250	26,918	73,607	173,353
Girls' shirts, blouses, sweaters	502,244	137,256	95,508	110,011	157,661
Girls' skirts and pants	372,199	71,612	101,979	117,612	81,446
Girls' accessories	266,817	129,796	30,542	55,206	49,316
Children under age 2	**4,483,199**	**928,821**	**1,157,747**	**1,364,136**	**1,029,904**
Infant dresses, outerwear	1,713,010	306,907	450,364	608,061	347,453
Infant underwear	1,895,746	395,996	533,707	532,853	431,638
Infant nightwear, loungewear	285,875	70,120	80,755	84,008	51,059
Infant accessories	440,584	105,499	57,978	104,410	171,360
Other apparel products and services	**5,788,136**	**1,354,654**	**1,116,593**	**1,941,794**	**1,372,874**
Jewelry and watches	2,691,713	652,817	514,295	774,077	750,697
Watches	242,153	58,824	64,449	78,008	40,847
Jewelry	2,449,560	593,993	449,588	696,470	709,850
Men's footwear	938,344	235,935	186,616	295,630	218,434
Boys' footwear	500,002	138,321	121,391	214,021	25,654
Women's footwear	988,793	143,436	131,744	497,650	217,936
Girls' footwear	369,956	160,061	76,614	55,206	74,970
TRANSPORTATION	**4,918,178**	**1,050,518**	**1,068,709**	**1,357,736**	**1,441,119**
Used cars	1,368,839	296,251	157,886	254,025	660,783
Airline fares	760,092	119,353	173,934	242,024	224,412
Ship fares	307,176	67,349	93,955	86,409	60,026
HEALTH CARE	**3,653,600**	**656,014**	**997,272**	**991,699**	**1,009,730**
Physician's services	344,172	26,641	92,402	114,811	109,840
Dental services	451,795	99,319	104,826	164,816	83,189
Care in convalescent or nursing home	581,841	134,059	272,289	86,009	89,416
Nonprescription vitamins	440,584	17,690	64,190	69,207	289,917
Prescription drugs	266,817	31,756	92,661	123,212	19,178
ENTERTAINMENT	**8,771,330**	**1,714,631**	**2,496,157**	**2,743,074**	**1,822,943**
Toys, games, hobbies, and tricycles	3,360,998	704,821	938,518	1,103,710	614,456
Other entertainment	5,410,332	1,009,810	1,557,380	1,639,364	1,208,737
Fees for recreational lessons	883,411	220,376	200,076	189,619	273,728
Community antenna or cable TV	714,128	174,340	147,533	253,625	138,732

	total consumer units	Northeast	Midwest	South	West
VCRs and videodisc players	$253,364	$32,183	$69,366	$77,208	$75,219
Video game hardware and software	238,790	56,053	59,531	68,807	54,297
Athletic gear, game tables, exercise equipment	739,913	69,267	271,513	273,227	128,271
Hunting and fishing equipment	343,050	26,215	126,568	94,809	96,639
Photographer fees	357,625	111,893	135,886	98,810	11,706
PERSONAL CARE PRODUCTS AND SERVICES	**2,371,084**	**542,416**	**576,414**	**778,878**	**471,490**
Cosmetics, perfume, bath preparation	1,404,713	295,611	345,020	494,049	269,743
Electric personal care appliances	371,077	87,810	86,190	102,410	94,148
EDUCATION	**20,614,419**	**5,664,356**	**5,619,976**	**4,533,253**	**4,797,835**
College tuition	14,330,766	4,046,273	4,416,675	2,496,250	3,371,910
Elementary and high school tuition	2,909,203	1,084,832	287,042	977,698	559,162
Other school tuition	497,760	103,155	61,602	194,019	139,479
Other school expenses including rentals	447,311	50,512	83,861	206,421	106,104
College books and supplies	1,337,448	217,393	344,503	349,635	425,661
Miscellaneous school supplies	827,357	107,844	381,774	206,821	132,007
ALL OTHER GIFTS	**9,390,166**	**2,394,089**	**2,424,719**	**2,468,247**	**2,103,894**
Gifts of trip expenses	4,977,595	1,300,946	1,164,476	1,106,111	1,406,249
Lotteries and gambling losses	320,629	14,919	278,242	8,401	20,175
Legal fees	652,469	19,608	287,819	271,627	73,725
Funeral expenses	2,830,727	1,007,679	435,611	909,291	477,716
Miscellaneous personal services	242,153	13,214	136,145	32,803	61,271

Note: Numbers may not add to total because of rounding. (–) means sample is too small to make a reliable estimate. Expenditures for items in a given category may not add to category total because categories with annual spending of less than $2.00 for the average household are omitted. Spending on gifts is also included in the product and service categories in other chapters.
Source: Calculations by New Strategist based on the 2002 Consumer Expenditure Survey

Table 6.20 Gifts for Non—Household Members: Market shares by region, 2002

(percentage of total annual spending on selected gifts of products and services for non—household members accounted for by consumer units by region, 2002)

	total consumer units	Northeast	Midwest	South	West
Share of total consumer units	100.0%	19.0%	23.1%	35.7%	22.2%
Share of total before-tax income	100.0	20.8	23.0	32.9	23.4
Share of total spending	100.0	19.8	23.0	32.7	24.4
Share of gifts spending	100.0	22.8	26.2	28.3	22.7
FOOD	**100.0%**	**29.1%**	**28.5%**	**24.8%**	**17.6%**
Cakes and cupcakes	100.0	20.0	26.8	20.3	32.7
Fresh fruit other than apples, bananas, and citrus	100.0	39.8	24.3	27.0	8.5
Candy and chewing gum	100.0	22.9	24.9	25.3	26.7
Board (including at school)	100.0	14.7	33.9	34.8	16.6
Catered affairs	100.0	51.6	27.9	12.4	8.2
ALCOHOLIC BEVERAGES	**100.0**	**16.4**	**29.5**	**25.3**	**28.8**
Beer and ale	100.0	15.5	29.3	31.1	24.1
Wine	100.0	17.6	25.7	21.5	35.0
HOUSING	**100.0**	**19.0**	**26.7**	**33.7**	**20.6**
Housekeeping supplies	**100.0**	**21.5**	**24.2**	**30.1**	**24.1**
Laundry and cleaning supplies	100.0	9.5	19.9	37.8	33.1
Other household products	100.0	18.4	27.6	30.8	23.2
Miscellaneous household products	100.0	15.1	28.5	37.0	19.5
Lawn and garden supplies	100.0	23.7	28.4	21.6	26.2
Postage and stationery	100.0	24.1	23.2	29.1	23.5
Stationery, stationery supplies, giftwrap	100.0	24.1	26.6	28.4	20.6
Postage	100.0	24.0	12.9	29.7	33.2
Household textiles	**100.0**	**23.3**	**26.6**	**29.6**	**20.4**
Bathroom linens	100.0	17.2	20.6	31.7	30.6
Bedroom linens	100.0	18.9	31.3	33.5	16.4
Appliances and miscellaneous housewares	**100.0**	**22.0**	**25.4**	**32.2**	**20.4**
Major appliances	100.0	20.5	34.6	21.9	23.0
Small appliances and miscellaneous housewares	100.0	22.8	20.4	37.9	18.9
China and other dinnerware	100.0	12.2	13.0	68.0	7.2
Nonelectric cookware	100.0	32.7	24.6	36.1	6.4
Tableware, nonelectric kitchenware	100.0	13.9	30.1	34.1	22.2
Small electric kitchen appliances	100.0	24.2	27.6	23.2	25.2
Miscellaneous household equipment	**100.0**	**18.2**	**29.5**	**32.6**	**19.8**
Infants' equipment	100.0	9.3	24.1	58.8	8.4
Outdoor equipment	100.0	24.1	26.5	30.0	19.1
Other household decorative items	100.0	15.7	33.9	34.0	16.5
Power tools	100.0	51.0	12.1	1.0	34.6
Indoor plants, fresh flowers	100.0	20.4	27.5	33.0	19.1
Computers and computer hardware	100.0	14.5	31.7	23.6	30.2
Miscellaneous household equipment	100.0	20.1	29.2	29.8	20.9
Other housing	**100.0**	**17.4**	**26.3**	**36.4**	**19.9**
Repair or maintenance services	100.0	5.6	15.1	58.7	20.6
Housing while attending school	100.0	13.8	34.2	28.9	23.1
Natural gas (renter)	100.0	30.1	27.1	27.1	15.6
Electricity (renter)	100.0	14.5	21.4	48.9	15.3
Water, sewer maintenance (renter)	100.0	13.8	19.1	49.8	17.5
Day-care centers, nurseries, and preschools	100.0	16.4	22.1	38.6	23.0

	total consumer units	Northeast	Midwest	South	West
APPAREL AND SERVICES	100.0%	22.7%	24.1%	28.3%	24.8%
Men and boys, aged 2 or older	100.0	20.3	25.9	29.3	24.5
Men's coats and jackets	100.0	21.6	32.4	20.3	25.5
Men's accessories	100.0	13.4	12.8	47.9	26.1
Men's sweaters and vests	100.0	33.0	25.0	20.5	21.4
Men's active sportswear	100.0	30.8	16.3	25.9	26.6
Men's shirts	100.0	17.9	26.2	29.1	26.8
Men's pants	100.0	19.3	37.0	21.8	21.8
Boys' shirts	100.0	18.2	33.3	31.9	16.6
Boys' pants	100.0	18.9	22.3	35.0	23.8
Women and girls, aged 2 or older	100.0	25.1	24.7	23.3	26.7
Women's coats and jackets	100.0	43.1	12.1	13.5	30.6
Women's dresses	100.0	11.8	31.0	37.8	19.6
Women's vests and sweaters	100.0	29.7	32.8	11.1	26.0
Women's shirts, tops, blouses	100.0	16.7	26.2	33.0	24.2
Women's pants	100.0	19.1	30.2	15.2	35.4
Women's active sportswear	100.0	37.3	29.8	7.5	25.0
Women's sleepwear	100.0	37.5	19.6	15.7	26.6
Women's accessories	100.0	12.9	23.3	40.4	23.7
Girls' dresses and suits	100.0	17.7	8.1	22.0	51.9
Girls' shirts, blouses, sweaters	100.0	27.3	19.0	21.9	31.4
Girls' skirts and pants	100.0	19.2	27.4	31.6	21.9
Girls' accessories	100.0	48.6	11.4	20.7	18.5
Children under age 2	100.0	20.7	25.8	30.4	23.0
Infant dresses, outerwear	100.0	17.9	26.3	35.5	20.3
Infant underwear	100.0	20.9	28.2	28.1	22.8
Infant nightwear, loungewear	100.0	24.5	28.2	29.4	17.9
Infant accessories	100.0	23.9	13.2	23.7	38.9
Other apparel products and services	100.0	23.4	19.3	33.5	23.7
Jewelry and watches	100.0	24.3	19.1	28.8	27.9
Watches	100.0	24.3	26.6	32.2	16.9
Jewelry	100.0	24.2	18.4	28.4	29.0
Men's footwear	100.0	25.1	19.9	31.5	23.3
Boys' footwear	100.0	27.7	24.3	42.8	5.1
Women's footwear	100.0	14.5	13.3	50.3	22.0
Girls' footwear	100.0	43.3	20.7	14.9	20.3
TRANSPORTATION	100.0	21.4	21.7	27.6	29.3
Used cars	100.0	21.6	11.5	18.6	48.3
Airline fares	100.0	15.7	22.9	31.8	29.5
Ship fares	100.0	21.9	30.6	28.1	19.5
HEALTH CARE	100.0	18.0	27.3	27.1	27.6
Physician's services	100.0	7.7	26.8	33.4	31.9
Dental services	100.0	22.0	23.2	36.5	18.4
Care in convalescent or nursing home	100.0	23.0	46.8	14.8	15.4
Nonprescription vitamins	100.0	4.0	14.6	15.7	65.8
Prescription drugs	100.0	11.9	34.7	46.2	7.2
ENTERTAINMENT	100.0	19.5	28.5	31.3	20.8
Toys, games, hobbies, and tricycles	100.0	21.0	27.9	32.8	18.3
Other entertainment	100.0	18.7	28.8	30.3	22.3
Fees for recreational lessons	100.0	24.9	22.6	21.5	31.0
Community antenna or cable TV	100.0	24.4	20.7	35.5	19.4

	total consumer units	Northeast	Midwest	South	West
VCRs and videodisc players	100.0%	12.7%	27.4%	30.5%	29.7%
Video game hardware and software	100.0	23.5	24.9	28.8	22.7
Athletic gear, game tables, exercise equipment	100.0	9.4	36.7	36.9	17.3
Hunting and fishing equipment	100.0	7.6	36.9	27.6	28.2
Photographer fees	100.0	31.3	38.0	27.6	3.3
PERSONAL CARE PRODUCTS AND SERVICES	**100.0**	**22.9**	**24.3**	**32.8**	**19.9**
Cosmetics, perfume, bath preparation	100.0	21.0	24.6	35.2	19.2
Electric personal care appliances	100.0	23.7	23.2	27.6	25.4
EDUCATION	**100.0**	**27.5**	**27.3**	**22.0**	**23.3**
College tuition	100.0	28.2	30.8	17.4	23.5
Elementary and high school tuition	100.0	37.3	9.9	33.6	19.2
Other school tuition	100.0	20.7	12.4	39.0	28.0
Other school expenses including rentals	100.0	11.3	18.7	46.1	23.7
College books and supplies	100.0	16.3	25.8	26.1	31.8
Miscellaneous school supplies	100.0	13.0	46.1	25.0	16.0
ALL OTHER GIFTS	**100.0**	**25.5**	**25.8**	**26.3**	**22.4**
Gifts of trip expenses	100.0	26.1	23.4	22.2	28.3
Lotteries and gambling losses	100.0	4.7	86.8	2.6	6.3
Legal fees	100.0	3.0	44.1	41.6	11.3
Funeral expenses	100.0	35.6	15.4	32.1	16.9
Miscellaneous personal services	100.0	5.5	56.2	13.5	25.3

Note: Numbers may not add to total because of rounding. (–) means sample is too small to make a reliable estimate. Expenditures for items in a given category may not add to category total because categories with annual spending of less than $2.00 for the average household are omitted. Spending on gifts is also included in the product and service categories in other chapters.
Source: Calculations by New Strategist based on the 2002 Consumer Expenditure Survey

Table 6.21 Gifts for Non—Household Members: Average spending by education, 2002

(average annual spending of consumer units (CU) on selected gifts of products and services for non–household members by education of consumer unit reference person, 2002)

	total consumer units	less than high school graduate	high school graduate	some college	associate's degree	college graduate		
						total	bachelor's degree	master's, professional, doctorate
Number of consumer units (in thousands, add 000)	112,108	17,075	31,961	23,260	10,395	29,417	19,082	10,335
Average number of persons per CU	2.5	2.6	2.5	2.4	2.6	2.5	2.5	2.5
Average before-tax income of CU	$49,430.00	$25,564.00	$39,618.00	$42,598.00	$54,860.00	$77,820.00	$69,408.00	$92,783.00
Average spending of CU, total	40,676.60	24,930.40	33,707.63	38,653.57	44,405.79	57,384.01	53,731.57	64,118.48
Gifts, average spending	1,036.24	445.44	703.82	935.74	1,068.46	1,785.08	1,521.99	2,270.91
FOOD	$82.18	$33.26	$41.70	$66.47	$70.25	$169.89	$135.45	$233.42
Cakes and cupcakes	2.41	0.26	1.20	1.42	8.11	3.65	2.45	5.84
Fresh fruit other than apples, bananas, and citrus	2.26	2.43	1.52	2.18	5.19	2.12	1.98	2.37
Candy and chewing gum	11.69	8.75	10.99	9.93	13.88	14.38	13.19	16.54
Board (including at school)	21.90	1.09	7.95	23.96	7.98	52.42	50.45	56.06
Catered affairs	26.19	8.34	8.50	12.79	15.71	70.07	40.65	124.38
ALCOHOLIC BEVERAGES	13.42	8.45	9.31	13.32	15.78	19.38	19.82	18.58
Beer and ale	4.73	4.69	4.44	5.89	4.11	4.42	4.22	4.78
Wine	5.84	3.43	4.33	3.63	5.96	10.05	10.15	9.85
HOUSING	258.69	115.08	177.08	231.05	331.73	420.19	383.12	488.54
Housekeeping supplies	42.48	17.15	33.47	43.46	58.82	58.21	52.42	68.76
Laundry and cleaning supplies	2.93	1.49	3.21	3.97	3.47	2.43	3.01	1.37
Other household products	11.69	4.62	10.33	9.88	16.90	16.17	13.14	21.68
Miscellaneous household products	5.85	2.91	5.57	6.00	9.84	6.23	5.92	6.79
Lawn and garden supplies	4.20	0.36	3.42	1.93	5.26	8.13	5.46	12.97
Postage and stationery	27.86	11.05	19.92	29.61	38.45	39.61	36.26	45.71
Stationery, stationery supplies, giftwrap	21.13	7.83	16.94	20.53	26.10	30.73	29.44	33.06
Postage	6.14	2.57	2.65	8.59	11.79	7.99	6.39	10.89
Household textiles	13.72	3.81	13.14	9.54	18.29	20.77	23.30	16.20
Bathroom linens	2.59	2.21	2.66	1.29	5.63	2.70	1.44	5.00
Bedroom linens	6.10	0.14	7.62	5.35	5.37	8.18	9.52	5.74
Appliances and miscellaneous housewares	23.98	11.11	12.77	23.47	49.69	34.54	31.11	40.80
Major appliances	8.41	0.74	3.56	9.35	20.45	12.86	8.23	21.28
Small appliances and miscellaneous housewares	15.57	10.37	9.21	14.12	29.24	21.68	22.87	19.52
China and other dinnerware	2.46	0.60	0.61	3.75	0.23	5.03	5.84	3.55
Nonelectric cookware	3.53	4.12	2.46	0.86	14.59	2.88	2.74	3.13
Tableware, nonelectric kitchenware	2.63	0.70	2.26	2.55	3.97	3.59	3.38	3.97
Small electric kitchen appliances	2.71	2.30	2.13	3.23	2.69	3.18	2.98	3.56
Miscellaneous household equipment	64.70	30.44	46.12	49.41	91.93	104.36	99.32	113.71
Infants' equipment	3.82	3.23	2.03	1.17	8.52	6.37	8.36	2.74
Outdoor equipment	2.07	0.32	2.73	2.47	0.95	2.30	2.89	1.24
Other household decorative items	25.76	11.98	18.71	20.56	37.96	39.53	36.29	45.42
Power tools	2.80	–	0.22	1.19	3.79	7.59	9.34	4.41
Indoor plants, fresh flowers	13.43	5.92	10.76	13.61	13.40	20.55	18.51	24.31
Computers and computer hardware	6.59	1.93	5.01	4.81	8.85	11.63	6.13	21.79
Miscellaneous household equipment	2.19	0.69	1.71	0.80	6.25	3.14	4.12	1.35
Other housing	113.80	52.56	71.59	105.18	113.00	202.31	176.98	249.07
Repair or maintenance services	4.51	0.58	3.39	6.39	18.71	1.51	1.90	0.79
Housing while attending school	39.93	3.45	12.92	33.12	24.58	101.28	81.74	137.37
Natural gas (renter)	3.62	4.30	5.11	2.52	4.12	2.29	2.88	1.18
Electricity (renter)	14.67	20.28	18.38	12.73	13.13	9.46	11.81	5.13
Water, sewer maintenance (renter)	3.04	4.90	3.26	2.74	2.32	2.20	2.81	1.08
Day-care centers, nurseries, and preschools	23.81	4.96	8.18	28.38	23.38	48.29	44.61	55.07

	total consumer units	less than high school graduate	high school graduate	some college	associate's degree	college graduate total	bachelor's degree	master's, professional, doctorate
APPAREL AND SERVICES	**$237.13**	**$132.31**	**$192.49**	**$223.11**	**$228.26**	**$350.38**	**$360.36**	**$332.45**
Men and boys, aged 2 or older	**63.74**	**29.84**	**51.75**	**63.73**	**81.94**	**87.11**	**82.70**	**95.24**
Men's coats and jackets	5.09	–	2.44	2.18	18.98	8.08	4.63	14.34
Men's accessories	4.45	0.55	2.82	7.49	3.44	6.16	7.29	4.09
Men's sweaters and vests	3.06	1.35	2.56	2.77	3.39	4.70	4.15	5.74
Men's active sportswear	2.76	4.59	2.67	0.95	4.24	2.80	2.21	3.86
Men's shirts	16.79	4.93	9.16	19.03	17.94	28.37	30.02	25.37
Men's pants	6.93	1.31	8.06	6.85	5.52	8.98	9.41	8.19
Boys' shirts	3.71	2.73	4.66	4.82	3.13	2.62	2.50	2.86
Boys' pants	3.76	2.64	5.09	2.70	6.16	2.94	2.64	3.49
Women and girls, aged 2 or older	**81.76**	**40.62**	**69.42**	**73.19**	**75.88**	**122.19**	**134.37**	**100.03**
Women's coats and jackets	5.62	1.08	5.14	11.39	7.66	3.65	4.13	2.77
Women's dresses	7.66	1.38	8.07	4.07	5.14	13.54	20.31	1.21
Women's vests and sweaters	8.50	2.53	4.79	10.76	7.00	14.03	13.81	14.44
Women's shirts, tops, blouses	9.06	4.02	9.67	7.61	12.98	10.68	8.60	14.49
Women's pants	6.62	0.56	5.22	7.19	4.61	11.17	13.32	7.25
Women's active sportswear	4.33	0.86	4.27	2.04	2.30	8.29	9.99	5.19
Women's sleepwear	6.45	1.14	5.54	3.56	6.61	11.89	15.61	5.13
Women's accessories	5.71	7.31	3.36	2.01	2.87	10.78	10.32	11.63
Girls' dresses and suits	2.98	9.27	1.58	2.33	3.45	1.69	1.28	2.42
Girls' shirts, blouses, sweaters	4.48	3.52	4.00	6.10	3.95	4.45	3.71	5.79
Girls' skirts and pants	3.32	2.03	4.01	3.03	3.41	3.52	3.22	4.08
Girls' accessories	2.38	0.61	0.40	1.19	1.34	6.40	6.49	6.24
Children under age 2	**39.99**	**37.72**	**37.43**	**35.27**	**36.89**	**48.53**	**50.46**	**45.10**
Infant dresses, outerwear	15.28	10.46	14.93	16.88	15.11	17.24	15.62	20.22
Infant underwear	16.91	22.84	15.31	12.72	17.43	18.48	21.05	13.79
Infant nightwear, loungewear	2.55	1.34	2.47	2.28	2.40	3.61	2.62	5.44
Infant accessories	3.93	2.42	3.03	2.36	0.78	7.62	9.54	4.12
Other apparel products and services	**51.63**	**24.12**	**33.89**	**50.92**	**33.55**	**92.55**	**92.84**	**92.09**
Jewelry and watches	24.01	6.16	13.96	18.23	11.93	54.14	52.31	57.51
Watches	2.16	0.99	1.86	1.78	2.18	3.46	3.84	2.75
Jewelry	21.85	5.18	12.10	16.45	9.76	50.68	48.47	54.76
Men's footwear	8.37	10.14	7.97	5.94	10.88	8.88	8.46	9.64
Boys' footwear	4.46	1.41	1.69	10.47	3.10	4.96	7.05	1.16
Women's footwear	8.82	2.56	7.48	9.32	4.55	14.14	13.85	14.65
Girls' footwear	3.30	3.07	1.74	4.06	0.54	5.31	5.57	4.83
TRANSPORTATION	**43.87**	**17.94**	**38.48**	**62.99**	**65.96**	**41.84**	**39.41**	**46.30**
Used cars	12.21	–	19.05	7.68	45.71	3.63	5.59	–
Airline fares	6.78	3.19	4.31	5.20	7.22	12.64	10.75	16.12
Ship fares	2.74	1.48	1.39	2.27	3.66	5.00	4.01	6.84
HEALTH CARE	**32.59**	**18.31**	**20.10**	**28.94**	**34.56**	**55.54**	**29.35**	**103.67**
Physician's services	3.07	0.50	1.88	1.90	2.22	7.06	3.05	14.48
Dental services	4.03	2.00	1.67	4.57	10.86	4.95	3.70	7.26
Care in convalescent or nursing home	5.19	0.12	7.48	1.35	9.69	7.09	–	20.18
Nonprescription vitamins	3.93	1.24	0.55	2.27	0.78	10.77	2.22	26.33
Prescription drugs	2.38	0.64	3.08	1.86	2.28	3.08	3.13	3.00
ENTERTAINMENT	**78.24**	**38.09**	**71.37**	**75.28**	**81.18**	**108.57**	**101.42**	**121.80**
Toys, games, hobbies, and tricycles	29.98	18.40	33.68	28.86	33.37	32.39	28.58	39.44
Other entertainment	48.26	19.69	37.69	46.42	47.81	76.18	72.84	82.36
Fees for recreational lessons	7.88	1.74	2.85	7.69	10.01	16.32	11.78	24.70
Community antenna or cable TV	6.37	7.17	7.40	6.44	6.21	4.79	5.92	2.71

	total consumer units	less than high school graduate	high school graduate	some college	associate's degree	college graduate		
						total	bachelor's degree	master's, professional, doctorate
VCRs and videodisc players	$2.26	$0.32	$1.68	$1.53	$2.60	$4.49	$4.53	$4.42
Video game hardware and software	2.13	1.10	1.74	2.53	2.88	2.57	2.49	2.71
Athletic gear, game tables, exercise equipment	6.60	3.12	6.28	3.50	1.55	12.30	16.56	4.55
Hunting and fishing equipment	3.06	0.54	2.26	4.90	7.28	2.54	2.82	2.04
Photographer fees	3.19	1.06	0.70	3.29	3.64	6.91	6.32	8.01
PERSONAL CARE PRODUCTS AND SERVICES	**21.15**	**13.73**	**15.91**	**31.03**	**17.72**	**24.18**	**22.97**	**26.39**
Cosmetics, perfume, bath preparation	12.53	7.53	7.47	20.26	9.22	15.70	15.18	16.64
Electric personal care appliances	3.31	2.72	5.17	3.48	2.51	1.82	2.43	0.73
EDUCATION	**183.88**	**20.26**	**75.12**	**125.14**	**150.46**	**454.53**	**326.12**	**691.64**
College tuition	127.83	10.41	48.07	89.03	76.56	331.44	213.47	549.27
Elementary and high school tuition	25.95	1.30	6.06	12.98	34.59	69.06	68.44	70.20
Other school tuition	4.44	2.37	3.10	1.44	15.17	5.68	4.10	8.61
Other school expenses including rentals	3.99	0.81	2.37	2.15	4.33	8.92	7.11	12.24
College books and supplies	11.93	0.77	4.87	13.53	10.02	25.48	19.74	36.08
Miscellaneous school supplies	7.38	2.83	8.30	4.63	5.98	10.97	10.75	11.38
ALL OTHER GIFTS	**83.76**	**47.55**	**61.34**	**77.23**	**71.08**	**138.19**	**101.82**	**205.33**
Gifts of trip expenses	44.40	16.71	22.40	49.42	40.04	81.93	66.80	109.87
Lotteries and gambling losses	2.86	0.14	7.96	1.01	0.55	0.97	1.09	0.74
Legal fees	5.82	–	2.74	12.34	3.06	8.38	7.19	10.56
Funeral expenses	25.25	28.13	26.42	9.59	21.87	35.87	17.87	69.11
Miscellaneous personal services	2.16	–	0.21	1.27	3.69	5.36	4.17	7.53

Note: (−) means sample is too small to make a reliable estimate. Expenditures for items in a given category may not add to category total because categories with annual spending of less than $2.00 for the average household are omitted. Spending on gifts is also included in the product and service categories in other chapters.
Source: Bureau of Labor Statistics, unpublished tables from the 2002 Consumer Expenditure Survey

Table 6.22 Gifts for Non–Household Members: Indexed spending by education, 2002

(indexed average annual spending of consumer units (CU) on selected gifts of products and services for non–household members by education of consumer unit reference person, 2002; index definition: an index of 100 is the average for all consumer units; an index of 132 means that spending by consumer units in that group is 32 percent above the average for all consumer units; an index of 68 indicates spending that is 32 percent below the average for all consumer units)

	total consumer units	less than high school graduate	high school graduate	some college	associate's degree	college graduate total	bachelor's degree	master's, professional, doctorate
Average spending of CU, total	$40,677	$24,930	$33,708	$38,654	$44,406	$57,384	$53,732	$64,118
Average spending of CU, index	100	61	83	95	109	141	132	158
Gifts, spending index	100	43	68	90	103	172	147	219
FOOD	**100**	**40**	**51**	**81**	**85**	**207**	**165**	**284**
Cakes and cupcakes	100	11	50	59	337	151	102	242
Fresh fruit other than apples, bananas, and citrus	100	108	67	96	230	94	88	105
Candy and chewing gum	100	75	94	85	119	123	113	141
Board (including at school)	100	5	36	109	36	239	230	256
Catered affairs	100	32	32	49	60	268	155	475
ALCOHOLIC BEVERAGES	**100**	**63**	**69**	**99**	**118**	**144**	**148**	**138**
Beer and ale	100	99	94	125	87	93	89	101
Wine	100	59	74	62	102	172	174	169
HOUSING	**100**	**44**	**68**	**89**	**128**	**162**	**148**	**189**
Housekeeping supplies	**100**	**40**	**79**	**102**	**138**	**137**	**123**	**162**
Laundry and cleaning supplies	100	51	110	135	118	83	103	47
Other household products	100	40	88	85	145	138	112	185
Miscellaneous household products	100	50	95	103	168	106	101	116
Lawn and garden supplies	100	9	81	46	125	194	130	309
Postage and stationery	100	40	72	106	138	142	130	164
Stationery, stationery supplies, giftwrap	100	37	80	97	124	145	139	156
Postage	100	42	43	140	192	130	104	177
Household textiles	**100**	**28**	**96**	**70**	**133**	**151**	**170**	**118**
Bathroom linens	100	85	103	50	217	104	56	193
Bedroom linens	100	2	125	88	88	134	156	94
Appliances and miscellaneous housewares	**100**	**46**	**53**	**98**	**207**	**144**	**130**	**170**
Major appliances	100	9	42	111	243	153	98	253
Small appliances and miscellaneous housewares	100	67	59	91	188	139	147	125
China and other dinnerware	100	24	25	152	9	204	237	144
Nonelectric cookware	100	117	70	24	413	82	78	89
Tableware, nonelectric kitchenware	100	27	86	97	151	137	129	151
Small electric kitchen appliances	100	85	79	119	99	117	110	131
Miscellaneous household equipment	**100**	**47**	**71**	**76**	**142**	**161**	**154**	**176**
Infants' equipment	100	85	53	31	223	167	219	72
Outdoor equipment	100	15	132	119	46	111	140	60
Other household decorative items	100	47	73	80	147	153	141	176
Power tools	100	–	8	43	135	271	334	158
Indoor plants, fresh flowers	100	44	80	101	100	153	138	181
Computers and computer hardware	100	29	76	73	134	176	93	331
Miscellaneous household equipment	100	32	78	37	285	143	188	62
Other housing	**100**	**46**	**63**	**92**	**99**	**178**	**156**	**219**
Repair or maintenance services	100	13	75	142	415	33	42	18
Housing while attending school	100	9	32	83	62	254	205	344
Natural gas (renter)	100	119	141	70	114	63	80	33
Electricity (renter)	100	138	125	87	90	64	81	35
Water, sewer maintenance (renter)	100	161	107	90	76	72	92	36
Day-care centers, nurseries, and preschools	100	21	34	119	98	203	187	231

	total consumer units	less than high school graduate	high school graduate	some college	associate's degree	college graduate total	college graduate bachelor's degree	college graduate master's, professional, doctorate
APPAREL AND SERVICES	**100**	**56**	**81**	**94**	**96**	**148**	**152**	**140**
Men and boys, aged 2 or older	**100**	**47**	**81**	**100**	**129**	**137**	**130**	**149**
Men's coats and jackets	100	–	48	43	373	159	91	282
Men's accessories	100	12	63	168	77	138	164	92
Men's sweaters and vests	100	44	84	91	111	154	136	188
Men's active sportswear	100	166	97	34	154	101	80	140
Men's shirts	100	29	55	113	107	169	179	151
Men's pants	100	19	116	99	80	130	136	118
Boys' shirts	100	74	126	130	84	71	67	77
Boys' pants	100	70	135	72	164	78	70	93
Women and girls, aged 2 or older	**100**	**50**	**85**	**90**	**93**	**149**	**164**	**122**
Women's coats and jackets	100	19	91	203	136	65	73	49
Women's dresses	100	18	105	53	67	177	265	16
Women's vests and sweaters	100	30	56	127	82	165	162	170
Women's shirts, tops, blouses	100	44	107	84	143	118	95	160
Women's pants	100	8	79	109	70	169	201	110
Women's active sportswear	100	20	99	47	53	191	231	120
Women's sleepwear	100	18	86	55	102	184	242	80
Women's accessories	100	128	59	35	50	189	181	204
Girls' dresses and suits	100	311	53	78	116	57	43	81
Girls' shirts, blouses, sweaters	100	79	89	136	88	99	83	129
Girls' skirts and pants	100	61	121	91	103	106	97	123
Girls' accessories	100	26	17	50	56	269	273	262
Children under age 2	**100**	**94**	**94**	**88**	**92**	**121**	**126**	**113**
Infant dresses, outerwear	100	68	98	110	99	113	102	132
Infant underwear	100	135	91	75	103	109	124	82
Infant nightwear, loungewear	100	53	97	89	94	142	103	213
Infant accessories	100	62	77	60	20	194	243	105
Other apparel products and services	**100**	**47**	**66**	**99**	**65**	**179**	**180**	**178**
Jewelry and watches	100	26	58	76	50	225	218	240
Watches	100	46	86	82	101	160	178	127
Jewelry	100	24	55	75	45	232	222	251
Men's footwear	100	121	95	71	130	106	101	115
Boys' footwear	100	32	38	235	70	111	158	26
Women's footwear	100	29	85	106	52	160	157	166
Girls' footwear	100	93	53	123	16	161	169	146
TRANSPORTATION	**100**	**41**	**88**	**144**	**150**	**95**	**90**	**106**
Used cars	100	–	156	63	374	30	46	–
Airline fares	100	47	64	77	106	186	159	238
Ship fares	100	54	51	83	134	182	146	250
HEALTH CARE	**100**	**56**	**62**	**89**	**106**	**170**	**90**	**318**
Physician's services	100	16	61	62	72	230	99	472
Dental services	100	50	41	113	269	123	92	180
Care in convalescent or nursing home	100	2	144	26	187	137	–	389
Nonprescription vitamins	100	32	14	58	20	274	56	670
Prescription drugs	100	27	129	78	96	129	132	126
ENTERTAINMENT	**100**	**49**	**91**	**96**	**104**	**139**	**130**	**156**
Toys, games, hobbies, and tricycles	100	61	112	96	111	108	95	132
Other entertainment	100	41	78	96	99	158	151	171
Fees for recreational lessons	100	22	36	98	127	207	149	313
Community antenna or cable TV	100	113	116	101	97	75	93	43

	total consumer units	less than high school graduate	high school graduate	some college	associate's degree	college graduate total	bachelor's degree	master's, professional, doctorate
VCRs and videodisc players	100	14	74	68	115	199	200	196
Video game hardware and software	100	52	82	119	135	121	117	127
Athletic gear, game tables, exercise equipment	100	47	95	53	23	186	251	69
Hunting and fishing equipment	100	18	74	160	238	83	92	67
Photographer fees	100	33	22	103	114	217	198	251
PERSONAL CARE PRODUCTS AND SERVICES	**100**	**65**	**75**	**147**	**84**	**114**	**109**	**125**
Cosmetics, perfume, bath preparation	100	60	60	162	74	125	121	133
Electric personal care appliances	100	82	156	105	76	55	73	22
EDUCATION	**100**	**11**	**41**	**68**	**82**	**247**	**177**	**376**
College tuition	100	8	38	70	60	259	167	430
Elementary and high school tuition	100	5	23	50	133	266	264	271
Other school tuition	100	53	70	32	342	128	92	194
Other school expenses including rentals	100	20	59	54	109	224	178	307
College books and supplies	100	6	41	113	84	214	165	302
Miscellaneous school supplies	100	38	112	63	81	149	146	154
ALL OTHER GIFTS	**100**	**57**	**73**	**92**	**85**	**165**	**122**	**245**
Gifts of trip expenses	100	38	50	111	90	185	150	247
Lotteries and gambling losses	100	5	278	35	19	34	38	26
Legal fees	100	–	47	212	53	144	124	181
Funeral expenses	100	111	105	38	87	142	71	274
Miscellaneous personal services	100	–	10	59	171	248	193	349

Note: (–) means sample is too small to make a reliable estimate. Categories with annual spending of less than $2.00 for the average household are omitted. Spending on gifts is also included in the product and service categories in other chapters.
Source: Calculations by New Strategist based on the 2002 Consumer Expenditure Survey

Table 6.23 Gifts for Non–Household Members: Total spending by education, 2002

(total annual spending on selected gifts of products and services for non–household members by consumer unit (CU) educational attainment group, 2002; numbers in thousands)

	total consumer units	less than high school graduate	high school graduate	some college	associate's degree	college graduate total	bachelor's degree	master's, professional, doctorate
Number of consumer units	112,108	17,075	31,961	23,260	10,395	29,417	19,082	10,335
Total spending of all CUs	$4,560,172,273	$425,686,580	$1,077,329,562	$899,082,038	$461,598,187	$1,688,065,422	$1,025,305,819	$662,664,491
Gifts, total spending	116,170,794	7,605,888	22,494,791	21,765,312	11,106,642	52,511,698	29,042,613	23,469,855
FOOD	**$9,213,035**	**$567,915**	**$1,332,774**	**$1,546,092**	**$730,249**	**$4,997,654**	**$2,584,657**	**$2,412,396**
Cakes and cupcakes	270,180	4,440	38,353	33,029	84,303	107,372	46,751	60,356
Fresh fruit other than apples, bananas, and citrus	253,364	41,492	48,581	50,707	53,950	62,364	37,782	24,494
Candy and chewing gum	1,310,543	149,406	351,251	230,972	144,283	423,016	251,692	170,941
Board (including at school)	2,455,165	18,612	254,090	557,310	82,952	1,542,039	962,687	579,380
Catered affairs	2,936,109	142,406	271,669	297,495	163,305	2,061,249	775,683	1,285,467
ALCOHOLIC BEVERAGES	**1,504,489**	**144,284**	**297,557**	**309,823**	**164,033**	**570,101**	**378,205**	**192,024**
Beer and ale	530,271	80,082	141,907	137,001	42,723	130,023	80,526	49,401
Wine	654,711	58,567	138,391	84,434	61,954	295,641	193,682	101,800
HOUSING	**29,001,219**	**1,964,991**	**5,659,654**	**5,374,223**	**3,448,333**	**12,360,729**	**7,310,696**	**5,049,061**
Housekeeping supplies	**4,762,348**	**292,836**	**1,069,735**	**1,010,880**	**611,434**	**1,712,364**	**1,000,278**	**710,635**
Laundry and cleaning supplies	328,476	25,442	102,595	92,342	36,071	71,483	57,437	14,159
Other household products	1,310,543	78,887	330,157	229,809	175,676	475,673	250,737	224,063
Miscellaneous household products	655,832	49,688	178,023	139,560	102,287	183,268	112,965	70,175
Lawn and garden supplies	470,854	6,147	109,307	44,892	54,678	239,160	104,188	134,045
Postage and stationery	3,123,329	188,679	636,663	688,729	399,688	1,165,207	691,913	472,413
Stationery, stationery supplies, giftwrap	2,368,842	133,697	541,419	477,528	271,310	903,984	561,774	341,675
Postage	688,343	43,883	84,697	199,803	122,557	235,042	121,934	112,548
Household textiles	**1,538,122**	**65,056**	**419,968**	**221,900**	**190,125**	**610,991**	**444,611**	**167,427**
Bathroom linens	290,360	37,736	85,016	30,005	58,524	79,426	27,478	51,675
Bedroom linens	683,859	2,391	243,543	124,441	55,821	240,631	181,661	59,323
Appliances and miscellaneous housewares	**2,688,350**	**189,703**	**408,142**	**545,912**	**516,528**	**1,016,063**	**593,641**	**421,668**
Major appliances	942,828	12,636	113,781	217,481	212,578	378,303	157,045	219,929
Small appliances and misc. housewares	1,745,522	177,068	294,361	328,431	303,950	637,761	436,405	201,739
China and other dinnerware	275,786	10,245	19,496	87,225	2,391	147,968	111,439	36,689
Nonelectric cookware	395,741	70,349	78,624	20,004	151,663	84,721	52,285	32,349
Tableware, nonelectric kitchenware	294,844	11,953	72,232	59,313	41,268	105,607	64,497	41,030
Small electric kitchen appliances	303,813	39,273	68,077	75,130	27,963	93,546	56,864	36,793
Miscellaneous household equipment	**7,253,388**	**519,763**	**1,474,041**	**1,149,277**	**955,612**	**3,069,958**	**1,895,224**	**1,175,193**
Infants' equipment	428,253	55,152	64,881	27,214	88,565	187,386	159,526	28,318
Outdoor equipment	232,064	5,464	87,254	57,452	9,875	67,659	55,147	12,815
Other household decorative items	2,887,902	204,559	597,990	478,226	394,594	1,162,854	692,486	469,416
Power tools	313,902	–	7,031	27,679	39,397	223,275	178,226	45,577
Indoor plants, fresh flowers	1,505,610	101,084	343,900	316,569	139,293	604,519	353,208	251,244
Computers and computer hardware	738,792	32,955	160,125	111,881	91,996	342,120	116,973	225,200
Miscellaneous household equipment	245,517	11,782	54,653	18,608	64,969	92,369	78,618	13,952
Other housing	**12,757,890**	**897,462**	**2,288,088**	**2,446,487**	**1,174,635**	**5,951,353**	**3,377,132**	**2,574,138**
Repair or maintenance services	505,607	9,904	108,348	148,631	194,490	44,420	36,256	8,165
Housing while attending school	4,476,472	58,909	412,936	770,371	255,509	2,979,354	1,559,763	1,419,719
Natural gas (renter)	405,831	73,423	163,321	58,615	42,827	67,365	54,956	12,195
Electricity (renter)	1,644,624	346,281	587,443	296,100	136,486	278,285	225,358	53,019
Water, sewer maintenance (renter)	340,808	83,668	104,193	63,732	24,116	64,717	53,620	11,162
Day-care centers, nurseries, and preschools	2,669,291	84,692	261,441	660,119	243,035	1,420,547	851,248	569,148

	total consumer units	less than high school graduate	high school graduate	some college	associate's degree	college graduate total	college graduate bachelor's degree	college graduate master's, professional, doctorate
APPAREL AND SERVICES	$26,584,170	$2,259,193	$6,152,173	$5,189,539	$2,372,763	$10,307,128	$6,876,390	$3,435,871
Men and boys, aged 2 or older	7,145,764	509,518	1,653,982	1,482,360	851,766	2,562,515	1,578,081	984,305
Men's coats and jackets	570,630	–	77,985	50,707	197,297	237,689	88,350	148,204
Men's accessories	498,881	9,391	90,130	174,217	35,759	181,209	139,108	42,270
Men's sweaters and vests	343,050	23,051	81,820	64,430	35,239	138,260	79,190	59,323
Men's active sportswear	309,418	78,374	85,336	22,097	44,075	82,368	42,171	39,893
Men's shirts	1,882,293	84,180	292,763	442,638	186,486	834,560	572,842	262,199
Men's pants	776,908	22,368	257,606	159,331	57,380	264,165	179,562	84,644
Boys' shirts	415,921	46,615	148,938	112,113	32,536	77,073	47,705	29,558
Boys' pants	421,526	45,078	162,681	62,802	64,033	86,486	50,376	36,069
Women and girls, aged 2 or older	9,165,950	693,587	2,218,733	1,702,399	788,773	3,594,463	2,564,048	1,033,810
Women's coats and jackets	630,047	18,441	164,280	264,931	79,626	107,372	78,809	28,628
Women's dresses	858,747	23,564	257,925	94,668	53,430	398,306	387,555	12,505
Women's vests and sweaters	952,918	43,200	153,093	250,278	72,765	412,721	263,522	149,237
Women's shirts, tops, blouses	1,015,698	68,642	309,063	177,009	134,927	314,174	164,105	149,754
Women's pants	742,155	9,562	166,836	167,239	47,921	328,588	254,172	74,929
Women's active sportswear	485,428	14,685	136,473	47,450	23,909	243,867	190,629	53,639
Women's sleepwear	723,097	19,466	177,064	82,806	68,711	349,768	297,870	53,019
Women's accessories	640,137	124,818	107,389	46,753	29,834	317,115	196,926	120,196
Girls' dresses and suits	334,082	158,285	50,498	54,196	35,863	49,715	24,425	25,011
Girls' shirts, blouses, sweaters	502,244	60,104	127,844	141,886	41,060	130,906	70,794	59,840
Girls' skirts and pants	372,199	34,662	128,164	70,478	35,447	103,548	61,444	42,167
Girls' accessories	266,817	10,416	12,784	27,679	13,929	188,269	123,842	64,490
Children under age 2	4,483,199	644,069	1,196,300	820,380	383,472	1,427,607	962,878	466,109
Infant dresses, outerwear	1,713,010	178,605	477,178	392,629	157,068	507,149	298,061	208,974
Infant underwear	1,895,746	389,993	489,323	295,867	181,185	543,626	401,676	142,520
Infant nightwear, loungewear	285,875	22,881	78,944	53,033	24,948	106,195	49,995	56,222
Infant accessories	440,584	41,322	96,842	54,894	8,108	224,158	182,042	42,580
Other apparel products and services	5,788,136	411,849	1,083,158	1,184,399	348,752	2,722,543	1,771,573	951,750
Jewelry and watches	2,691,713	105,182	446,176	424,030	124,012	1,592,636	998,179	594,366
Watches	242,153	16,904	59,447	41,403	22,661	101,783	73,275	28,421
Jewelry	2,449,560	88,449	386,728	382,627	101,455	1,490,854	924,905	565,945
Men's footwear	938,344	173,141	254,729	138,164	113,098	261,223	161,434	99,629
Boys' footwear	500,002	24,076	54,014	243,532	32,225	145,908	134,528	11,989
Women's footwear	988,793	43,712	239,068	216,783	47,297	415,956	264,286	151,408
Girls' footwear	369,956	52,420	55,612	94,436	5,613	156,204	106,287	49,918
TRANSPORTATION	4,918,178	306,326	1,229,859	1,465,147	685,654	1,230,807	752,022	478,511
Used cars	1,368,839	–	608,857	178,637	475,155	106,784	106,668	–
Airline fares	760,092	54,469	137,752	120,952	75,052	371,831	205,132	166,600
Ship fares	307,176	25,271	44,426	52,800	38,046	147,085	76,519	70,691
HEALTH CARE	3,653,600	312,643	642,416	673,144	359,251	1,633,820	560,057	1,071,429
Physician's services	344,172	8,538	60,087	44,194	23,077	207,684	58,200	149,651
Dental services	451,795	34,150	53,375	106,298	112,890	145,614	70,603	75,032
Care in convalescent or nursing home	581,841	2,049	239,068	31,401	100,728	208,567	–	208,560
Nonprescription vitamins	440,584	21,173	17,579	52,800	8,108	316,821	42,362	272,121
Prescription drugs	266,817	10,928	98,440	43,264	23,701	90,604	59,727	31,005
ENTERTAINMENT	8,771,330	650,387	2,281,057	1,751,013	843,866	3,193,804	1,935,296	1,258,803
Toys, games, hobbies, and tricycles	3,360,998	314,180	1,076,446	671,284	346,881	952,817	545,364	407,612
Other entertainment	5,410,332	336,207	1,204,610	1,079,729	496,985	2,240,987	1,389,933	851,191
Fees for recreational lessons	883,411	29,711	91,089	178,869	104,054	480,085	224,786	255,275
Community antenna or cable TV	714,128	122,428	236,511	149,794	64,553	140,907	112,965	28,008

	total consumer units	less than high school graduate	high school graduate	some college	associate's degree	college graduate total	bachelor's degree	master's, professional, doctorate
VCRs and videodisc players	$253,364	$5,464	$53,694	$35,588	$27,027	$132,082	$86,441	$45,681
Video game hardware and software	238,790	18,783	55,612	58,848	29,938	75,602	47,514	28,008
Athletic gear, game tables, exercise equipment	739,913	53,274	200,715	81,410	16,112	361,829	315,998	47,024
Hunting and fishing equipment	343,050	9,221	72,232	113,974	75,676	74,719	53,811	21,083
Photographer fees	357,625	18,100	22,373	76,525	37,838	203,271	120,598	82,783
PERSONAL CARE PRODUCTS AND SERVICES	**2,371,084**	**234,440**	**508,500**	**721,758**	**184,199**	**711,303**	**438,314**	**272,741**
Cosmetics, perfume, bath preparation	1,404,713	128,575	238,749	471,248	95,842	461,847	289,665	171,974
Electric personal care appliances	371,077	46,444	165,238	80,945	26,091	53,539	46,369	7,545
EDUCATION	**20,614,419**	**345,940**	**2,400,910**	**2,910,756**	**1,564,032**	**13,370,909**	**6,223,022**	**7,148,099**
College tuition	14,330,766	177,751	1,536,365	2,070,838	795,841	9,749,970	4,073,435	5,676,705
Elementary and high school tuition	2,909,203	22,198	193,684	301,915	359,563	2,031,538	1,305,972	725,517
Other school tuition	497,760	40,468	99,079	33,494	157,692	167,089	78,236	88,984
Other school expenses including rentals	447,311	13,831	75,748	50,009	45,010	262,400	135,673	126,500
College books and supplies	1,337,448	13,148	155,650	314,708	104,158	749,545	376,679	372,887
Miscellaneous school supplies	827,357	48,322	265,276	107,694	62,162	322,704	205,132	117,612
ALL OTHER GIFTS	**9,390,166**	**811,916**	**1,960,488**	**1,796,370**	**738,877**	**4,065,135**	**1,942,929**	**2,122,086**
Gifts of trip expenses	4,977,595	285,323	715,926	1,149,509	416,216	2,410,135	1,274,678	1,135,506
Lotteries and gambling losses	320,629	2,391	254,410	23,493	5,717	28,534	20,799	7,648
Legal fees	652,469	–	87,573	287,028	31,809	246,514	137,200	109,138
Funeral expenses	2,830,727	480,320	844,410	223,063	227,339	1,055,188	340,995	714,252
Miscellaneous personal services	242,153	–	6,712	29,540	38,358	157,675	79,572	77,823

Note: Numbers may not add to total because of rounding. (–) means sample is too small to make a reliable estimate. Expenditures for items in a given category may not add to category total because categories with annual spending of less than $2.00 for the average household are omitted. Spending on gifts is also included in the product and service categories in other chapters.
Source: Calculations by New Strategist based on the 2002 Consumer Expenditure Survey

Table 6.24 Gifts for Non—Household Members: Market shares by education, 2002

(percentage of total annual spending on selected gifts of products and services for non–household members accounted for by consumer unit educational attainment groups, 2002)

	total consumer units	less than high school graduate	high school graduate	some college	associate's degree	college graduate total	college graduate bachelor's degree	college graduate master's, professional, doctorate
Share of total consumer units	100.0%	15.2%	28.5%	20.7%	9.3%	26.2%	17.0%	9.2%
Share of total before-tax income	100.0	7.9	22.8	17.9	10.3	41.3	23.9	17.3
Share of total spending	100.0	9.3	23.6	19.7	10.1	37.0	22.5	14.5
Share of gifts spending	100.0	6.5	19.4	18.7	9.6	45.2	25.0	20.2
FOOD	100.0%	6.2%	14.5%	16.8%	7.9%	54.2%	28.1%	26.2%
Cakes and cupcakes	100.0	1.6	14.2	12.2	31.2	39.7	17.3	22.3
Fresh fruit other than apples, bananas, and citrus	100.0	16.4	19.2	20.0	21.3	24.6	14.9	9.7
Candy and chewing gum	100.0	11.4	26.8	17.6	11.0	32.3	19.2	13.0
Board (including at school)	100.0	0.8	10.3	22.7	3.4	62.8	39.2	23.6
Catered affairs	100.0	4.9	9.3	10.1	5.6	70.2	26.4	43.8
ALCOHOLIC BEVERAGES	100.0	9.6	19.8	20.6	10.9	37.9	25.1	12.8
Beer and ale	100.0	15.1	26.8	25.8	8.1	24.5	15.2	9.3
Wine	100.0	8.9	21.1	12.9	9.5	45.2	29.6	15.5
HOUSING	100.0	6.8	19.5	18.5	11.9	42.6	25.2	17.4
Housekeeping supplies	100.0	6.1	22.5	21.2	12.8	36.0	21.0	14.9
Laundry and cleaning supplies	100.0	7.7	31.2	28.1	11.0	21.8	17.5	4.3
Other household products	100.0	6.0	25.2	17.5	13.4	36.3	19.1	17.1
Miscellaneous household products	100.0	7.6	27.1	21.3	15.6	27.9	17.2	10.7
Lawn and garden supplies	100.0	1.3	23.2	9.5	11.6	50.8	22.1	28.5
Postage and stationery	100.0	6.0	20.4	22.1	12.8	37.3	22.2	15.1
Stationery, stationery supplies, giftwrap	100.0	5.6	22.9	20.2	11.5	38.2	23.7	14.4
Postage	100.0	6.4	12.3	29.0	17.8	34.1	17.7	16.4
Household textiles	100.0	4.2	27.3	14.4	12.4	39.7	28.9	10.9
Bathroom linens	100.0	13.0	29.3	10.3	20.2	27.4	9.5	17.8
Bedroom linens	100.0	0.3	35.6	18.2	8.2	35.2	26.6	8.7
Appliances and miscellaneous housewares	100.0	7.1	15.2	20.3	19.2	37.8	22.1	15.7
Major appliances	100.0	1.3	12.1	23.1	22.5	40.1	16.7	23.3
Small appliances and miscellaneous housewares	100.0	10.1	16.9	18.8	17.4	36.5	25.0	11.6
China and other dinnerware	100.0	3.7	7.1	31.6	0.9	53.7	40.4	13.3
Nonelectric cookware	100.0	17.8	19.9	5.1	38.3	21.4	13.2	8.2
Tableware, nonelectric kitchenware	100.0	4.1	24.5	20.1	14.0	35.8	21.9	13.9
Small electric kitchen appliances	100.0	12.9	22.4	24.7	9.2	30.8	18.7	12.1
Miscellaneous household equipment	100.0	7.2	20.3	15.8	13.2	42.3	26.1	16.2
Infants' equipment	100.0	12.9	15.2	6.4	20.7	43.8	37.3	6.6
Outdoor equipment	100.0	2.4	37.6	24.8	4.3	29.2	23.8	5.5
Other household decorative items	100.0	7.1	20.7	16.6	13.7	40.3	24.0	16.3
Power tools	100.0	–	2.2	8.8	12.6	71.1	56.8	14.5
Indoor plants, fresh flowers	100.0	6.7	22.8	21.0	9.3	40.2	23.5	16.7
Computers and computer hardware	100.0	4.5	21.7	15.1	12.5	46.3	15.8	30.5
Miscellaneous household equipment	100.0	4.8	22.3	7.6	26.5	37.6	32.0	5.7
Other housing	100.0	7.0	17.9	19.2	9.2	46.6	26.5	20.2
Repair or maintenance services	100.0	2.0	21.4	29.4	38.5	8.8	7.2	1.6
Housing while attending school	100.0	1.3	9.2	17.2	5.7	66.6	34.8	31.7
Natural gas (renter)	100.0	18.1	40.2	14.4	10.6	16.6	13.5	3.0
Electricity (renter)	100.0	21.1	35.7	18.0	8.3	16.9	13.7	3.2
Water, sewer maintenance (renter)	100.0	24.5	30.6	18.7	7.1	19.0	15.7	3.3
Day-care centers, nurseries, and preschools	100.0	3.2	9.8	24.7	9.1	53.2	31.9	21.3

	total consumer units	less than high school graduate	high school graduate	some college	associate's degree	college graduate total	bachelor's degree	master's, professional, doctorate
APPAREL AND SERVICES	100.0%	8.5%	23.1%	19.5%	8.9%	38.8%	25.9%	12.9%
Men and boys, aged 2 or older	100.0	7.1	23.1	20.7	11.9	35.9	22.1	13.8
Men's coats and jackets	100.0	–	13.7	8.9	34.6	41.7	15.5	26.0
Men's accessories	100.0	1.9	18.1	34.9	7.2	36.3	27.9	8.5
Men's sweaters and vests	100.0	6.7	23.9	18.8	10.3	40.3	23.1	17.3
Men's active sportswear	100.0	25.3	27.6	7.1	14.2	26.6	13.6	12.9
Men's shirts	100.0	4.5	15.6	23.5	9.9	44.3	30.4	13.9
Men's pants	100.0	2.9	33.2	20.5	7.4	34.0	23.1	10.9
Boys' shirts	100.0	11.2	35.8	27.0	7.8	18.5	11.5	7.1
Boys' pants	100.0	10.7	38.6	14.9	15.2	20.5	12.0	8.6
Women and girls, aged 2 or older	100.0	7.6	24.2	18.6	8.6	39.2	28.0	11.3
Women's coats and jackets	100.0	2.9	26.1	42.0	12.6	17.0	12.5	4.5
Women's dresses	100.0	2.7	30.0	11.0	6.2	46.4	45.1	1.5
Women's vests and sweaters	100.0	4.5	16.1	26.3	7.6	43.3	27.7	15.7
Women's shirts, tops, blouses	100.0	6.8	30.4	17.4	13.3	30.9	16.2	14.7
Women's pants	100.0	1.3	22.5	22.5	6.5	44.3	34.2	10.1
Women's active sportswear	100.0	3.0	28.1	9.8	4.9	50.2	39.3	11.0
Women's sleepwear	100.0	2.7	24.5	11.5	9.5	48.4	41.2	7.3
Women's accessories	100.0	19.5	16.8	7.3	4.7	49.5	30.8	18.8
Girls' dresses and suits	100.0	47.4	15.1	16.2	10.7	14.9	7.3	7.5
Girls' shirts, blouses, sweaters	100.0	12.0	25.5	28.3	8.2	26.1	14.1	11.9
Girls' skirts and pants	100.0	9.3	34.4	18.9	9.5	27.8	16.5	11.3
Girls' accessories	100.0	3.9	4.8	10.4	5.2	70.6	46.4	24.2
Children under age 2	100.0	14.4	26.7	18.3	8.6	31.8	21.5	10.4
Infant dresses, outerwear	100.0	10.4	27.9	22.9	9.2	29.6	17.4	12.2
Infant underwear	100.0	20.6	25.8	15.6	9.6	28.7	21.2	7.5
Infant nightwear, loungewear	100.0	8.0	27.6	18.6	8.7	37.1	17.5	19.7
Infant accessories	100.0	9.4	22.0	12.5	1.8	50.9	41.3	9.7
Other apparel products and services	100.0	7.1	18.7	20.5	6.0	47.0	30.6	16.4
Jewelry and watches	100.0	3.9	16.6	15.8	4.6	59.2	37.1	22.1
Watches	100.0	7.0	24.5	17.1	9.4	42.0	30.3	11.7
Jewelry	100.0	3.6	15.8	15.6	4.1	60.9	37.8	23.1
Men's footwear	100.0	18.5	27.1	14.7	12.1	27.8	17.2	10.6
Boys' footwear	100.0	4.8	10.8	48.7	6.4	29.2	26.9	2.4
Women's footwear	100.0	4.4	24.2	21.9	4.8	42.1	26.7	15.3
Girls' footwear	100.0	14.2	15.0	25.5	1.5	42.2	28.7	13.5
TRANSPORTATION	100.0	6.2	25.0	29.8	13.9	25.0	15.3	9.7
Used cars	100.0	–	44.5	13.1	34.7	7.8	7.8	–
Airline fares	100.0	7.2	18.1	15.9	9.9	48.9	27.0	21.9
Ship fares	100.0	8.2	14.5	17.2	12.4	47.9	24.9	23.0
HEALTH CARE	100.0	8.6	17.6	18.4	9.8	44.7	15.3	29.3
Physician's services	100.0	2.5	17.5	12.8	6.7	60.3	16.9	43.5
Dental services	100.0	7.6	11.8	23.5	25.0	32.2	15.6	16.6
Care in convalescent or nursing home	100.0	0.4	41.1	5.4	17.3	35.8	–	35.8
Nonprescription vitamins	100.0	4.8	4.0	12.0	1.8	71.9	9.6	61.8
Prescription drugs	100.0	4.1	36.9	16.2	8.9	34.0	22.4	11.6
ENTERTAINMENT	100.0	7.4	26.0	20.0	9.6	36.4	22.1	14.4
Toys, games, hobbies, and tricycles	100.0	9.3	32.0	20.0	10.3	28.3	16.2	12.1
Other entertainment	100.0	6.2	22.3	20.0	9.2	41.4	25.7	15.7
Fees for recreational lessons	100.0	3.4	10.3	20.2	11.8	54.3	25.4	28.9
Community antenna or cable TV	100.0	17.1	33.1	21.0	9.0	19.7	15.8	3.9

	total consumer units	less than high school graduate	high school graduate	some college	associate's degree	college graduate		
						total	bachelor's degree	master's, professional, doctorate
VCRs and videodisc players	100.0%	2.2%	21.2%	14.0%	10.7%	52.1%	34.1%	18.0%
Video game hardware and software	100.0	7.9	23.3	24.6	12.5	31.7	19.9	11.7
Athletic gear, game tables, exercise equipment	100.0	7.2	27.1	11.0	2.2	48.9	42.7	6.4
Hunting and fishing equipment	100.0	2.7	21.1	33.2	22.1	21.8	15.7	6.1
Photographer fees	100.0	5.1	6.3	21.4	10.6	56.8	33.7	23.1
PERSONAL CARE PRODUCTS AND SERVICES	**100.0**	**9.9**	**21.4**	**30.4**	**7.8**	**30.0**	**18.5**	**11.5**
Cosmetics, perfume, bath preparation	100.0	9.2	17.0	33.5	6.8	32.9	20.6	12.2
Electric personal care appliances	100.0	12.5	44.5	21.8	7.0	14.4	12.5	2.0
EDUCATION	**100.0**	**1.7**	**11.6**	**14.1**	**7.6**	**64.9**	**30.2**	**34.7**
College tuition	100.0	1.2	10.7	14.5	5.6	68.0	28.4	39.6
Elementary and high school tuition	100.0	0.8	6.7	10.4	12.4	69.8	44.9	24.9
Other school tuition	100.0	8.1	19.9	6.7	31.7	33.6	15.7	17.9
Other school expenses including rentals	100.0	3.1	16.9	11.2	10.1	58.7	30.3	28.3
College books and supplies	100.0	1.0	11.6	23.5	7.8	56.0	28.2	27.9
Miscellaneous school supplies	100.0	5.8	32.1	13.0	7.5	39.0	24.8	14.2
ALL OTHER GIFTS	**100.0**	**8.6**	**20.9**	**19.1**	**7.9**	**43.3**	**20.7**	**22.6**
Gifts of trip expenses	100.0	5.7	14.4	23.1	8.4	48.4	25.6	22.8
Lotteries and gambling losses	100.0	0.7	79.3	7.3	1.8	8.9	6.5	2.4
Legal fees	100.0	–	13.4	44.0	4.9	37.8	21.0	16.7
Funeral expenses	100.0	17.0	29.8	7.9	8.0	37.3	12.0	25.2
Miscellaneous personal services	100.0	–	2.8	12.2	15.8	65.1	32.9	32.1

Note: Numbers may not add to total because of rounding. (–) means sample is too small to make a reliable estimate. Expenditures for items in a given category may not add to category total because categories with annual spending of less than $2.00 for the average household are omitted. Spending on gifts is also included in the product and service categories in other chapters.
Source: Calculations by New Strategist based on the 2002 Consumer Expenditure Survey

Spending on Health Care, 2002

American households spent 14 percent more on out-of-pocket health care costs in 2002 than in 1997, after adjusting for inflation. Out-of-pocket spending on health insurance rose 19 percent during those years, while drug spending was up 36 percent. Spending on medical services fell by 0.6 percent, however, as managed care limited services. Out-of-pocket health care costs absorbed 5.8 percent of the household budget in 2002, up from 5.3 percent in 1997.

Not surprisingly, out-of-pocket health care spending rises with age, and peaks among householders aged 65 or older at more than $3,500 in 2002. Householders aged 65 to 74 spend more than any other age group on out-of-pocket health insurance costs ($1,921 in 2002, despite Medicare coverage). Householders aged 75 or older spend the most out-of-pocket on prescription drugs ($883). Householders aged 55 to 64 spend the most on medical services ($863).

Out-of-pocket spending on health insurance is highest for the most affluent households, in large part because their households are the largest. In 2002, households with incomes of $70,000 or more spent $1,550 out-of-pocket on health insurance. Households with incomes between $20,000 and $29,999 spend the most out-of-pocket on prescription drugs—29 percent more than the average household. Many are elderly retirees.

Married couples without children at home, most of them older empty-nesters, spend the most out-of-pocket on health care, $3,614 in 2002—54 percent more than the average household. Married couples with children at home spend just 16 percent more than the average household on health care overall, but they spend 42 percent more than average on physician services.

Blacks and Hispanics spend far less than the average household on almost every health care category. Black households spent $1,339 out-of-pocket on health care in 2002 versus the $2,350 spent by the average household. Hispanics spent only slightly more than blacks, at $1,366.

Average household spending on health care is about the same regardless of region. But some regions spend more than others on specific health care categories. Households in the South spend 18 percent more than average on prescription drugs, while those in the West spend 22 percent less than average on this item. Average household spending on dental services is 30 percent above average in the West, and 16 percent below average in the South.

College graduates spend the most on out-of-pocket health insurance costs, an average of $2,914 in 2002—21 percent more than the average household. They spend 44 percent more than average on medical services. But householders with no more than a high school diploma spend more than college graduates on prescription drugs, in large part because they are older. Households headed by high school graduates spent an average of $405 out-of-pocket on prescription drugs in 2002, while households headed by college graduates spent $350.

Table 7.1 Health Care: Average spending by age, 2002

(average annual out-of-pocket spending of consumer units (CU) on health care, by age of consumer unit reference person, 2002)

	total consumer units	under 25	25 to 34	35 to 44	45 to 54	55 to 64	65 to 74	75+
Number of consumer units (in thousands, add 000)	112,108	8,737	18,988	24,394	22,691	15,314	11,216	10,767
Average number of persons per CU	2.5	1.9	2.9	3.2	2.7	2.1	1.9	1.5
Average before-tax income of CU	$49,430.00	$20,773.00	$49,133.00	$61,532.00	$64,974.00	$53,162.00	$35,118.00	$23,890.00
Average spending of CU, total	40,676.60	24,229.46	40,318.29	48,330.48	48,748.24	44,330.04	32,242.52	23,758.89
Health care, average spending	2,350.32	640.23	1,416.55	1,979.69	2,550.43	3,007.06	3,588.05	3,583.79
HEALTH INSURANCE	**$1,167.71**	**$284.87**	**$761.86**	**$1,022.89**	**$1,180.34**	**$1,356.19**	**$1,920.75**	**$1,848.81**
Commercial health insurance	217.53	71.55	186.02	263.07	269.41	303.33	163.75	113.02
Traditional fee-for-service health plan (not BCBS)	68.27	21.90	41.46	51.56	81.84	113.73	88.01	77.22
Preferred-provider health plan (not BCBS)	149.26	49.65	144.55	211.51	187.57	189.60	75.73	35.80
Blue Cross, Blue Shield	**315.67**	**82.12**	**221.46**	**316.45**	**372.19**	**420.17**	**359.40**	**356.27**
Traditional fee-for-service health plan	53.76	13.92	27.42	36.50	73.45	92.77	55.25	73.09
Preferred-provider health plan	106.99	28.53	90.22	137.68	153.87	138.72	66.91	28.47
Health maintenance organization	101.53	29.06	87.77	124.15	121.21	139.72	73.06	67.16
Commercial Medicare supplement	47.35	9.47	9.62	13.34	17.87	41.18	157.14	178.24
Other BCBS health insurance	6.05	1.15	6.43	4.78	5.79	7.77	7.05	9.30
Health maintenance plans (HMOs)	**280.47**	**81.95**	**273.39**	**331.70**	**359.76**	**338.16**	**226.85**	**144.62**
Medicare payments	**186.87**	**13.91**	**21.61**	**32.57**	**50.98**	**129.48**	**740.76**	**759.25**
Commercial Medicare supplements/ other health insurance	**167.18**	**35.33**	**59.38**	**79.10**	**128.00**	**165.06**	**429.98**	**475.64**
Commercial Medicare supplement (not BCBS)	106.32	19.14	27.63	35.66	64.08	84.65	305.45	388.36
Other health insurance (not BCBS)	60.86	16.19	31.75	43.44	63.93	80.41	124.53	87.28
MEDICAL SERVICES	**589.87**	**195.61**	**390.81**	**555.71**	**767.62**	**863.16**	**635.35**	**527.41**
Physician's services	147.53	45.22	120.77	137.83	178.25	247.04	132.38	109.20
Dental services	226.99	40.58	105.41	231.37	290.27	316.55	316.97	228.24
Eye care services	34.20	11.44	16.24	51.84	38.75	32.76	29.30	41.90
Service by professionals other than physician	42.76	7.13	23.92	40.17	71.71	61.03	33.52	33.45
Lab tests, X-rays	26.79	20.53	16.28	20.65	35.83	43.38	29.41	18.89
Hospital room	36.57	31.34	46.45	18.94	49.26	54.91	30.70	16.61
Hospital services other than room	51.51	25.70	51.13	41.30	74.36	71.57	39.97	31.59
Care in convalescent or nursing home	12.46	–	1.60	1.53	16.71	22.77	14.29	40.93
Other medical services	9.46	13.67	9.00	4.75	12.48	13.14	8.80	6.60
DRUGS	**487.43**	**130.13**	**209.16**	**302.53**	**490.15**	**658.75**	**884.02**	**1,028.36**
Nonprescription drugs	64.45	41.84	45.23	60.01	71.10	63.67	92.18	87.05
Nonprescription vitamins	49.15	16.85	34.39	28.79	70.38	71.02	64.15	57.83
Prescription drugs	373.83	71.45	129.53	213.74	348.67	524.05	727.69	883.48
MEDICAL SUPPLIES	**105.31**	**29.61**	**54.72**	**98.56**	**112.32**	**128.95**	**147.93**	**179.21**
Eyeglasses and contact lenses	52.26	20.42	30.28	56.86	70.86	64.20	58.91	43.32
Hearing aids	14.98	0.12	0.60	2.52	4.64	22.22	33.66	72.65
Topicals and dressings	27.56	8.57	21.06	30.25	28.83	32.47	30.61	36.30
Medical equipment for general use	2.69	0.34	0.76	2.40	3.27	3.85	4.95	3.39
Supportive, convalescent medical equipment	5.21	0.10	1.09	5.50	3.56	3.96	9.75	16.48
Rental of medical equipment	1.06	–	0.25	0.22	0.35	0.79	6.40	1.57
Rental of supportive, convalescent medical equipment	1.55	0.06	0.68	0.80	0.81	1.46	3.65	5.50

Note: (–) means sample is too small to make a reliable estimate.
Source: Bureau of Labor Statistics, unpublished tables from the 2002 Consumer Expenditure Survey

Table 7.2 Health Care: Indexed spending by age, 2002

(indexed average annual out-of-pocket spending of consumer units (CU) on health care, by age of consumer unit reference person, 2002; index definition: an index of 100 is the average for all consumer units; an index of 132 means that spending by consumer units in that group is 32 percent above the average for all consumer units; an index of 68 indicates spending that is 32 percent below the average for all consumer units)

	total consumer units	under 25	25 to 34	35 to 44	45 to 54	55 to 64	65 to 74	75+
Average spending of CU, total	$40,677	$24,229	$40,318	$48,330	$48,748	$44,330	$32,243	$23,759
Average spending of CU, index	100	60	99	119	120	109	79	58
Health care, spending index	100	27	60	84	109	128	153	152
HEALTH INSURANCE	**100**	**24**	**65**	**88**	**101**	**116**	**164**	**158**
Commercial health insurance	100	33	86	121	124	139	75	52
Traditional fee-for-service health plan (not BCBS)	100	32	61	76	120	167	129	113
Preferred-provider health plan (not BCBS)	100	33	97	142	126	127	51	24
Blue Cross, Blue Shield	**100**	**26**	**70**	**100**	**118**	**133**	**114**	**113**
Traditional fee-for-service health plan	100	26	51	68	137	173	103	136
Preferred-provider health plan	100	27	84	129	144	130	63	27
Health maintenance organization	100	29	86	122	119	138	72	66
Commercial Medicare supplement	100	20	20	28	38	87	332	376
Other BCBS health insurance	100	19	106	79	96	128	117	154
Health maintenance plans (HMOs)	**100**	**29**	**97**	**118**	**128**	**121**	**81**	**52**
Medicare payments	**100**	**7**	**12**	**17**	**27**	**69**	**396**	**406**
Commercial Medicare supplements/ other health insurance	**100**	**21**	**36**	**47**	**77**	**99**	**257**	**285**
Commercial Medicare supplement (not BCBS)	100	18	26	34	60	80	287	365
Other health insurance (not BCBS)	100	27	52	71	105	132	205	143
MEDICAL SERVICES	**100**	**33**	**66**	**94**	**130**	**146**	**108**	**89**
Physician's services	100	31	82	93	121	167	90	74
Dental services	100	18	46	102	128	139	140	101
Eye care services	100	33	47	152	113	96	86	123
Service by professionals other than physician	100	17	56	94	168	143	78	78
Lab tests, X-rays	100	77	61	77	134	162	110	71
Hospital room	100	86	127	52	135	150	84	45
Hospital services other than room	100	50	99	80	144	139	78	61
Care in convalescent or nursing home	100	–	13	12	134	183	115	328
Other medical services	100	145	95	50	132	139	93	70
DRUGS	**100**	**27**	**43**	**62**	**101**	**135**	**181**	**211**
Nonprescription drugs	100	65	70	93	110	99	143	135
Nonprescription vitamins	100	34	70	59	143	144	131	118
Prescription drugs	100	19	35	57	93	140	195	236
MEDICAL SUPPLIES	**100**	**28**	**52**	**94**	**107**	**122**	**140**	**170**
Eyeglasses and contact lenses	100	39	58	109	136	123	113	83
Hearing aids	100	1	4	17	31	148	225	485
Topicals and dressings	100	31	76	110	105	118	111	132
Medical equipment for general use	100	13	28	89	122	143	184	126
Supportive, convalescent medical equipment	100	2	21	106	68	76	187	316
Rental of medical equipment	100	–	24	21	33	75	604	148
Rental of supportive, convalescent medical equipment	100	4	44	52	52	94	235	355

Note: (–) means sample is too small to make a reliable estimate.
Source: Calculations by New Strategist based on the 2002 Consumer Expenditure Survey

Table 7.3 Health Care: Total spending by age, 2002

(total annual out-of-pocket spending on health care, by consumer unit (CU) age groups, 2002; numbers in thousands)

	total consumer units	under 25	25 to 34	35 to 44	45 to 54	55 to 64	65 to 74	75+
Number of consumer units	112,108	8,737	18,988	24,394	22,691	15,314	11,216	10,767
Total spending of all CUs	$4,560,172,273	$211,692,792	$765,563,691	$1,178,973,729	$1,106,146,314	$678,870,233	$361,632,104	$255,811,969
Health care, total spending	263,489,675	5,593,690	26,897,451	48,292,558	57,871,807	46,050,117	40,243,569	38,586,667
HEALTH INSURANCE	**$130,909,633**	**$2,488,909**	**$14,466,198**	**$24,952,379**	**$26,783,095**	**$20,768,694**	**$21,543,132**	**$19,906,137**
Commercial health insurance	**24,386,853**	**625,132**	**3,532,148**	**6,417,330**	**6,113,182**	**4,645,196**	**1,836,620**	**1,216,886**
Traditional fee-for-service health plan (not BCBS)	7,653,613	191,340	787,242	1,257,755	1,857,031	1,741,661	987,120	831,428
Preferred-provider health plan (not BCBS)	16,733,240	433,792	2,744,715	5,159,575	4,256,151	2,903,534	849,388	385,459
Blue Cross, Blue Shield	**35,389,132**	**717,482**	**4,205,082**	**7,719,481**	**8,445,363**	**6,434,483**	**4,031,030**	**3,835,959**
Traditional fee-for-service health plan	6,026,926	121,619	520,651	890,381	1,666,654	1,420,680	619,684	786,960
Preferred-provider health plan	11,994,435	249,267	1,713,097	3,358,566	3,491,464	2,124,358	750,463	306,536
Health maintenance organization	11,382,325	253,897	1,666,577	3,028,515	2,750,376	2,139,672	819,441	723,112
Commercial Medicare supplement	5,308,314	82,739	182,665	325,416	405,488	630,631	1,762,482	1,919,110
Other BCBS health insurance	678,253	10,048	122,093	116,603	131,381	118,990	79,073	100,133
Health maintenance plans (HMOs)	**31,442,931**	**715,997**	**5,191,129**	**8,091,490**	**8,163,314**	**5,178,582**	**2,544,350**	**1,557,124**
Medicare payments	**20,949,622**	**121,532**	**410,331**	**794,513**	**1,156,787**	**1,982,857**	**8,308,364**	**8,174,845**
Commercial Medicare supplements/ other health insurance	**18,742,215**	**308,678**	**1,127,507**	**1,929,565**	**2,904,448**	**2,527,729**	**4,822,656**	**5,121,216**
Commercial Medicare supplement (not BCBS)	11,919,323	167,226	524,638	869,890	1,454,039	1,296,330	3,425,927	4,181,472
Other health insurance (not BCBS)	6,822,893	141,452	602,869	1,059,675	1,450,636	1,231,399	1,396,728	939,744
MEDICAL SERVICES	**66,129,146**	**1,709,045**	**7,420,700**	**13,555,990**	**17,418,065**	**13,218,432**	**7,126,086**	**5,678,623**
Physician's services	16,539,293	395,087	2,293,181	3,362,225	4,044,671	3,783,171	1,484,774	1,175,756
Dental services	25,447,395	354,547	2,001,525	5,644,040	6,586,517	4,847,647	3,555,136	2,457,460
Eye care services	3,834,094	99,951	308,365	1,264,585	879,276	501,687	328,629	451,137
Service by professionals other than physician	4,793,738	62,295	454,193	979,907	1,627,172	934,613	375,960	360,156
Lab tests, X-rays	3,003,373	179,371	309,125	503,736	813,019	664,321	329,863	203,389
Hospital room	4,099,790	273,818	881,993	462,022	1,117,759	840,892	344,331	178,840
Hospital services other than room	5,774,683	224,541	970,856	1,007,472	1,687,303	1,096,023	448,304	340,130
Care in convalescent or nursing home	1,396,866	–	30,381	37,323	379,167	348,700	160,277	440,693
Other medical services	1,060,542	119,435	170,892	115,872	283,184	201,226	98,701	71,062
DRUGS	**54,644,802**	**1,136,946**	**3,971,530**	**7,379,917**	**11,121,994**	**10,088,098**	**9,915,168**	**11,072,352**
Nonprescription drugs	7,225,361	365,556	858,827	1,463,884	1,613,330	975,042	1,033,891	937,267
Nonprescription vitamins	5,510,108	147,218	652,997	702,303	1,596,993	1,087,600	719,506	622,656
Prescription drugs	41,909,334	624,259	2,459,516	5,213,974	7,911,671	8,025,302	8,161,771	9,512,429
MEDICAL SUPPLIES	**11,806,093**	**258,703**	**1,039,023**	**2,404,273**	**2,548,653**	**1,974,740**	**1,659,183**	**1,929,554**
Eyeglasses and contact lenses	5,858,764	178,410	574,957	1,387,043	1,607,884	983,159	660,735	466,426
Hearing aids	1,679,378	1,048	11,393	61,473	105,286	340,277	377,531	782,223
Topicals and dressings	3,089,696	74,876	399,887	737,919	654,182	497,246	343,322	390,842
Medical equipment for general use	301,571	2,971	14,431	58,546	74,200	58,959	55,519	36,500
Supportive, convalescent medical equipment	584,083	874	20,697	134,167	80,780	60,643	109,356	177,440
Rental of medical equipment	118,834	–	4,747	5,367	7,942	12,098	71,782	16,904
Rental of supportive, convalescent medical equipment	173,767	524	12,912	19,515	18,380	22,358	40,938	59,219

Note: Numbers may not add to total because of rounding. (–) means sample is too small to make a reliable estimate.
Source: Calculations by New Strategist based on the 2002 Consumer Expenditure Survey

Table 7.4 Health Care: Market shares by age, 2002

(percentage of total annual out-of-pocket spending on health care accounted for by consumer unit age groups, 2002)

	total consumer units	under 25	25 to 34	35 to 44	45 to 54	55 to 64	65 to 74	75+
Share of total consumer units	100.0%	7.8%	16.9%	21.8%	20.2%	13.7%	10.0%	9.6%
Share of total before-tax income	100.0	3.3	16.8	27.1	26.6	14.7	7.1	4.6
Share of total spending	100.0	4.6	16.8	25.9	24.3	14.9	7.9	5.6
Share of health care spending	100.0	2.1	10.2	18.3	22.0	17.5	15.3	14.6
HEALTH INSURANCE	100.0%	1.9%	11.1%	19.1%	20.5%	15.9%	16.5%	15.2%
Commercial health insurance	100.0	2.6	14.5	26.3	25.1	19.0	7.5	5.0
Traditional fee-for-service health plan (not BCBS)	100.0	2.5	10.3	16.4	24.3	22.8	12.9	10.9
Preferred-provider health plan (not BCBS)	100.0	2.6	16.4	30.8	25.4	17.4	5.1	2.3
Blue Cross, Blue Shield	100.0	2.0	11.9	21.8	23.9	18.2	11.4	10.8
Traditional fee-for-service health plan	100.0	2.0	8.6	14.8	27.7	23.6	10.3	13.1
Preferred-provider health plan	100.0	2.1	14.3	28.0	29.1	17.7	6.3	2.6
Health maintenance organization	100.0	2.2	14.6	26.6	24.2	18.8	7.2	6.4
Commercial Medicare supplement	100.0	1.6	3.4	6.1	7.6	11.9	33.2	36.2
Other BCBS health insurance	100.0	1.5	18.0	17.2	19.4	17.5	11.7	14.8
Health maintenance plans (HMOs)	100.0	2.3	16.5	25.7	26.0	16.5	8.1	5.0
Medicare payments	100.0	0.6	2.0	3.8	5.5	9.5	39.7	39.0
Commercial Medicare supplements/ other health insurance	100.0	1.6	6.0	10.3	15.5	13.5	25.7	27.3
Commercial Medicare supplement (not BCBS)	100.0	1.4	4.4	7.3	12.2	10.9	28.7	35.1
Other health insurance (not BCBS)	100.0	2.1	8.8	15.5	21.3	18.0	20.5	13.8
MEDICAL SERVICES	100.0	2.6	11.2	20.5	26.3	20.0	10.8	8.6
Physician's services	100.0	2.4	13.9	20.3	24.5	22.9	9.0	7.1
Dental services	100.0	1.4	7.9	22.2	25.9	19.0	14.0	9.7
Eye care services	100.0	2.6	8.0	33.0	22.9	13.1	8.6	11.8
Service by professionals other than physician	100.0	1.3	9.5	20.4	33.9	19.5	7.8	7.5
Lab tests, X-rays	100.0	6.0	10.3	16.8	27.1	22.1	11.0	6.8
Hospital room	100.0	6.7	21.5	11.3	27.3	20.5	8.4	4.4
Hospital services other than room	100.0	3.9	16.8	17.4	29.2	19.0	7.8	5.9
Care in convalescent or nursing home	100.0	–	2.2	2.7	27.1	25.0	11.5	31.5
Other medical services	100.0	11.3	16.1	10.9	26.7	19.0	9.3	6.7
DRUGS	100.0	2.1	7.3	13.5	20.4	18.5	18.1	20.3
Nonprescription drugs	100.0	5.1	11.9	20.3	22.3	13.5	14.3	13.0
Nonprescription vitamins	100.0	2.7	11.9	12.7	29.0	19.7	13.1	11.3
Prescription drugs	100.0	1.5	5.9	12.4	18.9	19.1	19.5	22.7
MEDICAL SUPPLIES	100.0	2.2	8.8	20.4	21.6	16.7	14.1	16.3
Eyeglasses and contact lenses	100.0	3.0	9.8	23.7	27.4	16.8	11.3	8.0
Hearing aids	100.0	0.1	0.7	3.7	6.3	20.3	22.5	46.6
Topicals and dressings	100.0	2.4	12.9	23.9	21.2	16.1	11.1	12.6
Medical equipment for general use	100.0	1.0	4.8	19.4	24.6	19.6	18.4	12.1
Supportive, convalescent medical equipment	100.0	0.1	3.5	23.0	13.8	10.4	18.7	30.4
Rental of medical equipment	100.0	–	4.0	4.5	6.7	10.2	60.4	14.2
Rental of supportive, convalescent medical equipment	100.0	0.3	7.4	11.2	10.6	12.9	23.6	34.1

Note: Numbers may not add to total because of rounding. (–) means sample is too small to make a reliable estimate.
Source: Calculations by New Strategist based on the 2002 Consumer Expenditure Survey

Table 7.5 Health Care: Average spending by income, 2002

(average annual out-of-pocket spending on health care, by before-tax income of consumer units (CU), 2002; complete income reporters only)

	complete income reporters	under $10,000	$10,000–$19,999	$20,000–$29,999	$30,000–$39,999	$40,000–$49,999	$50,000–$69,999	$70,000 or more
Number of consumer units (in thousands, add 000)	92,388	10,933	15,075	12,312	10,727	8,873	13,521	20,947
Average number of persons per CU	2.5	1.7	1.9	2.3	2.5	2.6	2.8	3.1
Average before-tax income of CU	$49,430.00	$5,554.80	$14,724.33	$24,495.00	$34,423.00	$44,443.00	$58,933.00	$115,629.00
Average spending of CU, total	42,556.98	17,627.83	22,838.71	28,835.85	35,095.39	41,787.38	50,406.17	76,627.31
Health care, average spending	2,409.53	1,110.99	1,978.02	2,288.54	2,378.69	2,598.46	2,672.37	3,230.31
HEALTH INSURANCE	$1,184.63	$569.71	$1,018.28	$1,109.39	$1,180.20	$1,276.30	$1,313.14	$1,550.01
Commercial health insurance	216.91	50.20	96.08	156.14	209.16	280.56	271.93	368.08
Traditional fee-for-service health plan (not BCBS)	66.02	14.12	54.45	55.74	97.15	93.23	54.69	87.34
Preferred-provider health plan (not BCBS)	150.89	36.09	41.64	100.40	112.01	187.34	217.24	280.74
Blue Cross, Blue Shield	322.25	126.16	207.37	242.24	338.80	392.11	392.34	470.98
Traditional fee-for-service health plan	53.25	31.78	44.05	33.69	63.38	72.12	62.26	63.58
Preferred-provider health plan	108.63	35.03	37.37	59.30	85.59	149.07	145.44	198.23
Health maintenance organization	105.28	28.81	47.01	71.42	122.70	134.25	133.61	167.56
Commercial Medicare supplement	48.52	30.01	74.88	71.41	59.00	33.99	43.60	29.73
Other BCBS health insurance	6.56	0.53	4.07	6.42	8.13	2.68	7.43	11.87
Health maintenance plans (HMOs)	285.88	82.08	150.71	197.43	259.36	285.52	399.09	482.17
Medicare payments	191.71	216.70	354.24	291.90	200.09	143.29	106.59	73.97
Commercial Medicare supplements/ other health insurance	167.88	94.57	209.86	221.68	172.78	174.82	143.19	154.81
Commercial Medicare supplement (not BCBS)	103.90	77.28	165.60	173.21	118.48	90.03	63.20	57.30
Other health insurance (not BCBS)	63.99	17.29	44.26	48.47	54.30	84.78	79.99	97.51
MEDICAL SERVICES	604.80	197.70	338.14	455.21	589.74	715.71	733.66	974.37
Physician's services	152.59	45.16	89.23	111.34	157.02	148.47	207.93	242.27
Dental services	234.64	60.71	130.58	173.47	203.42	240.89	281.59	419.30
Eye care services	35.63	11.95	16.95	24.47	59.68	38.86	41.35	50.62
Service by professionals other than physician	42.94	17.54	20.24	22.63	33.33	45.39	55.75	80.09
Lab tests, X-rays	26.97	15.68	16.78	16.95	25.79	41.72	36.22	34.49
Hospital room	34.50	14.45	22.05	38.76	39.23	60.49	29.51	41.21
Hospital services other than room	50.56	25.28	33.99	50.52	46.20	83.89	64.21	55.01
Care in convalescent or nursing home	14.32	3.89	3.83	3.47	10.87	25.31	9.71	33.76
Other medical services	10.39	3.04	4.49	13.59	14.20	30.69	7.40	7.97
DRUGS	508.05	289.22	520.99	629.16	505.51	494.59	501.65	549.07
Nonprescription drugs	72.86	44.87	60.80	81.94	69.88	63.34	81.44	88.56
Nonprescription vitamins	47.50	29.76	31.32	45.48	43.31	39.16	50.16	72.03
Prescription drugs	387.68	214.59	428.87	501.74	392.32	392.09	370.05	388.48
MEDICAL SUPPLIES	112.06	54.37	100.60	94.79	103.25	111.85	123.92	156.87
Eyeglasses and contact lenses	56.03	23.03	28.66	36.96	58.17	61.81	69.10	92.18
Hearing aids	15.05	7.29	36.65	18.36	9.60	10.29	12.23	8.22
Topicals and dressings	30.06	20.52	19.52	24.06	19.17	32.71	34.76	46.95
Medical equipment for general use	2.99	0.90	3.72	2.12	5.37	1.65	2.73	3.60
Supportive, convalescent medical equipment	5.13	1.35	9.80	4.53	8.85	3.08	3.49	4.11
Rental of medical equipment	1.10	0.54	0.41	4.53	0.25	0.53	0.83	0.72
Rental of supportive, convalescent medical equipment	1.70	0.75	1.85	4.22	1.83	1.79	0.78	1.09

Source: Bureau of Labor Statistics, unpublished tables from the 2002 Consumer Expenditure Survey; calculations by New Strategist

Table 7.6 Health Care: Indexed spending by income, 2002

(indexed average annual out-of-pocket spending of consumer units (CU) on health care, by before-tax income of consumer unit, 2002; complete income reporters only; index definition: an index of 100 is the average for all consumer units; an index of 132 means that spending by consumer units in that group is 32 percent above the average for all consumer units; an index of 68 indicates spending that is 32 percent below the average for all consumer units)

	complete income reporters	under $10,000	$10,000–$19,999	$20,000–$29,999	$30,000–$39,999	$40,000–$49,999	$50,000–$69,999	$70,000 or more
Average spending of CU, total	$42,557	$17,628	$22,839	$28,836	$35,095	$41,787	$50,406	$76,627
Average spending of CU, index	100	41	54	68	82	98	118	180
Health care, spending index	100	46	82	95	99	108	111	134
HEALTH INSURANCE	100	48	86	94	100	108	111	131
Commercial health insurance	100	23	44	72	96	129	125	170
Traditional fee-for-service health plan (not BCBS)	100	21	82	84	147	141	83	132
Preferred-provider health plan (not BCBS)	100	24	28	67	74	124	144	186
Blue Cross, Blue Shield	100	39	64	75	105	122	122	146
Traditional fee-for-service health plan	100	60	83	63	119	135	117	119
Preferred-provider health plan	100	32	34	55	79	137	134	182
Health maintenance organization	100	27	45	68	117	128	127	159
Commercial Medicare supplement	100	62	154	147	122	70	90	61
Other BCBS health insurance	100	8	62	98	124	41	113	181
Health maintenance plans (HMOs)	100	29	53	69	91	100	140	169
Medicare payments	100	113	185	152	104	75	56	39
Commercial Medicare supplements/ other health insurance	100	56	125	132	103	104	85	92
Commercial Medicare supplement (not BCBS)	100	74	159	167	114	87	61	55
Other health insurance (not BCBS)	100	27	69	76	85	132	125	152
MEDICAL SERVICES	100	33	56	75	98	118	121	161
Physician's services	100	30	58	73	103	97	136	159
Dental services	100	26	56	74	87	103	120	179
Eye care services	100	34	48	69	167	109	116	142
Service by professionals other than physician	100	41	47	53	78	106	130	187
Lab tests, X-rays	100	58	62	63	96	155	134	128
Hospital room	100	42	64	112	114	175	86	119
Hospital services other than room	100	50	67	100	91	166	127	109
Care in convalescent or nursing home	100	27	27	24	76	177	68	236
Other medical services	100	29	43	131	137	295	71	77
DRUGS	100	57	103	124	100	97	99	108
Nonprescription drugs	100	62	83	112	96	87	112	122
Nonprescription vitamins	100	63	66	96	91	82	106	152
Prescription drugs	100	55	111	129	101	101	95	100
MEDICAL SUPPLIES	100	49	90	85	92	100	111	140
Eyeglasses and contact lenses	100	41	51	66	104	110	123	165
Hearing aids	100	48	244	122	64	68	81	55
Topicals and dressings	100	68	65	80	64	109	116	156
Medical equipment for general use	100	30	124	71	180	55	91	120
Supportive, convalescent medical equipment	100	26	191	88	173	60	68	80
Rental of medical equipment	100	49	38	412	23	48	75	65
Rental of supportive, convalescent medical equipment	100	44	109	248	108	105	46	64

Source: Calculations by New Strategist based on the 2002 Consumer Expenditure Survey

Table 7.7 Health Care: Total spending by income, 2002

(total annual out-of-pocket spending on health care, by before-tax income group of consumer units (CU), 2002; complete income reporters only; numbers in thousands)

	complete income reporters	under $10,000	$10,000– $19,999	$20,000– $29,999	$30,000– $39,999	$40,000– $49,999	$50,000– $69,999	$70,000 or more
Number of consumer units	92,388	10,933	15,075	12,312	10,727	8,873	13,521	20,947
Total spending of all CUs	$3,931,754,268	$192,725,059	$344,293,530	$355,026,985	$376,468,249	$370,779,423	$681,541,825	$1,605,112,263
Health care, total spending	222,611,658	12,146,501	29,818,677	28,176,504	25,516,208	23,056,136	36,133,115	67,665,304
HEALTH INSURANCE	$109,445,596	$6,228,662	$15,350,617	$13,658,810	$12,660,005	$11,324,610	$17,754,966	$32,468,059
Commercial health insurance	20,039,881	548,890	1,448,474	1,922,396	2,243,659	2,489,409	3,676,766	7,710,172
Traditional fee-for-service health plan (not BCBS)	6,099,456	154,352	820,876	686,271	1,042,128	827,230	739,463	1,829,511
Preferred-provider health plan (not BCBS)	13,940,425	394,538	627,678	1,236,125	1,201,531	1,662,268	2,937,302	5,880,661
Blue Cross, Blue Shield	29,772,033	1,379,269	3,126,137	2,982,459	3,634,308	3,479,192	5,304,829	9,865,618
Traditional fee-for-service health plan	4,919,661	347,411	664,001	414,791	679,877	639,921	841,817	1,331,810
Preferred-provider health plan	10,036,108	382,979	563,293	730,102	918,124	1,322,698	1,966,494	4,152,324
Health maintenance organization	9,726,609	314,994	708,639	879,323	1,316,203	1,191,200	1,806,541	3,509,879
Commercial Medicare supplement	4,482,666	328,112	1,128,838	879,200	632,893	301,593	589,516	622,754
Other BCBS health insurance	606,065	5,773	61,375	79,043	87,211	23,780	100,461	248,641
Health maintenance plans (HMOs)	26,411,881	897,357	2,272,021	2,430,758	2,782,155	2,533,419	5,396,096	10,100,015
Medicare payments	17,711,703	2,369,234	5,340,225	3,593,873	2,146,365	1,271,412	1,441,203	1,549,450
Commercial Medicare supplements/ other health insurance	15,510,097	1,033,881	3,163,690	2,729,324	1,853,411	1,551,178	1,936,072	3,242,805
Commercial Medicare supplement (not BCBS)	9,599,113	844,892	2,496,399	2,132,562	1,270,935	798,836	854,527	1,200,263
Other health insurance (not BCBS)	5,911,908	188,989	667,291	596,763	582,476	752,253	1,081,545	2,042,542
MEDICAL SERVICES	55,876,262	2,161,428	5,097,510	5,604,546	6,326,141	6,350,495	9,919,817	20,410,128
Physician's services	14,097,485	493,786	1,345,125	1,370,818	1,684,354	1,317,374	2,811,422	5,074,830
Dental services	21,677,920	663,730	1,968,541	2,135,763	2,182,086	2,137,417	3,807,378	8,783,077
Eye care services	3,291,784	130,696	255,482	301,275	640,187	344,805	559,093	1,060,337
Service by professionals other than physician	3,967,141	191,781	305,142	278,621	357,531	402,745	753,796	1,677,645
Lab tests, X-rays	2,491,704	171,389	252,931	208,688	276,649	370,182	489,731	722,462
Hospital room	3,187,386	157,987	332,374	477,213	420,820	536,728	399,005	863,226
Hospital services other than room	4,671,137	276,441	512,397	622,002	495,587	744,356	868,183	1,152,294
Care in convalescent or nursing home	1,322,996	42,491	57,758	42,723	116,602	224,576	131,289	707,171
Other medical services	959,911	33,205	67,760	167,320	152,323	272,312	100,055	166,948
DRUGS	46,937,723	3,162,062	7,853,896	7,746,218	5,422,606	4,388,497	6,782,810	11,501,369
Nonprescription drugs	6,731,390	490,586	916,527	1,008,845	749,603	562,016	1,101,150	1,855,066
Nonprescription vitamins	4,388,430	325,354	472,205	559,950	464,586	347,467	678,213	1,508,812
Prescription drugs	35,816,980	2,346,122	6,465,163	6,177,423	4,208,417	3,479,015	5,003,446	8,137,491
MEDICAL SUPPLIES	10,352,999	594,420	1,516,574	1,167,054	1,107,563	992,445	1,675,522	3,285,956
Eyeglasses and contact lenses	5,176,500	251,785	431,987	455,052	623,990	548,440	934,301	1,930,894
Hearing aids	1,390,439	79,722	552,523	226,048	102,979	91,303	165,362	172,184
Topicals and dressings	2,777,183	224,315	294,242	296,227	205,637	290,236	469,990	983,462
Medical equipment for general use	276,240	9,888	56,057	26,101	57,604	14,640	36,912	75,409
Supportive, convalescent medical equipment	473,950	14,743	147,736	55,773	94,934	27,329	47,188	86,092
Rental of medical equipment	101,627	5,859	6,223	55,773	2,682	4,703	11,222	15,082
Rental of supportive, convalescent medical equipment	157,060	8,185	27,876	51,957	19,630	15,883	10,546	22,832

Note: Numbers may not add to total because of rounding.
Source: Calculations by New Strategist based on the 2002 Consumer Expenditure Survey

Table 7.8 Health Care: Market shares by income, 2002

(percentage of total annual out-of-pocket spending on health care accounted for by before-tax income group of consumer units, 2002; complete income reporters only)

	complete income reporters	under $10,000	$10,000–$19,999	$20,000–$29,999	$30,000–$39,999	$40,000–$49,999	$50,000–$69,999	$70,000 or more
Share of total consumer units	100.0%	11.8%	16.3%	13.3%	11.6%	9.6%	14.6%	22.7%
Share of total before-tax income	100.0	1.3	4.9	6.6	8.1	8.6	17.4	53.0
Share of total spending	100.0	4.9	8.8	9.0	9.6	8.6	17.4	53.0
Share of health care spending	100.0	5.5	13.4	12.7	11.5	10.4	16.2	30.4
HEALTH INSURANCE	**100.0%**	**5.7%**	**14.0%**	**12.5%**	**11.6%**	**10.3%**	**16.2%**	**29.7%**
Commercial health insurance	**100.0**	**2.7**	**7.2**	**9.6**	**11.2**	**12.4**	**18.3**	**38.5**
Traditional fee-for-service health plan (not BCBS)	100.0	2.5	13.5	11.3	17.1	13.6	12.1	30.0
Preferred-provider health plan (not BCBS)	100.0	2.8	4.5	8.9	8.6	11.9	21.1	42.2
Blue Cross, Blue Shield	**100.0**	**4.6**	**10.5**	**10.0**	**12.2**	**11.7**	**17.8**	**33.1**
Traditional fee-for-service health plan	100.0	7.1	13.5	8.4	13.8	13.0	17.1	27.1
Preferred-provider health plan	100.0	3.8	5.6	7.3	9.1	13.2	19.6	41.4
Health maintenance organization	100.0	3.2	7.3	9.0	13.5	12.2	18.6	36.1
Commercial Medicare supplement	100.0	7.3	25.2	19.6	14.1	6.7	13.2	13.9
Other BCBS health insurance	100.0	1.0	10.1	13.0	14.4	3.9	16.6	41.0
Health maintenance plans (HMOs)	**100.0**	**3.4**	**8.6**	**9.2**	**10.5**	**9.6**	**20.4**	**38.2**
Medicare payments	**100.0**	**13.4**	**30.2**	**20.3**	**12.1**	**7.2**	**8.1**	**8.7**
Commercial Medicare supplements/ other health insurance	**100.0**	**6.7**	**20.4**	**17.6**	**11.9**	**10.0**	**12.5**	**20.9**
Commercial Medicare supplement (not BCBS)	100.0	8.8	26.0	22.2	13.2	8.3	8.9	12.5
Other health insurance (not BCBS)	100.0	3.2	11.3	10.1	9.9	12.7	18.3	34.5
MEDICAL SERVICES	**100.0**	**3.9**	**9.1**	**10.0**	**11.3**	**11.4**	**17.8**	**36.5**
Physician's services	100.0	3.5	9.5	9.7	11.9	9.3	19.9	36.0
Dental services	100.0	3.1	9.1	9.9	10.1	9.9	17.6	40.5
Eye care services	100.0	4.0	7.8	9.2	19.4	10.5	17.0	32.2
Service by professionals other than physician	100.0	4.8	7.7	7.0	9.0	10.2	19.0	42.3
Lab tests, X-rays	100.0	6.9	10.2	8.4	11.1	14.9	19.7	29.0
Hospital room	100.0	5.0	10.4	15.0	13.2	16.8	12.5	27.1
Hospital services other than room	100.0	5.9	11.0	13.3	10.6	15.9	18.6	24.7
Care in convalescent or nursing home	100.0	3.2	4.4	3.2	8.8	17.0	9.9	53.5
Other medical services	100.0	3.5	7.1	17.4	15.9	28.4	10.4	17.4
DRUGS	**100.0**	**6.7**	**16.7**	**16.5**	**11.6**	**9.3**	**14.5**	**24.5**
Nonprescription drugs	100.0	7.3	13.6	15.0	11.1	8.3	16.4	27.6
Nonprescription vitamins	100.0	7.4	10.8	12.8	10.6	7.9	15.5	34.4
Prescription drugs	100.0	6.6	18.1	17.2	11.7	9.7	14.0	22.7
MEDICAL SUPPLIES	**100.0**	**5.7**	**14.6**	**11.3**	**10.7**	**9.6**	**16.2**	**31.7**
Eyeglasses and contact lenses	100.0	4.9	8.3	8.8	12.1	10.6	18.0	37.3
Hearing aids	100.0	5.7	39.7	16.3	7.4	6.6	11.9	12.4
Topicals and dressings	100.0	8.1	10.6	10.7	7.4	10.5	16.9	35.4
Medical equipment for general use	100.0	3.6	20.3	9.4	20.9	5.3	13.4	27.3
Supportive, convalescent medical equipment	100.0	3.1	31.2	11.8	20.0	5.8	10.0	18.2
Rental of medical equipment	100.0	5.8	6.1	54.9	2.6	4.6	11.0	14.8
Rental of supportive, convalescent medical equipment	100.0	5.2	17.7	33.1	12.5	10.1	6.7	14.5

Note: Numbers may not add to total because of rounding.
Source: Calculations by New Strategist based on the 2002 Consumer Expenditure Survey

Table 7.9 Health Care: Average spending by household type, 2002

(average annual out-of-pocket spending of consumer units (CU) on health care, by type of consumer unit, 2002)

	total married couples	married couples, no children	married couples with children				single parent, at least one child <18	single person
			total	oldest child under 6	oldest child 6 to 17	oldest child 18 or older		
Number of consumer units (in thousands, add 000)	56,265	23,118	28,790	5,547	15,206	8,036	6,730	33,055
Average number of persons per CU	3.2	2.0	3.9	3.5	4.1	3.9	2.9	1.0
Average before-tax income of CU	$67,155.00	$58,967.00	$73,918.00	$67,587.00	$72,720.00	$81,042.00	$26,966.00	$27,042.00
Average spending of CU, total	52,333.70	45,557.33	57,835.01	52,778.62	58,103.75	60,859.78	30,185.38	24,189.90
Health care, average spending	3,109.60	3,614.27	2,716.28	2,232.75	2,676.20	3,126.68	1,252.25	1,521.70
HEALTH INSURANCE	**$1,551.14**	**$1,798.61**	**$1,361.93**	**$1,253.09**	**$1,342.97**	**$1,472.94**	**$577.76**	**$758.50**
Commercial health insurance	321.36	315.41	337.86	342.08	363.55	286.34	127.67	96.79
Traditional fee-for-service health plan (not BCBS)	92.59	114.33	76.61	82.78	75.96	73.61	39.21	43.12
Preferred-provider health plan (not BCBS)	228.77	201.09	261.24	259.30	287.59	212.73	88.46	53.67
Blue Cross, Blue Shield	**429.71**	**451.56**	**413.72**	**466.29**	**404.43**	**395.01**	**171.56**	**188.51**
Traditional fee-for-service health plan	70.71	82.84	59.62	81.05	54.32	54.85	15.55	44.45
Preferred-provider health plan	157.28	122.74	187.30	230.79	178.38	174.16	71.72	46.37
Health maintenance organization	139.31	134.39	139.87	142.02	153.25	113.06	63.47	47.40
Commercial Medicare supplement	53.94	102.86	17.90	3.34	9.53	43.78	14.87	47.29
Other BCBS health insurance	8.47	8.73	9.04	9.10	8.95	9.16	5.95	3.00
Health maintenance plans (HMOs)	**393.99**	**328.33**	**444.33**	**348.15**	**455.64**	**489.33**	**198.86**	**121.71**
Medicare payments	**200.00**	**384.50**	**43.19**	**10.46**	**11.83**	**125.12**	**39.85**	**201.58**
Commercial Medicare supplements/ other health insurance	**206.08**	**318.82**	**122.83**	**86.11**	**107.53**	**177.14**	**39.81**	**149.92**
Commercial Medicare supplement (not BCBS)	121.72	208.23	54.35	42.30	32.85	103.35	16.38	106.44
Other health insurance (not BCBS)	84.36	110.59	68.48	43.81	74.68	73.79	23.43	43.48
MEDICAL SERVICES	**807.83**	**828.40**	**806.27**	**632.71**	**814.98**	**909.31**	**410.62**	**329.58**
Physician's services	216.35	217.46	209.08	242.66	193.98	214.47	88.90	62.74
Dental services	313.58	321.61	317.18	123.89	352.18	384.38	165.26	124.68
Eye care services	43.30	37.48	49.67	19.16	50.61	68.94	20.33	27.32
Service by professionals other than physician	54.14	51.28	60.01	52.52	62.79	59.91	31.39	28.98
Lab tests, X-rays	35.85	45.85	30.65	22.60	32.51	32.70	15.70	16.76
Hospital room	48.92	47.64	48.57	72.89	38.87	50.13	40.71	22.52
Hospital services other than room	71.56	68.61	75.45	85.29	63.24	91.74	37.83	25.73
Care in convalescent or nursing home	10.70	23.19	2.26	2.17	1.73	3.32	6.45	12.35
Other medical services	3.14	–	6.32	–	11.81	–	–	8.49
DRUGS	**614.78**	**822.79**	**432.61**	**274.40**	**400.09**	**604.03**	**186.60**	**365.60**
Nonprescription drugs	77.64	82.70	73.19	65.46	68.58	88.09	47.89	42.92
Nonprescription vitamins	62.79	64.78	56.84	42.17	64.78	51.81	13.55	35.41
Prescription drugs	474.35	675.31	302.57	166.76	266.73	464.14	125.16	287.27
MEDICAL SUPPLIES	**135.85**	**164.48**	**115.47**	**72.55**	**118.15**	**140.40**	**77.27**	**68.02**
Eyeglasses and contact lenses	69.96	70.60	70.24	38.47	76.41	80.52	43.08	29.48
Hearing aids	16.75	34.50	4.82	2.06	3.61	9.03	0.98	16.74
Topicals and dressings	37.37	41.60	35.09	29.65	33.84	41.58	13.28	13.82
Medical equipment for general use	3.09	4.19	1.93	0.66	2.04	2.59	2.53	2.60
Supportive, convalescent medical equipment	5.55	7.89	2.23	0.86	1.70	4.18	16.96	3.47
Rental of medical equipment	1.60	3.10	0.48	0.43	0.34	0.77	0.05	0.50
Rental of supportive, convalescent medical equipment	1.54	2.59	0.68	0.42	0.21	1.73	0.39	1.41

Note: Average spending figures for total consumer units can be found on Average Spending by Age and Average Spending by Region tables. (–) means sample is too small to make a reliable estimate.
Source: Bureau of Labor Statistics, unpublished tables from the 2002 Consumer Expenditure Survey

Table 7.10 Health Care: Indexed spending by household type, 2002

(indexed average annual out-of-pocket spending of consumer units (CU) on health care, by type of consumer unit, 2002; index definition: an index of 100 is the average for all consumer units; an index of 132 means that spending by consumer units in that group is 32 percent above the average for all consumer units; an index of 68 indicates spending that is 32 percent below the average for all consumer units)

	total married couples	married couples, no children	married couples with children total	oldest child under 6	oldest child 6 to 17	oldest child 18 or older	single parent, at least one child <18	single person
Average spending of CU, total	$52,334	$45,557	$57,835	$52,779	$58,104	$60,860	$30,185	$24,190
Average spending of CU, index	129	112	142	130	143	150	74	59
Health care, spending index	132	154	116	95	114	133	53	65
HEALTH INSURANCE	**133**	**154**	**117**	**107**	**115**	**126**	**49**	**65**
Commercial health insurance	**148**	**145**	**155**	**157**	**167**	**132**	**59**	**44**
Traditional fee-for-service health plan (not BCBS)	136	167	112	121	111	108	57	63
Preferred-provider health plan (not BCBS)	153	135	175	174	193	143	59	36
Blue Cross, Blue Shield	**136**	**143**	**131**	**148**	**128**	**125**	**54**	**60**
Traditional fee-for-service health plan	132	154	111	151	101	102	29	83
Preferred-provider health plan	147	115	175	216	167	163	67	43
Health maintenance organization	137	132	138	140	151	111	63	47
Commercial Medicare supplement	114	217	38	7	20	92	31	100
Other BCBS health insurance	140	144	149	150	148	151	98	50
Health maintenance plans (HMOs)	**140**	**117**	**158**	**124**	**162**	**174**	**71**	**43**
Medicare payments	**107**	**206**	**23**	**6**	**6**	**67**	**21**	**108**
Commercial Medicare supplements/ other health insurance	**123**	**191**	**73**	**52**	**64**	**106**	**24**	**90**
Commercial Medicare supplement (not BCBS)	114	196	51	40	31	97	15	100
Other health insurance (not BCBS)	139	182	113	72	123	121	38	71
MEDICAL SERVICES	**137**	**140**	**137**	**107**	**138**	**154**	**70**	**56**
Physician's services	147	147	142	164	131	145	60	43
Dental services	138	142	140	55	155	169	73	55
Eye care services	127	110	145	56	148	202	59	80
Service by professionals other than physician	127	120	140	123	147	140	73	68
Lab tests, X-rays	134	171	114	84	121	122	59	63
Hospital room	134	130	133	199	106	137	111	62
Hospital services other than room	139	133	146	166	123	178	73	50
Care in convalescent or nursing home	86	186	18	17	14	27	52	99
Other medical services	33	–	67	–	125	–	–	90
DRUGS	**126**	**169**	**89**	**56**	**82**	**124**	**38**	**75**
Nonprescription drugs	120	128	114	102	106	137	74	67
Nonprescription vitamins	128	132	116	86	132	105	28	72
Prescription drugs	127	181	81	45	71	124	33	77
MEDICAL SUPPLIES	**129**	**156**	**110**	**69**	**112**	**133**	**73**	**65**
Eyeglasses and contact lenses	134	135	134	74	146	154	82	56
Hearing aids	112	230	32	14	24	60	7	112
Topicals and dressings	136	151	127	108	123	151	48	50
Medical equipment for general use	115	156	72	25	76	96	94	97
Supportive, convalescent medical equipment	107	151	43	17	33	80	326	67
Rental of medical equipment	151	292	45	41	32	73	5	47
Rental of supportive, convalescent medical equipment	99	167	44	27	14	112	25	91

Note: Spending index for total consumer units is 100. (–) means sample is too small to make a reliable estimate.
Source: Calculations by New Strategist based on the 2002 Consumer Expenditure Survey

Table 7.11 Health Care: Total spending by household type, 2002

(total annual out-of-pocket spending on health care, by consumer unit (CU) type, 2002; numbers in thousands)

	total married couples	married couples, no children	married couples with children total	oldest child under 6	oldest child 6 to 17	oldest child 18 or older	single parent, at least one child <18	single person
Number of consumer units	56,265	23,118	28,790	5,547	15,206	8,036	6,730	33,055
Total spending of all CUs	$2,944,555,631	$1,053,194,355	$1,665,069,938	$292,763,005	$883,525,623	$489,069,192	$203,147,607	$799,597,145
Health care, total spending	174,961,644	83,554,694	78,201,701	12,385,064	40,694,297	25,126,000	8,427,643	50,299,794
HEALTH INSURANCE	**$87,274,892**	**$41,580,266**	**$39,209,965**	**$6,950,890**	**$20,421,202**	**$11,836,546**	**$3,888,325**	**$25,072,218**
Commercial health insurance	**18,081,320**	**7,291,648**	**9,726,989**	**1,897,518**	**5,528,141**	**2,301,028**	**859,219**	**3,199,393**
Traditional fee-for-service health plan (not BCBS)	5,209,576	2,643,081	2,205,602	459,181	1,155,048	591,530	263,883	1,425,332
Preferred-provider health plan (not BCBS)	12,871,744	4,648,799	7,521,100	1,438,337	4,373,094	1,709,498	595,336	1,774,062
Blue Cross, Blue Shield	**24,177,633**	**10,439,164**	**11,910,999**	**2,586,511**	**6,149,763**	**3,174,300**	**1,154,599**	**6,231,198**
Traditional fee-for-service health plan	3,978,498	1,915,095	1,716,460	449,584	825,990	440,775	104,652	1,469,295
Preferred-provider health plan	8,849,359	2,837,503	5,392,367	1,280,192	2,712,446	1,399,550	482,676	1,532,760
Health maintenance organization	7,838,277	3,106,828	4,026,857	787,785	2,330,320	908,550	427,153	1,566,807
Commercial Medicare supplement	3,034,934	2,377,917	515,341	18,527	144,913	351,816	100,075	1,563,171
Other BCBS health insurance	476,565	201,820	260,262	50,478	136,094	73,610	40,044	99,165
Health maintenance plans (HMOs)	**22,167,847**	**7,590,333**	**12,792,261**	**1,931,188**	**6,928,462**	**3,932,256**	**1,338,328**	**4,023,124**
Medicare payments	**11,253,000**	**8,888,871**	**1,243,440**	**58,022**	**179,887**	**1,005,464**	**268,191**	**6,663,227**
Commercial Medicare supplements/ other health insurance	**11,595,091**	**7,370,481**	**3,536,276**	**477,652**	**1,635,101**	**1,423,497**	**267,921**	**4,955,606**
Commercial Medicare supplement (not BCBS)	6,848,576	4,813,861	1,564,737	234,638	499,517	830,521	110,237	3,518,374
Other health insurance (not BCBS)	4,746,515	2,556,620	1,971,539	243,014	1,135,584	592,976	157,684	1,437,231
MEDICAL SERVICES	**45,452,555**	**19,150,951**	**23,212,513**	**3,509,642**	**12,392,586**	**7,307,215**	**2,763,473**	**10,894,267**
Physician's services	12,172,933	5,027,240	6,019,413	1,346,035	2,949,660	1,723,481	598,297	2,073,871
Dental services	17,643,579	7,434,980	9,131,612	687,218	5,355,249	3,088,878	1,112,200	4,121,297
Eye care services	2,436,275	866,463	1,429,999	106,281	769,576	554,002	136,821	903,063
Service by professionals other than physician	3,046,187	1,185,491	1,727,688	291,328	954,785	481,437	211,255	957,934
Lab tests, X-rays	2,017,100	1,059,960	882,414	125,362	494,347	262,777	105,661	554,002
Hospital room	2,752,484	1,101,342	1,398,330	404,321	591,057	402,845	273,978	744,399
Hospital services other than room	4,026,323	1,586,126	2,172,206	473,104	961,627	737,223	254,596	850,505
Care in convalescent or nursing home	602,036	536,106	65,065	12,037	26,306	26,680	43,409	408,229
Other medical services	176,672	–	181,953	–	179,583	–	–	280,637
DRUGS	**34,590,597**	**19,021,259**	**12,454,842**	**1,522,097**	**6,083,769**	**4,853,985**	**1,255,818**	**12,084,908**
Nonprescription drugs	4,368,415	1,911,859	2,107,140	363,107	1,042,827	707,891	322,300	1,418,721
Nonprescription vitamins	3,532,879	1,497,584	1,636,424	233,917	985,045	416,345	91,192	1,170,478
Prescription drugs	26,689,303	15,611,817	8,710,990	925,018	4,055,896	3,729,829	842,327	9,495,710
MEDICAL SUPPLIES	**7,643,600**	**3,802,449**	**3,324,381**	**402,435**	**1,796,589**	**1,128,254**	**520,027**	**2,248,401**
Eyeglasses and contact lenses	3,936,299	1,632,131	2,022,210	213,393	1,161,890	647,059	289,928	974,461
Hearing aids	942,439	797,571	138,768	11,427	54,894	72,565	6,595	553,341
Topicals and dressings	2,102,623	961,709	1,010,241	164,469	514,571	334,137	89,374	456,820
Medical equipment for general use	173,859	96,864	55,565	3,661	31,020	20,813	17,027	85,943
Supportive, convalescent medical equipment	312,271	182,401	64,202	4,770	25,850	33,590	114,141	114,701
Rental of medical equipment	90,024	71,666	13,819	2,385	5,170	6,188	337	16,528
Rental of supportive, convalescent medical equipment	86,648	59,876	19,577	2,330	3,193	13,902	2,625	46,608

Note: Total spending figures for total consumer units can be found on Total Spending by Age and Total Spending by Region tables. Spending by type of consumer unit will not add to total because not all types of consumer units are shown. (–) means sample is too small to make a reliable estimate.
Source: Calculations by New Strategist based on the 2002 Consumer Expenditure Survey

Table 7.12 Health Care: Market shares by household type, 2002

(percentage of total annual out-of-pocket spending on health care accounted for by types of consumer units, 2002)

	total married couples	married couples, no children	married couples with children				single parent, at least one child <18	single person
			total	oldest child under 6	oldest child 6 to 17	oldest child 18 or older		
Share of total consumer units	50.2%	20.6%	25.7%	4.9%	13.6%	7.2%	6.0%	29.5%
Share of total before-tax income	68.2	24.6	38.4	6.8	20.0	11.8	3.3	16.1
Share of total spending	64.6	23.1	36.5	6.4	19.4	10.7	4.5	17.5
Share of health care spending	66.4	31.7	29.7	4.7	15.4	9.5	3.2	19.1
HEALTH INSURANCE	**66.7%**	**31.8%**	**30.0%**	**5.3%**	**15.6%**	**9.0%**	**3.0%**	**19.2%**
Commercial health insurance	**74.1**	**29.9**	**39.9**	**7.8**	**22.7**	**9.4**	**3.5**	**13.1**
Traditional fee-for-service health plan (not BCBS)	68.1	34.5	28.8	6.0	15.1	7.7	3.4	18.6
Preferred-provider health plan (not BCBS)	76.9	27.8	44.9	8.6	26.1	10.2	3.6	10.6
Blue Cross, Blue Shield	**68.3**	**29.5**	**33.7**	**7.3**	**17.4**	**9.0**	**3.3**	**17.6**
Traditional fee-for-service health plan	66.0	31.8	28.5	7.5	13.7	7.3	1.7	24.4
Preferred-provider health plan	73.8	23.7	45.0	10.7	22.6	11.7	4.0	12.8
Health maintenance organization	68.9	27.3	35.4	6.9	20.5	8.0	3.8	13.8
Commercial Medicare supplement	57.2	44.8	9.7	0.3	2.7	6.6	1.9	29.4
Other BCBS health insurance	70.3	29.8	38.4	7.4	20.1	10.9	5.9	14.6
Health maintenance plans (HMOs)	**70.5**	**24.1**	**40.7**	**6.1**	**22.0**	**12.5**	**4.3**	**12.8**
Medicare payments	**53.7**	**42.4**	**5.9**	**0.3**	**0.9**	**4.8**	**1.3**	**31.8**
Commercial Medicare supplements/ other health insurance	**61.9**	**39.3**	**18.9**	**2.5**	**8.7**	**7.6**	**1.4**	**26.4**
Commercial Medicare supplement (not BCBS)	57.5	40.4	13.1	2.0	4.2	7.0	0.9	29.5
Other health insurance (not BCBS)	69.6	37.5	28.9	3.6	16.6	8.7	2.3	21.1
MEDICAL SERVICES	**68.7**	**29.0**	**35.1**	**5.3**	**18.7**	**11.0**	**4.2**	**16.5**
Physician's services	73.6	30.4	36.4	8.1	17.8	10.4	3.6	12.5
Dental services	69.3	29.2	35.9	2.7	21.0	12.1	4.4	16.2
Eye care services	63.5	22.6	37.3	2.8	20.1	14.4	3.6	23.6
Service by professionals other than physician	63.5	24.7	36.0	6.1	19.9	10.0	4.4	20.0
Lab tests, X-rays	67.2	35.3	29.4	4.2	16.5	8.7	3.5	18.4
Hospital room	67.1	26.9	34.1	9.9	14.4	9.8	6.7	18.2
Hospital services other than room	69.7	27.5	37.6	8.2	16.7	12.8	4.4	14.7
Care in convalescent or nursing home	43.1	38.4	4.7	0.9	1.9	1.9	3.1	29.2
Other medical services	16.7	–	17.2	–	16.9	–	–	26.5
DRUGS	**63.3**	**34.8**	**22.8**	**2.8**	**11.1**	**8.9**	**2.3**	**22.1**
Nonprescription drugs	60.5	26.5	29.2	5.0	14.4	9.8	4.5	19.6
Nonprescription vitamins	64.1	27.2	29.7	4.2	17.9	7.6	1.7	21.2
Prescription drugs	63.7	37.3	20.8	2.2	9.7	8.9	2.0	22.7
MEDICAL SUPPLIES	**64.7**	**32.2**	**28.2**	**3.4**	**15.2**	**9.6**	**4.4**	**19.0**
Eyeglasses and contact lenses	67.2	27.9	34.5	3.6	19.8	11.0	4.9	16.6
Hearing aids	56.1	47.5	8.3	0.7	3.3	4.3	0.4	32.9
Topicals and dressings	68.1	31.1	32.7	5.3	16.7	10.8	2.9	14.8
Medical equipment for general use	57.7	32.1	18.4	1.2	10.3	6.9	5.6	28.5
Supportive, convalescent medical equipment	53.5	31.2	11.0	0.8	4.4	5.8	19.5	19.6
Rental of medical equipment	75.8	60.3	11.6	2.0	4.4	5.2	0.3	13.9
Rental of supportive, convalescent medical equipment	49.9	34.5	11.3	1.3	1.8	8.0	1.5	26.8

Note: Market share for total consumer units is 100.0%. Market shares by type of consumer unit will not add to total because not all types of consumer units are shown. (–) means sample is too small to make a reliable estimate.

Source: Calculations by New Strategist based on the 2002 Consumer Expenditure Survey

Table 7.13 Health Care: Average spending by race and Hispanic origin, 2002

(average annual out-of-pocket spending of consumer units (CU) on health care, by race and Hispanic origin of consumer unit reference person, 2002)

	total consumer units	race		Hispanic origin	
		black	white and other	Hispanic	non-Hispanic
Number of consumer units					
(in thousands, add 000)	112,108	13,554	98,553	10,500	101,608
Average number of persons per CU	2.5	2.7	2.5	3.3	2.4
Average before-tax income of CU	$49,430.00	$35,944.00	$51,177.00	$37,360.00	$50,742.00
Average spending of CU, total	40,676.60	30,135.94	42,134.55	34,742.47	41,294.67
Health care, average spending	2,350.32	1,339.34	2,489.63	1,365.88	2,451.87
HEALTH INSURANCE	$1,167.71	$746.79	$1,225.60	$670.75	$1,219.07
Commercial health insurance	217.53	105.69	232.91	111.16	228.52
Traditional fee-for-service health plan (not BCBS)	68.27	32.11	73.24	25.94	72.65
Preferred-provider health plan (not BCBS)	149.26	73.58	159.67	85.22	155.87
Blue Cross, Blue Shield	315.67	165.10	336.38	160.01	331.76
Traditional fee-for-service health plan	53.76	29.36	57.11	7.75	58.51
Preferred-provider health plan	106.99	42.49	115.86	41.07	113.80
Health maintenance organization	101.53	72.02	105.58	86.84	103.04
Commercial Medicare supplement	47.35	18.31	51.35	20.79	50.10
Other BCBS health insurance	6.05	2.91	6.48	3.56	6.31
Health maintenance plans (HMOs)	280.47	251.60	284.44	228.76	285.81
Medicare payments	186.87	140.68	193.22	109.00	194.91
Commercial Medicare supplements/ other health insurance	167.18	83.73	178.66	61.82	178.07
Commercial Medicare supplement (not BCBS)	106.32	55.81	113.27	43.44	112.82
Other health insurance (not BCBS)	60.86	27.92	65.39	18.38	65.25
MEDICAL SERVICES	589.87	247.44	636.97	357.68	613.85
Physician's services	147.53	57.08	159.97	102.85	152.15
Dental services	226.99	101.37	244.26	118.97	238.15
Eye care services	34.20	15.78	36.73	20.45	35.62
Service by professionals other than physician	42.76	11.42	47.08	14.70	45.66
Lab tests, X-rays	26.79	14.69	28.45	19.14	27.58
Hospital room	36.57	17.97	39.13	36.94	36.53
Hospital services other than room	51.51	26.13	55.00	35.63	53.15
Care in convalescent or nursing home	12.46	0.20	14.15	0.75	13.67
Other medical services	9.46	2.79	10.38	8.25	9.59
DRUGS	487.43	294.67	514.16	271.37	509.63
Nonprescription drugs	64.45	42.70	67.53	60.25	64.85
Nonprescription vitamins	49.15	17.26	53.67	39.04	50.10
Prescription drugs	373.83	234.72	392.96	172.08	394.68
MEDICAL SUPPLIES	105.31	50.43	112.89	66.08	109.33
Eyeglasses and contact lenses	52.26	27.33	55.69	32.45	54.30
Hearing aids	14.98	0.17	17.02	4.46	16.07
Topicals and dressings	27.56	18.83	28.80	23.62	27.94
Medical equipment for general use	2.69	0.57	2.98	2.19	2.74
Supportive, convalescent medical equipment	5.21	1.03	5.78	2.45	5.49
Rental of medical equipment	1.06	0.50	1.14	0.19	1.15
Rental of supportive, convalescent medical equipment	1.55	2.00	1.49	0.70	1.64

Note: Other races include Asians, Native Americans, and Pacific Islanders.
Source: Bureau of Labor Statistics, unpublished tables from the 2002 Consumer Expenditure Survey

(indexed average annual out-of-pocket spending of consumer units (CU) on health care, by race and Hispanic origin of consumer unit reference person, 2002; index definition: an index of 100 is the average for all consumer units; an index of 132 means that spending by consumer units in that group is 32 percent above the average for all consumer units; an index of 68 indicates spending that is 32 percent below the average for all consumer units)

	total consumer units	race		Hispanic origin	
		black	white and other	Hispanic	non-Hispanic
Average spending of CU, total	$40,677	$30,136	$42,135	$34,742	$41,295
Average spending of CU, index	100	74	104	85	102
Health care, spending index	100	57	106	58	104
HEALTH INSURANCE	**100**	**64**	**105**	**57**	**104**
Commercial health insurance	100	49	107	51	105
Traditional fee-for-service health plan (not BCBS)	100	47	107	38	106
Preferred-provider health plan (not BCBS)	100	49	107	57	104
Blue Cross, Blue Shield	100	52	107	51	105
Traditional fee-for-service health plan	100	55	106	14	109
Preferred-provider health plan	100	40	108	38	106
Health maintenance organization	100	71	104	86	101
Commercial Medicare supplement	100	39	108	44	106
Other BCBS health insurance	100	48	107	59	104
Health maintenance plans (HMOs)	**100**	**90**	**101**	**82**	**102**
Medicare payments	**100**	**75**	**103**	**58**	**104**
Commercial Medicare supplements/ other health insurance	**100**	**50**	**107**	**37**	**107**
Commercial Medicare supplement (not BCBS)	100	52	107	41	106
Other health insurance (not BCBS)	100	46	107	30	107
MEDICAL SERVICES	**100**	**42**	**108**	**61**	**104**
Physician's services	100	39	108	70	103
Dental services	100	45	108	52	105
Eye care services	100	46	107	60	104
Service by professionals other than physician	100	27	110	34	107
Lab tests, X-rays	100	55	106	71	103
Hospital room	100	49	107	101	100
Hospital services other than room	100	51	107	69	103
Care in convalescent or nursing home	100	2	114	6	110
Other medical services	100	29	110	87	101
DRUGS	**100**	**60**	**105**	**56**	**105**
Nonprescription drugs	100	66	105	93	101
Nonprescription vitamins	100	35	109	79	102
Prescription drugs	100	63	105	46	106
MEDICAL SUPPLIES	**100**	**48**	**107**	**63**	**104**
Eyeglasses and contact lenses	100	52	107	62	104
Hearing aids	100	1	114	30	107
Topicals and dressings	100	68	104	86	101
Medical equipment for general use	100	21	111	81	102
Supportive, convalescent medical equipment	100	20	111	47	105
Rental of medical equipment	100	47	108	18	108
Rental of supportive, convalescent medical equipment	100	129	96	45	106

Note: Other races include Asians, Native Americans, and Pacific Islanders.
Source: Calculations by New Strategist based on the 2002 Consumer Expenditure Survey

Table 7.15 Health Care: Total spending by race and Hispanic origin, 2002

(total annual out-of-pocket spending on health care, by consumer unit race and Hispanic origin groups, 2002; numbers in thousands)

	total consumer units	race black	race white and other	Hispanic origin Hispanic	Hispanic origin non-Hispanic
Number of consumer units	112,108	13,554	98,553	10,500	101,608
Total spending of all consumer units	$4,560,172,273	$408,462,531	$4,152,486,306	$364,795,935	$4,195,868,829
Health care, total spending	263,489,675	18,153,414	245,360,505	14,341,740	249,129,607
HEALTH INSURANCE	$130,909,633	$10,121,992	$120,786,557	$7,042,875	$123,867,265
Commercial health insurance	24,386,853	1,432,522	22,953,979	1,167,180	23,219,460
Traditional fee-for-service health plan (not BCBS)	7,653,613	435,219	7,218,022	272,370	7,381,821
Preferred-provider health plan (not BCBS)	16,733,240	997,303	15,735,958	894,810	15,837,639
Blue Cross, Blue Shield	35,389,132	2,237,765	33,151,258	1,680,105	33,709,470
Traditional fee-for-service health plan	6,026,926	397,945	5,628,362	81,375	5,945,084
Preferred-provider health plan	11,994,435	575,909	11,418,351	431,235	11,562,990
Health maintenance organization	11,382,325	976,159	10,405,226	911,820	10,469,688
Commercial Medicare supplement	5,308,314	248,174	5,060,697	218,295	5,090,561
Other BCBS health insurance	678,253	39,442	638,623	37,380	641,146
Health maintenance plans (HMOs)	31,442,931	3,410,186	28,032,415	2,401,980	29,040,582
Medicare payments	20,949,622	1,906,777	19,042,411	1,144,500	19,804,415
Commercial Medicare supplements/ other health insurance	18,742,215	1,134,876	17,607,479	649,110	18,093,337
Commercial Medicare supplement (not BCBS)	11,919,323	756,449	11,163,098	456,120	11,463,415
Other health insurance (not BCBS)	6,822,893	378,428	6,444,381	192,990	6,629,922
MEDICAL SERVICES	66,129,146	3,353,802	62,775,304	3,755,640	62,372,071
Physician's services	16,539,293	773,662	15,765,523	1,079,925	15,459,657
Dental services	25,447,395	1,373,969	24,072,556	1,249,185	24,197,945
Eye care services	3,834,094	213,882	3,619,852	214,725	3,619,277
Service by professionals other than physician	4,793,738	154,787	4,639,875	154,350	4,639,421
Lab tests, X-rays	3,003,373	199,108	2,803,833	200,970	2,802,349
Hospital room	4,099,790	243,565	3,856,379	387,870	3,711,740
Hospital services other than room	5,774,683	354,166	5,420,415	374,115	5,400,465
Care in convalescent or nursing home	1,396,866	2,711	1,394,525	7,875	1,388,981
Other medical services	1,060,542	37,816	1,022,980	86,625	974,421
DRUGS	54,644,802	3,993,957	50,672,010	2,849,385	51,782,485
Nonprescription drugs	7,225,361	578,756	6,655,284	632,625	6,589,279
Nonprescription vitamins	5,510,108	233,942	5,289,340	409,920	5,090,561
Prescription drugs	41,909,334	3,181,395	38,727,387	1,806,840	40,102,645
MEDICAL SUPPLIES	11,806,093	683,528	11,125,648	693,840	11,108,803
Eyeglasses and contact lenses	5,858,764	370,431	5,488,417	340,725	5,517,314
Hearing aids	1,679,378	2,304	1,677,372	46,830	1,632,841
Topicals and dressings	3,089,696	255,222	2,838,326	248,010	2,838,928
Medical equipment for general use	301,571	7,726	293,688	22,995	278,406
Supportive, convalescent medical equipment	584,083	13,961	569,636	25,725	557,828
Rental of medical equipment	118,834	6,777	112,350	1,995	116,849
Rental of supportive, convalescent medical equipment	173,767	27,108	146,844	7,350	166,637

Note: Other races include Asians, Native Americans, and Pacific Islanders. Numbers may not add to total because of rounding.
Source: Calculations by New Strategist based on the 2002 Consumer Expenditure Survey

Table 7.16 Health Care: Market shares by race and Hispanic origin, 2002

(percentage of total annual out-of-pocket spending on health care accounted for by consumer unit race and Hispanic origin groups, 2002)

	total consumer units	race		Hispanic origin	
		black	white and other	Hispanic	non-Hispanic
Share of total consumer units	100.0%	12.1%	87.9%	9.4%	90.6%
Share of total before-tax income	100.0	8.8	91.0	7.1	93.0
Share of total spending	100.0	9.0	91.1	8.0	92.0
Share of health care spending	100.0	6.9	93.1	5.4	94.6
HEALTH INSURANCE	100.0%	7.7%	92.3%	5.4%	94.6%
Commercial health insurance	100.0	5.9	94.1	4.8	95.2
Traditional fee-for-service health plan (not BCBS)	100.0	5.7	94.3	3.6	96.4
Preferred-provider health plan (not BCBS)	100.0	6.0	94.0	5.3	94.6
Blue Cross, Blue Shield	100.0	6.3	93.7	4.7	95.3
Traditional fee-for-service health plan	100.0	6.6	93.4	1.4	98.6
Preferred-provider health plan	100.0	4.8	95.2	3.6	96.4
Health maintenance organization	100.0	8.6	91.4	8.0	92.0
Commercial Medicare supplement	100.0	4.7	95.3	4.1	95.9
Other BCBS health insurance	100.0	5.8	94.2	5.5	94.5
Health maintenance plans (HMOs)	100.0	10.8	89.2	7.6	92.4
Medicare payments	100.0	9.1	90.9	5.5	94.5
Commercial Medicare supplements/ other health insurance	100.0	6.1	93.9	3.5	96.5
Commercial Medicare supplement (not BCBS)	100.0	6.3	93.7	3.8	96.2
Other health insurance (not BCBS)	100.0	5.5	94.5	2.8	97.2
MEDICAL SERVICES	100.0	5.1	94.9	5.7	94.3
Physician's services	100.0	4.7	95.3	6.5	93.5
Dental services	100.0	5.4	94.6	4.9	95.1
Eye care services	100.0	5.6	94.4	5.6	94.4
Service by professionals other than physician	100.0	3.2	96.8	3.2	96.8
Lab tests, X-rays	100.0	6.6	93.4	6.7	93.3
Hospital room	100.0	5.9	94.1	9.5	90.5
Hospital services other than room	100.0	6.1	93.9	6.5	93.5
Care in convalescent or nursing home	100.0	0.2	99.8	0.6	99.4
Other medical services	100.0	3.6	96.5	8.2	91.9
DRUGS	100.0	7.3	92.7	5.2	94.8
Nonprescription drugs	100.0	8.0	92.1	8.8	91.2
Nonprescription vitamins	100.0	4.2	96.0	7.4	92.4
Prescription drugs	100.0	7.6	92.4	4.3	95.7
MEDICAL SUPPLIES	100.0	5.8	94.2	5.9	94.1
Eyeglasses and contact lenses	100.0	6.3	93.7	5.8	94.2
Hearing aids	100.0	0.1	99.9	2.8	97.2
Topicals and dressings	100.0	8.3	91.9	8.0	91.9
Medical equipment for general use	100.0	2.6	97.4	7.6	92.3
Supportive, convalescent medical equipment	100.0	2.4	97.5	4.4	95.5
Rental of medical equipment	100.0	5.7	94.5	1.7	98.3
Rental of supportive, convalescent medical equipment	100.0	15.6	84.5	4.2	95.9

Note: Other races include Asians, Native Americans, and Pacific Islanders. Numbers may not add to total because of rounding.
Source: Calculations by New Strategist based on the 2002 Consumer Expenditure Survey

Table 7.17 Health Care: Average spending by region, 2002

(average annual out-of-pocket spending of consumer units (CU) on health care, by region in which consumer unit lives, 2002)

	total consumer units	Northeast	Midwest	South	West
Number of consumer units (in thousands, add 000)	112,108	21,313	25,883	40,004	24,907
Average number of persons per CU	2.5	2.5	2.5	2.5	2.6
Average before-tax income of CU	$49,430.00	$53,983.00	$49,197.00	$45,641.00	$52,016.00
Average spending of CU, total	40,676.60	42,390.20	40,601.14	37,280.55	44,728.34
Health care, average spending	2,350.32	2,207.26	2,382.67	2,430.74	2,310.07
HEALTH INSURANCE	**$1,167.71**	**$1,177.56**	**$1,184.89**	**$1,195.78**	**$1,096.34**
Commercial health insurance	217.53	120.30	257.94	251.89	203.55
Traditional fee-for-service health plan (not BCBS)	68.27	60.18	98.04	68.22	44.34
Preferred-provider health plan (not BCBS)	149.26	60.12	159.89	183.68	159.20
Blue Cross, Blue Shield	**315.67**	**325.17**	**317.10**	**348.09**	**253.99**
Traditional fee-for-service health plan	53.76	79.42	46.78	54.57	37.74
Preferred-provider health plan	106.99	63.99	125.78	127.40	91.46
Health maintenance organization	101.53	137.95	88.08	98.29	89.53
Commercial Medicare supplement	47.35	39.85	51.57	58.65	31.25
Other BCBS health insurance	6.05	3.95	4.89	9.19	4.01
Health maintenance plans (HMOs)	**280.47**	**381.83**	**243.11**	**229.22**	**314.85**
Medicare payments	**186.87**	**189.54**	**189.79**	**193.24**	**171.32**
Commercial Medicare supplements/ other health insurance	**167.18**	**160.73**	**176.96**	**173.34**	**152.64**
Commercial Medicare supplement (not BCBS)	106.32	107.31	116.58	113.46	83.34
Other health insurance (not BCBS)	60.86	53.42	60.38	59.88	69.30
MEDICAL SERVICES	**589.87**	**505.31**	**565.97**	**596.92**	**675.75**
Physician's services	147.53	118.55	148.26	160.66	150.48
Dental services	226.99	227.10	216.69	190.77	295.75
Eye care services	34.20	32.44	37.04	39.32	24.52
Service by professionals other than physician	42.76	35.29	38.42	40.42	57.44
Lab tests, X-rays	26.79	18.77	26.79	29.73	28.92
Hospital room	36.57	12.78	34.88	48.33	39.79
Hospital services other than room	51.51	31.06	37.72	68.28	56.41
Care in convalescent or nursing home	12.46	22.02	17.14	7.84	6.84
Other medical services	9.46	7.31	9.03	11.57	8.36
DRUGS	**487.43**	**417.78**	**519.31**	**545.62**	**420.58**
Nonprescription drugs	64.45	59.66	72.15	65.34	59.27
Nonprescription vitamins	49.15	42.43	50.63	37.80	71.57
Prescription drugs	373.83	315.69	396.53	442.48	289.74
MEDICAL SUPPLIES	**105.31**	**106.61**	**112.50**	**92.42**	**117.40**
Eyeglasses and contact lenses	52.26	55.69	63.42	42.79	52.93
Hearing aids	14.98	13.66	8.03	15.92	21.81
Topicals and dressings	27.56	28.47	29.70	25.95	27.13
Medical equipment for general use	2.69	2.46	2.99	2.39	3.04
Supportive, convalescent medical equipment	5.21	4.13	5.09	2.45	10.70
Rental of medical equipment	1.06	0.41	1.29	1.56	0.58
Rental of supportive, convalescent medical equipment	1.55	1.78	1.97	1.37	1.20

Source: Bureau of Labor Statistics, unpublished tables from the 2002 Consumer Expenditure Survey

Table 7.18 Health Care: Indexed spending by region, 2002

(indexed average annual out-of-pocket spending of consumer units (CU) on health care, by region in which consumer unit lives, 2002; index definition: an index of 100 is the average for all consumer units; an index of 132 means that spending by consumer units in that group is 32 percent above the average for all consumer units; an index of 68 indicates spending that is 32 percent below the average for all consumer units)

	total consumer units	Northeast	Midwest	South	West
Average spending of CU, total	$40,677	$42,390	$40,601	$37,281	$44,728
Average spending of CU, index	100	104	100	92	110
Health care, spending index	100	94	101	103	98
HEALTH INSURANCE	100	101	101	102	94
Commercial health insurance	100	55	119	116	94
Traditional fee-for-service health plan (not BCBS)	100	88	144	100	65
Preferred-provider health plan (not BCBS)	100	40	107	123	107
Blue Cross, Blue Shield	100	103	100	110	80
Traditional fee-for-service health plan	100	148	87	102	70
Preferred-provider health plan	100	60	118	119	85
Health maintenance organization	100	136	87	97	88
Commercial Medicare supplement	100	84	109	124	66
Other BCBS health insurance	100	65	81	152	66
Health maintenance plans (HMOs)	100	136	87	82	112
Medicare payments	100	101	102	103	92
Commercial Medicare supplements/ other health insurance	100	96	106	104	91
Commercial Medicare supplement (not BCBS)	100	101	110	107	78
Other health insurance (not BCBS)	100	88	99	98	114
MEDICAL SERVICES	100	86	96	101	115
Physician's services	100	80	100	109	102
Dental services	100	100	95	84	130
Eye care services	100	95	108	115	72
Service by professionals other than physician	100	83	90	95	134
Lab tests, X-rays	100	70	100	111	108
Hospital room	100	35	95	132	109
Hospital services other than room	100	60	73	133	110
Care in convalescent or nursing home	100	177	138	63	55
Other medical services	100	77	95	122	88
DRUGS	100	86	107	112	86
Nonprescription drugs	100	93	112	101	92
Nonprescription vitamins	100	86	103	77	146
Prescription drugs	100	84	106	118	78
MEDICAL SUPPLIES	100	101	107	88	111
Eyeglasses and contact lenses	100	107	121	82	101
Hearing aids	100	91	54	106	146
Topicals and dressings	100	103	108	94	98
Medical equipment for general use	100	91	111	89	113
Supportive, convalescent medical equipment	100	79	98	47	205
Rental of medical equipment	100	39	122	147	55
Rental of supportive, convalescent medical equipment	100	115	127	88	77

Source: Calculations by New Strategist based on the 2002 Consumer Expenditure Survey

Table 7.19 Health Care: Total spending by region, 2002

(total annual out-of-pocket spending on health care, by region in which consumer units live, 2002; numbers in thousands)

	total consumer units	Northeast	Midwest	South	West
Number of consumer units	112,108	21,313	25,883	40,004	24,907
Total spending of all consumer units	$4,560,172,273	$903,462,333	$1,050,879,307	$1,491,371,122	$1,114,048,764
Health care, total spending	263,489,675	47,043,332	61,670,648	97,239,323	57,536,913
HEALTH INSURANCE	**$130,909,633**	**$25,097,336**	**$30,668,508**	**$47,835,983**	**$27,306,540**
Commercial health insurance	**24,386,853**	**2,563,954**	**6,676,261**	**10,076,608**	**5,069,820**
Traditional fee-for-service health plan (not BCBS)	7,653,613	1,282,616	2,537,569	2,729,073	1,104,376
Preferred-provider health plan (not BCBS)	16,733,240	1,281,338	4,138,433	7,347,935	3,965,194
Blue Cross, Blue Shield	**35,389,132**	**6,930,348**	**8,207,499**	**13,924,992**	**6,326,129**
Traditional fee-for-service health plan	6,026,926	1,692,678	1,210,807	2,183,018	939,990
Preferred-provider health plan	11,994,435	1,363,819	3,255,564	5,096,510	2,277,994
Health maintenance organization	11,382,325	2,940,128	2,279,775	3,931,993	2,229,924
Commercial Medicare supplement	5,308,314	849,323	1,334,786	2,346,235	778,344
Other BCBS health insurance	678,253	84,186	126,568	367,637	99,877
Health maintenance plans (HMOs)	**31,442,931**	**8,137,943**	**6,292,416**	**9,169,717**	**7,841,969**
Medicare payments	**20,949,622**	**4,039,666**	**4,912,335**	**7,730,373**	**4,267,067**
Commercial Medicare supplements/ other health insurance	**18,742,215**	**3,425,638**	**4,580,256**	**6,934,293**	**3,801,804**
Commercial Medicare supplement (not BCBS)	11,919,323	2,287,098	3,017,440	4,538,854	2,075,749
Other health insurance (not BCBS)	6,822,893	1,138,540	1,562,816	2,395,440	1,726,055
MEDICAL SERVICES	**66,129,146**	**10,769,672**	**14,649,002**	**23,879,188**	**16,830,905**
Physician's services	16,539,293	2,526,656	3,837,414	6,427,043	3,748,005
Dental services	25,447,395	4,840,182	5,608,587	7,631,563	7,366,245
Eye care services	3,834,094	691,394	958,706	1,572,957	610,720
Service by professionals other than physician	4,793,738	752,136	994,425	1,616,962	1,430,658
Lab tests, X-rays	3,003,373	400,045	693,406	1,189,319	720,310
Hospital room	4,099,790	272,380	902,799	1,933,393	991,050
Hospital services other than room	5,774,683	661,982	976,307	2,731,473	1,405,004
Care in convalescent or nursing home	1,396,866	469,312	443,635	313,631	170,364
Other medical services	1,060,542	155,798	233,723	462,846	208,223
DRUGS	**54,644,802**	**8,904,145**	**13,441,301**	**21,826,982**	**10,475,386**
Nonprescription drugs	7,225,361	1,271,534	1,867,458	2,613,861	1,476,238
Nonprescription vitamins	5,510,108	904,311	1,310,456	1,512,151	1,782,594
Prescription drugs	41,909,334	6,728,301	10,263,386	17,700,970	7,216,554
MEDICAL SUPPLIES	**11,806,093**	**2,272,179**	**2,911,838**	**3,697,170**	**2,924,082**
Eyeglasses and contact lenses	5,858,764	1,186,921	1,641,500	1,711,771	1,318,328
Hearing aids	1,679,378	291,136	207,840	636,864	543,222
Topicals and dressings	3,089,696	606,781	768,725	1,038,104	675,727
Medical equipment for general use	301,571	52,430	77,390	95,610	75,717
Supportive, convalescent medical equipment	584,083	88,023	131,744	98,010	266,505
Rental of medical equipment	118,834	8,738	33,389	62,406	14,446
Rental of supportive, convalescent medical equipment	173,767	37,937	50,990	54,805	29,888

Note: Numbers may not add to total because of rounding.
Source: Calculations by New Strategist based on the 2002 Consumer Expenditure Survey

Table 7.20 Health Care: Market shares by region, 2002

(percentage of total annual out-of-pocket spending on health care accounted for by consumer units by region, 2002)

	total consumer units	Northeast	Midwest	South	West
Share of total consumer units	100.0%	19.0%	23.1%	35.7%	22.2%
Share of total before-tax income	100.0	20.8	23.0	32.9	23.4
Share of total spending	100.0	19.8	23.0	32.7	24.4
Share of health care spending	100.0	17.9	23.4	36.9	21.8
HEALTH INSURANCE	100.0%	19.2%	23.4%	36.5%	20.9%
Commercial health insurance	100.0	10.5	27.4	41.3	20.8
Traditional fee-for-service health plan (not BCBS)	100.0	16.8	33.2	35.7	14.4
Preferred-provider health plan (not BCBS)	100.0	7.7	24.7	43.9	23.7
Blue Cross, Blue Shield	100.0	19.6	23.2	39.3	17.9
Traditional fee-for-service health plan	100.0	28.1	20.1	36.2	15.6
Preferred-provider health plan	100.0	11.4	27.1	42.5	19.0
Health maintenance organization	100.0	25.8	20.0	34.5	19.6
Commercial Medicare supplement	100.0	16.0	25.1	44.2	14.7
Other BCBS health insurance	100.0	12.4	18.7	54.2	14.7
Health maintenance plans (HMOs)	100.0	25.9	20.0	29.2	24.9
Medicare payments	100.0	19.3	23.4	36.9	20.4
Commercial Medicare supplements/ other health insurance	100.0	18.3	24.4	37.0	20.3
Commercial Medicare supplement (not BCBS)	100.0	19.2	25.3	38.1	17.4
Other health insurance (not BCBS)	100.0	16.7	22.9	35.1	25.3
MEDICAL SERVICES	100.0	16.3	22.2	36.1	25.5
Physician's services	100.0	15.3	23.2	38.9	22.7
Dental services	100.0	19.0	22.0	30.0	28.9
Eye care services	100.0	18.0	25.0	41.0	15.9
Service by professionals other than physician	100.0	15.7	20.7	33.7	29.8
Lab tests, X-rays	100.0	13.3	23.1	39.6	24.0
Hospital room	100.0	6.6	22.0	47.2	24.2
Hospital services other than room	100.0	11.5	16.9	47.3	24.3
Care in convalescent or nursing home	100.0	33.6	31.8	22.5	12.2
Other medical services	100.0	14.7	22.0	43.6	19.6
DRUGS	100.0	16.3	24.6	39.9	19.2
Nonprescription drugs	100.0	17.6	25.8	36.2	20.4
Nonprescription vitamins	100.0	16.4	23.8	27.4	32.4
Prescription drugs	100.0	16.1	24.5	42.2	17.2
MEDICAL SUPPLIES	100.0	19.2	24.7	31.3	24.8
Eyeglasses and contact lenses	100.0	20.3	28.0	29.2	22.5
Hearing aids	100.0	17.3	12.4	37.9	32.3
Topicals and dressings	100.0	19.6	24.9	33.6	21.9
Medical equipment for general use	100.0	17.4	25.7	31.7	25.1
Supportive, convalescent medical equipment	100.0	15.1	22.6	16.8	45.6
Rental of medical equipment	100.0	7.4	28.1	52.5	12.2
Rental of supportive, convalescent medical equipment	100.0	21.8	29.3	31.5	17.2

Note: Numbers may not add to total because of rounding.
Source: Calculations by New Strategist based on the 2002 Consumer Expenditure Survey

Table 7.21 Health Care: Average spending by education, 2002

(average annual out-of-pocket spending of consumer units (CU) on health care, by education of consumer unit reference person, 2002)

	total consumer units	less than high school graduate	high school graduate	some college	associate's degree	college graduate total	bachelor's degree	master's, professional, doctorate
Number of consumer units (in thousands, add 000)	112,108	17,075	31,961	23,260	10,395	29,417	19,082	10,335
Average number of persons per CU	2.5	2.6	2.5	2.4	2.6	2.5	2.5	2.5
Average before-tax income of CU	$49,430.00	$25,564.00	$39,618.00	$42,598.00	$54,860.00	$77,820.00	$69,408.00	$92,783.00
Average spending of CU, total	40,676.60	24,930.40	33,707.63	38,653.57	44,405.79	57,384.01	53,731.57	64,118.48
Health care, average spending	2,350.32	1,796.82	2,207.91	2,149.29	2,534.99	2,913.92	2,740.29	3,234.14
HEALTH INSURANCE	**$1,167.71**	**$913.66**	**$1,132.51**	**$1,051.15**	**$1,247.52**	**$1,417.39**	**$1,349.46**	**$1,542.82**
Commercial health insurance	217.53	102.67	182.96	204.24	264.02	315.84	299.64	345.73
Traditional fee-for-service health plan (not BCBS)	68.27	40.45	68.22	66.07	91.33	78.07	63.02	105.87
Preferred-provider health plan (not BCBS)	149.26	62.22	114.74	138.17	172.69	237.76	236.63	239.86
Blue Cross, Blue Shield	**315.67**	**191.62**	**299.48**	**285.78**	**348.10**	**417.45**	**403.65**	**442.91**
Traditional fee-for-service health plan	53.76	30.22	52.68	53.70	47.56	70.82	60.90	89.13
Preferred-provider health plan	106.99	29.47	94.50	101.02	121.83	165.02	162.83	169.06
Health maintenance organization	101.53	56.15	96.56	91.52	113.27	137.02	138.56	134.17
Commercial Medicare supplement	47.35	71.42	50.25	35.87	55.44	36.46	32.19	44.34
Other BCBS health insurance	6.05	4.36	5.50	3.67	10.00	8.13	9.17	6.21
Health maintenance plans (HMOs)	**280.47**	**138.17**	**255.58**	**261.62**	**349.37**	**380.65**	**368.74**	**402.64**
Medicare payments	**186.87**	**325.08**	**218.40**	**146.17**	**130.93**	**124.34**	**118.01**	**136.02**
Commercial Medicare supplements/ other health insurance	**167.18**	**156.11**	**176.09**	**153.35**	**155.10**	**179.12**	**159.41**	**215.52**
Commercial Medicare supplement (not BCBS)	106.32	132.10	123.95	93.95	81.61	90.73	74.38	120.90
Other health insurance (not BCBS)	60.86	24.02	52.14	59.40	73.49	88.39	85.03	94.61
MEDICAL SERVICES	**589.87**	**330.10**	**489.15**	**550.24**	**680.16**	**849.02**	**764.38**	**1,005.39**
Physician's services	147.53	84.96	136.49	132.61	135.00	212.06	200.24	233.88
Dental services	226.99	96.11	185.63	216.79	280.21	337.14	311.33	384.80
Eye care services	34.20	16.27	23.33	40.79	41.45	48.63	45.73	53.96
Service by professionals other than physician	42.76	21.75	24.29	32.69	54.26	78.94	61.19	111.72
Lab tests, X-rays	26.79	19.33	21.57	32.19	33.96	29.97	25.78	37.71
Hospital room	36.57	37.63	35.05	23.91	50.61	42.65	34.79	57.17
Hospital services other than room	51.51	41.43	49.07	58.47	57.66	52.34	48.47	59.48
Care in convalescent or nursing home	12.46	2.77	8.44	3.44	11.98	29.75	18.18	51.13
Other medical services	9.46	9.85	5.27	9.35	15.03	11.91	9.95	15.54
DRUGS	**487.43**	**489.06**	**496.18**	**446.09**	**505.04**	**499.62**	**477.64**	**539.74**
Nonprescription drugs	64.45	57.48	61.93	61.88	64.06	72.28	69.35	77.61
Nonprescription vitamins	49.15	36.61	29.55	42.92	57.66	76.95	61.64	104.80
Prescription drugs	373.83	394.98	404.70	341.28	383.32	350.40	346.64	357.33
MEDICAL SUPPLIES	**105.31**	**64.00**	**90.08**	**101.81**	**102.26**	**147.88**	**148.81**	**146.20**
Eyeglasses and contact lenses	52.26	27.51	42.97	50.95	69.79	71.56	67.48	79.10
Hearing aids	14.98	5.75	16.33	13.90	1.32	24.55	28.58	17.12
Topicals and dressings	27.56	22.14	22.16	20.39	22.99	42.08	42.88	40.64
Medical equipment for general use	2.69	0.98	2.56	2.56	3.02	3.80	4.16	3.12
Supportive, convalescent medical equipment	5.21	3.51	3.54	10.58	3.81	4.26	3.79	5.12
Rental of medical equipment	1.06	3.46	0.77	0.68	0.27	0.57	0.83	0.07
Rental of supportive, convalescent medical equipment	1.55	0.65	1.75	2.76	1.06	1.07	1.09	1.03

Source: Bureau of Labor Statistics, unpublished tables from the 2002 Consumer Expenditure Survey

Table 7.22 Health Care: Indexed spending by education, 2002

(indexed average annual out-of-pocket spending of consumer units (CU) on health care, by education of consumer unit reference person, 2002; index definition: an index of 100 is the average for all consumer units; an index of 132 means that spending by consumer units in that group is 32 percent above the average for all consumer units; an index of 68 indicates spending that is 32 percent below the average for all consumer units)

	total consumer units	less than high school graduate	high school graduate	some college	associate's degree	college graduate total	bachelor's degree	master's, professional, doctorate
Average spending of CU, total	$40,677	$24,930	$33,708	$38,654	$44,406	$57,384	$53,732	$64,118
Average spending of CU, index	100	61	83	95	109	141	132	158
Health care, spending index	100	76	94	91	108	124	117	138
HEALTH INSURANCE	100	78	97	90	107	121	116	132
Commercial health insurance	100	47	84	94	121	145	138	159
Traditional fee-for-service health plan (not BCBS)	100	59	100	97	134	114	92	155
Preferred-provider health plan (not BCBS)	100	42	77	93	116	159	159	161
Blue Cross, Blue Shield	100	61	95	91	110	132	128	140
Traditional fee-for-service health plan	100	56	98	100	88	132	113	166
Preferred-provider health plan	100	28	88	94	114	154	152	158
Health maintenance organization	100	55	95	90	112	135	136	132
Commercial Medicare supplement	100	151	106	76	117	77	68	94
Other BCBS health insurance	100	72	91	61	165	134	152	103
Health maintenance plans (HMOs)	100	49	91	93	125	136	131	144
Medicare payments	100	174	117	78	70	67	63	73
Commercial Medicare supplements/ other health insurance	100	93	105	92	93	107	95	129
Commercial Medicare supplement (not BCBS)	100	124	117	88	77	85	70	114
Other health insurance (not BCBS)	100	39	86	98	121	145	140	155
MEDICAL SERVICES	100	56	83	93	115	144	130	170
Physician's services	100	58	93	90	92	144	136	159
Dental services	100	42	82	96	123	149	137	170
Eye care services	100	48	68	119	121	142	134	158
Service by professionals other than physician	100	51	57	76	127	185	143	261
Lab tests, X-rays	100	72	81	120	127	112	96	141
Hospital room	100	103	96	65	138	117	95	156
Hospital services other than room	100	80	95	114	112	102	94	115
Care in convalescent or nursing home	100	22	68	28	96	239	146	410
Other medical services	100	104	56	99	159	126	105	164
DRUGS	100	100	102	92	104	103	98	111
Nonprescription drugs	100	89	96	96	99	112	108	120
Nonprescription vitamins	100	74	60	87	117	157	125	213
Prescription drugs	100	106	108	91	103	94	93	96
MEDICAL SUPPLIES	100	61	86	97	97	140	141	139
Eyeglasses and contact lenses	100	53	82	97	134	137	129	151
Hearing aids	100	38	109	93	9	164	191	114
Topicals and dressings	100	80	80	74	83	153	156	147
Medical equipment for general use	100	36	95	95	112	141	155	116
Supportive, convalescent medical equipment	100	67	68	203	73	82	73	98
Rental of medical equipment	100	326	73	64	25	54	78	7
Rental of supportive, convalescent medical equipment	100	42	113	178	68	69	70	66

Source: Calculations by New Strategist based on the 2002 Consumer Expenditure Survey

Table 7.23 Health Care: Total spending by education, 2002

(total annual out-of-pocket spending on health care, by consumer unit (CU) educational attainment groups, 2002; numbers in thousands)

	total consumer units	less than high school graduate	high school graduate	some college	associate's degree	college graduate total	bachelor's degree	master's, professional, doctorate
Number of consumer units	112,108	17,075	31,961	23,260	10,395	29,417	19,082	10,335
Total spending of all CUs	$4,560,172,273	$425,686,580	$1,077,329,562	$899,082,038	$461,598,187	$1,688,065,422	$1,025,305,819	$662,664,491
Health care, total spending	263,489,675	30,680,702	70,567,012	49,992,485	26,351,221	85,718,785	52,290,214	33,424,837
HEALTH INSURANCE	**$130,909,633**	**$15,600,745**	**$36,196,152**	**$24,449,749**	**$12,967,970**	**$41,695,362**	**$25,750,396**	**$15,945,045**
Commercial health insurance	**24,386,853**	**1,753,090**	**5,847,585**	**4,750,622**	**2,744,488**	**9,291,065**	**5,717,730**	**3,573,120**
Traditional fee-for-service health plan (not BCBS)	7,653,613	690,684	2,180,379	1,536,788	949,375	2,296,585	1,202,548	1,094,166
Preferred-provider health plan (not BCBS)	16,733,240	1,062,407	3,667,205	3,213,834	1,795,113	6,994,186	4,515,374	2,478,953
Blue Cross, Blue Shield	**35,389,132**	**3,271,912**	**9,571,680**	**6,647,243**	**3,618,500**	**12,280,127**	**7,702,449**	**4,577,475**
Traditional fee-for-service health plan	6,026,926	516,007	1,683,705	1,249,062	494,386	2,083,312	1,162,094	921,159
Preferred-provider health plan	11,994,435	503,200	3,020,315	2,349,725	1,266,423	4,854,393	3,107,122	1,747,235
Health maintenance organization	11,382,325	958,761	3,086,154	2,128,755	1,177,442	4,030,717	2,644,002	1,386,647
Commercial Medicare supplement	5,308,314	1,219,497	1,606,040	834,336	576,299	1,072,544	614,250	458,254
Other BCBS health insurance	678,253	74,447	175,786	85,364	103,950	239,160	174,982	64,180
Health maintenance plans (HMOs)	**31,442,931**	**2,359,253**	**8,168,592**	**6,085,281**	**3,631,701**	**11,197,581**	**7,036,297**	**4,161,284**
Medicare payments	**20,949,622**	**5,550,741**	**6,980,282**	**3,399,914**	**1,361,017**	**3,657,710**	**2,251,867**	**1,405,767**
Commercial Medicare supplements/ other health insurance	**18,742,215**	**2,665,578**	**5,628,012**	**3,566,921**	**1,612,265**	**5,269,173**	**3,041,862**	**2,227,399**
Commercial Medicare supplement (not BCBS)	11,919,323	2,255,608	3,961,566	2,185,277	848,336	2,669,004	1,419,319	1,249,502
Other health insurance (not BCBS)	6,822,893	410,142	1,666,447	1,381,644	763,929	2,600,169	1,622,542	977,794
MEDICAL SERVICES	**66,129,146**	**5,636,458**	**15,633,723**	**12,798,582**	**7,070,263**	**24,975,621**	**14,585,899**	**10,390,706**
Physician's services	16,539,293	1,450,692	4,362,357	3,084,509	1,403,325	6,238,169	3,820,980	2,417,150
Dental services	25,447,395	1,641,078	5,932,920	5,042,535	2,912,783	9,917,647	5,940,799	3,976,908
Eye care services	3,834,094	277,810	745,650	948,775	430,873	1,430,549	872,620	557,677
Service by professionals other than physician	4,793,738	371,381	776,333	760,369	564,033	2,322,178	1,167,628	1,154,626
Lab tests, X-rays	3,003,373	330,060	689,399	748,739	353,014	881,627	491,934	389,733
Hospital room	4,099,790	642,532	1,120,233	556,147	526,091	1,254,635	663,863	590,852
Hospital services other than room	5,774,683	707,417	1,568,326	1,360,012	599,376	1,539,686	924,905	614,726
Care in convalescent or nursing home	1,396,866	47,298	269,751	80,014	124,532	875,156	346,911	528,429
Other medical services	1,060,542	168,189	168,434	217,481	156,237	350,356	189,866	160,606
DRUGS	**54,644,802**	**8,350,700**	**15,858,409**	**10,376,053**	**5,249,891**	**14,697,322**	**9,114,326**	**5,578,213**
Nonprescription drugs	7,225,361	981,471	1,979,345	1,439,329	665,904	2,126,261	1,323,337	802,099
Nonprescription vitamins	5,510,108	625,116	944,448	998,319	599,376	2,263,638	1,176,214	1,083,108
Prescription drugs	41,909,334	6,744,284	12,934,617	7,938,173	3,984,611	10,307,717	6,614,584	3,693,006
MEDICAL SUPPLIES	**11,806,093**	**1,092,800**	**2,879,047**	**2,368,101**	**1,062,993**	**4,350,186**	**2,839,592**	**1,510,977**
Eyeglasses and contact lenses	5,858,764	469,733	1,373,364	1,185,097	725,467	2,105,081	1,287,653	817,499
Hearing aids	1,679,378	98,181	521,923	323,314	13,721	722,187	545,364	176,935
Topicals and dressings	3,089,696	378,041	708,256	474,271	238,981	1,237,867	818,236	420,014
Medical equipment for general use	301,571	16,734	81,820	59,546	31,393	111,785	79,381	32,245
Supportive, convalescent medical equipment	584,083	59,933	113,142	246,091	39,605	125,316	72,321	52,915
Rental of medical equipment	118,834	59,080	24,610	15,817	2,807	16,768	15,838	723
Rental of supportive, convalescent medical equipment	173,767	11,099	55,932	64,198	11,019	31,476	20,799	10,645

Note: Numbers may not add to total because of rounding.
Source: Calculations by New Strategist based on the 2002 Consumer Expenditure Survey

Table 7.24 Health Care: Market shares by education, 2002

(percentage of total annual out-of-pocket spending on health care accounted for by consumer unit educational attainment groups, 2002)

	total consumer units	less than high school graduate	high school graduate	some college	associate's degree	college graduate total	bachelor's degree	master's, professional, doctorate
Share of total consumer units	100.0%	15.2%	28.5%	20.7%	9.3%	26.2%	17.0%	9.2%
Share of total before-tax income	100.0	7.9	22.8	17.9	10.3	41.3	23.9	17.3
Share of total spending	100.0	9.3	23.6	19.7	10.1	37.0	22.5	14.5
Share of health care spending	100.0	11.6	26.8	19.0	10.0	32.5	19.8	12.7
HEALTH INSURANCE	100.0%	11.9%	27.6%	18.7%	9.9%	31.9%	19.7%	12.2%
Commercial health insurance	100.0	7.2	24.0	19.5	11.3	38.1	23.4	14.7
Traditional fee-for-service health plan (not BCBS)	100.0	9.0	28.5	20.1	12.4	30.0	15.7	14.3
Preferred-provider health plan (not BCBS)	100.0	6.3	21.9	19.2	10.7	41.8	27.0	14.8
Blue Cross, Blue Shield	100.0	9.2	27.0	18.8	10.2	34.7	21.8	12.9
Traditional fee-for-service health plan	100.0	8.6	27.9	20.7	8.2	34.6	19.3	15.3
Preferred-provider health plan	100.0	4.2	25.2	19.6	10.6	40.5	25.9	14.6
Health maintenance organization	100.0	8.4	27.1	18.7	10.3	35.4	23.2	12.2
Commercial Medicare supplement	100.0	23.0	30.3	15.7	10.9	20.2	11.6	8.6
Other BCBS health insurance	100.0	11.0	25.9	12.6	15.3	35.3	25.8	9.5
Health maintenance plans (HMOs)	100.0	7.5	26.0	19.4	11.6	35.6	22.4	13.2
Medicare payments	100.0	26.5	33.3	16.2	6.5	17.5	10.7	6.7
Commercial Medicare supplements/ other health insurance	100.0	14.2	30.0	19.0	8.6	28.1	16.2	11.9
Commercial Medicare supplement (not BCBS)	100.0	18.9	33.2	18.3	7.1	22.4	11.9	10.5
Other health insurance (not BCBS)	100.0	6.0	24.4	20.3	11.2	38.1	23.8	14.3
MEDICAL SERVICES	100.0	8.5	23.6	19.4	10.7	37.8	22.1	15.7
Physician's services	100.0	8.8	26.4	18.6	8.5	37.7	23.1	14.6
Dental services	100.0	6.4	23.3	19.8	11.4	39.0	23.3	15.6
Eye care services	100.0	7.2	19.4	24.7	11.2	37.3	22.8	14.5
Service by professionals other than physician	100.0	7.7	16.2	15.9	11.8	48.4	24.4	24.1
Lab tests, X-rays	100.0	11.0	23.0	24.9	11.8	29.4	16.4	13.0
Hospital room	100.0	15.7	27.3	13.6	12.8	30.6	16.2	14.4
Hospital services other than room	100.0	12.3	27.2	23.6	10.4	26.7	16.0	10.6
Care in convalescent or nursing home	100.0	3.4	19.3	5.7	8.9	62.7	24.8	37.8
Other medical services	100.0	15.9	15.9	20.5	14.7	33.0	17.9	15.1
DRUGS	100.0	15.3	29.0	19.0	9.6	26.9	16.7	10.2
Nonprescription drugs	100.0	13.6	27.4	19.9	9.2	29.4	18.3	11.1
Nonprescription vitamins	100.0	11.3	17.1	18.1	10.9	41.1	21.3	19.7
Prescription drugs	100.0	16.1	30.9	18.9	9.5	24.6	15.8	8.8
MEDICAL SUPPLIES	100.0	9.3	24.4	20.1	9.0	36.8	24.1	12.8
Eyeglasses and contact lenses	100.0	8.0	23.4	20.2	12.4	35.9	22.0	14.0
Hearing aids	100.0	5.8	31.1	19.3	0.8	43.0	32.5	10.5
Topicals and dressings	100.0	12.2	22.9	15.4	7.7	40.1	26.5	13.6
Medical equipment for general use	100.0	5.5	27.1	19.7	10.4	37.1	26.3	10.7
Supportive, convalescent medical equipment	100.0	10.3	19.4	42.1	6.8	21.5	12.4	9.1
Rental of medical equipment	100.0	49.7	20.7	13.3	2.4	14.1	13.3	0.6
Rental of supportive, convalescent medical equipment	100.0	6.4	32.2	36.9	6.3	18.1	12.0	6.1

Note: Numbers may not add to total because of rounding.
Source: Calculations by New Strategist based on the 2002 Consumer Expenditure Survey

Spending on Household Operations, 2002

Americans are spending more on housing than ever before as homeownership rates reach record highs. In 2002, housing costs—including shelter, utilities, and all household operations (household services, housekeeping supplies, furniture, and equipment)—absorbed 32.7 percent of the expenditures of the average household. That figure was up from 32.4 percent in 1997. Not all housing categories are experiencing spending gains, however. For example, spending on household furnishings and equipment fell 10 percent between 1997 and 2002, after adjusting for inflation—despite the rise in homeownership. Spending on household services rose 15 percent during those years, while spending on housekeeping supplies rose 7 percent.

Overall housing costs are highest for householders aged 35 to 44, at $16,350 in 2002. The 35-to-44 age group spends the most on household services, $1,010 in 2002, because of the high cost of day care. Householders aged 45 to 54 spend the most on furnishings and equipment (including computer hardware). Householders aged 55 to 64 spend the most on housekeeping supplies. Householders aged 65 to 74 spend the most on postage.

Households with incomes of $70,000 or more spent $23,695 on housing in 2002, versus the $13,481 spent by the average income-reporting household. The most affluent households spend far more than average on just about every category of household operations. They account for 70 percent of household spending on outdoor furniture and 68 percent of spending on outdoor equipment such as grills.

Among household types, married couples with preschoolers spend the most on housing, $19,141 in 2002. Behind this figure is the high cost of housing for recent homebuyers, and many married couples with young children are new homeowners. In addition, these householders spend the most on day care. Married couples with preschoolers spent an average of $1,519 on day care centers in 2002.

Black and Hispanic householders spend less than average on housing, but they spend more on some household products and services. Hispanics spend 33 percent more than average on laundry and cleaning supplies. Blacks spend 45 percent more than average on home security system service fees.

Households in the West spend the most on housing, $15,297 in 2002, because of the high cost of housing in California and other Western states. Spending on housing is lowest in the South, at $11,766. Southern households spend the most on termite and pest control services, however. Households in the West spend the most on computer hardware and software. Midwesterners are the biggest spenders on water softening services.

Not surprisingly, college graduates (who dominate the nation's affluent households) spend the most on housing, an average of $19,111 in 2002. They spend far more than the average household on almost every category of household operations. They spend more than twice the average on housekeeping services and on outdoor furniture. They spend 23 percent less than average on window air conditioners.

Table 8.1 Housing: Household Operations: Average spending by age, 2002

(average annual spending of consumer units (CU) on household services, supplies, furnishings, and equipment, by age of consumer unit reference person, 2002)

	total consumer units	under 25	25 to 34	35 to 44	45 to 54	55 to 64	65 to 74	75+
Number of consumer units (in thousands, add 000)	112,108	8,737	18,988	24,394	22,691	15,314	11,216	10,767
Average number of persons per CU	2.5	1.9	2.9	3.2	2.7	2.1	1.9	1.5
Average before-tax income of CU	$49,430.00	$20,773.00	$49,133.00	$61,532.00	$64,974.00	$53,162.00	$35,118.00	$23,890.00
Average spending of CU, total	40,676.60	24,229.46	40,318.29	48,330.48	48,748.24	44,330.04	32,242.52	23,758.89
Housing, average spending	13,283.08	7,436.31	13,727.04	16,349.51	15,475.55	13,831.08	10,052.07	8,257.08
HOUSEHOLD SERVICES	**$705.71**	**$198.20**	**$895.24**	**$1,010.38**	**$612.82**	**$560.80**	**$486.39**	**$723.36**
Personal services	**331.02**	**98.89**	**649.96**	**579.88**	**165.23**	**79.43**	**78.93**	**362.87**
Babysitting and child care in your own home	35.91	6.44	79.69	82.39	18.21	1.80	0.22	0.35
Babysitting and child care, someone else's home	27.48	19.07	61.86	58.09	9.68	6.00	0.56	0.46
Day care centers, nurseries, and preschools	210.74	71.83	478.96	411.92	130.72	36.67	14.70	15.03
Other household services	**374.70**	**99.31**	**245.28**	**430.50**	**447.59**	**481.37**	**407.46**	**360.50**
Housekeeping services	79.90	2.44	29.12	96.20	100.65	105.36	88.16	106.83
Gardening, lawn care service	72.38	6.96	22.49	64.74	76.39	114.50	114.75	118.27
Water softening service	3.15	0.19	2.83	4.19	3.77	3.22	2.23	3.36
Nonclothing laundry and dry cleaning, sent out	1.72	0.73	1.54	1.46	1.81	2.19	1.98	2.28
Nonclothing laundry and dry cleaning, coin-operated	4.13	5.86	6.74	4.43	3.68	3.00	1.80	2.47
Termite/pest control services	13.25	1.17	8.26	11.51	14.11	17.13	19.80	21.63
Home security system service fee	17.40	4.35	15.34	20.73	20.94	20.17	18.89	11.06
Other home services	15.06	2.17	6.68	11.64	17.98	26.90	21.98	17.90
Termite/pest control products	0.68	0.20	0.38	0.65	0.59	0.99	0.79	1.34
Moving, storage, and freight express	33.13	16.71	32.41	49.72	35.06	30.61	29.45	13.51
Appliance repair, including service center	10.86	0.72	5.15	9.79	13.54	15.70	16.19	13.55
Reupholstering and furniture repair	7.40	1.06	0.98	7.20	6.25	21.69	7.17	6.73
Repairs/rentals of lawn/garden equipment, hand/power tools, etc.	3.62	0.45	1.66	3.65	3.72	5.34	5.93	4.53
Appliance rental	1.07	1.27	1.92	1.77	0.96	0.11	0.36	0.14
Repair of computer systems for nonbusiness use	2.53	0.68	0.41	3.09	4.78	2.87	1.55	2.35
Computer information services	107.29	53.88	109.13	138.15	141.37	110.59	75.04	34.54
HOUSEKEEPING SUPPLIES	**545.28**	**225.96**	**389.49**	**588.74**	**633.42**	**838.21**	**546.71**	**378.61**
Laundry and cleaning supplies	**130.57**	**77.18**	**124.88**	**152.11**	**147.24**	**138.95**	**132.36**	**85.01**
Soaps and detergents	72.89	48.58	75.31	86.49	81.81	69.99	68.91	45.96
Other laundry cleaning products	57.68	28.60	49.57	65.62	65.43	68.96	63.45	39.04
Other household products	**283.28**	**94.78**	**172.75**	**294.62**	**333.45**	**538.17**	**250.43**	**172.35**
Cleansing and toilet tissue, paper towels, and napkins	76.46	38.04	63.36	88.27	86.35	88.91	72.54	70.01
Miscellaneous household products	96.81	48.49	71.06	119.34	137.16	99.44	85.39	52.84
Lawn and garden supplies	110.01	8.25	38.34	87.02	109.94	349.82	92.50	49.51
Postage and stationery	**131.44**	**54.01**	**91.86**	**142.00**	**152.73**	**161.10**	**163.92**	**121.25**
Stationery, stationery supplies, giftwrap	60.20	25.71	50.11	74.05	75.03	65.63	54.95	40.89
Postage	69.12	27.56	40.06	67.05	73.43	91.75	107.52	79.74
Delivery services	2.12	0.74	1.69	0.90	4.27	3.73	1.46	0.61

	total consumer units	under 25	25 to 34	35 to 44	45 to 54	55 to 64	65 to 74	75+
HOUSEHOLD FURNISHINGS AND EQUIPMENT	**$1,518.36**	**$812.45**	**$1,469.49**	**$1,822.52**	**$1,900.13**	**$1,811.44**	**$1,130.57**	**$663.39**
Household textiles	**135.52**	**93.31**	**127.92**	**137.34**	**152.30**	**183.06**	**126.85**	**83.94**
Bathroom linens	22.35	17.56	21.44	25.03	25.67	23.10	21.99	13.79
Bedroom linens	65.98	67.37	65.30	61.91	77.10	84.95	59.45	30.38
Kitchen and dining room linens	10.11	1.42	8.45	12.64	7.99	15.93	12.42	8.18
Curtains and draperies	16.65	4.28	15.12	20.98	20.00	17.90	16.83	10.53
Slipcovers and decorative pillows	7.40	0.29	8.85	2.43	4.72	19.99	2.92	14.65
Sewing materials for household items	11.44	2.01	7.55	12.27	14.06	20.12	12.18	5.47
Other linens	1.59	0.37	1.20	2.09	2.76	1.09	1.07	0.94
Furniture	**401.28**	**170.35**	**471.70**	**523.70**	**452.57**	**483.53**	**242.47**	**127.43**
Mattresses and springs	52.91	33.54	70.55	65.01	54.28	47.15	45.32	23.33
Other bedroom furniture	68.33	27.17	88.78	100.54	82.01	65.23	29.24	9.04
Sofas	85.33	38.60	103.01	114.43	85.95	98.27	57.57	35.27
Living room chairs	39.21	11.17	34.22	34.27	49.14	60.52	39.06	30.92
Living room tables	18.03	10.12	17.40	20.62	22.36	28.12	11.16	3.35
Kitchen and dining room furniture	61.28	17.50	64.24	88.11	67.57	98.92	18.90	8.13
Infants' furniture	6.46	5.30	15.63	9.58	3.27	2.37	2.88	0.40
Outdoor furniture	16.79	2.61	11.30	24.81	20.65	24.10	15.37	2.73
Wall units, cabinets, and other furniture	52.94	24.35	66.57	66.32	67.35	58.85	22.95	14.27
Floor coverings	**40.49**	**8.05**	**29.98**	**44.20**	**58.92**	**53.35**	**33.42**	**27.12**
Wall-to-wall carpeting	21.69	3.15	17.14	19.76	32.61	24.98	23.93	19.18
Floor coverings, nonpermanent	18.79	4.89	12.83	24.44	26.31	28.37	9.49	7.94
Major appliances	**188.47**	**87.72**	**148.07**	**252.35**	**219.49**	**219.72**	**167.63**	**108.30**
Dishwashers (built-in), garbage disposals, range hoods	16.52	2.42	11.58	24.04	22.08	19.20	9.59	11.32
Refrigerators and freezers	52.08	25.15	40.22	69.52	52.00	65.53	51.72	36.76
Washing machines	22.30	9.55	25.83	28.53	19.17	26.22	23.01	12.55
Clothes dryers	17.05	10.19	18.33	24.46	16.60	21.22	9.35	6.59
Cooking stoves, ovens	30.95	9.88	19.30	49.45	36.01	29.65	34.41	14.30
Microwave ovens	10.50	6.36	8.98	12.16	11.47	11.97	11.41	7.64
Window air conditioners	7.90	5.91	5.62	9.66	11.76	5.35	5.86	7.22
Electric floor-cleaning equipment	22.80	7.19	15.35	25.04	42.66	27.11	12.17	6.41
Sewing machines	4.79	1.18	1.78	5.52	6.69	6.53	5.87	3.74
Miscellaneous household appliances	2.81	9.63	0.39	1.83	0.72	6.53	3.85	1.79
Small appliances and misc. housewares	**100.43**	**75.67**	**109.00**	**88.46**	**123.60**	**134.15**	**92.72**	**42.19**
Housewares	77.55	60.73	90.12	63.36	95.40	105.58	72.35	27.45
Plastic dinnerware	1.57	1.70	1.78	1.94	1.71	1.74	0.94	0.32
China and other dinnerware	14.51	24.48	24.65	7.87	13.72	13.38	15.75	4.89
Flatware	3.79	2.41	3.09	4.30	4.65	5.62	3.54	0.82
Glassware	6.51	2.23	5.58	6.68	10.33	8.52	5.18	1.64
Silver serving pieces	4.05	0.82	3.59	5.51	2.94	5.86	5.53	2.34
Other serving pieces	1.44	1.80	1.21	1.29	1.36	3.16	0.59	0.48
Nonelectric cookware	24.25	16.18	35.25	15.54	33.90	24.38	25.63	8.57
Tableware, nonelectric kitchenware	21.44	11.11	14.96	20.24	26.80	42.93	15.18	8.40
Small appliances	22.89	14.95	18.88	25.10	28.20	28.57	20.36	14.73
Small electric kitchen appliances	17.18	10.96	14.34	18.21	20.76	21.86	15.15	12.82
Portable heating and cooling equipment	5.70	3.98	4.54	6.89	7.43	6.71	5.21	1.92

	total consumer units	under 25	25 to 34	35 to 44	45 to 54	55 to 64	65 to 74	75+
Miscellaneous household equipment	**$652.17**	**$377.35**	**$582.83**	**$776.47**	**$893.25**	**$737.62**	**$467.48**	**$274.41**
Window coverings	13.91	2.22	15.86	13.13	18.78	17.20	15.58	5.07
Infants' equipment	12.96	4.28	16.80	16.67	24.01	6.09	3.60	0.49
Laundry and cleaning equipment	15.15	6.87	15.48	18.50	16.89	16.24	16.94	6.33
Outdoor equipment	31.52	2.09	9.76	50.22	71.84	20.07	7.60	7.42
Clocks	5.87	3.11	3.65	11.26	6.23	5.53	2.37	3.01
Lamps and lighting fixtures	11.74	5.38	7.53	14.84	16.02	18.48	8.29	2.32
Other household decorative items	144.94	77.12	128.94	157.14	186.12	185.63	115.74	85.02
Telephones and accessories	32.73	17.37	27.72	27.26	45.21	37.45	43.13	22.80
Lawn and garden equipment	48.16	7.68	35.43	81.75	47.21	55.78	42.44	24.48
Power tools	33.27	46.15	46.26	17.93	53.50	36.77	16.27	3.21
Office furniture for home use	10.57	6.05	11.07	12.41	13.80	13.40	4.19	4.97
Hand tools	8.05	3.63	9.81	10.23	9.12	8.74	4.77	3.82
Indoor plants and fresh flowers	49.78	21.24	35.68	50.36	65.51	68.69	51.74	34.41
Closet and storage items	9.98	2.40	7.76	16.55	11.84	10.46	6.49	4.03
Rental of furniture	4.60	5.81	9.17	6.89	2.99	2.50	0.84	0.63
Luggage	5.98	3.25	4.66	7.26	7.16	8.00	5.87	2.41
Computers and computer hardware, nonbusiness use	138.58	125.33	142.09	163.45	196.74	154.15	53.96	30.22
Computer software and accessories, nonbusiness use	17.67	15.56	19.33	22.76	20.88	17.43	11.53	4.92
Telephone answering devices	1.08	1.00	1.14	1.31	1.37	0.85	0.84	0.50
Calculators	1.44	2.37	0.76	2.00	2.71	0.61	0.47	0.13
Business equipment for home use	0.97	0.91	0.87	0.25	2.04	0.74	1.01	0.87
Other hardware	12.85	3.36	6.74	22.74	17.69	5.17	19.33	2.76
Smoke alarms	1.49	0.16	1.50	3.38	0.78	1.06	0.37	1.61
Other household appliances	9.23	2.52	8.51	9.07	14.24	10.65	8.87	4.13
Miscellaneous household equipment and parts	29.62	11.50	16.34	39.12	40.55	35.91	25.25	18.82

Note: Numbers may not add to total because not all categories are shown.
Source: Bureau of Labor Statistics, unpublished tables from the 2002 Consumer Expenditure Survey

Table 8.2 Housing: Household Operations: Indexed spending by age, 2002

(indexed average annual spending of consumer units (CU) on household services, supplies, furnishings, and equipment, by age of consumer unit reference person, 2002; index definition: an index of 100 is the average for all consumer units; an index of 132 means that spending by consumer units in that group is 32 percent above the average for all consumer units; an index of 68 indicates spending that is 32 percent below the average for all consumer units)

	total consumer units	under 25	25 to 34	35 to 44	45 to 54	55 to 64	65 to 74	75+
Average spending of CU, total	$40,677	$24,229	$40,318	$48,330	$48,748	$44,330	$32,243	$23,759
Average spending of CU, index	100	60	99	119	120	109	79	58
Housing, spending index	100	56	103	123	117	104	76	62
HOUSEHOLD SERVICES	**100**	**28**	**127**	**143**	**87**	**79**	**69**	**103**
Personal services	**100**	**30**	**196**	**175**	**50**	**24**	**24**	**110**
Babysitting and child care in your own home	100	18	222	229	51	5	1	1
Babysitting and child care, someone else's home	100	69	225	211	35	22	2	2
Day care centers, nurseries, and preschools	100	34	227	195	62	17	7	7
Other household services	**100**	**27**	**65**	**115**	**119**	**128**	**109**	**96**
Housekeeping services	100	3	36	120	126	132	110	134
Gardening, lawn care service	100	10	31	89	106	158	159	163
Water softening service	100	6	90	133	120	102	71	107
Nonclothing laundry and dry cleaning, sent out	100	42	90	85	105	127	115	133
Nonclothing laundry and dry cleaning, coin-operated	100	142	163	107	89	73	44	60
Termite/pest control services	100	9	62	87	106	129	149	163
Home security system service fee	100	25	88	119	120	116	109	64
Other home services	100	14	44	77	119	179	146	119
Termite/pest control products	100	29	56	96	87	146	116	197
Moving, storage, and freight express	100	50	98	150	106	92	89	41
Appliance repair, including service center	100	7	47	90	125	145	149	125
Reupholstering and furniture repair	100	14	13	97	84	293	97	91
Repairs/rentals of lawn/garden equipment, hand/power tools, etc.	100	12	46	101	103	148	164	125
Appliance rental	100	119	179	165	90	10	34	13
Repair of computer systems for nonbusiness use	100	27	16	122	189	113	61	93
Computer information services	100	50	102	129	132	103	70	32
HOUSEKEEPING SUPPLIES	**100**	**41**	**71**	**108**	**116**	**154**	**100**	**69**
Laundry and cleaning supplies	**100**	**59**	**96**	**116**	**113**	**106**	**101**	**65**
Soaps and detergents	100	67	103	119	112	96	95	63
Other laundry cleaning products	100	50	86	114	113	120	110	68
Other household products	**100**	**33**	**61**	**104**	**118**	**190**	**88**	**61**
Cleansing and toilet tissue, paper towels, and napkins	100	50	83	115	113	116	95	92
Miscellaneous household products	100	50	73	123	142	103	88	55
Lawn and garden supplies	100	7	35	79	100	318	84	45
Postage and stationery	**100**	**41**	**70**	**108**	**116**	**123**	**125**	**92**
Stationery, stationery supplies, giftwrap	100	43	83	123	125	109	91	68
Postage	100	40	58	97	106	133	156	115
Delivery services	100	35	80	42	201	176	69	29

	total consumer units	under 25	25 to 34	35 to 44	45 to 54	55 to 64	65 to 74	75+
HOUSEHOLD FURNISHINGS AND EQUIPMENT	**100**	**54**	**97**	**120**	**125**	**119**	**74**	**44**
Household textiles	**100**	**69**	**94**	**101**	**112**	**135**	**94**	**62**
Bathroom linens	100	79	96	112	115	103	98	62
Bedroom linens	100	102	99	94	117	129	90	46
Kitchen and dining room linens	100	14	84	125	79	158	123	81
Curtains and draperies	100	26	91	126	120	108	101	63
Slipcovers and decorative pillows	100	4	120	33	64	270	39	198
Sewing materials for household items	100	18	66	107	123	176	106	48
Other linens	100	23	75	131	174	69	67	59
Furniture	**100**	**42**	**118**	**131**	**113**	**120**	**60**	**32**
Mattresses and springs	100	63	133	123	103	89	86	44
Other bedroom furniture	100	40	130	147	120	95	43	13
Sofas	100	45	121	134	101	115	67	41
Living room chairs	100	28	87	87	125	154	100	79
Living room tables	100	56	97	114	124	156	62	19
Kitchen and dining room furniture	100	29	105	144	110	161	31	13
Infants' furniture	100	82	242	148	51	37	45	6
Outdoor furniture	100	16	67	148	123	144	92	16
Wall units, cabinets, and other furniture	100	46	126	125	127	111	43	27
Floor coverings	**100**	**20**	**74**	**109**	**146**	**132**	**83**	**67**
Wall-to-wall carpeting	100	15	79	91	150	115	110	88
Floor coverings, nonpermanent	100	26	68	130	140	151	51	42
Major appliances	**100**	**47**	**79**	**134**	**116**	**117**	**89**	**57**
Dishwashers (built-in), garbage disposals, range hoods	100	15	70	146	134	116	58	69
Refrigerators and freezers	100	48	77	133	100	126	99	71
Washing machines	100	43	116	128	86	118	103	56
Clothes dryers	100	60	108	143	97	124	55	39
Cooking stoves, ovens	100	32	62	160	116	96	111	46
Microwave ovens	100	61	86	116	109	114	109	73
Window air conditioners	100	75	71	122	149	68	74	91
Electric floor-cleaning equipment	100	32	67	110	187	119	53	28
Sewing machines	100	25	37	115	140	136	123	78
Miscellaneous household appliances	100	343	14	65	26	232	137	64
Small appliances and misc. housewares	**100**	**75**	**109**	**88**	**123**	**134**	**92**	**42**
Housewares	100	78	116	82	123	136	93	35
Plastic dinnerware	100	108	113	124	109	111	60	20
China and other dinnerware	100	169	170	54	95	92	109	34
Flatware	100	64	82	113	123	148	93	22
Glassware	100	34	86	103	159	131	80	25
Silver serving pieces	100	20	89	136	73	145	137	58
Other serving pieces	100	125	84	90	94	219	41	33
Nonelectric cookware	100	67	145	64	140	101	106	35
Tableware, nonelectric kitchenware	100	52	70	94	125	200	71	39
Small appliances	100	65	82	110	123	125	89	64
Small electric kitchen appliances	100	64	83	106	121	127	88	75
Portable heating and cooling equipment	100	70	80	121	130	118	91	34

	total consumer units	under 25	25 to 34	35 to 44	45 to 54	55 to 64	65 to 74	75+
Miscellaneous household equipment	**100**	**58**	**89**	**119**	**137**	**113**	**72**	**42**
Window coverings	100	16	114	94	135	124	112	36
Infants' equipment	100	33	130	129	185	47	28	4
Laundry and cleaning equipment	100	45	102	122	111	107	112	42
Outdoor equipment	100	7	31	159	228	64	24	24
Clocks	100	53	62	192	106	94	40	51
Lamps and lighting fixtures	100	46	64	126	136	157	71	20
Other household decorative items	100	53	89	108	128	128	80	59
Telephones and accessories	100	53	85	83	138	114	132	70
Lawn and garden equipment	100	16	74	170	98	116	88	51
Power tools	100	139	139	54	161	111	49	10
Office furniture for home use	100	57	105	117	131	127	40	47
Hand tools	100	45	122	127	113	109	59	47
Indoor plants and fresh flowers	100	43	72	101	132	138	104	69
Closet and storage items	100	24	78	166	119	105	65	40
Rental of furniture	100	126	199	150	65	54	18	14
Luggage	100	54	78	121	120	134	98	40
Computers and computer hardware, nonbusiness use	100	90	103	118	142	111	39	22
Computer software and accessories, nonbusiness use	100	88	109	129	118	99	65	28
Telephone answering devices	100	93	106	121	127	79	78	46
Calculators	100	165	53	139	188	42	33	9
Business equipment for home use	100	94	90	26	210	76	104	90
Other hardware	100	26	52	177	138	40	150	21
Smoke alarms	100	11	101	227	52	71	25	108
Other household appliances	100	27	92	98	154	115	96	45
Miscellaneous household equipment and parts	100	39	55	132	137	121	85	64

Source: Calculations by New Strategist based on the 2002 Consumer Expenditure Survey

Table 8.3 Housing: Household Operations: Total spending by age, 2002

(total annual spending on household services, supplies, furnishings, and equipment, by consumer unit (CU) age groups, 2002; numbers in thousands)

	total consumer units	under 25	25 to 34	35 to 44	45 to 54	55 to 64	65 to 74	75+
Number of consumer units	112,108	8,737	18,988	24,394	22,691	15,314	11,216	10,767
Total spending of all CUs	$4,560,172,273	$211,692,792	$765,563,691	$1,178,973,729	$1,106,146,314	$678,870,233	$361,632,104	$255,811,969
Housing, total spending	1,489,139,533	64,971,040	260,649,036	398,829,947	351,155,705	211,809,159	112,744,017	88,903,980
HOUSEHOLD SERVICES	**$79,115,737**	**$1,731,673**	**$16,998,817**	**$24,647,210**	**$13,905,499**	**$8,588,091**	**$5,455,350**	**$7,788,417**
Personal services	**37,109,990**	**864,002**	**12,341,440**	**14,145,593**	**3,749,234**	**1,216,391**	**885,279**	**3,907,021**
Babysitting and child care in your own home	4,025,798	56,266	1,513,154	2,009,822	413,203	27,565	2,468	3,768
Babysitting and child care, someone else's home	3,080,728	166,615	1,174,598	1,417,047	219,649	91,884	6,281	4,953
Day care centers, nurseries, and preschools	23,625,640	627,579	9,094,492	10,048,376	2,966,168	561,564	164,875	161,828
Other household services	**42,006,868**	**867,671**	**4,657,377**	**10,501,617**	**10,156,265**	**7,371,700**	**4,570,071**	**3,881,504**
Housekeeping services	8,957,429	21,318	552,931	2,346,703	2,283,849	1,613,483	988,803	1,150,239
Gardening, lawn care service	8,114,377	60,810	427,040	1,579,268	1,733,365	1,753,453	1,287,036	1,273,413
Water softening service	353,140	1,660	53,736	102,211	85,545	49,311	25,012	36,177
Nonclothing laundry and dry cleaning, sent out	192,826	6,378	29,242	35,615	41,071	33,538	22,208	24,549
Nonclothing laundry and dry cleaning, coin-operated	463,006	51,199	127,979	108,065	83,503	45,942	20,189	26,594
Termite/pest control services	1,485,431	10,222	156,841	280,775	320,170	262,329	222,077	232,890
Home security system service fee	1,950,679	38,006	291,276	505,688	475,150	308,883	211,870	119,083
Other home services	1,688,346	18,959	126,840	283,946	407,984	411,947	246,528	192,729
Termite/pest control products	76,233	1,747	7,215	15,856	13,388	15,161	8,861	14,428
Moving, storage, and freight express	3,714,138	145,995	615,401	1,212,870	795,546	468,762	330,311	145,462
Appliance repair, including service center	1,217,493	6,291	97,788	238,817	307,236	240,430	181,587	145,893
Reupholstering and furniture repair	829,599	9,261	18,608	175,637	141,819	332,161	80,419	72,462
Repairs/rentals of lawn/garden equipment, hand/power tools, etc.	405,831	3,932	31,520	89,038	84,411	81,777	66,511	48,775
Appliance rental	119,956	11,096	36,457	43,177	21,783	1,685	4,038	1,507
Repair of computer systems, nonbusiness use	283,633	5,941	7,785	75,377	108,463	43,951	17,385	25,302
Computer information services	12,028,067	470,750	2,072,160	3,370,031	3,207,827	1,693,575	841,649	371,892
HOUSEKEEPING SUPPLIES	**61,130,250**	**1,974,213**	**7,395,636**	**14,361,724**	**14,372,933**	**12,836,348**	**6,131,899**	**4,076,494**
Laundry and cleaning supplies	**14,637,942**	**674,322**	**2,371,221**	**3,710,571**	**3,341,023**	**2,127,880**	**1,484,550**	**915,303**
Soaps and detergents	8,171,552	424,443	1,429,986	2,109,837	1,856,351	1,071,827	772,895	494,851
Other laundry cleaning products	6,466,389	249,878	941,235	1,600,734	1,484,672	1,056,053	711,655	420,344
Other household products	**31,757,954**	**828,093**	**3,280,177**	**7,186,960**	**7,566,314**	**8,241,535**	**2,808,823**	**1,855,692**
Cleansing and toilet tissue, paper towels, and napkins	8,571,778	332,355	1,203,080	2,153,258	1,959,368	1,361,568	813,609	753,798
Miscellaneous household products	10,853,175	423,657	1,349,287	2,911,180	3,112,298	1,522,824	957,734	568,928
Lawn and garden supplies	12,333,001	72,080	728,000	2,122,766	2,494,649	5,357,143	1,037,480	533,074
Postage and stationery	**14,735,476**	**471,885**	**1,744,238**	**3,463,948**	**3,465,596**	**2,467,085**	**1,838,527**	**1,305,499**
Stationery, stationery supplies, giftwrap	6,748,902	224,628	951,489	1,806,376	1,702,506	1,005,058	616,319	440,263
Postage	7,748,905	240,792	760,659	1,635,618	1,666,200	1,405,060	1,205,944	858,561
Delivery services	237,669	6,465	32,090	21,955	96,891	57,121	16,375	6,568

	total consumer units	under 25	25 to 34	35 to 44	45 to 54	55 to 64	65 to 74	75+
HOUSEHOLD FURNISHINGS AND EQUIPMENT	**$170,220,303**	**$7,098,376**	**$27,902,676**	**$44,458,553**	**$43,115,850**	**$27,740,392**	**$12,680,473**	**$7,142,720**
Household textiles	**15,192,876**	**815,249**	**2,428,945**	**3,350,272**	**3,455,839**	**2,803,381**	**1,422,750**	**903,782**
Bathroom linens	2,505,614	153,422	407,103	610,582	582,478	353,753	246,640	148,477
Bedroom linens	7,396,886	588,612	1,239,916	1,510,233	1,749,476	1,300,924	666,791	327,101
Kitchen and dining room linens	1,133,412	12,407	160,449	308,340	181,301	243,952	139,303	88,074
Curtains and draperies	1,866,598	37,394	287,099	511,786	453,820	274,121	188,765	113,377
Slipcovers and decorative pillows	829,599	2,534	168,044	59,277	107,102	306,127	32,751	157,737
Sewing materials for household items	1,282,516	17,561	143,359	299,314	319,035	308,118	136,611	58,895
Other linens	178,252	3,233	22,786	50,983	62,627	16,692	12,001	10,121
Furniture	**44,986,698**	**1,488,348**	**8,956,640**	**12,775,138**	**10,269,266**	**7,404,778**	**2,719,544**	**1,372,039**
Mattresses and springs	5,931,634	293,039	1,339,603	1,585,854	1,231,667	722,055	508,309	251,194
Other bedroom furniture	7,660,340	237,384	1,685,755	2,452,573	1,860,889	998,932	327,956	97,334
Sofas	9,566,176	337,248	1,955,954	2,791,405	1,950,291	1,504,907	645,705	379,752
Living room chairs	4,395,755	97,592	649,769	835,982	1,115,036	926,803	438,097	332,916
Living room tables	2,021,307	88,418	330,391	503,004	507,371	430,630	125,171	36,069
Kitchen and dining room furniture	6,869,978	152,898	1,219,789	2,149,355	1,533,231	1,514,861	211,982	87,536
Infants' furniture	724,218	46,306	296,782	233,695	74,200	36,294	32,302	4,307
Outdoor furniture	1,882,293	22,804	214,564	605,215	468,569	369,067	172,390	29,394
Wall units, cabinets, and other furniture	5,934,998	212,746	1,264,031	1,617,810	1,528,239	901,229	257,407	153,645
Floor coverings	**4,539,253**	**70,333**	**569,260**	**1,078,215**	**1,336,954**	**817,002**	**374,839**	**292,001**
Wall-to-wall carpeting	2,431,623	27,522	325,454	482,025	739,954	382,544	268,399	206,511
Floor coverings, nonpermanent	2,106,509	42,724	243,616	596,189	597,000	434,458	106,440	85,490
Major appliances	**21,128,995**	**766,410**	**2,811,553**	**6,155,826**	**4,980,448**	**3,364,792**	**1,880,138**	**1,166,066**
Dishwashers (built-in), garbage disposals, range hoods	1,852,024	21,144	219,881	586,432	501,017	294,029	107,561	121,882
Refrigerators and freezers	5,838,585	219,736	763,697	1,695,871	1,179,932	1,003,526	580,092	395,795
Washing machines	2,500,008	83,438	490,460	695,961	434,986	401,533	258,080	135,126
Clothes dryers	1,911,441	89,030	348,050	596,677	376,671	324,963	104,870	70,955
Cooking stoves, ovens	3,469,743	86,322	366,468	1,206,283	817,103	454,060	385,943	153,968
Microwave ovens	1,177,134	55,567	170,512	296,631	260,266	183,309	127,975	82,260
Window air conditioners	885,653	51,636	106,713	235,646	266,846	81,930	65,726	77,738
Electric floor-cleaning equipment	2,556,062	62,819	291,466	610,826	967,998	415,163	136,499	69,016
Sewing machines	536,997	10,310	33,799	134,655	151,803	100,000	65,838	40,269
Miscellaneous household appliances	315,023	84,137	7,405	44,641	16,338	100,000	43,182	19,273
Small appliances and misc. housewares	**11,259,006**	**661,129**	**2,069,692**	**2,157,893**	**2,804,608**	**2,054,373**	**1,039,948**	**454,260**
Housewares	8,693,975	530,598	1,711,199	1,545,604	2,164,721	1,616,852	811,478	295,554
Plastic dinnerware	176,010	14,853	33,799	47,324	38,802	26,646	10,543	3,445
China and other dinnerware	1,626,687	213,882	468,054	191,981	311,321	204,901	176,652	52,651
Flatware	424,889	21,056	58,673	104,894	105,513	86,065	39,705	8,829
Glassware	729,823	19,484	105,953	162,952	234,398	130,475	58,099	17,658
Silver serving pieces	454,037	7,164	68,167	134,411	66,712	89,740	62,024	25,195
Other serving pieces	161,436	15,727	22,975	31,468	30,860	48,392	6,617	5,168
Nonelectric cookware	2,718,619	141,365	669,327	379,083	769,225	373,355	287,466	92,273
Tableware, nonelectric kitchenware	2,403,596	97,068	284,060	493,735	608,119	657,430	170,259	90,443
Small appliances	2,566,152	130,618	358,493	612,289	639,886	437,521	228,358	158,598
Small electric kitchen appliances	1,926,015	95,758	272,288	444,215	471,065	334,764	169,922	138,033
Portable heating and cooling equipment	639,016	34,773	86,206	168,075	168,594	102,757	58,435	20,673

	total consumer units	under 25	25 to 34	35 to 44	45 to 54	55 to 64	65 to 74	75+
Miscellaneous household equipment	**$73,113,474**	**$3,296,907**	**$11,066,776**	**$18,941,209**	**$20,268,736**	**$11,295,913**	**$5,243,256**	**$2,954,572**
Window coverings	1,559,422	19,396	301,150	320,293	426,137	263,401	174,745	54,589
Infants' equipment	1,452,920	37,394	318,998	406,648	544,811	93,262	40,378	5,276
Laundry and cleaning equipment	1,698,436	60,023	293,934	451,289	383,251	248,699	189,999	68,155
Outdoor equipment	3,533,644	18,260	185,323	1,225,067	1,630,121	307,352	85,242	79,891
Clocks	658,074	27,172	69,306	274,676	141,365	84,686	26,582	32,409
Lamps and lighting fixtures	1,316,148	47,005	142,980	362,007	363,510	283,003	92,981	24,979
Other household decorative items	16,248,934	673,797	2,448,313	3,833,273	4,223,249	2,842,738	1,298,140	915,410
Telephones and accessories	3,669,295	151,762	526,347	664,980	1,025,860	573,509	483,746	245,488
Lawn and garden equipment	5,399,121	67,100	672,745	1,994,210	1,071,242	854,215	476,007	263,576
Power tools	3,729,833	403,213	878,385	437,384	1,213,969	563,096	182,484	34,562
Office furniture for home use	1,184,982	52,859	210,197	302,730	313,136	205,208	46,995	53,512
Hand tools	902,469	31,715	186,272	249,551	206,942	133,844	53,500	41,130
Indoor plants and fresh flowers	5,580,736	185,574	677,492	1,228,482	1,486,487	1,051,919	580,316	370,492
Closet and storage items	1,118,838	20,969	147,347	403,721	268,661	160,184	72,792	43,391
Rental of furniture	515,697	50,762	174,120	168,075	67,846	38,285	9,421	6,783
Luggage	670,406	28,395	88,484	177,100	162,468	122,512	65,838	25,948
Computers and computer hardware, nonbusiness use	15,535,927	1,095,008	2,698,005	3,987,199	4,464,227	2,360,653	605,215	325,379
Computer software and accessories, nonbusiness use	1,980,948	135,948	367,038	555,207	473,788	266,923	129,320	52,974
Telephone answering devices	121,077	8,737	21,646	31,956	31,087	13,017	9,421	5,384
Calculators	161,436	20,707	14,431	48,788	61,493	9,342	5,272	1,400
Business equipment for home use	108,745	7,951	16,520	6,099	46,290	11,332	11,328	9,367
Other hardware	1,440,588	29,356	127,979	554,720	401,404	79,173	216,805	29,717
Smoke alarms	167,041	1,398	28,482	82,452	17,699	16,233	4,150	17,335
Other household appliances	1,034,757	22,017	161,588	221,254	323,120	163,094	99,486	44,468
Miscellaneous household equipment and parts	3,320,639	100,476	310,264	954,293	920,120	549,926	283,204	202,635

Note: Numbers may not add to total because of rounding and because not all categories are shown.
Source: Calculations by New Strategist based on the 2002 Consumer Expenditure Survey

Table 8.4 Housing: Household Operations: Market shares by age, 2002

(percentage of total annual spending on household services, supplies, furnishings, and equipment accounted for by consumer unit age groups, 2002)

	total consumer units	under 25	25 to 34	35 to 44	45 to 54	55 to 64	65 to 74	75+
Share of total consumer units	100.0%	7.8%	16.9%	21.8%	20.2%	13.7%	10.0%	9.6%
Share of total before-tax income	100.0	3.3	16.8	27.1	26.6	14.7	10.0	9.6
Share of total spending	100.0	4.6	16.8	27.1	26.6	14.7	7.1	4.6
Share of housing spending	100.0	4.4	17.5	26.8	23.6	14.2	7.6	6.0
HOUSEHOLD SERVICES	**100.0%**	**2.2%**	**21.5%**	**31.2%**	**17.6%**	**10.9%**	**6.9%**	**9.8%**
Personal services	**100.0**	**2.3**	**33.3**	**38.1**	**10.1**	**3.3**	**2.4**	**10.5**
Babysitting and child care in your own home	100.0	1.4	37.6	49.9	10.3	0.7	0.1	0.1
Babysitting and child care, someone else's home	100.0	5.4	38.1	46.0	7.1	3.0	0.2	0.2
Day care centers, nurseries, and preschools	100.0	2.7	38.5	42.5	12.6	2.4	0.7	0.7
Other household services	**100.0**	**2.1**	**11.1**	**25.0**	**24.2**	**17.5**	**10.9**	**9.2**
Housekeeping services	100.0	0.2	6.2	26.2	25.5	18.0	11.0	12.8
Gardening, lawn care service	100.0	0.7	5.3	19.5	21.4	21.6	15.9	15.7
Water softening service	100.0	0.5	15.2	28.9	24.2	14.0	7.1	10.2
Nonclothing laundry and dry cleaning, sent out	100.0	3.3	15.2	18.5	21.3	17.4	11.5	12.7
Nonclothing laundry and dry cleaning, coin-operated	100.0	11.1	27.6	23.3	18.0	9.9	4.4	5.7
Termite/pest control services	100.0	0.7	10.6	18.9	21.6	17.7	15.0	15.7
Home security system service fee	100.0	1.9	14.9	25.9	24.4	15.8	10.9	6.1
Other home services	100.0	1.1	7.5	16.8	24.2	24.4	14.6	11.4
Termite/pest control products	100.0	2.3	9.5	20.8	17.6	19.9	11.6	18.9
Moving, storage, and freight express	100.0	3.9	16.6	32.7	21.4	12.6	8.9	3.9
Appliance repair, including service center	100.0	0.5	8.0	19.6	25.2	19.7	14.9	12.0
Reupholstering and furniture repair	100.0	1.1	2.2	21.2	17.1	40.0	9.7	8.7
Repairs/rentals of lawn/garden equipment, hand/power tools, etc.	100.0	1.0	7.8	21.9	20.8	20.2	16.4	12.0
Appliance rental	100.0	9.3	30.4	36.0	18.2	1.4	3.4	1.3
Repair of computer systems for nonbusiness use	100.0	2.1	2.7	26.6	38.2	15.5	6.1	8.9
Computer information services	100.0	3.9	17.2	28.0	26.7	14.1	7.0	3.1
HOUSEKEEPING SUPPLIES	**100.0**	**3.2**	**12.1**	**23.5**	**23.5**	**21.0**	**10.0**	**6.7**
Laundry and cleaning supplies	**100.0**	**4.6**	**16.2**	**25.3**	**22.8**	**14.5**	**10.1**	**6.3**
Soaps and detergents	100.0	5.2	17.5	25.8	22.7	13.1	9.5	6.1
Other laundry cleaning products	100.0	3.9	14.6	24.8	23.0	16.3	11.0	6.5
Other household products	**100.0**	**2.6**	**10.3**	**22.6**	**23.8**	**26.0**	**8.8**	**5.8**
Cleansing and toilet tissue, paper towels, and napkins	100.0	3.9	14.0	25.1	22.9	15.9	9.5	8.8
Miscellaneous household products	100.0	3.9	12.4	26.8	28.7	14.0	8.8	5.2
Lawn and garden supplies	100.0	0.6	5.9	17.2	20.2	43.4	8.4	4.3
Postage and stationery	**100.0**	**3.2**	**11.8**	**23.5**	**23.5**	**16.7**	**12.5**	**8.9**
Stationery, stationery supplies, giftwrap	100.0	3.3	14.1	26.8	25.2	14.9	9.1	6.5
Postage	100.0	3.1	9.8	21.1	21.5	18.1	15.6	11.1
Delivery services	100.0	2.7	13.5	9.2	40.8	24.0	6.9	2.8

	total consumer units	under 25	25 to 34	35 to 44	45 to 54	55 to 64	65 to 74	75+
HOUSEHOLD FURNISHINGS AND EQUIPMENT	100.0%	4.2%	16.4%	26.1%	25.3%	16.3%	7.4%	4.2%
Household textiles	100.0	5.4	16.0	22.1	22.7	18.5	9.4	5.9
Bathroom linens	100.0	6.1	16.2	24.4	23.2	14.1	9.8	5.9
Bedroom linens	100.0	8.0	16.8	20.4	23.7	17.6	9.0	4.4
Kitchen and dining room linens	100.0	1.1	14.2	27.2	16.0	21.5	12.3	7.8
Curtains and draperies	100.0	2.0	15.4	27.4	24.3	14.7	10.1	6.1
Slipcovers and decorative pillows	100.0	0.3	20.3	7.1	12.9	36.9	3.9	19.0
Sewing materials for household items	100.0	1.4	11.2	23.3	24.9	24.0	10.7	4.6
Other linens	100.0	1.8	12.8	28.6	35.1	9.4	6.7	5.7
Furniture	100.0	3.3	19.9	28.4	22.8	16.5	6.0	3.0
Mattresses and springs	100.0	4.9	22.6	26.7	20.8	12.2	8.6	4.2
Other bedroom furniture	100.0	3.1	22.0	32.0	24.3	13.0	4.3	1.3
Sofas	100.0	3.5	20.4	29.2	20.4	15.7	6.7	4.0
Living room chairs	100.0	2.2	14.8	19.0	25.4	21.1	10.0	7.6
Living room tables	100.0	4.4	16.3	24.9	25.1	21.3	6.2	1.8
Kitchen and dining room furniture	100.0	2.2	17.8	31.3	22.3	22.1	3.1	1.3
Infants' furniture	100.0	6.4	41.0	32.3	10.2	5.0	4.5	0.6
Outdoor furniture	100.0	1.2	11.4	32.2	24.9	19.6	9.2	1.6
Wall units, cabinets, and other furniture	100.0	3.6	21.3	27.3	25.7	15.2	4.3	2.6
Floor coverings	100.0	1.5	12.5	23.8	29.5	18.0	8.3	6.4
Wall-to-wall carpeting	100.0	1.1	13.4	19.8	30.4	15.7	11.0	8.5
Floor coverings, nonpermanent	100.0	2.0	11.6	28.3	28.3	20.6	5.1	4.1
Major appliances	100.0	3.6	13.3	29.1	23.6	15.9	8.9	5.5
Dishwashers (built-in), garbage disposals, range hoods	100.0	1.1	11.9	31.7	27.1	15.9	5.8	6.6
Refrigerators and freezers	100.0	3.8	13.1	29.0	20.2	17.2	9.9	6.8
Washing machines	100.0	3.3	19.6	27.8	17.4	16.1	10.3	5.4
Clothes dryers	100.0	4.7	18.2	31.2	19.7	17.0	5.5	3.7
Cooking stoves, ovens	100.0	2.5	10.6	34.8	23.5	13.1	11.1	4.4
Microwave ovens	100.0	4.7	14.5	25.2	22.1	15.6	10.9	7.0
Window air conditioners	100.0	5.8	12.0	26.6	30.1	9.3	7.4	8.8
Electric floor-cleaning equipment	100.0	2.5	11.4	23.9	37.9	16.2	5.3	2.7
Sewing machines	100.0	1.9	6.3	25.1	28.3	18.6	12.3	7.5
Miscellaneous household appliances	100.0	26.7	2.4	14.2	5.2	31.7	13.7	6.1
Small appliances and misc. housewares	100.0	5.9	18.4	19.2	24.9	18.2	9.2	4.0
Housewares	100.0	6.1	19.7	17.8	24.9	18.6	9.3	3.4
Plastic dinnerware	100.0	8.4	19.2	26.9	22.0	15.1	6.0	2.0
China and other dinnerware	100.0	13.1	28.8	11.8	19.1	12.6	10.9	3.2
Flatware	100.0	5.0	13.8	24.7	24.8	20.3	9.3	2.1
Glassware	100.0	2.7	14.5	22.3	32.1	17.9	8.0	2.4
Silver serving pieces	100.0	1.6	15.0	29.6	14.7	19.8	13.7	5.5
Other serving pieces	100.0	9.7	14.2	19.5	19.1	30.0	4.1	3.2
Nonelectric cookware	100.0	5.2	24.6	13.9	28.3	13.7	10.6	3.4
Tableware, nonelectric kitchenware	100.0	4.0	11.8	20.5	25.3	27.4	7.1	3.8
Small appliances	100.0	5.1	14.0	23.9	24.9	17.0	8.9	6.2
Small electric kitchen appliances	100.0	5.0	14.1	23.1	24.5	17.4	8.8	7.2
Portable heating and cooling equipment	100.0	5.4	13.5	26.3	26.4	16.1	9.1	3.2

Miscellaneous household equipment	total consumer units	under 25	25 to 34	35 to 44	45 to 54	55 to 64	65 to 74	75+
	100.0%	4.5%	15.1%	25.9%	27.7%	15.4%	7.2%	4.0%
Window coverings	100.0	1.2	19.3	20.5	27.3	16.9	11.2	3.5
Infants' equipment	100.0	2.6	22.0	28.0	37.5	6.4	2.8	0.4
Laundry and cleaning equipment	100.0	3.5	17.3	26.6	22.6	14.6	11.2	4.0
Outdoor equipment	100.0	0.5	5.2	34.7	46.1	8.7	2.4	2.3
Clocks	100.0	4.1	10.5	41.7	21.5	12.9	4.0	4.9
Lamps and lighting fixtures	100.0	3.6	10.9	27.5	27.6	21.5	7.1	1.9
Other household decorative items	100.0	4.1	15.1	23.6	26.0	17.5	8.0	5.6
Telephones and accessories	100.0	4.1	14.3	18.1	28.0	15.6	13.2	6.7
Lawn and garden equipment	100.0	1.2	12.5	36.9	19.8	15.8	8.8	4.9
Power tools	100.0	10.8	23.6	11.7	32.5	15.1	4.9	0.9
Office furniture for home use	100.0	4.5	17.7	25.5	26.4	17.3	4.0	4.5
Hand tools	100.0	3.5	20.6	27.7	22.9	14.8	5.9	4.6
Indoor plants and fresh flowers	100.0	3.3	12.1	22.0	26.6	18.8	10.4	6.6
Closet and storage items	100.0	1.9	13.2	36.1	24.0	14.3	6.5	3.9
Rental of furniture	100.0	9.8	33.8	32.6	13.2	7.4	1.8	1.3
Luggage	100.0	4.2	13.2	26.4	24.2	18.3	9.8	3.9
Computers and computer hardware, nonbusiness use	100.0	7.0	17.4	25.7	28.7	15.2	3.9	2.1
Computer software and accessories, nonbusiness use	100.0	6.9	18.5	28.0	23.9	13.5	6.5	2.7
Telephone answering devices	100.0	7.2	17.9	26.4	25.7	10.8	7.8	4.4
Calculators	100.0	12.8	8.9	30.2	38.1	5.8	3.3	0.9
Business equipment for home use	100.0	7.3	15.2	5.6	42.6	10.4	10.4	8.6
Other hardware	100.0	2.0	8.9	38.5	27.9	5.5	15.0	2.1
Smoke alarms	100.0	0.8	17.1	49.4	10.6	9.7	2.5	10.4
Other household appliances	100.0	2.1	15.6	21.4	31.2	15.8	9.6	4.3
Miscellaneous household equipment and parts	100.0	3.0	9.3	28.7	27.7	16.6	8.5	6.1

Note: Numbers may not add to total because of rounding.
Source: Calculations by New Strategist based on the 2002 Consumer Expenditure Survey

Table 8.5 Housing: Household Operations: Average spending by income, 2002

(average annual spending on household services, supplies, furnishings, and equipment, by before-tax income of consumer units (CU), 2002; complete income reporters only)

	complete income reporters	under $10,000	$10,000–$19,999	$20,000–$29,999	$30,000–$39,999	$40,000–$49,999	$50,000–$69,999	$70,000 or more
Number of consumer units (in thousands, add 000)	92,388	10,933	15,075	12,312	10,727	8,873	13,521	20,947
Average number of persons per CU	2.5	1.7	1.9	2.3	2.5	2.6	2.8	3.1
Average before-tax income of CU	$49,430.00	$5,554.80	$14,724.33	$24,495.00	$34,423.00	$44,443.00	$58,933.00	$115,629.00
Average spending of CU, total	42,556.98	17,627.83	22,838.71	28,835.85	35,095.39	41,787.38	50,406.17	76,627.31
Housing, average spending	13,480.52	6,322.60	7,774.87	9,594.62	11,240.22	13,158.81	15,275.81	23,695.41
HOUSEHOLD SERVICES	$736.28	$196.52	$308.64	$476.82	$575.47	$687.80	$752.65	$1,570.52
Personal services	351.88	53.30	115.74	228.12	305.52	339.95	359.08	774.58
Babysitting and child care in your own home	36.27	5.99	8.83	6.91	6.50	13.12	32.28	116.72
Babysitting and child care, someone else's home	29.59	10.21	12.18	21.35	24.68	34.93	35.80	53.32
Day care centers, nurseries, and preschools	223.91	17.83	45.99	101.86	104.81	172.04	283.98	575.43
Other household services	384.39	143.22	192.91	248.70	269.95	347.85	393.57	795.94
Housekeeping services	80.49	21.01	31.89	33.21	36.66	49.90	48.50	230.35
Gardening, lawn care service	74.39	26.98	54.73	46.39	49.51	61.53	60.73	156.76
Water softening service	3.41	1.99	1.91	2.22	3.78	3.57	4.08	5.25
Nonclothing laundry and dry cleaning, sent out	1.63	0.97	0.85	1.14	1.02	1.21	1.43	3.43
Nonclothing laundry and dry cleaning, coin-operated	4.44	3.81	6.29	5.65	5.29	5.11	4.05	2.24
Termite/pest control services	13.94	3.15	8.22	9.66	8.12	18.84	15.01	26.42
Home security system service fee	17.49	4.37	6.40	11.07	11.67	13.96	20.90	38.37
Other home services	14.01	2.64	9.39	12.64	8.00	8.51	14.14	29.41
Termite/pest control products	0.79	0.27	0.20	0.95	0.95	1.25	0.50	1.31
Moving, storage, and freight express	35.28	29.92	17.50	34.94	37.95	33.57	34.15	51.17
Appliance repair, including service center	11.85	4.65	5.97	7.74	8.14	12.76	14.06	22.33
Reupholstering and furniture repair	8.07	6.19	2.60	5.72	4.24	8.61	11.92	13.60
Repairs/rentals of lawn/garden equipment, hand/power tools, etc.	4.01	0.60	2.82	2.21	3.58	3.86	4.03	7.98
Appliance rental	1.26	1.07	0.89	1.22	0.53	0.07	1.22	2.54
Repair of computer systems for nonbusiness use	2.77	1.23	1.67	0.92	1.78	3.37	4.43	4.63
Computer information services	109.21	34.36	40.61	72.03	87.51	120.30	153.77	197.14
HOUSEKEEPING SUPPLIES	606.10	316.72	348.81	432.33	489.72	522.98	1,045.91	847.36
Laundry and cleaning supplies	140.04	96.67	104.17	128.77	127.10	133.97	164.54	185.67
Soaps and detergents	77.96	54.39	59.28	70.28	74.94	71.94	92.06	101.78
Other laundry cleaning products	62.08	42.28	44.89	58.49	52.15	62.03	72.47	83.89
Other household products	322.05	140.67	160.55	192.50	240.30	242.11	696.98	441.20
Cleansing and toilet tissue, paper towels, and napkins	84.71	60.41	67.41	72.40	73.43	75.95	95.23	118.14
Miscellaneous household products	110.72	49.01	62.52	74.90	113.70	97.57	143.54	178.11
Lawn and garden supplies	126.62	31.24	30.63	45.20	53.16	68.58	458.21	144.96
Postage and stationery	144.01	79.38	84.10	111.06	122.33	146.90	184.39	220.49
Stationery, stationery supplies, giftwrap	66.63	28.62	28.90	44.06	53.74	61.05	77.73	126.03
Postage	75.19	50.01	53.82	66.30	65.93	85.23	104.16	89.93
Delivery services	2.19	0.75	1.39	0.71	2.66	0.63	2.50	4.52

	complete income reporters	under $10,000	$10,000– $19,999	$20,000– $29,999	$30,000– $39,999	$40,000– $49,999	$50,000– $69,999	$70,000 or more
HOUSEHOLD FURNISHINGS AND EQUIPMENT	**$1,601.59**	**$544.44**	**$661.94**	**$1,001.09**	**$1,197.58**	**$1,528.91**	**$1,770.12**	**$3,283.35**
Household textiles	**144.40**	**53.74**	**70.66**	**129.53**	**115.29**	**144.18**	**134.76**	**268.34**
Bathroom linens	25.17	10.87	13.87	13.17	14.92	15.80	31.95	51.70
Bedroom linens	67.55	25.34	34.98	84.34	64.45	81.81	50.85	105.11
Kitchen and dining room linens	12.14	4.55	5.26	6.96	11.65	9.14	14.06	23.87
Curtains and draperies	17.64	3.16	10.23	8.48	8.84	21.47	15.38	40.25
Slipcovers and decorative pillows	8.26	5.86	0.83	8.52	6.84	0.90	5.96	19.48
Sewing materials for household items	11.90	3.66	4.87	6.90	7.96	13.18	14.71	23.85
Other linens	1.74	0.31	0.62	1.16	0.63	1.87	1.84	4.07
Furniture	**399.18**	**103.89**	**117.11**	**240.32**	**260.68**	**342.90**	**424.82**	**927.91**
Mattresses and springs	56.75	21.73	18.27	42.14	38.67	42.57	66.99	119.97
Other bedroom furniture	68.06	17.14	13.12	27.16	50.42	50.09	68.07	174.86
Sofas	85.46	24.82	28.57	55.02	72.32	91.15	105.59	167.26
Living room chairs	37.95	10.59	17.27	31.76	24.88	27.40	34.02	84.44
Living room tables	16.95	4.39	7.77	10.59	9.14	11.20	17.65	39.86
Kitchen and dining room furniture	60.37	6.40	17.77	24.95	25.95	59.32	59.93	158.37
Infants' furniture	6.66	0.88	2.16	4.47	3.51	7.60	7.55	14.85
Outdoor furniture	15.95	2.18	1.78	4.39	6.13	11.10	13.21	49.01
Wall units, cabinets, and other furniture	51.03	15.74	10.42	39.83	29.67	42.48	51.82	119.29
Floor coverings	**42.45**	**10.03**	**25.76**	**23.49**	**25.04**	**16.13**	**34.98**	**107.41**
Wall-to-wall carpeting	23.01	0.68	17.79	16.02	14.41	10.65	19.95	54.10
Floor coverings, nonpermanent	19.45	9.34	7.96	7.46	10.63	5.48	15.03	53.30
Major appliances	**198.86**	**65.51**	**104.81**	**111.76**	**147.31**	**204.49**	**241.26**	**382.74**
Dishwashers (built-in), garbage disposals, range hoods	17.33	5.25	7.52	5.77	9.94	15.12	16.85	42.52
Refrigerators and freezers	52.39	17.22	26.03	31.06	40.85	71.31	63.15	93.23
Washing machines	23.73	9.82	16.22	17.78	18.33	24.60	32.97	36.33
Clothes dryers	17.72	3.84	9.79	13.38	13.10	18.17	23.93	31.38
Cooking stoves, ovens	32.10	9.59	19.06	11.61	21.60	32.13	26.18	74.46
Microwave ovens	10.78	6.22	9.81	8.50	10.00	9.28	12.33	15.24
Window air conditioners	8.18	3.97	6.31	10.13	7.55	9.90	9.72	9.17
Electric floor-cleaning equipment	28.30	8.00	4.25	10.87	14.20	20.50	45.37	64.81
Sewing machines	5.00	1.37	3.23	1.84	1.51	2.41	6.63	11.86
Miscellaneous household appliances	2.58	–	1.54	0.82	9.22	0.17	3.74	2.48
Small appliances and misc. housewares	**108.40**	**43.74**	**52.52**	**81.29**	**102.07**	**121.84**	**105.30**	**194.01**
Housewares	83.18	33.67	40.54	61.70	79.88	97.06	71.73	151.71
Plastic dinnerware	1.70	0.97	1.00	1.22	0.88	0.98	2.08	3.34
China and other dinnerware	13.24	5.51	3.86	7.83	16.24	29.73	6.42	22.52
Flatware	4.06	2.18	2.51	1.44	2.38	3.00	5.59	8.02
Glassware	7.97	3.57	4.26	4.58	5.03	6.53	7.82	16.77
Silver serving pieces	4.91	3.28	3.18	1.02	2.49	2.71	2.29	12.94
Other serving pieces	1.58	1.00	0.30	0.91	1.06	2.41	2.21	2.72
Nonelectric cookware	24.56	7.13	12.67	16.82	33.13	26.54	21.37	42.32
Tableware, nonelectric kitchenware	25.17	10.03	12.77	27.88	18.67	25.16	23.95	43.07
Small appliances	25.22	10.07	11.98	19.59	22.19	24.78	33.57	42.30
Small electric kitchen appliances	18.94	5.86	9.68	14.84	16.13	20.29	24.29	32.27
Portable heating and cooling equipment	6.27	4.21	2.30	4.74	6.06	4.49	9.28	10.04

	complete income reporters	under $10,000	$10,000–$19,999	$20,000–$29,999	$30,000–$39,999	$40,000–$49,999	$50,000–$69,999	$70,000 or more
Miscellaneous household equipment	**$708.30**	**$267.53**	**$291.08**	**$414.71**	**$547.19**	**$699.36**	**$829.00**	**$1,402.94**
Window coverings	15.00	6.21	4.08	4.62	12.97	14.80	14.27	35.13
Infants' equipment	11.66	4.48	11.10	7.93	13.32	5.40	17.67	15.63
Laundry and cleaning equipment	16.42	12.16	9.06	9.07	12.90	21.26	21.87	24.51
Outdoor equipment	39.37	1.61	15.35	6.00	14.64	29.69	27.39	117.30
Clocks	6.48	2.23	2.54	4.99	3.37	15.82	3.20	11.83
Lamps and lighting fixtures	12.49	4.39	3.68	5.08	5.45	8.95	14.43	31.25
Other household decorative items	164.40	62.40	62.35	123.18	94.32	149.95	177.42	340.17
Telephones and accessories	36.99	32.76	26.21	26.60	36.47	38.18	33.84	54.51
Lawn and garden equipment	49.32	2.85	15.23	27.51	45.51	44.68	83.96	92.49
Power tools	34.10	5.19	8.28	8.05	44.35	68.20	36.73	60.57
Office furniture for home use	11.31	4.90	1.87	6.91	3.97	7.43	14.50	27.36
Hand tools	8.70	1.91	4.25	5.54	7.87	9.80	12.84	14.58
Indoor plants and fresh flowers	52.38	19.30	21.44	32.04	39.26	47.81	60.44	107.32
Closet and storage items	12.29	3.39	5.51	10.04	5.86	7.27	14.89	26.09
Rental of furniture	5.00	5.85	7.82	4.52	4.97	7.69	4.14	2.25
Luggage	6.58	2.45	3.13	2.45	2.85	4.73	7.95	15.43
Computers and computer hardware, nonbusiness use	145.01	65.47	46.07	89.48	125.51	144.24	192.93	269.76
Computer software and accessories, nonbusiness use	19.22	8.75	8.85	10.73	18.15	15.21	20.94	38.26
Telephone answering devices	1.12	0.88	0.87	0.71	1.21	0.91	1.94	1.20
Calculators	1.48	0.67	0.86	0.78	0.75	1.09	1.96	2.99
Business equipment for home use	1.09	0.40	0.84	1.00	0.38	0.85	0.50	2.55
Other hardware	14.21	1.98	11.56	3.59	5.76	15.58	12.31	32.95
Smoke alarms	1.70	0.39	2.28	0.30	1.45	1.00	0.88	3.72
Other household appliances	9.54	2.75	3.73	4.00	8.72	7.72	13.39	19.22
Miscellaneous household equipment and parts	32.45	14.13	14.14	19.58	37.17	31.10	38.61	55.87

Note: Numbers may not add to total because not all categories are shown. (–) means sample is too small to make a reliable estimate.
Source: Bureau of Labor Statistics, unpublished tables from the 2002 Consumer Expenditure Survey; calculations by New Strategist

Table 8.6 Housing: Household Operations: Indexed spending by income, 2002

(indexed average annual spending of consumer units (CU) on household services, supplies, furnishings, and equipment, by before-tax income of consumer unit, 2002; complete income reporters only; index definition: an index of 100 is the average for all consumer units; an index of 132 means that spending by consumer units in that group is 32 percent above the average for all consumer units; an index of 68 indicates spending that is 32 percent below the average for all consumer units)

	complete income reporters	under $10,000	$10,000–$19,999	$20,000–$29,999	$30,000–$39,999	$40,000–$49,999	$50,000–$69,999	$70,000 or more
Average spending of CU, total	$42,557	$17,628	$22,839	$28,836	$35,095	$41,787	$50,406	$76,627
Average spending of CU, index	100	41	54	68	82	98	118	180
Housing, spending index	100	47	58	71	83	98	113	176
HOUSEHOLD SERVICES	**100**	**27**	**42**	**65**	**78**	**93**	**102**	**213**
Personal services	**100**	**15**	**33**	**65**	**87**	**97**	**102**	**220**
Babysitting and child care in your own home	100	17	24	19	18	36	89	322
Babysitting and child care, someone else's home	100	35	41	72	83	118	121	180
Day care centers, nurseries, and preschools	100	8	21	45	47	77	127	257
Other household services	**100**	**37**	**50**	**65**	**70**	**90**	**102**	**207**
Housekeeping services	100	26	40	41	46	62	60	286
Gardening, lawn care service	100	36	74	62	67	83	82	211
Water softening service	100	58	56	65	111	105	120	154
Nonclothing laundry and dry cleaning, sent out	100	60	52	70	63	74	88	210
Nonclothing laundry and dry cleaning, coin-operated	100	86	142	127	119	115	91	50
Termite/pest control services	100	23	59	69	58	135	108	190
Home security system service fee	100	25	37	63	67	80	119	219
Other home services	100	19	67	90	57	61	101	210
Termite/pest control products	100	34	25	120	120	158	63	166
Moving, storage, and freight express	100	85	50	99	108	95	97	145
Appliance repair, including service center	100	39	50	65	69	108	119	188
Reupholstering and furniture repair	100	77	32	71	53	107	148	169
Repairs/rentals of lawn/garden equipment, hand/power tools, etc.	100	15	70	55	89	96	100	199
Appliance rental	100	85	71	97	42	6	97	202
Repair of computer systems for nonbusiness use	100	44	60	33	64	122	160	167
Computer information services	100	31	37	66	80	110	141	181
HOUSEKEEPING SUPPLIES	**100**	**52**	**58**	**71**	**81**	**86**	**173**	**140**
Laundry and cleaning supplies	**100**	**69**	**74**	**92**	**91**	**96**	**117**	**133**
Soaps and detergents	100	70	76	90	96	92	118	131
Other laundry cleaning products	100	68	72	94	84	100	117	135
Other household products	**100**	**44**	**50**	**60**	**75**	**75**	**216**	**137**
Cleansing and toilet tissue, paper towels, and napkins	100	71	80	85	87	90	112	139
Miscellaneous household products	100	44	56	68	103	88	130	161
Lawn and garden supplies	100	25	24	36	42	54	362	114
Postage and stationery	**100**	**55**	**58**	**77**	**85**	**102**	**128**	**153**
Stationery, stationery supplies, giftwrap	100	43	43	66	81	92	117	189
Postage	100	67	72	88	88	113	139	120
Delivery services	100	34	63	32	121	29	114	206

	complete income reporters	under $10,000	$10,000– $19,999	$20,000– $29,999	$30,000– $39,999	$40,000– $49,999	$50,000– $69,999	$70,000 or more
HOUSEHOLD FURNISHINGS AND EQUIPMENT	**100**	**34**	**41**	**63**	**75**	**95**	**111**	**205**
Household textiles	**100**	**37**	**49**	**90**	**80**	**100**	**93**	**186**
Bathroom linens	100	43	55	52	59	63	127	205
Bedroom linens	100	38	52	125	95	121	75	156
Kitchen and dining room linens	100	37	43	57	96	75	116	197
Curtains and draperies	100	18	58	48	50	122	87	228
Slipcovers and decorative pillows	100	71	10	103	83	11	72	236
Sewing materials for household items	100	31	41	58	67	111	124	200
Other linens	100	18	36	67	36	107	106	234
Furniture	**100**	**26**	**29**	**60**	**65**	**86**	**106**	**232**
Mattresses and springs	100	38	32	74	68	75	118	211
Other bedroom furniture	100	25	19	40	74	74	100	257
Sofas	100	29	33	64	85	107	124	196
Living room chairs	100	28	46	84	66	72	90	223
Living room tables	100	26	46	62	54	66	104	235
Kitchen and dining room furniture	100	11	29	41	43	98	99	262
Infants' furniture	100	13	32	67	53	114	113	223
Outdoor furniture	100	14	11	28	38	70	83	307
Wall units, cabinets, and other furniture	100	31	20	78	58	83	102	234
Floor coverings	**100**	**24**	**61**	**55**	**59**	**38**	**82**	**253**
Wall-to-wall carpeting	100	3	77	70	63	46	87	235
Floor coverings, nonpermanent	100	48	41	38	55	28	77	274
Major appliances	**100**	**33**	**53**	**56**	**74**	**103**	**121**	**192**
Dishwashers (built-in), garbage disposals, range hoods	100	30	43	33	57	87	97	245
Refrigerators and freezers	100	33	50	59	78	136	121	178
Washing machines	100	41	68	75	77	104	139	153
Clothes dryers	100	22	55	76	74	103	135	177
Cooking stoves, ovens	100	30	59	36	67	100	82	232
Microwave ovens	100	58	91	79	93	86	114	141
Window air conditioners	100	48	77	124	92	121	119	112
Electric floor-cleaning equipment	100	28	15	38	50	72	160	229
Sewing machines	100	27	65	37	30	48	133	237
Miscellaneous household appliances	100	–	60	32	357	7	145	96
Small appliances and misc. housewares	**100**	**40**	**48**	**75**	**94**	**112**	**97**	**179**
Housewares	100	40	49	74	96	117	86	182
Plastic dinnerware	100	57	59	72	52	58	122	196
China and other dinnerware	100	42	29	59	123	225	48	170
Flatware	100	54	62	35	59	74	138	198
Glassware	100	45	53	57	63	82	98	210
Silver serving pieces	100	67	65	21	51	55	47	264
Other serving pieces	100	63	19	58	67	153	140	172
Nonelectric cookware	100	29	52	68	135	108	87	172
Tableware, nonelectric kitchenware	100	40	51	111	74	100	95	171
Small appliances	100	40	47	78	88	98	133	168
Small electric kitchen appliances	100	31	51	78	85	107	128	170
Portable heating and cooling equipment	100	67	37	76	97	72	148	160

	complete income reporters	under $10,000	$10,000–$19,999	$20,000–$29,999	$30,000–$39,999	$40,000–$49,999	$50,000–$69,999	$70,000 or more
Miscellaneous household equipment	**100**	**38**	**41**	**59**	**77**	**99**	**117**	**198**
Window coverings	100	41	27	31	86	99	95	234
Infants' equipment	100	38	95	68	114	46	152	134
Laundry and cleaning equipment	100	74	55	55	79	129	133	149
Outdoor equipment	100	4	39	15	37	75	70	298
Clocks	100	34	39	77	52	244	49	183
Lamps and lighting fixtures	100	35	29	41	44	72	116	250
Other household decorative items	100	38	38	75	57	91	108	207
Telephones and accessories	100	89	71	72	99	103	91	147
Lawn and garden equipment	100	6	31	56	92	91	170	188
Power tools	100	15	24	24	130	200	108	178
Office furniture for home use	100	43	16	61	35	66	128	242
Hand tools	100	22	49	64	90	113	148	168
Indoor plants and fresh flowers	100	37	41	61	75	91	115	205
Closet and storage items	100	28	45	82	48	59	121	212
Rental of furniture	100	117	156	90	99	154	83	45
Luggage	100	37	48	37	43	72	121	234
Computers and computer hardware, nonbusiness use	100	45	32	62	87	99	133	186
Computer software and accessories, nonbusiness use	100	46	46	56	94	79	109	199
Telephone answering devices	100	78	77	63	108	81	173	107
Calculators	100	45	58	53	51	74	132	202
Business equipment for home use	100	37	77	92	35	78	46	234
Other hardware	100	14	81	25	41	110	87	232
Smoke alarms	100	23	134	18	85	59	52	219
Other household appliances	100	29	39	42	91	81	140	201
Miscellaneous household equipment and parts	100	44	44	60	115	96	119	172

Note: (–) means sample is too small to make a reliable estimate.
Source: Calculations by New Strategist based on the 2002 Consumer Expenditure Survey

Table 8.7 Housing: Household Operations: Total spending by income, 2002

(total annual spending on household services, supplies, furnishings, and equipment, by before-tax income group of consumer units (CU), 2002; complete income reporters only; numbers in thousands)

	complete income reporters	under $10,000	$10,000–$19,999	$20,000–$29,999	$30,000–$39,999	$40,000–$49,999	$50,000–$69,999	$70,000 or more
Number of consumer units	92,388	10,933	15,075	12,312	10,727	8,873	13,521	20,947
Total spending of all CUs	$3,931,754,268	$192,725,059	$344,293,530	$355,026,985	$376,468,249	$370,779,423	$681,541,825	$1,605,112,263
Housing, total spending	1,245,438,282	69,124,997	117,206,161	118,128,961	120,573,840	116,758,121	206,544,227	496,347,753
HOUSEHOLD SERVICES	**$68,023,437**	**$2,148,513**	**$4,652,817**	**$5,870,608**	**$6,173,067**	**$6,102,849**	**$10,176,581**	**$32,897,682**
Personal services	**32,509,489**	**582,708**	**1,744,835**	**2,808,613**	**3,277,313**	**3,016,376**	**4,855,121**	**16,225,127**
Babysitting and child care in your own home	3,350,913	65,488	133,131	85,076	69,726	116,414	436,458	2,444,934
Babysitting and child care, someone else's home	2,733,761	111,625	183,670	262,861	264,742	309,934	484,052	1,116,894
Day care centers, nurseries, and preschools	20,686,597	194,935	693,318	1,254,100	1,124,297	1,526,511	3,839,694	12,053,532
Other household services	**35,513,023**	**1,565,875**	**2,908,062**	**3,061,994**	**2,895,754**	**3,086,473**	**5,321,460**	**16,672,555**
Housekeeping services	7,436,310	229,703	480,701	408,882	393,252	442,763	655,769	4,825,141
Gardening, lawn care service	6,872,743	295,016	824,985	571,154	531,094	545,956	821,130	3,283,652
Water softening service	315,043	21,748	28,747	27,333	40,548	31,677	55,166	109,972
Nonclothing laundry and dry cleaning, sent out	150,592	10,641	12,786	14,036	10,942	10,736	19,335	71,848
Nonclothing laundry and dry cleaning, coin-operated	410,203	41,655	94,866	69,563	56,746	45,341	54,760	46,921
Termite/pest control services	1,287,889	34,448	123,913	118,934	87,103	167,167	202,950	553,420
Home security system service fee	1,615,866	47,762	96,415	136,294	125,184	123,867	282,589	803,736
Other home services	1,294,356	28,903	141,512	155,624	85,816	75,509	191,187	616,051
Termite/pest control products	72,987	2,937	3,029	11,696	10,191	11,091	6,761	27,441
Moving, storage, and freight express	3,259,449	327,157	263,761	430,181	407,090	297,867	461,742	1,071,858
Appliance repair, including service center	1,094,798	50,810	90,013	95,295	87,318	113,219	190,105	467,747
Reupholstering and furniture repair	745,571	67,711	39,223	70,425	45,482	76,397	161,170	284,879
Repairs/rentals of lawn/garden equipment, hand/power tools, etc.	370,476	6,558	42,439	27,210	38,403	34,250	54,490	167,157
Appliance rental	116,409	11,684	13,463	15,021	5,685	621	16,496	53,205
Repair of computer systems, nonbusiness use	255,915	13,429	25,240	11,327	19,094	29,902	59,898	96,985
Computer information services	10,089,693	375,642	612,186	886,833	938,720	1,067,422	2,079,124	4,129,492
HOUSEKEEPING SUPPLIES	**55,996,367**	**3,462,698**	**5,258,385**	**5,322,847**	**5,253,226**	**4,640,402**	**14,141,749**	**17,749,650**
Laundry and cleaning supplies	**12,938,016**	**1,056,899**	**1,570,389**	**1,585,416**	**1,363,402**	**1,188,716**	**2,224,745**	**3,889,229**
Soaps and detergents	7,202,568	594,696	893,629	865,287	803,881	638,324	1,244,743	2,131,986
Other laundry cleaning products	5,735,447	462,202	676,690	720,129	559,413	550,392	979,867	1,757,244
Other household products	**29,753,555**	**1,537,958**	**2,420,272**	**2,370,060**	**2,577,698**	**2,148,242**	**9,423,867**	**9,241,816**
Cleansing and toilet tissue, paper towels, and napkins	7,826,187	660,469	1,016,162	891,389	787,684	673,904	1,287,605	2,474,679
Miscellaneous household products	10,229,199	535,858	942,427	922,169	1,219,660	865,739	1,940,804	3,730,870
Lawn and garden supplies	11,698,169	341,593	461,683	556,502	570,247	608,510	6,195,457	3,036,477
Postage and stationery	**13,304,796**	**867,879**	**1,267,795**	**1,367,371**	**1,312,234**	**1,303,444**	**2,493,137**	**4,618,604**
Stationery, stationery supplies, giftwrap	6,155,812	312,932	435,621	542,467	576,469	541,697	1,050,987	2,639,950
Postage	6,946,654	546,730	811,275	816,286	707,231	756,246	1,408,347	1,883,764
Delivery services	202,330	8,179	20,898	8,742	28,534	5,590	33,803	94,680

	complete income reporters	under $10,000	$10,000– $19,999	$20,000– $29,999	$30,000– $39,999	$40,000– $49,999	$50,000– $69,999	$70,000 or more
HOUSEHOLD FURNISHINGS AND EQUIPMENT	**$147,967,697**	**$5,952,355**	**$9,978,782**	**$12,325,420**	**$12,846,441**	**$13,566,018**	**$23,933,793**	**$68,776,332**
Household textiles	**13,340,827**	**587,584**	**1,065,125**	**1,594,773**	**1,236,716**	**1,279,309**	**1,822,090**	**5,620,918**
Bathroom linens	2,325,406	118,830	209,024	162,149	160,047	140,193	431,996	1,082,960
Bedroom linens	6,240,809	277,049	527,344	1,038,394	691,355	725,900	687,543	2,201,739
Kitchen and dining room linens	1,121,590	49,748	79,301	85,692	124,970	81,099	190,105	500,005
Curtains and draperies	1,629,724	34,537	154,272	104,406	94,827	190,503	207,953	843,117
Slipcovers and decorative pillows	763,125	64,048	12,440	104,898	73,373	7,986	80,585	408,048
Sewing materials for household items	1,099,417	40,012	73,417	84,953	85,387	116,946	198,894	499,586
Other linens	160,755	3,358	9,328	14,282	6,758	16,593	24,879	85,254
Furniture	**36,879,442**	**1,135,854**	**1,765,415**	**2,958,820**	**2,796,314**	**3,042,552**	**5,743,991**	**19,436,931**
Mattresses and springs	5,243,019	237,598	275,457	518,828	414,813	377,724	905,772	2,513,012
Other bedroom furniture	6,287,927	187,385	197,719	334,394	540,855	444,449	920,374	3,662,792
Sofas	7,895,478	271,358	430,682	677,406	775,777	808,774	1,427,682	3,503,595
Living room chairs	3,506,125	115,819	260,323	391,029	266,888	243,120	459,984	1,768,765
Living room tables	1,565,977	47,986	117,183	130,384	98,045	99,378	238,646	834,947
Kitchen and dining room furniture	5,577,464	69,954	267,840	307,184	278,366	526,346	810,314	3,317,376
Infants' furniture	615,304	9,654	32,506	55,035	37,652	67,435	102,084	311,063
Outdoor furniture	1,473,589	23,874	26,813	54,050	65,757	98,490	178,612	1,026,612
Wall units, cabinets, and other furniture	4,714,560	172,119	157,045	490,387	318,270	376,925	700,658	2,498,768
Floor coverings	**3,921,871**	**109,706**	**388,348**	**289,209**	**268,604**	**143,121**	**472,965**	**2,249,917**
Wall-to-wall carpeting	2,125,848	7,459	268,193	197,238	154,576	94,497	269,744	1,133,233
Floor coverings, nonpermanent	1,796,947	102,138	120,004	91,848	114,028	48,624	203,221	1,116,475
Major appliances	**18,372,278**	**716,261**	**1,580,065**	**1,375,989**	**1,580,194**	**1,814,440**	**3,262,076**	**8,017,255**
Dishwashers (built-in), garbage disposals, range hoods	1,601,084	57,451	113,374	71,040	106,626	134,160	227,829	890,666
Refrigerators and freezers	4,840,207	188,319	392,349	382,411	438,198	632,734	853,851	1,952,889
Washing machines	2,192,367	107,333	244,548	218,907	196,626	218,276	445,787	761,005
Clothes dryers	1,637,115	41,968	147,604	164,735	140,524	161,222	323,558	657,317
Cooking stoves, ovens	2,965,655	104,803	287,281	142,942	231,703	285,089	353,980	1,559,714
Microwave ovens	995,943	68,020	147,934	104,652	107,270	82,341	166,714	319,232
Window air conditioners	755,734	43,353	95,143	124,721	80,989	87,843	131,424	192,084
Electric floor-cleaning equipment	2,614,580	87,412	64,100	133,831	152,323	181,897	613,448	1,357,575
Sewing machines	461,940	14,962	48,730	22,654	16,198	21,384	89,644	248,431
Miscellaneous household appliances	238,361	–	23,170	10,096	98,903	1,508	50,569	51,949
Small appliances and misc. housewares	**10,014,859**	**478,163**	**791,787**	**1,000,842**	**1,094,905**	**1,081,086**	**1,423,761**	**4,063,927**
Housewares	7,684,834	368,091	611,213	759,650	856,873	861,213	969,861	3,177,869
Plastic dinnerware	157,060	10,645	15,063	15,021	9,440	8,696	28,124	69,963
China and other dinnerware	1,223,217	60,289	58,209	96,403	174,206	263,794	86,805	471,726
Flatware	375,095	23,862	37,899	17,729	25,530	26,619	75,582	167,995
Glassware	736,332	39,033	64,186	56,389	53,957	57,941	105,734	351,281
Silver serving pieces	453,625	35,901	47,870	12,558	26,710	24,046	30,963	271,054
Other serving pieces	145,973	10,905	4,504	11,204	11,371	21,384	29,881	56,976
Nonelectric cookware	2,269,049	77,959	190,943	207,088	355,386	235,489	288,944	886,477
Tableware, nonelectric kitchenware	2,325,406	109,606	192,539	343,259	200,273	223,245	323,828	902,187
Small appliances	2,330,025	110,072	180,574	241,192	238,032	219,873	453,900	886,058
Small electric kitchen appliances	1,749,829	64,047	145,892	182,710	173,027	180,033	328,425	675,960
Portable heating and cooling equipment	579,273	46,026	34,612	58,359	65,006	39,840	125,475	210,308

	complete income reporters	under $10,000	$10,000– $19,999	$20,000– $29,999	$30,000– $39,999	$40,000– $49,999	$50,000– $69,999	$70,000 or more
Miscellaneous household equipment	**$65,438,420**	**$2,924,928**	**$4,388,042**	**$5,105,910**	**$5,869,707**	**$6,205,421**	**$11,208,909**	**$29,387,384**
Window coverings	1,385,820	67,933	61,570	56,881	139,129	131,320	192,945	735,868
Infants' equipment	1,077,244	48,974	167,346	97,634	142,884	47,914	238,916	327,402
Laundry and cleaning equipment	1,517,011	132,997	136,567	111,670	138,378	188,640	295,704	513,411
Outdoor equipment	3,637,316	17,553	231,362	73,872	157,043	263,439	370,340	2,457,083
Clocks	598,674	24,423	38,268	61,437	36,150	140,371	43,267	247,803
Lamps and lighting fixtures	1,153,926	47,993	55,442	62,545	58,462	79,413	195,108	654,594
Other household decorative items	15,188,587	682,183	939,979	1,516,592	1,011,771	1,330,506	2,398,896	7,125,541
Telephones and accessories	3,417,432	358,185	395,161	327,499	391,214	338,771	457,551	1,141,821
Lawn and garden equipment	4,556,576	31,184	229,630	338,703	488,186	396,446	1,135,223	1,937,388
Power tools	3,150,431	56,789	124,773	99,112	475,742	605,139	496,626	1,268,760
Office furniture for home use	1,044,908	53,614	28,132	85,076	42,586	65,926	196,055	573,110
Hand tools	803,776	20,864	64,119	68,208	84,421	86,955	173,610	305,407
Indoor plants and fresh flowers	4,839,283	211,019	323,251	394,476	421,142	424,218	817,209	2,248,032
Closet and storage items	1,135,449	37,102	83,104	123,612	62,860	64,507	201,328	546,507
Rental of furniture	461,940	63,981	117,833	55,650	53,313	68,233	55,977	47,131
Luggage	607,913	26,821	47,219	30,164	30,572	41,969	107,492	323,212
Computers and computer hardware, nonbusiness use	13,397,184	715,818	694,448	1,101,678	1,346,346	1,279,842	2,608,607	5,650,663
Computer software and accessories, nonbusiness use	1,775,697	95,634	133,452	132,108	194,695	134,958	283,130	801,432
Telephone answering devices	103,475	9,599	13,064	8,742	12,980	8,074	26,231	25,136
Calculators	136,734	7,286	12,921	9,603	8,045	9,672	26,501	62,632
Business equipment for home use	100,703	4,389	12,631	12,312	4,076	7,542	6,761	53,415
Other hardware	1,312,833	21,699	174,214	44,200	61,788	138,241	166,444	690,204
Smoke alarms	157,060	4,231	34,349	3,694	15,554	8,873	11,898	77,923
Other household appliances	881,382	30,118	56,274	49,248	93,539	68,500	181,046	402,601
Miscellaneous household equipment and parts	2,997,991	154,502	213,162	241,069	398,723	275,950	522,046	1,170,309

Note: Numbers may not add to total because of rounding and because not all categories are shown. (–) means sample is too small to make a reliable estimate.
Source: Calculations by New Strategist based on the 2002 Consumer Expenditure Survey

Table 8.8 Housing: Household Operations: Market shares by income, 2002

(percentage of total annual spending on household services, supplies, furnishings, and equipment accounted for by before-tax income group of consumer units, 2002; complete income reporters only)

	complete income reporters	under $10,000	$10,000–$19,999	$20,000–$29,999	$30,000–$39,999	$40,000–$49,999	$50,000–$69,999	$70,000 or more
Share of total consumer units	100.0%	11.8%	16.3%	13.3%	11.6%	9.6%	14.6%	22.7%
Share of total before-tax income	100.0	1.3	4.9	6.6	8.1	8.6	17.4	53.0
Share of total spending	100.0	4.9	8.8	9.0	9.6	9.4	17.3	40.8
Share of housing spending	100.0	5.6	9.4	9.5	9.7	9.4	16.6	39.9
HOUSEHOLD SERVICES	100.0%	3.2%	6.8%	8.6%	9.1%	9.0%	15.0%	48.4%
Personal services	100.0	1.8	5.4	8.6	10.1	9.3	14.9	49.9
Babysitting and child care in your own home	100.0	2.0	4.0	2.5	2.1	3.5	13.0	73.0
Babysitting and child care, someone else's home	100.0	4.1	6.7	9.6	9.7	11.3	17.7	40.9
Day care centers, nurseries, and preschools	100.0	0.9	3.4	6.1	5.4	7.4	18.6	58.3
Other household services	100.0	4.4	8.2	8.6	8.2	8.7	15.0	46.9
Housekeeping services	100.0	3.1	6.5	5.5	5.3	6.0	8.8	64.9
Gardening, lawn care service	100.0	4.3	12.0	8.3	7.7	7.9	11.9	47.8
Water softening service	100.0	6.9	9.1	8.7	12.9	10.1	17.5	34.9
Nonclothing laundry and dry cleaning, sent out	100.0	7.1	8.5	9.3	7.3	7.1	12.8	47.7
Nonclothing laundry and dry cleaning, coin-operated	100.0	10.2	23.1	17.0	13.8	11.1	13.3	11.4
Termite/pest control services	100.0	2.7	9.6	9.2	6.8	13.0	15.8	43.0
Home security system service fee	100.0	3.0	6.0	8.4	7.7	7.7	17.5	49.7
Other home services	100.0	2.2	10.9	12.0	6.6	5.8	14.8	47.6
Termite/pest control products	100.0	4.0	4.2	16.0	14.0	15.2	9.3	37.6
Moving, storage, and freight express	100.0	10.0	8.1	13.2	12.5	9.1	14.2	32.9
Appliance repair, including service center	100.0	4.6	8.2	8.7	8.0	10.3	17.4	42.7
Reupholstering and furniture repair	100.0	9.1	5.3	9.4	6.1	10.2	21.6	38.2
Repairs/rentals of lawn/garden equipment, hand/power tools, etc.	100.0	1.8	11.5	7.3	10.4	9.2	14.7	45.1
Appliance rental	100.0	10.0	11.6	12.9	4.9	0.5	14.2	45.7
Repair of computer systems for nonbusiness use	100.0	5.2	9.9	4.4	7.5	11.7	23.4	37.9
Computer information services	100.0	3.7	6.1	8.8	9.3	10.6	20.6	40.9
HOUSEKEEPING SUPPLIES	100.0	6.2	9.4	9.5	9.4	8.3	25.3	31.7
Laundry and cleaning supplies	100.0	8.2	12.1	12.3	10.5	9.2	17.2	30.1
Soaps and detergents	100.0	8.3	12.4	12.0	11.2	8.9	17.3	29.6
Other laundry cleaning products	100.0	8.1	11.8	12.6	9.8	9.6	17.1	30.6
Other household products	100.0	5.2	8.1	8.0	8.7	7.2	31.7	31.1
Cleansing and toilet tissue, paper towels, and napkins	100.0	8.4	13.0	11.4	10.1	8.6	16.5	31.6
Miscellaneous household products	100.0	5.2	9.2	9.0	11.9	8.5	19.0	36.5
Lawn and garden supplies	100.0	2.9	3.9	4.8	4.9	5.2	53.0	26.0
Postage and stationery	100.0	6.5	9.5	10.3	9.9	9.8	18.7	34.7
Stationery, stationery supplies, giftwrap	100.0	5.1	7.1	8.8	9.4	8.8	17.1	42.9
Postage	100.0	7.9	11.7	11.8	10.2	10.9	20.3	27.1
Delivery services	100.0	4.0	10.3	4.3	14.1	2.8	16.7	46.8

	complete income reporters	under $10,000	$10,000–$19,999	$20,000–$29,999	$30,000–$39,999	$40,000–$49,999	$50,000–$69,999	$70,000 or more
HOUSEHOLD FURNISHINGS AND EQUIPMENT	**100.0%**	**4.0%**	**6.7%**	**8.3%**	**8.7%**	**9.2%**	**16.2%**	**46.5%**
Household textiles	**100.0**	**4.4**	**8.0**	**12.0**	**9.3**	**9.6**	**13.7**	**42.1**
Bathroom linens	100.0	5.1	9.0	7.0	6.9	6.0	18.6	46.6
Bedroom linens	100.0	4.4	8.4	16.6	11.1	11.6	11.0	35.3
Kitchen and dining room linens	100.0	4.4	7.1	7.6	11.1	7.2	16.9	44.6
Curtains and draperies	100.0	2.1	9.5	6.4	5.8	11.7	12.8	51.7
Slipcovers and decorative pillows	100.0	8.4	1.6	13.7	9.6	1.0	10.6	53.5
Sewing materials for household items	100.0	3.6	6.7	7.7	7.8	10.6	18.1	45.4
Other linens	100.0	2.1	5.8	8.9	4.2	10.3	15.5	53.0
Furniture	**100.0**	**3.1**	**4.8**	**8.0**	**7.6**	**8.2**	**15.6**	**52.7**
Mattresses and springs	100.0	4.5	5.3	9.9	7.9	7.2	17.3	47.9
Other bedroom furniture	100.0	3.0	3.1	5.3	8.6	7.1	14.6	58.3
Sofas	100.0	3.4	5.5	8.6	9.8	10.2	18.1	44.4
Living room chairs	100.0	3.3	7.4	11.2	7.6	6.9	13.1	50.4
Living room tables	100.0	3.1	7.5	8.3	6.3	6.3	15.2	53.3
Kitchen and dining room furniture	100.0	1.3	4.8	5.5	5.0	9.4	14.5	59.5
Infants' furniture	100.0	1.6	5.3	8.9	6.1	11.0	16.6	50.6
Outdoor furniture	100.0	1.6	1.8	3.7	4.5	6.7	12.1	69.7
Wall units, cabinets, and other furniture	100.0	3.7	3.3	10.4	6.8	8.0	14.9	53.0
Floor coverings	**100.0**	**2.8**	**9.9**	**7.4**	**6.8**	**3.6**	**12.1**	**57.4**
Wall-to-wall carpeting	100.0	0.4	12.6	9.3	7.3	4.4	12.7	53.3
Floor coverings, nonpermanent	100.0	5.7	6.7	5.1	6.3	2.7	11.3	62.1
Major appliances	**100.0**	**3.9**	**8.6**	**7.5**	**8.6**	**9.9**	**17.8**	**43.6**
Dishwashers (built-in), garbage disposals, range hoods	100.0	3.6	7.1	4.4	6.7	8.4	14.2	55.6
Refrigerators and freezers	100.0	3.9	8.1	7.9	9.1	13.1	17.6	40.3
Washing machines	100.0	4.9	11.2	10.0	9.0	10.0	20.3	34.7
Clothes dryers	100.0	2.6	9.0	10.1	8.6	9.8	19.8	40.2
Cooking stoves, ovens	100.0	3.5	9.7	4.8	7.8	9.6	11.9	52.6
Microwave ovens	100.0	6.8	14.9	10.5	10.8	8.3	16.7	32.1
Window air conditioners	100.0	5.7	12.6	16.5	10.7	11.6	17.4	25.4
Electric floor-cleaning equipment	100.0	3.3	2.5	5.1	5.8	7.0	23.5	51.9
Sewing machines	100.0	3.2	10.5	4.9	3.5	4.6	19.4	53.8
Miscellaneous household appliances	100.0	–	9.7	4.2	41.5	0.6	21.2	21.8
Small appliances and misc. housewares	**100.0**	**4.8**	**7.9**	**10.0**	**10.9**	**10.8**	**14.2**	**40.6**
Housewares	100.0	4.8	8.0	9.9	11.2	11.2	12.6	41.4
Plastic dinnerware	100.0	4.8	8.0	9.9	6.0	5.5	17.9	44.5
China and other dinnerware	100.0	6.8	9.6	9.6	14.2	21.6	7.1	38.6
Flatware	100.0	4.9	4.8	7.9	6.8	7.1	20.2	44.8
Glassware	100.0	6.4	10.1	4.7	7.3	7.9	14.4	47.7
Silver serving pieces	100.0	5.3	8.7	7.7	5.9	5.3	6.8	59.8
Other serving pieces	100.0	7.9	10.6	2.8	7.8	14.6	20.5	39.0
Nonelectric cookware	100.0	7.5	3.1	7.7	15.7	10.4	12.7	39.1
Tableware, nonelectric kitchenware	100.0	3.4	8.4	9.1	8.6	9.6	13.9	38.8
Small appliances	100.0	4.7	8.3	14.8	10.2	9.4	19.5	38.0
Small electric kitchen appliances	100.0	4.7	7.7	10.4	9.9	10.3	18.8	38.6
Portable heating and cooling equipment	100.0	3.7	8.3	10.4	11.2	6.9	21.7	36.3

	complete income reporters	under $10,000	$10,000– $19,999	$20,000– $29,999	$30,000– $39,999	$40,000– $49,999	$50,000– $69,999	$70,000 or more
Miscellaneous household equipment	**100.0%**	**4.5%**	**6.7%**	**7.8%**	**9.0%**	**9.5%**	**17.1%**	**44.9%**
Window coverings	100.0	4.9	4.4	4.1	10.0	9.5	13.9	53.1
Infants' equipment	100.0	4.5	15.5	9.1	13.3	4.4	22.2	30.4
Laundry and cleaning equipment	100.0	8.8	9.0	7.4	9.1	12.4	19.5	33.8
Outdoor equipment	100.0	0.5	6.4	2.0	4.3	7.2	10.2	67.6
Clocks	100.0	4.1	6.4	10.3	6.0	23.4	7.2	41.4
Lamps and lighting fixtures	100.0	4.2	4.8	5.4	5.1	6.9	16.9	56.7
Other household decorative items	100.0	4.5	6.2	10.0	6.7	8.8	15.8	46.9
Telephones and accessories	100.0	10.5	11.6	9.6	11.4	9.9	13.4	33.4
Lawn and garden equipment	100.0	0.7	5.0	7.4	10.7	8.7	24.9	42.5
Power tools	100.0	1.8	4.0	3.1	15.1	19.2	15.8	40.3
Office furniture for home use	100.0	5.1	2.7	8.1	4.1	6.3	18.8	54.8
Hand tools	100.0	2.6	8.0	8.5	10.5	10.8	21.6	38.0
Indoor plants and fresh flowers	100.0	4.4	6.7	8.2	8.7	8.8	16.9	46.5
Closet and storage items	100.0	3.3	7.3	10.9	5.5	5.7	17.7	48.1
Rental of furniture	100.0	13.9	25.5	12.0	11.5	14.8	12.1	10.2
Luggage	100.0	4.4	7.8	5.0	5.0	6.9	17.7	53.2
Computers and computer hardware, nonbusiness use	100.0	5.3	5.2	8.2	10.0	9.6	19.5	42.2
Computer software and accessories, nonbusiness use	100.0	5.4	7.5	7.4	11.0	7.6	15.9	45.1
Telephone answering devices	100.0	9.3	12.6	8.4	12.5	7.8	25.3	24.3
Calculators	100.0	5.3	9.5	7.0	5.9	7.1	19.4	45.8
Business equipment for home use	100.0	4.4	12.5	12.2	4.0	7.5	6.7	53.0
Other hardware	100.0	1.7	13.3	3.4	4.7	10.5	12.7	52.6
Smoke alarms	100.0	2.7	21.9	2.4	9.9	5.6	7.6	49.6
Other household appliances	100.0	3.4	6.4	5.6	10.6	7.8	20.5	45.7
Miscellaneous household equipment and parts	100.0	5.2	7.1	8.0	13.3	9.2	17.4	39.0

Note: Numbers may not add to total because of rounding. (–) means sample is too small to make a reliable estimate.
Source: Calculations by New Strategist based on the 2002 Consumer Expenditure Survey

Table 8.9 Housing: Household Operations: Average spending by household type, 2002

(average annual spending of consumer units (CU) on household services, supplies, furnishings, and equipment, by type of consumer unit, 2002)

	total married couples	married couples, no children	married couples with children				single parent, at least one child <18	single person
			total	oldest child under 6	oldest child 6 to 17	oldest child 18 or older		
Number of consumer units (in thousands, add 000)	56,265	23,118	28,790	5,547	15,206	8,036	6,730	33,055
Average number of persons per CU	3.2	2.0	3.9	3.5	4.1	3.9	2.9	1.0
Average before-tax income of CU	$67,155.00	$58,967.00	$73,918.00	$67,587.00	$72,720.00	$81,042.00	$26,966.00	$27,042.00
Average spending of CU, total	52,333.70	45,557.33	57,835.01	52,778.62	58,103.75	60,859.78	30,185.38	24,189.90
Housing, average spending	16,649.27	14,422.39	18,459.93	19,140.57	18,618.79	17,697.37	11,021.68	8,619.27
HOUSEHOLD SERVICES	**$942.88**	**$553.33**	**$1,263.54**	**$2,320.13**	**$1,220.68**	**$615.27**	**$814.42**	**$399.90**
Personal services	**462.61**	**68.33**	**775.95**	**1,912.19**	**705.47**	**124.95**	**571.40**	**134.35**
Babysitting and child care in your own home	59.38	0.38	109.77	253.81	108.56	12.62	71.18	0.20
Babysitting and child care, someone else's home	33.74	0.50	59.65	136.57	60.53	4.89	87.13	3.66
Day care centers, nurseries, and preschools	335.10	9.30	604.14	1,519.66	534.32	104.26	411.62	7.20
Other household services	**480.27**	**485.00**	**487.59**	**407.94**	**515.21**	**490.31**	**243.02**	**265.55**
Housekeeping services	109.00	105.59	118.46	84.79	131.08	117.83	54.10	54.24
Gardening, lawn care service	86.85	106.86	69.46	53.09	70.49	78.82	31.91	66.19
Water softening service	4.15	3.61	4.68	3.16	5.39	4.41	4.17	1.90
Nonclothing laundry and dry cleaning, sent out	1.71	2.08	1.33	1.74	1.09	1.51	0.45	2.14
Nonclothing laundry and dry cleaning, coin-operated	3.29	2.25	3.89	4.42	3.24	4.77	6.70	3.69
Termite/pest control services	17.18	20.20	16.39	20.72	14.70	16.59	4.75	8.28
Home security system service fee	23.88	24.24	24.96	24.60	28.02	19.41	13.02	9.49
Other home services	19.56	23.16	17.94	9.24	17.14	25.45	11.78	12.02
Termite/pest control products	0.77	1.21	0.52	0.58	0.59	0.35	0.42	0.34
Moving, storage, and freight express	36.24	36.78	36.96	48.40	42.91	17.79	25.67	27.68
Appliance repair, including service center	14.90	15.30	13.94	11.24	13.96	15.78	4.65	6.14
Reupholstering and furniture repair	9.48	13.47	7.56	9.46	6.30	8.65	0.75	7.30
Repairs/rentals of lawn/garden equipment, hand/power tools, etc.	5.22	5.35	5.51	3.15	6.21	5.81	1.16	2.21
Appliance rental	1.20	0.41	1.08	0.22	1.47	0.93	1.62	0.25
Repair of computer systems for nonbusiness use	3.49	3.14	4.03	1.11	4.10	5.91	1.75	1.29
Computer information services	142.03	119.91	159.69	129.53	168.17	164.46	77.37	62.16
HOUSEKEEPING SUPPLIES	**754.38**	**816.98**	**711.50**	**552.46**	**723.62**	**804.43**	**336.96**	**269.87**
Laundry and cleaning supplies	**169.42**	**139.73**	**191.91**	**155.71**	**194.86**	**212.67**	**119.92**	**63.83**
Soaps and detergents	93.57	74.33	108.42	89.37	112.70	113.93	76.32	34.99
Other laundry cleaning products	75.85	65.40	83.49	66.34	82.17	98.75	43.60	28.85
Other household products	**413.82**	**495.36**	**356.82**	**252.13**	**377.58**	**392.47**	**147.25**	**117.86**
Cleansing and toilet tissue, paper towels, and napkins	99.64	85.19	108.74	85.69	115.32	112.60	59.51	38.17
Miscellaneous household products	134.92	113.16	153.51	113.27	177.16	135.93	59.80	44.94
Lawn and garden supplies	179.27	297.01	94.57	53.18	85.10	143.94	27.93	34.75
Postage and stationery	**171.14**	**181.89**	**162.77**	**144.62**	**151.17**	**199.28**	**69.80**	**88.18**
Stationery, stationery supplies, giftwrap	82.71	83.98	83.49	74.53	82.93	91.21	32.50	31.45
Postage	85.25	94.41	75.87	70.09	65.90	100.02	35.76	55.61
Delivery services	3.18	3.51	3.41	–	2.35	8.04	1.54	1.12

	total married couples	married couples, no children	married couples with children				single parent, at least one child <18	single person
			total	oldest child under 6	oldest child 6 to 17	oldest child 18 or older		
HOUSEHOLD FURNISHINGS AND EQUIPMENT	**$2,103.57**	**$2,026.91**	**$2,211.95**	**$2,020.71**	**$2,271.15**	**$2,233.72**	**$886.05**	**$772.08**
Household textiles	**177.05**	**188.02**	**173.27**	**146.78**	**163.81**	**211.76**	**72.63**	**81.03**
Bathroom linens	30.87	26.09	35.41	19.58	29.08	59.73	11.66	11.87
Bedroom linens	83.08	91.87	77.72	85.76	64.55	98.10	37.43	35.38
Kitchen and dining room linens	14.48	14.10	14.35	5.37	18.79	12.11	4.81	5.12
Curtains and draperies	22.75	27.26	20.44	18.25	23.04	17.03	9.70	9.82
Slipcovers and decorative pillows	6.02	7.11	6.00	6.55	6.26	5.08	2.79	12.83
Sewing materials for household items	17.60	19.51	16.96	9.90	18.60	18.72	3.51	5.42
Other linens	2.24	2.09	2.40	1.38	3.50	1.00	2.73	0.58
Furniture	**573.79**	**589.58**	**578.27**	**540.34**	**619.97**	**525.57**	**231.62**	**179.44**
Mattresses and springs	72.51	66.04	80.14	74.41	88.27	68.74	31.37	30.40
Other bedroom furniture	89.00	72.47	105.00	123.21	112.02	79.15	72.79	31.84
Sofas	124.23	111.96	134.93	129.43	146.62	116.61	46.42	34.44
Living room chairs	56.98	77.68	42.11	35.15	40.21	50.51	12.18	19.33
Living room tables	24.32	25.70	24.18	17.46	26.45	24.54	9.95	9.56
Kitchen and dining room furniture	96.46	127.06	78.39	67.47	89.03	65.80	23.54	23.50
Infants' furniture	9.95	9.03	10.13	28.59	6.15	4.90	3.11	1.10
Outdoor furniture	26.61	26.52	28.65	13.80	29.80	36.74	5.98	5.57
Wall units, cabinets, and other furniture	73.73	73.13	74.74	50.83	81.43	78.58	26.28	23.71
Floor coverings	**63.92**	**78.08**	**58.41**	**40.79**	**67.05**	**54.22**	**14.76**	**15.07**
Wall-to-wall carpeting	34.92	41.85	32.97	25.61	34.28	35.59	9.32	7.63
Floor coverings, nonpermanent	29.00	36.24	25.43	15.19	32.76	18.64	5.44	7.45
Major appliances	**252.37**	**258.42**	**250.84**	**228.17**	**247.93**	**272.19**	**139.83**	**94.05**
Dishwashers (built-in), garbage disposals, range hoods	25.05	25.39	24.95	19.96	28.33	22.00	8.86	5.50
Refrigerators and freezers	70.86	73.18	68.99	66.39	69.69	69.44	32.46	28.10
Washing machines	28.83	26.75	29.79	34.53	27.22	31.40	22.50	13.07
Clothes dryers	22.12	20.02	23.73	28.79	21.24	24.94	21.19	8.27
Cooking stoves, ovens	40.79	42.49	41.77	26.64	43.12	49.65	12.51	12.57
Microwave ovens	13.09	12.61	13.70	12.97	13.11	15.35	7.38	7.36
Window air conditioners	9.83	7.15	10.91	8.39	10.85	12.80	7.25	4.97
Electric floor-cleaning equipment	30.84	38.67	25.66	27.60	24.60	26.34	23.90	10.05
Sewing machines	7.31	9.59	6.23	2.27	4.19	12.82	0.21	2.12
Miscellaneous household appliances	2.76	2.27	3.61	–	3.56	6.38	2.28	1.33
Small appliances and misc. housewares	**133.86**	**134.25**	**140.87**	**157.84**	**128.50**	**152.78**	**56.20**	**56.81**
Housewares	104.27	103.18	112.70	139.32	97.56	123.17	42.71	42.81
Plastic dinnerware	2.08	1.29	2.79	3.49	2.81	2.26	0.79	0.87
China and other dinnerware	16.04	17.82	15.79	9.04	14.51	23.29	4.46	12.61
Flatware	5.49	6.47	4.97	4.24	3.80	7.69	1.30	2.28
Glassware	8.12	6.13	9.91	5.96	7.54	17.56	4.51	3.33
Silver serving pieces	6.09	6.19	6.64	8.72	6.46	5.48	2.03	1.97
Other serving pieces	1.64	1.83	1.37	1.61	1.07	1.77	0.89	1.40
Nonelectric cookware	34.16	28.06	42.75	88.30	30.91	32.83	9.91	12.57
Tableware, nonelectric kitchenware	30.65	35.40	28.48	17.95	30.46	32.30	18.82	7.75
Small appliances	29.58	31.08	28.17	18.52	30.93	29.61	13.49	14.00
Small electric kitchen appliances	21.64	22.96	20.34	15.91	20.74	22.64	10.53	10.70
Portable heating and cooling equipment	7.94	8.12	7.83	2.61	10.19	6.97	2.96	3.30

	total married couples	married couples, no children	married couples with children				single parent, at least one child <18	single person
			total	oldest child under 6	oldest child 6 to 17	oldest child 18 or older		
Miscellaneous household equipment	**$902.58**	**$778.55**	**$1,010.28**	**$906.78**	**$1,043.91**	**$1,017.19**	**$371.02**	**$345.67**
Window coverings	18.85	13.25	23.66	34.11	21.37	20.79	2.52	8.13
Infants' equipment	19.61	9.30	25.69	48.10	11.23	38.05	7.18	1.99
Laundry and cleaning equipment	20.05	19.58	21.03	21.77	20.14	22.26	16.68	7.10
Outdoor equipment	56.77	39.19	71.92	34.33	95.21	53.13	7.30	3.24
Clocks	8.82	7.01	7.38	0.13	8.90	9.69	6.64	1.82
Lamps and lighting fixtures	16.77	20.60	14.22	9.61	15.03	15.85	3.92	6.59
Other household decorative items	201.92	180.19	222.20	252.87	216.02	211.94	68.47	73.60
Telephones and accessories	43.30	27.47	53.78	27.09	65.86	49.33	11.63	17.64
Lawn and garden equipment	69.09	65.07	77.51	72.35	83.50	69.73	15.59	20.00
Power tools	45.68	39.68	50.16	26.54	60.20	47.53	10.12	25.10
Office furniture for home use	15.20	14.80	15.44	9.45	19.81	11.33	6.84	5.95
Hand tools	11.21	11.93	11.07	10.98	10.56	12.08	4.03	3.71
Indoor plants and fresh flowers	66.99	72.57	63.28	52.56	60.07	76.75	18.22	32.06
Closet and storage items	13.82	10.06	15.49	28.52	12.17	12.52	9.47	4.83
Rental of furniture	3.37	1.62	4.99	5.64	5.77	3.06	18.93	2.35
Luggage	8.02	7.76	8.79	5.92	8.86	10.66	2.13	4.02
Computers and computer hardware, nonbusiness use	177.84	140.57	213.56	172.65	219.09	231.35	119.77	84.39
Computer software and accessories, nonbusiness use	23.27	18.42	27.45	24.18	28.05	28.58	7.95	11.05
Telephone answering devices	1.09	1.03	1.18	1.32	1.31	0.83	1.95	0.94
Calculators	1.90	0.70	2.77	1.29	2.59	4.15	2.58	0.80
Business equipment for home use	1.20	1.60	0.82	1.97	0.48	0.68	1.24	0.76
Other hardware	22.16	19.84	20.67	18.90	26.06	11.23	5.57	2.32
Smoke alarms	2.50	1.47	2.33	2.94	2.79	1.04	0.49	0.44
Other household appliances	14.43	15.32	14.97	4.68	13.96	23.97	1.38	4.06
Miscellaneous household equipment and parts	38.73	39.52	39.90	38.88	34.89	50.65	20.44	22.78

Note: Average spending figures for total consumer units can be found on Average Spending by Age and Average Spending by Region tables. Numbers may not add to total because not all categories are shown. (–) means sample is too small to make a reliable estimate.
Source: Bureau of Labor Statistics, unpublished tables from the 2002 Consumer Expenditure Survey

Table 8.10 Housing: Household Operations: Indexed spending by household type, 2002

(indexed average annual spending of consumer units (CU) on household services, supplies, furnishings, and equipment, by type of consumer unit, 2002; index definition: an index of 100 is the average for all consumer units; an index of 132 means that spending by consumer units in that group is 32 percent above the average for all consumer units; an index of 68 indicates spending that is 32 percent below the average for all consumer units)

	total married couples	married couples, no children	married couples with children				single parent, at least one child <18	single person
			total	oldest child under 6	oldest child 6 to 17	oldest child 18 or older		
Average spending of CU, total	$52,334	$45,557	$57,835	$52,779	$58,104	$60,860	$30,185	$24,190
Average spending of CU, index	129	112	142	130	143	150	74	59
Housing, spending index	125	109	139	144	140	133	83	65
HOUSEHOLD SERVICES	**134**	**78**	**179**	**329**	**173**	**87**	**115**	**57**
Personal services	**140**	**21**	**234**	**578**	**213**	**38**	**173**	**41**
Babysitting and child care in your own home	165	1	306	707	302	35	198	1
Babysitting and child care, someone else's home	123	2	217	497	220	18	317	13
Day care centers, nurseries, and preschools	159	4	287	721	254	49	195	3
Other household services	**128**	**129**	**130**	**109**	**137**	**131**	**65**	**71**
Housekeeping services	136	132	148	106	164	147	68	68
Gardening, lawn care service	120	148	96	73	97	109	44	91
Water softening service	132	115	149	100	171	140	132	60
Nonclothing laundry and dry cleaning, sent out	99	121	77	101	63	88	26	124
Nonclothing laundry and dry cleaning, coin-operated	80	54	94	107	78	115	162	89
Termite/pest control services	130	152	124	156	111	125	36	62
Home security system service fee	137	139	143	141	161	112	75	55
Other home services	130	154	119	61	114	169	78	80
Termite/pest control products	113	178	76	85	87	51	62	50
Moving, storage, and freight express	109	111	112	146	130	54	77	84
Appliance repair, including service center	137	141	128	103	129	145	43	57
Reupholstering and furniture repair	128	182	102	128	85	117	10	99
Repairs/rentals of lawn/garden equipment, hand/power tools, etc.	144	148	152	87	172	160	32	61
Appliance rental	112	38	101	21	137	87	151	23
Repair of computer systems for nonbusiness use	138	124	159	44	162	234	69	51
Computer information services	132	112	149	121	157	153	72	58
HOUSEKEEPING SUPPLIES	**138**	**150**	**130**	**101**	**133**	**148**	**62**	**49**
Laundry and cleaning supplies	**130**	**107**	**147**	**119**	**149**	**163**	**92**	**49**
Soaps and detergents	128	102	149	123	155	156	105	48
Other laundry cleaning products	132	113	145	115	142	171	76	50
Other household products	**146**	**175**	**126**	**89**	**133**	**139**	**52**	**42**
Cleansing and toilet tissue, paper towels, and napkins	130	111	142	112	151	147	78	50
Miscellaneous household products	139	117	159	117	183	140	62	46
Lawn and garden supplies	163	270	86	48	77	131	25	32
Postage and stationery	**130**	**138**	**124**	**110**	**115**	**152**	**53**	**67**
Stationery, stationery supplies, giftwrap	137	140	139	124	138	152	54	52
Postage	123	137	110	101	95	145	52	80
Delivery services	150	166	161	–	111	379	73	53

	total married couples	married couples, no children	married couples with children			single parent, at least one child <18	single person
			total	oldest child under 6	oldest child 6 to 17	oldest child 18 or older		

	total married couples	married couples, no children	total	oldest child under 6	oldest child 6 to 17	oldest child 18 or older	single parent, at least one child <18	single person
HOUSEHOLD FURNISHINGS AND EQUIPMENT	**139**	**133**	**146**	**133**	**150**	**147**	**58**	**51**
Household textiles	**131**	**139**	**128**	**108**	**121**	**156**	**54**	**60**
Bathroom linens	138	117	158	88	130	267	52	53
Bedroom linens	126	139	118	130	98	149	57	54
Kitchen and dining room linens	143	139	142	53	186	120	48	51
Curtains and draperies	137	164	123	110	138	102	58	59
Slipcovers and decorative pillows	81	96	81	89	85	69	38	173
Sewing materials for household items	154	171	148	87	163	164	31	47
Other linens	141	131	151	87	220	63	172	36
Furniture	**143**	**147**	**144**	**135**	**154**	**131**	**58**	**45**
Mattresses and springs	137	125	151	141	167	130	59	57
Other bedroom furniture	130	106	154	180	164	116	107	47
Sofas	146	131	158	152	172	137	54	40
Living room chairs	145	198	107	90	103	129	31	49
Living room tables	135	143	134	97	147	136	55	53
Kitchen and dining room furniture	157	207	128	110	145	107	38	38
Infants' furniture	154	140	157	443	95	76	48	17
Outdoor furniture	158	158	171	82	177	219	36	33
Wall units, cabinets, and other furniture	139	138	141	96	154	148	50	45
Floor coverings	**158**	**193**	**144**	**101**	**166**	**134**	**36**	**37**
Wall-to-wall carpeting	161	193	152	118	158	164	43	35
Floor coverings, nonpermanent	154	193	135	81	174	99	29	40
Major appliances	**134**	**137**	**133**	**121**	**132**	**144**	**74**	**50**
Dishwashers (built-in), garbage disposals, range hoods	152	154	151	121	171	133	54	33
Refrigerators and freezers	136	141	132	127	134	133	62	54
Washing machines	129	120	134	155	122	141	101	59
Clothes dryers	130	117	139	169	125	146	124	49
Cooking stoves, ovens	132	137	135	86	139	160	40	41
Microwave ovens	125	120	130	124	125	146	70	70
Window air conditioners	124	91	138	106	137	162	92	63
Electric floor-cleaning equipment	135	170	113	121	108	116	105	44
Sewing machines	153	200	130	47	87	268	4	44
Miscellaneous household appliances	98	81	128	–	127	227	81	47
Small appliances and misc. housewares	**133**	**134**	**140**	**157**	**128**	**152**	**56**	**57**
Housewares	134	133	145	180	126	159	55	55
Plastic dinnerware	132	82	178	222	179	144	50	55
China and other dinnerware	111	123	109	62	100	161	31	87
Flatware	145	171	131	112	100	203	34	60
Glassware	125	94	152	92	116	270	69	51
Silver serving pieces	150	153	164	215	160	135	50	49
Other serving pieces	114	127	95	112	74	123	62	97
Nonelectric cookware	141	116	176	364	127	135	41	52
Tableware, nonelectric kitchenware	143	165	133	84	142	151	88	36
Small appliances	129	136	123	81	135	129	59	61
Small electric kitchen appliances	126	134	118	93	121	132	61	62
Portable heating and cooling equipment	139	142	137	46	179	122	52	58

Miscellaneous household equipment	total married couples	married couples, no children	married couples with children				single parent, at least one child <18	single person
			total	oldest child under 6	oldest child 6 to 17	oldest child 18 or older		
Miscellaneous household equipment	**138**	**119**	**155**	**139**	**160**	**156**	**57**	**53**
Window coverings	136	95	170	245	154	149	18	58
Infants' equipment	151	72	198	371	87	294	55	15
Laundry and cleaning equipment	132	129	139	144	133	147	110	47
Outdoor equipment	180	124	228	109	302	169	23	10
Clocks	150	119	126	2	152	165	113	31
Lamps and lighting fixtures	143	175	121	82	128	135	33	56
Other household decorative items	139	124	153	174	149	146	47	51
Telephones and accessories	132	84	164	83	201	151	36	54
Lawn and garden equipment	143	135	161	150	173	145	32	42
Power tools	137	119	151	80	181	143	30	75
Office furniture for home use	144	140	146	89	187	107	65	56
Hand tools	139	148	138	136	131	150	50	46
Indoor plants and fresh flowers	135	146	127	106	121	154	37	64
Closet and storage items	138	101	155	286	122	125	95	48
Rental of furniture	73	35	108	123	125	67	412	51
Luggage	134	130	147	99	148	178	36	67
Computers and computer hardware, nonbusiness use	128	101	154	125	158	167	86	61
Computer software and accessories, nonbusiness use	132	104	155	137	159	162	45	63
Telephone answering devices	101	95	109	122	121	77	181	87
Calculators	132	49	192	90	180	288	179	56
Business equipment for home use	124	165	85	203	49	70	128	78
Other hardware	172	154	161	147	203	87	43	18
Smoke alarms	168	99	156	197	187	70	33	30
Other household appliances	156	166	162	51	151	260	15	44
Miscellaneous household equipment and parts	131	133	135	131	118	171	69	77

Note: Spending index for total consumer units is 100. (–) means sample is too small to make a reliable estimate.
Source: Calculations by New Strategist based on the 2002 Consumer Expenditure Survey

Table 8.11 Housing: Household Operations: Total spending by household type, 2002

(total annual spending on household services, supplies, furnishings, and equipment, by consumer unit (CU) type, 2002; numbers in thousands)

	total married couples	married couples, no children	married couples with children			single parent, at least one child <18	single person
			total	oldest child under 6	oldest child 6 to 17	oldest child 18 or older		
Number of consumer units	56,265	23,118	28,790	5,547	15,206	8,036	6,730	33,055
Total spending of all CUs	$2,944,555,631	$1,053,194,355	$1,665,069,938	$292,763,005	$883,525,623	$489,069,192	$203,147,607	$799,597,145
Housing, total spending	936,771,177	333,416,812	531,461,385	106,172,742	283,117,321	142,216,065	74,175,906	284,909,970
HOUSEHOLD SERVICES	**$53,051,143**	**$12,791,883**	**$36,377,317**	**$12,869,761**	**$18,561,660**	**$4,944,310**	**$5,481,047**	**$13,218,695**
Personal services	**26,028,752**	**1,579,653**	**22,339,601**	**10,606,918**	**10,727,377**	**1,004,098**	**3,845,522**	**4,440,939**
Babysitting and child care in your own home	3,341,016	8,785	3,160,278	1,407,884	1,650,763	101,414	479,041	6,611
Babysitting and child care, someone else's home	1,898,381	11,559	1,717,324	757,554	920,419	39,296	586,385	120,981
Day care centers, nurseries, and preschools	18,854,402	214,997	17,393,191	8,429,554	8,124,870	837,833	2,770,203	237,996
Other household services	**27,022,392**	**11,212,230**	**14,037,716**	**2,262,843**	**7,834,283**	**3,940,131**	**1,635,525**	**8,777,755**
Housekeeping services	6,132,885	2,441,030	3,410,463	470,330	1,993,202	946,882	364,093	1,792,903
Gardening, lawn care service	4,886,615	2,470,389	1,999,753	294,490	1,071,871	633,398	214,754	2,187,910
Water softening service	233,500	83,456	134,737	17,529	81,960	35,439	28,064	62,805
Nonclothing laundry and dry cleaning, sent out	96,213	48,085	38,291	9,652	16,575	12,134	3,029	70,738
Nonclothing laundry and dry cleaning, coin-operated	185,112	52,016	111,993	24,518	49,267	38,332	45,091	121,973
Termite/pest control services	966,633	466,984	471,868	114,934	223,528	133,317	31,968	273,695
Home security system service fee	1,343,608	560,380	718,598	136,456	426,072	155,979	87,625	313,692
Other home services	1,100,543	535,413	516,493	51,254	260,631	204,516	79,279	397,321
Termite/pest control products	43,324	27,973	14,971	3,217	8,972	2,813	2,827	11,239
Moving, storage, and freight express	2,039,044	850,280	1,064,078	268,475	652,489	142,960	172,759	914,962
Appliance repair, including service center	838,349	353,705	401,333	62,348	212,276	126,808	31,295	202,958
Reupholstering and furniture repair	533,392	311,399	217,652	52,475	95,798	69,511	5,048	241,302
Repairs/rentals of lawn/garden equipment, hand/power tools, etc.	293,703	123,681	158,633	17,473	94,429	46,689	7,807	73,052
Appliance rental	67,518	9,478	31,093	1,220	22,353	7,473	10,903	8,264
Repair of computer systems, nonbusiness use	196,365	72,591	116,024	6,157	62,345	47,493	11,778	42,641
Computer information services	7,991,318	2,772,079	4,597,475	718,503	2,557,193	1,321,601	520,700	2,054,699
HOUSEKEEPING SUPPLIES	**42,445,191**	**18,886,944**	**20,484,085**	**3,064,496**	**11,003,366**	**6,464,399**	**2,267,741**	**8,920,553**
Laundry and cleaning supplies	**9,532,416**	**3,230,278**	**5,525,089**	**863,723**	**2,963,041**	**1,709,016**	**807,062**	**2,109,901**
Soaps and detergents	5,264,716	1,718,361	3,121,412	495,735	1,713,716	915,541	513,634	1,156,594
Other laundry cleaning products	4,267,700	1,511,917	2,403,677	367,988	1,249,477	793,555	293,428	953,637
Other household products	**23,283,582**	**11,451,732**	**10,272,848**	**1,398,565**	**5,741,481**	**3,153,889**	**990,993**	**3,895,862**
Cleansing and toilet tissue, paper towels, and napkins	5,606,245	1,969,422	3,130,625	475,322	1,753,556	904,854	400,502	1,261,709
Miscellaneous household products	7,591,274	2,616,033	4,419,553	628,309	2,693,895	1,092,333	402,454	1,485,492
Lawn and garden supplies	10,086,627	6,866,277	2,722,670	294,989	1,294,031	1,156,702	187,969	1,148,661
Postage and stationery	**9,629,192**	**4,204,933**	**4,686,148**	**802,207**	**2,298,691**	**1,601,414**	**469,754**	**2,914,790**
Stationery, stationery supplies, giftwrap	4,653,678	1,941,450	2,403,677	413,418	1,261,034	732,964	218,725	1,039,580
Postage	4,796,591	2,182,570	2,184,297	388,789	1,002,075	803,761	240,665	1,838,189
Delivery services	178,923	81,144	98,174	–	35,734	64,609	10,364	37,022

HOUSEHOLD FURNISHINGS AND EQUIPMENT	total married couples	married couples, no children	married couples with children				single parent, at least one child <18	single person
			total	oldest child under 6	oldest child 6 to 17	oldest child 18 or older		
	$118,357,366	$46,858,105	$63,682,041	$11,208,878	$34,535,107	$17,950,174	$5,963,117	$25,521,104
Household textiles	9,961,718	4,346,646	4,988,443	814,189	2,490,895	1,701,703	488,800	2,678,447
Bathroom linens	1,736,901	603,149	1,019,454	108,610	442,190	479,990	78,472	392,363
Bedroom linens	4,674,496	2,123,851	2,237,559	475,711	981,547	788,332	251,904	1,169,486
Kitchen and dining room linens	814,717	325,964	413,137	29,787	285,721	97,316	32,371	169,242
Curtains and draperies	1,280,029	630,197	588,468	101,233	350,346	136,853	65,281	324,600
Slipcovers and decorative pillows	338,715	164,369	172,740	36,333	95,190	40,823	18,777	424,096
Sewing materials for household items	990,264	451,032	488,278	54,915	282,832	150,434	23,622	179,158
Other linens	126,034	48,317	69,096	7,655	53,221	8,036	18,373	19,172
Furniture	32,284,294	13,629,910	16,648,393	2,997,266	9,427,264	4,223,481	1,558,803	5,931,389
Mattresses and springs	4,079,775	1,526,713	2,307,231	412,752	1,342,234	552,395	211,120	1,004,872
Other bedroom furniture	5,007,585	1,675,361	3,022,950	683,446	1,703,376	636,049	489,877	1,052,471
Sofas	6,989,801	2,588,291	3,884,635	717,948	2,229,504	937,078	312,407	1,138,414
Living room chairs	3,205,980	1,795,806	1,212,347	194,977	611,433	405,898	81,971	638,953
Living room tables	1,368,365	594,133	696,142	96,851	402,199	197,203	66,964	316,006
Kitchen and dining room furniture	5,427,322	2,937,373	2,256,848	374,256	1,353,790	528,769	158,424	776,793
Infants' furniture	559,837	208,756	291,643	158,589	93,517	39,376	20,930	36,361
Outdoor furniture	1,497,212	613,089	824,834	76,549	453,139	295,243	40,245	184,116
Wall units, cabinets, and other furniture	4,148,418	1,690,619	2,151,765	281,954	1,238,225	631,469	176,864	783,734
Floor coverings	3,596,459	1,805,053	1,681,624	226,262	1,019,562	435,712	99,335	498,139
Wall-to-wall carpeting	1,964,774	967,488	949,206	142,059	521,262	286,001	62,724	252,210
Floor coverings, nonpermanent	1,631,685	837,796	732,130	84,259	498,149	149,791	36,611	246,260
Major appliances	14,199,598	5,974,154	7,221,684	1,265,659	3,770,024	2,187,319	941,056	3,108,823
Dishwashers (built-in), garbage disposals, range hoods	1,409,438	586,966	718,311	110,718	430,786	176,792	59,628	181,803
Refrigerators and freezers	3,986,938	1,691,775	1,986,222	368,265	1,059,706	558,020	218,456	928,846
Washing machines	1,622,120	618,407	857,654	191,538	413,907	252,330	151,425	432,029
Clothes dryers	1,244,582	462,822	683,187	159,698	322,975	200,418	142,609	273,365
Cooking stoves, ovens	2,295,049	982,284	1,202,558	147,772	655,683	398,987	84,192	415,501
Microwave ovens	736,509	291,518	394,423	71,945	199,351	123,353	49,667	243,285
Window air conditioners	553,085	165,294	314,099	46,539	164,985	102,861	48,793	164,283
Electric floor-cleaning equipment	1,735,213	893,973	738,751	153,097	374,068	211,668	160,847	332,203
Sewing machines	411,297	221,702	179,362	12,592	63,713	103,022	1,413	70,077
Miscellaneous household appliances	155,291	52,478	103,932	–	54,133	51,270	15,344	43,963
Small appliances and misc. housewares	7,531,633	3,103,592	4,055,647	875,538	1,953,971	1,227,740	378,226	1,877,855
Housewares	5,866,752	2,385,315	3,244,633	772,808	1,483,497	989,794	287,438	1,415,085
Plastic dinnerware	117,031	29,822	80,324	19,359	42,729	18,161	5,317	28,758
China and other dinnerware	902,491	411,963	454,594	50,145	220,639	187,158	30,016	416,824
Flatware	308,895	149,573	143,086	23,519	57,783	61,797	8,749	75,365
Glassware	456,872	141,713	285,309	33,060	114,653	141,112	30,352	110,073
Silver serving pieces	342,654	143,100	191,166	48,370	98,231	44,037	13,662	65,118
Other serving pieces	92,275	42,306	39,442	8,931	16,270	14,224	5,990	46,277
Nonelectric cookware	1,922,012	648,691	1,230,773	489,800	470,017	263,822	66,694	415,501
Tableware, nonelectric kitchenware	1,724,522	818,377	819,939	99,569	463,175	259,563	126,659	256,176
Small appliances	1,664,319	718,507	811,014	102,730	470,322	237,946	90,788	462,770
Small electric kitchen appliances	1,217,575	530,789	585,589	88,253	315,372	181,935	70,867	353,689
Portable heating and cooling equipment	446,744	187,718	225,426	14,478	154,949	56,011	19,921	109,082

	total married couples	married couples, no children	married couples with children				single parent, at least one child <18	single person
			total	oldest child under 6	oldest child 6 to 17	oldest child 18 or older		
Miscellaneous household equipment	**$50,783,664**	**$17,998,519**	**$29,085,961**	**$5,029,909**	**$15,873,695**	**$8,174,139**	**$2,496,965**	**$11,426,122**
Window coverings	1,060,595	306,314	681,171	189,208	324,952	167,068	16,960	268,737
Infants' equipment	1,103,357	214,997	739,615	266,811	170,763	305,770	48,321	65,779
Laundry and cleaning equipment	1,128,113	452,650	605,454	120,758	306,249	178,881	112,256	234,691
Outdoor equipment	3,194,164	905,994	2,070,577	190,429	1,447,763	426,953	49,129	107,098
Clocks	496,257	162,057	212,470	721	135,333	77,869	44,687	60,160
Lamps and lighting fixtures	943,564	476,231	409,394	53,307	228,546	127,371	26,382	217,832
Other household decorative items	11,361,029	4,165,632	6,397,138	1,402,670	3,284,800	1,703,150	460,803	2,432,848
Telephones and accessories	2,436,275	635,051	1,548,326	150,268	1,001,467	396,416	78,270	583,090
Lawn and garden equipment	3,887,349	1,504,288	2,231,513	401,325	1,269,701	560,350	104,921	661,100
Power tools	2,570,185	917,322	1,444,106	147,217	915,401	381,951	68,108	829,681
Office furniture for home use	855,228	342,146	444,518	52,419	301,231	91,048	46,033	196,677
Hand tools	630,731	275,798	318,705	60,906	160,575	97,075	27,122	122,634
Indoor plants and fresh flowers	3,769,192	1,677,673	1,821,831	291,550	913,424	616,763	122,621	1,059,743
Closet and storage items	777,582	232,567	445,957	158,200	185,057	100,611	63,733	159,656
Rental of furniture	189,613	37,451	143,662	31,285	87,739	24,590	127,399	77,679
Luggage	451,245	179,396	253,064	32,838	134,725	85,664	14,335	132,881
Computers and computer hardware, nonbusiness use	10,006,168	3,249,697	6,148,392	957,690	3,331,483	1,859,129	806,052	2,789,511
Computer software and accessories, nonbusiness use	1,309,287	425,834	790,286	134,126	426,528	229,669	53,504	365,258
Telephone answering devices	61,329	23,812	33,972	7,322	19,920	6,670	13,124	31,072
Calculators	106,904	16,183	79,748	7,156	39,384	33,349	17,363	26,444
Business equipment for home use	67,518	36,989	23,608	10,928	7,299	5,464	8,345	25,122
Other hardware	1,246,832	458,661	595,089	104,838	396,268	90,244	37,486	76,688
Smoke alarms	140,663	33,983	67,081	16,308	42,425	8,357	3,298	14,544
Other household appliances	811,904	354,168	430,986	25,960	212,276	192,623	9,287	134,203
Miscellaneous household equipment and parts	2,179,143	913,623	1,148,721	215,667	530,537	407,023	137,561	752,993

Note: Total spending figures for total consumer units can be found on Total Spending by Age and Total Spending by Region tables. Spending will not add to total because not all types of consumer units or categories are shown. (–) means sample is too small to make a reliable estimate.
Source: Calculations by New Strategist based on the 2002 Consumer Expenditure Survey

Table 8.12 Housing: Household Operations: Market shares by household type, 2002

(percentage of total annual spending on household services, supplies, furnishings, and equipment accounted for by types of consumer units, 2002)

	total married couples	married couples, no children	married couples with children				single parent, at least one child <18	single person
			total	oldest child under 6	oldest child 6 to 17	oldest child 18 or older		
Share of total consumer units	50.2%	20.6%	25.7%	4.9%	13.6%	7.2%	6.0%	29.5%
Share of total before-tax income	68.2	24.6	38.4	6.8	20.0	11.8	3.3	16.1
Share of total spending	64.6	23.1	36.5	6.4	19.4	10.7	4.5	17.5
Share of housing spending	62.9	22.4	35.7	7.1	19.0	9.6	5.0	19.1
HOUSEHOLD SERVICES	**67.1%**	**16.2%**	**46.0%**	**16.3%**	**23.5%**	**6.2%**	**6.9%**	**16.7%**
Personal services	**70.1**	**4.3**	**60.2**	**28.6**	**28.9**	**2.7**	**10.4**	**12.0**
Babysitting and child care in your own home	83.0	0.2	78.5	35.0	41.0	2.5	11.9	0.2
Babysitting and child care, someone else's home	61.6	0.4	55.7	24.6	29.9	1.3	19.0	3.9
Day care centers, nurseries, and preschools	79.8	0.9	73.6	35.7	34.4	3.5	11.7	1.0
Other household services	**64.3**	**26.7**	**33.4**	**5.4**	**18.7**	**9.4**	**3.9**	**20.9**
Housekeeping services	68.5	27.3	38.1	5.3	22.3	10.6	4.1	20.0
Gardening, lawn care service	60.2	30.4	24.6	3.6	13.2	7.8	2.6	27.0
Water softening service	66.1	23.6	38.2	5.0	23.2	10.0	7.9	17.8
Nonclothing laundry and dry cleaning, sent out	49.9	24.9	19.9	5.0	8.6	6.3	1.6	36.7
Nonclothing laundry and dry cleaning, coin-operated	40.0	11.2	24.2	5.3	10.6	8.3	9.7	26.3
Termite/pest control services	65.1	31.4	31.8	7.7	15.0	9.0	2.2	18.4
Home security system service fee	68.9	28.7	36.8	7.0	21.8	8.0	4.5	16.1
Other home services	65.2	31.7	30.6	3.0	15.4	12.1	4.7	23.5
Termite/pest control products	56.8	36.7	19.6	4.2	11.8	3.7	3.7	14.7
Moving, storage, and freight express	54.9	22.9	28.6	7.2	17.6	3.8	4.7	24.6
Appliance repair, including service center	68.9	29.1	33.0	5.1	17.4	10.4	2.6	16.7
Reupholstering and furniture repair	64.3	37.5	26.2	6.3	11.5	8.4	0.6	29.1
Repairs/rentals of lawn/garden equipment, hand/power tools, etc.	72.4	30.5	39.1	4.3	23.3	11.5	1.9	18.0
Appliance rental	56.3	7.9	25.9	1.0	18.6	6.2	9.1	6.9
Repair of computer systems for nonbusiness use	69.2	25.6	40.9	2.2	22.0	16.7	4.2	15.0
Computer information services	66.4	23.0	38.2	6.0	21.3	11.0	4.3	17.1
HOUSEKEEPING SUPPLIES	**69.4**	**30.9**	**33.5**	**5.0**	**18.0**	**10.6**	**3.7**	**14.6**
Laundry and cleaning supplies	**65.1**	**22.1**	**37.7**	**5.9**	**20.2**	**11.7**	**5.5**	**14.4**
Soaps and detergents	64.4	21.0	38.2	6.1	21.0	11.2	6.3	14.2
Other laundry cleaning products	66.0	23.4	37.2	5.7	19.3	12.3	4.5	14.7
Other household products	**73.3**	**36.1**	**32.3**	**4.4**	**18.1**	**9.9**	**3.1**	**12.3**
Cleansing and toilet tissue, paper towels, and napkins	65.4	23.0	36.5	5.5	20.5	10.6	4.7	14.7
Miscellaneous household products	69.9	24.1	40.7	5.8	24.8	10.1	3.7	13.7
Lawn and garden supplies	81.8	55.7	22.1	2.4	10.5	9.4	1.5	9.3
Postage and stationery	**65.3**	**28.5**	**31.8**	**5.4**	**15.6**	**10.9**	**3.2**	**19.8**
Stationery, stationery supplies, giftwrap	69.0	28.8	35.6	6.1	18.7	10.9	3.2	15.4
Postage	61.9	28.2	28.2	5.0	12.9	10.4	3.1	23.7
Delivery services	75.3	34.1	41.3	–	15.0	27.2	4.4	15.6

	total married couples	married couples, no children	married couples with children				single parent, at least one child <18	single person
			total	oldest child under 6	oldest child 6 to 17	oldest child 18 or older		
HOUSEHOLD FURNISHINGS AND EQUIPMENT	**69.5%**	**27.5%**	**37.4%**	**6.6%**	**20.3%**	**10.5%**	**3.5%**	**15.0%**
Household textiles	**65.6**	**28.6**	**32.8**	**5.4**	**16.4**	**11.2**	**3.2**	**17.6**
Bathroom linens	69.3	24.1	40.7	4.3	17.6	19.2	3.1	15.7
Bedroom linens	63.2	28.7	30.3	6.4	13.3	10.7	3.4	15.8
Kitchen and dining room linens	71.9	28.8	36.5	2.6	25.2	8.6	2.9	14.9
Curtains and draperies	68.6	33.8	31.5	5.4	18.8	7.3	3.5	17.4
Slipcovers and decorative pillows	40.8	19.8	20.8	4.4	11.5	4.9	2.3	51.1
Sewing materials for household items	77.2	35.2	38.1	4.3	22.1	11.7	1.8	14.0
Other linens	70.7	27.1	38.8	4.3	29.9	4.5	10.3	10.8
Furniture	**71.8**	**30.3**	**37.0**	**6.7**	**21.0**	**9.4**	**3.5**	**13.2**
Mattresses and springs	68.8	25.7	38.9	7.0	22.6	9.3	3.6	16.9
Other bedroom furniture	65.4	21.9	39.5	8.9	22.2	8.3	6.4	13.7
Sofas	73.1	27.1	40.6	7.5	23.3	9.8	3.3	11.9
Living room chairs	72.9	40.9	27.6	4.4	13.9	9.2	1.9	14.5
Living room tables	67.7	29.4	34.4	4.8	19.9	9.8	3.3	15.6
Kitchen and dining room furniture	79.0	42.8	32.9	5.4	19.7	7.7	2.3	11.3
Infants' furniture	77.3	28.8	40.3	21.9	12.9	5.4	2.9	5.0
Outdoor furniture	79.5	32.6	43.8	4.1	24.1	15.7	2.1	9.8
Wall units, cabinets, and other furniture	69.9	28.5	36.3	4.8	20.9	10.6	3.0	13.2
Floor coverings	**79.2**	**39.8**	**37.0**	**5.0**	**22.5**	**9.6**	**2.2**	**11.0**
Wall-to-wall carpeting	80.8	39.8	39.0	5.8	21.4	11.8	2.6	10.4
Floor coverings, nonpermanent	77.5	39.8	34.8	4.0	23.6	7.1	1.7	11.7
Major appliances	**67.2**	**28.3**	**34.2**	**6.0**	**17.8**	**10.4**	**4.5**	**14.7**
Dishwashers (built-in), garbage disposals, range hoods	76.1	31.7	38.8	6.0	23.3	9.5	3.2	9.8
Refrigerators and freezers	68.3	29.0	34.0	6.3	18.2	9.6	3.7	15.9
Washing machines	64.9	24.7	34.3	7.7	16.6	10.1	6.1	17.3
Clothes dryers	65.1	24.2	35.7	8.4	16.9	10.5	7.5	14.3
Cooking stoves, ovens	66.1	28.3	34.7	4.3	18.9	11.5	2.4	12.0
Microwave ovens	62.6	24.8	33.5	6.1	16.9	10.5	4.2	20.7
Window air conditioners	62.4	18.7	35.5	5.3	18.6	11.6	5.5	18.5
Electric floor-cleaning equipment	67.9	35.0	28.9	6.0	14.6	8.3	6.3	13.0
Sewing machines	76.6	41.3	33.4	2.3	11.9	19.2	0.3	13.0
Miscellaneous household appliances	49.3	16.7	33.0	–	17.2	16.3	4.9	14.0
Small appliances and misc. housewares	**66.9**	**27.6**	**36.0**	**7.8**	**17.4**	**10.9**	**3.4**	**16.7**
Housewares	67.5	27.4	37.3	8.9	17.1	11.4	3.3	16.3
Plastic dinnerware	66.5	16.9	45.6	11.0	24.3	10.3	3.0	16.3
China and other dinnerware	55.5	25.3	27.9	3.1	13.6	11.5	1.8	25.6
Flatware	72.7	35.2	33.7	5.5	13.6	14.5	2.1	17.7
Glassware	62.6	19.4	39.1	4.5	15.7	19.3	4.2	15.1
Silver serving pieces	75.5	31.5	42.1	10.7	21.6	9.7	3.0	14.3
Other serving pieces	57.2	26.2	24.4	5.5	10.1	8.8	3.7	28.7
Nonelectric cookware	70.7	23.9	45.3	18.0	17.3	9.7	2.5	15.3
Tableware, nonelectric kitchenware	71.7	34.0	34.1	4.1	19.3	10.8	5.3	10.7
Small appliances	64.9	28.0	31.6	4.0	18.3	9.3	3.5	18.0
Small electric kitchen appliances	63.2	27.6	30.4	4.6	16.4	9.4	3.7	18.4
Portable heating and cooling equipment	69.9	29.4	35.3	2.3	24.2	8.8	3.1	17.1

	total married couples	married couples, no children	married couples with children				single parent, at least one child <18	single person
			total	oldest child under 6	oldest child 6 to 17	oldest child 18 or older		
Miscellaneous household equipment	**69.5%**	**24.6%**	**39.8%**	**6.9%**	**21.7%**	**11.2%**	**3.4%**	**15.6%**
Window coverings	68.0	19.6	43.7	12.1	20.8	10.7	1.1	17.2
Infants' equipment	75.9	14.8	50.9	18.4	11.8	21.0	3.3	4.5
Laundry and cleaning equipment	66.4	26.7	35.6	7.1	18.0	10.5	6.6	13.8
Outdoor equipment	90.4	25.6	58.6	5.4	41.0	12.1	1.4	3.0
Clocks	75.4	24.6	32.3	0.1	20.6	11.8	6.8	9.1
Lamps and lighting fixtures	71.7	36.2	31.1	4.1	17.4	9.7	2.0	16.6
Other household decorative items	69.9	25.6	39.4	8.6	20.2	10.5	2.8	15.0
Telephones and accessories	66.4	17.3	42.2	4.1	27.3	10.8	2.1	15.9
Lawn and garden equipment	72.0	27.9	41.3	7.4	23.5	10.4	1.9	12.2
Power tools	68.9	24.6	38.7	3.9	24.5	10.2	1.8	22.2
Office furniture for home use	72.2	28.9	37.5	4.4	25.4	7.7	3.9	16.6
Hand tools	69.9	30.6	35.3	6.7	17.8	10.8	3.0	13.6
Indoor plants and fresh flowers	67.5	30.1	32.6	5.2	16.4	11.1	2.2	19.0
Closet and storage items	69.5	20.8	39.9	14.1	16.5	9.0	5.7	14.3
Rental of furniture	36.8	7.3	27.9	6.1	17.0	4.8	24.7	15.1
Luggage	67.3	26.8	37.7	4.9	20.1	12.8	2.1	19.8
Computers and computer hardware, nonbusiness use	64.4	20.9	39.6	6.2	21.4	12.0	5.2	18.0
Computer software and accessories, nonbusiness use	66.1	21.5	39.9	6.8	21.5	11.6	2.7	18.4
Telephone answering devices	50.7	19.7	28.1	6.0	16.5	5.5	10.8	25.7
Calculators	66.2	10.0	49.4	4.4	24.4	20.7	10.8	16.4
Business equipment for home use	62.1	34.0	21.7	10.0	6.7	5.0	7.7	23.1
Other hardware	86.6	31.8	41.3	7.3	27.5	6.3	2.6	5.3
Smoke alarms	84.2	20.3	40.2	9.8	25.4	5.0	2.0	8.7
Other household appliances	78.5	34.2	41.7	2.5	20.5	18.6	0.9	13.0
Miscellaneous household equipment and parts	65.6	27.5	34.6	6.5	16.0	12.3	4.1	22.7

Note: Market share for total consumer units is 100.0%. Market shares by type of consumer unit will not add to total because not all types of consumer units are shown. (–) means sample is too small to make a reliable estimate.
Source: Calculations by New Strategist based on the 2002 Consumer Expenditure Survey

Table 8.13 Housing: Household Operations: Average spending by race and Hispanic origin, 2002

(average annual spending of consumer units (CU) on household services, supplies, furnishings, and equipment, by race and Hispanic origin of consumer unit reference person, 2002)

	total consumer units	race		Hispanic origin	
		black	white and other	Hispanic	non-Hispanic
Number of consumer units (in thousands, add 000)	112,108	13,554	98,553	10,500	101,608
Average number of persons per CU	2.5	2.7	2.5	3.3	2.4
Average before-tax income of CU	$49,430.00	$35,944.00	$51,177.00	$37,360.00	$50,742.00
Average spending of CU, total	40,676.60	30,135.94	42,134.55	34,742.47	41,294.67
Housing, average spending	13,283.08	10,756.15	13,632.80	11,841.17	13,430.92
HOUSEHOLD SERVICES	**$705.71**	**$509.03**	**$732.76**	**$406.58**	**$736.62**
Personal services	**331.02**	**287.39**	**337.02**	**211.78**	**343.34**
Babysitting and child care in your own home	35.91	30.73	36.63	38.22	35.68
Babysitting and child care in someone else's home	27.48	20.81	28.40	47.12	25.45
Day care centers, nurseries, and preschools	210.74	232.42	207.75	122.35	219.87
Other household services	**374.70**	**221.65**	**395.75**	**194.80**	**393.28**
Housekeeping services	79.90	12.49	89.17	35.16	84.52
Gardening, lawn care service	72.38	41.12	76.68	30.89	76.67
Water softening service	3.15	2.00	3.31	3.74	3.09
Nonclothing laundry and dry cleaning, sent out	1.72	0.81	1.84	0.93	1.80
Nonclothing laundry and dry cleaning, coin-operated	4.13	6.01	3.87	11.34	3.39
Termite/pest control services	13.25	10.11	13.68	4.01	14.20
Home security system service fee	17.40	25.15	16.33	11.17	18.04
Other home services	15.06	4.18	16.56	5.23	16.08
Termite/pest control products	0.68	0.49	0.71	0.01	0.75
Moving, storage, and freight express	33.13	29.38	33.64	16.68	34.83
Appliance repair, including service center	10.86	6.27	11.50	5.42	11.43
Reupholstering and furniture repair	7.40	4.69	7.78	4.12	7.74
Repairs/rentals of lawn/garden equipment, hand/power tools, etc.	3.62	1.79	3.87	1.46	3.85
Appliance rental	1.07	2.14	0.92	0.16	1.16
Repair of computer systems for nonbusiness use	2.53	1.06	2.74	1.01	2.69
Computer information services	107.29	73.26	111.97	62.05	111.97
HOUSEKEEPING SUPPLIES	**545.28**	**312.73**	**578.22**	**470.62**	**552.33**
Laundry and cleaning supplies	**130.57**	**124.03**	**131.49**	**173.90**	**126.48**
Soaps and detergents	72.89	74.35	72.68	105.57	69.81
Other laundry cleaning products	57.68	49.67	58.81	68.33	56.67
Other household products	**283.28**	**123.98**	**305.84**	**225.08**	**288.77**
Cleansing and toilet tissue, paper towels, and napkins	76.46	59.80	78.82	99.41	74.30
Miscellaneous household products	96.81	46.54	103.92	69.33	99.40
Lawn and garden supplies	110.01	17.64	123.09	56.35	115.07
Postage and stationery	**131.44**	**64.72**	**140.89**	**71.64**	**137.08**
Stationery, stationery supplies, giftwrap	60.20	23.33	65.42	23.57	63.66
Postage	69.12	41.24	73.07	44.70	71.43
Delivery services	2.12	0.15	2.40	3.37	2.00

	total consumer units	race		Hispanic origin	
		black	white and other	Hispanic	non-Hispanic
HOUSEHOLD FURNISHINGS AND EQUIPMENT	**$1,518.36**	**$887.01**	**$1,606.41**	**$1,178.80**	**$1,552.96**
Household textiles	**135.52**	**67.99**	**145.02**	**140.76**	**135.15**
Bathroom linens	22.35	8.94	24.25	28.30	21.79
Bedroom linens	65.98	39.17	69.78	86.43	64.05
Kitchen and dining room linens	10.11	3.83	11.00	8.94	10.22
Curtains and draperies	16.65	8.73	17.74	10.50	17.28
Slipcovers and decorative pillows	7.40	2.17	8.14	0.29	8.07
Sewing materials for household items	11.44	4.52	12.40	3.69	12.24
Other linens	1.59	0.64	1.72	2.60	1.49
Furniture	**401.28**	**292.59**	**416.22**	**345.17**	**407.07**
Mattresses and springs	52.91	44.10	54.12	52.83	52.92
Other bedroom furniture	68.33	67.02	68.51	54.50	69.76
Sofas	85.33	64.61	88.17	88.16	85.03
Living room chairs	39.21	15.26	42.51	23.88	40.80
Living room tables	18.03	14.73	18.48	20.21	17.80
Kitchen and dining room furniture	61.28	46.77	63.27	50.48	62.39
Infants' furniture	6.46	4.87	6.68	6.20	6.48
Outdoor furniture	16.79	5.45	18.35	5.46	17.96
Wall units, cabinets, and other furniture	52.94	29.79	56.13	43.46	53.92
Floor coverings	**40.49**	**26.57**	**42.40**	**12.79**	**43.35**
Wall-to-wall carpeting	21.69	15.99	22.49	6.74	23.24
Floor coverings, nonpermanent	18.79	10.58	19.91	6.05	20.10
Major appliances	**188.47**	**173.42**	**190.57**	**148.29**	**192.57**
Dishwashers (built-in), garbage disposals, range hoods	16.52	6.94	17.84	5.10	17.71
Refrigerators and freezers	52.08	44.28	53.16	48.43	52.45
Washing machines	22.30	18.84	22.77	21.39	22.39
Clothes dryers	17.05	18.88	16.80	14.94	17.27
Cooking stoves, ovens	30.95	45.95	28.90	20.15	32.08
Microwave ovens	10.50	8.20	10.81	9.31	10.62
Window air conditioners	7.90	7.46	7.96	6.67	8.03
Electric floor-cleaning equipment	22.80	17.81	23.51	20.12	23.06
Sewing machines	4.79	5.08	4.75	2.06	5.07
Miscellaneous household appliances	2.81	–	3.21	0.13	3.07
Small appliances and misc. housewares	**100.43**	**50.93**	**107.41**	**91.09**	**101.39**
Housewares	77.55	34.83	83.59	76.06	77.69
Plastic dinnerware	1.57	0.83	1.67	2.06	1.51
China and other dinnerware	14.51	3.29	16.10	18.46	14.14
Flatware	3.79	2.81	3.92	3.33	3.83
Glassware	6.51	3.34	6.96	7.83	6.39
Silver serving pieces	4.05	0.89	4.49	1.02	4.33
Other serving pieces	1.44	0.63	1.55	0.67	1.52
Nonelectric cookware	24.25	13.79	25.73	25.46	24.13
Tableware, nonelectric kitchenware	21.44	9.25	23.17	17.23	21.84
Small appliances	22.89	16.10	23.82	15.04	23.70
Small electric kitchen appliances	17.18	11.41	17.98	12.01	17.72
Portable heating and cooling equipment	5.70	4.69	5.84	3.02	5.98

	total consumer units	race		Hispanic origin	
		black	white and other	Hispanic	non-Hispanic
Miscellaneous household equipment	**$652.17**	**$275.50**	**$704.79**	**$440.69**	**$673.43**
Window coverings	13.91	8.21	14.70	6.80	14.65
Infants' equipment	12.96	4.42	14.17	12.76	12.98
Laundry and cleaning equipment	15.15	8.80	16.05	19.01	14.79
Outdoor equipment	31.52	3.28	35.53	2.69	34.25
Clocks	5.87	9.70	5.32	8.62	5.61
Lamps and lighting fixtures	11.74	4.73	12.71	7.46	12.19
Other household decorative items	144.94	49.79	158.41	128.83	146.46
Telephones and accessories	32.73	21.65	34.30	30.88	32.91
Lawn and garden equipment	48.16	15.72	52.62	15.94	51.49
Power tools	33.27	4.50	37.34	30.41	33.54
Office furniture for home use	10.57	5.59	11.25	3.65	11.28
Hand tools	8.05	1.57	8.95	9.29	7.93
Indoor plants and fresh flowers	49.78	20.11	53.86	28.86	51.94
Closet and storage items	9.98	3.99	10.83	5.63	10.40
Rental of furniture	4.60	9.06	3.98	4.89	4.57
Luggage	5.98	4.28	6.22	4.13	6.18
Computers and computer hardware, nonbusiness use	138.58	62.66	149.02	76.78	144.97
Computer software and accessories, nonbusiness use	17.67	7.93	19.01	10.09	18.46
Telephone answering devices	1.08	0.80	1.12	1.22	1.07
Calculators	1.44	0.67	1.54	1.02	1.48
Business equipment for home use	0.97	0.72	1.01	0.83	0.99
Other hardware	12.85	2.13	14.37	4.89	13.61
Smoke alarms	1.49	0.33	1.65	4.24	1.21
Other household appliances	9.23	3.47	10.02	3.12	9.87
Miscellaneous household equipment and parts	29.62	21.39	30.78	18.67	30.65

Note: Other races include Asians, Native Americans, and Pacific Islanders. Numbers may not add to total because not all categories are shown. (–) means sample is too small to make a reliable estimate.
Source: Bureau of Labor Statistics, unpublished tables from the 2002 Consumer Expenditure Survey

Table 8.14 Housing: Household Operations: Indexed spending by race and Hispanic origin, 2002

(indexed average annual spending of consumer units (CU) on household services, supplies, furnishings, and equipment, by race and Hispanic origin of consumer unit reference person, 2002; index definition: an index of 100 is the average for all consumer units; an index of 132 means that spending by consumer units in that group is 32 percent above the average for all consumer units; an index of 68 indicates spending that is 32 percent below the average for all consumer units)

	total consumer units	race		Hispanic origin	
		black	white and other	Hispanic	non-Hispanic
Average spending of CU, total	$40,677	$30,136	$42,135	$34,742	$41,295
Average spending of CU, index	100	74	104	85	102
Housing, spending index	100	81	103	89	101
HOUSEHOLD SERVICES	**100**	**72**	**104**	**58**	**104**
Personal services	**100**	**87**	**102**	**64**	**104**
Babysitting and child care in your own home	100	86	102	106	99
Babysitting and child care in someone else's home	100	76	103	171	93
Day care centers, nurseries, and preschools	100	110	99	58	104
Other household services	**100**	**59**	**106**	**52**	**105**
Housekeeping services	100	16	112	44	106
Gardening, lawn care service	100	57	106	43	106
Water softening service	100	63	105	119	98
Nonclothing laundry and dry cleaning, sent out	100	47	107	54	105
Nonclothing laundry and dry cleaning, coin-operated	100	146	94	275	82
Termite/pest control services	100	76	103	30	107
Home security system service fee	100	145	94	64	104
Other home services	100	28	110	35	107
Termite/pest control products	100	72	104	1	110
Moving, storage, and freight express	100	89	102	50	105
Appliance repair, including service center	100	58	106	50	105
Reupholstering and furniture repair	100	63	105	56	105
Repairs/rentals of lawn/garden equipment, hand/power tools, etc.	100	49	107	40	106
Appliance rental	100	200	86	15	108
Repair of computer systems for nonbusiness use	100	42	108	40	106
Computer information services	100	68	104	58	104
HOUSEKEEPING SUPPLIES	**100**	**57**	**106**	**86**	**101**
Laundry and cleaning supplies	**100**	**95**	**101**	**133**	**97**
Soaps and detergents	100	102	100	145	96
Other laundry cleaning products	100	86	102	118	98
Other household products	**100**	**44**	**108**	**79**	**102**
Cleansing and toilet tissue, paper towels, and napkins	100	78	103	130	97
Miscellaneous household products	100	48	107	72	103
Lawn and garden supplies	100	16	112	51	105
Postage and stationery	**100**	**49**	**107**	**55**	**104**
Stationery, stationery supplies, giftwrap	100	39	109	39	106
Postage	100	60	106	65	103
Delivery services	100	7	113	159	94

	total consumer units	race black	race white and other	Hispanic origin Hispanic	Hispanic origin non-Hispanic
HOUSEHOLD FURNISHINGS AND EQUIPMENT	**100**	**58**	**106**	**78**	**102**
Household textiles	**100**	**50**	**107**	**104**	**100**
Bathroom linens	100	40	109	127	97
Bedroom linens	100	59	106	131	97
Kitchen and dining room linens	100	38	109	88	101
Curtains and draperies	100	52	107	63	104
Slipcovers and decorative pillows	100	29	110	4	109
Sewing materials for household items	100	40	108	32	107
Other linens	100	40	108	164	94
Furniture	**100**	**73**	**104**	**86**	**101**
Mattresses and springs	100	83	102	100	100
Other bedroom furniture	100	98	100	80	102
Sofas	100	76	103	103	100
Living room chairs	100	39	108	61	104
Living room tables	100	82	102	112	99
Kitchen and dining room furniture	100	76	103	82	102
Infants' furniture	100	75	103	96	100
Outdoor furniture	100	32	109	33	107
Wall units, cabinets, and other furniture	100	56	106	82	102
Floor coverings	**100**	**66**	**105**	**32**	**107**
Wall-to-wall carpeting	100	74	104	31	107
Floor coverings, nonpermanent	100	56	106	32	107
Major appliances	**100**	**92**	**101**	**79**	**102**
Dishwashers (built-in), garbage disposals, range hoods	100	42	108	31	107
Refrigerators and freezers	100	85	102	93	101
Washing machines	100	84	102	96	100
Clothes dryers	100	111	99	88	101
Cooking stoves, ovens	100	148	93	65	104
Microwave ovens	100	78	103	89	101
Window air conditioners	100	94	101	84	102
Electric floor-cleaning equipment	100	78	103	88	101
Sewing machines	100	106	99	43	106
Miscellaneous household appliances	100	–	114	5	109
Small appliances and misc. housewares	**100**	**51**	**107**	**91**	**101**
Housewares	100	45	108	98	100
Plastic dinnerware	100	53	106	131	96
China and other dinnerware	100	23	111	127	97
Flatware	100	74	103	88	101
Glassware	100	51	107	120	98
Silver serving pieces	100	22	111	25	107
Other serving pieces	100	44	108	47	106
Nonelectric cookware	100	57	106	105	100
Tableware, nonelectric kitchenware	100	43	108	80	102
Small appliances	100	70	104	66	104
Small electric kitchen appliances	100	66	105	70	103
Portable heating and cooling equipment	100	82	102	53	105

	total consumer units	race		Hispanic origin	
		black	white and other	Hispanic	non-Hispanic
Miscellaneous household equipment	**100**	**42**	**108**	**68**	**103**
Window coverings	100	59	106	49	105
Infants' equipment	100	34	109	98	100
Laundry and cleaning equipment	100	58	106	125	98
Outdoor equipment	100	10	113	9	109
Clocks	100	165	91	147	96
Lamps and lighting fixtures	100	40	108	64	104
Other household decorative items	100	34	109	89	101
Telephones and accessories	100	66	105	94	101
Lawn and garden equipment	100	33	109	33	107
Power tools	100	14	112	91	101
Office furniture for home use	100	53	106	35	107
Hand tools	100	20	111	115	99
Indoor plants and fresh flowers	100	40	108	58	104
Closet and storage items	100	40	109	56	104
Rental of furniture	100	197	87	106	99
Luggage	100	72	104	69	103
Computers and computer hardware, nonbusiness use	100	45	108	55	105
Computer software and accessories, nonbusiness use	100	45	108	57	104
Telephone answering devices	100	74	104	113	99
Calculators	100	47	107	71	103
Business equipment for home use	100	74	104	86	102
Other hardware	100	17	112	38	106
Smoke alarms	100	22	111	285	81
Other household appliances	100	38	109	34	107
Miscellaneous household equipment and parts	100	72	104	63	103

Note: Other races include Asians, Native Americans, and Pacific Islanders. (–) means sample is too small to make a reliable estimate.
Source: Calculations by New Strategist based on the 2002 Consumer Expenditure Survey

Table 8.15 Housing: Household Operations: Total spending by race and Hispanic origin, 2002

(total annual spending on household services, supplies, furnishings, and equipment, by consumer unit race and Hispanic origin groups, 2002; numbers in thousands)

	total consumer units	race black	race white and other	Hispanic origin Hispanic	Hispanic origin non-Hispanic
Number of consumer units	112,108	13,554	98,553	10,500	101,608
Total spending of all consumer units	$4,560,172,273	$408,462,531	$4,152,486,306	$364,795,935	$4,195,868,829
Housing, total spending	1,489,139,533	145,788,857	1,343,553,338	124,332,285	1,364,688,919
HOUSEHOLD SERVICES	**$79,115,737**	**$6,899,393**	**$72,215,696**	**$4,269,090**	**$74,846,485**
Personal services	**37,109,990**	**3,895,284**	**33,214,332**	**2,223,690**	**34,886,091**
Babysitting and child care in your own home	4,025,798	416,514	3,609,996	401,310	3,625,373
Babysitting and child care in someone else's home	3,080,728	282,059	2,798,905	494,760	2,585,924
Day care centers, nurseries, and preschools	23,625,640	3,150,221	20,474,386	1,284,675	22,340,551
Other household services	**42,006,868**	**3,004,244**	**39,002,350**	**2,045,400**	**39,960,394**
Housekeeping services	8,957,429	169,289	8,787,971	369,180	8,587,908
Gardening, lawn care service	8,114,377	557,340	7,557,044	324,345	7,790,285
Water softening service	353,140	27,108	326,210	39,270	313,969
Nonclothing laundry and dry cleaning, sent out	192,826	10,979	181,338	9,765	182,894
Nonclothing laundry and dry cleaning, coin-operated	463,006	81,460	381,400	119,070	344,451
Termite/pest control services	1,485,431	137,031	1,348,205	42,105	1,442,834
Home security system service fee	1,950,679	340,883	1,609,370	117,285	1,833,008
Other home services	1,688,346	56,656	1,632,038	54,915	1,633,857
Termite/pest control products	76,233	6,641	69,973	105	76,206
Moving, storage, and freight express	3,714,138	398,217	3,315,323	175,140	3,539,007
Appliance repair, including service center	1,217,493	84,984	1,133,360	56,910	1,161,379
Reupholstering and furniture repair	829,599	63,568	766,742	43,260	786,446
Repairs/rentals of lawn/garden equipment, hand/power tools, etc.	405,831	24,262	381,400	15,330	391,191
Appliance rental	119,956	29,006	90,669	1,680	117,865
Repair of computer systems for nonbusiness use	283,633	14,367	270,035	10,605	273,326
Computer information services	12,028,067	992,966	11,034,979	651,525	11,377,048
HOUSEKEEPING SUPPLIES	**61,130,250**	**4,238,742**	**56,985,316**	**4,941,510**	**56,121,147**
Laundry and cleaning supplies	**14,637,942**	**1,681,103**	**12,958,734**	**1,825,950**	**12,851,380**
Soaps and detergents	8,171,552	1,007,740	7,162,832	1,108,485	7,093,254
Other laundry cleaning products	6,466,389	673,227	5,795,902	717,465	5,758,125
Other household products	**31,757,954**	**1,680,425**	**30,141,450**	**2,363,340**	**29,341,342**
Cleansing and toilet tissue, paper towels, and napkins	8,571,778	810,529	7,767,947	1,043,805	7,549,474
Miscellaneous household products	10,853,175	630,803	10,241,628	727,965	10,099,835
Lawn and garden supplies	12,333,001	239,093	12,130,889	591,675	11,692,033
Postage and stationery	**14,735,476**	**877,215**	**13,885,132**	**752,220**	**13,928,425**
Stationery, stationery supplies, giftwrap	6,748,902	316,215	6,447,337	247,485	6,468,365
Postage	7,748,905	558,967	7,201,268	469,350	7,257,859
Delivery services	237,669	2,033	236,527	35,385	203,216

	total consumer units	race		Hispanic origin	
		black	white and other	Hispanic	non-Hispanic
HOUSEHOLD FURNISHINGS AND EQUIPMENT	**$170,220,303**	**$12,022,534**	**$158,316,525**	**$12,377,400**	**$157,793,160**
Household textiles	**15,192,876**	**921,536**	**14,292,156**	**1,477,980**	**13,732,321**
Bathroom linens	2,505,614	121,173	2,389,910	297,150	2,214,038
Bedroom linens	7,396,886	530,910	6,877,028	907,515	6,507,992
Kitchen and dining room linens	1,133,412	51,912	1,084,083	93,870	1,038,434
Curtains and draperies	1,866,598	118,326	1,748,330	110,250	1,755,786
Slipcovers and decorative pillows	829,599	29,412	802,221	3,045	819,977
Sewing materials for household items	1,282,516	61,264	1,222,057	38,745	1,243,682
Other linens	178,252	8,675	169,511	27,300	151,396
Furniture	**44,986,698**	**3,965,765**	**41,019,730**	**3,624,285**	**41,361,569**
Mattresses and springs	5,931,634	597,731	5,333,688	554,715	5,377,095
Other bedroom furniture	7,660,340	908,389	6,751,866	572,250	7,088,174
Sofas	9,566,176	875,724	8,689,418	925,680	8,639,728
Living room chairs	4,395,755	206,834	4,189,488	250,740	4,145,606
Living room tables	2,021,307	199,650	1,821,259	212,205	1,808,622
Kitchen and dining room furniture	6,869,978	633,921	6,235,448	530,040	6,339,323
Infants' furniture	724,218	66,008	658,334	65,100	658,420
Outdoor furniture	1,882,293	73,869	1,808,448	57,330	1,824,880
Wall units, cabinets, and other furniture	5,934,998	403,774	5,531,780	456,330	5,478,703
Floor coverings	**4,539,253**	**360,130**	**4,178,647**	**134,295**	**4,404,707**
Wall-to-wall carpeting	2,431,623	216,728	2,216,457	70,770	2,361,370
Floor coverings, nonpermanent	2,106,509	143,401	1,962,190	63,525	2,042,321
Major appliances	**21,128,995**	**2,350,535**	**18,781,245**	**1,557,045**	**19,566,653**
Dishwashers (built-in), garbage disposals, range hoods	1,852,024	94,065	1,758,186	53,550	1,799,478
Refrigerators and freezers	5,838,585	600,171	5,239,077	508,515	5,329,340
Washing machines	2,500,008	255,357	2,244,052	224,595	2,275,003
Clothes dryers	1,911,441	255,900	1,655,690	156,870	1,754,770
Cooking stoves, ovens	3,469,743	622,806	2,848,182	211,575	3,259,585
Microwave ovens	1,177,134	111,143	1,065,358	97,755	1,079,077
Window air conditioners	885,653	101,113	784,482	70,035	815,912
Electric floor-cleaning equipment	2,556,062	241,397	2,316,981	211,260	2,343,080
Sewing machines	536,997	68,854	468,127	21,630	515,153
Miscellaneous household appliances	315,023	–	316,355	1,365	311,937
Small appliances and misc. housewares	**11,259,006**	**690,305**	**10,585,578**	**956,445**	**10,302,035**
Housewares	8,693,975	472,086	8,238,045	798,630	7,893,926
Plastic dinnerware	176,010	11,250	164,584	21,630	153,428
China and other dinnerware	1,626,687	44,593	1,586,703	193,830	1,436,737
Flatware	424,889	38,087	386,328	34,965	389,159
Glassware	729,823	45,270	685,929	82,215	649,275
Silver serving pieces	454,037	12,063	442,503	10,710	439,963
Other serving pieces	161,436	8,539	152,757	7,035	154,444
Nonelectric cookware	2,718,619	186,910	2,535,769	267,330	2,451,801
Tableware, nonelectric kitchenware	2,403,596	125,375	2,283,473	180,915	2,219,119
Small appliances	2,566,152	218,219	2,347,532	157,920	2,408,110
Small electric kitchen appliances	1,926,015	154,651	1,771,983	126,105	1,800,494
Portable heating and cooling equipment	639,016	63,568	575,550	31,710	607,616

	total consumer units	race		Hispanic origin	
		black	white and other	Hispanic	non-Hispanic
Miscellaneous household equipment	**$73,113,474**	**$3,734,127**	**$69,459,169**	**$4,627,245**	**$68,425,875**
Window coverings	1,559,422	111,278	1,448,729	71,400	1,488,557
Infants' equipment	1,452,920	59,909	1,396,496	133,980	1,318,872
Laundry and cleaning equipment	1,698,436	119,275	1,581,776	199,605	1,502,782
Outdoor equipment	3,533,644	44,457	3,501,588	28,245	3,480,074
Clocks	658,074	131,474	524,302	90,510	570,021
Lamps and lighting fixtures	1,316,148	64,110	1,252,609	78,330	1,238,602
Other household decorative items	16,248,934	674,854	15,611,781	1,352,715	14,881,508
Telephones and accessories	3,669,295	293,444	3,380,368	324,240	3,343,919
Lawn and garden equipment	5,399,121	213,069	5,185,859	167,370	5,231,796
Power tools	3,729,833	60,993	3,679,969	319,305	3,407,932
Office furniture for home use	1,184,982	75,767	1,108,721	38,325	1,146,138
Hand tools	902,469	21,280	882,049	97,545	805,751
Indoor plants and fresh flowers	5,580,736	272,571	5,308,065	303,030	5,277,520
Closet and storage items	1,118,838	54,080	1,067,329	59,115	1,056,723
Rental of furniture	515,697	122,799	392,241	51,345	464,349
Luggage	670,406	58,011	613,000	43,365	627,937
Computers and computer hardware, nonbusiness use	15,535,927	849,294	14,686,368	806,190	14,730,112
Computer software and accessories, nonbusiness use	1,980,948	107,483	1,873,493	105,945	1,875,684
Telephone answering devices	121,077	10,843	110,379	12,810	108,721
Calculators	161,436	9,081	151,772	10,710	150,380
Business equipment for home use	108,745	9,759	99,539	8,715	100,592
Other hardware	1,440,588	28,870	1,416,207	51,345	1,382,885
Smoke alarms	167,041	4,473	162,612	44,520	122,946
Other household appliances	1,034,757	47,032	987,501	32,760	1,002,871
Miscellaneous household equipment and parts	3,320,639	289,920	3,033,461	196,035	3,114,285

Note: Other races include Asians, Native Americans, and Pacific Islanders. Numbers may not add to total because of rounding and because not all categories are shown. (–) means sample is too small to make a reliable estimate.
Source: Calculations by New Strategist based on the 2002 Consumer Expenditure Survey

Table 8.16 Housing: Household Operations: Market shares by race and Hispanic origin, 2002

(percentage of total annual spending on household services, supplies, furnishings, and equipment accounted for by consumer unit race and Hispanic origin groups, 2002)

	total consumer units	race		Hispanic origin	
		black	white and other	Hispanic	non-Hispanic
Share of total consumer units	**100.0%**	**12.1%**	**87.9%**	**9.4%**	**90.6%**
Share of total before-tax income	**100.0**	**8.8**	**91.0**	**7.1**	**93.0**
Share of total spending	**100.0**	**9.0**	**91.1**	**8.0**	**92.0**
Share of housing spending	**100.0**	**9.8**	**90.2**	**8.3**	**91.6**
HOUSEHOLD SERVICES	**100.0%**	**8.7%**	**91.3%**	**5.4%**	**94.6%**
Personal services	**100.0**	**10.5**	**89.5**	**6.0**	**94.0**
Babysitting and child care in your own home	100.0	10.3	89.7	10.0	90.1
Babysitting and child care in someone else's home	100.0	9.2	90.9	16.1	83.9
Day care centers, nurseries, and preschools	100.0	13.3	86.7	5.4	94.6
Other household services	**100.0**	**7.2**	**92.8**	**4.9**	**95.1**
Housekeeping services	100.0	1.9	98.1	4.1	95.9
Gardening, lawn care service	100.0	6.9	93.1	4.0	96.0
Water softening service	100.0	7.7	92.4	11.1	88.9
Nonclothing laundry and dry cleaning, sent out	100.0	5.7	94.0	5.1	94.8
Nonclothing laundry and dry cleaning, coin-operated	100.0	17.6	82.4	25.7	74.4
Termite/pest control services	100.0	9.2	90.8	2.8	97.1
Home security system service fee	100.0	17.5	82.5	6.0	94.0
Other home services	100.0	3.4	96.7	3.3	96.8
Termite/pest control products	100.0	8.7	91.8	0.1	100.0
Moving, storage, and freight express	100.0	10.7	89.3	4.7	95.3
Appliance repair, including service center	100.0	7.0	93.1	4.7	95.4
Reupholstering and furniture repair	100.0	7.7	92.4	5.2	94.8
Repairs/rentals of lawn/garden equipment, hand/power tools, etc.	100.0	6.0	94.0	3.8	96.4
Appliance rental	100.0	24.2	75.6	1.4	98.3
Repair of computer systems for nonbusiness use	100.0	5.1	95.2	3.7	96.4
Computer information services	100.0	8.3	91.7	5.4	94.6
HOUSEKEEPING SUPPLIES	**100.0**	**6.9**	**93.2**	**8.1**	**91.8**
Laundry and cleaning supplies	**100.0**	**11.5**	**88.5**	**12.5**	**87.8**
Soaps and detergents	100.0	12.3	87.7	13.6	86.8
Other laundry cleaning products	100.0	10.4	89.6	11.1	89.0
Other household products	**100.0**	**5.3**	**94.9**	**7.4**	**92.4**
Cleansing and toilet tissue, paper towels, and napkins	100.0	9.5	90.6	12.2	88.1
Miscellaneous household products	100.0	5.8	94.4	6.7	93.1
Lawn and garden supplies	100.0	1.9	98.4	4.8	94.8
Postage and stationery	**100.0**	**6.0**	**94.2**	**5.1**	**94.5**
Stationery, stationery supplies, giftwrap	100.0	4.7	95.5	3.7	95.8
Postage	100.0	7.2	92.9	6.1	93.7
Delivery services	100.0	0.9	99.5	14.9	85.5

	total consumer units	race		Hispanic origin	
		black	white and other	Hispanic	non-Hispanic
HOUSEHOLD FURNISHINGS AND EQUIPMENT	**100.0%**	**7.1%**	**93.0%**	**7.3%**	**92.7%**
Household textiles	**100.0**	**6.1**	**94.1**	**9.7**	**90.4**
Bathroom linens	100.0	4.8	95.4	11.9	88.4
Bedroom linens	100.0	7.2	93.0	12.3	88.0
Kitchen and dining room linens	100.0	4.6	95.6	8.3	91.6
Curtains and draperies	100.0	6.3	93.7	5.9	94.1
Slipcovers and decorative pillows	100.0	3.5	96.7	0.4	98.8
Sewing materials for household items	100.0	4.8	95.3	3.0	97.0
Other linens	100.0	4.9	95.1	15.3	84.9
Furniture	**100.0**	**8.8**	**91.2**	**8.1**	**91.9**
Mattresses and springs	100.0	10.1	89.9	9.4	90.7
Other bedroom furniture	100.0	11.9	88.1	7.5	92.5
Sofas	100.0	9.2	90.8	9.7	90.3
Living room chairs	100.0	4.7	95.3	5.7	94.3
Living room tables	100.0	9.9	90.1	10.5	89.5
Kitchen and dining room furniture	100.0	9.2	90.8	7.7	92.3
Infants' furniture	100.0	9.1	90.9	9.0	90.9
Outdoor furniture	100.0	3.9	96.1	3.0	96.9
Wall units, cabinets, and other furniture	100.0	6.8	93.2	7.7	92.3
Floor coverings	**100.0**	**7.9**	**92.1**	**3.0**	**97.0**
Wall-to-wall carpeting	100.0	8.9	91.2	2.9	97.1
Floor coverings, nonpermanent	100.0	6.8	93.1	3.0	97.0
Major appliances	**100.0**	**11.1**	**88.9**	**7.4**	**92.6**
Dishwashers (built-in), garbage disposals, range hoods	100.0	5.1	94.9	2.9	97.2
Refrigerators and freezers	100.0	10.3	89.7	8.7	91.3
Washing machines	100.0	10.2	89.8	9.0	91.0
Clothes dryers	100.0	13.4	86.6	8.2	91.8
Cooking stoves, ovens	100.0	17.9	82.1	6.1	93.9
Microwave ovens	100.0	9.4	90.5	8.3	91.7
Window air conditioners	100.0	11.4	88.6	7.9	92.1
Electric floor-cleaning equipment	100.0	9.4	90.6	8.3	91.7
Sewing machines	100.0	12.8	87.2	4.0	95.9
Miscellaneous household appliances	100.0	–	100.0	0.4	99.0
Small appliances and misc. housewares	**100.0**	**6.1**	**94.0**	**8.5**	**91.5**
Housewares	100.0	5.4	94.8	9.2	90.8
Plastic dinnerware	100.0	6.4	93.5	12.3	87.2
China and other dinnerware	100.0	2.7	97.5	11.9	88.3
Flatware	100.0	9.0	90.9	8.2	91.6
Glassware	100.0	6.2	94.0	11.3	89.0
Silver serving pieces	100.0	2.7	97.5	2.4	96.9
Other serving pieces	100.0	5.3	94.6	4.4	95.7
Nonelectric cookware	100.0	6.9	93.3	9.8	90.2
Tableware, nonelectric kitchenware	100.0	5.2	95.0	7.5	92.3
Small appliances	100.0	8.5	91.5	6.2	93.8
Small electric kitchen appliances	100.0	8.0	92.0	6.5	93.5
Portable heating and cooling equipment	100.0	9.9	90.1	5.0	95.1

	total consumer units	race		Hispanic origin	
		black	white and other	Hispanic	non-Hispanic
Miscellaneous household equipment	**100.0%**	**5.1%**	**95.0%**	**6.3%**	**93.6%**
Window coverings	100.0	7.1	92.9	4.6	95.5
Infants' equipment	100.0	4.1	96.1	9.2	90.8
Laundry and cleaning equipment	100.0	7.0	93.1	11.8	88.5
Outdoor equipment	100.0	1.3	99.1	0.8	98.5
Clocks	100.0	20.0	79.7	13.8	86.6
Lamps and lighting fixtures	100.0	4.9	95.2	6.0	94.1
Other household decorative items	100.0	4.2	96.1	8.3	91.6
Telephones and accessories	100.0	8.0	92.1	8.8	91.1
Lawn and garden equipment	100.0	3.9	96.1	3.1	96.9
Power tools	100.0	1.6	98.7	8.6	91.4
Office furniture for home use	100.0	6.4	93.6	3.2	96.7
Hand tools	100.0	2.4	97.7	10.8	89.3
Indoor plants and fresh flowers	100.0	4.9	95.1	5.4	94.6
Closet and storage items	100.0	4.8	95.4	5.3	94.4
Rental of furniture	100.0	23.8	76.1	10.0	90.0
Luggage	100.0	8.7	91.4	6.5	93.7
Computers and computer hardware, nonbusiness use	100.0	5.5	94.5	5.2	94.8
Computer software and accessories, nonbusiness use	100.0	5.4	94.6	5.3	94.7
Telephone answering devices	100.0	9.0	91.2	10.6	89.8
Calculators	100.0	5.6	94.0	6.6	93.2
Business equipment for home use	100.0	9.0	91.5	8.0	92.5
Other hardware	100.0	2.0	98.3	3.6	96.0
Smoke alarms	100.0	2.7	97.3	26.7	73.6
Other household appliances	100.0	4.5	95.4	3.2	96.9
Miscellaneous household equipment and parts	100.0	8.7	91.4	5.9	93.8

Note: Other races include Asians, Native Americans, and Pacific Islanders. Numbers may not add to total because of rounding. (–) means sample is too small to make a reliable estimate.
Source: Calculations by New Strategist based on the 2002 Consumer Expenditure Survey

Table 8.17 Housing: Household Operations: Average spending by region, 2002

(average annual spending of consumer units (CU) on household services, supplies, furnishings, and equipment, by region in which consumer unit lives, 2002)

	total consumer units	Northeast	Midwest	South	West
Number of consumer units (in thousands, add 000)	112,108	21,313	25,883	40,004	24,907
Average number of persons per CU	2.5	2.5	2.5	2.5	2.6
Average before-tax income of CU	$49,430.00	$53,983.00	$49,197.00	$45,641.00	$52,016.00
Average spending of CU, total	40,676.60	42,390.20	40,601.14	37,280.55	44,728.34
Housing, average spending	13,283.08	14,558.03	12,641.21	11,766.17	15,297.47
HOUSEHOLD SERVICES	$705.71	$804.16	$569.97	$690.25	$787.37
Personal services	331.02	432.30	259.58	336.59	309.64
Babysitting and child care in your own home	35.91	51.64	34.57	29.49	34.18
Babysitting and child care in someone else's home	27.48	29.82	28.05	21.34	34.75
Day care centers, nurseries, and preschools	210.74	293.56	181.69	181.83	216.48
Other household services	374.70	371.86	310.39	353.66	477.73
Housekeeping services	79.90	71.97	66.36	73.41	111.18
Gardening, lawn care service	72.38	70.98	51.67	73.52	93.27
Water softening service	3.15	2.18	5.08	2.18	3.55
Nonclothing laundry and dry cleaning, sent out	1.72	2.22	1.41	1.24	2.38
Nonclothing laundry and dry cleaning, coin-operated	4.13	6.41	3.33	2.73	5.27
Termite/pest control services	13.25	6.07	5.30	20.45	16.09
Home security system service fee	17.40	13.80	12.42	22.84	16.91
Other home services	15.06	21.51	11.02	9.63	22.49
Termite/pest control products	0.68	0.72	0.38	0.79	0.79
Moving, storage, and freight express	33.13	22.13	26.72	26.05	60.57
Appliance repair, including service center	10.86	10.76	11.46	10.21	11.38
Reupholstering and furniture repair	7.40	13.26	3.04	8.45	5.24
Repairs/rentals of lawn/garden equipment, hand/power tools, etc.	3.62	3.85	3.94	4.13	2.27
Appliance rental	1.07	0.61	1.58	0.81	1.33
Repair of computer systems for nonbusiness use	2.53	1.71	3.05	1.90	3.72
Computer information services	107.29	123.09	102.36	94.31	119.74
HOUSEKEEPING SUPPLIES	545.28	497.88	709.39	489.37	506.11
Laundry and cleaning supplies	130.57	118.39	136.00	137.35	124.80
Soaps and detergents	72.89	69.54	72.12	75.35	72.71
Other laundry cleaning products	57.68	48.86	63.89	62.01	52.09
Other household products	283.28	239.47	434.48	238.83	236.02
Cleansing and toilet tissue, paper towels, and napkins	76.46	81.55	77.15	74.25	74.84
Miscellaneous household products	96.81	88.16	109.52	102.10	82.80
Lawn and garden supplies	110.01	69.77	247.80	62.49	78.39
Postage and stationery	131.44	140.01	138.91	113.18	145.29
Stationery, stationery supplies, giftwrap	60.20	60.24	71.25	51.24	63.02
Postage	69.12	78.12	66.75	60.01	78.21
Delivery services	2.12	1.65	0.91	1.93	4.06

	total consumer units	Northeast	Midwest	South	West
HOUSEHOLD FURNISHINGS AND EQUIPMENT	**$1,518.36**	**$1,544.23**	**$1,583.43**	**$1,333.15**	**$1,727.03**
Household textiles	**135.52**	**122.40**	**129.15**	**115.23**	**186.09**
Bathroom linens	22.35	18.11	21.13	24.88	23.29
Bedroom linens	65.98	48.36	64.65	54.09	101.73
Kitchen and dining room linens	10.11	15.29	8.23	7.56	11.58
Curtains and draperies	16.65	19.46	15.08	14.09	19.98
Slipcovers and decorative pillows	7.40	6.92	4.12	6.22	13.08
Sewing materials for household items	11.44	12.10	14.74	6.96	14.66
Other linens	1.59	2.16	1.21	1.42	1.77
Furniture	**401.28**	**461.10**	**362.05**	**358.12**	**460.15**
Mattresses and springs	52.91	58.06	43.31	49.24	64.37
Other bedroom furniture	68.33	76.82	62.44	64.46	73.42
Sofas	85.33	88.71	80.48	77.87	99.44
Living room chairs	39.21	42.96	39.21	34.34	43.84
Living room tables	18.03	23.23	14.65	14.96	22.01
Kitchen and dining room furniture	61.28	75.38	50.73	58.75	64.24
Infants' furniture	6.46	7.44	5.64	6.46	6.47
Outdoor furniture	16.79	21.52	14.20	11.72	23.57
Wall units, cabinets, and other furniture	52.94	66.98	51.39	40.32	62.80
Floor coverings	**40.49**	**47.82**	**45.09**	**37.48**	**34.25**
Wall-to-wall carpeting	21.69	22.95	33.10	17.46	15.60
Floor coverings, nonpermanent	18.79	24.87	11.99	20.02	18.66
Major appliances	**188.47**	**188.64**	**196.40**	**162.62**	**221.68**
Dishwashers (built-in), garbage disposals, range hoods	16.52	18.50	13.97	14.47	20.79
Refrigerators and freezers	52.08	53.90	52.15	46.53	59.37
Washing machines	22.30	21.64	22.03	20.03	26.78
Clothes dryers	17.05	17.35	18.35	16.62	16.13
Cooking stoves, ovens	30.95	30.14	26.02	30.87	36.92
Microwave ovens	10.50	12.03	9.61	9.90	11.07
Window air conditioners	7.90	15.20	6.23	7.14	4.62
Electric floor-cleaning equipment	22.80	15.83	39.02	11.15	30.70
Sewing machines	4.79	3.38	5.18	3.07	8.34
Miscellaneous household appliances	2.81	–	2.24	2.29	6.69
Small appliances and misc. housewares	**100.43**	**90.93**	**101.25**	**88.65**	**126.80**
Housewares	77.55	65.71	76.23	71.39	99.09
Plastic dinnerware	1.57	1.89	1.66	0.96	2.16
China and other dinnerware	14.51	8.03	12.39	12.67	25.31
Flatware	3.79	3.22	3.42	3.53	5.07
Glassware	6.51	8.07	3.84	7.11	6.96
Silver serving pieces	4.05	4.46	2.20	5.28	3.62
Other serving pieces	1.44	1.51	1.66	1.14	1.62
Nonelectric cookware	24.25	22.55	23.33	20.89	32.03
Tableware, nonelectric kitchenware	21.44	15.97	27.74	19.80	22.31
Small appliances	22.89	25.23	25.02	17.26	27.71
Small electric kitchen appliances	17.18	18.58	18.26	12.87	21.79
Portable heating and cooling equipment	5.70	6.65	6.75	4.38	5.92

	total consumer units	Northeast	Midwest	South	West
Miscellaneous household equipment	**$652.17**	**$633.32**	**$749.48**	**$571.06**	**$698.05**
Window coverings	13.91	13.80	13.62	9.32	21.70
Infants' equipment	12.96	4.99	10.57	16.96	16.04
Laundry and cleaning equipment	15.15	14.80	16.09	15.06	14.63
Outdoor equipment	31.52	23.65	46.35	28.06	28.60
Clocks	5.87	3.56	5.96	6.97	6.03
Lamps and lighting fixtures	11.74	11.49	14.14	8.44	14.77
Other household decorative items	144.94	152.80	165.33	127.58	144.61
Telephones and accessories	32.73	22.24	43.39	34.15	28.65
Lawn and garden equipment	48.16	65.97	58.49	47.09	23.89
Power tools	33.27	28.30	39.47	34.59	29.10
Office furniture for home use	10.57	8.59	12.16	7.05	16.25
Hand tools	8.05	7.32	8.67	5.87	11.56
Indoor plants and fresh flowers	49.78	59.32	61.12	38.67	47.68
Closet and storage items	9.98	9.95	11.89	7.25	12.39
Rental of furniture	4.60	3.52	5.57	5.58	2.92
Luggage	5.98	6.52	5.59	5.06	7.42
Computers and computer hardware, nonbusiness use	138.58	134.95	144.63	114.13	174.67
Computer software and accessories, nonbusiness use	17.67	12.96	18.13	12.90	28.90
Telephone answering devices	1.08	0.74	1.20	1.19	1.08
Calculators	1.44	1.01	2.23	0.95	1.77
Business equipment for home use	0.97	0.52	0.91	1.19	1.07
Other hardware	12.85	13.64	14.62	7.49	18.87
Smoke alarms	1.49	0.66	1.08	2.51	0.99
Other household appliances	9.23	9.39	7.93	8.47	11.68
Miscellaneous household equipment and parts	29.62	22.66	40.33	24.51	32.77

Note: Numbers may not add to total because not all categories are shown. (–) means sample is too small to make a reliable estimate.
Source: Bureau of Labor Statistics, unpublished tables from the 2002 Consumer Expenditure Survey

Table 8.18   Housing: Household Operations: Indexed spending by region, 2002

(indexed average annual spending of consumer units (CU) on household services, supplies, furnishings, and equipment, by region in which consumer unit lives, 2002; index definition: an index of 100 is the average for all consumer units; an index of 132 means that spending by consumer units in that group is 32 percent above the average for all consumer units; an index of 68 indicates spending that is 32 percent below the average for all consumer units)

	total consumer units	Northeast	Midwest	South	West
Average spending of CU, total	**$40,677**	**$42,390**	**$40,601**	**$37,281**	**$44,728**
Average spending of CU, index	**100**	**104**	**100**	**92**	**110**
Housing, spending index	**100**	**110**	**95**	**89**	**115**
HOUSEHOLD SERVICES	**100**	**114**	**81**	**98**	**112**
Personal services	**100**	**131**	**78**	**102**	**94**
Babysitting and child care in your own home	100	144	96	82	95
Babysitting and child care in someone else's home	100	109	102	78	126
Day care centers, nurseries, and preschools	100	139	86	86	103
Other household services	**100**	**99**	**83**	**94**	**127**
Housekeeping services	100	90	83	92	139
Gardening, lawn care service	100	98	71	102	129
Water softening service	100	69	161	69	113
Nonclothing laundry and dry cleaning, sent out	100	129	82	72	138
Nonclothing laundry and dry cleaning, coin-operated	100	155	81	66	128
Termite/pest control services	100	46	40	154	121
Home security system service fee	100	79	71	131	97
Other home services	100	143	73	64	149
Termite/pest control products	100	106	56	116	116
Moving, storage, and freight express	100	67	81	79	183
Appliance repair, including service center	100	99	106	94	105
Reupholstering and furniture repair	100	179	41	114	71
Repairs/rentals of lawn/garden equipment, hand/power tools, etc.	100	106	109	114	63
Appliance rental	100	57	148	76	124
Repair of computer systems for nonbusiness use	100	68	121	75	147
Computer information services	100	115	95	88	112
HOUSEKEEPING SUPPLIES	**100**	**91**	**130**	**90**	**93**
Laundry and cleaning supplies	**100**	**91**	**104**	**105**	**96**
Soaps and detergents	100	95	99	103	100
Other laundry cleaning products	100	85	111	108	90
Other household products	**100**	**85**	**153**	**84**	**83**
Cleansing and toilet tissue, paper towels, and napkins	100	107	101	97	98
Miscellaneous household products	100	91	113	105	86
Lawn and garden supplies	100	63	225	57	71
Postage and stationery	**100**	**107**	**106**	**86**	**111**
Stationery, stationery supplies, giftwrap	100	100	118	85	105
Postage	100	113	97	87	113
Delivery services	100	78	43	91	192

	total consumer units	Northeast	Midwest	South	West
HOUSEHOLD FURNISHINGS AND EQUIPMENT	**100**	**102**	**104**	**88**	**114**
Household textiles	**100**	**90**	**95**	**85**	**137**
Bathroom linens	100	81	95	111	104
Bedroom linens	100	73	98	82	154
Kitchen and dining room linens	100	151	81	75	115
Curtains and draperies	100	117	91	85	120
Slipcovers and decorative pillows	100	94	56	84	177
Sewing materials for household items	100	106	129	61	128
Other linens	100	136	76	89	111
Furniture	**100**	**115**	**90**	**89**	**115**
Mattresses and springs	100	110	82	93	122
Other bedroom furniture	100	112	91	94	107
Sofas	100	104	94	91	117
Living room chairs	100	110	100	88	112
Living room tables	100	129	81	83	122
Kitchen and dining room furniture	100	123	83	96	105
Infants' furniture	100	115	87	100	100
Outdoor furniture	100	128	85	70	140
Wall units, cabinets, and other furniture	100	127	97	76	119
Floor coverings	**100**	**118**	**111**	**93**	**85**
Wall-to-wall carpeting	100	106	153	80	72
Floor coverings, nonpermanent	100	132	64	107	99
Major appliances	**100**	**100**	**104**	**86**	**118**
Dishwashers (built-in), garbage disposals, range hoods	100	112	85	88	126
Refrigerators and freezers	100	103	100	89	114
Washing machines	100	97	99	90	120
Clothes dryers	100	102	108	97	95
Cooking stoves, ovens	100	97	84	100	119
Microwave ovens	100	115	92	94	105
Window air conditioners	100	192	79	90	58
Electric floor-cleaning equipment	100	69	171	49	135
Sewing machines	100	71	108	64	174
Miscellaneous household appliances	100	–	80	81	238
Small appliances and misc. housewares	**100**	**91**	**101**	**88**	**126**
Housewares	100	85	98	92	128
Plastic dinnerware	100	120	106	61	138
China and other dinnerware	100	55	85	87	174
Flatware	100	85	90	93	134
Glassware	100	124	59	109	107
Silver serving pieces	100	110	54	130	89
Other serving pieces	100	105	115	79	113
Nonelectric cookware	100	93	96	86	132
Tableware, nonelectric kitchenware	100	74	129	92	104
Small appliances	100	110	109	75	121
Small electric kitchen appliances	100	108	106	75	127
Portable heating and cooling equipment	100	117	118	77	104

	total consumer units	Northeast	Midwest	South	West
Miscellaneous household equipment	**100**	**97**	**115**	**88**	**107**
Window coverings	100	99	98	67	156
Infants' equipment	100	39	82	131	124
Laundry and cleaning equipment	100	98	106	99	97
Outdoor equipment	100	75	147	89	91
Clocks	100	61	102	119	103
Lamps and lighting fixtures	100	98	120	72	126
Other household decorative items	100	105	114	88	100
Telephones and accessories	100	68	133	104	88
Lawn and garden equipment	100	137	121	98	50
Power tools	100	85	119	104	87
Office furniture for home use	100	81	115	67	154
Hand tools	100	91	108	73	144
Indoor plants and fresh flowers	100	119	123	78	96
Closet and storage items	100	100	119	73	124
Rental of furniture	100	77	121	121	63
Luggage	100	109	93	85	124
Computers and computer hardware, nonbusiness use	100	97	104	82	126
Computer software and accessories, nonbusiness use	100	73	103	73	164
Telephone answering devices	100	69	111	110	100
Calculators	100	70	155	66	123
Business equipment for home use	100	54	94	123	110
Other hardware	100	106	114	58	147
Smoke alarms	100	44	72	168	66
Other household appliances	100	102	86	92	127
Miscellaneous household equipment and parts	100	77	136	83	111

Note: (–) means sample is too small to make a reliable estimate.
Source: Calculations by New Strategist based on the 2002 Consumer Expenditure Survey

Table 8.19 Housing: Household Operations: Total spending by region, 2002

(total annual spending on household services, supplies, furnishings, and equipment, by region in which consumer units live, 2002; numbers in thousands)

	total consumer units	Northeast	Midwest	South	West
Number of consumer units	112,108	21,313	25,883	40,004	24,907
Total spending of all consumer units	$4,560,172,273	$903,462,333	$1,050,879,307	$1,491,371,122	$1,114,048,764
Housing, total spending	1,489,139,533	310,275,293	327,192,438	470,693,865	381,014,085
HOUSEHOLD SERVICES	**$79,115,737**	**$17,139,062**	**$14,752,534**	**$27,612,761**	**$19,611,025**
Personal services	**37,109,990**	**9,213,610**	**6,718,709**	**13,464,946**	**7,712,203**
Babysitting and child care in your own home	4,025,798	1,100,603	894,775	1,179,718	851,321
Babysitting and child care in someone else's home	3,080,728	635,554	726,018	853,685	865,518
Day care centers, nurseries, and preschools	23,625,640	6,256,644	4,702,682	7,273,927	5,391,867
Other household services	**42,006,868**	**7,925,452**	**8,033,824**	**14,147,815**	**11,898,821**
Housekeeping services	8,957,429	1,533,897	1,717,596	2,936,694	2,769,160
Gardening, lawn care service	8,114,377	1,512,797	1,337,375	2,941,094	2,323,076
Water softening service	353,140	46,462	131,486	87,209	88,420
Nonclothing laundry and dry cleaning, sent out	192,826	47,315	36,495	49,605	59,279
Nonclothing laundry and dry cleaning, coin-operated	463,006	136,616	86,190	109,211	131,260
Termite/pest control services	1,485,431	129,370	137,180	818,082	400,754
Home security system service fee	1,950,679	294,119	321,467	913,691	421,177
Other home services	1,688,346	458,443	285,231	385,239	560,158
Termite/pest control products	76,233	15,345	9,836	31,603	19,677
Moving, storage, and freight express	3,714,138	471,657	691,594	1,042,104	1,508,617
Appliance repair, including service center	1,217,493	229,328	296,619	408,441	283,442
Reupholstering and furniture repair	829,599	282,610	78,684	338,034	130,513
Repairs/rentals of lawn/garden equipment, hand/power tools, etc.	405,831	82,055	101,979	165,217	56,539
Appliance rental	119,956	13,001	40,895	32,403	33,126
Repair of computer systems for nonbusiness use	283,633	36,445	78,943	76,008	92,654
Computer information services	12,028,067	2,623,417	2,649,384	3,772,777	2,982,364
HOUSEKEEPING SUPPLIES	**61,130,250**	**10,611,316**	**18,361,141**	**19,576,757**	**12,605,682**
Laundry and cleaning supplies	**14,637,942**	**2,523,246**	**3,520,088**	**5,494,549**	**3,108,394**
Soaps and detergents	8,171,552	1,482,106	1,866,682	3,014,301	1,810,988
Other laundry cleaning products	6,466,389	1,041,353	1,653,665	2,480,648	1,297,406
Other household products	**31,757,954**	**5,103,824**	**11,245,646**	**9,554,155**	**5,878,550**
Cleansing and toilet tissue, paper towels, and napkins	8,571,778	1,738,075	1,996,873	2,970,297	1,864,040
Miscellaneous household products	10,853,175	1,878,954	2,834,706	4,084,408	2,062,300
Lawn and garden supplies	12,333,001	1,487,008	6,413,807	2,499,850	1,952,460
Postage and stationery	**14,735,476**	**2,984,033**	**3,595,408**	**4,527,653**	**3,618,738**
Stationery, stationery supplies, giftwrap	6,748,902	1,283,895	1,844,164	2,049,805	1,569,639
Postage	7,748,905	1,664,972	1,727,690	2,400,640	1,947,976
Delivery services	237,669	35,166	23,554	77,208	101,122

HOUSEHOLD FURNISHINGS AND EQUIPMENT	total consumer units	Northeast	Midwest	South	West
	$170,220,303	$32,912,174	$40,983,919	$53,331,333	$43,015,136
Household textiles	**15,192,876**	**2,608,711**	**3,342,789**	**4,609,661**	**4,634,944**
Bathroom linens	2,505,614	385,978	546,908	995,300	580,084
Bedroom linens	7,396,886	1,030,697	1,673,336	2,163,816	2,533,789
Kitchen and dining room linens	1,133,412	325,876	213,017	302,430	288,423
Curtains and draperies	1,866,598	414,751	390,316	563,656	497,642
Slipcovers and decorative pillows	829,599	147,486	106,638	248,825	325,784
Sewing materials for household items	1,282,516	257,887	381,515	278,428	365,137
Other linens	178,252	46,036	31,318	56,806	44,085
Furniture	**44,986,698**	**9,827,424**	**9,370,940**	**14,326,232**	**11,460,956**
Mattresses and springs	5,931,634	1,237,433	1,120,993	1,969,797	1,603,264
Other bedroom furniture	7,660,340	1,637,265	1,616,135	2,578,658	1,828,672
Sofas	9,566,176	1,890,676	2,083,064	3,115,111	2,476,752
Living room chairs	4,395,755	915,606	1,014,872	1,373,737	1,091,923
Living room tables	2,021,307	495,101	379,186	598,460	548,203
Kitchen and dining room furniture	6,869,978	1,606,574	1,313,045	2,350,235	1,600,026
Infants' furniture	724,218	158,569	145,980	258,426	161,148
Outdoor furniture	1,882,293	458,656	367,539	468,847	587,058
Wall units, cabinets, and other furniture	5,934,998	1,427,545	1,330,127	1,612,961	1,564,160
Floor coverings	**4,539,253**	**1,019,188**	**1,167,064**	**1,499,350**	**853,065**
Wall-to-wall carpeting	2,431,623	489,133	856,727	698,470	388,549
Floor coverings, nonpermanent	2,106,509	530,054	310,337	800,880	464,765
Major appliances	**21,128,995**	**4,020,484**	**5,083,421**	**6,505,450**	**5,521,384**
Dishwashers (built-in), garbage disposals, range hoods	1,852,024	394,291	361,586	578,858	517,817
Refrigerators and freezers	5,838,585	1,148,771	1,349,798	1,861,386	1,478,729
Washing machines	2,500,008	461,213	570,202	801,280	667,009
Clothes dryers	1,911,441	369,781	474,953	664,866	401,750
Cooking stoves, ovens	3,469,743	642,374	673,476	1,234,923	919,566
Microwave ovens	1,177,134	256,395	248,736	396,040	275,720
Window air conditioners	885,653	323,958	161,251	285,629	115,070
Electric floor-cleaning equipment	2,556,062	337,385	1,009,955	446,045	764,645
Sewing machines	536,997	72,038	134,074	122,812	207,724
Miscellaneous household appliances	315,023	–	57,978	91,609	166,628
Small appliances and misc. housewares	**11,259,006**	**1,937,991**	**2,620,654**	**3,546,355**	**3,158,208**
Housewares	8,693,975	1,400,477	1,973,061	2,855,886	2,468,035
Plastic dinnerware	176,010	40,282	42,966	38,404	53,799
China and other dinnerware	1,626,687	171,143	320,690	506,851	630,396
Flatware	424,889	68,628	88,520	141,214	126,278
Glassware	729,823	171,996	99,391	284,428	173,353
Silver serving pieces	454,037	95,056	56,943	211,221	90,163
Other serving pieces	161,436	32,183	42,966	45,605	40,349
Nonelectric cookware	2,718,619	480,608	603,850	835,684	797,771
Tableware, nonelectric kitchenware	2,403,596	340,369	717,994	792,079	555,675
Small appliances	2,566,152	537,727	647,593	690,469	690,173
Small electric kitchen appliances	1,926,015	395,996	472,624	514,851	542,724
Portable heating and cooling equipment	639,016	141,731	174,710	175,218	147,449

	total consumer units	Northeast	Midwest	South	West
Miscellaneous household equipment	**$73,113,474**	**$13,497,949**	**$19,398,791**	**$22,844,684**	**$17,386,331**
Window coverings	1,559,422	294,119	352,526	372,837	540,482
Infants' equipment	1,452,920	106,352	273,583	678,468	399,508
Laundry and cleaning equipment	1,698,436	315,432	416,457	602,460	364,389
Outdoor equipment	3,533,644	504,052	1,199,677	1,122,512	712,340
Clocks	658,074	75,874	154,263	278,828	150,189
Lamps and lighting fixtures	1,316,148	244,886	365,986	337,634	367,876
Other household decorative items	16,248,934	3,256,626	4,279,236	5,103,710	3,601,801
Telephones and accessories	3,669,295	474,001	1,123,063	1,366,137	713,586
Lawn and garden equipment	5,399,121	1,406,019	1,513,897	1,883,788	595,028
Power tools	3,729,833	603,158	1,021,602	1,383,738	724,794
Office furniture for home use	1,184,982	183,079	314,737	282,028	404,739
Hand tools	902,469	156,011	224,406	234,823	287,925
Indoor plants and fresh flowers	5,580,736	1,264,287	1,581,969	1,546,955	1,187,566
Closet and storage items	1,118,838	212,064	307,749	290,029	308,598
Rental of furniture	515,697	75,022	144,168	223,222	72,728
Luggage	670,406	138,961	144,686	202,420	184,810
Computers and computer hardware, nonbusiness use	15,535,927	2,876,189	3,743,458	4,565,657	4,350,506
Computer software and accessories, nonbusiness use	1,980,948	276,216	469,259	516,052	719,812
Telephone answering devices	121,077	15,772	31,060	47,605	26,900
Calculators	161,436	21,526	57,719	38,004	44,085
Business equipment for home use	108,745	11,083	23,554	47,605	26,650
Other hardware	1,440,588	290,709	378,409	299,630	469,995
Smoke alarms	167,041	14,067	27,954	100,410	24,658
Other household appliances	1,034,757	200,129	205,252	338,834	290,914
Miscellaneous household equipment and parts	3,320,639	482,953	1,043,861	980,498	816,202

Note: Numbers may not add to total because of rounding and because not all categories are shown. (–) means sample is too small to make a reliable estimate.
Source: Calculations by New Strategist based on the 2002 Consumer Expenditure Survey

Table 8.20 Housing: Household Operations: Market shares by region, 2002

(percentage of total annual spending on household services, supplies, furnishings, and equipment accounted for by consumer units by region, 2002)

	total consumer units	Northeast	Midwest	South	West
Share of total consumer units	**100.0%**	**19.0%**	**23.1%**	**35.7%**	**22.2%**
Share of total before-tax income	**100.0**	**20.8**	**23.0**	**32.9**	**23.4**
Share of total spending	**100.0**	**19.8**	**23.0**	**32.7**	**24.4**
Share of housing spending	**100.0**	**20.8**	**22.0**	**31.6**	**25.6**
HOUSEHOLD SERVICES	**100.0%**	**21.7%**	**18.6%**	**34.9%**	**24.8%**
Personal services	**100.0**	**24.8**	**18.1**	**36.3**	**20.8**
Babysitting and child care in your own home	100.0	27.3	22.2	29.3	21.1
Babysitting and child care in someone else's home	100.0	20.6	23.6	27.7	28.1
Day care centers, nurseries, and preschools	100.0	26.5	19.9	30.8	22.8
Other household services	**100.0**	**18.9**	**19.1**	**33.7**	**28.3**
Housekeeping services	100.0	17.1	19.2	32.8	30.9
Gardening, lawn care service	100.0	18.6	16.5	36.2	28.6
Water softening service	100.0	13.2	37.2	24.7	25.0
Nonclothing laundry and dry cleaning, sent out	100.0	24.5	18.9	25.7	30.7
Nonclothing laundry and dry cleaning, coin-operated	100.0	29.5	18.6	23.6	28.3
Termite/pest control services	100.0	8.7	9.2	55.1	27.0
Home security system service fee	100.0	15.1	16.5	46.8	21.6
Other home services	100.0	27.2	16.9	22.8	33.2
Termite/pest control products	100.0	20.1	12.9	41.5	25.8
Moving, storage, and freight express	100.0	12.7	18.6	28.1	40.6
Appliance repair, including service center	100.0	18.8	24.4	33.5	23.3
Reupholstering and furniture repair	100.0	34.1	9.5	40.7	15.7
Repairs/rentals of lawn/garden equipment, hand/power tools, etc.	100.0	20.2	25.1	40.7	13.9
Appliance rental	100.0	10.8	34.1	27.0	27.6
Repair of computer systems for nonbusiness use	100.0	12.8	27.8	26.8	32.7
Computer information services	100.0	21.8	22.0	31.4	24.8
HOUSEKEEPING SUPPLIES	**100.0**	**17.4**	**30.0**	**32.0**	**20.6**
Laundry and cleaning supplies	**100.0**	**17.2**	**24.0**	**37.5**	**21.2**
Soaps and detergents	100.0	18.1	22.8	36.9	22.2
Other laundry cleaning products	100.0	16.1	25.6	38.4	20.1
Other household products	**100.0**	**16.1**	**35.4**	**30.1**	**18.5**
Cleansing and toilet tissue, paper towels, and napkins	100.0	20.3	23.3	34.7	21.7
Miscellaneous household products	100.0	17.3	26.1	37.6	19.0
Lawn and garden supplies	100.0	12.1	52.0	20.3	15.8
Postage and stationery	**100.0**	**20.3**	**24.4**	**30.7**	**24.6**
Stationery, stationery supplies, giftwrap	100.0	19.0	27.3	30.4	23.3
Postage	100.0	21.5	22.3	31.0	25.1
Delivery services	100.0	14.8	9.9	32.5	42.5

	total consumer units	Northeast	Midwest	South	West
HOUSEHOLD FURNISHINGS AND EQUIPMENT	**100.0%**	**19.3%**	**24.1%**	**31.3%**	**25.3%**
Household textiles	**100.0**	**17.2**	**22.0**	**30.3**	**30.5**
Bathroom linens	100.0	15.4	21.8	39.7	23.2
Bedroom linens	100.0	13.9	22.6	29.3	34.3
Kitchen and dining room linens	100.0	28.8	18.8	26.7	25.4
Curtains and draperies	100.0	22.2	20.9	30.2	26.7
Slipcovers and decorative pillows	100.0	17.8	12.9	30.0	39.3
Sewing materials for household items	100.0	20.1	29.7	21.7	28.5
Other linens	100.0	25.8	17.6	31.9	24.7
Furniture	**100.0**	**21.8**	**20.8**	**31.8**	**25.5**
Mattresses and springs	100.0	20.9	18.9	33.2	27.0
Other bedroom furniture	100.0	21.4	21.1	33.7	23.9
Sofas	100.0	19.8	21.8	32.6	25.9
Living room chairs	100.0	20.8	23.1	31.3	24.8
Living room tables	100.0	24.5	18.8	29.6	27.1
Kitchen and dining room furniture	100.0	23.4	19.1	34.2	23.3
Infants' furniture	100.0	21.9	20.2	35.7	22.3
Outdoor furniture	100.0	24.4	19.5	24.9	31.2
Wall units, cabinets, and other furniture	100.0	24.1	22.4	27.2	26.4
Floor coverings	**100.0**	**22.5**	**25.7**	**33.0**	**18.8**
Wall-to-wall carpeting	100.0	20.1	35.2	28.7	16.0
Floor coverings, nonpermanent	100.0	25.2	14.7	38.0	22.1
Major appliances	**100.0**	**19.0**	**24.1**	**30.8**	**26.1**
Dishwashers (built-in), garbage disposals, range hoods	100.0	21.3	19.5	31.3	28.0
Refrigerators and freezers	100.0	19.7	23.1	31.9	25.3
Washing machines	100.0	18.4	22.8	32.1	26.7
Clothes dryers	100.0	19.3	24.8	34.8	21.0
Cooking stoves, ovens	100.0	18.5	19.4	35.6	26.5
Microwave ovens	100.0	21.8	21.1	33.6	23.4
Window air conditioners	100.0	36.6	18.2	32.3	13.0
Electric floor-cleaning equipment	100.0	13.2	39.5	17.5	29.9
Sewing machines	100.0	13.4	25.0	22.9	38.7
Miscellaneous household appliances	100.0	–	18.4	29.1	52.9
Small appliances and misc. housewares	**100.0**	**17.2**	**23.3**	**31.5**	**28.1**
Housewares	100.0	16.1	22.7	32.8	28.4
Plastic dinnerware	100.0	22.9	24.4	21.8	30.6
China and other dinnerware	100.0	10.5	19.7	31.2	38.8
Flatware	100.0	16.2	20.8	33.2	29.7
Glassware	100.0	23.6	13.6	39.0	23.8
Silver serving pieces	100.0	20.9	12.5	46.5	19.9
Other serving pieces	100.0	19.9	26.6	28.2	25.0
Nonelectric cookware	100.0	17.7	22.2	30.7	29.3
Tableware, nonelectric kitchenware	100.0	14.2	29.9	33.0	23.1
Small appliances	100.0	21.0	25.2	26.9	26.9
Small electric kitchen appliances	100.0	20.6	24.5	26.7	28.2
Portable heating and cooling equipment	100.0	22.2	27.3	27.4	23.1

Miscellaneous household equipment	total consumer units 100.0%	Northeast 18.5%	Midwest 26.5%	South 31.2%	West 23.8%
Window coverings	100.0	18.9	22.6	23.9	34.7
Infants' equipment	100.0	7.3	18.8	46.7	27.5
Laundry and cleaning equipment	100.0	18.6	24.5	35.5	21.5
Outdoor equipment	100.0	14.3	34.0	31.8	20.2
Clocks	100.0	11.5	23.4	42.4	22.8
Lamps and lighting fixtures	100.0	18.6	27.8	25.7	28.0
Other household decorative items	100.0	20.0	26.3	31.4	22.2
Telephones and accessories	100.0	12.9	30.6	37.2	19.4
Lawn and garden equipment	100.0	26.0	28.0	34.9	11.0
Power tools	100.0	16.2	27.4	37.1	19.4
Office furniture for home use	100.0	15.4	26.6	23.8	34.2
Hand tools	100.0	17.3	24.9	26.0	31.9
Indoor plants and fresh flowers	100.0	22.7	28.3	27.7	21.3
Closet and storage items	100.0	19.0	27.5	25.9	27.6
Rental of furniture	100.0	14.5	28.0	43.3	14.1
Luggage	100.0	20.7	21.6	30.2	27.6
Computers and computer hardware, nonbusiness use	100.0	18.5	24.1	29.4	28.0
Computer software and accessories, nonbusiness use	100.0	13.9	23.7	26.1	36.3
Telephone answering devices	100.0	13.0	25.7	39.3	22.2
Calculators	100.0	13.3	35.8	23.5	27.3
Business equipment for home use	100.0	10.2	21.7	43.8	24.5
Other hardware	100.0	20.2	26.3	20.8	32.6
Smoke alarms	100.0	8.4	16.7	60.1	14.8
Other household appliances	100.0	19.3	19.8	32.7	28.1
Miscellaneous household equipment and parts	100.0	14.5	31.4	29.5	24.6

Note: Numbers may not add to total because of rounding. (–) means sample is too small to make a reliable estimate.
Source: Calculations by New Strategist based on the 2002 Consumer Expenditure Survey

Table 8.21 Housing: Household Operations: Average spending by education, 2002

(average annual spending of consumer units (CU) on household services, supplies, furnishings, and equipment, by education of consumer unit reference person, 2002)

	total consumer units	less than high school graduate	high school graduate	some college	associate's degree	college graduate total	college graduate bachelor's degree	college graduate master's, professional, doctorate
Number of consumer units (in thousands, add 000)	112,108	17,075	31,961	23,260	10,395	29,417	19,082	10,335
Average number of persons per CU	2.5	2.6	2.5	2.4	2.6	2.5	2.5	2.5
Average before-tax income of CU	$49,430.00	$25,564.00	$39,618.00	$42,598.00	$54,860.00	$77,820.00	$69,408.00	$92,783.00
Average spending of CU, total	40,676.60	24,930.40	33,707.63	38,653.57	44,405.79	57,384.01	53,731.57	64,118.48
Housing, average spending	13,283.08	8,287.79	10,799.89	12,336.44	14,643.80	19,111.29	17,758.72	21,607.22
HOUSEHOLD SERVICES	**$705.71**	**$259.82**	**$426.86**	**$713.07**	**$789.31**	**$1,232.07**	**$1,087.66**	**$1,498.69**
Personal services	**331.02**	**126.06**	**195.23**	**372.49**	**391.11**	**543.49**	**497.55**	**628.30**
Babysitting and child care in your own home	35.91	20.89	11.74	23.29	39.59	79.59	77.48	83.47
Babysitting and child care in someone else's home	27.48	20.72	21.26	30.41	36.92	32.52	29.89	37.39
Day care centers, nurseries, and preschools	210.74	44.27	129.15	209.50	298.54	365.95	324.60	442.31
Other household services	**374.70**	**133.76**	**231.63**	**340.58**	**398.20**	**688.58**	**590.11**	**870.39**
Housekeeping services	79.90	17.98	30.03	54.23	78.99	190.64	136.90	289.87
Gardening, lawn care service	72.38	27.39	42.80	66.10	66.77	137.59	116.53	176.48
Water softening service	3.15	1.50	3.10	3.21	5.54	3.29	3.43	3.03
Nonclothing laundry and dry cleaning, sent out	1.72	0.75	0.88	1.52	1.03	3.59	3.57	3.63
Nonclothing laundry and dry cleaning, coin-operated	4.13	6.01	4.01	4.23	2.58	3.65	4.23	2.59
Termite/pest control services	13.25	8.29	6.25	13.89	15.84	22.30	22.87	21.26
Home security system service fee	17.40	7.86	13.52	13.89	17.13	30.02	27.73	34.23
Other home services	15.06	5.74	9.43	11.26	13.96	29.99	29.25	31.36
Termite/pest control products	0.68	0.53	0.28	0.60	0.87	1.21	0.80	1.97
Moving, storage, and freight express	33.13	10.46	21.16	44.72	26.62	52.43	39.64	76.05
Appliance repair, including service center	10.86	6.16	7.96	10.80	12.95	16.06	14.79	18.42
Reupholstering and furniture repair	7.40	2.48	2.80	3.31	4.36	19.58	15.99	26.20
Repairs/rentals of lawn/garden equipment, hand/power tools, etc.	3.62	1.67	3.73	2.16	7.27	4.50	4.27	4.94
Appliance rental	1.07	1.34	1.35	0.92	1.15	0.70	0.57	0.94
Repair of computer systems for nonbusiness use	2.53	1.14	1.69	1.45	5.19	4.18	3.56	5.32
Computer information services	107.29	34.24	81.51	107.32	135.72	167.64	164.99	172.53
HOUSEKEEPING SUPPLIES	**545.28**	**401.61**	**440.10**	**465.42**	**955.61**	**653.47**	**623.69**	**707.68**
Laundry and cleaning supplies	**130.57**	**130.41**	**127.76**	**126.22**	**133.20**	**135.75**	**136.95**	**133.57**
Soaps and detergents	72.89	72.43	72.80	72.62	68.98	74.57	77.95	68.43
Other laundry cleaning products	57.68	57.98	54.96	53.60	64.23	61.18	59.01	65.14
Other household products	**283.28**	**204.57**	**210.39**	**213.30**	**680.90**	**324.24**	**309.41**	**351.21**
Cleansing and toilet tissue, paper towels, and napkins	76.46	79.33	70.42	72.38	75.52	84.39	83.31	86.36
Miscellaneous household products	96.81	84.02	77.07	76.55	109.67	133.36	123.53	151.25
Lawn and garden supplies	110.01	41.22	62.89	64.37	495.71	106.49	102.58	113.60
Postage and stationery	**131.44**	**66.63**	**101.94**	**125.91**	**141.51**	**193.48**	**177.32**	**222.90**
Stationery, stationery supplies, giftwrap	60.20	26.01	44.49	57.43	59.68	94.75	93.63	96.79
Postage	69.12	39.96	56.71	67.15	76.02	95.08	81.77	119.31
Delivery services	2.12	0.66	0.75	1.33	5.81	3.65	1.92	6.80

	total consumer units	less than high school graduate	high school graduate	some college	associate's degree	college graduate total	bachelor's degree	master's, professional, doctorate
HOUSEHOLD FURNISHINGS AND EQUIPMENT	**$1,518.36**	**$819.01**	**$1,155.67**	**$1,353.23**	**$1,813.79**	**$2,315.36**	**$2,161.95**	**$2,597.98**
Household textiles	**135.52**	**83.74**	**103.54**	**139.17**	**126.78**	**195.94**	**180.04**	**225.12**
Bathroom linens	22.35	15.29	16.91	30.72	21.97	25.54	25.00	26.51
Bedroom linens	65.98	51.80	56.90	64.52	53.66	86.81	76.93	104.77
Kitchen and dining room linens	10.11	4.74	7.33	5.84	10.89	18.28	17.66	19.40
Curtains and draperies	16.65	5.82	10.56	12.75	17.16	32.45	23.69	48.63
Slipcovers and decorative pillows	7.40	1.14	2.32	14.29	6.11	11.16	15.24	3.74
Sewing materials for household items	11.44	4.42	8.10	9.89	15.41	18.97	19.46	18.07
Other linens	1.59	0.51	1.43	1.16	1.58	2.74	2.06	4.00
Furniture	**401.28**	**210.75**	**304.00**	**321.31**	**433.52**	**669.39**	**611.37**	**776.51**
Mattresses and springs	52.91	31.15	48.03	43.31	56.01	77.34	74.27	83.00
Other bedroom furniture	68.33	37.31	53.17	50.88	64.97	117.80	112.92	126.82
Sofas	85.33	61.05	69.22	66.63	104.23	125.01	114.97	143.56
Living room chairs	39.21	22.29	25.50	37.40	44.32	63.57	57.66	74.49
Living room tables	18.03	9.84	8.83	17.28	19.43	32.88	30.46	37.34
Kitchen and dining room furniture	61.28	26.55	46.02	49.54	48.05	111.97	95.70	142.01
Infants' furniture	6.46	3.40	4.12	4.87	5.94	12.22	12.57	11.55
Outdoor furniture	16.79	4.07	11.12	10.15	20.01	34.44	32.92	37.23
Wall units, cabinets, and other furniture	52.94	15.08	37.99	41.26	70.58	94.16	79.89	120.50
Floor coverings	**40.49**	**24.83**	**32.34**	**29.14**	**28.54**	**71.62**	**59.57**	**93.85**
Wall-to-wall carpeting	21.69	19.01	21.94	17.27	15.62	28.65	28.14	29.59
Floor coverings, nonpermanent	18.79	5.82	10.39	11.88	12.93	42.96	31.43	64.26
Major appliances	**188.47**	**112.11**	**141.23**	**202.60**	**269.49**	**243.52**	**220.95**	**285.24**
Dishwashers (built-in), garbage disposals, range hoods	16.52	3.24	8.23	18.30	25.26	28.77	22.51	40.31
Refrigerators and freezers	52.08	32.79	37.82	48.34	82.07	71.12	64.92	82.58
Washing machines	22.30	17.40	18.86	20.89	28.55	27.78	24.82	33.24
Clothes dryers	17.05	9.98	14.08	13.89	31.91	21.62	21.05	22.66
Cooking stoves, ovens	30.95	18.76	25.14	38.44	36.32	36.53	28.96	50.51
Microwave ovens	10.50	6.95	7.53	13.75	12.85	12.38	11.12	14.71
Window air conditioners	7.90	9.19	7.99	6.87	12.99	6.08	6.72	4.90
Electric floor-cleaning equipment	22.80	10.28	17.67	29.75	25.27	28.45	30.23	25.22
Sewing machines	4.79	2.17	3.43	4.47	9.41	6.40	6.88	5.52
Miscellaneous household appliances	2.81	0.83	0.23	6.74	4.06	3.28	2.54	4.61
Small appliances and misc. housewares	**100.43**	**70.32**	**79.94**	**77.41**	**128.86**	**144.62**	**140.16**	**152.81**
Housewares	77.55	56.46	59.50	55.47	101.22	114.76	112.90	118.17
Plastic dinnerware	1.57	0.82	0.75	2.19	2.71	1.98	1.76	2.40
China and other dinnerware	14.51	7.66	5.80	11.66	15.80	28.29	18.36	46.36
Flatware	3.79	1.94	1.98	4.40	4.54	6.08	6.45	5.40
Glassware	6.51	7.72	4.47	4.39	13.32	7.44	7.38	7.53
Silver serving pieces	4.05	2.37	1.62	1.82	6.43	8.17	11.02	2.98
Other serving pieces	1.44	0.43	0.83	1.11	1.71	2.84	2.12	4.16
Nonelectric cookware	24.25	26.55	23.10	14.03	30.61	29.54	35.34	18.99
Tableware, nonelectric kitchenware	21.44	8.96	20.95	15.87	26.11	30.42	30.47	30.34
Small appliances	22.89	13.86	20.44	21.94	27.63	29.85	27.26	34.64
Small electric kitchen appliances	17.18	10.06	13.71	17.34	21.56	23.41	21.05	27.78
Portable heating and cooling equipment	5.70	3.80	6.72	4.60	6.07	6.44	6.22	6.86

	total consumer units	less than high school graduate	high school graduate	some college	associate's degree	college graduate total	bachelor's degree	master's, professional, doctorate
Miscellaneous household equipment	**$652.17**	**$317.27**	**$494.62**	**$583.60**	**$826.60**	**$990.28**	**$949.86**	**$1,064.45**
Window coverings	13.91	4.34	9.45	15.04	9.70	24.92	25.88	23.14
Infants' equipment	12.96	8.70	11.31	8.36	14.41	19.47	26.12	7.37
Laundry and cleaning equipment	15.15	12.52	13.97	13.61	14.01	19.04	18.65	19.74
Outdoor equipment	31.52	11.01	13.76	19.06	57.76	60.29	45.84	86.58
Clocks	5.87	9.05	3.82	4.27	2.42	8.57	11.81	2.69
Lamps and lighting fixtures	11.74	3.88	6.26	11.52	8.91	23.45	19.60	30.54
Other household decorative items	144.94	66.96	105.12	120.97	172.76	231.37	223.42	245.83
Telephones and accessories	32.73	36.99	25.44	23.98	31.58	44.59	42.26	48.84
Lawn and garden equipment	48.16	25.47	53.40	44.22	93.53	42.71	39.74	48.21
Power tools	33.27	23.96	28.42	17.14	62.30	45.20	44.28	46.87
Office furniture for home use	10.57	1.48	7.15	10.89	16.43	17.22	18.77	14.36
Hand tools	8.05	3.99	7.90	8.50	12.03	8.83	9.70	7.22
Indoor plants and fresh flowers	49.78	20.23	36.76	46.27	50.37	83.65	75.33	99.00
Closet and storage items	9.98	3.90	4.87	10.85	14.23	16.24	15.32	17.91
Rental of furniture	4.60	8.56	4.97	5.03	1.74	2.56	1.64	4.26
Luggage	5.98	1.18	3.41	4.23	9.92	11.57	10.66	13.24
Computers and computer hardware, nonbusiness use	138.58	42.90	97.63	144.95	159.38	226.23	217.27	242.78
Computer software and accessories, nonbusiness use	17.67	4.30	10.08	17.64	21.71	32.28	32.53	31.83
Telephone answering devices	1.08	0.39	1.21	0.82	1.25	1.50	1.32	1.81
Calculators	1.44	0.53	0.88	1.84	2.02	2.05	2.50	1.21
Business equipment for home use	0.97	0.62	0.84	0.87	1.03	1.37	1.05	1.98
Other hardware	12.85	4.93	9.95	15.24	26.40	13.86	16.17	9.67
Smoke alarms	1.49	2.74	0.42	2.28	1.90	1.18	1.22	1.07
Other household appliances	9.23	3.70	10.59	5.65	6.85	14.65	13.76	16.28
Miscellaneous household equipment and parts	29.62	14.94	27.00	30.36	33.97	37.50	35.01	42.03

Note: Numbers may not add to total because not all categories are shown.
Source: Bureau of Labor Statistics, unpublished tables from the 2002 Consumer Expenditure Survey

Table 8.22 Housing: Household Operations: Indexed spending by education, 2002

(indexed average annual spending of consumer units (CU) on household services, supplies, furnishings, and equipment, by education of consumer unit reference person, 2002; index definition: an index of 100 is the average for all consumer units; an index of 132 means that spending by consumer units in that group is 32 percent above the average for all consumer units; an index of 68 indicates spending that is 32 percent below the average for all consumer units)

	total consumer units	less than high school graduate	high school graduate	some college	associate's degree	college graduate total	bachelor's degree	master's, professional, doctorate
Average spending of CU, total	$40,677	$24,930	$33,708	$38,654	$44,406	$57,384	$53,732	$64,118
Average spending of CU, index	100	61	83	95	109	141	132	158
Housing, spending index	100	62	81	93	110	144	134	163
HOUSEHOLD SERVICES	**100**	**37**	**60**	**101**	**112**	**175**	**154**	**212**
Personal services	**100**	**38**	**59**	**113**	**118**	**164**	**150**	**190**
Babysitting and child care in your own home	100	58	33	65	110	222	216	232
Babysitting and child care in someone else's home	100	75	77	111	134	118	109	136
Day care centers, nurseries, and preschools	100	21	61	99	142	174	154	210
Other household services	**100**	**36**	**62**	**91**	**106**	**184**	**157**	**232**
Housekeeping services	100	23	38	68	99	239	171	363
Gardening, lawn care service	100	38	59	91	92	190	161	244
Water softening service	100	48	98	102	176	104	109	96
Nonclothing laundry and dry cleaning, sent out	100	44	51	88	60	209	208	211
Nonclothing laundry and dry cleaning, coin-operated	100	146	97	102	62	88	102	63
Termite/pest control services	100	63	47	105	120	168	173	160
Home security system service fee	100	45	78	80	98	173	159	197
Other home services	100	38	63	75	93	199	194	208
Termite/pest control products	100	78	41	88	128	178	118	290
Moving, storage, and freight express	100	32	64	135	80	158	120	230
Appliance repair, including service center	100	57	73	99	119	148	136	170
Reupholstering and furniture repair	100	34	38	45	59	265	216	354
Repairs/rentals of lawn/garden equipment, hand/power tools, etc.	100	46	103	60	201	124	118	136
Appliance rental	100	125	126	86	107	65	53	88
Repair of computer systems for nonbusiness use	100	45	67	57	205	165	141	210
Computer information services	100	32	76	100	126	156	154	161
HOUSEKEEPING SUPPLIES	**100**	**74**	**81**	**85**	**175**	**120**	**114**	**130**
Laundry and cleaning supplies	**100**	**100**	**98**	**97**	**102**	**104**	**105**	**102**
Soaps and detergents	100	99	100	100	95	102	107	94
Other laundry cleaning products	100	101	95	93	111	106	102	113
Other household products	**100**	**72**	**74**	**75**	**240**	**114**	**109**	**124**
Cleansing and toilet tissue, paper towels, and napkins	100	104	92	95	99	110	109	113
Miscellaneous household products	100	87	80	79	113	138	128	156
Lawn and garden supplies	100	37	57	59	451	97	93	103
Postage and stationery	**100**	**51**	**78**	**96**	**108**	**147**	**135**	**170**
Stationery, stationery supplies, giftwrap	100	43	74	95	99	157	156	161
Postage	100	58	82	97	110	138	118	173
Delivery services	100	31	35	63	274	172	91	321

	total consumer units	less than high school graduate	high school graduate	some college	associate's degree	college graduate total	bachelor's degree	master's, professional, doctorate
HOUSEHOLD FURNISHINGS								
AND EQUIPMENT	**100**	**54**	**76**	**89**	**119**	**152**	**142**	**171**
Household textiles	**100**	**62**	**76**	**103**	**94**	**145**	**133**	**166**
Bathroom linens	100	68	76	137	98	114	112	119
Bedroom linens	100	79	86	98	81	132	117	159
Kitchen and dining room linens	100	47	73	58	108	181	175	192
Curtains and draperies	100	35	63	77	103	195	142	292
Slipcovers and decorative pillows	100	15	31	193	83	151	206	51
Sewing materials for household items	100	39	71	86	135	166	170	158
Other linens	100	32	90	73	99	172	130	252
Furniture	**100**	**53**	**76**	**80**	**108**	**167**	**152**	**194**
Mattresses and springs	100	59	91	82	106	146	140	157
Other bedroom furniture	100	55	78	74	95	172	165	186
Sofas	100	72	81	78	122	147	135	168
Living room chairs	100	57	65	95	113	162	147	190
Living room tables	100	55	49	96	108	182	169	207
Kitchen and dining room furniture	100	43	75	81	78	183	156	232
Infants' furniture	100	53	64	75	92	189	195	179
Outdoor furniture	100	24	66	60	119	205	196	222
Wall units, cabinets, and other furniture	100	28	72	78	133	178	151	228
Floor coverings	**100**	**61**	**80**	**72**	**70**	**177**	**147**	**232**
Wall-to-wall carpeting	100	88	101	80	72	132	130	136
Floor coverings, nonpermanent	100	31	55	63	69	229	167	342
Major appliances	**100**	**59**	**75**	**107**	**143**	**129**	**117**	**151**
Dishwashers (built-in), garbage disposals, range hoods	100	20	50	111	153	174	136	244
Refrigerators and freezers	100	63	73	93	158	137	125	159
Washing machines	100	78	85	94	128	125	111	149
Clothes dryers	100	59	83	81	187	127	123	133
Cooking stoves, ovens	100	61	81	124	117	118	94	163
Microwave ovens	100	66	72	131	122	118	106	140
Window air conditioners	100	116	101	87	164	77	85	62
Electric floor-cleaning equipment	100	45	78	130	111	125	133	111
Sewing machines	100	45	72	93	196	134	144	115
Miscellaneous household appliances	100	30	8	240	144	117	90	164
Small appliances and misc. housewares	**100**	**70**	**80**	**77**	**128**	**144**	**140**	**152**
Housewares	100	73	77	72	131	148	146	152
Plastic dinnerware	100	52	48	139	173	126	112	153
China and other dinnerware	100	53	40	80	109	195	127	320
Flatware	100	51	52	116	120	160	170	142
Glassware	100	119	69	67	205	114	113	116
Silver serving pieces	100	59	40	45	159	202	272	74
Other serving pieces	100	30	58	77	119	197	147	289
Nonelectric cookware	100	109	95	58	126	122	146	78
Tableware, nonelectric kitchenware	100	42	98	74	122	142	142	142
Small appliances	100	61	89	96	121	130	119	151
Small electric kitchen appliances	100	59	80	101	125	136	123	162
Portable heating and cooling equipment	100	67	118	81	106	113	109	120

	total consumer units	less than high school graduate	high school graduate	some college	associate's degree	college graduate		
						total	bachelor's degree	master's, professional, doctorate
Miscellaneous household equipment	**100**	**49**	**76**	**89**	**127**	**152**	**146**	**163**
Window coverings	100	31	68	108	70	179	186	166
Infants' equipment	100	67	87	65	111	150	202	57
Laundry and cleaning equipment	100	83	92	90	92	126	123	130
Outdoor equipment	100	35	44	60	183	191	145	275
Clocks	100	154	65	73	41	146	201	46
Lamps and lighting fixtures	100	33	53	98	76	200	167	260
Other household decorative items	100	46	73	83	119	160	154	170
Telephones and accessories	100	113	78	73	96	136	129	149
Lawn and garden equipment	100	53	111	92	194	89	83	100
Power tools	100	72	85	52	187	136	133	141
Office furniture for home use	100	14	68	103	155	163	178	136
Hand tools	100	50	98	106	149	110	120	90
Indoor plants and fresh flowers	100	41	74	93	101	168	151	199
Closet and storage items	100	39	49	109	143	163	154	179
Rental of furniture	100	186	108	109	38	56	36	93
Luggage	100	20	57	71	166	193	178	221
Computers and computer hardware, nonbusiness use	100	31	70	105	115	163	157	175
Computer software and accessories, nonbusiness use	100	24	57	100	123	183	184	180
Telephone answering devices	100	36	112	76	116	139	122	168
Calculators	100	37	61	128	140	142	174	84
Business equipment for home use	100	64	87	90	106	141	108	204
Other hardware	100	38	77	119	205	108	126	75
Smoke alarms	100	184	28	153	128	79	82	72
Other household appliances	100	40	115	61	74	159	149	176
Miscellaneous household equipment and parts	100	50	91	102	115	127	118	142

Source: Calculations by New Strategist based on the 2002 Consumer Expenditure Survey

Table 8.23 Housing: Household Operations: Total spending by education, 2002

(total annual spending on household services, supplies, furnishings, and equipment, by consumer unit (CU) educational attainment group, 2002; numbers in thousands)

	total consumer units	less than high school graduate	high school graduate	some college	associate's degree	college graduate total	bachelor's degree	master's, professional, doctorate
Number of consumer units	112,108	17,075	31,961	23,260	10,395	29,417	19,082	10,335
Total spending of all CUs	$4,560,172,273	$425,686,580	$1,077,329,562	$899,082,038	$461,598,187	$1,688,065,422	$1,025,305,819	$662,664,491
Housing, total spending	1,489,139,533	141,514,014	345,175,284	286,945,594	152,222,301	562,196,818	338,871,895	223,310,619
HOUSEHOLD SERVICES	**$79,115,737**	**$4,436,427**	**$13,642,872**	**$16,586,008**	**$8,204,877**	**$36,243,803**	**$20,754,728**	**$15,488,961**
Personal services	**37,109,990**	**2,152,475**	**6,239,746**	**8,664,117**	**4,065,588**	**15,987,845**	**9,494,249**	**6,493,481**
Babysitting and child care in your own home	4,025,798	356,697	375,222	541,725	411,538	2,341,299	1,478,473	862,662
Babysitting and child care in someone else's home	3,080,728	353,794	679,491	707,337	383,783	956,641	570,361	386,426
Day care centers, nurseries, and preschools	23,625,640	755,910	4,127,763	4,872,970	3,103,323	10,765,151	6,194,017	4,571,274
Other household services	**42,006,868**	**2,283,952**	**7,403,126**	**7,921,891**	**4,139,289**	**20,255,958**	**11,260,479**	**8,995,481**
Housekeeping services	8,957,429	307,009	959,789	1,261,390	821,101	5,608,057	2,612,326	2,995,806
Gardening, lawn care service	8,114,377	467,684	1,367,931	1,537,486	694,074	4,047,485	2,223,625	1,823,921
Water softening service	353,140	25,613	99,079	74,665	57,588	96,782	65,451	31,315
Nonclothing laundry and dry cleaning, sent out	192,826	12,806	28,126	35,355	10,707	105,607	68,123	37,516
Nonclothing laundry and dry cleaning, coin-operated	463,006	102,621	128,164	98,390	26,819	107,372	80,717	26,768
Termite/pest control services	1,485,431	141,552	199,756	323,081	164,657	655,999	436,405	219,722
Home security system service fee	1,950,679	134,210	432,113	323,081	178,066	883,098	529,144	353,767
Other home services	1,688,346	98,011	301,392	261,908	145,114	882,216	558,149	324,106
Termite/pest control products	76,233	9,050	8,949	13,956	9,044	35,595	15,266	20,360
Moving, storage, and freight express	3,714,138	178,605	676,295	1,040,187	276,715	1,542,333	756,410	785,977
Appliance repair, including service center	1,217,493	105,182	254,410	251,208	134,615	472,437	282,223	190,371
Reupholstering and furniture repair	829,599	42,346	89,491	76,991	45,322	575,985	305,121	270,777
Repairs/rentals of lawn/garden equipment, hand/power tools, etc.	405,831	28,515	119,215	50,242	75,572	132,377	81,480	51,055
Appliance rental	119,956	22,881	43,147	21,399	11,954	20,592	10,877	9,715
Repair of computer systems for nonbusiness use	283,633	19,466	54,014	33,727	53,950	122,963	67,932	54,982
Computer information services	12,028,067	584,648	2,605,141	2,496,263	1,410,809	4,931,466	3,148,339	1,783,098
HOUSEKEEPING SUPPLIES	**61,130,250**	**6,857,491**	**14,066,036**	**10,825,669**	**9,933,566**	**19,223,127**	**11,901,253**	**7,313,873**
Laundry and cleaning supplies	**14,637,942**	**2,226,751**	**4,083,337**	**2,935,877**	**1,384,614**	**3,993,358**	**2,613,280**	**1,380,446**
Soaps and detergents	8,171,552	1,236,742	2,326,761	1,689,141	717,047	2,193,626	1,487,442	707,224
Other laundry cleaning products	6,466,389	990,009	1,756,577	1,246,736	667,671	1,799,732	1,126,029	673,222
Other household products	**31,757,954**	**3,493,033**	**6,724,275**	**4,961,358**	**7,077,956**	**9,538,168**	**5,904,162**	**3,629,755**
Cleansing and toilet tissue, paper towels, and napkins	8,571,778	1,354,560	2,250,694	1,683,559	785,030	2,482,501	1,589,721	892,531
Miscellaneous household products	10,853,175	1,434,642	2,463,234	1,780,553	1,140,020	3,923,051	2,357,199	1,563,169
Lawn and garden supplies	12,333,001	703,832	2,010,027	1,497,246	5,152,905	3,132,616	1,957,432	1,174,056
Postage and stationery	**14,735,476**	**1,137,707**	**3,258,104**	**2,928,667**	**1,470,996**	**5,691,601**	**3,383,620**	**2,303,672**
Stationery, stationery supplies, giftwrap	6,748,902	444,121	1,421,945	1,335,822	620,374	2,787,261	1,786,648	1,000,325
Postage	7,748,905	682,317	1,812,508	1,561,909	790,228	2,796,968	1,560,335	1,233,069
Delivery services	237,669	11,270	23,971	30,936	60,395	107,372	36,637	70,278

	total consumer units	less than high school graduate	high school graduate	some college	associate's degree	college graduate total	bachelor's degree	master's, professional, doctorate
HOUSEHOLD FURNISHINGS AND EQUIPMENT	**$170,220,303**	**$13,984,596**	**$36,936,369**	**$31,476,130**	**$18,854,347**	**$68,110,945**	**$41,254,330**	**$26,850,123**
Household textiles	**15,192,876**	**1,429,861**	**3,309,242**	**3,237,094**	**1,317,878**	**5,763,967**	**3,435,523**	**2,326,615**
Bathroom linens	2,505,614	261,077	540,461	714,547	228,378	751,310	477,050	273,981
Bedroom linens	7,396,886	884,485	1,818,581	1,500,735	557,796	2,553,690	1,467,978	1,082,798
Kitchen and dining room linens	1,133,412	80,936	234,274	135,838	113,202	537,743	336,988	200,499
Curtains and draperies	1,866,598	99,377	337,508	296,565	178,378	954,582	452,053	502,591
Slipcovers and decorative pillows	829,599	19,466	74,150	332,385	63,513	328,294	290,810	38,653
Sewing materials for household items	1,282,516	75,472	258,884	230,041	160,187	558,040	371,336	186,753
Other linens	178,252	8,708	45,704	26,982	16,424	80,603	39,309	41,340
Furniture	**44,986,698**	**3,598,556**	**9,716,144**	**7,473,671**	**4,506,440**	**19,691,446**	**11,666,162**	**8,025,231**
Mattresses and springs	5,931,634	531,886	1,535,087	1,007,391	582,224	2,275,111	1,417,220	857,805
Other bedroom furniture	7,660,340	637,068	1,699,366	1,183,469	675,363	3,465,323	2,154,739	1,310,685
Sofas	9,566,176	1,042,429	2,212,340	1,549,814	1,083,471	3,677,419	2,193,858	1,483,693
Living room chairs	4,395,755	380,602	815,006	869,924	460,706	1,870,039	1,100,268	769,854
Living room tables	2,021,307	168,018	282,216	401,933	201,975	967,231	581,238	385,909
Kitchen and dining room furniture	6,869,978	453,341	1,470,845	1,152,300	499,480	3,293,821	1,826,147	1,467,673
Infants' furniture	724,218	58,055	131,679	113,276	61,746	359,476	239,861	119,369
Outdoor furniture	1,882,293	69,495	355,406	236,089	208,004	1,013,121	628,179	384,772
Wall units, cabinets, and other furniture	5,934,998	257,491	1,214,198	959,708	733,679	2,769,905	1,524,461	1,245,368
Floor coverings	**4,539,253**	**423,972**	**1,033,619**	**677,796**	**296,673**	**2,106,846**	**1,136,715**	**969,940**
Wall-to-wall carpeting	2,431,623	324,596	701,224	401,700	162,370	842,797	536,967	305,813
Floor coverings, nonpermanent	2,106,509	99,377	332,075	276,329	134,407	1,263,754	599,747	664,127
Major appliances	**21,128,995**	**1,914,278**	**4,513,852**	**4,712,476**	**2,801,349**	**7,163,628**	**4,216,168**	**2,947,955**
Dishwashers (built-in), garbage disposals, range hoods	1,852,024	55,323	263,039	425,658	262,578	846,327	429,536	416,604
Refrigerators and freezers	5,838,585	559,889	1,208,765	1,124,388	853,118	2,092,137	1,238,803	853,464
Washing machines	2,500,008	297,105	602,784	485,901	296,777	817,204	473,615	343,535
Clothes dryers	1,911,441	170,409	450,011	323,081	331,704	635,996	401,676	234,191
Cooking stoves, ovens	3,469,743	320,327	803,500	894,114	377,546	1,074,603	552,615	522,021
Microwave ovens	1,177,134	118,671	240,666	319,825	133,576	364,182	212,192	152,028
Window air conditioners	885,653	156,919	255,368	159,796	135,031	178,855	128,231	50,642
Electric floor-cleaning equipment	2,556,062	175,531	564,751	691,985	262,682	836,914	576,849	260,649
Sewing machines	536,997	37,053	109,626	103,972	97,817	188,269	131,284	57,049
Miscellaneous household appliances	315,023	14,172	7,351	156,772	42,204	96,488	48,468	47,644
Small appliances and misc. housewares	**11,259,006**	**1,200,714**	**2,554,962**	**1,800,557**	**1,339,500**	**4,254,287**	**2,674,533**	**1,579,291**
Housewares	8,693,975	964,055	1,901,680	1,290,232	1,052,182	3,375,895	2,154,358	1,221,287
Plastic dinnerware	176,010	14,002	23,971	50,939	28,170	58,246	33,584	24,804
China and other dinnerware	1,626,687	130,795	185,374	271,212	164,241	832,207	350,346	479,131
Flatware	424,889	33,126	63,283	102,344	47,193	178,855	123,079	55,809
Glassware	729,823	131,819	142,866	102,111	138,461	218,862	140,825	77,823
Silver serving pieces	454,037	40,468	51,777	42,333	66,840	240,337	210,284	30,798
Other serving pieces	161,436	7,342	26,528	25,819	17,775	83,544	40,454	42,994
Nonelectric cookware	2,718,619	453,341	738,299	326,338	318,191	868,978	674,358	196,262
Tableware, nonelectric kitchenware	2,403,596	152,992	669,583	369,136	271,413	894,865	581,429	313,564
Small appliances	2,566,152	236,660	653,283	510,324	287,214	878,097	520,175	358,004
Small electric kitchen appliances	1,926,015	171,775	438,185	403,328	224,116	688,652	401,676	287,106
Portable heating and cooling equipment	639,016	64,885	214,778	106,996	63,098	189,445	118,690	70,898

	total consumer units	less than high school graduate	high school graduate	some college	associate's degree	college graduate total	bachelor's degree	master's, professional, doctorate
Miscellaneous household equipment	**$73,113,474**	**$5,417,385**	**$15,808,550**	**$13,574,536**	**$8,592,507**	**$29,131,067**	**$18,125,229**	**$11,001,091**
Window coverings	1,559,422	74,106	302,031	349,830	100,832	733,072	493,842	239,152
Infants' equipment	1,452,920	148,553	361,479	194,454	149,792	572,749	498,422	76,169
Laundry and cleaning equipment	1,698,436	213,779	446,495	316,569	145,634	560,100	355,879	204,013
Outdoor equipment	3,533,644	187,996	439,783	443,336	600,415	1,773,551	874,719	894,804
Clocks	658,074	154,529	122,091	99,320	25,156	252,104	225,358	27,801
Lamps and lighting fixtures	1,316,148	66,251	200,076	267,955	92,619	689,829	374,007	315,631
Other household decorative items	16,248,934	1,143,342	3,359,740	2,813,762	1,795,840	6,806,211	4,263,300	2,540,653
Telephones and accessories	3,669,295	631,604	813,088	557,775	328,274	1,311,704	806,405	504,761
Lawn and garden equipment	5,399,121	434,900	1,706,717	1,028,557	972,244	1,256,400	758,319	498,250
Power tools	3,729,833	409,117	908,332	398,676	647,609	1,329,648	844,951	484,401
Office furniture for home use	1,184,982	25,271	228,521	253,301	170,790	506,561	358,169	148,411
Hand tools	902,469	68,129	252,492	197,710	125,052	259,752	185,095	74,619
Indoor plants and fresh flowers	5,580,736	345,427	1,174,886	1,076,240	523,596	2,460,732	1,437,447	1,023,165
Closet and storage items	1,118,838	66,593	155,650	252,371	147,921	477,732	292,336	185,100
Rental of furniture	515,697	146,162	158,846	116,998	18,087	75,308	31,294	44,027
Luggage	670,406	20,149	108,987	98,390	103,118	340,355	203,414	136,835
Computers and computer hardware, nonbusiness use	15,535,927	732,518	3,120,352	3,371,537	1,656,755	6,655,008	4,145,946	2,509,131
Computer software and accessories, nonbusiness use	1,980,948	73,423	322,167	410,306	225,675	949,581	620,737	328,963
Telephone answering devices	121,077	6,659	38,673	19,073	12,994	44,126	25,188	18,706
Calculators	161,436	9,050	28,126	42,798	20,998	60,305	47,705	12,505
Business equipment for home use	108,745	10,587	26,847	20,236	10,707	40,301	20,036	20,463
Other hardware	1,440,588	84,180	318,012	354,482	274,428	407,720	308,556	99,939
Smoke alarms	167,041	46,786	13,424	53,033	19,751	34,712	23,280	11,058
Other household appliances	1,034,757	63,178	338,467	131,419	71,206	430,959	262,568	168,254
Miscellaneous household equipment and parts	3,320,639	255,101	862,947	706,174	353,118	1,103,138	668,061	434,380

Note: Numbers may not add to total because of rounding and because not all categories are shown.
Source: Calculations by New Strategist based on the 2002 Consumer Expenditure Survey

Table 8.24 Housing: Household Operations: Market shares by education, 2002

(percentage of total annual spending on household services, supplies, furnishings, and equipment accounted for by consumer unit educational attainment groups, 2002)

	total consumer units	less than high school graduate	high school graduate	some college	associate's degree	college graduate total	bachelor's degree	master's, professional, doctorate
Share of total consumer units	100.0%	15.2%	28.5%	20.7%	9.3%	26.2%	17.0%	9.2%
Share of total before-tax income	100.0	7.9	22.8	17.9	10.3	41.3	23.9	17.3
Share of total spending	100.0	9.3	23.6	19.7	10.1	37.0	22.5	14.5
Share of housing spending	100.0	9.5	23.2	19.3	10.2	37.8	22.8	15.0
HOUSEHOLD SERVICES	**100.0%**	**5.6%**	**17.2%**	**21.0%**	**10.4%**	**45.8%**	**26.2%**	**19.6%**
Personal services	**100.0**	**5.8**	**16.8**	**23.3**	**11.0**	**43.1**	**25.6**	**17.5**
Babysitting and child care in your own home	100.0	8.9	9.3	13.5	10.2	58.2	36.7	21.4
Babysitting and child care in someone else's home	100.0	11.5	22.1	23.0	12.5	31.1	18.5	12.5
Day care centers, nurseries, and preschools	100.0	3.2	17.5	20.6	13.1	45.6	26.2	19.3
Other household services	**100.0**	**5.4**	**17.6**	**18.9**	**9.9**	**48.2**	**26.8**	**21.4**
Housekeeping services	100.0	3.4	10.7	14.1	9.2	62.6	29.2	33.4
Gardening, lawn care service	100.0	5.8	16.9	18.9	8.6	49.9	27.4	22.5
Water softening service	100.0	7.3	28.1	21.1	16.3	27.4	18.5	8.9
Nonclothing laundry and dry cleaning, sent out	100.0	6.6	14.6	18.3	5.6	54.8	35.3	19.5
Nonclothing laundry and dry cleaning, coin-operated	100.0	22.2	27.7	21.3	5.8	23.2	17.4	5.8
Termite/pest control services	100.0	9.5	13.4	21.8	11.1	44.2	29.4	14.8
Home security system service fee	100.0	6.9	22.2	16.6	9.1	45.3	27.1	18.1
Other home services	100.0	5.8	17.9	15.5	8.6	52.3	33.1	19.2
Termite/pest control products	100.0	11.9	11.7	18.3	11.9	46.7	20.0	26.7
Moving, storage, and freight express	100.0	4.8	18.2	28.0	7.5	41.5	20.4	21.2
Appliance repair, including service center	100.0	8.6	20.9	20.6	11.1	38.8	23.2	15.6
Reupholstering and furniture repair	100.0	5.1	10.8	9.3	5.5	69.4	36.8	32.6
Repairs/rentals of lawn/garden equipment, hand/power tools, etc.	100.0	7.0	29.4	12.4	18.6	32.6	20.1	12.6
Appliance rental	100.0	19.1	36.0	17.8	10.0	17.2	9.1	8.1
Repair of computer systems for nonbusiness use	100.0	6.9	19.0	11.9	19.0	43.4	24.0	19.4
Computer information services	100.0	4.9	21.7	20.8	11.7	41.0	26.2	14.8
HOUSEKEEPING SUPPLIES	**100.0**	**11.2**	**23.0**	**17.7**	**16.2**	**31.4**	**19.5**	**12.0**
Laundry and cleaning supplies	**100.0**	**15.2**	**27.9**	**20.1**	**9.5**	**27.3**	**17.9**	**9.4**
Soaps and detergents	100.0	15.1	28.5	20.7	8.8	26.8	18.2	8.7
Other laundry cleaning products	100.0	15.3	27.2	19.3	10.3	27.8	17.4	10.4
Other household products	**100.0**	**11.0**	**21.2**	**15.6**	**22.3**	**30.0**	**18.6**	**11.4**
Cleansing and toilet tissue, paper towels, and napkins	100.0	15.8	26.3	19.6	9.2	29.0	18.5	10.4
Miscellaneous household products	100.0	13.2	22.7	16.4	10.5	36.1	21.7	14.4
Lawn and garden supplies	100.0	5.7	16.3	12.1	41.8	25.4	15.9	9.5
Postage and stationery	**100.0**	**7.7**	**22.1**	**19.9**	**10.0**	**38.6**	**23.0**	**15.6**
Stationery, stationery supplies, giftwrap	100.0	6.6	21.1	19.8	9.2	41.3	26.5	14.8
Postage	100.0	8.8	23.4	20.2	10.2	36.1	20.1	15.9
Delivery services	100.0	4.7	10.1	13.0	25.4	45.2	15.4	29.6

	total consumer units	less than high school graduate	high school graduate	some college	associate's degree	college graduate total	bachelor's degree	master's, professional, doctorate
HOUSEHOLD FURNISHINGS AND EQUIPMENT	100.0%	8.2%	21.7%	18.5%	11.1%	40.0%	24.2%	15.8%
Household textiles	100.0	9.4	21.8	21.3	8.7	37.9	22.6	15.3
Bathroom linens	100.0	10.4	21.6	28.5	9.1	30.0	19.0	10.9
Bedroom linens	100.0	12.0	24.6	20.3	7.5	34.5	19.8	14.6
Kitchen and dining room linens	100.0	7.1	20.7	12.0	10.0	47.4	29.7	17.7
Curtains and draperies	100.0	5.3	18.1	15.9	9.6	51.1	24.2	26.9
Slipcovers and decorative pillows	100.0	2.3	8.9	40.1	7.7	39.6	35.1	4.7
Sewing materials for household items	100.0	5.9	20.2	17.9	12.5	43.5	29.0	14.6
Other linens	100.0	4.9	25.6	15.1	9.2	45.2	22.1	23.2
Furniture	100.0	8.0	21.6	16.6	10.0	43.8	25.9	17.8
Mattresses and springs	100.0	9.0	25.9	17.0	9.8	38.4	23.9	14.5
Other bedroom furniture	100.0	8.3	22.2	15.4	8.8	45.2	28.1	17.1
Sofas	100.0	10.9	23.1	16.2	11.3	38.4	22.9	15.5
Living room chairs	100.0	8.7	18.5	19.8	10.5	42.5	25.0	17.5
Living room tables	100.0	8.3	14.0	19.9	10.0	47.9	28.8	19.1
Kitchen and dining room furniture	100.0	6.6	21.4	16.8	7.3	47.9	26.6	21.4
Infants' furniture	100.0	8.0	18.2	15.6	8.5	49.6	33.1	16.5
Outdoor furniture	100.0	3.7	18.9	12.5	11.1	53.8	33.4	20.4
Wall units, cabinets, and other furniture	100.0	4.3	20.5	16.2	12.4	46.7	25.7	21.0
Floor coverings	100.0	9.3	22.8	14.9	6.5	46.4	25.0	21.4
Wall-to-wall carpeting	100.0	13.3	28.8	16.5	6.7	34.7	22.1	12.6
Floor coverings, nonpermanent	100.0	4.7	15.8	13.1	6.4	60.0	28.5	31.5
Major appliances	100.0	9.1	21.4	22.3	13.3	33.9	20.0	14.0
Dishwashers (built-in), garbage disposals, range hoods	100.0	3.0	14.2	23.0	14.2	45.7	23.2	22.5
Refrigerators and freezers	100.0	9.6	20.7	19.3	14.6	35.8	21.2	14.6
Washing machines	100.0	11.9	24.1	19.4	11.9	32.7	18.9	13.7
Clothes dryers	100.0	8.9	23.5	16.9	17.4	33.3	21.0	12.3
Cooking stoves, ovens	100.0	9.2	23.2	25.8	10.9	31.0	15.9	15.0
Microwave ovens	100.0	10.1	20.4	27.2	11.3	30.9	18.0	12.9
Window air conditioners	100.0	17.7	28.8	18.0	15.2	20.2	14.5	5.7
Electric floor-cleaning equipment	100.0	6.9	22.1	27.1	10.3	32.7	22.6	10.2
Sewing machines	100.0	6.9	20.4	19.4	18.2	35.1	24.4	10.6
Miscellaneous household appliances	100.0	4.5	2.3	49.8	13.4	30.6	15.4	15.1
Small appliances and misc. housewares	100.0	10.7	22.7	16.0	11.9	37.8	23.8	14.0
Housewares	100.0	11.1	21.9	14.8	12.1	38.8	24.8	14.0
Plastic dinnerware	100.0	8.0	13.6	28.9	16.0	33.1	19.1	14.1
China and other dinnerware	100.0	8.0	11.4	16.7	10.1	51.2	21.5	29.5
Flatware	100.0	7.8	14.9	24.1	11.1	42.1	29.0	13.1
Glassware	100.0	18.1	19.6	14.0	19.0	30.0	19.3	10.7
Silver serving pieces	100.0	8.9	11.4	9.3	14.7	52.9	46.3	6.8
Other serving pieces	100.0	4.5	16.4	16.0	11.0	51.8	25.1	26.6
Nonelectric cookware	100.0	16.7	27.2	12.0	11.7	32.0	24.8	7.2
Tableware, nonelectric kitchenware	100.0	6.4	27.9	15.4	11.3	37.2	24.2	13.0
Small appliances	100.0	9.2	25.5	19.9	11.2	34.2	20.3	14.0
Small electric kitchen appliances	100.0	8.9	22.8	20.9	11.6	35.8	20.9	14.9
Portable heating and cooling equipment	100.0	10.2	33.6	16.7	9.9	29.6	18.6	11.1

Miscellaneous household equipment	total consumer units	less than high school graduate	high school graduate	some college	associate's degree	college graduate total	bachelor's degree	master's, professional, doctorate
	100.0%	7.4%	21.6%	18.6%	11.8%	39.8%	24.8%	15.0%
Window coverings	100.0	4.8	19.4	22.4	6.5	47.0	31.7	15.3
Infants' equipment	100.0	10.2	24.9	13.4	10.3	39.4	34.3	5.2
Laundry and cleaning equipment	100.0	12.6	26.3	18.6	8.6	33.0	21.0	12.0
Outdoor equipment	100.0	5.3	12.4	12.5	17.0	50.2	24.8	25.3
Clocks	100.0	23.5	18.6	15.1	3.8	38.3	34.2	4.2
Lamps and lighting fixtures	100.0	5.0	15.2	20.4	7.0	52.4	28.4	24.0
Other household decorative items	100.0	7.0	20.7	17.3	11.1	41.9	26.2	15.6
Telephones and accessories	100.0	17.2	22.2	15.2	8.9	35.7	22.0	13.8
Lawn and garden equipment	100.0	8.1	31.6	19.1	18.0	23.3	14.0	9.2
Power tools	100.0	11.0	24.4	10.7	17.4	35.6	22.7	13.0
Office furniture for home use	100.0	2.1	19.3	21.4	14.4	42.7	30.2	12.5
Hand tools	100.0	7.5	28.0	21.9	13.9	28.8	20.5	8.3
Indoor plants and fresh flowers	100.0	6.2	21.1	19.3	9.4	44.1	25.8	18.3
Closet and storage items	100.0	6.0	13.9	22.6	13.2	42.7	26.1	16.5
Rental of furniture	100.0	28.3	30.8	22.7	3.5	14.6	6.1	8.5
Luggage	100.0	3.0	16.3	14.7	15.4	50.8	30.3	20.4
Computers and computer hardware, nonbusiness use	100.0	4.7	20.1	21.7	10.7	42.8	26.7	16.2
Computer software and accessories, nonbusiness use	100.0	3.7	16.3	20.7	11.4	47.9	31.3	16.6
Telephone answering devices	100.0	5.5	31.9	15.8	10.7	36.4	20.8	15.5
Calculators	100.0	5.6	17.4	26.5	13.0	37.4	29.6	7.7
Business equipment for home use	100.0	9.7	24.7	18.6	9.8	37.1	18.4	18.8
Other hardware	100.0	5.8	22.1	24.6	19.0	28.3	21.4	6.9
Smoke alarms	100.0	28.0	8.0	31.7	11.8	20.8	13.9	6.6
Other household appliances	100.0	6.1	32.7	12.7	6.9	41.6	25.4	16.3
Miscellaneous household equipment and parts	100.0	7.7	26.0	21.3	10.6	33.2	20.1	13.1

Note: Numbers may not add to total because of rounding.
Source: Calculations by New Strategist based on the 2002 Consumer Expenditure Survey

Spending on Shelter and Utilities, 2002

Housing is by far Americans' biggest expense. In 2002, housing costs—including shelter, utilities, and all household operations (household services, housekeeping supplies, furniture, and equipment)—absorbed 32.7 percent of the expenditures of the average household. That figure was up from 32.4 percent in 1997, despite the drop in interest rates. Spending on shelter rose 10 percent between 1997 and 2002, after adjusting for inflation. Spending on owned homes rose 17 percent while spending on rented homes fell 3 percent. Spending on other lodging, such as hotels and motels, rose 6 percent. Spending on utilities and fuels was down by 0.4 percent, thanks to falling energy prices during those years.

Housing costs are highest for householders aged 35 to 44, at $16,350 in 2002. This age group spends the most on owned homes—$7,105 in 2002. Close behind are householders aged 45 to 54, spending $6,787, most of it mortgage interest charges. Spending on maintenance and repair services for owned homes is greatest among householders aged 55 to 64, who also spend the most on owned vacation homes.

Households with incomes of $70,000 or more spent $23,695 on housing in 2002, versus the $13,481 spent by the average income-reporting household. The most affluent households account for a large share of the market in a number of shelter categories: 54 percent of the market for painting and wallpapering owned homes, 51 percent of the market for landscape maintenance of owned homes, 60 percent of the market for owned vacations homes, and 55 percent of the market for lodging on trips.

Among household types, married couples with preschoolers spend the most on housing, $19,141 in 2002. Behind this figure is the high cost of housing for recent homebuyers, and many married couples with young children are new homeowners. This household type spends more than twice the average on mortgage interest. Married couples without children at home (most of them empty nesters) spend more than twice the average on owned vacation homes and 68 percent more than average on lodging while on trips.

Black and Hispanic householders spend less than average on housing, but they spend more on some shelter categories. Blacks spend 31 percent more than the average household on rent, while Hispanics spend 70 percent more. Blacks spend 17 percent more than average on residential telephone service, while Hispanics spend nearly three times the average on phone cards.

Households in the West spend the most on housing, $15,297 in 2002, because of the high cost of housing in California and other Western states. Housing costs are lowest in the South, at $11,766. Western households spend 40 percent more than the average household on mortgage interest. Households in the Northeast spend 24 percent more than average on lodging on trips, while households in the South spend 23 percent more than average on electricity.

Not surprisingly, college graduates (who dominate the nation's affluent households) spend the most on housing, an average of $19,111 in 2002. They spend far more than the average household on almost every shelter category. They spend 72 percent more than average on mortgage interest, more than twice the average on lodging on trips, and more than double the average on owned vacation homes.

Table 9.1 Housing: Shelter and Utilities: Average spending by age, 2002

(average annual spending of consumer units (CU) on shelter and utilities, by age of consumer unit reference person, 2002)

	total consumer units	under 25	25 to 34	35 to 44	45 to 54	55 to 64	65 to 74	75+
Number of consumer units (in thousands, add 000)	112,108	8,737	18,988	24,394	22,691	15,314	11,216	10,767
Average number of persons per CU	2.5	1.9	2.9	3.2	2.7	2.1	1.9	1.5
Average before-tax income of CU	$49,430.00	$20,773.00	$49,133.00	$61,532.00	$64,974.00	$53,162.00	$35,118.00	$23,890.00
Average spending of CU, total	40,676.60	24,229.46	40,318.29	48,330.48	48,748.24	44,330.04	32,242.52	23,758.89
Housing, average spending	13,283.08	7,436.31	13,727.04	16,349.51	15,475.55	13,831.08	10,052.07	8,257.08
SHELTER	$7,829.41	$4,851.44	$8,470.23	$9,902.03	$9,223.01	$7,667.42	$5,298.58	$4,349.62
Owned dwellings*	5,164.96	830.26	4,700.64	7,105.47	6,786.54	5,594.55	3,848.81	2,447.13
Mortgage interest and charges	2,962.16	443.10	3,285.94	4,608.18	4,061.06	2,711.96	1,366.37	408.21
Mortgage interest	2,811.49	418.60	3,183.16	4,428.51	3,828.96	2,502.25	1,230.57	376.51
Interest paid, home equity loan	88.61	22.25	73.32	116.04	122.42	102.17	89.04	16.30
Interest paid, home equity line of credit	61.88	2.25	28.52	63.52	109.67	107.54	46.77	15.40
Property taxes	1,242.36	280.75	822.52	1,473.22	1,556.57	1,539.97	1,299.27	1,095.27
Maintenance, repairs, insurance, other expenses	960.43	106.41	592.18	1,024.08	1,168.90	1,342.62	1,183.16	943.64
Homeowner's insurance	283.30	33.42	190.44	294.53	352.13	371.89	356.77	276.85
Ground rent	40.96	11.36	35.33	34.19	39.20	53.42	49.56	67.29
Maintenance and repair services	519.60	43.43	280.39	546.76	632.32	784.35	638.00	528.82
Painting and papering	55.58	10.89	30.20	62.32	59.08	98.33	68.14	40.04
Plumbing and water heating	46.63	5.76	26.13	46.63	47.59	59.19	65.92	75.94
Heat, air conditioning, electrical work	86.28	4.02	53.27	78.51	126.76	104.76	123.49	78.46
Roofing and gutters	71.20	2.46	23.70	77.93	86.86	76.58	87.97	137.36
Other repair and maintenance services	214.77	18.56	108.09	240.95	249.76	377.28	243.09	168.39
Repair, replacement of hard-surface flooring	43.54	1.67	36.95	38.92	60.60	66.88	46.69	27.15
Repair of built-in appliances	1.62	0.08	2.05	1.50	1.69	1.32	2.71	1.48
Maintenance and repair materials	83.75	12.58	66.07	119.20	107.31	93.26	88.86	23.81
Paints, wallpaper, and supplies	14.71	2.85	13.70	21.82	19.25	16.89	9.03	3.24
Tools, equip. for painting, wallpapering	1.58	0.31	1.47	2.34	2.07	1.81	0.97	0.35
Plumbing supplies and equipment	5.62	0.22	5.42	6.25	6.43	8.47	5.80	3.03
Electrical supplies, heating, cooling equip.	3.46	0.16	2.41	2.67	4.24	4.69	8.04	1.62
Hard-surface flooring, repair, replacement	8.72	0.95	7.98	14.56	8.96	7.08	11.09	2.42
Roofing and gutters	5.29	0.67	5.32	7.32	8.76	3.54	4.80	0.04
Plaster, paneling, siding, windows, doors, screens, awnings	13.92	0.94	9.08	14.42	20.01	21.79	16.00	5.62
Patio, walk, fence, driveway, masonry, brick, and stucco materials	1.29	0.15	0.72	2.25	1.60	1.03	1.03	1.09
Landscape maintenance	4.73	0.05	4.37	7.43	7.14	4.67	2.12	0.77
Miscellaneous supplies and equipment	24.43	6.29	15.60	40.15	28.86	23.28	29.97	5.63
Insulation, other maintenance, repair	13.15	2.91	7.20	23.35	11.37	15.59	17.62	4.47
Finish basement, remodel rooms, build patios, walks, etc.	11.28	3.39	8.40	16.80	17.49	7.69	12.36	1.16
Property management and security	27.64	4.00	16.31	25.23	33.28	32.37	41.25	39.51
Property management	21.94	3.69	13.61	19.45	27.33	25.69	30.31	31.64
Management, upkeep services for security	5.71	0.31	2.70	5.78	5.96	6.68	10.94	7.87
Parking	5.17	1.61	3.63	4.17	4.65	7.33	8.72	7.36

	total consumer units	under 25	25 to 34	35 to 44	45 to 54	55 to 64	65 to 74	75+
Rented dwellings	**$2,159.89**	**$3,644.35**	**$3,476.20**	**$2,350.84**	**$1,732.87**	**$1,302.95**	**$905.16**	**$1,627.19**
Rent	2,104.66	3,568.54	3,397.78	2,297.90	1,678.66	1,259.94	868.94	1,585.05
Rent as pay	27.17	47.52	35.72	28.25	25.28	18.85	18.40	18.06
Maintenance, insurance, other expenses	28.06	28.28	42.70	24.69	28.93	24.16	17.82	24.08
Tenant's insurance	8.90	5.26	14.01	9.40	8.93	7.19	4.53	8.65
Maintenance and repair services	11.16	7.14	11.41	7.42	14.09	13.26	9.81	14.66
Maintenance and repair materials	8.00	15.88	17.28	7.87	5.91	3.71	3.49	0.77
Other lodging	**504.56**	**376.84**	**293.39**	**445.72**	**703.60**	**769.91**	**544.61**	**275.31**
Owned vacation homes	171.55	26.58	87.80	137.67	237.53	314.87	189.38	152.16
Mortgage interest and charges	71.98	10.48	56.75	76.82	105.10	130.28	37.86	20.65
Property taxes	63.76	9.42	22.33	38.58	85.18	106.67	95.78	98.40
Maintenance, insurance, and other expenses	35.81	6.68	8.72	22.28	47.25	77.91	55.74	33.10
Homeowner's insurance	9.70	1.96	4.96	9.65	11.38	10.07	21.20	8.38
Ground rent	2.93	–	2.06	0.62	0.34	6.04	6.91	8.97
Maintenance and repair services	16.76	1.12	0.61	8.37	29.53	42.46	17.95	12.24
Maintenance and repair materials	2.07	–	–	2.16	0.33	8.20	3.59	0.55
Property management and security	3.60	3.35	0.85	1.07	4.36	9.96	4.48	2.77
Property management	2.50	2.88	0.64	0.95	2.91	6.16	3.38	1.97
Management, upkeep services for security	1.10	0.48	0.21	0.12	1.45	3.80	1.10	0.80
Parking	0.76	0.25	0.24	0.41	1.31	1.18	1.62	0.19
Housing while attending school	80.14	257.06	15.66	31.81	174.86	87.50	24.11	8.03
Lodging on trips	252.87	93.20	189.92	276.23	291.21	367.54	331.13	115.12
UTILITIES, FUELS, AND PUBLIC SERVICES	**2,684.32**	**1,348.26**	**2,502.59**	**3,025.84**	**3,106.18**	**2,953.22**	**2,589.82**	**2,142.10**
Natural gas	**329.75**	**107.80**	**288.10**	**369.38**	**382.69**	**355.25**	**336.22**	**338.90**
Electricity	**981.09**	**470.64**	**864.22**	**1,105.26**	**1,137.50**	**1,112.11**	**985.47**	**799.47**
Fuel oil and other fuels	**88.41**	**21.36**	**54.58**	**86.14**	**89.90**	**126.56**	**114.63**	**122.92**
Fuel oil	45.98	7.58	23.88	47.75	47.08	65.68	59.43	67.75
Coal	0.07	–	–	0.09	0.08	0.21	–	–
Bottled/tank gas	35.27	11.60	26.15	32.60	36.03	51.67	42.90	43.79
Wood and other fuels	7.09	2.18	4.55	5.70	6.72	8.99	12.30	11.38
Telephone services	**956.74**	**640.94**	**1,032.44**	**1,095.80**	**1,108.93**	**980.99**	**793.94**	**578.81**
Residential telephone and pay phones	641.00	345.92	641.89	712.52	722.88	696.51	612.94	494.50
Cellular phone service	293.76	258.73	360.03	358.45	364.57	265.65	170.48	77.89
Pager service	1.71	0.30	2.03	1.62	2.44	2.73	1.05	0.18
Phone cards	20.28	35.99	28.49	23.21	19.04	16.09	9.47	6.25
Water and other public services	**328.33**	**107.52**	**263.26**	**369.25**	**387.16**	**378.30**	**359.55**	**301.99**
Water and sewerage maintenance	237.16	78.73	190.31	272.73	282.76	267.38	253.23	211.88
Trash and garbage collection	89.05	28.36	71.73	94.56	101.12	108.02	104.09	88.28
Septic tank cleaning	2.12	0.43	1.22	1.96	3.28	2.90	2.23	1.83

See appendix for information about mortgage principle reduction.
Note: (–) means sample is too small to make a reliable estimate.
Source: Bureau of Labor Statistics, unpublished tables from the 2002 Consumer Expenditure Survey

Table 9.2 Housing: Shelter and Utilities: Indexed spending by age, 2002

(indexed average annual spending of consumer units (CU) on shelter and utilities, by age of consumer unit reference person, 2002; index definition: an index of 100 is the average for all consumer units; an index of 132 means that spending by consumer units in that group is 32 percent above the average for all consumer units; an index of 68 indicates spending that is 32 percent below the average for all consumer units)

	total consumer units	under 25	25 to 34	35 to 44	45 to 54	55 to 64	65 to 74	75+
Average spending of CU, total	$40,677	$24,229	$40,318	$48,330	$48,748	$44,330	$32,243	$23,759
Average spending of CU, index	100	60	99	119	120	109	79	58
Housing, spending index	100	56	103	123	117	104	76	62
SHELTER	**100**	**62**	**108**	**126**	**118**	**98**	**68**	**56**
Owned dwellings*	**100**	**16**	**91**	**138**	**131**	**108**	**75**	**47**
Mortgage interest and charges	100	15	111	156	137	92	46	14
Mortgage interest	100	15	113	158	136	89	44	13
Interest paid, home equity loan	100	25	83	131	138	115	100	18
Interest paid, home equity line of credit	100	4	46	103	177	174	76	25
Property taxes	100	23	66	119	125	124	105	88
Maintenance, repairs, insurance, other expenses	100	11	62	107	122	140	123	98
Homeowner's insurance	100	12	67	104	124	131	126	98
Ground rent	100	28	86	83	96	130	121	164
Maintenance and repair services	100	8	54	105	122	151	123	102
Painting and papering	100	20	54	112	106	177	123	72
Plumbing and water heating	100	12	56	100	102	127	141	163
Heat, air conditioning, electrical work	100	5	62	91	147	121	143	91
Roofing and gutters	100	3	33	109	122	108	124	193
Other repair and maintenance services	100	9	50	112	116	176	113	78
Repair, replacement of hard-surface flooring	100	4	85	89	139	154	107	62
Repair of built-in appliances	100	5	127	93	104	81	167	91
Maintenance and repair materials	100	15	79	142	128	111	106	28
Paints, wallpaper, and supplies	100	19	93	148	131	115	61	22
Tools, equip. for painting, wallpapering	100	20	93	148	131	115	61	22
Plumbing supplies and equipment	100	4	96	111	114	151	103	54
Electrical supplies, heating, cooling equip.	100	5	70	77	123	136	232	47
Hard-surface flooring, repair, replacement	100	11	92	167	103	81	127	28
Roofing and gutters	100	13	101	138	166	67	91	1
Plaster, paneling, siding, windows, doors, screens, awnings	100	7	65	104	144	157	115	40
Patio, walk, fence, driveway, masonry, brick, and stucco materials	100	12	56	174	124	80	80	84
Landscape maintenance	100	1	92	157	151	99	45	16
Miscellaneous supplies and equipment	100	26	64	164	118	95	123	23
Insulation, other maintenance, repair	100	22	55	178	86	119	134	34
Finish basement, remodel rooms, build patios, walks, etc.	100	30	74	149	155	68	110	10
Property management and security	100	14	59	91	120	117	149	143
Property management	100	17	62	89	125	117	138	144
Management, upkeep services for security	100	5	47	101	104	117	192	138
Parking	100	31	70	81	90	142	169	142

	total consumer units	under 25	25 to 34	35 to 44	45 to 54	55 to 64	65 to 74	75+
Rented dwellings	**100**	**169**	**161**	**109**	**80**	**60**	**42**	**75**
Rent	100	170	161	109	80	60	41	75
Rent as pay	100	175	131	104	93	69	68	66
Maintenance, insurance, other expenses	100	101	152	88	103	86	64	86
Tenant's insurance	100	59	157	106	100	81	51	97
Maintenance and repair services	100	64	102	66	126	119	88	131
Maintenance and repair materials	100	199	216	98	74	46	44	10
Other lodging	**100**	**75**	**58**	**88**	**139**	**153**	**108**	**55**
Owned vacation homes	100	15	51	80	138	184	110	89
Mortgage interest and charges	100	15	79	107	146	181	53	29
Property taxes	100	15	35	61	134	167	150	154
Maintenance, insurance, and other expenses	100	19	24	62	132	218	156	92
Homeowner's insurance	100	20	51	99	117	104	219	86
Ground rent	100	–	70	21	12	206	236	306
Maintenance and repair services	100	7	4	50	176	253	107	73
Maintenance and repair materials	100	–	–	104	16	396	173	27
Property management and security	100	93	24	30	121	277	124	77
Property management	100	115	26	38	116	246	135	79
Management, upkeep services for security	100	44	19	11	132	345	100	73
Parking	100	33	32	54	172	155	213	25
Housing while attending school	100	321	20	40	218	109	30	10
Lodging on trips	100	37	75	109	115	145	131	46
UTILITIES, FUELS, AND PUBLIC SERVICES	**100**	**50**	**93**	**113**	**116**	**110**	**96**	**80**
Natural gas	**100**	**33**	**87**	**112**	**116**	**108**	**102**	**103**
Electricity	**100**	**48**	**88**	**113**	**116**	**113**	**100**	**81**
Fuel oil and other fuels	**100**	**24**	**62**	**97**	**102**	**143**	**130**	**139**
Fuel oil	100	16	52	104	102	143	129	147
Coal	100	–	–	129	114	300	–	–
Bottled/tank gas	100	33	74	92	102	146	122	124
Wood and other fuels	100	31	64	80	95	127	173	161
Telephone services	**100**	**67**	**108**	**115**	**116**	**103**	**83**	**60**
Residential telephone and pay phones	100	54	100	111	113	109	96	77
Cellular phone service	100	88	123	122	124	90	58	27
Pager service	100	18	119	95	143	160	61	11
Phone cards	100	177	140	114	94	79	47	31
Water and other public services	**100**	**33**	**80**	**112**	**118**	**115**	**110**	**92**
Water and sewerage maintenance	100	33	80	115	119	113	107	89
Trash and garbage collection	100	32	81	106	114	121	117	99
Septic tank cleaning	100	20	58	92	155	137	105	86

See appendix for information about mortgage principle reduction.
Note: (–) means sample is too small to make a reliable estimate.
Source: Calculations by New Strategist based on the 2002 Consumer Expenditure Survey

Table 9.3 Housing: Shelter and Utilities: Total spending by age, 2002

(total annual spending on shelter and utilities, by consumer unit (CU) age groups, 2002; numbers in thousands)

	total consumer units	under 25	25 to 34	35 to 44	45 to 54	55 to 64	65 to 74	75+
Number of consumer units	112,108	8,737	18,988	24,394	22,691	15,314	11,216	10,767
Total spending of all CUs	$4,560,172,273	$211,692,792	$765,563,691	$1,178,973,729	$1,106,146,314	$678,870,233	$361,632,104	$255,811,969
Housing, total spending	1,489,139,533	64,971,040	260,649,036	398,829,947	351,155,705	211,809,159	112,744,017	88,903,980
SHELTER	$877,739,496	$42,387,031	$160,832,727	$241,550,120	$209,279,320	$117,418,870	$59,428,873	$46,832,359
Owned dwellings*	579,033,336	7,253,982	89,255,752	173,330,835	153,993,379	85,674,939	43,168,253	26,348,249
Mortgage interest and charges	332,081,833	3,871,365	62,393,429	112,411,943	92,149,512	41,530,955	15,325,206	4,395,197
Mortgage interest	315,190,521	3,657,308	60,441,842	108,029,073	86,882,931	38,319,457	13,802,073	4,053,883
Interest paid, home equity loan	9,933,890	194,398	1,392,200	2,830,680	2,777,832	1,564,631	998,673	175,502
Interest paid, home equity line of credit	6,937,243	19,658	541,538	1,549,507	2,488,522	1,646,868	524,572	165,812
Property taxes	139,278,495	2,452,913	15,618,010	35,937,729	35,320,130	23,583,101	14,572,612	11,792,772
Maintenance, repairs, insurance, other expenses	107,671,886	929,704	11,244,314	24,981,408	26,523,510	20,560,883	13,270,323	10,160,172
Homeowner's insurance	31,760,196	291,991	3,616,075	7,184,765	7,990,182	5,695,123	4,001,532	2,980,844
Ground rent	4,591,944	99,252	670,846	834,031	889,487	818,074	555,865	724,511
Maintenance and repair services	58,251,317	379,448	5,324,045	13,337,663	14,347,973	12,011,536	7,155,808	5,693,805
Painting and papering	6,230,963	95,146	573,438	1,520,234	1,340,584	1,505,826	764,258	431,111
Plumbing and water heating	5,227,596	50,325	496,156	1,137,492	1,079,865	906,436	739,359	817,646
Heat, air conditioning, electrical work	9,672,678	35,123	1,011,491	1,915,173	2,876,311	1,604,295	1,385,064	844,779
Roofing and gutters	7,982,090	21,493	450,016	1,901,024	1,970,940	1,172,746	986,672	1,478,955
Other repair and maintenance services	24,077,435	162,159	2,052,413	5,877,734	5,667,304	5,777,666	2,726,497	1,813,055
Repair, replacement of hard-surface flooring	4,881,182	14,591	701,607	949,414	1,375,075	1,024,200	523,675	292,324
Repair of built-in appliances	181,615	699	38,925	36,591	38,348	20,214	30,395	15,935
Maintenance and repair materials	9,389,045	109,911	1,254,537	2,907,765	2,434,971	1,428,184	996,654	256,362
Paints, wallpaper, and supplies	1,649,109	24,900	260,136	532,277	436,802	258,653	101,280	34,885
Tools, equip. for painting, wallpapering	177,131	2,708	27,912	57,082	46,970	27,718	10,880	3,768
Plumbing supplies and equipment	630,047	1,922	102,915	152,463	145,903	129,710	65,053	32,624
Electrical supplies, heating, cooling equip.	387,894	1,398	45,761	65,132	96,210	71,823	90,177	17,443
Hard-surface flooring, repair, replacement	977,582	8,300	151,524	355,177	203,311	108,423	124,385	26,056
Roofing and gutters	593,051	5,854	101,016	178,564	198,773	54,212	53,837	431
Plaster, paneling, siding, windows, doors, screens, awnings	1,560,543	8,213	172,411	351,761	454,047	333,692	179,456	60,511
Patio, walk, fence, driveway, masonry, brick, and stucco materials	144,619	1,311	13,671	54,887	36,306	15,773	11,552	11,736
Landscape maintenance	530,271	437	82,978	181,247	162,014	71,516	23,778	8,291
Miscellaneous supplies and equipment	2,738,798	54,956	296,213	979,419	654,862	356,510	336,144	60,618
Insulation, other maintenance, repair	1,474,220	25,425	136,714	569,600	257,997	238,745	197,626	48,128
Finish basement, remodel rooms, build patios, walks, etc.	1,264,578	29,618	159,499	409,819	396,866	117,765	138,630	12,490
Property management and security	3,098,665	34,948	309,694	615,461	755,156	495,714	462,660	425,404
Property management	2,459,650	32,240	258,427	474,463	620,145	393,417	339,957	340,668
Management, upkeep services for security	640,137	2,708	51,268	140,997	135,238	102,298	122,703	84,736
Parking	579,598	14,067	68,926	101,723	105,513	112,252	97,804	79,245

	total consumer units	under 25	25 to 34	35 to 44	45 to 54	55 to 64	65 to 74	75+
Rented dwellings	**$242,140,948**	**$31,840,686**	**$66,006,086**	**$57,346,391**	**$39,320,553**	**$19,953,376**	**$10,152,275**	**$17,519,955**
Rent	235,949,223	31,178,334	64,517,047	56,054,973	38,090,474	19,294,721	9,746,031	17,066,233
Rent as pay	3,045,974	415,182	678,251	689,131	573,628	288,669	206,374	194,452
Maintenance, insurance, other expenses	3,145,750	247,082	810,788	602,288	656,451	369,986	199,869	259,269
Tenant's insurance	997,761	45,957	266,022	229,304	202,631	110,108	50,808	93,135
Maintenance and repair services	1,251,125	62,382	216,653	181,003	319,716	203,064	110,029	157,844
Maintenance and repair materials	896,864	138,744	328,113	191,981	134,104	56,815	39,144	8,291
Other lodging	**56,565,212**	**3,292,451**	**5,570,889**	**10,872,894**	**15,965,388**	**11,790,402**	**6,108,346**	**2,964,263**
Owned vacation homes	19,232,127	232,229	1,667,146	3,358,322	5,389,793	4,821,919	2,124,086	1,638,307
Mortgage interest and charges	8,069,534	91,564	1,077,569	1,873,947	2,384,824	1,995,108	424,638	222,339
Property taxes	7,148,006	82,303	424,002	941,121	1,932,819	1,633,544	1,074,268	1,059,473
Maintenance, insurance, and other expenses	4,014,587	58,363	165,575	543,498	1,072,150	1,193,114	625,180	356,388
Homeowner's insurance	1,087,448	17,125	94,180	235,402	258,224	154,212	237,779	90,227
Ground rent	328,476	–	39,115	15,124	7,715	92,497	77,503	96,580
Maintenance and repair services	1,878,930	9,785	11,583	204,178	670,065	650,232	201,327	131,788
Maintenance and repair materials	232,064	–	–	52,691	7,488	125,575	40,265	5,922
Property management and security	403,589	29,269	16,140	26,102	98,933	152,527	50,248	29,825
Property management	280,270	25,163	12,152	23,174	66,031	94,334	37,910	21,211
Management, upkeep services for security	123,319	4,194	3,987	2,927	32,902	58,193	12,338	8,614
Parking	85,202	2,184	4,557	10,002	29,725	18,071	18,170	2,046
Housing while attending school	8,984,335	2,245,933	297,352	775,973	3,967,748	1,339,975	270,418	86,459
Lodging on trips	28,348,750	814,288	3,606,201	6,738,355	6,607,846	5,628,508	3,713,954	1,239,497
UTILITIES, FUELS, AND PUBLIC SERVICES	**300,933,747**	**11,779,748**	**47,519,179**	**73,812,341**	**70,482,330**	**45,225,611**	**29,047,421**	**23,063,991**
Natural gas	**36,967,613**	**941,849**	**5,470,443**	**9,010,656**	**8,683,619**	**5,440,299**	**3,771,044**	**3,648,936**
Electricity	**109,988,038**	**4,111,982**	**16,409,809**	**26,961,712**	**25,811,013**	**17,030,853**	**11,053,032**	**8,607,893**
Fuel oil and other fuels	**9,911,468**	**186,622**	**1,036,365**	**2,101,299**	**2,039,921**	**1,938,140**	**1,285,690**	**1,323,480**
Fuel oil	5,154,726	66,226	453,433	1,164,814	1,068,292	1,005,824	666,567	729,464
Coal	7,848	–	–	2,195	1,815	3,216	–	–
Bottled/tank gas	3,954,049	101,349	496,536	795,244	817,557	791,274	481,166	471,487
Wood and other fuels	794,846	19,047	86,395	139,046	152,484	137,673	137,957	122,528
Telephone services	**107,258,208**	**5,599,893**	**19,603,971**	**26,730,945**	**25,162,731**	**15,022,881**	**8,904,831**	**6,232,047**
Residential telephone and pay phones	71,861,228	3,022,303	12,188,207	17,381,213	16,402,870	10,666,354	6,874,735	5,324,282
Cellular phone service	32,932,846	2,260,524	6,836,250	8,744,029	8,272,458	4,068,164	1,912,104	838,642
Pager service	191,705	2,621	38,546	39,518	55,366	41,807	11,777	1,938
Phone cards	2,273,550	314,445	540,968	566,185	432,037	246,402	106,216	67,294
Water and other public services	**36,808,420**	**939,402**	**4,998,781**	**9,007,485**	**8,785,048**	**5,793,286**	**4,032,713**	**3,251,526**
Water and sewerage maintenance	26,587,533	687,864	3,613,606	6,652,976	6,416,107	4,094,657	2,840,228	2,281,312
Trash and garbage collection	9,983,217	247,781	1,362,009	2,306,697	2,294,514	1,654,218	1,167,473	950,511
Septic tank cleaning	237,669	3,757	23,165	47,812	74,426	44,411	25,012	19,704

See appendix for information about mortgage principle reduction.
Note: Numbers may not add to total because of rounding. (–) means sample is too small to make a reliable estimate.
Source: Calculations by New Strategist based on the 2002 Consumer Expenditure Survey

Table 9.4 Housing: Shelter and Utilities: Market shares by age, 2002

(percentage of total annual spending on shelter and utilities accounted for by consumer unit age groups, 2002)

	total consumer units	under 25	25 to 34	35 to 44	45 to 54	55 to 64	65 to 74	75+
Share of total consumer units	100.0%	7.8%	16.9%	21.8%	20.2%	13.7%	10.0%	9.6%
Share of total before-tax income	100.0	3.3	16.8	27.1	26.6	14.7	7.1	4.6
Share of total spending	100.0	4.6	16.8	25.9	24.3	14.9	7.9	5.6
Share of housing spending	100.0	4.4	17.5	26.8	23.6	14.2	7.6	6.0
SHELTER	**100.0%**	**4.8%**	**18.3%**	**27.5%**	**23.8%**	**13.4%**	**6.8%**	**5.3%**
Owned dwellings*	**100.0**	**1.3**	**15.4**	**29.9**	**26.6**	**14.8**	**7.5**	**4.6**
Mortgage interest and charges	100.0	1.2	18.8	33.9	27.7	12.5	4.6	1.3
Mortgage interest	100.0	1.2	19.2	34.3	27.6	12.2	4.4	1.3
Interest paid, home equity loan	100.0	2.0	14.0	28.5	28.0	15.8	10.1	1.8
Interest paid, home equity line of credit	100.0	0.3	7.8	22.3	35.9	23.7	7.6	2.4
Property taxes	100.0	1.8	11.2	25.8	25.4	16.9	10.5	8.5
Maintenance, repairs, insurance, other expenses	100.0	0.9	10.4	23.2	24.6	19.1	12.3	9.4
Homeowner's insurance	100.0	0.9	11.4	22.6	25.2	17.9	12.6	9.4
Ground rent	100.0	2.2	14.6	18.2	19.4	17.8	12.1	15.8
Maintenance and repair services	100.0	0.7	9.1	22.9	24.6	20.6	12.3	9.8
Painting and papering	100.0	1.5	9.2	24.4	21.5	24.2	12.3	6.9
Plumbing and water heating	100.0	1.0	9.5	21.8	20.7	17.3	14.1	15.6
Heat, air conditioning, electrical work	100.0	0.4	10.5	19.8	29.7	16.6	14.3	8.7
Roofing and gutters	100.0	0.3	5.6	23.8	24.7	14.7	12.4	18.5
Other repair and maintenance services	100.0	0.7	8.5	24.4	23.5	24.0	11.3	7.5
Repair, replacement of hard-surface flooring	100.0	0.3	14.4	19.5	28.2	21.0	10.7	6.0
Repair of built-in appliances	100.0	0.4	21.4	20.1	21.1	11.1	16.7	8.8
Maintenance and repair materials	100.0	1.2	13.4	31.0	25.9	15.2	10.6	2.7
Paints, wallpaper, and supplies	100.0	1.5	15.8	32.3	26.5	15.7	6.1	2.1
Tools, equip. for painting, wallpapering	100.0	1.5	15.8	32.2	26.5	15.6	6.1	2.1
Plumbing supplies and equipment	100.0	0.3	16.3	24.2	23.2	20.6	10.3	5.2
Electrical supplies, heating, cooling equip.	100.0	0.4	11.8	16.8	24.8	18.5	23.2	4.5
Hard-surface flooring, repair, replacement	100.0	0.8	15.5	36.3	20.8	11.1	12.7	2.7
Roofing and gutters	100.0	1.0	17.0	30.1	33.5	9.1	9.1	0.1
Plaster, paneling, siding, windows, doors, screens, awnings	100.0	0.5	11.0	22.5	29.1	21.4	11.5	3.9
Patio, walk, fence, driveway, masonry, brick, and stucco materials	100.0	0.9	9.5	38.0	25.1	10.9	8.0	8.1
Landscape maintenance	100.0	0.1	15.6	34.2	30.6	13.5	4.5	1.6
Miscellaneous supplies and equipment	100.0	2.0	10.8	35.8	23.9	13.0	12.3	2.2
Insulation, other maintenance, repair	100.0	1.7	9.3	38.6	17.5	16.2	13.4	3.3
Finish basement, remodel rooms, build patios, walks, etc.	100.0	2.3	12.6	32.4	31.4	9.3	11.0	1.0
Property management and security	100.0	1.1	10.0	19.9	24.4	16.0	14.9	13.7
Property management	100.0	1.3	10.5	19.3	25.2	16.0	13.8	13.9
Management, upkeep services for security	100.0	0.4	8.0	22.0	21.1	16.0	19.2	13.2
Parking	100.0	2.4	11.9	17.6	18.2	19.4	16.9	13.7

	total consumer units	under 25	25 to 34	35 to 44	45 to 54	55 to 64	65 to 74	75+
Rented dwellings	**100.0%**	**13.1%**	**27.3%**	**23.7%**	**16.2%**	**8.2%**	**4.2%**	**7.2%**
Rent	100.0	13.2	27.3	23.8	16.1	8.2	4.1	7.2
Rent as pay	100.0	13.6	22.3	22.6	18.8	9.5	6.8	6.4
Maintenance, insurance, other expenses	100.0	7.9	25.8	19.1	20.9	11.8	6.4	8.2
Tenant's insurance	100.0	4.6	26.7	23.0	20.3	11.0	5.1	9.3
Maintenance and repair services	100.0	5.0	17.3	14.5	25.6	16.2	8.8	12.6
Maintenance and repair materials	100.0	15.5	36.6	21.4	15.0	6.3	4.4	0.9
Other lodging	**100.0**	**5.8**	**9.8**	**19.2**	**28.2**	**20.8**	**10.8**	**5.2**
Owned vacation homes	100.0	1.2	8.7	17.5	28.0	25.1	11.0	8.5
Mortgage interest and charges	100.0	1.1	13.4	23.2	29.6	24.7	5.3	2.8
Property taxes	100.0	1.2	5.9	13.2	27.0	22.9	15.0	14.8
Maintenance, insurance, and other expenses	100.0	1.5	4.1	13.5	26.7	29.7	15.6	8.9
Homeowner's insurance	100.0	1.6	8.7	21.6	23.7	14.2	21.9	8.3
Ground rent	100.0	–	11.9	4.6	2.3	28.2	23.6	29.4
Maintenance and repair services	100.0	0.5	0.6	10.9	35.7	34.6	10.7	7.0
Maintenance and repair materials	100.0	–	–	22.7	3.2	54.1	17.4	2.6
Property management and security	100.0	7.3	4.0	6.5	24.5	37.8	12.5	7.4
Property management	100.0	9.0	4.3	8.3	23.6	33.7	13.5	7.6
Management, upkeep services for security	100.0	3.4	3.2	2.4	26.7	47.2	10.0	7.0
Parking	100.0	2.6	5.3	11.7	34.9	21.2	21.3	2.4
Housing while attending school	100.0	25.0	3.3	8.6	44.2	14.9	3.0	1.0
Lodging on trips	100.0	2.9	12.7	23.8	23.3	19.9	13.1	4.4
UTILITIES, FUELS, AND PUBLIC SERVICES	**100.0**	**3.9**	**15.8**	**24.5**	**23.4**	**15.0**	**9.7**	**7.7**
Natural gas	**100.0**	**2.5**	**14.8**	**24.4**	**23.5**	**14.7**	**10.2**	**9.9**
Electricity	**100.0**	**3.7**	**14.9**	**24.5**	**23.5**	**15.5**	**10.0**	**7.8**
Fuel oil and other fuels	**100.0**	**1.9**	**10.5**	**21.2**	**20.6**	**19.6**	**13.0**	**13.4**
Fuel oil	100.0	1.3	8.8	22.6	20.7	19.5	12.9	14.2
Coal	100.0	–	–	28.0	23.1	41.0	–	–
Bottled/tank gas	100.0	2.6	12.6	20.1	20.7	20.0	12.2	11.9
Wood and other fuels	100.0	2.4	10.9	17.5	19.2	17.3	17.4	15.4
Telephone services	**100.0**	**5.2**	**18.3**	**24.9**	**23.5**	**14.0**	**8.3**	**5.8**
Residential telephone and pay phones	100.0	4.2	17.0	24.2	22.8	14.8	9.6	7.4
Cellular phone service	100.0	6.9	20.8	26.6	25.1	12.4	5.8	2.5
Pager service	100.0	1.4	20.1	20.6	28.9	21.8	6.1	1.0
Phone cards	100.0	13.8	23.8	24.9	19.0	10.8	4.7	3.0
Water and other public services	**100.0**	**2.6**	**13.6**	**24.5**	**23.9**	**15.7**	**11.0**	**8.8**
Water and sewerage maintenance	100.0	2.6	13.6	25.0	24.1	15.4	10.7	8.6
Trash and garbage collection	100.0	2.5	13.6	23.1	23.0	16.6	11.7	9.5
Septic tank cleaning	100.0	1.6	9.7	20.1	31.3	18.7	10.5	8.3

See appendix for information about mortgage principle reduction.
Note: Numbers may not add to total because of rounding. (–) means sample is too small to make a reliable estimate.
Source: Calculations by New Strategist based on the 2002 Consumer Expenditure Survey

Table 9.5 Housing: Shelter and Utilities: Average spending by income, 2002

(average annual spending on shelter and utilities, by before-tax income of consumer units (CU), 2002; complete income reporters only)

	complete income reporters	under $10,000	$10,000– $19,999	$20,000– $29,999	$30,000– $39,999	$40,000– $49,999	$50,000– $69,999	$70,000 or more
Number of consumer units								
(in thousands, add 000)	92,388	10,933	15,075	12,312	10,727	8,873	13,521	20,947
Average number of persons per CU	2.5	1.7	1.9	2.3	2.5	2.6	2.8	3.1
Average before-tax income of CU	$49,430.00	$5,554.80	$14,724.33	$24,495.00	$34,423.00	$44,443.00	$58,933.00	$115,629.00
Average spending of CU, total	42,556.98	17,627.83	22,838.71	28,835.85	35,095.39	41,787.38	50,406.17	76,627.31
Housing, average spending	13,480.52	6,322.60	7,774.87	9,594.62	11,240.22	13,158.81	15,275.81	23,695.41
SHELTER	**$7,853.70**	**$3,744.61**	**$4,482.34**	**$5,367.99**	**$6,451.40**	**$7,670.59**	**$8,580.84**	**$14,212.12**
Owned dwellings*	**5,147.99**	**1,285.52**	**1,858.77**	**2,511.20**	**3,546.62**	**4,719.85**	**6,046.99**	**11,502.17**
Mortgage interest and charges	2,946.74	569.02	612.18	1,167.09	1,840.50	2,728.49	3,641.21	7,124.67
Mortgage interest	2,787.30	535.32	565.78	1,083.12	1,747.73	2,571.40	3,447.94	6,760.56
Interest paid, home equity loan	93.86	24.38	34.51	58.05	59.53	85.65	116.83	200.12
Interest paid, home equity line of credit	65.36	9.32	11.90	24.62	33.09	71.41	76.43	163.87
Property taxes	1,209.37	403.33	654.26	690.03	846.27	1,029.82	1,335.48	2,515.46
Maintenance, repairs, insurance, other expenses	991.88	313.18	592.33	654.08	859.85	961.54	1,070.30	1,862.05
Homeowner's insurance	288.58	101.45	170.76	201.65	245.70	306.70	327.87	511.04
Ground rent	43.69	28.24	55.68	72.17	51.68	59.02	47.76	13.16
Maintenance and repair services	536.84	158.13	310.39	313.63	473.67	476.26	548.06	1,079.44
Painting and papering	53.92	22.22	25.39	27.92	48.94	34.56	34.87	129.31
Plumbing and water heating	50.84	26.67	51.29	29.17	46.24	66.48	41.58	77.59
Heat, air conditioning, electrical work	92.24	17.47	64.34	58.76	67.36	78.38	98.03	185.90
Roofing and gutters	68.81	32.53	51.80	26.02	90.97	76.34	50.10	122.69
Other repair and maintenance services	221.80	54.04	103.75	142.88	185.32	179.71	269.14	446.66
Repair, replacement of hard-surface flooring	47.47	4.60	12.78	27.81	33.43	38.84	52.42	114.02
Repair of built-in appliances	1.76	0.59	1.04	1.08	1.42	1.95	1.92	3.27
Maintenance and repair materials	89.57	16.00	29.02	43.07	62.41	85.91	123.15	192.64
Paints, wallpaper, and supplies	16.01	4.95	4.44	9.71	9.41	16.34	21.09	33.77
Tools, equip. for painting, wallpapering	1.72	0.53	0.48	1.04	1.01	1.76	2.27	3.63
Plumbing supplies and equipment	6.32	1.37	3.54	2.71	5.74	8.79	6.60	12.09
Electrical supplies, heating, cooling equip.	3.76	0.05	0.64	2.21	2.04	2.21	1.87	11.62
Hard-surface flooring, repair, replacement	9.68	0.03	1.94	5.03	5.29	15.57	13.17	20.54
Roofing and gutters	5.82	1.71	4.69	0.41	3.44	5.53	4.20	14.38
Plaster, paneling, siding, windows, doors, screens, awnings	15.64	3.10	4.41	7.56	9.87	10.86	27.70	32.20
Patio, walk, fence, driveway, masonry, brick, and stucco materials	1.23	0.01	0.97	0.34	2.66	0.90	1.49	1.81
Landscape maintenance	4.88	–	0.61	2.77	3.71	5.41	6.75	10.90
Miscellaneous supplies and equipment	24.50	4.24	7.30	11.28	19.24	18.55	38.01	51.71
Insulation, other maintenance, repair	13.23	1.07	2.44	9.40	8.41	11.02	18.95	29.32
Finish basement, remodel rooms, build patios, walks, etc.	11.27	3.18	4.86	1.87	10.83	7.53	19.07	22.39
Property management and security	27.89	7.52	22.59	17.98	19.83	27.53	20.21	57.41
Property management	22.30	5.65	17.45	15.22	15.93	21.15	17.43	45.55
Management, upkeep services for security	5.59	1.87	5.15	2.76	3.89	6.38	2.78	11.86
Parking	5.31	1.85	3.88	5.57	6.56	6.13	3.25	8.35

	complete income reporters	under $10,000	$10,000–$19,999	$20,000–$29,999	$30,000–$39,999	$40,000–$49,999	$50,000–$69,999	$70,000 or more
Rented dwellings	**$2,196.96**	**$2,195.02**	**$2,435.00**	**$2,640.20**	**$2,600.73**	**$2,604.37**	**$2,082.12**	**$1,460.93**
Rent	2,138.99	2,107.70	2,356.29	2,573.32	2,530.38	2,559.77	2,049.10	1,423.00
Rent as pay	28.10	68.07	48.61	38.33	23.78	12.29	4.83	10.40
Maintenance, insurance, other expenses	29.87	19.25	30.09	28.55	46.57	32.31	28.20	27.53
Tenant's insurance	9.61	5.55	7.01	7.25	8.90	12.81	15.39	10.29
Maintenance and repair services	12.13	5.68	18.55	14.38	21.30	7.55	6.90	10.17
Maintenance and repair materials	8.13	8.02	4.54	6.92	16.37	11.95	5.90	7.08
Other lodging	**508.75**	**264.07**	**188.57**	**216.59**	**304.05**	**346.37**	**451.72**	**1,249.02**
Owned vacation homes	167.44	20.55	57.55	69.81	131.68	109.27	135.54	444.14
Mortgage interest and charges	70.84	4.07	11.47	21.66	32.62	38.97	54.11	221.18
Property taxes	68.38	4.07	10.63	21.66	32.62	38.64	53.51	211.46
Maintenance, insurance, and other expenses	34.20	6.32	13.61	25.46	30.84	22.99	34.15	75.22
Homeowner's insurance	9.27	3.29	7.23	8.95	7.02	7.86	9.67	15.56
Ground rent	3.32	0.28	3.06	4.45	5.12	6.56	0.91	3.70
Maintenance and repair services	14.49	2.03	2.70	9.40	4.20	5.00	16.89	40.22
Maintenance and repair materials	2.42	–	0.09	0.78	12.57	0.46	2.09	2.15
Property management and security	3.85	0.52	0.51	1.88	1.60	3.01	4.28	10.38
Property management	2.69	0.39	0.40	1.67	1.03	2.65	0.60	8.37
Management, upkeep services for security	1.16	0.14	0.10	0.21	0.57	0.36	3.68	2.01
Parking	0.85	0.19	0.05	–	0.33	0.10	0.31	3.21
Housing while attending school	78.23	148.37	43.37	22.27	14.88	35.78	44.87	171.55
Lodging on trips	263.07	95.15	87.65	124.51	157.48	201.33	271.31	633.33
UTILITIES, FUELS, AND PUBLIC SERVICES	**2,682.85**	**1,520.32**	**1,973.13**	**2,316.38**	**2,526.05**	**2,748.53**	**3,126.29**	**3,782.06**
Natural gas	**323.39**	**161.92**	**228.45**	**278.83**	**319.27**	**340.05**	**341.86**	**485.30**
Electricity	**972.70**	**600.45**	**771.63**	**883.38**	**930.58**	**999.38**	**1,130.42**	**1,272.64**
Fuel oil and other fuels	**89.82**	**53.52**	**88.80**	**82.96**	**84.10**	**70.69**	**93.11**	**122.44**
Fuel oil	46.49	26.98	37.34	43.75	37.96	35.17	50.82	71.22
Coal	0.08	–	–	–	0.20	0.17	0.27	0.01
Bottled/tank gas	35.91	20.51	41.68	32.81	38.33	30.70	35.79	42.65
Wood and other fuels	7.35	6.04	9.79	6.40	7.61	4.65	6.24	8.57
Telephone services	**967.65**	**552.84**	**646.91**	**800.15**	**899.13**	**998.98**	**1,169.33**	**1,405.10**
Residential telephone and pay phones	640.42	411.75	502.71	580.16	616.90	671.39	730.70	834.93
Cellular phone service	304.19	119.00	121.85	193.24	258.03	305.40	419.43	546.03
Pager service	1.85	0.28	0.20	0.46	1.74	2.20	1.82	4.60
Phone cards	21.20	21.82	22.14	26.29	22.45	19.98	17.39	19.53
Water and other public services	**329.29**	**151.58**	**237.33**	**271.06**	**292.98**	**339.43**	**391.56**	**496.57**
Water and sewerage maintenance	237.00	112.46	170.74	201.45	216.93	240.27	281.46	350.78
Trash and garbage collection	89.99	37.76	65.22	68.22	74.73	96.26	107.87	141.51
Septic tank cleaning	2.30	1.37	1.37	1.39	1.32	2.90	2.24	4.29

See appendix for information about mortgage principle reduction.
Note: (–) means sample is too small to make a reliable estimate.
Source: Bureau of Labor Statistics, unpublished tables from the 2002 Consumer Expenditure Survey; calculations by New Strategist

Table 9.6 Housing: Shelter and Utilities: Indexed spending by income, 2002

(indexed average annual spending of consumer units (CU) on shelter and utilities, by before-tax income of consumer unit, 2002; complete income reporters only; index definition: an index of 100 is the average for all consumer units; an index of 132 means that spending by consumer units in that group is 32 percent above the average for all consumer units; an index of 68 indicates spending that is 32 percent below the average for all consumer units)

	complete income reporters	under $10,000	$10,000–$19,999	$20,000–$29,999	$30,000–$39,999	$40,000–$49,999	$50,000–$69,999	$70,000 or more
Average spending of CU, total	$42,557	$17,628	$22,839	$28,836	$35,095	$41,787	$50,406	$76,627
Average spending of CU, index	100	41	54	68	82	98	118	180
Housing, spending index	100	47	58	71	83	98	113	176
SHELTER	100	48	57	68	82	98	109	181
Owned dwellings*	100	25	36	49	69	92	117	223
Mortgage interest and charges	100	19	21	40	62	93	124	242
Mortgage interest	100	19	20	39	63	92	124	243
Interest paid, home equity loan	100	26	37	62	63	91	124	213
Interest paid, home equity line of credit	100	14	18	38	51	109	117	251
Property taxes	100	33	54	57	70	85	110	208
Maintenance, repairs, insurance, other expenses	100	32	60	66	87	97	108	188
Homeowner's insurance	100	35	59	70	85	106	114	177
Ground rent	100	65	127	165	118	135	109	30
Maintenance and repair services	100	29	58	58	88	89	102	201
Painting and papering	100	41	47	52	91	64	65	240
Plumbing and water heating	100	52	101	57	91	131	82	153
Heat, air conditioning, electrical work	100	19	70	64	73	85	106	202
Roofing and gutters	100	47	75	38	132	111	73	178
Other repair and maintenance services	100	24	47	64	84	81	121	201
Repair, replacement of hard-surface flooring	100	10	27	59	70	82	110	240
Repair of built-in appliances	100	33	59	61	81	111	109	186
Maintenance and repair materials	100	18	32	48	70	96	137	215
Paints, wallpaper, and supplies	100	31	28	61	59	102	132	211
Tools, equip. for painting, wallpapering	100	31	28	60	59	102	132	211
Plumbing supplies and equipment	100	22	56	43	91	139	104	191
Electrical supplies, heating, cooling equip.	100	1	17	59	54	59	50	309
Hard-surface flooring, repair, replacement	100	0	20	52	55	161	136	212
Roofing and gutters	100	29	81	7	59	95	72	247
Plaster, paneling, siding, windows, doors, screens, awnings	100	20	28	48	63	69	177	206
Patio, walk, fence, driveway, masonry, brick, and stucco materials	100	1	79	28	216	73	121	147
Landscape maintenance	100	–	12	57	76	111	138	223
Miscellaneous supplies and equipment	100	17	30	46	79	76	155	211
Insulation, other maintenance, repair	100	8	18	71	64	83	143	222
Finish basement, remodel rooms, build patios, walks, etc.	100	28	43	17	96	67	169	199
Property management and security	100	27	81	64	71	99	72	206
Property management	100	25	78	68	71	95	78	204
Management, upkeep services for security	100	33	92	49	70	114	50	212
Parking	100	35	73	105	124	115	61	157

	complete income reporters	under $10,000	$10,000–$19,999	$20,000–$29,999	$30,000–$39,999	$40,000–$49,999	$50,000–$69,999	$70,000 or more
Rented dwellings	**100**	**100**	**111**	**120**	**118**	**119**	**95**	**66**
Rent	100	99	110	120	118	120	96	67
Rent as pay	100	242	173	136	85	44	17	37
Maintenance, insurance, other expenses	100	64	101	96	156	108	94	92
Tenant's insurance	100	58	73	75	93	133	160	107
Maintenance and repair services	100	47	153	119	176	62	57	84
Maintenance and repair materials	100	99	56	85	201	147	73	87
Other lodging	**100**	**52**	**37**	**43**	**60**	**68**	**89**	**246**
Owned vacation homes	100	12	34	42	79	65	81	265
Mortgage interest and charges	100	6	16	31	46	55	76	312
Property taxes	100	6	16	32	48	57	78	309
Maintenance, insurance, and other expenses	100	18	40	74	90	67	100	220
Homeowner's insurance	100	35	78	97	76	85	104	168
Ground rent	100	9	92	134	154	198	27	111
Maintenance and repair services	100	14	19	65	29	35	117	278
Maintenance and repair materials	100	–	4	32	519	19	86	89
Property management and security	100	14	13	49	42	78	111	270
Property management	100	14	15	62	38	99	22	311
Management, upkeep services for security	100	12	9	18	49	31	317	173
Parking	100	22	6	–	39	12	36	378
Housing while attending school	100	190	55	28	19	46	57	219
Lodging on trips	100	36	33	47	60	77	103	241
UTILITIES, FUELS, AND PUBLIC SERVICES	**100**	**57**	**74**	**86**	**94**	**102**	**117**	**141**
Natural gas	**100**	**50**	**71**	**86**	**99**	**105**	**106**	**150**
Electricity	**100**	**62**	**79**	**91**	**96**	**103**	**116**	**131**
Fuel oil and other fuels	**100**	**60**	**99**	**92**	**94**	**79**	**104**	**136**
Fuel oil	100	58	80	94	82	76	109	153
Coal	100	–	–	–	250	213	338	13
Bottled/tank gas	100	57	116	91	107	85	100	119
Wood and other fuels	100	82	133	87	104	63	85	117
Telephone services	**100**	**57**	**67**	**83**	**93**	**103**	**121**	**145**
Residential telephone and pay phones	100	64	78	91	96	105	114	130
Cellular phone service	100	39	40	64	85	100	138	180
Pager service	100	15	11	25	94	119	98	249
Phone cards	100	103	104	124	106	94	82	92
Water and other public services	**100**	**46**	**72**	**82**	**89**	**103**	**119**	**151**
Water and sewerage maintenance	100	47	72	85	92	101	119	148
Trash and garbage collection	100	42	72	76	83	107	120	157
Septic tank cleaning	100	59	60	60	57	126	97	187

See appendix for information about mortgage principle reduction.
Note: (–) means sample is too small to make a reliable estimate.
Source: Calculations by New Strategist based on the 2002 Consumer Expenditure Survey

Table 9.7 Housing: Shelter and Utilities: Total spending by income, 2002

(total annual spending on shelter and utilities, by before-tax income group of consumer units (CU), 2002; complete income reporters only; numbers in thousands)

	complete income reporters	under $10,000	$10,000– $19,999	$20,000– $29,999	$30,000– $39,999	$40,000– $49,999	$50,000– $69,999	$70,000 or more
Number of consumer units	**92,388**	**10,933**	**15,075**	**12,312**	**10,727**	**8,873**	**13,521**	**20,947**
Total spending of all CUs	**$3,931,754,268**	**$192,725,059**	**$344,293,530**	**$355,026,985**	**$376,468,249**	**$370,779,423**	**$681,541,825**	**$1,605,112,263**
Housing, total spending	**1,245,438,282**	**69,124,997**	**117,206,161**	**118,128,961**	**120,573,840**	**116,758,121**	**206,544,227**	**496,347,753**
SHELTER	**$725,587,636**	**$40,939,810**	**$67,571,315**	**$66,090,693**	**$69,204,168**	**$68,061,145**	**$116,021,538**	**$297,701,278**
Owned dwellings*	**475,612,500**	**14,054,606**	**28,021,024**	**30,917,894**	**38,044,593**	**41,879,229**	**81,761,352**	**240,935,955**
Mortgage interest and charges	272,243,415	6,221,079	9,228,625	14,369,212	19,743,044	24,209,892	49,232,800	149,240,462
Mortgage interest	257,513,072	5,852,646	8,529,066	13,335,373	18,747,900	22,816,032	46,619,597	141,613,450
Interest paid, home equity loan	8,671,538	266,588	520,194	714,712	638,578	759,972	1,579,658	4,191,914
Interest paid, home equity line of credit	6,038,480	101,846	179,435	303,121	354,956	633,621	1,033,410	3,432,585
Property taxes	111,731,276	4,409,575	9,862,988	8,495,649	9,077,938	9,137,593	18,057,025	52,691,341
Maintenance, repairs, insurance, other expenses	91,637,809	3,423,990	8,929,412	8,053,033	9,223,611	8,531,744	14,471,526	39,004,361
Homeowner's insurance	26,661,329	1,109,154	2,574,257	2,482,715	2,635,624	2,721,349	4,433,130	10,704,755
Ground rent	4,036,432	308,762	839,420	888,557	554,371	523,684	645,763	275,663
Maintenance and repair services	49,597,574	1,728,805	4,679,117	3,861,413	5,081,058	4,225,855	7,410,319	22,611,030
Painting and papering	4,981,561	242,939	382,785	343,751	524,979	306,651	471,477	2,708,657
Plumbing and water heating	4,697,006	291,599	773,146	359,141	496,016	589,877	562,203	1,625,278
Heat, air conditioning, electrical work	8,521,869	191,041	969,957	723,453	722,571	695,466	1,325,464	3,894,047
Roofing and gutters	6,357,218	355,615	780,945	320,358	975,835	677,365	677,402	2,569,987
Other repair and maintenance services	20,491,658	590,785	1,564,085	1,759,139	1,987,928	1,594,567	3,639,042	9,356,187
Repair, replacement of hard-surface flooring	4,385,658	50,272	192,593	342,397	358,604	344,627	708,771	2,388,377
Repair of built-in appliances	162,603	6,443	15,606	13,297	15,232	17,302	25,960	68,497
Maintenance and repair materials	8,275,193	174,879	437,527	530,278	669,472	762,279	1,665,111	4,035,230
Paints, wallpaper, and supplies	1,479,132	54,144	66,970	119,550	100,941	144,985	285,158	707,380
Tools, equip. for painting, wallpapering	158,907	5,844	7,175	12,804	10,834	15,616	30,693	76,038
Plumbing supplies and equipment	583,892	14,974	53,342	33,366	61,573	77,994	89,239	253,249
Electrical supplies, heating, cooling equip.	347,379	494	9,700	27,210	21,883	19,609	25,284	243,404
Hard-surface flooring, repair, replacement	894,316	353	29,293	61,929	56,746	138,153	178,072	430,251
Roofing and gutters	537,698	18,650	70,630	5,048	36,901	49,068	56,788	301,218
Plaster, paneling, siding, windows, doors, screens, awnings	1,444,948	33,927	66,553	93,079	105,875	96,361	374,532	674,493
Patio, walk, fence, driveway, masonry, brick, and stucco materials	113,637	141	14,691	4,186	28,534	7,986	20,146	37,914
Landscape maintenance	450,853	–	9,173	34,104	39,797	48,003	91,267	228,322
Miscellaneous supplies and equipment	2,263,506	46,383	109,990	138,879	206,387	164,594	513,933	1,083,169
Insulation, other maintenance, repair	1,222,293	11,661	36,728	115,733	90,214	97,780	256,223	614,166
Finish basement, remodel rooms, build patios, walks, etc.	1,041,213	34,722	73,262	23,023	116,173	66,814	257,845	469,003
Property management and security	2,576,701	82,174	340,616	221,370	212,716	244,274	273,259	1,202,567
Property management	2,060,252	61,743	263,089	187,389	170,881	187,664	235,671	954,136
Management, upkeep services for security	516,449	20,431	77,607	33,981	41,728	56,610	37,588	248,431
Parking	490,580	20,178	58,475	68,578	70,369	54,391	43,943	174,907

	complete income reporters	under $10,000	$10,000– $19,999	$20,000– $29,999	$30,000– $39,999	$40,000– $49,999	$50,000– $69,999	$70,000 or more
Rented dwellings	**$202,972,740**	**$23,998,153**	**$36,707,550**	**$32,506,142**	**$27,898,031**	**$23,108,575**	**$28,152,345**	**$30,602,101**
Rent	197,617,008	23,043,500	35,521,028	31,682,716	27,143,386	22,712,839	27,705,881	29,807,581
Rent as pay	2,596,103	744,226	732,773	471,919	255,088	109,049	65,306	217,849
Maintenance, insurance, other expenses	2,759,630	210,459	453,669	351,508	499,556	286,687	381,292	576,671
Tenant's insurance	887,849	60,666	105,666	89,262	95,470	113,663	208,088	215,545
Maintenance and repair services	1,120,666	62,092	279,581	177,047	228,485	66,991	93,295	213,031
Maintenance and repair materials	751,114	87,700	68,502	85,199	175,601	106,032	79,774	148,305
Other lodging	**47,002,395**	**2,887,090**	**2,842,741**	**2,666,656**	**3,261,544**	**3,073,341**	**6,107,706**	**26,163,222**
Owned vacation homes	15,469,447	224,691	867,536	859,501	1,412,531	969,553	1,832,636	9,303,401
Mortgage interest and charges	6,544,766	44,488	172,887	266,678	349,915	345,781	731,621	4,633,057
Property taxes	6,317,491	44,488	160,306	266,678	349,915	342,853	723,509	4,429,453
Maintenance, insurance, and other expenses	3,159,670	69,045	205,223	313,464	330,821	203,990	461,742	1,575,633
Homeowner's insurance	856,437	35,940	108,937	110,192	75,304	69,742	130,748	325,935
Ground rent	306,728	3,102	46,154	54,788	54,922	58,207	12,304	77,504
Maintenance and repair services	1,338,702	22,176	40,643	115,733	45,053	44,365	228,370	842,488
Maintenance and repair materials	223,579	–	1,361	9,603	134,838	4,082	28,259	45,036
Property management and security	355,694	5,711	7,638	23,147	17,163	26,708	57,870	217,430
Property management	248,524	4,231	5,984	20,561	11,049	23,513	8,113	175,326
Management, upkeep services for security	107,170	1,481	1,574	2,586	6,114	3,194	49,757	42,103
Parking	78,530	2,045	721	–	3,540	887	4,192	67,240
Housing while attending school	7,227,513	1,622,165	653,828	274,188	159,618	317,476	606,687	3,593,458
Lodging on trips	24,304,511	1,040,233	1,321,378	1,532,967	1,689,288	1,786,401	3,668,383	13,266,364
UTILITIES, FUELS, AND PUBLIC SERVICES	**247,863,146**	**16,621,622**	**29,744,863**	**28,519,271**	**27,096,938**	**24,387,707**	**42,270,567**	**79,222,811**
Natural gas	**29,877,355**	**1,770,245**	**3,443,915**	**3,432,955**	**3,424,809**	**3,017,264**	**4,622,289**	**10,165,579**
Electricity	**89,865,808**	**6,564,703**	**11,632,363**	**10,876,175**	**9,982,332**	**8,867,499**	**15,284,409**	**26,657,990**
Fuel oil and other fuels	**8,298,290**	**585,175**	**1,338,695**	**1,021,404**	**902,141**	**627,232**	**1,258,940**	**2,564,751**
Fuel oil	4,295,118	294,964	562,883	538,650	407,197	312,063	687,137	1,491,845
Coal	7,391	–	–	–	2,145	1,508	3,651	209
Bottled/tank gas	3,317,653	224,219	628,253	403,957	411,166	272,401	483,917	893,390
Wood and other fuels	679,052	65,993	147,559	78,797	81,632	41,259	84,371	179,516
Telephone services	**89,399,248**	**6,044,241**	**9,752,192**	**9,851,447**	**9,644,968**	**8,863,950**	**15,810,511**	**29,432,630**
Residential telephone and pay phones	59,167,123	4,501,647	7,578,396	7,142,930	6,617,486	5,957,243	9,879,795	17,489,279
Cellular phone service	28,103,506	1,300,999	1,836,926	2,379,171	2,767,888	2,709,814	5,671,113	11,437,690
Pager service	170,918	3,086	3,081	5,664	18,665	19,521	24,608	96,356
Phone cards	1,958,626	238,549	333,780	323,682	240,821	177,283	235,130	409,095
Water and other public services	**30,422,445**	**1,657,257**	**3,577,778**	**3,337,291**	**3,142,796**	**3,011,762**	**5,294,283**	**10,401,652**
Water and sewerage maintenance	21,895,956	1,229,506	2,573,912	2,480,252	2,327,008	2,131,916	3,805,621	7,347,789
Trash and garbage collection	8,313,996	412,810	983,175	839,925	801,629	854,115	1,458,510	2,964,210
Septic tank cleaning	212,492	14,942	20,691	17,114	14,160	25,732	30,287	89,863

See appendix for information about mortgage principle reduction.
Note: Numbers may not add to total because of rounding. (–) means sample is too small to make a reliable estimate.
Source: Calculations by New Strategist based on the 2002 Consumer Expenditure Survey

Table 9.8 Housing: Shelter and Utilities: Market shares by income, 2002

(percentage of total annual spending on shelter and utilities accounted for by before-tax income group of consumer units, 2002; complete income reporters only)

	complete income reporters	under $10,000	$10,000–$19,999	$20,000–$29,999	$30,000–$39,999	$40,000–$49,999	$50,000–$69,999	$70,000 or more
Share of total consumer units	100.0%	11.8%	16.3%	13.3%	11.6%	9.6%	14.6%	22.7%
Share of total before-tax income	100.0	1.3	4.9	6.6	8.1	8.6	17.4	53.0
Share of total spending	100.0	4.9	8.8	9.0	9.6	9.4	17.3	40.8
Share of housing spending	100.0	5.6	9.4	9.5	9.7	9.4	16.6	39.9
SHELTER	100.0%	5.6%	9.3%	9.1%	9.5%	9.4%	16.0%	41.0%
Owned dwellings*	100.0	3.0	5.9	6.5	8.0	8.8	17.2	50.7
Mortgage interest and charges	100.0	2.3	3.4	5.3	7.3	8.9	18.1	54.8
Mortgage interest	100.0	2.3	3.3	5.2	7.3	8.9	18.1	55.0
Interest paid, home equity loan	100.0	3.1	6.0	8.2	7.4	8.8	18.2	48.3
Interest paid, home equity line of credit	100.0	1.7	3.0	5.0	5.9	10.5	17.1	56.8
Property taxes	100.0	3.9	8.8	7.6	8.1	8.2	16.2	47.2
Maintenance, repairs, insurance, other expenses	100.0	3.7	9.7	8.8	10.1	9.3	15.8	42.6
Homeowner's insurance	100.0	4.2	9.7	9.3	9.9	10.2	16.6	40.2
Ground rent	100.0	7.6	20.8	22.0	13.7	13.0	16.0	6.8
Maintenance and repair services	100.0	3.5	9.4	7.8	10.2	8.5	14.9	45.6
Painting and papering	100.0	4.9	7.7	6.9	10.5	6.2	9.5	54.4
Plumbing and water heating	100.0	6.2	16.5	7.6	10.6	12.6	12.0	34.6
Heat, air conditioning, electrical work	100.0	2.2	11.4	8.5	8.5	8.2	15.6	45.7
Roofing and gutters	100.0	5.6	12.3	5.0	15.4	10.7	10.7	40.4
Other repair and maintenance services	100.0	2.9	7.6	8.6	9.7	7.8	17.8	45.7
Repair, replacement of hard-surface flooring	100.0	1.1	4.4	7.8	8.2	7.9	16.2	54.5
Repair of built-in appliances	100.0	4.0	9.6	8.2	9.4	10.6	16.0	42.1
Maintenance and repair materials	100.0	2.1	5.3	6.4	8.1	9.2	20.1	48.8
Paints, wallpaper, and supplies	100.0	3.7	4.5	8.1	6.8	9.8	19.3	47.8
Tools, equip. for painting, wallpapering	100.0	3.7	4.5	8.1	6.8	9.8	19.3	47.9
Plumbing supplies and equipment	100.0	2.6	9.1	5.7	10.5	13.4	15.3	43.4
Electrical supplies, heating, cooling equip.	100.0	0.1	2.8	7.8	6.3	5.6	7.3	70.1
Hard-surface flooring, repair, replacement	100.0	0.0	3.3	6.9	6.3	15.4	19.9	48.1
Roofing and gutters	100.0	3.5	13.1	0.9	6.9	9.1	10.6	56.0
Plaster, paneling, siding, windows, doors, screens, awnings	100.0	2.3	4.6	6.4	7.3	6.7	25.9	46.7
Patio, walk, fence, driveway, masonry, brick, and stucco materials	100.0	0.1	12.9	3.7	25.1	7.0	17.7	33.4
Landscape maintenance	100.0	–	2.0	7.6	8.8	10.6	20.2	50.6
Miscellaneous supplies and equipment	100.0	2.0	4.9	6.1	9.1	7.3	22.7	47.9
Insulation, other maintenance, repair	100.0	1.0	3.0	9.5	7.4	8.0	21.0	50.2
Finish basement, remodel rooms, build patios, walks, etc.	100.0	3.3	7.0	2.2	11.2	6.4	24.8	45.0
Property management and security	100.0	3.2	13.2	8.6	8.3	9.5	10.6	46.7
Property management	100.0	3.0	12.8	9.1	8.3	9.1	11.4	46.3
Management, upkeep services for security	100.0	4.0	15.0	6.6	8.1	11.0	7.3	48.1
Parking	100.0	4.1	11.9	14.0	14.3	11.1	9.0	35.7

	complete income reporters	under $10,000	$10,000– $19,999	$20,000– $29,999	$30,000– $39,999	$40,000– $49,999	$50,000– $69,999	$70,000 or more
Rented dwellings	**100.0%**	**11.8%**	**18.1%**	**16.0%**	**13.7%**	**11.4%**	**13.9%**	**15.1%**
Rent	100.0	11.7	18.0	16.0	13.7	11.5	14.0	15.1
Rent as pay	100.0	28.7	28.2	18.2	9.8	4.2	2.5	8.4
Maintenance, insurance, other expenses	100.0	7.6	16.4	12.7	18.1	10.4	13.8	20.9
Tenant's insurance	100.0	6.8	11.9	10.1	10.8	12.8	23.4	24.3
Maintenance and repair services	100.0	5.5	24.9	15.8	20.4	6.0	8.3	19.0
Maintenance and repair materials	100.0	11.7	9.1	11.3	23.4	14.1	10.6	19.7
Other lodging	**100.0**	**6.1**	**6.0**	**5.7**	**6.9**	**6.5**	**13.0**	**55.7**
Owned vacation homes	100.0	1.5	5.6	5.6	9.1	6.3	11.8	60.1
Mortgage interest and charges	100.0	0.7	2.6	4.1	5.3	5.3	11.2	70.8
Property taxes	100.0	0.7	2.5	4.2	5.5	5.4	11.5	70.1
Maintenance, insurance, and other expenses	100.0	2.2	6.5	9.9	10.5	6.5	14.6	49.9
Homeowner's insurance	100.0	4.2	12.7	12.9	8.8	8.1	15.3	38.1
Ground rent	100.0	1.0	15.0	17.9	17.9	19.0	4.0	25.3
Maintenance and repair services	100.0	1.7	3.0	8.6	3.4	3.3	17.1	62.9
Maintenance and repair materials	100.0	–	0.6	4.3	60.3	1.8	12.6	20.1
Property management and security	100.0	1.6	2.1	6.5	4.8	7.5	16.3	61.1
Property management	100.0	1.7	2.4	8.3	4.4	9.5	3.3	70.5
Management, upkeep services for security	100.0	1.4	1.5	2.4	5.7	3.0	46.4	39.3
Parking	100.0	2.6	0.9	–	4.5	1.1	5.3	85.6
Housing while attending school	100.0	22.4	9.0	3.8	2.2	4.4	8.4	49.7
Lodging on trips	100.0	4.3	5.4	6.3	7.0	7.4	15.1	54.6
UTILITIES, FUELS, AND PUBLIC SERVICES	**100.0**	**6.7**	**12.0**	**11.5**	**10.9**	**9.8**	**17.1**	**32.0**
Natural gas	**100.0**	**5.9**	**11.5**	**11.5**	**11.5**	**10.1**	**15.5**	**34.0**
Electricity	**100.0**	**7.3**	**12.9**	**12.1**	**11.1**	**9.9**	**17.0**	**29.7**
Fuel oil and other fuels	**100.0**	**7.1**	**16.1**	**12.3**	**10.9**	**7.6**	**15.2**	**30.9**
Fuel oil	100.0	6.9	13.1	12.5	9.5	7.3	16.0	34.7
Coal	100.0	–	–	–	29.0	20.4	49.4	2.8
Bottled/tank gas	100.0	6.8	18.9	12.2	12.4	8.2	14.6	26.9
Wood and other fuels	100.0	9.7	21.7	11.6	12.0	6.1	12.4	26.4
Telephone services	**100.0**	**6.8**	**10.9**	**11.0**	**10.8**	**9.9**	**17.7**	**32.9**
Residential telephone and pay phones	100.0	7.6	12.8	12.1	11.2	10.1	16.7	29.6
Cellular phone service	100.0	4.6	6.5	8.5	9.8	9.6	20.2	40.7
Pager service	100.0	1.8	1.8	3.3	10.9	11.4	14.4	56.4
Phone cards	100.0	12.2	17.0	16.5	12.3	9.1	12.0	20.9
Water and other public services	**100.0**	**5.4**	**11.8**	**11.0**	**10.3**	**9.9**	**17.4**	**34.2**
Water and sewerage maintenance	100.0	5.6	11.8	11.3	10.6	9.7	17.4	33.6
Trash and garbage collection	100.0	5.0	11.8	10.1	9.6	10.3	17.5	35.7
Septic tank cleaning	100.0	7.0	9.7	8.1	6.7	12.1	14.3	42.3

See appendix for information about mortgage principle reduction.
Note: Numbers may not add to total because of rounding. (–) means sample is too small to make a reliable estimate.
Source: Calculations by New Strategist based on the 2002 Consumer Expenditure Survey

Table 9.9 Housing: Shelter and Utilities: Average spending by household type, 2002

(average annual spending of consumer units (CU) on shelter and utilities, by type of consumer unit, 2002)

	total married couples	married couples, no children	married couples with children				single parent, at least one child <18	single person
			total	oldest child under 6	oldest child 6 to 17	oldest child 18 or older		
Number of consumer units								
(in thousands, add 000)	56,265	23,118	28,790	5,547	15,206	8,036	6,730	33,055
Average number of persons per CU	3.2	2.0	3.9	3.5	4.1	3.9	2.9	1.0
Average before-tax income of CU	$67,155.00	$58,967.00	$73,918.00	$67,587.00	$72,720.00	$81,042.00	$26,966.00	$27,042.00
Average spending of CU, total	52,333.70	45,557.33	57,835.01	52,778.62	58,103.75	60,859.78	30,185.38	24,189.90
Housing, average spending	16,649.27	14,422.39	18,459.93	19,140.57	18,618.79	17,697.37	11,021.68	8,619.27
SHELTER	**$9,577.78**	**$8,109.94**	**$10,794.95**	**$11,268.58**	**$10,912.02**	**$10,246.50**	**$6,513.40**	**$5,465.33**
Owned dwellings*	**7,411.12**	**6,113.59**	**8,536.39**	**8,505.78**	**8,727.69**	**8,195.55**	**3,102.14**	**2,605.04**
Mortgage interest and charges	4,375.80	3,053.34	5,471.93	5,950.45	5,739.48	4,635.37	1,871.66	1,259.96
Mortgage interest	4,144.87	2,858.43	5,213.89	5,785.06	5,464.21	4,345.96	1,807.15	1,197.94
Interest paid, home equity loan	133.65	107.67	149.83	110.19	162.80	152.65	42.80	33.89
Interest paid, home equity line of credit	96.94	87.24	108.11	54.70	112.47	136.73	21.71	28.13
Property taxes	1,722.11	1,669.59	1,785.68	1,544.71	1,822.15	1,883.03	623.48	755.44
Maintenance, repairs, insurance, other expenses	1,313.21	1,390.67	1,278.78	1,010.61	1,166.07	1,677.15	607.00	589.63
Homeowner's insurance	383.42	389.88	381.59	286.37	390.08	431.25	174.16	181.43
Ground rent	37.79	42.76	35.80	39.52	36.95	31.06	42.37	46.36
Maintenance and repair services	729.96	806.36	689.16	531.87	583.03	998.55	345.76	290.05
Painting and papering	74.43	74.18	75.10	93.24	68.40	75.26	33.21	33.72
Plumbing and water heating	57.18	67.11	49.90	29.60	46.22	70.88	38.27	41.33
Heat, air conditioning, electrical work	116.37	121.15	108.56	103.58	87.11	152.57	53.99	54.47
Roofing and gutters	96.22	98.27	100.54	101.99	78.33	141.58	62.27	48.27
Other repair and maintenance services	324.37	382.22	290.22	146.45	250.88	463.91	124.73	88.72
Repair, replacement of hard-surface flooring	58.89	60.97	62.41	54.26	49.78	91.95	32.95	22.92
Repair of built-in appliances	2.51	2.47	2.41	2.75	2.30	2.40	0.34	0.62
Maintenance and repair materials	130.83	110.69	146.17	111.87	139.95	181.61	35.41	28.59
Paints, wallpaper, and supplies	22.18	18.00	26.31	24.02	26.60	27.35	9.52	6.08
Tools, equip. for painting, wallpapering	2.38	1.93	2.83	2.58	2.86	2.94	1.02	0.65
Plumbing supplies and equipment	8.26	8.20	7.63	7.27	7.36	8.41	5.01	2.07
Electrical supplies, heating, cooling equip.	5.60	2.39	8.09	2.38	2.93	21.80	0.58	1.61
Hard-surface flooring, repair, replacement	14.37	9.44	18.40	12.08	16.89	25.61	3.98	2.71
Roofing and gutters	8.59	6.88	9.38	6.56	11.51	7.28	0.05	2.49
Plaster, paneling, siding, windows, doors, screens, awnings	21.27	25.55	19.89	8.50	15.51	36.05	2.69	5.35
Patio, walk, fence, driveway, masonry, brick, and stucco materials	1.97	1.37	2.55	0.38	3.04	3.15	0.12	0.38
Landscape maintenance	7.06	6.79	7.67	5.62	10.93	2.91	0.91	3.04
Miscellaneous supplies and equipment	39.15	30.15	43.42	42.49	42.33	46.12	11.53	4.20
Insulation, other maintenance, repair	21.89	16.39	26.84	20.79	28.09	28.64	3.64	3.06
Finish basement, remodel rooms, build patios, walks, etc.	17.26	13.76	16.58	21.69	14.24	17.48	7.89	1.14
Property management and security	26.65	35.02	22.24	33.93	13.47	30.75	8.32	35.73
Property management	21.35	26.47	18.87	29.78	10.60	26.99	6.34	28.33
Management, upkeep services for security	5.29	8.55	3.37	4.16	2.87	3.77	1.98	7.40
Parking	4.55	5.96	3.82	7.04	2.60	3.92	0.98	7.48

	total married couples	married couples, no children	married couples with children				single parent, at least one child <18	single person
			total	oldest child under 6	oldest child 6 to 17	oldest child 18 or older		
Rented dwellings	**$1,451.41**	**$1,156.54**	**$1,610.86**	**$2,383.52**	**$1,600.44**	**$1,097.23**	**$3,280.23**	**$2,538.22**
Rent	1,408.69	1,113.64	1,572.49	2,350.74	1,557.00	1,064.60	3,179.92	2,473.71
Rent as pay	13.71	9.30	15.25	13.54	13.91	18.97	81.51	35.11
Maintenance, insurance, other expenses	29.02	33.60	23.12	19.24	29.53	13.66	18.81	29.40
Tenant's insurance	7.96	9.21	7.05	9.73	7.31	4.71	10.39	10.33
Maintenance and repair services	11.56	15.11	5.94	0.88	8.95	3.73	3.18	12.49
Maintenance and repair materials	9.50	9.28	10.13	8.63	13.27	5.22	5.23	6.57
Other lodging	**715.24**	**839.81**	**647.70**	**379.28**	**583.89**	**953.72**	**131.03**	**322.08**
Owned vacation homes	238.59	357.88	154.35	114.13	151.72	187.11	27.17	105.61
Mortgage interest and charges	98.53	137.48	70.51	61.83	69.12	79.13	6.88	41.13
Property taxes	95.26	135.61	65.90	61.58	62.01	76.26	6.88	40.10
Maintenance, insurance, and other expenses	49.40	84.31	24.53	12.48	26.68	28.78	9.86	24.39
Homeowner's insurance	11.55	14.15	9.65	7.87	7.98	14.02	1.07	7.23
Ground rent	4.47	8.68	0.65	–	1.24	–	–	2.10
Maintenance and repair services	23.50	44.82	9.29	1.52	13.18	7.28	7.58	11.52
Maintenance and repair materials	1.34	3.27	–	–	–	–	–	0.98
Property management and security	5.53	9.43	2.41	1.85	0.96	5.54	0.65	1.79
Property management	3.83	6.12	1.80	1.49	0.81	3.89	0.59	1.29
Management, upkeep services for security	1.70	3.30	0.61	0.36	0.14	1.65	0.05	0.50
Parking	0.94	1.38	0.71	1.23	0.42	0.90	–	0.78
Housing while attending school	101.02	57.29	146.50	19.91	69.45	379.67	25.85	85.53
Lodging on trips	375.64	424.64	346.85	245.25	362.72	386.94	78.02	130.93
UTILITIES, FUELS, AND PUBLIC SERVICES	**3,270.67**	**2,915.22**	**3,477.99**	**2,978.69**	**3,491.31**	**3,797.46**	**2,470.84**	**1,712.09**
Natural gas	**399.07**	**354.00**	**426.92**	**350.68**	**442.25**	**450.53**	**306.80**	**224.84**
Electricity	**1,199.41**	**1,087.86**	**1,261.64**	**1,040.51**	**1,284.65**	**1,370.73**	**961.05**	**599.79**
Fuel oil and other fuels	**111.11**	**114.08**	**107.37**	**78.07**	**105.62**	**130.92**	**50.34**	**62.56**
Fuel oil	58.07	55.17	60.75	47.37	58.09	75.01	20.50	35.43
Coal	0.09	0.06	0.13	–	0.01	0.45	–	0.06
Bottled/tank gas	44.50	50.31	38.62	25.60	39.00	46.87	26.67	21.55
Wood and other fuels	8.46	8.54	7.88	5.10	8.52	8.59	3.17	5.51
Telephone services	**1,135.48**	**970.33**	**1,234.20**	**1,128.50**	**1,203.58**	**1,365.11**	**913.08**	**624.40**
Residential telephone and pay phones	742.40	670.40	779.39	726.59	765.32	842.46	628.70	454.06
Cellular phone service	370.33	285.18	429.89	376.24	415.38	494.37	263.18	155.58
Pager service	2.24	1.25	2.66	2.01	1.10	6.04	1.15	0.77
Phone cards	20.51	13.50	22.27	23.65	21.78	22.24	20.05	13.98
Water and other public services	**425.59**	**388.96**	**447.86**	**380.92**	**455.21**	**480.17**	**239.57**	**200.50**
Water and sewerage maintenance	309.16	272.00	331.22	268.32	343.28	351.83	177.70	136.61
Trash and garbage collection	113.11	114.81	112.64	109.10	109.09	121.82	61.39	63.33
Septic tank cleaning	3.32	2.15	3.99	3.50	2.84	6.52	0.48	0.57

See appendix for information about mortgage principle reduction.

Note: Average spending figures for total consumer units can be found on Average Spending by Age and Average Spending by Region tables. (–) means sample is too small to make a reliable estimate.

Source: Bureau of Labor Statistics, unpublished tables from the 2002 Consumer Expenditure Survey

Table 9.10 Housing: Shelter and Utilities: Indexed spending by household type, 2002

(indexed average annual spending of consumer units (CU) on shelter and utilities, by type of consumer unit, 2002; index definition: an index of 100 is the average for all consumer units; an index of 132 means that spending by consumer units in that group is 32 percent above the average for all consumer units; an index of 68 indicates spending that is 32 percent below the average for all consumer units)

	total married couples	married couples, no children	married couples with children				single parent, at least one child <18	single person
			total	oldest child under 6	oldest child 6 to 17	oldest child 18 or older		
Average spending of CU, total	$52,334	$45,557	$57,835	$52,779	$58,104	$60,860	$30,185	$24,190
Average spending of CU, index	129	112	142	130	143	150	74	59
Housing, spending index	125	109	139	144	140	133	83	65
SHELTER	**122**	**104**	**138**	**144**	**139**	**131**	**83**	**70**
Owned dwellings*	**143**	**118**	**165**	**165**	**169**	**159**	**60**	**50**
Mortgage interest and charges	148	103	185	201	194	156	63	43
Mortgage interest	147	102	185	206	194	155	64	43
Interest paid, home equity loan	151	122	169	124	184	172	48	38
Interest paid, home equity line of credit	157	141	175	88	182	221	35	45
Property taxes	139	134	144	124	147	152	50	61
Maintenance, repairs, insurance, other expenses	137	145	133	105	121	175	63	61
Homeowner's insurance	135	138	135	101	138	152	61	64
Ground rent	92	104	87	96	90	76	103	113
Maintenance and repair services	140	155	133	102	112	192	67	56
Painting and papering	134	133	135	168	123	135	60	61
Plumbing and water heating	123	144	107	63	99	152	82	89
Heat, air conditioning, electrical work	135	140	126	120	101	177	63	63
Roofing and gutters	135	138	141	143	110	199	87	68
Other repair and maintenance services	151	178	135	68	117	216	58	41
Repair, replacement of hard-surface flooring	135	140	143	125	114	211	76	53
Repair of built-in appliances	155	152	149	170	142	148	21	38
Maintenance and repair materials	156	132	175	134	167	217	42	34
Paints, wallpaper, and supplies	151	122	179	163	181	186	65	41
Tools, equip. for painting, wallpapering	151	122	179	163	181	186	65	41
Plumbing supplies and equipment	147	146	136	129	131	150	89	37
Electrical supplies, heating, cooling equip.	162	69	234	69	85	630	17	47
Hard-surface flooring, repair, replacement	165	108	211	139	194	294	46	31
Roofing and gutters	162	130	177	124	218	138	1	47
Plaster, paneling, siding, windows, doors, screens, awnings	153	184	143	61	111	259	19	38
Patio, walk, fence, driveway, masonry, brick, and stucco materials	153	106	198	29	236	244	9	29
Landscape maintenance	149	144	162	119	231	62	19	64
Miscellaneous supplies and equipment	160	123	178	174	173	189	47	17
Insulation, other maintenance, repair	166	125	204	158	214	218	28	23
Finish basement, remodel rooms, build patios, walks, etc.	153	122	147	192	126	155	70	10
Property management and security	96	127	80	123	49	111	30	129
Property management	97	121	86	136	48	123	29	129
Management, upkeep services for security	93	150	59	73	50	66	35	130
Parking	88	115	74	136	50	76	19	145

	total married couples	married couples, no children	married couples with children				single parent, at least one child <18	single person
			total	oldest child under 6	oldest child 6 to 17	oldest child 18 or older		
Rented dwellings	**67**	**54**	**75**	**110**	**74**	**51**	**152**	**118**
Rent	67	53	75	112	74	51	151	118
Rent as pay	50	34	56	50	51	70	300	129
Maintenance, insurance, other expenses	103	120	82	69	105	49	67	105
Tenant's insurance	89	103	79	109	82	53	117	116
Maintenance and repair services	104	135	53	8	80	33	28	112
Maintenance and repair materials	119	116	127	108	166	65	65	82
Other lodging	**142**	**166**	**128**	**75**	**116**	**189**	**26**	**64**
Owned vacation homes	139	209	90	67	88	109	16	62
Mortgage interest and charges	137	191	98	86	96	110	10	57
Property taxes	149	213	103	97	97	120	11	63
Maintenance, insurance, and other expenses	138	235	69	35	75	80	28	68
Homeowner's insurance	119	146	99	81	82	145	11	75
Ground rent	153	296	22	–	42	–	–	72
Maintenance and repair services	140	267	55	9	79	43	45	69
Maintenance and repair materials	65	158	–	–	–	–	–	47
Property management and security	154	262	67	51	27	154	18	50
Property management	153	245	72	60	32	156	24	52
Management, upkeep services for security	155	300	55	33	13	150	5	45
Parking	124	182	93	162	55	118	–	103
Housing while attending school	126	71	183	25	87	474	32	107
Lodging on trips	149	168	137	97	143	153	31	52
UTILITIES, FUELS, AND PUBLIC SERVICES	**122**	**109**	**130**	**111**	**130**	**141**	**92**	**64**
Natural gas	**121**	**107**	**129**	**106**	**134**	**137**	**93**	**68**
Electricity	**122**	**111**	**129**	**106**	**131**	**140**	**98**	**61**
Fuel oil and other fuels	**126**	**129**	**121**	**88**	**119**	**148**	**57**	**71**
Fuel oil	126	120	132	103	126	163	45	77
Coal	129	86	186	–	14	643	–	86
Bottled/tank gas	126	143	109	73	111	133	76	61
Wood and other fuels	119	120	111	72	120	121	45	78
Telephone services	**119**	**101**	**129**	**118**	**126**	**143**	**95**	**65**
Residential telephone and pay phones	116	105	122	113	119	131	98	71
Cellular phone service	126	97	146	128	141	168	90	53
Pager service	131	73	156	118	64	353	67	45
Phone cards	101	67	110	117	107	110	99	69
Water and other public services	**130**	**118**	**136**	**116**	**139**	**146**	**73**	**61**
Water and sewerage maintenance	130	115	140	113	145	148	75	58
Trash and garbage collection	127	129	126	123	123	137	69	71
Septic tank cleaning	157	101	188	165	134	308	23	27

*See appendix for information about mortgage principle reduction.

Note: Spending index for total consumer units is 100. (–) means sample is too small to make a reliable estimate.

Source: Calculations by New Strategist based on the 2002 Consumer Expenditure Survey

Table 9.11 Housing: Shelter and Utilities: Total spending by household type, 2002

(total annual spending on shelter and utilities, by consumer unit (CU) type, 2002; numbers in thousands)

	total married couples	married couples, no children	married couples with children total	oldest child under 6	oldest child 6 to 17	oldest child 18 or older	single parent, at least one child <18	single person
Number of consumer units	56,265	23,118	28,790	5,547	15,206	8,036	6,730	33,055
Total spending of all CUs	$2,944,555,631	$1,053,194,355	$1,665,069,938	$292,763,005	$883,525,623	$489,069,192	$203,147,607	$799,597,145
Housing, total spending	936,771,177	333,416,812	531,461,385	106,172,742	283,117,321	142,216,065	74,175,906	284,909,970
SHELTER	**$538,893,792**	**$187,485,593**	**$310,786,611**	**$62,506,813**	**$165,928,176**	**$82,340,874**	**$43,835,182**	**$180,656,483**
Owned dwellings*	416,986,667	141,333,974	245,762,668	47,181,562	132,713,254	65,859,440	20,877,402	86,109,597
Mortgage interest and charges	246,204,387	70,587,114	157,536,865	33,007,146	87,274,533	37,249,833	12,596,272	41,647,978
Mortgage interest	233,211,111	66,081,185	150,107,893	32,089,728	83,088,777	34,924,135	12,162,120	39,597,907
Interest paid, home equity loan	7,519,817	2,489,115	4,313,606	611,224	2,475,537	1,226,695	288,044	1,120,234
Interest paid, home equity line of credit	5,454,329	2,016,814	3,112,487	303,421	1,710,219	1,098,762	146,108	929,837
Property taxes	96,894,519	38,597,582	51,409,727	8,568,506	27,707,613	15,132,029	4,196,020	24,971,069
Maintenance, repairs, insurance, other expenses	73,887,761	32,149,509	36,816,076	5,605,854	17,731,260	13,477,577	4,085,110	19,490,220
Homeowner's insurance	21,573,126	9,013,246	10,985,976	1,588,494	5,931,556	3,465,525	1,172,097	5,997,169
Ground rent	2,126,254	988,526	1,030,682	219,217	561,862	249,598	285,150	1,532,430
Maintenance and repair services	41,071,199	18,641,430	19,840,916	2,950,283	8,865,554	8,024,348	2,326,965	9,587,603
Painting and papering	4,187,804	1,714,893	2,162,129	517,202	1,040,090	604,789	223,503	1,114,615
Plumbing and water heating	3,217,233	1,551,449	1,436,621	164,191	702,821	569,592	257,557	1,366,163
Heat, air conditioning, electrical work	6,547,558	2,800,746	3,125,442	574,558	1,324,595	1,226,053	363,353	1,800,506
Roofing and gutters	5,413,818	2,271,806	2,894,547	565,739	1,191,086	1,137,737	419,077	1,595,565
Other repair and maintenance services	18,250,678	8,836,162	8,355,434	812,358	3,814,881	3,727,981	839,433	2,932,640
Repair, replacement of hard-surface flooring	3,313,446	1,409,504	1,796,784	300,980	756,955	738,910	221,754	757,621
Repair of built-in appliances	141,225	57,101	69,384	15,254	34,974	19,286	2,288	20,494
Maintenance and repair materials	7,361,150	2,558,931	4,208,234	620,543	2,128,080	1,459,418	238,309	945,042
Paints, wallpaper, and supplies	1,247,958	416,124	757,465	133,239	404,480	219,785	64,070	200,974
Tools, equip. for painting, wallpapering	133,911	44,618	81,476	14,311	43,489	23,626	6,865	21,486
Plumbing supplies and equipment	464,749	189,568	219,668	40,327	111,916	67,583	33,717	68,424
Electrical supplies, heating, cooling equip.	315,084	55,252	232,911	13,202	44,554	175,185	3,903	53,219
Hard-surface flooring, repair, replacement	808,528	218,234	529,736	67,008	256,829	205,802	26,785	89,579
Roofing and gutters	483,316	159,052	270,050	36,388	175,021	58,502	337	82,307
Plaster, paneling, siding, windows, doors, screens, awnings	1,196,757	590,665	572,633	47,150	235,845	289,698	18,104	176,844
Patio, walk, fence, driveway, masonry, brick, and stucco materials	110,842	31,672	73,415	2,108	46,226	25,313	808	12,561
Landscape maintenance	397,231	156,971	220,819	31,174	166,202	23,385	6,124	100,487
Miscellaneous supplies and equipment	2,202,775	697,008	1,250,062	235,692	643,670	370,620	77,597	138,831
Insulation, other maintenance, repair	1,231,641	378,904	772,724	115,322	427,137	230,151	24,497	101,148
Finish basement, remodel rooms, build patios, walks, etc.	971,134	318,104	477,338	120,314	216,533	140,469	53,100	37,683
Property management and security	1,499,462	809,592	640,290	188,210	204,825	247,107	55,994	1,181,055
Property management	1,201,258	611,933	543,267	165,190	161,184	216,892	42,668	936,448
Management, upkeep services for security	297,642	197,659	97,022	23,076	43,641	30,296	13,325	244,607
Parking	256,006	137,783	109,978	39,051	39,536	31,501	6,595	247,251

	total married couples	married couples, no children	married couples with children				single parent, at least one child <18	single person
			total	oldest child under 6	oldest child 6 to 17	oldest child 18 or older		
Rented dwellings	$81,663,584	$26,736,892	$46,376,659	$13,221,385	$24,336,291	$8,817,340	$22,075,948	$83,900,862
Rent	79,259,943	25,745,130	45,271,987	13,039,555	23,675,742	8,555,126	21,400,862	81,768,484
Rent as pay	771,393	214,997	439,048	75,106	211,515	152,443	548,562	1,160,561
Maintenance, insurance, other expenses	1,632,810	776,765	665,625	106,724	449,033	109,772	126,591	971,817
Tenant's insurance	447,869	212,917	202,970	53,972	111,156	37,850	69,925	341,458
Maintenance and repair services	650,423	349,313	171,013	4,881	136,094	29,974	21,401	412,857
Maintenance and repair materials	534,518	214,535	291,643	47,871	201,784	41,948	35,198	217,171
Other lodging	40,242,979	19,414,728	18,647,283	2,103,866	8,878,631	7,664,094	881,832	10,646,354
Owned vacation homes	13,424,266	8,273,470	4,443,737	633,079	2,307,054	1,503,616	182,854	3,490,939
Mortgage interest and charges	5,543,790	3,178,263	2,029,983	342,971	1,051,039	635,889	46,302	1,359,552
Property taxes	5,359,804	3,135,032	1,897,261	341,584	942,924	612,825	46,302	1,325,506
Maintenance, insurance, and other expenses	2,779,491	1,949,079	706,219	69,227	405,696	231,276	66,358	806,211
Homeowner's insurance	649,861	327,120	277,824	43,655	121,344	112,665	7,201	238,988
Ground rent	251,505	200,664	18,714	–	18,855		–	69,416
Maintenance and repair services	1,322,228	1,036,149	267,459	8,431	200,415	58,502	51,013	380,794
Maintenance and repair materials	75,395	75,596	–	–	–	–	–	32,394
Property management and security	311,145	218,003	69,384	10,262	14,598	44,519	4,375	59,168
Property management	215,495	141,482	51,822	8,265	12,317	31,260	3,971	42,641
Management, upkeep services for security	95,651	76,289	17,562	1,997	2,129	13,259	337	16,528
Parking	52,889	31,903	20,441	6,823	6,387	7,232	–	25,783
Housing while attending school	5,683,890	1,324,430	4,217,735	110,441	1,056,057	3,051,028	173,971	2,827,194
Lodging on trips	21,135,385	9,816,828	9,985,812	1,360,402	5,515,520	3,109,450	525,075	4,327,891
UTILITIES, FUELS, AND PUBLIC SERVICES	184,024,248	67,394,056	100,131,332	16,522,793	53,088,860	30,516,389	16,628,753	56,593,135
Natural gas	22,453,674	8,183,772	12,291,027	1,945,222	6,724,854	3,620,459	2,064,764	7,432,086
Electricity	67,484,804	25,149,147	36,322,616	5,771,709	19,534,388	11,015,186	6,467,867	19,826,058
Fuel oil and other fuels	6,251,604	2,637,301	3,091,182	433,054	1,606,058	1,052,073	338,788	2,067,921
Fuel oil	3,267,309	1,275,420	1,748,993	262,761	883,317	602,780	137,965	1,171,139
Coal	5,064	1,387	3,743	–	152	3,616	–	1,983
Bottled/tank gas	2,503,793	1,163,067	1,111,870	142,003	593,034	376,647	–	712,335
Wood and other fuels	476,002	197,428	226,865	28,290	129,555	69,029	21,334	182,133
Telephone services	63,887,782	22,432,089	35,532,618	6,259,790	18,301,637	10,970,024	6,145,028	20,639,542
Residential telephone and pay phones	41,771,136	15,498,307	22,438,638	4,030,395	11,637,456	6,770,009	4,231,151	15,008,953
Cellular phone service	20,836,617	6,592,791	12,376,533	2,087,003	6,316,268	3,972,757	1,771,201	5,142,697
Pager service	126,034	28,898	76,581	11,149	16,727	48,537	7,740	25,452
Phone cards	1,153,995	312,093	641,153	131,187	331,187	178,721	134,937	462,109
Water and other public services	23,945,821	8,991,977	12,893,889	2,112,963	6,921,923	3,858,646	1,612,306	6,627,528
Water and sewerage maintenance	17,394,887	6,288,096	9,535,824	1,488,371	5,219,916	2,827,306	1,195,921	4,515,644
Trash and garbage collection	6,364,134	2,654,178	3,242,906	605,178	1,658,823	978,946	413,155	2,093,373
Septic tank cleaning	186,800	49,704	114,872	19,415	43,185	52,395	3,230	18,841

See appendix for information about mortgage principle reduction.

Note: Total spending figures for total consumer units can be found on Total Spending by Age and Total Spending by Region tables. Spending by type of consumer unit will not add to total because not all types of consumer units are shown. (–) means sample is too small to make a reliable estimate.

Source: Calculations by New Strategist based on the 2002 Consumer Expenditure Survey

Table 9.12 Housing: Shelter and Utilities: Market shares by household type, 2002

(percentage of total annual spending on shelter and utilities accounted for by types of consumer units, 2002)

	total married couples	married couples, no children	married couples with children				single parent, at least one child <18	single person
			total	oldest child under 6	oldest child 6 to 17	oldest child 18 or older		
Share of total consumer units	50.2%	20.6%	25.7%	4.9%	13.6%	7.2%	6.0%	29.5%
Share of total before-tax income	68.2	24.6	38.4	6.8	20.0	11.8	3.3	16.1
Share of total spending	64.6	23.1	36.5	6.4	19.4	10.7	4.5	17.5
Share of housing spending	62.9	22.4	35.7	7.1	19.0	9.6	5.0	19.1
SHELTER	**61.4%**	**21.4%**	**35.4%**	**7.1%**	**18.9%**	**9.4%**	**5.0%**	**20.6%**
Owned dwellings*	**72.0**	**24.4**	**42.4**	**8.1**	**22.9**	**11.4**	**3.6**	**14.9**
Mortgage interest and charges	74.1	21.3	47.4	9.9	26.3	11.2	3.8	12.5
Mortgage interest	74.0	21.0	47.6	10.2	26.4	11.1	3.9	12.6
Interest paid, home equity loan	75.7	25.1	43.4	6.2	24.9	12.3	2.9	11.3
Interest paid, home equity line of credit	78.6	29.1	44.9	4.4	24.7	15.8	2.1	13.4
Property taxes	69.6	27.7	36.9	6.2	19.9	10.9	3.0	17.9
Maintenance, repairs, insurance, other expenses	68.6	29.9	34.2	5.2	16.5	12.5	3.8	18.1
Homeowner's insurance	67.9	28.4	34.6	5.0	18.7	10.9	3.7	18.9
Ground rent	46.3	21.5	22.4	4.8	12.2	5.4	6.2	33.4
Maintenance and repair services	70.5	32.0	34.1	5.1	15.2	13.8	4.0	16.5
Painting and papering	67.2	27.5	34.7	8.3	16.7	9.7	3.6	17.9
Plumbing and water heating	61.5	29.7	27.5	3.1	13.4	10.9	4.9	26.1
Heat, air conditioning, electrical work	67.7	29.0	32.3	5.9	13.7	12.7	3.8	18.6
Roofing and gutters	67.8	28.5	36.3	7.1	14.9	14.3	5.3	20.0
Other repair and maintenance services	75.8	36.7	34.7	3.4	15.8	15.5	3.5	12.2
Repair, replacement of hard-surface flooring	67.9	28.9	36.8	6.2	15.5	15.1	4.5	15.5
Repair of built-in appliances	77.8	31.4	38.2	8.4	19.3	10.6	1.3	11.3
Maintenance and repair materials	78.4	27.3	44.8	6.6	22.7	15.5	2.5	10.1
Paints, wallpaper, and supplies	75.7	25.2	45.9	8.1	24.5	13.3	3.9	12.2
Tools, equip. for painting, wallpapering	75.6	25.2	46.0	8.1	24.6	13.3	3.9	12.1
Plumbing supplies and equipment	73.8	30.1	34.9	6.4	17.8	10.7	5.4	10.9
Electrical supplies, heating, cooling equip.	81.2	14.2	60.0	3.4	11.5	45.2	1.0	13.7
Hard-surface flooring, repair, replacement	82.7	22.3	54.2	6.9	26.3	21.1	2.7	9.2
Roofing and gutters	81.5	26.8	45.5	6.1	29.5	9.9	0.1	13.9
Plaster, paneling, siding, windows, doors, screens, awnings	76.7	37.8	36.7	3.0	15.1	18.6	1.2	11.3
Patio, walk, fence, driveway, masonry, brick, and stucco materials	76.6	21.9	50.8	1.5	32.0	17.5	0.6	8.7
Landscape maintenance	74.9	29.6	41.6	5.9	31.3	4.4	1.2	19.0
Miscellaneous supplies and equipment	80.4	25.4	45.6	8.6	23.5	13.5	2.8	5.1
Insulation, other maintenance, repair	83.5	25.7	52.4	7.8	29.0	15.6	1.7	6.9
Finish basement, remodel rooms, build patios, walks, etc.	76.8	25.2	37.7	9.5	17.1	11.1	4.2	3.0
Property management and security	48.4	26.1	20.7	6.1	6.6	8.0	1.8	38.1
Property management	48.8	24.9	22.1	6.7	6.6	8.8	1.7	38.1
Management, upkeep services for security	46.5	30.9	15.2	3.6	6.8	4.7	2.1	38.2
Parking	44.2	23.8	19.0	6.7	6.8	5.4	1.1	42.7

	total married couples	married couples, no children	married couples with children				single parent, at least one child <18	single person
			total	oldest child under 6	oldest child 6 to 17	oldest child 18 or older		
Rented dwellings	**33.7%**	**11.0%**	**19.2%**	**5.5%**	**10.1%**	**3.6%**	**9.1%**	**34.6%**
Rent	33.6	10.9	19.2	5.5	10.0	3.6	9.1	34.7
Rent as pay	25.3	7.1	14.4	2.5	6.9	5.0	18.0	38.1
Maintenance, insurance, other expenses	51.9	24.7	21.2	3.4	14.3	3.5	4.0	30.9
Tenant's insurance	44.9	21.3	20.3	5.4	11.1	3.8	7.0	34.2
Maintenance and repair services	52.0	27.9	13.7	0.4	10.9	2.4	1.7	33.0
Maintenance and repair materials	59.6	23.9	32.5	5.3	22.5	4.7	3.9	24.2
Other lodging	**71.1**	**34.3**	**33.0**	**3.7**	**15.7**	**13.5**	**1.6**	**18.8**
Owned vacation homes	69.8	43.0	23.1	3.3	12.0	7.8	1.0	18.2
Mortgage interest and charges	68.7	39.4	25.2	4.3	13.0	7.9	0.6	16.8
Property taxes	75.0	43.9	26.5	4.8	13.2	8.6	0.6	18.5
Maintenance, insurance, and other expenses	69.2	48.5	17.6	1.7	10.1	5.8	1.7	20.1
Homeowner's insurance	59.8	30.1	25.5	4.0	11.2	10.4	0.7	22.0
Ground rent	76.6	61.1	5.7	–	5.7	–	–	21.1
Maintenance and repair services	70.4	55.1	14.2	0.4	10.7	3.1	2.7	20.3
Maintenance and repair materials	32.5	32.6	–	–	–	–	–	14.0
Property management and security	77.1	54.0	17.2	2.5	3.6	11.0	1.1	14.7
Property management	76.9	50.5	18.5	2.9	4.4	11.2	1.4	15.2
Management, upkeep services for security	77.6	61.9	14.2	1.6	1.7	10.8	0.3	13.4
Parking	62.1	37.4	24.0	8.0	7.5	8.5	–	30.3
Housing while attending school	63.3	14.7	46.9	1.2	11.8	34.0	1.9	31.5
Lodging on trips	74.6	34.6	35.2	4.8	19.5	11.0	1.9	15.3
UTILITIES, FUELS, AND PUBLIC SERVICES	**61.2**	**22.4**	**33.3**	**5.5**	**17.6**	**10.1**	**5.5**	**18.8**
Natural gas	**60.7**	**22.1**	**33.2**	**5.3**	**18.2**	**9.8**	**5.6**	**20.1**
Electricity	**61.4**	**22.9**	**33.0**	**5.2**	**17.8**	**10.0**	**5.9**	**18.0**
Fuel oil and other fuels	**63.1**	**26.6**	**31.2**	**4.4**	**16.2**	**10.6**	**3.4**	**20.9**
Fuel oil	63.4	24.7	33.9	5.1	17.1	11.7	2.7	22.7
Coal	64.5	17.7	47.7	–	1.9	46.1	–	25.3
Bottled/tank gas	63.3	29.4	28.1	3.6	15.0	9.5	4.5	18.0
Wood and other fuels	59.9	24.8	28.5	3.6	16.3	8.7	2.7	22.9
Telephone services	**59.6**	**20.9**	**33.1**	**5.8**	**17.1**	**10.2**	**5.7**	**19.2**
Residential telephone and pay phones	58.1	21.6	31.2	5.6	16.2	9.4	5.9	20.9
Cellular phone service	63.3	20.0	37.6	6.3	19.2	12.1	5.4	15.6
Pager service	65.7	15.1	39.9	5.8	8.7	25.3	4.0	13.3
Phone cards	50.8	13.7	28.2	5.8	14.6	7.9	5.9	20.3
Water and other public services	**65.1**	**24.4**	**35.0**	**5.7**	**18.8**	**10.5**	**4.4**	**18.0**
Water and sewerage maintenance	65.4	23.7	35.9	5.6	19.6	10.6	4.5	17.0
Trash and garbage collection	63.7	26.6	32.5	6.1	16.6	9.8	4.1	21.0
Septic tank cleaning	78.6	20.9	48.3	8.2	18.2	22.0	1.4	7.9

*See appendix for information about mortgage principle reduction.
Note: Market share for total consumer units is 100.0%. Market shares by type of consumer unit will not add to total because not all types of consumer units are shown. (–) means sample is too small to make a reliable estimate.
Source: Calculations by New Strategist based on the 2002 Consumer Expenditure Survey

Table 9.13 Housing: Shelter and Utilities: Average spending by race and Hispanic origin, 2002

(average annual spending of consumer units (CU) on shelter and utilities, by race and Hispanic origin of consumer unit reference person, 2002)

	total consumer units	race black	race white and other	Hispanic origin Hispanic	Hispanic origin non-Hispanic
Number of consumer units					
(in thousands, add 000)	112,108	13,554	98,553	10,500	101,608
Average number of persons per CU	2.5	2.7	2.5	3.3	2.4
Average before-tax income of CU	$49,430.00	$35,944.00	$51,177.00	$37,360.00	$50,742.00
Average spending of CU, total	40,676.60	30,135.94	42,134.55	34,742.47	41,294.67
Housing, average spending	13,283.08	10,756.15	13,632.80	11,841.17	13,430.92
SHELTER	$7,829.41	$6,279.04	$8,042.64	$7,372.46	$7,876.63
Owned dwellings*	5,164.96	3,222.50	5,432.11	3,566.61	5,330.13
Mortgage interest and charges	2,962.16	1,999.62	3,094.55	2,231.64	3,037.65
Mortgage interest	2,811.49	1,914.19	2,934.90	2,171.35	2,877.64
Interest paid, home equity loan	88.61	69.59	91.23	47.80	92.83
Interest paid, home equity line of credit	61.88	15.84	68.21	10.95	67.14
Property taxes	1,242.36	668.69	1,321.26	696.33	1,298.79
Maintenance, repairs, insurance, other expenses	960.43	554.20	1,016.30	638.64	993.68
Homeowner's insurance	283.30	185.66	296.73	181.25	293.85
Ground rent	40.96	6.33	45.73	50.36	39.99
Maintenance and repair services	519.60	316.19	547.58	333.05	538.88
Painting and papering	55.58	32.01	58.82	37.34	57.46
Plumbing and water heating	46.63	42.46	47.20	18.95	49.49
Heat, air conditioning, electrical work	86.28	56.65	90.35	25.00	92.61
Roofing and gutters	71.20	37.11	75.89	44.98	73.91
Other repair and maintenance services	214.77	129.36	226.51	170.89	219.30
Repair, replacement of hard-surface flooring	43.54	17.90	47.06	35.10	44.41
Repair of built-in appliances	1.62	0.71	1.74	0.79	1.70
Maintenance and repair materials	83.75	34.37	90.54	58.53	86.35
Paints, wallpaper, and supplies	14.71	11.62	15.13	11.31	15.06
Tools, equip. for painting, wallpapering	1.58	1.25	1.63	1.21	1.62
Plumbing supplies and equipment	5.62	2.78	6.02	6.81	5.50
Electrical supplies, heating, cooling equip.	3.46	1.12	3.78	2.12	3.60
Hard-surface flooring, repair, replacement	8.72	2.21	9.61	8.61	8.73
Roofing and gutters	5.29	2.94	5.61	1.86	5.64
Plaster, paneling, siding, windows, doors, screens, awnings	13.92	6.93	14.88	8.37	14.49
Patio, walk, fence, driveway, masonry, brick, and stucco materials	1.29	0.11	1.46	3.53	1.06
Landscape maintenance	4.73	0.75	5.28	0.65	5.15
Miscellaneous supplies and equipment	24.43	4.68	27.15	14.06	25.50
Insulation, other maintenance, repair	13.15	3.82	14.43	7.51	13.73
Finish basement, remodel rooms, build patios, walks, etc.	11.28	0.86	12.71	6.55	11.77
Property management and security	27.64	10.47	30.01	12.90	29.17
Property management	21.94	7.10	23.98	10.45	23.12
Management, upkeep services for security	5.71	3.37	6.03	2.45	6.04
Parking	5.17	1.18	5.72	2.55	5.44

	total consumer units	race		Hispanic origin	
		black	white and other	Hispanic	non-Hispanic
Rented dwellings	**$2,159.89**	**$2,852.11**	**$2,064.69**	**$3,644.64**	**$2,006.46**
Rent	2,104.66	2,760.71	2,014.44	3,576.28	1,952.59
Rent as pay	27.17	56.25	23.17	44.55	25.37
Maintenance, insurance, other expenses	28.06	35.15	27.09	23.81	28.50
Tenant's insurance	8.90	7.14	9.15	6.52	9.15
Maintenance and repair services	11.16	23.17	9.51	8.73	11.41
Maintenance and repair materials	8.00	4.84	8.44	8.57	7.94
Other lodging	**504.56**	**204.42**	**545.84**	**161.21**	**540.04**
Owned vacation homes	171.55	73.75	185.00	46.23	184.50
Mortgage interest and charges	71.98	42.02	76.11	19.06	77.45
Property taxes	63.76	18.41	69.99	18.35	68.45
Maintenance, insurance, and other expenses	35.81	13.32	38.90	8.82	38.60
Homeowner's insurance	9.70	9.80	9.68	3.06	10.38
Ground rent	2.93	–	3.34	3.32	2.89
Maintenance and repair services	16.76	1.25	18.89	0.22	18.47
Maintenance and repair materials	2.07	–	2.35	–	2.28
Property management and security	3.60	2.14	3.80	2.16	3.74
Property management	2.50	1.53	2.63	2.00	2.55
Management, upkeep services for security	1.10	0.62	1.16	0.16	1.20
Parking	0.76	0.12	0.84	0.07	0.83
Housing while attending school	80.14	46.19	84.81	22.40	86.10
Lodging on trips	252.87	84.49	276.03	92.58	269.44
UTILITIES, FUELS, AND PUBLIC SERVICES	**2,684.32**	**2,768.34**	**2,672.77**	**2,412.72**	**2,712.39**
Natural gas	**329.75**	**380.24**	**322.81**	**245.32**	**338.47**
Electricity	**981.09**	**1,033.84**	**973.83**	**808.39**	**998.93**
Fuel oil and other fuels	**88.41**	**29.97**	**96.45**	**45.81**	**92.81**
Fuel oil	45.98	16.37	50.05	17.70	48.90
Coal	0.07	–	0.07	–	0.07
Bottled/tank gas	35.27	9.16	38.86	24.68	36.37
Wood and other fuels	7.09	4.43	7.46	3.43	7.47
Telephone services	**956.74**	**1,050.33**	**943.87**	**1,021.11**	**950.09**
Residential telephone and pay phones	641.00	748.44	626.22	661.18	638.91
Cellular phone service	293.76	276.42	296.14	299.86	293.12
Pager service	1.71	3.86	1.41	1.50	1.73
Phone cards	20.28	21.61	20.10	58.57	16.32
Water and other public services	**328.33**	**273.97**	**335.81**	**292.09**	**332.08**
Water and sewerage maintenance	237.16	215.86	240.09	220.54	238.87
Trash and garbage collection	89.05	57.28	93.42	69.69	91.05
Septic tank cleaning	2.12	0.83	2.30	1.86	2.15

See appendix for information about mortgage principle reduction.
Note: Other races include Asians, Native Americans, and Pacific Islanders. (–) means sample is too small to make a reliable estimate.
Source: Bureau of Labor Statistics, unpublished tables from the 2002 Consumer Expenditure Survey

Table 9.14 Housing: Shelter and Utilities: Indexed spending by race and Hispanic origin, 2002

(indexed average annual spending of consumer units (CU) on shelter and utilities, by race and Hispanic origin of consumer unit reference person, 2002; index definition: an index of 100 is the average for all consumer units; an index of 132 means that spending by consumer units in that group is 32 percent above the average for all consumer units; an index of 68 indicates spending that is 32 percent below the average for all consumer units)

	total consumer units	race		Hispanic origin	
		black	white and other	Hispanic	non-Hispanic
Average spending of CU, total	$40,677	$30,136	$42,135	$34,742	$41,295
Average spending of CU, index	100	74	104	85	102
Housing, spending index	100	81	103	89	101
SHELTER	100	80	103	94	101
Owned dwellings*	100	62	105	69	103
Mortgage interest and charges	100	68	104	75	103
Mortgage interest	100	68	104	77	102
Interest paid, home equity loan	100	79	103	54	105
Interest paid, home equity line of credit	100	26	110	18	109
Property taxes	100	54	106	56	105
Maintenance, repairs, insurance, other expenses	100	58	106	66	103
Homeowner's insurance	100	66	105	64	104
Ground rent	100	15	112	123	98
Maintenance and repair services	100	61	105	64	104
Painting and papering	100	58	106	67	103
Plumbing and water heating	100	91	101	41	106
Heat, air conditioning, electrical work	100	66	105	29	107
Roofing and gutters	100	52	107	63	104
Other repair and maintenance services	100	60	105	80	102
Repair, replacement of hard-surface flooring	100	41	108	81	102
Repair of built-in appliances	100	44	107	49	105
Maintenance and repair materials	100	41	108	70	103
Paints, wallpaper, and supplies	100	79	103	77	102
Tools, equip. for painting, wallpapering	100	79	103	77	103
Plumbing supplies and equipment	100	49	107	121	98
Electrical supplies, heating, cooling equip.	100	32	109	61	104
Hard-surface flooring, repair, replacement	100	25	110	99	100
Roofing and gutters	100	56	106	35	107
Plaster, paneling, siding, windows, doors, screens, awnings	100	50	107	60	104
Patio, walk, fence, driveway, masonry, brick, and stucco materials	100	9	113	274	82
Landscape maintenance	100	16	112	14	109
Miscellaneous supplies and equipment	100	19	111	58	104
Insulation, other maintenance, repair	100	29	110	57	104
Finish basement, remodel rooms, build patios, walks, etc.	100	8	113	58	104
Property management and security	100	38	109	47	106
Property management	100	32	109	48	105
Management, upkeep services for security	100	59	106	43	106
Parking	100	23	111	49	105

	total consumer units	race		Hispanic origin	
		black	white and other	Hispanic	non-Hispanic
Rented dwellings	**100**	**132**	**96**	**169**	**93**
Rent	100	131	96	170	93
Rent as pay	100	207	85	164	93
Maintenance, insurance, other expenses	100	125	97	85	102
Tenant's insurance	100	80	103	73	103
Maintenance and repair services	100	208	85	78	102
Maintenance and repair materials	100	61	106	107	99
Other lodging	**100**	**41**	**108**	**32**	**107**
Owned vacation homes	100	43	108	27	108
Mortgage interest and charges	100	58	106	26	108
Property taxes	100	29	110	29	107
Maintenance, insurance, and other expenses	100	37	109	25	108
Homeowner's insurance	100	101	100	32	107
Ground rent	100	–	114	113	99
Maintenance and repair services	100	7	113	1	110
Maintenance and repair materials	100	–	114	–	110
Property management and security	100	59	106	60	104
Property management	100	61	105	80	102
Management, upkeep services for security	100	56	105	15	109
Parking	100	16	111	9	109
Housing while attending school	100	58	106	28	107
Lodging on trips	100	33	109	37	107
UTILITIES, FUELS, AND PUBLIC SERVICES	**100**	**103**	**100**	**90**	**101**
Natural gas	**100**	**115**	**98**	**74**	**103**
Electricity	**100**	**105**	**99**	**82**	**102**
Fuel oil and other fuels	**100**	**34**	**109**	**52**	**105**
Fuel oil	100	36	109	38	106
Coal	100	–	100	–	100
Bottled/tank gas	100	26	110	70	103
Wood and other fuels	100	62	105	48	105
Telephone services	**100**	**110**	**99**	**107**	**99**
Residential telephone and pay phones	100	117	98	103	100
Cellular phone service	100	94	101	102	100
Pager service	100	226	82	88	101
Phone cards	100	107	99	289	80
Water and other public services	**100**	**83**	**102**	**89**	**101**
Water and sewerage maintenance	100	91	101	93	101
Trash and garbage collection	100	64	105	78	102
Septic tank cleaning	100	39	108	88	101

See appendix for information about mortgage principle reduction.
Note: Other races include Asians, Native Americans, and Pacific Islanders. (–) means sample is too small to make a reliable estimate.
Source: Calculations by New Strategist based on the 2002 Consumer Expenditure Survey

Table 9.15 Housing: Shelter and Utilities: Total spending by race and Hispanic origin, 2002

(total annual spending on shelter and utilities, by consumer unit race and Hispanic origin groups, 2002; numbers in thousands)

| | total consumer units | race | | Hispanic origin | |
		black	white and other	Hispanic	non-Hispanic
Number of consumer units	112,108	13,554	98,553	10,500	101,608
Total spending of all consumer units	$4,560,172,273	$408,462,531	$4,152,486,306	$364,795,935	$4,195,868,829
Housing, total spending	1,489,139,533	145,788,857	1,343,553,338	124,332,285	1,364,688,919
SHELTER	**$877,739,496**	**$85,106,108**	**$792,626,300**	**$77,410,830**	**$800,328,621**
Owned dwellings*	**579,033,336**	**43,677,765**	**535,350,737**	**37,449,405**	**541,583,849**
Mortgage interest and charges	332,081,833	27,102,849	304,977,186	23,432,220	308,649,541
Mortgage interest	315,190,521	25,944,931	289,243,200	22,799,175	292,391,245
Interest paid, home equity loan	9,933,890	943,223	8,990,990	501,900	9,432,271
Interest paid, home equity line of credit	6,937,243	214,695	6,722,300	114,975	6,821,961
Property taxes	139,278,495	9,063,424	130,214,137	7,311,465	131,967,454
Maintenance, repairs, insurance, other expenses	107,671,886	7,511,627	100,159,414	6,705,720	100,965,837
Homeowner's insurance	31,760,196	2,516,436	29,243,632	1,903,125	29,857,511
Ground rent	4,591,944	85,797	4,506,829	528,780	4,063,304
Maintenance and repair services	58,251,317	4,285,639	53,965,652	3,497,025	54,754,519
Painting and papering	6,230,963	433,864	5,796,887	392,070	5,838,396
Plumbing and water heating	5,227,596	575,503	4,651,702	198,975	5,028,580
Heat, air conditioning, electrical work	9,672,678	767,834	8,904,264	262,500	9,409,917
Roofing and gutters	7,982,090	502,989	7,479,187	472,290	7,509,847
Other repair and maintenance services	24,077,435	1,753,345	22,323,240	1,794,345	22,282,634
Repair, replacement of hard-surface flooring	4,881,182	242,617	4,637,904	368,550	4,512,411
Repair of built-in appliances	181,615	9,623	171,482	8,295	172,734
Maintenance and repair materials	9,389,045	465,851	8,922,989	614,565	8,773,851
Paints, wallpaper, and supplies	1,649,109	157,497	1,491,107	118,755	1,530,216
Tools, equip. for painting, wallpapering	177,131	16,943	160,641	12,705	164,605
Plumbing supplies and equipment	630,047	37,680	593,289	71,505	558,844
Electrical supplies, heating, cooling equip.	387,894	15,180	372,530	22,260	365,789
Hard-surface flooring, repair, replacement	977,582	29,954	947,094	90,405	887,038
Roofing and gutters	593,051	39,849	552,882	19,530	573,069
Plaster, paneling, siding, windows, doors, screens, awnings	1,560,543	93,929	1,466,469	87,885	1,472,300
Patio, walk, fence, driveway, masonry, brick, and stucco materials	144,619	1,491	143,887	37,065	107,704
Landscape maintenance	530,271	10,166	520,360	6,825	523,281
Miscellaneous supplies and equipment	2,738,798	63,433	2,675,714	147,630	2,591,004
Insulation, other maintenance, repair	1,474,220	51,776	1,422,120	78,855	1,395,078
Finish basement, remodel rooms, build patios, walks, etc.	1,264,578	11,656	1,252,609	68,775	1,195,926
Property management and security	3,098,665	141,910	2,957,576	135,450	2,963,905
Property management	2,459,650	96,233	2,363,301	109,725	2,349,177
Management, upkeep services for security	640,137	45,677	594,275	25,725	613,712
Parking	579,598	15,994	563,723	26,775	552,748

	total consumer units	race		Hispanic origin	
		black	white and other	Hispanic	non-Hispanic
Rented dwellings	**$242,140,948**	**$38,657,499**	**$203,481,394**	**$38,268,720**	**$203,872,388**
Rent	235,949,223	37,418,663	198,529,105	37,550,940	198,398,765
Rent as pay	3,045,974	762,413	2,283,473	467,775	2,577,795
Maintenance, insurance, other expenses	3,145,750	476,423	2,669,801	250,005	2,895,828
Tenant's insurance	997,761	96,776	901,760	68,460	929,713
Maintenance and repair services	1,251,125	314,046	937,239	91,665	1,159,347
Maintenance and repair materials	896,864	65,601	831,787	89,985	806,768
Other lodging	**56,565,212**	**2,770,709**	**53,794,170**	**1,692,705**	**54,872,384**
Owned vacation homes	19,232,127	999,608	18,232,305	485,415	18,746,676
Mortgage interest and charges	8,069,534	569,539	7,500,869	200,130	7,869,540
Property taxes	7,148,006	249,529	6,897,724	192,675	6,955,068
Maintenance, insurance, and other expenses	4,014,587	180,539	3,833,712	92,610	3,922,069
Homeowner's insurance	1,087,448	132,829	953,993	32,130	1,054,691
Ground rent	328,476	–	328,476	34,860	293,647
Maintenance and repair services	1,878,930	16,943	1,861,666	2,310	1,876,700
Maintenance and repair materials	232,064	–	231,600	–	231,666
Property management and security	403,589	29,006	374,501	–	380,014
Property management	280,270	20,738	259,194	22,680	259,100
Management, upkeep services for security	123,319	8,403	114,321	21,000	121,930
Parking	85,202	1,626	82,785	1,680	84,335
Housing while attending school	8,984,335	626,059	8,358,280	735	8,748,449
Lodging on trips	28,348,750	1,145,177	27,203,585	235,200	27,377,260
UTILITIES, FUELS, AND PUBLIC SERVICES	**300,933,747**	**37,522,080**	**263,409,502**	**25,333,560**	**275,600,523**
Natural gas	**36,967,613**	**5,153,773**	**31,813,894**	**2,575,860**	**34,391,260**
Electricity	**109,988,038**	**14,012,667**	**95,973,868**	**8,488,095**	**101,499,279**
Fuel oil and other fuels	**9,911,468**	**406,213**	**9,505,437**	**481,005**	**9,430,238**
Fuel oil	5,154,726	221,879	4,932,578	185,850	4,968,631
Coal	7,848	–	6,899	–	7,113
Bottled/tank gas	3,954,049	124,155	3,829,770	259,140	3,695,483
Wood and other fuels	794,846	60,044	735,205	36,015	759,012
Telephone services	**107,258,208**	**14,236,173**	**93,021,220**	**10,721,655**	**96,536,745**
Residential telephone and pay phones	71,861,228	10,144,356	61,715,860	6,942,390	64,918,367
Cellular phone service	32,932,846	3,746,597	29,185,485	3,148,530	29,783,337
Pager service	191,705	52,318	138,960	15,750	175,782
Phone cards	2,273,550	292,902	1,980,915	614,985	1,658,243
Water and other public services	**36,808,420**	**3,713,389**	**33,095,083**	**3,066,945**	**33,741,985**
Water and sewerage maintenance	26,587,533	2,925,766	23,661,590	2,315,670	24,271,103
Trash and garbage collection	9,983,217	776,373	9,206,821	731,745	9,251,408
Septic tank cleaning	237,669	11,250	226,672	19,530	218,457

See appendix for information about mortgage principle reduction.

Note: Other races include Asians, Native Americans, and Pacific Islanders. Numbers may not add to total because of rounding. (–) means sample is too small to make a reliable estimate.

Source: Calculations by New Strategist based on the 2002 Consumer Expenditure Survey

Table 9.16 Housing: Shelter and Utilities: Market shares by race and Hispanic origin, 2002

(percentage of total annual spending on shelter and utilities accounted for by consumer unit race and Hispanic origin groups, 2002)

	total consumer units	race		Hispanic origin	
		black	white and other	Hispanic	non-Hispanic
Share of total consumer units	100.0%	12.1%	87.9%	9.4%	90.6%
Share of total before-tax income	100.0	8.8	91.0	7.1	93.0
Share of total spending	100.0	9.0	91.1	8.0	92.0
Share of housing spending	100.0	9.8	90.2	8.3	91.6
SHELTER	100.0%	9.7%	90.3%	8.8%	91.2%
Owned dwellings*	100.0	7.5	92.5	6.5	93.5
Mortgage interest and charges	100.0	8.2	91.8	7.1	92.9
Mortgage interest	100.0	8.2	91.8	7.2	92.8
Interest paid, home equity loan	100.0	9.5	90.5	5.1	95.0
Interest paid, home equity line of credit	100.0	3.1	96.9	1.7	98.3
Property taxes	100.0	6.5	93.5	5.2	94.8
Maintenance, repairs, insurance, other expenses	100.0	7.0	93.0	6.2	93.8
Homeowner's insurance	100.0	7.9	92.1	6.0	94.0
Ground rent	100.0	1.9	98.1	11.5	88.5
Maintenance and repair services	100.0	7.4	92.6	6.0	94.0
Painting and papering	100.0	7.0	93.0	6.3	93.7
Plumbing and water heating	100.0	11.0	89.0	3.8	96.2
Heat, air conditioning, electrical work	100.0	7.9	92.1	2.7	97.3
Roofing and gutters	100.0	6.3	93.7	5.9	94.1
Other repair and maintenance services	100.0	7.3	92.7	7.5	92.5
Repair, replacement of hard-surface flooring	100.0	5.0	95.0	7.6	92.4
Repair of built-in appliances	100.0	5.3	94.4	4.6	95.1
Maintenance and repair materials	100.0	5.0	95.0	6.5	93.4
Paints, wallpaper, and supplies	100.0	9.6	90.4	7.2	92.8
Tools, equip. for painting, wallpapering	100.0	9.6	90.7	7.2	92.9
Plumbing supplies and equipment	100.0	6.0	94.2	11.3	88.7
Electrical supplies, heating, cooling equip.	100.0	3.9	96.0	5.7	94.3
Hard-surface flooring, repair, replacement	100.0	3.1	96.9	9.2	90.7
Roofing and gutters	100.0	6.7	93.2	3.3	96.6
Plaster, paneling, siding, windows, doors, screens, awnings	100.0	6.0	94.0	5.6	94.3
Patio, walk, fence, driveway, masonry, brick, and stucco materials	100.0	1.0	99.5	25.6	74.5
Landscape maintenance	100.0	1.9	98.1	1.3	98.7
Miscellaneous supplies and equipment	100.0	2.3	97.7	5.4	94.6
Insulation, other maintenance, repair	100.0	3.5	96.5	5.3	94.6
Finish basement, remodel rooms, build patios, walks, etc.	100.0	0.9	99.1	5.4	94.6
Property management and security	100.0	4.6	95.4	4.4	95.7
Property management	100.0	3.9	96.1	4.5	95.5
Management, upkeep services for security	100.0	7.1	92.8	4.0	95.9
Parking	100.0	2.8	97.3	4.6	95.4

	total consumer units	race		Hispanic origin	
		black	white and other	Hispanic	non-Hispanic
Rented dwellings	**100.0%**	**16.0%**	**84.0%**	**15.8%**	**84.2%**
Rent	100.0	15.9	84.1	15.9	84.1
Rent as pay	100.0	25.0	75.0	15.4	84.6
Maintenance, insurance, other expenses	100.0	15.1	84.9	7.9	92.1
Tenant's insurance	100.0	9.7	90.4	6.9	93.2
Maintenance and repair services	100.0	25.1	74.9	7.3	92.7
Maintenance and repair materials	100.0	7.3	92.7	10.0	90.0
Other lodging	**100.0**	**4.9**	**95.1**	**3.0**	**97.0**
Owned vacation homes	100.0	5.2	94.8	2.5	97.5
Mortgage interest and charges	100.0	7.1	93.0	2.5	97.5
Property taxes	100.0	3.5	96.5	2.7	97.3
Maintenance, insurance, and other expenses	100.0	4.5	95.5	2.3	97.7
Homeowner's insurance	100.0	12.2	87.7	3.0	97.0
Ground rent	100.0	–	100.0	10.6	89.4
Maintenance and repair services	100.0	0.9	99.1	0.1	99.9
Maintenance and repair materials	100.0	–	99.8	–	99.8
Property management and security	100.0	7.2	92.8	5.6	94.2
Property management	100.0	7.4	92.5	7.5	92.4
Management, upkeep services for security	100.0	6.8	92.7	1.4	98.9
Parking	100.0	1.9	97.2	0.9	99.0
Housing while attending school	100.0	7.0	93.0	2.6	97.4
Lodging on trips	100.0	4.0	96.0	3.4	96.6
UTILITIES, FUELS, AND PUBLIC SERVICES	**100.0**	**12.5**	**87.5**	**8.4**	**91.6**
Natural gas	**100.0**	**13.9**	**86.1**	**7.0**	**93.0**
Electricity	**100.0**	**12.7**	**87.3**	**7.7**	**92.3**
Fuel oil and other fuels	**100.0**	**4.1**	**95.9**	**4.9**	**95.1**
Fuel oil	100.0	4.3	95.7	3.6	96.4
Coal	100.0	–	87.9	–	90.6
Bottled/tank gas	100.0	3.1	96.9	6.6	93.5
Wood and other fuels	100.0	7.6	92.5	4.5	95.5
Telephone services	**100.0**	**13.3**	**86.7**	**10.0**	**90.0**
Residential telephone and pay phones	100.0	14.1	85.9	9.7	90.3
Cellular phone service	100.0	11.4	88.6	9.6	90.4
Pager service	100.0	27.3	72.5	8.2	91.7
Phone cards	100.0	12.9	87.1	27.0	72.9
Water and other public services	**100.0**	**10.1**	**89.9**	**8.3**	**91.7**
Water and sewerage maintenance	100.0	11.0	89.0	8.7	91.3
Trash and garbage collection	100.0	7.8	92.2	7.3	92.7
Septic tank cleaning	100.0	4.7	95.4	8.2	91.9

*See appendix for information about mortgage principle reduction.

Note: Other races include Asians, Native Americans, and Pacific Islanders. Numbers may not add to total because of rounding. (–) means sample is too small to make a reliable estimate.

Source: Calculations by New Strategist based on the 2002 Consumer Expenditure Survey

Table 9.17 Housing: Shelter and Utilities: Average spending by region, 2002

(average annual spending of consumer units (CU) on shelter and utilities, by region in which consumer unit lives, 2002)

	total consumer units	Northeast	Midwest	South	West
Number of consumer units					
(in thousands, add 000)	112,108	21,313	25,883	40,004	24,907
Average number of persons per CU	2.5	2.5	2.5	2.5	2.6
Average before-tax income of CU	$49,430.00	$53,983.00	$49,197.00	$45,641.00	$52,016.00
Average spending of CU, total	40,676.60	42,390.20	40,601.14	37,280.55	44,728.34
Housing, average spending	13,283.08	14,558.03	12,641.21	11,766.17	15,297.47
SHELTER	$7,829.41	$8,961.50	$7,096.54	$6,478.27	$9,792.35
Owned dwellings*	5,164.96	5,793.22	4,943.66	4,322.43	6,210.52
Mortgage interest and charges	2,962.16	2,844.06	2,643.74	2,529.97	4,088.29
Mortgage interest	2,811.49	2,635.76	2,470.97	2,427.94	3,931.78
Interest paid, home equity loan	88.61	127.32	104.88	55.63	91.56
Interest paid, home equity line of credit	61.88	80.79	67.88	46.00	64.94
Property taxes	1,242.36	1,945.67	1,316.49	906.32	1,103.23
Maintenance, repairs, insurance, other expenses	960.43	1,003.49	983.44	886.14	1,018.99
Homeowner's insurance	283.30	248.30	284.80	311.36	266.65
Ground rent	40.96	16.56	30.45	33.79	84.30
Maintenance and repair services	519.60	579.02	553.76	450.35	544.48
Painting and papering	55.58	66.58	31.29	51.57	77.83
Plumbing and water heating	46.63	55.50	50.04	43.18	41.04
Heat, air conditioning, electrical work	86.28	70.31	84.73	100.42	78.83
Roofing and gutters	71.20	61.97	78.19	75.56	64.81
Other repair and maintenance services	214.77	286.41	279.50	130.63	221.34
Repair, replacement of hard-surface flooring	43.54	36.14	28.71	47.84	58.36
Repair of built-in appliances	1.62	2.11	1.31	1.15	2.27
Maintenance and repair materials	83.75	103.01	89.42	66.41	89.22
Paints, wallpaper, and supplies	14.71	13.85	16.04	12.84	17.07
Tools, equip. for painting, wallpapering	1.58	1.49	1.72	1.38	1.83
Plumbing supplies and equipment	5.62	3.52	5.63	6.28	6.36
Electrical supplies, heating, cooling equip.	3.46	4.14	3.97	2.38	4.09
Hard-surface flooring, repair, replacement	8.72	13.41	7.27	6.05	10.48
Roofing and gutters	5.29	9.93	5.16	4.35	2.94
Plaster, paneling, siding, windows, doors, screens, awnings	13.92	10.67	16.55	11.78	17.38
Patio, walk, fence, driveway, masonry, brick, and stucco materials	1.29	0.51	1.64	0.61	2.70
Landscape maintenance	4.73	4.83	8.06	2.64	4.54
Miscellaneous supplies and equipment	24.43	40.65	23.37	18.10	21.83
Insulation, other maintenance, repair	13.15	21.29	11.61	9.51	13.63
Finish basement, remodel rooms, build patios, walks, etc.	11.28	19.36	11.76	8.59	8.20
Property management and security	27.64	50.17	21.32	19.35	28.26
Property management	21.94	40.52	18.09	14.93	21.28
Management, upkeep services for security	5.71	9.65	3.23	4.42	6.98
Parking	5.17	6.44	3.69	4.88	6.09

	total consumer units	Northeast	Midwest	South	West
Rented dwellings	**$2,159.89**	**$2,566.68**	**$1,656.75**	**$1,743.54**	**$3,003.37**
Rent	2,104.66	2,508.71	1,610.52	1,692.27	2,934.79
Rent as pay	27.17	26.93	17.14	24.87	41.47
Maintenance, insurance, other expenses	28.06	31.04	29.10	26.40	27.11
Tenant's insurance	8.90	8.26	13.01	7.72	7.07
Maintenance and repair services	11.16	13.58	9.35	10.99	11.24
Maintenance and repair materials	8.00	9.20	6.73	7.69	8.80
Other lodging	**504.56**	**601.61**	**496.12**	**412.30**	**578.46**
Owned vacation homes	171.55	202.55	154.33	151.17	195.66
Mortgage interest and charges	71.98	84.49	58.07	53.76	105.01
Property taxes	63.76	73.04	68.58	56.79	62.00
Maintenance, insurance, and other expenses	35.81	45.02	27.68	40.62	28.64
Homeowner's insurance	9.70	9.57	6.91	12.44	8.30
Ground rent	2.93	0.36	3.60	1.55	6.66
Maintenance and repair services	16.76	24.32	13.34	19.60	9.28
Maintenance and repair materials	2.07	2.18	0.53	3.98	0.51
Property management and security	3.60	7.29	2.48	2.75	2.94
Property management	2.50	4.39	1.65	2.31	2.06
Management, upkeep services for security	1.10	2.90	0.83	0.45	0.88
Parking	0.76	1.31	0.83	0.29	0.96
Housing while attending school	80.14	84.65	90.45	53.70	108.02
Lodging on trips	252.87	314.41	251.35	207.43	274.79
UTILITIES, FUELS, AND PUBLIC SERVICES	**2,684.32**	**2,750.26**	**2,681.88**	**2,775.12**	**2,484.60**
Natural gas	**329.75**	**450.15**	**457.91**	**202.61**	**297.74**
Electricity	**981.09**	**860.75**	**905.20**	**1,203.20**	**806.18**
Fuel oil and other fuels	**88.41**	**237.70**	**76.99**	**47.49**	**38.26**
Fuel oil	45.98	196.39	10.38	13.39	6.60
Coal	0.07	0.27	–	–	0.06
Bottled/tank gas	35.27	28.76	62.16	28.70	23.46
Wood and other fuels	7.09	12.29	4.45	5.39	8.14
Telephone services	**956.74**	**951.83**	**934.23**	**986.85**	**935.98**
Residential telephone and pay phones	641.00	673.71	623.17	661.08	599.29
Cellular phone service	293.76	254.65	288.03	306.75	312.30
Pager service	1.71	1.40	2.92	1.57	0.93
Phone cards	20.28	22.07	20.11	17.45	23.47
Water and other public services	**328.33**	**249.83**	**307.55**	**334.97**	**406.44**
Water and sewerage maintenance	237.16	181.76	218.65	250.19	282.86
Trash and garbage collection	89.05	63.96	86.87	83.64	121.49
Septic tank cleaning	2.12	4.11	2.04	1.14	2.09

*See appendix for information about mortgage principle reduction.
Note: (–) means sample is too small to make a reliable estimate.
Source: Bureau of Labor Statistics, unpublished tables from the 2002 Consumer Expenditure Survey

Table 9.18 Housing: Shelter and Utilities: Indexed spending by region, 2002

(indexed average annual spending of consumer units (CU) on shelter and utilities, by region in which consumer unit lives, 2002; index definition: an index of 100 is the average for all consumer units; an index of 132 means that spending by consumer units in that group is 32 percent above the average for all consumer units; an index of 68 indicates spending that is 32 percent below the average for all consumer units)

	total consumer units	Northeast	Midwest	South	West
Average spending of CU, total	$40,677	$42,390	$40,601	$37,281	$44,728
Average spending of CU, index	100	104	100	92	110
Housing, spending index	100	110	95	89	115
SHELTER	**100**	**114**	**91**	**83**	**125**
Owned dwellings*	**100**	**112**	**96**	**84**	**120**
Mortgage interest and charges	100	96	89	85	138
Mortgage interest	100	94	88	86	140
Interest paid, home equity loan	100	144	118	63	103
Interest paid, home equity line of credit	100	131	110	74	105
Property taxes	100	157	106	73	89
Maintenance, repairs, insurance, other expenses	100	104	102	92	106
Homeowner's insurance	100	88	101	110	94
Ground rent	100	40	74	82	206
Maintenance and repair services	100	111	107	87	105
Painting and papering	100	120	56	93	140
Plumbing and water heating	100	119	107	93	88
Heat, air conditioning, electrical work	100	81	98	116	91
Roofing and gutters	100	87	110	106	91
Other repair and maintenance services	100	133	130	61	103
Repair, replacement of hard-surface flooring	100	83	66	110	134
Repair of built-in appliances	100	130	81	71	140
Maintenance and repair materials	100	123	107	79	107
Paints, wallpaper, and supplies	100	94	109	87	116
Tools, equip. for painting, wallpapering	100	94	109	87	116
Plumbing supplies and equipment	100	63	100	112	113
Electrical supplies, heating, cooling equip.	100	120	115	69	118
Hard-surface flooring, repair, replacement	100	154	83	69	120
Roofing and gutters	100	188	98	82	56
Plaster, paneling, siding, windows, doors, screens, awnings	100	77	119	85	125
Patio, walk, fence, driveway, masonry, brick, and stucco materials	100	40	127	47	209
Landscape maintenance	100	102	170	56	96
Miscellaneous supplies and equipment	100	166	96	74	89
Insulation, other maintenance, repair	100	162	88	72	104
Finish basement, remodel rooms, build patios, walks, etc.	100	172	104	76	73
Property management and security	100	182	77	70	102
Property management	100	185	82	68	97
Management, upkeep services for security	100	169	57	77	122
Parking	100	125	71	94	118

	total consumer units	Northeast	Midwest	South	West
Rented dwellings	**100**	**119**	**77**	**81**	**139**
Rent	100	119	77	80	139
Rent as pay	100	99	63	92	153
Maintenance, insurance, other expenses	100	111	104	94	97
Tenant's insurance	100	93	146	87	79
Maintenance and repair services	100	122	84	98	101
Maintenance and repair materials	100	115	84	96	110
Other lodging	**100**	**119**	**98**	**82**	**115**
Owned vacation homes	100	118	90	88	114
Mortgage interest and charges	100	117	81	75	146
Property taxes	100	115	108	89	97
Maintenance, insurance, and other expenses	100	126	77	113	80
Homeowner's insurance	100	99	71	128	86
Ground rent	100	12	123	53	227
Maintenance and repair services	100	145	80	117	55
Maintenance and repair materials	100	105	26	192	25
Property management and security	100	203	69	76	82
Property management	100	176	66	92	82
Management, upkeep services for security	100	264	75	41	80
Parking	100	172	109	38	126
Housing while attending school	100	106	113	67	135
Lodging on trips	100	124	99	82	109
UTILITIES, FUELS, AND PUBLIC SERVICES	**100**	**102**	**100**	**103**	**93**
Natural gas	**100**	**137**	**139**	**61**	**90**
Electricity	**100**	**88**	**92**	**123**	**82**
Fuel oil and other fuels	**100**	**269**	**87**	**54**	**43**
Fuel oil	100	427	23	29	14
Coal	100	386	–	–	86
Bottled/tank gas	100	82	176	81	67
Wood and other fuels	100	173	63	76	115
Telephone services	**100**	**99**	**98**	**103**	**98**
Residential telephone and pay phones	100	105	97	103	93
Cellular phone service	100	87	98	104	106
Pager service	100	82	171	92	54
Phone cards	100	109	99	86	116
Water and other public services	**100**	**76**	**94**	**102**	**124**
Water and sewerage maintenance	100	77	92	105	119
Trash and garbage collection	100	72	98	94	136
Septic tank cleaning	100	194	96	54	99

See appendix for information about mortgage principle reduction.
Note: (–) means sample is too small to make a reliable estimate.
Source: Calculations by New Strategist based on the 2002 Consumer Expenditure Survey

Table 9.19 Housing: Shelter and Utilities: Total spending by region, 2002

(total annual spending on shelter and utilities, by region in which consumer units live, 2002; numbers in thousands)

	total consumer units	Northeast	Midwest	South	West
Number of consumer units	112,108	21,313	25,883	40,004	24,907
Total spending of all consumer units	$4,560,172,273	$903,462,333	$1,050,879,307	$1,491,371,122	$1,114,048,764
Housing, total spending	1,489,139,533	310,275,293	327,192,438	470,693,865	381,014,085
SHELTER	**$877,739,496**	**$190,996,450**	**$183,679,745**	**$259,156,713**	**$243,898,061**
Owned dwellings*	579,033,336	123,470,898	127,956,752	172,914,490	154,685,422
Mortgage interest and charges	332,081,833	60,615,451	68,427,922	101,208,920	101,827,039
Mortgage interest	315,190,521	56,175,953	63,956,117	97,127,312	97,928,844
Interest paid, home equity loan	9,933,890	2,713,571	2,714,609	2,225,423	2,280,485
Interest paid, home equity line of credit	6,937,243	1,721,877	1,756,938	1,840,184	1,617,461
Property taxes	139,278,495	41,468,065	34,074,711	36,256,425	27,478,150
Maintenance, repairs, insurance, other expenses	107,671,886	21,387,382	25,454,378	35,449,145	25,379,984
Homeowner's insurance	31,760,196	5,292,018	7,371,478	12,455,645	6,641,452
Ground rent	4,591,944	352,943	788,137	1,351,735	2,099,660
Maintenance and repair services	58,251,317	12,340,653	14,332,970	18,015,801	13,561,363
Painting and papering	6,230,963	1,419,020	809,879	2,063,006	1,938,512
Plumbing and water heating	5,227,596	1,182,872	1,295,185	1,727,373	1,022,183
Heat, air conditioning, electrical work	9,672,678	1,498,517	2,193,067	4,017,202	1,963,419
Roofing and gutters	7,982,090	1,320,767	2,023,792	3,022,702	1,614,223
Other repair and maintenance services	24,077,435	6,104,256	7,234,299	5,225,723	5,512,915
Repair, replacement of hard-surface flooring	4,881,182	770,252	743,101	1,913,791	1,453,573
Repair of built-in appliances	181,615	44,970	33,907	46,005	56,539
Maintenance and repair materials	9,389,045	2,195,452	2,314,458	2,656,666	2,222,203
Paints, wallpaper, and supplies	1,649,109	295,185	415,163	513,651	425,162
Tools, equip. for painting, wallpapering	177,131	31,756	44,519	55,206	45,580
Plumbing supplies and equipment	630,047	75,022	145,721	251,225	158,409
Electrical supplies, heating, cooling equip.	387,894	88,236	102,756	95,210	101,870
Hard-surface flooring, repair, replacement	977,582	285,807	188,169	242,024	261,025
Roofing and gutters	593,051	211,638	133,556	174,017	73,227
Plaster, paneling, siding, windows, doors, screens, awnings	1,560,543	227,410	428,364	471,247	432,884
Patio, walk, fence, driveway, masonry, brick, and stucco materials	144,619	10,870	42,448	24,402	67,249
Landscape maintenance	530,271	102,942	208,617	105,611	113,078
Miscellaneous supplies and equipment	2,738,798	866,373	604,886	724,072	543,720
Insulation, other maintenance, repair	1,474,220	453,754	300,502	380,438	339,482
Finish basement, remodel rooms, build patios, walks, etc.	1,264,578	412,620	304,384	343,634	204,237
Property management and security	3,098,665	1,069,273	551,826	774,077	703,872
Property management	2,459,650	863,603	468,223	597,260	530,021
Management, upkeep services for security	640,137	205,670	83,602	176,818	173,851
Parking	579,598	137,256	95,508	195,220	151,684

	total consumer units	Northeast	Midwest	South	West
Rented dwellings	$242,140,948	$54,703,651	$42,881,660	$69,748,574	$74,804,937
Rent	235,949,223	53,468,136	41,685,089	67,697,569	73,096,815
Rent as pay	3,045,974	573,959	443,635	994,899	1,032,893
Maintenance, insurance, other expenses	3,145,750	661,556	753,195	1,056,106	675,229
Tenant's insurance	997,761	176,045	336,738	308,831	176,092
Maintenance and repair services	1,251,125	289,431	242,006	439,644	279,955
Maintenance and repair materials	896,864	196,080	174,193	307,631	219,182
Other lodging	56,565,212	12,822,114	12,841,074	16,493,649	14,407,703
Owned vacation homes	19,232,127	4,316,948	3,994,523	6,047,405	4,873,304
Mortgage interest and charges	8,069,534	1,800,735	1,503,026	2,150,615	2,615,484
Property taxes	7,148,006	1,556,702	1,775,056	2,271,827	1,544,234
Maintenance, insurance, and other expenses	4,014,587	959,511	716,441	1,624,962	713,336
Homeowner's insurance	1,087,448	203,965	178,852	497,650	206,728
Ground rent	328,476	7,673	93,179	62,006	165,881
Maintenance and repair services	1,878,930	518,332	345,279	784,078	231,137
Maintenance and repair materials	232,064	46,462	13,718	159,216	12,703
Property management and security	403,589	155,372	64,190	110,011	73,227
Property management	280,270	93,564	42,707	92,409	51,308
Management, upkeep services for security	123,319	61,808	21,483	18,002	21,918
Parking	85,202	27,920	21,483	11,601	23,911
Housing while attending school	8,984,335	1,804,145	2,341,117	2,148,215	2,690,454
Lodging on trips	28,348,750	6,701,020	6,505,692	8,298,030	6,844,195
UTILITIES, FUELS, AND PUBLIC SERVICES	300,933,747	58,616,291	69,415,100	111,015,900	61,883,932
Natural gas	36,967,613	9,594,047	11,852,085	8,105,210	7,415,810
Electricity	109,988,038	18,345,165	23,429,292	48,132,813	20,079,525
Fuel oil and other fuels	9,911,468	5,066,100	1,992,732	1,899,790	952,942
Fuel oil	5,154,726	4,185,660	268,666	535,654	164,386
Coal	7,848	5,755	–	–	1,494
Bottled/tank gas	3,954,049	612,962	1,608,887	1,148,115	584,318
Wood and other fuels	794,846	261,937	115,179	215,622	202,743
Telephone services	107,258,208	20,286,353	24,180,675	39,477,947	23,312,454
Residential telephone and pay phones	71,861,228	14,358,781	16,129,509	26,445,844	14,926,516
Cellular phone service	32,932,846	5,427,355	7,455,080	12,271,227	7,778,456
Pager service	191,705	29,838	75,578	62,806	23,164
Phone cards	2,273,550	470,378	520,507	698,070	584,567
Water and other public services	36,808,420	5,324,627	7,960,317	13,400,140	10,123,201
Water and sewerage maintenance	26,587,533	3,873,851	5,659,318	10,008,601	7,045,194
Trash and garbage collection	9,983,217	1,363,179	2,248,456	3,345,935	3,025,951
Septic tank cleaning	237,669	87,596	52,801	45,605	52,056

*See appendix for information about mortgage principle reduction.

Note: Numbers may not add to total because of rounding. (–) means sample is too small to make a reliable estimate.

Source: Calculations by New Strategist based on the 2002 Consumer Expenditure Survey

Table 9.20 Housing: Shelter and Utilities: Market shares by region, 2002

(percentage of total annual spending on shelter and utilities accounted for by consumer units by region, 2002)

	total consumer units	Northeast	Midwest	South	West
Share of total consumer units	100.0%	19.0%	23.1%	35.7%	22.2%
Share of total before-tax income	100.0	20.8	23.0	32.9	23.4
Share of total spending	100.0	19.8	23.0	32.7	24.4
Share of housing spending	100.0	20.8	22.0	31.6	25.6
SHELTER	**100.0%**	**21.8%**	**20.9%**	**29.5%**	**27.8%**
Owned dwellings*	**100.0**	**21.3**	**22.1**	**29.9**	**26.7**
Mortgage interest and charges	100.0	18.3	20.6	30.5	30.7
Mortgage interest	100.0	17.8	20.3	30.8	31.1
Interest paid, home equity loan	100.0	27.3	27.3	22.4	23.0
Interest paid, home equity line of credit	100.0	24.8	25.3	26.5	23.3
Property taxes	100.0	29.8	24.5	26.0	19.7
Maintenance, repairs, insurance, other expenses	100.0	19.9	23.6	32.9	23.6
Homeowner's insurance	100.0	16.7	23.2	39.2	20.9
Ground rent	100.0	7.7	17.2	29.4	45.7
Maintenance and repair services	100.0	21.2	24.6	30.9	23.3
Painting and papering	100.0	22.8	13.0	33.1	31.1
Plumbing and water heating	100.0	22.6	24.8	33.0	19.6
Heat, air conditioning, electrical work	100.0	15.5	22.7	41.5	20.3
Roofing and gutters	100.0	16.5	25.4	37.9	20.2
Other repair and maintenance services	100.0	25.4	30.0	21.7	22.9
Repair, replacement of hard-surface flooring	100.0	15.8	15.2	39.2	29.8
Repair of built-in appliances	100.0	24.8	18.7	25.3	31.1
Maintenance and repair materials	100.0	23.4	24.7	28.3	23.7
Paints, wallpaper, and supplies	100.0	17.9	25.2	31.1	25.8
Tools, equip. for painting, wallpapering	100.0	17.9	25.1	31.2	25.7
Plumbing supplies and equipment	100.0	11.9	23.1	39.9	25.1
Electrical supplies, heating, cooling equip.	100.0	22.7	26.5	24.5	26.3
Hard-surface flooring, repair, replacement	100.0	29.2	19.2	24.8	26.7
Roofing and gutters	100.0	35.7	22.5	29.3	12.3
Plaster, paneling, siding, windows, doors, screens, awnings	100.0	14.6	27.4	30.2	27.7
Patio, walk, fence, driveway, masonry, brick, and stucco materials	100.0	7.5	29.4	16.9	46.5
Landscape maintenance	100.0	19.4	39.3	19.9	21.3
Miscellaneous supplies and equipment	100.0	31.6	22.1	26.4	19.9
Insulation, other maintenance, repair	100.0	30.8	20.4	25.8	23.0
Finish basement, remodel rooms, build patios, walks, etc.	100.0	32.6	24.1	27.2	16.2
Property management and security	100.0	34.5	17.8	25.0	22.7
Property management	100.0	35.1	19.0	24.3	21.5
Management, upkeep services for security	100.0	32.1	13.1	27.6	27.2
Parking	100.0	23.7	16.5	33.7	26.2

	total consumer units	Northeast	Midwest	South	West
Rented dwellings	**100.0%**	**22.6%**	**17.7%**	**28.8%**	**30.9%**
Rent	100.0	22.7	17.7	28.7	31.0
Rent as pay	100.0	18.8	14.6	32.7	33.9
Maintenance, insurance, other expenses	100.0	21.0	23.9	33.6	21.5
Tenant's insurance	100.0	17.6	33.7	31.0	17.6
Maintenance and repair services	100.0	23.1	19.3	35.1	22.4
Maintenance and repair materials	100.0	21.9	19.4	34.3	24.4
Other lodging	**100.0**	**22.7**	**22.7**	**29.2**	**25.5**
Owned vacation homes	100.0	22.4	20.8	31.4	25.3
Mortgage interest and charges	100.0	22.3	18.6	26.7	32.4
Property taxes	100.0	21.8	24.8	31.8	21.6
Maintenance, insurance, and other expenses	100.0	23.9	17.8	40.5	17.8
Homeowner's insurance	100.0	18.8	16.4	45.8	19.0
Ground rent	100.0	2.3	28.4	18.9	50.5
Maintenance and repair services	100.0	27.6	18.4	41.7	12.3
Maintenance and repair materials	100.0	20.0	5.9	68.6	5.5
Property management and security	100.0	38.5	15.9	27.3	18.1
Property management	100.0	33.4	15.2	33.0	18.3
Management, upkeep services for security	100.0	50.1	17.4	14.6	17.8
Parking	100.0	32.8	25.2	13.6	28.1
Housing while attending school	100.0	20.1	26.1	23.9	29.9
Lodging on trips	100.0	23.6	22.9	29.3	24.1
UTILITIES, FUELS, AND PUBLIC SERVICES	**100.0**	**19.5**	**23.1**	**36.9**	**20.6**
Natural gas	**100.0**	**26.0**	**32.1**	**21.9**	**20.1**
Electricity	**100.0**	**16.7**	**21.3**	**43.8**	**18.3**
Fuel oil and other fuels	**100.0**	**51.1**	**20.1**	**19.2**	**9.6**
Fuel oil	100.0	81.2	5.2	10.4	3.2
Coal	100.0	73.3	–	–	19.0
Bottled/tank gas	100.0	15.5	40.7	29.0	14.8
Wood and other fuels	100.0	33.0	14.5	27.1	25.5
Telephone services	**100.0**	**18.9**	**22.5**	**36.8**	**21.7**
Residential telephone and pay phones	100.0	20.0	22.4	36.8	20.8
Cellular phone service	100.0	16.5	22.6	37.3	23.6
Pager service	100.0	15.6	39.4	32.8	12.1
Phone cards	100.0	20.7	22.9	30.7	25.7
Water and other public services	**100.0**	**14.5**	**21.6**	**36.4**	**27.5**
Water and sewerage maintenance	100.0	14.6	21.3	37.6	26.5
Trash and garbage collection	100.0	13.7	22.5	33.5	30.3
Septic tank cleaning	100.0	36.9	22.2	19.2	21.9

See appendix for information about mortgage principle reduction.

Note: Numbers may not add to total because of rounding. (–) means sample is too small to make a reliable estimate.

Source: Calculations by New Strategist based on the 2002 Consumer Expenditure Survey

Table 9.21 Housing: Shelter and Utilities: Average spending by education, 2002

(average annual spending of consumer units (CU) on shelter and utilities, by education of consumer unit reference person, 2002)

	total consumer units	less than high school graduate	high school graduate	some college	associate's degree	college graduate total	bachelor's degree	master's, professional, doctorate
Number of consumer units (in thousands, add 000)	112,108	17,075	31,961	23,260	10,395	29,417	19,082	10,335
Average number of persons per CU	2.5	2.6	2.5	2.4	2.6	2.5	2.5	2.5
Average before-tax income of CU	$49,430.00	$25,564.00	$39,618.00	$42,598.00	$54,860.00	$77,820.00	$69,408.00	$92,783.00
Average spending of CU, total	40,676.60	24,930.40	33,707.63	38,653.57	44,405.79	57,384.01	53,731.57	64,118.48
Housing, average spending	13,283.08	8,287.79	10,799.89	12,336.44	14,643.80	19,111.29	17,758.72	21,607.22
SHELTER	**$7,829.41**	**$4,596.60**	**$6,179.90**	**$7,289.87**	**$8,183.43**	**$11,799.52**	**$10,867.29**	**$13,520.76**
Owned dwellings*	5,164.96	2,194.02	3,902.31	4,509.68	5,858.02	8,534.47	7,711.12	10,054.68
Mortgage interest and charges	2,962.16	1,015.77	2,098.08	2,654.69	3,496.57	5,085.02	4,655.36	5,878.34
Mortgage interest	2,811.49	969.18	1,969.07	2,523.54	3,303.74	4,849.86	4,440.19	5,606.26
Interest paid, home equity loan	88.61	32.50	87.40	78.29	126.36	117.32	104.81	140.42
Interest paid, home equity line of credit	61.88	13.15	41.56	52.85	66.42	117.76	110.36	131.41
Property taxes	1,242.36	666.30	999.95	984.52	1,284.97	2,028.93	1,744.30	2,554.47
Maintenance, repairs, insurance, other expenses	960.43	511.95	804.28	870.47	1,076.47	1,420.52	1,311.46	1,621.88
Homeowner's insurance	283.30	168.05	256.62	264.26	303.74	387.03	353.43	449.09
Ground rent	40.96	56.06	54.01	50.31	45.04	9.19	10.94	5.96
Maintenance and repair services	519.60	237.51	395.46	463.31	588.70	838.30	785.15	936.45
Painting and papering	55.58	18.48	26.82	40.20	40.00	126.01	116.81	142.99
Plumbing and water heating	46.63	22.26	37.72	36.11	55.76	75.55	72.46	81.25
Heat, air conditioning, electrical work	86.28	38.13	73.14	84.38	128.16	115.19	108.31	127.90
Roofing and gutters	71.20	56.15	60.15	61.89	74.21	98.23	83.10	126.15
Other repair and maintenance services	214.77	88.72	163.11	202.08	232.10	347.97	323.13	393.83
Repair, replacement of hard-surface flooring	43.54	13.42	33.03	37.49	58.02	72.10	77.24	62.60
Repair of built-in appliances	1.62	0.35	1.50	1.16	0.45	3.25	4.09	1.71
Maintenance and repair materials	83.75	39.34	78.34	68.07	112.74	117.55	108.05	135.09
Paints, wallpaper, and supplies	14.71	5.67	14.08	12.77	18.26	20.92	21.80	19.29
Tools, equip. for painting, wallpapering	1.58	0.61	1.51	1.37	1.96	2.25	2.34	2.07
Plumbing supplies and equipment	5.62	5.71	4.30	3.96	5.47	8.38	6.07	12.65
Electrical supplies, heating, cooling equip.	3.46	0.94	4.64	1.18	3.61	5.39	6.44	3.46
Hard-surface flooring, repair, replacement	8.72	3.73	8.88	8.55	9.98	11.12	11.06	11.23
Roofing and gutters	5.29	5.75	4.82	5.45	9.83	3.79	5.41	0.80
Plaster, paneling, siding, windows, doors, screens, awnings	13.92	6.27	14.44	6.92	21.72	20.56	15.45	29.99
Patio, walk, fence, driveway, masonry, brick, and stucco materials	1.29	0.78	1.15	0.35	3.19	1.82	1.37	2.66
Landscape maintenance	4.73	0.76	3.63	4.42	3.75	8.81	8.05	10.23
Miscellaneous supplies and equipment	24.43	9.11	20.89	23.09	34.97	34.51	30.06	42.72
Insulation, other maintenance, repair	13.15	6.88	8.18	8.58	19.90	23.42	19.42	30.79
Finish basement, remodel rooms, build patios, walks, etc.	11.28	2.23	12.71	14.51	15.07	11.09	10.64	11.93
Property management and security	27.64	9.20	16.82	20.04	19.30	59.07	45.70	83.77
Property management	21.94	8.11	14.65	15.01	16.57	45.24	33.18	67.51
Management, upkeep services for security	5.71	1.09	2.17	5.03	2.72	13.83	12.51	16.26
Parking	5.17	1.79	3.03	4.48	6.94	9.37	8.20	11.53

	total consumer units	less than high school graduate	high school graduate	some college	associate's degree	college graduate		
						total	bachelor's degree	master's, professional, doctorate
Rented dwellings	**$2,159.89**	**$2,278.72**	**$1,987.37**	**$2,315.11**	**$1,892.56**	**$2,250.10**	**$2,369.25**	**$2,030.09**
Rent	2,104.66	2,205.92	1,941.21	2,256.84	1,843.87	2,195.31	2,314.85	1,974.60
Rent as pay	27.17	46.70	23.74	28.60	6.62	25.68	26.15	24.80
Maintenance, insurance, other expenses	28.06	26.09	22.42	29.67	42.07	29.11	28.25	30.69
Tenant's insurance	8.90	4.38	6.21	9.32	11.67	13.14	12.21	14.88
Maintenance and repair services	11.16	15.43	8.41	11.79	22.85	7.02	7.38	6.37
Maintenance and repair materials	8.00	6.28	7.79	8.56	7.55	8.94	8.67	9.45
Other lodging	**504.56**	**123.86**	**290.22**	**465.09**	**432.86**	**1,014.95**	**786.92**	**1,435.99**
Owned vacation homes	171.55	64.21	110.06	125.15	127.56	352.89	248.88	544.93
Mortgage interest and charges	71.98	19.31	30.80	54.56	46.32	170.15	121.01	260.89
Property taxes	69.57	19.14	30.80	46.58	46.32	167.35	117.44	259.48
Maintenance, insurance, and other expenses	35.81	20.66	34.01	27.63	25.93	56.51	46.03	75.87
Homeowner's insurance	9.70	5.16	10.18	9.71	11.78	11.06	9.16	14.57
Ground rent	2.93	0.67	1.28	5.05	1.64	4.83	6.90	1.00
Maintenance and repair services	16.76	6.16	18.63	9.56	8.60	29.46	21.19	44.73
Maintenance and repair materials	2.07	6.33	1.25	1.57	0.71	1.36	1.90	0.37
Property management and security	3.60	2.23	2.56	1.42	2.49	7.63	4.97	12.53
Property management	2.50	1.84	1.98	1.18	1.69	4.77	4.37	5.53
Management, upkeep services for security	1.10	0.39	0.58	0.24	0.80	2.85	0.61	7.00
Parking	0.76	0.12	0.11	0.33	0.71	2.17	1.91	2.66
Housing while attending school	80.14	5.54	31.29	124.38	41.94	155.02	115.35	228.27
Lodging on trips	252.87	54.11	148.87	215.55	263.36	507.04	422.69	662.79
UTILITIES, FUELS, AND PUBLIC SERVICES	**2,684.32**	**2,210.75**	**2,597.37**	**2,514.85**	**2,901.67**	**3,110.87**	**3,018.12**	**3,282.11**
Natural gas	**329.75**	**252.02**	**315.49**	**292.78**	**350.33**	**412.32**	**398.99**	**436.92**
Electricity	**981.09**	**884.83**	**997.08**	**918.05**	**1,044.52**	**1,047.01**	**1,023.44**	**1,090.52**
Fuel oil and other fuels	**88.41**	**92.53**	**96.74**	**73.62**	**99.63**	**84.70**	**72.60**	**107.05**
Fuel oil	45.98	39.34	47.48	34.91	49.40	55.74	46.28	73.21
Coal	0.07	0.11	0.06	0.09	–	0.06	0.01	0.14
Bottled/tank gas	35.27	42.99	41.84	31.56	43.00	23.87	21.87	27.55
Wood and other fuels	7.09	10.09	7.37	7.06	7.23	5.04	4.44	6.14
Telephone services	**956.74**	**725.10**	**886.37**	**925.22**	**1,041.75**	**1,162.54**	**1,131.84**	**1,219.24**
Residential telephone and pay phones	641.00	548.45	621.82	592.44	674.96	741.95	718.53	785.20
Cellular phone service	293.76	143.29	244.41	313.00	348.33	400.21	393.62	412.37
Pager service	1.71	1.52	1.65	1.29	3.54	1.56	1.24	2.16
Phone cards	20.28	31.85	18.49	18.50	14.92	18.82	18.45	19.50
Water and other public services	**328.33**	**256.27**	**301.68**	**305.18**	**365.44**	**404.30**	**391.26**	**428.39**
Water and sewerage maintenance	237.16	193.45	220.44	218.58	267.41	284.69	278.32	296.45
Trash and garbage collection	89.05	61.85	79.27	84.10	94.53	117.44	110.46	130.32
Septic tank cleaning	2.12	0.97	1.97	2.50	3.50	2.18	2.48	1.63

*See appendix for information about mortgage principle reduction.
Note: (–) means sample is too small to make a reliable estimate.
Source: Bureau of Labor Statistics, unpublished tables from the 2002 Consumer Expenditure Survey

Table 9.22 Housing: Shelter and Utilities: Indexed spending by education, 2002

(indexed average annual spending of consumer units (CU) on shelter and utilities, by education of consumer unit reference person, 2002; index definition: an index of 100 is the average for all consumer units; an index of 132 means that spending by consumer units in that group is 32 percent above the average for all consumer units; an index of 68 indicates spending that is 32 percent below the average for all consumer units)

	total consumer units	less than high school graduate	high school graduate	some college	associate's degree	college graduate total	bachelor's degree	master's, professional, doctorate
Average spending of CU, total	$40,677	$24,930	$33,708	$38,654	$44,406	$57,384	$53,732	$64,118
Average spending of CU, index	100	61	83	95	109	141	132	158
Housing, spending index	100	62	81	93	110	144	134	163
SHELTER	**100**	**59**	**79**	**93**	**105**	**151**	**139**	**173**
Owned dwellings*	100	42	76	87	113	165	149	195
Mortgage interest and charges	100	34	71	90	118	172	157	198
Mortgage interest	100	34	70	90	118	173	158	199
Interest paid, home equity loan	100	37	99	88	143	132	118	158
Interest paid, home equity line of credit	100	21	67	85	107	190	178	212
Property taxes	100	54	80	79	103	163	140	206
Maintenance, repairs, insurance, other expenses	100	53	84	91	112	148	137	169
Homeowner's insurance	100	59	91	93	107	137	125	159
Ground rent	100	137	132	123	110	22	27	15
Maintenance and repair services	100	46	76	89	113	161	151	180
Painting and papering	100	33	48	72	72	227	210	257
Plumbing and water heating	100	48	81	77	120	162	155	174
Heat, air conditioning, electrical work	100	44	85	98	149	134	126	148
Roofing and gutters	100	79	84	87	104	138	117	177
Other repair and maintenance services	100	41	76	94	108	162	150	183
Repair, replacement of hard-surface flooring	100	31	76	86	133	166	177	144
Repair of built-in appliances	100	22	93	72	28	201	252	106
Maintenance and repair materials	100	47	94	81	135	140	129	161
Paints, wallpaper, and supplies	100	39	96	87	124	142	148	131
Tools, equip. for painting, wallpapering	100	39	96	87	124	142	148	131
Plumbing supplies and equipment	100	102	77	70	97	149	108	225
Electrical supplies, heating, cooling equip.	100	27	134	34	104	156	186	100
Hard-surface flooring, repair, replacement	100	43	102	98	114	128	127	129
Roofing and gutters	100	109	91	103	186	72	102	15
Plaster, paneling, siding, windows, doors, screens, awnings	100	45	104	50	156	148	111	215
Patio, walk, fence, driveway, masonry, brick, and stucco materials	100	60	89	27	247	141	106	206
Landscape maintenance	100	16	77	93	79	186	170	216
Miscellaneous supplies and equipment	100	37	86	95	143	141	123	175
Insulation, other maintenance, repair	100	52	62	65	151	178	148	234
Finish basement, remodel rooms, build patios, walks, etc.	100	20	113	129	134	98	94	106
Property management and security	100	33	61	73	70	214	165	303
Property management	100	37	67	68	76	206	151	308
Management, upkeep services for security	100	19	38	88	48	242	219	285
Parking	100	35	59	87	134	181	159	223

	total consumer units	less than high school graduate	high school graduate	some college	associate's degree	college graduate		
						total	bachelor's degree	master's, professional, doctorate
Rented dwellings	100	106	92	107	88	104	110	94
Rent	100	105	92	107	88	104	110	94
Rent as pay	100	172	87	105	24	95	96	91
Maintenance, insurance, other expenses	100	93	80	106	150	104	101	109
Tenant's insurance	100	49	70	105	131	148	137	167
Maintenance and repair services	100	138	75	106	205	63	66	57
Maintenance and repair materials	100	79	97	107	94	112	108	118
Other lodging	100	25	58	92	86	201	156	285
Owned vacation homes	100	37	64	73	74	206	145	318
Mortgage interest and charges	100	27	43	76	64	236	168	362
Property taxes	100	28	44	67	67	241	169	373
Maintenance, insurance, and other expenses	100	58	95	77	72	158	129	212
Homeowner's insurance	100	53	105	100	121	114	94	150
Ground rent	100	23	44	172	56	165	235	34
Maintenance and repair services	100	37	111	57	51	176	126	267
Maintenance and repair materials	100	306	60	76	34	66	92	18
Property management and security	100	62	71	39	69	212	138	348
Property management	100	74	79	47	68	191	175	221
Management, upkeep services for security	100	35	53	22	73	259	55	636
Parking	100	16	14	43	93	286	251	350
Housing while attending school	100	7	39	155	52	193	144	285
Lodging on trips	100	21	59	85	104	201	167	262
UTILITIES, FUELS, AND PUBLIC SERVICES	100	82	97	94	108	116	112	122
Natural gas	100	76	96	89	106	125	121	133
Electricity	100	90	102	94	106	107	104	111
Fuel oil and other fuels	100	105	109	83	113	96	82	121
Fuel oil	100	86	103	76	107	121	101	159
Coal	100	157	86	129	–	86	14	200
Bottled/tank gas	100	122	119	89	122	68	62	78
Wood and other fuels	100	142	104	100	102	71	63	87
Telephone services	100	76	93	97	109	122	118	127
Residential telephone and pay phones	100	86	97	92	105	116	112	122
Cellular phone service	100	49	83	107	119	136	134	140
Pager service	100	89	96	75	207	91	73	126
Phone cards	100	157	91	91	74	93	91	96
Water and other public services	100	78	92	93	111	123	119	130
Water and sewerage maintenance	100	82	93	92	113	120	117	125
Trash and garbage collection	100	69	89	94	106	132	124	146
Septic tank cleaning	100	46	93	118	165	103	117	77

See appendix for information about mortgage principle reduction.
Note: (–) means sample is too small to make a reliable estimate.
Source: Calculations by New Strategist based on the 2002 Consumer Expenditure Survey

Table 9.23 Housing: Shelter and Utilities: Total spending by education, 2002

(total annual spending on shelter and utilities, by consumer unit (CU) educational attainment group, 2002; numbers in thousands)

	total consumer units	less than high school graduate	high school graduate	some college	associate's degree	college graduate total	bachelor's degree	master's, professional, doctorate
Number of consumer units	112,108	17,075	31,961	23,260	10,395	29,417	19,082	10,335
Total spending of all CUs	$4,560,172,273	$425,686,580	$1,077,329,562	$899,082,038	$461,598,187	$1,688,065,422	$1,025,305,819	$662,664,491
Housing, total spending	1,489,139,533	141,514,014	345,175,284	286,945,594	152,222,301	562,196,818	338,871,895	223,310,619
SHELTER	$877,739,496	$78,486,945	$197,515,784	$169,562,376	$85,066,755	$347,106,480	$207,369,628	$139,737,055
Owned dwellings*	579,033,336	37,462,892	124,721,730	104,895,157	60,894,118	251,058,504	147,143,592	103,915,118
Mortgage interest and charges	332,081,833	17,344,273	67,056,735	61,748,089	36,346,845	149,586,033	88,833,580	60,752,644
Mortgage interest	315,190,521	16,548,749	62,933,446	58,697,540	34,342,377	142,668,332	84,727,706	57,940,697
Interest paid, home equity loan	9,933,890	554,938	2,793,391	1,821,025	1,313,512	3,451,202	1,999,984	1,451,241
Interest paid, home equity line of credit	6,937,243	224,536	1,328,299	1,229,291	690,436	3,464,146	2,105,890	1,358,122
Property taxes	139,278,495	11,377,073	31,959,402	22,899,935	13,357,263	59,685,034	33,284,733	26,400,447
Maintenance, repairs, insurance, other expenses	107,671,886	8,741,546	25,705,593	20,247,132	11,189,906	41,787,437	25,025,280	16,762,130
Homeowner's insurance	31,760,196	2,869,454	8,201,832	6,146,688	3,157,377	11,385,262	6,744,151	4,641,345
Ground rent	4,591,944	957,225	1,726,214	1,170,211	468,191	270,342	208,757	61,597
Maintenance and repair services	58,251,317	4,055,483	12,639,297	10,776,591	6,119,537	24,660,271	14,982,232	9,678,211
Painting and papering	6,230,963	315,546	857,194	935,052	415,800	3,706,836	2,228,968	1,477,802
Plumbing and water heating	5,227,596	380,090	1,205,569	839,919	579,625	2,222,454	1,382,682	839,719
Heat, air conditioning, electrical work	9,672,678	651,070	2,337,628	1,962,679	1,332,223	3,388,544	2,066,771	1,321,847
Roofing and gutters	7,982,090	958,761	1,922,454	1,439,561	771,413	2,889,632	1,585,714	1,303,760
Other repair and maintenance services	24,077,435	1,514,894	5,213,159	4,700,381	2,412,680	10,236,233	6,165,967	4,070,233
Repair, replacement of hard-surface flooring	4,881,182	229,147	1,055,672	872,017	603,118	2,120,966	1,473,894	646,971
Repair of built-in appliances	181,615	5,976	47,942	26,982	4,678	95,605	78,045	17,673
Maintenance and repair materials	9,389,045	671,731	2,503,825	1,583,308	1,171,932	3,457,968	2,061,810	1,396,155
Paints, wallpaper, and supplies	1,649,109	96,815	450,011	297,030	189,813	615,404	415,988	199,362
Tools, equip. for painting, wallpapering	177,131	10,416	48,261	31,866	20,374	66,188	44,652	21,393
Plumbing supplies and equipment	630,047	97,498	137,432	92,110	56,861	246,514	115,828	130,738
Electrical supplies, heating, cooling equip.	387,894	16,051	148,299	27,447	37,526	158,558	122,888	35,759
Hard-surface flooring, repair, replacement	977,582	63,690	283,814	198,873	103,742	327,117	211,047	116,062
Roofing and gutters	593,051	98,181	154,052	126,767	102,183	111,490	103,234	8,268
Plaster, paneling, siding, windows, doors, screens, awnings	1,560,543	107,060	461,517	160,959	225,779	604,814	294,817	309,947
Patio, walk, fence, driveway, masonry, brick, and stucco materials	144,619	13,319	36,755	8,141	33,160	53,539	26,142	27,491
Landscape maintenance	530,271	12,977	116,018	102,809	38,981	259,164	153,610	105,727
Miscellaneous supplies and equipment	2,738,798	155,553	667,665	537,073	363,513	1,015,181	573,605	441,511
Insulation, other maintenance, repair	1,474,220	117,476	261,441	199,571	206,861	688,946	370,572	318,215
Finish basement, remodel rooms, build patios, walks, etc.	1,264,578	38,077	406,224	337,503	156,653	326,235	203,032	123,297
Property management and security	3,098,665	157,090	537,584	466,130	200,624	1,737,662	872,047	865,763
Property management	2,459,650	138,478	468,229	349,133	172,245	1,330,825	633,141	697,716
Management, upkeep services for security	640,137	18,612	69,355	116,998	28,274	406,837	238,716	168,047
Parking	579,598	30,564	96,842	104,205	72,141	275,637	156,472	119,163

	total consumer units	less than high school graduate	high school graduate	some college	associate's degree	college graduate total	bachelor's degree	master's, professional, doctorate
Rented dwellings	**$242,140,948**	**$38,909,144**	**$63,518,333**	**$53,849,459**	**$19,673,161**	**$66,191,192**	**$45,210,029**	**$20,980,980**
Rent	235,949,223	37,666,084	62,043,013	52,494,098	19,167,029	64,579,434	44,171,968	20,407,491
Rent as pay	3,045,974	797,403	758,754	665,236	68,815	755,429	498,994	256,308
Maintenance, insurance, other expenses	3,145,750	445,487	716,566	690,124	437,318	856,329	539,067	317,181
Tenant's insurance	997,761	74,789	198,478	216,783	121,310	386,539	232,991	153,785
Maintenance and repair services	1,251,125	263,467	268,792	274,235	237,526	206,507	140,825	65,834
Maintenance and repair materials	896,864	107,231	248,976	199,106	78,482	262,988	165,441	97,666
Other lodging	**56,565,212**	**2,114,910**	**9,275,721**	**10,817,993**	**4,499,580**	**29,856,784**	**15,016,007**	**14,840,957**
Owned vacation homes	19,232,127	1,096,386	3,517,628	2,910,989	1,325,986	10,380,965	4,749,128	5,631,852
Mortgage interest and charges	8,069,534	329,718	984,399	1,269,066	481,496	5,005,303	2,309,113	2,696,298
Property taxes	7,799,354	326,816	984,399	1,083,451	481,496	4,922,935	2,240,990	2,681,726
Maintenance, insurance, and other expenses	4,014,587	352,770	1,086,994	642,674	269,542	1,662,355	878,344	784,116
Homeowner's insurance	1,087,448	88,107	325,363	225,855	122,453	325,352	174,791	150,581
Ground rent	328,476	11,440	40,910	117,463	17,048	142,084	131,666	10,335
Maintenance and repair services	1,878,930	105,182	595,433	222,366	89,397	866,625	404,348	462,285
Maintenance and repair materials	232,064	108,085	39,951	36,518	7,380	40,007	36,256	3,824
Property management and security	403,589	38,077	81,820	33,029	25,884	224,452	94,838	129,498
Property management	280,270	31,418	63,283	27,447	17,568	140,319	83,388	57,153
Management, upkeep services for security	123,319	6,659	18,537	5,582	8,316	83,838	11,640	72,345
Parking	85,202	2,049	3,516	7,676	7,380	63,835	36,447	27,491
Housing while attending school	8,984,335	94,596	1,000,060	2,893,079	435,966	4,560,223	2,201,109	2,359,170
Lodging on trips	28,348,750	923,928	4,758,034	5,013,693	2,737,627	14,915,596	8,065,771	6,849,935
UTILITIES, FUELS, AND PUBLIC SERVICES	**300,933,747**	**37,748,556**	**83,014,543**	**58,495,411**	**30,162,860**	**91,512,463**	**57,591,766**	**33,920,607**
Natural gas	**36,967,613**	**4,303,242**	**10,083,376**	**6,810,063**	**3,641,680**	**12,129,217**	**7,613,527**	**4,515,568**
Electricity	**109,988,038**	**15,108,472**	**31,867,674**	**21,353,843**	**10,857,785**	**30,799,893**	**19,529,282**	**11,270,524**
Fuel oil and other fuels	**9,911,468**	**1,579,950**	**3,091,907**	**1,712,401**	**1,035,654**	**2,491,620**	**1,385,353**	**1,106,362**
Fuel oil	5,154,726	671,731	1,517,508	812,007	513,513	1,639,704	883,115	756,625
Coal	7,848	1,878	1,918	2,093	–	1,765	191	1,447
Bottled/tank gas	3,954,049	734,054	1,337,248	734,086	446,985	702,184	417,323	284,729
Wood and other fuels	794,846	172,287	235,553	164,216	75,156	148,262	84,724	63,457
Telephone services	**107,258,208**	**12,381,083**	**28,329,272**	**21,520,617**	**10,828,991**	**34,198,439**	**21,597,771**	**12,600,845**
Residential telephone and pay phones	71,861,228	9,364,784	19,873,989	13,780,154	7,016,209	21,825,943	13,710,989	8,115,042
Cellular phone service	32,932,846	2,446,677	7,811,588	7,280,380	3,620,890	11,772,978	7,511,057	4,261,844
Pager service	191,705	25,954	52,736	30,005	36,798	45,891	23,662	22,324
Phone cards	2,273,550	543,839	590,959	430,310	155,093	553,628	352,063	201,533
Water and other public services	**36,808,420**	**4,375,810**	**9,641,994**	**7,098,487**	**3,798,749**	**11,893,293**	**7,466,023**	**4,427,411**
Water and sewerage maintenance	26,587,533	3,303,159	7,045,483	5,084,171	2,779,727	8,374,726	5,310,902	3,063,811
Trash and garbage collection	9,983,217	1,056,089	2,533,548	1,956,166	982,639	3,454,732	2,107,798	1,346,857
Septic tank cleaning	237,669	16,563	62,963	58,150	36,383	64,129	47,323	16,846

See appendix for information about mortgage principle reduction.
Note: Numbers may not add to total because of rounding. (–) means sample is too small to make a reliable estimate.
Source: Calculations by New Strategist based on the 2002 Consumer Expenditure Survey

Table 9.24 Housing: Shelter and Utilities: Market shares by education, 2002

(percentage of total annual spending on shelter and utilities accounted for by consumer unit educational attainment groups, 2002)

	total consumer units	less than high school graduate	high school graduate	some college	associate's degree	college graduate total	bachelor's degree	master's, professional, doctorate
Share of total consumer units	100.0%	15.2%	28.5%	20.7%	9.3%	26.2%	17.0%	9.2%
Share of total before-tax income	100.0	7.9	22.8	17.9	10.3	41.3	23.9	17.3
Share of total spending	100.0	9.3	23.6	19.7	10.1	37.0	22.5	14.5
Share of housing spending	100.0	9.5	23.2	19.3	10.2	37.8	22.8	15.0
SHELTER	100.0%	8.9%	22.5%	19.3%	9.7%	39.5%	23.6%	15.9%
Owned dwellings*	100.0	6.5	21.5	18.1	10.5	43.4	25.4	17.9
Mortgage interest and charges	100.0	5.2	20.2	18.6	10.9	45.0	26.8	18.3
Mortgage interest	100.0	5.3	20.0	18.6	10.9	45.3	26.9	18.4
Interest paid, home equity loan	100.0	5.6	28.1	18.3	13.2	34.7	20.1	14.6
Interest paid, home equity line of credit	100.0	3.2	19.1	17.7	10.0	49.9	30.4	19.6
Property taxes	100.0	8.2	22.9	16.4	9.6	42.9	23.9	19.0
Maintenance, repairs, insurance, other expenses	100.0	8.1	23.9	18.8	10.4	38.8	23.2	15.6
Homeowner's insurance	100.0	9.0	25.8	19.4	9.9	35.8	21.2	14.6
Ground rent	100.0	20.8	37.6	25.5	10.2	5.9	4.5	1.3
Maintenance and repair services	100.0	7.0	21.7	18.5	10.5	42.3	25.7	16.6
Painting and papering	100.0	5.1	13.8	15.0	6.7	59.5	35.8	23.7
Plumbing and water heating	100.0	7.3	23.1	16.1	11.1	42.5	26.4	16.1
Heat, air conditioning, electrical work	100.0	6.7	24.2	20.3	13.8	35.0	21.4	13.7
Roofing and gutters	100.0	12.0	24.1	18.0	9.7	36.2	19.9	16.3
Other repair and maintenance services	100.0	6.3	21.7	19.5	10.0	42.5	25.6	16.9
Repair, replacement of hard-surface flooring	100.0	4.7	21.6	17.9	12.4	43.5	30.2	13.3
Repair of built-in appliances	100.0	3.3	26.4	14.9	2.6	52.6	43.0	9.7
Maintenance and repair materials	100.0	7.2	26.7	16.9	12.5	36.8	22.0	14.9
Paints, wallpaper, and supplies	100.0	5.9	27.3	18.0	11.5	37.3	25.2	12.1
Tools, equip. for painting, wallpapering	100.0	5.9	27.2	18.0	11.5	37.4	25.2	12.1
Plumbing supplies and equipment	100.0	15.5	21.8	14.6	9.0	39.1	18.4	20.8
Electrical supplies, heating, cooling equip.	100.0	4.1	38.2	7.1	9.7	40.9	31.7	9.2
Hard-surface flooring, repair, replacement	100.0	6.5	29.0	20.3	10.6	33.5	21.6	11.9
Roofing and gutters	100.0	16.6	26.0	21.4	17.2	18.8	17.4	1.4
Plaster, paneling, siding, windows, doors, screens, awnings	100.0	6.9	29.6	10.3	14.5	38.8	18.9	19.9
Patio, walk, fence, driveway, masonry, brick, and stucco materials	100.0	9.2	25.4	5.6	22.9	37.0	18.1	19.0
Landscape maintenance	100.0	2.4	21.9	19.4	7.4	48.9	29.0	19.9
Miscellaneous supplies and equipment	100.0	5.7	24.4	19.6	13.3	37.1	20.9	16.1
Insulation, other maintenance, repair	100.0	8.0	17.7	13.5	14.0	46.7	25.1	21.6
Finish basement, remodel rooms, build patios, walks, etc.	100.0	3.0	32.1	26.7	12.4	25.8	16.1	9.8
Property management and security	100.0	5.1	17.3	15.0	6.5	56.1	28.1	27.9
Property management	100.0	5.6	19.0	14.2	7.0	54.1	25.7	28.4
Management, upkeep services for security	100.0	2.9	10.8	18.3	4.4	63.6	37.3	26.3
Parking	100.0	5.3	16.7	18.0	12.4	47.6	27.0	20.6

	total consumer units	less than high school graduate	high school graduate	some college	associate's degree	college graduate total	bachelor's degree	master's, professional, doctorate
Rented dwellings	**100.0%**	**16.1%**	**26.2%**	**22.2%**	**8.1%**	**27.3%**	**18.7%**	**8.7%**
Rent	100.0	16.0	26.3	22.2	8.1	27.4	18.7	8.6
Rent as pay	100.0	26.2	24.9	21.8	2.3	24.8	16.4	8.4
Maintenance, insurance, other expenses	100.0	14.2	22.8	21.9	13.9	27.2	17.1	10.1
Tenant's insurance	100.0	7.5	19.9	21.7	12.2	38.7	23.4	15.4
Maintenance and repair services	100.0	21.1	21.5	21.9	19.0	16.5	11.3	5.3
Maintenance and repair materials	100.0	12.0	27.8	22.2	8.8	29.3	18.4	10.9
Other lodging	**100.0**	**3.7**	**16.4**	**19.1**	**8.0**	**52.8**	**26.5**	**26.2**
Owned vacation homes	100.0	5.7	18.3	15.1	6.9	54.0	24.7	29.3
Mortgage interest and charges	100.0	4.1	12.2	15.7	6.0	62.0	28.6	33.4
Property taxes	100.0	4.2	12.6	13.9	6.2	63.1	28.7	34.4
Maintenance, insurance, and other expenses	100.0	8.8	27.1	16.0	6.7	41.4	21.9	19.5
Homeowner's insurance	100.0	8.1	29.9	20.8	11.3	29.9	16.1	13.8
Ground rent	100.0	3.5	12.5	35.8	5.2	43.3	40.1	3.1
Maintenance and repair services	100.0	5.6	31.7	11.8	4.8	46.1	21.5	24.6
Maintenance and repair materials	100.0	46.6	17.2	15.7	3.2	17.2	15.6	1.6
Property management and security	100.0	9.4	20.3	8.2	6.4	55.6	23.5	32.1
Property management	100.0	11.2	22.6	9.8	6.3	50.1	29.8	20.4
Management, upkeep services for security	100.0	5.4	15.0	4.5	6.7	68.0	9.4	58.7
Parking	100.0	2.4	4.1	9.0	8.7	74.9	42.8	32.3
Housing while attending school	100.0	1.1	11.1	32.2	4.9	50.8	24.5	26.3
Lodging on trips	100.0	3.3	16.8	17.7	9.7	52.6	28.5	24.2
UTILITIES, FUELS, AND PUBLIC SERVICES	**100.0**	**12.5**	**27.6**	**19.4**	**10.0**	**30.4**	**19.1**	**11.3**
Natural gas	**100.0**	**11.6**	**27.3**	**18.4**	**9.9**	**32.8**	**20.6**	**12.2**
Electricity	**100.0**	**13.7**	**29.0**	**19.4**	**9.9**	**28.0**	**17.8**	**10.2**
Fuel oil and other fuels	**100.0**	**15.9**	**31.2**	**17.3**	**10.4**	**25.1**	**14.0**	**11.2**
Fuel oil	100.0	13.0	29.4	15.8	10.0	31.8	17.1	14.7
Coal	100.0	23.9	24.4	26.7	–	22.5	2.4	18.4
Bottled/tank gas	100.0	18.6	33.8	18.6	11.3	17.8	10.6	7.2
Wood and other fuels	100.0	21.7	29.6	20.7	9.5	18.7	10.7	8.0
Telephone services	**100.0**	**11.5**	**26.4**	**20.1**	**10.1**	**31.9**	**20.1**	**11.7**
Residential telephone and pay phones	100.0	13.0	27.7	19.2	9.8	30.4	19.1	11.3
Cellular phone service	100.0	7.4	23.7	22.1	11.0	35.7	22.8	12.9
Pager service	100.0	13.5	27.5	15.7	19.2	23.9	12.3	11.6
Phone cards	100.0	23.9	26.0	18.9	6.8	24.4	15.5	8.9
Water and other public services	**100.0**	**11.9**	**26.2**	**19.3**	**10.3**	**32.3**	**20.3**	**12.0**
Water and sewerage maintenance	100.0	12.4	26.5	19.1	10.5	31.5	20.0	11.5
Trash and garbage collection	100.0	10.6	25.4	19.6	9.8	34.6	21.1	13.5
Septic tank cleaning	100.0	7.0	26.5	24.5	15.3	27.0	19.9	7.1

*See appendix for information about mortgage principle reduction.

Note: Numbers may not add to total because of rounding. (–) means sample is too small to make a reliable estimate.

Source: Calculations by New Strategist based on the 2002 Consumer Expenditure Survey

Spending on Personal Care, Reading, Education, and Tobacco, 2002

The average household spent 11 percent less on personal care products and services in 2002 than in 1997, after adjusting for inflation. Spending on reading material also fell during those years—down a substantial 24 percent as television and the Internet cut household spending on books and newspapers. Not surprisingly, spending on education rose 18 percent as college tuition soared. The average household spent 8 percent more on tobacco in 2002 than in 1997 as cigarette prices rose.

Spending on personal care products and services is highest among householders aged 35 to 44, at $615 in 2002. This is the age when household size peaks. The biggest spenders on reading material are householders aged 55 to 64. This age group spends 40 percent more than the average household on magazine subscriptions. Householders aged 65 or older are the biggest spenders on newspaper subscriptions, however. Education spending is greatest for the youngest householders, who are most likely to be paying their way through college. Householders aged 45 to 54 (the parents of college students) are the second biggest spenders on education.

Households with incomes of $70,000 or more spend 63 percent more than the average household on personal care products and services. This high-income group spends 80 percent more than the average household on reading material and more than twice the average on education. Households with incomes below $50,000 account for the 61 percent majority of spending on tobacco products and smoking supplies.

Not surprisingly, spending on education is highest among married couples with children aged 18 or older at home because many have children in college. Couples with school-aged or older children at home spend the most on personal care products and services because they have the largest households. Married couples without children at home spend the most on reading material—particularly on newspaper and magazine subscriptions. Tobacco spending is highest for couples with adult children at home.

Black and Hispanic householders spend about an average amount on personal care products and services, but on a number of individual personal care items their spending is well above average. Blacks spend more than four times the average on wigs and hairpieces, for example. Hispanics spend 23 percent more than average on hair care products. Black and Hispanic householders spend less than average on reading material, education, and tobacco.

Households in the Northeast spend the most on newspapers, while households in the West spend the most on books. Spending on tobacco is greatest in the Midwest, 23 percent above average. Average household spending on education is 35 percent below average in the South.

College graduates spend more than other householders on personal care products and services, reading material, and education. They spend 91 percent more than the average household on college tuition and more than twice the average on books not purchased through book clubs. Householders with a high school diploma spend the most on tobacco, 37 percent more than the average household.

Table 10.1 Personal Care, Reading, Education, Tobacco: Average spending by age, 2002

(average annual spending of consumer units (CU) on personal care, reading, education, and tobacco products, by age of consumer unit reference person, 2002)

	total consumer units	under 25	25 to 34	35 to 44	45 to 54	55 to 64	65 to 74	75+
Number of consumer units (in thousands, add 000)	112,108	8,737	18,988	24,394	22,691	15,314	11,216	10,767
Average number of persons per CU	2.5	1.9	2.9	3.2	2.7	2.1	1.9	1.5
Average before-tax income of CU	$49,430.00	$20,773.00	$49,133.00	$61,532.00	$64,974.00	$53,162.00	$35,118.00	$23,890.00
Average spending of CU, total	40,676.60	24,229.46	40,318.29	48,330.48	48,748.24	44,330.04	32,242.52	23,758.89
PERSONAL CARE PRODUCTS AND SERVICES	**$525.80**	**$329.38**	**$487.53**	**$614.64**	**$588.30**	**$556.56**	**$508.65**	**$389.55**
Personal care products	**276.65**	**199.15**	**260.97**	**344.16**	**309.10**	**277.92**	**257.03**	**160.24**
Hair care products	53.57	41.15	54.63	73.46	62.76	42.17	41.73	24.49
Hair accessories	6.57	6.53	7.85	8.87	7.08	3.96	4.50	3.69
Wigs and hairpieces	1.32	1.57	0.91	1.59	1.49	1.73	0.94	0.73
Oral hygiene products	27.33	15.89	23.23	33.34	30.00	28.98	28.20	21.27
Shaving products	15.09	7.50	18.02	17.78	16.75	17.68	11.97	5.69
Cosmetics, perfume, and bath products	129.13	90.08	120.36	150.78	142.65	146.04	131.45	70.46
Deodorants, feminine hygiene, misc. products	30.29	32.27	29.66	37.83	29.89	25.49	23.17	27.53
Electric personal care appliances	13.34	4.17	6.29	20.53	18.48	11.88	15.07	6.38
Personal care services	**249.15**	**130.23**	**226.56**	**270.47**	**279.20**	**278.65**	**251.63**	**229.31**
READING	**138.57**	**56.68**	**103.06**	**134.57**	**166.64**	**181.44**	**160.71**	**133.51**
Newspaper subscriptions	43.88	5.60	16.72	33.10	48.35	66.74	73.55	74.41
Newspaper, nonsubscription	11.30	5.92	8.69	13.39	12.63	12.41	13.76	8.60
Magazine subscriptions	16.59	6.82	11.22	14.30	19.35	23.16	21.76	18.57
Magazines, nonsubscription	9.35	8.82	11.63	11.10	10.67	7.85	7.70	2.83
Books purchased through book clubs	6.62	1.67	5.37	7.69	7.49	6.32	6.84	8.75
Books not purchased through book clubs	50.38	27.78	49.13	54.53	66.99	64.63	36.97	20.17
EDUCATION	**751.95**	**1,663.52**	**571.41**	**738.35**	**1,208.24**	**589.41**	**288.58**	**112.15**
College tuition	444.45	1,304.63	375.98	282.97	670.56	435.40	140.10	86.52
Elementary and high school tuition	128.94	4.32	46.33	229.46	296.06	29.53	66.42	2.33
Other school tuition	25.53	9.93	19.19	36.22	42.47	20.84	20.27	1.55
Other school expenses including rentals	25.77	26.99	21.70	39.26	41.84	16.07	4.88	3.11
Books, supplies for college	57.93	265.85	49.53	34.97	71.51	34.34	15.30	5.41
Books, supplies for elementary, high school	16.14	4.57	13.88	35.19	21.79	7.72	2.76	0.35
Books, supplies for day care, nursery school	3.39	1.78	3.74	5.92	5.29	0.84	0.89	0.58
Miscellaneous school expenses and supplies	49.80	45.46	41.06	74.35	58.70	44.67	37.96	12.30
TOBACCO PRODUCTS AND SMOKING SUPPLIES	**320.49**	**285.68**	**315.27**	**375.83**	**415.01**	**360.52**	**220.31**	**80.83**
Cigarettes	291.89	259.31	280.77	347.75	383.70	327.02	199.59	64.05
Other tobacco products	26.27	21.99	32.94	25.51	29.21	32.04	17.12	14.84
Smoking accessories	2.33	4.38	1.56	2.56	2.10	1.45	3.60	1.94

Source: Bureau of Labor Statistics, unpublished tables from the 2002 Consumer Expenditure Survey

Table 10.2 Personal Care, Reading, Education, Tobacco: Indexed spending by age, 2002

(indexed average annual spending of consumer units (CU) on personal care, reading, education, and tobacco products, by age of consumer unit reference person, 2002; index definition: an index of 100 is the average for all consumer units; an index of 132 means that spending by consumer units in that group is 32 percent above the average for all consumer units; an index of 68 indicates spending that is 32 percent below the average for all consumer units)

	total consumer units	under 25	25 to 34	35 to 44	45 to 54	55 to 64	65 to 74	75+
Average spending of CU, total	$40,677	$24,229	$40,318	$48,330	$48,748	$44,330	$32,243	$23,759
Average spending of CU, index	100	60	99	119	120	109	79	58
PERSONAL CARE PRODUCTS AND SERVICES	**100**	**63**	**93**	**117**	**112**	**106**	**97**	**74**
Personal care products	**100**	**72**	**94**	**124**	**112**	**100**	**93**	**58**
Hair care products	100	77	102	137	117	79	78	46
Hair accessories	100	99	119	135	108	60	68	56
Wigs and hairpieces	100	119	69	120	113	131	71	55
Oral hygiene products	100	58	85	122	110	106	103	78
Shaving products	100	50	119	118	111	117	79	38
Cosmetics, perfume, and bath products	100	70	93	117	110	113	102	55
Deodorants, feminine hygiene, misc. products	100	107	98	125	99	84	76	91
Electric personal care appliances	100	31	47	154	139	89	113	48
Personal care services	**100**	**52**	**91**	**109**	**112**	**112**	**101**	**92**
READING	**100**	**41**	**74**	**97**	**120**	**131**	**116**	**96**
Newspaper subscriptions	100	13	38	75	110	152	168	170
Newspaper, nonsubscription	100	52	77	118	112	110	122	76
Magazine subscriptions	100	41	68	86	117	140	131	112
Magazines, nonsubscription	100	94	124	119	114	84	82	30
Books purchased through book clubs	100	25	81	116	113	95	103	132
Books not purchased through book clubs	100	55	98	108	133	128	73	40
EDUCATION	**100**	**221**	**76**	**98**	**161**	**78**	**38**	**15**
College tuition	100	294	85	64	151	98	32	19
Elementary and high school tuition	100	3	36	178	230	23	52	2
Other school tuition	100	39	75	142	166	82	79	6
Other school expenses including rentals	100	105	84	152	162	62	19	12
Books, supplies for college	100	459	85	60	123	59	26	9
Books, supplies for elementary, high school	100	28	86	218	135	48	17	2
Books, supplies for day care, nursery school	100	53	110	175	156	25	26	17
Miscellaneous school expenses and supplies	100	91	82	149	118	90	76	25
TOBACCO PRODUCTS AND SMOKING SUPPLIES	**100**	**89**	**98**	**117**	**129**	**112**	**69**	**25**
Cigarettes	100	89	96	119	131	112	68	22
Other tobacco products	100	84	125	97	111	122	65	56
Smoking accessories	100	188	67	110	90	62	155	83

Source: Calculations by New Strategist based on the 2002 Consumer Expenditure Survey

Table 10.3 Personal Care, Reading, Education, Tobacco: Total spending by age, 2002

(total annual spending on personal care, reading, education, and tobacco products, by consumer unit (CU) age groups, 2002; numbers in thousands)

	total consumer units	under 25	25 to 34	35 to 44	45 to 54	55 to 64	65 to 74	75+
Number of consumer units	112,108	8,737	18,988	24,394	22,691	15,314	11,216	10,767
Total spending of all CUs	$4,560,172,273	$211,692,792	$765,563,691	$1,178,973,729	$1,106,146,314	$678,870,233	$361,632,104	$255,811,969
PERSONAL CARE PRODUCTS AND SERVICES	**$58,946,386**	**$2,877,793**	**$9,257,220**	**$14,993,528**	**$13,349,115**	**$8,523,160**	**$5,705,018**	**$4,194,285**
Personal care products	31,014,678	1,739,974	4,955,298	8,395,439	7,013,788	4,256,067	2,882,848	1,725,304
Hair care products	6,005,626	359,528	1,037,314	1,791,983	1,424,087	645,791	468,044	263,684
Hair accessories	736,550	57,053	149,056	216,375	160,652	60,643	50,472	39,730
Wigs and hairpieces	147,983	13,717	17,279	38,786	33,810	26,493	10,543	7,860
Oral hygiene products	3,063,912	138,831	441,091	813,296	680,730	443,800	316,291	229,014
Shaving products	1,691,710	65,528	342,164	433,725	380,074	270,752	134,256	61,264
Cosmetics, perfume, and bath products	14,476,506	787,029	2,285,396	3,678,127	3,236,871	2,236,457	1,474,343	758,643
Deodorants, feminine hygiene, misc. products	3,395,751	281,943	563,184	922,825	678,234	390,354	259,875	296,416
Electric personal care appliances	1,495,521	36,433	119,435	500,809	419,330	181,930	169,025	68,693
Personal care services	27,931,708	1,137,820	4,301,921	6,597,845	6,335,327	4,267,246	2,822,282	2,468,981
READING	**15,534,806**	**495,213**	**1,956,903**	**3,282,701**	**3,781,228**	**2,778,572**	**1,802,523**	**1,437,502**
Newspaper subscriptions	4,919,299	48,927	317,479	807,441	1,097,110	1,022,056	824,937	801,172
Newspaper, nonsubscription	1,266,820	51,723	165,006	326,636	286,587	190,047	154,332	92,596
Magazine subscriptions	1,859,872	59,586	213,045	348,834	439,071	354,672	244,060	199,943
Magazines, nonsubscription	1,048,210	77,060	220,830	270,773	242,113	120,215	86,363	30,471
Books purchased through book clubs	742,155	14,591	101,966	187,590	169,956	96,784	76,717	94,211
Books not purchased through book clubs	5,648,001	242,714	932,880	1,330,205	1,520,070	989,744	414,656	217,170
EDUCATION	**84,299,611**	**14,534,174**	**10,849,933**	**18,011,310**	**27,416,174**	**9,026,225**	**3,236,713**	**1,207,519**
College tuition	49,826,401	11,398,552	7,139,108	6,902,770	15,215,677	6,667,716	1,571,362	931,561
Elementary and high school tuition	14,455,206	37,744	879,714	5,597,447	6,717,897	452,222	744,967	25,087
Other school tuition	2,862,117	86,758	364,380	883,551	963,687	319,144	227,348	16,689
Other school expenses including rentals	2,889,023	235,812	412,040	957,708	949,391	246,096	54,734	33,485
Books, supplies for college	6,494,416	2,322,731	940,476	853,058	1,622,633	525,883	171,605	58,249
Books, supplies for elementary, high school	1,809,423	39,928	263,553	858,425	494,437	118,224	30,956	3,768
Books, supplies for day care, nursery school	380,046	15,552	71,015	144,412	120,035	12,864	9,982	6,245
Miscellaneous school expenses and supplies	5,582,978	397,184	779,647	1,813,694	1,331,962	684,076	425,759	132,434
TOBACCO PRODUCTS AND SMOKING SUPPLIES	**35,929,493**	**2,495,986**	**5,986,347**	**9,167,997**	**9,416,992**	**5,521,003**	**2,470,997**	**870,297**
Cigarettes	32,723,204	2,265,591	5,331,261	8,483,014	8,706,537	5,007,984	2,238,601	689,626
Other tobacco products	2,945,077	192,127	625,465	622,291	662,804	490,661	192,018	159,782
Smoking accessories	261,212	38,268	29,621	62,449	47,651	22,205	40,378	20,888

Note: Numbers may not add to total because of rounding.
Source: Calculations by New Strategist based on the 2002 Consumer Expenditure Survey

Table 10.4 Personal Care, Reading, Education, Tobacco: Market shares by age, 2002

(percentage of total annual spending on personal care, reading, education, and tobacco products accounted for by consumer unit age groups, 2002)

	total consumer units	under 25	25 to 34	35 to 44	45 to 54	55 to 64	65 to 74	75+
Share of total consumer units	100.0%	7.8%	16.9%	21.8%	20.2%	13.7%	10.0%	9.6%
Share of total before-tax income	100.0	3.3	16.8	27.1	26.6	14.7	7.1	4.6
Share of total spending	100.0	4.6	16.8	25.9	24.3	14.9	7.9	5.6
PERSONAL CARE PRODUCTS AND SERVICES	100.0%	4.9%	15.7%	25.4%	22.6%	14.5%	9.7%	7.1%
Personal care products	100.0	5.6	16.0	27.1	22.6	13.7	9.3	5.6
Hair care products	100.0	6.0	17.3	29.8	23.7	10.8	7.8	4.4
Hair accessories	100.0	7.7	20.2	29.4	21.8	8.2	6.9	5.4
Wigs and hairpieces	100.0	9.3	11.7	26.2	22.8	17.9	7.1	5.3
Oral hygiene products	100.0	4.5	14.4	26.5	22.2	14.5	10.3	7.5
Shaving products	100.0	3.9	20.2	25.6	22.5	16.0	7.9	3.6
Cosmetics, perfume, and bath products	100.0	5.4	15.8	25.4	22.4	15.4	10.2	5.2
Deodorants, feminine hygiene, misc. products	100.0	8.3	16.6	27.2	20.0	11.5	7.7	8.7
Electric personal care appliances	100.0	2.4	8.0	33.5	28.0	12.2	11.3	4.6
Personal care services	100.0	4.1	15.4	23.6	22.7	15.3	10.1	8.8
READING	100.0	3.2	12.6	21.1	24.3	17.9	11.6	9.3
Newspaper subscriptions	100.0	1.0	6.5	16.4	22.3	20.8	16.8	16.3
Newspaper, nonsubscription	100.0	4.1	13.0	25.8	22.6	15.0	12.2	7.3
Magazine subscriptions	100.0	3.2	11.5	18.8	23.6	19.1	13.1	10.8
Magazines, nonsubscription	100.0	7.4	21.1	25.8	23.1	11.5	8.2	2.9
Books purchased through book clubs	100.0	2.0	13.7	25.3	22.9	13.0	10.3	12.7
Books not purchased through book clubs	100.0	4.3	16.5	23.6	26.9	17.5	7.3	3.8
EDUCATION	100.0	17.2	12.9	21.4	32.5	10.7	3.8	1.4
College tuition	100.0	22.9	14.3	13.9	30.5	13.4	3.2	1.9
Elementary and high school tuition	100.0	0.3	6.1	38.7	46.5	3.1	5.2	0.2
Other school tuition	100.0	3.0	12.7	30.9	33.7	11.2	7.9	0.6
Other school expenses including rentals	100.0	8.2	14.3	33.1	32.9	8.5	1.9	1.2
Books, supplies for college	100.0	35.8	14.5	13.1	25.0	8.1	2.6	0.9
Books, supplies for elementary, high school	100.0	2.2	14.6	47.4	27.3	6.5	1.7	0.2
Books, supplies for day care, nursery school	100.0	4.1	18.7	38.0	31.6	3.4	2.6	1.6
Miscellaneous school expenses and supplies	100.0	7.1	14.0	32.5	23.9	12.3	7.6	2.4
TOBACCO PRODUCTS AND SMOKING SUPPLIES	100.0	6.9	16.7	25.5	26.2	15.4	6.9	2.4
Cigarettes	100.0	6.9	16.3	25.9	26.6	15.3	6.8	2.1
Other tobacco products	100.0	6.5	21.2	21.1	22.5	16.7	6.5	5.4
Smoking accessories	100.0	14.7	11.3	23.9	18.2	8.5	15.5	8.0

Note: Numbers may not add to total because of rounding.
Source: Calculations by New Strategist based on the 2002 Consumer Expenditure Survey

Table 10.5 Personal Care, Reading, Education, Tobacco: Average spending by income, 2002

(average annual spending on personal care, reading, education, and tobacco products, by before-tax income of consumer units (CU), 2002; complete income reporters only)

	complete income reporters	under $10,000	$10,000– $19,999	$20,000– $29,999	$30,000– $39,999	$40,000– $49,999	$50,000– $69,999	$70,000 or more
Number of consumer units								
(in thousands, add 000)	92,388	10,933	15,075	12,312	10,727	8,873	13,521	20,947
Average number of persons per CU	2.5	1.7	1.9	2.3	2.5	2.6	2.8	3.1
Average before-tax income of CU	$49,430.00	$5,554.80	$14,724.33	$24,495.00	$34,423.00	$44,443.00	$58,933.00	$115,629.00
Average spending of CU, total	42,556.98	17,627.83	22,838.71	28,835.85	35,095.39	41,787.38	50,406.17	76,627.31
PERSONAL CARE PRODUCTS								
AND SERVICES	**$561.52**	**$269.23**	**$367.12**	**$431.59**	**$464.23**	**$551.23**	**$655.45**	**$915.14**
Personal care products	310.26	158.07	211.08	234.97	262.22	313.67	377.66	476.18
Hair care products	59.87	38.43	34.07	55.16	55.52	67.04	73.10	81.69
Hair accessories	7.70	5.40	5.66	6.55	7.54	6.78	8.74	10.71
Wigs and hairpieces	1.41	1.49	1.25	1.48	1.13	1.20	1.23	1.79
Oral hygiene products	29.78	18.89	23.74	26.33	25.48	32.19	33.69	39.86
Shaving products	16.62	7.36	7.91	10.74	12.62	17.47	25.45	26.78
Cosmetics, perfume, and bath products	145.22	60.99	100.92	89.28	118.79	155.19	178.23	237.59
Deodorants, feminine hygiene, misc. products	34.05	14.82	30.93	32.67	33.91	30.33	35.67	46.39
Electric personal care appliances	15.60	10.70	6.60	12.76	7.23	3.48	21.55	31.38
Personal care services	**251.26**	**111.16**	**156.04**	**196.62**	**202.01**	**237.56**	**277.79**	**438.96**
READING	**145.33**	**59.39**	**84.97**	**105.58**	**108.82**	**140.02**	**170.05**	**261.94**
Newspaper subscriptions	45.49	19.81	35.04	35.78	35.05	40.97	49.51	76.78
Newspaper, nonsubscription	11.90	4.95	8.56	13.71	11.33	12.42	15.22	14.81
Magazine subscriptions	17.91	6.61	10.27	14.21	13.40	16.62	21.66	31.93
Magazines, nonsubscription	9.86	5.10	4.93	6.42	7.56	8.63	13.15	17.50
Books purchased through book clubs	6.94	1.43	4.25	5.45	7.07	7.46	9.29	10.82
Books not purchased through book clubs	52.71	21.47	21.79	29.68	34.29	53.77	60.76	108.57
EDUCATION	**771.44**	**851.08**	**410.16**	**310.99**	**387.97**	**536.23**	**618.58**	**1,653.13**
College tuition	456.55	674.06	279.83	206.90	235.21	296.73	304.09	896.43
Elementary and high school tuition	122.48	15.63	17.06	13.60	23.71	95.31	109.86	388.34
Other school tuition	28.14	1.37	13.71	5.85	19.00	11.58	44.93	66.47
Other school expenses including rentals	25.92	8.81	13.31	13.06	15.73	28.36	29.62	53.28
Books, supplies for college	60.97	115.35	48.98	31.14	32.47	42.61	48.78	89.00
Books, supplies for elementary, high school	16.76	3.68	6.33	9.97	16.82	14.83	20.42	33.49
Books, supplies for day care, nursery school	3.92	1.04	0.66	1.94	5.74	2.67	6.14	7.10
Miscellaneous school expenses and supplies	56.70	31.14	30.29	28.53	39.29	44.15	54.74	119.02
TOBACCO PRODUCTS AND								
SMOKING SUPPLIES	**333.51**	**224.88**	**271.50**	**364.43**	**390.43**	**401.05**	**421.57**	**302.13**
Cigarettes	303.29	210.59	248.33	337.96	359.00	367.14	388.35	260.37
Other tobacco products	27.58	11.32	19.99	24.49	30.06	29.18	31.26	39.03
Smoking accessories	2.64	2.98	3.19	1.97	1.37	4.72	1.96	2.73

Source: Bureau of Labor Statistics, unpublished tables from the 2002 Consumer Expenditure Survey; calculations by New Strategist

Table 10.6 Personal Care, Reading, Education, Tobacco: Indexed spending by income, 2002

(indexed average annual spending of consumer units (CU) on personal care, reading, education, and tobacco products, by before-tax income of consumer unit, 2002; complete income reporters only; index definition: an index of 100 is the average for all consumer units; an index of 132 means that spending by consumer units in that group is 32 percent above the average for all consumer units; an index of 68 indicates spending that is 32 percent below the average for all consumer units)

	complete income reporters	under $10,000	$10,000–$19,999	$20,000–$29,999	$30,000–$39,999	$40,000–$49,999	$50,000–$69,999	$70,000 or more
Average spending of CU, total	$42,557	$17,628	$22,839	$28,836	$35,095	$41,787	$50,406	$76,627
Average spending of CU, index	100	41	54	68	82	98	118	180
PERSONAL CARE PRODUCTS AND SERVICES	**100**	**48**	**65**	**77**	**83**	**98**	**117**	**163**
Personal care products	**100**	**51**	**68**	**76**	**85**	**101**	**122**	**153**
Hair care products	100	64	57	92	93	112	122	136
Hair accessories	100	70	73	85	98	88	114	139
Wigs and hairpieces	100	105	89	105	80	85	87	127
Oral hygiene products	100	63	80	88	86	108	113	134
Shaving products	100	44	48	65	76	105	153	161
Cosmetics, perfume, and bath products	100	42	69	61	82	107	123	164
Deodorants, feminine hygiene, misc. products	100	44	91	96	100	89	105	136
Electric personal care appliances	100	69	42	82	46	22	138	201
Personal care services	**100**	**44**	**62**	**78**	**80**	**95**	**111**	**175**
READING	**100**	**41**	**58**	**73**	**75**	**96**	**117**	**180**
Newspaper subscriptions	100	44	77	79	77	90	109	169
Newspaper, nonsubscription	100	42	72	115	95	104	128	124
Magazine subscriptions	100	37	57	79	75	93	121	178
Magazines, nonsubscription	100	52	50	65	77	88	133	177
Books purchased through book clubs	100	21	61	79	102	107	134	156
Books not purchased through book clubs	100	41	41	56	65	102	115	206
EDUCATION	**100**	**110**	**53**	**40**	**50**	**70**	**80**	**214**
College tuition	100	148	61	45	52	65	67	196
Elementary and high school tuition	100	13	14	11	19	78	90	317
Other school tuition	100	5	49	21	68	41	160	236
Other school expenses including rentals	100	34	51	50	61	109	114	206
Books, supplies for college	100	189	80	51	53	70	80	146
Books, supplies for elementary, high school	100	22	38	59	100	88	122	200
Books, supplies for day care, nursery school	100	27	17	49	146	68	157	181
Miscellaneous school expenses and supplies	100	55	53	50	69	78	97	210
TOBACCO PRODUCTS AND SMOKING SUPPLIES	**100**	**67**	**81**	**109**	**117**	**120**	**126**	**91**
Cigarettes	100	69	82	111	118	121	128	86
Other tobacco products	100	41	72	89	109	106	113	142
Smoking accessories	100	113	121	75	52	179	74	103

Source: Calculations by New Strategist based on the 2002 Consumer Expenditure Survey

Table 10.7 Personal Care, Reading, Education, Tobacco: Total spending by income, 2002

(total annual spending on personal care, reading, education, and tobacco products, by before-tax income group of consumer units (CU), 2002; complete income reporters only; numbers in thousands)

	complete income reporters	under $10,000	$10,000–$19,999	$20,000–$29,999	$30,000–$39,999	$40,000–$49,999	$50,000–$69,999	$70,000 or more
Number of consumer units	92,388	10,933	15,075	12,312	10,727	8,873	13,521	20,947
Total spending of all CUs	$3,931,754,268	$192,725,059	$344,293,530	$355,026,985	$376,468,249	$370,779,423	$681,541,825	$1,605,112,263
PERSONAL CARE PRODUCTS								
AND SERVICES	**$51,877,710**	**$2,943,445**	**$5,534,291**	**$5,313,736**	**$4,979,795**	**$4,891,064**	**$8,862,339**	**$19,169,438**
Personal care products	**28,664,301**	**1,728,151**	**3,182,056**	**2,892,951**	**2,812,834**	**2,783,194**	**5,106,341**	**9,974,542**
Hair care products	5,531,270	420,115	513,645	679,130	595,563	594,846	988,385	1,711,160
Hair accessories	711,388	59,023	85,256	80,644	80,882	60,159	118,174	224,342
Wigs and hairpieces	130,267	16,263	18,828	18,222	12,122	10,648	16,631	37,495
Oral hygiene products	2,751,315	206,485	357,894	324,175	273,324	285,622	455,522	834,947
Shaving products	1,535,489	80,454	119,197	132,231	135,375	155,011	344,109	560,961
Cosmetics, perfume, and bath products	13,416,585	666,771	1,521,376	1,099,215	1,274,260	1,377,001	2,409,848	4,976,798
Deodorants, feminine hygiene, misc. products	3,145,811	161,999	466,195	402,233	363,753	269,118	482,294	971,731
Electric personal care appliances	1,441,253	117,009	99,514	157,101	77,556	30,878	291,378	657,317
Personal care services	**23,213,409**	**1,215,294**	**2,352,235**	**2,420,785**	**2,166,961**	**2,107,870**	**3,755,999**	**9,194,895**
READING	**13,426,748**	**649,364**	**1,280,899**	**1,299,901**	**1,167,312**	**1,242,397**	**2,299,246**	**5,486,857**
Newspaper subscriptions	4,202,730	216,608	528,158	440,523	375,981	363,527	669,425	1,608,311
Newspaper, nonsubscription	1,099,417	54,108	128,972	168,798	121,537	110,203	205,790	310,225
Magazine subscriptions	1,654,669	72,247	154,849	174,954	143,742	147,469	292,865	668,838
Magazines, nonsubscription	910,946	55,789	74,340	79,043	81,096	76,574	177,801	366,573
Books purchased through book clubs	641,173	15,676	64,087	67,100	75,840	66,193	125,610	226,647
Books not purchased through book clubs	4,869,771	234,780	328,525	365,420	367,829	477,101	821,536	2,274,216
EDUCATION	**71,271,799**	**9,304,882**	**6,183,157**	**3,828,909**	**4,161,754**	**4,757,969**	**8,363,820**	**34,628,114**
College tuition	42,179,741	7,369,492	4,218,388	2,547,353	2,523,098	2,632,885	4,111,601	18,777,519
Elementary and high school tuition	11,315,682	170,877	257,114	167,443	254,337	845,686	1,485,417	8,134,558
Other school tuition	2,599,798	14,995	206,648	72,025	203,813	102,749	607,499	1,392,347
Other school expenses including rentals	2,394,697	96,313	200,633	160,795	168,736	251,638	400,492	1,116,056
Books, supplies for college	5,632,896	1,261,090	738,399	383,396	348,306	378,079	659,554	1,864,283
Books, supplies for elementary, high school	1,548,423	40,243	95,364	122,751	180,428	131,587	276,099	701,515
Books, supplies for day care, nursery school	362,161	11,363	9,951	23,885	61,573	23,691	83,019	148,724
Miscellaneous school expenses and supplies	5,238,400	340,438	456,662	351,261	421,464	391,743	740,140	2,493,112
TOBACCO PRODUCTS AND								
SMOKING SUPPLIES	**30,812,322**	**2,458,583**	**4,092,903**	**4,486,862**	**4,188,143**	**3,558,517**	**5,700,048**	**6,328,717**
Cigarettes	28,020,357	2,302,393	3,743,556	4,160,964	3,850,993	3,257,633	5,250,880	5,453,970
Other tobacco products	2,548,061	123,753	301,329	301,521	322,454	258,914	422,666	817,561
Smoking accessories	243,904	32,547	48,018	24,255	14,696	41,881	26,501	57,185

Note: Numbers may not add to total because of rounding.
Source: Calculations by New Strategist based on the 2002 Consumer Expenditure Survey

Table 10.8 Personal Care, Reading, Education, Tobacco: Market shares by income, 2002

(percentage of total annual spending on personal care, reading, education, and tobacco products accounted for by before-tax income group of consumer units, 2002; complete income reporters only)

	complete income reporters	under $10,000	$10,000–$19,999	$20,000–$29,999	$30,000–$39,999	$40,000–$49,999	$50,000–$69,999	$70,000 or more
Share of total consumer units	100.0%	11.8%	16.3%	13.3%	11.6%	9.6%	14.6%	22.7%
Share of total before-tax income	100.0	1.3	4.9	6.6	8.1	8.6	17.4	53.0
Share of total spending	100.0	4.9	8.8	9.0	9.6	9.4	17.3	40.8
PERSONAL CARE PRODUCTS								
AND SERVICES	100.0%	5.7%	10.7%	10.2%	9.6%	9.4%	17.1%	37.0%
Personal care products	100.0	6.0	11.1	10.1	9.8	9.7	17.8	34.8
Hair care products	100.0	7.6	9.3	12.3	10.8	10.8	17.9	30.9
Hair accessories	100.0	8.3	12.0	11.3	11.4	8.5	16.6	31.5
Wigs and hairpieces	100.0	12.5	14.5	14.0	9.3	8.2	12.8	28.8
Oral hygiene products	100.0	7.5	13.0	11.8	9.9	10.4	16.6	30.3
Shaving products	100.0	5.2	7.8	8.6	8.8	10.1	22.4	36.5
Cosmetics, perfume, and bath products	100.0	5.0	11.3	8.2	9.5	10.3	18.0	37.1
Deodorants, feminine hygiene, misc. products	100.0	5.1	14.8	12.8	11.6	8.6	15.3	30.9
Electric personal care appliances	100.0	8.1	6.9	10.9	5.4	2.1	20.2	45.6
Personal care services	100.0	5.2	10.1	10.4	9.3	9.1	16.2	39.6
READING	100.0	4.8	9.5	9.7	8.7	9.3	17.1	40.9
Newspaper subscriptions	100.0	5.2	12.6	10.5	8.9	8.6	15.9	38.3
Newspaper, nonsubscription	100.0	4.9	11.7	15.4	11.1	10.0	18.7	28.2
Magazine subscriptions	100.0	4.4	9.4	10.6	8.7	8.9	17.7	40.4
Magazines, nonsubscription	100.0	6.1	8.2	8.7	8.9	8.4	19.5	40.2
Books purchased through book clubs	100.0	2.4	10.0	10.5	11.8	10.3	19.6	35.3
Books not purchased through book clubs	100.0	4.8	6.7	7.5	7.6	9.8	16.9	46.7
EDUCATION	100.0	13.1	8.7	5.4	5.8	6.7	11.7	48.6
College tuition	100.0	17.5	10.0	6.0	6.0	6.2	9.7	44.5
Elementary and high school tuition	100.0	1.5	2.3	1.5	2.2	7.5	13.1	71.9
Other school tuition	100.0	0.6	7.9	2.8	7.8	4.0	23.4	53.6
Other school expenses including rentals	100.0	4.0	8.4	6.7	7.0	10.5	16.7	46.6
Books, supplies for college	100.0	22.4	13.1	6.8	6.2	6.7	11.7	33.1
Books, supplies for elementary, high school	100.0	2.6	6.2	7.9	11.7	8.5	17.8	45.3
Books, supplies for day care, nursery school	100.0	3.1	2.7	6.6	17.0	6.5	22.9	41.1
Miscellaneous school expenses and supplies	100.0	6.5	8.7	6.7	8.0	7.5	14.1	47.6
TOBACCO PRODUCTS AND								
SMOKING SUPPLIES	100.0	8.0	13.3	14.6	13.6	11.5	18.5	20.5
Cigarettes	100.0	8.2	13.4	14.8	13.7	11.6	18.7	19.5
Other tobacco products	100.0	4.9	11.8	11.8	12.7	10.2	16.6	32.1
Smoking accessories	100.0	13.3	19.7	9.9	6.0	17.2	10.9	23.4

Note: Numbers may not add to total because of rounding.
Source: Calculations by New Strategist based on the 2002 Consumer Expenditure Survey

Table 10.9 Personal Care, Reading, Education, Tobacco: Average spending by household type, 2002

(average annual spending of consumer units (CU) on personal care, reading, education, and tobacco products, by type of consumer unit, 2002)

	total married couples	married couples, no children	married couples with children				single parent, at least one child <18	single person
			total	oldest child under 6	oldest child 6 to 17	oldest child 18 or older		
Number of consumer units								
(in thousands, add 000)	56,265	23,118	28,790	5,547	15,206	8,036	6,730	33,055
Average number of persons per CU	3.2	2.0	3.9	3.5	4.1	3.9	2.9	1.0
Average before-tax income of CU	$67,155.00	$58,967.00	$73,918.00	$67,587.00	$72,720.00	$81,042.00	$26,966.00	$27,042.00
Average spending of CU, total	52,333.70	45,557.33	57,835.01	52,778.62	58,103.75	60,859.78	30,185.38	24,189.90
PERSONAL CARE PRODUCTS								
AND SERVICES	**$662.10**	**$608.25**	**$711.22**	**$549.43**	**$757.28**	**$735.74**	**$427.50**	**$310.50**
Personal care products	**346.58**	**294.35**	**389.04**	**295.66**	**430.53**	**375.01**	**245.50**	**149.44**
Hair care products	65.02	47.48	76.73	58.85	83.34	76.69	60.16	27.86
Hair accessories	7.34	4.46	9.51	12.93	9.96	6.11	11.44	3.75
Wigs and hairpieces	1.30	1.45	0.87	0.39	0.98	1.01	3.58	0.87
Oral hygiene products	34.84	31.40	38.22	34.05	37.74	42.25	24.68	14.13
Shaving products	20.15	17.57	23.32	15.81	26.20	23.09	10.52	8.03
Cosmetics, perfume, and bath products	163.07	144.10	179.21	133.00	200.95	169.84	97.20	72.00
Deodorants, feminine hygiene, misc. products	36.62	29.80	41.15	33.68	45.47	38.04	33.56	17.78
Electric personal care appliances	18.24	18.09	20.04	6.96	25.89	17.99	4.35	5.03
Personal care services	**315.52**	**313.90**	**322.18**	**253.77**	**326.76**	**360.72**	**182.00**	**161.06**
READING	**174.09**	**192.14**	**166.19**	**132.49**	**168.96**	**184.22**	**71.85**	**107.92**
Newspaper subscriptions	58.31	72.86	47.85	31.62	45.68	63.15	11.53	32.84
Newspaper, nonsubscription	12.73	13.16	12.51	13.26	10.83	15.15	8.37	9.84
Magazine subscriptions	21.61	26.45	18.70	15.30	20.50	17.65	5.85	13.01
Magazines, nonsubscription	10.70	9.60	11.88	9.48	11.92	13.46	6.94	7.29
Books purchased through book clubs	7.23	6.82	7.80	7.94	8.00	7.33	5.07	5.95
Books not purchased through book clubs	62.98	62.57	67.04	54.89	71.34	67.28	32.28	38.74
EDUCATION	**951.73**	**489.91**	**1,365.97**	**336.22**	**1,246.38**	**2,303.42**	**453.64**	**562.34**
College tuition	516.07	356.07	666.30	203.78	333.71	1,614.87	148.54	428.34
Elementary and high school tuition	217.88	21.01	390.20	16.65	577.79	293.11	119.28	23.40
Other school tuition	34.32	25.93	42.13	25.15	46.12	46.31	20.92	9.17
Other school expenses including rentals	36.05	11.92	56.36	14.47	67.99	63.28	34.10	10.05
Books, supplies for college	54.69	36.92	70.36	32.53	29.52	173.76	30.63	65.29
Books, supplies for elementary, high school	25.43	1.89	43.81	4.26	69.21	23.04	31.99	0.87
Books, supplies for day care, nursery school	5.01	1.04	8.36	5.77	12.60	2.13	1.83	1.21
Miscellaneous school expenses and supplies	62.28	35.13	88.45	33.60	109.45	86.92	66.36	24.02
TOBACCO PRODUCTS AND								
SMOKING SUPPLIES	**335.68**	**285.62**	**343.77**	**274.64**	**318.32**	**439.69**	**262.41**	**210.03**
Cigarettes	301.12	254.14	306.89	230.54	283.48	403.88	253.08	188.14
Other tobacco products	31.71	28.05	34.28	42.16	32.37	32.48	8.31	20.47
Smoking accessories	2.86	3.43	2.60	1.94	2.47	3.33	1.02	1.42

Note: Average spending figures for total consumer units can be found on Average Spending by Age and Average Spending by Region tables.
Source: Bureau of Labor Statistics, unpublished tables from the 2002 Consumer Expenditure Survey

Table 10.10 Personal Care, Reading, Education, Tobacco: Indexed spending by household type, 2002

(indexed average annual spending of consumer units (CU) on personal care, reading, education, and tobacco products, by type of consumer unit, 2002; index definition: an index of 100 is the average for all consumer units; an index of 132 means that spending by consumer units in that group is 32 percent above the average for all consumer units; an index of 68 indicates spending that is 32 percent below the average for all consumer units)

	total married couples	married couples, no children	married couples with children				single parent, at least one child <18	single person
			total	oldest child under 6	oldest child 6 to 17	oldest child 18 or older		
Average spending of CU, total	$52,334	$45,557	$57,835	$52,779	$58,104	$60,860	$30,185	$24,190
Average spending of CU, index	129	112	142	130	143	150	74	59
PERSONAL CARE PRODUCTS AND SERVICES	**126**	**116**	**135**	**104**	**144**	**140**	**81**	**59**
Personal care products	**125**	**106**	**141**	**107**	**156**	**136**	**89**	**54**
Hair care products	121	89	143	110	156	143	112	52
Hair accessories	112	68	145	197	152	93	174	57
Wigs and hairpieces	98	110	66	30	74	77	271	66
Oral hygiene products	127	115	140	125	138	155	90	52
Shaving products	134	116	155	105	174	153	70	53
Cosmetics, perfume, and bath products	126	112	139	103	156	132	75	56
Deodorants, feminine hygiene, misc. products	121	98	136	111	150	126	111	59
Electric personal care appliances	137	136	150	52	194	135	33	38
Personal care services	**127**	**126**	**129**	**102**	**131**	**145**	**73**	**65**
READING	**126**	**139**	**120**	**96**	**122**	**133**	**52**	**78**
Newspaper subscriptions	133	166	109	72	104	144	26	75
Newspaper, nonsubscription	113	116	111	117	96	134	74	87
Magazine subscriptions	130	159	113	92	124	106	35	78
Magazines, nonsubscription	114	103	127	101	127	144	74	78
Books purchased through book clubs	109	103	118	120	121	111	77	90
Books not purchased through book clubs	125	124	133	109	142	134	64	77
EDUCATION	**127**	**65**	**182**	**45**	**166**	**306**	**60**	**75**
College tuition	116	80	150	46	75	363	33	96
Elementary and high school tuition	169	16	303	13	448	227	93	18
Other school tuition	134	102	165	99	181	181	82	36
Other school expenses including rentals	140	46	219	56	264	246	132	39
Books, supplies for college	94	64	121	56	51	300	53	113
Books, supplies for elementary, high school	158	12	271	26	429	143	198	5
Books, supplies for day care, nursery school	148	31	247	170	372	63	54	36
Miscellaneous school expenses and supplies	125	71	178	67	220	175	133	48
TOBACCO PRODUCTS AND SMOKING SUPPLIES	**105**	**89**	**107**	**86**	**99**	**137**	**82**	**66**
Cigarettes	103	87	105	79	97	138	87	64
Other tobacco products	121	107	130	160	123	124	32	78
Smoking accessories	123	147	112	83	106	143	44	61

Note: Spending index for total consumer units is 100.
Source: Calculations by New Strategist based on the 2002 Consumer Expenditure Survey

Table 10.11 Personal Care, Reading, Education, Tobacco: Total spending by household type, 2002

(total annual spending on personal care, reading, education, and tobacco products, by consumer unit (CU) type, 2002; numbers in thousands)

	total married couples	married couples, no children	married couples with children				single parent, at least one child <18	single person
			total	oldest child under 6	oldest child 6 to 17	oldest child 18 or older		
Number of consumer units	56,265	23,118	28,790	5,547	15,206	8,036	6,730	33,055
Total spending of all CUs	$2,944,555,631	$1,053,194,355	$1,665,069,938	$292,763,005	$883,525,623	$489,069,192	$203,147,607	$799,597,145
PERSONAL CARE PRODUCTS AND SERVICES	**$37,253,057**	**$14,061,524**	**$20,476,024**	**$3,047,688**	**$11,515,200**	**$5,912,407**	**$2,877,075**	**$10,263,578**
Personal care products	**19,500,324**	**6,804,783**	**11,200,462**	**1,640,026**	**6,546,639**	**3,013,580**	**1,652,215**	**4,939,739**
Hair care products	3,658,350	1,097,643	2,209,057	326,441	1,267,268	616,281	404,877	920,912
Hair accessories	412,985	103,106	273,793	71,723	151,452	49,100	76,991	123,956
Wigs and hairpieces	73,145	33,521	25,047	2,163	14,902	8,116	24,093	28,758
Oral hygiene products	1,960,273	725,905	1,100,354	188,875	573,874	339,521	166,096	467,067
Shaving products	1,133,740	406,183	671,383	87,698	398,397	185,551	70,800	265,432
Cosmetics, perfume, and bath products	9,175,134	3,331,304	5,159,456	737,751	3,055,646	1,364,834	654,156	2,379,960
Deodorants, feminine hygiene, misc. products	2,060,424	688,916	1,184,709	186,823	691,417	305,689	225,859	587,718
Electric personal care appliances	1,026,274	418,205	576,952	38,607	393,683	144,568	29,276	166,267
Personal care services	**17,752,733**	**7,256,740**	**9,275,562**	**1,407,662**	**4,968,713**	**2,898,746**	**1,224,860**	**5,323,838**
READING	**9,795,174**	**4,441,893**	**4,784,610**	**734,922**	**2,569,206**	**1,480,392**	**483,551**	**3,567,296**
Newspaper subscriptions	3,280,812	1,684,377	1,377,602	175,396	694,610	507,473	77,597	1,085,526
Newspaper, nonsubscription	716,253	304,233	360,163	73,553	164,681	121,745	56,330	325,261
Magazine subscriptions	1,215,887	611,471	538,373	84,869	311,723	141,835	39,371	430,046
Magazines, nonsubscription	602,036	221,933	342,025	52,586	181,256	108,165	46,706	240,971
Books purchased through book clubs	406,796	157,665	224,562	44,043	121,648	58,904	34,121	196,677
Books not purchased through book clubs	3,543,570	1,446,493	1,930,082	304,475	1,084,796	540,662	217,244	1,280,551
EDUCATION	**53,549,088**	**11,325,739**	**39,326,276**	**1,865,012**	**18,952,454**	**18,510,283**	**3,052,997**	**18,588,149**
College tuition	29,036,679	8,231,626	19,182,777	1,130,368	5,074,394	12,977,095	999,674	14,158,779
Elementary and high school tuition	12,259,018	485,709	11,233,858	92,358	8,785,875	2,355,432	802,754	773,487
Other school tuition	1,931,015	599,450	1,212,923	139,507	701,301	372,147	140,792	303,114
Other school expenses including rentals	2,028,353	275,567	1,622,604	80,265	1,033,856	508,518	229,493	332,203
Books, supplies for college	3,077,133	853,517	2,025,664	180,444	448,881	1,396,335	206,140	2,158,161
Books, supplies for elementary, high school	1,430,819	43,693	1,261,290	23,630	1,052,407	185,149	215,293	28,758
Books, supplies for day care, nursery school	281,888	24,043	240,684	32,006	191,596	17,117	12,316	39,997
Miscellaneous school expenses and supplies	3,504,184	812,135	2,546,476	186,379	1,664,297	698,489	446,603	793,981
TOBACCO PRODUCTS AND SMOKING SUPPLIES	**18,887,035**	**6,602,963**	**9,897,138**	**1,523,428**	**4,840,374**	**3,533,349**	**1,766,019**	**6,942,542**
Cigarettes	16,942,517	5,875,209	8,835,363	1,278,805	4,310,597	3,245,580	1,703,228	6,218,968
Other tobacco products	1,784,163	648,460	986,921	233,862	492,218	261,009	55,926	676,636
Smoking accessories	160,918	79,295	74,854	10,761	37,559	26,760	6,865	46,938

Note: Total spending figures for total consumer units can be found on Total Spending by Age and Total Spending by Region tables. Spending by type of consumer unit will not add to total because not all types of consumer units are shown.
Source: Calculations by New Strategist based on the 2002 Consumer Expenditure Survey

Table 10.12 Personal Care, Reading, Education, Tobacco: Market shares by household type, 2002

(percentage of total annual spending on personal care, reading, education, and tobacco products accounted for by types of consumer units, 2002)

	total married couples	married couples, no children	married couples with children				single parent, at least one child <18	single person
			total	oldest child under 6	oldest child 6 to 17	oldest child 18 or older		
Share of total consumer units	50.2%	20.6%	25.7%	4.9%	13.6%	7.2%	6.0%	29.5%
Share of total before-tax income	68.2	24.6	38.4	6.8	20.0	11.8	3.3	16.1
Share of total spending	64.6	23.1	36.5	6.4	19.4	10.7	4.5	17.5
PERSONAL CARE PRODUCTS AND SERVICES	**63.2%**	**23.9%**	**34.7%**	**5.2%**	**19.5%**	**10.0%**	**4.9%**	**17.4%**
Personal care products	**62.9**	**21.9**	**36.1**	**5.3**	**21.1**	**9.7**	**5.3**	**15.9**
Hair care products	60.9	18.3	36.8	5.4	21.1	10.3	6.7	15.3
Hair accessories	56.1	14.0	37.2	9.7	20.6	6.7	10.5	16.8
Wigs and hairpieces	49.4	22.7	16.9	1.5	10.1	5.5	16.3	19.4
Oral hygiene products	64.0	23.7	35.9	6.2	18.7	11.1	5.4	15.2
Shaving products	67.0	24.0	39.7	5.2	23.5	11.0	4.2	15.7
Cosmetics, perfume, and bath products	63.4	23.0	35.6	5.1	21.1	9.4	4.5	16.4
Deodorants, feminine hygiene, misc. products	60.7	20.3	34.9	5.5	20.4	9.0	6.7	17.3
Electric personal care appliances	68.6	28.0	38.6	2.6	26.3	9.7	2.0	11.1
Personal care services	**63.6**	**26.0**	**33.2**	**5.0**	**17.8**	**10.4**	**4.4**	**19.1**
READING	**63.1**	**28.6**	**30.8**	**4.7**	**16.5**	**9.5**	**3.1**	**23.0**
Newspaper subscriptions	66.7	34.2	28.0	3.6	14.1	10.3	1.6	22.1
Newspaper, nonsubscription	56.5	24.0	28.4	5.8	13.0	9.6	4.4	25.7
Magazine subscriptions	65.4	32.9	28.9	4.6	16.8	7.6	2.1	23.1
Magazines, nonsubscription	57.4	21.2	32.6	5.0	17.3	10.3	4.5	23.0
Books purchased through book clubs	54.8	21.2	30.3	5.9	16.4	7.9	4.6	26.5
Books not purchased through book clubs	62.7	25.6	34.2	5.4	19.2	9.6	3.8	22.7
EDUCATION	**63.5**	**13.4**	**46.7**	**2.2**	**22.5**	**22.0**	**3.6**	**22.1**
College tuition	58.3	16.5	38.5	2.3	10.2	26.0	2.0	28.4
Elementary and high school tuition	84.8	3.4	77.7	0.6	60.8	16.3	5.6	5.4
Other school tuition	67.5	20.9	42.4	4.9	24.5	13.0	4.9	10.6
Other school expenses including rentals	70.2	9.5	56.2	2.8	35.8	17.6	7.9	11.5
Books, supplies for college	47.4	13.1	31.2	2.8	6.9	21.5	3.2	33.2
Books, supplies for elementary, high school	79.1	2.4	69.7	1.3	58.2	10.2	11.9	1.6
Books, supplies for day care, nursery school	74.2	6.3	63.3	8.4	50.4	4.5	3.2	10.5
Miscellaneous school expenses and supplies	62.8	14.5	45.6	3.3	29.8	12.5	8.0	14.2
TOBACCO PRODUCTS AND SMOKING SUPPLIES	**52.6**	**18.4**	**27.5**	**4.2**	**13.5**	**9.8**	**4.9**	**19.3**
Cigarettes	51.8	18.0	27.0	3.9	13.2	9.9	5.2	19.0
Other tobacco products	60.6	22.0	33.5	7.9	16.7	8.9	1.9	23.0
Smoking accessories	61.6	30.4	28.7	4.1	14.4	10.2	2.6	18.0

Note: Market share for total consumer units is 100.0%. Market shares by type of consumer unit will not add to total because not all types of consumer units are shown.
Source: Calculations by New Strategist based on the 2002 Consumer Expenditure Survey

Table 10.13 Personal Care, Reading, Education, Tobacco: Average spending by race and Hispanic origin, 2002

(average annual spending of consumer units (CU) on personal care, reading, education, and tobacco products, by race and Hispanic origin of consumer unit reference person, 2002)

	total consumer units	race		Hispanic origin	
		black	white and other	Hispanic	non-Hispanic
Number of consumer units					
(in thousands, add 000)	112,108	13,554	98,553	10,500	101,608
Average number of persons per CU	2.5	2.7	2.5	3.3	2.4
Average before-tax income of CU	$49,430.00	$35,944.00	$51,177.00	$37,360.00	$50,742.00
Average spending of CU, total	40,676.60	30,135.94	42,134.55	34,742.47	41,294.67
PERSONAL CARE PRODUCTS					
AND SERVICES	**$525.80**	**$487.63**	**$531.32**	**$491.64**	**$529.49**
Personal care products	**276.65**	**214.54**	**285.47**	**293.59**	**275.06**
Hair care products	53.57	45.21	54.75	65.93	52.40
Hair accessories	6.57	8.66	6.27	7.90	6.44
Wigs and hairpieces	1.32	5.76	0.71	0.84	1.37
Oral hygiene products	27.33	20.71	28.27	33.97	26.70
Shaving products	15.09	7.27	16.20	12.14	15.37
Cosmetics, perfume, and bath products	129.13	93.83	134.13	132.14	128.85
Deodorants, feminine hygiene, misc. products	30.29	30.28	30.29	29.16	30.40
Electric personal care appliances	13.34	2.81	14.84	11.51	13.52
Personal care services	**249.15**	**273.09**	**245.86**	**198.04**	**254.43**
READING	**138.57**	**66.70**	**148.46**	**60.35**	**146.65**
Newspaper subscriptions	43.88	17.93	47.45	15.30	46.83
Newspaper, nonsubscription	11.30	10.96	11.35	9.01	11.54
Magazine subscriptions	16.59	7.70	17.81	7.35	17.54
Magazines, nonsubscription	9.35	5.89	9.82	5.28	9.77
Books purchased through book clubs	6.62	4.19	6.95	2.31	7.06
Books not purchased through book clubs	50.38	19.89	54.57	20.75	53.44
EDUCATION	**751.95**	**462.84**	**791.71**	**487.53**	**779.22**
College tuition	444.45	257.29	470.20	262.53	463.25
Elementary and high school tuition	128.94	61.39	138.23	92.30	132.73
Other school tuition	25.53	17.04	26.69	8.82	27.25
Other school expenses including rentals	25.77	20.88	26.45	23.70	25.99
Books, supplies for college	57.93	36.34	60.90	38.22	59.97
Books, supplies for elementary, high school	16.14	17.68	15.93	16.24	16.13
Books, supplies for day care, nursery school	3.39	2.67	3.49	1.76	3.56
Miscellaneous school expenses and supplies	49.80	49.56	49.83	43.97	50.35
TOBACCO PRODUCTS AND					
SMOKING SUPPLIES	**320.49**	**210.04**	**335.69**	**186.17**	**334.36**
Cigarettes	291.89	194.83	305.24	173.39	304.13
Other tobacco products	26.27	13.48	28.03	12.05	27.74
Smoking accessories	2.33	1.72	2.42	0.73	2.49

Note: Other races include Asians, Native Americans, and Pacific Islanders.
Source: Bureau of Labor Statistics, unpublished tables from the 2002 Consumer Expenditure Survey

Table 10.14 Personal Care, Reading, Education, Tobacco: Indexed spending by race and Hispanic origin, 2002

(indexed average annual spending of consumer units (CU) on personal care, reading, education, and tobacco products, by race and Hispanic origin of consumer unit reference person, 2002; index definition: an index of 100 is the average for all consumer units; an index of 132 means that spending by consumer units in that group is 32 percent above the average for all consumer units; an index of 68 indicates spending that is 32 percent below the average for all consumer units)

	total consumer units	race		Hispanic origin	
		black	white and other	Hispanic	non-Hispanic
Average spending of CU, total	$40,677	$30,136	$42,135	$34,742	$41,295
Average spending of CU, index	**100**	**74**	**104**	**85**	**102**
PERSONAL CARE PRODUCTS AND SERVICES	**100**	**93**	**101**	**94**	**101**
Personal care products	**100**	**78**	**103**	**106**	**99**
Hair care products	100	84	102	123	98
Hair accessories	100	132	95	120	98
Wigs and hairpieces	100	436	54	64	104
Oral hygiene products	100	76	103	124	98
Shaving products	100	48	107	80	102
Cosmetics, perfume, and bath products	100	73	104	102	100
Deodorants, feminine hygiene, misc. products	100	100	100	96	100
Electric personal care appliances	100	21	111	86	101
Personal care services	**100**	**110**	**99**	**79**	**102**
READING	**100**	**48**	**107**	**44**	**106**
Newspaper subscriptions	100	41	108	35	107
Newspaper, nonsubscription	100	97	100	80	102
Magazine subscriptions	100	46	107	44	106
Magazines, nonsubscription	100	63	105	56	104
Books purchased through book clubs	100	63	105	35	107
Books not purchased through book clubs	100	39	108	41	106
EDUCATION	**100**	**62**	**105**	**65**	**104**
College tuition	100	58	106	59	104
Elementary and high school tuition	100	48	107	72	103
Other school tuition	100	67	105	35	107
Other school expenses including rentals	100	81	103	92	101
Books, supplies for college	100	63	105	66	104
Books, supplies for elementary, high school	100	110	99	101	100
Books, supplies for day care, nursery school	100	79	103	52	105
Miscellaneous school expenses and supplies	100	100	100	88	101
TOBACCO PRODUCTS AND SMOKING SUPPLIES	**100**	**66**	**105**	**58**	**104**
Cigarettes	100	67	105	59	104
Other tobacco products	100	51	107	46	106
Smoking accessories	100	74	104	31	107

Note: Other races include Asians, Native Americans, and Pacific Islanders.
Source: Calculations by New Strategist based on the 2002 Consumer Expenditure Survey

Table 10.15 Personal Care, Reading, Education, Tobacco: Total spending by race and Hispanic origin, 2002

(total annual spending on personal care, reading, education, and tobacco products, by consumer unit race and Hispanic origin groups, 2002; numbers in thousands)

	total consumer units	race		Hispanic origin	
		black	white and other	Hispanic	non-Hispanic
Number of consumer units	112,108	13,554	98,553	10,500	101,608
Total spending of all consumer units	$4,560,172,273	$408,462,531	$4,152,486,306	$364,795,935	$4,195,868,829
PERSONAL CARE PRODUCTS					
AND SERVICES	**$58,946,386**	**$6,609,337**	**$52,363,180**	**$5,162,220**	**$53,800,420**
Personal care products	**31,014,678**	**2,907,875**	**28,133,925**	**3,082,695**	**27,948,296**
Hair care products	6,005,626	612,776	5,395,777	692,265	5,324,259
Hair accessories	736,550	117,378	617,927	82,950	654,356
Wigs and hairpieces	147,983	78,071	69,973	8,820	139,203
Oral hygiene products	3,063,912	280,703	2,786,093	356,685	2,712,934
Shaving products	1,691,710	98,538	1,596,559	127,470	1,561,715
Cosmetics, perfume, and bath products	14,476,506	1,271,772	13,218,914	1,387,470	13,092,191
Deodorants, feminine hygiene, misc. products	3,395,751	410,415	2,985,170	306,180	3,088,883
Electric personal care appliances	1,495,521	38,087	1,462,527	120,855	1,373,740
Personal care services	**27,931,708**	**3,701,462**	**24,230,241**	**2,079,420**	**25,852,123**
READING	**15,534,806**	**904,052**	**14,631,178**	**633,675**	**14,900,813**
Newspaper subscriptions	4,919,299	243,023	4,676,340	160,650	4,758,303
Newspaper, nonsubscription	1,266,820	148,552	1,118,577	94,605	1,172,556
Magazine subscriptions	1,859,872	104,366	1,755,229	77,175	1,782,204
Magazines, nonsubscription	1,048,210	79,833	967,790	55,440	992,710
Books purchased through book clubs	742,155	56,791	684,943	24,255	717,352
Books not purchased through book clubs	5,648,001	269,589	5,378,037	217,875	5,429,932
EDUCATION	**84,299,611**	**6,273,333**	**78,025,396**	**5,119,065**	**79,174,986**
College tuition	49,826,401	3,487,309	46,339,621	2,756,565	47,069,906
Elementary and high school tuition	14,455,206	832,080	13,622,981	969,150	13,486,430
Other school tuition	2,862,117	230,960	2,630,380	92,610	2,768,818
Other school expenses including rentals	2,889,023	283,008	2,606,727	248,850	2,640,792
Books, supplies for college	6,494,416	492,552	6,001,878	401,310	6,093,432
Books, supplies for elementary, high school	1,809,423	239,635	1,569,949	170,520	1,638,937
Books, supplies for day care, nursery school	380,046	36,189	343,950	18,480	361,724
Miscellaneous school expenses and supplies	5,582,978	671,736	4,910,896	461,685	5,115,963
TOBACCO PRODUCTS AND					
SMOKING SUPPLIES	**35,929,493**	**2,846,882**	**33,083,257**	**1,954,785**	**33,973,651**
Cigarettes	32,723,204	2,640,726	30,082,318	1,820,595	30,902,041
Other tobacco products	2,945,077	182,708	2,762,441	126,525	2,818,606
Smoking accessories	261,212	23,313	238,498	7,665	253,004

Note: Other races include Asians, Native Americans, and Pacific Islanders. Numbers may not add to total because of rounding.
Source: Calculations by New Strategist based on the 2002 Consumer Expenditure Survey

Table 10.16 Personal Care, Reading, Education, Tobacco: Market shares by race and Hispanic origin, 2002

(percentage of total annual spending on personal care, reading, education, and tobacco products accounted for by consumer unit race and Hispanic origin groups, 2002)

	total consumer units	race		Hispanic origin	
		black	white and other	Hispanic	non-Hispanic
Share of total consumer units	100.0%	12.1%	87.9%	9.4%	90.6%
Share of total before-tax income	100.0	8.8	91.0	7.1	93.0
Share of total spending	100.0	9.0	91.1	8.0	92.0
PERSONAL CARE PRODUCTS AND SERVICES	**100.0%**	**11.2%**	**88.8%**	**8.8%**	**91.3%**
Personal care products	100.0	9.4	90.7	9.9	90.1
Hair care products	100.0	10.2	89.8	11.5	88.7
Hair accessories	100.0	15.9	83.9	11.3	88.8
Wigs and hairpieces	100.0	52.8	47.3	6.0	94.1
Oral hygiene products	100.0	9.2	90.9	11.6	88.5
Shaving products	100.0	5.8	94.4	7.5	92.3
Cosmetics, perfume, and bath products	100.0	8.8	91.3	9.6	90.4
Deodorants, feminine hygiene, misc. products	100.0	12.1	87.9	9.0	91.0
Electric personal care appliances	100.0	2.5	97.8	8.1	91.9
Personal care services	**100.0**	**13.3**	**86.7**	**7.4**	**92.6**
READING	**100.0**	**5.8**	**94.2**	**4.1**	**95.9**
Newspaper subscriptions	100.0	4.9	95.1	3.3	96.7
Newspaper, nonsubscription	100.0	11.7	88.3	7.5	92.6
Magazine subscriptions	100.0	5.6	94.4	4.1	95.8
Magazines, nonsubscription	100.0	7.6	92.3	5.3	94.7
Books purchased through book clubs	100.0	7.7	92.3	3.3	96.7
Books not purchased through book clubs	100.0	4.8	95.2	3.9	96.1
EDUCATION	**100.0**	**7.4**	**92.6**	**6.1**	**93.9**
College tuition	100.0	7.0	93.0	5.5	94.5
Elementary and high school tuition	100.0	5.8	94.2	6.7	93.3
Other school tuition	100.0	8.1	91.9	3.2	96.7
Other school expenses including rentals	100.0	9.8	90.2	8.6	91.4
Books, supplies for college	100.0	7.6	92.4	6.2	93.8
Books, supplies for elementary, high school	100.0	13.2	86.8	9.4	90.6
Books, supplies for day care, nursery school	100.0	9.5	90.5	4.9	95.2
Miscellaneous school expenses and supplies	100.0	12.0	88.0	8.3	91.6
TOBACCO PRODUCTS AND SMOKING SUPPLIES	**100.0**	**7.9**	**92.1**	**5.4**	**94.6**
Cigarettes	100.0	8.1	91.9	5.6	94.4
Other tobacco products	100.0	6.2	93.8	4.3	95.7
Smoking accessories	100.0	8.9	91.3	2.9	96.9

Note: Other races include Asians, Native Americans, and Pacific Islanders. Numbers may not add to total because of rounding.
Source: Calculations by New Strategist based on the 2002 Consumer Expenditure Survey

Table 10.17 Personal Care, Reading, Education, Tobacco: Average spending by region, 2002

(average annual spending of consumer units (CU) on personal care, reading, education, and tobacco products, by region in which consumer unit lives, 2002)

	total consumer units	Northeast	Midwest	South	West
Number of consumer units (in thousands, add 000)	112,108	21,313	25,883	40,004	24,907
Average number of persons per CU	2.5	2.5	2.5	2.5	2.6
Average before-tax income of CU	$49,430.00	$53,983.00	$49,197.00	$45,641.00	$52,016.00
Average spending of CU, total	40,676.60	42,390.20	40,601.14	37,280.55	44,728.34
PERSONAL CARE PRODUCTS AND SERVICES	**$525.80**	**$518.08**	**$516.58**	**$509.49**	**$568.61**
Personal care products	**276.65**	**253.17**	**276.77**	**273.57**	**301.98**
Hair care products	53.57	49.36	58.35	48.64	60.17
Hair accessories	6.57	5.61	6.91	6.34	7.42
Wigs and hairpieces	1.32	1.43	1.20	1.51	1.06
Oral hygiene products	27.33	27.34	24.68	27.18	30.29
Shaving products	15.09	18.51	14.04	14.43	14.25
Cosmetics, perfume, and bath products	129.13	110.93	123.72	131.05	147.61
Deodorants, feminine hygiene, misc. products	30.29	27.85	35.79	28.73	29.23
Electric personal care appliances	13.34	12.14	12.08	15.70	11.95
Personal care services	**249.15**	**264.91**	**239.81**	**235.92**	**266.63**
READING	**138.57**	**165.12**	**149.49**	**103.00**	**161.64**
Newspaper subscriptions	43.88	55.86	50.18	33.89	43.13
Newspaper, nonsubscription	11.30	20.49	13.12	7.66	7.40
Magazine subscriptions	16.59	17.17	20.35	12.31	19.04
Magazines, nonsubscription	9.35	9.24	11.04	7.43	10.75
Books purchased through book clubs	6.62	7.09	7.07	4.37	9.34
Books not purchased through book clubs	50.38	54.99	46.94	36.88	71.68
EDUCATION	**751.95**	**1,061.99**	**717.85**	**487.25**	**947.29**
College tuition	444.45	688.53	444.21	231.46	577.95
Elementary and high school tuition	128.94	204.21	112.47	102.46	124.18
Other school tuition	25.53	24.45	16.07	19.32	46.24
Other school expenses including rentals	25.77	22.45	25.54	22.77	33.69
Books, supplies for college	57.93	60.69	51.31	40.59	90.31
Books, supplies for elementary, high school	16.14	13.55	16.14	18.33	14.83
Books, supplies for day care, nursery school	3.39	2.69	1.91	4.07	4.43
Miscellaneous school expenses and supplies	49.80	45.41	50.20	48.26	55.67
TOBACCO PRODUCTS AND SMOKING SUPPLIES	**320.49**	**315.49**	**395.57**	**320.64**	**246.55**
Cigarettes	291.89	295.89	367.64	286.55	218.31
Other tobacco products	26.27	17.93	24.61	31.88	26.14
Smoking accessories	2.33	1.67	3.32	2.20	2.10

Source: Bureau of Labor Statistics, unpublished tables from the 2002 Consumer Expenditure Survey

Table 10.18   Personal Care, Reading, Education, Tobacco: Indexed spending by region, 2002

(indexed average annual spending of consumer units (CU) on personal care, reading, education, and tobacco products, by region in which consumer unit lives, 2002; index definition: an index of 100 is the average for all consumer units; an index of 132 means that spending by consumer units in that group is 32 percent above the average for all consumer units; an index of 68 indicates spending that is 32 percent below the average for all consumer units)

	total consumer units	Northeast	Midwest	South	West
Average spending of CU, total	**$40,677**	**$42,390**	**$40,601**	**$37,281**	**$44,728**
Average spending of CU, index	**100**	**104**	**100**	**92**	**110**
PERSONAL CARE PRODUCTS AND SERVICES	**100**	**99**	**98**	**97**	**108**
Personal care products	**100**	**92**	**100**	**99**	**109**
Hair care products	100	92	109	91	112
Hair accessories	100	85	105	96	113
Wigs and hairpieces	100	108	91	114	80
Oral hygiene products	100	100	90	99	111
Shaving products	100	123	93	96	94
Cosmetics, perfume, and bath products	100	86	96	101	114
Deodorants, feminine hygiene, misc. products	100	92	118	95	97
Electric personal care appliances	100	91	91	118	90
Personal care services	**100**	**106**	**96**	**95**	**107**
READING	**100**	**119**	**108**	**74**	**117**
Newspaper subscriptions	100	127	114	77	98
Newspaper, nonsubscription	100	181	116	68	65
Magazine subscriptions	100	103	123	74	115
Magazines, nonsubscription	100	99	118	79	115
Books purchased through book clubs	100	107	107	66	141
Books not purchased through book clubs	100	109	93	73	142
EDUCATION	**100**	**141**	**95**	**65**	**126**
College tuition	100	155	100	52	130
Elementary and high school tuition	100	158	87	79	96
Other school tuition	100	96	63	76	181
Other school expenses including rentals	100	87	99	88	131
Books, supplies for college	100	105	89	70	156
Books, supplies for elementary, high school	100	84	100	114	92
Books, supplies for day care, nursery school	100	79	56	120	131
Miscellaneous school expenses and supplies	100	91	101	97	112
TOBACCO PRODUCTS AND SMOKING SUPPLIES	**100**	**98**	**123**	**100**	**77**
Cigarettes	100	101	126	98	75
Other tobacco products	100	68	94	121	100
Smoking accessories	100	72	142	94	90

Source: Calculations by New Strategist based on the 2002 Consumer Expenditure Survey

Table 10.19 Personal Care, Reading, Education, Tobacco: Total spending by region, 2002

(total annual spending on personal care, reading, education, and tobacco products, by region in which consumer units live, 2002; numbers in thousands)

	total consumer units	Northeast	Midwest	South	West
Number of consumer units	112,108	21,313	25,883	40,004	24,907
Total spending of all consumer units	$4,560,172,273	$903,462,333	$1,050,879,307	$1,491,371,122	$1,114,048,764
PERSONAL CARE PRODUCTS AND SERVICES	**$58,946,386**	**$11,041,839**	**$13,370,640**	**$20,381,638**	**$14,162,369**
Personal care products	**31,014,678**	**5,395,812**	**7,163,638**	**10,943,894**	**7,521,416**
Hair care products	6,005,626	1,052,010	1,510,273	1,945,795	1,498,654
Hair accessories	736,550	119,566	178,852	253,625	184,810
Wigs and hairpieces	147,983	30,478	31,060	60,406	26,401
Oral hygiene products	3,063,912	582,697	638,792	1,087,309	754,433
Shaving products	1,691,710	394,504	363,397	577,258	354,925
Cosmetics, perfume, and bath products	14,476,506	2,364,251	3,202,245	5,242,524	3,676,522
Deodorants, feminine hygiene, misc. products	3,395,751	593,567	926,353	1,149,315	728,032
Electric personal care appliances	1,495,521	258,740	312,667	628,063	297,639
Personal care services	**27,931,708**	**5,646,027**	**6,207,002**	**9,437,744**	**6,640,953**
READING	**15,534,806**	**53,519,203**	**3,869,250**	**4,120,412**	**4,025,967**
Newspaper subscriptions	4,919,299	1,190,544	1,298,809	1,355,736	1,074,239
Newspaper, nonsubscription	1,266,820	436,703	339,585	306,431	184,312
Magazine subscriptions	1,859,872	365,944	526,719	492,449	474,229
Magazines, nonsubscription	1,048,210	196,932	285,748	297,230	267,750
Books purchased through book clubs	742,155	151,109	182,993	174,817	232,631
Books not purchased through book clubs	5,648,001	1,172,002	1,214,948	1,475,348	1,785,334
EDUCATION	**84,299,611**	**22,634,193**	**18,580,112**	**19,491,949**	**23,594,152**
College tuition	49,826,401	14,674,640	11,497,487	9,259,326	14,395,001
Elementary and high school tuition	14,455,206	4,352,328	2,911,061	4,098,810	3,092,951
Other school tuition	2,862,117	521,103	415,940	772,877	1,151,700
Other school expenses including rentals	2,889,023	478,477	661,052	910,891	839,117
Books, supplies for college	6,494,416	1,293,486	1,328,057	1,623,762	2,249,351
Books, supplies for elementary, high school	1,809,423	288,791	417,752	733,273	369,371
Books, supplies for day care, nursery school	380,046	57,332	49,437	162,816	110,338
Miscellaneous school expenses and supplies	5,582,978	967,823	1,299,327	1,930,593	1,386,573
TOBACCO PRODUCTS AND SMOKING SUPPLIES	**35,929,493**	**6,724,038**	**10,238,538**	**12,826,883**	**6,140,821**
Cigarettes	32,723,204	6,306,304	9,515,626	11,463,146	5,437,447
Other tobacco products	2,945,077	382,142	636,981	1,275,328	651,069
Smoking accessories	261,212	35,593	85,932	88,009	52,305

Note: Numbers may not add to total because of rounding.
Source: Calculations by New Strategist based on the 2002 Consumer Expenditure Survey

Table 10.20 Personal Care, Reading, Education, Tobacco: Market shares by region, 2002

(percentage of total annual spending on personal care, reading, education, and tobacco products accounted for by consumer units by region, 2002)

	total consumer units	Northeast	Midwest	South	West
Share of total consumer units	100.0%	19.0%	23.1%	35.7%	22.2%
Share of total before-tax income	100.0	20.8	23.0	32.9	23.4
Share of total spending	100.0	19.8	23.0	32.7	24.4
PERSONAL CARE PRODUCTS AND SERVICES	**100.0%**	**18.7%**	**22.7%**	**34.6%**	**24.0%**
Personal care products	100.0	17.4	23.1	35.3	24.3
Hair care products	100.0	17.5	25.1	32.4	25.0
Hair accessories	100.0	16.2	24.3	34.4	25.1
Wigs and hairpieces	100.0	20.6	21.0	40.8	17.8
Oral hygiene products	100.0	19.0	20.8	35.5	24.6
Shaving products	100.0	23.3	21.5	34.1	21.0
Cosmetics, perfume, and bath products	100.0	16.3	22.1	36.2	25.4
Deodorants, feminine hygiene, misc. products	100.0	17.5	27.3	33.8	21.4
Electric personal care appliances	100.0	17.3	20.9	42.0	19.9
Personal care services	**100.0**	**20.2**	**22.2**	**33.8**	**23.8**
READING	**100.0**	**22.7**	**24.9**	**26.5**	**25.9**
Newspaper subscriptions	100.0	24.2	26.4	27.6	21.8
Newspaper, nonsubscription	100.0	34.5	26.8	24.2	14.5
Magazine subscriptions	100.0	19.7	28.3	26.5	25.5
Magazines, nonsubscription	100.0	18.8	27.3	28.4	25.5
Books purchased through book clubs	100.0	20.4	24.7	23.6	31.3
Books not purchased through book clubs	100.0	20.8	21.5	26.1	31.6
EDUCATION	**100.0**	**26.8**	**22.0**	**23.1**	**28.0**
College tuition	100.0	29.5	23.1	18.6	28.9
Elementary and high school tuition	100.0	30.1	20.1	28.4	21.4
Other school tuition	100.0	18.2	14.5	27.0	40.2
Other school expenses including rentals	100.0	16.6	22.9	31.5	29.0
Books, supplies for college	100.0	19.9	20.4	25.0	34.6
Books, supplies for elementary, high school	100.0	16.0	23.1	40.5	20.4
Books, supplies for day care, nursery school	100.0	15.1	13.0	42.8	29.0
Miscellaneous school expenses and supplies	100.0	17.3	23.3	34.6	24.8
TOBACCO PRODUCTS AND SMOKING SUPPLIES	**100.0**	**18.7**	**28.5**	**35.7**	**17.1**
Cigarettes	100.0	19.3	29.1	35.0	16.6
Other tobacco products	100.0	13.0	21.6	43.3	22.1
Smoking accessories	100.0	13.6	32.9	33.7	20.0

Note: Numbers may not add to total because of rounding.
Source: Calculations by New Strategist based on the 2002 Consumer Expenditure Survey

Table 10.21 Personal Care, Reading, Education, Tobacco: Average spending by education, 2002

(average annual spending of consumer units (CU) on personal care, reading, education, and tobacco products, by education of consumer unit reference person, 2002)

	total consumer units	less than high school graduate	high school graduate	some college	associate's degree	college graduate total	bachelor's degree	master's, professional, doctorate
Number of consumer units (in thousands, add 000)	112,108	17,075	31,961	23,260	10,395	29,417	19,082	10,335
Average number of persons per CU	2.5	2.6	2.5	2.4	2.6	2.5	2.5	2.5
Average before-tax income of CU	$49,430.00	$25,564.00	$39,618.00	$42,598.00	$54,860.00	$77,820.00	$69,408.00	$92,783.00
Average spending of CU, total	40,676.60	24,930.40	33,707.63	38,653.57	44,405.79	57,384.01	53,731.57	64,118.48
PERSONAL CARE PRODUCTS AND SERVICES	**$525.80**	**$350.34**	**$453.24**	**$529.74**	**$535.14**	**$691.26**	**$673.60**	**$723.91**
Personal care products	**276.65**	**201.70**	**234.78**	**292.09**	**280.47**	**343.29**	**344.63**	**340.84**
Hair care products	53.57	46.14	45.22	60.18	70.03	56.06	58.22	52.14
Hair accessories	6.57	4.10	5.49	7.83	7.98	7.53	8.93	4.98
Wigs and hairpieces	1.32	2.05	1.19	1.50	1.81	0.73	0.67	0.85
Oral hygiene products	27.33	23.83	23.41	24.92	24.71	35.47	35.62	35.20
Shaving products	15.09	12.34	14.22	11.32	14.72	20.06	20.75	18.80
Cosmetics, perfume, and bath products	129.13	79.02	103.13	141.88	122.53	172.79	170.83	176.36
Deodorants, feminine hygiene, misc. products	30.29	25.38	29.69	31.23	29.27	32.92	31.50	35.50
Electric personal care appliances	13.34	8.83	12.42	13.22	9.42	17.73	18.11	17.03
Personal care services	**249.15**	**148.64**	**218.46**	**237.65**	**254.67**	**347.97**	**328.97**	**383.06**
READING	**138.57**	**55.25**	**96.46**	**127.34**	**137.58**	**241.89**	**204.42**	**311.06**
Newspaper subscriptions	43.88	23.91	38.69	39.24	42.83	65.15	57.49	79.28
Newspaper, nonsubscription	11.30	8.66	11.36	10.30	11.05	13.65	12.95	14.96
Magazine subscriptions	16.59	5.34	12.18	16.28	16.93	28.03	23.30	36.77
Magazines, nonsubscription	9.35	4.28	6.65	10.11	11.56	13.83	13.15	15.07
Books purchased through book clubs	6.62	2.52	4.72	6.91	5.91	11.07	8.50	15.83
Books not purchased through book clubs	50.38	10.51	22.74	44.31	48.94	108.85	88.53	146.38
EDUCATION	**751.95**	**120.20**	**306.35**	**952.95**	**746.07**	**1,442.31**	**1,277.75**	**1,745.99**
College tuition	444.45	53.37	171.96	613.79	403.94	847.94	768.17	995.22
Elementary and high school tuition	128.94	11.82	39.00	97.99	135.64	316.75	253.10	434.28
Other school tuition	25.53	8.18	11.77	22.17	51.28	44.10	38.28	54.84
Other school expenses including rentals	25.77	6.66	13.74	24.59	30.85	49.08	46.78	53.33
Books, supplies for college	57.93	7.96	22.61	117.99	56.55	78.31	73.47	87.25
Books, supplies for elementary, high school	16.14	11.75	12.85	15.34	18.23	22.15	21.63	23.11
Books, supplies for day care, nursery school	3.39	0.85	1.68	2.79	4.43	6.82	5.62	9.02
Miscellaneous school expenses and supplies	49.80	19.61	32.74	58.28	45.15	77.15	70.68	88.93
TOBACCO PRODUCTS AND SMOKING SUPPLIES	**320.49**	**354.16**	**440.59**	**339.77**	**288.64**	**166.64**	**186.24**	**130.46**
Cigarettes	291.89	328.67	412.40	307.43	261.73	137.97	153.84	108.67
Other tobacco products	26.27	22.34	26.62	28.54	24.80	26.91	30.14	20.93
Smoking accessories	2.33	3.15	1.57	3.80	2.11	1.76	2.25	0.86

Source: Bureau of Labor Statistics, unpublished tables from the 2002 Consumer Expenditure Survey

Table 10.22 Personal Care, Reading, Education, Tobacco: Indexed spending by education, 2002

(indexed average annual spending of consumer units (CU) on personal care, reading, education, and tobacco products, by education of consumer unit reference person, 2002; index definition: an index of 100 is the average for all consumer units; an index of 132 means that spending by consumer units in that group is 32 percent above the average for all consumer units; an index of 68 indicates spending that is 32 percent below the average for all consumer units)

	total consumer units	less than high school graduate	high school graduate	some college	associate's degree	college graduate total	bachelor's degree	master's, professional, doctorate
Average spending of CU, total	$40,677	$24,930	$33,708	$38,654	$44,406	$57,384	$53,732	$64,118
Average spending of CU, index	100	61	83	95	109	141	132	158
PERSONAL CARE PRODUCTS AND SERVICES	100	67	86	101	102	131	128	138
Personal care products	100	73	85	106	101	124	125	123
Hair care products	100	86	84	112	131	105	109	97
Hair accessories	100	62	84	119	121	115	136	76
Wigs and hairpieces	100	155	90	114	137	55	51	64
Oral hygiene products	100	87	86	91	90	130	130	129
Shaving products	100	82	94	75	98	133	138	125
Cosmetics, perfume, and bath products	100	61	80	110	95	134	132	137
Deodorants, feminine hygiene, misc. products	100	84	98	103	97	109	104	117
Electric personal care appliances	100	66	93	99	71	133	136	128
Personal care services	100	60	88	95	102	140	132	154
READING	100	40	70	92	99	175	148	224
Newspaper subscriptions	100	54	88	89	98	148	131	181
Newspaper, nonsubscription	100	77	101	91	98	121	115	132
Magazine subscriptions	100	32	73	98	102	169	140	222
Magazines, nonsubscription	100	46	71	108	124	148	141	161
Books purchased through book clubs	100	38	71	104	89	167	128	239
Books not purchased through book clubs	100	21	45	88	97	216	176	291
EDUCATION	100	16	41	127	99	192	170	232
College tuition	100	12	39	138	91	191	173	224
Elementary and high school tuition	100	9	30	76	105	246	196	337
Other school tuition	100	32	46	87	201	173	150	215
Other school expenses including rentals	100	26	53	95	120	190	182	207
Books, supplies for college	100	14	39	204	98	135	127	151
Books, supplies for elementary, high school	100	73	80	95	113	137	134	143
Books, supplies for day care, nursery school	100	25	50	82	131	201	166	266
Miscellaneous school expenses and supplies	100	39	66	117	91	155	142	179
TOBACCO PRODUCTS AND SMOKING SUPPLIES	100	111	137	106	90	52	58	41
Cigarettes	100	113	141	105	90	47	53	37
Other tobacco products	100	85	101	109	94	102	115	80
Smoking accessories	100	135	67	163	91	76	97	37

Source: Calculations by New Strategist based on the 2002 Consumer Expenditure Survey

Table 10.23 Personal Care, Reading, Education, Tobacco: Total spending by education, 2002

(total annual spending on personal care, reading, education, and tobacco products, by consumer unit (CU) educational attainment group, 2002; numbers in thousands)

	total consumer units	less than high school graduate	high school graduate	some college	associate's degree	college graduate total	college graduate bachelor's degree	college graduate master's, professional, doctorate
Number of consumer units	112,108	17,075	31,961	23,260	10,395	29,417	19,082	10,335
Total spending of all CUs	$4,560,172,273	$425,686,580	$1,077,329,562	$899,082,038	$461,598,187	$1,688,065,422	$1,025,305,819	$662,664,491
PERSONAL CARE PRODUCTS								
AND SERVICES	**$58,946,386**	**$5,982,056**	**$14,486,004**	**$12,321,752**	**$5,562,780**	**$20,334,795**	**$12,853,635**	**$7,481,610**
Personal care products	**31,014,678**	**3,444,028**	**7,503,804**	**6,794,013**	**2,915,486**	**10,098,562**	**6,576,230**	**3,522,581**
Hair care products	6,005,626	787,841	1,445,276	1,399,787	727,962	1,649,117	1,110,954	538,867
Hair accessories	736,550	70,008	175,466	182,126	82,952	221,510	170,402	51,468
Wigs and hairpieces	147,983	35,004	38,034	34,890	18,815	21,474	12,785	8,785
Oral hygiene products	3,063,912	406,897	748,207	579,639	256,860	1,043,421	679,701	363,792
Shaving products	1,691,710	210,706	454,485	263,303	153,014	590,105	395,952	194,298
Cosmetics, perfume, and bath products	14,476,506	1,349,267	3,296,138	3,300,129	1,273,699	5,082,963	3,259,778	1,822,681
Deodorants, feminine hygiene, misc. products	3,395,751	433,364	948,922	726,410	304,262	968,408	601,083	366,893
Electric personal care appliances	1,495,521	150,772	396,956	307,497	97,921	521,563	345,575	176,005
Personal care services	**27,931,708**	**2,538,028**	**6,982,200**	**5,527,739**	**2,647,295**	**10,236,233**	**6,277,406**	**3,958,925**
READING	**15,534,806**	**943,394**	**3,082,958**	**2,961,928**	**1,430,144**	**7,115,678**	**3,900,742**	**3,214,805**
Newspaper subscriptions	4,919,299	408,263	1,236,571	912,722	445,218	1,916,518	1,097,024	819,359
Newspaper, nonsubscription	1,266,820	147,870	363,077	239,578	114,865	401,542	247,112	154,612
Magazine subscriptions	1,859,872	91,181	389,285	378,673	175,987	824,559	444,611	380,018
Magazines, nonsubscription	1,048,210	73,081	212,541	235,159	120,166	406,837	250,928	155,748
Books purchased through book clubs	742,155	43,029	150,856	160,727	61,434	325,646	162,197	163,603
Books not purchased through book clubs	5,648,001	179,458	726,793	1,030,651	508,731	3,202,040	1,689,329	1,512,837
EDUCATION	**84,299,611**	**2,052,415**	**9,791,252**	**22,165,617**	**7,755,398**	**42,428,433**	**24,382,026**	**18,044,807**
College tuition	49,826,401	911,293	5,496,014	14,276,755	4,198,956	24,943,851	14,658,220	10,285,599
Elementary and high school tuition	14,455,206	201,827	1,246,479	2,279,247	1,409,978	9,317,835	4,829,654	4,488,284
Other school tuition	2,862,117	139,674	376,181	515,674	533,056	1,297,290	730,459	566,771
Other school expenses including rentals	2,889,023	113,720	439,144	571,963	320,686	1,443,786	892,656	551,166
Books, supplies for college	6,494,416	135,917	722,638	2,744,447	587,837	2,303,645	1,401,955	901,729
Books, supplies for elementary, high school	1,809,423	200,631	410,699	356,808	189,501	651,587	412,744	238,842
Books, supplies for day care, nursery school	380,046	14,514	53,694	64,895	46,050	200,624	107,241	93,222
Miscellaneous school expenses and supplies	5,582,978	334,841	1,046,403	1,355,593	469,334	2,269,522	1,348,716	919,092
TOBACCO PRODUCTS AND								
SMOKING SUPPLIES	**35,929,493**	**6,047,282**	**14,081,697**	**7,903,050**	**3,000,413**	**4,902,049**	**3,553,832**	**1,348,304**
Cigarettes	32,723,204	5,612,040	13,180,716	7,150,822	2,720,683	4,058,663	2,935,575	1,123,104
Other tobacco products	2,945,077	381,456	850,802	663,840	257,796	791,611	575,131	216,312
Smoking accessories	261,212	53,786	50,179	88,388	21,933	51,774	42,935	8,888

Note: Numbers may not add to total because of rounding.
Source: Calculations by New Strategist based on the 2002 Consumer Expenditure Survey

Table 10.24 Personal Care, Reading, Education, Tobacco: Market shares by education, 2002

(percentage of total annual spending on personal care, reading, education, and tobacco products accounted for by consumer unit educational attainment groups, 2002)

	total consumer units	less than high school graduate	high school graduate	some college	associate's degree	college graduate total	bachelor's degree	master's, professional, doctorate
Share of total consumer units	100.0%	15.2%	28.5%	20.7%	9.3%	26.2%	17.0%	9.2%
Share of total before-tax income	100.0	7.9	22.8	17.9	10.3	41.3	23.9	17.3
Share of total spending	100.0	9.3	23.6	19.7	10.1	37.0	22.5	14.5
PERSONAL CARE PRODUCTS								
AND SERVICES	**100.0%**	**10.1%**	**24.6%**	**20.9%**	**9.4%**	**34.5%**	**21.8%**	**12.7%**
Personal care products	**100.0**	**11.1**	**24.2**	**21.9**	**9.4**	**32.6**	**21.2**	**11.4**
Hair care products	100.0	13.1	24.1	23.3	12.1	27.5	18.5	9.0
Hair accessories	100.0	9.5	23.8	24.7	11.3	30.1	23.1	7.0
Wigs and hairpieces	100.0	23.7	25.7	23.6	12.7	14.5	8.6	5.9
Oral hygiene products	100.0	13.3	24.4	18.9	8.4	34.1	22.2	11.9
Shaving products	100.0	12.5	26.9	15.6	9.0	34.9	23.4	11.5
Cosmetics, perfume, and bath products	100.0	9.3	22.8	22.8	8.8	35.1	22.5	12.6
Deodorants, feminine hygiene, misc. products	100.0	12.8	27.9	21.4	9.0	28.5	17.7	10.8
Electric personal care appliances	100.0	10.1	26.5	20.6	6.5	34.9	23.1	11.8
Personal care services	**100.0**	**9.1**	**25.0**	**19.8**	**9.5**	**36.6**	**22.5**	**14.2**
READING	**100.0**	**6.1**	**19.8**	**19.1**	**9.2**	**45.8**	**25.1**	**20.7**
Newspaper subscriptions	100.0	8.3	25.1	18.6	9.1	39.0	22.3	16.7
Newspaper, nonsubscription	100.0	11.7	28.7	18.9	9.1	31.7	19.5	12.2
Magazine subscriptions	100.0	4.9	20.9	20.4	9.5	44.3	23.9	20.4
Magazines, nonsubscription	100.0	7.0	20.3	22.4	11.5	38.8	23.9	14.9
Books purchased through book clubs	100.0	5.8	20.3	21.7	8.3	43.9	21.9	22.0
Books not purchased through book clubs	100.0	3.2	12.9	18.2	9.0	56.7	29.9	26.8
EDUCATION	**100.0**	**2.4**	**11.6**	**26.3**	**9.2**	**50.3**	**28.9**	**21.4**
College tuition	100.0	1.8	11.0	28.7	8.4	50.1	29.4	20.6
Elementary and high school tuition	100.0	1.4	8.6	15.8	9.8	64.5	33.4	31.0
Other school tuition	100.0	4.9	13.1	18.0	18.6	45.3	25.5	19.8
Other school expenses including rentals	100.0	3.9	15.2	19.8	11.1	50.0	30.9	19.1
Books, supplies for college	100.0	2.1	11.1	42.3	9.1	35.5	21.6	13.9
Books, supplies for elementary, high school	100.0	11.1	22.7	19.7	10.5	36.0	22.8	13.2
Books, supplies for day care, nursery school	100.0	3.8	14.1	17.1	12.1	52.8	28.2	24.5
Miscellaneous school expenses and supplies	100.0	6.0	18.7	24.3	8.4	40.7	24.2	16.5
TOBACCO PRODUCTS AND								
SMOKING SUPPLIES	**100.0**	**16.8**	**39.2**	**22.0**	**8.4**	**13.6**	**9.9**	**3.8**
Cigarettes	100.0	17.2	40.3	21.9	8.3	12.4	9.0	3.4
Other tobacco products	100.0	13.0	28.9	22.5	8.8	26.9	19.5	7.3
Smoking accessories	100.0	20.6	19.2	33.8	8.4	19.8	16.4	3.4

Note: Numbers may not add to total because of rounding.
Source: Calculations by New Strategist based on the 2002 Consumer Expenditure Survey

CHAPTER
11

Spending on Transportation, 2002

Transportation is the second largest household expenditure category, consuming 19.1 percent of the average household budget in 2002—up from 18.5 percent in 1997. Household spending on transportation rose 8 percent between 1997 and 2002, to $7,759 after adjusting for inflation. Spending on new cars and trucks rose a substantial 28 percent during these years as rebates and no-interest loans lured buyers. Spending on used cars and trucks climbed a smaller 13 percent. Spending on vehicle rentals and leasing fell 14 percent as the popularity of leasing declined. Spending on gasoline and motor oil was stable during the 1997-to-2002 time period. As Americans cut back on their travel following the September 11, 2001, terrorist attacks, spending on public transportation fell 11 percent.

Householders aged 35 to 44 spend the most on transportation, $9,400 in 2002, or 21 percent more than the average household. These are also the largest households, which accounts for their above-average spending. Householders aged 55 to 64 spend the most on new cars, however, while those aged 45 to 54 spend the most on used cars. Spending on public transportation peaks in the 55-to-64 age group. Householders aged 55 to 64 also spend 36 percent more than average on airline fares and 74 percent more on intercity train fares. They spend more than twice the average on ship fares.

Households with incomes of $70,000 or more spend 69 percent more than the average household on transportation. Affluent households control 44 percent of spending on new cars and trucks. They account for 63 percent of spending on new motorcycles and for half of spending on airline fares.

Married couples with children aged 18 or older at home spend the most on transportation because they are more likely to have two or more cars. In 2002, this household type spent more than twice the average on new cars. Married couples without children at home (most of them empty-nesters) spend 36 percent more than the average household on airline fares and nearly three times the average on ship fares.

Blacks and Hispanics spend less than the average household on transportation, but on some categories their spending is well above average. Hispanics spend 25 percent more than average on used trucks, while blacks spend 23 percent more than average on vehicle finance charges. Black and Hispanic households spend 60 to 92 percent more than average on intracity mass transit fares.

Households in the West spend the most on transportation, $8,449 in 2002. Households in the South spend the most on new trucks, however—14 percent more than the average household. Households in the Northeast spend 57 percent more than the average household on public transportation.

Because they dominate affluent households, college graduates spend 29 percent more than average on transportation. They spend 50 percent more than average on new cars and twice the average on public transportation. Households headed by college graduates control 55 percent of the market for airline fares and 57 percent of the market for ship fares.

Table 11.1 Transportation: Average spending by age, 2002

(average annual spending of consumer units (CU) on transportation, by age of consumer unit reference person, 2002)

	total consumer units	under 25	25 to 34	35 to 44	45 to 54	55 to 64	65 to 74	75+
Number of consumer units								
(in thousands, add 000)	112,108	8,737	18,988	24,394	22,691	15,314	11,216	10,767
Average number of persons per CU	2.5	1.9	2.9	3.2	2.7	2.1	1.9	1.5
Average before-tax income of CU	$49,430.00	$20,773.00	$49,133.00	$61,532.00	$64,974.00	$53,162.00	$35,118.00	$23,890.00
Average spending of CU, total	40,676.60	24,229.46	40,318.29	48,330.48	48,748.24	44,330.04	32,242.52	23,758.89
Transportation, average spending	7,759.29	5,101.90	8,423.07	9,399.89	9,173.39	8,448.62	5,730.69	3,177.83
VEHICLE PURCHASES	$3,664.93	$2,635.02	$4,268.90	$4,591.97	$4,202.68	$3,881.56	$2,429.84	$1,180.26
Cars and trucks, new	1,752.96	663.94	1,739.49	2,393.58	1,966.43	2,079.81	1,351.97	711.89
New cars	883.08	532.32	789.03	997.89	1,026.46	1,151.52	769.17	508.15
New trucks	869.88	131.61	950.46	1,395.68	939.97	928.29	582.81	203.74
Cars and trucks, used	1,842.29	1,917.15	2,454.23	2,115.23	2,108.51	1,763.01	1,042.90	468.37
Used cars	1,113.46	1,215.74	1,315.16	1,189.73	1,348.44	1,143.17	789.66	301.81
Used trucks	728.82	701.42	1,139.07	925.50	760.07	619.84	253.24	166.56
Other vehicles	69.68	53.93	75.19	83.16	127.74	38.74	34.97	–
New motorcycles	36.26	33.30	41.46	35.58	63.62	18.46	34.97	–
Used motorcycles	33.42	20.63	33.73	47.58	64.12	20.28	–	–
GASOLINE AND MOTOR OIL	1,235.06	903.03	1,256.79	1,472.79	1,494.67	1,292.37	969.76	575.24
Gasoline	1,125.01	803.85	1,153.23	1,356.47	1,371.63	1,157.54	848.63	533.36
Diesel fuel	10.86	2.00	10.46	14.58	10.15	10.45	21.20	1.66
Gasoline on trips	88.24	86.71	80.63	89.54	98.99	113.71	92.77	36.40
Motor oil	10.05	9.60	11.65	11.30	12.91	9.51	6.24	3.46
Motor oil on trips	0.89	0.88	0.81	0.90	1.00	1.15	0.94	0.37
OTHER VEHICLE EXPENSES	2,470.55	1,339.31	2,505.26	2,934.96	3,055.40	2,734.97	1,944.81	1,211.70
Vehicle finance charges	397.04	216.66	516.47	528.69	479.38	370.05	216.76	87.18
Automobile finance charges	193.12	138.60	253.45	231.92	232.99	188.16	120.77	41.45
Truck finance charges	182.89	73.43	242.16	265.51	219.68	160.89	77.37	43.63
Motorcycle and plane finance charges	2.36	1.53	3.08	4.42	3.31	0.22	0.53	–
Other vehicle finance charges	18.67	3.09	17.77	26.84	23.40	20.78	18.08	2.09
Maintenance and repairs	697.30	394.44	608.61	843.38	847.87	832.05	553.07	407.80
Coolant, additives, brake, transmission fluids	3.82	3.71	4.20	4.82	4.72	3.27	2.28	1.47
Tires—purchased, replaced, installed	89.93	55.95	89.94	103.48	112.37	97.84	75.10	43.69
Parts, equipment, and accessories	41.70	34.72	37.50	43.94	53.75	49.43	36.27	18.91
Vehicle audio equipment, excl. labor	12.32	2.02	48.23	11.02	7.17	–	–	–
Vehicle products	4.92	1.78	2.09	8.66	3.78	10.05	2.14	1.94
Miscellaneous auto repair, servicing	43.69	20.97	20.10	63.51	38.11	93.30	27.26	16.56
Body work and painting	31.24	19.87	19.31	36.21	42.74	31.70	24.97	31.92
Clutch, transmission repair	48.68	26.71	47.61	60.61	68.34	40.63	31.03	29.78
Drive shaft and rear-end repair	6.51	1.57	9.54	7.73	7.38	9.07	2.62	1.04
Brake work	57.73	32.01	47.65	76.39	68.83	70.00	39.10	32.62
Repair to steering or front-end	16.91	16.41	15.05	18.15	18.21	21.18	19.38	6.45
Repair to engine cooling system	21.68	5.17	16.14	25.09	28.18	26.06	18.58	20.40
Motor tune-up	49.69	30.32	37.26	63.87	59.66	61.18	41.88	25.98
Lube, oil change, and oil filters	65.07	38.59	61.55	70.49	78.00	76.36	62.52	39.83
Front-end alignment, wheel balance, rotation	11.90	11.13	9.16	11.63	16.70	15.37	9.58	5.33
Shock absorber replacement	4.82	1.77	1.46	6.38	8.41	5.43	3.58	2.58
Gas tank repair, replacement	4.32	–	4.06	3.74	7.15	2.81	2.17	8.24
Tire repair and other repair work	39.83	14.72	28.67	47.90	48.81	56.21	35.43	23.95
Vehicle air conditioning repair	17.00	4.47	12.06	18.43	19.66	22.37	22.18	13.97
Exhaust system repair	12.56	13.76	12.15	11.25	15.16	12.04	10.47	12.74

	total consumer units	under 25	25 to 34	35 to 44	45 to 54	55 to 64	65 to 74	75+
Electrical system repair	$28.42	$11.74	$21.25	$33.85	$34.81	$30.93	$32.28	$21.25
Motor repair, replacement	76.62	45.20	58.63	106.31	95.66	80.83	49.48	48.71
Auto repair service policy	7.93	1.86	5.00	9.91	10.26	15.99	4.76	0.45
Vehicle insurance	**893.50**	**478.79**	**871.99**	**986.86**	**1,125.08**	**991.15**	**798.94**	**528.01**
Vehicle rental, leases, licenses, other charges	**482.71**	**249.41**	**508.20**	**576.03**	**603.08**	**541.72**	**376.04**	**188.72**
Leased and rented vehicles	324.48	142.27	362.55	390.19	416.29	364.43	235.52	98.69
Rented vehicles	41.33	15.02	33.38	45.29	53.27	60.97	37.19	18.95
Auto rental	6.76	2.85	6.14	5.95	9.75	6.62	5.65	7.90
Auto rental on trips	28.28	5.53	22.72	31.73	34.78	49.23	25.11	8.54
Truck rental	2.21	4.84	0.44	2.94	3.02	1.14	1.72	1.87
Truck rental on trips	3.55	0.80	3.94	3.87	4.77	3.73	4.43	0.65
Leased vehicles	283.15	127.24	329.16	344.91	363.02	303.46	198.33	79.73
Car lease payments	149.63	70.41	188.80	134.16	202.52	170.20	129.20	60.41
Truck lease payments	114.24	46.72	119.88	188.52	133.14	112.23	57.53	12.91
Vehicle registration, state	72.82	39.06	64.33	84.64	85.24	85.51	72.47	44.52
Vehicle registration, local	7.76	4.26	6.17	10.11	9.16	8.25	7.19	5.04
Driver's license	6.26	6.02	5.98	5.90	7.66	6.82	5.60	4.70
Vehicle inspection	9.26	4.80	7.81	10.76	10.97	10.68	9.72	5.95
Parking fees	29.25	34.37	31.12	38.96	34.30	27.11	14.53	7.56
Parking fees in home city, excl. residence	24.24	30.99	27.20	32.38	28.42	21.18	10.01	5.47
Parking fees on trips	5.01	3.38	3.92	6.58	5.89	5.93	4.51	2.09
Tolls	10.59	5.38	12.45	13.72	12.90	11.55	5.43	3.19
Tolls on trips	3.94	3.08	3.75	4.33	4.49	4.95	4.44	0.98
Towing charges	5.60	7.19	7.55	5.60	6.76	5.06	2.88	2.00
Automobile service clubs	12.75	2.99	6.49	11.83	15.30	17.36	18.28	16.09
PUBLIC TRANSPORTATION	**388.75**	**224.54**	**392.12**	**400.18**	**420.64**	**539.72**	**386.28**	**210.62**
Airline fares	243.57	138.30	239.99	257.73	278.73	332.29	233.42	113.46
Intercity bus fares	11.48	7.38	10.01	11.77	9.61	15.54	16.82	9.38
Intracity mass transit fares	49.97	48.49	59.99	73.27	54.05	39.92	24.12	13.36
Local transportation on trips	10.91	5.81	9.37	10.57	11.79	15.39	11.79	9.39
Taxi fares and limousine service on trips	6.41	3.41	5.50	6.21	6.92	9.04	6.92	5.52
Taxi fares and limousine service	18.95	10.04	23.10	9.98	16.38	38.32	27.88	7.48
Intercity train fares	16.09	8.23	12.65	12.04	17.26	28.06	20.60	13.58
Ship fares	29.74	2.83	29.97	16.74	22.76	60.65	44.56	35.91
School bus	1.64	0.05	1.55	1.88	3.14	0.52	0.18	2.53

Note: (–) means sample is too small to make a reliable estimate.
Source: Bureau of Labor Statistics, unpublished tables from the 2002 Consumer Expenditure Survey

Table 11.2 Transportation: Indexed spending by age, 2002

(indexed average annual spending of consumer units (CU) on transportation, by age of consumer unit reference person, 2002; index definition: an index of 100 is the average for all consumer units; an index of 132 means that spending by consumer units in that group is 32 percent above the average for all consumer units; an index of 68 indicates spending that is 32 percent below the average for all consumer units)

	total consumer units	under 25	25 to 34	35 to 44	45 to 54	55 to 64	65 to 74	75+
Average spending of CU, total	$40,677	$24,229	$40,318	$48,330	$48,748	$44,330	$32,243	$23,759
Average spending of CU, index	100	60	99	119	120	109	79	58
Transportation, spending index	100	66	109	121	118	109	74	41
VEHICLE PURCHASES	100	72	116	125	115	106	66	32
Cars and trucks, new	100	38	99	137	112	119	77	41
New cars	100	60	89	113	116	130	87	58
New trucks	100	15	109	160	108	107	67	23
Cars and trucks, used	100	104	133	115	114	96	57	25
Used cars	100	109	118	107	121	103	71	27
Used trucks	100	96	156	127	104	85	35	23
Other vehicles	100	77	108	119	183	56	50	–
New motorcycles	100	92	114	98	175	51	96	–
Used motorcycles	100	62	101	142	192	61	–	–
GASOLINE AND MOTOR OIL	100	73	102	119	121	105	79	47
Gasoline	100	71	103	121	122	103	75	47
Diesel fuel	100	18	96	134	93	96	195	15
Gasoline on trips	100	98	91	101	112	129	105	41
Motor oil	100	96	116	112	128	95	62	34
Motor oil on trips	100	99	91	101	112	129	106	42
OTHER VEHICLE EXPENSES	100	54	101	119	124	111	79	49
Vehicle finance charges	100	55	130	133	121	93	55	22
Automobile finance charges	100	72	131	120	121	97	63	21
Truck finance charges	100	40	132	145	120	88	42	24
Motorcycle and plane finance charges	100	65	131	187	140	9	22	–
Other vehicle finance charges	100	17	95	144	125	111	97	11
Maintenance and repairs	100	57	87	121	122	119	79	58
Coolant, additives, brake, transmission fluids	100	97	110	126	124	86	60	38
Tires—purchased, replaced, installed	100	62	100	115	125	109	84	49
Parts, equipment, and accessories	100	83	90	105	129	119	87	45
Vehicle audio equipment, excl. labor	100	16	391	89	58	–	–	–
Vehicle products	100	36	42	176	77	204	43	39
Miscellaneous auto repair, servicing	100	48	46	145	87	214	62	38
Body work and painting	100	64	62	116	137	101	80	102
Clutch, transmission repair	100	55	98	125	140	83	64	61
Drive shaft and rear-end repair	100	24	147	119	113	139	40	16
Brake work	100	55	83	132	119	121	68	57
Repair to steering or front-end	100	97	89	107	108	125	115	38
Repair to engine cooling system	100	24	74	116	130	120	86	94
Motor tune-up	100	61	75	129	120	123	84	52
Lube, oil change, and oil filters	100	59	95	108	120	117	96	61
Front-end alignment, wheel balance, rotation	100	94	77	98	140	129	81	45
Shock absorber replacement	100	37	30	132	174	113	74	54
Gas tank repair, replacement	100	–	94	87	166	65	50	191
Tire repair and other repair work	100	37	72	120	123	141	89	60
Vehicle air conditioning repair	100	26	71	108	116	132	130	82
Exhaust system repair	100	110	97	90	121	96	83	101

	total consumer units	under 25	25 to 34	35 to 44	45 to 54	55 to 64	65 to 74	75+
Electrical system repair	100	41	75	119	122	109	114	75
Motor repair, replacement	100	59	77	139	125	105	65	64
Auto repair service policy	100	23	63	125	129	202	60	6
Vehicle insurance	**100**	**54**	**98**	**110**	**126**	**111**	**89**	**59**
Vehicle rental, leases, licenses, other charges	**100**	**52**	**105**	**119**	**125**	**112**	**78**	**39**
Leased and rented vehicles	100	44	112	120	128	112	73	30
Rented vehicles	100	36	81	110	129	148	90	46
Auto rental	100	42	91	88	144	98	84	117
Auto rental on trips	100	20	80	112	123	174	89	30
Truck rental	100	219	20	133	137	52	78	85
Truck rental on trips	100	23	111	109	134	105	125	18
Leased vehicles	100	45	116	122	128	107	70	28
Car lease payments	100	47	126	90	135	114	86	40
Truck lease payments	100	41	105	165	117	98	50	11
Vehicle registration, state	100	54	88	116	117	117	100	61
Vehicle registration, local	100	55	80	130	118	106	93	65
Driver's license	100	96	96	94	122	109	89	75
Vehicle inspection	100	52	84	116	118	115	105	64
Parking fees	100	118	106	133	117	93	50	26
Parking fees in home city, excl. residence	100	128	112	134	117	87	41	23
Parking fees on trips	100	67	78	131	118	118	90	42
Tolls	100	51	118	130	122	109	51	30
Tolls on trips	100	78	95	110	114	126	113	25
Towing charges	100	128	135	100	121	90	51	36
Automobile service clubs	100	23	51	93	120	136	143	126
PUBLIC TRANSPORTATION	**100**	**58**	**101**	**103**	**108**	**139**	**99**	**54**
Airline fares	100	57	99	106	114	136	96	47
Intercity bus fares	100	64	87	103	84	135	147	82
Intracity mass transit fares	100	97	120	147	108	80	48	27
Local transportation on trips	100	53	86	97	108	141	108	86
Taxi fares and limousine service on trips	100	53	86	97	108	141	108	86
Taxi fares and limousine service	100	53	122	53	86	202	147	39
Intercity train fares	100	51	79	75	107	174	128	84
Ship fares	100	10	101	56	77	204	150	121
School bus	100	3	95	115	191	32	11	154

Note: (–) means sample is too small to make a reliable estimate.
Source: Calculations by New Strategist based on the 2002 Consumer Expenditure Survey

Table 11.3 Transportation: Total spending by age, 2002

(total annual spending on transportation, by consumer unit (CU) age groups, 2002; numbers in thousands)

	total consumer units	under 25	25 to 34	35 to 44	45 to 54	55 to 64	65 to 74	75+
Number of consumer units	112,108	8,737	18,988	24,394	22,691	15,314	11,216	10,767
Total spending of all CUs	$4,560,172,273	$211,692,792	$765,563,691	$1,178,973,729	$1,106,146,314	$678,870,233	$361,632,104	$255,811,969
Transportation, total spending	869,878,483	44,575,300	159,937,253	229,300,917	208,153,392	129,382,167	64,275,419	34,215,696
VEHICLE PURCHASES	$410,867,972	$23,022,170	$81,057,873	$112,016,516	$95,363,012	$59,442,210	$27,253,085	$12,707,859
Cars and trucks, new	196,520,840	5,800,844	33,029,436	58,388,991	44,620,263	31,850,210	15,163,696	7,664,920
New cars	99,000,333	4,650,880	14,982,102	24,342,529	23,291,404	17,634,377	8,627,011	5,471,251
New trucks	97,520,507	1,149,877	18,047,334	34,046,218	21,328,859	14,215,833	6,536,797	2,193,669
Cars and trucks, used	206,535,447	16,750,140	46,600,919	51,598,921	47,844,200	26,998,735	11,697,166	5,042,940
Used cars	124,827,774	10,621,920	24,972,258	29,022,274	30,597,452	17,506,505	8,856,827	3,249,588
Used trucks	81,706,553	6,128,307	21,628,661	22,576,647	17,246,748	9,492,230	2,840,340	1,793,352
Other vehicles	7,811,685	471,186	1,427,708	2,028,605	2,898,548	593,264	392,224	–
New motorcycles	4,065,036	290,942	787,242	867,939	1,443,601	282,696	392,224	–
Used motorcycles	3,746,649	180,244	640,465	1,160,667	1,454,947	310,568	–	–
GASOLINE AND MOTOR OIL	138,460,106	7,889,773	23,863,929	35,927,239	33,915,557	19,791,354	10,876,828	6,193,609
Gasoline	126,122,621	7,023,237	21,897,531	33,089,729	31,123,656	17,726,568	9,518,234	5,742,687
Diesel fuel	1,217,493	17,474	198,614	355,665	230,314	160,031	237,779	17,873
Gasoline on trips	9,892,410	757,585	1,531,002	2,184,239	2,246,182	1,741,355	1,040,508	391,919
Motor oil	1,126,685	83,875	221,210	275,652	292,941	145,636	69,988	37,254
Motor oil on trips	99,776	7,689	15,380	21,955	22,691	17,611	10,543	3,984
OTHER VEHICLE EXPENSES	276,968,419	11,701,551	47,569,877	71,595,414	69,330,081	41,883,331	21,812,989	13,046,374
Vehicle finance charges	44,511,360	1,892,958	9,806,732	12,896,864	10,877,612	5,666,946	2,431,180	938,667
Automobile finance charges	21,650,297	1,210,948	4,812,509	5,657,456	5,286,776	2,881,482	1,354,556	446,292
Truck finance charges	20,503,432	641,558	4,598,134	6,476,851	4,984,759	2,463,869	867,782	469,764
Motorcycle and plane finance charges	264,575	13,368	58,483	107,821	75,107	3,369	5,944	–
Other vehicle finance charges	2,093,056	26,997	337,417	654,735	530,969	318,225	202,785	22,503
Maintenance and repairs	78,172,908	3,446,222	11,556,287	20,573,412	19,239,018	12,742,014	6,203,233	4,390,783
Coolant, additives, brake, transmission fluids	428,253	32,414	79,750	117,579	107,102	50,077	25,572	15,827
Tires—purchased, replaced, installed	10,081,872	488,835	1,707,781	2,524,291	2,549,788	1,498,322	842,322	470,410
Parts, equipment, and accessories	4,674,904	303,349	712,050	1,071,872	1,219,641	756,971	406,804	203,604
Vehicle audio equipment, excl. labor	1,381,171	17,649	915,791	268,822	162,694	–	–	–
Vehicle products	551,571	15,552	39,685	211,252	85,772	153,906	24,002	20,888
Miscellaneous auto repair, servicing	4,897,999	183,215	381,659	1,549,263	864,754	1,428,796	305,748	178,302
Body work and painting	3,502,254	173,604	366,658	883,307	969,813	485,454	280,064	343,683
Clutch, transmission repair	5,457,417	233,365	904,019	1,478,520	1,550,703	622,208	348,032	320,641
Drive shaft and rear-end repair	729,823	13,717	181,146	188,566	167,460	138,898	29,386	11,198
Brake work	6,471,995	279,671	904,778	1,863,458	1,561,822	1,071,980	438,546	351,220
Repair to steering or front-end	1,895,746	143,374	285,769	442,751	413,203	324,351	217,366	69,447
Repair to engine cooling system	2,430,501	45,170	306,466	612,045	639,432	399,083	208,393	219,647
Motor tune-up	5,570,647	264,906	707,493	1,558,045	1,353,745	936,911	469,726	279,727
Lube, oil change, and oil filters	7,294,868	337,161	1,168,711	1,719,533	1,769,898	1,169,377	701,224	428,850
Front-end alignment, wheel balance, rotation	1,334,085	97,243	173,930	283,702	378,940	235,376	107,449	57,388
Shock absorber replacement	540,361	15,464	27,722	155,634	190,831	83,155	40,153	27,779
Gas tank repair, replacement	484,307	–	77,091	91,234	162,241	43,032	24,339	88,720
Tire repair and other repair work	4,465,262	128,609	544,386	1,168,473	1,107,548	860,800	397,383	257,870
Vehicle air conditioning repair	1,905,836	39,054	228,995	449,581	446,105	342,574	248,771	150,415
Exhaust system repair	1,408,076	120,221	230,704	274,433	343,996	184,381	117,432	137,172

	total consumer units	under 25	25 to 34	35 to 44	45 to 54	55 to 64	65 to 74	75+
Electrical system repair	$3,186,109	$102,572	$403,495	$825,737	$789,874	$473,662	$362,052	$228,799
Motor repair, replacement	8,589,715	394,912	1,113,266	2,593,326	2,170,621	1,237,831	554,968	524,461
Auto repair service policy	889,016	16,251	94,940	241,745	232,810	244,871	53,388	4,845
Vehicle insurance	**100,168,498**	**4,183,188**	**16,557,346**	**24,073,463**	**25,529,190**	**15,178,471**	**8,960,911**	**5,685,084**
Vehicle rental, leases, licenses, other charges	**54,115,653**	**2,179,095**	**9,649,702**	**14,051,676**	**13,684,488**	**8,295,900**	**4,217,665**	**2,031,948**
Leased and rented vehicles	36,376,804	1,243,013	6,884,099	9,518,295	9,446,036	5,580,881	2,641,592	1,062,595
Rented vehicles	4,633,424	131,230	633,819	1,104,804	1,208,750	933,695	417,123	204,035
Auto rental	757,850	24,900	116,586	145,144	221,237	101,379	63,370	85,059
Auto rental on trips	3,170,414	48,316	431,407	774,022	789,193	753,908	281,634	91,950
Truck rental	247,759	42,287	8,355	71,718	68,527	17,458	19,292	20,134
Truck rental on trips	397,983	6,990	74,813	94,405	108,236	57,121	49,687	6,999
Leased vehicles	31,743,380	1,111,696	6,250,090	8,413,735	8,237,287	4,647,186	2,224,469	858,453
Car lease payments	16,774,720	615,172	3,584,934	3,272,699	4,595,381	2,606,443	1,449,107	650,434
Truck lease payments	12,807,218	408,193	2,276,281	4,598,757	3,021,080	1,718,690	645,256	139,002
Vehicle registration, state	8,163,705	341,267	1,221,498	2,064,708	1,934,181	1,309,500	812,824	479,347
Vehicle registration, local	869,958	37,220	117,156	246,623	207,850	126,341	80,643	54,266
Driver's license	701,796	52,597	113,548	143,925	173,813	104,441	62,810	50,605
Vehicle inspection	1,038,120	41,938	148,296	262,479	248,920	163,554	109,020	64,064
Parking fees	3,279,159	300,291	590,907	950,390	778,301	415,163	162,968	81,399
Parking fees in home city, excl. residence	2,717,498	270,760	516,474	789,878	644,878	324,351	112,272	58,895
Parking fees on trips	561,661	29,531	74,433	160,513	133,650	90,812	50,584	22,503
Tolls	1,187,224	47,005	236,401	334,686	292,714	176,877	60,903	34,347
Tolls on trips	441,706	26,910	71,205	105,626	101,883	75,804	49,799	10,552
Towing charges	627,805	62,819	143,359	136,606	153,391	77,489	32,302	21,534
Automobile service clubs	1,429,377	26,124	123,232	288,581	347,172	265,851	205,028	173,241
PUBLIC TRANSPORTATION	**43,581,985**	**1,961,806**	**7,445,575**	**9,761,991**	**9,544,742**	**8,265,272**	**4,332,516**	**2,267,746**
Airline fares	27,306,146	1,208,327	4,556,930	6,287,066	6,324,662	5,088,689	2,618,039	1,221,624
Intercity bus fares	1,287,000	64,479	190,070	287,117	218,061	237,980	188,653	100,994
Intracity mass transit fares	5,602,037	423,657	1,139,090	1,787,348	1,226,449	611,335	270,530	143,847
Local transportation on trips	1,223,098	50,762	177,918	257,845	267,527	235,682	132,237	101,102
Taxi fares and limousine service on trips	718,612	29,793	104,434	151,487	157,022	138,439	77,615	59,434
Taxi fares and limousine service	2,124,447	87,719	438,623	243,452	371,679	586,832	312,702	80,537
Intercity train fares	1,803,818	71,906	240,198	293,704	391,647	429,711	231,050	146,216
Ship fares	3,334,092	24,726	569,070	408,356	516,447	928,794	499,785	386,643
School bus	183,857	437	29,431	45,861	71,250	7,963	2,019	27,241

Note: Numbers may not add to total because of rounding. (–) means sample is too small to make a reliable estimate.
Source: Calculations by New Strategist based on the 2002 Consumer Expenditure Survey

Table 11.4 Transportation: Market shares by age, 2002

(percentage of total annual spending on transportation accounted for by consumer unit age groups, 2002)

	total consumer units	under 25	25 to 34	35 to 44	45 to 54	55 to 64	65 to 74	75+
Share of total consumer units	100.0%	7.8%	16.9%	21.8%	20.2%	13.7%	10.0%	9.6%
Share of total before-tax income	100.0	3.3	16.8	27.1	26.6	14.7	7.1	4.6
Share of total spending	100.0	4.6	16.8	25.9	24.3	14.9	7.9	5.6
Share of transportation spending	100.0	5.1	18.4	26.4	23.9	14.9	7.4	3.9
VEHICLE PURCHASES	100.0%	5.6%	19.7%	27.3%	23.2%	14.5%	6.6%	3.1%
Cars and trucks, new	100.0	3.0	16.8	29.7	22.7	16.2	7.7	3.9
New cars	100.0	4.7	15.1	24.6	23.5	17.8	8.7	5.5
New trucks	100.0	1.2	18.5	34.9	21.9	14.6	6.7	2.2
Cars and trucks, used	100.0	8.1	22.6	25.0	23.2	13.1	5.7	2.4
Used cars	100.0	8.5	20.0	23.2	24.5	14.0	7.1	2.6
Used trucks	100.0	7.5	26.5	27.6	21.1	11.6	3.5	2.2
Other vehicles	100.0	6.0	18.3	26.0	37.1	7.6	5.0	–
New motorcycles	100.0	7.2	19.4	21.4	35.5	7.0	9.6	–
Used motorcycles	100.0	4.8	17.1	31.0	38.8	8.3	–	–
GASOLINE AND MOTOR OIL	100.0	5.7	17.2	25.9	24.5	14.3	7.9	4.5
Gasoline	100.0	5.6	17.4	26.2	24.7	14.1	7.5	4.6
Diesel fuel	100.0	1.4	16.3	29.2	18.9	13.1	19.5	1.5
Gasoline on trips	100.0	7.7	15.5	22.1	22.7	17.6	10.5	4.0
Motor oil	100.0	7.4	19.6	24.5	26.0	12.9	6.2	3.3
Motor oil on trips	100.0	7.7	15.4	22.0	22.7	17.7	10.6	4.0
OTHER VEHICLE EXPENSES	100.0	4.2	17.2	25.8	25.0	15.1	7.9	4.7
Vehicle finance charges	100.0	4.3	22.0	29.0	24.4	12.7	5.5	2.1
Automobile finance charges	100.0	5.6	22.2	26.1	24.4	13.3	6.3	2.1
Truck finance charges	100.0	3.1	22.4	31.6	24.3	12.0	4.2	2.3
Motorcycle and plane finance charges	100.0	5.1	22.1	40.8	28.4	1.3	2.2	–
Other vehicle finance charges	100.0	1.3	16.1	31.3	25.4	15.2	9.7	1.1
Maintenance and repairs	100.0	4.4	14.8	26.3	24.6	16.3	7.9	5.6
Coolant, additives, brake, transmission fluids	100.0	7.6	18.6	27.5	25.0	11.7	6.0	3.7
Tires—purchased, replaced, installed	100.0	4.8	16.9	25.0	25.3	14.9	8.4	4.7
Parts, equipment, and accessories	100.0	6.5	15.2	22.9	26.1	16.2	8.7	4.4
Vehicle audio equipment, excl. labor	100.0	1.3	66.3	19.5	11.8	–	–	–
Vehicle products	100.0	2.8	7.2	38.3	15.6	27.9	4.4	3.8
Miscellaneous auto repair, servicing	100.0	3.7	7.8	31.6	17.7	29.2	6.2	3.6
Body work and painting	100.0	5.0	10.5	25.2	27.7	13.9	8.0	9.8
Clutch, transmission repair	100.0	4.3	16.6	27.1	28.4	11.4	6.4	5.9
Drive shaft and rear-end repair	100.0	1.9	24.8	25.8	22.9	19.0	4.0	1.5
Brake work	100.0	4.3	14.0	28.8	24.1	16.6	6.8	5.4
Repair to steering or front-end	100.0	7.6	15.1	23.4	21.8	17.1	11.5	3.7
Repair to engine cooling system	100.0	1.9	12.6	25.2	26.3	16.4	8.6	9.0
Motor tune-up	100.0	4.8	12.7	28.0	24.3	16.8	8.4	5.0
Lube, oil change, and oil filters	100.0	4.6	16.0	23.6	24.3	16.0	9.6	5.9
Front-end alignment, wheel balance, rotation	100.0	7.3	13.0	21.3	28.4	17.6	8.1	4.3
Shock absorber replacement	100.0	2.9	5.1	28.8	35.3	15.4	7.4	5.1
Gas tank repair, replacement	100.0	–	15.9	18.8	33.5	8.9	5.0	18.3
Tire repair and other repair work	100.0	2.9	12.2	26.2	24.8	19.3	8.9	5.8
Vehicle air conditioning repair	100.0	2.0	12.0	23.6	23.4	18.0	13.1	7.9
Exhaust system repair	100.0	8.5	16.4	19.5	24.4	13.1	8.3	9.7

	total consumer units	under 25	25 to 34	35 to 44	45 to 54	55 to 64	65 to 74	75+
Electrical system repair	100.0%	3.2%	12.7%	25.9%	24.8%	14.9%	11.4%	7.2%
Motor repair, replacement	100.0	4.6	13.0	30.2	25.3	14.4	6.5	6.1
Auto repair service policy	100.0	1.8	10.7	27.2	26.2	27.5	6.0	0.5
Vehicle insurance	**100.0**	**4.2**	**16.5**	**24.0**	**25.5**	**15.2**	**8.9**	**5.7**
Vehicle rental, leases, licenses, other charges	**100.0**	**4.0**	**17.8**	**26.0**	**25.3**	**15.3**	**7.8**	**3.8**
Leased and rented vehicles	100.0	3.4	18.9	26.2	26.0	15.3	7.3	2.9
Rented vehicles	100.0	2.8	13.7	23.8	26.1	20.2	9.0	4.4
Auto rental	100.0	3.3	15.4	19.2	29.2	13.4	8.4	11.2
Auto rental on trips	100.0	1.5	13.6	24.4	24.9	23.8	8.9	2.9
Truck rental	100.0	17.1	3.4	28.9	27.7	7.0	7.8	8.1
Truck rental on trips	100.0	1.8	18.8	23.7	27.2	14.4	12.5	1.8
Leased vehicles	100.0	3.5	19.7	26.5	25.9	14.6	7.0	2.7
Car lease payments	100.0	3.7	21.4	19.5	27.4	15.5	8.6	3.9
Truck lease payments	100.0	3.2	17.8	35.9	23.6	13.4	5.0	1.1
Vehicle registration, state	100.0	4.2	15.0	25.3	23.7	16.0	10.0	5.9
Vehicle registration, local	100.0	4.3	13.5	28.3	23.9	14.5	9.3	6.2
Driver's license	100.0	7.5	16.2	20.5	24.8	14.9	8.9	7.2
Vehicle inspection	100.0	4.0	14.3	25.3	24.0	15.8	10.5	6.2
Parking fees	100.0	9.2	18.0	29.0	23.7	12.7	5.0	2.5
Parking fees in home city, excl. residence	100.0	10.0	19.0	29.1	23.7	11.9	4.1	2.2
Parking fees on trips	100.0	5.3	13.3	28.6	23.8	16.2	9.0	4.0
Tolls	100.0	4.0	19.9	28.2	24.7	14.9	5.1	2.9
Tolls on trips	100.0	6.1	16.1	23.9	23.1	17.2	11.3	2.4
Towing charges	100.0	10.0	22.8	21.8	24.4	12.3	5.1	3.4
Automobile service clubs	100.0	1.8	8.6	20.2	24.3	18.6	14.3	12.1
PUBLIC TRANSPORTATION	**100.0**	**4.5**	**17.1**	**22.4**	**21.9**	**19.0**	**9.9**	**5.2**
Airline fares	100.0	4.4	16.7	23.0	23.2	18.6	9.6	4.5
Intercity bus fares	100.0	5.0	14.8	22.3	16.9	18.5	14.7	7.8
Intracity mass transit fares	100.0	7.6	20.3	31.9	21.9	10.9	4.8	2.6
Local transportation on trips	100.0	4.2	14.5	21.1	21.9	19.3	10.8	8.3
Taxi fares and limousine service on trips	100.0	4.1	14.5	21.1	21.9	19.3	10.8	8.3
Taxi fares and limousine service	100.0	4.1	20.6	11.5	17.5	27.6	14.7	3.8
Intercity train fares	100.0	4.0	13.3	16.3	21.7	23.8	12.8	8.1
Ship fares	100.0	0.7	17.1	12.2	15.5	27.9	15.0	11.6
School bus	100.0	0.2	16.0	24.9	38.8	4.3	1.1	14.8

Note: Numbers may not add to total because of rounding. (–) means sample is too small to make a reliable estimate.
Source: Calculations by New Strategist based on the 2002 Consumer Expenditure Survey

Table 11.5 Transportation: Average spending by income, 2002

(average annual spending on transportation, by before-tax income of consumer unit (CU), 2002; complete income reporters only)

	complete income reporters	under $10,000	$10,000–$19,999	$20,000–$29,999	$30,000–$39,999	$40,000–$49,999	$50,000–$69,999	$70,000 or more
Number of consumer units (in thousands, add 000)	92,388	10,933	15,075	12,312	10,727	8,873	13,521	20,947
Average number of persons per CU	2.5	1.7	1.9	2.3	2.5	2.6	2.8	3.1
Average before-tax income of CU	$49,430.00	$5,554.80	$14,724.33	$24,495.00	$34,423.00	$44,443.00	$58,933.00	$115,629.00
Average spending of CU, total	42,556.98	17,627.83	22,838.71	28,835.85	35,095.39	41,787.38	50,406.17	76,627.31
Transportation, average spending	7,984.45	2,727.38	4,326.79	5,274.88	7,040.88	8,651.32	10,555.48	13,486.91
VEHICLE PURCHASES	**$3,778.32**	**$1,188.62**	**$2,222.88**	**$2,323.45**	**$3,343.00**	**$4,291.97**	**$5,190.59**	**$6,198.28**
Cars and trucks, new	**1,767.41**	**373.46**	**899.92**	**761.68**	**1,446.01**	**2,054.33**	**2,263.82**	**3,433.03**
New cars	901.55	146.06	480.45	472.81	832.06	1,169.65	1,155.33	1,609.14
New trucks	865.85	227.39	419.47	288.87	613.95	884.69	1,108.49	1,823.89
Cars and trucks, used	**1,939.39**	**814.86**	**1,310.64**	**1,525.18**	**1,860.15**	**2,173.75**	**2,811.11**	**2,600.89**
Used cars	1,178.40	643.47	829.75	1,000.70	1,053.94	1,417.76	1,475.91	1,583.28
Used trucks	760.98	171.40	480.90	524.48	806.22	755.99	1,335.20	1,017.61
Other vehicles	**71.52**	**0.29**	**12.32**	**36.59**	**36.84**	**63.88**	**115.65**	**164.36**
New motorcycles	37.01	–	12.32	–	19.90	40.20	37.76	102.76
Used motorcycles	34.52	0.29	–	36.59	16.94	23.68	77.89	61.60
GASOLINE AND MOTOR OIL	**1,252.40**	**536.35**	**718.09**	**986.64**	**1,261.41**	**1,289.11**	**1,592.36**	**1,927.30**
Gasoline	1,134.98	484.39	661.10	898.46	1,138.98	1,170.74	1,448.40	1,735.13
Diesel fuel	10.71	1.46	3.67	6.38	11.42	10.35	16.63	19.11
Gasoline on trips	95.23	45.24	46.04	72.14	96.53	96.60	112.62	157.82
Motor oil	10.52	4.80	6.80	8.93	13.51	10.44	13.58	13.64
Motor oil on trips	0.96	0.45	0.47	0.73	0.98	0.98	1.14	1.59
OTHER VEHICLE EXPENSES	**2,550.01**	**835.37**	**1,215.99**	**1,733.62**	**2,172.30**	**2,688.38**	**3,301.97**	**4,526.95**
Vehicle finance charges	**403.49**	**88.60**	**140.78**	**225.73**	**371.72**	**452.23**	**593.41**	**734.44**
Automobile finance charges	200.45	46.66	85.32	125.61	185.84	249.17	291.04	335.95
Truck finance charges	183.13	38.94	51.01	94.60	171.94	184.32	278.55	349.12
Motorcycle and plane finance charges	2.52	0.17	0.38	0.56	2.10	2.32	4.66	5.38
Other vehicle finance charges	17.39	2.83	4.08	4.97	11.84	16.42	19.16	43.99
Maintenance and repairs	**732.49**	**296.82**	**385.15**	**571.08**	**613.60**	**759.24**	**917.93**	**1,228.04**
Coolant, additives, brake, transmission fluids	4.08	2.79	3.26	3.29	4.78	4.61	5.15	4.53
Tires—purchased, replaced, installed	93.71	40.48	41.46	82.33	71.80	100.14	130.17	150.73
Parts, equipment, and accessories	42.74	14.80	27.50	42.99	54.03	48.88	60.70	48.15
Vehicle audio equipment, excl. labor	15.44	–	–	14.09	9.05	12.59	–	47.83
Vehicle products	5.51	1.17	1.97	2.06	4.32	2.85	13.30	9.00
Miscellaneous auto repair, servicing	47.19	11.66	19.57	53.01	25.98	33.31	38.58	100.56
Body work and painting	32.35	11.35	19.17	24.01	14.67	22.80	48.09	60.65
Clutch, transmission repair	49.63	41.58	33.25	23.32	48.52	52.38	67.01	69.27
Drive shaft and rear-end repair	7.03	2.01	1.91	7.11	6.89	4.58	12.59	10.79
Brake work	61.91	19.08	33.20	46.16	45.35	69.52	80.22	107.62
Repair to steering or front-end	17.67	9.54	9.44	18.19	16.37	12.33	22.22	27.54
Repair to engine cooling system	22.99	9.18	15.60	24.05	16.39	25.58	31.11	31.93
Motor tune-up	50.89	18.02	28.96	30.55	36.79	47.96	54.72	101.78
Lube, oil change, and oil filters	68.33	26.68	39.25	51.43	63.87	69.66	86.10	111.17
Front-end alignment, wheel balance, rotation	13.17	6.35	7.54	9.39	8.89	12.23	20.94	20.55
Shock absorber replacement	5.57	1.06	1.98	4.00	3.42	3.85	12.38	8.87
Gas tank repair, replacement	4.72	–	1.32	8.87	2.75	1.50	6.91	7.67
Tire repair and other repair work	41.17	18.44	23.43	28.26	44.22	48.90	43.41	67.12
Vehicle air conditioning repair	17.68	7.56	12.45	12.12	15.21	15.10	21.49	29.91
Exhaust system repair	13.23	9.25	6.39	7.57	9.90	15.84	19.99	19.78

	complete income reporters	under $10,000	$10,000–$19,999	$20,000–$29,999	$30,000–$39,999	$40,000–$49,999	$50,000–$69,999	$70,000 or more
Electrical system repair	$30.83	$10.41	$18.83	$23.43	$29.72	$26.74	$46.17	$46.90
Motor repair, replacement	77.70	33.46	36.38	50.12	72.75	110.39	87.02	129.42
Auto repair service policy	8.94	1.95	2.29	4.76	7.93	17.47	9.66	16.26
Vehicle insurance	**919.59**	**324.08**	**519.58**	**707.32**	**877.34**	**1,024.41**	**1,160.09**	**1,465.06**
Vehicle rental, leases, licenses, other charges	**494.44**	**125.88**	**170.48**	**229.48**	**309.64**	**452.50**	**630.55**	**1,099.41**
Leased and rented vehicles	323.83	58.96	78.33	114.79	163.87	273.79	422.68	800.95
Rented vehicles	43.69	7.70	9.69	19.61	19.75	37.68	52.16	110.44
Auto rental	7.03	2.10	2.66	3.29	4.04	8.78	9.84	13.90
Auto rental on trips	30.13	4.44	4.98	13.20	13.76	22.16	30.64	83.02
Truck rental	2.04	0.29	1.23	0.60	1.08	2.29	3.30	3.98
Truck rental on trips	3.92	0.87	0.82	2.51	0.87	3.25	8.13	7.69
Leased vehicles	280.14	51.26	68.65	95.17	144.11	236.11	370.53	690.52
Car lease payments	148.71	33.96	37.74	60.87	68.44	127.30	193.36	361.46
Truck lease payments	113.00	11.34	25.04	33.62	61.13	95.34	169.93	273.32
Vehicle registration, state	78.75	27.79	43.07	52.75	77.52	81.28	102.64	130.47
Vehicle registration, local	8.09	3.24	5.09	5.37	8.11	10.23	11.51	11.27
Driver's license	6.80	4.51	4.55	5.46	7.34	6.75	8.50	9.07
Vehicle inspection	10.09	3.30	6.11	8.50	9.72	9.84	12.57	16.14
Parking fees	29.93	14.81	12.39	13.52	15.47	24.93	33.66	67.18
Parking fees in home city, excl. residence	24.81	13.14	10.28	11.83	12.47	21.27	28.52	54.43
Parking fees on trips	5.11	1.68	2.10	1.69	3.01	3.65	5.14	12.76
Tolls	12.62	3.42	3.46	9.16	8.63	15.74	9.63	27.87
Tolls on trips	4.19	1.81	1.67	2.37	3.66	5.27	4.52	7.93
Towing charges	6.11	3.85	5.77	7.10	5.17	9.27	6.74	5.68
Automobile service clubs	14.01	4.18	10.06	10.46	10.14	15.40	18.10	22.85
PUBLIC TRANSPORTATION	**403.72**	**167.04**	**169.82**	**231.17**	**264.17**	**381.87**	**470.56**	**834.39**
Airline fares	254.06	85.16	92.09	125.94	145.12	237.30	306.32	563.23
Intercity bus fares	12.71	5.27	8.33	9.63	12.36	13.68	18.86	17.36
Intracity mass transit fares	51.12	38.59	43.35	44.93	45.56	48.13	43.69	75.81
Local transportation on trips	11.66	4.74	5.72	4.65	6.53	11.80	10.94	26.70
Taxi fares and limousine service on trips	6.85	2.79	3.36	2.73	3.84	6.93	6.43	15.68
Taxi fares and limousine service	19.69	20.24	6.08	5.04	16.69	29.10	8.93	42.11
Intercity train fares	15.51	4.94	5.60	11.01	17.69	9.62	10.81	35.20
Ship fares	30.19	4.34	4.32	25.35	13.48	23.56	62.62	55.59
School bus	1.92	0.97	0.98	1.89	2.90	1.74	1.96	2.68

Note: (–) means sample is too small to make a reliable estimate.
Source: Bureau of Labor Statistics, unpublished tables from the 2002 Consumer Expenditure Survey; calculations by New Strategist

Table 11.6 Transportation: Indexed spending by income, 2002

(indexed average annual spending of consumer units (CU) on transportation, by before-tax income of consumer unit, 2002; complete income reporters only; index definition: an index of 100 is the average for all consumer units; an index of 132 means that spending by consumer units in that group is 32 percent above the average for all consumer units; an index of 68 indicates spending that is 32 percent below the average for all consumer units)

	complete income reporters	under $10,000	$10,000–$19,999	$20,000–$29,999	$30,000–$39,999	$40,000–$49,999	$50,000–$69,999	$70,000 or more
Average spending of CU, total	$42,557	$17,628	$22,839	$28,836	$35,095	$41,787	$50,406	$76,627
Average spending of CU, index	100	41	54	68	82	98	118	180
Transportation, spending index	100	34	54	66	88	108	132	169
VEHICLE PURCHASES	100	31	59	61	88	114	137	164
Cars and trucks, new	100	21	51	43	82	116	128	194
New cars	100	16	53	52	92	130	128	178
New trucks	100	26	48	33	71	102	128	211
Cars and trucks, used	100	42	68	79	96	112	145	134
Used cars	100	55	70	85	89	120	125	134
Used trucks	100	23	63	69	106	99	175	134
Other vehicles	100	0	17	51	52	89	162	230
New motorcycles	100	–	33	–	54	109	102	278
Used motorcycles	100	1	–	106	49	69	226	178
GASOLINE AND MOTOR OIL	100	43	57	79	101	103	127	154
Gasoline	100	43	58	79	100	103	128	153
Diesel fuel	100	14	34	60	107	97	155	178
Gasoline on trips	100	48	48	76	101	101	118	166
Motor oil	100	46	65	85	128	99	129	130
Motor oil on trips	100	47	48	76	102	102	119	166
OTHER VEHICLE EXPENSES	100	33	48	68	85	105	129	178
Vehicle finance charges	100	22	35	56	92	112	147	182
Automobile finance charges	100	23	43	63	93	124	145	168
Truck finance charges	100	21	28	52	94	101	152	191
Motorcycle and plane finance charges	100	7	15	22	83	92	185	213
Other vehicle finance charges	100	16	23	29	68	94	110	253
Maintenance and repairs	100	41	53	78	84	104	125	168
Coolant, additives, brake, transmission fluids	100	68	80	81	117	113	126	111
Tires—purchased, replaced, installed	100	43	44	88	77	107	139	161
Parts, equipment, and accessories	100	35	64	101	126	114	142	113
Vehicle audio equipment, excl. labor	100	–	–	91	59	82	–	310
Vehicle products	100	21	36	37	78	52	241	163
Miscellaneous auto repair, servicing	100	25	41	112	55	71	82	213
Body work and painting	100	35	59	74	45	70	149	187
Clutch, transmission repair	100	84	67	47	98	106	135	140
Drive shaft and rear-end repair	100	29	27	101	98	65	179	153
Brake work	100	31	54	75	73	112	130	174
Repair to steering or front-end	100	54	53	103	93	70	126	156
Repair to engine cooling system	100	40	68	105	71	111	135	139
Motor tune-up	100	35	57	60	72	94	108	200
Lube, oil change, and oil filters	100	39	57	75	93	102	126	163
Front-end alignment, wheel balance, rotation	100	48	57	71	68	93	159	156
Shock absorber replacement	100	19	36	72	61	69	222	159
Gas tank repair, replacement	100	–	28	188	58	32	146	163
Tire repair and other repair work	100	45	57	69	107	119	105	163
Vehicle air conditioning repair	100	43	70	69	86	85	122	169
Exhaust system repair	100	70	48	57	75	120	151	150

	complete income reporters	under $10,000	$10,000– $19,999	$20,000– $29,999	$30,000– $39,999	$40,000– $49,999	$50,000– $69,999	$70,000 or more
Electrical system repair	100	34	61	76	96	87	150	152
Motor repair, replacement	100	43	47	65	94	142	112	167
Auto repair service policy	100	22	26	53	89	195	108	182
Vehicle insurance	**100**	**35**	**57**	**77**	**95**	**111**	**126**	**159**
Vehicle rental, leases, licenses, other charges	**100**	**25**	**34**	**46**	**63**	**92**	**128**	**222**
Leased and rented vehicles	100	18	24	35	51	85	131	247
Rented vehicles	100	18	22	45	45	86	119	253
Auto rental	100	30	38	47	57	125	140	198
Auto rental on trips	100	15	17	44	46	74	102	276
Truck rental	100	14	60	29	53	112	162	195
Truck rental on trips	100	22	21	64	22	83	207	196
Leased vehicles	100	18	25	34	51	84	132	246
Car lease payments	100	23	25	41	46	86	130	243
Truck lease payments	100	10	22	30	54	84	150	242
Vehicle registration, state	100	35	55	67	98	103	130	166
Vehicle registration, local	100	40	63	66	100	126	142	139
Driver's license	100	66	67	80	108	99	125	133
Vehicle inspection	100	33	61	84	96	98	125	160
Parking fees	100	49	41	45	52	83	112	224
Parking fees in home city, excl. residence	100	53	41	48	50	86	115	219
Parking fees on trips	100	33	41	33	59	71	101	250
Tolls	100	27	27	73	68	125	76	221
Tolls on trips	100	43	40	57	87	126	108	189
Towing charges	100	63	94	116	85	152	110	93
Automobile service clubs	100	30	72	75	72	110	129	163
PUBLIC TRANSPORTATION	**100**	**41**	**42**	**57**	**65**	**95**	**117**	**207**
Airline fares	100	34	36	50	57	93	121	222
Intercity bus fares	100	41	66	76	97	108	148	137
Intracity mass transit fares	100	75	85	88	89	94	85	148
Local transportation on trips	100	41	49	40	56	101	94	229
Taxi fares and limousine service on trips	100	41	49	40	56	101	94	229
Taxi fares and limousine service	100	103	31	26	85	148	45	214
Intercity train fares	100	32	36	71	114	62	70	227
Ship fares	100	14	14	84	45	78	207	184
School bus	100	51	51	98	151	91	102	140

Note: (–) means sample is too small to make a reliable estimate.
Source: Calculations by New Strategist based on the 2002 Consumer Expenditure Survey

Table 11.7 Transportation: Total spending by income, 2002

(total annual spending on transportation, by before-tax income group of consumer units (CU), 2002; complete income reporters only; numbers in thousands)

	complete income reporters	under $10,000	$10,000– $19,999	$20,000– $29,999	$30,000– $39,999	$40,000– $49,999	$50,000– $69,999	$70,000 or more
Number of consumer units	92,388	10,933	15,075	12,312	10,727	8,873	13,521	20,947
Total spending of all CUs	$3,931,754,268	$192,725,059	$344,293,530	$355,026,985	$376,468,249	$370,779,423	$681,541,825	$1,605,112,263
Transportation, total spending	737,667,367	29,818,464	65,226,316	64,944,323	75,527,520	76,763,162	142,720,645	282,510,304
VEHICLE PURCHASES	**$349,071,428**	**$12,995,198**	**$33,509,986**	**$28,606,316**	**$35,860,361**	**$38,082,650**	**$70,181,967**	**$129,835,371**
Cars and trucks, new	**163,287,475**	**4,083,085**	**13,566,334**	**9,377,804**	**15,511,349**	**18,228,070**	**30,609,110**	**71,911,679**
New cars	83,292,401	1,596,924	7,242,795	5,821,237	8,925,508	10,378,304	15,621,217	33,706,656
New trucks	79,994,150	2,486,091	6,323,539	3,556,567	6,585,842	7,849,854	14,987,893	38,205,024
Cars and trucks, used	**179,176,363**	**8,908,901**	**19,757,969**	**18,778,016**	**19,953,829**	**19,287,684**	**38,009,018**	**54,480,843**
Used cars	108,870,019	7,035,064	12,508,473	12,320,618	11,305,614	12,579,784	19,955,779	33,164,966
Used trucks	70,305,420	1,873,908	7,249,496	6,457,398	8,648,322	6,707,899	18,053,239	21,315,877
Other vehicles	**6,607,590**	**3,173**	**185,682**	**450,496**	**395,183**	**566,807**	**1,563,704**	**3,442,849**
New motorcycles	3,419,280	–	185,682	–	213,467	356,695	510,553	2,152,514
Used motorcycles	3,189,234	3,173	–	450,496	181,715	210,113	1,053,151	1,290,335
GASOLINE AND MOTOR OIL	**115,706,731**	**5,863,866**	**10,825,134**	**12,147,512**	**13,531,145**	**11,438,273**	**21,530,300**	**40,371,153**
Gasoline	104,858,532	5,295,830	9,966,141	11,061,840	12,217,838	10,387,976	19,583,816	36,345,768
Diesel fuel	989,475	15,976	55,362	78,551	122,502	91,836	224,854	400,297
Gasoline on trips	8,798,109	494,572	694,085	888,188	1,035,477	857,132	1,522,735	3,305,856
Motor oil	971,922	52,519	102,532	109,946	144,922	92,634	183,615	285,717
Motor oil on trips	88,692	4,970	7,015	8,988	10,512	8,696	15,414	33,306
OTHER VEHICLE EXPENSES	**235,590,324**	**9,133,113**	**18,331,095**	**21,344,329**	**23,302,262**	**23,853,996**	**44,645,936**	**94,826,022**
Vehicle finance charges	**37,277,634**	**968,688**	**2,122,326**	**2,779,188**	**3,987,440**	**4,012,637**	**8,023,497**	**15,384,315**
Automobile finance charges	18,519,175	510,165	1,286,179	1,546,510	1,993,506	2,210,885	3,935,152	7,037,145
Truck finance charges	16,919,014	425,755	768,901	1,164,715	1,844,400	1,635,471	3,766,275	7,313,017
Motorcycle and plane finance charges	232,818	1,863	5,725	6,895	22,527	20,585	63,008	112,695
Other vehicle finance charges	1,606,627	30,943	61,441	61,191	127,008	145,695	259,062	921,459
Maintenance and repairs	**67,673,286**	**3,245,095**	**5,806,187**	**7,031,137**	**6,582,087**	**6,736,737**	**12,411,332**	**25,723,754**
Coolant, additives, brake, transmission fluids	376,943	30,501	49,183	40,506	51,275	40,905	69,633	94,890
Tires—purchased, replaced, installed	8,657,679	442,614	624,967	1,013,647	770,199	888,542	1,760,029	3,157,341
Parts, equipment, and accessories	3,948,663	161,858	414,592	529,293	579,580	433,712	820,725	1,008,598
Vehicle audio equipment, excl. labor	1,426,471	–	–	173,476	97,079	111,711		1,001,895
Vehicle products	509,058	12,767	29,626	25,363	46,341	25,288	179,829	188,523
Miscellaneous auto repair, servicing	4,359,790	127,449	294,977	652,659	278,687	295,560	521,640	2,106,430
Body work and painting	2,988,752	124,078	288,977	295,611	157,365	202,304	650,225	1,270,436
Clutch, transmission repair	4,585,216	454,644	501,312	287,116	520,474	464,768	906,042	1,450,999
Drive shaft and rear-end repair	649,488	21,929	28,789	87,538	73,909	40,638	170,229	226,018
Brake work	5,719,741	208,568	500,523	568,322	486,469	616,851	1,084,655	2,254,316
Repair to steering or front-end	1,632,496	104,253	142,300	223,955	175,601	109,404	300,437	576,880
Repair to engine cooling system	2,124,000	100,378	235,219	296,104	175,816	226,971	420,638	668,838
Motor tune-up	4,701,625	197,015	436,539	376,132	394,646	425,549	739,869	2,131,986
Lube, oil change, and oil filters	6,312,872	291,747	591,633	633,206	685,133	618,093	1,164,158	2,328,678
Front-end alignment, wheel balance, rotation	1,216,750	69,466	113,667	115,610	95,363	108,517	283,130	430,461
Shock absorber replacement	514,601	11,561	29,919	49,248	36,686	34,161	167,390	185,800
Gas tank repair, replacement	436,071	–	19,879	109,207	29,499	13,310	93,430	160,663
Tire repair and other repair work	3,803,614	201,634	353,193	347,937	474,348	433,890	586,947	1,405,963
Vehicle air conditioning repair	1,633,420	82,632	187,702	149,221	163,158	133,982	290,566	626,525
Exhaust system repair	1,222,293	101,091	96,393	93,202	106,197	140,548	270,285	414,332

	complete income reporters	under $10,000	$10,000–$19,999	$20,000–$29,999	$30,000–$39,999	$40,000–$49,999	$50,000–$69,999	$70,000 or more
Electrical system repair	$2,848,322	$113,828	$283,823	$288,470	$318,806	$237,264	$624,265	$982,414
Motor repair, replacement	7,178,548	365,792	548,382	617,077	780,389	979,490	1,176,597	2,710,961
Auto repair service policy	825,949	21,361	34,529	58,605	85,065	155,011	130,613	340,598
Vehicle insurance	**84,959,081**	**3,543,177**	**7,832,609**	**8,708,524**	**9,411,226**	**9,089,590**	**15,685,577**	**30,688,612**
Vehicle rental, leases, licenses, other charges	**45,680,323**	**1,376,224**	**2,569,973**	**2,825,358**	**3,321,508**	**4,015,033**	**8,525,667**	**23,029,341**
Leased and rented vehicles	29,918,006	644,584	1,180,899	1,413,294	1,757,833	2,429,339	5,715,056	16,777,500
Rented vehicles	4,036,432	84,203	146,068	241,438	211,858	334,335	705,255	2,313,387
Auto rental	649,488	22,923	40,105	40,506	43,337	77,905	133,047	291,163
Auto rental on trips	2,783,650	48,596	75,064	162,518	147,604	196,626	414,283	1,739,020
Truck rental	188,472	3,140	18,552	7,387	11,585	20,319	44,619	83,369
Truck rental on trips	362,161	9,544	12,427	30,903	9,332	28,837	109,926	161,082
Leased vehicles	25,881,574	560,381	1,034,831	1,171,733	1,545,868	2,095,004	5,009,936	14,464,322
Car lease payments	13,739,019	371,315	568,994	749,431	734,156	1,129,533	2,614,421	7,571,503
Truck lease payments	10,439,844	123,990	377,533	413,929	655,742	845,952	2,297,624	5,725,234
Vehicle registration, state	7,275,555	303,826	649,262	649,458	831,557	721,197	1,387,795	2,732,955
Vehicle registration, local	747,419	35,441	76,683	66,115	86,996	90,771	155,627	236,073
Driver's license	628,238	49,310	68,535	67,224	78,736	59,893	114,929	189,989
Vehicle inspection	932,195	36,088	92,117	104,652	104,266	87,310	169,959	338,085
Parking fees	2,765,173	161,969	186,730	166,458	165,947	221,204	455,117	1,407,219
Parking fees in home city, excl. residence	2,292,146	143,633	154,973	145,651	133,766	188,729	385,619	1,140,145
Parking fees on trips	472,103	18,337	31,677	20,807	32,288	32,386	69,498	267,284
Tolls	1,165,937	37,439	52,111	112,778	92,574	139,661	130,207	583,793
Tolls on trips	387,106	19,774	25,111	29,179	39,261	46,761	61,115	166,110
Towing charges	564,491	42,048	86,984	87,415	55,459	82,253	91,132	118,979
Automobile service clubs	1,294,356	45,674	151,702	128,784	108,772	136,644	244,730	478,639
PUBLIC TRANSPORTATION	**37,298,883**	**1,826,216**	**2,560,101**	**2,846,165**	**2,833,752**	**3,388,333**	**6,362,442**	**17,477,967**
Airline fares	23,472,095	931,022	1,388,222	1,550,573	1,556,702	2,105,563	4,141,753	11,797,979
Intercity bus fares	1,174,251	57,609	125,516	118,565	132,586	121,383	255,006	363,640
Intracity mass transit fares	4,722,875	421,900	653,484	553,178	488,722	427,057	590,732	1,587,992
Local transportation on trips	1,077,244	51,845	86,170	57,251	70,047	104,701	147,920	559,285
Taxi fares and limousine service on trips	632,858	30,477	50,672	33,612	41,192	61,490	86,940	328,449
Taxi fares and limousine service	1,819,120	221,282	91,729	62,052	179,034	258,204	120,743	882,078
Intercity train fares	1,432,938	54,023	84,468	135,555	189,761	85,358	146,162	737,334
Ship fares	2,789,194	47,408	65,087	312,109	144,600	209,048	846,685	1,164,444
School bus	177,385	10,651	14,751	23,270	31,108	15,439	26,501	56,138

Note: Numbers may not add to total because of rounding. (–) means sample is too small to make a reliable estimate.
Source: Calculations by New Strategist based on the 2002 Consumer Expenditure Survey

Table 11.8 Transportation: Market shares by income, 2002

(percentage of total annual spending on transportation accounted for by before-tax income group of consumer units, 2002; complete income reporters only)

	complete income reporters	under $10,000	$10,000– $19,999	$20,000– $29,999	$30,000– $39,999	$40,000– $49,999	$50,000– $69,999	$70,000 or more
Share of total consumer units	100.0%	11.8%	16.3%	13.3%	11.6%	9.6%	14.6%	22.7%
Share of total before-tax income	100.0	1.3	4.9	6.6	8.1	8.6	17.4	53.0
Share of total spending	100.0	4.9	8.8	9.0	9.6	9.4	17.3	40.8
Share of transportation spending	100.0	4.0	8.8	8.8	10.2	10.4	19.3	38.3
VEHICLE PURCHASES	**100.0%**	**3.7%**	**9.6%**	**8.2%**	**10.3%**	**10.9%**	**20.1%**	**37.2%**
Cars and trucks, new	**100.0**	**2.5**	**8.3**	**5.7**	**9.5**	**11.2**	**18.7**	**44.0**
New cars	100.0	1.9	8.7	7.0	10.7	12.5	18.8	40.5
New trucks	100.0	3.1	7.9	4.4	8.2	9.8	18.7	47.8
Cars and trucks, used	**100.0**	**5.0**	**11.0**	**10.5**	**11.1**	**10.8**	**21.2**	**30.4**
Used cars	100.0	6.5	11.5	11.3	10.4	11.6	18.3	30.5
Used trucks	100.0	2.7	10.3	9.2	12.3	9.5	25.7	30.3
Other vehicles	**100.0**	**0.0**	**2.8**	**6.8**	**6.0**	**8.6**	**23.7**	**52.1**
New motorcycles	100.0	–	5.4	–	6.2	10.4	14.9	63.0
Used motorcycles	100.0	0.1	–	14.1	5.7	6.6	33.0	40.5
GASOLINE AND MOTOR OIL	**100.0**	**5.1**	**9.4**	**10.5**	**11.7**	**9.9**	**18.6**	**34.9**
Gasoline	100.0	5.1	9.5	10.5	11.7	9.9	18.7	34.7
Diesel fuel	100.0	1.6	5.6	7.9	12.4	9.3	22.7	40.5
Gasoline on trips	100.0	5.6	7.9	10.1	11.8	9.7	17.3	37.6
Motor oil	100.0	5.4	10.5	11.3	14.9	9.5	18.9	29.4
Motor oil on trips	100.0	5.6	7.9	10.1	11.9	9.8	17.4	37.6
OTHER VEHICLE EXPENSES	**100.0**	**3.9**	**7.8**	**9.1**	**9.9**	**10.1**	**19.0**	**40.3**
Vehicle finance charges	**100.0**	**2.6**	**5.7**	**7.5**	**10.7**	**10.8**	**21.5**	**41.3**
Automobile finance charges	100.0	2.8	6.9	8.4	10.8	11.9	21.2	38.0
Truck finance charges	100.0	2.5	4.5	6.9	10.9	9.7	22.3	43.2
Motorcycle and plane finance charges	100.0	0.8	2.5	3.0	9.7	8.8	27.1	48.4
Other vehicle finance charges	100.0	1.9	3.8	3.8	7.9	9.1	16.1	57.4
Maintenance and repairs	**100.0**	**4.8**	**8.6**	**10.4**	**9.7**	**10.0**	**18.3**	**38.0**
Coolant, additives, brake, transmission fluids	100.0	8.1	13.0	10.7	13.6	10.9	18.5	25.2
Tires—purchased, replaced, installed	100.0	5.1	7.2	11.7	8.9	10.3	20.3	36.5
Parts, equipment, and accessories	100.0	4.1	10.5	13.4	14.7	11.0	20.8	25.5
Vehicle audio equipment, excl. labor	100.0	–	–	12.2	6.8	7.8	–	70.2
Vehicle products	100.0	2.5	5.8	5.0	9.1	5.0	35.3	37.0
Miscellaneous auto repair, servicing	100.0	2.9	6.8	15.0	6.4	6.8	12.0	48.3
Body work and painting	100.0	4.2	9.7	9.9	5.3	6.8	21.8	42.5
Clutch, transmission repair	100.0	9.9	10.9	6.3	11.4	10.1	19.8	31.6
Drive shaft and rear-end repair	100.0	3.4	4.4	13.5	11.4	6.3	26.2	34.8
Brake work	100.0	3.6	8.8	9.9	8.5	10.8	19.0	39.4
Repair to steering or front-end	100.0	6.4	8.7	13.7	10.8	6.7	18.4	35.3
Repair to engine cooling system	100.0	4.7	11.1	13.9	8.3	10.7	19.8	31.5
Motor tune-up	100.0	4.2	9.3	8.0	8.4	9.1	15.7	45.3
Lube, oil change, and oil filters	100.0	4.6	9.4	10.0	10.9	9.8	18.4	36.9
Front-end alignment, wheel balance, rotation	100.0	5.7	9.3	9.5	7.8	8.9	23.3	35.4
Shock absorber replacement	100.0	2.2	5.8	9.6	7.1	6.6	32.5	36.1
Gas tank repair, replacement	100.0	–	4.6	25.0	6.8	3.1	21.4	36.8
Tire repair and other repair work	100.0	5.3	9.3	9.1	12.5	11.4	15.4	37.0
Vehicle air conditioning repair	100.0	5.1	11.5	9.1	10.0	8.2	17.8	38.4
Exhaust system repair	100.0	8.3	7.9	7.6	8.7	11.5	22.1	33.9

	complete income reporters	under $10,000	$10,000–$19,999	$20,000–$29,999	$30,000–$39,999	$40,000–$49,999	$50,000–$69,999	$70,000 or more
Electrical system repair	100.0%	4.0%	10.0%	10.1%	11.2%	8.3%	21.9%	34.5%
Motor repair, replacement	100.0	5.1	7.6	8.6	10.9	13.6	16.4	37.8
Auto repair service policy	100.0	2.6	4.2	7.1	10.3	18.8	15.8	41.2
Vehicle insurance	**100.0**	**4.2**	**9.2**	**10.3**	**11.1**	**10.7**	**18.5**	**36.1**
Vehicle rental, leases, licenses, other charges	**100.0**	**3.0**	**5.6**	**6.2**	**7.3**	**8.8**	**18.7**	**50.4**
Leased and rented vehicles	100.0	2.2	3.9	4.7	5.9	8.1	19.1	56.1
Rented vehicles	100.0	2.1	3.6	6.0	5.2	8.3	17.5	57.3
Auto rental	100.0	3.5	6.2	6.2	6.7	12.0	20.5	44.8
Auto rental on trips	100.0	1.7	2.7	5.8	5.3	7.1	14.9	62.5
Truck rental	100.0	1.7	9.8	3.9	6.1	10.8	23.7	44.2
Truck rental on trips	100.0	2.6	3.4	8.5	2.6	8.0	30.4	44.5
Leased vehicles	100.0	2.2	4.0	4.5	6.0	8.1	19.4	55.9
Car lease payments	100.0	2.7	4.1	5.5	5.3	8.2	19.0	55.1
Truck lease payments	100.0	1.2	3.6	4.0	6.3	8.1	22.0	54.8
Vehicle registration, state	100.0	4.2	8.9	8.9	11.4	9.9	19.1	37.6
Vehicle registration, local	100.0	4.7	10.3	8.8	11.6	12.1	20.8	31.6
Driver's license	100.0	7.8	10.9	10.7	12.5	9.5	18.3	30.2
Vehicle inspection	100.0	3.9	9.9	11.2	11.2	9.4	18.2	36.3
Parking fees	100.0	5.9	6.8	6.0	6.0	8.0	16.5	50.9
Parking fees in home city, excl. residence	100.0	6.3	6.8	6.4	5.8	8.2	16.8	49.7
Parking fees on trips	100.0	3.9	6.7	4.4	6.8	6.9	14.7	56.6
Tolls	100.0	3.2	4.5	9.7	7.9	12.0	11.2	50.1
Tolls on trips	100.0	5.1	6.5	7.5	10.1	12.1	15.8	42.9
Towing charges	100.0	7.4	15.4	15.5	9.8	14.6	16.1	21.1
Automobile service clubs	100.0	3.5	11.7	9.9	8.4	10.6	18.9	37.0
PUBLIC TRANSPORTATION	**100.0**	**4.9**	**6.9**	**7.6**	**7.6**	**9.1**	**17.1**	**46.9**
Airline fares	100.0	4.0	5.9	6.6	6.6	9.0	17.6	50.3
Intercity bus fares	100.0	4.9	10.7	10.1	11.3	10.3	21.7	31.0
Intracity mass transit fares	100.0	8.9	13.8	11.7	10.3	9.0	12.5	33.6
Local transportation on trips	100.0	4.8	8.0	5.3	6.5	9.7	13.7	51.9
Taxi fares and limousine service on trips	100.0	4.8	8.0	5.3	6.5	9.7	13.7	51.9
Taxi fares and limousine service	100.0	12.2	5.0	3.4	9.8	14.2	6.6	48.5
Intercity train fares	100.0	3.8	5.9	9.5	13.2	6.0	10.2	51.5
Ship fares	100.0	1.7	2.3	11.2	5.2	7.5	30.4	41.7
School bus	100.0	6.0	8.3	13.1	17.5	8.7	14.9	31.6

Note: Numbers may not add to total because of rounding. (−) means sample is too small to make a reliable estimate.
Source: Calculations by New Strategist based on the 2002 Consumer Expenditure Survey

Table 11.9 Transportation: Average spending by household type, 2002

(average annual spending of consumer units (CU) on transportation, by type of consumer unit, 2002)

	total married couples	married couples, no children	married couples with children			single parent, at least one child <18	single person
			total	oldest child under 6	oldest child 6 to 17	oldest child 18 or older		
Number of consumer units								
(in thousands, add 000)	56,265	23,118	28,790	5,547	15,206	8,036	6,730	33,055
Average number of persons per CU	3.2	2.0	3.9	3.5	4.1	3.9	2.9	1.0
Average before-tax income of CU	$67,155.00	$58,967.00	$73,918.00	$67,587.00	$72,720.00	$81,042.00	$26,966.00	$27,042.00
Average spending of CU, total	52,333.70	45,557.33	57,835.01	52,778.62	58,103.75	60,859.78	30,185.38	24,189.90
Transportation, average spending	10,198.83	8,592.34	11,425.16	10,466.89	11,203.18	12,506.26	5,548.96	3,890.15
VEHICLE PURCHASES	**$4,794.94**	**$3,898.03**	**$5,513.48**	**$5,390.97**	**$5,512.27**	**$5,600.35**	**$2,833.16**	**$1,661.83**
Cars and trucks, new	**2,397.78**	**2,220.35**	**2,643.50**	**2,668.48**	**2,556.18**	**2,791.49**	**1,186.31**	**791.26**
New cars	1,184.97	1,140.02	1,233.47	962.15	990.76	1,880.00	592.51	445.79
New trucks	1,212.81	1,080.33	1,410.03	1,706.33	1,565.41	911.50	593.80	345.47
Cars and trucks, used	**2,296.10**	**1,617.21**	**2,725.67**	**2,531.45**	**2,830.70**	**2,661.02**	**1,592.87**	**845.78**
Used cars	1,280.54	1,026.86	1,423.71	1,453.01	1,296.53	1,644.12	1,123.42	597.60
Used trucks	1,015.56	590.35	1,301.96	1,078.44	1,534.16	1,016.90	469.45	248.17
Other vehicles	**101.06**	**60.47**	**144.31**	**191.04**	**125.40**	**147.84**	**53.98**	**24.79**
New motorcycles	55.36	34.08	80.82	125.20	42.36	122.97	51.52	6.96
Used motorcycles	45.70	26.39	63.49	65.84	83.04	24.87	2.46	17.83
GASOLINE AND MOTOR OIL	**1,620.91**	**1,345.06**	**1,807.44**	**1,494.06**	**1,760.87**	**2,111.88**	**912.06**	**646.13**
Gasoline	1,471.82	1,187.60	1,661.39	1,370.47	1,613.81	1,952.24	854.16	580.25
Diesel fuel	15.32	12.68	18.31	10.06	18.18	24.27	6.62	4.02
Gasoline on trips	119.03	133.08	111.21	99.67	113.79	114.30	45.72	56.40
Motor oil	13.53	10.37	15.40	12.85	13.94	19.91	5.11	4.89
Motor oil on trips	1.20	1.34	1.12	1.01	1.15	1.15	0.46	0.57
OTHER VEHICLE EXPENSES	**3,287.41**	**2,817.93**	**3,648.85**	**3,175.52**	**3,491.06**	**4,273.50**	**1,644.61**	**1,306.25**
Vehicle finance charges	**564.03**	**439.22**	**649.29**	**621.76**	**640.94**	**684.09**	**252.64**	**142.84**
Automobile finance charges	251.94	217.29	268.94	291.85	224.56	337.11	155.00	86.32
Truck finance charges	278.40	190.74	343.15	311.08	376.27	302.61	85.68	50.41
Motorcycle and plane finance charges	2.85	1.20	4.23	2.71	5.14	3.55	1.52	1.50
Other vehicle finance charges	30.83	29.99	32.97	16.13	34.97	40.82	10.44	4.62
Maintenance and repairs	**899.72**	**803.74**	**992.51**	**827.22**	**974.08**	**1,140.95**	**448.21**	**437.13**
Coolant, additives, brake, transmission fluids	4.98	3.74	5.65	4.05	5.33	7.35	3.09	1.97
Tires—purchased, replaced, installed	119.46	108.42	129.02	102.97	124.27	155.97	54.07	48.64
Parts, equipment, and accessories	56.39	50.72	59.27	45.77	53.46	79.59	19.91	19.24
Vehicle audio equipment, excl. labor	15.65	–	31.52	75.05	9.70	43.02	1.23	11.09
Vehicle products	7.60	6.34	8.95	2.19	11.41	9.01	1.11	2.16
Miscellaneous auto repair, servicing	56.22	54.51	58.93	32.32	78.34	39.78	20.74	27.92
Body work and painting	41.59	38.55	44.91	22.39	46.75	56.96	21.10	17.89
Clutch, transmission repair	62.93	45.10	77.40	50.11	81.06	89.32	23.03	31.88
Drive shaft and rear-end repair	7.63	5.72	10.31	2.79	11.09	14.01	3.64	6.07
Brake work	74.51	66.76	82.82	72.58	77.90	99.22	41.23	32.44
Repair to steering or front-end	21.33	20.62	22.66	13.07	19.87	34.55	13.59	12.41
Repair to engine cooling system	25.40	21.09	29.31	22.58	30.39	31.91	19.15	17.51
Motor tune-up	62.22	65.59	57.65	61.24	56.48	57.37	27.27	33.91
Lube, oil change, and oil filters	84.02	82.89	86.57	72.96	83.53	101.72	44.35	41.59
Front-end alignment, wheel balance, rotation	14.55	14.37	14.41	8.35	13.07	21.12	9.92	8.31
Shock absorber replacement	7.77	4.18	10.99	6.89	11.59	12.67	3.12	1.25
Gas tank repair, replacement	6.08	3.84	8.66	5.70	10.47	7.25	3.35	1.19
Tire repair and other repair work	51.01	53.59	53.31	40.94	57.16	54.57	18.41	29.64
Vehicle air conditioning repair	22.37	22.91	21.65	22.97	20.55	22.82	12.09	9.85
Exhaust system repair	13.29	14.40	12.39	6.55	12.83	15.57	10.02	8.26

	total married couples	married couples, no children	married couples with children				single parent, at least one child <18	single person
			total	oldest child under 6	oldest child 6 to 17	oldest child 18 or older		
Electrical system repair	$34.35	$32.66	$36.79	$23.95	$36.07	$47.02	$27.76	$19.63
Motor repair, replacement	99.44	79.29	115.73	127.01	105.13	128.00	65.29	48.09
Auto repair service policy	10.95	8.43	13.62	4.80	17.61	12.15	4.75	6.21
Vehicle insurance	**1,156.80**	**1,014.73**	**1,246.53**	**993.07**	**1,140.02**	**1,623.04**	**642.52**	**485.95**
Vehicle rental, leases, licenses, other charges	**666.86**	**560.24**	**760.52**	**733.47**	**736.03**	**825.41**	**301.24**	**240.33**
Leased and rented vehicles	463.14	374.85	538.24	520.30	514.65	595.28	198.91	135.65
Rented vehicles	57.04	63.40	52.13	31.65	58.62	54.01	15.90	23.15
Auto rental	7.46	7.79	6.88	3.65	6.55	9.74	5.82	4.21
Auto rental on trips	41.17	48.97	35.12	22.65	38.39	37.51	8.99	15.82
Truck rental	2.22	1.49	2.79	0.70	4.25	1.47	0.49	0.90
Truck rental on trips	5.60	4.72	6.56	4.65	8.56	4.11	0.60	1.41
Leased vehicles	406.10	311.45	486.11	488.66	456.03	541.27	183.01	112.50
Car lease payments	203.60	177.61	234.21	281.27	185.68	293.56	85.64	68.02
Truck lease payments	177.82	110.23	228.04	180.78	253.95	211.64	58.81	40.05
Vehicle registration, state	99.23	92.67	106.33	85.29	112.03	110.06	37.42	42.33
Vehicle registration, local	9.63	7.82	11.22	14.00	11.11	9.50	7.16	5.29
Driver's license	8.09	7.82	8.30	7.50	7.42	10.53	4.49	4.15
Vehicle inspection	12.26	10.73	12.82	14.62	10.63	15.73	5.74	5.35
Parking fees	34.03	29.61	39.47	47.51	38.68	35.39	17.14	25.35
Parking fees in home city, excl. residence	26.84	21.76	32.47	41.64	31.38	28.20	15.11	22.38
Parking fees on trips	7.19	7.85	6.99	5.87	7.30	7.19	2.03	2.97
Tolls	13.48	9.46	16.84	21.19	16.12	15.06	14.00	6.28
Tolls on trips	5.00	4.96	5.20	6.20	5.12	4.67	1.90	2.71
Towing charges	5.37	3.69	6.86	9.17	5.07	8.68	8.44	3.86
Automobile service clubs	16.63	18.62	15.23	7.68	15.20	20.52	6.04	9.36
PUBLIC TRANSPORTATION	**495.58**	**531.31**	**455.38**	**406.34**	**438.98**	**520.53**	**159.13**	**275.95**
Airline fares	325.59	331.60	311.83	273.51	309.78	342.15	75.87	167.99
Intercity bus fares	13.70	13.32	13.90	10.48	11.57	20.67	2.96	10.18
Intracity mass transit fares	47.83	32.68	53.19	60.30	45.62	62.60	43.18	38.61
Local transportation on trips	13.06	13.10	13.18	9.92	11.60	18.41	2.63	9.95
Taxi fares and limousine service on trips	7.67	7.70	7.74	5.83	6.81	10.81	1.54	5.85
Taxi fares and limousine service	18.62	22.68	16.60	6.72	18.53	20.03	18.99	22.93
Intercity train fares	20.96	29.40	15.07	8.45	14.30	21.12	2.86	11.75
Ship fares	46.44	80.72	21.07	31.14	18.27	19.43	7.78	7.96
School bus	1.71	0.11	2.80	–	2.50	5.30	3.32	0.72

Note: Average spending figures for total consumer units can be found on Average Spending by Age and Average Spending by Region tables. (–) means sample is too small to make a reliable estimate.
Source: Bureau of Labor Statistics, unpublished tables from the 2002 Consumer Expenditure Survey

Table 11.10 Transportation: Indexed spending by household type, 2002

(indexed average annual spending of consumer units (CU) on transportation, by type of consumer unit, 2002; index definition: an index of 100 is the average for all consumer units; an index of 132 means that spending by consumer units in that group is 32 percent above the average for all consumer units; an index of 68 indicates spending that is 32 percent below the average for all consumer units)

	total married couples	married couples, no children	married couples with children total	oldest child under 6	oldest child 6 to 17	oldest child 18 or older	single parent, at least one child <18	single person
Average spending of CU, total	$52,334	$45,557	$57,835	$52,779	$58,104	$60,860	$30,185	$24,190
Average spending of CU, index	129	112	142	130	143	150	74	59
Transportation, spending index	131	111	147	135	144	161	72	50
VEHICLE PURCHASES	**131**	**106**	**150**	**147**	**150**	**153**	**77**	**45**
Cars and trucks, new	**137**	**127**	**151**	**152**	**146**	**159**	**68**	**45**
New cars	134	129	140	109	112	213	67	50
New trucks	139	124	162	196	180	105	68	40
Cars and trucks, used	**125**	**88**	**148**	**137**	**154**	**144**	**86**	**46**
Used cars	115	92	128	130	116	148	101	54
Used trucks	139	81	179	148	210	140	64	34
Other vehicles	**145**	**87**	**207**	**274**	**180**	**212**	**77**	**36**
New motorcycles	153	94	223	345	117	339	142	19
Used motorcycles	137	79	190	197	248	74	7	53
GASOLINE AND MOTOR OIL	**131**	**109**	**146**	**121**	**143**	**171**	**74**	**52**
Gasoline	131	106	148	122	143	174	76	52
Diesel fuel	141	117	169	93	167	223	61	37
Gasoline on trips	135	151	126	113	129	130	52	64
Motor oil	135	103	153	128	139	198	51	49
Motor oil on trips	135	151	126	113	129	129	52	64
OTHER VEHICLE EXPENSES	**133**	**114**	**148**	**129**	**141**	**173**	**67**	**53**
Vehicle finance charges	**142**	**111**	**164**	**157**	**161**	**172**	**64**	**36**
Automobile finance charges	130	113	139	151	116	175	80	45
Truck finance charges	152	104	188	170	206	165	47	28
Motorcycle and plane finance charges	121	51	179	115	218	150	64	64
Other vehicle finance charges	165	161	177	86	187	219	56	25
Maintenance and repairs	**129**	**115**	**142**	**119**	**140**	**164**	**64**	**63**
Coolant, additives, brake, transmission fluids	130	98	148	106	140	192	81	52
Tires—purchased, replaced, installed	133	121	143	115	138	173	60	54
Parts, equipment, and accessories	135	122	142	110	128	191	48	46
Vehicle audio equipment, excl. labor	127	–	256	609	79	349	10	90
Vehicle products	154	129	182	45	232	183	23	44
Miscellaneous auto repair, servicing	129	125	135	74	179	91	47	64
Body work and painting	133	123	144	72	150	182	68	57
Clutch, transmission repair	129	93	159	103	167	183	47	65
Drive shaft and rear-end repair	117	88	158	43	170	215	56	93
Brake work	129	116	143	126	135	172	71	56
Repair to steering or front-end	126	122	134	77	118	204	80	73
Repair to engine cooling system	117	97	135	104	140	147	88	81
Motor tune-up	125	132	116	123	114	115	55	68
Lube, oil change, and oil filters	129	127	133	112	128	156	68	64
Front-end alignment, wheel balance, rotation	122	121	121	70	110	177	83	70
Shock absorber replacement	161	87	228	143	240	263	65	26
Gas tank repair, replacement	141	89	200	132	242	168	78	28
Tire repair and other repair work	128	135	134	103	144	137	46	74
Vehicle air conditioning repair	132	135	127	135	121	134	71	58
Exhaust system repair	106	115	99	52	102	124	80	66

	total married couples	married couples, no children	married couples with children				single parent, at least one child <18	single person
			total	oldest child under 6	oldest child 6 to 17	oldest child 18 or older		
Electrical system repair	121	115	129	84	127	165	98	69
Motor repair, replacement	130	103	151	166	137	167	85	63
Auto repair service policy	138	106	172	61	222	153	60	78
Vehicle insurance	**129**	**114**	**140**	**111**	**128**	**182**	**72**	**54**
Vehicle rental, leases, licenses, other charges	**138**	**116**	**158**	**152**	**152**	**171**	**62**	**50**
Leased and rented vehicles	143	116	166	160	159	183	61	42
Rented vehicles	138	153	126	77	142	131	38	56
Auto rental	110	115	102	54	97	144	86	62
Auto rental on trips	146	173	124	80	136	133	32	56
Truck rental	100	67	126	32	192	67	22	41
Truck rental on trips	158	133	185	131	241	116	17	40
Leased vehicles	143	110	172	173	161	191	65	40
Car lease payments	136	119	157	188	124	196	57	45
Truck lease payments	156	96	200	158	222	185	51	35
Vehicle registration, state	136	127	146	117	154	151	51	58
Vehicle registration, local	124	101	145	180	143	122	92	68
Driver's license	129	125	133	120	119	168	72	66
Vehicle inspection	132	116	138	158	115	170	62	58
Parking fees	116	101	135	162	132	121	59	87
Parking fees in home city, excl. residence	111	90	134	172	129	116	62	92
Parking fees on trips	144	157	140	117	146	144	41	59
Tolls	127	89	159	200	152	142	132	59
Tolls on trips	127	126	132	157	130	119	48	69
Towing charges	96	66	123	164	91	155	151	69
Automobile service clubs	130	146	119	60	119	161	47	73
PUBLIC TRANSPORTATION	**127**	**137**	**117**	**105**	**113**	**134**	**41**	**71**
Airline fares	134	136	128	112	127	140	31	69
Intercity bus fares	119	116	121	91	101	180	26	89
Intracity mass transit fares	96	65	106	121	91	125	86	77
Local transportation on trips	120	120	121	91	106	169	24	91
Taxi fares and limousine service on trips	120	120	121	91	106	169	24	91
Taxi fares and limousine service	98	120	88	35	98	106	100	121
Intercity train fares	130	183	94	53	89	131	18	73
Ship fares	156	271	71	105	61	65	26	27
School bus	104	7	171	–	152	323	202	44

Note: Spending index for total consumer units is 100. (–) means sample is too small to make a reliable estimate.
Source: Calculations by New Strategist based on the 2002 Consumer Expenditure Survey

Table 11.11 Transportation: Total spending by household type, 2002

(total annual spending on transportation, by consumer unit (CU) type, 2002; numbers in thousands)

	total married couples	married couples, no children	married couples with children total	oldest child under 6	oldest child 6 to 17	oldest child 18 or older	single parent, at least one child <18	single person
Number of consumer units	56,265	23,118	28,790	5,547	15,206	8,036	6,730	33,055
Total spending of all CUs	$2,944,555,631	$1,053,194,355	$1,665,069,938	$292,763,005	$883,525,623	$489,069,192	$203,147,607	$799,597,145
Transportation, total spending	573,837,170	198,637,716	328,930,356	58,059,839	170,355,555	100,500,305	37,344,501	128,588,908
VEHICLE PURCHASES	**$269,787,299**	**$90,114,658**	**$158,733,089**	**$29,903,711**	**$83,819,578**	**$45,004,413**	**$19,067,167**	**$54,931,791**
Cars and trucks, new	**134,911,092**	**51,330,051**	**76,106,365**	**14,802,059**	**38,869,273**	**22,432,414**	**7,983,866**	**26,155,099**
New cars	66,672,337	26,354,982	35,511,601	5,337,046	15,065,497	15,107,680	3,987,592	14,735,588
New trucks	68,238,755	24,975,069	40,594,764	9,465,013	23,803,624	7,324,814	3,996,274	11,419,511
Cars and trucks, used	**129,190,067**	**37,386,661**	**78,472,039**	**14,041,953**	**43,043,624**	**21,383,957**	**10,720,015**	**27,957,258**
Used cars	72,049,583	23,738,949	40,988,611	8,059,846	19,715,035	13,212,148	7,560,617	19,753,668
Used trucks	57,140,483	13,647,711	37,483,428	5,982,107	23,328,437	8,171,808	3,159,399	8,203,259
Other vehicles	**5,686,141**	**1,397,945**	**4,154,685**	**1,059,699**	**1,906,832**	**1,188,042**	**363,285**	**819,433**
New motorcycles	3,114,830	787,861	2,326,808	694,484	644,126	988,187	346,730	230,063
Used motorcycles	2,571,311	610,084	1,827,877	365,214	1,262,706	199,855	16,556	589,371
GASOLINE AND MOTOR OIL	**91,200,501**	**31,095,097**	**52,036,198**	**8,287,551**	**26,775,789**	**16,971,068**	**6,138,164**	**21,357,827**
Gasoline	82,811,952	27,454,937	47,831,418	7,601,997	24,539,595	15,688,201	5,748,497	19,180,164
Diesel fuel	861,980	293,136	527,145	55,803	276,445	195,034	44,553	132,881
Gasoline on trips	6,697,223	3,076,543	3,201,736	552,869	1,730,291	918,515	307,696	1,864,302
Motor oil	761,265	239,734	443,366	71,279	211,972	159,997	34,390	161,639
Motor oil on trips	67,518	30,978	32,245	5,602	17,487	9,241	3,096	18,841
OTHER VEHICLE EXPENSES	**184,966,124**	**65,144,906**	**105,050,392**	**17,614,609**	**53,085,058**	**34,341,846**	**11,068,225**	**43,178,094**
Vehicle finance charges	**31,735,148**	**10,153,888**	**18,693,059**	**3,448,903**	**9,746,134**	**5,497,347**	**1,700,267**	**4,721,576**
Automobile finance charges	14,175,404	5,023,310	7,742,783	1,618,892	3,414,659	2,709,016	1,043,150	2,853,308
Truck finance charges	15,664,176	4,409,527	9,879,289	1,725,561	5,721,562	2,431,774	576,626	1,666,303
Motorcycle and plane finance charges	160,355	27,742	121,782	15,032	78,159	28,528	10,230	49,583
Other vehicle finance charges	1,734,650	693,309	949,206	89,473	531,754	328,030	70,261	152,714
Maintenance and repairs	**50,622,746**	**18,580,861**	**28,574,363**	**4,588,589**	**14,811,860**	**9,168,674**	**3,016,453**	**14,449,332**
Coolant, additives, brake, transmission fluids	280,200	86,461	162,664	22,465	81,048	59,065	20,796	65,118
Tires—purchased, replaced, installed	6,721,417	2,506,454	3,714,486	571,175	1,889,650	1,253,375	363,891	1,607,795
Parts, equipment, and accessories	3,172,783	1,172,545	1,706,383	253,886	812,913	639,585	133,994	635,978
Vehicle audio equipment, excl. labor	880,547	–	907,461	416,302	147,498	345,709	8,278	366,580
Vehicle products	427,614	146,568	257,671	12,148	173,500	72,404	7,470	71,399
Miscellaneous auto repair, servicing	3,163,218	1,260,162	1,696,595	179,279	1,191,238	319,672	139,580	922,896
Body work and painting	2,340,061	891,199	1,292,959	124,197	710,881	457,731	142,003	591,354
Clutch, transmission repair	3,540,756	1,042,622	2,228,346	277,960	1,232,598	717,776	154,992	1,053,793
Drive shaft and rear-end repair	429,302	132,235	296,825	15,476	168,635	112,584	24,497	200,644
Brake work	4,192,305	1,543,358	2,384,388	402,601	1,184,547	797,332	277,478	1,072,304
Repair to steering or front-end	1,200,132	476,693	652,381	72,499	302,143	277,644	91,461	410,213
Repair to engine cooling system	1,429,131	487,559	843,835	125,251	462,110	256,429	128,880	578,793
Motor tune-up	3,500,808	1,516,310	1,659,744	339,698	858,835	461,025	183,527	1,120,895
Lube, oil change, and oil filters	4,727,385	1,916,251	2,492,350	404,709	1,270,157	817,422	298,476	1,374,757
Front-end alignment, wheel balance, rotation	818,656	332,206	414,864	46,317	198,742	169,720	66,762	274,687
Shock absorber replacement	437,179	96,633	316,402	38,219	176,238	101,816	20,998	41,319
Gas tank repair, replacement	342,091	88,773	249,321	31,618	159,207	58,261	22,546	39,335
Tire repair and other repair work	2,870,078	1,238,894	1,534,795	227,094	869,175	438,525	123,899	979,750
Vehicle air conditioning repair	1,258,648	529,633	623,304	127,415	312,483	183,382	81,366	325,592
Exhaust system repair	747,762	332,899	356,708	36,333	195,093	125,121	67,435	273,034

	total married couples	married couples, no children	married couples with children				single parent, at least one child <18	single person
			total	oldest child under 6	oldest child 6 to 17	oldest child 18 or older		
Electrical system repair	$1,932,703	$755,034	$1,059,184	$132,851	$548,480	$377,853	$186,825	$648,870
Motor repair, replacement	5,594,992	1,833,026	3,331,867	704,524	1,598,607	1,028,608	439,402	1,589,615
Auto repair service policy	616,102	194,885	392,120	26,626	267,778	97,637	31,968	205,272
Vehicle insurance	**65,087,352**	**23,458,528**	**35,887,599**	**5,508,559**	**17,335,144**	**13,042,749**	**4,324,160**	**16,063,077**
Vehicle rental, leases, licenses, other charges	**37,520,878**	**12,951,628**	**21,895,371**	**4,068,558**	**11,192,072**	**6,632,995**	**2,027,345**	**7,944,108**
Leased and rented vehicles	26,058,572	8,665,782	15,495,930	2,886,104	7,825,768	4,783,670	1,338,664	4,483,911
Rented vehicles	3,209,356	1,465,681	1,500,823	175,563	891,376	434,024	107,007	765,223
Auto rental	419,737	180,089	198,075	20,247	99,599	78,271	39,169	139,162
Auto rental on trips	2,316,430	1,132,088	1,011,105	125,640	583,758	301,430	60,503	522,930
Truck rental	124,908	34,446	80,324	3,883	64,626	11,813	3,298	29,750
Truck rental on trips	315,084	109,117	188,862	25,794	130,163	33,028	4,038	46,608
Leased vehicles	22,849,217	7,200,101	13,995,107	2,710,597	6,934,392	4,349,646	1,231,657	3,718,688
Car lease payments	11,455,554	4,105,988	6,742,906	1,560,205	2,823,450	2,359,048	576,357	2,248,401
Truck lease payments	10,005,042	2,548,297	6,565,272	1,002,787	3,861,564	1,700,739	395,791	1,323,853
Vehicle registration, state	5,583,176	2,142,345	3,061,241	473,104	1,703,528	884,442	251,837	1,399,218
Vehicle registration, local	541,832	180,783	323,024	77,658	168,939	76,342	48,187	174,861
Driver's license	455,184	180,783	238,957	41,603	112,829	84,619	30,218	137,178
Vehicle inspection	689,809	248,056	369,088	81,097	161,640	126,406	38,630	176,844
Parking fees	1,914,698	684,524	1,136,341	263,538	588,168	284,394	115,352	837,944
Parking fees in home city, excl. residence	1,510,153	503,048	934,811	230,977	477,164	226,615	101,690	739,771
Parking fees on trips	404,545	181,476	201,242	32,561	111,004	57,779	13,662	98,173
Tolls	758,452	218,696	484,824	117,541	245,121	121,022	94,220	207,585
Tolls on trips	281,325	114,665	149,708	34,391	77,855	37,528	12,787	89,579
Towing charges	302,143	85,305	197,499	50,866	77,094	69,752	56,801	127,592
Automobile service clubs	935,687	430,457	438,472	42,601	231,131	164,899	40,649	309,395
PUBLIC TRANSPORTATION	**27,883,809**	**12,282,825**	**13,110,390**	**2,253,968**	**6,675,130**	**4,182,979**	**1,070,945**	**9,121,527**
Airline fares	18,319,321	7,665,929	8,977,586	1,517,160	4,710,515	2,749,517	510,605	5,552,909
Intercity bus fares	770,831	307,932	400,181	58,133	175,933	166,104	19,921	336,500
Intracity mass transit fares	2,691,155	755,496	1,531,340	334,484	693,698	503,054	290,601	1,276,254
Local transportation on trips	734,821	302,846	379,452	55,026	176,390	147,943	17,700	328,897
Taxi fares and limousine service on trips	431,553	178,009	222,835	32,339	103,553	86,869	10,364	193,372
Taxi fares and limousine service	1,047,654	524,316	477,914	37,276	281,767	160,961	127,803	757,951
Intercity train fares	1,179,314	679,669	433,865	46,872	217,446	169,720	19,248	388,396
Ship fares	2,612,947	1,866,085	606,605	172,734	277,814	156,139	52,359	263,118
School bus	96,213	2,543	80,612	–	38,015	42,591	22,344	23,800

Note: Total spending figures for total consumer units can be found on Total Spending by Age and Total Spending by Region tables. Spending by type of consumer unit will not add to total because not all types of consumer units are shown. (–) means sample is too small to make a reliable estimate.
Source: Calculations by New Strategist based on the 2002 Consumer Expenditure Survey

Table 11.12 Transportation: Market shares by household type, 2002

(percentage of total annual spending on transportation accounted for by types of consumer units, 2002)

	total married couples	married couples, no children	married couples with children				single parent, at least one child <18	single person
			total	oldest child under 6	oldest child 6 to 17	oldest child 18 or older		
Share of total consumer units	50.2%	20.6%	25.7%	4.9%	13.6%	7.2%	6.0%	29.5%
Share of total before-tax income	68.2	24.6	38.4	6.8	20.0	11.8	3.3	16.1
Share of total spending	64.6	23.1	36.5	6.4	19.4	10.7	4.5	17.5
Share of transportation spending	66.0	22.8	37.8	6.7	19.6	11.6	4.3	14.8
VEHICLE PURCHASES	**65.7%**	**21.9%**	**38.6%**	**7.3%**	**20.4%**	**11.0%**	**4.6%**	**13.4%**
Cars and trucks, new	**68.6**	**26.1**	**38.7**	**7.5**	**19.8**	**11.4**	**4.1**	**13.3**
New cars	67.3	26.6	35.9	5.4	15.2	15.3	4.0	14.9
New trucks	70.0	25.6	41.6	9.7	24.4	7.5	4.1	11.7
Cars and trucks, used	**62.6**	**18.1**	**38.0**	**6.8**	**20.8**	**10.4**	**5.2**	**13.5**
Used cars	57.7	19.0	32.8	6.5	15.8	10.6	6.1	15.8
Used trucks	69.9	16.7	45.9	7.3	28.6	10.0	3.9	10.0
Other vehicles	**72.8**	**17.9**	**53.2**	**13.6**	**24.4**	**15.2**	**4.7**	**10.5**
New motorcycles	76.6	19.4	57.2	17.1	15.8	24.3	8.5	5.7
Used motorcycles	68.6	16.3	48.8	9.7	33.7	5.3	0.4	15.7
GASOLINE AND MOTOR OIL	**65.9**	**22.5**	**37.6**	**6.0**	**19.3**	**12.3**	**4.4**	**15.4**
Gasoline	65.7	21.8	37.9	6.0	19.5	12.4	4.6	15.2
Diesel fuel	70.8	24.1	43.3	4.6	22.7	16.0	3.7	10.9
Gasoline on trips	67.7	31.1	32.4	5.6	17.5	9.3	3.1	18.8
Motor oil	67.6	21.3	39.4	6.3	18.8	14.2	3.1	14.3
Motor oil on trips	67.7	31.0	32.3	5.6	17.5	9.3	3.1	18.9
OTHER VEHICLE EXPENSES	**66.8**	**23.5**	**37.9**	**6.4**	**19.2**	**12.4**	**4.0**	**15.6**
Vehicle finance charges	**71.3**	**22.8**	**42.0**	**7.7**	**21.9**	**12.4**	**3.8**	**10.6**
Automobile finance charges	65.5	23.2	35.8	7.5	15.8	12.5	4.8	13.2
Truck finance charges	76.4	21.5	48.2	8.4	27.9	11.9	2.8	8.1
Motorcycle and plane finance charges	60.6	10.5	46.0	5.7	29.5	10.8	3.9	18.7
Other vehicle finance charges	82.9	33.1	45.4	4.3	25.4	15.7	3.4	7.3
Maintenance and repairs	**64.8**	**23.8**	**36.6**	**5.9**	**18.9**	**11.7**	**3.9**	**18.5**
Coolant, additives, brake, transmission fluids	65.4	20.2	38.0	5.2	18.9	13.8	4.9	15.2
Tires—purchased, replaced, installed	66.7	24.9	36.8	5.7	18.7	12.4	3.6	15.9
Parts, equipment, and accessories	67.9	25.1	36.5	5.4	17.4	13.7	2.9	13.6
Vehicle audio equipment, excl. labor	63.8	–	65.7	30.1	10.7	25.0	0.6	26.5
Vehicle products	77.5	26.6	46.7	2.2	31.5	13.1	1.4	12.9
Miscellaneous auto repair, servicing	64.6	25.7	34.6	3.7	24.3	6.5	2.8	18.8
Body work and painting	66.8	25.4	36.9	3.5	20.3	13.1	4.1	16.9
Clutch, transmission repair	64.9	19.1	40.8	5.1	22.6	13.2	2.8	19.3
Drive shaft and rear-end repair	58.8	18.1	40.7	2.1	23.1	15.4	3.4	27.5
Brake work	64.8	23.8	36.8	6.2	18.3	12.3	4.3	16.6
Repair to steering or front-end	63.3	25.1	34.4	3.8	15.9	14.6	4.8	21.6
Repair to engine cooling system	58.8	20.1	34.7	5.2	19.0	10.6	5.3	23.8
Motor tune-up	62.8	27.2	29.8	6.1	15.4	8.3	3.3	20.1
Lube, oil change, and oil filters	64.8	26.3	34.2	5.5	17.4	11.2	4.1	18.8
Front-end alignment, wheel balance, rotation	61.4	24.9	31.1	3.5	14.9	12.7	5.0	20.6
Shock absorber replacement	80.9	17.9	58.6	7.1	32.6	18.8	3.9	7.6
Gas tank repair, replacement	70.6	18.3	51.5	6.5	32.9	12.0	4.7	8.1
Tire repair and other repair work	64.3	27.7	34.4	5.1	19.5	9.8	2.8	21.9
Vehicle air conditioning repair	66.0	27.8	32.7	6.7	16.4	9.6	4.3	17.1
Exhaust system repair	53.1	23.6	25.3	2.6	13.9	8.9	4.8	19.4

	total married couples	married couples, no children	married couples with children				single parent, at least one child <18	single person
			total	oldest child under 6	oldest child 6 to 17	oldest child 18 or older		
Electrical system repair	60.7%	23.7%	33.2%	4.2%	17.2%	11.9%	5.9%	20.4%
Motor repair, replacement	65.1	21.3	38.8	8.2	18.6	12.0	5.1	18.5
Auto repair service policy	69.3	21.9	44.1	3.0	30.1	11.0	3.6	23.1
Vehicle insurance	**65.0**	**23.4**	**35.8**	**5.5**	**17.3**	**13.0**	**4.3**	**16.0**
Vehicle rental, leases, licenses, other charges	**69.3**	**23.9**	**40.5**	**7.5**	**20.7**	**12.3**	**3.7**	**14.7**
Leased and rented vehicles	71.6	23.8	42.6	7.9	21.5	13.2	3.7	12.3
Rented vehicles	69.3	31.6	32.4	3.8	19.2	9.4	2.3	16.5
Auto rental	55.4	23.8	26.1	2.7	13.1	10.3	5.2	18.4
Auto rental on trips	73.1	35.7	31.9	4.0	18.4	9.5	1.9	16.5
Truck rental	50.4	13.9	32.4	1.6	26.1	4.8	1.3	12.0
Truck rental on trips	79.2	27.4	47.5	6.5	32.7	8.3	1.0	11.7
Leased vehicles	72.0	22.7	44.1	8.5	21.8	13.7	3.9	11.7
Car lease payments	68.3	24.5	40.2	9.3	16.8	14.1	3.4	13.4
Truck lease payments	78.1	19.9	51.3	7.8	30.2	13.3	3.1	10.3
Vehicle registration, state	68.4	26.2	37.5	5.8	20.9	10.8	3.1	17.1
Vehicle registration, local	62.3	20.8	37.1	8.9	19.4	8.8	5.5	20.1
Driver's license	64.9	25.8	34.0	5.9	16.1	12.1	4.3	19.5
Vehicle inspection	66.4	23.9	35.6	7.8	15.6	12.2	3.7	17.0
Parking fees	58.4	20.9	34.7	8.0	17.9	8.7	3.5	25.6
Parking fees in home city, excl. residence	55.6	18.5	34.4	8.5	17.6	8.3	3.7	27.2
Parking fees on trips	72.0	32.3	35.8	5.8	19.8	10.3	2.4	17.5
Tolls	63.9	18.4	40.8	9.9	20.6	10.2	7.9	17.5
Tolls on trips	63.7	26.0	33.9	7.8	17.6	8.5	2.9	20.3
Towing charges	48.1	13.6	31.5	8.1	12.3	11.1	9.0	20.3
Automobile service clubs	65.5	30.1	30.7	3.0	16.2	11.5	2.8	21.6
PUBLIC TRANSPORTATION	**64.0**	**28.2**	**30.1**	**5.2**	**15.3**	**9.6**	**2.5**	**20.9**
Airline fares	67.1	28.1	32.9	5.6	17.3	10.1	1.9	20.3
Intercity bus fares	59.9	23.9	31.1	4.5	13.7	12.9	1.5	26.1
Intracity mass transit fares	48.0	13.5	27.3	6.0	12.4	9.0	5.2	22.8
Local transportation on trips	60.1	24.8	31.0	4.5	14.4	12.1	1.4	26.9
Taxi fares and limousine service on trips	60.1	24.8	31.0	4.5	14.4	12.1	1.4	26.9
Taxi fares and limousine service	49.3	24.7	22.5	1.8	13.3	7.6	6.0	35.7
Intercity train fares	65.4	37.7	24.1	2.6	12.1	9.4	1.1	21.5
Ship fares	78.4	56.0	18.2	5.2	8.3	4.7	1.6	7.9
School bus	52.3	1.4	43.8	–	20.7	23.2	12.2	12.9

Note: Market share for total consumer units is 100.0%. Market shares by type of consumer unit will not add to total because not all types of consumer units are shown. (–) means sample is too small to make a reliable estimate.
Source: Calculations by New Strategist based on the 2002 Consumer Expenditure Survey

Table 11.13 Transportation: Average spending by race and Hispanic origin, 2002

(average annual spending by consumer units (CU) on transportation, by race and Hispanic origin of consumer unit reference person, 2002)

	total consumer units	race		Hispanic origin	
		black	white and other	Hispanic	non-Hispanic
Number of consumer units (in thousands, add 000)	112,108	13,554	98,553	10,500	101,608
Average number of persons per CU	2.5	2.7	2.5	3.3	2.4
Average before-tax income of CU	$49,430.00	$35,944.00	$51,177.00	$37,360.00	$50,742.00
Average spending of CU, total	40,676.60	30,135.94	42,134.55	34,742.47	41,294.67
Transportation, average spending	7,759.29	5,447.13	8,077.47	6,768.97	7,861.31
VEHICLE PURCHASES	**$3,664.93**	**$2,420.14**	**$3,836.12**	**$3,129.59**	**$3,720.24**
Cars and trucks, new	**1,752.96**	**999.59**	**1,856.57**	**1,148.94**	**1,815.38**
New cars	883.08	740.57	902.68	555.32	916.95
New trucks	869.88	259.03	953.89	593.63	898.42
Cars and trucks, used	**1,842.29**	**1,409.59**	**1,901.80**	**1,899.54**	**1,836.37**
Used cars	1,113.46	1,032.80	1,124.56	990.82	1,126.14
Used trucks	728.82	376.78	777.24	908.73	710.23
Other vehicles	**69.68**	**10.95**	**77.76**	**81.11**	**68.50**
New motorcycles	36.26	10.72	39.77	50.78	34.75
Used motorcycles	33.42	0.23	37.99	30.33	33.74
GASOLINE AND MOTOR OIL	**1,235.06**	**924.54**	**1,277.76**	**1,261.05**	**1,232.37**
Gasoline	1,125.01	875.17	1,159.38	1,180.08	1,119.32
Diesel fuel	10.86	2.07	12.07	9.07	11.05
Gasoline on trips	88.24	40.65	94.79	59.79	91.19
Motor oil	10.05	6.25	10.57	11.51	9.89
Motor oil on trips	0.89	0.41	0.96	0.60	0.92
OTHER VEHICLE EXPENSES	**2,470.55**	**1,874.55**	**2,552.70**	**2,061.77**	**2,512.51**
Vehicle finance charges	**397.04**	**334.60**	**405.63**	**407.13**	**396.00**
Automobile finance charges	193.12	236.73	187.12	185.02	193.96
Truck finance charges	182.89	97.32	194.66	209.61	180.13
Motorcycle and plane finance charges	2.36	–	2.68	0.91	2.51
Other vehicle finance charges	18.67	0.55	21.17	11.59	19.41
Maintenance and repairs	**697.30**	**498.82**	**724.78**	**528.62**	**714.43**
Coolant, additives, brake, transmission fluids	3.82	2.63	3.99	5.53	3.64
Tires—purchased, replaced, installed	89.93	66.57	93.14	70.18	91.97
Parts, equipment, and accessories	41.70	18.65	44.87	42.90	41.57
Vehicle audio equipment, excl. labor	12.32	–	14.07	0.89	13.40
Vehicle products	4.92	0.36	5.57	5.11	4.91
Miscellaneous auto repair, servicing	43.69	17.23	47.44	22.13	45.73
Body work and painting	31.24	21.62	32.57	25.49	31.84
Clutch, transmission repair	48.68	42.34	49.55	40.04	49.57
Drive shaft and rear-end repair	6.51	6.46	6.52	0.33	7.15
Brake work	57.73	48.05	59.06	47.61	58.77
Repair to steering or front-end	16.91	5.51	18.48	13.02	17.32
Repair to engine cooling system	21.68	20.02	21.90	13.17	22.56
Motor tune-up	49.69	42.82	50.63	34.23	51.29
Lube, oil change, and oil filters	65.07	47.00	67.56	54.54	66.16
Front-end alignment, wheel balance, rotation	11.90	9.62	12.21	5.84	12.52
Shock absorber replacement	4.82	2.72	5.11	4.50	4.86
Gas tank repair, replacement	4.32	4.63	4.28	2.86	4.46
Tire repair and other repair work	39.83	27.37	41.54	24.05	41.46
Vehicle air conditioning repair	17.00	11.25	17.79	12.45	17.47
Exhaust system repair	12.56	8.58	13.11	8.86	12.95

	total consumer units	race		Hispanic origin	
		black	white and other	Hispanic	non-Hispanic
Electrical system repair	$28.42	$33.23	$27.76	$14.90	$29.82
Motor repair, replacement	76.62	61.27	78.73	74.20	76.87
Auto repair service policy	7.93	0.90	8.89	5.78	8.15
Vehicle insurance	**893.50**	**691.81**	**921.24**	**799.19**	**903.25**
Vehicle rental, leases, licenses, other charges	**482.71**	**349.33**	**501.06**	**326.83**	**498.84**
Leased and rented vehicles	324.48	241.67	335.87	190.39	338.34
Rented vehicles	41.33	25.77	43.47	22.05	43.32
Auto rental	6.76	5.88	6.88	4.78	6.96
Auto rental on trips	28.28	12.85	30.40	12.62	29.90
Truck rental	2.21	2.84	2.12	0.99	2.33
Truck rental on trips	3.55	3.57	3.55	3.66	3.54
Leased vehicles	283.15	215.90	292.40	168.35	295.01
Car lease payments	149.63	127.65	152.65	77.66	157.06
Truck lease payments	114.24	80.70	118.86	84.06	117.36
Vehicle registration, state	72.82	42.66	76.96	61.95	73.94
Vehicle registration, local	7.76	8.94	7.60	8.80	7.65
Driver's license	6.26	4.87	6.45	4.59	6.43
Vehicle inspection	9.26	8.13	9.41	11.72	9.00
Parking fees	29.25	19.36	30.61	22.04	30.00
Parking fees in home city, excl. residence	24.24	17.30	25.20	18.79	24.80
Parking fees on trips	5.01	2.06	5.42	3.25	5.20
Tolls	10.59	9.08	10.80	13.94	10.27
Tolls on trips	3.94	2.72	4.11	2.61	4.08
Towing charges	5.60	5.72	5.58	4.90	5.67
Automobile service clubs	12.75	6.18	13.65	5.89	13.46
PUBLIC TRANSPORTATION	**388.75**	**227.91**	**410.88**	**316.56**	**396.18**
Airline fares	243.57	96.32	263.82	155.36	252.68
Intercity bus fares	11.48	7.49	12.03	13.35	11.29
Intracity mass transit fares	49.97	79.83	45.87	96.10	45.21
Local transportation on trips	10.91	3.72	11.90	5.94	11.42
Taxi fares and limousine service on trips	6.41	2.18	6.99	3.49	6.71
Taxi fares and limousine service	18.95	16.82	19.25	15.47	19.27
Intercity train fares	16.09	6.18	17.46	8.57	16.87
Ship fares	29.74	12.63	32.09	15.31	31.23
School bus	1.64	2.73	1.49	2.98	1.50

Note: Other races include Asians, Native Americans, and Pacific Islanders. (–) means sample is too small to make a reliable estimate.
Source: Bureau of Labor Statistics, unpublished tables from the 2002 Consumer Expenditure Survey

Table 11.14 Transportation: Indexed spending by race and Hispanic origin, 2002

(indexed average annual spending of consumer units (CU) on transportation, by race and Hispanic origin of consumer unit reference person, 2002; index definition: an index of 100 is the average for all consumer units; an index of 132 means that spending by consumer units in that group is 32 percent above the average for all consumer units; an index of 68 indicates spending that is 32 percent below the average for all consumer units)

	total consumer units	race black	race white and other	Hispanic origin Hispanic	Hispanic origin non-Hispanic
Average spending of CU, total	$40,677	$30,136	$42,135	$34,742	$41,295
Average spending of CU, index	100	74	104	85	102
Transportation, spending index	100	70	104	87	101
VEHICLE PURCHASES	100	66	105	85	102
Cars and trucks, new	100	57	106	66	104
New cars	100	84	102	63	104
New trucks	100	30	110	68	103
Cars and trucks, used	100	77	103	103	100
Used cars	100	93	101	89	101
Used trucks	100	52	107	125	97
Other vehicles	100	16	112	116	98
New motorcycles	100	30	110	140	96
Used motorcycles	100	1	114	91	101
GASOLINE AND MOTOR OIL	100	75	103	102	100
Gasoline	100	78	103	105	99
Diesel fuel	100	19	111	84	102
Gasoline on trips	100	46	107	68	103
Motor oil	100	62	105	115	98
Motor oil on trips	100	46	108	67	103
OTHER VEHICLE EXPENSES	100	76	103	83	102
Vehicle finance charges	100	84	102	103	100
Automobile finance charges	100	123	97	96	100
Truck finance charges	100	53	106	115	98
Motorcycle and plane finance charges	100	–	114	39	106
Other vehicle finance charges	100	3	113	62	104
Maintenance and repairs	100	72	104	76	102
Coolant, additives, brake, transmission fluids	100	69	104	145	95
Tires—purchased, replaced, installed	100	74	104	78	102
Parts, equipment, and accessories	100	45	108	103	100
Vehicle audio equipment, excl. labor	100	–	114	7	109
Vehicle products	100	7	113	104	100
Miscellaneous auto repair, servicing	100	39	109	51	105
Body work and painting	100	69	104	82	102
Clutch, transmission repair	100	87	102	82	102
Drive shaft and rear-end repair	100	99	100	5	110
Brake work	100	83	102	82	102
Repair to steering or front-end	100	33	109	77	102
Repair to engine cooling system	100	92	101	61	104
Motor tune-up	100	86	102	69	103
Lube, oil change, and oil filters	100	72	104	84	102
Front-end alignment, wheel balance, rotation	100	81	103	49	105
Shock absorber replacement	100	56	106	93	101
Gas tank repair, replacement	100	107	99	66	103
Tire repair and other repair work	100	69	104	60	104
Vehicle air conditioning repair	100	66	105	73	103
Exhaust system repair	100	68	104	71	103

	total consumer units	race		Hispanic origin	
		black	white and other	Hispanic	non-Hispanic
Electrical system repair	100	117	98	52	105
Motor repair, replacement	100	80	103	97	100
Auto repair service policy	100	11	112	73	103
Vehicle insurance	**100**	**77**	**103**	**89**	**101**
Vehicle rental, leases, licenses, other charges	**100**	**72**	**104**	**68**	**103**
Leased and rented vehicles	100	74	104	59	104
Rented vehicles	100	62	105	53	105
Auto rental	100	87	102	71	103
Auto rental on trips	100	45	107	45	106
Truck rental	100	129	96	45	105
Truck rental on trips	100	101	100	103	100
Leased vehicles	100	76	103	59	104
Car lease payments	100	85	102	52	105
Truck lease payments	100	71	104	74	103
Vehicle registration, state	100	59	106	85	102
Vehicle registration, local	100	115	98	113	99
Driver's license	100	78	103	73	103
Vehicle inspection	100	88	102	127	97
Parking fees	100	66	105	75	103
Parking fees in home city, excl. residence	100	71	104	78	102
Parking fees on trips	100	41	108	65	104
Tolls	100	86	102	132	97
Tolls on trips	100	69	104	66	104
Towing charges	100	102	100	88	101
Automobile service clubs	100	48	107	46	106
PUBLIC TRANSPORTATION	**100**	**59**	**106**	**81**	**102**
Airline fares	100	40	108	64	104
Intercity bus fares	100	65	105	116	98
Intracity mass transit fares	100	160	92	192	90
Local transportation on trips	100	34	109	54	105
Taxi fares and limousine service on trips	100	34	109	54	105
Taxi fares and limousine service	100	89	102	82	102
Intercity train fares	100	38	109	53	105
Ship fares	100	42	108	51	105
School bus	100	166	91	182	91

Note: Other races include Asians, Native Americans, and Pacific Islanders. (–) means sample is too small to make a reliable estimate.
Source: Calculations by New Strategist based on the 2002 Consumer Expenditure Survey

Table 11.15 Transportation: Total spending by race and Hispanic origin, 2002

(total annual spending on transportation, by consumer unit race and Hispanic origin groups, 2002; numbers in thousands)

	total consumer units	race — black	race — white and other	Hispanic origin — Hispanic	Hispanic origin — non-Hispanic
Number of consumer units	112,108	13,554	98,553	10,500	101,608
Total spending of all consumer units	$4,560,172,273	$408,462,531	$4,152,486,306	$364,795,935	$4,195,868,829
Transportation, total spending	869,878,483	73,830,400	796,058,901	71,074,185	798,771,986
VEHICLE PURCHASES	**$410,867,972**	**$32,802,578**	**$378,061,134**	**$32,860,695**	**$378,006,146**
Cars and trucks, new	**196,520,840**	**13,548,443**	**182,970,543**	**12,063,870**	**184,457,131**
New cars	99,000,333	10,037,686	88,961,822	5,830,860	93,169,456
New trucks	97,520,507	3,510,893	94,008,721	6,233,115	91,286,659
Cars and trucks, used	**206,535,447**	**19,105,583**	**187,428,095**	**19,945,170**	**186,589,883**
Used cars	124,827,774	13,998,571	110,828,762	10,403,610	114,424,833
Used trucks	81,706,553	5,106,876	76,599,334	9,541,665	72,165,050
Other vehicles	**7,811,685**	**148,416**	**7,663,481**	**851,655**	**6,960,148**
New motorcycles	4,065,036	145,299	3,919,453	533,190	3,530,878
Used motorcycles	3,746,649	3,117	3,744,028	318,465	3,428,254
GASOLINE AND MOTOR OIL	**138,460,106**	**12,531,215**	**125,927,081**	**13,241,025**	**125,218,651**
Gasoline	126,122,621	11,862,054	114,260,377	12,390,840	113,731,867
Diesel fuel	1,217,493	28,057	1,189,535	95,235	1,122,768
Gasoline on trips	9,892,410	550,970	9,341,839	627,795	9,265,634
Motor oil	1,126,685	84,713	1,041,705	120,855	1,004,903
Motor oil on trips	99,776	5,557	94,611	6,300	93,479
OTHER VEHICLE EXPENSES	**276,968,419**	**25,407,651**	**251,576,243**	**21,648,585**	**255,291,116**
Vehicle finance charges	**44,511,360**	**4,535,168**	**39,976,053**	**4,274,865**	**40,236,768**
Automobile finance charges	21,650,297	3,208,638	18,441,237	1,942,710	19,707,888
Truck finance charges	20,503,432	1,319,075	19,184,327	2,200,905	18,302,649
Motorcycle and plane finance charges	264,575	–	264,122	9,555	255,036
Other vehicle finance charges	2,093,056	7,455	2,086,367	121,695	1,972,211
Maintenance and repairs	**78,172,908**	**6,761,006**	**71,429,243**	**5,550,510**	**72,591,803**
Coolant, additives, brake, transmission fluids	428,253	35,647	393,226	58,065	369,853
Tires—purchased, replaced, installed	10,081,872	902,290	9,179,226	736,890	9,344,888
Parts, equipment, and accessories	4,674,904	252,782	4,422,073	450,450	4,223,845
Vehicle audio equipment, excl. labor	1,381,171	–	1,381,171	9,345	1,361,547
Vehicle products	551,571	4,879	548,940	53,655	498,895
Miscellaneous auto repair, servicing	4,897,999	233,535	4,675,354	232,365	4,646,534
Body work and painting	3,502,254	293,037	3,209,871	267,645	3,235,199
Clutch, transmission repair	5,457,417	573,876	4,883,301	420,420	5,036,709
Drive shaft and rear-end repair	729,823	87,559	642,566	3,465	726,497
Brake work	6,471,995	651,270	5,820,540	499,905	5,971,502
Repair to steering or front-end	1,895,746	74,683	1,821,259	136,710	1,759,851
Repair to engine cooling system	2,430,501	271,351	2,158,311	138,285	2,292,276
Motor tune-up	5,570,647	580,382	4,989,738	359,415	5,211,474
Lube, oil change, and oil filters	7,294,868	637,038	6,658,241	572,670	6,722,385
Front-end alignment, wheel balance, rotation	1,334,085	130,389	1,203,332	61,320	1,272,132
Shock absorber replacement	540,361	36,867	503,606	47,250	493,815
Gas tank repair, replacement	484,307	62,755	421,807	30,030	453,172
Tire repair and other repair work	4,465,262	370,973	4,093,892	252,525	4,212,668
Vehicle air conditioning repair	1,905,836	152,483	1,753,258	130,725	1,775,092
Exhaust system repair	1,408,076	116,293	1,292,030	93,030	1,315,824

	total consumer units	race		Hispanic origin	
		black	white and other	Hispanic	non-Hispanic
Electrical system repair	$3,186,109	$450,399	$2,735,831	$156,450	$3,029,951
Motor repair, replacement	8,589,715	830,454	7,759,078	779,100	7,810,607
Auto repair service policy	889,016	12,199	876,136	60,690	828,105
Vehicle insurance	**100,168,498**	**9,376,793**	**90,790,966**	**8,391,495**	**91,777,426**
Vehicle rental, leases, licenses, other charges	**54,115,653**	**4,734,819**	**49,380,966**	**3,431,715**	**50,686,135**
Leased and rented vehicles	36,376,804	3,275,595	33,100,996	1,999,095	34,378,051
Rented vehicles	4,633,424	349,287	4,284,099	231,525	4,401,659
Auto rental	757,850	79,698	678,045	50,190	707,192
Auto rental on trips	3,170,414	174,169	2,996,011	132,510	3,038,079
Truck rental	247,759	38,493	208,932	10,395	236,747
Truck rental on trips	397,983	48,388	349,863	38,430	359,692
Leased vehicles	31,743,380	2,926,309	28,816,897	1,767,675	29,975,376
Car lease payments	16,774,720	1,730,168	15,044,115	815,430	15,958,552
Truck lease payments	12,807,218	1,093,808	11,714,010	882,630	11,924,715
Vehicle registration, state	8,163,705	578,214	7,584,639	650,475	7,512,896
Vehicle registration, local	869,958	121,173	749,003	92,400	777,301
Driver's license	701,796	66,008	635,667	48,195	653,339
Vehicle inspection	1,038,120	110,194	927,384	123,060	914,472
Parking fees	3,279,159	262,405	3,016,707	231,420	3,048,240
Parking fees in home city, excl. residence	2,717,498	234,484	2,483,536	197,295	2,519,878
Parking fees on trips	561,661	27,921	534,157	34,125	528,362
Tolls	1,187,224	123,070	1,064,372	146,370	1,043,514
Tolls on trips	441,706	36,867	405,053	27,405	414,561
Towing charges	627,805	77,529	549,926	51,450	576,117
Automobile service clubs	1,429,377	83,764	1,345,248	61,845	1,367,644
PUBLIC TRANSPORTATION	**43,581,985**	**3,089,092**	**40,493,457**	**3,323,880**	**40,255,057**
Airline fares	27,306,146	1,305,521	26,000,252	1,631,280	25,674,309
Intercity bus fares	1,287,000	101,519	1,185,593	140,175	1,147,154
Intracity mass transit fares	5,602,037	1,082,016	4,520,626	1,009,050	4,593,698
Local transportation on trips	1,223,098	50,421	1,172,781	62,370	1,160,363
Taxi fares and limousine service on trips	718,612	29,548	688,885	36,645	681,790
Taxi fares and limousine service	2,124,447	227,978	1,897,145	162,435	1,957,986
Intercity train fares	1,803,818	83,764	1,720,735	89,985	1,714,127
Ship fares	3,334,092	171,187	3,162,566	160,755	3,173,218
School bus	183,857	37,002	146,844	31,290	152,412

Note: Other races include Asians, Native Americans, and Pacific Islanders. Numbers may not add to total because of rounding. (−) means sample is too small to make a reliable estimate.
Source: Calculations by New Strategist based on the 2002 Consumer Expenditure Survey

Table 11.16 Transportation: Market shares by race and Hispanic origin, 2002

(percentage of total annual spending on transportation accounted for by consumer unit race and Hispanic origin groups, 2002)

	total consumer units	race black	race white and other	Hispanic origin Hispanic	Hispanic origin non-Hispanic
Share of total consumer units	100.0%	12.1%	87.9%	9.4%	90.6%
Share of total before-tax income	100.0	8.8	91.0	7.1	93.0
Share of total spending	100.0	9.0	91.1	8.0	92.0
Share of transportation spending	100.0	8.5	91.5	8.2	91.8
VEHICLE PURCHASES	100.0%	8.0%	92.0%	8.0%	92.0%
Cars and trucks, new	100.0	6.9	93.1	6.1	93.9
New cars	100.0	10.1	89.9	5.9	94.1
New trucks	100.0	3.6	96.4	6.4	93.6
Cars and trucks, used	100.0	9.3	90.7	9.7	90.3
Used cars	100.0	11.2	88.8	8.3	91.7
Used trucks	100.0	6.3	93.7	11.7	88.3
Other vehicles	100.0	1.9	98.1	10.9	89.1
New motorcycles	100.0	3.6	96.4	13.1	86.9
Used motorcycles	100.0	0.1	99.9	8.5	91.5
GASOLINE AND MOTOR OIL	100.0	9.1	90.9	9.6	90.4
Gasoline	100.0	9.4	90.6	9.8	90.2
Diesel fuel	100.0	2.3	97.7	7.8	92.2
Gasoline on trips	100.0	5.6	94.4	6.3	93.7
Motor oil	100.0	7.5	92.5	10.7	89.2
Motor oil on trips	100.0	5.6	94.8	6.3	93.7
OTHER VEHICLE EXPENSES	100.0	9.2	90.8	7.8	92.2
Vehicle finance charges	100.0	10.2	89.8	9.6	90.4
Automobile finance charges	100.0	14.8	85.2	9.0	91.0
Truck finance charges	100.0	6.4	93.6	10.7	89.3
Motorcycle and plane finance charges	100.0	–	99.8	3.6	96.4
Other vehicle finance charges	100.0	0.4	99.7	5.8	94.2
Maintenance and repairs	100.0	8.6	91.4	7.1	92.9
Coolant, additives, brake, transmission fluids	100.0	8.3	91.8	13.6	86.4
Tires—purchased, replaced, installed	100.0	8.9	91.0	7.3	92.7
Parts, equipment, and accessories	100.0	5.4	94.6	9.6	90.4
Vehicle audio equipment, excl. labor	100.0	–	100.0	0.7	98.6
Vehicle products	100.0	0.9	99.5	9.7	90.4
Miscellaneous auto repair, servicing	100.0	4.8	95.5	4.7	94.9
Body work and painting	100.0	8.4	91.7	7.6	92.4
Clutch, transmission repair	100.0	10.5	89.5	7.7	92.3
Drive shaft and rear-end repair	100.0	12.0	88.0	0.5	99.5
Brake work	100.0	10.1	89.9	7.7	92.3
Repair to steering or front-end	100.0	3.9	96.1	7.2	92.8
Repair to engine cooling system	100.0	11.2	88.8	5.7	94.3
Motor tune-up	100.0	10.4	89.6	6.5	93.6
Lube, oil change, and oil filters	100.0	8.7	91.3	7.9	92.2
Front-end alignment, wheel balance, rotation	100.0	9.8	90.2	4.6	95.4
Shock absorber replacement	100.0	6.8	93.2	8.7	91.4
Gas tank repair, replacement	100.0	13.0	87.1	6.2	93.6
Tire repair and other repair work	100.0	8.3	91.7	5.7	94.3
Vehicle air conditioning repair	100.0	8.0	92.0	6.9	93.1
Exhaust system repair	100.0	8.3	91.8	6.6	93.4

	total consumer units	race		Hispanic origin	
		black	white and other	Hispanic	non-Hispanic
Electrical system repair	100.0%	14.1%	85.9%	4.9%	95.1%
Motor repair, replacement	100.0	9.7	90.3	9.1	90.9
Auto repair service policy	100.0	1.4	98.6	6.8	93.1
Vehicle insurance	**100.0**	**9.4**	**90.6**	**8.4**	**91.6**
Vehicle rental, leases, licenses, other charges	**100.0**	**8.7**	**91.3**	**6.3**	**93.7**
Leased and rented vehicles	100.0	9.0	91.0	5.5	94.5
Rented vehicles	100.0	7.5	92.5	5.0	95.0
Auto rental	100.0	10.5	89.5	6.6	93.3
Auto rental on trips	100.0	5.5	94.5	4.2	95.8
Truck rental	100.0	15.5	84.3	4.2	95.6
Truck rental on trips	100.0	12.2	87.9	9.7	90.4
Leased vehicles	100.0	9.2	90.8	5.6	94.4
Car lease payments	100.0	10.3	89.7	4.9	95.1
Truck lease payments	100.0	8.5	91.5	6.9	93.1
Vehicle registration, state	100.0	7.1	92.9	8.0	92.0
Vehicle registration, local	100.0	13.9	86.1	10.6	89.3
Driver's license	100.0	9.4	90.6	6.9	93.1
Vehicle inspection	100.0	10.6	89.3	11.9	88.1
Parking fees	100.0	8.0	92.0	7.1	93.0
Parking fees in home city, excl. residence	100.0	8.6	91.4	7.3	92.7
Parking fees on trips	100.0	5.0	95.1	6.1	94.1
Tolls	100.0	10.4	89.7	12.3	87.9
Tolls on trips	100.0	8.3	91.7	6.2	93.9
Towing charges	100.0	12.3	87.6	8.2	91.8
Automobile service clubs	100.0	5.9	94.1	4.3	95.7
PUBLIC TRANSPORTATION	**100.0**	**7.1**	**92.9**	**7.6**	**92.4**
Airline fares	100.0	4.8	95.2	6.0	94.0
Intercity bus fares	100.0	7.9	92.1	10.9	89.1
Intracity mass transit fares	100.0	19.3	80.7	18.0	82.0
Local transportation on trips	100.0	4.1	95.9	5.1	94.9
Taxi fares and limousine service on trips	100.0	4.1	95.9	5.1	94.9
Taxi fares and limousine service	100.0	10.7	89.3	7.6	92.2
Intercity train fares	100.0	4.6	95.4	5.0	95.0
Ship fares	100.0	5.1	94.9	4.8	95.2
School bus	100.0	20.1	79.9	17.0	82.9

Note: Other races include Asians, Native Americans, and Pacific Islanders. Numbers may not add to total because of rounding. (–) means sample is too small to make a reliable estimate.
Source: Calculations by New Strategist based on the 2002 Consumer Expenditure Survey

Table 11.17 Transportation: Average spending by region, 2002

(average annual spending of consumer units (CU) on transportation, by region in which consumer unit lives, 2002)

	total consumer units	Northeast	Midwest	South	West
Number of consumer units (in thousands, add 000)	112,108	21,313	25,883	40,004	24,907
Average number of persons per CU	2.5	2.5	2.5	2.5	2.6
Average before-tax income of CU	$49,430.00	$53,983.00	$49,197.00	$45,641.00	$52,016.00
Average spending of CU, total	40,676.60	42,390.20	40,601.14	37,280.55	44,728.34
Transportation, average spending	7,759.29	7,185.37	8,132.69	7,393.43	8,449.48
VEHICLE PURCHASES	$3,664.93	$3,036.38	$4,034.45	$3,591.24	$3,937.12
Cars and trucks, new	1,752.96	1,602.60	1,611.79	1,796.37	1,958.60
New cars	883.08	920.92	794.40	808.23	1,063.08
New trucks	869.88	681.67	817.40	988.14	895.52
Cars and trucks, used	1,842.29	1,371.51	2,313.81	1,741.81	1,916.51
Used cars	1,113.46	929.45	1,312.19	1,032.82	1,193.93
Used trucks	728.82	442.06	1,001.62	708.99	722.58
Other vehicles	69.68	62.28	108.84	53.06	62.00
New motorcycles	36.26	45.70	63.61	19.55	26.58
Used motorcycles	33.42	16.58	45.23	33.51	35.42
GASOLINE AND MOTOR OIL	1,235.06	1,081.41	1,269.48	1,238.37	1,325.44
Gasoline	1,125.01	1,010.07	1,147.04	1,134.81	1,184.75
Diesel fuel	10.86	4.45	10.23	10.71	17.25
Gasoline on trips	88.24	60.11	98.77	82.08	111.28
Motor oil	10.05	6.18	12.44	9.94	11.03
Motor oil on trips	0.89	0.61	1.00	0.83	1.12
OTHER VEHICLE EXPENSES	2,470.55	2,455.88	2,486.83	2,299.10	2,741.89
Vehicle finance charges	397.04	298.36	396.18	452.41	393.43
Automobile finance charges	193.12	167.94	185.14	218.76	181.78
Truck finance charges	182.89	119.00	184.52	215.20	183.97
Motorcycle and plane finance charges	2.36	2.67	3.92	1.01	2.63
Other vehicle finance charges	18.67	8.76	22.60	17.45	25.05
Maintenance and repairs	697.30	592.97	686.90	644.31	883.17
Coolant, additives, brake, transmission fluids	3.82	2.54	4.88	3.46	4.39
Tires—purchased, replaced, installed	89.93	78.94	81.22	91.44	105.97
Parts, equipment, and accessories	41.70	24.81	38.72	38.68	64.08
Vehicle audio equipment, excl. labor	12.32	3.88	7.81	8.54	30.40
Vehicle products	4.92	4.36	7.52	4.46	3.47
Miscellaneous auto repair, servicing	43.69	21.16	56.68	51.52	37.53
Body work and painting	31.24	31.25	25.66	32.52	34.98
Clutch, transmission repair	48.68	56.66	43.98	38.86	62.51
Drive shaft and rear-end repair	6.51	4.49	5.60	6.04	9.96
Brake work	57.73	65.08	56.05	46.05	71.93
Repair to steering or front-end	16.91	19.22	20.35	11.68	19.78
Repair to engine cooling system	21.68	19.08	23.45	15.62	31.78
Motor tune-up	49.69	47.92	39.78	42.43	73.17
Lube, oil change, and oil filters	65.07	55.46	73.43	59.99	72.77
Front-end alignment, wheel balance, rotation	11.90	12.39	14.87	10.08	11.31
Shock absorber replacement	4.82	5.59	5.82	3.10	5.91
Gas tank repair, replacement	4.32	6.09	3.10	3.18	5.85
Tire repair and other repair work	39.83	34.81	38.60	30.47	60.44
Vehicle air conditioning repair	17.00	7.66	15.07	22.85	17.60
Exhaust system repair	12.56	19.30	12.03	8.05	14.60

	total consumer units	Northeast	Midwest	South	West
Electrical system repair	$28.42	$26.45	$33.82	$24.31	$31.09
Motor repair, replacement	76.62	41.15	69.57	84.41	101.78
Auto repair service policy	7.93	4.70	8.89	6.57	11.87
Vehicle insurance	**893.50**	**921.06**	**875.91**	**861.38**	**939.80**
Vehicle rental, leases, licenses, other charges	**482.71**	**643.49**	**527.84**	**340.99**	**525.49**
Leased and rented vehicles	324.48	466.76	357.98	226.56	325.19
Rented vehicles	41.33	46.04	38.87	31.78	55.20
Auto rental	6.76	8.74	5.16	4.98	9.58
Auto rental on trips	28.28	33.04	26.45	19.50	40.22
Truck rental	2.21	1.83	2.54	2.55	1.63
Truck rental on trips	3.55	1.61	4.43	4.28	3.13
Leased vehicles	283.15	420.72	319.11	194.78	269.99
Car lease payments	149.63	231.81	156.68	101.70	148.95
Truck lease payments	114.24	152.04	145.50	83.16	99.34
Vehicle registration, state	72.82	41.73	95.59	49.31	113.51
Vehicle registration, local	7.76	5.14	6.16	11.63	5.46
Driver's license	6.26	9.31	6.16	5.07	5.66
Vehicle inspection	9.26	16.81	3.14	7.66	11.73
Parking fees	29.25	47.69	33.08	14.89	32.57
Parking fees in home city, excl. residence	24.24	41.61	27.86	11.53	26.03
Parking fees on trips	5.01	6.08	5.22	3.36	6.54
Tolls	10.59	25.69	4.82	9.30	5.38
Tolls on trips	3.94	8.62	2.92	3.36	1.92
Towing charges	5.60	3.74	5.75	5.62	6.99
Automobile service clubs	12.75	18.00	12.23	7.59	17.08
PUBLIC TRANSPORTATION	**388.75**	**611.70**	**341.93**	**264.72**	**445.04**
Airline fares	243.57	292.68	223.95	182.30	320.32
Intercity bus fares	11.48	14.09	9.91	9.87	13.47
Intracity mass transit fares	49.97	152.83	24.75	16.39	42.09
Local transportation on trips	10.91	15.15	11.72	8.15	10.86
Taxi fares and limousine service on trips	6.41	8.90	6.88	4.79	6.38
Taxi fares and limousine service	18.95	52.72	9.43	12.86	8.90
Intercity train fares	16.09	24.67	16.70	9.94	18.01
Ship fares	29.74	48.67	36.75	18.78	23.84
School bus	1.64	2.00	1.82	1.62	1.18

Source: Bureau of Labor Statistics, unpublished tables from the 2002 Consumer Expenditure Survey

Table 11.18 Transportation: Indexed spending by region, 2002

(indexed average annual spending of consumer units (CU) on transportation, by region in which consumer unit lives, 2002; index definition: an index of 100 is the average for all consumer units; an index of 132 means that spending by consumer units in that group is 32 percent above the average for all consumer units; an index of 68 indicates spending that is 32 percent below the average for all consumer units)

	total consumer units	Northeast	Midwest	South	West
Average spending of CU, total	$40,677	$42,390	$40,601	$37,281	$44,728
Average spending of CU, index	100	104	100	92	110
Transportation, spending index	100	93	105	95	109
VEHICLE PURCHASES	100	83	110	98	107
Cars and trucks, new	100	91	92	102	112
New cars	100	104	90	92	120
New trucks	100	78	94	114	103
Cars and trucks, used	100	74	126	95	104
Used cars	100	83	118	93	107
Used trucks	100	61	137	97	99
Other vehicles	100	89	156	76	89
New motorcycles	100	126	175	54	73
Used motorcycles	100	50	135	100	106
GASOLINE AND MOTOR OIL	100	88	103	100	107
Gasoline	100	90	102	101	105
Diesel fuel	100	41	94	99	159
Gasoline on trips	100	68	112	93	126
Motor oil	100	61	124	99	110
Motor oil on trips	100	69	112	93	126
OTHER VEHICLE EXPENSES	100	99	101	93	111
Vehicle finance charges	100	75	100	114	99
Automobile finance charges	100	87	96	113	94
Truck finance charges	100	65	101	118	101
Motorcycle and plane finance charges	100	113	166	43	111
Other vehicle finance charges	100	47	121	93	134
Maintenance and repairs	100	85	99	92	127
Coolant, additives, brake, transmission fluids	100	66	128	91	115
Tires—purchased, replaced, installed	100	88	90	102	118
Parts, equipment, and accessories	100	59	93	93	154
Vehicle audio equipment, excl. labor	100	31	63	69	247
Vehicle products	100	89	153	91	71
Miscellaneous auto repair, servicing	100	48	130	118	86
Body work and painting	100	100	82	104	112
Clutch, transmission repair	100	116	90	80	128
Drive shaft and rear-end repair	100	69	86	93	153
Brake work	100	113	97	80	125
Repair to steering or front-end	100	114	120	69	117
Repair to engine cooling system	100	88	108	72	147
Motor tune-up	100	96	80	85	147
Lube, oil change, and oil filters	100	85	113	92	112
Front-end alignment, wheel balance, rotation	100	104	125	85	95
Shock absorber replacement	100	116	121	64	123
Gas tank repair, replacement	100	141	72	74	135
Tire repair and other repair work	100	87	97	77	152
Vehicle air conditioning repair	100	45	89	134	104
Exhaust system repair	100	154	96	64	116

	total consumer units	Northeast	Midwest	South	West
Electrical system repair	100	93	119	86	109
Motor repair, replacement	100	54	91	110	109
Auto repair service policy	100	59	112	83	150
Vehicle insurance	**100**	**103**	**98**	**96**	**105**
Vehicle rental, leases, licenses, other charges	**100**	**133**	**109**	**71**	**109**
Leased and rented vehicles	100	144	110	70	100
Rented vehicles	100	111	94	77	134
Auto rental	100	129	76	74	142
Auto rental on trips	100	117	94	69	142
Truck rental	100	83	115	115	74
Truck rental on trips	100	45	125	121	88
Leased vehicles	100	149	113	69	95
Car lease payments	100	155	105	68	100
Truck lease payments	100	133	127	73	87
Vehicle registration, state	100	57	131	68	156
Vehicle registration, local	100	66	79	150	70
Driver's license	100	149	98	81	90
Vehicle inspection	100	182	34	83	127
Parking fees	100	163	113	51	111
Parking fees in home city, excl. residence	100	172	115	48	107
Parking fees on trips	100	121	104	67	131
Tolls	100	243	46	88	51
Tolls on trips	100	219	74	85	49
Towing charges	100	67	103	100	125
Automobile service clubs	100	141	96	60	134
PUBLIC TRANSPORTATION	**100**	**157**	**88**	**68**	**114**
Airline fares	100	120	92	75	132
Intercity bus fares	100	123	86	86	117
Intracity mass transit fares	100	306	50	33	84
Local transportation on trips	100	139	107	75	100
Taxi fares and limousine service on trips	100	139	107	75	100
Taxi fares and limousine service	100	278	50	68	47
Intercity train fares	100	153	104	62	112
Ship fares	100	164	124	63	80
School bus	100	122	111	99	72

Source: Calculations by New Strategist based on the 2002 Consumer Expenditure Survey

Table 11.19 Transportation: Total spending by region, 2002

(total annual spending on transportation, by region in which consumer units live, 2002; numbers in thousands)

	total consumer units	Northeast	Midwest	South	West
Number of consumer units	112,108	21,313	25,883	40,004	24,907
Total spending of all consumer units	$4,560,172,273	$903,462,333	$1,050,879,307	$1,491,371,122	$1,114,048,764
Transportation, total spending	869,878,483	153,141,791	210,498,415	295,766,774	210,451,198
VEHICLE PURCHASES	$410,867,972	$64,714,367	$104,423,669	$143,663,965	$98,061,848
Cars and trucks, new	196,520,840	34,156,214	41,717,961	71,861,985	48,782,850
New cars	99,000,333	19,627,568	20,561,455	32,332,433	26,478,134
New trucks	97,520,507	14,528,433	21,156,764	39,529,553	22,304,717
Cars and trucks, used	206,535,447	29,230,993	59,888,344	69,679,367	47,734,515
Used cars	124,827,774	19,809,368	33,963,414	41,316,931	29,737,215
Used trucks	81,706,553	9,421,625	25,924,930	28,362,436	17,997,300
Other vehicles	7,811,685	1,327,374	2,817,106	2,122,612	1,544,234
New motorcycles	4,065,036	974,004	1,646,418	782,078	662,028
Used motorcycles	3,746,649	353,370	1,170,688	1,340,534	882,206
GASOLINE AND MOTOR OIL	138,460,106	23,048,091	32,857,951	49,539,753	33,012,734
Gasoline	126,122,621	21,527,622	29,688,836	45,396,939	29,508,568
Diesel fuel	1,217,493	94,843	264,783	428,443	429,646
Gasoline on trips	9,892,410	1,281,124	2,556,464	3,283,528	2,771,651
Motor oil	1,126,685	131,714	321,985	397,640	274,724
Motor oil on trips	99,776	13,001	25,883	33,203	27,896
OTHER VEHICLE EXPENSES	276,968,419	52,342,170	64,366,621	91,973,196	68,292,254
Vehicle finance charges	44,511,360	6,358,947	10,254,327	18,098,210	9,799,161
Automobile finance charges	21,650,297	3,579,305	4,791,979	8,751,275	4,527,594
Truck finance charges	20,503,432	2,536,247	4,775,931	8,608,861	4,582,141
Motorcycle and plane finance charges	264,575	56,906	101,461	40,404	65,505
Other vehicle finance charges	2,093,056	186,702	584,956	698,070	623,920
Maintenance and repairs	78,172,908	12,637,970	17,779,033	25,774,977	21,997,115
Coolant, additives, brake, transmission fluids	428,253	54,135	126,309	138,414	109,342
Tires—purchased, replaced, installed	10,081,872	1,682,448	2,102,217	3,657,966	2,639,395
Parts, equipment, and accessories	4,674,904	528,776	1,002,190	1,547,355	1,596,041
Vehicle audio equipment, excl. labor	1,381,171	82,694	202,146	341,634	757,173
Vehicle products	551,571	92,925	194,640	178,418	86,427
Miscellaneous auto repair, servicing	4,897,999	450,983	1,467,048	2,061,006	934,760
Body work and painting	3,502,254	666,031	664,158	1,300,930	871,247
Clutch, transmission repair	5,457,417	1,207,595	1,138,334	1,554,555	1,556,937
Drive shaft and rear-end repair	729,823	95,695	144,945	241,624	248,074
Brake work	6,471,995	1,387,050	1,450,742	1,842,184	1,791,561
Repair to steering or front-end	1,895,746	409,636	526,719	467,247	492,660
Repair to engine cooling system	2,430,501	406,652	606,956	624,862	791,544
Motor tune-up	5,570,647	1,021,319	1,029,626	1,697,370	1,822,445
Lube, oil change, and oil filters	7,294,868	1,182,019	1,900,589	2,399,840	1,812,482
Front-end alignment, wheel balance, rotation	1,334,085	264,068	384,880	403,240	281,698
Shock absorber replacement	540,361	119,140	150,639	124,012	147,200
Gas tank repair, replacement	484,307	129,796	80,237	127,213	145,706
Tire repair and other repair work	4,465,262	741,906	999,084	1,218,922	1,505,379
Vehicle air conditioning repair	1,905,836	163,258	390,057	914,091	438,363
Exhaust system repair	1,408,076	411,341	311,372	322,032	363,642

	total consumer units	Northeast	Midwest	South	West
Electrical system repair	$3,186,109	$563,729	$875,363	$972,497	$774,359
Motor repair, replacement	8,589,715	877,030	1,800,680	3,376,738	2,535,034
Auto repair service policy	889,016	100,171	230,100	262,826	295,646
Vehicle insurance	**100,168,498**	**19,630,552**	**22,671,179**	**34,458,646**	**23,407,599**
Vehicle rental, leases, licenses, other charges	**54,115,653**	**13,714,702**	**13,662,083**	**13,640,964**	**13,088,379**
Leased and rented vehicles	36,376,804	9,948,056	9,265,596	9,063,306	8,099,507
Rented vehicles	4,633,424	981,251	1,006,072	1,271,327	1,374,866
Auto rental	757,850	186,276	133,556	199,220	238,609
Auto rental on trips	3,170,414	704,182	684,605	780,078	1,001,760
Truck rental	247,759	39,003	65,743	102,010	40,598
Truck rental on trips	397,983	34,314	114,662	171,217	77,959
Leased vehicles	31,743,380	8,966,805	8,259,524	7,791,979	6,724,641
Car lease payments	16,774,720	4,940,567	4,055,348	4,068,407	3,709,898
Truck lease payments	12,807,218	3,240,429	3,765,977	3,326,733	2,474,261
Vehicle registration, state	8,163,705	889,391	2,474,156	1,972,597	2,827,194
Vehicle registration, local	869,958	109,549	159,439	465,247	135,992
Driver's license	701,796	198,424	159,439	202,820	140,974
Vehicle inspection	1,038,120	358,272	81,273	306,431	292,159
Parking fees	3,279,159	1,016,417	856,210	595,660	811,221
Parking fees in home city, excl. residence	2,717,498	886,834	721,100	461,246	648,329
Parking fees on trips	561,661	129,583	135,109	134,413	162,892
Tolls	1,187,224	547,531	124,756	372,037	134,000
Tolls on trips	441,706	183,718	75,578	134,413	47,821
Towing charges	627,805	79,711	148,827	224,822	174,100
Automobile service clubs	1,429,377	383,634	316,549	303,630	425,412
PUBLIC TRANSPORTATION	**43,581,985**	**13,037,162**	**8,850,174**	**10,589,859**	**11,084,611**
Airline fares	27,306,146	6,237,889	5,796,498	7,292,729	7,978,210
Intercity bus fares	1,287,000	300,300	256,501	394,839	335,497
Intracity mass transit fares	5,602,037	3,257,266	640,604	655,666	1,048,336
Local transportation on trips	1,223,098	322,892	303,349	326,033	270,490
Taxi fares and limousine service on trips	718,612	189,686	178,075	191,619	158,907
Taxi fares and limousine service	2,124,447	1,123,621	244,077	514,451	221,672
Intercity train fares	1,803,818	525,792	432,246	397,640	448,575
Ship fares	3,334,092	1,037,304	951,200	751,275	593,783
School bus	183,857	42,626	47,107	64,806	29,390

Note: Numbers may not add to total because of rounding.
Source: Calculations by New Strategist based on the 2002 Consumer Expenditure Survey

Table 11.20 Transportation: Market shares by region, 2002

(percentage of total annual spending on transportation accounted for by consumer units by region, 2002)

	total consumer units	Northeast	Midwest	South	West
Share of total consumer units	100.0%	19.0%	23.1%	35.7%	22.2%
Share of total before-tax income	100.0	20.8	23.0	32.9	23.4
Share of total spending	100.0	19.8	23.0	32.7	24.4
Share of transportation spending	100.0	17.6	24.2	34.0	24.2
VEHICLE PURCHASES	100.0%	15.8%	25.4%	35.0%	23.9%
Cars and trucks, new	100.0	17.4	21.2	36.6	24.8
New cars	100.0	19.8	20.8	32.7	26.7
New trucks	100.0	14.9	21.7	40.5	22.9
Cars and trucks, used	100.0	14.2	29.0	33.7	23.1
Used cars	100.0	15.9	27.2	33.1	23.8
Used trucks	100.0	11.5	31.7	34.7	22.0
Other vehicles	100.0	17.0	36.1	27.2	19.8
New motorcycles	100.0	24.0	40.5	19.2	16.3
Used motorcycles	100.0	9.4	31.2	35.8	23.5
GASOLINE AND MOTOR OIL	100.0	16.6	23.7	35.8	23.8
Gasoline	100.0	17.1	23.5	36.0	23.4
Diesel fuel	100.0	7.8	21.7	35.2	35.3
Gasoline on trips	100.0	13.0	25.8	33.2	28.0
Motor oil	100.0	11.7	28.6	35.3	24.4
Motor oil on trips	100.0	13.0	25.9	33.3	28.0
OTHER VEHICLE EXPENSES	100.0	18.9	23.2	33.2	24.7
Vehicle finance charges	100.0	14.3	23.0	40.7	22.0
Automobile finance charges	100.0	16.5	22.1	40.4	20.9
Truck finance charges	100.0	12.4	23.3	42.0	22.3
Motorcycle and plane finance charges	100.0	21.5	38.3	15.3	24.8
Other vehicle finance charges	100.0	8.9	27.9	33.4	29.8
Maintenance and repairs	100.0	16.2	22.7	33.0	28.1
Coolant, additives, brake, transmission fluids	100.0	12.6	29.5	32.3	25.5
Tires—purchased, replaced, installed	100.0	16.7	20.9	36.3	26.2
Parts, equipment, and accessories	100.0	11.3	21.4	33.1	34.1
Vehicle audio equipment, excl. labor	100.0	6.0	14.6	24.7	54.8
Vehicle products	100.0	16.8	35.3	32.3	15.7
Miscellaneous auto repair, servicing	100.0	9.2	30.0	42.1	19.1
Body work and painting	100.0	19.0	19.0	37.1	24.9
Clutch, transmission repair	100.0	22.1	20.9	28.5	28.5
Drive shaft and rear-end repair	100.0	13.1	19.9	33.1	34.0
Brake work	100.0	21.4	22.4	28.5	27.7
Repair to steering or front-end	100.0	21.6	27.8	24.6	26.0
Repair to engine cooling system	100.0	16.7	25.0	25.7	32.6
Motor tune-up	100.0	18.3	18.5	30.5	32.7
Lube, oil change, and oil filters	100.0	16.2	26.1	32.9	24.8
Front-end alignment, wheel balance, rotation	100.0	19.8	28.8	30.2	21.1
Shock absorber replacement	100.0	22.0	27.9	22.9	27.2
Gas tank repair, replacement	100.0	26.8	16.6	26.3	30.1
Tire repair and other repair work	100.0	16.6	22.4	27.3	33.7
Vehicle air conditioning repair	100.0	8.6	20.5	48.0	23.0
Exhaust system repair	100.0	29.2	22.1	22.9	25.8

	total consumer units	Northeast	Midwest	South	West
Electrical system repair	100.0%	17.7%	27.5%	30.5%	24.3%
Motor repair, replacement	100.0	10.2	21.0	39.3	29.5
Auto repair service policy	100.0	11.3	25.9	29.6	33.3
Vehicle insurance	**100.0**	**19.6**	**22.6**	**34.4**	**23.4**
Vehicle rental, leases, licenses, other charges	**100.0**	**25.3**	**25.2**	**25.2**	**24.2**
Leased and rented vehicles	100.0	27.3	25.5	24.9	22.3
Rented vehicles	100.0	21.2	21.7	27.4	29.7
Auto rental	100.0	24.6	17.6	26.3	31.5
Auto rental on trips	100.0	22.2	21.6	24.6	31.6
Truck rental	100.0	15.7	26.5	41.2	16.4
Truck rental on trips	100.0	8.6	28.8	43.0	19.6
Leased vehicles	100.0	28.2	26.0	24.5	21.2
Car lease payments	100.0	29.5	24.2	24.3	22.1
Truck lease payments	100.0	25.3	29.4	26.0	19.3
Vehicle registration, state	100.0	10.9	30.3	24.2	34.6
Vehicle registration, local	100.0	12.6	18.3	53.5	15.6
Driver's license	100.0	28.3	22.7	28.9	20.1
Vehicle inspection	100.0	34.5	7.8	29.5	28.1
Parking fees	100.0	31.0	26.1	18.2	24.7
Parking fees in home city, excl. residence	100.0	32.6	26.5	17.0	23.9
Parking fees on trips	100.0	23.1	24.1	23.9	29.0
Tolls	100.0	46.1	10.5	31.3	11.3
Tolls on trips	100.0	41.6	17.1	30.4	10.8
Towing charges	100.0	12.7	23.7	35.8	27.7
Automobile service clubs	100.0	26.8	22.1	21.2	29.8
PUBLIC TRANSPORTATION	**100.0**	**29.9**	**20.3**	**24.3**	**25.4**
Airline fares	100.0	22.8	21.2	26.7	29.2
Intercity bus fares	100.0	23.3	19.9	30.7	26.1
Intracity mass transit fares	100.0	58.1	11.4	11.7	18.7
Local transportation on trips	100.0	26.4	24.8	26.7	22.1
Taxi fares and limousine service on trips	100.0	26.4	24.8	26.7	22.1
Taxi fares and limousine service	100.0	52.9	11.5	24.2	10.4
Intercity train fares	100.0	29.1	24.0	22.0	24.9
Ship fares	100.0	31.1	28.5	22.5	17.8
School bus	100.0	23.2	25.6	35.2	16.0

Note: Numbers may not add to total because of rounding.
Source: Calculations by New Strategist based on the 2002 Consumer Expenditure Survey

Table 11.21 Transportation: Average spending by education, 2002

(average annual spending of consumer units (CU) on transportation, by education of consumer unit reference person, 2002)

	total consumer units	less than high school graduate	high school graduate	some college	associate's degree	college graduate total	bachelor's degree	master's, professional, doctorate
Number of consumer units								
(in thousands, add 000)	112,108	17,075	31,961	23,260	10,395	29,417	19,082	10,335
Average number of persons per CU	2.5	2.6	2.5	2.4	2.6	2.5	2.5	2.5
Average before-tax income of CU	$49,430.00	$25,564.00	$39,618.00	$42,598.00	$54,860.00	$77,820.00	$69,408.00	$92,783.00
Average spending of CU, total	40,676.60	24,930.40	33,707.63	38,653.57	44,405.79	57,384.01	53,731.57	64,118.48
Transportation, average spending	7,759.29	4,826.20	6,982.76	7,742.68	8,546.28	10,034.92	9,677.87	10,693.55
VEHICLE PURCHASES	$3,664.93	$2,374.89	$3,351.39	$3,848.28	$3,744.38	$4,581.30	$4,507.26	$4,718.00
Cars and trucks, new	1,752.96	890.92	1,457.09	1,797.06	1,744.42	2,542.92	2,326.05	2,943.35
New cars	883.08	565.49	627.83	857.06	1,003.12	1,322.92	1,152.29	1,637.96
New trucks	869.88	325.43	829.26	940.00	741.30	1,220.00	1,173.76	1,305.38
Cars and trucks, used	1,842.29	1,465.65	1,816.56	1,979.42	1,851.02	1,977.34	2,113.65	1,725.66
Used cars	1,113.46	931.46	1,083.26	1,176.39	1,047.94	1,225.31	1,256.96	1,166.88
Used trucks	728.82	534.19	733.30	803.03	803.07	752.03	856.69	558.78
Other vehicles	69.68	18.32	77.74	71.80	148.94	61.04	67.56	49.00
New motorcycles	36.26	–	36.54	33.44	97.66	37.52	44.72	24.23
Used motorcycles	33.42	18.32	41.20	38.37	51.28	23.52	22.84	24.77
GASOLINE AND MOTOR OIL	1,235.06	901.86	1,212.25	1,228.50	1,429.94	1,389.56	1,355.36	1,452.71
Gasoline	1,125.01	845.35	1,121.20	1,112.53	1,303.30	1,238.36	1,215.74	1,280.11
Diesel fuel	10.86	9.50	14.12	9.05	7.73	10.65	11.44	9.21
Gasoline on trips	88.24	36.05	64.79	96.30	105.51	131.55	118.62	155.41
Motor oil	10.05	10.60	11.48	9.65	12.34	7.67	8.36	6.41
Motor oil on trips	0.89	0.36	0.65	0.97	1.07	1.33	1.20	1.57
OTHER VEHICLE EXPENSES	2,470.55	1,395.75	2,201.21	2,368.85	2,983.39	3,282.31	3,169.98	3,489.43
Vehicle finance charges	397.04	225.70	394.52	417.89	501.64	445.78	456.54	425.92
Automobile finance charges	193.12	116.72	174.97	198.69	239.41	236.42	230.29	247.74
Truck finance charges	182.89	103.92	195.34	191.83	239.31	188.19	209.64	148.59
Motorcycle and plane finance charges	2.36	0.43	3.82	2.69	3.29	1.29	1.70	0.54
Other vehicle finance charges	18.67	4.62	20.39	24.67	19.63	19.88	14.91	29.06
Maintenance and repairs	697.30	395.73	573.42	669.11	855.88	970.49	912.56	1,077.22
Coolant, additives, brake, transmission fluids	3.82	3.86	4.42	4.17	4.26	2.72	2.78	2.60
Tires—purchased, replaced, installed	89.93	54.67	83.53	93.92	101.07	110.27	111.33	108.31
Parts, equipment, and accessories	41.70	35.49	47.08	42.16	55.23	34.30	36.06	31.05
Vehicle audio equipment, excl. labor	12.32	0.56	4.67	22.70	50.58	6.96	5.66	9.31
Vehicle products	4.92	2.86	5.26	2.43	3.24	7.83	4.07	14.69
Miscellaneous auto repair, servicing	43.69	14.75	30.64	33.26	69.30	70.47	67.82	75.30
Body work and painting	31.24	13.11	24.23	31.92	32.61	48.37	46.02	52.70
Clutch, transmission repair	48.68	28.07	48.97	45.75	57.84	59.41	55.19	67.21
Drive shaft and rear-end repair	6.51	2.52	3.89	8.08	5.38	10.84	9.50	13.32
Brake work	57.73	27.88	42.80	57.52	66.01	88.51	80.44	103.41
Repair to steering or front-end	16.91	7.62	15.43	16.10	23.04	22.39	19.29	28.12
Repair to engine cooling system	21.68	11.80	17.77	26.06	22.03	28.06	25.17	33.39
Motor tune-up	49.69	24.25	32.76	43.71	51.56	86.91	74.79	109.30
Lube, oil change, and oil filters	65.07	32.64	55.38	65.07	74.26	91.18	85.73	101.26
Front-end alignment, wheel balance, rotation	11.90	8.48	9.79	12.77	15.81	14.11	13.40	15.42
Shock absorber replacement	4.82	2.82	4.37	2.13	3.16	9.20	7.85	11.70
Gas tank repair, replacement	4.32	7.50	2.24	4.24	0.74	6.05	4.90	8.14
Tire repair and other repair work	39.83	20.57	32.33	31.96	45.92	63.22	58.17	72.55
Vehicle air conditioning repair	17.00	9.25	10.42	14.78	27.74	26.60	27.82	24.35
Exhaust system repair	12.56	6.70	8.49	12.67	19.41	17.89	14.92	23.37

	total consumer units	less than high school graduate	high school graduate	some college	associate's degree	college graduate total	bachelor's degree	master's, professional, doctorate
Electrical system repair	$28.42	$15.62	$27.24	$24.70	$31.56	$38.96	$37.29	$42.04
Motor repair, replacement	76.62	57.56	56.09	65.73	88.84	114.28	113.51	115.69
Auto repair service policy	7.93	7.15	5.65	7.27	6.29	11.95	10.84	13.99
Vehicle insurance	**893.50**	**616.51**	**870.82**	**833.58**	**1,038.76**	**1,074.98**	**1,030.61**	**1,156.90**
Vehicle rental, leases, licenses, other charges	**482.71**	**157.81**	**362.46**	**448.26**	**587.11**	**791.06**	**770.27**	**829.39**
Leased and rented vehicles	324.48	73.44	241.13	295.16	418.28	550.80	545.43	560.72
Rented vehicles	41.33	8.28	21.72	34.22	46.21	85.73	73.95	107.47
Auto rental	6.76	1.22	3.38	5.92	6.10	14.54	15.23	13.29
Auto rental on trips	28.28	3.81	13.66	23.09	31.60	61.30	48.07	85.74
Truck rental	2.21	1.22	1.97	1.34	2.28	3.70	4.70	1.86
Truck rental on trips	3.55	1.72	2.20	3.51	5.79	5.33	5.73	4.59
Leased vehicles	283.15	65.16	219.41	260.94	372.07	465.07	471.48	453.25
Car lease payments	149.63	23.67	90.96	152.44	172.24	276.26	275.93	276.87
Truck lease payments	114.24	39.50	108.45	99.75	166.60	156.88	171.49	129.90
Vehicle registration, state	72.82	43.97	65.21	71.83	84.20	94.58	93.74	96.14
Vehicle registration, local	7.76	5.24	7.67	9.15	6.75	8.58	8.54	8.63
Driver's license	6.26	4.43	6.15	6.73	6.95	6.83	7.17	6.20
Vehicle inspection	9.26	7.85	8.16	8.30	10.86	11.47	11.33	11.74
Parking fees	29.25	6.12	10.91	28.85	22.01	65.49	55.84	83.31
Parking fees in home city, excl. residence	24.24	5.10	8.47	24.65	16.73	54.82	47.27	68.76
Parking fees on trips	5.01	1.03	2.44	4.20	5.28	10.67	8.57	14.55
Tolls	10.59	4.99	5.18	6.28	12.35	21.28	19.34	24.80
Tolls on trips	3.94	1.39	2.57	3.40	3.90	7.34	6.11	9.63
Towing charges	5.60	4.10	6.00	6.51	5.22	5.44	5.63	5.09
Automobile service clubs	12.75	6.27	9.49	12.06	16.58	19.25	17.14	23.14
PUBLIC TRANSPORTATION	**388.75**	**153.70**	**217.91**	**297.04**	**388.57**	**781.75**	**645.27**	**1,033.41**
Airline fares	243.57	63.99	124.44	192.29	253.67	514.20	432.87	664.36
Intercity bus fares	11.48	9.92	8.26	8.83	10.74	18.26	15.21	23.88
Intracity mass transit fares	49.97	50.35	38.19	37.00	31.90	79.19	78.63	80.23
Local transportation on trips	10.91	2.07	4.97	9.89	12.01	22.89	18.64	30.75
Taxi fares and limousine service on trips	6.41	1.22	2.92	5.81	7.06	13.44	10.94	18.06
Taxi fares and limousine service	18.95	11.22	10.84	12.17	24.78	33.90	21.10	57.21
Intercity train fares	16.09	5.03	9.50	12.05	16.38	32.78	29.25	39.30
Ship fares	29.74	8.58	18.07	16.83	31.28	64.35	37.60	113.74
School bus	1.64	1.33	0.72	2.16	0.75	2.73	1.02	5.89

Note: (–) means sample is too small to make a reliable estimate.
Source: Bureau of Labor Statistics, unpublished tables from the 2002 Consumer Expenditure Survey

Table 11.22 Transportation: Indexed spending by education, 2002

(indexed average annual spending of consumer units (CU) on transportation, by education of consumer unit reference person, 2002; index definition: an index of 100 is the average for all consumer units; an index of 132 means that spending by consumer units in that group is 32 percent above the average for all consumer units; an index of 68 indicates spending that is 32 percent below the average for all consumer units)

	total consumer units	less than high school graduate	high school graduate	some college	associate's degree	college graduate total	bachelor's degree	master's, professional, doctorate
Average spending of CU, total	$40,677	$24,930	$33,708	$38,654	$44,406	$57,384	$53,732	$64,118
Average spending of CU, index	100	61	83	95	109	141	132	158
Transportation, spending index	100	62	90	100	110	129	125	138
VEHICLE PURCHASES	**100**	**65**	**91**	**105**	**102**	**125**	**123**	**129**
Cars and trucks, new	**100**	**51**	**83**	**103**	**100**	**145**	**133**	**168**
New cars	100	64	71	97	114	150	130	185
New trucks	100	37	95	108	85	140	135	150
Cars and trucks, used	**100**	**80**	**99**	**107**	**100**	**107**	**115**	**94**
Used cars	100	84	97	106	94	110	113	105
Used trucks	100	73	101	110	110	103	118	77
Other vehicles	**100**	**26**	**112**	**103**	**214**	**88**	**97**	**70**
New motorcycles	100	–	101	92	269	103	123	67
Used motorcycles	100	55	123	115	153	70	68	74
GASOLINE AND MOTOR OIL	**100**	**73**	**98**	**99**	**116**	**113**	**110**	**118**
Gasoline	100	75	100	99	116	110	108	114
Diesel fuel	100	87	130	83	71	98	105	85
Gasoline on trips	100	41	73	109	120	149	134	176
Motor oil	100	105	114	96	123	76	83	64
Motor oil on trips	100	40	73	109	120	149	135	176
OTHER VEHICLE EXPENSES	**100**	**56**	**89**	**96**	**121**	**133**	**128**	**141**
Vehicle finance charges	**100**	**57**	**99**	**105**	**126**	**112**	**115**	**107**
Automobile finance charges	100	60	91	103	124	122	119	128
Truck finance charges	100	57	107	105	131	103	115	81
Motorcycle and plane finance charges	100	18	162	114	139	55	72	23
Other vehicle finance charges	100	25	109	132	105	106	80	156
Maintenance and repairs	**100**	**57**	**82**	**96**	**123**	**139**	**131**	**154**
Coolant, additives, brake, transmission fluids	100	101	116	109	112	71	73	68
Tires—purchased, replaced, installed	100	61	93	104	112	123	124	120
Parts, equipment, and accessories	100	85	113	101	132	82	86	74
Vehicle audio equipment, excl. labor	100	5	38	184	411	56	46	76
Vehicle products	100	58	107	49	66	159	83	299
Miscellaneous auto repair, servicing	100	34	70	76	159	161	155	172
Body work and painting	100	42	78	102	104	155	147	169
Clutch, transmission repair	100	58	101	94	119	122	113	138
Drive shaft and rear-end repair	100	39	60	124	83	167	146	205
Brake work	100	48	74	100	114	153	139	179
Repair to steering or front-end	100	45	91	95	136	132	114	166
Repair to engine cooling system	100	54	82	120	102	129	116	154
Motor tune-up	100	49	66	88	104	175	151	220
Lube, oil change, and oil filters	100	50	85	100	114	140	132	156
Front-end alignment, wheel balance, rotation	100	71	82	107	133	119	113	130
Shock absorber replacement	100	59	91	44	66	191	163	243
Gas tank repair, replacement	100	174	52	98	17	140	113	188
Tire repair and other repair work	100	52	81	80	115	159	146	182
Vehicle air conditioning repair	100	54	61	87	163	156	164	143
Exhaust system repair	100	53	68	101	155	142	119	186

	total consumer units	less than high school graduate	high school graduate	some college	associate's degree	college graduate total	bachelor's degree	master's, professional, doctorate
Electrical system repair	100	55	96	87	111	137	131	148
Motor repair, replacement	100	75	73	86	116	149	148	151
Auto repair service policy	100	90	71	92	79	151	137	176
Vehicle insurance	**100**	**69**	**97**	**93**	**116**	**120**	**115**	**129**
Vehicle rental, leases, licenses, other charges	**100**	**33**	**75**	**93**	**122**	**164**	**160**	**172**
Leased and rented vehicles	100	23	74	91	129	170	168	173
Rented vehicles	100	20	53	83	112	207	179	260
Auto rental	100	18	50	88	90	215	225	197
Auto rental on trips	100	13	48	82	112	217	170	303
Truck rental	100	55	89	61	103	167	213	84
Truck rental on trips	100	48	62	99	163	150	161	129
Leased vehicles	100	23	77	92	131	164	167	160
Car lease payments	100	16	61	102	115	185	184	185
Truck lease payments	100	35	95	87	146	137	150	114
Vehicle registration, state	100	60	90	99	116	130	129	132
Vehicle registration, local	100	68	99	118	87	111	110	111
Driver's license	100	71	98	108	111	109	115	99
Vehicle inspection	100	85	88	90	117	124	122	127
Parking fees	100	21	37	99	75	224	191	285
Parking fees in home city, excl. residence	100	21	35	102	69	226	195	284
Parking fees on trips	100	21	49	84	105	213	171	290
Tolls	100	47	49	59	117	201	183	234
Tolls on trips	100	35	65	86	99	186	155	244
Towing charges	100	73	107	116	93	97	101	91
Automobile service clubs	100	49	74	95	130	151	134	181
PUBLIC TRANSPORTATION	**100**	**40**	**56**	**76**	**100**	**201**	**166**	**266**
Airline fares	100	26	51	79	104	211	178	273
Intercity bus fares	100	86	72	77	94	159	132	208
Intracity mass transit fares	100	101	76	74	64	158	157	161
Local transportation on trips	100	19	46	91	110	210	171	282
Taxi fares and limousine service on trips	100	19	46	91	110	210	171	282
Taxi fares and limousine service	100	59	57	64	131	179	111	302
Intercity train fares	100	31	59	75	102	204	182	244
Ship fares	100	29	61	57	105	216	126	382
School bus	100	81	44	132	46	166	62	359

Note: (–) means sample is too small to make a reliable estimate.
Source: Calculations by New Strategist based on the 2002 Consumer Expenditure Survey

Table 11.23 Transportation: Total spending by education, 2002

(total annual spending on transportation, by consumer unit (CU) educational attainment group, 2002; numbers in thousands)

	total consumer units	less than high school graduate	high school graduate	some college	associate's degree	college graduate total	college graduate bachelor's degree	college graduate master's, professional, doctorate
Number of consumer units	112,108	17,075	31,961	23,260	10,395	29,417	19,082	10,335
Total spending of all CUs	$4,560,172,273	$425,686,580	$1,077,329,562	$899,082,038	$461,598,187	$1,688,065,422	$1,025,305,819	$662,664,491
Transportation, total spending	869,878,483	82,407,365	223,175,992	180,094,737	88,838,581	295,197,242	184,673,115	110,517,839
VEHICLE PURCHASES	$410,867,972	$40,551,247	$107,113,776	$89,510,993	$38,922,830	$134,768,102	$86,007,535	$48,760,530
Cars and trucks, new	196,520,840	15,212,459	46,570,053	41,799,616	18,133,246	74,805,078	44,385,686	30,419,522
New cars	99,000,333	9,655,742	20,066,075	19,935,216	10,427,432	38,916,338	21,987,998	16,928,317
New trucks	97,520,507	5,556,717	26,503,979	21,864,400	7,705,814	35,888,740	22,397,688	13,491,102
Cars and trucks, used	206,535,447	25,025,974	58,059,074	46,041,309	19,241,353	58,167,411	40,332,669	17,834,696
Used cars	124,827,774	15,904,680	34,622,073	27,362,831	10,893,336	36,044,944	23,985,311	12,059,705
Used trucks	81,706,553	9,121,294	23,437,001	18,678,478	8,347,913	22,122,467	16,347,359	5,774,991
Other vehicles	7,811,685	312,814	2,484,648	1,670,068	1,548,231	1,795,614	1,289,180	506,415
New motorcycles	4,065,036	–	1,167,855	777,814	1,015,176	1,103,726	853,347	250,417
Used motorcycles	3,746,649	312,814	1,316,793	892,486	533,056	691,888	435,833	255,998
GASOLINE AND MOTOR OIL	138,460,106	15,399,260	38,744,722	28,574,910	14,864,226	40,876,687	25,862,980	15,013,758
Gasoline	126,122,621	14,434,351	35,834,673	25,877,448	13,547,804	36,428,836	23,198,751	13,229,937
Diesel fuel	1,217,493	162,213	451,289	210,503	80,353	313,291	218,298	95,185
Gasoline on trips	9,892,410	615,554	2,070,753	2,239,938	1,096,776	3,869,806	2,263,507	1,606,162
Motor oil	1,126,685	180,995	366,912	224,459	128,274	225,628	159,526	66,247
Motor oil on trips	99,776	6,147	20,775	22,562	11,123	39,125	22,898	16,226
OTHER VEHICLE EXPENSES	276,968,419	23,832,431	70,352,873	55,099,451	31,012,339	96,555,713	60,489,558	36,063,259
Vehicle finance charges	44,511,360	3,853,828	12,609,254	9,720,121	5,214,548	13,113,510	8,711,696	4,401,883
Automobile finance charges	21,650,297	1,992,994	5,592,216	4,621,529	2,488,667	6,954,767	4,394,394	2,560,393
Truck finance charges	20,503,432	1,774,434	6,243,262	4,461,966	2,487,627	5,535,985	4,000,350	1,535,678
Motorcycle and plane finance charges	264,575	7,342	122,091	62,569	34,200	37,948	32,439	5,581
Other vehicle finance charges	2,093,056	78,887	651,685	573,824	204,054	584,810	284,513	300,335
Maintenance and repairs	78,172,908	6,757,090	18,327,077	15,563,499	8,896,873	28,548,904	17,413,470	11,133,069
Coolant, additives, brake, transmission fluids	428,253	65,910	141,268	96,994	44,283	80,014	53,048	26,871
Tires—purchased, replaced, installed	10,081,872	933,490	2,669,702	2,184,579	1,050,623	3,243,813	2,124,399	1,119,384
Parts, equipment, and accessories	4,674,904	605,992	1,504,724	980,642	574,116	1,009,003	688,097	320,902
Vehicle audio equipment, excl. labor	1,381,171	9,562	149,258	528,002	525,779	204,742	108,004	96,219
Vehicle products	551,571	48,835	168,115	56,522	33,680	230,335	77,664	151,821
Miscellaneous auto repair, servicing	4,897,999	251,856	979,285	773,628	720,374	2,073,016	1,294,141	778,226
Body work and painting	3,502,254	223,853	774,415	742,459	338,981	1,422,900	878,154	544,655
Clutch, transmission repair	5,457,417	479,295	1,565,130	1,064,145	601,247	1,747,664	1,053,136	694,615
Drive shaft and rear-end repair	729,823	43,029	124,328	187,941	55,925	318,880	181,279	137,662
Brake work	6,471,995	476,051	1,367,931	1,337,915	686,174	2,603,699	1,534,956	1,068,742
Repair to steering or front-end	1,895,746	130,112	493,158	374,486	239,501	658,647	368,092	290,620
Repair to engine cooling system	2,430,501	201,485	567,947	606,156	229,002	825,441	480,294	345,086
Motor tune-up	5,570,647	414,069	1,047,042	1,016,695	535,966	2,556,631	1,427,143	1,129,616
Lube, oil change, and oil filters	7,294,868	557,328	1,770,000	1,513,528	771,933	2,682,242	1,635,900	1,046,522
Front-end alignment, wheel balance, rotation	1,334,085	144,796	312,898	297,030	164,345	415,074	255,699	159,366
Shock absorber replacement	540,361	48,152	139,670	49,544	32,848	270,636	149,794	120,920
Gas tank repair, replacement	484,307	128,063	71,593	98,622	7,692	177,973	93,502	84,127
Tire repair and other repair work	4,465,262	351,233	1,033,299	743,390	477,338	1,859,743	1,110,000	749,804
Vehicle air conditioning repair	1,905,836	157,944	333,034	343,783	288,357	782,492	530,861	251,657
Exhaust system repair	1,408,076	114,403	271,349	294,704	201,767	526,270	284,703	241,529

	total consumer units	less than high school graduate	high school graduate	some college	associate's degree	college graduate total	bachelor's degree	master's, professional, doctorate
Electrical system repair	$3,186,109	$266,712	$870,618	$574,522	$328,066	$1,146,086	$711,568	$434,483
Motor repair, replacement	8,589,715	982,837	1,792,692	1,528,880	923,492	3,361,775	2,165,998	1,195,656
Auto repair service policy	889,016	122,086	180,580	169,100	65,385	351,533	206,849	144,587
Vehicle insurance	**100,168,498**	**10,526,908**	**27,832,278**	**19,389,071**	**10,797,910**	**31,622,687**	**19,666,100**	**11,956,562**
Vehicle rental, leases, licenses, other charges	**54,115,653**	**2,694,606**	**11,584,584**	**10,426,528**	**6,103,008**	**23,270,612**	**14,698,292**	**8,571,746**
Leased and rented vehicles	36,376,804	1,253,988	7,706,756	6,865,422	4,348,021	16,202,884	10,407,895	5,795,041
Rented vehicles	4,633,424	141,381	694,193	795,957	480,353	2,521,919	1,411,114	1,110,702
Auto rental	757,850	20,832	108,028	137,699	63,410	427,723	290,619	137,352
Auto rental on trips	3,170,414	65,056	436,587	537,073	328,482	1,803,262	917,272	886,123
Truck rental	247,759	20,832	62,963	31,168	23,701	108,843	89,685	19,223
Truck rental on trips	397,983	29,369	70,314	81,643	60,187	156,793	109,340	47,438
Leased vehicles	31,743,380	1,112,607	7,012,563	6,069,464	3,867,668	13,680,964	8,996,781	4,684,339
Car lease payments	16,774,720	404,165	2,907,173	3,545,754	1,790,435	8,126,740	5,265,296	2,861,451
Truck lease payments	12,807,218	674,463	3,466,170	2,320,185	1,731,807	4,614,939	3,272,372	1,342,517
Vehicle registration, state	8,163,705	750,788	2,084,177	1,670,766	875,259	2,782,260	1,788,747	993,607
Vehicle registration, local	869,958	89,473	245,141	212,829	70,166	252,398	162,960	89,191
Driver's license	701,796	75,642	196,560	156,540	72,245	200,918	136,818	64,077
Vehicle inspection	1,038,120	134,039	260,802	193,058	112,890	337,413	216,199	121,333
Parking fees	3,279,159	104,499	348,695	671,051	228,794	1,926,519	1,065,539	861,009
Parking fees in home city, excl. residence	2,717,498	87,083	270,710	573,359	173,908	1,612,640	902,006	710,635
Parking fees on trips	561,661	17,587	77,985	97,692	54,886	313,879	163,533	150,374
Tolls	1,187,224	85,204	165,558	146,073	128,378	625,994	369,046	256,308
Tolls on trips	441,706	23,734	82,140	79,084	40,541	215,921	116,591	99,526
Towing charges	627,805	70,008	191,766	151,423	54,262	160,028	107,432	52,605
Automobile service clubs	1,429,377	107,060	303,310	280,516	172,349	566,277	327,065	239,152
PUBLIC TRANSPORTATION	**43,581,985**	**2,624,428**	**6,964,622**	**6,909,150**	**4,039,185**	**22,996,740**	**12,313,042**	**10,680,292**
Airline fares	27,306,146	1,092,629	3,977,227	4,472,665	2,636,900	15,126,221	8,260,025	6,866,161
Intercity bus fares	1,287,000	169,384	263,998	205,386	111,642	537,154	290,237	246,800
Intracity mass transit fares	5,602,037	859,726	1,220,591	860,620	331,601	2,329,532	1,500,418	829,177
Local transportation on trips	1,223,098	35,345	158,846	230,041	124,844	673,355	355,688	317,801
Taxi fares and limousine service on trips	718,612	20,832	93,326	135,141	73,389	395,364	208,757	186,650
Taxi fares and limousine service	2,124,447	191,582	346,457	283,074	257,588	997,236	402,630	591,265
Intercity train fares	1,803,818	85,887	303,630	280,283	170,270	964,289	558,149	406,166
Ship fares	3,334,092	146,504	577,535	391,466	325,156	1,892,984	717,483	1,175,503
School bus	183,857	22,710	23,012	50,242	7,796	80,308	19,464	60,873

Note: Numbers may not add to total because of rounding. (–) means sample is too small to make a reliable estimate.
Source: Calculations by New Strategist based on the 2002 Consumer Expenditure Survey

Table 11.24 Transportation: Market shares by education, 2002

(percentage of total annual spending on transportation accounted for by consumer unit educational attainment groups, 2002)

	total consumer units	less than high school graduate	high school graduate	some college	associate's degree	college graduate total	bachelor's degree	master's, professional, doctorate
Share of total consumer units	100.0%	15.2%	28.5%	20.7%	9.3%	26.2%	17.0%	9.2%
Share of total before-tax income	100.0	7.9	22.8	17.9	10.3	41.3	23.9	17.3
Share of total spending	100.0	9.3	23.6	19.7	10.1	37.0	22.5	14.5
Share of transportation spending	100.0	9.5	25.7	20.7	10.2	33.9	21.2	12.7
VEHICLE PURCHASES	100.0%	9.9%	26.1%	21.8%	9.5%	32.8%	20.9%	11.9%
Cars and trucks, new	100.0	7.7	23.7	21.3	9.2	38.1	22.6	15.5
New cars	100.0	9.8	20.3	20.1	10.5	39.3	22.2	17.1
New trucks	100.0	5.7	27.2	22.4	7.9	36.8	23.0	13.8
Cars and trucks, used	100.0	12.1	28.1	22.3	9.3	28.2	19.5	8.6
Used cars	100.0	12.7	27.7	21.9	8.7	28.9	19.2	9.7
Used trucks	100.0	11.2	28.7	22.9	10.2	27.1	20.0	7.1
Other vehicles	100.0	4.0	31.8	21.4	19.8	23.0	16.5	6.5
New motorcycles	100.0	–	28.7	19.1	25.0	27.2	21.0	6.2
Used motorcycles	100.0	8.3	35.1	23.8	14.2	18.5	11.6	6.8
GASOLINE AND MOTOR OIL	100.0	11.1	28.0	20.6	10.7	29.5	18.7	10.8
Gasoline	100.0	11.4	28.4	20.5	10.7	28.9	18.4	10.5
Diesel fuel	100.0	13.3	37.1	17.3	6.6	25.7	17.9	7.8
Gasoline on trips	100.0	6.2	20.9	22.6	11.1	39.1	22.9	16.2
Motor oil	100.0	16.1	32.6	19.9	11.4	20.0	14.2	5.9
Motor oil on trips	100.0	6.2	20.8	22.6	11.1	39.2	22.9	16.3
OTHER VEHICLE EXPENSES	100.0	8.6	25.4	19.9	11.2	34.9	21.8	13.0
Vehicle finance charges	100.0	8.7	28.3	21.8	11.7	29.5	19.6	9.9
Automobile finance charges	100.0	9.2	25.8	21.3	11.5	32.1	20.3	11.8
Truck finance charges	100.0	8.7	30.4	21.8	12.1	27.0	19.5	7.5
Motorcycle and plane finance charges	100.0	2.8	46.1	23.6	12.9	14.3	12.3	2.1
Other vehicle finance charges	100.0	3.8	31.1	27.4	9.7	27.9	13.6	14.3
Maintenance and repairs	100.0	8.6	23.4	19.9	11.4	36.5	22.3	14.2
Coolant, additives, brake, transmission fluids	100.0	15.4	33.0	22.6	10.3	18.7	12.4	6.3
Tires—purchased, replaced, installed	100.0	9.3	26.5	21.7	10.4	32.2	21.1	11.1
Parts, equipment, and accessories	100.0	13.0	32.2	21.0	12.3	21.6	14.7	6.9
Vehicle audio equipment, excl. labor	100.0	0.7	10.8	38.2	38.1	14.8	7.8	7.0
Vehicle products	100.0	8.9	30.5	10.2	6.1	41.8	14.1	27.5
Miscellaneous auto repair, servicing	100.0	5.1	20.0	15.8	14.7	42.3	26.4	15.9
Body work and painting	100.0	6.4	22.1	21.2	9.7	40.6	25.1	15.6
Clutch, transmission repair	100.0	8.8	28.7	19.5	11.0	32.0	19.3	12.7
Drive shaft and rear-end repair	100.0	5.9	17.0	25.8	7.7	43.7	24.8	18.9
Brake work	100.0	7.4	21.1	20.7	10.6	40.2	23.7	16.5
Repair to steering or front-end	100.0	6.9	26.0	19.8	12.6	34.7	19.4	15.3
Repair to engine cooling system	100.0	8.3	23.4	24.9	9.4	34.0	19.8	14.2
Motor tune-up	100.0	7.4	18.8	18.3	9.6	45.9	25.6	20.3
Lube, oil change, and oil filters	100.0	7.6	24.3	20.7	10.6	36.8	22.4	14.3
Front-end alignment, wheel balance, rotation	100.0	10.9	23.5	22.3	12.3	31.1	19.2	11.9
Shock absorber replacement	100.0	8.9	25.8	9.2	6.1	50.1	27.7	22.4
Gas tank repair, replacement	100.0	26.4	14.8	20.4	1.6	36.7	19.3	17.4
Tire repair and other repair work	100.0	7.9	23.1	16.6	10.7	41.6	24.9	16.8
Vehicle air conditioning repair	100.0	8.3	17.5	18.0	15.1	41.1	27.9	13.2
Exhaust system repair	100.0	8.1	19.3	20.9	14.3	37.4	20.2	17.2

	total consumer units	less than high school graduate	high school graduate	some college	associate's degree	college graduate total	bachelor's degree	master's, professional, doctorate
Electrical system repair	100.0%	8.4%	27.3%	18.0%	10.3%	36.0%	22.3%	13.6%
Motor repair, replacement	100.0	11.4	20.9	17.8	10.8	39.1	25.2	13.9
Auto repair service policy	100.0	13.7	20.3	19.0	7.4	39.5	23.3	16.3
Vehicle insurance	**100.0**	**10.5**	**27.8**	**19.4**	**10.8**	**31.6**	**19.6**	**11.9**
Vehicle rental, leases, licenses, other charges	**100.0**	**5.0**	**21.4**	**19.3**	**11.3**	**43.0**	**27.2**	**15.8**
Leased and rented vehicles	100.0	3.4	21.2	18.9	12.0	44.5	28.6	15.9
Rented vehicles	100.0	3.1	15.0	17.2	10.4	54.4	30.5	24.0
Auto rental	100.0	2.7	14.3	18.2	8.4	56.4	38.3	18.1
Auto rental on trips	100.0	2.1	13.8	16.9	10.4	56.9	28.9	27.9
Truck rental	100.0	8.4	25.4	12.6	9.6	43.9	36.2	7.8
Truck rental on trips	100.0	7.4	17.7	20.5	15.1	39.4	27.5	11.9
Leased vehicles	100.0	3.5	22.1	19.1	12.2	43.1	28.3	14.8
Car lease payments	100.0	2.4	17.3	21.1	10.7	48.4	31.4	17.1
Truck lease payments	100.0	5.3	27.1	18.1	13.5	36.0	25.6	10.5
Vehicle registration, state	100.0	9.2	25.5	20.5	10.7	34.1	21.9	12.2
Vehicle registration, local	100.0	10.3	28.2	24.5	8.1	29.0	18.7	10.3
Driver's license	100.0	10.8	28.0	22.3	10.3	28.6	19.5	9.1
Vehicle inspection	100.0	12.9	25.1	18.6	10.9	32.5	20.8	11.7
Parking fees	100.0	3.2	10.6	20.5	7.0	58.8	32.5	26.3
Parking fees in home city, excl. residence	100.0	3.2	10.0	21.1	6.4	59.3	33.2	26.2
Parking fees on trips	100.0	3.1	13.9	17.4	9.8	55.9	29.1	26.8
Tolls	100.0	7.2	13.9	12.3	10.8	52.7	31.1	21.6
Tolls on trips	100.0	5.4	18.6	17.9	9.2	48.9	26.4	22.5
Towing charges	100.0	11.2	30.5	24.1	8.6	25.5	17.1	8.4
Automobile service clubs	100.0	7.5	21.2	19.6	12.1	39.6	22.9	16.7
PUBLIC TRANSPORTATION	**100.0**	**6.0**	**16.0**	**15.9**	**9.3**	**52.8**	**28.3**	**24.5**
Airline fares	100.0	4.0	14.6	16.4	9.7	55.4	30.2	25.1
Intercity bus fares	100.0	13.2	20.5	16.0	8.7	41.7	22.6	19.2
Intracity mass transit fares	100.0	15.3	21.8	15.4	5.9	41.6	26.8	14.8
Local transportation on trips	100.0	2.9	13.0	18.8	10.2	55.1	29.1	26.0
Taxi fares and limousine service on trips	100.0	2.9	13.0	18.8	10.2	55.0	29.1	26.0
Taxi fares and limousine service	100.0	9.0	16.3	13.3	12.1	46.9	19.0	27.8
Intercity train fares	100.0	4.8	16.8	15.5	9.4	53.5	30.9	22.5
Ship fares	100.0	4.4	17.3	11.7	9.8	56.8	21.5	35.3
School bus	100.0	12.4	12.5	27.3	4.2	43.7	10.6	33.1

Note: Numbers may not add to total because of rounding. (–) means sample is too small to make a reliable estimate.
Source: Calculations by New Strategist based on the 2002 Consumer Expenditure Survey

Appendix A

About the Consumer Expenditure Survey

History

The Consumer Expenditure Survey (CEX) is an ongoing study of the day-to-day spending of American households. In taking the survey, government interviewers collect spending data on products and services as well as the amount and sources of household income, changes in saving and debt, and demographic and economic characteristics of household members. Data collection for the CEX is done by the Bureau of the Census, under contract with the Bureau of Labor Statistics (BLS). The BLS is responsible for analysis and release of the survey data.

Since the late 19th century, the federal government has conducted expenditure surveys about every ten years. Although the results have been used for a variety of purposes, their primary application is to track consumer prices. Beginning in 1980, the CEX became a continuous survey with annual release of data (with a lag time of about two years between data collection and release). The survey is used to update prices for the market basket of products and services used in calculating the Consumer Price Index.

Description of the Consumer Expenditure Survey

The CEX is two surveys: an interview survey and a diary survey. In the interview portion of the survey, respondents are asked each quarter for five consecutive quarters to report their expenditures for the previous three months. The purchase of big-ticket items such as houses, cars, and major appliances, or recurring expenses such as insurance premiums, utility payments, and rent are recorded by the interview survey. About 95 percent of all expenditures are covered by the interview component.

Expenditures on small, frequently purchased items are recorded during a two-week period by the diary survey. These detailed records include expenses for food and beverages purchased in grocery stores and at restaurants, as well as other items such as tobacco, housekeeping supplies, nonprescription drugs, and personal care products and services. The diary survey is intended to capture expenditures respondents are likely to forget or recall incorrectly over longer periods of time.

The average spending figures shown in this book are the integrated data from both the diary and interview components of the survey. Integrated data provide a more complete accounting of consumer expenditures than either component of the survey is designed to do alone.

Data Collection and Processing

Two separate, nationally representative samples are used for the interview and diary surveys. For the interview survey, about 7,500 consumer units are interviewed on a rotating panel basis each quarter for five consecutive quarters. Another 7,500 consumer units keep weekly diaries of spending for two consecutive weeks. Data collection is carried out in 105 areas of the country.

The data are reviewed, audited, and cleaned by the BLS, and then weighted to reflect the number and characteristics of all U.S. consumer units. As with any sample survey, the CEX is subject to two major types of error. Nonsampling error occurs when respondents misinterpret questions or interviewers are inconsistent in the way they ask questions or record answers. Respondents may forget items, recall expenses incorrectly, or deliberately give wrong answers. A respondent may remember how much he or she spent at the grocery store but forget the items picked up at a local convenience store. Most surveys of alcohol consumption or spending on alcohol suffer from this type of underreporting, for example. Nonsampling error can also be caused by mistakes during the various stages of data processing and refinement.

Sampling error occurs when a sample does not accurately represent the population it is supposed to represent. This kind of error is present in every sample-based survey and is minimized by using a proper sampling procedure. Standard error tables documenting the extent of sampling error in the CEX are available from the BLS at http://www.bls.gov/cex/csxstnderror.htm.

Although the CEX is the best source of information about the spending behavior of American households, it should be treated with caution because of the above problems. Comparisons with consumption data from other sources show that CEX data tend to underestimate expenditures except for rent, fuel, telephone service, furniture, transportation, and personal care services. Despite these problems, the data reveal important spending patterns by demographic segment that can be used to better understand consumer behavior.

The Definition of Consumer Units

The CEX uses consumer units as its sampling unit instead of households, which are the sampling units used by the Census Bureau. The term household is used interchangeably with the term consumer unit in this book for convenience, although they are not exactly the same. Some households contain more than one consumer unit.

Consumer units are defined by the BLS as either: 1) members of a household who are related by blood, marriage, adoption, or other legal arrangements; 2) a person living alone or sharing a household with others or living as a roomer in a private home or lodging house or in permanent living quarters in a hotel or motel, but who is financially independent; or 3) two persons or more living together who pool their income to make joint expenditure decisions. The BLS defines financial independence in terms of the three major expenses categories: housing, food, and other living expenses. To be considered financially independent, at least two of the three major expense categories have to be provided by the respondent.

The Census Bureau uses households as its sampling unit in the decennial census and in the monthly Current Population Survey. The Census Bureau's household consists of all persons who occupy a housing unit. A house, an apartment or other groups of rooms, or a single room is regarded as a housing unit when it is occupied or intended for occupancy as separate living quarters; that is, when the occupants do not live and eat with any other persons in the structure and there is direct access from the outside or through a common hall.

The definition goes on to specify that a household includes the related family members and all the unrelated persons, if any, such as lodgers, foster children, wards, or employees who share the housing unit. A person living alone in a housing unit or a group of unrelated persons sharing a housing unit as partners is also counted as a household. The count of households excludes group quarters.

Because there can be more than one consumer unit in a household, consumer units outnumber households by several million. Most of the excess consumer units are headed by young adults, under age 25.

For More Information

If you want to know more about the Consumer Expenditure Survey, contact the CEX specialists at the Bureau of Labor Statistics at (202) 691-6900, or visit the Consumer Expenditure Survey home page at http://www.bls.gov/cex/. The CEX web site includes news releases, technical documentation, and current and historical CEX data. The detailed average spending data shown in Chapters 2 through 11 of *Household Spending* are available only by special request from the BLS.

Reduction of Mortgage Principle

The spending statistics reported by the Consumer Expenditure Survey do not include the amount households spend to reduce their mortgage principle. Since the survey treats home equity as an asset, principle reduction is regarded as asset accumulation rather than an expenditure.

The table below shows the average 2002 reduction of mortgage principle for owned homes for the six major demographic variables shown in the book: age of reference person, average before-tax income of consumer unit, type of consumer unit, and race and Hispanic origin of reference person, region, and educational attainment of consumer unit reference person. Adding these amounts to expenditures for the category "owned dwellings" gives a more complete picture of the amount households devote to housing.

(average annual reduction in mortgage principle for owned homes, by age of consumer unit (cu) reference person, average before-tax income of consumer unit, type of consumer unit, race and Hispanic origin of consumer unit reference person, region in which consumer unit lives, and educational attainment of consumer unit reference person, 2002)

	total consumer units	under 25	25 to 34	35 to 44	45 to 54	55 to 64	65 or older total	65 to 74	75 or older
• Age of reference person	−$996.78	−$113.06	−$773.23	−$1,400.10	−$1,529.24	−$1,233.19	−$379.21	−$590.20	−$159.44

	complete income reporters	under $10,000	$10,000– $19,999	$20,000– $29,999	$30,000– $39,999	$30,000– $49,999	$50,000– $69,999	$70,000 or more	
• Before-tax income of consumer unit	−$982.24	−$246.35	−$266.87	−$410.34	−$629.61	−$849.36	−$1,154.97	−$2,342.70	

	total married couples	married couples, no children	married couples with children total	oldest child under age 6	oldest child 6 to 17	oldest child 18 or older	single parent with child under 18	single person
• Type of consumer unit	−$1,478.54	−$1,135.41	−$1,779.14	−$1,594.66	−$1,827.98	−$1,814.09	−$613.43	−$419.16

	total consumer units	black	white and other	Hispanic	non-Hispanic
• Race/Hispanic origin of reference person	−$996.78	−$625.10	−$1,047.90	−$639.73	−$1,033.68

	total consumer units	Northeast	Midwest	South	West
• Region in which consumer unit lives	−$996.78	−$1,033.60	−$988.23	−$852.40	−$1,206.05

	total consumer units	less than high school graduate	high school graduate	some college	associate's degree	college graduate total	bachelor's degree	master's, professional, doctorate
• Educational attainment of reference person	−$996.78	−$362.02	−$709.31	−$841.97	−$1,188.03	−$1,732.38	−$1,523.26	−$2,118.49

Source: Bureau of Labor Statistics, 2002 Consumer Expenditure Survey

Appendix C

Percent Reporting Expenditure and Amount Spent, Average Quarter 2002

(percent of consumer units reporting expenditure and amount spent by purchasers during an average quarter, 2002)

	percent reporting expenditure during quarter	average amount spent per quarter
FOOD	**99.50%**	**$1,319.50**
Food at home	**98.95**	**973.90**
Grocery stores	98.34	901.80
Convenience stores	27.81	239.27
Food prepared by cu on trips	13.27	77.62
Food away from home	**81.42**	**428.93**
Meals at restaurants, carryouts, and other	77.68	317.67
Board (including at school)	1.47	791.50
Catered affairs	1.38	1,250.00
Food on trips	27.17	194.60
School lunches	9.70	154.64
Meals as pay	2.04	280.15
ALCOHOLIC BEVERAGES	**42.12**	**196.55**
At home	**33.64**	**131.11**
Beer and wine	32.61	111.17
Other alcoholic beverages	9.46	83.01
Away from home	**27.77**	**139.31**
Alcoholic beverages at restaurants, taverns	21.97	138.78
Alcoholic beverages purchased on trips	12.34	66.41
HOUSING	**99.51**	**3,114.78**
Shelter	**97.42**	**2,009.19**
OWNED DWELLINGS	**66.52**	**1,941.13**
Mortgage interest and charges	41.31	1,792.64
Mortgage interest	38.72	1,815.27
Interest paid, home equity loan	4.33	511.61
Interest paid, home equity line of credit	3.47	445.82
Prepayment penalty charge	0.02	225.00
Property taxes	65.12	476.95
Maintenance, repairs, insurance, other expenses	36.99	649.11
Homeowners and related insurance	25.60	276.66
Ground rent	1.46	701.37
Maintenance and repair services	12.89	1,007.76
Painting and papering	1.66	837.05
Plumbing and water heating	3.32	351.13
Heat, air conditioning, electrical work	3.87	557.36
Roofing and gutters	1.00	1,780.00
Other repair and maintenance services	4.85	1,107.06
Repair/replacement of hard surface flooring	0.74	1,470.95
Repair of built-in appliances	0.40	101.25

	percent reporting expenditure during quarter	average amount spent per quarter
Maintenance and repair materials	6.64%	$315.32
Paints, wallpaper and supplies	2.74	134.22
Tools/equipment for painting, wallpapering	2.74	14.42
Plumbing supplies and equipment	0.98	143.37
Electrical supplies, heating/cooling equipment	0.44	196.59
Hard surface flooring, repair and replacement	0.48	454.17
Roofing and gutters	0.27	489.81
Plaster, paneling, siding, windows, doors, screens, awnings	1.08	322.22
Patio, walk, fence, driveway, masonry, brick, and stucco work	0.43	75.00
Landscape maintenance	0.43	275.00
Miscellaneous supplies and equipment	1.77	345.06
Insulation, other maintenance/repair	1.41	233.16
Finish basement, remodel rooms, build patios, walks, etc.	0.39	723.08
Property management and security	3.78	182.80
Property management	3.49	157.16
Management and upkeep services for security	1.12	127.46
Parking	1.07	120.79
RENTED DWELLINGS	**31.79**	**1,698.56**
Rent	31.35	1,678.36
Rent as pay	0.72	943.40
Maintenance, insurance, and other expenses	3.64	192.72
Tenant's insurance	2.40	92.71
Maintenance and repair services	0.54	516.67
Repair or maintenance services	0.50	529.00
Repair and replacement of hard surface flooring	0.03	425.00
Repair of built-in appliances	0.02	87.50
Maintenance and repair materials	0.92	217.39
Paint, wallpaper, and supplies	0.34	74.26
Painting and wallpapering	0.34	8.09
Plastering, paneling, roofing, gutters, etc.	0.11	204.55
Plumbing supplies and equipment	0.17	117.65
Electrical supplies, heating and cooling equipment	0.05	150.00
Miscellaneous supplies and equipment	0.27	339.81
Insulation, other maintenance and repair	0.16	170.31
Materials for additions, finishing basements, remodeling rooms	0.11	552.27
Hard surface flooring	0.10	182.50
Landscape maintenance	0.05	245.00
OTHER LODGING	**20.67**	**610.26**
Owned vacation homes	4.92	871.70
Mortgage interest and charges	1.30	1,384.23
Mortgage interest	1.26	1,380.36
Interest paid, home equity loan	0.02	1,812.50
Interest paid, home equity line of credit	0.03	808.33
Property taxes	4.30	370.70
Maintenance, insurance and other expenses	1.54	581.33
Homeowners and related insurance	0.88	275.57
Ground rent	0.06	1,220.83
Maintenance and repair services	0.59	710.17
Maintenance and repair materials	0.09	575.00

	percent reporting expenditure during quarter	average amount spent per quarter
Property management and security	0.49%	$183.67
Property management	0.44	142.05
Management and upkeep services for security	0.25	110.00
Parking	0.15	126.67
Housing while attending school	1.33	1,506.39
Lodging on out-of-town trips	16.23	389.51
Utilities, fuels, public services	**97.64**	**687.30**
Natural gas	49.94	165.07
Electricity	91.19	268.97
Fuel oil and other fuels	9.09	243.15
Fuel oil	3.48	330.32
Coal	0.01	175.00
Bottled gas	5.24	168.27
Wood and other fuels	0.87	203.74
Telephone services	95.35	250.85
Telephone services in home city, excl. mobile car phones	91.81	174.55
Cellular phone service	43.41	169.18
Pager service	0.61	70.08
Phone cards	10.87	46.64
Water and other public services	61.30	133.90
Water and sewerage maintenance	55.06	107.68
Trash and garbage collection	38.06	58.49
Septic tank cleaning	0.32	165.63
Household services	**55.49**	**317.67**
Personal services	8.70	951.21
Babysitting and child care in your own home	2.06	435.80
Babysitting and child care in someone else's home	1.20	572.50
Care for elderly, invalids, handicapped, etc.	0.35	3,576.43
Adult day care centers	0.15	1,135.00
Day care centers, nursery and preschools	5.97	882.50
Other household services	52.44	178.34
Housekeeping services	5.65	353.54
Gardening, lawn care service	11.94	151.55
Water softening service	0.98	80.36
Nonclothing laundry and dry cleaning, sent out	1.01	42.57
Nonclothing laundry and dry cleaning, coin-operated	5.22	19.78
Termite/pest control services	2.27	145.93
Home security system service fee	4.67	93.15
Other home services	2.13	176.76
Termite/pest control products	0.41	41.46
Moving, storage, and freight express	2.30	360.11
Appliance repair, including service center	2.27	119.60
Reupholstering and furniture repair	0.59	313.56
Repairs/rentals of lawn/garden equipment, hand/power tools, etc.	0.94	96.28
Appliance rental	0.16	167.19
Rental of office equipment for nonbusiness use	0.04	256.25
Repair of computer systems for nonbusiness use	0.46	137.50
Computer information services	35.70	75.13

	percent reporting expenditure during quarter	average amount spent per quarter
Household furnishings and equipment	**52.55%**	**$561.02**
Household textiles	17.98	115.04
Bathroom linens	6.17	47.24
Bedroom linens	9.05	100.91
Kitchen and dining room linens	2.10	32.50
Curtains and draperies	2.39	174.16
Slipcovers and decorative pillows	0.78	68.27
Sewing materials for household items	4.28	66.82
Other linens	0.73	54.45
Furniture	11.54	869.32
Mattress and springs	2.09	632.89
Other bedroom furniture	2.27	752.53
Sofas	2.19	974.09
Living room chairs	2.14	458.06
Living room tables	1.60	281.72
Kitchen and dining room furniture	1.74	880.46
Infants' furniture	0.79	204.43
Outdoor furniture	1.66	252.86
Wall units, cabinets, and other furniture	2.86	462.76
Floor coverings	3.27	309.56
Wall-to-wall carpeting (renter)	0.06	270.83
Wall-to-wall carpeting, replacement (owner)	0.42	1,252.38
Floor coverings, nonpermanent	2.85	164.82
Major appliances	8.41	524.44
Dishwashers (built-in), garbage disposals, range hoods (renter)	0.09	344.44
Dishwashers (built-in), garbage disposals, range hoods (owner)	0.88	434.09
Refrigerators and freezers (renter)	0.40	348.75
Refrigerators and freezers (owner)	1.60	726.56
Washing machines (renter)	0.30	368.33
Washing machines (owner)	0.90	496.67
Clothes dryers (renter)	0.24	330.21
Clothes dryers (owner)	0.80	433.75
Cooking stoves, ovens (renter)	0.21	340.48
Cooking stoves, ovens (owner)	0.92	763.32
Microwave ovens (renter)	0.64	83.59
Microwave ovens (owner)	1.24	168.55
Portable dishwasher (renter)	0.01	625.00
Portable dishwasher (owner)	0.04	318.75
Window air conditioners (renter)	0.21	217.86
Window air conditioners (owner)	0.48	316.15
Electric floor cleaning equipment	1.65	205.61
Sewing machines	0.36	332.64
Small appliances and miscellaneous housewares	15.92	84.72
Housewares	9.38	82.81
Plastic dinnerware	1.42	27.64
China and other dinnerware	2.93	79.27
Flatware	1.62	58.49
Glassware	2.45	41.33
Silver serving pieces	0.11	100.00
Other serving pieces	0.78	46.15
Nonelectric cookware	3.18	82.55

	percent reporting expenditure during quarter	average amount spent per quarter
Small appliances	8.66%	$66.08
Small electric kitchen appliances	7.34	58.51
Portable heating and cooling equipment	1.62	87.96
Miscellaneous household equipment	37.66	281.72
Window coverings	1.44	241.49
Infants' equipment	0.73	104.45
Outdoor equipment	0.83	209.04
Clocks	1.35	69.26
Lamps and lighting fixtures	2.83	103.71
Other household decorative items	9.27	145.23
Telephones and accessories	4.60	71.74
Lawn and garden equipment	2.81	428.47
Power tools	2.27	177.64
Small miscellaneous furnishings	1.29	204.84
Hand tools	2.63	76.52
Indoor plants and fresh flowers	17.08	72.86
Closet and storage items	1.96	53.57
Rental of furniture	0.40	287.50
Luggage	1.53	97.71
Computers and computer hardware, nonbusiness use	4.66	743.45
Computer software and accessories, nonbusiness use	4.26	103.70
Telephone answering devices	0.54	50.00
Calculators	0.91	39.56
Business equipment for home use	0.23	105.43
Smoke alarms (owner)	0.37	74.32
Smoke alarms (renter)	0.06	162.50
Other household appliances (owner)	1.10	181.82
Other household appliances (renter)	0.38	80.92
APPAREL AND SERVICES	**78.17**	**412.97**
Men and boys'	**39.85**	**216.50**
MEN'S APPAREL	**33.42**	**197.80**
Suits	2.23	369.51
Sportcoats and tailored jackets	1.59	167.45
Coats and jackets	5.13	122.37
Underwear	8.76	29.42
Hosiery	8.95	17.63
Nightwear	2.17	34.33
Accessories	5.96	37.42
Sweaters and vests	4.49	87.31
Active sportswear	3.72	64.78
Shirts	17.69	77.26
Pants	18.06	91.39
Shorts and shorts sets	5.40	53.75
Uniforms	0.99	81.06
Costumes	1.05	151.19
BOYS' (AGED 2 TO 15) APPAREL	**12.48**	**161.60**
Coats and jackets	2.38	67.02
Sweaters	1.44	63.37
Shirts	6.60	62.77
Underwear	3.78	28.57
Nightwear	1.16	30.39
Hosiery	3.85	15.78

	percent reporting expenditure during quarter	average amount spent per quarter
Accessories	1.62%	$21.76
Suits, sportcoats, and vests	0.64	92.58
Pants	6.85	82.41
Shorts and shorts sets	3.50	61.86
Uniforms	1.67	50.15
Active sportswear	0.95	101.05
Costumes	1.23	75.61
Women and girls'	**49.64**	**261.67**
WOMEN'S APPAREL	**44.82**	**235.17**
Coats and jackets	7.38	115.85
Dresses	10.30	124.10
Sportcoats and tailored jackets	1.49	108.72
Sweaters and vests	10.44	80.17
Shirts, blouses, and tops	23.01	73.19
Skirts	6.92	61.71
Pants	21.44	85.38
Shorts and shorts sets	7.32	54.58
Active sportswear	5.11	58.86
Nightwear	7.75	39.77
Undergarments	14.27	45.81
Hosiery	14.60	20.62
Suits	4.12	176.03
Accessories	8.79	44.34
Uniforms	1.63	93.87
Costumes	1.72	136.92
GIRLS' (AGED 2 TO 15) APPAREL	**13.39**	**182.90**
Coats and jackets	2.55	63.63
Dresses and suits	3.07	74.35
Shirts, blouses, and sweaters	7.87	78.59
Skirts and pants	7.01	85.84
Shorts and shorts sets	3.26	63.50
Active sportswear	1.81	46.41
Underwear and nightwear	5.19	36.75
Hosiery	3.84	16.28
Accessories	2.21	24.77
Uniforms	1.03	115.78
Costumes	1.61	74.53
Children under age two	14.57	121.04
Coats, jackets, and snowsuits	1.74	34.91
Outerwear including dresses	8.77	67.59
Underwear	8.48	98.76
Nightwear and loungewear	3.38	30.10
Accessories	4.70	36.33
Footwear	**30.86**	**101.09**
Men's	11.53	91.39
Boys'	5.54	63.72
Women's	17.70	78.04
Girls'	5.82	57.04
Other apparel products and services	**44.79**	**129.08**
Material for making clothes	1.56	48.72
Sewing patterns and notions	2.14	19.39
Watches	4.30	79.19

	percent reporting expenditure during quarter	average amount spent per quarter
Jewelry	8.16%	$274.66
Shoe repair and other shoe services	1.18	30.51
Coin-operated apparel laundry and dry cleaning	15.54	60.46
Apparel alteration, repair, and tailoring services	3.47	42.22
Clothing rental	0.54	123.15
Watch and jewelry repair	2.94	46.68
Professional laundry, dry cleaning	21.90	79.55
Clothing storage	0.09	152.78
TRANSPORTATION	**93.79**	**2,049.64**
Vehicle purchases	**6.65**	**13,777.93**
Cars and trucks, new	1.90	23,065.26
New cars	1.03	21,433.98
New trucks	0.87	24,996.55
Cars and trucks, used	4.62	9,969.10
Used cars	3.07	9,067.26
Used trucks	1.61	11,317.08
Other vehicles	0.20	8,710.00
New motorcycles	0.09	10,072.22
Used motorcycles	0.11	7,595.45
Gasoline and motor oil	**89.32**	**345.68**
Gasoline	88.33	318.41
Diesel fuel	1.24	218.95
Gasoline on out-of-town trips	24.79	88.99
Motor oil	12.79	19.64
Motor oil on out-of-town trips	24.79	0.90
Other vehicle expenses	**80.47**	**748.27**
Vehicle finance charges	33.55	295.86
Automobile finance charges	20.68	233.46
Truck finance charges	15.77	289.93
Motorcycle and plane finance charges	0.54	109.26
Other vehicle finance charges	1.49	313.26
Maintenance and repairs	53.91	299.51
Coolant, additives, brake, transmission fluids	8.04	11.88
Tires	8.35	269.25
Parts, equipment, and accessories	11.03	94.51
Vehicle audio equipment	0.14	275.00
Body work and painting	1.40	557.86
Clutch, transmission repair	1.87	650.80
Drive shaft and rear-end repair	0.35	465.00
Brake work	5.76	250.56
Repair to steering or front-end	1.32	320.27
Repair to engine cooling system	2.30	235.65
Motor tune-up	5.34	232.63
Lube, oil change, and oil filters	34.08	47.73
Front-end alignment, wheel balance, rotation	2.58	115.31
Shock absorber replacement	0.35	344.29
Repair tires and other repair work	6.38	156.07
Exhaust system repair	1.35	232.59
Electrical system repair	3.09	229.94
Motor repair, replacement	3.09	619.90

	percent reporting expenditure during quarter	average amount spent per quarter
Auto repair service policy	0.43%	$461.05
Vehicle accessories, including labor	0.69	299.64
Vehicle audio equipment, including labor	0.33	303.79
Vehicle air conditioning repair	1.35	314.81
Vehicle insurance	52.08	428.91
Vehicle rental, leases, licenses, other charges	41.20	286.48
Leased and rented vehicles	8.48	956.60
Rented vehicles	3.66	282.31
Auto rental	0.76	222.37
Auto rental, out-of-town trips	2.61	270.88
Truck rental	0.21	263.10
Truck rental, out-of-town trips	0.25	355.00
Leased vehicles	5.20	1,361.30
Car lease payments	3.17	1,180.05
Cash downpayment (car lease)	0.11	2,529.55
Termination fee (car lease)	0.04	800.00
Truck lease payments	2.34	1,220.51
Cash downpayment (truck lease)	0.06	2,050.00
Termination fee (truck lease)	0.06	808.33
Vehicle registration, state	16.07	113.29
Vehicle registration, local	2.11	91.94
Driver's license	5.95	26.30
Vehicle inspection	6.65	34.81
Parking fees	12.69	57.62
Parking fees in home city, excluding residence	10.17	59.59
Parking fees, out-of-town trips	3.56	35.18
Tolls on out-of-town trips	7.87	12.52
Towing charges	1.41	99.29
Automobile service clubs	4.27	74.65
Public transportation	**18.84**	**505.48**
Airline fares	10.09	603.49
Intercity bus fares	4.28	67.06
Intracity mass transit fares	7.40	168.82
Local transportation on out-of-town trips	5.39	50.60
Taxi fares and limousine service on trips	5.39	29.73
Taxi fares and limousine service	2.93	94.88
Intercity train fares	4.05	99.32
Ship fares	2.63	282.70
School bus	0.24	170.83
HEALTH CARE	**78.98**	**698.77**
Health insurance	**62.91**	**464.04**
Commercial health insurance	12.89	421.90
Traditional fee for service health plan (not BCBS)	4.18	408.31
Preferred provider health plan (not BCBS)	8.93	417.86
Blue Cross, Blue Shield	17.17	459.62
Traditional fee for service health plan	2.56	525.00
Preferred provider health plan	5.79	461.96
Health maintenance organization	6.09	416.79
Commercial Medicare supplement	2.56	462.40
Other BCBS health insurance	0.82	184.45
Health maintenance plans (HMOs)	17.80	393.92

	percent reporting expenditure during quarter	average amount spent per quarter
Medicare payments	22.15%	$210.91
Commercial Medicare supplements/other health insurance	14.07	297.05
Commercial Medicare supplement (not BCBS)	6.53	407.04
Other health insurance (not BCBS)	8.17	186.23
Medical services	**43.83**	**335.54**
Physician's services	28.97	127.31
Dental services	16.12	352.03
Eye care services	6.85	124.82
Service by professionals other than physician	4.84	220.87
Lab tests, x-rays	4.32	155.03
Hospital room	2.01	454.85
Hospital services other than room	4.08	315.63
Care in convalescent or nursing home	0.21	1,483.33
Other medical services	1.12	211.16
Prescription drugs	**48.09**	**194.34**
Medical supplies	**9.10**	**213.57**
Eyeglasses and contact lenses	7.21	181.21
Hearing aids	0.60	624.17
Medical equipment for general use	0.74	90.88
Supportive/convalescent medical equipment	0.74	176.01
Rental of medical equipment	0.23	115.22
Rental of supportive, convalescent medical equipment	0.38	101.97
ENTERTAINMENT	**89.67**	**547.11**
Fees and admissions	**51.26**	**264.18**
Recreation expenses, out of town trips	10.36	61.87
Social, recreation, civic club membership	13.02	207.22
Fees for participant sports	11.92	157.40
Participant sports, out-of-town trips	5.35	137.85
Movie, theater, opera, ballet	34.10	72.07
Movie, other admissions, out-of-town trips	11.18	101.90
Admission to sports events	7.71	117.32
Admission to sports events, out-of-town trips	11.18	33.97
Fees for recreational lessons	7.46	277.11
Other entertainment services, out-of-town trips	10.36	61.87
Television, radios, sound equipment	**81.60**	**210.14**
Televisions	74.04	183.57
Community antenna or cable TV	67.89	140.77
Black and white TV	0.11	181.82
Color TV, console	0.81	1,192.28
Color TV, portable, table model	2.83	345.76
VCRs and video disc players	2.85	203.95
Video cassettes, tapes, and discs	15.98	51.83
Video game hardware and software	4.74	123.73
Repair of TV, radio, and sound equipment	0.55	113.64
Rental of televisions	0.06	191.67
Radios and sound equipment	40.18	88.51
Radios	1.30	87.88
Tape recorders and players	0.35	73.57
Sound components and component systems	1.79	281.98
Compact disc, tape, record, video mail order clubs	2.59	63.03

	percent reporting expenditure during quarter	average amount spent per quarter
Records, CDs, audio tapes, needles	17.77%	$51.31
Rental of VCR, radio, sound equipment	0.03	208.33
Musical instruments and accessories	1.60	387.81
Rental and repair of musical instruments	0.39	78.21
Rental of video cassettes, tapes, discs, films	29.09	33.80
Sound equipment accessories	1.01	169.06
Satellite dishes	0.12	208.33
Pets, toys, and playground equipment	**39.96**	**192.11**
Pets	29.19	159.47
Pet purchase, supplies, and medicines	24.49	94.74
Pet services	4.87	112.68
Veterinary services	8.86	201.58
Toys, games, hobbies, and tricycles	17.54	167.25
Playground equipment	0.42	210.71
Other entertainment supplies, equipment, services	**34.39**	**310.93**
Unmotored recreational vehicles	0.17	6,932.35
Boat without motor and boat trailers	0.11	3,670.45
Trailer and other attachable campers	0.06	12,912.50
Motorized recreational vehicles	0.32	13,296.09
Motorized camper	0.03	33,375.00
Other vehicle	0.14	6,333.93
Motor boats	0.15	15,778.33
Rental of recreational vehicles	0.23	216.30
Rental of noncamper trailer	0.01	300.00
Boat and trailer rental, out-of-town trips	0.05	70.00
Rental of camper on out-of-town trips	0.03	691.67
Rental of other vehicles, out-of-town trips	0.10	130.00
Rental of boat	0.02	200.00
Rental of other RVs	0.03	175.00
Outboard motors	0.04	443.75
Docking and landing fees	0.55	302.73
Sports, recreation, exercise equipment	11.49	245.43
Athletic gear, game tables, exercise equipment	5.97	192.50
Bicycles	1.49	225.67
Camping equipment	1.12	108.93
Hunting and fishing equipment	2.04	213.48
Winter sports equipment	0.48	283.85
Water sports equipment	0.64	349.61
Other sports equipment	1.64	222.87
Rental and repair of miscellaneous sports equipment	0.33	156.82
Photographic equipment and supplies	28.82	76.53
Film	20.74	21.38
Film processing	20.73	32.08
Repair and rental of photographic equipment	0.05	60.00
Photographic equipment	2.33	250.43
Photographer fees	3.37	151.48
PERSONAL CARE PRODUCTS AND SERVICES	**74.01**	**86.16**
Wigs and hairpieces	0.61	54.10
Electric personal care appliances	3.12	39.50
Personal care services	73.40	84.74

	percent reporting expenditure during quarter	average amount spent per quarter
READING	**53.88%**	**$64.24**
Newspaper subscriptions	24.39	44.98
Newspaper, nonsubscriptions	16.79	16.83
Magazine subscriptions	9.37	44.26
Magazines, nonsubscriptions	12.58	18.58
Books purchased through book clubs	2.90	57.07
Books not purchased through book clubs	21.61	58.28
Encyclopedia and other reference book sets	0.08	103.13
EDUCATION	**16.08**	**1,091.67**
College tuition	5.25	2,116.43
Elementary/high school tuition	1.94	1,661.60
Other schools tuition	0.99	644.70
Other school expenses including rentals	3.77	170.89
Books, supplies for college	4.61	314.15
Books, supplies for elementary, high school	4.49	89.87
Books, supplies for day care, nursery school	0.76	111.51
TOBACCO PRODUCTS AND SMOKING SUPPLIES	**24.23**	**328.27**
Cigarettes	21.70	336.28
Other tobacco products	3.68	178.46
FINANCIAL PRODUCTS AND SERVICES		
Miscellaneous financial products and services	**47.74**	**400.11**
Lotteries and gambling losses	17.23	87.96
Legal fees	2.99	1,111.96
Funeral expenses	2.19	889.38
Safe deposit box rental	2.61	36.78
Checking accounts, other bank service charges	18.35	35.30
Cemetery lots, vaults, and maintenance fees	0.85	472.06
Accounting fees	5.95	243.07
Finance charges, except mortgage and vehicles	8.13	834.47
Occupational expenses	5.33	180.39
Expenses for other properties	5.14	320.96
Interest paid, home equity line of credit (other property)	0.04	2,668.75
Credit card memberships	1.32	53.41
Shopping club membership fees	3.33	44.82
Cash contributions	**51.52**	**619.71**
Support for college students	2.19	866.89
Alimony expenditures	0.30	1,765.00
Child support expenditures	3.80	1,254.93
Gifts to non-household members of stocks, bonds and mutual funds	0.43	1,408.72
Cash contributions to charities	18.69	184.08
Cash contributions to religious organizations	34.48	404.07
Cash contributions to educational organizations	2.63	317.68
Cash contributions to political organizations	1.45	187.93
Other cash gifts	12.45	453.33
Personal insurance and pensions	**77.33**	**1,260.38**
Life and other personal insurance	36.82	275.74
Life, endowment, annuity, other personal insurance	36.03	271.75
Other nonhealth insurance	2.13	169.72

	percent reporting expenditure during quarter	average amount spent per quarter
Pensions and Social Security	**67.97%**	**$1,284.58**
Deductions for government retirement	2.72	638.60
Deductions for railroad retirement	0.04	1,381.25
Deductions for private pensions	9.48	1,029.48
Nonpayroll deposit to retirement plans	8.57	1,243.06
Deductions for Social Security	67.50	964.56
PERSONAL TAXES	**57.81**	**1,079.51**
Federal income taxes	53.59	859.57
State and local income taxes	36.96	342.57
Other taxes	15.00	245.40
GIFTS	**35.45**	**512.65**
Food	**1.34**	**910.82**
Housing	**14.60**	**285.86**
Household textiles	2.45	73.88
Appliances and miscellaneous housewares	2.65	130.94
Major appliances	0.47	289.36
Small appliances and miscellaneous housewares	2.28	92.54
Miscellaneous household equipment	7.50	106.73
Other housing	4.93	577.08
Apparel and services	**19.86**	**197.97**
Males aged two or older	6.17	159.97
Females aged two or older	7.53	169.19
Children under age two	9.87	86.37
Other apparel products and services	4.98	164.31
Jewelry and watches	2.55	235.39
All other apparel products and services	2.73	79.85
Transportation	**1.06**	**992.92**
Health care	**1.65**	**391.67**
Entertainment	**9.58**	**169.75**
Toys, games, hobbies, and tricycles	5.73	130.80
Other entertainment	4.75	184.58
Education	**2.93**	**1,505.97**
All other gifts	**5.07**	**218.93**

Source: Calculations by New Strategist based on the 2002 Consumer Expenditure Survey

Spending by Product and Service, 2002 Ranking

(average annual spending of consumer units on products and services, ranked by amount spent, 2002)

Mortgage interest	$2,962.16
Social Security	2,604.32
Rent	2,104.66
Federal income taxes	1,842.57
Property taxes	1,242.36
Gasoline and motor oil	1,235.06
Health insurance	1,167.71
Used cars	1,113.46
Electricity	981.09
Vehicle insurance	893.50
New cars	883.08
New trucks	869.88
Used trucks	728.82
Vehicle maintenance and repairs	697.30
Residential telephone and pay phones	641.00
Apparel, women's	586.91
Cash contributions to church, religious organizations	557.29
Television sets	543.66
Maintenance and repair services, owned homes	519.60
Dinner at full-service restaurants	518.02
State and local income taxes	506.45
Tuition, college	444.45
Retirement accounts, nonpayroll deposits	426.12
Finance charges, vehicle	397.04
Life, endowment, annuity, other personal insurance	391.65
Pensions, deductions for private	390.38
Cable service and community antenna	382.28
Lunch at fast food restaurants and take-outs	377.71
Drugs, prescription	373.83
Natural gas	329.75
Apparel, men's	319.48
Cellular phone service	293.76
Cigarettes	291.89
Homeowner's insurance	283.30
Vehicle leasing	283.15
Finance charges, except mortgage and vehicles	271.37
Lodging on trips	252.87
Personal care services	249.15
Airline fares	243.57
Water and sewerage maintenance	237.16
Beef	231.17
Dental services	226.99
Lunch at full-service restaurants	224.82
Dinner at fast food restaurants and take-outs	213.33
Food purchased from restaurants on trips	211.49
Day care centers, nurseries, and preschools	210.74

Child support expenditures	$190.75
Medicare payments	186.87
Snacks at fast food restaurants and take-outs	185.69
Fresh fruits	178.20
Fresh vegetables	174.88
Vacation homes, owned	171.55
Pork	167.34
Physician's services	147.53
Decorative items for the home	144.94
Poultry	144.13
Shoes, women's	141.64
Computers and computer hardware, nonbusiness use	138.58
Cash contributions to charities	137.62
Legal fees	132.99
Postage	131.44
Laundry and cleaning supplies	130.57
Cosmetics, perfume, and bath products	129.13
Tuition, elementary and high school	128.94
Carbonated drinks	125.04
Fish and seafood	120.97
Toys, games, hobbies, and tricycles	117.34
Apparel, girls'	117.21
Milk, fresh	114.63
Beer and ale at home	112.34
Lawn and garden supplies	110.01
Social, recreation, civic club membership	107.92
Computer information services	107.29
Shoes, men's	102.90
Pet food	102.56
Movie, theater, opera, ballet tickets	98.30
Cheese	95.64
Motorboats	94.67
Apparel, boys'	89.98
Jewelry	89.65
Trash and garbage collection	89.05
Home equity loan, line of credit interest	88.61
Breakfast at fast food restaurants and take-outs	87.83
Cereals, ready-to-eat and cooked	87.66
Breakfast at full-service restaurants	87.08
Sofas	85.33
Fats and oils	85.16
Bread	83.83
Maintenance and repair materials, owned homes	83.75
Fees for recreational lessons	82.69
Apparel, infants'	82.60
State and local registration	80.58
Housing while attending school	80.14
Housekeeping services	79.90
Funeral expenses	77.91
Lunch at employer and school cafeterias	77.76
Wine at home	77.75
Cleansing and toilet tissue, paper towels, and napkins	76.46
Potato chips and other snacks	76.37
Cash support for college students	75.94
Candy and chewing gum	75.44
Fees for participant sports	75.05

Gardening, lawn care service	$72.38
Veterinary services	71.44
Laundry and dry cleaning of apparel, professional	69.69
Deductions for government retirement	69.48
Whiskey and other alcoholic beverages at restaurants, bars	69.16
Catered affairs	69.00
Lunch meats (cold cuts)	68.99
Bedroom furniture, except mattress and springs	68.33
Bedroom linens	65.98
Drugs, nonprescription	64.45
Kitchen and dining room furniture	61.28
Athletic gear, game tables, exercise equipment	60.51
Stationery, stationery supplies, giftwrap	60.20
School lunches	60.00
Fruit juice, canned and bottled	59.74
Ice cream and related products	58.74
Books, supplies for college	57.93
Accounting fees	57.85
Vegetables, canned and dried	55.58
Hair care products	53.57
Wall units, cabinets, and other furniture	52.94
Mattresses and springs	52.91
Beer and ale at restaurants, bars	52.86
Pet purchase, supplies, and medicines	52.29
Eyeglasses and contact lenses	52.26
Refrigerators and freezers	52.08
Hospital services other than room	51.51
Books, except book clubs	50.38
Care for elderly, invalids, handicapped, etc.	50.07
Mass transit fares, intracity	49.97
Plants and fresh flowers, indoor	49.78
Vitamins, nonprescription	49.15
Lawn and garden equipment	48.16
Lottery and gambling losses	46.94
Board (including at school)	46.54
Cookies	46.31
Fuel oil	45.98
Newspaper subscriptions	43.88
Medical services by professionals other than physician	42.76
Coffee	41.59
Vehicle rental	41.33
Biscuits and rolls	41.04
Ground rent	40.96
Motorized camper	40.05
Rental of video cassettes, tapes, discs, films	39.33
Living room chairs	39.21
Occupational expenses	38.46
Sauces and gravies	37.78
Laundry and dry cleaning of apparel, coin-operated	37.58
Shoes, boys'	36.87
Snacks at vending machines, mobile vendors	36.71
Hospital room	36.57
Records, CDs, audio tapes, needles	36.47
New motorcycles	36.26
Admission to sports events	36.18
Babysitting and child care, own home	35.91

Soups, canned and packaged	$ 35.82
Cakes and cupcakes	35.73
Hunting and fishing equipment	35.68
Bottled/tank gas	35.27
Eye care services	34.20
Eggs	33.75
Used motorcycles	33.42
Cash contributions to educational institutions	33.42
Power tools	33.27
Video cassettes, tapes, and discs	33.13
Moving, storage, and freight express	33.13
Alcoholic beverages on trips	32.78
Telephones and accessories	32.73
Shoes, girls'	31.76
Baby food	31.57
Outdoor equipment	31.52
Trailer and other attachable campers	30.99
Cooking stoves, ovens	30.95
Deodorants, feminine hygiene, misc. products	30.29
Snacks at full-service restaurants	30.17
Frozen meals	29.88
Ship fares	29.74
Parking fees	29.25
Vegetables, frozen	27.85
Property management, owned home	27.64
Topicals and dressings	27.56
Pasta, cornmeal, and other cereal products	27.54
Babysitting and child care, other home	27.48
Oral hygiene products	27.33
Salad dressings	27.01
Lab tests, X-rays	26.79
Film processing	26.60
Tobacco products, except cigarettes	26.27
Checking accounts, other bank service charges	25.91
Wine at restaurants, bars	25.85
Sweetrolls, coffee cakes, doughnuts	25.84
Recreation expenses on trips	25.64
Bakery products, frozen and refrigerated	25.64
Musical instruments and accessories	24.82
Crackers	24.36
Nonelectric cookware	24.25
Gifts to non–CU members of stocks, bonds, mutual funds	24.23
Nuts	24.16
Video game hardware and software	23.46
Photographic equipment	23.34
VCRs and video disc players	23.25
Meals as pay	22.86
Electric floor-cleaning equipment	22.80
Bathroom linens	22.35
Washing machines	22.30
Fruit juice, fresh	22.20
Jams, preserves, other sweets	22.06
Pet services	21.95
Floor coverings, wall-to-wall	21.69
Prepared salads	21.46
Tableware, nonelectric kitchenware	21.44

Alimony	$21.18
Salt, spices, and other seasonings	21.14
Frankfurters	20.95
Photographer's fees	20.42
Phone cards	20.28
Sound components and component systems	20.19
Fruit-flavored drinks, noncarbonated	18.95
Taxi fares and limousine service	18.95
Floor coverings, nonpermanent	18.79
Butter	18.48
Baking needs	18.19
Living room tables	18.03
Rice	17.82
Film	17.74
Computer software and accessories, nonbusiness use	17.67
Home security system service fee	17.40
Small electric kitchen appliances	17.18
Clothes dryers	17.05
Outdoor furniture	16.79
Curtains and draperies	16.65
Magazine subscriptions	16.59
Dishwashers (built-in), garbage disposals, range hoods	16.52
Boat without motor and boat trailers	16.15
Books, supplies for elementary, high school	16.14
Train fares, intercity	16.09
Cemetery lots, vaults, and maintenance fees	16.05
Tea	15.86
Sugar	15.56
Laundry and cleaning equipment	15.15
Shaving products	15.09
Fruit, canned	15.06
Hearing aids	14.98
China and other dinnerware	14.51
Window coverings	13.91
Whiskey at home	13.90
Watches	13.62
Bicycles	13.45
Electric personal care appliances	13.34
Termite/pest control services	13.25
Infants' equipment	12.96
Peanut butter	12.89
Automobile service clubs	12.75
Cream	12.52
Convalescent or nursing home care	12.46
Flour mixes, prepared	12.40
Lamps and lighting fixtures	11.74
Bus fares, intercity	11.48
Sewing materials for household items	11.44
Newspaper, nonsubscription	11.30
Maintenance and repair services, rented homes	11.16
Local transportation on trips	10.91
Cash contributions to political organizations	10.90
Appliance repair, including service center	10.86
Tolls	10.59
Office furniture for home use	10.57
Microwave ovens	10.50

Prepared desserts	$10.32
Snacks at employer and school cafeterias	10.11
Kitchen and dining room linens	10.11
Closet and storage items	9.98
Margarine	9.86
Pies, tarts, turnovers	9.82
Olives, pickles, relishes	9.70
Camping equipment	9.59
Magazines, nonsubscription	9.35
Nondairy cream and imitation milk	9.33
Vehicle inspection	9.26
Water sports equipment	8.95
Tenant's insurance	8.90
Flour	8.65
Sewing patterns and notions	8.20
Hand tools	8.05
Maintenance and repair materials, rented homes	8.00
Lamb and organ meats	7.99
Air conditioners, window	7.90
Slipcovers and decorative pillows	7.40
Reupholstering and furniture repair	7.40
Vegetable juices	7.23
Wood and other fuels	7.09
Adult day care centers	6.81
Docking and landing fees	6.66
Books purchased through book clubs	6.62
Hair accessories	6.57
Compact disc, tape, record, video mail order clubs	6.53
Glassware	6.51
Infants' furniture	6.46
Taxi fares and limousine service on trips	6.41
Driver's license	6.26
Fruit, dried	6.06
Luggage	5.98
Sound equipment accessories	5.97
Shopping club membership fees	5.97
Clocks	5.87
Apparel repair and tailoring	5.86
Management and upkeep services for security, owned home	5.71
Portable heating and cooling equipment	5.70
Towing charges	5.60
Lunch at vending machines, mobile vendors	5.50
Watch and jewelry repair	5.49
Winter sports equipment	5.45
Tape recorders and players	5.31
Parking, owned home	5.17
Material for making clothes	5.11
Breakfast at employer and school cafeterias	5.11
Pinball, electronic video games	4.84
Sewing machines	4.79
Rental of furniture	4.60
Artificial sweeteners	4.33
Laundry and dry cleaning, nonapparel, coin-operated	4.13
Silver serving pieces	4.05
Radios	3.98
Tolls on trips	3.94

Safe deposit box rental	$3.84
Flatware	3.79
Repairs/rentals of lawn/garden equip., hand/power tools, etc.	3.62
Playground equipment	3.54
Bread and cracker products	3.50
Books, supplies for day care, nursery school	3.39
Fruit juice, frozen	3.35
Dinner at employer and school cafeterias	3.32
Water softening service	3.15
Credit card memberships	2.82
Fruit, frozen	2.79
Medical equipment	2.69
Clothing rental	2.66
Repair of computer systems for nonbusiness use	2.53
Repair of TV, radio, and sound equipment	2.50
Smoking accessories	2.33
Deductions for railroad retirement	2.21
Septic tank cleaning	2.12
Delivery services	2.12
Rental and repair of miscellaneous sports equipment	2.07
Rental of recreational vehicles	1.99
Dinner at vending machines, mobile vendors	1.87
Laundry and dry cleaning, nonapparel, sent out	1.72
Pager service	1.71
School bus	1.64
Plastic dinnerware	1.57
Fireworks	1.52
Smoke alarms	1.49
Shoe repair and other shoe services	1.44
Calculators	1.44
Breakfast at vending machines, mobile vendors	1.40
Wigs and hairpieces	1.32
Souvenirs	1.25
Rental and repair of musical instruments	1.22
Visual goods	1.19
Telephone answering devices	1.08
Appliance rental	1.07
Rental of medical equipment	1.06
Business equipment for home use	0.97
Outboard motors	0.71
Termite/pest control products	0.68
Nonalcoholic beer	0.64
Clothing storage	0.55
Rental of television sets	0.46
Rental of VCR, radio, sound equipment	0.25
Repair and rental of photographic equipment	0.12
Coal	0.07

Note: Ranking does not show miscellaneous categories or gift spending, which is included in each product and service category.
Source: Calculations by New Strategist based on the 2002 Consumer Expenditure Survey

Glossary

age The age of the reference person, also called the householder or head of household.

alcoholic beverages Includes beer and ale, wine, whiskey, gin, vodka, rum, and other alcoholic beverages.

apparel, accessories, and related services Includes the following:

• *men's and boys' apparel* Includes coats, jackets, sweaters, vests, sport coats, tailored jackets, slacks, shorts and short sets, sportswear, shirts, underwear, nightwear, hosiery, uniforms, and other accessories.

• *women's and girls' apparel* Includes coats, jackets, furs, sport coats, tailored jackets, sweaters, vests, blouses, shirts, dresses, dungarees, culottes, slacks, shorts, sportswear, underwear, nightwear, uniforms, hosiery, and other accessories.

• *infants' apparel* Includes coats, jackets, snowsuits, underwear, diapers, dresses, crawlers, sleeping garments, hosiery, footwear, and other accessories for children.

• *footwear* Includes articles such as shoes, slippers, boots, and other similar items. It excludes footwear for babies and footwear used for sports such as bowling or golf shoes.

• *other apparel products and services* Includes material for making clothes, shoe repair, alterations and sewing patterns and notions, clothing rental, clothing storage, dry cleaning, sent-out laundry, watches, jewelry, and repairs to watches and jewelry.

average spending The average amount spent per household. The Bureau of Labor Statistics calculates the average for all households in a segment, not just for those who purchased an item. For items purchased by most households—such as bread—average spending figures are an accurate account of actual spending. For products and services purchased by few households during a year's time—such as cars—the average amount spent is much less than what purchasers spend. See the Percent Reporting Appendix for the percentage of consumer units reporting an expenditure and the average amount spent by purchasers.

baby boom People born from 1946 through 1964, aged 38 to 56 in 2002.

baby bust People born from 1965 through 1976, aged 26 to 37 in 2001. Also known as Generation X.

cash contributions Includes cash contributed to persons or organizations outside the consumer unit including alimony and child support payments, care of students away from home, and contributions to religious, educational, charitable, or political organizations.

complete income reporters Respondents who provided values for major sources of income, such as wages and salaries, self-employment income, and Social Security income. Even complete income reporters may not have given a full accounting of all income from all sources.

consumer unit Defined as follows:

• All members of a household who are related by blood, marriage, adoption, or other legal arrangements.

• A person living alone or sharing a household with others or living as a roomer in a private home or lodging house or in permanent living quarters in a hotel or motel, but who is financially independent.

• Two persons or more living together who pool their income to make joint expenditure decisions. Financial independence is determined by the three major expense categories: housing, food, and other living expenses. To be considered financially independent, at least two of the three major expense categories have to be provided by the respondent. For convenience, called households in the text of this book.

consumer unit, composition of The classification of interview households by type according to: (1) relationship of other household members to the reference person; (2) age of the children to the reference person; and (3) combination of relationship to the reference person and age of the children. Stepchildren and adopted children are included with the reference person's own children.

earner A consumer unit member aged 14 or older who worked at least one week during the 12 months prior to the interview date.

education Includes tuition, fees, books, supplies, and equipment for public and private nursery schools, elementary and high schools, colleges and universities, and other schools.

education of reference person The number of years of formal education of the reference person based on the highest grade completed. If the respondent was enrolled at the time of interview, the grade being attended is the one recorded. Those not reporting their education are classified under no school or not reported.

entertainment Includes the following:

• *fees and admissions* Includes fees for participant sports; admissions to sporting events, movies, concerts, plays; health, swimming, tennis, and country club memberships, and other social recreational and fraternal organizations; recreational lessons or instructions; and recreational expenses on trips.

• *television, radio, and sound equipment* Includes television sets, video recorders, video cassettes, tapes, discs, disc players, video game hardware, video game cartridges, cable TV, radios, phonographs, tape recorders and players, sound components, records and tapes, and records and tapes through record clubs, musical instruments, and rental and repair of TV and sound equipment.

• *pets, toys, hobbies, and playground equipment* Includes pet food, pet services, veterinary expenses, toys, games, hobbies, and playground equipment.

• *other entertainment equipment and services* Includes indoor exercise equipment, athletic shoes, bicycles, trailers, campers, camping equipment, rental of cameras and trailers, hunting and fishing equipment, sports equipment, winter sports equipment, water sports equipment, boats, boat motors and boat trailers, rental of boat, landing and docking fees, rental and repair of sports equipment, photographic equipment, film and film processing, photographer fees, repair and rental of photo equipment, fireworks, pinball and electronic video games.

expenditure The transaction cost including excise and sales taxes of goods and services acquired during the survey period. The full cost of each purchase is recorded even though full payment may not have been made at the date of purchase. Expenditure estimates include gifts. Excluded from expenditures are purchases or portions of purchases directly assignable to business purposes and periodic credit or installment payments on goods and services already acquired.

federal income tax Includes federal income tax withheld in the survey year to pay for income earned in survey year plus additional tax paid in survey year to cover any underpayment or under withholding of tax in the year prior to the survey.

financial products and services Includes union dues, professional dues and fees, other occupational expenses, funerals, cemetery lots, and unclassified fees and personal services.

food Includes the following:

• *food-at-home* Refers to the total expenditures for food at grocery stores or other food stores during the interview period. It is calculated by multiplying the number of visits to a grocery or other food store by the average amount spent per visit. It excludes the purchase of nonfood items.

• *food-away-from-home* Includes all meals (breakfast, lunch, brunch, and dinner) at restaurants, carryouts, and vending machines, including tips, plus meals as pay, special catered affairs such as weddings, bar mitzvahs, and confirmations, and meals away from home on trips.

generation X People born from 1965 through 1976, aged 26 to 37 in 2002. Also known as the baby bust.

gifts for non-household members Includes gift expenditures for people outside of the consumer unit. The amount spent on gifts is also included in individual product and service categories.

health care Includes the following:

• *health insurance* Includes health maintenance plans (HMOs), Blue Cross/Blue Shield, commercial health insurance, Medicare, Medicare supplemental insurance, and other health insurance.

• *medical services* Includes hospital room and services, physicians' services, services of a practitioner other than a physician, eye and dental care, lab tests, X-rays, nursing, therapy services, care in convalescent or nursing home, and other medical care.

• *drugs* Includes prescription and non-prescription drugs, internal and respiratory over-the-counter drugs.

• *medical supplies* Includes eyeglasses and contact lenses, topicals and dressings, antiseptics, bandages, cotton, first aid kits, contraceptives; medical equipment for general use such as syringes, ice bags, thermometers, vaporizers, heating pads; supportive or convalescent medical equipment such as hearing aids, braces, canes, crutches, and walkers.

Hispanic origin The self-identified Hispanic origin of the consumer unit reference person. All consumer units are included in one of two Hispanic origin groups based on the reference person's Hispanic origin: Hispanic or non-Hispanic. Hispanics may be of any race.

household According to the Census Bureau, all the people who occupy a household. A group of unrelated people who share a housing unit as roommates or unmarried partners is also counted as a household. Households do not include group quarters such as college dormitories, prisons, or nursing homes. A household may contain more than one consumer unit. The terms "household" and "consumer unit" are used interchangeably in this book.

household furnishings and equipment Includes the following:

• *household textiles* Includes bathroom, kitchen, dining room, and other linens, curtains and drapes, slipcovers and decorative pillows, and sewing materials.

• *furniture* Includes living room, dining room, kitchen, bedroom, nursery, porch, lawn, and other outdoor furniture.

• *carpet, rugs, and other floor coverings* Includes installation and replacement of wall-to-wall carpets, room-size rugs, and other soft floor coverings.

• *major appliances* Includes refrigerators, freezers, dishwashers, stoves, ovens, garbage disposals, vacuum cleaners, microwaves, air-conditioners, sewing machines, washing machines and dryers, and floor cleaning equipment.

• *small appliances and miscellaneous housewares* Includes small electrical kitchen appliances, portable heating and cooling equipment, china and other dinnerware, flatware, glassware, silver and other serving pieces, nonelectric cookware, and plastic dinnerware. Excludes personal care appliances.

• *miscellaneous household equipment* Includes typewriters, luggage, lamps and other light fixtures, window coverings, clocks, lawn mowers and gardening equipment, other hand and power tools, telephone answering devices, telephone accessories, computers and computer hardware for home use, calculators, office equipment for home use, floral arrangements and house plants, rental of furniture, closet and storage items, household decorative items, infants' equipment, outdoor equipment, smoke alarms, other household appliances and small miscellaneous furnishing.

household services Includes the following:

• *personal services* Includes baby sitting, day care, and care of elderly and handicapped persons.

• *other household services* Includes housekeeping services, gardening and lawn care services, coin-operated laundry and dry-cleaning of household textiles, termite and pest control products, moving, storage, and freight expenses, repair of household appliances and other household equipment, reupholstering and furniture repair, rental and repair of lawn and gardening tools, and rental of other household equipment.

housekeeping supplies Includes soaps, detergents, other laundry cleaning products, cleansing and toilet tissue, paper towels, napkins, and miscellaneous household products; lawn and garden supplies, postage, stationery, stationery supplies, and gift wrap.

housing tenure "Owner" includes households living in their own homes, cooperatives, condominiums, or townhouses. "Renter" includes households paying rent as well as families living rent free in lieu of wages.

income before taxes The total money earnings and selected money receipts accruing to a consumer unit during the 12 months prior to the interview date. Income includes the following components:

• *wages and salaries* Includes total money earnings for all members of the consumer unit aged 14 or older from all jobs, including civilian wages and salaries, Armed Forces pay and allowances, piece-rate payments, commissions, tips, National Guard or Reserve pay (received for training periods), and cash bonuses before deductions for taxes, pensions, union dues, etc.

• *self-employment income* Includes net business and farm income, which consists of net income (gross receipts minus operating expenses) from a profession or unincorporated business or from the operation of a farm by an owner, tenant, or sharecropper. If the business or farm is a partnership, only an appropriate share of net income is recorded. Losses are also recorded.

• *Social Security, private and government retirement* Includes the following: payments by the federal government made under retirement, survivor, and disability insurance programs to retired persons, dependents of deceased insured workers, or to disabled workers; and private pensions or retirement benefits received by retired persons or their survivors, either directly or through an insurance company.

• *interest, dividends, rental income, and other property income* Includes interest income on savings or bonds; payments made by a corporation to its stockholders, periodic receipts from estates or trust funds; net income or loss from the rental of property, real estate, or farms, and net income or loss from roomers or boarders.

• *unemployment and workers' compensation and veterans' benefits* Includes income from unemployment compensation and workers' compensation, and veterans' payments including educational benefits, but excluding military retirement.

• *public assistance, supplemental security income, and food stamps* Includes public assistance or welfare, including money received from job training grants; supplemental security income paid by federal, state, and local welfare agencies to low-income persons who are aged 65 or older, blind, or disabled; and the value of food stamps obtained.

• *regular contributions for support* Includes alimony and child support as well as any regular contributions from persons outside the consumer unit.

• *other income* Includes money income from care of foster children, cash scholarships, fellowships, or stipends not based on working; and meals and rent as pay.

indexed spending The indexed spending figures compare the spending of each demographic segment with that of the average household. To compute an index, the amount spent on an item by a demographic segment is divided by the amount spent on the item by the average household. That figure is then multiplied by 100. An index of 100 is the average for all households. An index of 132 means average spending by households in a segment is 32 percent above average (100 plus 32). An index of 75 means average spending by households in a segment is 25 percent below average (100 minus 25). Indexed spending figures identify the consumer units that spend the most on a product or service.

life and other personal insurance Includes premiums from whole life and term insurance; endowments; income and other life insurance; mortgage guarantee insurance; mortgage life insurance; premiums for personal life liability, accident and disability; and other non-health insurance other than homes and vehicles.

market share The market share is the percentage of total household spending on an item that is accounted for by a demographic segment. Market shares are calculated by dividing a demographic segment's total spending on an item by the total spending of all households on the item. Total spending on an item for all households is calculated by multiplying average spending by the total number of households (112,108,000 in 2002). Total spending on an item for each demographic segment is calculated by multiplying the segment's average spending by the number of households in the segment. Market shares reveal the demographic segments that account for the largest share of spending on a product or service.

metropolitan statistical area (MSA) As defined by the Office of Management and Budget, a large population nucleus, together with adjacent communities which have a high degree of economic and social integration with the nucleus.

millennial generation People born from 1977 though 1994, and aged 8 through 25 in 2002.

occupation The occupation in which the reference person received the most earnings during the survey period. The occupational categories follow those of the Census of Population. Categories shown in the tables include the following:

• *self-employed* Includes all occupational categories; the reference person is self-employed in own business, professional practice, or farm.

• *wage and salary earners, managers and professionals* Includes executives, administrators, managers, and professional specialties such as architects, engineers, natural and social scientists, lawyers, teachers, writers, health diagnosis and treatment workers, entertainers, and athletes.

• *wage and salary earners, technical, sales, and clerical workers* Includes technicians and related support work-

ers; sales representatives, sales workers, cashiers, and sales-related occupations; and administrative support, including clerical.

• *retired* People who did not work either full- or part-time during the survey period.

personal care Includes products for the hair, oral hygiene products, shaving needs, cosmetics and bath products, suntan lotions and hand creams, electric personal care appliances, incontinence products, other personal care products, personal care services such as hair care services (haircuts, bleaching, tinting, coloring, conditioning treatments, permanents, press, and curls), styling and other services for wigs and hairpieces, body massages or slenderizing treatments, facials, manicures, pedicures, shaves, electrolysis.

race The self-identified race of the consumer unit reference person. All consumer units are included in one of two racial groups based on the reference person's race: black or "white and other." The "other" group includes American Indians, Alaskan natives, Asians, and Pacific Islanders. Hispanics may be of any race.

reading Includes subscriptions for newspapers, magazines, and books through book clubs; purchase of single-copy newspapers and magazines, books, and encyclopedias and other reference books.

reference person The first member mentioned by the respondent when asked to "Start with the name of the person or one of the persons who owns or rents the home." It is with respect to this person that the relationship of other consumer unit members is determined. Also called the householder or head of household.

region Consumer units are classified according to their address at the time of their participation in the survey. The four major census regions of the United States are the following state groupings:

• *Northeast* Connecticut, Maine, Massachusetts, New Hampshire, New Jersey, New York, Pennsylvania, Rhode Island, and Vermont.

• *Midwest* Illinois, Indiana, Iowa, Kansas, Michigan, Minnesota, Missouri, Nebraska, North Dakota, Ohio, South Dakota, and Wisconsin.

• *South* Alabama, Arkansas, Delaware, District of Columbia, Florida, Georgia, Kentucky, Louisiana, Maryland, Mississippi, North Carolina, Oklahoma, South Carolina, Tennessee, Texas, Virginia, and West Virginia.

• *West* Alaska, Arizona, California, Colorado, Hawaii, Idaho, Montana, Nevada, New Mexico, Oregon, Utah, Washington, and Wyoming.

retirement, pensions, and Social Security Includes all Social Security contributions paid by employees; employees' contributions to railroad retirement, government retirement and private pensions programs; retirement programs for self-employed.

shelter Includes the following:

• *owned dwellings* Includes interest on mortgages, property taxes and insurance, refinancing and prepayment charges, ground rent, expenses for property management/security, homeowners' insurance, fire insurance and extended coverage, landscaping expenses for repairs and maintenance contracted out (including periodic maintenance and service contracts), and expenses of materials for owner-performed repairs and maintenance for dwellings used or maintained by the consumer unit, but not dwellings maintained for business or rent.

• *rented dwellings* Includes rent paid for dwellings, rent received as pay, parking fees, maintenance, and other expenses.

• *other lodging* Includes all expenses for vacation homes, school, college, hotels, motels, cottages, trailer camps, and other lodging while out of town.

• *utilities, fuels, and public services* Includes natural gas, electricity, fuel oil, coal, bottled gas, wood, and other fuels; telephone services; water, garbage and trash collection, sewerage maintenance, septic tank cleaning, and other public services.

size of consumer unit The number of people whose usual place of residence at the time of the interview is in the consumer unit.

state and local income taxes Includes state and local income taxes withheld in the survey year to pay for income earned in survey year plus additional taxes paid in the survey year to cover any underpayment or under withholding of taxes in the year prior to the survey.

tobacco and smoking supplies Includes cigarettes, cigars, snuff, loose smoking tobacco, chewing tobacco, and smoking accessories such as cigarette or cigar holders, pipes, flints, lighters, pipe cleaners, and other smoking products and accessories.

transportation Includes the following:

• *vehicle purchases (net outlay)* Includes the net outlay (purchase price minus trade-in value) on new and used domestic and imported cars and trucks and other vehicles, including motorcycles and private planes.

• *gasoline and motor oil* Includes gasoline, diesel fuel, and motor oil.

• *other vehicle expenses* Includes vehicle finance charges, maintenance and repairs, vehicle insurance, and vehicle rental licenses and other charges.

• *vehicle finance charges* Includes the dollar amount of interest paid for a loan contracted for the purchase of vehicles described above.

• *maintenance and repairs* Includes tires, batteries, tubes, lubrication, filters, coolant, additives, brake and transmission fluids, oil change, brake adjustment and repair, front-end alignment, wheel balancing, steering repair, shock absorber replacement, clutch and transmission repair, electrical system repair, repair to cooling system, drive train repair, drive shaft and rear-end repair, tire repair, other maintenance and services, and auto repair policies.

• *vehicle insurance* Includes the premium paid for insuring cars, trucks, and other vehicles.

• *vehicle rental, licenses, and other charges* Includes leased and rented cars, trucks, motorcycles, and aircraft, inspection fees, state and local registration, drivers' license fees, parking fees, towing charges, and tolls on trips.

• *public transportation* Includes fares for mass transit, buses, trains, airlines, taxis, private school buses, and fares paid on trips for trains, boats, taxis, buses, and trains.

Index

hearing aids, 466–489
high school tuition, 616–639
    gifts of, 392–463
hobbies, 218–265
    gifts of, 2–165, 392–463
home equity loan/line of credit, interest paid, 566–613
hosiery, 168–215
hospital room, 466–489
hospital services, other than room, 466–489
    gifts of, 392–463
hot dogs. *See* Frankfurters.
hotels. *See* Lodging on trips.
housecleaning. *See* Housekeeping services.
household services, 2–165, 492–563
household textiles, 2–165, 492–563
    gifts of, 2–165, 392–463
housekeeping services, 492–563
housekeeping supplies, 2–165, 492–563
    gifts of, 2–165, 392–463
housing, 2–165, 492–563, 566–613
    gifts of, 2–165, 392–463
    while attending school, 566–613
    while attending school, gifts of, 392–463
hunting equipment, 218–265
    gifts of, 392–463

ice cream, 294–389
infants'
    apparel, 2–165, 168–215
    apparel, gifts of, 2–165, 392–463
    equipment, 492–563
    equipment, gifts of, 392–463
    furniture, 492–563
insulation, for housing, 566–613
insurance
    health, 466–489
    homeowners and related, 566–613
    life and other personal, 2–165, 268–291
    nonhealth, 268–291
    tenants, 566–613
    vehicle, 2–165, 642–689
interest
    home equity loan/line of credit, 566–613
    mortgage, 2–165, 566–613
    vehicle, 2–165, 642–689

jams and preserves, 294–389
jewelry, 168–215
    gifts of, 2–165, 392–463

kitchen
    appliances, small electric, 492–563
    appliances, small, gifts of, 392–463
    furniture, 492–563
    linens, 492–563
kitchenware, nonelectric, 492–563
    gifts of, 392–463

lab tests, X-rays, 466–489
lamb, 294–389
lamps and lighting fixtures, 492–563
landscape maintenance, 492–563
laundry and cleaning supplies, 2–165, 492–563
    gifts of, 392–463

laundry and dry cleaning
    apparel, coin-operated, 168–215
    apparel, professional, 168–215
    nonapparel, 492–563
lawn and garden
    equipment, 492–563
    service, 492–563
    supplies, 492–563
    supplies, gifts of, 392–463
leasing
    car, 642–689
    truck, 642–689
legal fees, 268–291
lessons, recreational, 218–265
    gifts of, 392–463
lettuce, 294–389
life insurance. *See* Insurance.
lights. *See* Lamps and lighting fixtures.
limousine service. *See* Taxi fares and limousine service.
linens
    bathroom, 492–563
    bedroom, 492–563
    gifts of, 392–463
    kitchen and dining room, 492–563
liverwurst, 294–389
living room
    chairs, 492–563
    tables, 492–563
lodging on trips, 566–613
lottery losses, 268–291
    gifts of, 392–463
luggage, 492–563
lunch
    at restaurants, 294–389
    at school, 294–389
lunch meats, 294–389

magazines
    nonsubscription, 616–639
    subscription, 616–639
maintenance and repairs for housing, 2–165, 566–613
    gifts of, 392–463
    owned homes, 566–613
    rented homes, 566–613
    vacation homes, 566–613
margarine, 294–389
mass transit fares, intracity, 642–689
material for making clothes, 168–215
mattresses and springs, 492–563
meals as pay, 294–389
meats, 2–165, 294–389
medical
    equipment, 466–489
    services, 2–165, 466–489
    supplies, 2–165, 466–489
Medicare, commercial supplements, 466–489
memberships
    credit card, 268–291
    social, recreation, and civic club, 218–265
men's apparel, 2–165, 168–215
    gifts of, 2–165, 392–463
microwave ovens, 492–563
milk
    fresh, 2–165, 294–389
    imitation, 294–389